Symbol	Description	Page
a_i	Action i in a decision analysis	828
A^c	Complement of event A	128
A, B	Events	119
$A \cup B$	Union of events A and B	127
$A \cap B$	Intersection of events A and B	127
α (alpha)	Probability of rejecting H_0 if in fact H_0 is true (Type I error)	285
b	Number of blocks in a randomized block design	691
β (beta)	Probability of accepting H_0 if in fact H_0 is false (Type II error)	286
β_0	y-intercept in regression models	397
$\hat{\beta}_0$	Least squares estimator of β_0	401
β_1	Slope of straight-line regression model	397
$\hat{\beta}_1$	Least squares estimator of β_1	401
β_i	Coefficient of independent variable x_i in a multiple regression model	450
$\hat{\beta}_i$	Least squares estimator of β_i	452
C_t	Cyclical effect in a time series	628
CS	Cost of sampling	889
χ^2 (chi square)	Probability distribution of various test statistics	755
df	Degrees of freedom for the t, χ^2, and F distributions	302
$E(n_{ij})$	Expected count in cell (i, j) of a contingency table	800
$\hat{E}(n_{ij})$	Estimated expected count in cell (i, j) of a contingency table	801
$E(x)$	Expected value of the random variable x	168
$EOL(a_i)$	Expected opportunity loss for action i in a decision analysis	880
ENGS	Expected net gain of sampling in a decision analysis	889
$EP(a_i)$	Expected payoff for action i in a decision analysis	838
EPNS	Expected payoff for no sampling in a decision analysis	888
EPS	Expected payoff of sampling in a decision analysis	888
$EU(a_i)$	Expected utility for action i in a decision analysis	851
EVPI	Expected value of perfect information in a decision analysis	881
EVSI	Expected value of sample information	888
ε (epsilon)	Random error component in regression models	397
f_i	Frequency for category i in a qualitative data set	17
$f(x)$	Probability density function for a continuous random variable x	210
F	Test statistic used to compare two variances, to compare k population means, and to test several terms in a multiple regression	353
F_r	Test statistic for the Friedman nonparametric analysis of variance	761
F_α	Value of F distribution with area α to its right	354
H	Test statistic for the Kruskal–Wallis nonparametric analysis of variance	754
H_a	Alternative (or research) hypothesis	288
H_0	Null hypothesis	288

Continued inside back cover

THIRD EDITION

Statistics for Business and Economics

THIRD EDITION

Statistics for Business and Economics

James T. McClave
College of Business Administration
University of Florida

P. George Benson
School of Management
University of Minnesota

Dellen Publishing Company
San Francisco

Collier Macmillan Publishers
London

divisions of Macmillan, Inc.

Copyright 1985 by Dellen Publishing Company, a division of Macmillan, Inc.

Printed in the United States of America

Permissions: Dellen Publishing Company
               400 Pacific Avenue
               San Francisco, California 94133

Orders: Dellen Publishing Company
          c/o Macmillan Publishing Company
          Front and Brown Streets
          Riverside, New Jersey 08075

Collier Macmillan Canada, Inc.

Library of Congress Cataloging in Publication Data

McClave, James T.
    Statistics for business and economics.

    Includes index.
    1. Commercial statistics.   2. Economics — Statistical
methods.   3. Statistics.   I. Benson, P. George,
1946 –   II. Title.
HF1017.M36   1985   519.5   84 – 26030

Printing   2 3 4 5 6 7 8   Year 5 6 7 8 9 0

ISBN 0-02-378770-8

CONTENTS

Chapter 9   **Two Samples: Estimation and Tests of Hypotheses**   **333**

Chapter 10   **Simple Linear Regression**   **395**

Chapter 11   **Multiple Regression**   **449**

PREFACE

The third edition of *Statistics for Business and Economics* maintains the same objectives as the second, namely to introduce students to the basic concepts of statistics and to show them how these concepts can be used in making inferences from business and economic data. The text is designed so that the early chapters can be used for a one-quarter (or a one-semester) introductory course for all undergraduates. The remainder of the text can be used as a second-quarter (semester) follow-up course, with emphasis on special applications such as regression analysis, time series, analysis of variance, or one of the other methodologies included in the later chapters. As in the second edition, we have maintained a unified approach to the subject, attempting both to provide an overall picture of statistics and its role in business and the sciences, and to provide the student with some methodology that will be relevant and useful in other college courses and subsequent fields of employment.

We have maintained the same level of presentation in the third edition. In addition to making important changes in the featured boxes and in wording (which improves the readability of the text), the following major changes or additions have been made:

1. **Chapter 2: Graphical Descriptions of Data** New Section 2.4 explains how to construct stem and leaf displays as a means of describing quantitative data. This section leads naturally to a discussion of relative frequency histograms in Section 2.5.

2. **Chapter 3: Numerical Descriptive Measures** New Section 3.10 explains how to use z-scores and box plots to identify outliers. Then this concept is used to introduce the notion of a rare event and to provide a brief introduction to statistical inference in Section 3.11.

3. **Chapter 6: Continuous Random Variables** In the second edition, all the examples in Section 6.2 were concerned with finding areas under the normal curve between two values of the standard normal random variable z or between two values of a normal random variable x. We have added an example that deals with the reverse problem, finding a value z_0 corresponding to an area under the normal curve.

4. **Chapter 8: Estimation and a Test of an Hypothesis: Single Sample** We have added the definition of a point estimator. We have also expanded our discussion of the role of the Type II error in testing hypotheses by showing, in new Example 8.3, how to calculate β. Since calculating β helps in understanding its meaning, we have added two exercises at the end of the section. The values of β obtained in the solutions are those shown in Figure 8.7.

5. **Chapter 13: Index Numbers and Time Series** We have added a substantial amount of new material and have split the old Chapter 13 into two chapters. The new Chapter 13 covers methods for describing time series. In addition, it presents some of the important types of index numbers used to describe business and economic phenomena. The focus of the new Chapter 14 is forecasting. It introduces the student to time series models, explains how these models are fit to time series data, and shows how to use the time series prediction equation for forecasting.

6. Chapter 15: Analysis of Variance This chapter has been greatly expanded by adding two new sections, many new examples, and corresponding exercises. New Section 15.3 explains how to perform an analysis of variance for a two-factor factorial experiment. Particular stress is placed on the importance of detecting factor interactions. New Section 15.4 presents Tukey's method for making multiple comparisons about a set of population means.

7. Particular effort was made in preparing the third edition to add exercises that were based on real-life situations, data sets, and/or research results that were reported by the news media or in research journals. A total of 236 new conceptual exercises of this type were added in this edition.

8. Twenty-three new case studies were added in this edition to place greater emphasis on the relevance of statistics to problem-solving in the real world.

In addition to the changes listed above, the third edition of *Statistics for Business and Economics* retains the features of the second. The material is presented in a manner that permits flexibility in the amount of time devoted to particular topics. Sections that are not prerequisite to succeeding sections and chapters are marked "(Optional)." For example, an instructor who wishes to devote more time at the beginning of the course to descriptive statistics might wish to cover all topics in Chapters 2 and 3. In contrast, an instructor who wishes to move rapidly into statistical inference might omit the optional sections (2.2, 2.3, 2.6, and 2.7) and devote only one or two lectures to these chapters.

We have included several features in this text that make it different from most introductory business statistics texts currently available. These features, which assist the student in achieving an overview of statistics and an understanding of its relevance in the solution of business problems, are as follows:

1. Case Studies (See the list of case studies on page xvii.) Many important concepts are emphasized by the inclusion of case studies, which consist of brief summaries of actual business applications of the concepts and are often drawn directly from the business literature. These case studies allow the student to see business applications of important statistical concepts immediately after the introduction of the concepts. The case studies also help to answer by example the often asked questions, "Why should I study statistics? Of what relevance is statistics to business?" Finally, the case studies constantly remind the student that each concept is related to the dominant theme — statistical inference.

2. Where We've Been . . . Where We're Going . . . The first page of each chapter is a "unification" page. Our purpose is to allow the student to see how the chapter fits into the scheme of statistical inference. First, we briefly show how the material presented in previous chapters helps us to achieve our goal (Where We've Been). Then, we indicate what the next chapter (or chapters) contributes to the overall objective (Where We're Going). This feature allows us to point out that we are constructing the foundation block by block, with each chapter an important component in the structure of statistical inference. Furthermore, this feature provides a series of brief résumés of the material covered as well as glimpses of future topics.

3. Many Examples and Exercises We believe that most students learn by
doing. The text contains many worked examples to demonstrate how to solve various
types of problems. We then provide the student with a large number (more than 1,300) of
exercises. The answers for most are included at the end of the text. The exercises are of
two types:

    a. Learning the Mechanics These exercises are intended to be straightfor-
ward applications of the new concepts. They are introduced in a few words and are
unhampered by a barrage of background information designed to make them "practical," but which often detracts from instructional objectives. Thus, with a minimum of
labor, the student can recheck his or her ability to comprehend a concept or a
definition.

    b. Applying the Concepts The mechanical exercises described above are
followed by realistic exercises that allow the student to see applications of statistics
to the solution of problems encountered in business and economics. Once the
mechanics are mastered, these exercises develop the student's skills at compre-
hending realistic problems that describe situations to which the techniques may be
applied.

4. On Your Own . . . The chapters end with an exercise entitled "On Your
Own . . . ." The intent of this exercise is to give the student some hands-on experience
with a business application of the statistical concepts introduced in the chapter. In most
cases, the student is required to collect, analyze, and interpret data relating to some
business phenomenon.

5. A Simple, Clear Style We have tried to achieve a simple and clear writing style.
Subjects that are tangential to our objective have been avoided, even though some may
be of academic interest to those well-versed in statistics. We have not taken an encyclo-
pedic approach in the presentation of material.

**6. An Extensive Coverage of Multiple Regression Analysis and
Model Building** This topic represents one of the most useful statistical tools for
the solution of business problems. Although an entire text could be devoted to regression
modeling, we feel that we have presented a coverage that is understandable, usable, and
much more comprehensive than the presentations in other introductory business statistics texts. We devote three chapters to discussing the major types of inferences that can
be derived from a regression analysis, showing how these results appear in computer
printouts and, most important, selecting multiple regression models to be used in an
analysis. Thus, the instructor has the choice of a one-chapter coverage of simple regression, a two-chapter treatment of simple and multiple regression, or a complete three-
chapter coverage of simple regression, multiple regression, and model building. The
following two chapters on index numbers and time series analysis are closely tied to the
three chapters on multiple regression analysis because they present an introduction to
forecasting based on time-dependent data. This extensive coverage of such useful
statistical tools will provide added evidence to the student of the relevance of statistics to
the solution of business problems.

7. Footnotes and Appendix A Although the text is designed for students with a
noncalculus background, footnotes explain the role of calculus in various derivations.

Footnotes are also used to inform the student about some of the theory underlying certain results. Appendix A presents some useful counting rules for the instructor who wishes to place greater emphasis on probability. Consequently, we think the footnotes and Appendix A provide an opportunity for flexibility in the mathematical and theoretical level at which the material is presented.

8. **Decision Analysis**   We have included a two-chapter treatment of decision analysis. In Chapter 18 the classic decision problem in presented. In addition to the standard expected payoff criterion using prior information, several other decision-making criteria are presented. This includes a rather complete introduction to the role of utility functions in decision analysis. In Chapter 19 Bayes' Rule is used both to compute the expected value of sample information before it is purchased and to revise the prior probabilities after sample information is obtained. Throughout both chapters we stress (by setting off in boxes) a step-by-step approach for all calculations. This allows the student to devote time to understanding the concepts and philosophies of decision analysis and to avoid being caught up in the necessary tedious calculations that accompany these analyses.

9. **Supplementary Material**   A solutions manual, a study guide, and a 3,000 item test bank are available.

Acknowledgments

As with the first and second editions, we owe thanks to the many people who assisted in reviewing and preparing this edition. Chief among these are the reviewers and the people who assisted in the preparation of exercises for the text and the test bank. Their names are listed below. We particularly acknowledge the editorial assistance of Susan L. Reiland, the outstanding administrative support of Jane Oas Benson, and the typing and assistance of Brenda Dobson and Patricia Brager. Without these four, we never could have completed this work.

Gordon J. Alexander
University of Minnesota

Larry M. Austin
Texas Tech University

Clarence Bayne
Concordia University

Carl Bedell
Philadelphia College of Textiles and Science

David M. Bergman
University of Minnesota

Atul Bhatia
University of Minnesota

Jim Branscome
University of Texas at Arlington

Francis J. Brewerton
Middle Tennessee State University

Daniel Brick
College of St. Thomas

Robert W. Brobst
University of Texas at Arlington

Michael Broida
Miami University of Ohio

Larry Claypool
Oklahoma State University

Edward R. Clayton
Virginia Polytechnic Institute and State University

Ken Constantine
University of New Hampshire

Jim Daly
California State Polytechnic Institute

Dileep Dhavale
University of Northern Iowa

Carol Eger
Stanford University

Robert Elrod
Georgia State University

Douglas A. Elvers
University of North Carolina at Chapel Hill

Susan Flach
University of Minnesota

Alan E. Gelfand
University of Connecticut

Michael E. Hanna
University of Texas at Arlington

Don Holbert
Oklahoma State University

James Holstein
University of Missouri

Warren M. Holt
Southeastern Massachusetts University

Steve Hora
Texas Tech University

Marius Janson
University of Missouri

Ross H. Johnson
Madison College

Timothy J. Killeen
University of Connecticut

Richard W. Kulp
Wright-Patterson AFB, Air Force Institute of Technology

Martin Labbe
State University of New York College at New Paltz

James Lackritz
California State University at San Diego

Philip Levine
William Patterson College

Eddie M. Lewis
University of Southern Mississippi

Pi-Erh Lin
Florida State University

Paula M. Oas
University of Minnesota

William M. Partian
Fordham College

Vijay Pisharody
University of Minnesota

P. V. Rao
University of Florida

Jayant Saraph
University of Minnesota

Craig Slinkman
University of Texas at Arlington

Charles Sommer
State University of New York at Brockport

Donald N. Steinnes
University of Minnesota at Duluth

Virgil F. Stone
Texas A and I University

Chipei Tseng
Northern Illinois University

Pankaj Vaish
University of Minnesota

Charles F. Warnock
Colorado State University

William J. Weida
United States Air Force Academy

T. J. Wharton
University of New Hampshire

Edna White
Texas A & M University

James Willis
Louisiana State University

Douglas A. Wolfe
Ohio State University

Fike Zahroon
Moorhead State University

CASE STUDIES

THIRD EDITION

Statistics for Business and Economics

CHAPTER 1

What Is Statistics?

Where We're Going . . .

Statistics? Is it a field of study, a group of numbers that summarize some business operation, or, as the title of a recent book (Tanur et al., 1978) suggests, ''a guide to the unknown''? We attempt to answer this question in Chapter 1. Throughout the remainder of the text, we will show you how statistics can be used to aid in making business decisions.

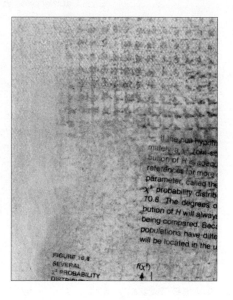

Contents

1.1
Statistics:
What Is It?

What does statistics mean to you? Does it bring to mind batting averages, the Dow Jones Average, unemployment figures, numerical distortions of facts (lying with statistics!), or simply a college requirement you have to complete? We hope to convince you that statistics is a meaningful, useful science with a broad, almost limitless scope of application to business and economic problems. We also want to show that statistics lie only when they are misapplied. Finally, our objective is to paint a unified picture of statistics to leave you with the impression that your time was well spent studying a subject that will prove useful to you in many ways.

Statistics means "numerical descriptions" to most people. The Dow Jones Average, monthly unemployment figures, and the fraction of women executives in a particular industry are all statistical descriptions of large sets of data collected on some phenomenon. Most often, the purpose of calculating these numbers goes beyond the description of the particular set of data. Frequently, the data are regarded as a sample selected from some larger set of data. For example, a sampling of unpaid accounts for a large merchandiser would allow you to calculate an estimate of the average value of unpaid accounts. This estimate could be used as an audit check on the total value of all unpaid accounts held by the merchandiser. So, the applications of statistics to business can be divided into two broad areas: (1) describing large masses of data and (2) making inferences (estimates, decisions, predictions, etc.) about some set of data based on sampling. Let us examine some case studies that illustrate applications of statistics in business and government.

Case Study 1.1
The Consumer Price Index

A data set of interest to virtually all Americans is the set of prices charged for goods and services in the U.S. economy. The general upward movement in this set of prices is referred to as *inflation;* the general downward movement is referred to as *deflation.* In order to *estimate* the change in prices over time, the Bureau of Labor Statistics (BLS) of the U.S. Department of Labor developed the Consumer Price Index (CPI). Each month, the BLS collects price data about a specific collection of goods and services (called a *market basket*) from eighty-five urban areas around the country. Statistical procedures are used to compute the CPI from this sample price data and other information about consumers' spending habits. By comparing the level of the CPI at different points in time, it is possible to *estimate* the rate of inflation (or deflation) over particular time intervals and to compare the purchasing power of a dollar at different points in time.

One major use of the CPI as an index of inflation is as an indicator of the success or failure of government economic policies. A second use of the CPI is to escalate income payments. Millions of workers have *escalator clauses* in their collective bargaining contracts; these clauses call for increases in wage rates based on increases in the CPI. In addition, the incomes of Social Security beneficiaries and retired military and federal civil service employees are tied to the CPI. It has been estimated that a 1% increase in the CPI can trigger an increase of over $1 billion in income payments. Thus, it can be said that the very livelihoods of millions of Americans depend on the behavior of a statistical estimator, the CPI (U.S. Department of Labor, 1978). [*Note:* We will discuss the Consumer Price Index in greater detail in Chapter 13.]

Case Study 1.2
Taste-Preference
Scores for Beer

Two sets of data of interest to a firm's marketing department are (1) the set of taste-preference scores given by consumers to its product and to competitors' products when all brands are clearly labeled and (2) the taste-preference scores given by the same set of consumers when all brand labels have been removed and the consumer's only means of product identification is taste. With such information, the marketing department should be able to determine whether taste preference arose because of perceived physical differences in the products or as a result of the consumer's image of the brand (brand image is, of course, largely a result of a firm's marketing efforts). Such a determination should help the firm develop marketing strategies for its product.

A study using these two types of data was conducted by Ralph Allison and Kenneth Uhl (1965) in an effort to determine whether beer drinkers could distinguish among major brands of unlabeled beer. A sample of 326 beer drinkers was randomly selected from the set of beer drinkers identified as males who drank beer at least three times a week. During the first week of the study, each of the 326 participants was given a six-pack of unlabeled beer containing three major brands and was asked to taste-rate each beer on a scale from 1 (poor) to 10 (excellent). During the second week, the same set of drinkers was given a six-pack containing six major brands. This time, however, each bottle carried its usual label. Again, the drinkers were asked to taste-rate each beer from 1 to 10. From a statistical analysis of the two sets of data yielded by the study, Allison and Uhl concluded that the 326 beer drinkers studied could not distinguish among brands by taste on an overall basis. This result enabled them to infer statistically that such was also the case for beer drinkers in general. Their results also indicated that brand labels and their associations did significantly influence the tasters' evaluations. These findings suggest that physical differences in the products have less to do with their success or failure in the marketplace than the image of the brand in the consumers' minds. As to the benefits of such a study, Allison and Uhl note, ''to the extent that product images, and their changes, are believed to be a result of advertising . . . the ability of firms' advertising programs to influence product images can be more thoroughly examined.''

Case Study 1.3
Monitoring the
Unemployment Rate

The employment status (employed or unemployed) of each individual in the U.S. work force is a set of data that is of interest to economists, businesspeople, and sociologists. These data provide information on the social and economic health of our society. In order to obtain information about the employment status of the work force, the U.S. Bureau of the Census conducts what is known as the *Current Population Survey*. Each month approximately 1,500 interviewers visit about 82,000 of the 79.1 million households in the United States and question the occupants over 14 years of age about their employment status. Their responses enable the Bureau of the Census to *estimate* the percentage of people in the labor force who are unemployed (the *unemployment rate*). Thus, a *statistical estimator* serves as a monthly indicator of the nation's economic welfare.

Perhaps you are wondering how a reliable estimate of this percentage can be obtained from a sample that includes only about .1% of the households in the United States. The answer lies in the method used to select the sample of households. The method was designed to enable the Bureau of the Census to control the precision of their estimate while obtaining a sample that is representative of the set of all households in the country. That reliable estimates of nationwide characteristics can be obtained from relatively small sample sizes is an illustration of the power of statistics (U.S. Department of Commerce, 1978). [*Note:*   We will discuss sampling methods in detail in Chapter 20.]

Case Study 1.4
Auditing Parts and
Equipment for
Airline Maintenance

During the 1950's, the United Airlines Maintenance Base at San Francisco was responsible for the maintenance and overhaul of all United Airlines aircraft (Hunz, 1956). Their storeroom received, stored, and distributed all the parts needed for maintenance of the aircraft. To control the stock of spare parts and to determine the value of parts on hand, counts of the number of each item in stock, called *inventory counts,* were taken. It was the responsibility of the Auditing Division of United Airlines to verify the accuracy of the inventory counts. Thus, a set of data of interest to the accountants of the Auditing Division was the presence or absence of an error in counting the stock of each item in the storeroom's physical inventory. The accountants did not verify the accuracy of the counts by recounting all the inventory item groups but by sampling a small number of these groups and recounting them. If they found a large number of discrepancies between the original counts and their test counts, they inferred that many of the rest of the item counts (those not sampled and recounted) were also in error and concluded that the original inventory counts were unacceptable and would have to be done again. If they found only a small number of discrepancies, they inferred that most of the item counts not rechecked were accurate and concluded that the original inventory counts were satisfactory. Prior to the use of this inferential statistical procedure the Auditing Division verified inventory counts by recounting *all* the items in stock. The inferential procedure enabled them to do the same quality verification work as before, but at a substantial reduction in work-hours.

Case Study 1.5
The Decennial
Census of the
United States

The following description is quoted from the U.S. Bureau of the Census, *Statistical Abstract of the United States: 1981:*

> The U.S. Constitution provides for a census of the population every 10 years, primarily to establish a basis for apportionment of members of the House of Representatives among the states. For over a century after the first census in 1790, the census organization was a temporary one, created only for each decennial census. In 1902, the Bureau of the Census was established as a permanent federal agency, responsible for enumerating the population and also for compiling statistics on other subjects.
>
> The census of the population is a complete count. That is, an attempt is made to account for every person, for each person's residence, and for other characteristics (sex, age, family relationships, etc.). Since the 1940 census, however, some data have been obtained from representative samples of the population rather than a complete count. In the 1980 census, two sampling rates were employed. For most of the country, one in every six households (about 17%) received the long form or sample questionnaire; in areas estimated to have fewer than 2,500 inhabitants, every other household (50%) received the sample questionnaire to enhance the reliability of sample data in small areas. Exact agreement is not expected between sample data and the complete census count.

Why study statistics in a business program? The quantification of business research and business operations (quality control, statistical auditing, forecasting, etc.) has been truly astounding over the past several decades. Econometric modeling, market surveys, and the creation of indexes like the Consumer Price Index all represent relatively recent attempts to quantify economic behavior. It is extremely important that today's business graduate understand the methods and language of statistics, since the alternative is to be swamped by a flood of numbers that are more confusing than enlightening to the untutored mind. The business student should develop a discerning sense of rational thought that will distill the information contained in these numbers so it can be used to make intelligent decisions, inferences, and generalizations. We believe that the study of statistics is essential to the ability to operate effectively in the modern business environment.

1.2 The Elements of Statistics

Although applications of statistics abound in almost every area of human endeavor, there are certain elements common to all statistical problems. The foundation of every statistical problem is a *population:*

Definition 1.1

The *population* is a set of data that characterizes some phenomenon (in our situation, some business phenomenon).

Our definition of *population* is broader than the usual one. We are not just referring to a group of people. For example, the employment status of every person in the U.S. labor force is a population, as is the weekly profit figure for the entire time (past and future) a firm is in business. Other examples of populations are the number of errors on each page in an accountant's ledger and the daily Dow Jones Average, past and future. Thus, we think of a population as being a large — perhaps infinitely large — collection of measurements.

The second element of a statistical problem is the *sample:*

Definition 1.2

A *sample* is a subset of data selected from the population.

The sample is a subset (part of) the population.* The collections of daily Dow Jones Averages for the past 5 years, the monthly unemployment figures for the past 18 months, the weekly sales of a firm over the past year, and the number of errors per page on 10 pages of a 100-page ledger are all samples of the respective populations.

---

* In everyday usage, the word *sample* implies a collection of objects — e.g., a sample of 1,200 people from a city, or a sample of 10 transistors from a day's production. When selecting people or objects from some group, we will sometimes use this terminology; that is, we will speak of a sample of objects rather than the collection of measurements made on the objects. Whether we are speaking of a collection of measurements (our definition) or the collection of objects on which the measurements are made (everyday usage) will be clear from the context of the discussion.

The usefulness of the sample is clarified by considering the third element of a statistical problem — the *inference:*

Definition 1.3

A *statistical inference* is a decision, estimate, prediction, or generalization about the population based on information contained in a sample.

That is, we use the information in the smaller set of measurements (the sample) to make decisions, predictions, or generalizations about the large or whole set of measurements (the population). For example, we might use the number of accounting errors in a 10-page sample of a ledger to estimate the number of errors on all 100 pages of the ledger. Or we could use the past 18 months' unemployment figures to predict the next month's unemployment rate. We might try to infer this year's total sales from last year's weekly sales figures. Finally, we could predict the Dow Jones Average a year from now based on the sample of daily Dow Jones Averages over the past 5 years. In each case, we are using the information in a sample to make inferences about the corresponding population.

The preceding definitions identify three of the four elements of a statistical problem. The fourth, and perhaps the most important, is the topic of Section 1.3.

1.3 Statistics: Witchcraft or Science?

We have identified the primary objective of statistics as making inferences about a population based on information contained in a sample. However, inference-making constitutes only part of our story. The only way we could be completely certain that an inference about a population is correct would be to include the entire population in our sample. Since it may be too costly, time-consuming, or even impossible to do this, we sample only a portion of the observations in the population. This introduces an element of uncertainty associated with inferences based on this partial information about the population. Consequently, we will want to measure and report the *reliability* of each inference made; this is the fourth element of a statistical problem.

The measure of reliability that accompanies an inference separates the science of statistics from the art of fortune-telling. A palm reader, like a statistician, may examine a sample (your hand) and make inferences about the population (your life). However, no measure of reliability can be attached to the reader's inferences. On the other hand, we always assess the reliability of our statistical inferences. For example, if we use a sample of previous profit figures to predict a firm's future profits, we will give a *bound* on our *prediction error.* This bound is simply a number that the error of our prediction is not likely to exceed. Thus, the uncertainty of our prediction is measured by the size of the bound on the prediction errors. The reliability of our statistical inferences will be discussed throughout this text. For now, we simply want you to realize that an inference is incomplete without a measure of its reliability.

We conclude with a summary of the elements of a statistical problem.

1.4
The Role of Statistics in Managerial Decision-Making

Managers frequently rely on input from statistical analyses to help them make decisions. The role statistics can play in managerial decision-making is indicated in the flow diagram in Figure 1.1. Every managerial decision-making problem begins with a real-world problem. This problem is then formulated in managerial terms and framed as a managerial question. The next sequence of steps (proceeding counterclockwise around the flow diagram) identifies the role that statistics can play in this process. The managerial question is translated into a statistical question, the sample data are collected and analyzed, and the statistical question is answered. The next step in the process is using the answer to the statistical question to reach an answer to the managerial question. The answer to the managerial question will suggest a

Figure 1.1 Flow Diagram Showing the Role of Statistics in Managerial Decision-Making
Source: Chervany, Benson, & Iyer (1980).

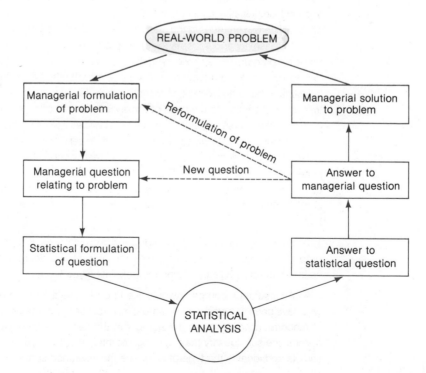

reformulation of the original managerial problem, suggest a new managerial question, or lead to the solution of the managerial problem.

One of the most difficult steps in the decision-making process — one that requires a cooperative effort among managers and statisticians — is the translation of the managerial question into statistical terms (that is, into a question about a population of data). This question must be formulated so that, when answered, it will provide the key to the answer to the managerial question. Thus, like the game of chess, you must formulate the statistical question with the end result, the solution to the managerial question, in mind.

**Exercises
1.1 – 1.11**

Applying the Concepts

1.1 The Food and Drug Administration is responsible for setting tolerance limits (upper limits) for contaminants in food. For the pesticide DDT, the limit is 5 parts per million (ppm). In order to investigate the extent of DDT contamination of Great Lakes fish, the Michigan Department of Agriculture examined a sample of 209 fish caught in the five Great Lakes. The catch consisted of lake trout, whitefish, chubs, coho salmon, and Chinook salmon. They found that only 1 fish (a lake trout) in the sample had more than 5 ppm of DDT ("Level of Tainted Fish . . . ," 1982). Identify the population, the sample, and the nature of the statistical inference Michigan's Department of Agriculture wants to make.

1.2 A problem frequently faced by the management-training specialist is the lack of management enthusiasm for in-plant training programs. Robert J. House (1962) studied the effects of certain changes in the management-training program of a large engineering firm on the enthusiasm for and acceptance of the program by management trainees. In particular, he made the program more challenging and less permissive by increasing the requirements that had to be met for graduation and using a more authoritative teaching style. In order to investigate the effectiveness of these changes, he gave the revised program to fifty-one trainees and compared their rate of absences with that of a class of forty-nine trainees who had taken the course under the old teaching policies. He found that the number of absences per person in his trainee group was significantly lower than that for the group trained under the old policies. He concluded that the revised teaching policies should increase class attendance in future courses as well. Thus, instead of speculating informally about the effectiveness of the revised teaching policies, House used statistical analysis to formally assess their impact. Identify the populations studied by House, the two samples, and the inference made by House.

1.3 Suppose you work for a major public opinion pollster and you wish to estimate the proportion of adult citizens who think the president is doing a good job in handling the nation's economy. Clearly define the population you wish to sample.

1.4 An insurance company would like to determine the proportion of all medical doctors who have been involved in one or more malpractice suits. The company selects 500 doctors at random and determines the number in the sample who have ever been involved in a malpractice suit. Identify the population of interest to the insurance company. Describe the sample and identify the type of inference the insurance company wishes to make.

1.5 *Corporate merger* is a means through which one firm (the bidder) acquires control of the assets of another firm (the target). Carol E. Eger (1982) identified a total of 497 mergers between firms listed on the New York Stock Exchange that resulted in the delisting of the acquired (target) firms' stock during the period 1958–1980. She sampled 38 of these mergers and evaluated the effects of the merger on the value of the holdings of the bidder firms' bondholders. In particular, she wanted to learn whether the value of the holdings increased or decreased as a result of the merger. Identify the population studied, the sample used, and the types of inferences we might wish to make about the population.

1.6 *Job-sharing* is an innovative employment alternative that originated in Sweden and is becoming very popular in the United States. Firms that offer job-sharing plans allow two or more persons to work part-time, sharing one full-time job on different days. For example, two job-sharers might alternate work weeks, with one working while the other is off. Job-sharers never work at the same time and may not even know each other. Job-sharing is particularly attractive to working mothers and to people who frequently lose their jobs due to fluctuations in the economy ("Your Job in the 1980's," 1980). In order to evaluate employers' satisfaction with job-sharing plans, a government agency contacted 100 firms that offer job-sharing. Each firm's director of personnel was asked whether the firm was satisfied with the productivity of workers with shared jobs. Describe the population from which the sample was selected and the type of inference the government agency wishes to make.

1.7 The checking of all accounts payable invoices for errors is a costly and time-consuming procedure. A method for effectively and economically checking for errors involves selecting a portion of the invoices and using the percentage of examined invoices that possess errors to estimate the percentage of all invoices that are in error. Identify the population, sample, and type of statistical inference to be made for this problem.

1.8 To compute their yearly income, trading stamp companies must determine their liability for unredeemed stamps. This requires an estimate of the fraction of all stamps issued that have not been redeemed. Davidson and colleagues (1967) have developed a method for estimating this fraction by studying the time lapse between the issue and redemption of a small percentage of the stamps in circulation. Identify the population, sample, and type of statistical inference to be made for this problem.

1.9 In the mid-1960's, engineers at the Whirlpool Corporation noted that the problem of household garbage disposal was one that few households had satisfactorily solved. Before undertaking a costly research project to attempt to devise a product to solve the problem, Whirlpool conducted a survey of households to determine what proportion of households were in fact concerned about the problem of garbage disposal. It was determined that the proportion was large enough that Whirlpool would probably be able to successfully market whatever product evolved from their research efforts; thus, they proceeded with a research study. The product that resulted was the portable trash compactor (McGuire, 1973). Identify the population of interest to Whirlpool. Describe the sample and the nature of the inference made by Whirlpool.

The next two exercises are designed to examine your current thinking on the subject of reliability. We will formally address this subject in subsequent chapters.

1.10 Refer to Case Study 1.3. Suppose you were asked to assess the reliability of the monthly estimate of the percentage of workers in the labor force who are unemployed. What information do you think would help you in making your assessment?

1.11 Refer to Exercise 1.8. Suppose you were an accountant for a trading stamp company and were responsible for preparing the firm's end-of-year income statement. You would be interested in knowing the firm's liability for unredeemed stamps. Suppose the firm's statistician estimated the fraction of stamps unredeemed out of all those sold during the year to be $\frac{1}{12}$. Suppose also that the statistician failed to give you an indication of the reliability of this estimate (a very serious oversight for a statistician). Since the reliability of your income statement would depend on the reliability of the statistician's estimate, you would be interested in knowing the reliability of the estimate. What information would help you measure the reliability of the statistician's estimate?

FIGURE 10.8
SEVERAL
PROBABILITY
DISTRIBUTIONS

On Your Own . . .

If you could start your own business right now, what kind would it be? Identify a set of business data that would be of interest to you and your firm. Is the data set you identified a sample or a population? How could you use this data set to help your business operate more efficiently?

References

Allison, R. I., & Uhl, K. P. "Influence of beer brand identification on taste perception." *Journal of Marketing Research,* Aug. 1965, 36–39.

Careers in statistics. Washington, D.C.: American Statistical Association and the Institute of Mathematical Statistics, 1974.

Chervany, N. L., Benson, P. G., & Iyer, R. K. "The planning stage in statistical reasoning." *The American Statistician,* Nov. 1980, 222–226.

Davidson, H. J., Neter, J., & Petras, A. S. "Estimating the liability for unredeemed stamps." *Journal of Accounting Research,* 1967, *5,* 186–207.

Eger, C. E. "Corporate mergers: An analytical analysis of the role of risky debt." Unpublished Ph.D. dissertation. University of Minnesota, 1982.

House, R. J. "An experiment in the use of management training standards." *Journal of the Academy of Management,* 1962, 5.

Hunz, E. "Application of statistical sampling to inventory audits." *The Internal Auditor,* 1956, *13,* 38.

"Level of tainted fish falls in Great Lakes." *Minneapolis Tribune,* Oct. 24, 1982, 15c.

McGuire, E. P. *Evaluating new product proposals.* New York: National Industrial Conference Board, 1973, p. 42.

Tanur, J. M., Mosteller, F., Kruskal, W. H., Link, R. F., Pieters, R. S., & Rising, G. R. *Statistics: A guide to the unknown.* San Francisco: Holden-Day, 1978.

U.S. Bureau of the Census. *Statistical abstract of the United States: 1981.* 102d ed. Washington, D.C.: U.S. Government Printing Office, 1981.

U.S. Department of Commerce. *An error profile: Employment as measured by the current population survey.* Statistical Policy Working Paper 3. Washington, D.C.: U.S. Government Printing Office, 1978.

U.S. Department of Labor. *The Consumer Price Index: Concepts and content over the years.* Bureau of Labor Statistics, Report 517. Washington, D.C.: U.S. Government Printing Office, May 1978.

Willis, R. E., & Chervany, N. L. *Statistical analysis and modeling for management decision-making.* Belmont, Calif.: Wadsworth, 1974, Chapter 1.

"Your job in the 1980's." *Consumers Digest,* Nov.–Dec. 1980, 32–36.

CHAPTER 2

Graphical Descriptions of Data

Where We've Been . . .

By examining typical examples of the use of statistics in business, we listed four elements that are common to every business statistical problem: a population, a sample, an inference, and a measure of the reliability of the inference. The last two elements identify the goal of statistics — using sample data to make an inference (a decision, estimate, or prediction) about a population.

Where We're Going . . .

Before we make an inference, we must be able to describe a data set. Graphical methods that provide a compact description of a data set are the topic of this chapter.

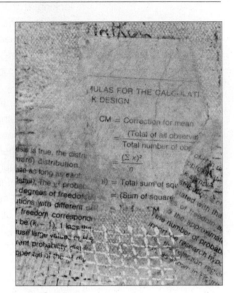

Contents

Before we can use the information in a sample to make inferences about a population, we must be able to extract the relevant information from the sample. That is, we need methods to summarize and describe the sample measurements. For example, if we look at last year's sales for 100 randomly selected companies, we are unlikely to extract much information by looking at the set of 100 sales figures. We would get a clearer picture of the data by calculating the average sales for all 100 companies, by determining the highest and lowest company sales, by drawing a graph showing the average monthly sales over the 12-month period, or in general, by using some technique that will extract and summarize relevant information from the data and, at the same time, allow us to obtain a clearer understanding of the sample.

In this chapter we first define two different types of business data and then present some graphical methods for describing data of each type. You will see that graphical methods for describing data are intuitively appealing descriptive techniques and that they can be used to describe either a sample or a population. However, as we will begin to demonstrate in Chapter 3, numerical methods for describing data are the keys that unlock the door to population inference-making.

As you will subsequently see, some of the descriptive measures discussed in this chapter are primarily of interest for describing large data sets. If statistical inference is your goal, only Sections 2.1, 2.4, and 2.5 are essential. For this reason, Sections 2.2, 2.3, 2.6, and 2.7 are marked "optional."

2.1 Types of Business Data

Although the number of business phenomena that can be measured is almost limitless, business data can generally be classified as one of two types: *quantitative* or *qualitative.*

Definition 2.1

Quantitative data are observations that are measured on a numerical scale.

The most common type of business data is quantitative data, since many business phenomena are measured on numerical scales. Examples of quantitative business data are:

1. The daily Dow Jones Industrial Average
2. The monthly unemployment percentage
3. Last year's sales for selected firms
4. The number of women executives in an industry

The measurements in these examples are all numerical.

All data that are not quantitative are qualitative (or categorical).

Definition 2.2

If each measurement in a data set falls into one and only one of a set of categories, the data set is called *qualitative* (or *categorical*).

Qualitative data are observations that are nonnumerical. Examples of qualitative business data are:

1. The political party affiliations of fifty randomly selected business executives — each executive would have one and only one political party affiliation
2. The brand of gasoline last purchased by seventy-four randomly selected automobile owners — again, each measurement would fall into one and only one category
3. The state in which each of thirty-two randomly selected firms in the United States has its highest yearly sales

Notice that each of the examples has nonnumerical, or qualitative, measurements.

As you would expect, the method used for summarizing the information in a sample of measurements depends on the type of business data being collected. We devote the remainder of this chapter to the presentation of graphical methods for describing quantitative and qualitative data sets.

Exercises 2.1–2.5

2.1 A food products company is considering marketing a new snack food. To see how consumers react to the product, the company conducted a taste test using 100 randomly selected shoppers at a suburban shopping mall. The shoppers were asked to taste the snack food and then fill out a short questionnaire that requested the following information:

a. What is your age?
b. Are you the person who typically does the food shopping for your household?
c. How many people are in your family?
d. How would you rate the taste of the snack food on a scale of 1 to 10, where 1 is least tasty?
e. Would you purchase this snack food if it were available on the market?
f. If you answered yes to question e, how often would you purchase it?

Each of these questions generates a data set of interest to the company. Classify the data in each data set as either quantitative or qualitative. Justify your classification.

2.2 Classify the following examples of business data as either qualitative or quantitative. Justify your classification.

a. Ten college freshmen were asked to indicate the brand of jeans they preferred.
b. Fifteen television cable companies were asked how many hours of sports programs they carry in a typical week.
c. Fifty executives were asked what percentage of their workday was spent in meetings.
d. The number of long-distance phone calls made from each of 100 public telephone booths on a particular day was recorded.

2.3 Classify the following examples of business data as either qualitative or quantitative:

a. The brand of pocket calculator purchased by twenty business statistics students
b. The list price of pocket calculators purchased by twenty business statistics students
c. The number of automobiles purchased during the past 5 years by the heads of fifty randomly selected households

d. The month indicated by each of forty-one randomly selected business firms as the month during which it had the highest sales

e. The depth of tread remaining on each of 137 randomly selected automobile tires after 20,000 miles of wear

2.4 Classify the following examples of business data as either qualitative or quantitative:

a. The brand of stereo speaker for which each of twenty-five college students indicated a preference

b. The loss (in dollars) incurred in each of the last 5 years by a department store as a result of shoplifting

c. The color of interior house paint (other than white) that each of the five largest manufacturers of paint says generates the most sales revenue for the firm

2.5 Classify the following examples of business data as either qualitative or quantitative:

a. The number of corporate mergers during each of the last 15 years

b. The change in the Consumer Price Index during each of the last 6 months

c. The length of time before each of thirty dry-cell batteries goes dead

d. The American automobile manufacturer that each of twenty-five service station mechanics indicated as producing the most reliable cars

2.2 Graphical Methods for Describing Qualitative Data: The Bar Chart (Optional)

As we noted in Section 2.1, a qualitative observation falls into one and only one of a group of categories. For example, suppose a women's clothing store located in the downtown area of a large city wants to open a branch in the suburbs. To obtain some information about the geographic distribution of its present customers, the store manager conducts a survey in which each customer is asked to identify her place of residence with regard to the city's four quadrants: northwest (NW), northeast (NE), southwest (SW), or southeast (SE). Out-of-town customers are excluded from the survey.

The results of the survey—the responses of $n = 30$ randomly selected resident customers—might appear as in Table 2.1. (Note that the symbol n is used here and throughout the text to represent the sample size—i.e., the number of measurements in a sample.) You can see that each of the thirty measurements falls in one and only one of the four possible categories representing the four quadrants of the city.

Table 2.1

Customer Residence Survey: $n = 30$

CUSTOMER	RESIDENCE	CUSTOMER	RESIDENCE	CUSTOMER	RESIDENCE
1	NW	11	NW	21	NE
2	SE	12	SE	22	NW
3	SE	13	SW	23	SW
4	NW	14	NW	24	SE
5	SW	15	SW	25	SW
6	NW	16	NE	26	NW
7	NE	17	NE	27	NW
8	SW	18	NW	28	SE
9	NW	19	NW	29	NE
10	SE	20	SW	30	SW

A natural and useful technique for summarizing qualitative data is to tabulate the *frequency* or *relative frequency* of each category.

Definition 2.3

The *frequency* for a category is the total number of measurements that fall in the category. The frequency for a particular category, say category i, will be denoted by the symbol f_i.

Definition 2.4

The *relative frequency* for a category is the frequency of that category divided by the total number of measurements; that is, the relative frequency for category i is

$$\text{Relative frequency} = \frac{f_i}{n}$$

where

n = Total number of measurements in the sample

f_i = Frequency for the ith category

The frequency for a category is the total number of measurements in that category, whereas the relative frequency for a category is the *proportion* of measurements in the category. Table 2.2 shows the frequency and relative frequency for the customer residences listed in Table 2.1. Note that the sum of the frequencies should always equal the total number of measurements in the sample and the sum of the relative frequencies should always equal 1 (except for rounding errors), as in Table 2.2.

Table 2.2

Frequencies and Relative Frequencies for Customer Residence Survey

CATEGORY	FREQUENCY	RELATIVE FREQUENCY
NE	5	5/30 = .167
NW	11	11/30 = .367
SE	6	6/30 = .200
SW	8	8/30 = .267
Total	30	1

A common means of graphically presenting the frequencies or relative frequencies for qualitative data is the *bar chart.* For this type of chart the frequencies (or relative frequencies) are represented by bars of equal width — one bar for each category. The height of the bar for a given category is proportional to the category frequency (or relative frequency). Usually the bars are placed in a vertical position with the base of the bar on the horizontal axis of the graph. The order of the bars on the horizontal axis is unimportant. Both a frequency bar chart and a relative frequency bar chart for the customer residence example are shown in Figure 2.1 at the top of the next page.

Figure 2.1 Bar Charts for Customer Residence Example

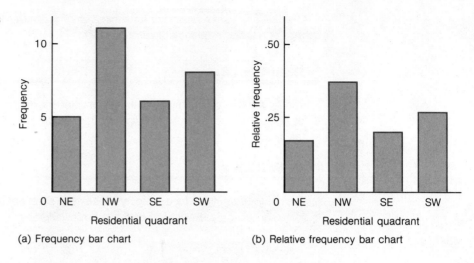

(a) Frequency bar chart

(b) Relative frequency bar chart

Case Study 2.1

How Americans Keep Fit

A recent article in the *Minneapolis Star and Tribune* (Winegar, 1983) described the fitness craze in the United States and the big business it has become:

> Two decades ago, fewer than one in four adult Americans exercised regularly; today around 72 million adults (approximately one out of three) claim to exercise on a regular basis, according to the President's Council on Physical Fitness and Sports.
>
> . . . more than 500 major U.S. corporations have created on-site fitness programs for their employees and thousands of smaller companies are cooperating with local fitness resources such as YWCA's or park and recreation offices to gain employee access to the exercise facilities.

Figure 2.2 How Americans Keep Fit
Source: Winegar (1983).

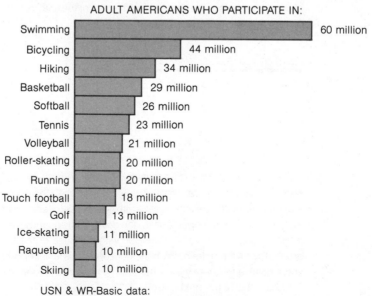

ADULT AMERICANS WHO PARTICIPATE IN:

Swimming — 60 million
Bicycling — 44 million
Hiking — 34 million
Basketball — 29 million
Softball — 26 million
Tennis — 23 million
Volleyball — 21 million
Roller-skating — 20 million
Running — 20 million
Touch football — 18 million
Golf — 13 million
Ice-skating — 11 million
Raquetball — 10 million
Skiing — 10 million

USN & WR-Basic data:
President's Council on Physical Fitness and Sports

The fitness fad has created mini-booms in the fashion industry's exercise/dance-wear market as well as in the development and marketing of weight-training equipment and machines such as Nautilus, Universal, and Olympic.

[The fitness boom has generated] an estimated $30 billion annually in sales of sports and health equipment, memberships, books, records, company fitness programs, health foods and diet aids.

The author of the article used the *bar chart* shown in Figure 2.2 to describe the athletic activities of Americans.

Case Study 2.2
Impact of Electronic Data Processing on Occupation Structure

George E. Delehanty (1966) examined the impact on occupation structure of the introduction of electronic data processing techniques and equipment into the large clerical operations of five large life insurance companies. He used a series of relative frequency bar charts to illustrate the changing pattern of one of the companies' (referred to as company B) work force distribution. Two of these bar charts are presented in Figure 2.3. The firm's various occupational levels are characterized by salary classes and are referred to as "job grades." The workers with the lowest salaries are in job grade 1. Notice that between December 1959 and June 1965 the proportion of workers in the lower job grades (1, 2, 3, and 4) decreased, while the proportion of workers in the higher grades (5, 6, and 7) increased. The bar charts of Figure 2.3 effectively illustrate this change. The reader can easily detect the change in firm B's occupation structure without having to dig through a morass of numbers.

Figure 2.3 Bar Charts Describing Company B's Home Office Work Force by Grade
Source: Delehanty (1966).

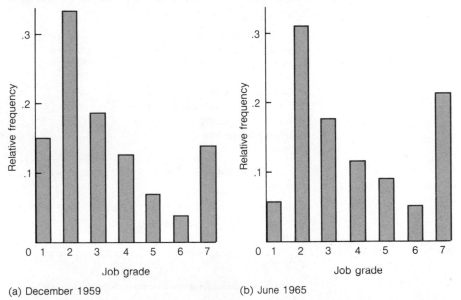

(a) December 1959   (b) June 1965

Based on the information in Figure 2.3, other data about company B, and information about the four other life insurance companies studied, Delehanty concluded (subject to certain qualifications discussed in the article) that "adaptation to punched-card and computer data processing has been associated with reduced requirements for low level clerical workers and increased requirements for higher level clerical manpower." He continues, "higher levels of staff, technicians, and top management have generally experienced sharp increases in employment."

Exercises 2.6–2.11

Learning the Mechanics

2.6 The popularity of automated bank tellers has been steadily increasing since their inception in the early 1970's. By the end of 1982, there were 35,721 automatic teller machines in the United States. Although they are popular as a means for withdrawing cash, bank officials have become concerned about the public's general reluctance to deposit funds through the machines. The table illustrates this problem. Construct a relative frequency bar chart for the data.

TYPE OF TRANSACTION	NUMBER OF TRANSACTIONS DURING 1982 (Billions)
Withdrawal	2.35
Deposit	.59
Transfer or other transaction	.16

Source: *Minneapolis Star and Tribune,* Mar. 12, 1984, p. 3M.

2.7 A questionnaire sent to the chief executives of some of the country's largest industrial corporations and commercial banking companies by *Fortune* magazine revealed the information given in the table concerning their main career emphasis. Construct a relative frequency bar chart for the data.

MAIN CAREER EMPHASIS	FREQUENCY
Legal	109
Financial	202
Marketing, distribution	223
Engineering, research and development	59
Production operations	149
General management	42
Other	30

Source: "A Group Profile of the *Fortune 500* Chief Executive," *Fortune,* May 1976.

2.8 The table lists the number of new housing units authorized (i.e., building permits granted) during 1980 for a sample of seven states. Construct a relative frequency bar chart for the data.

STATE	NUMBER OF HOUSING UNITS AUTHORIZED (Thousands)
Alaska	2.2
California	144.4
Florida	174.2
Kansas	10.9
New York	24.5
Ohio	31.2
Texas	127.5

Source: U.S. Bureau of the Census (1981), p. 756.

Applying the Concepts

2.9 A *bond* is a promissory note issued by a business or government unit in exchange for a specified amount of money. Typically, the note promises to repay the bondholder (*lender*) the face value of the bond (*par value*) at some future date (*maturity date*) plus a specified number of dollars in interest each year. Since the early 1900's, bonds have been given quality ratings that indicate the likelihood that the issuing firm will default on promises to bondholders. One of the major rating agencies is Moody's Investors Service. Moody's rating categories are shown here:

High Quality	Investment Grade	Substandard	Speculative
Aaa, Aa	A, Baa	Ba, B	Caa, Ca, C

The ratings run from triple A bonds (which are extremely safe) to C bonds (which have a high probability of default) (Brigham, 1982). The table lists the maturity dates and the Moody rating for a sample of bonds listed in *Moody's Bond Record*. Construct a bar chart to describe the bond ratings of this sample of bonds.

BOND ISSUER	MATURITY DATE	RATING
Beatrice Foods	1994	Aaa
Caterpillar Tractor	1986	Aa
Continental Group	1990	A
Control Data	1987	Baa
Diamond Shamrock	1994	A
Eastern Airlines	2002	B
Eaton	1992	A
Essex Chemical	1998	B
Food Fair Stores	1996	Caa
General Electric	2004	Aaa
General Signal	1999	Aa
Johns-Manville	2004	Ca
Marathon Oil	2006	A
Norton Simon	1998	Baa
Pepsico	1985	A
Pillsbury	1991	A
Singer	1999	Ba
Sun Oil	1990	Aa
Xerox	1999	Aa

Source: *Moody's Bond Record*, Moody's Investors Service, Vol. 49, No. 12, Dec. 1982.

2.10 During the 1970's the prices of single-family houses in the United States soared to record levels. The price of a typical new single-family home jumped from $23,400 in 1970 to $64,500 in 1980 (U.S. Bureau of the Census, 1981). No longer able to afford a house, many people opted for condominium living. As the demand for condominiums increased, owners of apartments found it more profitable to convert their apartments to condominiums. For her analysis of the condominium conversion market in the seven-county Minneapolis – St. Paul metropolitan area, Mary L. Bochnak (1982) constructed the following table to describe the stock of condominiums in Dakota and Ramsey counties as of December 31, 1980:

COUNTY	CITY	NUMBER OF APARTMENTS CONVERTED TO CONDOMINIUMS	NUMBER OF CONDOMINIUMS CONSTRUCTED
Dakota	Burnsville	409	135
	Eagan	8	128
	Farmington	0	36
	Inver Grove Heights	0	84
	Lilydale	0	139
	Mendota Heights	0	200
	West St. Paul	66	8
Ramsey	Little Canada	511	101
	Maplewood	0	252
	Mounds View	385	0
	New Brighton	54	0
	Roseville	767	30
	St. Anthony	0	148
	St. Paul	832	443
	Shoreview	192	8

Source: Bochnak (1982).

a. Construct a frequency bar chart for the number of apartments converted to condominiums in the cities of Ramsey county.

b. Construct a relative frequency bar chart for the total number of condominiums in the cities of Ramsey county. Do the same for the cities of Dakota county.

c. According to your graphs of part b, which city in each county had the largest share of the county's stock of condominiums?

d. Using your graph of part a as a starting point, create a bar chart that *also* reflects the number of condominiums constructed and the total number of condominiums in the cities of Ramsey county.

2.11 Are we running out of oil? The data in the table describe the new barrels of oil added to the reserves of the four largest U.S. oil companies in 1982 and the barrels of oil withdrawn from these reserves in the same year.

COMPANY	BARRELS ADDED (Millions)	BARRELS WITHDRAWN (Millions)
Exxon	124	270
Texaco	55	127
Socal	57	121
Mobil	34	103

Source: *U.S. News and World Report,* Jan. 23, 1984, p. 59.

a. Construct two relative frequency bar charts for the data, one for barrels added and one for barrels withdrawn.

b. Combine the bar charts you constructed in part a by plotting the eight relative frequencies on the same bar chart. You can do this by drawing two bars side by side for each company listed on the horizontal axis of your chart. Such a chart facilitates comparison of the two data sets.

c. In 1982, were these four oil companies able to find oil as quickly as they used it? Explain your answer making reference to your bar charts.

2.3 Graphical Methods for Describing Qualitative Data: The Pie Chart (Optional)

A second method of describing qualitative data sets — the pie chart — is often used in newspaper and magazine articles to depict budgets and other economic information. A complete circle (the pie) represents the total number of measurements. This is partitioned into a number of slices, with one slice for each category. The size of a slice is proportional to the relative frequency of a particular category. For example, since a complete circle spans 360°, if the relative frequency for a category is .30, the slice assigned to that category is 30% of 360 or (.30)(360) = 108°. See Figure 2.4.

Figure 2.5 shows a pie chart for the customer residence data of Section 2.2. Notice that the sizes of the slices are proportional to the relative frequencies assigned to the four categories. A compass and calculator are needed if the pie chart is to be precisely drawn, which makes it somewhat inconvenient to construct. However, even if we only approximate the size of the wedges, the pie chart provides a useful picture of a qualitative data set.

Figure 2.4 The Portion of a Pie Chart Corresponding to a Relative Frequency of .30

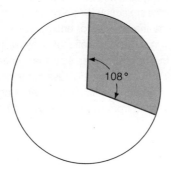

Figure 2.5 Pie Chart for Customer Residence Survey

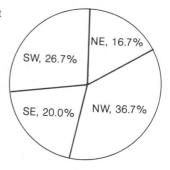

Case Study 2.3
Statistical Abstract of the United States

Each year the Bureau of the Census (U.S. Department of Commerce) publishes a 1,000-plus-page book entitled, *Statistical Abstract of the United States* (hereafter referred to as the *Statistical Abstract*). This book, published yearly since 1878, contains a "summary of statistics on the social, political, and economic organization of the United States. It is designed to serve as a convenient volume for statistical reference and as a guide to other statistical publications and [data] sources" (*Statistical Abstract,* 1981, p. v).

The vast majority of the data included in the *Statistical Abstract* are reported using summary tables such as Table 2.3. However, beginning with the 1981 edition, the *Statistical*

Table 2.3

Money in Circulation, by Denomination: 1960 to 1980 (in millions of dollars, as of December 31)

DENOMINATION	1960	1965	1970	1973	1974	1975	1976	1977	1978	1979	1980
Total[1]	32,869	42,056	57,093	72,497	79,743	86,547	93,717	103,811	114,645	125,600	137,244
Coin and small currency	23,521	29,842	39,639	48,288	51,606	54,865	57,645	62,543	66,693	70,693	73,893
Coin	2,427	4,027	6,281	7,759	8,332	8,959	9,483	10,071	10,739	11,658	12,419
$1[2]	1,533	1,908	2,310	2,639	2,720	2,809	2,858	3,038	3,194	3,308	3,499
$2	88	127	136	135	135	135	637	650	661	671	677
$5	2,246	2,618	3,161	3,614	3,718	3,841	3,905	4,190	4,393	4,549	4,635
$10	6,691	7,794	9,170	10,226	10,503	10,777	10,775	11,361	11,661	11,894	11,924
$20	10,536	13,369	18,581	23,915	26,197	28,344	29,987	33,233	36,045	38,613	40,739
Large currency	9,348	12,214	17,454	24,210	28,137	31,681	36,072	41,269	47,952	54,907	63,352
$50	2,815	3,540	4,896	6,514	7,444	8,157	9,026	10,079	11,279	12,585	13,731
$100	5,954	8,135	12,084	17,288	20,298	23,139	26,668	30,818	36,306	41,960	49,264
$500	249	245	215	185	179	175	172	169	167	164	163
$1,000	316	288	252	216	209	204	200	197	194	192	189
$5,000	3	3	3	2	2	2	2	2	2	2	2
$10,000	10	4	4	4	4	4	4	4	4	4	3

[1] Outside Treasury and Federal Reserve banks.   [2] Paper currency only; $1 silver coins reported under coin.

Source: 1960–1973, Board of Governors of the Federal Reserve System, *Federal Reserve Bulletin,* monthly; thereafter, U.S. Department of the Treasury, *Monthly Statement of United States Currency and Coin,* Form 1028.

Abstract began making extensive use of graphical descriptions of data in a section called "Recent Trends." Graphics employed include bar charts, pie charts, and time series graphs (we will discuss time series graphs in Section 2.7 and again in Chapter 13). For example, the pie charts in Figure 2.6 describe the sources of energy used to produce electricity in the United States in 1970 and 1980. In addition, the effects of the oil crisis and our resulting desire to reduce our dependence on foreign oil are reflected in the decrease in the proportion of total electricity production provided by oil and the increase in the proportion provided by coal. Notice, however, that while oil's proportion has decreased since 1970, the total number of kilowatt-hours of electricity produced from oil has increased since 1970.

Figure 2.6   Electric Energy Production, by Source of Energy

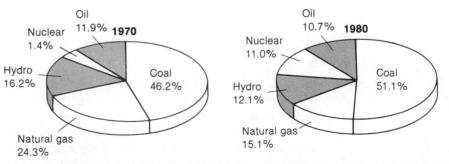

TOTAL PRODUCTION: 1,640 billion kWh   TOTAL PRODUCTION: 2,350 billion kWh

Exercises 2.12–2.19

Learning the Mechanics

2.12 The disk-memory market for personal computers is booming. Demand continues to outpace whatever manufacturers can supply. Even though more than eighty companies build disk memories, the data in the table indicate the market is dominated by a handful of firms. Construct a pie chart to describe the data.

FLOPPY DISK DRIVES 1983 TOTAL SALES: 4.7 MILLION UNITS	
Company	Market share
Tandon	53%
Shugart	18%
Alps Electric	16%
Others	13%

Source: *Business Week*, Feb. 6, 1984, p. 69.

2.13 The table describes the 1981 earnings of tobacco growers by states.

EARNINGS OF THE TOP TOBACCO GROWING STATES	
North Carolina	$1.3 billion
Kentucky	766 million
Tennessee	252 million
Virginia	243 million
South Carolina	240 million
Georgia	191 million
Maryland	43 million
Florida	41 million
Connecticut	37 million
Indiana	31 million

Source: *USA Today*, Mar. 19, 1983, p. 1.

a. Construct a pie chart to describe the data.
b. In your opinion, would this data set be most effectively summarized using a pie chart or a bar chart? Explain.

Applying the Concepts

2.14 When describing monetary data sets, newspapers and magazines sometimes employ a *dollar chart* rather than a pie chart. The dollar charts shown on the next page accompanied a series of articles in the *Minneapolis Star and Tribune* devoted to describing and analyzing President Reagan's proposed federal budget for 1984.

a. Convert the two dollar charts to pie charts.
b. Social insurance tax totals $242.9 billion and is less than the outlay for income security (Social Security, Medicare, etc.), which totals $282.4 billion. Is the proportion of total

receipts due to the social insurance tax also less than the proportion of outlays due to income security? Explain.

Dollar Charts to Describe the 1984 Federal Budget
Source: "The 1984 Federal Budget" (1983).

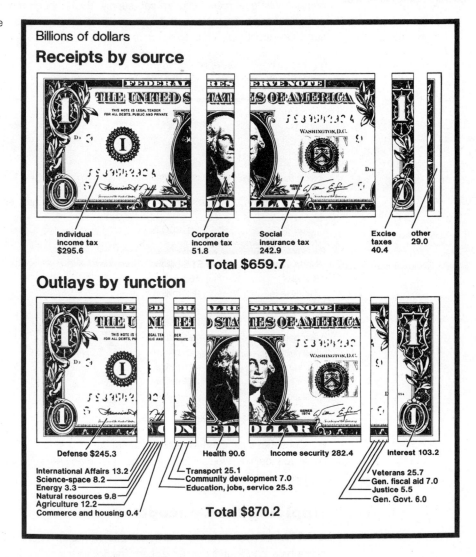

Billions of dollars

Receipts by source

Individual income tax $295.6

Corporate income tax 51.8

Social insurance tax 242.9

Excise taxes 40.4

other 29.0

Total $659.7

Outlays by function

Defense $245.3

International Affairs 13.2
Science-space 8.2
Energy 3.3
Natural resources 9.8
Agriculture 12.2
Commerce and housing 0.4

Transport 25.1
Community development 7.0
Education, jobs, service 25.3

Health 90.6

Income security 282.4

Interest 103.2

Veterans 25.7
Gen. fiscal aid 7.0
Justice 5.5
Gen. Govt. 6.0

Total $870.2

2.15 From 1950 to 1980 the number of people living in suburbs in the United States grew by 66.3 million while the number living in central cities grew by only 18 million. As a result of its population growth, suburbia has become a center for jobs, shopping, and entertainment. The business ventures that once existed only in cities, now thrive in the suburbs. The table describes the growth of suburbia.

	U.S. POPULATION (MILLIONS)		
	1960	*1970*	*1980*
Suburbs	54.9	75.6	101.5
Cities	58.0	63.8	67.9
Other	66.4	63.8	57.1

Source: *U.S. News and World Report,* Mar. 12, 1984, p. 59.

a. For each year listed in the table, construct a pie chart to describe the residences of the U.S. population.

b. Using the information displayed in your pie charts, describe the relative shift in the population between cities and suburbs over the period 1960–1980.

2.16 Although Wendy's and Burger King have increased their market share more than McDonald's in recent years, McDonald's still dominates the fast-food hamburger market, as shown in the pie chart.

1983 Market Share (Percentage Point Change in Market Share Since 1981) Source: *Business Week,* Jan. 30, 1984, p. 46.

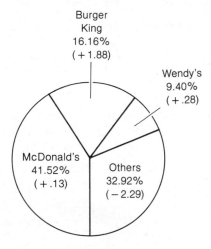

Burger King
16.16%
(+1.88)

Wendy's
9.40%
(+.28)

McDonald's
41.52%
(+.13)

Others
32.92%
(−2.29)

a. The market shares portrayed in the pie chart were based on 1983 sales. McDonald's 1983 sales were $8.16 billion. Find Burger King's and Wendy's 1983 sales.

b. Construct a pie chart that displays the market shares for the 1981 fast-food hamburger market.

2.17 In recent years, big-name chain stores such as J. C. Penney, Sears, Montgomery Ward, Target, and others have entered the $13-billion-a-year jewelry market. In fact, J. C. Penney has become the fourth-largest retail jewelry merchant in the United States, behind Zale's, Gordon Jewelry, and Best Products. Relying on heavy advertising and deep discounting, these retailers have brought mass-merchandising techniques to the jewelry business. As a result, Americans are changing the way they shop for jewelry, as illustrated by the chart at the top of the next page.

a. Construct a pie chart to describe the retail jewelry market in 1978.

b. Repeat part a for the 1982 jewelry market.

Where Consumers Buy
Jewelry
Source: *Business Week,*
Feb. 6, 1984, p. 56.

SHARE OF RETAIL JEWELRY MARKET, %

◄ Others

◄ Catalog showrooms
and discount stores

◄ Department and general
merchandise stores

◄ Jewelry stores

1978   1982

Data: Intergold Corp. N.W. Ayer, *Accent*

2.18 Refer to Exercise 2.17.

a. Construct relative frequency bar charts to characterize the two sets of market-share data.

b. With which graphical presentation do you find it easiest to compare the two market-share data sets: the graph given in Exercise 2.17, the pie charts you constructed in Exercise 2.17, or the bar charts of part a of this exercise? Explain your reasoning.

2.19 Consider the pie chart shown here.

The Breakfast Cereal Dollar:
Where It Goes

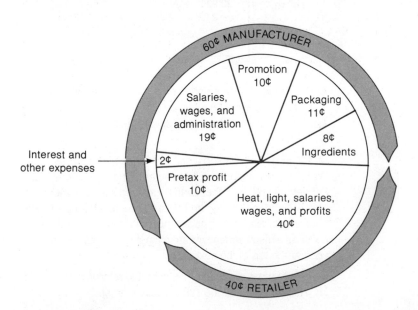

60¢ MANUFACTURER

Promotion
10¢

Salaries,
wages, and
administration
19¢

Packaging
11¢

8¢
Ingredients

Interest and
other expenses → 2¢

Pretax profit
10¢

Heat, light, salaries,
wages, and profits
40¢

40¢ RETAILER

a. What is the pie chart attempting to portray?

b. What does the pie chart tell you about the relationship between the cost of the ingredients in a box of cereal and the cost of the cereal's packaging?

c. According to the pie chart, how much do the ingredients in a $1.75 box of cereal cost the manufacturer?

2.4 Graphical Methods for Describing Quantitative Data: Stem and Leaf Displays

Quantitative data sets are those that consist of numerical measurements. Thus, a quantitative sample is simply a list of numerical values that result from observations taken on some variable x. Most business data are quantitative, so methods for summarizing quantitative data are especially important.

One set of quantitative data of interest to financial managers is the set of the daily *price-earnings ratios* of corporate common stocks. The price-earnings ratio for a common stock is the cost of one share of stock divided by the company's annual earnings per share. For example, if the price-earnings ratio for a stock is 10, the current company annual earnings represent a 10% return on the cost of the stock. Some portion (perhaps none) of the earnings is paid to the stockholder as a dividend; the remainder is reinvested in new plants, equipment, advertising, etc., in order to increase the future earnings of the company. A stock with a demonstrated high rate of growth in earnings usually sells at a premium — a high price-earnings ratio — because investors expect the company's annual earnings to grow and the price of the stock to rise proportionately. Conversely, the stock of a company that possesses a slow growth in earnings will usually sell at a low price-earnings ratio, almost as if it were a financial asset with a fixed rate of return.

In this section we present the price-earnings ratios of the stocks of some companies selected from the high-growth computer and peripheral equipment industry. We use this data set to show you how to construct a stem and leaf display to organize the information in a data set and to make it easy to understand.

Table 2.4 (page 30) gives the price-earnings ratios of the common stocks of twenty-nine companies that manufacture computers or computer peripheral equipment.

Figure 2.7 Stem and Leaf Display for the Computer Stock Price-Earnings Ratios

Stem	Leaf
0	7.4 8.6
1	8.8 7.9 1.4 0.7 9.0 9.2 1.9 2.6 8.4 1.4 4.3 0.3
2	3.6 0.1 6.5 7.7 3.8 5.6 6.1 9.4 2.5
3	5.5 7.3 5.3 3.1 8.6
4.5	1.4

Figure 2.7 shows a stem and leaf display for the data. To construct this display, we first partition a typical observation into a *stem* and a *leaf*. For our display we chose the stem portion of an observation to represent all digits at or to the left of the tens digit place. The remaining portion of the observation, to the right of the stem, is called the *leaf*. The stems and leaves for the price-earnings ratios 14.3, 35.3, and 8.6 are shown here:

Stem	Leaf		Stem	Leaf		Stem	Leaf
1	4.3		3	5.3		0	8.6

Figure 2.8 Alternative Stem and Leaf Display for the Computer Stock Price-Earnings Ratios

Stem	Leaf		
7	.4		
8	.6		
9			
10	.7	.3	
11	.4	.9	.4
12	.6		
13			
14	.3		
15			
16			
17	.9		
18	.8	.4	
19	.0	.2	
20	.1		
21			
22	.5		
23	.6	.8	
24			
25	.6		
26	.5	.1	
27	.7		
28			
29	.4		
30			
31			
32			
33	.1		
34			
35	.5	.3	
36			
37	.3		
38	.6		
39			
40			
41	.4		

Table 2.4 The Price-Earnings Ratios for Twenty-Nine Computer Stocks, Jan. 31, 1984

COMPANY	PRICE-EARNINGS RATIO	COMPANY	PRICE-EARNINGS RATIO
Amdahl	18.8	Gerber Scientific	27.7
Apple	23.6	Hewlett-Packard	23.8
Applied Magnetics	20.1	Honeywell	11.9
Atlas	7.4	IBM	12.6
Barry Wright	17.9	Intergraph	38.6
Burroughs	11.4	Mohawk Data	18.4
Commodore	8.6	NCR	11.4
Computer Vision	35.5	Paradyne	25.6
Control Data	10.7	Prime Computer	26.1
Cray Research	37.3	SCI Systems	29.4
Data General	35.3	Sperry	14.3
Datapoint	33.1	Tandem Computers	41.4
Dataproducts	26.5	Telex	10.3
Digital Equipment	19.0	Wang Labs	22.5
Electronic Memory	19.2		

After choosing the stem and leaf for an observation, we list the set of possible stems for the data set in a column from the smallest (0) to the largest (4). Then the leaf for each observation is recorded in the row of the display corresponding to the observation's stem. For example, the leaf (8.8) of the first observation in Table 2.4 (for Amdahl) is written in the row next to stem 1 in Figure 2.7. Similarly, the leaf (3.6) for the second observation in Table 2.4 (for Apple Computer) is recorded in the row of Figure 2.7 corresponding to stem 2. The stem and leaf display in Figure 2.7 presents a compact picture of the data set. You can see at a glance that almost all the twenty-nine price-earnings ratios fell in the stem rows 1 and 2. The twelve leaves in stem row 1 indicate that twelve of the twenty-nine price-earnings ratios were equal to or greater than 10 but less than 20. Similarly, the nine leaves in stem row 2 indicate that nine of the price-earnings ratios were in the 20's. Only two stocks had price-earnings ratios less than 10 (those in stem row 0), only five were in the 30's, and only one was 40 or more.

A more detailed picture of the data set can be obtained by increasing the number of possible stems in the display. To do this, we could choose the stem to be all digits to the left of the decimal point. For example, a price-earnings ratio of 20.2 would partition into

Stem	Leaf
20	.2

The complete stem and leaf display for the data in Table 2.4 for this choice of stem and leaf is shown in Figure 2.8.

Both of the stem and leaf displays shown in Figures 2.7 and 2.8 provide good graphical descriptions of the data set of Table 2.4. The stem and leaf display shown in Figure 2.8 contains many more stem rows than are contained in the display in Figure 2.7. As a consequence, many stem rows contain no leaves, and none contain more than 3. The resulting display shows a less compact picture of the data set than the one in Figure 2.7, but it has the advantage of showing the spread in the price-earnings ratios and the clusterings of observations over the interval from 7.4 to 41.4.

In addition to providing a good graphical picture of the data set, a stem and leaf display possesses two other advantages. First, if you want to recover the original data from a stem and leaf display, you can readily reconstruct the values of the observations by recombining the leaves with the stems. Second, the construction of the display automatically arranges the observations in ordered sets. This makes it easy to arrange the observations from smallest to largest and, for example, to find the observation in the middle of this ordered arrangement.

One disadvantage of the stem and leaf display is that it is awkward (although possible) to control the number of stems. Thus, in our example it is possible to define the stem so that the number of stems falls between 5 (Figure 2.7) and 35 (Figure 2.8), but some of the simplicity of the procedure is lost in the process. A more obvious disadvantage is that the stem and leaf display is unsuitable when the number of observations in the data set is large. Then the number of leaves in the stem rows becomes too large. To obtain a graphical description of large data sets, we display the data using a *relative frequency histogram*. This graphical method, which bears a similarity to the stem and leaf display, is discussed in Section 2.5.

How to Construct a Stem and Leaf Display

1. Define the stem and leaf you wish to use. You will probably wish to choose the stem so that the number of possible stems in the display is not too large.
2. Write the stems in a column from the smallest stem at the top to the largest at the bottom.
3. Record the leaf for each observation in the row corresponding to its stem.

**Exercises
2.20 – 2.26**

Learning the Mechanics

2.20 Construct a stem and leaf display for the following measurements:

26	33	24	11	8	35	39	16	28	26
34	41	20	17	29	19	29	25	45	50

2.21 Construct a stem and leaf display for the following measurements:

.02	.08	.14	.32	.27	.08	.01	.11	.20	.06
.01	.03	.12	.22	.42	.33	.18	.09	.02	.07

2.22 Construct a stem and leaf display for the following measurements using the leftmost two digits of each number as the stem:

1,050	1,530	2,111	1,786	1,633	1,819	1,899
1,763	1,312	1,400	1,219	1,101	1,375	1,701
1,301	1,256	1,492	1,616	1,907	1,777	1,339
1,781	1,662	1,831	1,790	1,788	1,769	1,344

2.23 Production processes may be classified as *make-to-stock processes* or *make-to-order processes.* Make-to-stock processes are designed to produce a standardized product that can be sold to customers from the firm's inventory. Make-to-order processes are designed to produce products according to customer specifications. The McDonald's and Burger King fast-food chains are classic examples of these two types of processes. McDonald's produces and stocks standardized hamburgers; Burger King — whose slogan is "Have It Your Way" — makes hamburgers according to the ingredients specified by the customer (Schroeder, 1981). In general, performance of make-to-order processes is measured by delivery time — the time from receipt of an order until the product is delivered to the customer. The data in the table are a sample of the delivery times from last year for a particular make-to-order firm. The delivery times marked by an asterisk are associated with customers who subsequently placed additional orders with the firm.

DELIVERY TIMES (Days)				
50*	64*	56*	43*	64*
82*	65*	49*	32*	63*
44*	71	54*	51*	102
49*	73*	50*	39*	86
33*	95	59*	51*	68

a. Construct a stem and leaf display for the data.

b. Circle the individual leaves of your stem and leaf display that are associated with customers who did not place a subsequent order.

c. Concerned that they are losing potential repeat customers due to long delivery times, management would like to establish a guideline for the maximum tolerable delivery time. Using your stem and leaf display of part b, suggest a guideline. Explain your reasoning.

2.24 In a manufacturing plant a *work center* is a specific production facility that consists of one or more people and/or machines and is treated as one unit for the purposes of capacity requirements planning and job scheduling. If jobs arrive at a particular work center at a faster rate than they depart, the work center impedes the overall production process and is referred to as a *bottleneck* (Fogarty and Hoffmann, 1983). The data in the table were collected by an operations manager for use in investigating a potential bottleneck work center.

NUMBER OF ITEMS ARRIVING AT WORK CENTER PER HOUR			NUMBER OF ITEMS DEPARTING WORK CENTER PER HOUR		
155	115	156	156	109	127
150	159	163	148	135	119
172	143	159	140	127	115
166	148	175	122	99	106
151	161	138	171	123	135
148	129	135	125	107	152
140	152	139	111	137	161

a. Construct a stem and leaf display for the two sets of measurements.

b. Do your stem and leaf displays suggest that the work center may be a bottleneck? Explain.

2.25 Typically, the more attractive a corporate common stock is to an investor, the higher the stock's price-earnings ratio. For example, if investors expect the stock's future earnings per share to increase, the price of the stock will be bid up and a high price-earnings ratio will result. Thus, the level of a stock's price-earnings ratio is a function of both the current financial performance of the firm and an investor's expectation of future performance (Spiro, 1982). The table contains the price-earnings (P/E) ratios for samples of firms from the electronics industry and the auto parts industry.

AUTO PARTS		ELECTRONICS	
Firm	*P/E ratio*	*Firm*	*P/E ratio*
Lear Siegler	11	AMP	28
Purolator	15	Raytheon	13
Easco	14	General Instrument	14
Genuine Parts	15	Intel	55
Federal-Mogul	12	Avnet	27
PPG Industries	12	Perkin Elmer	24
A.O. Smith	35	TRW	15
Borg-Warner	12	Motorola	26
Hoover Universal	12	Hewlett-Packard	22
Libbey-Owens-Ford	23	Honeywell	13
Dana	23	American District	11
Champion Spark Plug	18	Corning Glass Works	15
Dayco	39	Gould	18
Sheller-Globe	15	EG&G	22
Arvin Industries	16	Varian Associates	26

Source: *Forbes,* Jan. 2, 1984, pp. 274–290.

a. Construct a stem and leaf display for each of these data sets.
b. What do your stem and leaf displays suggest about the level of the P/E ratios of firms in the electronics industry as compared to firms in the auto parts industry? Explain.

2.26 The table contains the top salary offer received by each of a sample of thirty MBA students who graduated from the University of Minnesota in 1983 and had 1 year or less work experience prior to entering the MBA program. Salaries offered to students who majored in management information systems (MIS) are indicated with an asterisk; offers made to students who majored in accounting are indicated with two asterisks.

SALARY OFFERS TO 1983 MBA GRADUATES				
$30,100	$25,800	$28,905	$31,200*	$26,800
25,300	19,900	24,330	27,500*	30,540
26,850	17,784**	20,730**	22,890	28,900*
24,985	24,920	24,960**	26,855	21,605
23,700	35,004	26,000*	21,445	25,000*
25,200*	22,303	23,755	24,600*	23,895**

Source: Placement Office, School of Management, University of Minnesota.

a. Construct a stem and leaf display for the data.

b. Circle the individual leaves of your stem and leaf display that are associated with MIS graduates. Draw boxes around the individual leaves associated with accounting graduates. What does the pattern of circles and boxes suggest about the relative magnitudes of the starting salaries in MIS and accounting? Explain.

2.5 Graphical Methods for Describing Quantitative Data: Frequency Histograms and Polygons

The computer stock price-earnings ratios are graphically described in Figure 2.9 using a *relative frequency histogram.* The resulting image is similar to what you would obtain if you rotated the stem and leaf display in Figure 2.7 counterclockwise 90°. The stems, now called *measurement classes,* are located on the horizontal axis of the figure. The class intervals are contiguous and of equal width, and the endpoints of the classes are chosen so that no observation can fall on the point of division between two classes. The data in a stem row are now replaced by a rectangle rising vertically over a class interval with a height equal to the proportion of the total number of observations (called the *class relative frequency*) falling in the class interval.

The information provided by the relative frequency histogram is similar to that conveyed by the stem and leaf display except that the exact values of the original observations can no longer be reconstructed from the histogram. On the plus side, the relative frequency histogram gives clearly and precisely the proportion of price-earnings ratios falling in each class interval. Also, you can choose the number of classes and thereby have greater control over the quality of your pictorial description of the data. In Figure 2.9 you can see at a glance that all the computer stock price-earnings ratios fell between 7.35 and 42.35. The class interval 7.35 – 12.35 contains the largest class frequency, .241. Most of the price-earnings ratios fell in the first four classes, between 7.35 and 27.35.

Relative frequency histograms can also be used to visually compare two data sets. Table 2.5 gives the price-earnings ratios for thirty-four electrical utility stocks with no exposure to the

Figure 2.9 Relative Frequency Histogram for the Computer Stock Price-Earnings Ratios in Table 2.4

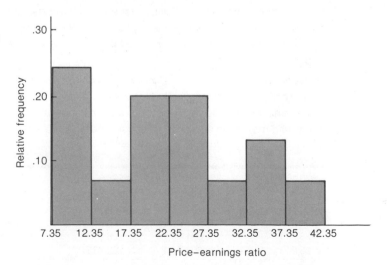

Table 2.5

Price-Earnings Ratios for Thirty-Four Electrical Utility Stocks

COMPANY	PRICE-EARNINGS RATIO	COMPANY	PRICE-EARNINGS RATIO
Allegheny Power	7.5	Montana-Dakota	7.5
Central Illinois Light	7.5	Montana Power	7.4
Central Illinois P.S.	7.2	Nevada Power	11.0
Citizens Utilities	13.8	Northern Indiana P.S.	8.8
C.P. National	7.9	Oklahoma G&E	7.6
Empire District	6.7	Orange & Rockland	8.0
Hawaiian Electric	11.0	Otter Tail	8.4
Idaho Power	7.4	Potomac Electric	9.8
Interstate Power	7.6	St. Joseph L&P	6.3
Iowa Public Service	9.2	Savannah Electric	5.6
Iowa Southern	6.3	Sierra Pacific	8.6
Ipalco	7.1	So. Indiana G&E	6.9
Kansas P&L	6.2	SW Public Service	8.3
Kentucky Utilities	6.6	TECO	8.2
Louisville G&E	8.3	Texas-New Mexico	6.4
Minnesota P&L	7.3	Tucson Electric	7.4
Missouri Public Serv.	5.8	Utah P&L	9.8

financial risks associated with nuclear power plants. These companies' earnings grow slowly from year to year, they are viewed as relatively secure, and high percentages of their earnings are paid annually to the stockholders. A relative frequency histogram for the low-growth electrical utility price-earnings ratios is shown in Figure 2.10. To aid in comparing the price-earnings ratios for computer and electrical utility stocks, we have used the same class intervals as were used in Figure 2.9. You can see from the shapes and locations of the relative frequency histograms that the utility stocks (Figure 2.10) command much lower price-earnings ratios than the computer stocks (Figure 2.9) and that they are much less variable.

Figure 2.10 Relative Frequency Histogram for the Electrical Utility Stock Price-Earnings Ratios in Table 2.5

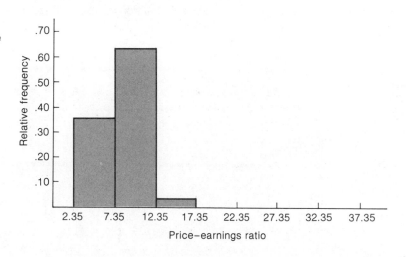

To construct the relative frequency histogram for the computer stock price-earnings ratio data (Table 2.4), we first choose the *class interval width* and then define the measurement classes. We will usually choose between five and twenty classes for the histogram; the larger the amount of data, the larger the number of classes. Suppose we wanted seven classes to span the distance between the smallest and the largest price-earnings ratios. Then the class width would be

$$\frac{\text{Largest measurement} - \text{Smallest measurement}}{\text{Number of intervals}} = \frac{41.4 - 7.4}{7} = 4.86$$

or, rounding upward so as to be certain of including the extreme observations,

Class interval width ≈ 5.0

By locating the lower boundary of the first class interval at 7.35 (a value arbitrarily selected slightly below the smallest measurement) and adding 5.0, we find the upper boundary to be 12.35. Adding 5.0 again, we find the upper boundary of the second class to be 17.35. Continuing this process, we obtain the seven class intervals shown in Table 2.6. Note that each boundary falls on a .05 value (one significant digit more than the measurements), which guarantees that no measurement will fall on a class boundary.

Table 2.6

Measurement Classes, Frequencies, and Relative Frequencies for the Price-Earnings Ratios in Table 2.4

CLASS	MEASUREMENT CLASS	CLASS FREQUENCY	CLASS RELATIVE FREQUENCY
1	7.35–12.35	7	7/29 = .241
2	12.35–17.35	2	2/29 = .069
3	17.35–22.35	6	6/29 = .207
4	22.35–27.35	6	6/29 = .207
5	27.35–32.35	2	2/29 = .069
6	32.35–37.35	4	4/29 = .138
7	37.35–42.35	2	2/29 = .069
Total		29	1.0

The next step is to find the *class frequencies* and calculate the *class relative frequencies.* These quantities are defined as follows:

Definition 2.5

The *class frequency* for a given class, say class i, is equal to the total number of measurements that fall in that class. The class frequency for class i is denoted by the symbol f_i.

Definition 2.6

The *class relative frequency* for a given class, say class i, is equal to the class frequency divided by the total number n of measurements, i.e.,

Relative frequency for class $i = \dfrac{f_i}{n}$

The class frequencies and relative frequencies for the price-earnings ratios are shown in the third and fourth columns of Table 2.6.

The final step in the construction of a histogram is to plot the measurement classes on a horizontal axis and the frequency (or relative frequency) of each class on a vertical axis. Unlike the bar chart, the frequency (or relative frequency) is not plotted as a vertical line over a single point, but instead as a rectangle with a base width equal to that of the measurement class and a height equal to the frequency (or relative frequency). The result is the relative frequency histogram shown in Figure 2.9.

The steps for constructing histograms for quantitative data sets are summarized in the box.

How to Construct a Histogram

1. Arrange the data in increasing order, from the smallest to the largest measurement.

2. Divide the interval from the smallest to the largest measurement into between five and twenty equal subintervals, making sure that:

  a. Each measurement falls into one and only one measurement class.

  b. No measurement falls on a measurement class boundary.

  Use a small number of measurement classes if you have a small amount of data; use a larger number of classes for a larger amount of data.

3. Compute the frequency (or relative frequency) of measurements in each measurement class.

4. Using a vertical axis of about three-fourths the length of the horizontal axis, plot each frequency (or relative frequency) as a rectangle over the corresponding measurement class.

By looking at a histogram (say the relative frequency histogram in Figure 2.9), you can see two important facts. First, note the total area under the histogram, and then note the proportion of the total area that falls over a particular interval of the horizontal axis. You will see that the proportion of the total area that falls above an interval is equal to the relative frequency of the measurements that fall in the interval.* For example, the relative frequency for the class interval 7.35 – 12.35 is .241. Consequently, the rectangle above the interval contains .241 of the total area under the histogram.

Second, you can imagine the appearance of the relative frequency histogram for a very large set of data (say a population). As the number of measurements in a data set is increased, you can obtain a better description of the data by decreasing the width of the class intervals. When the class intervals become small enough, a relative frequency histogram will (for all practical purposes) appear as a smooth curve (see Figure 2.11 on page 38).

Another method of graphing the frequencies (or relative frequencies) for the measurement classes is the *frequency* (or *relative frequency*) *polygon.* To construct the frequency

* Some histograms are constructed with all class intervals of equal width except the first and last, which are open-ended. The proportionality between area and relative frequency will not hold for these histograms. We will restrict our attention to histograms that possess equal-sized class intervals, because later we will want to establish a correspondence between relative frequency histograms and probability distributions.

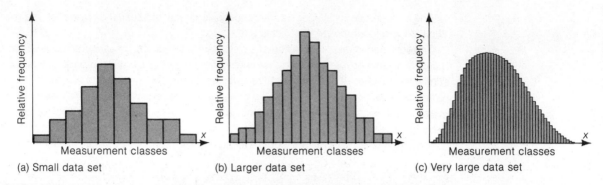

(a) Small data set   (b) Larger data set   (c) Very large data set

Figure 2.11 The Effect of the Size of a Data Set on the Outline of a Histogram

polygon, we form measurement classes precisely as for the frequency histogram. We then place a dot at the midpoint of each measurement class at a height equal to the frequency of the class. Then neighboring dots are connected by straight lines. The first and last dots are connected by a line segment to the horizontal axis at a point one-half class interval width below the lowest measurement class and above the highest measurement class, respectively.

Case Study 2.4
Appraising the Market Value of an Asset

The *market value* of an asset is the price negotiated by a willing buyer and a willing seller of the asset, each acting rationally in his or her own self-interest. The *book value* of an asset is the value of the asset as shown in its owner's accounting records. Generally speaking, it is the amount the owner paid for the asset, less any depreciation expense (Davidson, Stickney, & Weil, 1979).

Robert R. Sterling and Raymond Radosevich (1969) examined the hypothesis that accountants generally agree on the book value of a depreciable asset, but do not agree on its current market value. A questionnaire was prepared in which the installment purchase of a depreciable asset was described and the respondent was asked to determine the market value of the asset. The questionnaire also contained a series of questions relating to the book value of the asset. These questions enabled Sterling and Radosevich to calculate a book value for the asset for each of the respondents. The questionnaire was mailed to 500 randomly

Figure 2.12 Frequency Histograms for Book and Market Values as Assessed by CPA's

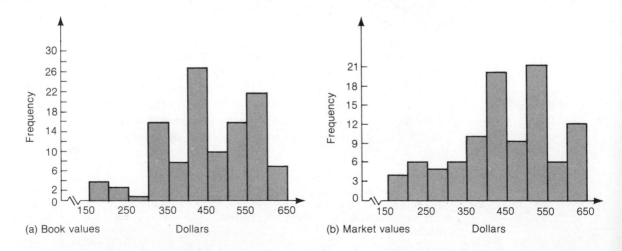

(a) Book values   (b) Market values

selected Certified Public Accountants (CPA's) in the United States; 114 and 99 usable book value and market value responses, respectively, were returned.

The frequency distributions of book values and market values obtained from the returned questionnaires appear in Figure 2.12. In both histograms, the intervals from $150 to $200 and $600 to $650 include all responses less than $200 and greater than $600, respectively. The histograms suggest disagreement among the CPA's as to both the book value and the market value of the asset. Thus, Sterling and Radosevich rejected the hypothesis that accountants tend to agree on book values and to disagree on market values.

Note that decisions based on a visual comparison of histograms are risky because they are subject to an unknown probability of error. For example, we might wonder whether disagreement among the CPA's really exists or whether the difference we see in the histograms is due to random variation that would be present from sample to sample. We will begin to answer questions of this type in Chapter 7.

Exercises 2.27–2.34

Learning the Mechanics

2.27 One of the three basic operating units in the gas industry is the producer who explores and drills for the gas. Recently, producers have experienced sharp cost increases. To offset these increases, the producers charge higher prices at the wellhead when drilling. The following is a sample of wellhead prices (in cents per thousand cubic feet) for twenty-five gas producers last year:

47	53	58	52	55
56	57	54	49	57
62	51	54	59	61
60	62	53	57	63
58	59	60	58	56

a. Construct a relative frequency histogram for the data. Use six class intervals, each with a width of 3¢. Begin the first interval at 46.5.

b. What proportion of wellhead prices exceeds 55¢? Now examine the total area under the relative frequency histogram. What proportion of this area lies to the right of 55¢?

c. Explain the correspondence between areas under the relative frequency histogram and relative frequencies.

2.28 The annual incomes for thirty randomly selected secretaries are recorded below (in thousands of dollars):

9.8	10.1	13.2	15.4	10.9	13.6
11.2	9.7	12.6	10.3	11.0	17.6
8.9	9.4	8.9	10.6	10.4	10.9
10.5	10.2	11.8	8.1	12.1	12.0
13.2	12.2	12.4	14.5	10.5	9.7

Construct a relative frequency histogram for the data. Use a class interval width equal to 1.2, and use 8.05 as the lower boundary of the first class. The intervals will then be 8.05–9.25, 9.25–10.45, etc.

2.29 A large company is interested in determining the length of service of its employees. Twenty-five employees are randomly chosen, and the length of service (in years) is recorded for each. The data are as follows:

3.1	1.8	6.4	10.2	11.2
15.6	11.6	6.8	1.5	2.9
3.4	7.2	0.5	7.7	8.4
0.7	3.9	8.2	8.0	5.5
10.3	12.1	3.9	0.9	4.3

Construct a relative frequency histogram for the data.

2.30 Twenty-four economists were asked to project the percentage change in the Consumer Price Index between now (September) and January 1 next year. The following are their projections:

+ 2%	− 5%	+ 7%	+ 4%	+ 4%	+ 0%
+1%	+ 3%	− 1%	− 1%	− 2%	− 2%
+ 4%	− 1%	+ 5%	+ 6%	+ 6%	+ 5%
+ 2%	+ 6%	+ 8%	+ 12%	+ 3%	− 4%

a. Construct a relative frequency histogram for the data.
b. How might you summarize these twenty-four predictions without using a graph or a table?

Applying the Concepts

2.31 Considering the climate, is it economically feasible to start an orange grove in northern Florida? If the temperature falls below 32°F, oil-burning smudge pots must be lit to keep the orange trees from freezing. Suppose a prospective grower decides that a grove would be economically feasible if the pots have to be lit an average of 15 days or less each year. The grower selects 20 years since 1900 at random and obtains the total number of days per year that the temperature fell below 32°F:

20	15	13	25	12	13	18
14	6	13	9	14	16	10
28	16	17	12	11	15	

a. Construct a relative frequency histogram for the data.
b. Based on the sample data, estimate the proportion of years in which the pots have to be lit 15 days or less. [*Note:* We will show you how to evaluate the reliability of this estimate in Chapter 8.]

2.32 In order to better understand the interactions that take place between salespeople and customers, Ronald P. Willett and Allan L. Pennington (1966) monitored the interactions of appliance salespeople and customers on the floor of a large department store. Part of their research involved observing the length of time customers and salespeople interacted prior to the close of the sale or the departure of the customer. The data below, adapted from the article, are the lengths of time (in minutes) from the first customer–salesperson contact to the close of the sale or the customer's departure for 132 customers who completed their appliance purchase either at the time they were observed or within the following 2 weeks. Instances where a purchase was made by the customer at the time he or she was observed are denoted with an asterisk.

1.0*	33.3	37.0	40.1	6.0*	1.7	4.5*	3.0	5.1*	7.4*
0.7	15.0*	9.7	27.2*	10.9	18.7*	13.3*	30.0*	41.3*	44.4*
15.0	12.3	7.0*	16.2	7.4*	17.6*	14.9	15.1*	32.2	1.9*
5.4*	8.4	8.1*	15.5	14.0*	40.0	6.1	28.7	38.1	30.5
7.6	7.9	4.1*	25.4*	12.2*	22.3	7.8*	29.2	30.5	34.6*
7.0*	10.3	10.0*	21.9	0.4*	25.6*	3.3	26.4*	39.2*	42.3
1.1	10.1*	41.6	17.4*	14.9	20.1*	9.0*	27.7	42.1	48.6
11.1	31.8	11.0*	25.1*	12.0*	16.9*	26.0	27.7	47.6*	35.1
15.0*	35.4	49.1*	30.0*	14.2	19.2*	39.9	23.0	43.1	38.2
12.8*	10.9*	13.0	20.6*	7.7	50.1	8.0*	24.8	35.0*	8.1*
118.4	8.9*	77.1	60.2*	105.2*	11.0	15.9	20.1*	3.2	8.8
18.0*	0.8	7.9*	12.5	69.1	11.1	30.0	12.4	1.5	14.2*
17.7*	0.9	13.5	8.4	81.0	10.5	26.2	18.4	6.0	15.9
66.1*	98.2								

a. Construct a relative frequency histogram for each of the following data sets:
  (1) The complete set of 132 times
  (2) The set of times associated with customers who made appliance purchases at the time they were being observed
  (3) The set of times asssociated with customers who made the appliance purchases at a later date

b. Describe any differences you detect between the histograms of parts a(2) and a(3).

c. Suggest possible explanations for the differences you noted in part b.

2.33 The ability to fill a customer's order on time depends to a great extent on being able to estimate how long it will take to produce the product in question. In most production processes, the time required to complete a particular task will be shorter each time the task is undertaken. Furthermore, it has been observed that in most cases the task time will decrease at a decreasing rate the more times the task is undertaken. Thus, in order to estimate how long it will take to produce a particular product, a manufacturer may want to study the relationship between production time per unit and the number of units that have been produced. The line or curve characterizing this relationship is called a *learning curve* (Chase & Aquilano, 1977). Twenty-five employees, all of whom were performing the same production task for the tenth time, were observed. Each person's task-completion time (in minutes) was recorded. The same twenty-five employees were observed again the thirtieth time they performed the same task and the fiftieth time they performed the task. The resulting completion times are as shown in the table.

TENTH PERFORMANCE		THIRTIETH PERFORMANCE		FIFTIETH PERFORMANCE	
15	19	16	11	10	8
21	20	10	10	5	10
30	22	12	13	7	8
17	20	9	12	9	7
18	19	7	8	8	8
22	18	11	20	11	6
33	17	8	7	12	5
41	16	9	6	9	6
10	20	5	9	7	4
14	22	15	10	6	15
18	19	10	10	8	7
25	24	11	11	14	20
23		9		9	

a. Construct frequency histograms for each of the three data sets.

b. Compare the histograms. Does it appear that the relationship between task completion time and the number of times the task is performed is in agreement with the observations noted above about production processes in general? Explain.

2.34 Construct relative frequency histograms for each of the two data sets in Exercise 2.24. Compare them with each other and with the corresponding stem and leaf displays of Exercise 2.24. Do they convey the same information about the data sets? Explain.

2.6 Cumulative Relative Frequency Distributions (Optional)

A *cumulative relative frequency distribution,* another graphical method for describing quantitative data sets, is shown for the twenty-nine computer price-earnings ratios (Table 2.4) in Figure 2.13.

The cumulative relative frequency histogram is constructed in the same manner as the relative frequency histogram except that the height of the rectangle constructed over an interval is the proportion of all observations less than or equal to those in a particular class. If the classes are numbered 1, 2, 3, . . . , from the smallest to the largest values of x, then the cumulative frequency for class 3 would equal the sum of the class frequencies corresponding to classes 1, 2, and 3:

Cumulative frequency for class 3 $= f_1 + f_2 + f_3$

Figure 2.13 Cumulative Relative Frequency Histogram for the Computer Price-Earnings Ratios in Table 2.4

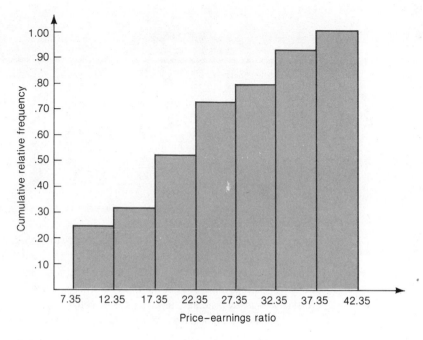

Similarly,

$$\text{Cumulative relative frequency for class 3} = \frac{f_1 + f_2 + f_3}{n}$$

where n is the total number of measurements in the sample.

Definition 2.7

The *class cumulative frequency* for a given class, say class i, is equal to the sum of the class frequencies up to and including the frequency for class i, i.e.,

Class cumulative frequency for class $i = f_1 + f_2 + \cdots + f_i$

Definition 2.8

The *class cumulative relative frequency* for a given class, say class i, is equal to the class cumulative frequency divided by the total number n of measurements, i.e.,

$$\text{Class cumulative relative frequency for class } i = \frac{\text{Class cumulative frequency}}{n}$$

The cumulative frequencies and cumulative relative frequencies can be calculated by adding two more columns to a table used to tabulate and calculate the class frequencies and class relative frequencies. For example, Table 2.6, which was used to calculate the relative

Table 2.7

Cumulative Frequencies and
Cumulative Relative
Frequencies for the Price-
Earnings Ratios

CLASS NUMBER	MEASUREMENT CLASS	CLASS FREQUENCY	CLASS CUMULATIVE FREQUENCY	CLASS RELATIVE FREQUENCY	CLASS CUMULATIVE RELATIVE FREQUENCY
1	7.35–12.35	7	7	7/29 = .241	7/29 = .241
2	12.35–17.35	2	9	2/29 = .069	9/29 = .310
3	17.35–22.35	6	15	6/29 = .207	15/29 = .517
4	22.35–27.35	6	21	6/29 = .207	21/29 = .724
5	27.35–32.35	2	23	2/29 = .069	23/29 = .793
6	32.35–37.35	4	27	4/29 = .138	27/29 = .931
7	37.35–42.35	2	29	2/29 = .069	29/29 = 1.000
	Total	29		1.000	

frequencies for the computer stock price-earnings ratios, is reproduced with the two new columns (the shaded columns) in Table 2.7.

You can see that the cumulative relative frequency for a class is calculated by summing the frequencies of all classes up to and including that particular class and dividing by the total number of measurements, $n = 29$. Note also that the cumulative relative frequency for a particular class is always larger than that for the class to its left. As a result, the cumulative relative frequency histogram always rises as you move to the right. Finally, when you reach the last class, the cumulative relative frequency will equal 1.

How to Construct a Cumulative Relative Frequency Distribution

1. Add two columns to the table used to calculate the class relative frequencies: a column for the class cumulative frequency and one for the class cumulative relative frequency.

2. Calculate the cumulative frequency and the cumulative relative frequency for each class.

3. Construct a graph by plotting the class cumulative relative frequency as a rectangle over the corresponding measurement class.

**Exercises
2.35–2.38**

Learning the Mechanics

2.35 Use the relative frequency distribution you prepared for Exercise 2.27 to construct a cumulative relative frequency distribution.

2.36 Use the relative frequency distribution you prepared for Exercise 2.28 to construct a cumulative relative frequency distribution.

2.37 Use the relative frequency distribution you prepared for Exercise 2.29 to construct a cumulative relative frequency distribution.

Applying the Concepts

2.38 Refer to the cumulative relative frequency distribution from Exercise 2.36.

a. Find the proportion of the thirty annual incomes that are less than $14,050.

b. Find the proportion that exceed $14,050.

2.7 Distorting the Truth with Pictures (Optional)

While it may be true in telling a story that a picture is worth a thousand words, it is also true that pictures can be used to convey a colored and distorted message to the viewer. So the old adage "Let the buyer (reader) beware" applies. Examine relative frequency histograms and, in general, all graphical descriptions with care.

We will mention a few of the pitfalls to watch for when analyzing a chart or graph. But first we should mention the *time series graph,* which is often the object of distortion. This type of graph records the behavior of some business variable over time, with the business variable plotted on the vertical axis and the time plotted on the horizontal axis. Examples of business variables commonly graphed as time series abound: economic indexes, profit, sales, supply, demand, etc. We will treat the subject of time series more completely in Chapters 13 and 14. For now, we will simply use some time series graphs to demonstrate several ways pictures may be distorted.

One common way to change the impression conveyed by a graph is to change the scale on the vertical axis, the horizontal axis, or both. For example, if you want to show that the change in firm A's market share over time is moderate, you could pack in a large number of units per inch on the vertical axis. That is, make the distance between successive units on the vertical scale small, as shown in Figure 2.14. You can see that the change in the firm's market share over time appears to be minimal.

Figure 2.14 Firm A's Market Share from 1979 to 1984—Packed Vertical Axis

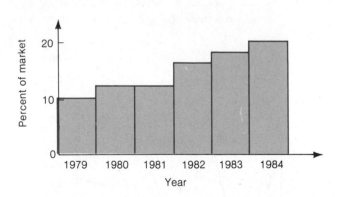

To make the changes in firm A's market share appear large, you could increase the distance between successive units on the vertical axis. That is, you stretch the vertical axis by graphing only a few units per inch, as shown in Figure 2.15 (page 46). The telltale sign of stretching is a long vertical axis, but this is often hidden by starting the vertical axis at some

Figure 2.15 Firm A's Market Share from 1979 to 1984 — Stretched Vertical Axis

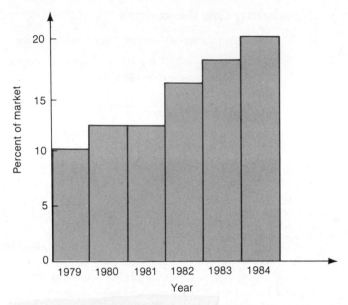

point above 0, as shown in Figure 2.16(a). Or, the same effect can be achieved by using a broken line for the vertical axis, as shown in Figure 2.16(b).

Stretching the horizontal axis (increasing the distance between successive units) may also lead you to incorrect conclusions. For example, Figure 2.17(a) depicts rental income in the United States from the first quarter of 1978 to the first quarter of 1980. If you increase the length of the horizontal axis, as in Figure 2.17(b), the change in the rental income over time seems to be less pronounced.

The changes in categories indicated by a bar chart can also be emphasized or deemphasized by stretching or shrinking the vertical axis. Another method of achieving visual distortion

Figure 2.16 Daily Stock Sales on the New York Stock Exchange from May to July 1979

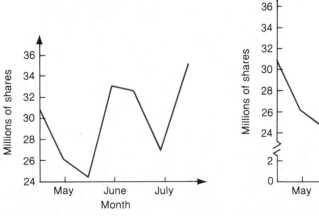

(a) Vertical axis started at a point greater than 0

(b) Gap in vertical axis

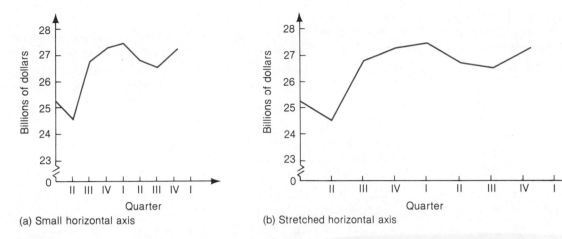

(a) Small horizontal axis

(b) Stretched horizontal axis

Figure 2.17 Rental Income from the First Quarter of 1978 to the First Quarter of 1980

with bar charts is by making the width of the bars proportional to their height. For example, look at the bar chart in Figure 2.18(a), which depicts the percentage of a year's total automobile sales attributable to each of the four major manufacturers. Now suppose we make the width as well as the height grow as the market share grows. This is shown in Figure 2.18(b). The reader may tend to equate the *area* of the bars with the relative market share of each manufacturer. In fact, the true relative market share is proportional only to the height of the bars.

Sometimes, as noted by Zelazny (1975), we do not need to manipulate the graph to distort the impression it creates. Modifying the verbal description that accompanies the graph can change the interpretation that will be made by the viewer. Figure 2.19 provides a good illustration of this ploy.

We have presented only a few of the ways that graphs can be used to convey misleading pictures of business phenomena. However, the lesson is clear. Examine all graphical descriptions of data with care. Particularly, check the axes and the size of the units on each axis. Ignore visual changes and concentrate on the actual numerical changes indicated by the graph or chart.

Figure 2.18 Relative Share of the Automobile Market for Each of Four Major Manufacturers

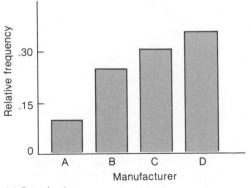

(a) Bar chart

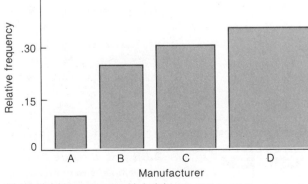

(b) Width of bars grows with height

Figure 2.19 Changing the Verbal Description to Change a Viewer's Interpretation
Source: Reprinted by permission of the publisher, from "Grappling with Graphics," by Gene Zelazny, *Management Review*, Oct. 1975, p. 7. © 1975 by AMACOM, a division of American Management Associations. All rights reserved.

Production continues to decline for second year

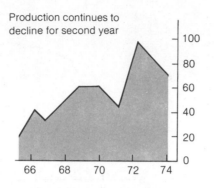

For our production, we need not even change the chart, so we can't be accused of fudging the data. Here we'll simply change the title so that for the Senate subcommittee, we'll indicate that we're not doing as well as in the past. . . .

1974: 3rd best year for production

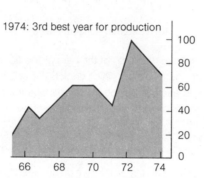

Whereas for the general public, we'll tell them that we're still in the prime years.

Summary

Business data can be classified as one of two types: *qualitative* or *quantitative*. In a qualitative data set each observation falls into one of a set of categories, whereas in a quantitative data set each observation is measured on a numerical scale.

Since we want to use sample data to make inferences about the population from which it is drawn, it is important for us to be able to describe the data. Graphical methods are important and useful tools for describing both types of data. The *bar chart* and *pie chart* are useful graphical methods for describing qualitative data. *Stem and leaf displays* and *relative frequency histograms* are graphical techniques used to describe quantitative data sets.

Our ultimate goal is to use the sample to make inferences about the population. We must be wary of using graphical techniques to accomplish this goal, since they do not lend themselves to a measure of reliability for an inference. Therefore, we need to develop numerical measures to describe a data set. This is the purpose of the next chapter.

Supplementary Exercises 2.39 – 2.54

[*Note: Starred (*) exercises refer to optional sections in this chapter.*]

2.39 According to estimates of the International Data Corporation, 85,000 word processing keyboards were sold by U.S. manufacturers in 1979. The table shows each manufacturer's market share. Construct a relative frequency bar chart for the data.

COMPANY	MARKET SHARE	COMPANY	MARKET SHARE
Artec	1%	Wang	16%
Wordstream	1%	NBI	4%
Four-Phase	2%	Vydec	4%
A.B. Dick	2%	Lexitron	4%
Digital Equipment	3%	Olivetti	4%
CPT	4%	3M	3%
Xerox	4%	Burroughs	3%
AM International	6%	Datapoint	2%
IBM	8%	Micom	1%
Lanier/AES	13%	Others	15%

Source: *Fortune,* Sept. 22, 1980, p. 56.

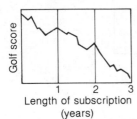

Golf score

Length of subscription
(years)

1   2   3

*2.40 A graph similar to the one shown here appeared in a recent advertisement for a well-known golf magazine. One person might interpret the graph's message as being the longer you subscribe to the magazine, the better golfer you should become. Another person might interpret it as indicating that if you subscribe for 3 years, your game should improve dramatically.

a. Explain why the graph can be interpreted in more than one way.

b. How could the graph be altered to rectify the current distortion?

2.41 Classify the following examples of data as either qualitative or quantitative.

a. The style of music preferred by thirty randomly selected radio listeners

b. The length of time it takes each of fifteen telephone installers to hook up a wall telephone

c. The population of each of ten randomly selected cities in the United States

2.42 A questionnaire sent to the chief executives of the country's 500 largest industrial corporations and commercial banking companies by *Fortune* magazine revealed the information given in the table concerning their educational backgrounds. Construct a relative frequency bar chart for the data.

LEVEL OF EDUCATION	PERCENT
High school or less	4.5
Attended college	9.3
College graduate	27.9
Postgraduate study	18.6
Master's degree	24.2
Doctorate	15.5

Source: "A Group Profile of the *Fortune* 500 Chief Executive," May 1976.

*2.43 Construct a pie chart for the data in Exercise 2.42.

*2.44 If it is not examined carefully, the graphical description of U.S. peanut production shown at the top of the next page can be misleading.

Source: *Gainesville Sun,* Sept. 11, 1976.

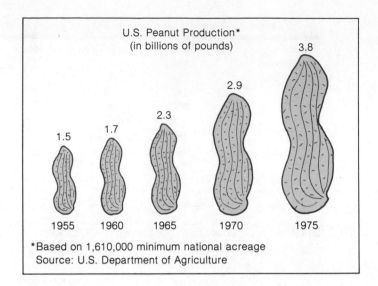

U.S. Peanut Production*
(in billions of pounds)

3.8

2.9

2.3

1.7

1.5

1955   1960   1965   1970   1975

*Based on 1,610,000 minimum national acreage
Source: U.S. Department of Agriculture

a. Explain why the graph may mislead some readers.

b. Construct an undistorted graph of U.S. peanut production for the given years.

2.45 The following is a list of the lengths (in inches) of thirty randomly selected golf tees produced by a machine designed to produce tees 1.5 inches long:

1.49	1.47	1.52	1.50	1.51	1.54
1.55	1.52	1.48	1.49	1.50	1.51
1.51	1.50	1.53	1.54	1.52	1.55
1.51	1.50	1.50	1.49	1.51	1.57
1.51	1.53	1.47	1.50	1.51	1.49

Construct a relative frequency histogram for the data.

*2.46 Refer to Exercise 2.45. Construct a cumulative frequency distribution and a cumulative relative frequency distribution for the data on tee lengths.

*2.47 In experimenting with a new technique for imprinting paper napkins with designs, names, etc., a paper products company discovered that four different results were possible:
(A) Imprint successful
(B) Imprint smeared
(C) Imprint off-center to the left
(D) Imprint off-center to the right
To test the reliability of the technique, they imprinted 1,000 napkins and obtained the results shown in the graph (letters defined as above).

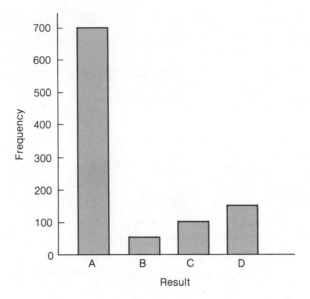

a. What type of graphical tool is the figure?

b. What information does the graph convey to you?

c. From the information provided by the graph, how might you numerically describe the reliability of the imprinting technique?

*2.48 On a recent Friday, six of the major luxury hotels in Atlanta reported that the following number of rooms were occupied:

HOTEL	NUMBER OF ROOMS OCCUPIED
Atlanta Hilton	801
Fairmont	389
Hyatt Regency	699
Marriott	542
Omni International	521
Peachtree Plaza	1,002

a. Construct a relative frequency bar chart for the data.

b. Is it possible to determine which hotel had the greatest percentage of its rooms filled on that Friday? Explain.

c. What other information about the hotels would make the data more meaningful?

*2.49 Businesses planning international expansion should be aware of the impending surge in the population of the world. It took until 1800 for the world's population to reach 1 billion. But between 1984 and 2000, the population is expected to grow from 4.6 billion to 6.1 billion.

That's a jump of 1.5 billion in just 16 years. The table describes the expected increase in more detail.

LOCATION	POPULATION (MILLIONS)	
	1984	*2000*
Africa	513	851
Asia	2,730	3,564
Europe	489	511
Latin America	390	564
North America	259	302
Oceania	24	29
USSR	272	309
Total	4,677	6,130

Source: *U.S. News & World Report,* Jan. 9, 1984, p. 53.

a. Construct two relative frequency bar charts, one for the 1984 data and one for the 2000 data.
b. Use the information on your bar charts to describe the pattern of shifts in population concentrations that are expected between 1984 and 2000.

*2.50

Regional Share of Single Family Housing Starts in the United States
Source: U.S. Bureau of the Census, *Statistical Abstract of the United States: 1979.*

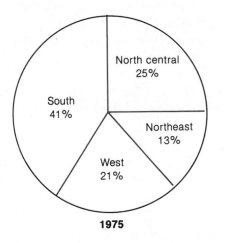

1975

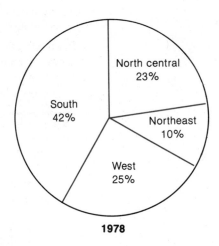

1978

a. What type of graphical tool is shown here?
b. What are the figures attempting to describe?
c. Suppose you were given the number of housing starts for each region in 1975 and 1978. Explain how you would construct the above figures using this information.
d. Compare the two figures.

2.51 Use one of the graphical methods presented in this chapter to depict the data set given in the table.

RENT ($)	PERCENT OF RENTERS IN EACH RENT CLASS
Less than 80	8
80 – 99	5
100 – 119	7
120 – 149	12
150 – 199	26
200 – 299	32
300 and over	10

Source: U.S. Bureau of the Census, *Statistical Abstract of the United States: 1979.*

*2.52 One measure of the value of the equity of a firm is the total value of the stock issued by the firm. This total is determined by multiplying the number of shares of stock issued by the current market value of a share of stock. In a recent survey commissioned by *Business Week* and conducted by Louis Harris & Associates, top executives of more than 600 U.S. corporations were asked the following:

Question: Do you feel that the current price of your company's stock is an accurate indicator of the real value of your company? If not, does the stock price undervalue the company or overvalue it?

RESPONSE	PERCENTAGE OF SAMPLE
Assigns real value	32%
Undervalues	60%
Overvalues	2%
Not sure	6%

Source: *Business Week,* Feb. 20, 1984, p. 14.

a. Construct a pie chart for the data.
b. Assume the Harris organization received responses from 700 executives. Construct a frequency bar chart for the above data.

2.53 A manufacturer of industrial wheels is losing many profitable orders because of the long time it takes the firm's marketing, engineering, and accounting departments to develop price quotes for potential customers. To remedy this problem the firm's management would like to set guidelines for the length of time each department should spend developing price quotes. To help develop these guidelines, fifty requests for price quotes were randomly selected from the set of all price quotes made last year; the processing time was determined for each price quote for each department. These times are displayed in the table. Notice that the price quotes are also classified by whether they were "lost" (i.e., whether or not the customer placed an order after receiving the price quote).

Price Quote Processing Times (in Days)

REQUEST NUMBER	MARKETING	ENGINEERING	ACCOUNTING	LOST?	REQUEST NUMBER	MARKETING	ENGINEERING	ACCOUNTING	LOST?
1	7.0	6.2	0.1	No	26	0.6	2.2	0.5	No
2	0.4	5.2	0.1	No	27	6.0	1.8	0.2	No
3	2.4	4.6	0.6	No	28	5.8	0.6	0.5	No
4	6.2	13.0	0.8	Yes	29	7.8	7.2	2.2	Yes
5	4.7	0.9	0.5	No	30	3.2	6.9	0.1	No
6	1.3	0.4	0.1	No	31	11.0	1.7	3.3	No
7	7.3	6.1	0.1	No	32	6.2	1.3	2.0	No
8	5.6	3.6	3.8	No	33	6.9	6.0	10.5	Yes
9	5.5	9.6	0.5	No	34	5.4	0.4	8.4	No
10	5.3	4.8	0.8	No	35	6.0	7.9	0.4	No
11	6.0	2.6	0.1	No	36	4.0	1.8	18.2	Yes
12	2.6	11.3	1.0	No	37	4.5	1.3	0.3	No
13	2.0	0.6	0.8	No	38	2.2	4.8	0.4	No
14	0.4	12.2	1.0	No	39	3.5	7.2	7.0	Yes
15	8.7	2.2	3.7	No	40	0.1	0.9	14.4	No
16	4.7	9.6	0.1	No	41	2.9	7.7	5.8	No
17	6.9	12.3	0.2	Yes	42	5.4	3.8	0.3	No
18	0.2	4.2	0.3	No	43	6.7	1.3	0.1	No
19	5.5	3.5	0.4	No	44	2.0	6.3	9.9	Yes
20	2.9	5.3	22.0	No	45	0.1	12.0	3.2	No
21	5.9	7.3	1.7	No	46	6.4	1.3	6.2	No
22	6.2	4.4	0.1	No	47	4.0	2.4	13.5	Yes
23	4.1	2.1	30.0	Yes	48	10.0	5.3	0.1	No
24	5.8	0.6	0.1	No	49	8.0	14.4	1.9	Yes
25	5.0	3.1	2.3	No	50	7.0	10.0	2.0	No

a. Use a graphical technique to describe each of the following:
   (1) The processing time of the marketing department
   (2) The processing time of the engineering department
   (3) The processing time of the accounting department
   (4) The total processing time for individual price quotes
b. Using your results from part a, develop "maximum processing time" guidelines for each department that, if followed, will help the firm reduce the number of lost orders.

*2.54 Referring to Exercise 2.53, construct a cumulative frequency distribution for the total processing time data set. It is said that a frequency distribution answers the question: How many measurements fell in class i? What question does your cumulative frequency distribution answer about the total processing time data set?

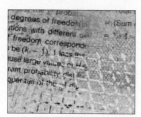

On Your Own . . .

Utilizing the data sources listed here, sources suggested by your instructor, or your own resourcefulness, find two real business-oriented data sets: one quantitative and one qualitative. Describe both data sets graphically using one or more of the graphical techniques presented in this chapter. These data sets and your graphs will be referred to in "On Your Own" sections in later chapters, so choose data sets of interest to you and be sure to keep copies of the data sets and your graphs.

Suggested Secondary Data Sources*

Board of Governors of the Federal Reserve System. *Federal Reserve Bulletin* (monthly).
Business Week (magazine).
Dun & Bradstreet's *Million dollar directory* (yearly).
Dun & Bradstreet's *Middle market directory* (yearly).
Forbes (magazine).
Fortune (magazine).
Standard & Poor's trade and securities statistics (monthly supplements).
Standard & Poor's Corporation. *Industry surveys.*
Target group index. Axiom Press (yearly).
U.S. Bureau of the Census. *Census of manufacturers.*
U.S. Bureau of the Census. *County business patterns.*
U.S. Bureau of the Census. *Statistical abstract of the United States* (yearly).
U.S. Department of Commerce, Office of Business Economics. *Business statistics.*
U.S. Department of Commerce, Office of Business Economics. *Survey of current business* (monthly).
U.S. Department of Labor. *Monthly labor review.*
U.S. Department of Labor, Bureau of Labor Statistics. *Employment and earnings.*
U.S. Department of Labor, Bureau of Labor Statistics. *National survey of professional, administrative, technical, and clerical pay.*
Wall Street Journal (daily).
Your state's statistical abstract.

Guides to Finding Secondary Data

Business Periodical Index.
Coman. *Sources of business information.*
Encyclopedia of business information sources. Detroit: Gale Research Co.
Funk and Scott Index of Corporations and Industries.
Funk and Scott Index International: Industries, countries, companies.
Guide to special issues and indexes of periodicals.
Houser and Leonard. *Government statistics for business use.*
New York Times Index.
Statistics sources, edited by Paul Wasserman. Detroit: Gale Research Co.
U.S. Bureau of the Census. *Directory of non-federal statistics for states and local areas.*
Wall Street Journal Index.
Your local chamber of commerce.

* *Primary data* are data you (or someone in your organization) collect for the study at hand. *Secondary data* are data collected by someone outside your organization for purposes other than the study at hand.

References

Bochnak, M. L. "An analysis of the residential condominium conversion market." Unpublished Ph.D. dissertation. School of Management, University of Minnesota, 1982.

Brigham, E. F. *Financial management theory and practice.* 3d ed. Chicago: Dryden Press, 1982. Chapter 13.

Chase, R. B., & Aquilano, N. J. *Production and operations management.* Rev. ed. Homewood, Ill.: Richard D. Irwin, 1977.

Chou, Ya-lun. *Statistical analysis.* 2d ed. New York: Holt, Rinehart and Winston, 1975. Chapter 2.

Davidson, S., Stickney, C. P., & Weil, R. L. *Financial accounting,* 2d ed. Chicago: Dryden Press, 1979.

Delehanty, G. E. "Office automation and the occupation structure." *Industrial Management Review,* Spring 1966, 99–109.

Dodd, P. "Merger proposals, management discretion, and stockholder wealth." *Journal of Financial Economics 8,* 105–137.

Eger, C. E. "Corporate mergers: An empirical analysis of the role of risky debt." Unpublished Ph.D. dissertation. School of Management, University of Minnesota, 1982.

Fogarty, D. W., & Hoffmann, T. R. *Production and inventory management.* Cincinnati, Ohio: South-Western, 1983.

Harper, D. V. *Transportation in America.* 2d ed. Englewood Cliffs, N.J.: Prentice-Hall, 1982. Chapter 5.

Huff, D. *How to lie with statistics.* New York: Norton, 1954.

Journal of Financial Economics, June 1982, *10,* 119.

MBA Executive, Jan. 1980, 3–14.

Neter, J., Wasserman, W., & Whitmore, G. A. *Applied statistics.* 2d ed. Boston: Allyn & Bacon, 1982. Chapter 3.

Schroeder, R. G. *Operations management.* New York: McGraw-Hill, 1981. Chapter 5.

Spiro, H. T. *Finance for the nonfinancial manager.* New York: Wiley, 1982. Chapter 17.

Sterling, R. R., & Radosevich, R. "A valuation experiment." *Journal of Accounting Research,* Spring 1969, 90–95.

"The 1984 federal budget." *Minneapolis Star and Tribune,* Feb. 1, 1983, 4a.

U.S. Bureau of the Census. *Statistical abstract of the United States: 1981.* 102d ed. Washington, D.C.: U.S. Government Printing Office, 1981.

Willett, R. P., & Pennington, A. L. "Customer and salesman: The anatomy of choice and influence in a retail setting." *Science, Technology and Marketing,* Proceedings of the 1966 Fall Conference of the American Marketing Association, Raymond M. Haas (ed.), pp. 598–616.

Winegar, K. "No longer a fad, fitness has grown into healthy obsession." *Minneapolis Star and Tribune,* Jan. 5, 1983, 1c.

Zelazny, G. "Grappling with graphics." *Management Review,* Oct. 1975, 7.

CHAPTER 3

Numerical Descriptive Measures

Where We've Been . . .

As we noted in Chapter 1, the goal of this course is to teach you how to use sample data to make inferences about a population data set. The first step in arriving at this goal is to learn how to describe a data set. As you learned in Chapter 2, graphical methods are advantageous because they convey a rapid and easily understood description of data sets.

Where We're Going . . .

There is a major drawback to using a graphical descriptive method for making an inference about a population from which a sample was selected. Namely, it is difficult to provide a measure of the reliability of the inference. How similar will the graphical description of the sample data be to the corresponding figure for the population? To answer this question, statisticians use one or more numbers to create a mental image of a data set. These numbers, called *numerical descriptive measures,* are the topic of this chapter.

Contents

Several types of numerical descriptive measures have been developed to characterize and help us create a mental picture of the relative frequency distribution of a data set. The two most important of these are measures of central tendency and measures of variation. Measures of central tendency are numbers computed from the data set that help us locate the "center" of a relative frequency distribution. Similarly, measures of variation describe the spread or dispersion of a set of data and therefore of its relative frequency distribution.

Numerical descriptive measures also have been devised to measure the *skewness* of a distribution (the tendency for a relative frequency distribution to stretch out in one direction) and the *kurtosis* (peakedness) of a distribution, as well as other characteristics of a data set. These measures do not play an important role in the statistical methods discussed in this text; thus, they are omitted from the discussion.

Numerical descriptive measures can be calculated for any data set, either for a sample or for a population. If statistical inference is our goal, as is often the case, we will ultimately use sample numerical descriptive measures to make inferences about the corresponding measures for the population.

3.1 The Mode: A Measure of Central Tendency

If you visualize a relative frequency distribution, one measure of central tendency that immediately comes to mind is the value of x that locates the peak of the distribution—that is, the value of x that occurs with the greatest frequency. This value of x is called the *mode*.

Definition 3.1
The *mode* is the measurement that occurs with greatest frequency in the data set.

Because it emphasizes data concentration, the mode has applications in marketing as well as in the description of large data sets collected by state and federal agencies. For example, a retailer of men's clothing would be interested in the modal neck size and sleeve length of potential customers. The modal income class of the laborers in the United States is of interest to the Labor Department. Thus, the mode provides a useful measure of central tendency for many business applications.

Unless the data set is rather large, the mode may not be very meaningful. For example, consider the price-earnings ratio measurements for the twenty-nine computer companies we used in the previous chapter. If you were to reexamine these data (presented in Table 2.4), you would find that only one of the twenty-nine measurements (11.4) is duplicated in this sample. All the other measurements appear with the same frequency (once). Thus, although there is only one mode for the sample, this information is of no practical use for data description. We can calculate a more meaningful mode by constructing a relative frequency histogram for the data. The interval containing the most measurements is called the *modal class* and the mode is taken to be the midpoint of this class interval.* Figure 3.1 shows the relative frequency histogram for the twenty-nine price-earnings ratios. The modal class, the

---

* There are several definitions for the mode of a relative frequency histogram. Our definition is one of the simplest, but it is adequate for an introductory discussion of the mode.

Figure 3.1 Histogram for Computer Price-Earnings Ratio Data: The Modal Class

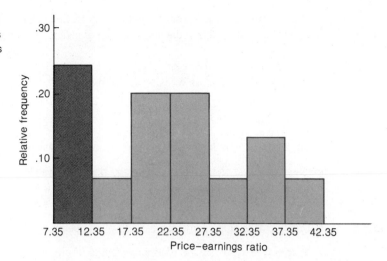

one corresponding to the interval 7.35 – 12.35 (darkly shaded in Figure 3.1), lies to the left side of the distribution. The mode is the midpoint of this interval; that is, $\frac{1}{2}(7.35 + 12.35) = 9.85$. In the sense that the mode measures data concentration, it provides a measure of central tendency of the data.

3.2 The Arithmetic Mean: A Measure of Central Tendency

The most popular and best understood measure of central tendency for a quantitative data set is the *arithmetic mean* (or simply the *mean*):

Definition 3.2

The *mean* of a set of quantitative data is equal to the sum of the measurements divided by the number of measurements contained in the data set.

Or, in nontechnical terms, the mean is the average value of the data set.

Before calculating the mean (or other numerical descriptive measures) of data sets, we present some shorthand notation that will simplify our calculation instructions. Remember that such notation is used for only one reason — to avoid having to repeat the same verbal descriptions over and over. If you mentally substitute the verbal definition of a symbol each time you read it, you will soon become accustomed to its use.

We will denote the measurements of a data set as follows:

$$x_1, x_2, x_3, \ldots, x_n$$

where x_1 is the first measurement in the data set, x_2 is the second measurement in the data set, x_3 is the third measurement in the data set, . . . , and x_n is the nth (and last) measurement in the data set. Thus, if we have five measurements in a set of data, we will write x_1, x_2, x_3, x_4, x_5 to represent the measurements. If the actual numbers are 5, 3, 8, 5, and 4, we have $x_1 = 5$, $x_2 = 3$, $x_3 = 8$, $x_4 = 5$, and $x_5 = 4$.

To calculate the mean of a set of measurements, we must sum them and divide by n, the number of measurements in the set. The sum of measurements $x_1, x_2, \ldots, x_n$ is

$$x_1 + x_2 + \cdots + x_n$$

To shorten the notation, we will write this sum as

$$x_1 + x_2 + \cdots + x_n = \sum_{i=1}^{n} x_i$$

where Σ is the symbol for the summation. Verbally translate $\sum_{i=1}^{n} x_i$ as follows: "The sum of the measurements, whose typical member is x_i, beginning with the member x_1 and ending with the member x_n." The typical member will always appear following the Σ, the subscript of the first member of the summation will always appear below the Σ symbol, and the subscript of the last member of the summation will always appear above the Σ. For example, $\sum_{i=2}^{5} x_i = x_2 + x_3 + x_4 + x_5$, where the typical element x_i follows the Σ symbol, the first element to appear in the sum is identified by the subscript 2 (shown below the Σ symbol), and the last element to appear in the sum is identified by the subscript 5 (shown above the Σ symbol).

Finally, we will denote the mean of a sample of measurements by $\bar{x}$ (read "x-bar"), and represent the formula for its calculation as follows:

$$\bar{x} = \frac{\sum_{i=1}^{n} x_i}{n}$$

Example 3.1   Calculate the mean of the following five sample measurements: 5, 3, 8, 5, 6

Solution   Using the definition of sample mean and the shorthand notation, we find

$$\bar{x} = \frac{\sum_{i=1}^{5} x_i}{5} = \frac{5 + 3 + 8 + 5 + 6}{5} = \frac{27}{5} = 5.4$$

       ∎

Example 3.2   Calculate the mean for the sample of twenty-nine computer stock price-earnings ratios of Table 2.4 (reproduced here):

18.8	8.6	26.5	12.6	29.4	7.4	37.3	27.7	11.4	10.3
23.6	35.5	19.0	38.6	14.3	17.9	35.3	23.8	25.6	22.5
20.1	10.7	19.2	18.4	41.4	11.4	33.1	11.9	26.1	

Solution   Using the above data, we have

$$\bar{x} = \frac{\sum_{i=1}^{29} x_i}{29} = \frac{18.8 + 23.6 + \cdots + 22.5}{29} = \frac{638.4}{29} = 22.01$$

Glancing at the data set, you can see that the smallest price-earnings ratio is 7.4, the largest is 41.4, and the mean, 22.01, falls near the middle of this data set. Investing equal amounts of money in each of these twenty-nine computer stocks would allow you to invest in companies with relatively low and relatively high price-earnings ratios. The mean price-earnings ratio for the group as a whole is 22.01. ▪

The sample mean will play an important role in accomplishing our objective of making inferences about populations based on sample information. For this reason, it is important to use a different symbol when we want to discuss the ***mean of a population*** of measurements —i.e., the mean of the entire set of measurements in which we are interested. We use the Greek letter μ (mu) for the population mean. We will adopt a general policy of using Greek letters to represent population numerical descriptive measures and Roman letters to represent corresponding descriptive measures for the sample.

$$\bar{x} = \text{Sample mean} \qquad \mu = \text{Population mean}$$

The sample mean, $\bar{x}$, will often be used to estimate (make an inference about) the population mean, μ. For example, the population of all computer stock price-earnings ratios has a mean equal to some value, μ. Our sample of twenty-nine price-earnings ratios has a mean of $\bar{x} = 22.01$. If, as is usually the case, we did not have access to the population of measurements, we could use $\bar{x}$ as an estimator or approximator for μ. Then we would need to know something about the reliability of our inference. That is, we would need to know how accurately we might expect $\bar{x}$ to estimate μ. In Chapter 8, we will find that this accuracy depends on two factors:

1. The size of the sample—the larger the sample, the more accurate the estimate will tend to be
2. The variability or spread of the data—all other factors remaining constant, the more variable the data, the less accurate the estimate

In summary, the mean provides a valuable measure of the central tendency for a set of measurements. It is a very common tool in business and economic research, and therefore the mean will be the focus of much of our discussion of inferential statistics.

Case Study 3.1

Hotels: A Rational
Method for
Overbooking

The most outstanding characteristic of the general hotel reservation system is the option of the prospective guest, without penalty, to change or cancel his reservation or even to "no-show" (fail to arrive without notice). Overbooking (taking reservations in excess of the hotel capacity) is practiced widely throughout the industry as a compensating economic measure. This has motivated our research into the problem of determining policies for overbooking which are based on some set of rational criteria.

So said Marvin Rothstein (1974) in an article that appeared in *Decision Sciences,* a journal published by the American Institute for Decision Sciences. In this paper Rothstein introduces a method for scientifically determining hotel booking policies and applies it to the booking problems of the 133-room Sheraton Pocono Inn at Stroudsburg, Pennsylvania.

From the Sheraton Pocono Inn's records, the number of reservations, walk-ins (people without reservations who expect to be accommodated), cancellations, and no-shows were tabulated for each day during the period August 1–28, 1971. The inn's records for this period included approximately 3,100 guest histories. From the tabulated data, the mean or average number of room reservations per day for each of the 7 days of the week were computed. These appear in Table 3.1. In applying his booking policy decision method to the Sheraton's data, Rothstein used the means listed in Table 3.1 to help portray the inn's demand for rooms.

Table 3.1

Mean Number of Room Reservations, August 1–28, 1971, 133 Rooms

SUNDAY	MONDAY	TUESDAY	WEDNESDAY	THURSDAY	FRIDAY	SATURDAY
138	126	149	160	150	150	169

The mean number of Saturday reservations during the period August 1–28, 1971, is 169. This may be interpreted as an estimate of μ, the mean number of rooms demanded via reservations (walk-ins also contribute to the demand for rooms) on a Saturday during 1971. If the reservation data for all Saturdays during 1971 had been tabulated, μ could have been computed. But, since only the August data are available, they were used to estimate μ. Can you think of some problems associated with using August's data to estimate the mean for the entire year?

Case Study 3.2

Measuring Investors' Reactions to a Corporate Selloff Announcement: The General Electric/ Utah International Case

In 1976, General Electric Company (GE) acquired Utah International Inc., an Australian mining company, in exchange for common stock valued at $2.17 billion. At the time, this was said to be the largest merger in U.S. history. In the Friday, January 28, 1983, edition of the *Wall Street Journal,* GE announced that it "agreed tentatively to sell most of its Utah International Inc. mining unit to an Australian natural resources company [Broken Hill Proprietary Co.] for $2.4 billion." When a parent firm sells a subsidiary, division, product line, or some other asset to another firm, the transaction is referred to as a *selloff* (or sometimes a *divestiture*). Payment is generally in the form of cash and/or marketable securities.

A question of interest to financial analysts with respect to GE's proposed selloff would be: How will investors interpret this information? As good news for GE? As bad news? Financial theory suggests that if investors perceive the announcement as good news, the stock's daily rate of return* will jump up on the day of the announcement or the following day, then subside to the preannouncement level. Downward movement at the time of the announcement is an indication that the selloff is viewed as bad news. No movement suggests that the announcement contained little if any new information for investors.

Before examining GE's rates of return during the period in question, it is helpful to note that in studying stock prices (or rates of return) we make a distinction between (1) sampling from a population of prices and (2) sampling a consecutive series of prices. In the first case, we sample from a finite set of *existing* prices. For example, we might draw a sample of 20 closing

---

* If no dividends have been declared on the day in question, a stock's rate of return on day t is defined as $(P_t - P_{t-1})/P_{t-1}$, where P_t is the closing price of the stock on day t and P_{t-1} is its closing price the day before.

prices from the last 100 closing prices of GE stock. This sample provides information about the population of 100 prices. In the second case, we think of prices as being generated or produced over time by a theoretical price-generating *process* in the same sense that manufactured goods are produced over time by a production *process.* Thus, when we observe a consecutive series of prices, we say we are sampling from the price-generating process. For example, we might decide to sample the next 20 closing prices of GE stock. This sample will provide information about the characteristics of the price-generating process.

One method that can be used to examine the effects of GE's announcement on GE's rates of return involves sampling GE's sequence of closing prices from, say, 20 days before the announcement to 20 days after the announcement. From these data, the daily rates of return over this period can be calculated. Then, GE's mean rate of return just prior to the announcement, $\bar{r}_1$, can be obtained, as well as the mean rate of return following the announcement, $\bar{r}_3$. These means can be compared to the rate of return on the announcement day (and/or the mean rate of return for, say, the announcement day and the day following, $\bar{r}_2$) to examine the effect the announcement had on GE's rate of return. Table 3.2 shows both the rates of return during the period in question and the sample means described above. The fact that $\bar{r}_1$ and $\bar{r}_3$ are of approximately the same magnitude, while $\bar{r}_2$ is much larger, suggests that GE's selloff announcement was taken as good news by investors. For other more sophisticated approaches to using mean rates of return to study the effects of announcements such as GE's, see Brown and Warner (1980).

Table 3.2

Rates of Return on GE's Common Stock

DATE	RATE OF RETURN		DATE	RATE OF RETURN	
12/31/82	−.0078		1/28/83*	.0459	$\bar{r}_2 = .0424$
1/3/83	−.0329		1/31/83	.0389	
1/4/83	.0204		2/1/83	−.0254	
1/5/83	−.0067		2/2/83	−.0062	
1/6/83	.0255		2/3/83	−.0025	
1/7/83	.0131		2/4/83	.0050	
1/10/83	.0259		2/7/83	.0249	
1/11/83	−.0126		2/8/83	−.0121	
1/12/83	−.0038		2/9/83	.0074	
1/13/83	−.0077		2/10/83	.0110	
1/14/83	−.0052	$\bar{r}_1 = -.0017$	2/11/83	−.0084	$\bar{r}_3 = .0026$
1/17/83	.0026		2/14/83	.0097	
1/18/83	.0000		2/15/83	−.0169	
1/19/83	−.0091		2/16/83	−.0024	
1/20/83	−.0065		2/17/83	.0000	
1/21/83	−.0118		2/18/83	.0197	
1/24/83	−.0200		2/22/83	.0012	
1/25/83	−.0163		2/23/83	.0301	
1/26/83	−.0080		2/24/83	.0164	
1/27/83	.0270		2/25/83	−.0011	
			2/28/83	−.0014	

* Date selloff plans were announced in the *Wall Street Journal.*

3.3
The Median: Another Measure of Central Tendency

Another very important measure of central tendency is the *median* of a set of measurements:

Definition 3.3

The *median* of a data set is a number such that half the measurements fall below the median and half fall above.

The median is of most value in describing large data sets. If the data set is characterized by a relative frequency histogram (see Figure 3.2), the median is the point on the x-axis such that half the area under the histogram lies above the median and half lies below. [*Note:* In Section 2.5, we observed that the relative frequency associated with a particular interval on the x-axis is proportional to the area under the histogram that lies above the interval.]

Figure 3.2 Location of the Median

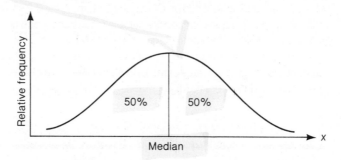

For a small, or even a large but finite, number of measurements, there may be many numbers that satisfy the property indicated in Figure 3.2. For this reason, we will arbitrarily calculate the median of a data set as follows:

Calculating a Median

Rank the n measurements in the data set from the smallest to the largest. The smallest will receive rank 1; the next largest, rank 2; . . . ; and the largest, rank n.

1. If the number, n, of measurements is odd, the median is the measurement in the middle of the ranking—i.e., the measurement with rank equal to $(n + 1)/2$.
2. If the number, n, of measurements is even, the median is the mean of the two middle measurements in the ranking—i.e., halfway between the measurement ranked $n/2$ and the measurement ranked $(n/2) + 1$.

Example 3.3 Consider the following sample of $n = 7$ measurements: 5, 7, 4, 5, 20, 6, 2

a. Calculate the median of this sample.
b. Eliminate the last measurement (the 2), and calculate the median of the remaining $n = 6$ measurements.

Solution   **a.** The seven measurements in the sample are first ranked in ascending order:

2, 4, 5, 5, 6, 7, 20

Since the number of measurements is odd, the median is the middle measurement. Thus, the median of this sample is 5.

b. After removing the 2 from the set of measurements, we rank the sample measurements in ascending order as follows:

4, 5, 5, 6, 7, 20

Now the number of measurements is even, so we average the middle two measurements. The median is $(5 + 6)/2 = 5.5$.   ■

In certain situations, the median may be a better measure of central tendency than the mean. In particular, the median is less sensitive than the mean to extremely large or small measurements. To illustrate, note that all but one of the measurements in Example 3.3a center about $x = 5$. The single large measurement, $x = 20$, does not affect the value of the median, 5, but it shifts the mean, $\bar{x} = 7$, to the right of most of the measurements.

As another example, if you were interested in computing a measure of central tendency of the incomes of a company's employees, the mean might be misleading. If all blue- and white-collar employees' incomes are included in the data set, the high incomes of a few executives will influence the mean more than the median. Thus, the median will provide a more accurate picture of the typical income for an employee. Similarly, the median yearly sales for a set of companies would locate the middle of the sales data. However, the very large yearly sales of a few companies would greatly influence the mean, making it deceptively large. That is, the mean could exceed a vast majority of the sample measurements, making it a misleading measure of central tendency.

For a numerical example, we have arranged the twenty-nine computer stock price-earnings ratios in ascending order in Table 3.3.

Table 3.3

Price-Earnings Ratio Data in Ascending Order

7.4	11.9	19.0	25.6	35.3
8.6	12.6	19.2	26.1	35.5
10.3	14.3	20.1	26.5	37.3
10.7	17.9	22.5	27.7	38.6
11.4	18.4	23.6	29.4	41.4
11.4	18.8	23.8	33.1	

Since the number of measurements is odd, the median equals the measurement with rank equal to $(n + 1)/2 = (29 + 1)/2 = 15$, i.e., 20.1.

Note that the median is smaller than the mean (22.01) for this sample. This fact indicates that the data are *skewed* to the right—i.e., that the measurements tend to *tail off* to the right. This is because the mean is affected more than the median by extreme (large or small) observations. Consequently, if a distribution tails out in one direction, the mean will shift toward this tail. This skewness is evident in Figure 3.3, where we show the mode, mean, and median for the price-earnings ratio data.

A comparison of the mean and the median gives us a general method for detecting skewness in data sets, as shown in the box.

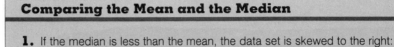

Comparing the Mean and the Median

1. If the median is less than the mean, the data set is skewed to the right:

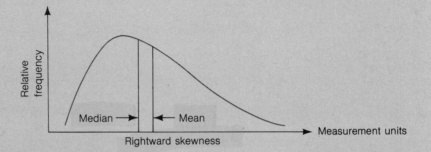

2. The median will equal the mean when the data set is symmetric:

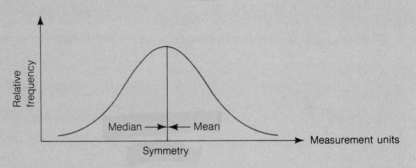

3. If the median is greater than the mean, the data set is skewed to the left:

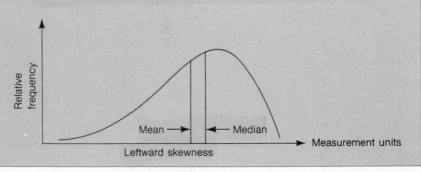

Figure 3.3 Computer Stock Price-Earnings Ratio Data: Mode, Mean, and Median

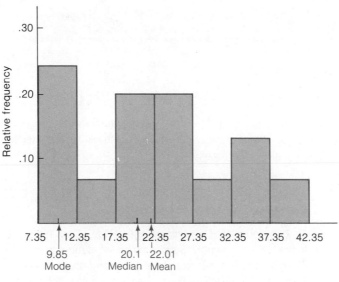

Price–earnings ratio

Case Study 3.3
The Delphi Technique for Obtaining a Consensus of Opinion

George T. Milkovich, Anthony J. Annoni, and Thomas A. Mahoney (1972) explain the delphi technique as follows:

> The delphi technique, a set of procedures originally developed by the Rand Corporation in the late 1940's, is designed to obtain the most reliable consensus of opinion of a group of experts. Essentially, the delphi is a series of intensive interrogations of each individual expert (by a series of questionnaires) concerning some primary question interspersed with controlled feedback. The procedures are designed to avoid direct confrontation of the experts with one another.
>
> The interaction among the experts is accomplished through an intermediary who gathers the data requests of the experts and summarizes them along with the experts' answers to the primary question. This mode of controlled interaction among the experts is a deliberate attempt to avoid the disadvantages associated with more conventional use of experts such as in round table discussions or direct confrontation of opposing views. The developers of the delphi argue the procedures are more conducive to independent thought and allow more gradual formulation to a considered opinion.

This article presents a study of the usefulness of the delphi procedure in projecting labor requirements in a low profit margin national retail firm. Seven company executives formed the panel of experts. Five questionnaires submitted at approximately 8-day intervals were used to interrogate the seven experts. On questionnaires 2–5, they were each asked the primary question: "How many buyers will the firm need 1 year from now?" Their individual responses along with the median response of the group for each questionnaire appear in Table 3.4.

Note that the median response increased from 35 on questionnaire 2 to 38 on questionnaires 4 and 5. This increase indicates an upward shift in the distribution of the experts' estimates as to the number of buyers the firm would need a year from now.

Table 3.4
Projected Demand
for Buyers

QUESTIONNAIRE	\[EXPERTS\] A	B	C	D	E	F	G	MEDIAN
2	55	35	33	35	55	33	32	35
3	45	35	41	35	41	34	32	35
4	45	38	41	35	41	34	34	38
5	45	38	41	35	45	34	34	38

One conclusion of the study was that the delphi technique provided closer estimates of the actual number of buyers (37) needed by the firm 1 year later than did other more conventional estimating techniques.

Exercises 3.1–3.10

Learning the Mechanics

3.1 According to *Consumers' Digest* (Nov.–Dec. 1980), sugar is the leading food additive in the U.S. food supply. Sugar may be listed more than once on a product's ingredient list since it goes by different names depending on its source (e.g., sucrose, corn sweetener, fructose, and dextrose). Thus, when you read a product's label you may have to total up the sugar in the product to see how much sweetener it contains. The table gives a list of candy bars and the percentage of sugar they contain relative to their weight.

BRAND	PERCENTAGE OF SUGAR BY WEIGHT	BRAND	PERCENTAGE OF SUGAR BY WEIGHT
Baby Ruth	23.7	Power House	30.6
Butterfinger	29.5	Bit-O-Honey	23.5
Mr. Goodbar	34.2	Chunky	38.4
Milk Duds	36.0	Milk Chocolate Covered	
Mello Mint	79.6	Raisinettes	24.7
M & M Plain Chocolate		Oh Henry!	31.2
Candies	52.2	Borden Cracker Jack	14.7
Mars Chocolate Almond	36.4	Good & Plenty Licorice	28.2
Milky Way	26.8	Nestle's Crunch	43.5
Marathon	36.7	Planter Jumbo Block	
Snickers	28.0	Peanut Candy	21.5
3 Musketeers	36.1	Switzer Licorice	8.4
Junior Mints	45.3	Switzer Red Licorice	2.8
Pom Poms	29.5	Tootsie Pop Drops	54.1
Sugar Babies	41.0	Tootsie Roll	21.1
Sugar Daddy	22.0	Fancy Fruit Lifesavers	77.6
Almond Joy	20.0	Spear-O-Mint Lifesavers	67.6

Source: *National Confectioners Association Brand Name Guide to Sugar* (Nelson Hall Paperback)
Secondary Source: *Consumers' Digest*, Nov.–Dec. 1980, p. 11.

a. Calculate the mean percentage of sugar per bar for the candy bars listed.
b. Find the median for the data set.

c. Construct a relative frequency histogram for the data set. Indicate the location of the mean and median of the data set on your histogram.

3.2 Revenues of the top 100 U.S. firms in the data processing industry grew from $55.6 billion in 1980 to $67.8 billion in 1981, an increase of 21.9%. Of these 100 firms, the revenues for the top seven manufacturers of microcomputers are shown in the table.

RANK	COMPANY	1981 REVENUES ($ millions)	1980 REVENUES ($ millions)	% CHANGE
1	Apple Computer Inc.	401.1	165.2	142.7
2	Tandy Corp.	293.0	149.6	95.8
3	Hewlett-Packard Co.	235.0	200.0	17.5
4	Commodore International Ltd.	140.0	104.0	34.6
5	Gould (SEL)	140.0	100.0	40.0
6	Cado Systems Corp.	68.2	50.6	34.7
7	Cromemco Inc.	59.0	45.0	31.1

Source: *Datamation,* June 1982, p. 116.

a. Calculate the mean and median percentage change in revenues for these seven firms.
b. Will the median of a data set always be equal to an actual value in the data set as was the case in part a? Explain.

3.3 Thirty stocks were selected from the New York Stock Exchange Composite Transactions Table published in the July 1, 1983, *Wall Street Journal.* These stocks are listed in the table (using the *Wall Street Journal* abbreviations) along with their closing prices on June 30, 1983, and the change in each closing price from June 29 to June 30.

STOCK	CLOSING PRICE	NET CHANGE	STOCK	CLOSING PRICE	NET CHANGE
ACF	$34\frac{1}{2}$	0	Kroger	$41\frac{5}{8}$	$+\frac{1}{2}$
Alcoa	37	$-\frac{7}{8}$	MCA	$39\frac{1}{2}$	$+\frac{1}{4}$
ATT	$63\frac{1}{2}$	$+\frac{3}{8}$	Munsng	$14\frac{5}{8}$	$-\frac{1}{4}$
Avon	$34\frac{1}{8}$	$+\frac{1}{8}$	NwstAir	$51\frac{1}{4}$	0
Bnk Am	$22\frac{5}{8}$	$+\frac{1}{4}$	PepsiCo	$35\frac{5}{8}$	$+\frac{3}{8}$
Boeing	$45\frac{3}{4}$	$-\frac{5}{8}$	Polarid	$30\frac{3}{4}$	$+\frac{5}{8}$
CBS	$66\frac{7}{8}$	$-\frac{1}{8}$	RepAir	$7\frac{5}{8}$	0
Chryslr	32	$+\frac{1}{8}$	Revlon	$35\frac{1}{4}$	0
Citicrp	$39\frac{1}{2}$	$+1$	Seagrm	$31\frac{7}{8}$	$+\frac{1}{8}$
ColgPal	$23\frac{1}{8}$	$+\frac{1}{8}$	SouPac	72	$+\frac{1}{2}$
DeltaAr	$42\frac{1}{2}$	$+\frac{1}{8}$	Tndycft	$19\frac{3}{8}$	$-\frac{3}{8}$
Exxon	$33\frac{3}{4}$	0	ToroCo	$12\frac{3}{8}$	$+\frac{3}{8}$
FdExp	$70\frac{1}{4}$	$-\frac{3}{4}$	USSteel	$24\frac{3}{8}$	0
GnMills	$55\frac{1}{4}$	$+\frac{3}{8}$	Upjohn	$64\frac{1}{4}$	$+\frac{5}{8}$
Hershy	$53\frac{3}{4}$	$+1\frac{1}{2}$	WinDix	$57\frac{1}{4}$	$+\frac{1}{2}$

a. Construct a relative frequency histogram for the net change in closing price for the sample of stocks.

b. Calculate the mean, median, and mode for the net change data and locate them on your histogram of part a.

c. According to your histogram of part a, what is the modal class of the net change data set?

3.4 The table lists the mean age for each team in the National Basketball Association (NBA) along with the number of players on each team at the start of the 1982–1983 season. What was the population mean age at the start of the 1982–1983 season? [*Hint:* $\sum_{i=1}^{n} x_i = n\bar{x}$]

TEAM	NUMBER OF PLAYERS	MEAN AGE	TEAM	NUMBER OF PLAYERS	MEAN AGE
1. Indiana	12	24.720	13. San Antonio	12	26.25
2. Portland	12	24.724	14. Los Angeles	13	26.42
3. Golden State	15	24.96	15. New York	14	26.45
4. Dallas	13	25.17	16. Cleveland	14	26.48
5. New Jersey	13	25.26	17. San Diego	13	26.71
6. Kansas City	12	25.27	18. Boston	12	26.94
7. Chicago	12	25.32	19. Seattle	11	27.09
8. Detroit	13	25.65	20. Atlanta	12	27.12
9. Philadelphia	12	25.96	21. Denver	11	27.59
10. Phoenix	13	26.10	22. Houston	12	29.21
11. Washington	13	26.10	23. Milwaukee	13	29.72
12. Utah	11	26.13			

Source: *Basketball Weekly,* Vol. 16, No. 5, Jan. 3, 1983, pp. 10–11.

Applying the Concepts

3.5 According to the American Automobile Association, as of July 1, 1983, the average price of self-service unleaded gasoline in the United States was 13.1¢ per gallon cheaper than the average price of full-service unleaded gas. The table lists the average price of full-service unleaded gas in each of a sample of twenty states:

STATE	PRICE	STATE	PRICE
Alaska	$1.160	New Hampshire	$1.324
Arkansas	1.336	New Jersey	1.190
California	1.479	New York	1.336
Connecticut	1.350	Oklahoma	1.348
Delaware	1.234	Oregon	1.309
Maine	1.306	Pennsylvania	1.271
Massachusetts	1.275	Rhode Island	1.310
Missouri	1.346	Texas	1.347
Montana	1.278	Utah	1.339
Nevada	1.449	Vermont	1.329

Source: *USA Today,* July 1, 1983, p. 4A.

a. Calculate the mean, median, and mode of this data set.

b. Eliminate the highest price from the data set and repeat part a. What effect does dropping this measurement have on the measures of central tendency calculated in part a?

c. Arrange the twenty prices in order from low to high. Next, eliminate the lowest two prices and the highest two prices from the data set and calculate the mean of the remaining prices. The result is called an *80% trimmed mean* since it is calculated using the central 80% of the values in the data set. An advantage of the trimmed mean is that it is not as sensitive as the arithmetic mean to extreme observations in the data set.

3.6 At the end of 1982, McDonald's had 7,300 restaurants and total sales for the year of $7.8 billion. Burger King had 3,400 restaurants and total sales of $2.4 billion. McDonald's opens new restaurants at the rate of 500 per year and Burger King at the rate of 200 per year (*Minneapolis Tribune,* July 3, 1983).

a. Calculate the average sales per restaurant for McDonald's in 1982 and compare it with the average sales per restaurant for Burger King in 1982.

b. On average, how many restaurants does McDonald's open per month? Per week? Per day?

3.7 Refer to Exercise 3.3. Find the mean closing price for the sample of stocks on June 29.

3.8 In 1972, Kroger Corporation, the second largest supermarket chain in the United States, made a major strategic decision. Instead of continuing to hold prices high and trying to attract customers with weekend specials and heavy advertising, Kroger decided to emphasize price competition all week long. Its new strategy involved selling "brand-name groceries for less, on average, than its competitors were doing, and to advertise this fact strenuously" ("Keeping Up," 1979). For the situation described, explain what is meant by "on average" in the above quote.

3.9 Refer to Case Study 3.3. Practitioners of the delphi technique frequently use the median of the set of responses given by the panel of experts on the last questionnaire to describe "the opinion of the experts." Why do you suppose the median response is used rather than the mean response?

3.10 An *invoice* is a document that indicates the seller has completed his or her part of a sales contract. It states the names of the buyer and the seller and indicates what product or products have been shipped or delivered to the buyer, the date and method of shipment, and the prices, total sale figure, and terms of payment (Vatter, 1971).

A mail-order firm is interested in describing the size (in dollars) of the orders it received during the past fiscal year. To do so, the firm's accounting office randomly selected 100 invoices from the collection of all invoices written last year and recorded the "total sale" figure listed on each. These figures, rounded to the nearest dollar, are listed at the top of the next page.

a. Check the direction of skewness of the data set by comparing the median and mean.

b. Verify your answer to part a by constructing a frequency histogram of the data set. Locate the median and the mean of the data set on your histogram.

c. Suppose two more invoices were examined and their total sale figures, $20 and $250, were included in the data set. How would this affect the median and mean of the data set?

1	21	31	33	41	42	44	23	22	5
11	25	8	20	20	8	43	19	45	20
15	30	10	30	29	9	80	25	48	19
17	25	22	28	35	32	88	21	48	36
34	32	24	27	43	18	75	24	126	26
39	40	36	28	52	33	66	35	49	34
15	19	11	24	55	27	92	45	2	33
30	30	12	29	55	58	7	110	10	33
38	29	27	37	44	58	90	24	63	70
10	30	28	28	29	19	20	13	12	6

3.4 The Range: A Measure of Variability

In the preceding sections, we presented some methods for measuring the central tendency of a quantitative data set. However, central tendency tells only part of the story. Our information is incomplete without a measure of the *variability* or *spread* of the data set. Note that in describing a data set, we refer to either the sample or the population. Ultimately (in Chapter 8), we will use the sample numerical descriptive measures (statistics) to make inferences about the corresponding descriptive measures for the population from which the sample was selected.

If you examine the two histograms in Figure 3.4, you will notice that both hypothetical data sets are symmetric, with equal modes, medians, and means. However, in data set 1 in Figure 3.4(a), the measurements occur with almost equal frequency in the measurement classes, while in data set 2 in Figure 3.4(b), most of the measurements are clustered about the center. For this reason, a measure of variability is needed, along with a measure of central tendency, to describe a data set.

Figure 3.4

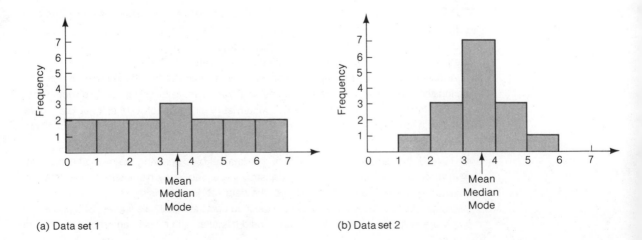

(a) Data set 1

(b) Data set 2

Perhaps the simplest measure of the variability of a quantitative data set is its *range.*

Definition 3.4

The *range* of a data set is equal to the largest measurement minus the smallest measurement.

The range measures the spread of the data by measuring the distance between the smallest and largest measurements. For example, stock A may vary in price during a given year from $32 to $36, while stock B may vary from $10 to $58, as shown in Figure 3.5. The range in price of stock A is $36 − $32 = $4, while that for stock B is $58 − $10 = $48. A comparison of ranges tells us that the price of stock B was much more variable than the price of stock A.

Figure 3.5 Ranges of Stock Prices for Two Companies

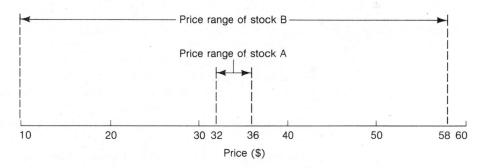

The range is not always a satisfactory measure of variability. For example, suppose we are comparing the profit margin (as a percentage of the total bid price) per construction job for 100 construction jobs for each of two cost estimators working for a large construction company. We find that the profit margins range from −10% (loss) to +40% (profit) for both cost estimators and therefore that the ranges for the two data sets, 40% − (−10%) = 50%, are equal. Because of this, we might be inclined to conclude that there is little or no difference in the performance of the two estimators.

But, suppose the histograms for the two sets of 100 profit margin measurements appear as shown in Figure 3.6 (next page). Although the ranges are equal and all central tendency measures are the same for these two symmetric data sets, there is an obvious difference between the two sets of measurements. The difference is that estimator B's profit margins tend to be more stable—i.e., to pile up or to cluster about the center of the data set. In contrast, estimator A's profit margins are more spread out over the range, indicating a higher incidence of some high profit margins, but also a greater risk of losses. Thus, even though the ranges are equal, the profit margin record of estimator A is more variable than that of estimator B, indicating a distinct difference in their cost estimating characteristics. We therefore need to develop more informative numerical measures of variability than the range.

Figure 3.6 Profit Margin Histograms for Two Cost Estimators

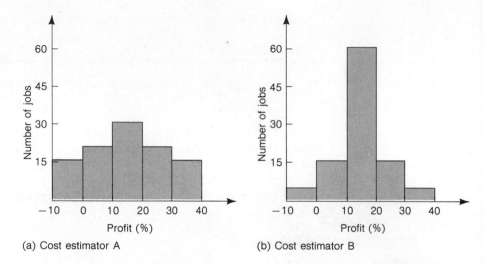

(a) Cost estimator A

(b) Cost estimator B

Case Study 3.4
More on the Delphi Technique

You will recall from Case Study 3.3 that the delphi technique is a set of procedures that may be used to obtain a consensus opinion from a group of experts through a series of questionnaires. Case Study 3.3 illustrated the use of the median as a measure of central tendency for the distribution of expert opinions elicited by the questionnaires. As a measure of variability of the data (i.e., the opinions), Milkovich et al. (1972) used the range. Table 3.4, showing the experts' opinions, is repeated here as Table 3.5, with the addition of the range of the distribution of opinions of each questionnaire in the right-hand column.

The range of 23 on questionnaire 2 indicates that at that time the experts' opinions were widely dispersed. The decrease in the range to 11 following questionnaire 4 indicates that as the experts received more information about the firm's needs and learned about one another's opinions, the variability in the distribution of their opinions decreased. Milkovich et al. noted that the decrease in the range was an indication that the experts' opinions were converging.

Table 3.5
Projected Demand for Buyers

QUESTIONNAIRE	EXPERTS							MEDIAN	RANGE
	A	B	C	D	E	F	G		
2	55	35	33	35	55	33	32	35	23
3	45	35	41	35	41	34	32	35	13
4	45	38	41	35	41	34	34	38	11
5	45	38	41	35	45	34	34	38	11

3.5 Variance and Standard Deviation

Recall that we represent the n measurements in a sample by the symbols $x_1, x_2, \ldots, x_n$ and we represent their mean by $\bar{x}$. What would be the interpretation of $x_1 - \bar{x}$? It is the distance, or *deviation,* between the first sample measurement, x_1, and the sample mean, $\bar{x}$. If we were to calculate this distance for *every* measurement in the sample, we would create a set of distances from the mean:

$$x_1 - \bar{x}, \; x_2 - \bar{x}, \; x_3 - \bar{x}, \; \ldots, \; x_n - \bar{x}$$

What information do these distances contain? If they tend to be large, the interpretation is that the data are spread out or highly variable. If the distances are mostly small, the data are clustered around the mean $\bar{x}$ and therefore do not exhibit much variability. As a simple example, consider the two samples in Table 3.6, which have five measurements (we have ordered the numbers for convenience). You will note that both samples have a mean of 3. However, a glance at the distances shows that sample 1 has greater variability — i.e., more large distances from $\bar{x}$ — than sample 2, which is clustered around $\bar{x}$. You can see this clearly by looking at these distances in Figure 3.7. Thus, the distances provide information about the variability of the sample measurements.

Table 3.6

	SAMPLE 1	SAMPLE 2
MEASUREMENTS	1, 2, 3, 4, 5	2, 3, 3, 3, 4
MEAN	$\bar{x} = \dfrac{1+2+3+4+5}{5} = \dfrac{15}{5}$ $= 3$	$\bar{x} = \dfrac{2+3+3+3+4}{5} = \dfrac{15}{5}$ $= 3$
DISTANCES FROM $\bar{x}$	$1-3, 2-3, 3-3, 4-3, 5-3$ or $-2, \quad -1, \quad 0, \quad 1, \quad 2$	$2-3, 3-3, 3-3, 3-3, 4-3$ or $-1, \quad 0, \quad 0, \quad 0, \quad 1$

The next step is to condense the information on distances from $\bar{x}$ into a single numerical measure of variability. Simply averaging the distances from $\bar{x}$ will not help. For example, in samples 1 and 2 the negative and positive distances cancel, so that the average distance is 0. Since this is true for any data set — i.e., the sum of the deviations, $\sum_{i=1}^{n} (x_i - \bar{x})$, is always 0 — we gain no information by averaging the distances from $\bar{x}$.

Figure 3.7 Distances from the Mean for Two Data Sets

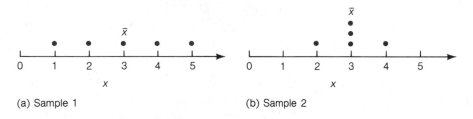

(a) Sample 1   (b) Sample 2

There are two methods for dealing with the fact that positive and negative distances from the mean cancel. The first is to treat all the distances as though they were positive, ignoring the sign of the negative distances. We will not pursue this line of thought because the resulting measure of variability (the mean of the absolute values of the distances) is difficult to interpret. A second method of eliminating the minus signs associated with the distances is to square them. The quantity we can calculate from the squared distances will provide a meaningful description of the variability of a data set.

To use the squared distances calculated from a data set, we first calculate the *sample variance:*

Definition 3.5

The *sample variance* for a sample of n measurements is equal to the sum of the squared distances from the mean divided by $(n-1)$. In symbols, using s^2 to represent the sample variance,

$$s^2 = \frac{\sum_{i=1}^{n}(x_i - \bar{x})^2}{n-1}$$

Referring to the two samples in Table 3.6, you can calculate the variance for sample 1 as follows:

$$s^2 = \frac{(1-3)^2 + (2-3)^2 + (3-3)^2 + (4-3)^2 + (5-3)^2}{5-1}$$

$$= \frac{4+1+0+1+4}{4} = 2.5$$

The second step in finding a meaningful measure of data variability is to calculate the *standard deviation* of the data set:

Definition 3.6

The *sample standard deviation, s,* is defined as the positive square root of the sample variance, s^2. Thus,

$$s = \sqrt{s^2} = \sqrt{\frac{\sum_{i=1}^{n}(x_i - \bar{x})^2}{n-1}}$$

The *population variance,* denoted by the symbol σ^2 (sigma squared), is the average of the squared distances of the observations from the mean, μ, and σ (sigma) is the square root of this quantity. Since we never really compute σ^2 or σ from the population (the object of sampling is to avoid this costly procedure), we simply denote these two quantities by their respective symbols.

$$s^2 = \text{Sample variance}$$
$$\sigma^2 = \text{Population variance}$$
$$s = \text{Sample standard deviation}$$
$$\sigma = \text{Population standard deviation}$$

Notice that, in contrast to the variance, the standard deviation is expressed in the original units of measurement. For example, if the original measurements are in dollars, the standard deviation will be expressed in dollars. Second, you may wonder why we use the divisor $(n - 1)$ instead of n when calculating the sample variance. This is because by using the divisor $(n - 1)$ you obtain a better estimate of σ^2 than you do by dividing the sum of the squared distances by n. Since we will ultimately want to use sample statistics to make inferences about numerical descriptive measures of the corresponding population, $(n - 1)$ is preferred to n when defining the sample variance.

Example 3.4 Calculate the standard deviation of the following sample: 2, 3, 3, 3, 4

Solution For this set of data, $\bar{x} = 3$. Then,

$$s = \sqrt{\frac{(2 - 3)^2 + (3 - 3)^2 + (3 - 3)^2 + (3 - 3)^2 + (4 - 3)^2}{5 - 1}}$$

$$= \sqrt{\frac{2}{4}} = \sqrt{0.5} = 0.71$$

Example 3.4 may have raised two thoughts in your mind. First, calculating s^2 and s can be very tedious if $\bar{x}$ is a number that contains a large number of significant figures or if there are a large number of measurements in a data set. Second, we have not explained how a sample standard deviation can be used to describe the variability of a data set. Fortunately, we have an easier method for calculating s^2 and s, and this method will be explained in Section 3.6. The interpretation of s will be the subject of Section 3.7.

3.6 Calculation Formulas for Variance and Standard Deviation

As the number of measurements in the sample becomes larger, the sample variance becomes more difficult to calculate. We must calculate the distance between each measurement and the mean, square it, sum the squared distances, and finally divide by $(n - 1)$. Fortunately, there is a shortcut formula for computing the sample variance:

Shortcut Formula for Sample Variance

$$s^2 = \frac{(\text{Sum of squares of sample measurements}) - \dfrac{(\text{Sum of sample measurements})^2}{n}}{n - 1}$$

$$= \frac{\displaystyle\sum_{i=1}^{n} x_i^2 - \dfrac{\left(\displaystyle\sum_{i=1}^{n} x_i\right)^2}{n}}{n - 1}$$

Note that the formula requires only the sum of the sample measurements, $\displaystyle\sum_{i=1}^{n} x_i$, and the sum of the squares of the sample measurements, $\displaystyle\sum_{i=1}^{n} x_i^2$. Be careful when you calculate these two sums. Rounding the values of x^2 that appear in $\sum_{i=1}^{n} x_i^2$ or rounding the quantity $\left(\sum_{i=1}^{n} x_i\right)^2 \Big/ n$ can lead to substantial errors in the calculation of s^2.

Example 3.5   Use the shortcut formula to compute the variances of these two samples of five measurements each:

   Sample 1:   1, 2, 3, 4, 5   Sample 2:   2, 3, 3, 3, 4

Solution   We first work with sample 1. The two quantities needed are

$$\sum_{i=1}^{5} x_i = 1 + 2 + 3 + 4 + 5 = 15$$

and

$$\sum_{i=1}^{5} x_i^2 = 1^2 + 2^2 + 3^2 + 4^2 + 5^2 = 1 + 4 + 9 + 16 + 25 = 55$$

Then the sample variance for sample 1 is

$$s^2 = \frac{\sum_{i=1}^{5} x_i^2 - \dfrac{\left(\sum_{i=1}^{5} x_i\right)^2}{5}}{5 - 1} = \frac{55 - \dfrac{(15)^2}{5}}{4} = \frac{55 - 45}{4} = \frac{10}{4} = 2.5$$

Similarly, for sample 2 we get

$$\sum_{i=1}^{5} x_i = 2 + 3 + 3 + 3 + 4 = 15$$

and

$$\sum_{i=1}^{5} x_i^2 = 2^2 + 3^2 + 3^2 + 3^2 + 4^2 = 4 + 9 + 9 + 9 + 16 = 47$$

Then the variance for sample 2 is

$$s^2 = \frac{\sum_{i=1}^{5} x_i^2 - \dfrac{\left(\sum_{i=1}^{5} x_i\right)^2}{5}}{5 - 1} = \frac{47 - \dfrac{(15)^2}{5}}{4} = \frac{47 - 45}{4} = \frac{2}{4} = 0.5$$

Note that these results agree with our calculations in the previous section.   ■

Example 3.6   The computer stock price-earnings measurements of Table 2.4 are repeated here. Calculate the sample variance, s^2, and the standard deviation, s, for these measurements.

18.8	8.6	26.5	12.6	29.4
23.6	35.5	19.0	38.6	14.3
20.1	10.7	19.2	18.4	41.4
7.4	37.3	27.7	11.4	10.3
17.9	35.3	23.8	25.6	22.5
11.4	33.1	11.9	26.1	

Solution   The calculation of the sample variance, s^2, would be very tedious for this sample if we tried to use the formula

$$s^2 = \frac{\sum_{i=1}^{29}(x_i - \bar{x})^2}{29 - 1}$$

because it would be necessary to compute all twenty-nine squared distances from the mean. However, for the shortcut formula we need compute only

$$\sum_{i=1}^{29} x_i = 18.8 + 23.6 + \cdots + 22.5 = 638.4$$

and

$$\sum_{i=1}^{29} x_i^2 = (18.8)^2 + (23.6)^2 + \cdots + (22.5)^2 = 16{,}757.42$$

Then

$$s^2 = \frac{\sum_{i=1}^{29} x_i^2 - \frac{\left(\sum_{i=1}^{29} x_i\right)^2}{29}}{29 - 1} = \frac{16{,}757.42 - \frac{(638.4)^2}{29}}{28} = 96.5648$$

The standard deviation is

$$s = \sqrt{s^2} = \sqrt{96.5648} = 9.83$$

Notice that we retained all the decimal places in the calculation of the sum of squares of the observations. This was done to reduce rounding error in the calculations, even though the original data were accurate to only one decimal place.* ■

---

* The accuracy of the original data has nothing to do with the degree of accuracy used in computing s^2 and s. Theoretically, s^2 and s should be computed without rounding error, but this is often impossible in practice. It is reasonable to retain twice as many decimal places in s^2 as you want to have in s. For example, if you want to calculate s to the nearest hundredth, you should calculate s^2 to the nearest ten-thousandth.

**Exercises
3.11–3.25**

Learning the Mechanics

3.11 Given the following information about two data sets, compute $\bar{x}$, the sample variance, and the standard deviation for each:

a. $n = 25$, $\sum_{i=1}^{n} x_i^2 = 1,000$, $\sum_{i=1}^{n} x_i = 50$

b. $n = 80$, $\sum_{i=1}^{n} x_i^2 = 270$, $\sum_{i=1}^{n} x_i = 100$

3.12 For each of the following data sets compute $\sum_{i=1}^{n} x_i$, $\sum_{i=1}^{n} x_i^2$, and $\left(\sum_{i=1}^{n} x_i\right)^2$:

a. 5, 9, 6, 3, 7   **b.** 3, 1, 4, 3, 0, −2
c. 90, 12, 40, 15   **d.** −1, 4, 1, 0, 5
e. 1, 0, 0, 1, 0, 10

3.13 Compute $\bar{x}$, s^2, and s for each of the data sets in Exercise 3.12.

3.14 Compute $\bar{x}$, s^2, and s for each of the following data sets.

a. 4, 3, 6, 0, 5   **b.** 3, 7, 7, 1, 2, 6
c. 4, 1, 1, 5, 6, 3   **d.** 3, 0, 1, 5

3.15 Compute $\bar{x}$, s^2, and s for each of the following data sets:

a. 10, 1, 0, 0, 20   **b.** 5, 9, −1, 100

3.16 Compute $\bar{x}$, s^2, and s for each of the following data sets. If appropriate, specify the units in which your answer is expressed.

a. 3, 1, 10, 10, 4
b. 8 feet, 10 feet, 32 feet, 5 feet
c. −1, −4, −3, 1, −4, −4
d. $\frac{1}{5}$ ounce, $\frac{1}{5}$ ounce, $\frac{1}{5}$ ounce, $\frac{2}{5}$ ounce, $\frac{1}{5}$ ounce, $\frac{4}{5}$ ounce

3.17 The range, variance, and standard deviation provide information about the variation in a data set.

a. Describe the information each conveys.
b. Discuss the advantages and disadvantages of using each to measure the variability of a data set.

3.18 Using only integers between 0 and 10, construct two data sets with at least ten observations each that have the same mean but different variances. Construct dot diagrams for each of your data sets (see Figure 3.7), and mark the mean of each data set on its dot diagram.

3.19 Using only integers between 0 and 10, construct two data sets with at least ten observations each that have the same range but different variances. Construct a dot diagram for each of your data sets (see Figure 3.7).

3.20 Using only integers between 0 and 10, construct two data sets with at least ten observations each that have the same range but different means. Construct a dot diagram for each of your data sets (see Figure 3.7), and mark the mean of each data set on its dot diagram.

3.21 The ten states with the highest percentages of total land devoted to state parks are listed below (data from *USA Today,* June 23, 1983).

New York	9.40%	New Mexico	2.10%
Connecticut	6.09%	South Dakota	1.84%
New Jersey	5.25%	New Hampshire	1.82%
Massachusetts	4.66%	Rhode Island	1.77%
South Carolina	3.25%	Pennsylvania	1.02%

a. Calculate the range of this data set.
b. Calculate the variance and standard deviation.
c. Can the variance of a data set ever be smaller than the standard deviation? Explain.
d. Can the variance of a data set ever be negative? Explain.

3.22 Refer to Exercise 3.21. If the percentage of land in Pennsylvania devoted to state parks were 0.90% instead of 1.02%, would the variance of the data set increase or decrease? Why? If instead of 1.02% or 0.90%, Pennsylvania's percentage were 3.0%, how would the resulting variance of the data set compare with the original variance calculated in part b of Exercise 3.21? Explain.

Applying the Concepts

3.23 The Consumer Price Index (CPI) measures the price change of a constant market basket of goods and services. The Bureau of Labor Statistics publishes a national CPI (called the U.S. City Average Index) as well as separate indexes for each of twenty-eight different cities in the United States. The national index and some of the city indexes are published monthly; the remainder of the city indexes are published bimonthly. The CPI is used as a measure of inflation during periods of rising prices and as a measure of deflation during periods of declining prices. The CPI is employed in cost-of-living escalator clauses of many labor contracts to adjust wages for changes in the cost of living. Changes in the CPI automatically trigger changes in workers' hourly wage rates (U.S. Department of Labor, 1978). For example, in the printing industry of Minneapolis and St. Paul, hourly wages are adjusted every 6 months (based on October and April values of the CPI) by 4¢ for every point change in the Minneapolis/St. Paul CPI.

The table at the top of the next page lists the published values of the U.S. City Average Index and Minneapolis/St. Paul Index during 1981 and the first half of 1982.

a. Calculate the mean values for the U.S. City Average Index and the Minneapolis/St. Paul Index.
b. Find the ranges of the U.S. City Average Index and the Minneapolis/St. Paul Index.
c. The standard deviation of the U.S. City Average Index over the 18 months described in the table is 8.48. Calculate the standard deviation for the Minneapolis/St. Paul Index over the time period described in the table.

d. Which index displayed the greater variation about its mean over the time period in question? Justify your response.

MONTH	U.S. CITY AVERAGE INDEX	MINNEAPOLIS/ ST. PAUL	MONTH	U.S. CITY AVERAGE INDEX	MINNEAPOLIS/ ST. PAUL
January	260.7	—	October	279.7	291.6
February	263.5	262.4	November	280.4	—
March	265.2	—	December	281.1	298.3
April	266.8	267.3	January	282.1	—
May	269.1	—	February	282.9	305.3
June	271.4	276.6	March	282.5	—
July	274.6	—	April	283.7	301.2
August	276.5	287.0	May	286.5	—
September	279.1	—	June	290.1	303.8

3.24 In order to set an appropriate price for a product, it is necessary to be able to estimate its cost of production. One element of the cost is based on the length of time it takes workers to produce the product. The most widely used technique for making such measurements is the *time study*. In a time study, the task to be studied is divided into measurable parts and each is timed with a stopwatch or filmed for later analysis. For each worker, this process is repeated many times for each subtask. Then the average and standard deviation of the time required to complete each subtask are computed for each worker. A worker's overall time to complete the task under study is then determined by adding his or her subtask-time averages (Chase & Aquilano, 1977). The data (in minutes) given in the table are the result of a time study of a production operation involving two subtasks.

REPETITION	WORKER A		WORKER B	
	Subtask 1	Subtask 2	Subtask 1	Subtask 2
1	30	2	31	7
2	28	4	30	2
3	31	3	32	6
4	38	3	30	5
5	25	2	29	4
6	29	4	30	1
7	30	3	31	4

a. Find the overall time it took each worker to complete the manufacturing operation under study.
b. For each worker, find the standard deviation of the seven times for subtask 1.
c. In the context of this problem, what are the standard deviations you computed in part b measuring?
d. Repeat part b for subtask 2.
e. If you could choose workers similar to A or workers similar to B to perform subtasks 1 and 2, which type would you assign to each subtask? Explain your decisions on the basis of your answers to parts a–d.

3.25 The table lists the yearly steel production for 1974–1980 for the five leading steel-producing countries in Europe.

Steel Production (thousands of tons)	1974	1975	1976	1977	1978	1979	1980
Germany	53.2	40.4	42.4	39.0	41.3	46.0	43.8
Italy	23.8	21.8	23.5	23.3	24.3	24.0	26.5
France	27.0	21.5	23.2	22.1	22.8	23.4	23.2
United Kingdom	22.4	19.8	22.4	20.4	20.3	21.6	11.3
Belgium	16.2	11.6	12.2	11.3	12.6	13.4	12.3

Source: U.S. Bureau of the Census, *Statistical Abstract of the United States.*

a. Measure the variation of each country's yearly steel production using the range.
b. Repeat part a using the variance as your measure of variation.
c. Rank the countries in terms of the variability of their production using your results from part a.
d. Rank the countries in terms of the variability of their production using your results from part b.
e. Do your two sets of rankings agree? Will the range and standard deviation always yield rankings that agree? Explain.

3.7 Interpreting the Standard Deviation

As we have seen, if we are comparing the variability of two samples selected from a population, the sample with the larger standard deviation is the more variable of the two. Thus, we know how to interpret the standard deviation on a relative or comparative basis, but we have not explained how it provides a measure of variability for a single sample.

One way to interpret the standard deviation as a measure of variability of a data set would be to answer questions such as the following: How many measurements are within 1 standard deviation of the mean? How many measurements are within 2 standard deviations? For a specific data set, we can answer the questions by counting the number of measurements in each of the intervals. However, if we are interested in obtaining a general answer to these questions, the problem is more difficult.

Table 3.7

Aids to the Interpretation of a Standard Deviation

1. A rule (from Chebyshev's theorem) that applies to any sample of measurements, regardless of the shape of the frequency distribution:
   a. It is possible that none of the measurements will fall within the interval $\bar{x} \pm s$ or $(\bar{x} - s, \bar{x} + s)$ — i.e., within 1 standard deviation of the mean.
   b. At least $\frac{3}{4}$ of the measurements will fall within $(\bar{x} - 2s, \bar{x} + 2s)$ — i.e., within 2 standard deviations of the mean.
   c. At least $\frac{8}{9}$ of the measurements will fall within $(\bar{x} - 3s, \bar{x} + 3s)$ — i.e., within 3 standard deviations of the mean.
2. A rule of thumb, called the Empirical Rule, that applies to samples with frequency distributions that are mound-shaped:
   a. Approximately 68% of the measurements will fall within the interval $\bar{x} \pm s$ or $(\bar{x} - s, \bar{x} + s)$ — i.e., within 1 standard deviation of the mean.
   b. Approximately 95% of the measurements will fall within $(\bar{x} - 2s, \bar{x} + 2s)$ — i.e., within 2 standard deviations of the mean.
   c. Essentially all the measurements will fall within $(\bar{x} - 3s, \bar{x} + 3s)$ — i.e., within 3 standard deviations of the mean.

In Table 3.7, we present two sets of guidelines to help answer the questions of how many measurements fall within 1, 2, and 3 standard deviations of the mean. The first set, which applies to any sample, is derived from a theorem proved by the Russian mathematician, Chebyshev. The second set, the Empirical Rule, is based on empirical evidence that has accumulated over time and applies to samples that possess mound-shaped frequency distributions — those that are approximately symmetric, with a clustering of measurements about the midpoint of the distribution (the mean, median, and mode should all be about the same) and that tail off as we move away from the center of the histogram. Thus, the histogram will have the appearance of a mound or bell, as shown in Figure 3.8. The percentages given for the various intervals (particularly the interval $\bar{x} - 2s$ to $\bar{x} + 2s$) in Table 3.7 provide remarkably good approximations even when the distribution of the data is slightly skewed or asymmetric.*

Figure 3.8 Histogram of a Mound-Shaped Sample

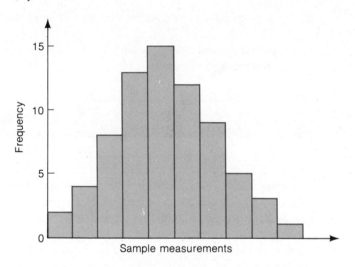

Example 3.7   The price-earnings ratio data for twenty-nine computer companies (Table 2.4) are repeated here:

18.8	8.6	26.5	12.6	29.4
23.6	35.5	19.0	38.6	14.3
20.1	10.7	19.2	18.4	41.4
7.4	37.3	27.7	11.4	10.3
17.9	35.3	23.8	25.6	22.5
11.4	33.1	11.9	26.1	

We have previously shown that the mean and standard deviation of these data are 22.01 and 9.83, respectively. Calculate the fraction of the twenty-nine measurements that lie within the intervals $\bar{x} \pm s$, $\bar{x} \pm 2s$, and $\bar{x} \pm 3s$, and compare the results with those in Table 3.7.

* It is our intention to imply that the Empirical Rule of Table 3.7 not only applies to normal distributions of data but also applies very well to mound-shaped distributions of large data sets and to distributions that possess a moderate degree of skewness.

Solution We first form the interval

$$(\bar{x} - s, \bar{x} + s) = (22.01 - 9.83, 22.01 + 9.83) = (12.18, 31.84)$$

A check of the measurements shows that sixteen of the twenty-nine measurements—approximately 55%—are within 1 standard deviation of the mean.
The interval

$$(\bar{x} - 2s, \bar{x} + 2s) = (22.01 - 19.66, 22.01 + 19.66) = (2.35, 41.67)$$

contains twenty-nine measurements, or all of the $n = 29$ measurements.
The 3 standard deviation interval around $\bar{x}$,

$$(\bar{x} - 3s, \bar{x} + 3s) = (22.01 - 29.49, 22.01 + 29.49) = (-7.48, 51.50)$$

also contains all the measurements.

Considering the small amount of data in our data set, these 1, 2, and 3 standard deviation percentages (55, 100, and 100) agree fairly well with the approximations of 68%, 95%, and 100% given by the Empirical Rule of Table 3.7 for mound-shaped distributions. If you look at the frequency histogram for this data set in Figure 2.9, you will note that, although the distribution is not really mound-shaped, it is not extremely skewed. Thus, we get reasonably good results from the mound-shaped approximations. Of course, we know from Table 3.7 that no matter what the shape of the distribution may be, we would expect at least 75% and 89% ($\frac{8}{9}$) of the measurements to lie within 2 and 3 standard deviations of $\bar{x}$, respectively.

■

Example 3.8 The aids for interpreting the value of a standard deviation (Table 3.7) can be put to an immediate practical use as a check on the calculation of a standard deviation. Suppose you have a data set for which the smallest measurement is 20 and the largest is 80. You have calculated the standard deviation of the data set to be $s = 190$. How can you use Table 3.7 to provide a rough check on your calculated value of s?

Solution The larger the number of measurements in a data set, the greater will be the tendency for very large or very small measurements (extreme values) to appear in the data set. But from Table 3.7 you know that most of the measurements (approximately 95% if the distribution is mound-shaped) will be within 2 standard deviations of the mean (see Figure 3.9). And,

Figure 3.9 The Relation Between the Range and the Standard Deviation

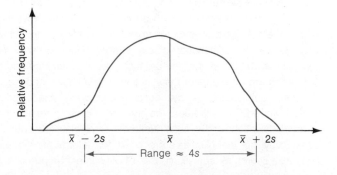

regardless of how many measurements are in the data set, almost all of them will fall within 3 standard deviations of the mean. Consequently, we would expect the range to be between 4 and 6 standard deviations—i.e., between $4s$ and $6s$. For the given data set, the range is

Range = Largest measurement − Smallest measurement
$$= 80 - 20 = 60$$

Then if we let the range equal $6s$, we obtain

Range $= 6s$
$$60 = 6s$$
$$s = 10$$

Or, if we let the range equal $4s$, we obtain a larger (and more conservative) value for s, namely,

Range $= 4s$
$$60 = 4s$$
$$s = 15$$

Now you can see that it does not make much difference whether you let the range equal $4s$ (which is more realistic for most data sets) or $6s$ (which is reasonable for large data sets). It is clear that your calculated value, $s = 190$, is too large, and you should check your calculations. ■

Case Study 3.5
Becoming More
Sensitive to
Customer Needs

The degree of sensitization on the part of a firm to the needs and wants of its consumers is frequently an important factor in determining the firm's overall success. Namias (1964) presents a procedure for achieving such sensitivity. The procedure uses the rate of consumer complaints about a product to determine when and when not to conduct a search for specific causes of consumer complaints. For simplification, we will discuss Namias's paper as if the procedure described used the number of complaints per 10,000 units of a product sold to determine when and when not to conduct a search for specific causes of consumer complaints. The details of the procedure are discussed in Case Study 3.6.

Namias's procedure, given our simplification, makes use of the *distribution* of the number of consumer complaints received about a product per 10,000 units of the product sold. To visualize such a distribution, imagine that a company produces its product in lots of 10,000 units and keeps track of the number of complaints received about items in each lot. The company's complaint records will show a series of numbers, perhaps 100, 96, 145, 201, etc., each of which is the number of complaints received about a particular lot of 10,000 units. This series of numbers is a quantitative data set from which a relative frequency histogram can be drawn. The histogram constructed from this data set is a representation of the distribution of interest—i.e., the distribution of the number of consumer complaints received about a product per 10,000 units of the product sold. The variance and standard deviation of this distribution are measures of the variation in the number of consumer complaints received. Namias determined that this distribution was mound-shaped. Accordingly, it can be said that approximately 95% of the time the number of complaints about a product will be within 2 standard deviations of the mean number of complaints. It is upon this fact, as we shall see in Case Study 3.6, that Namias's procedure for determining when it would be worthwhile to conduct a search for specific causes of consumer complaints is founded.

If it could not have been determined that the distribution of the number of complaints was mound-shaped, it could have been said only that at least 75% of the time the number of complaints about a product will be within 2 standard deviations of the mean number of complaints.

Exercises 3.26–3.38

Learning the Mechanics

3.26 Given a data set with a largest value of 760 and a smallest value of 135, what would you estimate the standard deviation to be? Explain the logic behind the procedure you used to estimate the standard deviation.

3.27 As a result of government and consumer pressure, automobile manufacturers in the United States are deeply involved in research to improve their products' gas mileage. One manufacturer, hoping to achieve 40 miles per gallon on one of its compact models, measured the mileage obtained by thirty test versions of the model with the following results (rounded to the nearest mile for convenience):

40	40	42	41	40	37
38	41	41	38	40	41
39	41	39	43	41	40
35	39	42	37	41	44
40	37	36	39	38	40

a. If the manufacturer would be satisfied with a (population) mean of 40 miles per gallon, how would it react to the above test data?
b. Compute $\bar{x}$, s^2, and s for the data set.
c. Use the information in Table 3.7 to check your calculation of s in part b.
d. What percentage of the measurements would you expect to find in the intervals $\bar{x} \pm s$, $\bar{x} \pm 2s$, and $\bar{x} \pm 3s$?
e. Count the number of measurements that actually fall within the intervals of part d, and express each interval count as a percentage of the total number of measurements. Compare these results with your answer to part d.

3.28 A manufacturer of video recorders is disturbed because retailers were complaining that they were not receiving shipments of recorders as fast as they had been promised. The manufacturer decided to run a check on the distribution network. Each of the fifty warehouses owned by the manufacturer throughout the country had been instructed to maintain at least 200 recorders in stock at all times so that a supply would always be readily available for retailers. The manufacturer checked the inventories of twenty of these warehouses and obtained the following numbers of video recorders in stock:

40	10	44	142	14
301	175	0	38	202
220	32	400	78	16
99	0	176	5	86

a. What is the mean number of recorders in stock for the twenty warehouses checked?

b. Compute s^2 and s for the data set.

c. Use the information in Table 3.7 to check your calculation of s in part b.

d. What percentage of the measurements would you expect to find in the intervals $\bar{x} \pm s$, $\bar{x} \pm 2s$, and $\bar{x} \pm 3s$?

e. Count the number of measurements that actually fall within the intervals of part d, and express each interval count as a percentage of the total number of measurements. Compare these results with your answers to part d.

3.29 Twenty-five mergers were sampled from the population of mergers that occurred between firms (excluding railroads) listed on the New York Stock Exchange during the period 1958–1960. For each merger, the ratio of the target firm's sales for the preceding year to the bidder firm's sales was calculated. (See Exercise 1.5 for definitions of target and bidder firms.) The twenty-five sales ratios are listed below (Eger, 1982, p. 133):

.16	.14	.18	.15	.14
.05	.10	.05	.02	.30
.03	.08	.32	.34	.04
.06	.02	.14	.07	.10
.04	.09	.29	.79	.02

a. Calculate $\bar{x}$, s^2, and s for this data set.

b. What percentage of the measurements would you expect to find in the intervals $\bar{x} \pm s$, $\bar{x} \pm 2s$, and $\bar{x} \pm 3s$?

c. Use the information in Table 3.7 to check your calculation of s in part a.

d. What percentage of measurements actually fall in the intervals of part b? Compare these results with the results of part b.

Applying the Concepts

3.30 Following World War II, births in the United States soared to record levels: from about 2.9 million in 1945 to 3.6 million in 1950 to over 4 million a year during the period 1955–1964, before declining in the mid-1960's (*Statistical Abstract of the United States: 1981*, p. 58). People born during this period are frequently referred to as belonging to the "baby boom" generation. The identification of demographic patterns such as this are vitally important to both business and government. For example, government can use such information to help predict tax revenues; and business can use it to predict spending patterns within the population (Curley, 1983). During the first 3 months of 1982 (i.e., the first quarter of 1982), the number of births in the United States declined 1% from the same period in 1981. However, in California, births declined 7.97%, from 105,244 to 96,851. The table on the next page lists the percentage change in the number of births between the first quarter of 1981 and the first quarter of 1982 for all fifty states and the District of Columbia.

a. Would it be appropriate to use the Empirical Rule to describe this data set? Justify your answer.

STATE	PERCENTAGE CHANGE IN NUMBER OF BIRTHS	STATE	PERCENTAGE CHANGE IN NUMBER OF BIRTHS
Alabama	−13.00	Montana	−1.00
Alaska	−1.47	Nebraska	−1.48
Arizona	4.36	Nevada	4.79
Arkansas	−4.89	New Hampshire	1.51
California	−7.97	New Jersey	−9.25
Colorado	8.40	New Mexico	63.41
Connecticut	7.96	New York	5.94
Delaware	−0.79	North Carolina	1.50
District of Columbia	−6.57	North Dakota	−0.67
Florida	9.28	Ohio	−9.34
Georgia	7.82	Oklahoma	13.02
Hawaii	3.17	Oregon	−7.93
Idaho	−5.21	Pennsylvania	0.31
Illinois	−1.65	Rhode Island	5.60
Indiana	−6.76	South Carolina	−6.14
Iowa	−5.33	South Dakota	−3.70
Kansas	1.86	Tennessee	−0.77
Kentucky	−7.20	Texas	4.90
Louisiana	−1.61	Utah	1.45
Maine	−9.17	Vermont	2.92
Maryland	10.08	Virginia	2.58
Massachusetts	4.13	Washington	−9.21
Michigan	−5.30	West Virginia	−9.02
Minnesota	1.59	Wisconsin	−10.21
Mississippi	−2.61	Wyoming	−1.98
Missouri	−4.16		

Source: *USA Today*, July 7, 1983, p. 4A.

b. According to Chebyshev's theorem, what percentage of the measurements in the data set will fall more than 2 standard deviations from the mean of the data set?

c. What percentage of measurements actually fall more than 2 standard deviations from the mean? Compare your answers to parts a and b.

3.31 A company that bottles sparkling water has determined that it lost an average of 30.4 cases a week last year due to breakage in transit. The standard deviation of the number of cases lost per week was 3.8 cases. With only this information, what can you say about the number of weeks last year that the company lost more than 38 cases due to breakage in transit? Justify your answer.

3.32 A chemical company produces a substance composed of 98% cracked corn particles and 2% zinc phosphide for use in controlling rat populations in sugarcane fields. Production must be carefully controlled to maintain the zinc phosphide at 2% because too much zinc phosphide will damage the sugarcane and too little will be ineffective in controlling the rat population. Records from past production indicate that the distribution of the actual percentage of zinc phosphide present in the substance is approximately mound-shaped, with a mean of 2.0% and a standard deviation of 0.08%. If the production line is operating correctly and a batch is chosen at random from a day's production, what is the approximate probability that it will contain less than 1.84% zinc phosphide?

3.33 In 1979, when the airlines were deregulated, there was hope that more airline companies would enter the market. The table contains some recent annual revenue data for the new entrants.

COMPANY	REVENUES ($ millions)	PROFITS ($ millions)	PASSENGER MILES (millions)
People Express	292	10.4	3,700
New York Air	130	4.5	657
Midway	104	−15.0	648
Muse Air	73	− 2.0	651
Jet America	60	− 8.0	610
American International	53	−11.8	295
Northeastern International	46	− 0.8	498
Air 1	20	−21.0	95
American West	18	− 6.3	351

Source: *New York Times*, Mar. 11, 1984.

a. Find the sample mean and variance for revenues, profits, and passenger miles flown.

b. Use the results of part a to sketch the distribution for each of the variables — revenue, profits, and passenger miles flown.

3.34 For 50 randomly selected days, the number of vehicles that used a certain road was ascertained by a city engineer. The mean was 385; the standard deviation was 15. Suppose you are interested in the proportion of days that there were between 340 and 430 vehicles using the road. What does Chebyshev's theorem tell you about this proportion?

3.35 A boat dealer has determined that the frequency distribution of the number of outboard motor sales per month over the last 5 years is mound-shaped, with a sample mean of 30 and a sample variance of 4. Approximately what percentage of the recorded monthly sales figures of the past 5 years would be expected to be greater than 34? Less than 26? Greater than 36?

3.36 Solar energy is considered by many to be the energy of the future. A recent survey was taken to compare the cost of solar energy with the cost of gas or electric energy. Results of the survey revealed that the average monthly utility bill of a three-bedroom house using gas or electric energy was $125 and the standard deviation was $15.

a. If nothing is known about the distribution of utility bills, what can you say about the fraction of all three-bedroom homes with gas or electric energy that have bills between $80 and $170?

b. If it is reasonable to assume that the distribution of utility bills is mound-shaped, approximately what proportion of three-bedroom homes would have monthly bills less than $110?

c. Suppose that three houses with solar energy units had the following utility bills: $78, $92, $87. Does this suggest that solar energy units might result in lower utility bills? Explain. [*Note:* We will present a statistical method for testing this conjecture in Chapter 8.]

3.37 When it is working properly, a machine that fills 25-pound bags of flour dispenses an average of 25 pounds per fill; the standard deviation of the amount of fill is 0.1 pound. To monitor the performance of the machine, an inspector weighs the contents of a bag coming off the machine's conveyor belt every half-hour during the day. If the contents of two consecutive bags fall more than 2 standard deviations from the mean (using the mean and standard deviation given above), the filling process is said to be out of control and the machine is shut down briefly for adjustments. The data given in the table are the weights measured by the inspector yesterday. Assume the machine is never shut down for more than 15 minutes at a time. At what times yesterday was the process shut down for adjustment? Justify your answer.

TIME	WEIGHT (pounds)	TIME	WEIGHT (pounds)
8:00 A.M.	25.10	12:30 P.M.	25.06
8:30	25.15	1:00	24.95
9:00	24.81	1:30	24.80
9:30	24.75	2:00	24.95
10:00	25.00	2:30	25.21
10:30	25.05	3:00	24.90
11:00	25.23	3:30	24.71
11:30	25.25	4:00	25.31
12:00	25.01	4:30	25.15
		5:00	25.20

3.38 A buyer for a lumber company must determine whether to buy a piece of land containing 5,000 pine trees. If 1,000 of the trees are at least 40 feet tall, the buyer will purchase the land; otherwise, he will not. The owner of the land reports that the distribution of the heights of the trees has a mean of 30 feet, and a standard deviation of 3 feet. Based on this information, what should the buyer decide?

3.8 Calculating a Mean and Standard Deviation from Grouped Data (Optional)

If your data have been grouped in classes of equal width and arranged in a frequency table, you can use the following formulas to calculate $\bar{x}$, s^2, and s:

Formulas for Calculating a Mean and Standard Deviation from Grouped Data

$\bar{x}_i =$ Midpoint of the ith class

$f_i =$ Frequency of the ith class

$k =$ Number of classes

$$\bar{x} = \frac{\sum\limits_{i=1}^{k} x_i f_i}{n} \qquad s^2 = \frac{\sum\limits_{i=1}^{k} x_i^2 f_i - \frac{\left(\sum\limits_{i=1}^{k} x_i f_i\right)^2}{n}}{n-1} \qquad s = \sqrt{s^2}$$

Example 3.9   Compute the mean and standard deviation for the computer stock price-earnings ratio data from Table 2.4 using the grouping shown in the frequency table, Table 2.6.

Solution   The seven class intervals, midpoints, and frequencies are listed in the table.

CLASS	CLASS MIDPOINT x_i	CLASS FREQUENCY f_i
7.35–12.35	9.85	7
12.35–17.35	14.85	2
17.35–22.35	19.85	6
22.35–27.35	24.85	6
27.35–32.35	29.85	2
32.35–37.35	34.85	4
37.35–42.35	39.85	2
		$n = 29$

Substituting the class midpoints and frequencies into the formulas, we obtain

$$\bar{x} = \frac{\sum\limits_{i=1}^{k} x_i f_i}{n} = \frac{(9.85)(7) + (14.85)(2) + \cdots + (39.85)(2)}{29} = \frac{645.65}{29} = 22.26$$

Now,

$$s^2 = \frac{\sum\limits_{i=1}^{k} x_i^2 f_i - \frac{\left(\sum\limits_{i=1}^{k} x_i f_i\right)^2}{n}}{n - 1}$$

and we found $\sum\limits_{i=1}^{k} x_i f_i = 645.65$ when we calculated $\bar{x}$. Therefore,

$$s^2 = \frac{[(9.85)^2(7) + (14.85)^2(2) + \cdots + (39.85)^2(2)] - (645.65)^2/29}{29 - 1}$$

$$= \frac{17,005.653 - 14,374.618}{28} = 93.9655$$

$$s = \sqrt{93.9655} = 9.69$$ ■

You will notice that the values of $\bar{x}$, s^2, and s from the formulas for grouped data usually do not agree with those obtained for the raw data ($\bar{x} = 22.01$ and $s = 9.83$). This is because we have substituted the value of the class midpoint for each value of x in a class interval. Only when every value of x in each class is equal to its respective class midpoint will the formulas for grouped and for ungrouped data give exactly the same answers for $\bar{x}$, s^2, and s. Otherwise, the formulas for grouped data will give only approximations to these numerical descriptive measures.

3.9 Measures of Relative Standing

As we have seen, numerical measures of central tendency and variability describe the general nature of a data set (either a sample or a population). We may also be interested in describing the relative location of a particular measurement within a data set. Descriptive measures of the relationship of a measurement to the rest of the data are called *measures of relative standing.*

One measure of the relative standing of a particular measurement is its *percentile ranking:*

Definition 3.7
Let $x_1, x_2, \ldots, x_n$ be a set of n measurements arranged in increasing (or decreasing) order. The *pth percentile* is a number x such that $p\%$ of the measurements fall below the pth percentile and $(100 - p)\%$ fall above it.

For example, if oil company A reports that its yearly sales are in the 90th percentile of all companies in the industry, the implication is that 90% of all oil companies have yearly sales less than company A's, and only 10% have yearly sales exceeding company A's. This is demonstrated in Figure 3.10.

Figure 3.10 Relative Frequency Distribution for Yearly Sales of Oil Companies

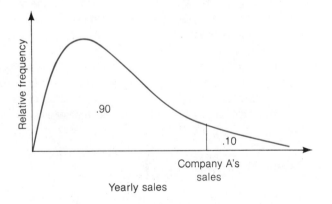

A less precise measure of the relative location of an observation is based on three particular percentiles, the *quartiles* of a data set. The quartiles are values of x that partition the data set into four groups, each containing 25% of the measurements. The lower quartile, Q_L, is the 25th percentile; the middle quartile is the median, M; and the upper quartile, Q_U, is the 75th percentile (see Figure 3.11 on the next page). Knowing that you achieved a test score "in the upper quartile" gives you an approximate location of your score relative to the other test scores. You know that it is in the top 25% of the scores. In addition, the quartiles enable you to construct a mental picture of the relative frequency distribution for the complete set of test scores. The median locates its center, and the lower and upper quartiles provide an indication of its spread.

Figure 3.11 The Quartiles for a Data Set

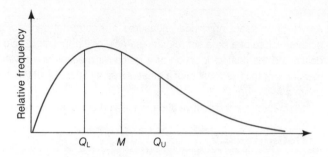

Definition 3.8

The *lower quartile* is the 25th percentile of a data set, the *middle quartile* is the median, and the *upper quartile* is the 75th percentile.

There are a number of methods for determining the quartiles of a data set. One relatively easy method is to rank the data and choose Q_L as the observation with rank equal to $\frac{1}{4}(n+1)$. Since $\frac{1}{4}(n+1)$ may be a fraction, we round to the nearest integer. For example, if $n = 26$, then $\frac{1}{4}(n+1) = \frac{1}{4}(26+1) = 6.75$. Rounding upward, we would select Q_L as the measurement with rank equal to 7. Approximately 25% (actually, $\frac{7}{26}$ or 27%) of the measurements will be less than or equal to Q_L.

Similarly, to find Q_U, we calculate $\frac{3}{4}(n+1)$ and round to the nearest integer. This integer is the rank of the measurement that we select as Q_U. For example, $\frac{3}{4}(n+1) = \frac{3}{4}(26+1) = 20.25$. Rounding downward, we would select Q_U as the measurement with rank 20. Approximately 25% ($\frac{7}{26}$ or 27%) of the measurements will be equal to or larger than Q_U.

Calculating Quartiles

Rank the n measurements in the data set from the smallest to the largest. The smallest will receive rank 1; the next largest, rank 2; . . . ; and the largest, rank n.

1. To find Q_L, calculate $\frac{1}{4}(n+1)$ and round to the nearest integer. The measurement with this rank is Q_L. [If $\frac{1}{4}(n+1)$ equals an integer plus $\frac{1}{2}$, round upward.]
2. To find Q_U, calculate $\frac{3}{4}(n+1)$ and round to the nearest integer. The measurement with this rank is Q_U. [If $\frac{3}{4}(n+1)$ equals an integer plus $\frac{1}{2}$, round downward.]

Example 3.10　　Find the lower and upper quartiles for the twenty-nine computer stock price-earnings ratios given in Table 2.4.

Solution　　The easiest way to find Q_L and Q_U is to obtain their values from the stem and leaf display shown in Figure 2.7. If the observations are ranked from the smallest to the largest, then Q_L is the observation with rank equal to

$$\tfrac{1}{4}(n+1) = \tfrac{1}{4}(29+1) = 7.5 \text{ or } 8$$

Similarly, Q_U will be the observation with rank equal to

$$\tfrac{3}{4}(n+1) = \tfrac{3}{4}(29+1) = 22.5 \text{ or } 22$$

Looking at the stem and leaf display in Figure 2.7 (page 29), you can see that two observations fall in stem row 0, and therefore that Q_L will be the observation with the sixth smallest leaf in stem row 1. This leaf is 2.6, and therefore,

$$Q_L = 12.6$$

To find Q_U, we start from the largest stem (4) and move upward through the stem and leaf display. Since the observation with rank 22 is the eighth from the largest observation, Q_U will be the one with the second largest leaf in stem row 2. Since this leaf is 7.7,

$$Q_U = 27.7 \qquad\qquad \blacksquare$$

Another measure of relative standing in popular use is the **z-score**. As you can see in Definition 3.9, the z-score makes use of the mean and standard deviation of the data set in order to specify the location of a measurement:

Definition 3.9

The *sample z-score* for a measurement x is

$$z = \frac{x - \bar{x}}{s}$$

The *population z-score* for a measurement x is

$$z = \frac{x - \mu}{\sigma}$$

Note that the z-score is calculated by subtracting $\bar{x}$ (or μ) from the measurement x and then dividing the result by s (or σ). The result, the z-score, represents the distance between a given measurement, x, and the mean, expressed in standard deviations.

Example 3.11 Suppose 200 steelworkers are selected, and the annual income of each is determined. The mean and standard deviation are $\bar{x} = \$14,000$ and $s = \$2,000$. Suppose Joe Smith's annual income is $12,000. What is his sample z-score?

Figure 3.12 Annual Income of Steelworkers

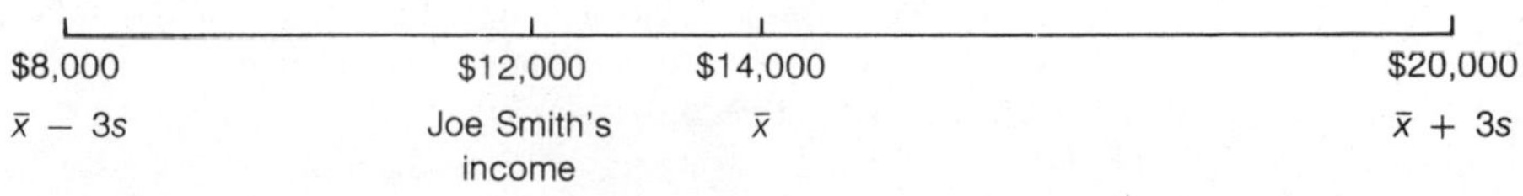

$8,000		$12,000	$14,000		$20,000
$\bar{x} - 3s$		Joe Smith's income	$\bar{x}$		$\bar{x} + 3s$

Solution   Joe Smith's annual income lies below the mean income of the 200 steelworkers (Figure 3.12). We compute

$$z = \frac{x - \bar{x}}{s} = \frac{\$12,000 - \$14,000}{\$2,000} = -1.0$$

which tells us that Joe Smith's annual income is 1.0 standard deviation *below* the sample mean, or, in short, his sample z-score is -1.0. ■

The numerical value of the z-score reflects the relative standing of the measurement. A large positive z-score implies that the measurement is larger than almost all other measurements, whereas a large negative z-score indicates that the measurement is smaller than almost every other measurement. If a z-score is 0 or near 0, the measurement is located near the middle of the sample or population.

We can be more specific if we know that the frequency distribution of the measurements is mound-shaped. In this case, the following interpretation of the z-scores can be given:

Interpretation of z-Scores for Mound-Shaped Distributions of Data

1. Approximately 68% of the measurements will have a z-score between -1 and 1.

2. Approximately 95% of the measurements will have a z-score between -2 and 2.

3. All or almost all the measurements will have a z-score between -3 and 3.

Note that this interpretation of z-scores is identical to that given in Table 3.7 for samples that exhibit mound-shaped frequency distributions. The statement that a measurement falls in the interval $(\mu - \sigma, \mu + \sigma)$ is identical to the statement that a measurement has a population z-score between -1 and 1, since all measurements between $(\mu - \sigma)$ and $(\mu + \sigma)$ are within 1 standard deviation of μ (see Figure 3.13).

Figure 3.13   Population z-Scores for a Mound-Shaped Distribution

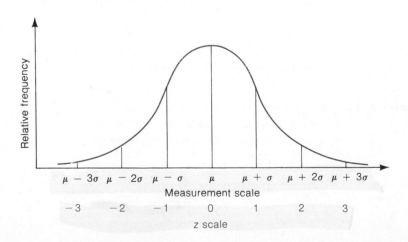

3.10 Detecting Outliers

An *outlier* is an observation that falls far out in the tail of a distribution and may be a faulty observation. Suppose, for example, that you were to sample the weekly sales of fifty salespersons in a company and found that all but one of the sales ranged from $3,000 to $5,000. The sales for the single exception were $750. If the object of the sampling is to learn something about the weekly sales of full-time salespersons, then the $750 observation is suspect and merits investigation. A further check of company records might indicate that the salesperson worked only a partial week because of sickness, etc. If so, this observation is not from the population of interest to you, and it should be deleted from the sample. If the investigation does not provide a reason for eliminating this observation from the sample, then it should not be deleted. Even though extreme values are improbable, their occurrence is not impossible.

The most obvious test for an outlier is to calculate its z-score (Section 3.9). For example, if the z-score for an observation is 4.2, we know that it lies more than 4 standard deviations away from the sample mean. The Empirical Rule (Table 3.7) tells us that a z-score this large is highly improbable and points to the possibility of a faulty observation.

A second method for detecting outliers, known as a *box plot*, is based on the *interquartile range,* IQR, the distance between the upper and lower quartiles,

$$IQR = Q_U - Q_L$$

This rule-of-thumb procedure locates a box on the x-axis above the middle 50% of the observations—i.e., between the lower and upper quartiles. A box plot for the twenty-nine price-earnings ratios of Table 2.4 is shown in Figure 3.14.

In Example 3.10, we found Q_L and Q_U for the twenty-nine price-earnings ratios to be 12.6 and 27.7, respectively. Therefore, the interquartile range is

$$IQR = Q_U - Q_L = 27.7 - 12.6 = 15.1$$

The box plot in Figure 3.14 locates a box over the x-axis between Q_L and Q_U. Fifty percent of the observations lie between Q_L and Q_U—i.e., within the box. A vertical line is drawn inside the box to locate the median. If the data set is symmetric, the median will fall at the center of the box. If the data set is skewed to the left or right, the median will fall toward the right or left side of the box, respectively. To detect outliers, two sets of limits are constructed. *Inner*

Figure 3.14 A Box Plot for the Twenty-Nine Computer Stock Price-Earnings Ratios of Table 2.4

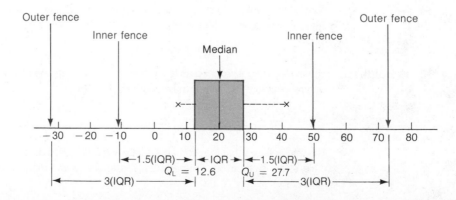

fences are located a distance of 1.5(IQR) = 1.5(15.1) = 22.65 below Q_L and above Q_U (see Figure 3.14). Any observations falling outside the inner fences are suspect outliers. Similarly, *outer fences* are located a distance of 3(IQR) = 3(15.1) = 45.3 below Q_L and above Q_U (see Figure 3.14). Any observations outside the outer fences are beyond the point of suspicion and are designated as outliers.

Suspect outliers — those observations between the inner and outer fences — are located on the box plot using small circles. Outliers — those observations that fall outside the outer fences — are located with solid dots. To further highlight extreme values, "whiskers" are added to the box plot. The value in the region between Q_L and the lower inner fence that is closest to the inner fence is marked with an $\times$ and joined to the box with a dashed line — a whisker. In our example, the $\times$ is located at 7.4. Similarly, an $\times$ with attached whisker is located at 41.4, the most extreme value in the region between Q_U and the upper inner fence.

Since our data set consists of price-earnings ratios, none can be less than 0 and therefore none can fall below the lower inner fence, -10.1. The largest price-earnings ratio in the data set, 41.4, comes close to the upper inner fence but it does not fall above it. Therefore, there is no evidence to indicate a suspect outlier in the computer stock price-earnings ratios.

The z-score and box-plot methods both establish rule-of-thumb limits outside of which an observation is deemed to be an outlier. Since both methods locate the limits a specified distance from the center (relatively speaking) of the data set, it should be possible to compare the ability of the two methods to detect outliers. In fact, we might expect the two rules of thumb to produce similar results. (We will lead you through this comparison for a particular type of data in Exercise 6.19.)

3.11 Outliers, Rare Events, and Statistical Inference

The object of a method for detecting outliers is to identify faulty sample observations — i.e., observations that do not belong to the population you are attempting to sample. As the following example illustrates, the logic employed in detecting outliers is the basis for one of the two methods for making statistical inferences about population parameters. We will introduce the logic here, and then develop it further in Chapter 8.

Example 3.12

Suppose a female bank employee believes her salary is low as a result of sex discrimination. To try to substantiate her belief, she collects information on the salaries of her male counterparts in the banking business. She finds that their salaries have a mean of $24,000 and a standard deviation of $2,000. Her salary is $17,000. Does this information support her claim of sex discrimination?

Solution   The analysis might proceed as follows: First, we calculate the z-score for the woman's salary with respect to those of her male counterparts. Thus,

$$z = \frac{\$17,000 - \$24,000}{\$2,000} = -3.5$$

The implication is that the woman's salary is 3.5 standard deviations *below* the mean of the male salary distribution. Furthermore, if a check of the male salary data shows that the

Figure 3.15 Male Salary Distribution

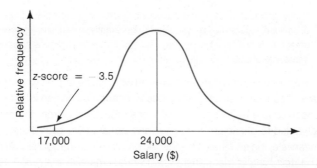

frequency distribution is mound-shaped, we can infer that very few salaries in this distribution should have a z-score less than -3, as shown in Figure 3.15. Therefore, a z-score of -3.5 represents either a measurement from a distribution different from the male salary distribution or a very unusual (highly improbable) measurement for the male salary distribution.

Well, which of the two situations do you think prevails? Do you think the woman's salary is simply an unusually low one in the distribution of salaries, or do you think her claim of salary discrimination is justified? Most people would probably conclude that her salary does not come from the male salary distribution. However, the careful investigator should require more information before inferring sex discrimination as the cause. We would want to know more about the data collection technique the woman used, and more about her competence at her job. Also, perhaps other factors like the length of employment should be considered in the analysis. ■

The above exemplifies an approach to statistical inference that might be called the *rare event approach.* An experimenter hypothesizes a specific frequency distribution to describe a population of measurements. Then a sample of measurements is drawn from the population. If the experimenter finds it unlikely that the sample came from the hypothesized distribution, the hypothesis is concluded to be false. Thus, in Example 3.12 the woman believes her salary reflects sex discrimination. She hypothesizes that her salary should be just another measurement in the distribution of her male counterparts' salaries if no discrimination exists. However, it is so unlikely that the sample (in this case, her salary) came from the male frequency distribution that she rejects that hypothesis, concluding that the distribution from which her salary was drawn is different from the distribution for the men.

This rare event approach to inference-making is discussed further in later chapters. Proper application of the approach requires a knowledge of probability, the subject of our next chapter.

Case Study 3.6

Deciding When to Respond to Consumer Complaints

Now we will finish the discussion, begun in Case Study 3.5, of a method proposed by Namias (1964) to determine when and when not to conduct a search for specific causes of consumer complaints.

The rate of consumer complaints about a product may change or vary as a result of merely chance or fate, or it may be due to some specific cause, such as a decline in the quality of the product. Concerning the former, Namias (1964) says:

In any operation or production process, variability in the output or product will occur, and no two operational results may be expected to be exactly alike. Complete constancy of consumer rates of complaint is not possible, for the vagaries of fate and chance operate even within the most rigid framework of quality or operation control.

Namias provides a decision rule with which to determine when the observed variation in the rate of consumer complaints is due to chance and when it is due to specific causes. If the observed rate is 2 standard deviations or less away from the mean rate of complaint, it is attributed to chance. If the observed rate is farther than 2 standard deviations above the mean rate, it is attributed to a specific problem in the production or distribution of the product. The reasoning is that if there are no problems with the production and distribution of the product, 95% of the time the rate of complaint should be within 2 standard deviations of the mean rate. If the production and distribution processes were operating normally, it would be very unlikely for a rate higher than 2 standard deviations above the mean to occur. Instead, it is more likely that the high complaint rate is caused by abnormal operation of the production and/or distribution process; that is, something specific is wrong with the process.

Namias recommends searching for the cause (or causes) only if the observed variation in the rate of complaints is determined by the rule to be the result of a specific cause (or causes). The degree of variability due to chance must be tolerated. Namias says,

> As long as the results exhibit chance variability, the causes are common, and there is no need to attempt to improve the product by making specific changes. Indeed this may only create more variability, not less, and it may inject trouble where none existed, with waste of time and money. . . . On the other hand, time and money are again wasted through failure to recognize specific conditions when they arise. It is therefore economical to look for a specific cause when there is more variability than is expected on the basis of chance alone.

Namias collected data from the records of a beverage company for a 2-week period to demonstrate the effectiveness of the rule. Consumer complaints concerned chipped bottles that looked dangerous. For one of the firm's brands the mean complaint rate was determined to be 26.01 and the rate 2 standard deviations above the mean was determined to be 48.78 complaints per 10,000 bottles sold. The complaint rate observed during the 2 weeks under study was 93.12 complaints per 10,000 bottles sold. Since 93.12 is many more than 2 standard deviations above the mean rate, it was concluded that the high rate of complaints must have been caused by some specific problem in the production or distribution of the particular brand of beverage and that a search for the problem would probably be worthwhile. The problem was traced to rough handling of the bottled beverage in the warehouse by newly hired workers. As a result, a training program for new workers was instituted.

Exercises 3.39 – 3.63

Learning the Mechanics

3.39 What is the 75th percentile of a data set?

3.40 What is another name for the 50th percentile?

3.41 Find the lower quartile, the median, and the upper quartile of the following set of ordered measurements:

1	31	43	49	52	55	59	66	72	89
12	31	45	50	52	55	59	67	76	92
20	33	46	50	53	56	60	68	76	96
24	39	47	51	53	57	62	69	82	103
28	40	48	52	53	58	63	71	84	109

3.42 Find the lower and upper quartiles of the following set of sample measurements:

1.11	1.24	1.35	1.31	1.55	1.49
1.72	1.66	1.40	2.00	1.24	1.14
1.55	1.26	1.30	1.86	1.25	1.28
1.39	1.65	1.46	1.41	1.31	2.10
1.36	1.33	1.50	1.12	1.38	1.82

3.43 In each of the following compute the z-score for the x value, and note whether your result is a sample z-score or a population z-score:

a. $x = 31$, $s = 7$, $\bar{x} = 24$ **b.** $x = 95$, $s = 4$, $\bar{x} = 101$
c. $x = 5$, $\mu = 2$, $\sigma = 1.7$ **d.** $\mu = 17$, $\sigma = 5$, $x = 14$

3.44 Consider the following data set:

31	5	20	16	25	2	7	14
16	37	31	2	4	19	74	7

a. Calculate $\bar{x}$ and s for the data set.
b. Suppose you were to draw an additional observation, and its value was 91. Calculate the z-score for this observation, and explain why you would or would not classify it as an outlier.
c. Construct a box plot for the sixteen observations. Would you classify any of the observations as outliers? Explain.

3.45 Consider the following data set:

0	5	6	3	1	2	3	2	1	8
1	7	1	5	4	4	3	1	6	0
5	0	20	5	2					

a. Calculate $\bar{x}$ and s for the data set.
b. Suppose you were to draw an additional observation, and its value was 91. Calculate the z-score for this observation, and explain why you would or would not classify it as an outlier.
c. Construct a box plot for the twenty-five observations. Would you classify any of the observations as outliers? Explain.

3.46 Suppose a box plot or z-score suggested an observation was an outlier. Should the observation be removed from your sample? Explain.

3.47 Construct a box plot for the following measurements and identify any outliers that exist:

21	42	30	65
51	35	28	10
34	55	44	49
47	99	33	34
32	33	33	72

3.48 Refer to Exercise 3.47. Find and interpret the z-scores associated with the outliers you identified.

3.49 Consider the following two sample data sets:

SAMPLE A			SAMPLE B		
121	171	158	171	152	170
173	184	163	168	169	171
157	85	145	190	183	185
165	172	196	140	173	206
170	159	172	172	174	169
161	187	100	199	151	180
142	166	171	167	170	188

a. Construct a box plot for each data set.
b. Using the information reflected in your box plots, describe the similarities and differences of the two data sets.
c. Identify any outliers that may exist in the two data sets.

Applying the Concepts

3.50 *Forbes'* "36th Annual Report on American Industry" (*Forbes,* Jan. 2, 1984) ranks the 998 U.S. companies with revenues over $450 million in 1983 in terms of profitability as measured by average return on equity over the previous 5 years. Textron fell at the upper quartile of *Forbes'* profitability distribution. Describe Textron's position within the profitability distribution.

3.51 The table at the top of the next page contains the top salary offer received by each member of a sample of fifty undergraduate business majors (excluding accounting majors) who graduated from the School of Management at the University of Minnesota in 1983.

a. Find the lower quartile, the median, and the upper quartile of this data set.
b. What proportion of the salary offers in the sample fall above the upper quartile? At or below the upper quartile?

SALARY OFFERS TO 1983 GRADUATES _($ thousands)_									
20.1	16.8	19.6	15.7	17.3	18.1	13.4	13.7	14.9	15.2
16.9	16.5	15.6	15.5	15.1	15.0	15.9	15.9	15.2	16.8
16.1	16.0	14.3	17.0	16.1	18.5	14.8	15.7	15.4	17.6
14.9	15.8	16.8	16.0	16.7	12.6	14.2	16.0	16.3	16.0
15.9	14.7	13.8	17.5	15.0	24.1	15.9	18.2	14.8	17.9

Source: Placement Office, School of Management, University of Minnesota.

c. Find and interpret the z-scores associated with the highest salary offer, the lowest salary offer, and the mean salary offer.

3.52 The College Placement Council regularly surveys 185 placement offices at 160 colleges and universities in the United States to determine beginning salary offers received by graduating students in different fields of study. In July 1983, they reported that 3,272 offers were received by undergraduate general business majors during the 1982–1983 academic year. Ten percent of these offers were for more than $1,916 per month; 50% for more than $1,500 per month; and 10% for less than $1,083 per month (*CPC Salary Survey,* 1983). Use percentiles to describe the relative standing of each of the above-mentioned salary offers within the 1982–1983 population of offers to general business students.

3.53 The table lists the unemployment rate in 1980 for a sample of nine countries.

COUNTRY	PERCENT UNEMPLOYED
Australia	6.1
Canada	7.5
France	6.6
Germany	3.3
Great Britain	7.5
Italy	3.9
Japan	2.0
Sweden	2.0
United States	7.1

Source: *Statistical Abstract of the United States: 1981,* p. 882.

a. Calculate the mean and standard deviation of this data set.

b. Calculate the z-scores of the unemployment rates of the United States, Australia, and Japan.

c. Describe the information conveyed by the sign (positive or negative) of the z-scores you calculated in part b.

3.54 One of the ways the federal government raises money is through sale of securities such as Treasury bonds, Treasury bills ("T-bills"), and U.S. savings bonds. Treasury bonds and bills are marketable (i.e., they can be traded in the securities market) long-term and short-term notes, respectively. U.S. savings bonds are nonmarketable notes; they can be purchased and redeemed only from the U.S. Treasury. On June 30, 1983, the interest rate on 3-month T-bills was 8.75%. Within the next week, the *Wall Street Journal* sampled seventeen economists and asked them to forecast the interest rate of 3-month T-bills on September 30, 1983 (T-bills are offered for sale weekly by the government, and their interest rates typically vary with each offering). The forecasts obtained are listed in the table.

ECONOMIST	INTEREST RATE FORECAST (%)	ECONOMIST	INTEREST RATE FORECAST (%)
Alan Greenspan	8.70	Robert Parry	8.50
Timothy Howard	8.75	John Paulus	9.50
Lacy H. Hunt	9.35	Norman Robertson	8.50
Edward Hyman	7.80	Francis Schott	8.50
David Jones	9.25	Stuart Schweitzer	9.00
Irwin Kellner	8.25	Allen Sinai	9.15
Alan Lerner	9.25	Thomas Thompson	9.25
Donald Maude	7.70	John Wilson	10.00
Anne Parker Mills	8.50		

Source: *Wall Street Journal*, July 5, 1983, p. 2.

a. Calculate the z-scores of Alan Greenspan's forecast and John Wilson's forecast. What do the z-scores tell you about their forecasts relative to the forecasts of the other economists?

b. Write a sentence or two that summarizes the seventeen forecasts. In your summary, use a measure of central tendency and a measure of variability.

3.55 For small data sets, the interpretation of percentiles given in Definition 3.7 is often modified as follows: The pth percentile is a number x such that at least p% of the measurements are less than or equal to x and at least $(100 - p)$% are greater than or equal to x. Consider the following data set:

5   8   31   12   40
26   30   8   31   20

a. Show that the 55th percentile of this data set is 26.

b. Specify all the measurements in the data set that could be interpreted as the 40th percentile.

3.56 In *Fortune* magazine's 1983 ranking of the 500 largest industrial corporations in the United States, Control Data Corporation ranked 80th in terms of 1982 sales. In 1981, it ranked 144th. Describe Control Data Corporation's position in each year's sales distribution in terms of percentiles.

3.57 A parking lot owner's accountant determined the owner's receipts for each of 100 randomly chosen days from the past year. The mean and standard deviation for the 100 days were $360 and $25, respectively. Yesterday's receipts amounted to $370.

a. Find the sample z-score for yesterday's receipts.

b. How many standard deviations away from the mean is the value of yesterday's receipts?

c. Would you consider yesterday's receipts to be unusually high? Why or why not?

3.58 A firm's earnings per share (E/S) of common stock is a measure used by investors to monitor the financial performance of a firm. Thirty firms were sampled from *Fortune* magazine's 1983 listing of the 500 largest industrial corporations in the United States, and their earnings per share are recorded in the table.

FIRM	E/S	FIRM	E/S
Illinois Tool Works	$3.26	Dow Jones	$1.39
Dayco	.25	United Brands	.06
Reynolds Metals	.26	Washington Post	3.70
Scott Paper	1.61	Avon Products	2.75
Phelps Dodge	−3.59	Reichhold Chemicals	.25
Westmoreland Coal	1.14	Genesco	−.09
Avery International	2.98	Warner Communications	3.96
Warner-Lambert	2.20	Asarco	−3.88
Burroughs	2.80	Snap-on Tools	1.84
General Electric	8.00	McCormick	2.02
Cooper Industries	2.76	Exxon	4.82
Lockheed	10.96	Georgia-Pacific	1.44
Kellogg	2.98	Crown Cork & Seal	3.15
Midland-Ross	.10	E.I. duPont de Nemours	3.75
Oxford Industries	5.66	United Merchants & Manufacturers	14.12

Source: *Fortune,* May 1983, pp. 226–254.

a. Use a box plot to identify outliers that may exist in this data set.

b. For each outlier identified in part a, determine how many standard deviations it lies from the mean of the E/S data set.

3.59 A manufacturer of minicomputer systems is interested in improving its customer support services. As a first step, its marketing department has been charged with the responsibility of summarizing the extent of customer problems in terms of system down time. The forty most recent customers were surveyed to determine the amount of down time (in hours) they had experienced during the previous month. These data are listed in the table.

CUSTOMER NUMBER	DOWN TIME	CUSTOMER NUMBER	DOWN TIME	CUSTOMER NUMBER	DOWN TIME	CUSTOMER NUMBER	DOWN TIME
230	12	240	24	250	4	260	34
231	16	241	15	251	10	261	26
232	5	242	13	252	15	262	17
233	16	243	8	253	7	263	11
234	21	244	2	254	20	264	64
235	29	245	11	255	9	265	19
236	38	246	22	256	22	266	18
237	14	247	17	257	18	167	24
238	47	248	31	258	28	268	49
239	0	249	10	259	19	269	50

a. Construct a box plot to describe these data.

b. Use your box plot to determine which customers are having unusually lengthy down times.

c. Find and interpret the z-scores associated with customers you identified in part b.

3.60 A hydraulic metal stamping machine is set to produce disks that are between 15.75 and 16.25 centimeters in diameter. At the start of each work shift, thirty disks are sampled from the production process and measured by an inspector to be sure the machine is operating properly. The measurements shown in the table were obtained at the start of the current work shift.

DISK DIAMETERS (Centimeters)				
16.22	15.95	15.92	16.05	16.10
15.82	16.15	16.05	15.96	16.02
15.74	16.07	16.13	16.00	16.09
16.01	16.13	16.19	15.84	15.92
16.13	16.25	15.94	16.04	16.07
16.00	15.99	16.24	16.09	16.02

a. Construct a box plot for these data. What does your box plot reveal about the current operation of the stamping machine?

b. Does your box plot indicate that the set of thirty measurements contains any outliers? Explain.

3.61 It is known that the frequency distribution of the number of video cassette recorders (VCRs) sold each week by a large department store in Atlanta is mound-shaped, with a mean of 35 and a variance of 9.

a. Approximately what percentage of the measurements in the frequency distribution should fall between 32 and 38? Between 26 and 44?

b. If the z-score for last week's sales was -1.33, how many VCRs did the store sell last week?

c. If it is known that the number of VCRs sold each week by a rival department store has a mound-shaped frequency distribution with a mean of 35 and a standard deviation of 2, for which store is it more likely that more than 41 VCRs will be sold in a week? Why?

3.62 Suppose that 40 and 90 are two elements of a population data set and that their z-scores are -2 and 3, respectively. Using just this information, is it possible to determine the population's mean and standard deviation? If so, find them. If not, explain why it is not possible.

3.63 Corporate advertising seeks as a primary goal the creation of a favorable and enduring impression of a firm. Its major thrust is in establishing a recognizable corporate identity, which is more than just marketing its products or creating positive public relations. In an article titled "When to Advertise Your Company" (*Harvard Business Review*, Mar.–Apr. 1982), Thomas F. Garbett provides data on corporate advertising by company size for 1979. The table gives the *Fortune 500* industries' average corporate advertising budgets. Calculate the mean average corporate advertising budget for all *Fortune 500* companies.

FORTUNE 500 INDUSTRIES	NUMBER OF COMPANIES	AVERAGE CORPORATE ADVERTISING BUDGET ($ thousands)
1–50	50	5,210
51–100	50	1,971
101–200	100	965
201–300	100	418
301–400	100	243
401–500	100	238

Summary

Numerical methods for describing quantitative data sets can be grouped as follows:

1. Measures of central tendency
2. Measures of variability

The mode, mean, and median of a data set are measures of central tendency. The *mode* is the most frequently observed member of the data set. The *mean* is the average of the data, obtained by summing the n measurements in the data set and dividing by n. The *median* is a number in the data set chosen so that half the measurements in the data set fall below the median and half fall above. The relationship between the mean and median provides information about the *skewness* of the frequency distribution. For making inferences about the population, the sample mean will usually be preferred to the other measures of central tendency.

The numerical description of a set of data requires more than a measure of central tendency. The *variability* of the data set must also be described. The *range, absolute deviation, variance,* and *standard deviation* all represent numerical measures of variability. Of these, the variance and standard deviation are used most commonly, especially when the ultimate objective is to make inferences about a population.

The mean and standard deviation may be used to make statements about the fraction of measurements in a given interval. For example, we know that at least 75% of the measurements in a data set will lie within 2 standard deviations of the mean. If the frequency distribution of the data set is mound-shaped, approximately 95% of the measurements will lie within 2 standard deviations of the mean.

Measures of relative standing provide still another dimension on which to describe a data set. The objective of these measures is to describe the location of a specific measurement relative to the rest of the data set. *Percentiles, quartiles,* and *z-scores* are important examples of measures of relative standing. *Outliers* in a data set may be detected through the construction of a *box plot.*

According to the *rare event* concept of statistical inference, if the chance that a particular sample came from a hypothetical population is very small, we can conclude either that the sample is extremely rare or that the hypothesized population is not the one from which the sample was drawn. The more unlikely it is that the sample came from the hypothesized population, the more strongly we favor the conclusion that the hypothesized population is not the true one. We need to be able to assess accurately the rarity of a sample, and this requires a knowledge of probability, the subject of Chapter 4.

Supplementary Exercises 3.64–3.90

[*Note:*　*Starred (*) exercises refer to the optional section in this chapter.*]

3.64 Compute $\sum_{i=1}^{n} x_i^2$, $\sum_{i=1}^{n} x_i$, and $\left(\sum_{i=1}^{n} x_i\right)^2$ for each of the following data sets:

a. 11, 1, 2, 8, 7　　　　**b.** 15, 15, 2, 6, 12
c. −1, 2, 0, −4, −8, 13　**d.** 100, 0, 0, 2

3.65 Compute s^2 and s for each of the data sets in Exercise 3.64.

3.66 Compute s^2 for each of the following data sets:

a. $\sum_{i=1}^{n} x_i^2 = 246$,　$\sum_{i=1}^{n} x_i = 63$,　$n = 22$

b. $\sum_{i=1}^{n} x_i^2 = 666$,　$\sum_{i=1}^{n} x_i = 106$,　$n = 25$

c. $\sum_{i=1}^{n} x_i^2 = 76$,　$\sum_{i=1}^{n} x_i = 11$,　$n = 7$

3.67 For each of the following data sets, compute $\bar{x}$, s^2, and s:

a. 13, 1, 10, 3, 3　　　　**b.** 13, 6, 6, 0
c. 1, 0, 1, 10, 11, 11, 15　**d.** 3, 3, 3, 3

3.68 Compute the range for each of the data sets in Exercise 3.67.

3.69 For each of the following data sets, compute $\bar{x}$, s^2, and s. If appropriate, specify the units in which your answers are expressed.

a. 4, 6, 6, 5, 6, 7
b. −$1, $4, −$3, $0, −$3, −$6
c. $\frac{3}{5}$ pound, $\frac{4}{5}$ pound, $\frac{2}{5}$ pound, $\frac{1}{5}$ pound, $\frac{1}{16}$ pound

3.70 What is the best measure of the variability of a quantitative data set? Why?

*3.71 Compute the mean and variance of the following data sets:

a.

CLASS	CLASS FREQUENCY
1–5	2
6–10	5
11–15	12
16–20	6

b.

CLASS	CLASS FREQUENCY
0.25–0.50	0
0.50–0.75	5
0.75–1.00	12
1.00–1.25	8
1.25–1.50	6
1.50–1.75	2

3.72 Under what circumstances might the standard deviation be preferred to the variance as a measure of the variation in a data set?

3.73 In reference to a measurement or observation, what is a measure of relative standing?

3.74 How does a z-score locate a measurement within a set of measurements? Explain.

3.75 "The genesis of the modern R&D [research and development] laboratory in America is commonly traced to 1876, when Thomas Edison opened his famed laboratory in Menlo Park and Alexander Graham Bell established an analogous facility in Boston. Wherever the starting point is placed, the idea spread rapidly until research and development came to be big business" (Scherer, 1980). The table lists the expenditures on R&D by industry group in 1975.

INDUSTRY GROUP	EXPENDITURES ON R&D ($ millions)
Food and tobacco products	367
Textiles and apparel	64
Lumber, wood products, and furniture	68
Paper and allied products	253
Chemicals and drugs	2,650
Petroleum refining and extraction	700
Rubber products	283
Stone, clay, and glass products	186
Primary metals	365
Fabricated metal products	311
Machinery	2,658
Electrical equipment and communications	5,530
Motor vehicles and other transportation equipment	2,367
Aircraft and missiles	5,729
Instruments	1,034
Nonmanufacturing industries	739

Source: U.S. National Science Foundation, *Research and Development in Industry, 1975* (Washington, D.C.: U.S. Government Printing Office, 1977, p. 29).

a. Compute the median of the R&D expenditures for this data set.
b. What was the average amount spent per industry group on R&D in 1975?
c. Explain why the mode cannot be effectively used as a measure of central tendency in the R&D expenditures data set.

3.76 A quality control inspector is interested in determining whether a metal lathe used to produce machine bearings is properly adjusted. He plans to do so by using thirty bearings selected randomly from the last 2,000 bearings produced by the machine to estimate the average diameter of bearings being produced. Define and explain the meanings of the following symbols *in the context of this problem:*

a. μ **b.** $\bar{x}$ **c.** σ **d.** s **e.** $\mu + 2\sigma$

3.77 One hundred management trainees were given an examination in basic accounting. Their test scores were found to have a mean and variance of 75 and 36, respectively.

a. Make a statement about the percentage of the test scores that would be expected to fall between 69 and 81.

b. If a grade of 63 was required to pass the test, make a statement about the percentage of the trainees who would be expected to fail.

3.78 Redo Exercise 3.77 assuming that the distribution of test scores was determined to be mound-shaped.

3.79 The Environmental Protection Agency (EPA) says it receives more complaints about the noise from motorcycles than from any other vehicles. As a result, on December 24, 1980, the EPA issued standards to limit the noise from motorcycles built after January 1, 1983. The regulations will be phased in from 1983 to 1986. By January 1, 1986, the noise level of all street motorcycles and small off-the-road motorcycles must not exceed 80 decibels. The agency said that "the 80-decibel limit should, on the average, reduce the noise from new street motorcycles by 5 decibels and by 2 to 7 decibels on new off-road motorcycles . . ." ("EPA Makes Itself Heard," 1980). Carefully explain, in the context of the situation described, what is meant by "on the average" in the quote above.

3.80 The following is a list of the number of defective bottles produced by a particular bottle-making machine during each of the last 10 hours:

2, 6, 4, 5, 8, 10, 1, 3, 6, 6

a. Determine the mean, median, mode, range, variance, and standard deviation of this data set. Specify the units of each measure.

b. As a check on your calculation of s in part a, use the range of the data to help you determine an approximate value for s. [*Hint:* Refer to Example 3.8.]

c. Which of the measures in part a are measures of variability and which are measures of central tendency?

3.81 The vice-president in charge of sales for the conglomerate you work for has asked you to evaluate the sales records of two of the firm's divisions. You note that the range of monthly sales for division A over the last 2 years is $50,000 and the range for division B is only $30,000. You compute each division's mean monthly sales for the same time period and discover that both divisions have a mean of $110,000. Assume that is all the information you have about the division's sales records. Would you be willing to say which of the divisions has a more consistent sales record? Why or why not?

3.82 Refer to Exercise 3.81.

a. Estimate the standard deviation of the monthly sales distribution of division B.

b. Based on your estimate in part a, would you say it is more likely that division B's sales next month will be over $120,000 or under $90,000?

c. Is it possible for division B's sales next month to be over $160,000? Explain.

3.83 Before purchasing stock in an electronics firm, the management of a mutual fund wants information concerning the price movements of the firm's stock during the past year. Thirty days of the past year were randomly selected and the closing price (to the nearest dollar) was recorded for each day:

$33	$20	$45	$41	$52	$36
21	33	41	36	49	26
51	28	32	35	32	28
50	35	48	29	50	28
33	39	30	30	28	29

The mutual fund's management has decided it should purchase the stock only if the mean closing price for last year is $41 or more.

a. Define the terms *mean, median,* and *mode* in the context of this problem.

b. Construct a relative frequency histogram for the data.

c. Compute the mean, median, and mode for the data set and locate them on the histogram.

d. Do you think the mutual fund should purchase the firm's stock? [*Note:* Simply looking at the sample and using your intuition could lead you to an erroneous conclusion. We will learn how to use the sample mean to make decisions about a population mean in Chapters 8 and 9.]

3.84 The manufacturers of an amazing new gadget claim in an advertisement for sales personnel that their first-year salespeople earn an average of $35,000. You call their main office and demand to know the standard deviation of first-year salespeople's incomes. The assistant personnel manager's secretary tells you the standard deviation is $9,000. What can be said about the fraction of the manufacturer's salespeople who make between $8,000 and $62,000 during their first year?

3.85 To help evaluate the impact of a proposed change in its credit policy, a department store wants to obtain a description of the ages of its accounts receivable. Accordingly, the store's internal auditor sampled thirty accounts and determined the number of days since each account had a balance of zero. The data are given in the table.

ACCOUNT NUMBER	AGE (Days)	ACCOUNT NUMBER	AGE (Days)
133	8	3333	80
398	10	3621	15
502	22	3981	0
553	12	4310	7
992	0	4322	45
1009	7	4480	28
1351	25	4618	0
1667	28	5021	38
1993	15	5118	9
2210	36	5226	18
2312	63	5438	21
2425	6	5506	3
2788	0	5872	110
3001	42	6095	54
3110	0	6204	0

a. Find the z-scores for the ages of account numbers 5021 and 5872.

b. Locate the ages of account numbers 5021 and 5872 on a box plot of the data. Do you consider both accounts to be outliers in terms of their ages? Explain.

3.86 Suppose you used the following formula as a measure of the variability (V) of a data set:

$$V = \frac{\sum_{i=1}^{n}(x_i - \bar{x})}{n}$$

What information can be learned about the variability of a data set using this formula? Using the data of Exercise 3.64, find V.

3.87 Many firms use on-the-job training to teach their employees computer programming. Suppose you work in the personnel department of a firm that just finished training a group of its employees to program and you have been requested to review the performance of one of the trainees on the final test that was given to all trainees. The mean and standard deviation of the test scores are 80 and 5, respectively, and the distribution of scores is mound-shaped.

a. The employee in question scored 65 on the final test. Compute the employee's z-score.

b. Approximately what percentage of the trainees will have z-scores equal to or less than the employee of part a?

c. If a trainee was arbitrarily selected from those who had taken the final test, is it more likely that he or she would score 90 or above, or 65 or below?

3.88 *Chebyshev's theorem* (mentioned in Table 3.7) states that at least $1 - (1/K^2)$ of a set of measurements will lie within K standard deviations of the mean of the data set. Use Chebyshev's theorem to state the fraction of a set of measurements that will lie within

a. 2 standard deviations of the mean μ $(K = 2)$

b. 3 standard deviations of the mean

c. 1.5 standard deviations of the mean

3.89 Seven workdays in June were selected, and the number of machine breakdowns per day in the woodworking shop of a furniture company was recorded. This procedure was repeated in August after the firm had replaced ten of its oldest machines. The data are listed in the table.

JUNE	8	3	0	0	10	4	9
AUGUST	0	3	4	11	3	3	2

a. Which month exhibits more variability in the number of machines that break down per day as measured by the range? As measured by s^2? In this case, which measure, s^2 or the range, do you feel better represents the variability of the data sets? Explain.

b. Add 3 to each of the numbers of breakdowns per day in June and recompute s^2 for June. Compare your result with that obtained in part a. What is the effect on s^2 of adding a constant to each of the sample measurements?

c. Multiply each of the numbers of breakdowns per day in June by 3 and recompute s^2 for June. Compare your result with that obtained in part a. What is the effect on s^2 of multiplying each sample measurement by a constant?

3.90 Economic theory suggests that the vigor of competition in an industry is related to the number of firms in the industry. As a measure of competitiveness, however, the number of firms in an industry does not take into consideration the extent to which a few firms may dominate that industry. For example, in an industry with 100 firms, each may produce 1% of industry output, or three firms may dominate, producing 75% compared to the other ninety-seven firms' 25%. The *market concentration ratio* is a measure of competitiveness that reflects such inequalities among firms in an industry. The market concentration ratio is usually defined as the percentage of total industry sales contributed by the largest few firms (usually three or four). A high concentration ratio indicates an industry dominated by a few firms. A low concentration ratio indicates an industry with much competition among many firms. The table contains 1970 three-firm market concentration ratios for twelve industries in each of six different countries. Answer the following questions using the methods from Chapters 2 and 3 that you deem appropriate.

INDUSTRY	UNITED STATES	CANADA	UNITED KINGDOM	SWEDEN	FRANCE	WEST GERMANY
Brewing	39	89	47	70	63	17
Cigarettes	68	90	94	100	100	94
Fabric weaving	30	67	28	50	23	16
Paints	26	40	40	92	14	32
Petroleum refining	25	64	79	100	60	47
Shoes (except rubber)	17	18	17	37	13	20
Glass bottles	65	100	73	100	84	93
Cement	20	65	86	100	81	54
Ordinary steel	42	80	39	63	84	56
Antifriction bearings	43	89	82	100	80	90
Refrigerators	64	75	65	89	100	72
Storage batteries	54	73	75	100	94	82

Source: F. M. Scherer, Alan Beckenstein, Erich Kaufer, & R. D. Murphy, *The Economics of Multiplant Operation: An International Comparisons Study* (Cambridge, Mass.: Harvard University Press, 1975). Reprinted by permission.

a. For each of the six countries, characterize the magnitude and variability of the sample of twelve market concentration ratios.

b. For each of the twelve industries, characterize the magnitude and variability of the sample of six market concentration ratios.

c. Which nation has on average the most competition within its industries? The least competition?

d. Which are the three most competitive industries? The three least competitive industries?

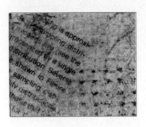

On Your Own . . .

1. Find the variance, standard deviation, and range of the quantitative data set you found for the "On Your Own" section in Chapter 2.

2. Use Table 3.7 to describe the distribution of this data set.

3. Count the actual number of observations that fall within 1, 2, and 3 standard deviations of the mean of the data set and compare these counts with the description of the data set you developed above.

References

Brown, S. J., & Warner, J. B. "Measuring security price performance," *Journal of Financial Economics*, Sept. 1980, *8*, 205–258.

Chase, R. B., & Aquilano, N. J. *Production and operations management*, Rev. ed. Homewood, Ill.: Richard D. Irwin, 1977. Chapter 11.

Consumer's Digest, Nov.–Dec. 1980.

CPC Salary Survey. Bethlehem, Pa.: The College Placement Council, Report No. 3, July 1983.

Curley, J. "Some think a 'baby boom' spending spree could lead to strong economic recovery." *Wall Street Journal*, Jan. 24, 1983, 25.

Eger, C. E. "Corporate mergers: An empirical analysis of the role of risky debt." Unpublished Ph.D. dissertation, School of Management, University of Minnesota, 1982.

"EPA makes itself heard on cycle noise." *Minneapolis Star*, Dec. 25, 1980, 29A.

"The *Fortune* directory of the 500 largest U.S. industrial corporations." *Fortune*, May 1983, 226–254.

"Keeping up." *Fortune*, Aug. 13, 1979, 100.

Mendenhall, W. *Introduction to probability and statistics*, 6th ed. Boston: Duxbury, 1983. Chapter 3.

Milkovich, G. T., Annoni, A. J., & Mahoney, T. A. "The use of the delphi procedures in manpower forecasting." *Management Science*, Dec. 1972, *19*, part I, 381–388.

Namias, J. "A method to detect specific causes of consumer complaints." *Journal of Marketing Research*, Aug. 1964, 63–68.

Neter, J., Wasserman, W., & Whitmore, G. A. *Applied statistics*. Boston: Allyn & Bacon, 1982. Chapter 3.

Postlewaite, S. "Salad bars sprout as fast-food battle turns from the burger." *Minneapolis Tribune*, July 3, 1983, 7D.

Rothstein, M. "Hotel overbooking as a Markovian sequential decision process." *Decision Sciences*, July 1974, *5*, 389–405.

Scherer, F. M. *Industrial market structure and economic performance*. 2d ed. Chicago: Rand McNally, 1980, pp. 408–409.

U.S. Bureau of the Census. *Statistical abstract of the United States: 1981*. 102d ed. Washington, D.C.: U.S. Government Printing Office, 1981.

U.S. Department of Labor. *The Consumer Price Index: Concepts and content over the years*. Bureau of Labor Statistics, Report 517, May 1978.

Vatter, W. J. *Accounting measurements for financial reports*. Homewood, Ill.: Richard D. Irwin, 1971, p. 78.

CHAPTER 4

Probability

Where We've Been . . .

In Chapter 1, we identified inference from a sample to a population as the goal of statistics. In Chapters 2 and 3, we learned how to describe a set of measurements using graphical and numerical descriptive methods.

Where We're Going . . .

We now begin to consider the problem of making an inference. What permits us to make the inferential jump from sample to population and then to give a measure of reliability for the inference? As you will subsequently see, the answer is *probability*. This chapter is devoted to a study of probability — what it is and some of the basic concepts of the theory that surrounds it.

Contents

You will recall that statistics is concerned with inferences about a population based on sample information. Understanding how this will be accomplished is easier if you understand the relationship between population and sample. This understanding is enhanced by reversing the statistical procedure of making inferences from sample to population. In this chapter we assume the population *known* and calculate the chances of obtaining various samples from the population. Thus, probability is the "reverse" of statistics: In probability we use the population information to infer the probable nature of the sample.

Probability plays an important role in decision-making. To illustrate, suppose you have an opportunity to invest in an oil exploration company. Past records show that for ten out of ten previous oil drillings (a sample of the company's experiences), all ten resulted in dry wells. What do you conclude? Do you think the chances are better than 50–50 that the company will hit a producing well? Should you invest in this company? We think your answer to these questions will be an emphatic no. If the company's exploratory prowess is sufficient to hit a producing well 50% of the time, a record of ten dry wells out of ten drilled is an event that is just too *improbable.* Do you agree?

As another illustration, suppose you are playing poker with what your opponents assure you is a well-shuffled deck of cards. In three consecutive five-card hands, the person on your right is dealt four aces. Based on this sample of three deals, do you think the cards are being adequately shuffled? Again, we think your answer will be no and that you will reach this conclusion because dealing three hands of four aces is just too *improbable,* assuming that the cards were properly shuffled.

Note that the decision concerning the potential success of the oil drilling company and the decision concerning the card shuffling were both based on probabilities—namely, the probabilities of certain sample results. Both situations were contrived so you could easily conclude that the probabilities of the sample results were small. Unfortunately, the probabilities of many observed sample results are not so easy to evaluate. For these cases, we will need the assistance of a theory of probability.

4.1 Events, Sample Spaces, and Probability

Most sets of data that are of interest to the business community are generated by some *experiment:*

Definition 4.1

An *experiment* is the process of making an observation or taking a measurement.

Our definition of *experiment* is broader than that used in the physical sciences, where we might picture test tubes, microscopes, and other equipment. Examples of statistical experiments in business are recording whether a customer prefers one of two brands of coffee (say, brand A or brand B), measuring the change in the Dow Jones Average from one day to the next, recording the weekly sales of a business firm, and counting the number of errors on a page of an accountant's ledger.

An experimental outcome is called an *event:*

Definition 4.2

An *event* is an outcome of the experiment.

Thus, if the experiment is to observe the up face following the toss of a die, three examples of events are observing an even number, observing a number less than 4, and observing a 6. If the experiment is counting the number of errors on a page of an accountant's ledger, three examples of events are observing no errors, observing fewer than five errors, and observing more than ten errors. Our goal is to be able to calculate the probability that a particular event occurs when an experiment is performed.

The calculation of event probabilities is made easier by listing the most basic outcomes of the experiment:

Definition 4.3

A *simple event* is an event that cannot be decomposed into two or more other events.

In Table 4.1 we present three examples of experiments and their simple events. We begin with simple coin and dice examples because they are most likely to be familiar to you. Experiment a in Table 4.1 is to observe the result of the toss of a single coin. You will undoubtedly agree that the most basic possible outcomes of this experiment are Observe a head and Observe a tail. Experiment b in Table 4.1 is to observe the result of tossing a single die. Note that the events Observe a 1, Observe a 2, etc., cannot be further decomposed into

---

Table 4.1
Experiments and Their
Simple Events

a. Experiment: Observe the up face on a coin
   Simple events: 1. Observe a head
                    2. Observe a tail
b. Experiment: Observe the up face on a die
   Simple events: 1. Observe a 1
                    2. Observe a 2
                    3. Observe a 3
                    4. Observe a 4
                    5. Observe a 5
                    6. Observe a 6
c. Experiment: Observe the up faces on two coins
   Simple events: 1. Observe H_1, H_2
                    2. Observe H_1, T_2
                    3. Observe T_1, H_2
                    4. Observe T_1, T_2
   (where H_1 means "Head on coin 1," H_2 means
   "Head on coin 2," etc.)

more basic events. Therefore, they are simple events. However, the event Observe an even number can be decomposed into Observe a 2, Observe a 4, and Observe a 6. Thus, Observe an even number is not a simple event. The reasoning is similar for experiment c in Table 4.1.

Simple events possess an important property. If the experiment is conducted once, you can observe one and only one simple event. For example, if you toss a coin and observe a head, you cannot observe a tail on the same toss. If you toss a die and observe a 2, you cannot also observe a 6. That is, for a single experiment, one and only one of the simple events must occur. To demonstrate that this property does not hold for all events, consider the event Observe an even number. It is possible for us to Observe an even number *and* Observe a 2 on the same toss.

The collection of all the simple events of an experiment is called the *sample space:*

Definition 4.4

The *sample space* of an experiment is the collection of all its simple events.

For example, there are six simple events associated with experiment b in Table 4.1. These six simple events comprise the sample space for the experiment. Similarly, for experiment c in Table 4.1, there are four simple events in the sample space.

A graphical method, called the *Venn diagram,* is useful for presenting the sample space and its simple events. The sample space is shown as a closed figure, labeled *S*. This figure contains a set of points, called *sample points,* with each point representing a simple event. Figure 4.1 shows the Venn diagram for each of the three experiments in Table 4.1. Note that the number of sample points in a sample space *S* is equal to the number of simple events associated with the respective experiment: two for experiment a, six for experiment b, and four for experiment c.

Now that we have defined the terms *simple event* and *sample space,* we are prepared to define the *probabilities of simple events.* The probability of a simple event is a number that measures the likelihood that the event will occur when the experiment is performed. This number is usually taken to be the relative frequency of the occurrence of a simple event in a very long series of repetitions of an experiment. Or, when this information is not available, we select the number based on experience. For example, if we are assigning probabilities to the two simple events in the coin toss experiment (Observe a head and Observe a tail), we might reason that if we toss a balanced coin a very large number of times, the simple events Observe a head and Observe a tail will occur with the same relative frequency of .5. Thus, the probability of each simple event is .5.

In other cases we may choose the probability based on general information about the experiment. For example, if the experiment is observing whether a business venture succeeds or fails (the simple events), we may assess the probability of success by considering the personnel managing the venture, the general state of the economy at the time, the success of similar ventures, and any other information deemed pertinent.[*] If we finally decide

Figure 4.1   Venn Diagrams for the Three Experiments from Table 4.1

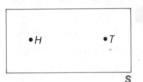

(a) Experiment: Observe the up face on a coin

(b) Experiment: Observe the up face on a die

(c) Experiment: Observe the up faces on two coins

---

[*] For a text that deals in detail with subjective evaluation of probabilities, see Winkler (1972).

that the venture has an 80% chance of succeeding, we assign a probability of .8 to the simple event Success. We believe that .8 is a reasonably accurate measure of the likelihood of the occurrence of the simple event Success. If it is not, we may be misled on any decisions based on this probability or based on any calculations in which it appears.

No matter how you assign the probabilities to simple events, the probabilities assigned must obey two rules:

> **1.** All simple event probabilities *must* lie in the interval from 0 to 1.
> **2.** The probabilities of all the simple events within a sample space must sum to 1.

Figure 4.2 Die Toss Experiment with Event *A*: Observe an Even Number

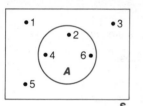

To find the probability of any event, you should recall that an event is any outcome of an experiment. Let us examine this statement in greater detail. Consider the die-tossing experiment and the event Observe an even number. Notice that you could just as easily define this event by saying "Observe a 2, Observe a 4, or Observe a 6," since the event will occur if and only if one of these three simple events occurs. Consequently, you can think of the event Observe an even number as the collection of the three simple events Observe a 2, Observe a 4, and Observe a 6. This event, which we will denote by the symbol *A*, can be represented in a Venn diagram by a closed figure inside the sample space *S*. This closed figure *A* will contain the simple events that constitute event *A*, as shown in Figure 4.2.

To summarize, we have demonstrated that an event can be defined in words or as a specific set of simple events. This leads us to the following definition of an *event:*

> ## Definition 4.5
>
> An *event* is a specific collection of simple events.

How do you decide which simple events belong to the set associated with an event *A*? Test each simple event in the sample space *S*. If event *A* occurs when a particular simple event occurs, then that simple event is in the event *A*. For example, in the die toss experiment, the event Observe an even number (event *A*) will occur if the simple event Observe a 2 occurs. By the same reasoning, the simple events Observe a 4 and Observe a 6 are in event *A*.

Now return to our original objective—finding the probability of any event. Consider the problem of finding the probability of observing an even number (event *A*) in the single toss of a die. You will recall that *A* will occur if one of the three simple events, toss a 2, 4, or 6, occurs. Since two or more simple events cannot occur at the same time, we can easily calculate the probability of event *A* by summing the probabilities of the three simple events. We would attach a probability equal to $\frac{1}{6}$ to each of the simple events (if the die is fair), so the probability of observing an even number (event *A*), denoted by the symbol $P(A)$, would be

$$P(A) = P(\text{Observe a 2}) + P(\text{Observe a 4}) + P(\text{Observe a 6})$$
$$= \tfrac{1}{6} + \tfrac{1}{6} + \tfrac{1}{6} = \tfrac{1}{2}$$

The previous example leads us to a general procedure for finding the probability of an event A:

> The probability of an event A is calculated by summing the probabilities of the simple events in A.

Thus, we can summarize the steps for calculating the probability of any event:*

Steps for Calculating Probabilities of Events

1. Define the experiment.
2. List the simple events.
3. Assign probabilities to the simple events.
4. Determine the collection of simple events contained in the event of interest.
5. Sum the simple event probabilities to obtain the event probability.

Example 4.1   Consider the experiment of tossing two coins. Assume both coins are fair.

a. List the simple events and assign them reasonable probabilities.
b. Consider the events

   A: {Observe exactly one head} B: {Observe at least one head}

   and calculate $P(A)$ and $P(B)$.

Solution   **a.** The simple events are

Figure 4.3 Venn Diagram of the Two-Coin Toss

$$H_1, H_2 \qquad H_1, T_2 \qquad T_1, H_2 \qquad T_1, T_2$$

where H_1 denotes Observe a head on coin 1, H_2 denotes Observe a head on coin 2, etc. If both coins are fair, we can again use the concept of relative frequency in a long series of experimental repetitions to conclude that each simple event should be assigned a probability of $\frac{1}{4}$.

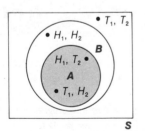

b. We use a Venn diagram to show the events A: {Observe exactly one head} and B: {Observe at least one head} (Figure 4.3). Then we may calculate the probabilities by adding the appropriate simple event probabilities:

$$P(A) = P(H_1, T_2) + P(T_1, H_2) = \tfrac{1}{4} + \tfrac{1}{4} = \tfrac{1}{2}$$
$$P(B) = P(H_1, H_2) + P(H_1, T_2) + P(T_1, H_2) = \tfrac{1}{4} + \tfrac{1}{4} + \tfrac{1}{4} = \tfrac{3}{4}$$ ■

Example 4.2   A bank wishes to divide its service windows into two groups corresponding to the type of customer account: commercial or personal. One problem facing the bank is deciding how to apportion the service windows to the categories of service. At this stage of our study, we do not have the tools to solve this problem, but we can say that one of the important factors affecting the solution is the proportion of the two types of customers that enter the bank at a

* A thorough treatment of this topic can be found in the text by Feller (1968).

particular time. To illustrate, what is the probability that an incoming customer will have a commercial account? What is the probability that the next two customers will have commercial accounts? What is the probability for the general case of k customers? Explain how you might attempt to solve this problem. [*Note:* For this example we use the term *customer* to refer only to people who seek teller service.]

Solution   The experiment corresponding to the entrance of a single customer is analogous to the coin-tossing experiment illustrated in Figure 4.1(a). A customer has either a commercial (consider this a head) or a personal (consider this a tail) account, and there are no other possible outcomes. Consequently, there are two simple events in the sample space:

Experiment: Observe the type of account a single customer has

Simple events: 1. C: {The customer has a commercial account}
                            2. P: {The customer has a personal account}

The difference between this problem and the coin-tossing problem becomes apparent when we attempt to assign probabilities to the two simple events. What probability should we assign to the simple event C? Some people might say .5, as for the coin-tossing experiment, but you can see that finding the probability of simple event C, $P(C)$, is not so easy. Suppose a check of the bank's records showed that 95% of its accounts are personal. Then, at first glance, it would appear that $P(C)$ is .05. But this may not be correct, because the probability will depend on how frequently the two types of customers use the accounts — i.e., how many times per week, on the average, they seek banking service. So the important point to note is that here is a case where equal probabilities are not assigned to the simple events. How can we find these probabilities? A good procedure might be to monitor the system for a period of time and ask incoming customers which type of service they desire. Then the proportions of the two types of customers could be used to approximate the probabilities of the two simple events.

The experiment corresponding to the entrance of the next two customers is similar to the experiment of Example 4.1, tossing two coins, except that the probability that a single customer possesses a commercial account is not .5. We will learn how to find the probabilities of the simple events for this experiment, or for the general case of k customers, in Section 4.5.   ■

Example 4.3   You have the capital to invest in two of four ventures, each of which requires approximately the same amount of investment capital. Unknown to you, two of the investments will eventually fail and two will be successful. You research the four ventures because you think that your research should increase your probability of a successful choice over a purely random selection, and you eventually decide on two. What is the lower limit of your probability of selecting the two best out of four? That is, if you used no information and selected two ventures at random, what is the probability that you would select the two successful ventures? At least one?

Solution   Denote the two successful enterprises as S_1 and S_2 and the two failing enterprises as F_1 and F_2. The experiment involves a random selection of two out of the four ventures, and each possible pair of ventures represents a simple event. The six simple events that make up the sample space are

1. S_1, S_2 3. S_1, F_2 5. S_2, F_2
2. S_1, F_1 4. S_2, F_1 6. F_1, F_2

The next step is to assign probabilities to the simple events. If we assume that the choice of any one pair is as likely as any other, then the probability of each simple event is $\frac{1}{6}$. Now check to see which simple events result in the choice of two successful ventures. Only one such simple event exists—namely, S_1, S_2. Therefore, the probability of choosing two successful ventures out of the four is

$$P(S_1, S_2) = \tfrac{1}{6}$$

The event of selecting at least one of the two successful ventures includes all the simple events except F_1, F_2.

$$\begin{aligned} P(\text{Select at least one success}) \\ &= P(S_1, S_2) + P(S_1, F_1) + P(S_1, F_2) + P(S_2, F_1) + P(S_2, F_2) \\ &= \tfrac{1}{6} + \tfrac{1}{6} + \tfrac{1}{6} + \tfrac{1}{6} + \tfrac{1}{6} = \tfrac{5}{6} \end{aligned}$$

Therefore, the worst that you could do in selecting two ventures out of four may not be too bad. With a random selection, the probability of selecting two successful ventures will be at least $\frac{1}{6}$ and the probability of selecting at least one successful venture out of two is at least $\frac{5}{6}$. ■

The preceding examples have one thing in common: The number of simple events in each of the sample spaces was small; hence the simple events were easy to identify and list. How can we manage this when the simple events run into the thousands or millions? For example, suppose you wish to select 5 people from a group of 1,000. Then each different group of 5 people would represent a simple event. How can you determine the number of simple events associated with this experiment?

One method of determining the number of simple events for a complex experiment is to develop a counting system. Start by examining a simple version of the experiment. For example, see if you can develop a system for counting the number of ways to select 2 people from a total of 4 (this is exactly what was done in Example 4.3). If the people are represented by the symbols C_1, C_2, C_3, and C_4, the simple events could be listed in the following pattern:

C_1, C_2 C_2, C_3 C_3, C_4
C_1, C_3 C_2, C_4
C_1, C_4

Note the pattern and now try a more complex situation—say, sampling 3 people out of 5. List the simple events and observe the pattern. Finally, see if you can deduce the pattern for the general case. Perhaps you can program a computer to produce the matching and counting for the number of samples of 5 selected from a total of 1,000.

A second method of determining the number of simple events for an experiment is to use ***combinatorial mathematics.*** This branch of mathematics is concerned with developing counting rules for given situations. For example, there is a simple rule for finding the number of different samples of 5 people selected from 1,000. This rule is given by the formula

$$\binom{N}{n} = \frac{N!}{n!(N-n)!}$$

where N is the number of elements in the population; n is the number of elements in the sample; and the factorial symbol (!) means that, say, $n! = n(n-1)(n-2) \cdots \cdot 3 \cdot 2 \cdot 1$. Thus, $5! = 5 \cdot 4 \cdot 3 \cdot 2 \cdot 1$. (The quantity 0! is defined to be equal to 1.)

Example 4.4　Find the number of different samples when selecting two elements from a group of four.

Solution　For this example, $N = 4$, $n = 2$, and

$$\binom{4}{2} = \frac{4!}{2!2!} = \frac{4 \cdot 3 \cdot 2 \cdot 1}{(2 \cdot 1)(2 \cdot 1)} = 6$$

You can see that this agrees with the number of simple events obtained above and in Example 4.3. ■

Example 4.5　Suppose you plan to invest equal amounts of money in each of five common stocks. If you have chosen twenty stocks from which to make the selection, how many different samples of five stocks can be selected from the twenty?

Solution　For this example, $N = 20$ and $n = 5$. Then the number of different samples of five that can be selected from the twenty stocks is

$$\binom{20}{5} = \frac{20!}{5!(20-5)!} = \frac{20!}{5!15!}$$

$$= \frac{20 \cdot 19 \cdot 18 \cdots \cdot 3 \cdot 2 \cdot 1}{(5 \cdot 4 \cdot 3 \cdot 2 \cdot 1)(15 \cdot 14 \cdot 13 \cdots \cdot 3 \cdot 2 \cdot 1)} = 15,504$$ ■

The symbol $\binom{N}{n}$, meaning the *number of combinations of N elements taken n at a time,* is just one of a large number of counting rules that have been developed by combinatorial mathematicians. If you are interested in learning more about combinatorial mathematics, you will find a few of the basic counting rules in Appendix A. Others can be found in the reference books listed at the end of this chapter.

**Exercises
4.1–4.16**

Learning the Mechanics

4.1 What is the difference between a *simple event* and an *event*?

4.2 An experiment results in one of the following simple events: E_1, E_2, E_3, E_4, and E_5.

a. Find $P(E_3)$ if $P(E_1) = .1$, $P(E_2) = .3$, $P(E_4) = .1$, and $P(E_5) = .1$.
b. Find $P(E_3)$ if $P(E_1) = P(E_3)$, $P(E_2) = .1$, $P(E_4) = .2$, and $P(E_5) = .2$.
c. Find $P(E_3)$ if $P(E_1) = P(E_2) = P(E_4) = P(E_5) = .1$.

4.3 An experiment results in one of the following simple events: E_1, E_2, E_3, and E_4.

a. It is known that $P(E_1) = P(E_2) = P(E_3) = P(E_4)$. Find $P(E_1)$.
b. It is known that $P(E_2) = P(E_3) = P(E_4) = .2$. Find $P(E_1)$.

4.4 Compute each of the following:

a. $\begin{pmatrix} 10 \\ 3 \end{pmatrix}$ **b.** $\begin{pmatrix} 6 \\ 2 \end{pmatrix}$ **c.** $\begin{pmatrix} 8 \\ 3 \end{pmatrix}$ **d.** $\begin{pmatrix} 5 \\ 5 \end{pmatrix}$ **e.** $\begin{pmatrix} 4 \\ 0 \end{pmatrix}$

4.5 Compute each of the following:

a. $\begin{pmatrix} 5 \\ 2 \end{pmatrix}$ **b.** $\begin{pmatrix} 7 \\ 5 \end{pmatrix}$ **c.** $\begin{pmatrix} 6 \\ 4 \end{pmatrix}$ **d.** $\begin{pmatrix} 10 \\ 10 \end{pmatrix}$ **e.** $\begin{pmatrix} 10 \\ 0 \end{pmatrix}$

Applying the Concepts

4.6 The population of the amounts of 500 automobile loans made by a bank last year can be described as follows:

AMOUNT OF LOAN ($)			
Under 1,000	1,000–3,999	4,000–5,999	6,000 or more
27	99	298	76

For the purpose of checking the accuracy of the bank's records, an auditor will randomly select one of these loans for inspection (i.e., each loan has an equal probability of being selected).

a. List the simple events in this experiment.
b. What is the probability that the loan selected will be for $6,000 or more?
c. What is the probability that the loan will be for less than $4,000?

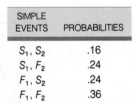

SIMPLE EVENTS	PROBABILITIES
S_1, S_2	.16
S_1, F_2	.24
F_1, S_2	.24
F_1, F_2	.36

4.7 A cigarette manufacturer has decided to market two new brands. An analysis of current market conditions and a review of the firm's past successes and failures with new brands have led the manufacturer to believe that the simple events and the probabilities of their occurrence in this marketing experiment are as listed in the table (S_1: Brand 1 succeeds, F_1: Brand 1 fails, etc.). Find the probability of each of the following events:

A: {Both new brands are successful in the first year}

B: {At least one new brand is successful in the first year}

4.8 Of six cars produced at a particular factory between 8 and 10 A.M. last Monday morning, three are known to be lemons. Three of the six cars were shipped to dealer A and the other three to dealer B. Just by chance, dealer A received all three lemons. What is the probability of this event occurring if, in fact, the three cars shipped to dealer A were selected at random from the six produced?

4.9 A buyer for a large metropolitan department store must choose two firms from the four available to supply the store's fall line of men's slacks. The buyer has not dealt with any of the four firms before and considers their products equally attractive. Unknown to the buyer, two of the four firms are having serious financial problems that may result in their not being able to

SIMPLE EVENTS	PROBABILITIES
G_1, G_2	$\frac{1}{6}$
G_1, P_1	$\frac{1}{6}$
G_1, P_2	$\frac{1}{6}$
G_2, P_1	$\frac{1}{6}$
G_2, P_2	$\frac{1}{6}$
P_1, P_2	$\frac{1}{6}$

deliver the slacks as soon as promised. The four firms are identified as G_1 and G_2 (firms in good financial condition) and P_1 and P_2 (firms in poor financial condition). Simple events identify the pair of firms selected. If the probability of the buyer selecting a particular pair from among the four is the same for each pair, the table gives the simple events and their probabilities for this buying experiment. Find the probability of each of the following events:

A: {Buyer selects two firms in good financial condition}

B: {Buyer selects at least one firm in poor financial condition}

4.10 Simulate the experiment in Exercise 4.9 by marking four poker chips (or cards), one corresponding to each of the four firms. Mix the chips, randomly draw two, and record the results. Replace the chips. Now repeat the experiment a large number of times (at least 100).

a. Calculate the proportion of times event A occurs. How does this proportion compare with $P(A)$? Should the proportion equal $P(A)$? Explain.

b. Calculate the proportion of times event B occurs and compare that with $P(B)$.

4.11 The Value Line Survey, a service for common stock investors, provides its subscribers with up-to-date evaluations of the prospects and risks associated with the purchase of a large number of common stocks. Each stock is ranked 1 (highest) to 5 (lowest) according to Value Line's estimate of the stock's potential for price appreciation during the next 12 months and according to its safety as an investment.

Suppose you plan to purchase stock in three electrical utility companies from among seven that possess rankings of 2 for price appreciation. Unknown to you, two of the companies will experience serious difficulties with their nuclear facilities during the coming year. If you randomly select the three companies from among the seven, what is the probability that:

a. You select none of the companies with prospective nuclear difficulties?

b. You select one of the companies with prospective nuclear difficulties?

c. You select both of the companies with prospective nuclear difficulties?

4.12 You are a lawyer for a client who has committed a felony, and there are seven judges who could hear your motion to set bail. Four judges are strict, and the other three are lenient. As you walk into the courtroom, judge A (a strict judge) is leaving to go home.

a. What is the probability of drawing a lenient judge for your client?

b. What is the probability of drawing a lenient judge for your client if the probability of getting judge B (a strict judge) is .3, the probability of getting judge C (a strict judge) is .4, and the probabilities of getting any of the other four judges are equally likely?

c. Suppose you know that judge D (a lenient judge) never follows judge A. What is the probability of drawing a lenient judge for your client if the probabilities in part b are valid?

4.13 A firm's accounting department believes the firm will make a profit in the first quarter of the year in one of the ranges listed in the table at the top of the next page, with probability as noted. Find the probability of each of the following events:

A: {The firm makes $99,999 or less}

B: {The firm makes over $149,999}

C: {The firm makes between $100,000 and $149,999}

PROFIT RANGE ($)	PROBABILITY
Under 75,000	.10
75,000 – 99,999	.15
100,000 – 124,999	.25
125,000 – 149,999	.35
150,000 – 174,999	.10
175,000 or over	.05

4.14 Before placing a person in a highly skilled position, a company gives applicants a series of three examinations. The first is a physical examination, and each applicant is classified as satisfactory or unsatisfactory. The other two are verbal and quantitative examinations, and the scores are used to classify each applicant as high, medium, or low in each area. Thus, each individual will receive a health score, a verbal score, and a quantitative score.

a. List the different sets of classifications that can result from this battery of examinations.
b. If all applicants who take the examinations are equally qualified, and all the variation in test scores is due to random variation in the types of test questions, what is the probability that an applicant receives the lowest classification on all three examinations?
c. If an applicant scores in the highest category on at least two of the three examinations, the applicant will get a position. What is the probability that a randomly selected applicant will get a position?

4.15 In May 1983, the unemployment rate in the United States ranged from 5.0% in South Dakota to 18.2% in West Virginia. The nationwide unemployment rate was 9.8%. The table lists the May 1983 and May 1982 unemployment rates for the fifteen Atlantic coast states. Suppose one of these fifteen states is to be selected and the direction of change in its unemployment rate from May 1982 to May 1983 is to be observed. Assume that each state has an equal probability of being selected.

STATE	MAY 1983 (%)	MAY 1982 (%)
Connecticut	6.3	6.6
Delaware	6.8	7.3
Florida	8.7	7.3
Georgia	7.1	7.4
Maine	9.6	8.6
Maryland	6.6	8.0
Massachusetts	6.5	8.6
New Hampshire	5.6	7.3
New Jersey	7.5	9.7
New York	8.5	7.9
North Carolina	8.4	8.8
Pennsylvania	12.1	13.0
Rhode Island	8.6	10.0
South Carolina	10.1	11.0
Virginia	6.0	7.5

Source: *USA Today*, July 20, 1983, p. 4A.

a. What is the probability that Pennsylvania will be selected? Florida? Virginia?

b. What is the probability of selecting a state that had no change in its unemployment rate?

c. What is the probability of selecting a state whose unemployment rate has increased? Decreased?

d. What is the probability of selecting a state whose unemployment rate increased 1% or more? Decreased 1% or more?

4.16 Corporation G, a manufacturer of razor blades, supplied a consumer with one pack of each of the three top name brands — G, S, and W — and asked him to use them and rank them in order of preference. The corporation was hoping the consumer would prefer its brand and rank it first, thereby giving them some material for an advertising campaign. If the consumer did not prefer one blade more than any other, but was still required to rank the blades, what is the probability that:

a. The consumer ranked brand G first? [*Hint:* One of the possible rankings would be G S W; i.e., G ranked 1, S ranked 2, and W ranked 3.]

b. The consumer ranked brand G last?

c. The consumer ranked brand G last and brand W second?

d. The consumer ranked brand W first, brand G second, and brand S third?

4.2 Compound Events

An event can often be viewed as a composition of two or more other events. Such an event, called a *compound event,* can be formed (composed) in two ways:

Definition 4.6

The *union* of two events A and B is the event that occurs if either A or B or both occur on a single performance of the experiment. We will denote the union of events A and B by the symbol $A \cup B$.

Definition 4.7

The *intersection* of two events A and B is the event that occurs if both A and B occur on a single performance of the experiment. We will write $A \cap B$ for the intersection of events A and B.

Example 4.6 Consider the die-toss experiment. Define the following events:

A: {Toss an even number}

B: {Toss a number less than or equal to 3}

a. Describe $A \cup B$ for this experiment.

b. Describe $A \cap B$ for this experiment.

c. Calculate $P(A \cup B)$ and $P(A \cap B)$ assuming the die is fair.

Solution

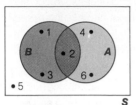

a. The union of A and B is the event that occurs if we observe an even number, a number less than or equal to 3, or both on a single throw of the die. Consequently, the simple events in the event A ∪ B are those for which A occurs, B occurs, or both A and B occur. Testing the simple events in the entire sample space, we find that the collection of simple events in the union of A and B is

$$A \cup B = \{1, 2, 3, 4, 6\}$$

b. The intersection of A and B is the event that occurs if we observe *both* an even number and a number less than or equal to 3 on a single throw of the die. Testing the simple events to see which imply the occurrence of *both* events A and B, we see that the intersection contains only one simple event:

$$A \cap B = \{2\}$$

In other words, the intersection of A and B is the simple event Observe a 2.

c. Recalling that the probability of an event is the sum of the probabilities of the simple events of which the event is composed, we have

$$P(A \cup B) = P(1) + P(2) + P(3) + P(4) + P(6)$$
$$= \tfrac{1}{6} + \tfrac{1}{6} + \tfrac{1}{6} + \tfrac{1}{6} + \tfrac{1}{6} = \tfrac{5}{6}$$

and

$$P(A \cap B) = P(2) = \tfrac{1}{6}$$ ■

4.3 Complementary Events

A very useful concept in the calculation of event probabilities is the notion of *complementary events:*

> ### Definition 4.8
>
> The *complement* of any event A is the event that A does not occur. We will denote the complement of A by A^c.

Since an event A is a collection of simple events, the simple events included in A^c are just those that are not in A. Figure 4.4 demonstrates this. You will note from the figure that all simple events in S are included in either A or A^c, and that *no* simple event is in both A and A^c. This leads us to conclude that the probabilities of an event and its complement *must sum to 1:*

> The sum of the probabilities of complementary events equals 1; i.e.,
>
> $$P(A) + P(A^c) = 1$$

Figure 4.4   Venn Diagram of Complementary Events

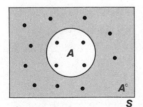

In many probability problems, it will be easier to calculate the probability of the complement of the event of interest than the event itself. Then, since

$$P(A) + P(A^c) = 1$$

we can calculate $P(A)$ by using the relationship

$$P(A) = 1 - P(A^c)$$

Example 4.7 Consider the experiment of tossing two fair coins. Calculate the probability of event A: {Observe at least one head} by using the complementary relationship.

Solution We know that the event A: {Observe at least one head} consists of the simple events

$$A = \{H_1, H_2; \quad H_1, T_2; \quad T_1, H_2\}$$

The complement of A is defined as the event that occurs when A does not occur. Therefore,

$$A^c = \{T_1, T_2\}$$

This complementary relationship is shown in Figure 4.5. Assuming the coins are balanced,

$$P(A^c) = P(T_1, T_2) = \tfrac{1}{4}$$

and

$$P(A) = 1 - P(A^c) = 1 - \tfrac{1}{4} = \tfrac{3}{4}$$

Figure 4.5 Complementary Events in the Toss of Two Coins

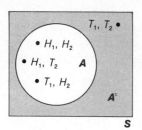

Exercises 4.17–4.33

Learning the Mechanics

4.17 Consider the Venn diagram shown, where $P(E_1) = P(E_2) = P(E_3) = \tfrac{1}{5}$, $P(E_4) = P(E_5) = \tfrac{1}{20}$, $P(E_6) = \tfrac{1}{10}$, and $P(E_7) = \tfrac{1}{5}$. Find each of the following probabilities:

a. $P(A)$ **b.** $P(B)$
c. $P(A \cup B)$ **d.** $P(A \cap B)$
e. $P(A^c)$ **f.** $P(B^c)$
g. $P(A \cup A^c)$ **h.** $P(A^c \cap B)$

Exercise 4.17

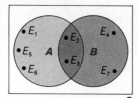

4.18 Consider the Venn diagram shown, where $P(E_1) = .13$, $P(E_2) = .05$, $P(E_3) = P(E_4) = .2$, $P(E_5) = .06$, $P(E_6) = .3$, and $P(E_7) = .06$. Find each of the following probabilities:

a. $P(A^c)$ **b.** $P(B^c)$
c. $P(A^c \cap B)$ **d.** $P(A \cup B)$
e. $P(A \cap B)$ **f.** $P(A^c \cup B^c)$

Exercise 4.18

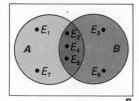

4.19 Two dice are tossed and the following events are defined:

   A: {The total number of dots on the upper faces of the two dice is equal to 5}

   B: {At least one of the two dice has three dots on the upper face}

a. Identify the simple events in each of the following events: A, B, $A \cap B$, and $A \cup B$.
b. Find $P(A)$ and $P(B)$ by summing the probabilities of the appropriate simple events.
c. Find $P(A \cap B)$ and $P(A \cup B)$ by summing the probabilities of the appropriate simple events.

4.20 Three coins are tossed and the following events are defined:

> A: {Observe at least one head}
>
> B: {Observe exactly two heads}
>
> C: {Observe exactly two tails}

Assume that the coins are balanced. Calculate the following probabilities by summing the probabilities of the appropriate simple events:

a. $P(A \cup B)$ **b.** $P(A \cap B)$ **c.** $P(A \cap C)$ **d.** $P(B \cap C)$

Applying the Concepts

4.21 A state energy agency mailed questionnaires on energy conservation to 1,000 home-owners in the state capital. Five hundred questionnaires were returned. Suppose that an experiment consists of randomly selecting one of the returned questionnaires. Consider the events:

> A: {The home is constructed of brick}
>
> B: {The home is more than 30 years old}
>
> C: {The home is heated with oil}

Describe each of the following events in terms of unions, intersections, and complements (i.e., $A \cup B$, $A \cap B$, A^c, etc.):

a. The home is more than 30 years old and is heated with oil.
b. The home is not constructed of brick.
c. The home is heated with oil or is more than 30 years old.
d. The home is constructed of brick and is not heated with oil.

4.22 Identifying managerial prospects who are both talented and motivated is difficult. A personnel manager constructed the table shown here to define nine combinations of talent-motivation levels. The numbers in the table are the manager's estimates of the probabilities that a managerial prospect will be classified in the respective categories.

		TALENT		
		High	Medium	Low
	High	.05	.16	.05
MOTIVATION	Medium	.19	.32	.05
	Low	.11	.05	.02

Suppose the personnel manager has decided to hire a new manager. Define the following events:

> A: {Prospect places in the high motivation category}
>
> B: {Prospect places in the high talent category}

C: {Prospect rates medium or better in both categories}

D: {Prospect rates low in at least one of the categories}

E: {Prospect places high in both categories}

a. Does the sum of the probabilities in the table equal 1?

b. Find the probability of each event defined above.

c. Find $P(A \cup B)$, $P(A \cap B)$, and $P(A \cup C)$.

d. Find $P(A^c)$ and explain what this means from a practical point of view.

4.23 After completing an inventory of three warehouses, a golf club shaft manufacturer described its stock of 12,246 shafts with the percentages given in the table. Suppose a shaft is selected at random from the 12,246 currently in stock and the warehouse number and type of shaft are observed.

		TYPE OF SHAFT		
		Regular	Stiff	Extra stiff
	1	19%	8%	3%
WAREHOUSE	2	14%	8%	2%
	3	28%	18%	0%

a. List all the simple events for this experiment.

b. What is the set of all simple events called?

c. Let C be the event that the shaft selected is from warehouse 3. Find $P(C)$ by summing the probabilities of the simple events in C.

d. Let F be the event that the shaft chosen is an extra stiff type. Find $P(F)$.

e. Let A be the event that the shaft selected is from warehouse 1. Find $P(A)$.

f. Let D be the event that the shaft selected is a regular type. Find $P(D)$.

g. Let E be the event that the shaft selected is a stiff type. Find $P(E)$.

4.24 Refer to Exercise 4.23. Describe the characteristics of a golf club shaft portrayed by the following events:

a. $A \cap F$ **b.** $C \cup E$ **c.** $C \cap D$ **d.** $A \cup F$ **e.** $A \cup D$

4.25 Refer to Exercise 4.23. Find the probabilities of the following events:

a. $A \cup C$ **b.** $A \cap F$ **c.** $C \cup E$ **d.** $C \cap F$ **e.** $D \cap E$

4.26 Refer to Exercise 4.23. Describe the characteristics of a golf club shaft portrayed by the following events:

a. $A \cup E$ **b.** $A \cap E$ **c.** $C \cap A$ **d.** $C \cup F$

4.27 Refer to Exercise 4.6, in which a bank's loan records were being audited. Suppose each of the 500 automobile loans made by the bank last year is now classified according to two characteristics: amount of loan and length of loan. As before, an auditor is planning to choose one loan at random for inspection.

		AMOUNT OF LOAN ($)		
		Under 1,000	1,000–3,999	4,000–5,999	6,000 or more
	12	25	4	0	0
LENGTH OF	24	2	15	1	0
LOAN	36	0	27	92	2
(MONTHS)	42	0	53	93	50
	48	0	0	112	24

a. List the simple events in this experiment.

b. What is the probability that the loan selected will be for $6,000 or more? Does your answer agree with your answer to part b in Exercise 4.6?

c. What is the probability that the loan selected is a 3-year loan for more than $5,999?

d. What is the probability that the loan selected is a 3- or 4-year loan?

e. What is the probability that the loan selected is a 42-month loan for $1,000 or more?

4.28 A large research and development corporation is interested in providing an in-house continuing education program for its employees. It compiled the given table of percentages describing its 5,000 employees' current education level.

	HIGHEST DEGREE OBTAINED			
	High school diploma	Bachelor's	Master's	Ph.D.
MALES	5%	20%	12%	11%
FEMALES	18%	15%	14%	5%

Suppose an employee is selected at random from the firm's 5,000 employees and the following events are defined:

A: {Employee chosen is a male}

B: {Employee chosen is a female}

C: {Highest degree obtained by the chosen employee is Ph.D.}

D: {Highest degree obtained by the chosen employee is master's}

E: {Highest degree obtained by the chosen employee is bachelor's}

F: {Highest degree obtained by the chosen employee is high school diploma}

Describe the characteristics of an employee portrayed by the following events:

a. $A \cup C$ **b.** $B \cup F$ **c.** $A \cap D$ **d.** $E \cap B$

4.29 Refer to Exercise 4.28. Find the probabilities of the following events by summing the probabilities of the appropriate simple events:

a. A, B, C, D, E, F **b.** $A \cup B$ **c.** $B \cap C$

d. $A \cap F$ **e.** $A \cap B$ **f.** $C \cap D$

4.30 Whether purchases are made by cash or credit card is of concern to merchandisers because they must pay a certain percentage of the sale value to the credit agency. To better understand the relationship between types of purchase (credit or cash) and types of merchandise, a department store analyzed 10,000 sales and placed them in the categories shown in the table. Suppose a single sale is selected at random from the 10,000 and the following events are defined:

A: {Sale was paid by credit card}

B: {Merchandise purchased was women's wear}

C: {Merchandise purchased was menswear}

D: {Merchandise purchased was sportswear}

		TYPE OF MERCHANDISE			
		Women's wear	Menswear	Sportswear	Household
TYPE OF	Cash	4%	7%	12%	7%
PURCHASE	Credit card	37%	11%	4%	18%

Describe the characteristics of a sale implied by the following events:

a. $A \cup B$ **b.** $B \cup C$ **c.** $B \cap A$ **d.** $C \cap A$

4.31 Refer to Exercise 4.30. Find the probabilities of the following events by summing the probabilities of the appropriate simple events:

a. A, B, C, D **b.** $A \cup B$ **c.** $B \cup C$ **d.** $B \cap A$ **e.** $C \cap A$

4.32 Refer to Exercise 4.30. The following events are defined:

A: {Sale was paid by credit card}

B: {Merchandise purchased was women's wear}

a. Describe the events A^c and B^c.
b. Find $P(A^c)$.
c. Find $P(B^c)$.
d. Find the probability that the sale was in neither menswear nor women's wear.
e. Find the probability that the sale was *not* a credit card purchase in the sportswear department.

4.33 The types of occupations of the 97,270,000 employed workers in the United States in 1980 are described in the table on the next page, and their relative frequencies are listed. Assume a worker is to be selected at random from this population (i.e., so that each worker in the population has an equal probability of being selected) and his or her occupation is to be determined. Also, assume each worker in the population has only one occupation.

OCCUPATION	RELATIVE FREQUENCY
White-collar workers	.522
Professional and technical	.161
Managers and administrators	.112
Salesworkers	.063
Clerical workers	.186
Blue-collar workers	.317
Craft and kindred workers	.129
Operatives, excluding transport	.106
Transport equipment operatives	.036
Nonfarm laborers	.046
Service workers	.133
Farm workers	.028

Source: *Statistical Abstract of the United States: 1981*, p. 401.

a. What is the probability that the worker will be a manager or an administrator?
b. What is the probability that the worker will be a white-collar worker or a blue-collar worker?
c. What is the probability that the worker will be a clerical worker and a salesworker?
d. What is the probability that the worker will not be a blue-collar worker?

4.4 Conditional Probability

Figure 4.6 Reduced Sample Space for the Die-Toss Experiment — Given That Event *B* Has Occurred

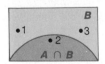

The probabilities we assign to the simple events of an experiment are measures of our belief that they will occur when the experiment is performed. When we assign these probabilities, we should make no assumptions other than those contained in or implied by the definition of the experiment. However, at times we will want to make assumptions other than those implied by the experimental description, and these extra assumptions may alter the probabilities we assign to the simple events of an experiment.

For example, we have shown that the probability of observing an even number (event *A*) on a toss of a fair die is $\frac{1}{2}$. However, suppose you are given the information that on a particular throw of the die the result was a number less than or equal to 3 (event *B*). Would you still believe that the probability of observing an even number on that throw of the die is equal to $\frac{1}{2}$? If you reason that making the assumption that *B* has occurred reduces the sample space from six simple events to three simple events (namely, those contained in event *B*), the reduced sample space is as shown in Figure 4.6.

Since the only even number of the three numbers in the reduced sample space *B* is the number 2 and since the die is fair, we conclude that the probability that *A* occurs *given that B occurs* is one in three, or $\frac{1}{3}$. We will use the symbol $P(A|B)$ to represent the probability of event *A* given that event *B* occurs. For the die-toss example,

$$P(A|B) = \frac{1}{3}$$

To get the probability of event *A* given that event *B* occurs, we proceed as follows: We divide the probability of the part of *A* that falls within the reduced sample space *B* — namely,

$P(A \cap B)$ — by the total probability of the reduced sample space — namely, $P(B)$. Thus, for the die-toss example with event A: {Observe an even number} and event B: {Observe a number less than or equal to 3}, we find

$$P(A|B) = \frac{P(A \cap B)}{P(B)} = \frac{P(2)}{P(1) + P(2) + P(3)} = \frac{\frac{1}{6}}{\frac{3}{6}} = \frac{1}{3}$$

This formula for $P(A|B)$ is true in general:

> To find the *conditional probability that event A occurs given that event B occurs,* divide the probability that *both* A and B occur by the probability that B occurs; that is,
>
> $$P(A|B) = \frac{P(A \cap B)}{P(B)}$$

Example 4.8

Suppose you are interested in the probability of the sale of a large piece of earth-moving equipment. A single prospect is contacted. Let F be the event that the buyer has sufficient money (or credit) to buy the product and let F^c denote the complement of F (the event that the prospect does not have the financial capability to buy the product). Similarly, let B be the event that the buyer wishes to buy the product and let B^c be the complement of that event. Then the four simple events associated with the experiment are shown in Figure 4.7, and their probabilities are given in Table 4.2.

Table 4.2

Probabilities of Customer Desire to Buy and Ability to Finance

		DESIRE	
		To buy, B	Not to buy, B^c
ABLE TO	Yes, F	.2	.1
FINANCE	No, F^c	.4	.3

Find the probability that a single prospect will buy, given that the prospect is able to finance the purchase.

Solution

Figure 4.7 Sample Space for Contacting a Sales Prospect

Suppose you consider the large collection of prospects for the sale of your product and randomly select one person from this collection. What is the probability that the person selected will buy the product? In order to buy the product, the customer must be financially able and have the desire to buy, so this probability would correspond to the entry in Table 4.2 below B and next to F, or $P(B \cap F) = .2$. This is called the *unconditional probability* of the event $B \cap F$.

In contrast, suppose you know that the prospect selected has the financial capability for purchasing the product. Now you are seeking the probability that the customer will buy given (the condition) that the customer has the financial ability to pay. This probability, the *conditional probability* of B given that F has occurred and denoted by the symbol $P(B|F)$, would be determined by considering only the simple events in the reduced sample space containing the simple events $B \cap F$ and $B^c \cap F$ — i.e., simple events that imply the prospect is financially

Figure 4.8 Subspace (Shaded) Containing Sample Points Implying a Financially Able Prospect

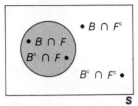

able to buy (this subspace is shaded in Figure 4.8). From our definition of conditional probability,

$$P(B|F) = \frac{P(B \cap F)}{P(F)}$$

where $P(F)$ is the sum of the probabilities of the two simple events corresponding to $B \cap F$ and $B^c \cap F$ (given in Table 4.2). Then

$$P(F) = P(B \cap F) + P(B^c \cap F) = .2 + .1 = .3$$

and the conditional probability that a prospect buys, given that the prospect is financially able, is

$$P(B|F) = \frac{P(B \cap F)}{P(F)} = \frac{.2}{.3} = .667$$

As we would expect, the probability that the prospect will buy, given that he or she is financially able, is higher than the unconditional probability of selecting a prospect who will buy.   ■

Example 4.9   The investigation of consumer product complaints by the Federal Trade Commission has generated much interest by manufacturers in the quality of their products. A manufacturer of an electromechanical kitchen aid conducted an analysis of a large number of consumer complaints and found that they fell into the six categories shown in Table 4.3. If a consumer complaint is received, what is the probability that the cause of the complaint was product appearance, given that the complaint originated prior to the end of the guarantee period?

Table 4.3

Distribution of Product Complaints

	REASON FOR COMPLAINT		
	Electrical	Mechanical	Appearance
DURING GUARANTEE PERIOD	18%	13%	32%
AFTER GUARANTEE PERIOD	12%	22%	3%

Solution   Let A represent the event that the cause of a particular complaint was product appearance and let B represent the event that the complaint occurred during the guarantee period. Checking Table 4.3, you can see that $(18 + 13 + 32)\% = 63\%$ of the complaints occurred during the guarantee time. Hence, $P(B) = .63$. The percentage of complaints that were caused by appearance, A, *and* occurred during the guarantee period, B, is 32%. Therefore, $P(A \cap B) = .32$. Using these probability values, we can calculate the conditional probability $P(A|B)$ that the cause of a complaint is appearance given that the complaint occurred prior to the termination of the guarantee time:

$$P(A|B) = \frac{P(A \cap B)}{P(B)} = \frac{.32}{.63} = .51$$

Consequently, you can see that slightly more than half of the complaints that occurred during the guarantee period were due to scratches, dents, or other imperfections in the surface of the kitchen devices.   ■

You will see in later chapters that conditional probability plays a key role in many business applications of statistics. For example, we may be interested in the probability that a particular stock gains 10% during the next year. We may estimate this probability (a statistical problem) by using information like the past performance of the stock or the general state of the economy at present. However, our probability estimate may change drastically if we assume the Gross National Product will increase by 10% in the next year. We would then be estimating the *conditional probability* that our stock gains 10% in the next year given that the GNP gains 10% in the same year. Thus, the probability of any event that is calculated or estimated based on an assumption that some other event occurs concurrently is a conditional probability.

Case Study 4.1
Purchase Patterns and the Conditional Probability of Purchasing

In his doctoral dissertation Alfred A. Kuehn (1958) examined sequential purchase data to gain some insight into consumer brand switching. He analyzed the frozen orange juice purchases of approximately 600 Chicago families during 1950–1952. The data were collected by the *Chicago Tribune* Consumer Panel. Kuehn was interested in determining the influence of a consumer's last four orange juice purchases on the next purchase. Thus, sequences of five purchases were analyzed.

Table 4.4 contains a summary of the data collected for Snow Crop brand orange juice and part of Kuehn's analysis of the data. In the column labeled "Previous Purchase Pattern" an S stands for the purchase of Snow Crop by a consumer and an O stands for the purchase of a brand other than Snow Crop. Thus, for example, SSSO is used to represent the purchase of Snow Crop three times in a row followed by the purchase of some other brand of frozen orange juice. The column labeled "Sample Size" lists the number of occurrences of the

Table 4.4

Observed Approximate Probability of Purchasing Snow Crop, Given the Four Previous Brand Purchases

PREVIOUS PURCHASE PATTERN S = Snow Crop O = Other brand	SAMPLE SIZE	FREQUENCY	OBSERVED APPROXIMATE PROBABILITY OF PURCHASE
SSSS	1,047	844	.806
OSSS	277	191	.690
SOSS	206	137	.665
SSOS	222	132	.595
SSSO	296	144	.486
OOSS	248	137	.552
SOOS	138	78	.565
OSOS	149	74	.497
SOSO	163	66	.405
OSSO	181	75	.414
SSOO	256	78	.305
OOOS	500	165	.330
OOSO	404	77	.191
OSOO	433	56	.129
SOOO	557	86	.154
OOOO	8,442	405	.048

purchase sequences in the first column. The column labeled "Frequency" lists the number of times the associated purchase sequence in the first column led to the next purchase (i.e., the fifth purchase in the sequence) being Snow Crop.

The column labeled "Observed Approximate Probability of Purchase" contains the relative frequency with which each sequence of the first column led to the next purchase being Snow Crop. These relative frequencies, which give approximate probabilities, are computed for each sequence of the first column by dividing the frequency of the sequence by the sample size of the sequence. Notice that these approximate probabilities are really conditional probabilities. For the sequences of five purchases analyzed, each of the entries in the fourth column is the approximate probability that the next purchase is Snow Crop, given that the previous four purchases were as noted in the first column. For example, .806 is the approximate probability that the next purchase will be Snow Crop given that the previous four purchases were also Snow Crop.

An examination of the approximate probabilities in the fourth column indicates that both the most recent brand purchased and the number of times a brand is purchased have an effect on the next brand purchased. It appears that the influence on the next brand of orange juice purchased by the second most recent purchase is not so strong as the most recent purchase, but is stronger than the third most recent purchase. In general, it appears that the probability of a particular consumer purchasing Snow Crop the next time he or she buys orange juice is inversely related to the number of consecutive purchases of another brand he or she made since last purchasing Snow Crop and is directly proportional to the number of Snow Crop purchases among the four purchases.

Kuehn, of course, goes on to conduct a more formal statistical analysis of these data, which we will not pursue here. We simply want you to see that probability is a basic tool for making inferences about populations using sample data.

4.5 Probabilities of Unions and Intersections

Since unions and intersections of events are themselves events, we can always calculate their probabilities by adding the probabilities of the simple events that constitute them. However, if we know the probabilities of certain events related to the union or intersection, sometimes it is simpler to use special formulas to calculate their probabilities.

The union of two events will often contain many simple events, since the union occurs if either one or both of the events occur. By studying the Venn diagram in Figure 4.9, you can see that the probability of the union of two events A and B can be obtained by summing $P(A)$ and $P(B)$ and subtracting the probability corresponding to $A \cap B$. Therefore, the formula for calculating the probability of the union of two events is as given in the box.

Figure 4.9 Venn Diagram of Union

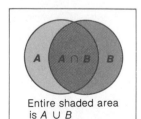

Entire shaded area is $A \cup B$

Additive Rule of Probability

The probability of the union of events A and B is the sum of the probabilities of events A and B minus the probability of the intersection of events A and B, i.e.,

$$P(A \cup B) = P(A) + P(B) - P(A \cap B)$$

Note that we must subtract the probability of the intersection because, when we add the probabilities of A and B, the intersection probability is counted twice.

Example 4.10 Consider the die-toss experiment. Define the events

  A: {Observe an even number}

  B: {Observe a number less than or equal to 3}

Assuming the die is fair, calculate the probability of the union of A and B by using the additive rule of probability.

Solution The formula for the probability of a union requires that we calculate the following:

$$P(A) = P(2) + P(4) + P(6) = \tfrac{1}{6} + \tfrac{1}{6} + \tfrac{1}{6} = \tfrac{3}{6}$$
$$P(B) = P(1) + P(2) + P(3) = \tfrac{1}{6} + \tfrac{1}{6} + \tfrac{1}{6} = \tfrac{3}{6}$$
$$P(A \cap B) = P(2) = \tfrac{1}{6}$$

Now we can calculate the probability of $A \cup B$.

$$P(A \cup B) = P(A) + P(B) - P(A \cap B) = \tfrac{3}{6} + \tfrac{3}{6} - \tfrac{1}{6} = \tfrac{5}{6}$$ ∎

If two events A and B do not intersect — i.e., when $A \cap B$ contains no simple events — we call the events A and B *mutually exclusive* events:

Definition 4.9

Events A and B are *mutually exclusive* if $A \cap B$ contains no simple events.

Figure 4.10 Venn Diagram of Mutually Exclusive Events

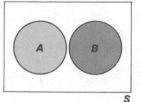

      S

Figure 4.10 shows a Venn diagram of two mutually exclusive events. The events A and B have no simple events in common; i.e., A and B cannot occur simultaneously, and $P(A \cap B) = 0$. Thus, we have the following important relationship:

If two events A and B are mutually exclusive, the probability of the union of A and B equals the sum of the probabilities of A and B; i.e.,

$$P(A \cup B) = P(A) + P(B)$$

Now we will develop a formula for calculating the probability of an intersection. Actually, we have already developed the formula in another context. You will recall that the formula for calculating the conditional probability of A given B is

$$P(A|B) = \frac{P(A \cap B)}{P(B)}$$

If we multiply both sides of this equation by $P(B)$, we get a formula for the probability of the intersection of events A and B:

Multiplicative Rule of Probability

$P(A \cap B) = P(B)P(A|B)$ or equivalently $P(A \cap B) = P(A)P(B|A)$

The second expression in the box is obtained by multiplying both sides of the equation $P(B|A) = P(A \cap B)/P(A)$ by $P(A)$.

Before working an example, we emphasize that the intersection often contains only a few simple events, in which case the probability is easy to calculate by summing the appropriate simple event probabilities. However, the formula for calculating intersection probabilities plays a very important role in an area of statistics known as *Bayesian statistics.* (More complete discussions of Bayesian statistics are contained in Chapter 19 and in the references at the end of this chapter.)

Example 4.11   Suppose an investment firm is interested in the following events:

    A: {Common stock in XYZ Corporation gains 10% next year}

    B: {Gross National Product gains 10% next year}

The firm has assigned the following probabilities on the basis of available information:

    $P(A|B) = .8$ $P(B) = .3$

That is, the investment company believes the probability is .8 that XYZ common stock will gain 10% in the next year *assuming that* the GNP gains 10% in the same time period. In addition, the company believes the probability is only .3 that the GNP will gain 10% in the next year. Use the formula for calculating the probability of an intersection to determine the probability that XYZ common stock *and* the GNP gain 10% in the next year.

Solution   We want to calculate $P(A \cap B)$. The formula is

    $P(A \cap B) = P(B)P(A|B) = (.3)(.8) = .24$

Thus, according to this investment firm, the probability is .24 that both XYZ common stock and the GNP will gain 10% in the next year.   ■

In the previous section we showed that the probability of an event A may be substantially altered by the assumption that the event B has occurred. However, this will not always be the case. In some instances the assumption that event B has occurred will not alter the probability of event A at all. When this is true, we call events A and B *independent:*

Definition 4.10

Events A and B are *independent* if the assumption that B has occurred does not alter the probability that A occurs; i.e., events A and B are independent if

$P(A|B) = P(A)$

Equivalently, events A and B are *independent* if

$P(B|A) = P(B)$

Events that are not independent are said to be *dependent*.

Example 4.12

Suppose that we decide to change the definition of event B in the die-toss experiment to {Observe a number less than or equal to 4} but we let event A remain an even number. Are events A and B independent (assuming a fair die)?

Solution

The Venn diagram for this experiment is shown in Figure 4.11. We first calculate

$$P(A) = \tfrac{1}{2}$$
$$P(B) = P(1) + P(2) + P(3) + P(4) = \tfrac{4}{6} = \tfrac{2}{3}$$
$$P(A \cap B) = P(2) + P(4) = \tfrac{2}{6} = \tfrac{1}{3}$$

Figure 4.11 Die-Toss Experiment, Example 4.12

Now assuming B has occurred, the conditional probability of A is

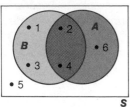

$$P(A|B) = \frac{P(A \cap B)}{P(B)} = \frac{\tfrac{1}{3}}{\tfrac{2}{3}} = \tfrac{1}{2} = P(A)$$

Thus, the assumption of the occurrence of event B does not alter the probability of observing an even number — it remains $\tfrac{1}{2}$. Therefore, the events A and B are independent. Note that if we calculate the conditional probability of B given A, our conclusion is the same:

$$P(B|A) = \frac{P(A \cap B)}{P(A)} = \frac{\tfrac{1}{3}}{\tfrac{1}{2}} = \tfrac{2}{3} = P(B)$$ ■

Example 4.13

Refer to the consumer product complaint study in Example 4.9. The percentages of complaints of various types in the pre- and post-guarantee periods are shown in Table 4.3. Define the following events:

A: {Cause of complaint is product appearance}

B: {Complaint occurred during the guarantee term}

Are A and B independent events?

Solution Events A and B are independent if $P(A|B) = P(A)$. We calculated $P(A|B)$ in Example 4.9 to be .51, and from Table 4.3 we can see that

$$P(A) = .32 + .03 = .35$$

Therefore, $P(A|B)$ is not equal to $P(A)$, and A and B are not independent events. ∎

We will make three final points about independence. The first is that the property of independence, unlike the mutually exclusive property, cannot be shown on or gleaned from a Venn diagram. In general, the only way to check for independence is by performing the calculations of the probabilities in the definition.

The second point concerns the relationship between the mutually exclusive and independence properties. Suppose that events A and B are mutually exclusive, as shown in Figure 4.10. Are these events independent or dependent? That is, does the assumption that B occurs alter the probability of the occurrence of A? It certainly does, because if we assume that B has occurred, it is impossible for A to have occurred simultaneously. Thus, mutually exclusive events are dependent events.

The third point is that the probability of the intersection of independent events is very easy to calculate. Referring to the formula for calculating the probability of an intersection, we find

$$P(A \cap B) = P(B)P(A|B)$$

Thus, since $P(A|B) = P(A)$ when A and B are independent, we have the following useful rule:

> *If events A and B are independent,* the probability of the intersection of A and B equals the product of the probabilities of A and B; i.e.,
>
> $$P(A \cap B) = P(A)P(B)$$

In the die-toss experiment, we showed in Example 4.12 that the events A: {Observe an even number} and B: {Observe a number less than or equal to 4} are independent if the die is fair. Thus,

$$P(A \cap B) = P(A)P(B) = (\tfrac{1}{2})(\tfrac{2}{3}) = \tfrac{1}{3}$$

This agrees with the result

$$P(A \cap B) = P(2) + P(4) = \tfrac{2}{6} = \tfrac{1}{3}$$

that we obtained in the example.

Example 4.14 In Example 4.2, a bank considered the problem of apportioning its service windows according to two types of accounts: personal or commercial. In the example, we attempted the smaller problem of finding the probability that one, two, or, in general, k customers arriving at the bank possessed a commercial account. We are now ready to find the probability that both of two customers arriving at the bank possess commercial accounts. Suppose a study of arriving customers showed that 20% of arriving customers intend to utilize their commercial accounts at the bank.

a. If two customers arrive at the bank, what is the probability that they will both utilize a commercial account?

b. If k customers arrive at the bank, what is the probability that all will utilize commercial accounts?

Solution   **a.** Let C_1 be the event that customer 1 will utilize a commercial account and let C_2 be a similar event for customer 2. The event that *both* customers will utilize commercial accounts is the intersection $C_1 \cap C_2$. Then, since it is not unreasonable to assume that the service requirements of the customers would be independent of one another, the probability that both will utilize commercial accounts is

$$P(C_1 \cap C_2) = P(C_1)P(C_2) = (.2)(.2) = (.2)^2 = .04$$

b. Let C_i represent the event that the ith customer will utilize a commercial account. Then the event that all three of three arriving customers will utilize a commercial account is the intersection of the event $C_1 \cap C_2$ (from part a) with the event C_3. Assuming independence of the events, C_1, C_2, and C_3, we have

$$P(C_1 \cap C_2 \cap C_3) = P(C_1 \cap C_2)P(C_3)$$
$$= (.2)^2(.2) = (.2)^3 = .008$$

Noting the pattern, you can see that the probability that all k out of k arriving customers will utilize a commercial account is the probability of $C_1 \cap C_2 \cap \cdots \cap C_k$, or

$$P(C_1 \cap C_2 \cap \cdots \cap C_k) = (.2)^k \qquad \text{for } k = 1, 2, 3, \ldots \qquad \blacksquare$$

Exercises 4.34–4.50

Learning the Mechanics

4.34 An experiment results in one of three mutually exclusive events, A, B, or C. It is known that $P(A) = .40$, $P(B) = .25$, and $P(C) = .35$. Find each of the following probabilities:

a. $P(A \cup B)$ **b.** $P(A \cap C)$ **c.** $P(A|B)$ **d.** $P(B \cup C)$

4.35 Refer to Exercise 4.34. Are B and C independent events? Explain.

4.36 An experiment results in one of five simple events, with the following probabilities: $P(E_1) = .22$, $P(E_2) = .31$, $P(E_3) = .15$, $P(E_4) = .22$, and $P(E_5) = .10$. The following events have been defined:

$$A = \{E_1, E_3\} \qquad B = \{E_2, E_3, E_4\} \qquad C = \{E_1, E_5\}$$

Find each of the following probabilities:

a. $P(A)$ **b.** $P(B)$ **c.** $P(A \cap B)$
d. $P(A|B)$ **e.** $P(B \cap C)$ **f.** $P(C|B)$

4.37 Refer to Exercise 4.36. Which of the following pairs of events are independent? Explain.

a. A and B **b.** A and C **c.** B and C

4.38 Three coins are tossed and the following events are defined:

   A: {Observe at least one head}

   B: {Observe exactly two heads}

   C: {Observe exactly two tails}

   D: {Observe at most one head}

   E: {Observe at least two tails}

Use the formulas of this section to calculate the following:

a. $P(A \cup B)$ **b.** $P(A \cap B)$ **c.** $P(A \cup C)$

d. $P(C \cap A)$ **e.** $P(A^c \cap C)$ **f.** $P(D \cap E)$

4.39 Use the events defined in Exercise 4.38 to find the following:

a. $P(B|A)$ **b.** $P(C|D)$ **c.** $P(C|E)$

4.40 If $P(R) = \frac{1}{3}$, $P(S) = \frac{1}{3}$, and events R and S are mutually exclusive, find $P(R|S)$ and $P(S|R)$.

4.41 Two dice are tossed and the following events are defined:

   A: {Sum of the numbers showing is an odd number}

   B: {Sum of the numbers showing is 8, 9, 10, or 11}

Are events *A* and *B* independent? Why?

Applying the Concepts

4.42 The table describes the 88.4 million U.S. federal tax returns filed with the Internal Revenue Service (IRS) in 1982 and the percentage of those returns that were audited by the IRS.

INCOME	NUMBER OF TAX FILERS (Millions)	PERCENTAGE AUDITED
Under $10,000	35.0	1.33
$10,000–$24,999	32.4	3.02
$25,000–$49,999	17.7	2.90
$50,000 or more	3.3	5.68

a. If a tax filer were to be randomly selected from this population of tax filers (i.e., each tax filer has an equal probability of being selected), what is the probability that the tax filer would have been audited?

b. If a tax filer were to be randomly selected from the population of tax filers described in the table (i.e., each tax filer has an equal probability of being selected), what is the probability that the tax filer had an income of $10,000–$24,999 in 1982 *and* was audited? What is the probability that the tax filer had an income of $50,000 or more in 1982 *or* was not audited?

c. Refer to part b. If it were known that the randomly selected tax filer had been audited, what is the probability that the person had an income of $50,000 or more? Under $10,000?

d. What is the probability that a tax filer with an income of $50,000 or more in 1982 would have been audited?

4.43 A particular automatic sprinkler system for high-rise apartment buildings, office buildings, and hotels has two different types of activation devices for each sprinkler head. One type has a reliability of .91 (i.e., the probability that it will activate the sprinkler when it should is .91). The other type, which operates independently of the first type, has a reliability of .87. Suppose a serious fire starts near a particular sprinkler head.

a. What is the probability that the sprinkler head will be activated?

b. What is the probability that the sprinkler head will not be activated?

c. What is the probability that both activation devices will work properly?

d. What is the probability that only the device with reliability .91 will work properly?

4.44 Which of the following sets of events are mutually exclusive?

a. The rate of inflation will increase next year.
   The rate of inflation will decrease next year.
   The rate of inflation will be the same next year as this year.

b. Sales will increase by 10,000 units.
   Sales will increase by at least 5,000 units.
   Sales will decrease by 1,000 units.

c. The consultant's fee will be at least $400 a day.
   The consultant's fee will be at least $600 a day.
   The consultant's fee will be at least $800 a day.

4.45 A soft drink bottler has two quality control inspectors independently check each case of soft drinks for chipped or cracked bottles before the cases leave the bottling plant. Having observed the work of the two trusted inspectors over several years, the bottler has determined that the probability of a defective case getting by the first inspector is .05 and the probability of a defective case getting by the second inspector is .10. What is the probability that a defective case gets by both inspectors?

4.46 A fast-food restaurant chain with 700 outlets in the United States describes the geographic location of its restaurants with the given table of percentages. A restaurant is to be chosen at random from the 700 to test market a new style of chicken.

		REGION			
		NE	SE	SW	NW
POPULATION OF CITY	Under 10,000	5%	6%	3%	0%
	10,000–100,000	10%	15%	12%	5%
	Over 100,000	25%	4%	5%	10%

a. Given the restaurant chosen is in a city with a population over 100,000, what is the probability that it is located in the Northeast?

b. Given the restaurant chosen is in the Southeast, what is the probability that it is located in a city with a population under 10,000?

c. If the restaurant selected is located in the Southwest, what is the probability that the city it is in has a population of 100,000 or less?

d. If the restaurant selected is located in the Northwest, what is the probability that the city it is in has a population of 10,000 or more?

4.47 Refer to Exercise 4.46. The following events are defined:

   A: {Population of city where chosen restaurant is located is over 100,000}

   B: {Chosen restaurant is located in the Northeast}

Are A and B independent events? Explain.

4.48 An article in *Business Week* (Sept. 12, 1983) reports on the problems that evolve from the failure to inform patients adequately of the proper application of prescription drugs and the precautions needed to avoid potential side effects. This failure results in numerous cases of serious illness and, in some cases, even death. One study revealed that 300,000 U.S. hospital admissions each year are caused by adverse reactions to prescription drugs. Another study concluded that 7% of all hospital admissions are related to drug-induced problems resulting from imprudent prescriptions. One method of increasing patients' awareness of the problem is for physicians to provide PMI (Patient Medication Instruction) sheets. However, the American Medical Association has found that only 20% of doctors who prescribe drugs frequently distribute such sheets to their patients. Assume that 20% of all patients receive the PMI sheet with their prescriptions and that 12% of all patients receive the PMI sheet and are hospitalized because of a drug-related problem. What is the probability that a person will be hospitalized for a drug-related problem given that the person has received the PMI sheet?

4.49 Even with strong advertising programs, new products are often unsuccessful. A company that produces a variety of household items found that only 18% of the new products it introduced over the last 10 years have become profitable. When two new products were introduced during the same year, only 5% of the time did both products become profitable. Suppose the company plans to introduce two new products, A and B, next year. If the percentages just cited define the probabilities of success, what is the probability that:

a. Product A will become profitable?

b. Product B will not become profitable?

c. At least one of the two products will become profitable?

d. Neither of the two products will become profitable?

e. Either product A or product B (but not both) will become profitable?

4.50 Refer to Exercise 4.49.

a. What is the probability that product A becomes profitable, given that product B is profitable?

b. Given that at least one of the products will be profitable, what is the probability that the profitable product is A?

4.6 Random Sampling

How a sample is selected from a population is of vital importance in statistical inference because the probability of an observed sample will be used to infer the characteristics of the sampled population. To illustrate, suppose you deal yourself 4 cards from a deck of 52 cards, and all 4 cards are aces. Do you conclude that your deck is an ordinary bridge deck, containing only 4 aces, or do you conclude that the deck is stacked with more than 4 aces? It depends on how the cards were drawn. If the 4 aces were always placed on the top of a standard bridge deck, drawing 4 aces would not be unusual—it would be certain. On the other hand, if the cards were thoroughly mixed, drawing 4 aces in a sample of 4 cards would be highly improbable. The point, of course, is that, in order to use the observed sample of 4 cards to make inferences about the population (the deck of 52 cards), you need to know how the sample was selected from the deck.

One of the simplest and most frequently used sampling procedures (implied in the previous examples and exercises) produces what is known as a *random sample.*

Definition 4.11

If *n* elements are selected from a population in such a way that every possible combination of *n* elements in the population has an equal probability of being selected, the *n* elements are said to be a *random sample.**

If a population is not too large and the elements can be marked on slips of paper or poker chips, you can physically mix the slips of paper or chips and remove *n* elements from the total. Then the elements that appear on the slips or chips selected would indicate the population elements to be included in the sample. Such a procedure would not guarantee a random sample because it is often difficult to achieve a thorough mix, but it provides a reasonably good approximation to random sampling.

Many samplers use a table of random numbers (see Table I in Appendix B). Random-number tables are constructed in such a way that every digit occurs with (approximately) equal probability. To use a table of random numbers, we number the *N* elements in the population from 1 to *N*. Then we turn to Table I and haphazardly select a number in the table. Proceeding from this number across the row or down the column (either will do), remove and record *n* numbers from the table. Use only the necessary number of digits in each random number to identify the element to be included in the sample. We illustrate this procedure with an example below.

Example 4.15

Suppose you wish to randomly sample 5 households (we will keep the number in the sample small to simplify our example) from a population of 100,000 households. Use Table I to select a random sample.

Solution

First, number the households in the population from 1 to 100,000. Then, turn to a page of Table I, say, the first page. A reproduction of part of the first page of Table I is shown in Figure

---

* Strictly speaking, this is a *simple random sample.* There are many different types of random samples. The simple random sample is the most frequently employed.

Figure 4.12 Reproduction of Part of Table I, Appendix B

COLUMN ROW	1	2	3	4	5	6
1	10480	15011	01536	02011	81647	91646
2	22368	46573	25595	85393	30995	89198
3	24130	48360	22527	97265	76393	64809
4	42167	93093	06243	61680	07856	16376
5	37570	39975	81837	16656	06121	91782
6	77921	06907	11008	42751	27756	53498
7	99562	72905	56420	69994	98872	31016
8	96301	91977	05463	07972	18876	20922
9	89579	14342	63661	10281	17453	18103
10	85475	36857	53342	53988	53060	59533
11	28918	69578	88231	33276	70997	79936
12	63553	40961	48235	03427	49626	69445
13	09429	93969	52636	92737	88974	33488
14	10365	61129	87529	85689	48237	52267
15	07119	97336	71048	08178	77233	13916

4.12. Now, commence with the random number that appears in the third row, second column. This number is 48360. Proceed down the second column to obtain the remaining four random numbers. The five selected random numbers are shaded in Figure 4.12. Using the first five digits to represent the households from 1 to 99,999 and the number 00000 to represent household 100,000, you can see that the households numbered

48,360   93,093   39,975   6,907   72,905

should be included in your sample.   ■

Case Study 4.2
The 1970 Draft Lottery

From 1948 through the early years of the Vietnam War, the Selective Service System drafted men into military service by age — oldest first, starting with 25-year-olds. A network of local draft boards was used to implement the selection process. Then, on the evening of December 1, 1969, in an attempt to overcome what many believed were inequities in this system, the Selective Service System conducted a lottery to determine the order of selection for 1970. Such lotteries had been used during World Wars I and II, but it had been 37 years since the last one.

The objective of the lottery was to randomly order the induction sequence of men between the ages of 19 and 26. To do this, the 366 possible days in a year were written on slips of paper and placed in egg-shaped capsules that were stored in monthly lots. The monthly lots were placed one by one into a wooden box that was turned end over end several times to mix the numbers. The capsules were then dumped into a large glass bowl and drawn one by one to obtain the order of induction. All men born on the first day drawn would be inducted first; those born on the second day drawn would be drafted next, etc. Thus, the lottery assigned a rank to each of the 366 birthdays. The results of the lottery are shown in Table 4.5.

In order to generate a random sequence of numbers with this procedure, it is necessary for each (remaining) capsule in the bowl to have an equal probability of being selected on each

Table 4.5

1970 Draft Lottery Results

1	Sept. 14	46	Nov. 11	91	Feb. 7	136	Mar. 11	181	Feb. 8	226	May 29
2	April 24	47	Nov. 27	92	Jan. 26	137	June 25	182	Nov. 23	227	July 19
3	Dec. 30	48	Aug. 8	93	July 1	138	Oct. 13	183	May 20	228	June 2
4	Feb. 14	49	Sept. 3	94	Oct. 28	139	Mar. 6	184	Sept. 8	229	Oct. 29
5	Oct. 18	50	July 7	95	Dec. 24	140	Jan. 18	185	Nov. 20	230	Nov. 24
6	Sept. 6	51	Nov. 7	96	Dec. 16	141	Aug. 18	186	Jan. 21	231	April 14
7	Oct. 26	52	Jan. 25	97	Nov. 8	142	Aug. 12	187	July 20	232	Sept. 4
8	Sept. 7	53	Dec. 22	98	July 17	143	Nov. 17	188	July 5	233	Sept. 27
9	Nov. 22	54	Aug. 5	99	Nov. 29	144	Feb. 2	189	Feb. 17	234	Oct. 7
10	Dec. 6	55	May 16	100	Dec. 31	145	Aug. 4	190	July 18	235	Jan. 17
11	Aug. 31	56	Dec. 5	101	Jan. 5	146	Nov. 18	191	April 29	236	Feb. 24
12	Dec. 7	57	Feb. 23	102	Aug. 15	147	April 7	192	Oct. 20	237	Oct. 11
13	July 8	58	Jan. 19	103	May 30	148	April 16	193	July 31	238	Jan. 14
14	April 11	59	Jan. 24	104	June 19	149	Sept. 25	194	Jan. 9	239	Mar. 20
15	July 12	60	June 21	105	Dec. 8	150	Feb. 11	195	Sept. 24	240	Dec. 19
16	Dec. 29	61	Aug. 29	106	Aug. 9	151	Sept. 29	196	Oct. 24	241	Oct. 19
17	Jan. 15	62	April 21	107	Nov. 16	152	Feb. 13	197	May 9	242	Sept. 12
18	Sept. 26	63	Sept. 20	108	March 1	153	July 22	198	Aug. 14	243	Oct. 21
19	Nov. 1	64	June 27	109	June 23	154	Aug. 17	199	Jan. 8	244	Oct. 3
20	June 4	65	May 10	110	June 6	155	May 6	200	Mar. 19	245	Aug. 26
21	Aug. 10	66	Nov. 12	111	Aug. 1	156	Nov. 21	201	Oct. 23	246	Sept. 18
22	June 26	67	July 25	112	May 17	157	Dec. 3	202	Oct. 4	247	June 22
23	July 24	68	Feb. 12	113	Sept. 15	158	Sept. 11	203	Nov. 19	248	July 11
24	Oct. 5	69	June 13	114	Aug. 6	159	Jan. 2	204	Sept. 21	249	June 1
25	Feb. 19	70	Dec. 21	115	July 3	160	Sept. 22	205	Feb. 27	250	May 21
26	Dec. 14	71	Sept. 10	116	Aug. 23	161	Sept. 2	206	June 10	251	Jan. 3
27	July 21	72	Oct. 12	117	Oct. 22	162	Dec. 23	207	Sept. 16	252	April 23
28	June 5	73	June 17	118	Jan. 23	163	Dec. 13	208	April 30	253	April 6
29	Mar. 2	74	April 27	119	Sept. 23	164	Jan. 30	209	June 30	254	Oct. 16
30	Mar. 31	75	May 19	120	July 16	165	Dec. 4	210	Feb. 4	255	Sept. 17
31	May 24	76	Nov. 6	121	Jan. 16	166	Mar. 16	211	Jan. 31	256	Mar. 23
32	April 1	77	Jan. 28	122	Mar. 7	167	Aug. 28	212	Feb. 16	257	Sept. 28
33	Mar. 17	78	Dec. 27	123	Dec. 28	168	Aug. 7	213	Mar. 8	258	Mar. 24
34	Nov. 2	79	Oct. 31	124	April 13	169	Mar. 15	214	Feb. 5	259	Mar. 13
35	May 7	80	Nov. 9	125	Oct. 2	170	Mar. 26	215	Jan. 4	260	April 17
36	Aug. 24	81	April 4	126	Nov. 13	171	Oct. 15	216	Feb. 10	261	Aug. 3
37	May 11	82	Sept. 5	127	Nov. 14	172	July 23	217	Mar. 30	262	April 28
38	Oct. 30	83	April 3	128	Dec. 18	173	Dec. 26	218	April 10	263	Sept. 9
39	Dec. 11	84	Dec. 25	129	Dec. 1	174	Nov. 30	219	April 9	264	Oct. 27
40	May 3	85	June 7	130	May 15	175	Sept. 13	220	Oct. 10	265	Mar. 22
41	Dec. 10	86	Feb. 1	131	Nov. 15	176	Oct. 25	221	Jan. 12	266	Nov. 4
42	July 13	87	Oct. 6	132	Nov. 25	177	Sept. 19	222	Jan. 28	267	Mar. 3
43	Dec. 9	88	July 28	133	May 12	178	May 14	223	Mar. 28	268	Mar. 27
44	Aug. 16	89	Feb. 15	134	June 11	179	Feb. 25	224	Jan. 6	269	April 5
45	Aug. 2	90	April 18	135	Dec. 20	180	June 15	225	Sept. 1	270	July 29

continued

Table 4.5 (continued)

271 April 2	287 July 30	303 July 26	319 May 23	335 June 9	351 April 25
272 June 12	288 Oct. 17	304 Dec. 17	320 Dec. 15	336 April 19	352 Aug. 27
273 April 15	289 July 27	305 Jan. 1	321 May 8	337 Jan. 22	353 June 29
274 June 16	290 Feb. 22	306 Jan. 7	322 July 15	338 Feb. 9	354 Mar. 14
275 Mar. 4	291 Aug. 21	307 Aug. 13	323 Mar. 10	339 Aug. 22	355 Jan. 27
276 May 4	292 Feb. 18	308 May 28	324 Aug. 11	340 April 26	356 June 14
277 July 9	293 Mar. 5	309 Nov. 26	325 Jan. 10	341 June 18	357 May 26
278 May 18	294 Oct. 14	310 Nov. 5	326 May 22	342 Oct. 9	358 June 24
279 July 4	295 May 13	311 Aug. 19	327 July 6	343 Mar. 25	359 Oct. 1
280 Jan. 20	296 May 27	312 April 8	328 Dec. 2	344 Aug. 20	360 June 20
281 Nov. 28	297 Feb. 3	313 May 31	329 Jan. 11	345 April 20	361 May 25
282 Nov. 10	298 May 2	314 Dec. 12	330 May 1	346 April 12	362 Mar. 29
283 Oct. 8	299 Feb. 28	315 Sept. 30	331 July 14	347 Feb. 6	363 Feb. 21
284 July 10	300 Mar. 12	316 April 22	332 Mar. 18	348 Nov. 3	364 May 5
285 Feb. 29	301 June 3	317 Mar. 9	333 Aug. 30	349 Jan. 29	365 Feb. 26
286 Aug. 25	302 Feb. 20	318 Jan. 13	334 Mar. 21	350 July 2	366 June 8

draw. That is, by means of thorough mixing, each capsule must have an equal opportunity to come to rest precisely where the sampler's hand closes within the bowl. Although this type of mixing is almost impossible to achieve, it can be approximated. Unfortunately, this was apparently not the case in the 1970 lottery. Even though the sequence of dates in Table 4.5 may appear to be random, there is ample statistical evidence to indicate a nonrandom selection of induction dates.* (In fact, it can be shown that the odds against observing the sequence of dates in Table 4.5 are 50,000 to 1.) Thus, this case study emphasizes the value of using a random-number table in the selection of a random sample. Most important, it points out the problems that may be encountered when attempting to acquire a random sample by a mechanical selection process.

Exercises 4.51 – 4.56

Learning the Mechanics

4.51 Suppose you wish to draw a sample of $n = 2$ elements from a population that contains $N = 10$ elements.

a. How many different samples of $n = 2$ elements can be selected?

b. If random sampling is employed, what is the probability of drawing a particular pair of elements in your sample?

4.52 Use Table I, Appendix B, to select a random sample of size $n = 20$ from among the digits, 0, 1, 2, . . . , 9. (Digits may repeat themselves.) Explain your procedure.

4.53 Suppose that a population contains $N = 200,000$ elements. Use Table I, Appendix B, to select a random sample of $n = 10$ elements from the population. Explain how you selected your sample.

---

* Statistical tests to detect nonrandomness in a sequence of numbers are beyond the scope of this text.

Applying the Concepts

4.54 To ascertain the effectiveness of their advertising campaigns, firms frequently conduct telephone interviews with consumers. Random samples of telephone numbers may be randomly or systematically selected from telephone directories, or a recent innovation called *random-digit dialing* may be employed. This approach involves using a random number generator to mechanically create the sample of phone numbers to be called. An advantage of random-digit dialing is that it makes it possible to obtain a representative sample from the population of all households with telephones, whereas with telephone directory sampling, it is only possible to obtain a sample from the population of households that have *listed* telephone numbers (Glasser & Metzger, 1972).

a. Explain how the random-number table (Table I) could be used to generate a sample of seven-digit telephone numbers.

b. Use the procedure you described in part a to generate a sample of 10 seven-digit telephone numbers.

c. Use the procedure you described in part a to generate 5 seven-digit telephone numbers whose first three digits are 373.

4.55 When a company sells shares of stock to investors, the transaction is said to take place in the *primary market*. To enable investors to resell the stock when they wish, *secondary markets* called *stock exchanges* were created. Stock exchange transactions involve buyers and sellers exchanging cash for shares of stock, with none of the proceeds going to the companies that issued the shares (Greenleaf, Foster, & Prinsky, 1982). The results of the previous business day's transactions for stocks traded on the New York Stock Exchange (NYSE) and five regional exchanges — the Midwest, Pacific, Philadelphia, Boston, and Cincinnati stock exchanges — are summarized each business day in the NYSE – Composite Transactions table in the *Wall Street Journal*.

a. Examine the NYSE – Composite Transactions table in a recent issue of the *Wall Street Journal* and explain how to draw a random sample of stocks from the table.

b. Use the procedure you described in part a to draw a random sample of twenty stocks from a recent NYSE – Composite Transactions table. For each stock in the sample, list its name (i.e., the abbreviation given in the table), its sales volume, and its closing price.

4.56 Using the random-number table (Table I, Appendix B), draw a random sample of five nonbusiness telephone subscribers from page 1 of your local telephone directory.

a. List your sample.

b. Describe the procedure you employed to obtain the sample.

c. Based on your experiences with one page of the telephone directory, what problems do you suppose would be encountered in drawing a random sample of size 1,000 from the entire directory?

Summary

We have developed some of the basic tools of probability that enable us to assess the probabilities of various sample outcomes, given a specific population structure. Although many of the examples we presented were of no practical importance, they accomplished their purpose if you now understand the concepts and definitions necessary for a basic knowledge of probability.

In the next several chapters, we will present probability models that can be used to solve practical business problems. You will see that for most applications, we will need to make inferences about unknown aspects of these probability models; i.e., we will need to apply inferential statistics to the problem.

Supplementary Exercises 4.57–4.85

4.57 What are the two rules that probabilities assigned to simple events must obey?

4.58 How are simple events and compound events related?

4.59 Are mutually exclusive events also dependent events? Explain.

4.60 Given that $P(A \cap B) = .4$ and $P(A|B) = .8$, find $P(B)$.

4.61 A manufacturer of electronic digital watches claims that the probability of its watch running more than 1 minute slow or 1 minute fast after 1 year of use is .05. A consumer protection agency has purchased four of the manufacturer's watches with the intention of testing the claim.

a. Assuming that the manufacturer's claim is correct, what is the probability that all four of the watches are as accurate as claimed?

b. Assuming that the manufacturer's claim is correct, what is the probability that exactly two of the four watches fail to meet the claim?

c. Suppose that three of the four tested watches failed to meet the claim. What inference can be made about the manufacturer's claim? Explain.

d. Suppose that all four tested watches failed to meet the claim. Is it necessarily true that the manufacturer's claim is false? Explain.

4.62 The state legislature has appropriated $1 million to be distributed in the form of grants to individuals and organizations engaged in the research and development of alternative energy sources. You have been hired by the state's energy agency to assemble a panel of five energy experts whose task it will be to determine which individuals and organizations should receive the grant money. You have identified eleven equally qualified individuals who are willing to serve on the panel. How many different panels of five experts could be formed from these eleven individuals?

4.63 A research and development company surveyed all 200 of its employees over the age of 60 and obtained the information given in the table. One of these 200 employees is selected at random.

| | UNDER 20 YEARS WITH COMPANY | | OVER 20 YEARS WITH COMPANY | |
	Technical staff	Nontechnical staff	Technical staff	Nontechnical staff
PLAN TO RETIRE AT AGE 65	31	5	45	12
PLAN TO RETIRE AT AGE 68	59	25	15	8

a. What is the probability that the person selected is on the technical staff?

b. If the person selected has over 20 years of service with the company, what is the probability that the person plans to retire at age 68?

c. If the person selected is on the technical staff, what is the probability that the person has been with the company less than 20 years?

d. What is the probability that the person selected has over 20 years with the company, is on the nontechnical staff, and plans to retire at age 65?

4.64 Refer to Exercise 4.63.

a. Consider the events A: {Plan to retire at age 68} and B: {On the technical staff}. Are events A and B independent? Explain.

b. Consider the event D: {Plan to retire at age 68 *and* on the technical staff}. Describe the complement of event D.

c. Consider the event E: {On the nontechnical staff}. Are events B and E mutually exclusive? Explain.

4.65 The set of securities (stocks, bonds, etc.) held by an individual or an organization is referred to as its *portfolio*. An investor wants to invest $2,000 in each of five different common stocks and has identified ten different stocks that she believes would be sound investments. How many different portfolios of five stocks could she form from among her list of ten stocks?

4.66 An advertising agency was interested in whether one of its client's advertisements in the latest issue of a nutrition magazine was noticed by readers of the magazine. Accordingly, it asked 1,500 of the magazine's subscribers who said they had read the latest issue whether they had noticed the advertisement. The table of percentages describes their responses. Suppose one of the 1,500 readers is chosen at random.

		NOTICED THE AD	DID NOT NOTICE THE AD
	Under 30	25%	5%
AGE GROUP	30–50	20%	15%
	Over 50	10%	25%

a. List all the simple events for this experiment.

b. What is the set of simple events in part a called?

c. For each of the simple events in part a, find the probability that it will occur.

4.67 Refer to Exercise 4.66. The following events are defined:

A: {Reader questioned was under 30}

B: {Reader questioned was between 30 and 50}

C: {Reader questioned noticed the advertisement}

D: {Reader questioned did not notice the advertisement}

Describe a reader portrayed by each of the following events:

a. $A \cap C$ **b.** $B \cup D$ **c.** $A \cap B$

4.68 Refer to Exercises 4.66 and 4.67. Find the probabilities of the following events:

a. $A \cup C$ **b.** $A \cap D$ **c.** $B \cup C$ **d.** $C \cap D$ **e.** $D \cup C$

4.69 Refer to Exercise 4.66. The following events are defined:

   E: {Reader questioned was over 50}

   F: {Reader questioned was over 50 *and* did not notice the advertisement}

Describe the following events:

a. E^c **b.** F^c

4.70 Refer to Exercises 4.66 and 4.67. Show that $P(B^c) = 1 - P(B)$.

4.71 Insurance companies use *mortality tables* to help them determine how large a premium to charge a particular individual for a particular life insurance policy. The table shows the probability of survival to age 65 for persons of the specified ages.

AGE	PROBABILITY OF SURVIVAL TO AGE 65	AGE	PROBABILITY OF SURVIVAL TO AGE 65
0	.72	40	.77
10	.74	45	.79
20	.74	50	.81
30	.75	55	.85
35	.76	60	.90

Source: U. S. Department of Health, Education, and Welfare, Public Health Service, National Center for Health Statistics, *United States Life Tables: 1969–71* (1973).

a. For a person 20 years old, what is the probability that he or she will die before age 65?

b. Describe in words the trend indicated by the increasing probabilities in the second and fourth columns.

4.72 Explain why the following statement is or is not valid: If an individual is chosen at random from all U.S. citizens living in the fifty states, the probability that this individual lives in New Hampshire is $\frac{1}{50}$.

4.73 A manufacturer of 35 mm cameras knows that a shipment of thirty cameras sent to a large discount store contains six defective cameras. The manufacturer also knows that the store will choose two of the cameras at random, test them, and accept the shipment if neither is defective.

a. What is the probability that the first camera chosen by the store will be defective?

b. Given that the first camera chosen passed inspection, what is the probability that the second camera chosen will fail inspection?

c. What is the probability that the shipment will be accepted?

4.74 Your firm has decided to market two new products. The manager of the Marketing Department believes the probability of product A being accepted by the public and product B not being accepted is .3, of product B being accepted and product A not being accepted is .4, and of both products A and B being accepted is .2. Given these probabilities the manager has concluded that the probability of both products failing is .01. Do you agree with this conclusion? Explain.

4.75 Suppose only two daily newspapers are available in your town — a local paper and one from a nearby city — and that 1,000 people in town subscribe to a daily paper. Assume that 65% of the people in town who subscribe to a daily newspaper subscribe to the local paper and 40% of those who subscribe to a daily paper subscribe to the city paper.

a. Use a Venn diagram to describe the population of newspaper subscribers.

b. If one of the 1,000 subscribers is chosen at random, what is the probability that he or she subscribes to both newspapers?

4.76 Six people apply for two identical positions in a company. Four are minority applicants and the remainder are nonminority. Define the following events:

A: {Both persons selected for the positions are nonminority candidates}

B: {Both persons selected for the positions are minority candidates}

C: {At least one of the persons selected is a minority candidate}

If all the applicants are equally qualified and the choice is therefore a random selection of two applicants from the six available, find the following:

a. $P(A)$　　**b.** $P(B)$　　**c.** $P(C)$　　**d.** $P(B|C)$

e. For the purpose of identification, assume that the minority candidates are numbered 1, 2, 3, and 4. Define the event D: {Minority candidate 1 is selected}. Find $P(D|C)$.

4.77 The table of percentages describing the location of a fast-food restaurant chain's franchises (Exercise 4.46) is reproduced here.

		REGION			
		NE	SE	SW	NW
	Under 10,000	5%	6%	3%	0%
POPULATION	10,000–100,000	10%	15%	12%	5%
OF CITY	Over 100,000	25%	4%	5%	10%

A restaurant is to be chosen at random from the 700 to test market a new style of chicken. The following events are defined:

A: {Chosen restaurant is in the Southeast}

B: {Chosen restaurant is in city of population under 10,000}

C: {Chosen restaurant is in city of population of 10,000 or over}

D: {Chosen restaurant is in the Northeast}

a. Find $P(A|B)$.　　**b.** Find $P(B|A)$.

c. Find $P(A|C)$.　　**d.** Find $P(C|D)$.

4.78 Refer to Exercise 4.77. Show that the following is true:

$$P(A \cap B) = P(A)P(B|A) = P(B)P(A|B) = .06$$

4.79 Suppose there are 500 applicants for five equivalent positions at a factory and the company is able to narrow the field to thirty equally qualified applicants. Seven of the finalists are minority candidates. Assume that the five who are chosen are selected at random from this final group of thirty.

a. What is the probability that none of the minority candidates is hired?

b. What is the probability that no more than one minority candidate is hired?

4.80 How can you show that two events are mutually exclusive?

4.81 According to David Dreman (*Forbes,* Oct. 27, 1980, pp. 202–203), investment in *new issues* (the stock of newly formed companies) can be both suicidal and rewarding. Dreman based his comments on a Securities and Exchange Commission study of 500 new issues that went public during the 1961–1962 stock boom. The commission found that of the 500 companies, 43% went bankrupt, 25% were operating at a loss, and only 20% showed any profitability. Only 12 companies out of the 500 appeared to have outstanding prospects. Suppose that, back in 1961, you had invested $1,000 in each of 3 of these new issues and that, because the prospects of the stocks were unknown, for all practical purposes the 3 stocks were randomly selected from among the 500 new issues. What is the probability that:

a. All 3 of the new issues would be among the 12 with outstanding prospects?

b. All 3 of the new issues would be from among the 43% that went bankrupt?

c. At least 1 of the 3 would be among the 12 with outstanding prospects?

4.82 The probability that a microcomputer salesperson sells a computer to a prospective customer on the first visit to the customer is .4. If the salesperson fails to make the sale on the first visit, the probability that the sale will be made on the second visit is .65. The salesperson never visits a prospective customer more than twice. What is the probability that the salesperson will make a sale to a particular customer?

4.83 A credit counselor claims that the probability that at least two local firms go bankrupt next year is .15, and the probability that exactly two local firms go bankrupt is .20. Can this statement be true? Explain.

4.84 Use a Venn diagram to show that

$$P(A \cap B^c) = P(A) - P(A \cap B)$$

4.85 A fair coin is flipped twenty times and twenty heads are observed. In such cases it is often said that a tail is due on the next flip. Is this statement true or false? Explain.

On Your Own . . .

Obtain a standard bridge deck of 52 cards and think of the cards as the 52 items your firm produces each day. Let the 4 aces and 4 kings in the deck represent defective items.

a. If one item is randomly sampled from a day's production, what is the probability of its being defective?

b. Shuffle the cards, draw one, and record whether it is a defective item. Then replace the card and repeat the process. After each draw, recalculate the proportion of the draws that have resulted in a defective item. Construct a graph with the proportion of defectives on the *y*-axis and the number of draws on the *x*-axis. Notice how the proportion defective stabilizes as the number of draws increases.

c. Draw a horizontal line on the graph in part b at a height equal to the probability you calculated in part a. Compare the calculated proportion of defectives to this probability. As the number of draws is increased, does the calculated proportion of defectives more closely approach the actual probability of drawing a defective?

References

"Drawing tonight will determine who is drafted," *New York Times,* Dec. 1, 1969, p. 1.

Feller, W. *An introduction to probability theory and its applications.* 3d ed. Vol. 1. New York: Wiley, 1968. Chapters 1, 4, and 5.

Glasser, G. J., & Metzger, G. D. "Random-digit dialing as a method of telephone sampling." *Journal of Marketing Research,* Feb. 1972, *9*, 59–64.

Greenleaf, J., Foster, R., & Prinsky, R. "Understanding financial data in the *Wall Street Journal.*" *Wall Street Journal,* Special Education Edition, 1982, 19.

Kuehn, A. A. "An analysis of the dynamics of consumer behavior and its implications for marketing management." Unpublished doctoral dissertation, Graduate School of Industrial Administration, Carnegie Institute of Technology, 1958.

Parzen, E. *Modern probability theory and its applications.* New York: Wiley, 1960. Chapters 1 and 2.

"Random or not? Judge studies lottery protest," *The National Observer,* Jan. 12, 1970, p. 2.

Williams, B. *A sampler on sampling.* New York: Wiley, 1978. Pp. 5–8.

Winkler, R. L. *An introduction to Bayesian inference and decision.* New York: Holt, Rinehart and Winston, 1972. Chapter 2.

Winkler, R. L., & Hays, W. L. *Statistics: Probability, inference, and decision.* 2d ed. New York: Holt, Rinehart and Winston, 1975. Chapters 1 and 2.

CHAPTER 5

Discrete Random Variables

Where We've Been . . .

By illustration, we indicated in Chapter 4 how probability would be used to make an inference about a population from information contained in a sample. We also noted that probability would be used to measure the reliability of the inference.

Where We're Going . . .

Most experimental events in Chapter 4 were described in words or denoted by capital letters. In real life, most sample observations are numerical — in other words, they are quantitative data. In this chapter, we will learn that business data are observed values of random variables. We will study several important random variables and will learn how to find the probabilities of specific numerical outcomes.

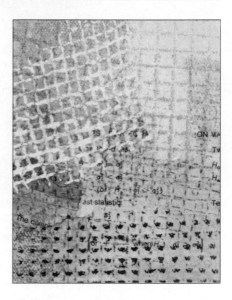

Contents

You may have noticed that most of the examples of business experiments given in Chapter 4 generated quantitative (numerical) data. This is frequently true; observations on many types of phenomena are numerical measurements. The Consumer Price Index, unemployment rate, number of sales made in a week, and yearly profit of a company are all examples of numerical measurements of some business phenomena. Thus, most business experiments have simple events that correspond to values of some numerical variable.

Definition 5.1

A *random variable* is a rule that assigns one (and only one) numerical value to each simple event of an experiment.*

The term *random variable* is more meaningful than the simpler term *variable* because the adjective *random* indicates that the experiment may result in one of the several possible values of the variable, according to the *random* outcome of the experiment. For example, if the experiment is to count the number of customers who use the drive-up window of a bank each day, the random variable (the number of customers) will vary from day to day, partly because of the random phenomena that influence whether customers use the drive-up window. Thus, the possible values of this random variable range from zero to the maximum number of customers the window could possibly serve in a day.

We define two different types of random variables, **discrete** and **continuous,** in Section 5.1. Then we spend the remainder of the chapter discussing specific types of discrete random variables and the aspects that make them important to the business statistician.

5.1 Two Types of Random Variables

Assigning one unit of probability to the simple events in a sample space, and consequently to the values of a random variable, is not always as easy as the examples in Chapter 4 may lead you to believe. If the number of simple events is finite, the job is easy. If the number of simple events is infinite but you can list them in order (we call this **countable**), the task is still not too difficult. But if the simple events are numerical and correspond to the infinitely large number of points contained in a line interval, the task is impossible. Why? Because you cannot assign a small portion of probability to each of the simple events in this infinitely large set — the sum of the probabilities will exceed 1 (the sum will be infinitely large). The consequences of this mathematical fact are important. We will have to use two different probability models, depending on whether the number of simple events in a sample space (or equivalently, the values that a random variable can assume) are countable or they correspond to the infinitely large number of points contained in one or more intervals on a line.

---

* By *experiment,* we mean an experiment that yields random outcomes (as defined in Chapter 4).

> **Definition 5.2**
>
> Random variables that can assume a *countable* number of values are called *discrete.*
>
> **Definition 5.3**
>
> Random variables that can assume values corresponding to any of the points contained in one or more intervals on a line are called *continuous.*

Examples of discrete random variables are:

1. The number of sales made by a salesperson in a given week: $x = 0, 1, 2, \ldots$
   [*Note:* Theoretically, x could become very large.]
2. The number of people in a sample of 500 who favor a particular product over all competitors: $x = 0, 1, 2, \ldots , 499, 500$.
3. The number of bids received in a bond offering: $x = 0, 1, 2, \ldots$
   [*Note:* Theoretically, x could become very large.]
4. The number of errors on a page of an accountant's ledger: $x = 0, 1, 2, \ldots$
5. The number of customers waiting to be served in a restaurant at a particular time: $x = 0, 1, 2, \ldots$

Note that each of the examples of discrete random variables begins with the words "the number of." This is very common because the discrete random variables most frequently observed in business are counts.

Examples of continuous random variables are:

1. The length of time between arrivals at a hospital clinic: $0 \leq x < \infty$ (infinity).
2. For a new apartment complex, the length of time from completion until a specified number of apartments are rented: $0 \leq x < \infty$.
3. The amount of carbonated beverage loaded into a 12-ounce can in a can filling operation: $0 \leq x \leq 12$.
4. The depth at which a successful oil drilling venture first strikes oil.
5. The weight of a food item bought in a supermarket.

In Section 5.2 we will discuss how to find the probability distribution for a discrete random variable. Then, several discrete random variables that play important roles in business decisions will be presented in subsequent sections. Probability distributions for some useful continuous random variables will be the subject of Chapter 6.

Exercises 5.1 – 5.10

Applying the Concepts

5.1 What is a random variable?

5.2 How do discrete and continuous random variables differ?

5.3 Which of the following describe continuous random variables, and which describe discrete random variables? Justify your answers.

a. The number of houses sold by a real estate developer
b. The amount of natural gas used per month for heating an apartment building
c. The exact amount of milk in a quart container
d. The number of accidents per week at a manufacturing plant

5.4 Which of the following describe continuous random variables, and which describe discrete random variables?

a. The number of people per day who report for work at a manufacturing plant
b. The number of errors found in an audit of a company's financial records
c. The length of time a customer waits for service at a supermarket checkout counter
d. The number of automobiles recalled by General Motors next year
e. The actual number of ounces of cola drink in a 12-ounce bottle

5.5 Give two examples of a business-oriented random variable. Do the same for a continuous random variable.

5.6 Give an example of a discrete random variable that would be of interest to a real estate salesperson.

5.7 Give an example of a continuous random variable that would be of interest to an economist.

5.8 Give an example of a discrete random variable that would be of interest to the manager of a hotel.

5.9 Suppose you were the manager of a clothing store. Give two examples of discrete random variables that would be of interest to you.

5.10 Suppose you were a stockbroker. Give an example of a continuous random variable that would be of interest to you.

5.2 Probability Distributions for Discrete Random Variables

Since a random variable assigns a numerical value to each of the simple events associated with an experiment, a complete description of a random variable requires that we specify its *probability distribution.* Note that each simple event is assigned one and only one value of the random variable, and hence, the values of the random variable represent mutually exclusive events.

> ### Definition 5.4
>
> The *probability distribution* of a discrete random variable is a graph, table, or formula that specifies the probability associated with each possible value the random variable can assume.

To illustrate, consider Example 5.1.

Example 5.1 Recall the experiment of tossing two coins (Chapter 4), and let x be the number of heads observed. Find the probability distribution for the random variable x, assuming the two coins are fair.

Solution Recall from Chapter 4 that the sample space and simple events for this experiment are as shown in Figure 5.1, and the probability associated with each of the four simple events is $\frac{1}{4}$. The random variable x can assume values 0, 1, 2. Then, identifying the probabilities of the simple events associated with each of these values of x, we have

Figure 5.1 Venn Diagram for the Two-Coin Toss Experiment

| H_1, H_2
•
$x = 2$ | T_1, H_2
•
$x = 1$ |
| H_1, T_2
•
$x = 1$ | T_1, T_2
•
$x = 0$ |

S

$$P(x = 0) = P(T_1, T_2) = \frac{1}{4}$$
$$P(x = 1) = P(T_1, H_2) + P(H_1, T_2) = \frac{1}{4} + \frac{1}{4} = \frac{1}{2}$$
$$P(x = 2) = P(H_1, H_2) = \frac{1}{4}$$

We will denote the probability distribution of x by the symbol $p(x)$. Then, for this example, $p(0) = \frac{1}{4}$, $p(1) = \frac{1}{2}$, and $p(2) = \frac{1}{4}$. Table 5.1 shows the probability distribution of x in tabular form, and Figure 5.2 shows it in two alternative graphical forms. Figure 5.2(a) shows the probabilities concentrated at the points, $x = 0$, 1, and 2. The heights of the vertical line segments give the probabilities that correspond to each of these values of x. The probability distribution in Figure 5.2(b) is shown as a histogram with one class corresponding to each of the three values of x. Although the probabilities for discrete random variables are, in fact, concentrated at specific points, the probability histogram will be a convenient way of viewing the probability distribution for a discrete random variable when we attempt to approximate certain probabilities in Section 6.5.

Table 5.1 Probability Distribution: Tabular Form

x	0	1	2
$p(x)$	$\frac{1}{4}$	$\frac{1}{2}$	$\frac{1}{4}$

Figure 5.2 Probability Distribution: Graphical Forms

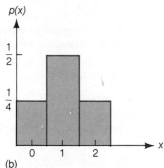

We could also present the probability distribution for x as a formula, but this would unnecessarily complicate a very simple example. We will give the formulas for the probability distributions of some discrete random variables later in this chapter.

Example 5.1 illustrates how the probability distribution for a discrete random variable can be derived, but for many practical examples of business random variables, the task is much more difficult. Fortunately, experiments and associated discrete random variables with identical characteristics are found in many different areas of business. That is, although the data may be collected in an area of accounting, marketing, economics, or management, for all practical purposes the data may represent observed values of the same type of random variable. This fact simplifies the problem for the business statistician. All that must be done is to define the nature of these often repeated experiments, define the type of random variable, and give the probability distribution of the random variable. Two requirements must be satisfied by all probability distributions for discrete random variables:

Requirements for the Probability Distribution of a Discrete Random Variable _x_

1. $p(x) \geq 0$ for all values of x $1 \geq p(x) \geq 0$

2. $\sum_{\text{All } x} p(x) = 1$

In Sections 5.4–5.7 we will describe four important types of discrete random variables, give their probability distributions, and explain where and how they can be applied in business. (Mathematical derivations of the probability distributions will be omitted, but these details can be found in the references at the end of the chapter.)

But first, in Section 5.3, we will discuss some descriptive measures of these sometimes complex probability distributions. Since probability distributions are analogous to the relative frequency distributions of Chapter 2, it should be no surprise that the mean and standard deviation are useful descriptive measures.

Case Study 5.1
Assessing the Effects of the Deadly Dutch Elm Disease

Since 1930 when the Dutch elm disease fungus was first discovered in the U.S. on the east coast, it has spread westward destroying elm trees all across the continent. It has been called ''. . . the most destructive and widespread plague of trees of our time'' (Webster, 1978). The fungus is spread primarily by English bark beetles which breed in diseased elm trees. Because of a lack of an effective chemical treatment, the major tactic in combating Dutch elm disease is a sanitation program which involves the removal of the diseased elm trees before they become a breeding ground for the fungus-carrying beetle (Chervany et al., 1980).

At the start of 1977, the city of Minneapolis had approximately 200,000 elms and had not lost more than 7,200 elms in any single year to Dutch elm disease. Since a major reforestation program had recently been inaugurated, this loss rate was not overly alarming. In 1977, however, Minneapolis lost 31,475 elms, approximately 16% of the existing elm population.

Prior to the 1978 growing season the Minneapolis Park and Recreation Board (Park Board), the organization responsible for managing the city's Dutch Elm Disease Sanitation Program, hired a team of management scientists to help in the design and operation of a sanitation program capable of dealing with the increased disease incidence. An integral part of the program proposed by the team involved forecasting the number of elms to be lost in the coming growing season. This information would enable the Park Board to plan staffing, evaluate potential bottlenecks in the elm removal operation, and inform the citizenry of the extent of the damage to the urban forest expected during the next year.

Because of the scarcity of historical data, the forecast was developed from the opinions of four disease experts. Each expert developed a discrete probability distribution to represent his beliefs regarding the number of elms that would be infected by the disease during the 1978 growing season. These four probability distributions were combined (by averaging using equal weights) to obtain a single discrete probability distribution reflecting the beliefs of all the experts regarding the number of elms to be infected. A slightly modified version of this probability distribution appears in the table.

NUMBER OF ELMS THAT WILL BE INFECTED IN 1978 x	$p(x)$
5,000– 9,999	.02
10,000–14,999	.07
15,000–19,999	.16
20,000–24,999	.17
25,000–29,999	.12
30,000–34,999	.13
35,000–39,999	.11
40,000–44,999	.08
45,000–49,999	.07
50,000 or more	.07

This distribution can be used to make probabilistic forecasts of the number of trees that will be infected in 1978. It indicates that, according to the combined opinions of the disease experts, it is most likely that the number of trees to be infected will be between 20,000 and 24,999. Furthermore, probability statements like the following can be made about the number of trees to be infected, x:

$$P(15,000 \leq x \leq 29,999) = .45$$
$$P(15,000 \leq x \leq 39,999) = .69$$
$$P(10,000 \leq x \leq 49,999) = .91$$
$$P(x < 15,000) = .09$$
$$P(x \geq 40,000) = .22$$

It is interesting to note that the actual number of losses to Dutch elm disease in 1978 was 20,817 trees, which is within the modal interval of the forecast distribution (Chervany et al., 1980).

Exercises 5.11–5.19

Learning the Mechanics

5.11 Three coins are tossed. Let x equal the number of heads observed.

a. Identify the simple events associated with this experiment and assign a value of x to each simple event, assuming the coins are fair.

b. Calculate $p(x)$ for each value of x.

c. Display the probability distribution of x in graphical form.

5.12 A die is tossed. Let x be the number of spots observed on the upturned face of the die.

a. Find the probability distribution of x and display it in tabular form.
b. Display the probability distribution of x in graphical form.

5.13 Explain why each of the following is or is not a valid probability distribution for a random variable x.

a.

x	0	1	2	3
$p(x)$	.1	.3	.3	.2

b.

x	-2	-1	0
$p(x)$	.25	.50	.25

c.

x	4	9	20
$p(x)$	$-.3$	.4	.3

d.

x	2	3	5	6
$p(x)$	.15	.15	.45	.35

5.14 The random variable x has the following discrete probability distribution:

x	0	1	2	3	4
$p(x)$	.10	.10	.25	.25	.30

a. Find $P(x \leq 0)$. **b.** Find $P(x < 0)$. **c.** Find $P(x = 2)$.
d. Find $P(x \leq 3)$. **e.** Find $P(x > 0)$. **f.** Find $P(2 \leq x \leq 4)$.

5.15 The random variable x has the following discrete probability distribution:

x	-2	-1	0	1	2
$p(x)$	.05	.20	.40	.20	.15

a. Find $P(x \leq 0)$. **b.** Find $P(x > -1)$. **c.** Find $P(-1 \leq x \leq 1)$.
d. Find $P(x < 2)$. **e.** Find $P(-1 < x < 2)$. **f.** Find $P(x < 1)$.

Applying the Concepts

5.16 A group of marketing managers were polled to assess the probabilities associated with the number, x, of sales that a company might expect per month for a new super-computer that was in the planning stages. These probabilities are shown here.

x	0	1	2	3	4	5	6	7	8
$p(x)$	.02	.08	.15	.19	.24	.17	.10	.04	.01

a. Display the probability distribution for x in graphical form.
b. Based on the marketing managers' probability distribution for x, what is the probability that the company will sell more than three computers per month? More than four?

5.17 Experience has shown that a builder of custom houses makes a profit on 95% of his contracts. Assume the event that the builder makes a profit on any one job is independent of whether he makes a profit on any other. The builder typically contracts to build three houses per month. Let x equal the number of houses per month that result in a profit.

a. Find $p(x)$.
b. Graph $p(x)$.
c. Find the probability that $x \geq 2$.

5.18 Coach "Bear" Bryant of the University of Alabama, a legendary figure in college football, was known for his winning seasons. He consistently won nine or more games per season. Suppose x represents the number of games won up to the halfway mark (six games) in a twelve-game season. If Coach Bryant and his team had a probability of .70 of winning any one game (and the winning or losing of any one game was independent of the outcome of any other), then the probability distribution of x (we show how to calculate these probabilities in Section 5.4) is:

x	0	1	2	3	4	5	6
$p(x)$	.001	.010	.060	.185	.324	.302	.118

Find the probability that the number of games won by Coach Bryant in the first half of a randomly selected season is:

a. 6   **b.** 5   **c.** Less than or equal to 4

5.19 Suppose the product development manager for your firm plans to market two new products. She thinks it is possible that both will fail consumer market tests, it is more likely that one will pass, and it is even more likely that neither will fail the market tests. Let x represent the number of the two new products that pass market tests. Display in tabular form a possible representation of the product manager's probability distribution for x.

5.3 Expected Values of Discrete Random Variables

If a discrete random variable, x, was observed a very large number of times and if the data generated were arranged in a relative frequency distribution, the relative frequency distribution would be indistinguishable from the probability distribution for the random variable. Thus, the probability distribution for a random variable is a theoretical model for the relative frequency distribution of a population. To the extent that the two distributions are equivalent (and we will assume they are), the probability distribution for x possesses a mean μ and a variance σ^2 that are identical to the corresponding descriptive measures for the population. The purpose of this section is to explain how you can find the mean value — or *expected value,* as it is called — for a random variable. We will illustrate the procedure with an example.

Examine the probability distribution for x (the number of heads observed in the toss of two coins) in Figure 5.3 (next page). Try to locate the mean of the distribution intuitively. We may reason as follows that the mean μ of this distribution is equal to 1: In a large number of experiments, $\frac{1}{4}$ should result in $x = 0$, $\frac{1}{2}$ in $x = 1$, and $\frac{1}{4}$ in $x = 2$ heads. Therefore, the average number of heads is

$$\mu = 0(\tfrac{1}{4}) + 1(\tfrac{1}{2}) + 2(\tfrac{1}{4})$$
$$= 0 + \tfrac{1}{2} + \tfrac{1}{2} = 1$$

Figure 5.3 Probability
Distribution for a Two-Coin
Toss

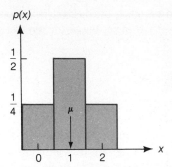

Note that to obtain the mean of the random variable x, we multiply each possible value of x by its probability $p(x)$, and then we sum this product over all possible values of x. Another term often used as a substitute for the *mean of x* is the *expected value of x,* denoted by $E(x)$:

> ## Definition 5.5
>
> The *expected value* of a discrete random variable x is
>
> $$\mu = E(x) = \sum_{\text{All } x} x p(x)$$

Example 5.2   Suppose you work for an insurance company and you sell a $10,000 whole life insurance policy at an annual premium of $290. Actuarial tables show that the probability of death during the next year for a person of your customer's age, sex, health, etc., is .001. What is the expected gain (amount of money made by the company) for a policy of this type?

Solution   The experiment is to observe whether the customer survives the upcoming year. The probabilities associated with the two simple events, Live and Die, are .999 and .001, respectively. The random variable you are interested in is the gain, x, which can assume the following values:

GAIN x	SIMPLE EVENT	PROBABILITY
$290	Customer lives	.999
$290 − $10,000	Customer dies	.001

If the customer lives, the company gains the $290 premium as profit. If the customer dies, the gain is negative because the company must pay $10,000, for a net "gain" of $(290 − 10,000)$. The expected gain is therefore

$$\mu = E(x) = \sum_{\text{All } x} x p(x)$$
$$= (290)(.999) + (290 - 10,000)(.001)$$
$$= 290(.999 + .001) - 10,000(.001)$$
$$= 290 - 10 = \$280$$

In other words, if the company were to sell a very large number of 1-year $10,000 policies to customers possessing the characteristics described above, it would (on the average) net $280 per sale in the next year. ∎

We want to measure the variability as well as the central tendency of a probability distribution. The **population variance**, σ^2, is defined as the average squared distance of x from the population mean, μ. Since x is a random variable, the squared distance, $(x - \mu)^2$, is also a random variable. Applying the same logic used to find the mean value of x, we find the mean value of $(x - \mu)^2$ by multiplying all possible values of $(x - \mu)^2$ by $p(x)$ and then summing over all possible x values.* This quantity,

$$E[(x - \mu)^2] = \sum_{\text{All } x} (x - \mu)^2 p(x)$$

is also called the **expected value of the squared distance from the mean**; i.e., $\sigma^2 = E[(x - \mu)^2]$. The **standard deviation** of x is defined as the square root of the variance.

Definition 5.6

The **variance** of a discrete random variable x is

$$\sigma^2 = E[(x - \mu)^2] = \sum_{\text{All } x} (x - \mu)^2 p(x)$$

Example 5.3

Suppose you invest a fixed sum of money in each of five business ventures. Assume you know that 70% of such ventures are successful, the outcomes of the ventures are independent of one another, and the probability distribution for the number, x, of successful ventures out of five is:

x	0	1	2	3	4	5
$p(x)$	.002	.029	.132	.309	.360	.168

a. Find $\mu = E(x)$.
b. Find $\sigma = \sqrt{E[(x - \mu)^2]}$.
c. Graph $p(x)$. Locate μ and the interval $\mu \pm 2\sigma$ on the graph. Explain how μ and σ can be used to describe $p(x)$.

Solution

a. Applying the formula, we obtain

$$\mu = E(x) = \sum_{\text{All } x} xp(x)$$

$$= 0(.002) + 1(.029) + 2(.132) + 3(.309) + 4(.360) + 5(.168)$$

$$= 3.50$$

---

* It can be shown that $E[(x - \mu)^2] = E(x^2) - \mu^2$, where $E(x^2) = \sum_{\text{All } x} x^2 p(x)$. Note the similarity between this expression and the shortcut formula $\sum_{i=1}^{n} (x_i - \bar{x})^2 = \sum_{i=1}^{n} x^2 - (\Sigma x)^2 / n$ given in Chapter 3.

b. Now we calculate the variance of x:

$$\sigma^2 = E[(x - \mu)^2] = \sum_{\text{All } x} (x - \mu)^2 p(x)$$

$$= (0 - 3.5)^2(.002) + (1 - 3.5)^2(.029) + (2 - 3.5)^2(.132)$$
$$+ (3 - 3.5)^2(.309) + (4 - 3.5)^2(.360) + (5 - 3.5)^2(.168)$$

$$= 1.05$$

Thus, the standard deviation is

$$\sigma = \sqrt{\sigma^2} = \sqrt{1.05} = 1.02$$

c. The graph of $p(x)$ is shown in Figure 5.4. Note that the mean μ and the interval $\mu \pm 2\sigma$ are shown on the graph. We can use μ and σ to describe the probability distribution in the same way that we used $\bar{x}$ and s to describe a relative frequency distribution in Chapter 3. Note particularly that $\mu = 3.5$ locates the probability distribution along the x-axis. If the investment is made in the five ventures, we expect to obtain a number x of successes near 3.5. Similarly, $\sigma = 1.02$ measures the spread of the probability distribution. Since this distribution is a theoretical relative frequency distribution that is moderately mound-shaped (see Figure 5.4), we expect (see Table 3.7) at least 75% and, more likely, near 95% of observed x values to fall in the interval $\mu \pm 2\sigma$—i.e., between 1.46 and 5.54. Compare this with the actual probability that x falls in the interval $\mu \pm 2\sigma$. From Figure 5.4

Figure 5.4 Graph of $p(x)$ for Example 5.3

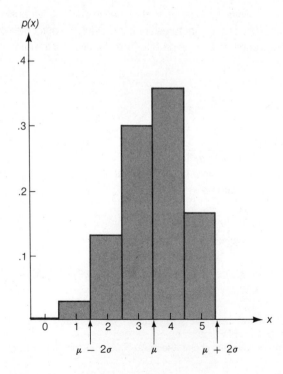

you can see that this probability includes the sum of $p(x)$ for all values of x except $p(0) = .002$ and $p(1) = .029$. Therefore, 96.9% of the probability distribution lies within 2 standard deviations of the mean. This percentage is consistent with Table 3.7. ■

Case Study 5.2
Portfolio Selection

Investors — be they large corporations, banks, pension funds, mutual funds, or individuals — seldom hold a single financial asset; rather, they hold portfolios of financial assets. Thus, the investor should be less concerned with the rate of return achieved by, say, a particular stock in the portfolio (rate of return is defined in Case Study 3.2) than in the overall rate of return of the portfolio. Since the future rate of return of a portfolio is uncertain, a probability distribution can be used to characterize a portfolio's future rate of return. Two examples of such distributions are shown in Figure 5.5. Alternatively, we might use just the mean and standard deviation of the probability distribution to characterize the future rate of return. Notice that portfolios A and B have the same mean, but that A has the greater standard deviation. As a result, A has the higher probability of yielding a negative rate of return. Accordingly, it should not be surprising that the standard deviation of a portfolio's rate of return distribution is frequently used as a measure of the risk associated with the portfolio — the higher the standard deviation, the greater the risk of the portfolio (i.e., the greater the uncertainty of the portfolio's rate of return) and vice versa.

Typically, an investor can choose from among many different assets to form a portfolio. Or put another way, there are many different portfolios for the investor to choose among. But which portfolio should the investor select? This problem was addressed by Harry M. Markowitz (1952) in a classic article published in the *Journal of Finance*. Characterizing portfolios by the mean and standard deviation of their rates of return, Markowitz proposed a two-step procedure for choosing among portfolios. First, the set of all possible portfolios — the *feasible set* — must be reduced to an *efficient set* of portfolios. An efficient portfolio is one that provides the highest possible mean rate of return for any given degree of risk (i.e., any given standard deviation) or the lowest possible degree of risk for any given mean rate of return. Second, from the efficient set, the investor should choose the portfolio that best suits his or her needs.

Figure 5.5 Rate of Return Distributions

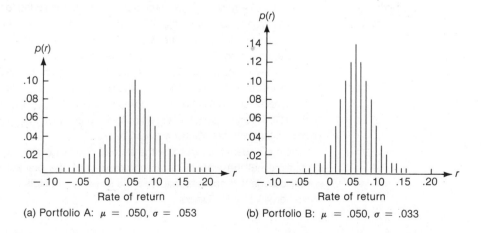

(a) Portfolio A: $\mu = .050$, $\sigma = .053$

(b) Portfolio B: $\mu = .050$, $\sigma = .033$

Figure 5.6 Efficient
Set of Portfolios

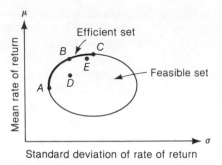

The graph in Figure 5.6 shows the mean and standard deviation of the rate of return for various portfolios. Portfolios identified by a value of μ and σ that fall within the ellipse represent the feasible set of portfolios for a particular investor. The efficient set of portfolios is denoted by the boundary line *ABC* and is sometimes called the *efficient frontier.* Portfolios to the left of *ABC* are not obtainable because they fall outside the feasible set. Portfolios to the right of *ABC* are not efficient because there always exists a portfolio on the efficient frontier that could provide (1) a higher mean return for a given level of standard deviation of returns (compare points *B* and *D*), or (2) a lower standard deviation (lower degree of risk) for a given mean return (compare points *B* and *E*). For details on how to determine the efficient set of portfolios for an investor, see Elton and Gruber (1981).

This case study illustrates that the probability distribution for the rate of return of a portfolio of financial assets provides a useful way to characterize the likelihood that the portfolio will yield an overall gain or loss. It also demonstrates that the process of selecting a portfolio of financial assets can be improved by comparing the means and standard deviations of the rates of return of alternative portfolios.

Case Study 5.3
A Restaurant Chain
Fights Sales Tax
Claim

The June 1, 1977, business section of the Orlando, Florida, *Sentinel Star* featured the following headline: "Red Lobster to Fight Tax Claim." According to the *Sentinel Star,* the Red Lobster Inns of America, a national seafood chain, has decided to take the state of Florida to court. The dispute concerns the 4% sales tax levied on most purchases in the state and mainly focuses on the state's "bracket collection system." According to the bracket system, a merchant must collect 1¢ for sales between 10¢ and 25¢, 2¢ for sales between 26¢ and 50¢, 3¢ for sales between 51¢ and 75¢, and 4¢ for sales between 76¢ and 99¢. Red Lobster contends that if this system is followed, merchants will always collect more than 4%. That is, if a sale is made for $10.41, 4% will be collected on the $10, but more than 4% will be collected on the 41¢. This, they contend, will amount to more than 4% on the total sale and therefore is not consistent with the 4% tax required by law.

Concrete evidence supplied by the state of Florida tax records does indeed support the contention that the amount of tax collected using the bracket system exceeds the 4% specified by law. It appears that the state sales tax receipts exceeded expected revenue (based on 4%) by $9.5 million.

What percent sales tax should the state expect to receive using the bracket system for computing the tax? (As noted, the tax on the whole-dollar portion of the sale will be 4%.) Using the formula for calculating expected values, you can show (see Exercise 5.126) that the expected tax paid on the cents portion of a sale is 4.6%.

<table>
<tr><td></td><td colspan="2">**Exercises**
5.20–5.34</td></tr>
</table>

Learning the Mechanics

5.20 Describe the differences in the meanings of the symbols μ, $\bar{x}$, and $E(x)$.

5.21 Consider the following probability distribution for the random variable x:

x	1	2	3	5	12
$p(x)$	.05	.15	.40	.30	.10

a. Find $E(x)$.
b. Graph $p(x)$ and locate $E(x)$ on the graph.

5.22 Consider the following probability distribution for the random variable x:

x	−2	−1	0	1	2
$p(x)$	.05	.20	.20	.30	.25

a. Find μ.
b. Graph $p(x)$ and locate μ on the graph.

5.23 Consider the following probability distribution for the random variable x:

x	10	20	30	40	50	60
$p(x)$	.10	.25	.30	.20	.10	.05

a. Find μ, σ^2, and σ.
b. Graph $p(x)$.
c. Locate μ and the interval $\mu \pm 2\sigma$ on your graph. What is the probability that x will fall within the interval $\mu \pm 2\sigma$?

5.24 Consider the following probability distribution for the random variable x:

x	.1	.2	.3	.4	.5
$p(x)$	.05	.30	.35	.20	.10

a. Find μ, σ^2, and σ.
b. Graph $p(x)$.
c. Locate μ and the interval $\mu \pm \sigma$ on your graph. What is the probability that x will fall within the interval $\mu \pm \sigma$?
d. Locate the interval $\mu \pm 3\sigma$ on your graph. What is the probability that x falls within this interval?

Applying the Concepts

5.25 The economic risks taken by businesses can be classified as being either *pure risks* or *speculative risks*. A pure risk is faced when there is a chance of incurring an economic loss but no chance of gain. A speculative risk is faced when there is a chance of gain as well as a chance of loss. Risk is sometimes measured by computing the variance or standard deviation of the probability distribution that describes the potential gains or losses of the firm. This follows from the fact that the greater the variation in potential outcomes, the greater the uncertainty faced by the firm; the smaller the variation, the more predictable the firm's gains or losses (Williams & Heins, 1976). The two discrete probability distributions given in the table were developed from historical data. They describe the potential total physical damage losses next year to the fleets of delivery trucks of two different firms. Both firms have ten trucks, and both have the same expected loss next year.

FIRM A		FIRM B	
Loss next year	Probability	Loss next year	Probability
$ 0	.01	$ 0	.00
500	.01	200	.01
1,000	.01	700	.02
1,500	.02	1,200	.02
2,000	.35	1,700	.15
2,500	.30	2,200	.30
3,000	.25	2,700	.30
3,500	.02	3,200	.15
4,000	.01	3,700	.02
4,500	.01	4,200	.02
5,000	.01	4,700	.01

a. Verify that both firms have the same expected total physical damage loss.

b. Compute the standard deviation of both probability distributions, and determine which firm faces the greater risk of physical damage to its fleet next year.

c. Was part b concerned with measuring speculative risk or pure risk? Explain.

5.26 A stock market analyst believes that the probability of stock ABC increasing in price by the close of business tomorrow is .6, the probability of it decreasing in price is .2, and the probability of tomorrow's price remaining the same as today's is .2. Assume that when stock ABC's price changes, it does so by exactly $2.

a. Based on the analyst's assumptions, what is the expected change in price of ABC at the close of business tomorrow?

b. Can the change in ABC's price at the close of business tomorrow actually equal its expected value? Explain.

5.27 Some managers believe frequent job changes will lead to more rapid advancement than if they remained at the same company. Other managers rarely leave their employers, changing no more than once every 7 years. An article on why and when managers move provides data on the average time between moves for 1,191 managers (John F. Veige, "Do

Managers on the Move Get Anywhere," *Harvard Business Review,* Mar.–Apr. 1981). The data are shown in the table. Assume the average time between moves, x, for each of the twelve time intervals is the midpoint of the interval (except for our estimated value of x for the last interval). These values are shown in the second column of the table. The percentages shown in the third column can be viewed as the approximate probabilities of the respective values of x.

AVERAGE TIME BETWEEN MOVES (Years)	x	MANAGERS WHO MOVE AT THIS RATE (%)
1–2	1.5	5.5
2–3	2.5	21.1
3–4	3.5	22.6
4–5	4.5	14.7
5–6	5.5	10.0
6–7	6.5	7.9
7–8	7.5	4.6
8–9	8.5	3.0
9–10	9.5	2.8
10–11	10.5	2.7
11–12	11.5	2.2
12 and over	15.5	2.9

a. Find the mean length of time managers stay on the job.

b. Find σ.

c. Find the approximate probability that the length of time a manager stays on the job falls within the interval $\mu \pm 2\sigma$.

5.28 To project the inventory required for a particular type of microwave oven, an appliance dealer analyzed the weekly number of sales over a long period of time. The appropriate probability distribution of the number, x, of sales per week is shown in the table.

x	0	1	2	3	4	5	6	7
$p(x)$	.01	.07	.18	.34	.24	.12	.03	.01

a. Find the expected number of sales per week.

b. Find σ^2 and σ.

c. Graph $p(x)$, and locate the interval $\mu \pm 2\sigma$ on the graph.

d. Find the probability that x falls in the interval $\mu \pm 2\sigma$.

PROFIT CONTRIBUTION x	$p(x)$
−$5,000*	.2
$10,000	.5
$30,000	.3

* A negative profit is a loss.

5.29 A company's marketing and accounting departments have determined that if the company markets its newly developed line of party favors, the probability distribution shown in the table will describe the contribution of the new line to the firm's profit during the next 6 months. The company has decided it should market the new line of party favors if the expected contribution to profit for the next 6 months is over $10,000. Based on the probability distribution, should the company market the new line?

5.30 Suppose you own a company that bonds financial managers. Based on past experience, you assess the probability that you will have to forfeit any particular bond to be .001. How much should you charge for a $1 million bond in order to break even on all such bonds?

5.31 A rock concert producer has scheduled an outdoor concert for Saturday, May 24. If it does not rain, the producer expects to make a $20,000 profit from the concert. If it does rain, the producer will be forced to cancel the concert and will lose $12,000 (rock star's fee, advertising costs, stadium rental, administrative costs, etc.). The producer has learned from the U.S. Weather Bureau that the probability of rain on May 24 is .4. Find the producer's expected profit from the concert.

5.32 Refer to Exercise 5.31. For a fee of $1,000, an insurance company has offered to insure the producer against all losses resulting from a rained-out concert. If the producer buys the insurance, what is the producer's expected profit from the concert?

5.33 Refer to Exercises 5.31 and 5.32. Assuming the Weather Bureau's forecast is accurate, do you believe the insurance company has charged too much or too little for the insurance policy? Explain.

5.34 One of the primary responsibilities of the personnel department of a firm is to maintain accurate and up-to-date professional and personal profiles of current employees and potential employees. Such information is utilized to match people to project assignments within the firm (Misshauk, 1979). A company is interested in hiring a person with an MBA degree and at least 2 years experience in a marketing department of a computer products firm. The company's personnel department has determined that it will cost the company $1,000 per job candidate to collect the required background information and to interview the candidate. As a result, it was decided to interview a maximum of three candidates. That is, the company will hire the first qualified person it finds, but will interview no more than three candidates. The company has received job applications from four persons who appear to be qualified but, unknown to the company, only one actually possesses the required background. Candidates to be interviewed will be randomly selected from the pool of four applicants.

a. Construct the probability distribution for the total cost to the firm of the interviewing strategy.

b. What is the probability that the firm's interviewing strategy will result in none of the four applicants being hired?

c. Calculate the mean of the probability distribution you constructed in part a.

d. What is the expected total cost of the interviewing strategy?

5.4 The Binomial Random Variable

A common source of business data is an opinion or preference survey. Many of these surveys result in dichotomous responses—i.e., responses that admit one of two possible alternatives, such as Yes–No. The number of Yes responses (or No responses) will usually have a *binomial probability distribution.* For example, suppose a random sample of consumers is selected from the totality of potential consumers of a particular product. The number of consumers in the sample who prefer the product to its competition is a random variable that has a binomial probability distribution.

All experiments that have the characteristics of the coin-tossing experiments of Chapter 4 and the preceding sections of this chapter yield *binomial random variables.* Imagine an experiment that is equivalent to tossing a coin n times. You are interested in observing the number of heads, x, in the n tosses. For such an experiment, x is a binomial random variable. In general, to decide whether a discrete random variable has a binomial probability distribution, check it against the characteristics listed in the box.

Characteristics of a Binomial Random Variable

1. The experiment consists of n identical trials.
2. There are only two possible outcomes on each trial. We denote one outcome by S (for Success) and the other by F (for Failure).
3. The probability of S remains the same from trial to trial. This probability is denoted by p, and the probability of F is denoted by q. Note that $p + q = 1$.
4. The trials are independent.
5. The binomial random variable x is the number of S's in n trials.

Example 5.4

For each of the following examples, decide whether x is a binomial random variable:

a. You randomly select three bonds out of a possible ten for an investment portfolio. Unknown to you, eight of the ten will maintain their present value, and the other two will lose value due to a change in their ratings. Let x be the number of the three bonds you select that lose value.

b. Before marketing a new product on a large scale, many companies conduct a consumer preference survey to determine whether the product is likely to be successful. Suppose a company develops a new diet soda and then conducts a taste-preference survey with 100 randomly chosen consumers stating their preference among the new soda and the two leading sellers. Let x be the number of the 100 who choose the new brand over the two others.

c. Some surveys are conducted using a method of sampling other than simple random sampling (defined in Chapter 4). For example, suppose a television cable company is trying to decide whether to establish a branch in a particular city. The company plans to conduct a survey to determine the fraction of households in the city that would use the cable television service. The sampling method is to choose a city block at random and then to survey every household on that block. This sampling technique is called *cluster sampling* and is discussed in Chapter 20. Suppose ten blocks are sampled in this manner, producing a total of 124 household responses. Let x be the number of the 124 households that would use the cable television service.

Solution

a. In checking the binomial characteristics, a problem arises with independence (characteristic 4 in the box). Suppose the first bond you picked was one of the two that will lose value. This reduces the chance that the second bond you pick will lose value, since now only one of the nine remaining bonds are in that category. Thus, the choices you make are dependent, and therefore x, the number of the three bonds you select that lose value, is *not* a binomial random variable.

b. Surveys that produce dichotomous responses and use random sampling techniques are classic examples of binomial experiments. In our example, each randomly selected consumer either states a preference for the new diet soda or does not. The sample of 100 consumers is a very small proportion of the totality of potential consumers, so the response of one would be, for all practical purposes, independent of another. Thus, x is a binomial random variable.

c. This example is a survey with dichotomous responses (Yes or No to the cable service), but the sampling method is not simple random sampling. Again, the binomial characteristic of independent trials would probably not be satisfied. The responses of households within a particular block would almost surely be dependent, since households within a block tend to be similar with respect to income, race, and general interests. Thus, the binomial model would not be satisfactory for x if the cluster sampling technique was used.   ■

The probability distribution for the binomial random variable is shown (in formula form) in the box.

The Binomial Probability Distribution

$$p(x) = \binom{n}{x} p^x q^{n-x} \qquad (x = 0, 1, 2, \ldots, n)$$

where

$p =$ Probability of a success on a single trial

$q = 1 - p$

$n =$ Number of trials

$x =$ Number of successes in n trials

$$\binom{n}{x} = \frac{n!}{x!(n-x)!}$$

As noted in Chapter 4, the symbol 5! means $5 \cdot 4 \cdot 3 \cdot 2 \cdot 1 = 120$. Similarly, $n! = n(n-1)(n-2) \cdot \ \cdots \ \cdot 3 \cdot 2 \cdot 1$, and remember, $0! = 1$.

The mean, variance, and standard deviation for the binomial random variable x are shown in the box.

Mean, Variance, and Standard Deviation for a Binomial Random Variable

Mean: $\mu = np$

Variance: $\sigma^2 = npq$

Standard deviation: $\sigma = \sqrt{npq}$

As we demonstrated in Chapter 3, the mean and standard deviation provide measures of the central tendency and variability, respectively, of a distribution. Thus, we can use μ and σ to obtain a rough visualization of the probability distribution for x when the calculation of the probabilities is too tedious. To illustrate the use of the binomial probability distribution, consider Example 5.5.

Example 5.5   A machine that produces stampings for automobile engines is malfunctioning and producing 10% defectives. The defective and nondefective stampings proceed from the machine in a random manner. If five stampings are collected randomly, find the probability that three of them are defective.

Solution   Let x equal the number of defectives in $n = 5$ trials. Then x is a binomial random variable with p, the probability that a single stamping will be defective, equal to .1, and $q = 1 - p = 1 - .1 = .9$. The probability distribution for x is given by the expression

$$p(x) = \binom{n}{x} p^x q^{n-x} = \binom{5}{x} (.1)^x (.9)^{5-x}$$

$$= \frac{5!}{x!(5-x)!} (.1)^x (.9)^{5-x} \qquad (x = 0, 1, 2, 3, 4, 5)$$

To find the probability of observing $x = 3$ defectives in a sample of $n = 5$, substitute $x = 3$ into the formula for $p(x)$ to obtain

$$p(3) = \frac{5!}{3!(5-3)!} (.1)^3 (.9)^{5-3} = \frac{5!}{3!2!} (.1)^3 (.9)^2$$

$$= \frac{5 \cdot 4 \cdot 3 \cdot 2 \cdot 1}{(3 \cdot 2 \cdot 1)(2 \cdot 1)} (.1)^3 (.9)^2$$

$$= .0081$$ ■

Example 5.6   Refer to Example 5.5 and find the values of $p(0)$, $p(1)$, $p(2)$, $p(4)$, and $p(5)$. Graph $p(x)$. Calculate the mean μ and standard deviation σ. Locate μ and the interval $\mu - 2\sigma$ to $\mu + 2\sigma$ on the graph. If the experiment were to be repeated many times, what proportion of the x observations would fall within the interval $\mu - 2\sigma$ to $\mu + 2\sigma$?

Solution   Again, $n = 5$, $p = .1$, and $q = .9$. Then, substituting into the formula for $p(x)$:

$$p(0) = \frac{5!}{0!(5-0)!} (.1)^0 (.9)^{5-0} = \frac{5 \cdot 4 \cdot 3 \cdot 2 \cdot 1}{(1)(5 \cdot 4 \cdot 3 \cdot 2 \cdot 1)} (1)(.9)^5$$

$$= .59049$$

$$p(1) = \frac{5!}{1!(5-1)!} (.1)^1 (.9)^{5-1} = 5(.1)(.9)^4$$

$$= .32805$$

$$p(2) = \frac{5!}{2!(5-2)!} (.1)^2 (.9)^{5-2} = (10)(.1)^2 (.9)^3$$

$$= .07290$$

$$p(4) = \frac{5!}{4!(5-4)!}(.1)^4(.9)^{5-4} = 5(.1)^4(.9)$$

$$= .00045$$

$$p(5) = \frac{5!}{5!(5-5)!}(.1)^5(.9)^{5-5} = (.1)^5$$

$$= .00001$$

The graph of $p(x)$ is shown as a probability histogram in Figure 5.7 [$p(3)$ is taken from Example 5.5 to be .0081].

Figure 5.7 The Binomial Distribution: $n = 5$, $p = .1$

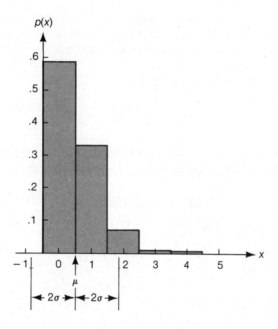

To calculate the values of μ and σ, substitute $n = 5$ and $p = .1$ into the following formulas:

$$\mu = np = (5)(.1) = .5 \qquad \sigma = \sqrt{npq} = \sqrt{(5)(.1)(.9)} = \sqrt{.45} = .67$$

To find the interval $\mu - 2\sigma$ to $\mu + 2\sigma$, we calculate

$$\mu - 2\sigma = .5 - 2(.67) = -.84 \qquad \mu + 2\sigma = .5 + 2(.67) = 1.84$$

If the experiment were to be repeated a large number of times, what proportion of the x observations would fall within the interval $\mu - 2\sigma$ to $\mu + 2\sigma$? You can see from Figure 5.7 that all observations equal to 0 or 1 will fall within the interval. The probabilities corresponding to these values are .5905 and .3280, respectively. Consequently, you would expect .5905 + .3280 = .9185, or approximately 91.9%, of the observations to fall within the interval $\mu - 2\sigma$ to $\mu + 2\sigma$. This again emphasizes that for most probability distributions, observations rarely fall more than 2 standard deviations from μ. ∎

f. $n = 10$

k \ p	0.01	0.05	0.10	0.20	0.30	0.40	0.50	0.60	0.70	0.80	0.90	0.95	0.99
0	.904	.599	.349	.107	.028	.006	.001	.000	.000	.000	.000	.000	.000
1	.996	.914	.736	.376	.149	.046	.011	.002	.000	.000	.000	.000	.000
2	1.000	.988	.930	.678	.383	.167	.055	.012	.002	.000	.000	.000	.000
3	1.000	.999	.987	.879	.650	.382	.172	.055	.011	.001	.000	.000	.000
4	1.000	1.000	.998	.967	.850	.633	.377	.166	.047	.006	.000	.000	.000
5	1.000	1.000	1.000	.994	.953	.834	.623	.367	.150	.033	.002	.000	.000
6	1.000	1.000	1.000	.999	.989	.945	.828	.618	.350	.121	.013	.001	.000
7	1.000	1.000	1.000	1.000	.998	.988	.945	.833	.617	.322	.070	.012	.000
8	1.000	1.000	1.000	1.000	1.000	.998	.989	.954	.851	.624	.264	.086	.004
9	1.000	1.000	1.000	1.000	1.000	1.000	.999	.994	.972	.893	.651	.401	.096

Figure 5.8 Reproduction of Part of Table II, Appendix B

Calculating all the binomial probabilities is tedious when n is large. You can often avoid this calculation by using Table II in Appendix B, part of which is shown in Figure 5.8. Because we will have greater use for the sums of the binomial probabilities than for the probabilities corresponding to specific values of x, the entries in Table II are the cumulative sums

$$P(x \leq k) = p(0) + p(1) + p(2) + \cdots + p(k)$$

for values of k equal to 0, 1, 2, . . . , $(n - 1)$. Note that all entries at $k = n$ would be 1.000 $[P(x \leq n) = 1]$, so we omit this row from the binomial tables.

The part of Table II shown in Figure 5.8 corresponds to $n = 10$ trials. Values of p are shown across the top row and values of a number, k, are shown at the left. To find $P(x \leq 2)$ for $n = 10$ and $p = .1$, find the intersection of the column corresponding to $p = .1$ and the row corresponding to $k = 2$. The recorded value is

$$P(x \leq 2) = .930$$

You can also use Table II to find the probabilities associated with specific values of x. Remember that the entries in the table are the sums of the binomial probabilities from $x = 0$ to $x = k$. Therefore, to find the probability that x is exactly 2 for $n = 10$ and $p = .1$, go to Table II and subtract the entry in row 1 from the entry in row 2 in the column corresponding to $p = .1$. That is,

$$p(2) = \sum_{x=0}^{2} p(x) - \sum_{x=0}^{1} p(x)$$
$$= .930 - .736 = .194$$

Example 5.7 Suppose a poll of twenty employees is taken in a large company. The purpose is to determine x, the number who favor unionization. Suppose that 60% of all the company's employees favor unionization.

   a. Find the mean and standard deviation of x.

   b. Use Table II of Appendix B to find the probability that $x < 10$.

   c. Use Table II to find the probability that $x > 12$.

   d. Use Table II to find the probability that $x = 11$.

Solution   **a.** The number of employees polled is presumably small compared with the total number of employees in this company. Thus, we may treat x, the number of the twenty who favor unionization, as a binomial random variable. The value of p is the fraction of the total employees who favor unionization; i.e., $p = .6$. Therefore, we calculate the mean and variance:

$$\mu = np = 20(.6) = 12 \qquad \sigma^2 = npq = 20(.6)(.4) = 4.8$$

The standard deviation is then

$$\sigma = \sqrt{4.8} = 2.19$$

   b. The tabulated value is

$$P(x \le 9) = .128$$

   c. To find the probability

$$P(x > 12) = \sum_{x=13}^{20} p(x)$$

we use the fact that for all probability distributions, $\sum_{\text{All } x} p(x) = 1$. Therefore,

$$P(x > 12) = 1 - P(x \le 12)$$

$$= 1 - \sum_{x=0}^{12} p(x)$$

Consulting Table II, we find the entry in row $k = 12$, column $p = .6$ to be .584. Thus,

$$P(x > 12) = 1 - .584 = .416$$

   d. To find the probability that exactly eleven employees favor unionization, recall that the entries in Table II are cumulative probabilities and use the relationship

$$P(x = 11) = [p(0) + p(1) + \cdots + p(10) + p(11)]$$
$$- [p(0) + p(1) + \cdots + p(9) + p(10)]$$
$$= P(x \le 11) - P(x \le 10)$$

Then

$$P(x = 11) = .404 - .245 = .159$$

The probability distribution for x in this example is shown in Figure 5.9. Note that the interval $\mu \pm 2\sigma$ is (7.6, 16.4).   ■

Figure 5.9 The Binomial Probability Distribution for x in Example 5.7: $n = 20$, $p = .6$

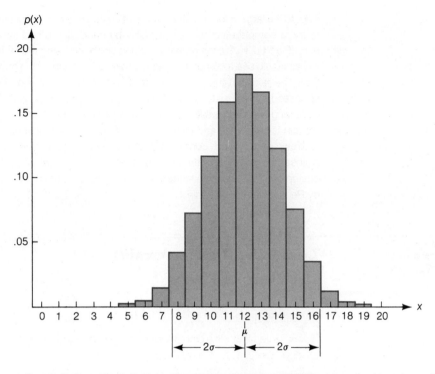

Case Study 5.4

Evaluating Customer Response to a New Sales Program

Arthur A. Brown, Frank T. Hulswit, and John D. Kettelle (1956) were asked by a large firm to study, and perhaps determine reasons for and solutions to, its lack of growth over the prior 5 years. In their article, Brown et al. refer to the firm as "Penstock Press, a large commercial printing company."

The primary concern of the study was Penstock's sales operations. Accordingly, Brown et al. conducted an experiment to study the sales effectiveness of Penstock's salespeople. The salespeople were instructed to increase their sales efforts toward all of Penstock's customers, but in particular toward sixty of the larger customers, for a 4-month experimental period. At the end of the 4-month period it was determined that the probability of a customer making a genuinely positive response to the increased sales effort merely by chance was .25. Of Penstock's sixty large customers, it was noted that twenty-four made what appeared to be genuinely positive responses. But before concluding that the increased sales effort toward the sixty large customers had paid off, Brown et al. felt it was important to determine how likely it would be for twenty-four or more of the sixty customers to make positive responses merely by chance. Assuming that the probability of a positive response occurring by chance (.25) is the same for each of the sixty customers and that the response of one customer does not affect that of another, the number of positive responses observed has a binomial probability distribution. Accordingly, the probability of twenty-four or more positive responses from the sixty customers can be determined as follows:

$$P(x \geq 24) = \sum_{x=24}^{60} \binom{60}{x}.25^x(.75)^{60-x} = .004$$

(Due to the large value of n, the number of customers in the experiment, it would be unrealistic to try to compute the above probability by hand. If you had access to binomial tables for $n = 60$ and $p = .25$, the probability could be found using the tables. Otherwise, it would be necessary to use a computer or an approximation such as the one we will discuss in Section 6.5.) The fact that the probability of observing twenty-four or more genuinely positive responses from the sixty customers merely by chance is only .004 indicates that in actually observing twenty-four such responses either a very rare event has occurred or the responses were in fact genuine and the increased sales effort did influence the increase in sales.

Brown et al. (1956) concluded that the number of positive responses could not be explained by chance, but that they in fact "implied deliberate continuing business from the customers," i.e., genuine responses. The authors noted that this conclusion was supported by Penstock's salespeople.

Exercises 5.35–5.52

Learning the Mechanics

5.35 Compute the following:

a. $\dfrac{5!}{3!(5-3)!}$ **b.** $\dbinom{6}{3}$ **c.** $\dbinom{8}{0}$ **d.** $\dbinom{5}{5}$ **e.** $\dbinom{6}{1}$

5.36 Given that x is a binomial random variable with $n = 5$ and $p = .2$, calculate the values for $p(x)$, $x = 0, 1, 2, 3, 4, 5$. Graph $p(x)$.

5.37 Given that x is a binomial random variable, compute $p(x)$ for each of the following cases:

a. $n = 6$, $x = 3$, $p = .3$
b. $n = 4$, $x = 2$, $q = .6$
c. $n = 2$, $x = 0$, $p = .8$

5.38 Given that x is a binomial random variable, $n = 6$, and $p = .4$:

a. Display $p(x)$ in tabular form.
b. Compute the mean and variance of x.
c. Graph $p(x)$ and locate $E(x)$ and the interval $\mu \pm 2\sigma$ on the graph.
d. What is the probability that x falls within the interval $\mu \pm 2\sigma$?

5.39 Given that x is a binomial random variable, $n = 5$, and $p = .5$:

a. Display $p(x)$ in tabular form.
b. Compute the mean and variance of x.
c. Graph $p(x)$ and locate $E(x)$ and the interval $\mu \pm 2\sigma$ on the graph.
d. What is the probability that x falls within the interval $\mu \pm 2\sigma$?

5.40 Use the results of Exercise 5.39 to find the following probabilities:

a. $P(x \leq 3)$ **b.** $P(x \leq 5)$ **c.** $P(x < 2)$

5.41 Given that x is a binomial random variable with $n = 15$ and $p = .4$, use Table II, Appendix B, to find the following probabilities:

a. $P(x \leq 1)$ **b.** $P(x \geq 3)$ **c.** $P(x \leq 5)$
d. $P(x < 10)$ **e.** $P(x > 10)$ **f.** $P(x = 6)$

5.42 The binomial probability distribution is a family of probability distributions, with each single distribution depending on the values of n and p. Assume that x is a binomial random variable with $n = 4$.

a. Determine the value of p such that the probability distribution of x is symmetric.
b. Determine a value of p such that the probability distribution of x is skewed to the right.
c. Determine a value of p such that the probability distribution of x is skewed to the left.
d. Graph each of the binomial distributions you obtained in parts a, b, and c. Locate the mean for each distribution on its graph.
e. In general, for what values of p will a binomial distribution be symmetric? Skewed to the right? Skewed to the left?

Applying the Concepts

5.43 Your firm's accountant believes that 10% of the company's invoices contain arithmetic errors. To check this theory, the accountant randomly samples twenty-five invoices and finds that seven contain errors. What is the probability that of the twenty-five invoices written, seven or more would contain errors if the accountant's theory was valid? What assumptions do you have to make to solve this problem using the methodology of this chapter?

5.44 A particular system in a space vehicle must work properly in order for the space ship to reenter Earth's atmosphere. One particular component of the system operates successfully only 85% of the time. To increase the reliability of the system, four of the components will be installed in such a way that the system will operate successfully if at least one component is working successfully. What is the probability that the system will fail? Assume the components operate independently.

5.45 According to the "January" theory, if the stock market is up in January, it will be up for the whole year (and vice versa). Believe it or not, this indicator of stock market behavior has been correct for 29 of the last 34 years and 100% correct in odd-numbered years ("Heard on the Street," *Wall Street Journal,* Feb. 1, 1984). Suppose there is no truth whatever in this theory and that stock prices are just as likely to move up or down in any given year, regardless of the direction of movement in January.

a. Find the probability of perfect agreement between the January and annual movements in stock prices over a period of 15 years.
b. What is the probability of perfect agreement between the January and annual movements in stock prices in at least 10 of 15 years?

5.46 A problem of considerable economic impact on the economy is the burgeoning cost of Medicare and other public-funded medical services. One aspect of this problem concerns the high percentage of people seeking medical treatment who, in fact, have no physical basis for their ailments. One conservative estimate is that the percentage of people who seek medical assistance and who have no real physical ailment is 10%, and some doctors believe that it may be as high as 40%. Suppose we were to randomly sample the records of a doctor and found that five of fifteen patients seeking medical assistance were physically healthy.

a. What is the probability of observing five or more physically healthy patients in a sample of fifteen if the proportion, p, that the doctor normally sees is 10%?

b. What is the probability of observing five or more physically healthy patients in a sample of fifteen if the proportion, p, that the doctor normally sees is 40%?

c. Why might your answer to part a make you believe that p is larger than .10?

5.47 According to the U.S. Golf Association (USGA), "The weight of the [golf] ball shall not be greater than 1.620 ounces avoirdupois, and the size not less than 1.680 inches in diameter. The velocity of the ball shall be not greater than 250 feet per second" (USGA, 1982). The USGA periodically checks the specifications of golf balls sold in the United States by randomly sampling balls from pro shops around the country. Two dozen of each kind are sampled, and if more than three do not meet size and/or velocity requirements, that kind of ball is removed from the USGA's approved-ball list (*Golf World*, Sept. 10, 1982).

a. What assumptions must be made and what information must be known in order to use the binomial probability distribution to calculate the probability that the USGA will remove a particular kind of golf ball from its approved-ball list?

b. Suppose 10% of all balls produced by a particular manufacturer are less than 1.680 inches in diameter, and assume that the number of such balls, x, in a sample of two dozen balls can be adequately characterized by a binomial probability distribution. Find the mean and standard deviation of the binomial distribution.

c. Refer to part b. If x has a binomial distribution, then so does the number, y, of balls in the sample that meet the USGA's minimum diameter. [*Note:* $x + y = 24$.] Describe the distribution of y. In particular, what are p, q, and n? Also, find $E(y)$ and the standard deviation of y.

5.48 A problem of great concern to a manufacturer is the cost of repair and replacement required under a product's guarantee agreement. Assume it is known that 10% of all electronic pocket calculators purchased are returned for repair while their guarantee is still in effect. If a firm purchased twenty-five pocket calculators for its salespeople, what is the probability that five or more of these calculators will need repair while their guarantees are still in effect?

5.49 Suppose you are a purchasing officer for a company. You have purchased 50,000 electrical switches and have been guaranteed by the supplier that the shipment will contain no more than 0.1% defectives. To check the shipment, you randomly sample 500 switches, test them, and find that four are defective. Assuming the supplier's claim is true, compute μ and σ for the number of defectives in a sample of 500 switches. If the supplier's claim is true, is it likely that you would have found four defective switches in the sample? Based on this sample, what inference would you make concerning the supplier's guarantee?

5.50 Many firms utilize sampling plans to control the quality of manufactured items ready for shipment or the quality of items that have been purchased. To illustrate the use of a sampling plan, suppose you are shipping electrical fuses in lots, each containing 10,000 fuses. The plan specifies that you will randomly sample twenty-five fuses from each lot and accept (and ship) the lot if the number of defective fuses, x, in the sample is less than 3. If $x \geq 3$, you will reject the lot and hold it for a complete reinspection. What is the probability of accepting a lot ($x = 0$, 1, or 2) if the actual fraction defective in the lot is:

a. 1   **b.** 0.8   **c.** 0.5   **d.** 0.2   **e.** 0.05   **f.** 0

Construct a graph showing $P(A)$, the probability of lot acceptance, as a function of the lot fraction detective, p. This graph is called the *operating characteristic curve* for the sampling plan.

5.51 Refer to Exercise 5.50. Suppose the sampling plan called for sampling $n = 25$ fuses and accepting a lot if $x \leq 3$. Calculate the quantities specified in Exercise 5.50, and construct the operating characteristic curve for this sampling plan. Compare this curve with the curve obtained in Exercise 5.50. (Note how the curve characterizes the ability of the plan to screen bad lots from shipment.)

5.52 After a costly study, a market analyst claims that 12% of all consumers in a particular sales region prefer a certain noncarbonated beverage. To check the validity of this figure, you decide to conduct a survey in the region. You randomly sample $n = 400$ customers and find that $x = 31$ prefer the beverage. Compute μ and σ for the random variable x. Based on a sample of 400, is it likely that you would observe a value of $x \leq 31$ if the market analyst's claim was true? Explain. Do the results of your survey agree with the 12% estimate given by the market analyst?

5.5 The Poisson Random Variable (Optional)

A type of probability distribution useful in describing the number of events that will occur in a specific period of time or in a specific area or volume is the *Poisson distribution* (named after the eighteenth-century physicist and mathematician, Siméon Poisson). The following are typical examples of random variables for which the Poisson probability distribution provides a good model:

1. The number of industrial accidents in a given manufacturing plant per month observed by a plant safety supervisor
2. The number of noticeable surface defects (scratches, dents, etc.) found by quality inspectors on a new automobile (or any manufactured product)
3. The parts per million of some toxicant found in the water or air emission from a manufacturing plant (a random variable of great interest to both the business community and the Environmental Protection Agency)
4. The number of arithmetic errors per 100 invoices (or per 1,000 invoices, etc.) in the accounting records of a company
5. The number of customer arrivals per unit time at a service counter (a service station, a hospital clinic, a supermarket checkout counter, etc.)
6. The number of death claims per day received by an insurance company
7. The number of breakdowns of an electronic computer per month

The characteristics of the Poisson random variable are usually rather difficult to verify for practical examples. The examples given above satisfy them well enough that the Poisson distribution provides a good model in many instances. As with all probability models, the real test of the adequacy of the Poisson model is whether it provides a reasonable approximation to reality — that is, whether empirical data support it.

Characteristics of a Poisson Random Variable

1. The experiment consists of counting the number of times a particular event occurs during a given unit of time or in a given area or volume (or weight, distance, or any other unit of measurement).

2. The probability that an event occurs in a given unit of time, area, or volume is the same for all the units.

3. The number of events that occur in one unit of time, area, or volume is independent of the number that occur in other units.

4. The mean (or expected) number of events in each unit will be denoted by the Greek letter lambda, λ.

The Poisson probability distribution also provides a good approximation to a binomial probability distribution with mean

$$\lambda = np$$

when n is large and p is small (say, $np \leq 7$). (See Exercise 5.58.)

In Table III of Appendix B you will find values of $e^{-\lambda}$ for various values of λ. These will aid in calculating Poisson probabilities.

The probability distribution, mean, and variance for a Poisson random variable are shown in the box.

Probability Distribution, Mean, and Variance for a Poisson Random Variable

$$p(x) = \frac{\lambda^x e^{-\lambda}}{x!} \qquad (x = 0, 1, 2, \ldots)$$

$$\mu = \lambda \qquad \sigma^2 = \lambda$$

where

$\lambda =$ Mean number of events during the given time period

$e = 2.71828 \ldots$

Example 5.8   Suppose the number, x, of a company's employees who are absent on Mondays has (approximately) a Poisson probability distribution. Furthermore, assume that the average number of Monday absentees is 2.5.

a. Find the mean and standard deviation of x, the number of employees absent on Monday.
b. Find the probability that exactly five employees are absent on a given Monday.
c. Find the probability that two or more employees are absent on a Monday.

Solution   **a.** The mean and variance of a Poisson random variable are both equal to λ. Thus, for this example

$$\mu = \lambda = 2.5 \qquad \sigma^2 = \lambda = 2.5$$

Then the standard deviation is

$$\sigma = \sqrt{2.5} = 1.58$$

b. We want the probability that exactly five employees are absent on Monday. The probability distribution for x is

$$p(x) = \frac{\lambda^x e^{-\lambda}}{x!}$$

Then, since $\lambda = 2.5$, $x = 5$, and $e^{-2.5} = .082085$ (from Table III),

$$p(5) = \frac{(2.5)^5 e^{-2.5}}{5!} = \frac{(2.5)^5(.082085)}{5 \cdot 4 \cdot 3 \cdot 2 \cdot 1} = .067$$

c. To find the probability that two or more employees are absent on Monday, we need to find

$$P(x \geq 2) = p(2) + p(3) + p(4) + \cdots = \sum_{x=2}^{\infty} p(x)$$

In order to find the probability of this event, we must use its complement. Thus,

$$P(x \geq 2) = 1 - P(x \leq 1) = 1 - [p(0) + p(1)]$$
$$= 1 - \frac{(2.5)^0 e^{-2.5}}{0!} - \frac{(2.5)^1 e^{-2.5}}{1!}$$
$$= 1 - \frac{1(.082085)}{1} - \frac{2.5(.082085)}{1}$$
$$= 1 - .287 = .713$$

Figure 5.10   Poisson Probability Distribution for x in Example 5.8

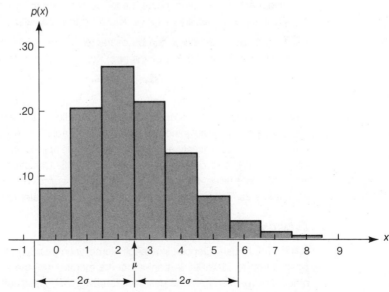

According to our Poisson model, the probability that two or more employees are absent on a Monday is .713.

The probability distribution for x is shown in Figure 5.10 for x values between 0 and 9. The mean $\mu = 2.5$ and the interval $\mu \pm 2\sigma$ or $(-.7, 5.7)$ are indicated. ■

**Exercises
5.53–5.67**

Learning the Mechanics

5.53 Use Table III in Appendix B to compute each of the following:

a. $e^{-3.0}$ **b.** $e^{-4.5}$ **c.** $e^{-1.7}$ **d.** $e^{-6.0}$

e. $\dfrac{(3)^2 e^{-3}}{2!}$ **f.** $\dfrac{(2.5)^3 e^{-2.5}}{3!}$ **g.** $\dfrac{(8.6)^4 e^{-8.6}}{4!}$

5.54 Given that x is a random variable for which a Poisson probability distribution provides a good characterization, compute the following:

a. $P(x \le 2)$, when $\lambda = 1$ **b.** $P(x = 1)$, when $\lambda = 4$
c. $P(x \ge 1)$, when $\lambda = 2$ **d.** $P(x = 0)$, when $\lambda = 8$

5.55 Given that x is a random variable for which a Poisson probability distribution with $\lambda = 2$ provides a good characterization:

a. Graph $p(x)$ for $x = 0, 1, 2, \ldots, 9, 10$.
b. Find μ and σ for x, and locate μ and the interval $\mu \pm 2\sigma$ on the graph.
c. What is the probability that x will fall within the interval $\mu \pm 2\sigma$?

5.56 Given that x is a random variable for which a Poisson probability distribution with $\lambda = 4$ provides a good characterization:

a. Graph $p(x)$ for $x = 0, 1, 2, \ldots, 9, 10$.
b. Find μ and σ for x, and locate μ and the interval $\mu \pm 2\sigma$ on the graph.
c. What is the probability that x will fall within the interval $\mu \pm 2\sigma$?

5.57 A random variable x can be characterized by a Poisson distribution with mean 6. Which of the following values of x is (are) *not* within 2 standard deviations of the mean?

a. 1 **b.** 5 **c.** 12 **d.** 2 **e.** 11 **f.** 7

5.58 As mentioned in the text, when n is large, p is small, and $np \le 7$, the Poisson probability distribution provides a good approximation to the binomial probability distribution. Since we provide exact binomial probabilities (Table II in Appendix B) for relatively small values of n, you can investigate the adequacy of the approximation for $n = 25$. Use Table II to find $p(0)$, $p(1)$, and $p(2)$ for $n = 25$ and $p = .05$. Calculate the corresponding Poisson approximations using $\lambda = \mu = np$. Note that these approximations are reasonably good for n as small as 25. To use the approximation, we would prefer to have $n \ge 100$.

Applying the Concepts

5.59 The Federal Deposit Insurance Corporation (FDIC), established in 1933, insures deposits of up to $100,000 in banks that are members of the Federal Reserve System (and others that voluntarily join the insurance fund) against losses due to bank failure or theft. From

1975 through 1980 the average number of bank failures per year among insured banks was 10.33 (*Statistical Abstract of the United States: 1981,* p. 510). Assume the number of bank failures per year, x, among insured banks can be adequately characterized by a Poisson probability distribution with mean 10.33.

a. In 1976, sixteen insured banks failed. Find $p(16)$.
b. Find the expected value and standard deviation of x.
c. How far (in standard deviations) does $x = 16$ lie above the mean of the Poisson distribution? That is, find the z-score for $x = 16$.
d. In 1977, six insured banks failed. Find $P(x \leq 6)$.

5.60 The National Transportation Safety Board is responsible for investigating aviation accidents. In 1979, 208.9 billion passenger miles were flown by commercial airlines in the United States. During this period there were 279 fatalities. In 1980, 200.1 billion passenger miles were flown and there were 13 fatalities. Based on data from 1975 to 1980, it is known that the average number of fatalities per 100 million passenger miles flown is approximately .043 (*Statistical Abstract of the United States: 1981,* p. 641). Assuming that airlines fly approximately 17 billion passenger miles per month, the mean number of fatalities for a 1-month period is 7.31 (170 times the mean per 100 million miles). Suppose the probability distribution for x, the number of fatalities per month, can be approximated by a Poisson probability distribution.

a. What is the probability that no fatalities will occur during any given month?
b. Find $E(x)$ and the standard deviation of x.
c. Use your answers to part b to describe the probability that as many as 20 fatalities will occur in any given month.

5.61 The Department of Commerce in a particular state has determined that the number of small businesses that declare bankruptcy per month has approximately a Poisson distribution with a mean equal to 6.5.

a. Find the probability of at least five bankruptcies occurring next month.
b. Find the probability of exactly four bankruptcies occurring next month.

5.62 The safety supervisor at a large manufacturing plant believes the expected number of industrial accidents per month to be 3.4. What is the probability of exactly two accidents occurring next month? Three or more? What assumptions do you need to make to solve this problem using the methodology of this chapter?

5.63 As a check on the quality of the wooden doors produced by a company, its owner requested that each door undergo inspection for defects before leaving the plant. The plant's quality control inspector found that 1 square foot of door surface contains on the average 0.5 minor flaw. Subsequently, 1 square foot of each door's surface was examined for flaws. The owner decided to have all doors reworked that were found to have two or more minor flaws in the square foot of surface that was inspected. What is the probability that a door will fail inspection and be sent back for reworking? What is the probability that a door will pass inspection?

5.64 A can company reports that the number of breakdowns per 8-hour shift on its machine-operated assembly line follows a Poisson distribution with a mean of 1.5. What is the probability of exactly two breakdowns during the midnight shift? What is the probability of fewer than two breakdowns during the afternoon shift? Of no breakdowns during three consecutive 8-hour shifts? (Assume the machine operates independently across shifts.)

5.65 The random variable x, the number of people who arrive at a cashier's counter in a bank during a specified period of time, often possesses (approximately) a Poisson probability distribution. If the mean arrival rate, λ, is known, the Poisson probability distribution can be used to aid in the design of the customer service facility. Suppose you estimate that the mean number of arrivals per minute for cashier service at a bank is one person per minute. What is the probability that in a given minute, the number of arrivals will equal three or more? Can you tell the bank manager that the number of arrivals will rarely exceed three per minute?

5.66 The probability that a health insurance company must pay a major medical claim for a policy is .001. If a group of 1,000 policyholders represents a random sample of all possible policyholders, what is the probability that the insurance company will have to pay at least one major medical claim in this sample? [*Hint:*   See Exercise 5.58.]

5.67 Give examples of two random variables of interest to a banker for which the Poisson probability distribution might provide a good model.

5.6
The Hyper-geometric Random Variable (Optional)

The *hypergeometric probability distribution* provides a realistic model for some types of enumerative (count) data. The characteristics of the hypergeometric distribution are listed in the box.

Characteristics of a Hypergeometric Random Variable

1. The experiment consists of randomly drawing n elements without replacement from a set of N elements, r of which are S's (for Success) and $(N - r)$ of which are F's (for Failure).
2. The hypergeometric random variable x is the number of S's in the draw of n elements.

Note that both the hypergeometric and binomial characteristics stipulate that each draw or trial results in one of two outcomes. The basic difference between these random variables is that the hypergeometric trials are dependent, while the binomial trials are independent. The draws are dependent because the probability of drawing an S (or an F) is dependent on what occurred on preceding draws.

To illustrate the dependence between trials, we note that the probability of drawing an S on the first draw is r/N. Then, the probability of drawing an S on the second draw depends on the outcome of the first. It will be either $(r - 1)/(N - 1)$ or $r/(N - 1)$, depending on whether the first draw was an S or an F. Consequently, the results of the draws represent dependent events.

For example, suppose we define x as the number of women hired in a random selection of three applicants from a total of six men and four women. This random variable satisfies the characteristics of a hypergeometric random variable with $N = 10$ and $n = 3$. The possible outcomes on each trial are either selection of a female (S) or selection of a male (F). Another example of a hypergeometric random variable is the number, x, of defective television picture tubes in a random selection of $n = 4$ from a shipment of $N = 8$ tubes. And, as a third example, suppose $n = 5$ stocks are randomly selected from a list of $N = 15$ stocks. Then, the number x of the five selected companies that pay regular dividends to stockholders is a hypergeometric random variable.

Probability Distribution, Mean, and Variance of the Hypergeometric Random Variable

$$p(x) = \frac{\binom{r}{x}\binom{N-r}{n-x}}{\binom{N}{n}} \qquad [x = \text{Maximum}[0, n - (N - r)], \ldots , \text{Minimum}(r, n)]$$

$$\mu = \frac{nr}{N} \qquad \sigma^2 = \frac{r(N-r)n(N-n)}{N^2(N-1)}$$

where

$N = $ Total number of elements

$r \ = $ Number of S's in the N elements

$n = $ Number of elements drawn

$x = $ Number of S's drawn in the n elements

Example 5.9

Suppose, as we mentioned earlier, an employer randomly selects three new employees from a total of ten applicants, six men and four women. Let x be the number of women who are hired.

a. Find the mean and standard deviation of x.

b. Find the probability that no women are hired.

Solution

a. Since x is a hypergeometric random variable with $N = 10$, $n = 3$, and $r = 4$, the mean and variance are

$$\mu = \frac{nr}{N} = \frac{(3)(4)}{10} = 1.2$$

$$\sigma^2 = \frac{r(N-r)n(N-n)}{N^2(N-1)} = \frac{4(10-4)3(10-3)}{(10)^2(10-1)}$$

$$= \frac{(4)(6)(3)(7)}{(100)(9)} = .56$$

The standard deviation is

$$\sigma = \sqrt{.56} = .75$$

b. The probability that no women are hired by the employer, assuming the selection is truly random, is

$$P(x = 0) = p(0) = \frac{\binom{4}{0}\binom{10-4}{3-0}}{\binom{10}{3}}$$

$$= \frac{\dfrac{4!}{0!(4-0)!}\dfrac{6!}{3!(6-3)!}}{\dfrac{10!}{3!(10-3)!}} = \frac{(1)(20)}{120} = \frac{1}{6}$$

The entire probability distribution for x is shown in Figure 5.11. The mean $\mu = 1.2$ and the interval $\mu \pm 2\sigma = (-.3, 2.7)$ are indicated. You can see that if this random variable were to be observed over and over again a large number of times, most of the values of x would fall within the interval $\mu \pm 2\sigma$.

Figure 5.11   Probability Distribution for x in Example 5.9

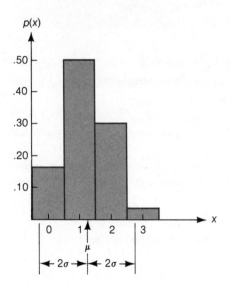

■

Exercises 5.68 – 5.82

Learning the Mechanics

5.68 Explain the difference between sampling with replacement and sampling without replacement.

5.69 How do binomial and hypergeometric random variables differ? In what respects are they similar?

5.70 Given that x is a hypergeometric random variable with $N = 8$, $n = 3$, and $r = 5$, compute the following:

a. $P(x = 1)$ **b.** $P(x = 0)$ **c.** $P(x = 3)$ **d.** $P(x \geq 4)$

5.71 Given that x is a hypergeometric random variable, compute $p(x)$ for each of the following cases:

a. $N = 5$, $n = 3$, $r = 3$, $x = 1$
b. $N = 9$, $n = 5$, $r = 3$, $x = 3$
c. $N = 4$, $n = 2$, $r = 2$, $x = 2$
d. $N = 4$, $n = 2$, $r = 2$, $x = 0$

5.72 Given that x is a hypergeometric random variable with $N = 10$, $n = 5$, and $r = 7$:

a. Display the probability distribution for x in tabular form.
b. Compute the mean and variance of x.
c. Graph $p(x)$ and locate μ and the interval $\mu \pm 2\sigma$ on the graph.
d. What is the probability that x will fall within the interval $\mu \pm 2\sigma$?

5.73 Given that x is a hypergeometric random variable with $N = 12$, $n = 8$, and $r = 6$:

a. Display the probability distribution for x in tabular form.
b. Compute μ and σ for x.
c. Graph $p(x)$ and locate μ and the interval $\mu \pm 2\sigma$ on the graph.
d. What is the probability that x will fall within the interval $\mu \pm 2\sigma$?

5.74 Use the results of Exercise 5.73 to find the following probabilities:

a. $P(x = 1)$ **b.** $P(x = 4)$ **c.** $P(x \le 4)$
d. $P(x \ge 5)$ **e.** $P(x < 3)$ **f.** $P(x \ge 8)$

5.75 Suppose you plan to sample 10 items from a population of 100 items and would like to determine the probability of observing 4 defective items in the sample. Which probability distribution should you use to compute this probability under the following conditions? Justify your answers.

a. The sample is drawn without replacement.
b. The sample is drawn with replacement.

Applying the Concepts

5.76 Suppose you are purchasing cases of wine (twelve bottles per case) and that periodically, you select a test case to determine the adequacy of the sealing process. To do this, you randomly select and test three bottles in the case. If a case contains one spoiled bottle of wine, what is the probability it will appear in your sample?

5.77 If you are purchasing small lots of a manufactured product and it is very costly to test a single item, it may be desirable to test a sample of items from the lot rather than every item in the lot. Such a sampling plan would be based on a hypergeometric probability distribution. For example, suppose each lot contains ten items. You decide to sample four items per lot and reject the lot if you observe one or more defectives. If the lot contains one defective item, what is the probability that you will accept the lot? What is the probability that you will accept the lot if it contains two defective items? Three? Four?

5.78 Construct an operating characteristic curve for the sampling plan in Exercise 5.77 by plotting the probability of lot acceptance, $P(A)$, versus the lot fraction defective. (Use the probabilities of lot acceptance calculated in Exercise 5.77.)

5.79 Refer to Exercises 5.77 and 5.78. Suppose we were to change the *acceptance number* for the sampling plan to 2 (i.e., we will accept the lot if the number, x, of defectives in the sample is $x \leq 2$). Construct an operating characteristic curve for this sampling plan, and compare it with the operating characteristic curve in Exercise 5.78. Which sampling plan is more likely to detect lots containing defectives? Explain how this is apparent in the comparison of the operating characteristic curves.

5.80 A marketing manager wants to fill the vacancies for four district managers from among the company's existing sales personnel. Twelve salespersons are judged to be suitable for the district managerial positions, eight men and four women. If the marketing manager randomly selects four persons from this group of twelve, find the probability distribution for the number, x, of women selected for the district managerial positions. Present the probability distribution in both graphical and tabular form.

5.81 A nursery advertises that it has ten elm trees for sale. Unknown to the nursery, three of the trees have already been infected with Dutch elm disease and will die within a year. If a buyer purchases two trees, what is the probability that both trees will be healthy? What is the probability that at least one of the trees is infected?

5.82 A curious event was recently described in the *Minneapolis Star and Tribune* (May 27, 1983). The Minneapolis Community Development Agency (MCDA) makes home improvement grants each year to homeowners in depressed neighborhoods within the city. Of the $708,000 granted in 1983, $233,000 was awarded by the city council using a "random selection" of 140 homeowners' applications from among a total of 743 applications — 601 from the north side and 142 from the south side of Minneapolis. Oddly, all 140 grants awarded were from the north side, clearly a highly improbable outcome if, in fact, the 140 winners were randomly selected from among the 743 applicants.

a. Suppose the 140 winning applications were randomly selected from among the total of 743, and let x equal the number in the sample from the north side. Find the mean and standard deviation of x.

b. Use the results of part a to support a contention that the grant winners were not randomly selected.

5.7 The Geometric Random Variable (Optional)

Another common discrete random variable that has many business applications is the *geometric random variable.* Like the binomial random variable, it arises naturally from a discussion of a coin-tossing experiment (whether the coin is balanced or unbalanced). But instead of tossing the coin a fixed number of times and observing the number, x, of heads, we toss the coin and count the number, x, of tosses until the first head appears. Like the binomial experiment, we assume that the tosses are independent of each other. The geometric random variable has the characteristics listed in the box.

> ## Characteristics of the Geometric Random Variable
>
> **1.** The experiment consists of a sequence of independent trials.
> **2.** Each trial results in one of two outcomes. We denote one of them by S and the other by F.
> **3.** The probability of S remains the same from trial to trial. We will denote this probability by p.
> **4.** The geometric random variable x is defined to be the number of trials until the first S is observed.

The probability distribution for the geometric random variable provides a good model for the length of time a customer must wait for some type of servicing. For this application, the time must be measured in whole units (minutes, hours, etc.). Then, x is equal to the number of time units a customer must wait until being served.

> ## Probability Distribution, Mean, and Variance of a Geometric Random Variable
>
> $$p(x) = q^{x-1}p \qquad (x = 1, 2, 3, 4, \ldots)$$
>
> $$\mu = \frac{1}{p} \qquad \sigma^2 = \frac{q}{p^2}$$
>
> where
>
> p = Probability of an S outcome
>
> $q = 1 - p$
>
> x = Number of trials until the first S is observed

The number of job applicants interviewed by an employer until the first suitable prospect is found is another discrete random variable that might be modeled by a geometric probability distribution. Or, for a sequence of independent drillings for oil, x could represent the number of drillings until the first successful well is hit.

Example 5.10 Let x be the number of days until the closing price of a certain stock shows a gain over the previous day's closing price. Assume that x is a geometric random variable, with p, the probability of a gain in price from one day to the next, equal to .5.

a. Find the mean and standard deviation of x.
b. Find the probability that more than 2 days pass before a gain in price from one day to the next is observed.

Solution **a.** The mean and variance for this geometric random variable are

$$\mu = \frac{1}{p} = \frac{1}{.5} = 2 \qquad \sigma^2 = \frac{q}{p^2} = \frac{.5}{(.5)(.5)} = 2$$

Then the standard deviation is

$$\sigma = \sqrt{\sigma^2} = \sqrt{2} = 1.41$$

b. To find the probability that more than 2 days pass before a gain in price is observed, we must find

$$P(x > 2) = p(3) + p(4) + p(5) + \cdots$$

Since this sum is never-ending, we use the complementary relationship:

$$P(x > 2) = 1 - P(x \le 2)$$
$$= 1 - [p(1) + p(2)]$$

Now,

$$p(1) = q^{1-1}p = (.5)^0(.5) = .5$$
$$p(2) = q^{2-1}p = (.5)^1(.5) = .25$$

Thus,

$$P(x > 2) = 1 - (.5 + .25) = .25$$

There is a .25 probability that more than 2 days will pass before the stock shows a gain in its closing price from one day to the next.

Figure 5.12 Probability Distribution for x in Example 5.10

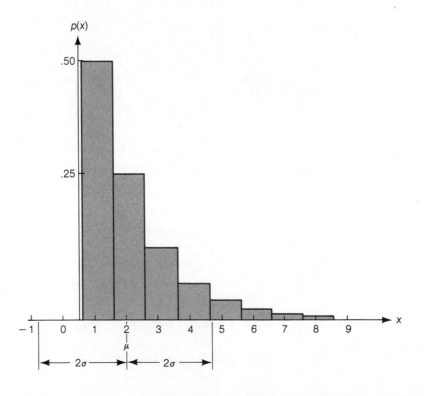

The probability distribution for x is shown in Figure 5.12. The expected value of x and the interval $\mu \pm 2\sigma$ are indicated. Note that the geometric probabilities will always decrease as x increases.   ■

Exercises
5.83–5.92

Learning the Mechanics

5.83 Given that x is a geometric random variable with $p = .2$, compute the following:

a. $P(x = 2)$ **b.** $P(x = 3)$ **c.** $P(x \leq 3)$
d. $P(x \geq 1)$ **e.** $P(x = 4)$ **f.** $P(x > 2)$

5.84 Given that x is a geometric random variable with $p = .7$:

a. Graph $p(x)$, $x = 1, 2, \ldots$.
b. Compute the mean and variance of x. Locate μ and the interval $\mu \pm 2\sigma$ on the graph.
c. What is the probability that x will fall within the interval $\mu \pm 2\sigma$?

5.85 Given that x is a geometric random variable with $p = .3$:

a. Graph $p(x)$, $x = 1, 2, \ldots$.
b. Compute the expected value and variance of x. Locate μ and the interval $\mu \pm \sigma$ on your graph.
c. What is the probability that x will fall within the interval $\mu \pm \sigma$?

5.86 Use the results of Exercise 5.85 to find the following probabilities:

a. $P(x \leq 2)$ **b.** $P(x > 3)$ **c.** $P(x > 0)$ **d.** $P(1 \leq x \leq 6)$

Applying the Concepts

5.87 In 1976, the median price of houses sold to first-time buyers in the United States was $37,670. By 1980, the median price had risen to $61,450. Suppose a large number of the 1980 first-time buyers are going to be randomly selected and interviewed. Let x be the number of interviews conducted until a home buyer whose house costs over $61,450 is found.

a. What is the probability that $x = 4$?
b. What is the probability that $x \leq 4$?
c. Find the expected value and standard deviation of x.
d. Using your answers to part c, describe the likelihood that x will be as large as 7.

5.88 If the probability that a customer will be served by a clerk during any given minute he or she is in the store is .3, what is the probability that the customer will have to wait 4 or more minutes to be served?

5.89 A company that produces food products has determined that the probability that a new cold breakfast cereal obtains more than a 3% market share in its first year on the market is .09. If the company markets one new cold cereal every other year, what is the probability that it will have to wait more than 6 years before marketing a cereal that acquires a market share of more than 3% in its first year?

5.90 The manufacturer of a price-reading optical scanner claims that the probability of it misreading the price of a product (i.e., misreading the bar code on a product's label) is .001. At the time one of the scanners was installed in a supermarket, the store manager tested the performance of the scanner.

a. If the manufacturer's claim is true, what is the probability that the scanner would not misread a price until after the fifth price was read?

b. If in fact the third price was misread, what inference can be made about the manufacturer's claim? Explain.

c. What assumptions must you make in arriving at the solutions for parts a and b?

5.91 Ten percent of the light bulbs produced by a company are defective. If an inspector tests light bulbs randomly selected from the production line, what is the probability that the first defective bulb will be observed on or after the fourth test? What is the expected number of tests the inspector will have to perform before the first defective bulb is observed?

5.92 An oil company has determined that the probability of striking oil on any particular drilling is .2. Accordingly, what is the probability that it would drill four dry wells before striking oil on the fifth drilling?

Summary

In the business world, observations taken on discrete random variables (those that can assume a countable number of values) often have the characteristics of a *binomial, Poisson, hypergeometric,* or *geometric random variable.* In this chapter, we gave the identifying characteristics for each of these random variables, indicated some business data for which the probability models would be appropriate, and gave the formulas for their probability distributions, means, and variances.

Using the probability distribution for a random variable, we were able to calculate the probabilities of specific sample observations. When the probabilities were difficult to calculate, the means and standard deviations provided numerical descriptive measures that enabled us to visualize the probability distributions and thereby to make some approximate probability statements about sample observations.

Supplementary Exercises 5.93–5.126

[*Note: Starred (*) exercises refer to optional sections in this chapter.*]

5.93 Given that x is a binomial random variable, compute $p(x)$ for each of the following cases:

a. $n = 4$, $x = 2$, $p = .2$ **b.** $n = 5$, $x = 4$, $p = .4$
c. $n = 3$, $x = 0$, $p = .5$

***5.94** Given that x is a hypergeometric random variable, compute $p(x)$ for each of the following cases:

a. $N = 8$, $n = 5$, $r = 3$, $x = 2$
b. $N = 6$, $n = 2$, $r = 2$, $x = 2$
c. $N = 5$, $n = 4$, $r = 4$, $x = 3$

*5.95 Given that x is a geometric random variable, compute $p(x)$ for each of the following cases:

a. $p = .3$, $x = 3$　　**b.** $p = .6$, $x = 4$　　**c.** $p = .8$, $x = 2$

*5.96 Given that x is a Poisson random variable, compute $p(x)$ for each of the following cases:

a. $\lambda = 3$, $x = 2$　　**b.** $\lambda = 2$, $x = 3$　　**c.** $\lambda = .5$, $x = 3$

*5.97 Given that x is a random variable for which a Poisson probability distribution with $\lambda = 4$ provides a good characterization, compute the following:

a. $P(x = 0)$　　**b.** $P(x = 3)$　　**c.** $P(x = 1)$
d. $P(x = 5)$　　**e.** $P(x \le 2)$　　**f.** $P(x \ge 2)$

*5.98 Given that x is a geometric random variable with $p = .3$, compute the following:

a. $P(x = 1)$　　**b.** $P(x = 2, 3, \text{ or } 4)$　　**c.** $P(x \le 2)$
d. $P(x = 4)$　　**e.** $P(x > 4)$　　　　　　**f.** $P(x = 1, 2, \text{ or } 5)$

*5.99 Given that x is a geometric random variable with $p = .4$:

a. Graph $p(x)$ for $x = 1, 2, \ldots, 7$.
b. Compute μ and σ for $p(x)$. Locate μ and the interval $\mu \pm 2\sigma$ on the graph.
c. What is the probability that x will fall within the interval $\mu \pm 2\sigma$?

5.100 Which of the following describe discrete random variables, and which describe continuous random variables?

a. The number of damaged inventory items
b. The average monthly sales revenue generated by a salesperson over the past year
c. The number of square feet of warehouse space a company rents
d. The length of time a firm must wait before its copying machine is fixed

5.101 Variables x, y, and z are three discrete random variables with the same mean and the same range. Their probability distributions are shown in the figures. Which has the largest variance? The next largest? The smallest? Explain.

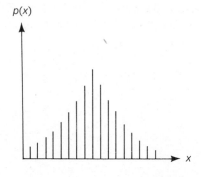
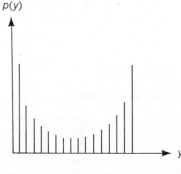
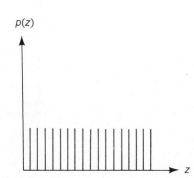

5.102 It is known that for each of two stocks it is equally likely for the stocks to increase, remain the same, or decrease in price by the close of business tomorrow. If only these two stocks are observed and x represents the number of stocks that increase in price by the close of business tomorrow, find the probability distribution for x and display it in tabular form. (Assume the stocks are independent.)

5.103 A shipment of 200 circuit boards contains 20 defectives. One board is randomly selected from the shipment, examined for defects, and placed back in the crate with the rest of the shipment. This sampling procedure is repeated four more times. (This type of sampling is referred to as sampling with replacement.) Let x be the number of defective boards found in the sample of size 5.

a. Determine the probability distribution for x and display it graphically.
b. Compute the mean and variance for x. Locate the mean on your graph of part a.

5.104 The Environmental Protection Agency (EPA) tested 842 in-use automobiles to determine whether there were differences between the cars' actual gas mileage and the mileage projected in the EPA's mileage guide. For highway driving, they found that only 68% of the cars tested had fuel economies within 2 miles per gallon of the mileage guide's projection (*Environmental News*, 1978). Assume this figure holds for the population of cars currently in use for which the EPA has determined projected gas mileages. Suppose the EPA is planning to select twenty cars at random from this population and test their fuel economies to determine how many are within 2 miles per gallon of their EPA projections.

a. Decide whether the following statement is true or false and explain: The number of cars in the sample of twenty that have mileages within 2 miles per gallon of their EPA projections is not a binomial random variable but, for convenience, could be treated as a binomial random variable.
b. What is the probability (approximately) that fewer than ten of the twenty cars selected will be within 2 miles per gallon of their EPA projections? (For convenience, use 70% as an approximation to 68%.)

*5.105 If 20% of the finished products coming off an assembly line are defective, what is the probability that more than three randomly selected finished products would have to be inspected before a defective product is found?

5.106 The owner of construction company A makes bids on jobs so that, if it is awarded the job, company A will make a $10,000 profit. The owner of construction company B makes bids on jobs so that, if it is awarded the job, company B will make a $15,000 profit. Each company describes the probability distribution of the number of jobs the company is awarded per year as shown in the table.

COMPANY A		COMPANY B	
x	p(x)	x	p(x)
2	.05	2	.15
3	.15	3	.30
4	.20	4	.30
5	.35	5	.20
6	.25	6	.05

a. Find the expected number of jobs each will be awarded in a year.

b. What is the expected profit for each company?

c. Find the variance and standard deviation of the distribution of the number of jobs awarded per year for each company.

d. Graph $p(x)$ for both companies A and B. For each company, what proportion of the time will x fall in the interval $\mu \pm 2\sigma$?

5.107 The state highway patrol has determined that one out of every six calls for help originating from roadside call boxes is a hoax. Five calls for help have been received and five tow trucks dispatched. What is the probability that none of the calls was a hoax? That only three of the callers really needed assistance? What assumptions do you have to make to solve this problem?

5.108 Refer to Exercise 5.107. If the highway patrol answers 10,000 calls for help next year, and each call costs the patrol about $20 (labor, gas, etc.), approximately how much money will be wasted answering false alarms?

*5.109 Refer to Exercise 5.108. The highway patrol has determined that the expected number of calls for help per hour is 1.1. What is the probability that in the next hour more than two calls for help will be received? Exactly three calls?

5.110 An advertisement for a laundry soap claims that the soap is preferred over all others by 30% of American women. Assuming this claim is true, what is the probability that fewer than four women in a random sample of twenty-five prefer the advertiser's brand? What is the probability that the number of women, x, preferring the brand takes a value in the interval $3 \le x \le 13$? If a sample of twenty-five American women was taken and only three preferred the brand, what inference would you make? Why?

*5.111 By mistake, a manufacturer of tape recorders includes three defective recorders in a shipment of ten going out to a small retailer. The retailer has decided to accept the shipment of recorders only if none are found to be defective. Upon receipt of the shipment, the retailer examines only five of the recorders. What is the probability that the shipment will be rejected? If the retailer inspects six of the recorders, what is the probability the shipment will be accepted?

5.112 A manufacturer considers a production lot unacceptable if 10% or more of the units in the lot are defective. In such cases the company wants to scrap (not ship) the entire lot. A company quality control inspector has proposed the following criterion for determining whether to reject a lot: In a sample of ten units from a lot, if two or more are defective, reject the entire lot. If the lot currently under examination is 11% defective, what is the probability that this decision rule will lead the quality control inspector to the correct decision?

5.113 When the price of grain is low, many farmers participate in government-financed, on-farm storage programs rather than selling their grain. But storage invites insect infestations, and grain elevators penalize farmers who sell them insect-infested grain. In 1982, the U.S. Grain Marketing Research Laboratory estimated that 80% of the storage bins of corn in the country were infested with insects, and it has been estimated that the economic loss to farmers in the state of Minnesota is $12.6 million annually (*Minneapolis Tribune,* Aug. 8, 1982). Suppose twenty storage bins of corn are randomly selected and examined for insect infestation.

a. What is the probability (approximately) that less than one-half of the bins are infested?

b. What assumptions did you make in answering part a?

c. Why is your answer to part a an approximation?

d. Would you be surprised if all twenty of the bins were infested? Explain.

*5.114 You have determined that one out of five customers who enter your furniture store makes a purchase. What is the probability that of the first four customers in a day the fourth is the initial customer to make a purchase?

*5.115 A wholesale office equipment outlet claims that on an average it sells 2.5 typewriters per day. If it has only 5 typewriters in stock at the close of business today and does not expect to receive a shipment of new typewriters until some time after the close of business tomorrow, what is the probability that the outlet's current supply of typewriters will not be sufficient to meet tomorrow's demand?

5.116 If the probability of a customer responding to one of your marketing department's mail questionnaires is .6, what is the probability that, of twenty questionnaires mailed, more than fifteen will be returned?

*5.117 Large bakeries typically have fleets of delivery trucks. It was determined by one such bakery that the expected number of delivery truck breakdowns per day was 1.5. What is the probability that there will be exactly two breakdowns today and exactly three tomorrow? Less than two today and more than two tomorrow? Assume that the number of breakdowns is independent from day to day.

*5.118 Of the thirty-eight numbers on the roulette wheel, eighteen are colored black. A gambler decides to place money on a black number. If the gambler does not win in either of the first two spins of the wheel, he will leave the casino; otherwise, he will continue playing. Let x equal the number of spins until the gambler achieves the first win.

a. Find the probability that the gambler loses at the roulette wheel and hence leaves the casino (i.e., the probability that $x > 2$).

b. Find the probability that the gambler remains betting at the roulette table after two spins of the wheel.

c. If the gambler always plays black, what is the expected number of spins before he achieves the first win [i.e., find $E(x)$]? Find σ^2, the variance of x.

d. Is it likely that x would exceed five? Explain. (Assume the gambler will play the game until he achieves the first win.)

5.119 A sales manager has determined that a salesperson makes a sale to 70% of the retailers visited. If the salesperson visits five retailers today and twenty tomorrow, what is the probability that she makes exactly four sales today *and* more than ten tomorrow?

5.120 Refer to Exercise 5.119. If the salesperson visits four retailers today and five tomorrow, what is the probability that in these two days she will make exactly two sales?

5.121 A large cigarette manufacturer has determined that the probability of a new brand of cigarettes obtaining a large enough market share to make production profitable is .3. If, over the next 3 years, this manufacturer introduces one new brand a year, what is the probability that at least one new brand will obtain sufficient market share to make its production profitable? What is the probability that all three new brands will obtain sufficient market share? What assumptions do you have to make to solve this problem?

5.122 If it is known that 5% of the finished products coming off an assembly line are defective, what is the probability that one of the next four products coming off the line is defective? What assumptions do you have to make to solve this problem using the methodology of this chapter?

*5.123 A small life insurance company has determined that on the average it receives five death claims per day. What is the probability that the company will receive three claims or less on a particular day? Exactly five claims? What assumptions must you make to find these probabilities?

5.124 In recent years, the use of the telephone as a data collection instrument for public opinion polls has been steadily increasing. However, one of the major factors bearing on the extent to which the telephone will become an acceptable data collection tool in the future is the refusal rate—i.e., the percentage of the eligible subjects actually contacted who refuse to take part in the poll. Suppose that past records indicate a refusal rate of 20% in a large city. A poll of twenty-five city residents is to be taken, and x is the number of residents contacted by telephone who refuse to take part in the poll.

a. Find the mean and variance of x.
b. Find $P(x \le 5)$.
c. Find $P(x > 10)$.

5.125 Suppose you are an airport manager. In looking over your records for the past year, you note that 60% of the time the 8:10 P.M. flight from Atlanta is 20 or more minutes late. If you assume that the probability of the 8:10 P.M. flight being 20 or more minutes late on each day during the upcoming 5-day period is .6, what is the probability that the plane will be 20 or more minutes late exactly three times in the next 5 days? At least three times in the next 5 days?

5.126 [*Warning:* This exercise is realistic, but the computations involved are tedious.] Refer to Case Study 5.3—the Red Lobster sales tax problem. Let $x = 0, 1, 2, \ldots, 99$ be the number of cents (exceeding whole dollars) involved in a sale, and assume that the sales tax is assessed using the bracket system listed in the table. Suppose that x has a probability distribution $p(x) = .01, x = 0, 1, 2, \ldots, 99$ (an assumption that might be fairly accurate for restaurant sales). Find the expected value of the percentage of tax paid on the cents portion of a sale. [*Hint:* You can write the percent tax—call it y—for each value of x. You also know the probabilities associated with each value of x and, consequently, each value of y. Then the expected percentage of tax paid is $E(y) = \Sigma y p(y)$.]

Values of x	Tax (¢)
0, 1, . . . , 9	0
10, 11, . . . , 25	1
26, 27, . . . , 50	2
51, 52, . . . , 75	3
76, 77, . . . , 99	4

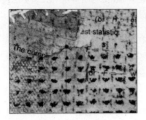

On Your Own . . .

To control the quality of incoming or outgoing large lots of manufactured items, manufacturers use a quality control lot acceptance sampling plan. For example, if each lot consists of 1,000 items, the plan will call for the selection of a random sample of n items (n is usually small) from each lot. The items in each sample are carefully inspected, the number of defectives recorded, and the lot considered to be of acceptable quality if the number of defectives is less than or equal to some specified number, a. The number a is called the *acceptance number* for the plan.

To illustrate, simulate sampling from a large lot of items that contains 10% defectives. Place ten poker chips (or marbles, etc.) in a bowl and mark one of the ten as defective. Randomly select a sample of five items from a lot by selecting a chip from the ten, replacing it, and repeating the process four more times. Count the number of times, x, that you observe the defective chip. This process is equivalent to selecting a random sample of $n = 5$ items from a large lot containing 10% defectives.

If you choose $a = 1$ as the acceptance number for the plan, then you will accept only lots for which $x \leq 1$.

By choosing n and a, you change the ability of a sampling plan to screen out bad lots. To investigate the properties of a sampling plan with $n = 5$ and $a = 1$, simulate the process of sampling from 100 lots.

a. Collect the 100 values of x obtained from the simulation, and construct a relative frequency histogram for x. Note that this histogram is an approximation to $p(x)$. Estimate the proportion of lots that will be accepted by the plan by dividing the number of lots accepted by 100.

b. Calculate the exact values of $p(x)$ for $n = 5$ and $p = .1$, and compare these with the results of part a.

References   Brandt, S. "Report: State's grain bins seriously infested." *Minneapolis Tribune,* Aug. 8, 1982, 1A.

Brigham, E. F. *Financial management theory and practice.* 2d ed. Hinsdale, Ill.: Dryden Press, 1979. Chapter 5.

Brown, A. A., Hulswit, F. T., & Kettelle, J. D. "A study of sales operations." *Operations Research,* June 1956, *4,* 296–308.

Cassano, D. "Shuffle of grants to fix up homes puts north on top." *Minneapolis Star and Tribune,* May 27, 1983, 1.

Chervany, N. L., Anderson, J. C., Benson, P. G., & Hill, A. V. "A management science approach to a Dutch elm disease sanitation program." *Interfaces,* Apr. 1980, *10,* 108.

Elton, E. J., & Gruber, M. J. *Modern portfolio theory and investment analysis.* New York: Wiley, 1981.

Environmental Protection Agency. *Environment News.* New England Regional Office, Boston, Jan. 1978, 11–12.

"Golf balls," *Golf World,* Sept. 10, 1982, 5.

Hogg, R. V., & Craig, A. T. *Introduction to mathematical statistics.* 4th ed. New York: Macmillan, 1978. Chapter 1.

Markowitz, H. M. "Portfolio selection." *Journal of Finance, 6,* Mar. 1952.

Mendenhall, W. *Introduction to probability and statistics.* 6th ed. Boston: Duxbury, 1983. Chapters 5 and 6.

Misshauk, M. J. *Management theory and practice.* Boston: Little, Brown, 1979. Chapter 13.

Parzen, E. *Modern probability theory and its applications.* New York: Wiley, 1960. Chapters 3, 4, 6, and 7.

U.S. Golf Association. *The rules of golf.* 1982, 10.

Webster, A. H. "Straight answers about Dutch elm disease." *Flower and Garden,* May 1978, 28–33, 46–47.

Williams, C. A., Jr., & Heins, R. M. *Risk management and insurance.* New York: McGraw-Hill, 1976. Pp. 10, 65, 66.

Willis, R. E., & Chervany, N. L. *Statistical analysis and modeling for management decision-making.* Belmont, Calif.: Wadsworth, 1974. Chapter 5.

CHAPTER 6

Continuous Random Variables

Where We've Been . . .

Because sample data represent observed values of random variables, we needed to find the probabilities associated with specific random variables. As noted in Chapter 5, this task depends on whether a random variable is discrete or continuous. The probability theory of Chapter 4 provided the mechanism for finding the probabilities associated with discrete random variables. Finding and describing this set of probabilities — the probability distribution for a discrete random variable — was the subject of Chapter 5.

Where We're Going . . .

Since business data are derived from observations on continuous as well as discrete random variables, we need to know probability distributions associated with continuous random variables and also how to use the mean and standard deviation to describe these distributions. Chapter 6 addresses this problem and, in particular, introduces the normal probability distribution. As you will see, the normal probability distribution is one of the most useful distributions in business statistics.

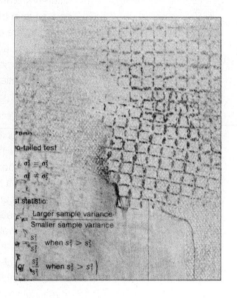

Contents

In this chapter we will consider some continuous random variables that are prevalent in business. Recall that a continuous random variable is one that can assume any value within some interval or intervals on a line. For example, the length of time between a consumer's purchase of new automobiles, the thickness of sheets of steel produced in a rolling mill, and the length of time between consumer complaints are all continuous random variables. The methodology we use to describe continuous random variables will necessarily be somewhat different from that used to describe discrete random variables. We will first discuss the general form of continuous probability distributions, and then we will present three specific types that are used in making business decisions. The normal probability distribution, which plays a basic and important role in both the theory and applications of statistics, is essential to the study of most of the subsequent chapters. The other two distributions — the uniform and the exponential — have business applications, but a study of these topics is optional.

6.1
Continuous
Probability
Distributions

The graphical form of the probability distribution for a continuous random variable, x, will be a smooth curve that might appear as shown in Figure 6.1. This curve, a function of x, is denoted by the symbol $f(x)$ and is variously called a *probability density function,* a *frequency function,* or a *probability distribution.*

The areas under a probability distribution correspond to probabilities for x. For example, the area A between the two points a and b, as shown in Figure 6.1, is the probability that x assumes a value between a and b $(a < x < b)$. Because areas over intervals represent probabilities, it follows that the total area under a probability distribution, the probability assigned to all values of x, should equal 1. Note that probability distributions for continuous random variables will have different shapes depending on the relative frequency distributions of real data that the probability distribution is supposed to model.

The areas under most probability distributions are obtained by the use of calculus* or other numerical methods. Because this is often a difficult procedure, we give the areas for some of

Figure 6.1   A Probability Distribution $f(x)$ for a Continuous Random Variable x

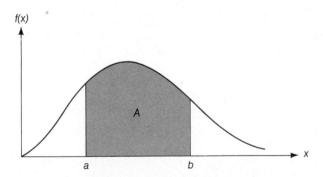

* Students with knowledge of calculus should note that the probability that x assumes a value in the interval $a < x < b$ is $P(a < x < b) = \int_a^b f(x)\,dx$, assuming the integral exists. Similar to the requirements for a discrete probability distribution, we require $f(x) \geq 0$ and $\int_{-\infty}^{\infty} f(x)\,dx = 1$.

the most common probability distributions in tabular form in Appendix B. Then, to find the area between two values of *x*, say *x = a* and *x = b*, you can simply consult the appropriate table.

For each of the continuous random variables presented in this chapter, we will give the formula for the probability distribution along with its mean and standard deviation. These two numbers, μ and σ, will enable you to make some approximate probability statements about a random variable even when you do not have access to a table of areas under the probability distribution.

6.2
The Normal
Distribution

One of the most commonly observed continuous random variables has a *bell-shaped* probability distribution, as shown in Figure 6.2. It is known as a *normal random variable,* and its probability distribution is called a *normal distribution.*

You will see during the remainder of this text that the normal distribution plays a very important role in the science of statistical inference. Many business phenomena generate random variables with probability distributions that are very well approximated by a normal distribution. For example, the percentage of monthly gain (or loss) of a stock's price may be a normal random variable, and the probability distribution for the yearly sales of a corporation might be approximated by a normal probability distribution. The normal distribution might also provide an accurate model for the probability distribution of the weights of loads of produce shipped to a supermarket. You can determine the adequacy of the normal approximation to an existing population of data by comparing the relative frequency distribution of a sample of the data (at least 200 measurements) to the normal probability distribution.

Figure 6.2   A Normal
Probability Distribution

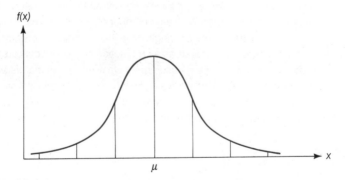

The normal distribution is perfectly symmetric about its mean, μ, as can be seen in the examples in Figure 6.3 (next page). Its spread is determined by the value of its standard deviation, σ.

The formula for the normal probability distribution is shown in the next box. Note that the mean μ and the variance σ^2 appear in this formula, so that no separate formulas for μ and σ^2 are necessary. To graph the normal curve we will have to know the numerical values of μ and σ.

Figure 6.3 Several Normal Distributions, with Different Means and Standard Deviations

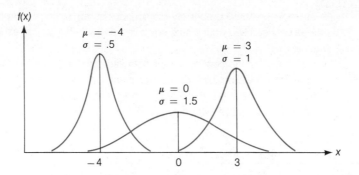

Probability Distribution for a Normal Random Variable x

$$f(x) = \frac{1}{\sigma\sqrt{2\pi}}\, e^{-(1/2)[(x-\mu)/\sigma]^2}$$

where

μ = Mean of the normal random variable, x

σ^2 = Variance of the normal random variable, x

$\pi = 3.1416 \ldots$

$e = 2.71828 \ldots$

Computing the area over intervals under the normal probability distribution is a difficult task.* Consequently, we will use the computer areas listed in Table IV of Appendix B. Although there is an infinitely large number of normal curves — one for each pair of values for μ and σ — we have formed a single table that will apply to any normal curve. This was done by constructing the table of areas as a function of the z-score (presented in Section 3.9). The population z-score for a measurement was defined as the *distance* between the measurement and the population mean, divided by the population standard deviation. Thus, the z-score gives the distance between a measurement and the mean in units equal to the standard deviation. In symbolic form, the z-score for the measurement x is

$$z = \frac{x - \mu}{\sigma}$$

To illustrate the use of Table IV, suppose we know that the length of time between charges of a pocket calculator has a normal distribution, with a mean of 50 hours and a standard deviation of 15 hours. If we were to observe the length of time that elapses before the need for the next charge, what is the probability that this measurement would assume a value between

---

* The student with knowledge of calculus should note that there is not a closed-form expression for $P(a < x < b) = \int_a^b f(x)\, dx$ for the normal probability distribution. However, the value of this definite integral can be obtained to any desired degree of accuracy by approximation procedures. The areas in Table IV of Appendix B were obtained by using such a procedure.

Figure 6.4 Normal Distribution: $\mu = 50$, $\sigma = 15$

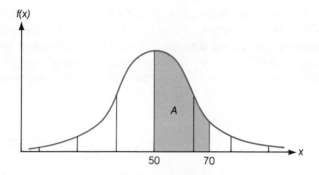

50 and 70 hours? This probability is the area under the normal probability distribution between 50 and 70, as shown in the shaded area, A, of Figure 6.4.

The first step in finding the area A is to calculate the z-score corresponding to the measurement 70. We calculate

$$z = \frac{x - \mu}{\sigma} = \frac{70 - 50}{15} = \frac{20}{15} = 1.33$$

Figure 6.5 Reproduction of Part of Table IV, Appendix B

Thus, the measurement 70 is 1.33 standard deviations above the mean, 50. The second step is to refer to Table IV (a partial reproduction of this table is shown in Figure 6.5). Note that

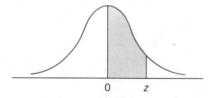

z	.00	.01	.02	.03	.04	.05	.06	.07	.08	.09
0.0	.0000	.0040	.0080	.0120	.0160	.0199	.0239	.0279	.0319	.0359
0.1	.0398	.0438	.0478	.0517	.0557	.0596	.0636	.0675	.0714	.0753
0.2	.0793	.0832	.0871	.0910	.0948	.0987	.1026	.1064	.1103	.1141
0.3	.1179	.1217	.1255	.1293	.1331	.1368	.1406	.1443	.1480	.1517
0.4	.1554	.1591	.1628	.1664	.1700	.1736	.1772	.1808	.1844	.1879
0.5	.1915	.1950	.1985	.2019	.2054	.2088	.2123	.2157	.2190	.2224
0.6	.2257	.2291	.2324	.2357	.2389	.2422	.2454	.2486	.2517	.2549
0.7	.2580	.2611	.2642	.2673	.2704	.2734	.2764	.2794	.2823	.2852
0.8	.2881	.2910	.2939	.2967	.2995	.3023	.3051	.3078	.3106	.3133
0.9	.3159	.3186	.3212	.3238	.3264	.3289	.3315	.3340	.3365	.3389
1.0	.3413	.3438	.3461	.3485	.3508	.3531	.3554	.3577	.3599	.3621
1.1	.3643	.3665	.3686	.3708	.3729	.3749	.3770	.3790	.3810	.3830
1.2	.3849	.3869	.3888	.3907	.3925	.3944	.3962	.3980	.3997	.4015
1.3	.4032	.4049	.4066	.4082	.4099	.4115	.4131	.4147	.4162	.4177
1.4	.4192	.4207	.4222	.4236	.4251	.4265	.4279	.4292	.4306	.4319
1.5	.4332	.4345	.4357	.4370	.4382	.4394	.4406	.4418	.4429	.4441

z-scores are listed in the left-hand column of the table. To find the area corresponding to a z-score of 1.33, we first locate the value 1.3 in the left-hand column. Since this column lists z values to one decimal place only, we refer to the top row of the table to get the second decimal place, .03. Finally, we locate the number where the row labeled z = 1.3 and the column labeled .03 meet. This number represents the area between the mean, μ, and the measurement that has a z-score of 1.33:

$A = .4082$

Thus, the probability that the calculator operates between 50 and 70 hours before needing a charge is .4082.

Example 6.1   Suppose you have a normal random variable x with $\mu = 50$ and $\sigma = 15$. Find the probability that x will fall within the interval $30 < x < 50$.

Solution   The solution to this example can be seen from Figure 6.6. Note that both x = 30 and x = 70 lie the same distance from the mean, $\mu = 50$; x = 30 lies below the mean and x = 70 lies above it. Then, because the normal curve is symmetric about the mean, the area representing the probability that x falls between x = 30 and $\mu = 50$ is equal to the area representing the probability that it falls between $\mu = 50$ and x = 70. The probability (from Table IV) is .4082 (obtained in the previous discussion).

Figure 6.6   Normal Probability Distribution: $\mu = 50, \sigma = 15$

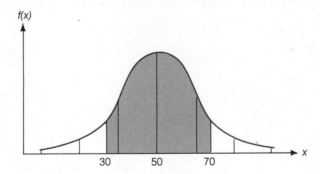

Because x = 30 lies to the left of the mean, the corresponding z-score should be negative and of the same numerical value as the z-score corresponding to x = 70. Checking, we obtain

$$z = \frac{x - \mu}{\sigma} = \frac{30 - 50}{15} = -1.33$$ ■

In finding areas (probabilities) under the normal curve, it is easier to show the locations of the z-scores rather than the corresponding values of x. For example, the z-scores corresponding to x = 30 and x = 70 are located on the distribution of z-scores at the points shown in Figure 6.7. The distribution of z-scores, known as a *standard normal distribution,* always has a mean equal to 0 and a standard deviation equal to 1.

Figure 6.7 A
Distribution of z-Scores (A
Standard Normal Distribution)

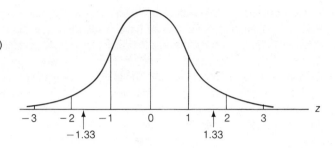

Example 6.2 Use Table IV in Appendix B to determine the area to the right of the z-score 1.64 for the standard normal distribution; i.e., find $P(z > 1.64)$.

Figure 6.8 Standard
Normal Distribution:
$\mu = 0, \sigma = 1$

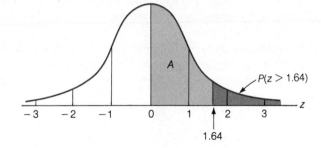

Solution The probability that a normal random variable will fall more than 1.64 standard deviations to the right of its mean is indicated in Figure 6.8. Because the normal distribution is symmetric, half of the total probability (.5) lies to the right of the mean and half to the left. Therefore, the desired probability is

$$P(z > 1.64) = .5 - A$$

where A is the area between $\mu = 0$ and $z = 1.64$, as shown in the figure. Referring to Table IV, we find that the area A corresponding to $z = 1.64$ is .4495. So,

$$P(z > 1.64) = .5 - A = .5 - .4495 = .0505$$ ■

Example 6.3 Find the total area to the right of $z = -.74$ for the standard normal distribution. This area is $P(z > -.74)$.

Figure 6.9 Standard
Normal Distribution:
$\mu = 0, \sigma = 1$

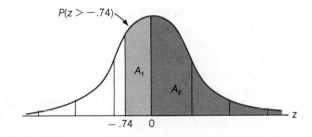

Solution   The standard normal distribution is shown in Figure 6.9, with the area to the right of $-.74$, $P(z > -.74)$, shaded. Note that we have divided the total shaded area corresponding to $P(z > -.74)$ into two parts: the area to the left of $z = 0$, A_1, and the area to the right of $z = 0$, A_2. Whenever the desired area overlaps the mean, it is necessary to make this division and to find the areas separately in Table IV. The area A_2 is easy to find, since it is all the area to the right of the mean. Thus, $A_2 = .5$. The area A_1 is the area between $z = 0$ and $z = -.74$. Therefore, we can find A_1 directly from Table IV (remember, we ignore the sign of the z value). We find $A_1 = .2704$. Then the total area, A, to the right of $z = -.74$ is the sum of the areas A_1 and A_2:

$$P(z > -.74) = A_1 + A_2 = .2704 + .5 = .7704$$ ∎

Example 6.4   Find the total area to the right of $z = 1.96$ and to the left of $z = -1.96$. To put this in probabilistic terminology, find the probability that a normal random variable lies more than 1.96 standard deviations away from the mean.

Solution   The requested probability $P(z > 1.96 \text{ or } z < -1.96)$ is the sum of the two areas A_1 and A_2 shown in Figure 6.10. Because the normal distribution is symmetric, the areas lying to the right of $z = 1.96$ and to the left of $z = -1.96$ must be equal. Therefore, $A_1 = A_2$.

Figure 6.10   Standard Normal Distribution: $\mu = 0, \sigma = 1$

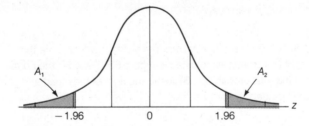

Checking Table IV, we find the area corresponding to $z = 1.96$ to be .4750. This is the area between $z = 0$ and $z = 1.96$. Therefore,

$$A_2 = .5 - .4750 = .0250$$

And, because of the symmetry of the normal distribution,

$$P(z > 1.96 \text{ or } z < -1.96) = A_1 + A_2 = .0250 + .0250 = .0500$$ ∎

Example 6.5   Suppose an automobile manufacturer introduces a new model that has an advertised mean in-city mileage of 27 miles per gallon. Although such advertisements seldom report any measure of variability, suppose you write the manufacturer for the details of the tests, and you find that the standard deviation is 3 miles per gallon. This information leads you to formulate a probability model for the random variable x, the in-city mileage for this car model. You believe that the probability distribution of x can be approximated by a normal distribution with a mean of 27 and a standard deviation of 3.

Figure 6.11 Normal Probability Distribution for x in Example 6.5: $\mu = 27$ Miles per Gallon, $\sigma = 3$ Miles per Gallon

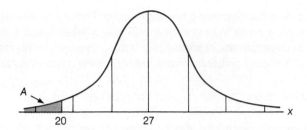

a. If you were to buy this model of automobile, what is the probability you would purchase one that averages less than 20 miles per gallon for in-city driving?

b. Suppose you purchase one of these new models, and it does get less than 20 miles per gallon for in-city driving. Should you conclude that your probability model is incorrect?

Solution   **a.** The probability model proposed for x, the in-city mileage, is shown in Figure 6.11. We are interested in finding the area, A, to the left of 20, since this area corresponds to the probability that a measurement chosen from this distribution falls below 20. Or in other words, if this model is correct, the area A represents the fraction of cars that can be expected to get less than 20 miles per gallon for in-city driving. To find A, we first calculate the z value corresponding to $x = 20$. That is,

$$z = \frac{x - \mu}{\sigma} = \frac{20 - 27}{3} = -\frac{7}{3} = -2.33$$

Because of the symmetry of the normal distribution about its mean and because Table IV provides only areas to the right of the mean, we look up 2.33 in Table IV, and find that the corresponding area is .4901. This is the area between $z = 0$ and $z = -2.33$, so we find

$$A = .5 - .4901 = .0099 \approx .01$$

According to this probability model, you should have only about a 1% chance of purchasing a car of this make with an in-city mileage under 20 miles per gallon.

b. Now you are asked to make an inference based on a sample — the car you purchased. You are getting less than 20 miles per gallon for in-city driving. What do you infer? We think you will agree that one of two possibilities is true:

The probability model is correct, and you simply were unfortunate to have purchased one of the cars in the 1% that get less than 20 miles per gallon in the city.

The probability model is incorrect. That is, if the manufacturer meant that the in-city mileage for the cars has a normal distribution with a mean equal to 27 and $\sigma = 3$, the claim is false.

You have no way of knowing with certainty which possibility is the correct one, but the evidence points to the second one. We are again relying on the rare event approach to statistical inference that we introduced earlier. The basic idea is that the sample (one measurement in this case) was so unlikely to have been drawn from the proposed probability model that it casts serious doubt on the model. We would be inclined to believe that the model is somehow in error. Perhaps the assumption of a normal distribution is unwarranted, or the mean of 27 is an overestimate, or the standard deviation of 3 is an underestimate, or some combination of these errors was made. At any rate, the form of the actual probability model certainly merits further investigation. ■

Example 6.6   Find the value of z, call it z_0, such that $P(z \geq z_0) = .10$.

Solution   This example reverses the questions posed in Examples 6.1–6.5. Rather than finding an area under the normal curve over a specific interval on the z- or x-axis, we are given a specific area under the normal curve and asked to find the value of z that bounds the interval. Specifically, we want to find the value of z_0 that places an area of .10 in the upper tail of the z distribution (see Figure 6.12).

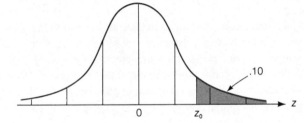

Figure 6.12 Standard Normal Distribution for Example 6.6

Since half of the area under the normal curve lies to the right of the mean, $z = 0$, the area between $z = 0$ and z_0 is $(.5 - .1) = .4$. Thus, z_0 is the value of z in Table IV of Appendix B that corresponds to an area equal to .4000. Examining the body of Table IV, we find that the tabulated area nearest to .4000 is .3997. Since the value of z corresponding to this area is 1.28, the value of z_0 such that $P(z \geq z_0) = .10$ is $z_0 \approx 1.28$. ■

Case Study 6.1
Evaluating an
Investment's Risk

Frederick S. Hillier (1963) described several ways a business firm can easily, but effectively, evaluate risky investment projects. He noted that, up to the time of his writing,

such procedures as have been suggested for dealing with risk have tended to be either quite simplified or somewhat theoretical. Thus, these procedures have tended to provide management with only a portion of the information required for a sound decision, or they have assumed the availability of information which is almost impossible to obtain.

In one of his approaches to handling risk, Hillier assumes that the cash flow from an investment to the firm in the ith future year after the investment is made is normally distributed, and shows that the present worth, P, of the proposed investment is therefore normally distributed with mean μ_P and variance σ_P^2. He points out that by describing P with a probability distribution as he has done, management is provided with information about P and, as a result, with some basis upon which to evaluate the risk of the investment decision.

Hillier provides an example of how management can evaluate the risk of an investment by assuming its present worth is normally distributed:

Suppose that, on the basis of the forecasts regarding prospective cash flow from a proposed investment of \$10,000, it is determined that $\mu_P = \$1,000$ and $\sigma_P = \$2,000$. Ordinarily, the current procedure would be to approve the investment since $\mu_P > 0$. However, with additional information available ($\sigma_P = \$2,000$) regarding the considerable risk of the investment, the executive can analyze the situation further. Using widely available tables for the normal distribution, he could note that the probability that $P < 0$, so that the investment won't pay, is 0.31. Furthermore, the probability is 0.16, 0.023, and 0.0013, respectively, that the investment will lose the present worth equivalent of at least $1,000, $3,000, and $5,000, respectively. Considering the financial status of the firm, the executive can use this and similar information to make his decision. Suppose, instead, that the executive is attempting to choose between this investment and a second investment with $\mu_P = \$500$ and $\sigma_P = \$500$. By conducting a similar analysis for the second investment, the executive can decide whether the greater expected earnings of the first investment justifies the greater risk. A useful technique for making this comparison is to superimpose the drawing of the probability distribution of P for the second investment upon the corresponding drawing for the first investment. This same approach generalizes to the comparison of more than two investments.

Exercises 6.1–6.19

Learning the Mechanics

6.1 Use Table IV in Appendix B to calculate the area under the standard normal distribution between the following pairs of z-scores:

a. $z = 0$ and $z = 2$ **b.** $z = 0$ and $z = 3.0$
c. $z = 0$ and $z = 1.5$ **d.** $z = 0$ and $z = .80$

6.2 Repeat Exercise 6.1 for each of the following pairs of z-scores:

a. $z = -1$ and $z = 1.5$ **b.** $z = -2$ and $z = 2$
c. $z = -.5$ and $z = 1.5$ **d.** $z = -3$ and $z = 3$

6.3 Repeat Exercise 6.1 for each of the following pairs of z-scores:

a. $z = -1.5$ and $z = -1.0$ **b.** $z = -.45$ and $z = .90$
c. $z = -2$ and $z = 0$ **d.** $z = -3$ and $z = 1.4$
e. $z = .5$ and $z = 1.5$ **f.** $z = -2$ and $z = -.5$

6.4 Find each of the following probabilities:

a. $P(z \geq 3)$ **b.** $P(z \leq -1.6)$ **c.** $P(z \geq 1.645)$
d. $P(z \geq 0)$ **e.** $P(z \leq -1.0)$ **f.** $P(z \leq -1.645)$

6.5 Find each of the following probabilities:

a. $P(-1 \leq z \leq 1)$ **b.** $P(-1.96 \leq z \leq 1.96)$
c. $P(-1.645 \leq z \leq 1.645)$ **d.** $P(-2 \leq z \leq 2)$

6.6 Find a value of z, call it z_0, such that

a. $P(z \geq z_0) = .05$ **b.** $P(z \geq z_0) = .025$
c. $P(z \leq z_0) = .025$ **d.** $P(z \geq z_0) = .10$

6.7 Suppose the random variable x is best described by a normal distribution with $\mu = 30$ and $\sigma = 4$. Find the z-score that corresponds to each of the following x values:

a. $x = 20$ **b.** $x = 30$ **c.** $x = 27.5$
d. $x = 15$ **e.** $x = 35$ **f.** $x = 25$

6.8 Refer to Exercise 6.7. How many standard deviations away from the mean of x are each of the following x values?

a. $x = 25$ **b.** $x = 37.5$ **c.** $x = 30$ **d.** $x = 36$

6.9 Find a value of z, call it z_0, such that

a. $P(z \leq z_0) = .0301$ **b.** $P(-z_0 \leq z \leq z_0) = .95$
c. $P(-z_0 \leq z \leq z_0) = .90$ **d.** $P(-z_0 \leq z \leq z_0) = .6826$
e. $P(z_0 \leq z \leq 0) = .1628$ **f.** $P(-.75 \leq z \leq z_0) = .7026$

6.10 Suppose the continuous random variable x has a normal probability distribution with mean 120 and variance 36. Draw a rough sketch (i.e., a graph) of the frequency function of x. Locate μ and the interval $\mu \pm 2\sigma$ on the graph. Find the following probabilities:

a. $P(\mu - 2\sigma \leq x \leq \mu + 2\sigma)$ **b.** $P(x \geq 128)$ **c.** $P(x \leq 108)$
d. $P(112 \leq x \leq 130)$ **e.** $P(114 \leq x \leq 116)$ **f.** $P(115 \leq x \leq 128)$

Applying the Concepts

6.11 Ideally, a worker seeking a new job in a particular industry should acquire information about wage rates offered by all firms in the industry. However, this information-search could be time-consuming and costly. In particular, the longer an unemployed worker searches for a higher wage, the greater will be the loss in income. Therefore, workers may not find it worthwhile to search until they find the highest available wage rate. The result is that managers may not have to pay top dollar to attract workers. These factors help explain the existing disparity in wage rates among firms (Blair & Kenny, 1982). Suppose the distribution of wage rates nationwide that would be offered to a particular skilled worker can be approximated by a normal distribution with $\mu = \$10.50$ per hour and $\sigma = \$1.25$ per hour. In addition, assume that the worker is offered $12.00 per hour by the first firm contacted.

a. Suppose the worker were to undertake a nationwide job search. What proportion of the wage rates that would be offered to the worker would be greater than $12.00 per hour?

b. If the worker were to complete a nationwide job search and then randomly select one of the many job offers received, what is the probability that the wage rate would be more than $10.00 per hour?

c. The *median*, call it x_m, of a continuous random variable x is the value such that $P(x \geq x_m) = P(x \leq x_m) = .5$. That is, the median is the value x_m such that half the area under the probability distribution lies above x_m and half lies below it. Find the median of the random variable corresponding to the wage rate and compare it to the mean wage rate.

6.12 According to recent studies in the banking industry, "insider loans" were the principal cause of more than half of all bank failures over the past 15 years. (An *insider loan* is money borrowed by directors and stockholders from the nationally chartered bank with which they are affiliated.) If it is known that the amount of money tied up in outstanding insider loans of nationally chartered banks across the country is approximately normally distributed with a mean of $500,000 and a standard deviation of $142,000, find the probability that a nationally chartered bank selected at random has insider loans totaling at least $900,000.

6.13 The *monthly rate of return* of a stock is a measure investors frequently use for evaluating the behavior of a stock over time. A stock's monthly rate of return generally reflects the amount of money an investor makes (or loses if the return is negative) for every dollar invested in the stock in a given month. Thus, stocks with high average monthly rates of return typically offer more lucrative investment opportunities than stocks with low average monthly rates of return. Eugene Fama (1976) has demonstrated that the probability distribution for the monthly rate of return of a stock can be approximated by a normal probability distribution. Suppose the monthly rates of return to stock ABC are normally distributed with mean .05 and standard deviation .03, and the monthly rates of return to stock XYZ are normally distributed with mean .07 and standard deviation .05. Assume that you have $100 invested in each stock.

a. Over the long run, which stock will yield the higher average monthly rate of return? Why?
b. Suppose you plan to hold each stock for only 1 month. What is the expected value of each investment at the end of 1 month?
c. Which stock offers greater protection against incurring a loss on your investment next month? Why?

6.14 Do security analysts do a good job of forecasting corporate earnings growth and advising their clientele? David Dreman, a *Forbes* columnist, addresses this question in an article titled "Astrology Might Be Better" (*Forbes,* Mar. 26, 1984). The basis of Dreman's article is a study by Professors Michael Sandretto of Harvard and Sudhir Milkrishnamurthi of the Massachusetts Institute of Technology. The study surveys security analysts' forecasts of annual earnings for the (then) current year for more than 769 companies with five or more forecasts per company per year. The average forecast error for this large number of forecasts was plus or minus 31.3%. To apply this information to a practical situation, suppose the population of analysts' forecast errors is normally distributed with a mean of 31.3% and a standard deviation of 10%.

a. If you obtain a security analyst's forecast for a particular company, what is the probability that it will be in error by more than 50%?
b. If three analysts make the forecast, what is the probability that at least one of the analysts will err by more than 50%?

6.15 In a survey of 2,000 long-distance telephone calls reported in the *Orlando Sentinel* (Mar. 12, 1984), it was found that seven of eight long-distance phone companies were overcharging (charging for additional time) for a given call and that six were charging for unconnected calls. Suppose that the additional time being charged to a long-distance phone call has a normal distribution with a mean of 25 seconds and a standard deviation of 8 seconds.

a. Find the probability that a given long-distance call will be overcharged by at least 40 seconds.
b. By no more than 10 seconds.

6.16 A company that sells annuities must base the annual payout on the probability distribution of the length of life of the participants in the plan. Suppose the probability distribution of the lifetimes of the participants in the plan is approximately a normal distribution with $\mu = 68$ years and $\sigma = 3.5$ years.

a. What proportion of the plan participants would receive payments beyond age 70?

b. Beyond age 75?

6.17 A machine used to regulate the amount of dye dispensed for mixing shades of paint can be set so that it discharges an average of μ milliliters of dye per can of paint. The amount of dye discharged is known to have a normal distribution with variance equal to .160. If more than 6 milliliters of dye are discharged when making a particular shade of blue paint, the shade is unacceptable. Determine the setting for μ so that no more than 1% of the cans of paint will be unacceptable.

6.18 A machine for filling quart milk cartons can be adjusted so that the mean of the distribution of fills (in ounces) is equal to some predetermined mean value, μ. Suppose the distribution of fills is approximately normal with a standard deviation equal to 0.6 ounce.

a. What percentage of the cartons will contain less than 32 ounces if μ is set at 32 ounces?

b. If μ is set at 33 ounces?

c. What setting should the dairy choose for μ if management wants to underfill (less than 32 ounces) only 5% of all cartons?

6.19 What relationship exists between the z-score and the box-plot methods (Section 3.10) for detecting outliers? Although the answer depends on the underlying distribution of the population being sampled, we will assume for this exercise that the population distribution is normal.

a. What are the z-scores corresponding to the lower and upper quartiles, Q_L and Q_U, of the population distribution?

b. In terms of standard deviations, specify the width of the interquartile range of the population distribution.

c. What are the z-scores corresponding to the inner fences?

d. What are the z-scores corresponding to the outer fences?

e. If an observation is randomly selected from the population, what is the probability that its z-score is less than -3 or greater than 3?

f. Refer to part e. What is the probability that the observation will fall outside the population inner fences?

g. Refer to parts e and f. What is the probability that the observation will fall outside the population outer fences?

h. Is there much difference between the z-score and box-plot methods for detecting outliers if the underlying population distribution is normal? Explain.

6.3
The Uniform
Distribution
(Optional)

Perhaps the simplest of all the continuous probability distributions is the *uniform distribution*. The frequency function has a rectangular shape, as shown in Figure 6.13. Note that the possible values of x consist of all points on the real line between point c and point d. The height of $f(x)$ is constant in that interval and equals $1/(d - c)$. Therefore, the total area under $f(x)$ is given by

$$\text{Total area of rectangle} = (\text{Base})(\text{Height}) = (d - c)\left(\frac{1}{d - c}\right) = 1$$

Figure 6.13 The Uniform Probability Distribution

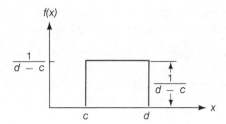

The uniform probability distribution provides a model for continuous random variables that are *evenly distributed* over a certain interval. That is, a uniform random variable is one that is just as likely to assume a value in one interval as it is to assume a value in any other interval of equal size. There is no clustering of values around any value; instead, there is an even spread over the entire region of possible values.

The uniform distribution is sometimes referred to as the ***randomness distribution,*** since one way of generating a uniform random variable is to perform an experiment in which a point is *randomly* selected on the horizontal axis between the points c and d. If we were to repeat this experiment infinitely often, we would create a uniform probability distribution like that shown in Figure 6.13. The random selection of points on a line can also be used to generate random numbers such as those in Table I of Appendix B. Recall that random numbers are selected in such a way that every digit has an equal probability of selection. Therefore, random numbers are realizations of a uniform random variable. (Random numbers were used to draw random samples in Section 4.6.)

The formulas for the uniform probability distribution and its mean and standard deviation are shown in the box.

Probability Distribution, Mean, and Standard Deviation of a Uniform Random Variable x

$$f(x) = \frac{1}{d-c} \quad (c \leq x \leq d) \qquad \mu = \frac{c+d}{2} \qquad \sigma = \frac{d-c}{\sqrt{12}}$$

Suppose the interval $a < x < b$ lies within the domain of x; i.e., it falls within the larger interval $c < x < d$. Then the probability that x assumes a value within the interval $a < x < b$ is the area of the rectangle over the interval — namely,[*]

$$\frac{b-a}{d-c}$$

Example 6.7 Suppose the research department of a steel manufacturer believes that one of the company's rolling machines is producing sheets of steel of varying thickness. The thickness is a

---

[*] The student who has knowledge of calculus should note that

$$P(a < x < b) = \int_a^b f(x)\, dx = \int_a^b 1/(d-c)\, dx = (b-a)/(d-c)$$

uniform random variable with values between 150 and 200 millimeters. Any sheets less than 160 millimeters thick must be scrapped because they are unacceptable to buyers.

a. Calculate the mean and standard deviation of x, the thickness of the sheets produced by this machine. Then graph the probability distribution and show the mean on the horizontal axis. Also show 1 and 2 standard deviation intervals around the mean.

b. Calculate the fraction of steel sheets produced by this machine that have to be scrapped.

Solution   **a.** To calculate the mean and standard deviation for x, we substitute 150 and 200 millimeters for c and d, respectively, in the formulas. Thus,

$$\mu = \frac{c+d}{2} = \frac{150 + 200}{2} = 175 \text{ millimeters}$$

and

$$\sigma = \frac{d-c}{\sqrt{12}} = \frac{200 - 150}{\sqrt{12}} = \frac{50}{3.464} = 14.43$$

The uniform probability distribution is

$$f(x) = \frac{1}{d-c} = \frac{1}{200 - 150} = \frac{1}{50}$$

The graph of this function is shown in Figure 6.14. The mean and the 1 and 2 standard deviation intervals around the mean are shown on the horizontal axis.

Figure 6.14 Distribution for x in Example 6.7

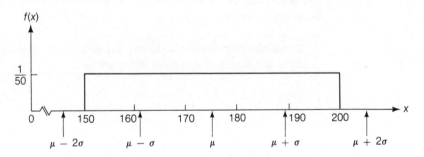

b. To find the fraction of steel sheets produced by the machine that have to be scrapped, we must find the probability that x, the thickness, is less than 160 millimeters. As indicated in Figure 6.15, we need to calculate the area under the frequency function $f(x)$

Figure 6.15 Probability That Sheet Thickness, x, Is Between 150 and 160 Millimeters

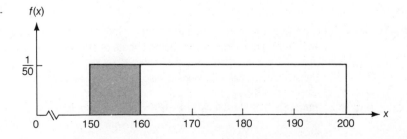

between the points $x = 150$ and $x = 160$. This is the area of a rectangle with base $160 - 150 = 10$ and height $\frac{1}{50}$. The fraction that has to be scrapped is then

$$P(x < 160) = (\text{Base})(\text{Height}) = (10)\left(\frac{1}{50}\right) = \frac{1}{5}$$

That is, 20% of all the sheets made by this machine must be scrapped.   ■

**Exercises
6.20–6.28**

Learning the Mechanics

6.20 Suppose x is a random variable best described by a uniform probability distribution with $c = 20$ and $d = 45$.

a. Find $f(x)$.
b. Find the mean and variance of x.
c. Graph $f(x)$ and locate μ and the interval $\mu \pm 2\sigma$ on the graph. Find the probability that x assumes a value within the interval $\mu \pm 2\sigma$.

6.21 Refer to Exercise 6.20. Find the following:

a. $P(20 \le x \le 35)$
b. $P(25 \le x \le 30)$
c. $P(x \ge 40)$
d. $P(x \le 25)$
e. $P(x \le 15)$
f. $P(10 \le x \le 40)$
g. $P(x \ge 36)$

6.22 Suppose x is a random variable best described by a uniform probability distribution with $c = 2$ and $d = 5$.

a. Find $f(x)$.
b. Find the mean and variance of x.
c. Graph $f(x)$ and locate μ and the interval $\mu \pm \sigma$. Find the probability that x assumes a value within the interval $\mu \pm \sigma$.

6.23 Use the probability distribution of Exercise 6.22 to find the value of a that makes each of the following probability statements true:

a. $P(x \ge a) = .5$ **b.** $P(x \le a) = .2$
c. $P(x \le a) = 0$ **d.** $P(2.5 \le x \le a) = .5$

Applying the Concepts

6.24 As we noted in this section, random numbers are values of a uniform random variable. Construct a relative frequency histogram for the data set listed at the top of the next page. (It was created by the random-number generator of the Minitab computer package.) Except for the expected variation in relative frequencies among the class intervals, does your histogram suggest that the data are observations on a uniform random variable? Explain.

38.8759	35.6438	55.6267	87.4506	60.8422	11.2159	69.2875
88.3734	95.3660	57.8870	50.7119	.7434	12.0605	71.6829
12.4337	98.0716	38.6584	78.3936	94.1727	.8413	23.0278
47.0121	31.8792	21.5478	71.8318	88.2612	93.3017	96.1009
62.6626	11.7828	64.5788	46.7404	28.6777	23.0892	75.1015
44.0466	43.3629	32.9847	87.7819	28.9622		

6.25 Rapid advances in technology in recent years have led to the development of extremely complex equipment and, consequently, to the need to evaluate the equipment's reliability. The *reliability* of a piece of equipment is frequently defined to be the probability, p, that the equipment performs its intended function successfully for a given period of time under specific conditions (Martz & Waller, 1982). Because p varies from one point in time to another, some reliability analysts treat p as if it were a random variable. Suppose an analyst characterizes the total uncertainty about the reliability of a particular robotic device used in an automobile assembly line using the following distribution:

$$f(p) = \begin{cases} 1 & 0 \leq p \leq 1 \\ 0 & \text{otherwise} \end{cases}$$

a. Graph the analyst's probability distribution for p.
b. Find the mean and variance of p.
c. According to the analyst's probability distribution for p, what is the probability that p is greater than .95? Less than .95?
d. Suppose the analyst receives the additional information that p is definitely between .90 and .95, but that there is complete uncertainty about where it lies between these values. Describe the probability distribution the analyst should now use to describe p.

6.26 The manager of a large department store with three floors reports that the time a customer on the second floor must wait for an elevator has a uniform distribution ranging from 0 to 4 minutes. Find the mean and variance of x, the time a customer on the second floor waits for an elevator. If it takes the elevator 15 seconds to go from floor to floor, find the probability that a hurried customer can reach the first floor in less than 1.5 minutes after pushing the second floor elevator button.

6.27 A bus is scheduled to stop at a certain bus stop every half hour on the hour and half hour. At the end of the day, buses still stop about every 30 minutes, but due to delays earlier in the day, they are equally likely to stop at any time during any given half hour. If you arrive at a bus stop at the end of the day, what is the probability that you will have to wait more than 20 minutes for the bus (no matter when you show up)? How long do you expect to wait for the bus?

6.28 The manager of a local soft drink bottling company believes that when a new beverage-dispensing machine is set to dispense 7 ounces, it in fact dispenses an amount at random anywhere between 6.5 and 7.5 ounces.

a. Is the amount dispensed by the beverage machine a discrete or continuous random variable? Explain.

b. Graph the frequency function for x, the amount of beverage the manager believes is dispensed by the new machine when it is set to dispense 7 ounces.

c. Find the mean and standard deviation for the distribution graphed in part b, and locate the mean and the interval $\mu \pm 2\sigma$ on the graph.

6.4
The
Exponential
Distribution
(Optional)

Another important probability distribution that is useful for describing business data is the *exponential probability distribution*. Two business phenomena with frequency functions that might be well approximated by the exponential distribution are the length of time between arrivals at a fast-food drive-through restaurant and the length of time between the filing of claims in a small insurance office. Note that in each of these examples, the measurements are the lengths of time between certain events. For this reason, the exponential distribution is sometimes called the *waiting time distribution*.

The formula for the exponential probability distribution is shown in the box, along with the mean and standard deviation of this frequency function.

Probability Distribution, Mean, and Standard Deviation for an Exponential Random Variable x

$$f(x) = \lambda e^{-\lambda x} \qquad (x > 0) \qquad \mu = \frac{1}{\lambda} \qquad \sigma = \frac{1}{\lambda}$$

Unlike the normal distribution, which has a shape and location determined by the values of the two quantities μ and σ, the shape of the exponential distribution is governed by a single

Figure 6.16 Exponential Distributions

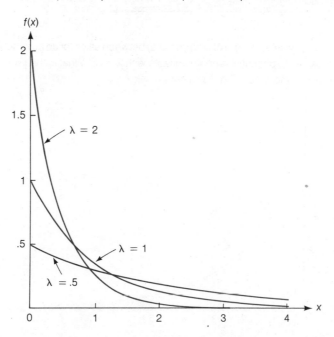

quantity, λ. Further, it is a probability distribution with the property that its mean equals its standard deviation. Exponential distributions corresponding to $\lambda = .5, 1,$ and 2 are shown in Figure 6.16.

To calculate probabilities for exponential random variables, we need to be able to find areas under the exponential probability distribution. Suppose we want to find the area, A, to the right of some number, a, as shown in Figure 6.17. This area can be calculated by using the following formula:

Finding the Area, A, to the Right of a Number, a, for an Exponential Distribution

$A = P(x \geq a) = e^{-\lambda a}$

Use Table III in Appendix B to find the value of $e^{-\lambda a}$ after substituting the appropriate numerical values for λ and a.

Figure 6.17 The Area, A, to the Right of a Number, a, for an Exponential Distribution

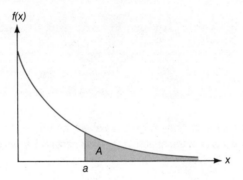

Example 6.8　Suppose the length of time (in days) between sales for an automobile salesperson is modeled as an exponential random variable with $\lambda = .5$. What is the probability that the salesperson goes more than 5 days without a sale?

Figure 6.18 Exponential Distribution for Example 6.8: $\lambda = .5$

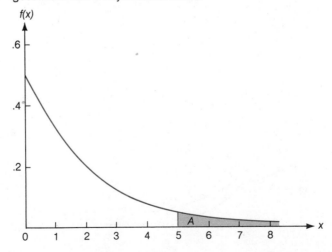

Solution   The probability we want is the area, A, to the right of $a = 5$ in Figure 6.18. To find this probability, use the formula given for area:

$$A = e^{-\lambda a} = e^{-(.5)(5)} = e^{-2.5}$$

Referring to Table III, we find

$$A = e^{-2.5} = .082085$$

That is, our model indicates that the automobile salesperson has a probability of about .08 of going more than 5 days without a sale. ∎

Example 6.9   A microwave oven manufacturer is trying to determine the length of warranty period it should attach to its magnetron tube, the most critical component in the oven. Preliminary testing has shown that the length of life (in years), x, of a magnetron tube has an exponential probability distribution with $\lambda = .16$.

a. Find the mean and standard deviation of x.

b. If a warranty period of 5 years is attached to the magnetron tube, what fraction of tubes must the manufacturer plan to replace (assuming the exponential model with $\lambda = .16$ is correct)?

c. Find the probability that the length of life of a magnetron tube will fall within the interval $\mu \pm 2\sigma$.

Solution   **a.** Using the formulas for the mean and standard deviation for an exponential random variable, we find

$$\mu = \frac{1}{\lambda} = \frac{1}{.16} = 6.25 \text{ years}$$

Also, since $\mu = \sigma$, $\sigma = 6.25$ years.

b. To find the fraction of tubes that will have to be replaced before the 5-year warranty period expires, we need to find the area between 0 and 5 under the distribution. This area, A, is shown in Figure 6.19. To find the required probability, we recall the formula

$$P(x > a) = e^{-\lambda a}$$

Figure 6.19 Exponential Distribution for Example 6.9: $\lambda = .16$

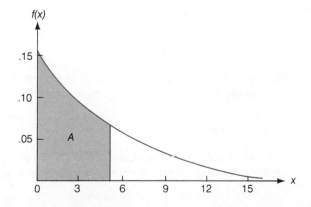

Using this formula and Table III of Appendix B, we find

$$P(x > 5) = e^{-\lambda(5)} = e^{-(.16)(5)} = e^{-.80} = .449329$$

To find the area A, we use the complementary relationship:

$$P(x \le 5) = 1 - P(x > 5) = 1 - .449329 = .550671$$

So, approximately 55% of the magnetron tubes will have to be replaced during the 5-year warranty period.

c. We would expect the probability that the life of a magnetron tube, x, falls within the interval $\mu \pm 2\sigma$ to be quite large (near .95 if we think the Empirical Rule in Table 3.7 might apply). A graph of the exponential distribution showing the interval from $\mu - 2\sigma$ to $\mu + 2\sigma$ is shown in Figure 6.20. Since the point $\mu - 2\sigma$ lies below $x = 0$, we need to find only the area between $x = 0$ and $a = \mu + 2\sigma = 6.25 + 2(6.25) = 18.75$. This area, A, which is shaded in Figure 6.20, is

$$A = 1 - P(x > 18.75)$$
$$= 1 - e^{-\lambda(18.75)} = 1 - e^{-(.16)(18.75)} = 1 - e^{-3}$$

Figure 6.20 Exponential Distribution for Example 6.9: $\lambda = .16$

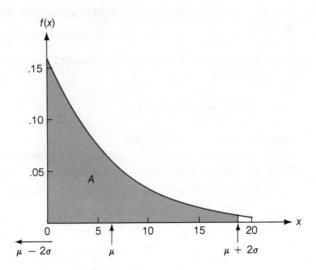

Checking Table III (Appendix B) for the value of e^{-3}, we find $e^{-3} = .049787$. Therefore, the probability that the life, x, of a magnetron tube falls within the interval $\mu \pm 2\sigma$ is

$$A = 1 - e^{-3}$$
$$= 1 - .049787 = .950213$$

You can see that this probability agrees very well with the Empirical Rule even though this probability distribution is not mound-shaped (it is strongly skewed to the right). ∎

Case Study 6.2

Queueing Theory

The formation of waiting lines, or *queues,* is a phenomenon that occurs whenever the demand for a service exceeds its supply. We see this daily at bank-teller windows, supermarket checkout counters, traffic lights, etc. If long queues develop, it may be an indication that not enough service is being provided. If no queues develop, it may be an indication that too much service is being provided. Either situation can prove costly to the service provider. To assist in planning service capacity, an area of study known as *queueing theory* has been employed to model the characteristics of waiting lines.

In the basic structure assumed by most queueing models, *customers* seeking service are generated over time by an *input source.* These customers enter the *queueing system,* join a queue, and await service. Members of the queue are selected for service by some rule (for example, first-come, first-served or random sampling) known as the *service discipline.* A chosen customer is served by the *service mechanism* and then leaves the queueing system. This process is illustrated in Figure 6.21.

Figure 6.21 Basic Queueing System

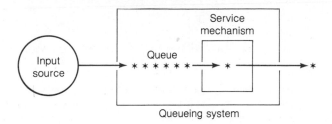

Queueing system

To complete the basic queueing model, certain assumptions must be made to model probabilistically the arrivals to and departures from the queueing system. It has been found that the *interarrival time* (the time between arrivals) to many real queues can be reasonably approximated by an exponential probability distribution. Furthermore, when the specific service required differs among individual customers, the exponential distribution has proved to provide an adequate approximation to the time required to service a customer (i.e., the time that elapses between when service begins and when it ends). Thus, the exponential distribution can be used to describe both the input source and the service mechanism. A more detailed description of the basic queueing theory model and its various assumptions can be found in Hillier and Lieberman (1983).

After developing a queueing model, we can answer such questions as: (1) What is the expected number of customers in the queueing system? (2) What is the expected length of the queue? (3) What is the expected waiting time in the system for an individual customer? (4) What is the expected waiting time in the queue for an individual customer? (5) Are the rates of arrival and departure such that the queue will continue to grow without bound?

W. Blaker Bolling (1972) describes how queueing theory was used to model the emergency room of the Richmond Memorial Hospital in Richmond, Virginia. The input source was the local population of Richmond (including visitors). The service mechanism consisted of eight fully staffed treatment tables. Thus, since it was possible to service eight patients simultaneously, the system was more complex than that described in Figure 6.21. In general, the service discipline was first-come, first-served, unless a serious emergency occurred. However, in modeling the system, a first-come, first-served discipline was assumed for simplicity. Historical data indicated that both interarrival times and service times could be adequately modeled with exponential distributions.

One use of the model was to project the capacity (number of staffed tables) needed to prevent the queue from growing without bound. For example, for the period between 8 and 9 P.M. in August 1972, the interarrival-time distribution was projected to be exponential with mean 5.96 minutes (.0993 hour), and the service-time distribution was projected to be exponential with mean 58 minutes (.9666 hour). Accordingly, the arrival rate was projected to be 10.07 per hour (i.e., $\lambda = 10.07$ for the interarrival-time distribution), and the service rate was projected to be 1.0345 patients per table per hour (i.e., $\lambda = 1.0345$ for the service-time distribution). Since there were just eight service tables, arrivals would exceed departures and, theoretically, the waiting room queue could grow without bound as long as rates of arrival and departure remained unchanged. It was determined through further analysis with the queueing model that it would be necessary to staff at least two more treatment tables to prevent this situation from occurring.

Case Study 6.3
Assessing the Reliability of Computer Software

In a discussion about the reliability of computer software, G. J. Schick (1974) says the following:

Custom software . . . is expensive to develop and requires extensive testing — the goal being to certify that the software is in error-free condition, ready to support the mission for which it was designed. Similar economies should also be expected from an integrated statistical software test program. Traditionally, there are never enough time or resources to test all possible branches and data combinations in a computer program of reasonable size.

Current practice is to design and develop a software system and then to test it to detect errors, until the amount of time and expense required to discover remaining errors is too great to justify further testing. . . . In principle, few large real-time computer programs ever have been tested completely and unequivocally in the sense that every logical data path has been successfully executed under every logical combination for the data at hand for all possible options. One management objective would be to test every logical path in the computer program at least once with some kind of numerical check. At the present state of the art, such a degree of testing is neither feasible nor realistic. In practice, the contractor must be willing to release and the customer willing to accept a level of risk associated with a program that has been less than completely checked.

In finding and correcting errors in a computer program (*debugging*) and determining the program's reliability, Schick and others have noted the importance of the distribution of the time until the next program error is found. If this distribution is assumed to be exponential, with

$$f(x) = \lambda\, e^{-\lambda x} \qquad (x > 0, \quad \lambda > 0)$$

then, as Schick points out, its mean, $1/\lambda$, would be the average time required to find the next error.

In his article, Schick describes a method relevant to software reliability for estimating the parameter, λ, of the exponential distribution. Using computer debugging data supplied by the U.S. Navy, Schick demonstrates how this estimation procedure and the exponential distribution can be used to estimate the reliability of a computer program. [*Note:* The model used by Schick to represent the distribution for the time until the next error is based on the exponential distribution, but it is slightly more complicated because he assumes that λ varies. For our purposes, however, nothing is lost by assuming the distribution to be exponential.]

After twenty-six program errors were found, Schick estimated λ to be .042. Accordingly, $1/\lambda = 23.8$ days. This means that the average time it would take to find the next (twenty-seventh) error would be about 24 days. Thus, the probability of it taking, say, 60 or more days to find the next error is

$$P(x \geq 60) = e^{-(.042)(60)} = .08046$$

Over the next 290 days, five more errors were detected. Since this is a rate of about one error every 60 days and since $P(x \geq 60) \approx .08$, it seems unlikely that an exponential distribution with $\lambda = .042$ is an appropriate representation of the distribution for the time until the next error. Based on the number of new errors found and the length of time it took to find them, Schick reestimated λ. He found $\lambda = .0036$. Thus, $1/\lambda = 278$ days, meaning that on average the next error (thirty-second) would not occur for 278 days. At this point, the length of time and, therefore, the cost required to find any remaining program errors may be prohibitive. Debugging should probably be discontinued.

Exercises 6.29–6.38

Applying the Mechanics

6.29 The random variables x and y have exponential distributions with $\lambda = 3$ and $\lambda = .75$, respectively. Using Table III in Appendix B, carefully plot both distributions on the same set of axes.

6.30 Suppose x has an exponential distribution with $\lambda = 3$. Find the following probabilities:

a. $P(x > 2)$ **b.** $P(x > 1.5)$ **c.** $P(x > 3)$ **d.** $P(x > .45)$

6.31 Suppose x has an exponential distribution with $\lambda = 2.5$. Find the following probabilities:

a. $P(x \leq 3)$ **b.** $P(x \leq 4)$ **c.** $P(x \leq 1.6)$ **d.** $P(x \leq .4)$

6.32 Suppose the random variable x is best approximated by an exponential probability distribution with $\lambda = 2$. Find the mean and variance of x. Find the probability that x will assume a value within the interval $\mu \pm 2\sigma$.

Applying the Concepts

6.33 The shelf-life of a product is a random variable that is related to consumer acceptance and, ultimately, to sales and profit. Suppose the shelf-life of bread is best approximated by an exponential distribution with mean equal to 2 days. What fraction of the loaves stocked today would you expect to still be saleable (i.e., not stale) 3 days from now?

6.34 An article in the Jacksonville, Florida, *Times Union* (Mar. 11, 1984) reports on the unexplained crash of a small plane on takeoff and the resulting injury to its 24-year-old student pilot. The article notes that Shields Aviation, the renter of the plane, inspects (and presumably performs maintenance) on the aircraft every 100 flight hours. The plane had flown 30 hours since its last inspection. Suppose that x, the time between malfunctions for this particular plane, has an exponential distribution with mean equal to 300 hours. What is the probability that a plane of this type will malfunction within 30 hours after the last inspection?

6.35 The probability distribution of the length of service time is important in the design of service facilities, and it has a definite effect on sales. Suppose the time an individual has to wait in line to be served at a fast-food hamburger franchise has an exponential distribution with mean equal to 1 minute. What is the probability that an individual would have to wait more than 2 minutes before being served? Less than 30 seconds?

6.36 As discussed in Case Study 6.2, Bolling (1972) used an exponential distribution with mean 58 minutes to model the service-time distribution of each of the eight treatment tables in the emergency room of Richmond Memorial Hospital.

a. Using this distribution, find the probability that it will take more than 58 minutes to treat a patient in the emergency room. More than 1.5 hours.

b. What is the probability that each of the next three patients will require more than 58 minutes for treatment?

c. Recall from part c of Exercise 6.11 that the median, x_m, of a continuous random variable x is the value such that $P(x \geq x_m) = P(x \leq x_m) = .5$. Is the median time required to treat a patient more or less than 58 minutes?

d. Using Table III in Appendix B, approximate the median of the service-time distribution.

6.37 In Case Study 6.3, the exponential distribution was used to help evaluate the reliability of a computer program. After twenty-six program errors were found, the time (in days) required to find the next error was determined to have an exponential distribution with $\lambda = .042$.

a. Graph this exponential distribution, and locate its mean and the interval $\mu \pm \sigma$ on your graph.

b. What is the mean time required to find the twenty-seventh program error?

c. What is the probability that it will take less than 30 days to find the twenty-seventh error?

d. Find the probability that the time required to find the twenty-seventh error is within the interval $\mu \pm \sigma$.

e. Find the probability that the time required to find the twenty-seventh error is within the interval $\mu \pm 2\sigma$. How does your answer compare with the approximate probability provided by the Empirical Rule of Chapter 3?

6.38 The following is a sample of the lengths of time between arrivals (rounded to the nearest minute) at the emergency room of a hospital:

8	9	28	3	22	7	5	3	4
23	6	4	5	7	10	5	1	9
14	4	2	6	12	4	1	10	5
3	3	14	18	13	18	15	12	1
5	9	26	37	8	1	19	1	8
11	16	3	31	21				

a. Draw a relative frequency histogram for the data. Does it appear that an exponential distribution could be used to characterize the length of time between arrivals? Explain.

b. If you were asked to model the length of time between arrivals for this emergency room, discuss how you would estimate λ.

6.5 Approximating a Binomial Distribution with a Normal Distribution

When a binomial random variable can assume a large number of values, the calculation of its probabilities may become very tedious. To contend with this problem, we provide tables in Appendix B to give the probabilities for some values of n and p, but these tables are by necessity incomplete. For example, the binomial table (Table II) can be used only for $n = 5, 6, 7, 8, 9, 10, 15, 20,$ or 25. To get around this limitation, we seek approximation procedures for calculating the probabilities associated with binomial random variables.

When n is large, a normal probability distribution can provide a good approximation to the probability histogram of a binomial random variable. To show how the approximation works, we refer to Example 5.7, in which we used the binomial distribution to model the number x of twenty employees who favor unionization. We assumed that 60% of all the company's employees favored unionization. The mean and standard deviation of x were found to be $\mu = 12$ and $\sigma = 2.19$. The binomial distribution for $n = 20$ and $p = .6$ is shown in Figure 6.22, and the approximating normal distribution with mean $\mu = 12$ and standard deviation $\sigma = 2.19$ is superimposed.

As part of Example 5.7, we used Table II to find the probability that $x < 10$. This probability, which is shaded in Figure 6.22, was found to equal .128. To find the normal approximation,

Figure 6.22 Binomial Distribution for $n = 20$, $p = .6$ and Normal Distribution with $\mu = 12$, $\sigma = 2.19$

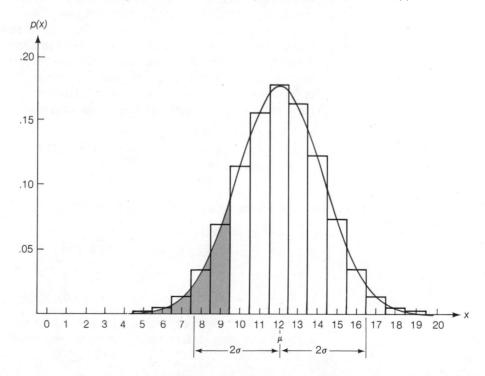

we first note that $P(0 \leq x < 10)$ corresponds to the area to the left of $x = 9.5$ on the normal curve in the figure. We use $x = 9.5$ rather than $x = 9$ or $x = 10$ so that all the binomial probability corresponding to $x = 9$ is included in the approximating normal curve area, but none of that corresponding to $x = 10$ is included. We thus calculate

$$z = \frac{x - \mu}{\sigma} = \frac{9.5 - 12}{2.19} = -1.14$$

From Table IV of Appendix B we find that the area between $z = 0$ and $z = -1.14$ is .3729. Thus, the approximating normal probability is the area to the left of $x = 9.5$, or

$$P(x \leq 9) \approx .5 - .3729 = .1271$$

You can see that the approximation differs only slightly from the exact value, .128.

You may be wondering how large n should be in order for the normal distribution to provide an adequate approximation to the binomial. We will, as a rule of thumb, require that the interval $\mu \pm 3\sigma$ lie completely within the range of values for x—i.e., within the interval from 0 to n. In the example above, $\mu \pm 3\sigma = 12 \pm 3(2.19) = 12 \pm 6.57 = (5.43, 18.57)$. This lies within the interval from 0 to 20, so the normal approximation should be adequate.

Example 6.10

The pocket calculator has become relatively inexpensive because its solid-state circuitry is stamped by machine, thus making mass production feasible. A problem with anything that is mass-produced is quality control. The process must somehow be monitored to be sure the rate of defective items is kept at an acceptable level.

One method of dealing with this problem is *lot acceptance sampling,* in which a sample of the items produced is selected, and each item in the sample is carefully tested. The lot of items is then accepted or rejected, based on the number of defectives in the sample. For example, suppose a manufacturer of calculators chooses 200 stamped circuits from the day's production and determines x, the number of defective circuits in the sample. Suppose that up to a 6% rate of defectives is considered acceptable for the process.

a. Find the mean and standard deviation of x, assuming the defective rate is 6%.

b. Use the normal approximation to determine the probability that twenty or more defectives are observed in the sample of 200 circuits—i.e., that $x \geq 20$.

Solution

a. The random variable x is binomial, with $n = 200$ and the fraction defective $p = .06$. Thus,

$$\mu = np = 200(.06) = 12$$
$$\sigma = \sqrt{npq} = \sqrt{200(.06)(.94)} = \sqrt{11.28} = 3.36$$

Note that

$$\mu \pm 3\sigma = 12 \pm 3(3.36) = 12 \pm 10.08 = (1.92, 22.08)$$

lies completely within the range from 0 to 200, so a normal probability distribution should provide an adequate approximation to this binomial distribution.

Figure 6.23 Normal Approximation to the Binomial Distribution with $n = 200$, $p = .06$

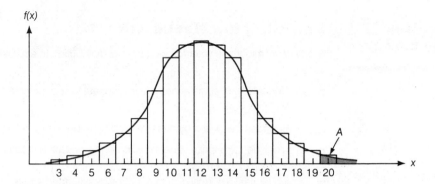

b. To find the approximating area corresponding to $x \geq 20$, refer to Figure 6.23. Note that we want to include all of the binomial probability histogram from 20 to 200, inclusive. But in order to include the entire rectangle corresponding to $x = 20$, we must begin the approximating area at $x = 19.5$. Thus, the z value is

$$z = \frac{x - \mu}{\sigma} = \frac{19.5 - 12}{3.36} = \frac{7.5}{3.36} = 2.23$$

Referring to Table IV of Appendix B, we observe that the area to the right of the mean corresponding to $z = 2.23$ (see Figure 6.24) is .4871. So, the area A is

$$A = .5 - .4871 = .0129$$

Figure 6.24 Standard Normal Distribution

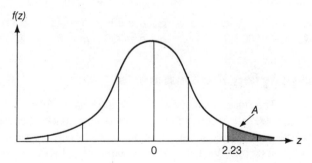

Thus, the normal approximation to the binomial probability is

$$P(x \geq 20) \approx .0129$$

In other words, the probability is extremely small that twenty or more defectives would be observed in a sample of 200 circuits, *if in fact the true defective rate is 6%*. If the manufacturer were to observe $x \geq 20$, the likely reason is that the process is producing more than the acceptable 6% defectives. ∎

**Exercises
6.39–6.52**

Learning the Mechanics

6.39 Why might you want to use a normal distribution to approximate a binomial distribution?

6.40 Under what circumstances is it appropriate to approximate a binomial distribution with a normal distribution?

6.41 Suppose that x is a binomial random variable with $p = .4$ and $n = 25$.

a. Would it be appropriate to approximate the probability distribution of x with a normal distribution? Explain.
b. Assuming that a normal distribution provides an adequate approximation to the distribution of x, what are the mean and variance of the approximating normal distribution?
c. Use Table II of Appendix B to find the exact value of $P(9 \le x \le 14)$.
d. Use the normal approximation to find $P(9 \le x \le 14)$.

6.42 Assume that x is a binomial random variable with $n = 25$ and $p = .5$. Use Table II of Appendix B and the normal approximation to find the exact and approximate values, respectively, for the following probabilities:

a. $P(x \le 12)$ **b.** $P(x \ge 15)$ **c.** $P(x > 13)$

6.43 Assume that x is a binomial random variable with $n = 100$ and $p = .45$. Use a normal approximation to find the following:

a. $P(x \le 45)$ **b.** $P(40 \le x \le 50)$ **c.** $P(x \ge 38)$

6.44 Assume that x is a binomial random variable with n and p as specified in parts a–f. For which cases would it be appropriate to use a normal distribution to approximate the binomial distribution?

a. $n = 50$, $p = .01$ **b.** $n = 20$, $p = .45$ **c.** $n = 10$, $p = .4$
d. $n = 1,000$, $p = .1$ **e.** $n = 200$, $p = .8$ **f.** $n = 35$, $p = .7$

Applying the Concepts

6.45 The *Statistical Abstract of the United States: 1981* reports that 22.5% of the country's 79,108,000 households are inhabited by one person. If 1,000 randomly selected homes are to participate in a Nielsen survey to determine television ratings, find the approximate probability that no more than 250 of these homes are inhabited by one person.

6.46 It is against the law to discriminate against job applicants because of race, religion, sex, or age. Forty percent of the individuals who apply for an accountant's position in a large corporation are over 45 years of age. If the company decides to choose fifty of a very large number of applicants for closer credential screening, claiming that the selection will be random and not age-biased, what is the approximate probability that fewer than fifteen of those chosen are over 45 years of age? (Assume that the applicant pool is large enough so that x, the number in the sample over 45 years of age, has a binomial probability distribution.)

6.47 The Department of Labor is interested in the fraction of the employed work force in the United States who feel in danger of losing their jobs during the next year. A random sample of

100 members of the work force is taken and x, the number who feel their jobs are in danger, is observed.

a. What type of random variable is x? Justify your answer.

b. Assuming 30% of the work force feels insecure about their jobs, what are the mean and standard deviation of the random variable x?

c. What is the approximate probability that no more than fifteen workers will feel that their jobs are in danger?

6.48 In May 1983, after an extensive investigation by the Consumer Product Safety Commission, Honeywell agreed to recall 770,000 potentially defective smoke detectors. The commission suggested that about 40% of the Honeywell detectors were defective. However, Honeywell found only four defectives in a random sample of 2,000 detectors and claimed the recall was not justified (Gross, 1983). Let x be the number of defective smoke detectors found in a random sample of 2,000 detectors.

a. What assumptions must be made in order to characterize x as a binomial random variable? Do these assumptions appear to be satisfied?

b. Assume that the conditions of part a hold. Determine the approximate probability of finding four or fewer defective smoke detectors in a random sample of 2,000 if, in fact, 40% of all detectors are defective.

c. Assume that Honeywell's sample data have been reported accurately. Is it *likely* that 40% of their detectors are defective? Explain.

d. Refer to part c. Is it *possible* that 40% of Honeywell's detectors are defective? Explain.

6.49 The percentage of fat in the bodies of American men is an approximate normal random variable with mean equal to 15% and standard deviation equal to 2%. If these values were used to describe the body fat of men in the U.S. Army and if 20% or more body fat is characterized as obese, what is the approximate probability that a random sample of 10,000 Army men will contain fewer than fifty who would be characterized as obese? Suppose the Army actually were to check the percentage of body fat for a random sample of 10,000 men. If only thirty contained 20% or more body fat, would you conclude that the Army was successful in reducing the percentage of obese men below the percentage in the general population? Explain your reasoning.

6.50 An advertising agency was hired to introduce a new product. It claimed that after its campaign, 30% of all consumers were familiar with the product. To check the claim, the manufacturer of the product surveyed 2,000 consumers. Of this number, 527 consumers had learned about the product through sources attributable to the campaign. What is the approximate probability that as few as 527 (i.e., 527 or fewer) would have learned about the product if the campaign was really 30% effective?

6.51 A credit card company claims that 80% of all clothing purchases in excess of $20 are made with credit cards. A random check of 100 clothing purchases in excess of $20 showed that seventy-three had been made with credit cards. If in fact 80% of all clothing purchases in excess of $20 are made with credit cards and if x is the number in a sample of 100 that make credit card purchases, find approximate values for:

a. $P(x \le 73)$

b. $P(75 \le x \le 85)$

6.52 To check on the effectiveness of a new production process, 700 photoflash devices were randomly selected from a large number that had been produced. If the process actually produces 6% defectives, what is the approximate probability that:

a. More than fifty defectives appear in the sample of 700?
b. The number of defectives in the sample of 700 is forty-five or less?

Summary

Many *continuous random variables* in business applications have probability distributions that are well approximated by the *normal, uniform,* or *exponential probability distributions*. In this chapter we showed the graphical shape of each probability distribution, gave its mean and variance, and pointed out some practical applications of each probability model. In addition, we showed that the normal probability distribution provides a good approximation for the binomial distribution when n is sufficiently large.

Supplementary Exercises 6.53–6.76

[*Note: Starred (*) exercises refer to optional sections in this chapter.*]

*6.53 Assume that x is a random variable best described by a uniform distribution with $c = 10$ and $d = 90$.

a. Find $f(x)$.
b. Find the mean and standard deviation of x.
c. Graph the probability distribution for x, and locate its mean and the interval $\mu \pm 2\sigma$ on the graph.
d. Find $P(x \leq 60)$.
e. Find $P(x \geq 90)$.
f. Find $P(x \leq 80)$.
g. Find $P(\mu - \sigma \leq x \leq \mu + \sigma)$.
h. Find $P(x > 75)$.

*6.54 Suppose x has an exponential distribution with $\lambda = .3$. Find the following probabilities:

a. $P(x \leq 2)$ **b.** $P(x > 3)$ **c.** $P(x = 1)$
d. $P(x \leq 7)$ **e.** $P(4 \leq x \leq 12)$ **f.** $P(x = 2.5)$

6.55 Use Table IV of Appendix B to calculate the area under the standard normal distribution between the following pairs of z-scores:

a. -1.96 and 1.96 **b.** -1.645 and 1.645 **c.** -3 and 3
d. -3 and 2.5 **e.** 1.5 and 2.5 **f.** -1.5 and 2.5

6.56 Use Table IV of Appendix B to find the following probabilities:

a. $P(z \geq .4)$ **b.** $P(z \leq .3)$
c. $P(z \geq -3.05)$ **d.** $P(-1.75 \leq z \leq -.25)$

6.57 Find a value of z, call it z_0, such that

a. $P(z \geq z_0) = .5517$ **b.** $P(z \leq z_0) = .5080$
c. $P(z \geq z_0) = .1492$ **d.** $P(z_0 \leq z \leq .59) = .4773$

6.58 The random variable x has a normal distribution with $\mu = 75$ and $\sigma = 10$. Find the following probabilities:

a. $P(x \le 80)$ **b.** $P(x \ge 85)$ **c.** $P(70 \le x \le 75)$
d. $P(x > 80)$ **e.** $P(x = 78)$ **f.** $P(x \le 110)$

6.59 Assume that x is a binomial random variable with $n = 50$ and $p = .6$. Find approximate values for the following probabilities:

a. $P(x \le 35)$ **b.** $P(25 \le x \le 40)$
c. $P(x \ge 20)$ **d.** $P(40 \le x \le 50)$

6.60 The metropolitan airport commission is considering the establishment of limitations on noise pollution around a local airport. At the present time, the noise level per jet takeoff in one neighborhood near the airport is approximately normally distributed with a mean of 100 decibels and a standard deviation of 6 decibels.

a. What is the probability that a randomly selected jet will generate a noise level greater than 108 decibels in this neighborhood?
b. What is the probability that a randomly selected jet will generate a noise level of exactly 100 decibels?
c. Suppose a regulation is passed that requires jet noise in this neighborhood to be lower than 105 decibels 95% of the time. Assuming the standard deviation of the noise distribution remains the same, how much will the mean level of noise have to be lowered to comply with the regulation?

6.61 Suppose the present value of a risky investment is approximately normally distributed with mean $10,000 and standard deviation $4,000. What is the probability that the present value of the investment is less than $1,000? Greater than $20,000?

*6.62 Blending feeders are used to break up tobacco that has been aged in tightly packed hogsheads. One cigarette manufacturer determined that the time between breakdowns for each of its blending feeders is best represented by an exponential distribution with mean equal to 100 hours of operation. Suppose a particular feeder was just repaired and put back into service. What is the probability that it will not break down for at least 50 more hours? What is the probability that it will break down within the next 100 hours?

6.63 E. Brewer and P. Kaeser (1963) conducted a study of the factors that affect the level of production of workers paid on a piecework basis (i.e., paid according to the number of items they produce or process). Their study involved observing the performance of thirty-six quality control inspectors at a paper mill in England over an 8-week period. The inspectors were responsible for detecting and sorting out paper with defects such as holes, spots, creases, and rust marks. Part of the study entailed computing and analyzing the average hourly earnings for each inspector for each week of the 8-week observation period. Brewer and Kaeser constructed a frequency histogram of the average earnings data and noted that the histogram could be approximated by a normal distribution.

a. How many observations are there in the average earnings data set?
b. Suppose the average earnings histogram can be approximated by a normal distribution with $\mu = \$7.65$ and $\sigma = \$1.25$. Approximately what proportion of the weekly average earnings are over $8.50 per hour?

c. Using the normal distribution of part b, is it possible to determine approximately how many inspectors averaged over $8.50 per hour for the 8-week period? If so, how many? If not, why not?

6.64 On December 28, 1980, before millions of television viewers, the Schlitz Brewing Co. conducted a "live" taste test between its beer, Schlitz, and Anheuser-Busch's Budweiser. The taste test was conducted using a panel of 100 "loyal Budweiser drinkers." The panelists were required to sign affidavits stating that they drink at least two six-packs of Budweiser per week. The two beers were served to the tasters without labels and in identical opaque mugs, making it virtually impossible to identify a brand by sight. Since it is against broadcasting industry regulations, the panel was not shown tasting the beers. Instead, the commercial began after both beers had been tasted but before the tasters had indicated their preferences. When the master of ceremonies, a former National Football League referee, signaled the tasters to reveal their preferences, a scoreboard indicated the percentage of the panel that preferred the taste of Schlitz. According to *Fortune* magazine, "there really is no great difference between its beer [Schlitz] and those of other American brewers. Most American beers — unlike most European brands — are subtly flavored, and it requires a trained palate to distinguish among them. Probably no more than one person in a hundred has such a palate" ("Schlitz's Crafty Taste Test," 1981). The scoreboard indicated that 46% of the panel preferred Schlitz. In light of the *Fortune* quote, is the fact that 46% preferred Schlitz surprising? Was Schlitz taking much of a chance by conducting the taste test on "live television"? Explain.

6.65 A loan officer in a large bank has been assigned to screen sixty loan applications during the next week. If her past record indicates that she turns down 20% of the applicants, what is the approximate probability that forty-one or more of the sixty applications will be approved? What is the approximate probability that between forty-five and fifty (inclusive) of the applications will be approved?

6.66 It is quite common for the standard deviation of a random variable to increase proportionally as the mean increases. When this occurs, the *coefficient of variation,*

$$CV = \frac{\sigma}{\mu}$$

the ratio of σ to μ, is the *proportionality constant.* To illustrate, the error (in dollars) in assessing the value of a house increases as the house increases in value. Suppose that long experience with assessors in your part of the country has shown that the coefficient of variation is .08 and that the probability distribution of assessed valuations on the same house by many different assessors is approximately normal with a mean we will call the *true value* of the house. Suppose the true value of your house is $50,000, and it is being assessed for taxation purposes. What is the probability that the assessor will assess your house in excess of $55,000?

6.67 As noted in Exercise 6.66, it is sometimes true that the larger the mean of a random variable, the larger will be its standard deviation. A measure of the relative variability of different data sets can be obtained by computing the coefficient of variation $(s/\bar{x})$ for each.

The following data sets reflect the numbers of checks (in thousands) processed per week by three different banks over the last 6 weeks:

BANK 1	BANK 2	BANK 3
20	60	100
10	63	92
18	58	81
25	65	110
31	70	105
12	54	129

Rank each of these data sets in terms of variability using the:

a. Range   **b.** Standard deviation   **c.** Coefficient of variation

*6.68 It is believed that the length of time a viewer can recall the details after viewing a particular television commercial follows an exponential distribution with a mean of 2 days.

a. How long after the commercial is aired will half the viewing audience be unable to recall details of the commercial?

b. What proportion of viewers will be able to recall details of the commercial after 5 days?

c. Five people who live in different parts of the country were exposed to the commercial at the same time. Four days later, all were able to recall details of the commercial. Is it likely that the exponential distribution described above is an appropriate characterization of the length of recall time? Explain.

6.69 A firm believes the internal rate of return for its proposed investment can best be described by a normal distribution with a mean of 15% and a standard deviation of 3%. What is the probability that the internal rate of return for the investment will be:

a. Greater than 20% or less than 10%?

b. At least 6%?

c. More than 16.5%?

*6.70 Assume that the length of the active life of baking yeast has an exponential distribution with a mean equal to 6 months. If the expiration date marked on a package of yeast is based on a life of 6 months, what is the probability that a package of the yeast will lose its potency before its expiration date?

*6.71 On the average, the main chute fails in one of every 1,000 parachutes. Suppose that during a lifetime, a professional parachutist makes 4,000 jumps, and let x equal the number of times the main chute fails. What is the approximate probability that the parachutist's main chute fails on at least one jump? [*Note:* Because n is large and p is so small, the Poisson probability distribution will also provide a good approximation to this probability. (See Exercise 5.58.) If you covered Section 5.5, find the Poisson approximation to $P(x > 0)$.]

*6.72 The Poisson probability distribution, like the binomial, can be approximated by a normal probability distribution in some situations. The approximation, using $\mu = \lambda$ and $\sigma = \sqrt{\lambda}$, will be good when λ is large (large enough so that the distance between $x = 0$ and λ is at least $3\sigma = 3\sqrt{\lambda}$; i.e., $\lambda \geq 9$). The number of union complaints per month at a particular manufacturing plant has a Poisson probability distribution with $\mu = 40$ complaints per month. Use the normal approximation to the Poisson probability distribution to find:

a. The approximate probability that the number of complaints in a given month will be less than thirty-five.

b. The approximate probability that the number of complaints in a given month will exceed forty.

c. What is the approximate probability that in each of 3 consecutive months, the number of complaints will exceed forty?

*6.73 The number of serious accidents per month in a manufacturing plant has (approximately) a Poisson probability distribution with a mean of 2.

a. If an accident occurs today, what is the probability that the next serious accident will not occur within the next month? [*Note:* If x, the number of events per unit time, has a Poisson distribution with mean λ, then it can be shown that the time between adjacent pairs of events has an exponential probability distribution with mean $1/\lambda$.]

b. What is the probability that more than one accident will occur within the next month?

6.74 A company has a lump-sum incentive plan for salespeople that is dependent on their level of sales. If they sell less than $100,000 per year, they receive a $1,000 bonus; from $100,000 to $200,000, they receive $5,000; and above $200,000, they receive $10,000. If the annual sales per salesperson has approximately a normal distribution with $\mu = \$180,000$ and $\sigma = \$50,000$:

a. Find p_1, the proportion of salespeople who receive a $1,000 bonus.

b. Find p_2, the proportion of salespeople who receive a $5,000 bonus.

c. Find p_3, the proportion of salespeople who receive a $10,000 bonus.

d. What is the mean value of the bonus payout for the company? [*Hint:* Review the definition for the expected value of a random variable in Chapter 5.]

6.75 The probability distribution of the number of people per month who open a savings account in a large banking system is approximately normal with $\mu = 1,280$ and $\sigma = 265$.

a. If the bank gives a $10 gift to each new account holder, what proportion of all months will the bank's payout for gifts exceed $15,000?

b. What is the bank's mean monthly payout for gifts?

6.76 Contrary to our intuition, very reliable decisions concerning the proportion of a large group of consumers who favor a particular product or a particular social issue can be based on relatively small samples. For example, suppose the target population of consumers contains 50,000,000 people and we want to decide whether the proportion of consumers, p, in the population who favor some product (or issue) is as large as some value, say .2. Suppose you randomly select a sample as small as 1,600 from the 50,000,000 and you observe the number, x, of consumers in the sample who favor the new product. Assuming that $p = .2$, find the mean and standard deviation of x. Suppose that 400 (or 25%) of the sample of 1,600 consumers favor the new product. Why might this sample result lead you to conclude that p (the proportion of consumers who favor the product in the population of

50,000,000) is larger than .2? [*Hint:* Compare the observed value of x with the values of μ and σ calculated on the assumption that $p = .2$.]

6.77 *Simulation* has been defined as "the process of designing a model of a real system and conducting experiments with this model for the purpose either of understanding the behavior of the system or of evaluating various strategies (within the limits imposed by a criterion or set of criteria) for the operation of the system" (Shannon, 1975). In Case Study 6.2, we saw that the Richmond Memorial Hospital used queueing theory to simulate the flow of patients in its emergency room. In that case, an exponential probability distribution was used to model the interarrival times of patients arriving at the emergency room. In general, after we have modeled the arrival process, we can use a computer to simulate arrivals. For Case Study 6.2, this is conceptually equivalent to drawing a random sample of interarrival times from a population of interarrival times whose relative frequency distribution is characterized by an exponential distribution. Many statistical computer packages are available for performing such simulations. For this exercise, Minitab was used to simulate a random sample of size $n = 48$ from a continuous probability distribution described in this chapter. Plot a relative frequency histogram for the accompanying data set, and describe the probability distribution from which it appears the data were sampled. [*Note:* A statistical test is available to test whether sample data have been selected from a specified population probability distribution. However, the test is beyond the scope of this text.]

.49809	.12027	.62005	.22538	.37436	.04148	.67047	.51957
.28542	.02330	.06551	.17087	.19405	.05575	1.83394	.01557
.01218	.05462	.08064	.81027	.45986	.29073	.14429	1.54523
.39153	.94809	.03960	.40591	.16163	.61685	.09053	.40320
.34805	.20736	1.15085	.52765	.29120	.09520	.16720	.49599
.08638	.00107	.32537	.16684	.04859	.29705	.18021	.05824

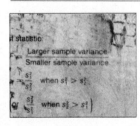

On Your Own . . .

For large values of n the computational effort involved in working with the binomial probability distribution is considerable. Fortunately, in many instances the normal distribution provides a good approximation to the binomial distribution. This exercise was designed to demonstrate how well the normal distribution approximates the binomial distribution.

a. Suppose the random variable x has a binomial probability distribution with $n = 10$ and $p = .5$. Using the binomial distribution, find the probability that x takes on a value in each of the following intervals: $\mu \pm \sigma$, $\mu \pm 2\sigma$, and $\mu \pm 3\sigma$.

b. Approximate the probabilities requested in part a using a normal approximation to the given binomial distribution.

c. Determine the magnitude of the difference between each of the three probabilities as determined by the binomial distribution and by the normal approximation.

d. Letting x have a binomial distribution with $n = 20$ and $p = .5$, repeat parts a, b, and c. Notice that the probability estimates provided by the normal distribution are more accurate for $n = 20$ than for $n = 10$.

References

Blair, R. D., & Kenny, L. W. *Microeconomics for managerial decision making.* New York: McGraw-Hill, 1982. Chapter 10.

Bolling, W. B. "Queuing model of a hospital emergency room." *Industrial Engineering,* Sept. 1972, 26–31.

Brewer, E., & Kaeser, P. "A comparative analysis of incentive plans." *Journal of Industrial Relations,* July 1963, *11,* 183–198.

Fama, E. F. *Foundations of finance.* New York: Basic Books, 1976. Chapter 1.

Gross, S. "Honeywell smoke detectors recalled after 18-month probe." *Minneapolis Star and Tribune,* May 25, 1983, 1A.

Hillier, F. S. "The derivation of probabilistic information for the evaluation of risky investments." *Management Science,* Apr. 1963, *9,* 443–457.

Hillier, F. S., & Lieberman, G. J. *Introduction to operations research.* 3d ed. San Francisco: Holden-Day, 1983. Chapter 10.

Hogg, R. V., & Craig, A. T. *Introduction to mathematical statistics.* 4th ed. New York: Macmillan, 1978. Chapter 1.

Lindgren, B. W. *Statistical theory.* 3d ed. New York: Macmillan, 1976. Chapters 2 and 3.

Martz, H. F., & Waller, R. A. *Bayesian reliability analysis.* New York: Wiley, 1982. Pp. 1 and 256.

Mood, A. M., Graybill, F. A., & Boes, D. C. *Introduction to the theory of statistics.* 3d ed. New York: McGraw-Hill, 1974. Chapter 3.

Neter, J., Wasserman W., & Whitmore G. A. *Applied statistics.* 2d ed. Boston: Allyn & Bacon, 1982. Chapter 7.

Schick, G. J. "The search for a software reliability model." *Decision Sciences,* Oct. 1974, *5,* 529.

"Schlitz's crafty taste test." *Fortune,* Jan. 26, 1981, 32–34.

Shannon, R. E. *Systems simulation: The art and science.* Englewood Cliffs, N.J.: Prentice-Hall, 1975. Chapter 1.

Winkler, R. L., & Hays, W. *Statistics: Probability, inference, and decision.* 2d ed. New York: Holt, Rinehart and Winston, 1975. Chapter 3.

CHAPTER 7

Sampling Distributions

Where We've Been . . .

We have learned in earlier chapters that the objective of most statistical investigations is inference — that is, making decisions about or estimating some numerical descriptive measure (a parameter) of a population based on sample data. To make the decision or to estimate the population parameter, we use sample data to compute sample statistics (Chapter 3) such as the sample mean or variance.

Where We're Going . . .

Because sample measurements are observed values of random variables, the value we compute for a sample statistic will vary in a random manner from sample to sample. In other words, since sample statistics are computed from random variables, they themselves are random variables, and they have probability distributions that are either discrete or continuous, as discussed in Chapters 5 and 6. The probability distribution of a sample statistic is called a *sampling distribution* because it characterizes the distribution of values of the statistic over a very large number of samples. Sampling distributions are the topic of this chapter. We will discuss why many sampling distributions tend to be approximately normal, and you will see how sampling distributions can be used to evaluate the accuracy of parameter estimates.

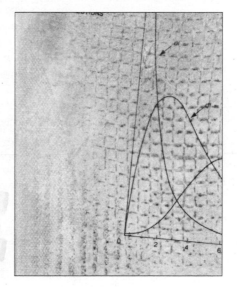

Contents

In Chapters 5 and 6 we assumed that we knew the probability distribution of a random variable, and based on this knowledge, we were able to compute the mean, variance, and probability that the random variable assumed specific values. However, in most practical business applications, this information will not be available. To illustrate, in Example 5.7, we calculated the probability that the binomial random variable x (the number of twenty polled employees who favor unionization) assumed specific values. To do this, it was necessary to assume some value for p, the proportion of the employees in the population who favor unionization. Thus, for the purpose of illustration we assumed $p = .6$, but in all likelihood, the exact value of p would be unknown. In fact, the probable purpose of taking the poll was to estimate p. Similarly, when we modeled the in-city gas mileage of a certain automobile model in Example 6.5, we used the normal probability distribution with an *assumed* mean and standard deviation of 27 and 3 miles per gallon, respectively. In reality, the true mean and standard deviation are unknown quantities that would have to be estimated.

Numerical quantities that describe probability distributions are called *parameters*. Thus, p (the probability of a success in a binomial experiment) and μ and σ (the mean and standard deviation of a normal distribution) are examples of parameters. Since probability distributions are used to characterize populations, it follows that parameters are also numerical descriptive measures of populations.

Definition 7.1

A *parameter* is a numerical descriptive measure of a population.

We often use the information contained in a sample to make inferences about the parameters of a population. In order to make such inferences, we must compute *sample statistics* that will aid in making these inferences.

Definition 7.2

A *sample statistic* is a quantity calculated from the observations in a sample.

Some examples of useful sample statistics we have already discussed are the sample mean, $\bar{x}$; sample median; sample variance, s^2; and the sample standard deviation, s. Before we can use these and other sample statistics to make inferences about population parameters, we have to be able to evaluate their properties. How can we decide which sample statistic contains the most information about a population parameter? One purpose of this chapter is to answer this question.

7.1 Introduction to Sampling Distributions

If we want to estimate a parameter of a population — say, the population mean, μ — there are a number of sample statistics that we could use for the estimate. Two possibilities are the sample mean, $\bar{x}$, and the sample median, m. Which of these do you think will provide a better estimate of μ?

Before answering this question, consider the following example: Toss a fair die and let x equal the number of dots showing on the up face. Suppose the die is tossed three times,

Figure 7.1 Comparing the Sample Mean ($\bar{x}$) and Sample Median (m) as Estimators of the Population Mean (μ)

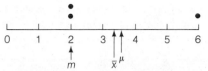

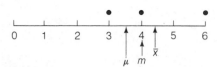

(a) Sample 1: $\bar{x}$ is closer than m to μ

(b) Sample 2: m is closer than $\bar{x}$ to μ

producing the sample measurements 2, 2, 6. The sample mean is $\bar{x} = 3.33$ and the sample median is $m = 2$. Since the population mean of x is $\mu = 3.5$, you can see that for this sample of three measurements, the sample mean $\bar{x}$ provides an estimate that falls closer to μ than does the sample median [see Figure 7.1(a)].

Now suppose we toss the die three more times and obtain the sample measurements 3, 4, 6. The mean and median of this sample are $\bar{x} = 4.33$ and $m = 4$, respectively. This time m is closer to μ [see Figure 7.1(b)].

This simple example illustrates an important point: Neither the sample mean nor the sample median will *always* fall closer to the population mean. Consequently, we cannot compare these two sample statistics or, in general, any two sample statistics on the basis of their performance for a single sample. Instead, we need to recognize that sample statistics are themselves random variables because different samples can lead to different values for the sample statistics. As random variables, sample statistics must be judged and compared on the basis of their probability distributions—i.e., the collection of values and associated probabilities of each statistic that would be obtained if the sampling experiment were repeated a *very large number of times*. We will illustrate this concept with an example.

Suppose it is known that in a certain part of Canada the daily high temperature recorded for all past months of January has a mean of $\mu = 10°F$ and a standard deviation of $\sigma = 5°F$. Consider an experiment consisting of randomly selecting twenty-five daily high temperatures from the records of past months of January and calculating the sample mean, $\bar{x}$. If this experiment were repeated a very large number of times, the value of $\bar{x}$ would vary from sample to sample. For example, the first sample of twenty-five temperature measurements might have a mean of $\bar{x} = 9.8$; the second sample, a mean of $\bar{x} = 11.4$; the third sample, a mean of $\bar{x} = 10.5$; etc. If the sampling experiment were repeated a very large number of times and the resulting values of $\bar{x}$ were displayed in a histogram, the histogram would be the approximate probability distribution of $\bar{x}$. If $\bar{x}$ is a good estimator of μ, we would expect the values of $\bar{x}$ to cluster around μ as shown in Figure 7.2. This probability distribution is called a *sampling distribution* because it describes the potential outcomes of $\bar{x}$ in repeated sampling.

Figure 7.2 Sampling Distribution for $\bar{x}$ Based on a Sample of $n = 25$ Measurements

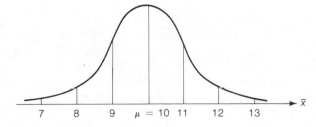

In actual practice, the sampling distribution of a statistic is obtained mathematically or (approximately) by simulating the sampling on a computer using the procedure described above.

> ### Definition 7.3
>
> The *sampling distribution* for a sample statistic calculated from a sample of n measurements is the probability distribution of the statistic.

If $\bar{x}$ has been calculated from a sample of $n = 25$ measurements selected from a population with mean $\mu = 10$ and standard deviation $\sigma = 5$, the sampling distribution (Figure 7.2) provides all the information you may wish to know about its behavior. For example, the probability that you will draw a sample of twenty-five measurements and obtain a value of $\bar{x}$ in the interval $9 \le \bar{x} \le 10$ will be the area under the sampling distribution over that interval. Note that you do not need to know the value of μ in order to make probability statements about the difference between $\bar{x}$ and μ.

Since the properties of a statistic are typified by its sampling distribution, it follows that, to compare two statistics, you compare their sampling distributions. For example, if you have two statistics, A and B, for estimating the same parameter (for purposes of illustration, suppose the parameter is the population variance σ^2) and if their sampling distributions are as shown in Figure 7.3, you would choose statistic A in preference to statistic B. You would make this choice because the sampling distribution for statistic A centers over σ^2 and has less spread (variation) than the sampling distribution for statistic B. When you draw a single sample in a practical sampling situation, the probability is higher that statistic A will fall closer to σ^2.

Figure 7.3 Two Sampling Distributions for Estimating the Population Variance, σ^2

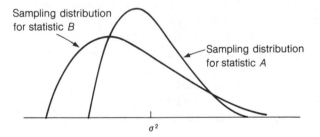

Sampling distribution for statistic B

Sampling distribution for statistic A

σ^2

Remember that in practice we will not know the numerical value of the unknown parameter, σ^2, so we will not know whether statistic A or statistic B is closer to σ^2 for particular samples. We have to rely on our theoretical knowledge of the sampling distributions to choose the better sample statistic and then use it sample after sample.

To show how two statistics can be compared, we will generate approximations to the sampling distributions for two statistics in the following example.

Example 7.1 Suppose we perform the following experiment: Take a sample of eleven measurements from the uniform distribution shown in Figure 7.4. Calculate the two sample statistics

$$\bar{x} = \text{Sample mean} = \frac{\sum_{i=1}^{11} x_i}{11}$$

$m = \text{Median} = \text{Sixth sample measurement when the eleven measurements are arranged in ascending order}$

Figure 7.4 Uniform Distribution from 0 to 1

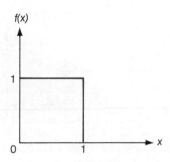

In this particular example we *know* that the population mean is $\mu = .5$. The objective will be to find out which sample statistic contains more information about μ. We use a computer to generate 1,000 samples, each with $n = 11$ observations. Then, we compute $\bar{x}$ and m for each sample. Our goal is to find the resulting approximate sampling distributions for $\bar{x}$ and m.

Table 7.1
First Ten Samples of $n = 11$ Measurements from a Uniform Distribution

SAMPLE	MEASUREMENTS										
1	.217	.786	.757	.125	.139	.919	.506	.771	.138	.516	.419
2	.303	.703	.812	.650	.848	.392	.988	.469	.632	.012	.065
3	.383	.547	.383	.584	.098	.676	.091	.535	.256	.163	.390
4	.218	.376	.248	.606	.610	.055	.095	.311	.086	.165	.665
5	.144	.069	.485	.739	.491	.054	.953	.179	.865	.429	.648
6	.426	.563	.186	.896	.628	.075	.283	.549	.295	.522	.674
7	.643	.828	.465	.672	.074	.300	.319	.254	.708	.384	.534
8	.616	.049	.324	.700	.803	.399	.557	.975	.569	.023	.072
9	.093	.835	.534	.212	.201	.041	.889	.728	.466	.142	.574
10	.957	.253	.983	.904	.696	.766	.880	.485	.035	.881	.732

Solution The first ten of the 1,000 samples generated are presented in Table 7.1. For each of the 1,000 samples we compute the sample mean, $\bar{x}$, and the sample median, m. For example, the first computer-generated sample from the uniform distribution (arranged in ascending order) contained the following measurements: .125, .138, .139, .217, .419, .506, .516, .757, .771, .786, .919. The sample mean, $\bar{x}$, and median, m, computed for this sample are

$$\bar{x} = \frac{.125 + .138 + \cdots + .919}{11} = .481$$

$m = \text{Sixth ordered measurement} = .506$

Figure 7.5   Approximate Sampling Distributions for $\bar{x}$ and m, Example 7.1

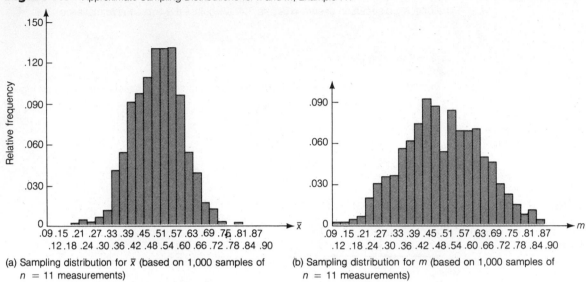

(a) Sampling distribution for $\bar{x}$ (based on 1,000 samples of $n = 11$ measurements)

(b) Sampling distribution for m (based on 1,000 samples of $n = 11$ measurements)

The relative frequency histograms for $\bar{x}$ and m for the 1,000 samples of size $n = 11$ are shown in Figure 7.5.

You can see that the values of $\bar{x}$ tend to cluster around μ to a greater extent than do the values of m. Thus, on the basis of the observed sampling distributions, we conclude that $\bar{x}$ contains more information about μ than m does — at least for samples of $n = 11$ measurements from the uniform distribution.   ■

We will not always have to simulate repeated sampling on a computer to find sampling distributions. Many sampling distributions can be derived mathematically, but the theory necessary to do this is beyond the scope of this text. Consequently, when we need to know the properties of a statistic, we will present its sampling distribution and describe its properties. Several of the important properties of sampling distributions are discussed in the next section.

7.2 Properties of Sampling Distributions: Unbiasedness and Minimum Variance

The simplest type of statistic used to make inferences about a population parameter is a *point estimator.* A point estimator is a rule or formula that tells us how to use the sample data to calculate a single number that can be used as an estimate of the value of some population parameter. For example, the sample mean, $\bar{x}$, is a point estimator of the population mean, μ. Similarly, the sample variance, s^2, is a point estimator of the population variance, σ^2.

Often, many different point estimators can be found to estimate the same parameter. Each will have a sampling distribution that provides information about the point estimator. By examining the sampling distribution, we can determine how large the difference between an estimate and the true value of the parameter — called the *error of estimation* — is likely to be.

Definition 7.4

A *point estimator* of a population parameter is a rule or formula that tells us how to use the sample data to calculate a single number that can be used as an *estimate* of the population parameter.

We can also determine whether an estimator is likely to overestimate or to underestimate a parameter.

Since the sampling distribution of a point estimator (or of any statistic) describes its behavior, we look to the sampling distribution to identify characteristics or properties that we would want an estimator to have. As a first consideration, we would like the sampling distribution to center over the parameter we want to estimate. One way to express centrality is in terms of the mean of the sampling distribution. Consequently, we say that a statistic is *unbiased* if its sampling distribution has a mean equal to the parameter it is intended to estimate. When this occurs, the sampling distribution of the statistic will be centered over the parameter as shown in Figure 7.6(a). If the mean of a sampling distribution is not equal to the parameter it is intended to estimate, the statistic is said to be *biased.* The amount of bias is the difference between the mean of the sampling distribution and the value of the parameter you wish to estimate. The sampling distribution for a biased statistic is shown in Figure 7.6(b).

Definition 7.5

If a sample statistic has a sampling distribution with a mean equal to the population parameter the statistic is intended to estimate, the statistic is said to be an *unbiased* estimator of the parameter.

If the mean of the sampling distribution is not equal to the parameter, the statistic is said to be a *biased* estimator of the parameter.

Figure 7.6 Sampling Distributions for Unbiased and Biased Estimators

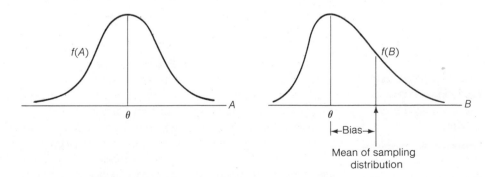

(a) Unbiased sample statistic for the parameter θ (b) Biased sample statistic for the parameter θ

The standard deviation of a sampling distribution measures another important property of a statistic — the spread of the estimates generated by repeated sampling. Suppose two statistics, A and B, are both unbiased estimators of the population parameter called θ (theta). Note that θ could be any parameter, such as μ, σ^2, or σ. Since the means of the two sampling distributions are the same, we turn to their standard deviations to decide which will provide estimates that fall closer to the unknown population parameter we are estimating. Naturally, we will choose the sample statistic that has the smaller standard deviation. Figure 7.7 depicts sampling distributions for A and B. Note that the standard deviation of the distribution of A is smaller than the standard deviation for B, indicating that over a large number of samples, the values of A cluster more closely around the unknown population parameter than do the values of B. Therefore, we would choose statistic A instead of statistic B as an estimator of θ.

Figure 7.7 Sampling Distributions for Two Unbiased Estimators

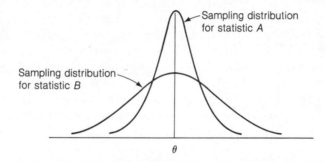

In summary, to make an inference about a population parameter, use the sample statistic with a sampling distribution that is unbiased and has a small standard deviation (usually smaller than the standard deviation of other unbiased sample statistics). How to find this sample statistic will not concern us, because the "best" statistic for estimating a particular parameter is a matter of record. We will simply present an unbiased estimator with its standard deviation for each population parameter we consider. [*Note:* The standard deviation of the sampling distribution for a statistic is usually called the *standard error* of the statistic.]

7.3
The Sampling Distribution of the Sample Mean

Estimating the mean useful life of automobiles, the mean monthly sales for all automobile dealers in a large city, and the mean breaking strength of a new plastic are practical problems with something in common. In each, we are interested in making an inference about the mean, μ, of some population. Because many practical business problems involve estimating μ, it is particularly important to have a sample statistic that is a good estimator of μ. As we mentioned in Chapter 3, the sample mean, $\bar{x}$, is generally a good choice as an estimator of μ. The mean and standard deviation of the sampling distribution of this useful statistic are related to the mean, μ, and standard deviation, σ, of the sampled population as described in the box.

The Mean and Standard Deviation of the Sampling Distribution of $\bar{x}$

Regardless of the shape of the population relative frequency distribution,

1. The mean of the sampling distribution of $\bar{x}$ will equal μ, the mean of the sampled population; i.e., $\mu_{\bar{x}} = \mu$.

2. The standard deviation of the sampling distribution of $\bar{x}$ will equal σ, the standard deviation of the sampled population, divided by the square root of the sample size, n; i.e.,

$$\sigma_{\bar{x}} = \frac{\sigma}{\sqrt{n}} * \quad = \quad \text{STANDARD ERROR} = \sqrt{\frac{\sigma^2}{n}}$$

n = SIZE OF THE SAMPLES   ie $\bar{x}$ FROM 100 SAMPLES OF SIZE = 10 $n = 10$

For example, suppose the sampled population has the uniform probability distribution shown in Figure 7.8(a). The mean and standard deviation of this probability distribution are $\mu = .5$ and $\sigma = .29$ (refer to Section 6.3 for the formulas for μ and σ). Now suppose a sample

Figure 7.8

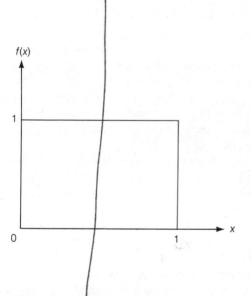

$f(x)$

1

0   1 x

(a) Relative frequency distribution of the sampled population

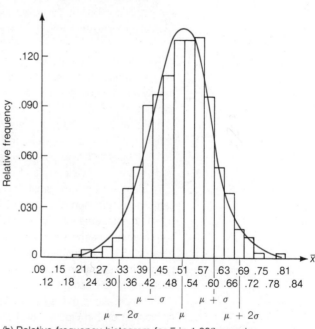

(b) Relative frequency histogram for $\bar{x}$ in 1,000 samples from a uniform distribution

* If the sample size, n, is large relative to the number, N, of elements in the population, $\sigma/\sqrt{n}$ must be multiplied by a finite population correction factor, $\sqrt{(N-n)/(N-1)}$. For most sampling situations, this correction factor will be close to 1 and can be ignored.   SEE CLASS NOTES

IF $\frac{n}{N} \geq .05$ WEEK 5 PG. 32

of eleven measurements is selected from this population. The sampling distribution of the sample mean for samples of size 11 will also have a mean of .5, with a standard deviation

$$\sigma_{\bar{x}} = \frac{\sigma}{\sqrt{n}} = \frac{.29}{\sqrt{11}} = .09$$

(That is, the standard error of $\bar{x}$ is $\sigma/\sqrt{n} = .09$.)

What can be said about the shape of the sampling distribution of $\bar{x}$? Two important theorems provide this information.

Theorem 7.1

If a random sample of n observations is selected from a normal population, the sampling distribution of $\bar{x}$ will be a normal distribution.

Theorem 7.2: Central Limit Theorem

If a random sample of n observations is selected from a population (any population), then, when n is sufficiently large, the sampling distribution of $\bar{x}$ will be approximately a normal distribution. The larger the sample size, n, the better will be the normal approximation to the sampling distribution of $\bar{x}$.*

The theorems indicate that $\bar{x}$ is an unbiased estimator of the population mean, μ [i.e., $E(\bar{x}) = \mu$], and that its sampling distribution, for sufficiently large samples, will be approximately a normal distribution. How large must the sample size, n, be so that $\bar{x}$ has a normal sampling distribution? This depends on the shape of the relative frequency distribution of the sampled population. Generally speaking, the greater the skewness of the sampled population distribution, the larger must be the sample size to obtain an adequate normal approximation to the sampling distribution of $\bar{x}$. But for some practical situations, n may be fairly small and the sampling distribution of $\bar{x}$ will be approximately normal.

To demonstrate how small n can be and still achieve approximate normality for the sampling distribution of $\bar{x}$, recall Example 7.1, in which we generated 1,000 samples of $n = 11$ measurements from a uniform distribution. The relative frequency histogram for the 1,000 sample means is shown in Figure 7.8(b), and the normal probability distribution with a mean of .5 and a standard deviation of .09 is superimposed. You can see that this normal probability distribution approximates the computer-generated sampling distribution very well, even though the sample size is only $n = 11$.

The implications of the Central Limit Theorem are apparent by comparing the sampling distribution of $\bar{x}$ in Figure 7.8(b) with the distribution of the sampled population in Figure 7.8(a). In this situation, the population relative frequency distribution is not skewed and, as a

---

* Also, because of the Central Limit Theorem, the sum of the identically distributed independent random variables, $\sum_{i=1}^{n} x_i$, will have a sampling distribution that will be approximately normal for large samples. This distribution will have a mean equal to $n\mu$ and a variance equal to $n\sigma^2$.

result, a very small sample size proved large enough to apply the Central Limit Theorem. The sampling distribution of $\bar{x}$ is approximately normal, even though the distribution of the sampled population is decidedly nonnormal. You will also note that the mean of the sampling distribution is equal to the mean of the distribution of the sampled population, but that the variability of the sampling distribution is substantially less than the variability of the sampled population.

In most real-life applications, the shape of the population distribution will *not* be known. In such cases, we typically require $n \geq 30$ in order to invoke the Central Limit Theorem.

Example 7.2   Suppose we have selected a random sample of $n = 25$ observations from a population with mean equal to 80 and standard deviation equal to 5. It is known that the population is not extremely skewed.

a. Sketch the relative frequency distributions for the population and for the sampling distribution of the sample mean, $\bar{x}$.

b. Find the probability that $\bar{x}$ will be larger than 82.

Solution   **a.** We do not know the exact shape of the population relative frequency distribution, but we do know that it should be centered about $\mu = 80$, its spread should be measured by $\sigma = 5$, and it is not highly skewed. One possibility is shown in Figure 7.9(a). We know that the sampling distribution of $\bar{x}$ will be approximately normal since the sampled population distribution is not extremely skewed (because of the Central Limit Theorem), and it will have mean and standard deviation

$$\mu_{\bar{x}} = \mu = 80 \quad \text{and} \quad \sigma_{\bar{x}} = \frac{\sigma}{\sqrt{n}} = \frac{5}{\sqrt{25}} = 1$$

The sampling distribution of $\bar{x}$ is shown in Figure 7.9(b).

Figure 7.9 A Population Relative Frequency Distribution and the Sampling Distribution for $\bar{x}$

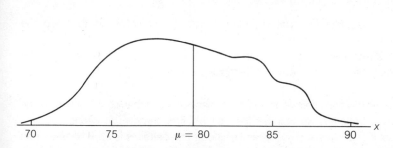

(a) Population relative frequency distribution

(b) Sampling distribution of $\bar{x}$

b. The probability that $\bar{x}$ will exceed 82 is equal to the darker shaded area in Figure 7.10 (next page). To find this area, we need to find the z-value corresponding to $\bar{x} = 82$. Remember that z is the difference between a normally distributed random variable and its mean, expressed in units of its standard deviation. Since $\bar{x}$ is a normally distributed

Figure 7.10   The Sampling Distribution of $\bar{x}$

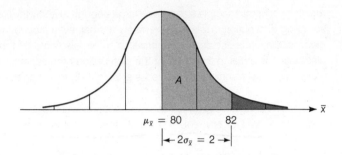

$$\mu_{\bar{x}} = 80 \qquad\qquad 82$$
$$\leftarrow 2\sigma_{\bar{x}} = 2 \rightarrow$$

random variable with mean $\mu_{\bar{x}} = \mu$ and standard deviation $\sigma_{\bar{x}} = \sigma/\sqrt{n}$, it follows that the z value corresponding to the sample mean, $\bar{x}$, is

$$z = \frac{\bar{x} - \mu_{\bar{x}}}{\sigma_{\bar{x}}}$$

Therefore, for $\bar{x} = 82$, we have

$$z = \frac{\bar{x} - \mu_{\bar{x}}}{\sigma_{\bar{x}}} = \frac{82 - 80}{1} = 2$$

The area A in Figure 7.10 corresponding to $z = 2$ is given in the table of areas under the normal curve (see Table IV, Appendix B) as .4772. Therefore, the tail area corresponding to the probability that $\bar{x}$ exceeds 82 is

$$P(\bar{x} > 82) = P(z > 2) = .5 - .4772 = .0228 \qquad\qquad ■$$

Example 7.3   A manufacturer of automobile batteries claims that the distribution of the lifetimes of its best battery has a mean of 54 months and a standard deviation of 6 months. Suppose a consumer group decides to check the claim by purchasing a sample of fifty of these batteries and subjecting them to tests that determine their lifetimes.

   a. Assuming the manufacturer's claim is true, describe the sampling distribution of the mean lifetime of a sample of fifty batteries.

   b. Assuming the manufacturer's claim is true, what is the probability that the consumer group's sample has a mean lifetime of 52 months or less?

Solution   **a.** Even though we have no information about the shape of the probability distribution of the lifetimes of the batteries, we can use the Central Limit Theorem to deduce that the sampling distribution for a sample mean lifetime of fifty batteries is approximately normally distributed. Furthermore, the mean of this sampling distribution is the same as the mean of the sampled population, which is $\mu = 54$ months, according to the manufacturer's claim. Finally, the standard deviation of the sampling distribution is given by

$$\sigma_{\bar{x}} = \frac{\sigma}{\sqrt{n}} = \frac{6}{\sqrt{50}} = 0.85 \text{ month}$$

Figure 7.11 Sampling Distribution of $\bar{x}$ in Example 7.3

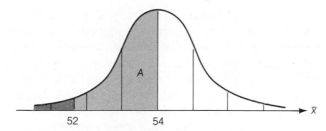

Thus, if we assume the claim is true, the sampling distribution of the mean lifetime of the fifty batteries is approximately normal with mean 54 months and standard deviation 0.85 month. The sampling distribution is shown in Figure 7.11.

b. If the manufacturer's claim is true, the probability that the consumer group observes a mean battery lifetime of 52 months or less for their sample of fifty batteries, $P(\bar{x} \le 52)$, is equivalent to the darker shaded area in Figure 7.11. Since the sampling distribution is approximately normal, we can find this area by computing the z value:

$$z = \frac{\bar{x} - \mu_{\bar{x}}}{\sigma_{\bar{x}}} = \frac{\bar{x} - \mu}{\sigma_{\bar{x}}} = \frac{52 - 54}{.85} = -2.35$$

where $\mu_{\bar{x}}$, the mean of the sampling distribution of $\bar{x}$, is equal to μ, the mean of the sampled population.

The area A shown in Figure 7.11 between $\bar{x} = 52$ and 54 is found in Table IV of Appendix B to be .4906, so the area to the left of 52 is

$$P(\bar{x} \le 52) = .5 - A = .5 - .4906 = .0094$$

Thus, the probability that the consumer group will observe a sample mean of 52 or less is only .0094 if the manufacturer's claim is true. If the fifty tested batteries do result in a mean of 52 months or less, the consumer group will have strong evidence that the manufacturer's claim is untrue, because such an event is very unlikely to occur if the claim is true. (This is still another application of the rare event approach to statistical inference.) ∎

In addition to providing a very useful approximation for the sampling distribution of a sample mean, the Central Limit Theorem offers an explanation for the fact that many relative frequency distributions of data are mound-shaped. Many of the macroscopic measurements we take in business research are really means or sums of many microscopic phenomena. For example, a year's sales of a company is the total of the many individual sales the company made during the year. Thus, the year's sales for a sample of similar companies may have a mound-shaped relative frequency distribution. Similarly, the length of time a construction company takes to complete a house might be viewed as the total of the time each of the large number of distinct jobs necessary to build the house takes to complete. The monthly profit of a firm can be viewed as the sum of the profits of all the transactions of the firm for that month. If we adopt viewpoints like these, the Central Limit Theorem offers some explanation for the frequent occurrence of mound-shaped distributions in nature.

Case Study 7.1
Evaluating the
Condition of Rental
Cars

In the winter of 1976, National Car Rental Systems, Inc., commissioned USAC Properties, Inc. [the performance testing/endorsement arm of the United States Automobile Club (USAC)] to conduct a survey of the general condition of the cars rented to the public by Hertz, Avis, National, and Budget Rent-A-Car.* National was interested in comparing the conditions of the cars they rented with those of the other leading car rental companies.

It was decided that teams of USAC officials would evaluate each company's cars on appearance and cleanliness, accessory performance, mechanical functions, and vehicle safety using a demerit point system designed specifically for this survey. Each car would start with a score of 100 points and would lose points for each discrepancy noted by the inspectors.

If all cars in each company's fleet were inspected and graded, one measure of the overall condition of each company's cars would be the mean of all scores received by each company. Such a survey, however, besides being virtually impossible to conduct logistically, would not yield results of sufficient consequence to justify its cost. It was therefore decided that the mean score each company would receive if all its cars were inspected (referred to below as a company's *fleet mean score*) would have to be estimated. Accordingly, ten major airports were randomly chosen, and ten cars from each company were randomly rented for inspection from each airport by USAC officials; i.e., a sample of size $n = 100$ cars from each company's fleet was drawn and inspected. In the analysis of USAC's inspection results, each company's mean score, $\bar{x}$, was used to estimate the company's unknown fleet mean score. (The use of a sample mean to estimate a population mean will be discussed in detail in Chapter 8.) As we have seen in this chapter, $\bar{x}$ is a random variable with a sampling distribution that has a mean equal to the mean of the population from which the sample was drawn. Thus, in the context of this case, the mean of the sampling distribution of $\bar{x}$ is the unknown fleet mean score. Since the sample size used by USAC was 100, the statisticians who evaluated USAC's inspection results were able to invoke the Central Limit Theorem and assume the sampling distribution of $\bar{x}$ to be approximately normally distributed. This assumption enabled comparisons of fleet mean scores for Hertz, Avis, National, and Budget Rent-A-Car to be made using the conventional large-sample testing procedures that will be presented in Chapters 8 and 9.

Case Study 7.2
Reducing
Investment Risk
Through
Diversification

In Case Study 5.2, it was noted that the variance of the monthly rate of return of a security is used by many investors as a measure of the risk or uncertainty involved in investing in the security. In this case study, we demonstrate that an investor can reduce investment risk by investing in more than one security — that is, by *diversifying* investments.

A number of studies by financial analysts have shown that the total risk (total variation) of a stock, as measured by the variance of the stock's rates of return over time, is comprised of two components: *systematic risk* and *unsystematic risk*. Systematic risk (systematic variability) is the portion of total risk caused by factors that simultaneously influence the prices of all stocks. Examples of such factors are changes in federal economic policies and changes in the national political climate. These factors explain why the prices of all stocks tend to move

* Information by personal communication with Rajiv Tandon, Corporate Vice President and General Manager of the Car Rental Division, National Car Rental Systems, Inc., Minneapolis, Minn.

together over time (i.e., generally upward or generally downward). Unsystematic risk (unsystematic variability) is the portion of the total risk of a particular stock due to factors that influence the firm in question but generally do not influence other firms. Examples of such factors are labor strikes, management errors, and lawsuits (Francis, 1980). Although the proportions of systematic and unsystematic risk vary from firm to firm, it has been determined that, for many of the stocks listed on the New York Stock Exchange, systematic risk comprises about 25% and unsystematic risk comprises about 75% of the stock's total risk (Blume, 1971). As is demonstrated in this case study, an investor can use diversification to reduce the unsystematic portion of the total investment risk.

Suppose an investor is considering investing a total of $5,000 in one or more of five different stocks. We will denote the monthly rates of return of these stocks by r_1, r_2, r_3, r_4, and r_5. For simplicity, we will assume these monthly returns are independent and identically distributed random variables with mean $\mu = 10\%$ and standard deviation $\sigma = 4\%$. Suppose the investor has narrowed the choice to two options: (1) invest $5,000 in stock 1 or (2) invest $1,000 in each of the five stocks.

Under the first option, the investor's monthly rate of return is r_1. Under the second option, since equal amounts of money were invested in each stock, the investor's monthly rate of return is $\bar{r} = \sum_{i=1}^{5} r_i/5$. If the first option is chosen, the investor's expected monthly rate of return, $E(r_i)$, is $\mu = 10\%$ and the risk, as measured by the variance of the stock's rate of return, is $\sigma^2 = 16$. If the second option is chosen, the investor's expected monthly rate of return, $E(\bar{r})$, can be shown to be the same as in the first option. However, since the numerator of $\bar{r}$ is the sum of $n = 5$ independent and identically distributed random variables, each with mean μ and variance σ^2, the variance of $\bar{r}$ is $\sigma_{\bar{r}}^2 = \sigma^2/n$. Accordingly, the risk faced by the investor is $\frac{16}{5} = 3.2$ and is lower than under the first option. Thus, the uncertainty faced by the investor is lower if the investor diversifies, rather than putting "all the eggs in one basket." For a more detailed discussion of risk reduction through diversification, see Sharpe (1981) and Elton and Gruber (1981).

7.4 The Relation Between Sample Size and a Sampling Distribution

Suppose you draw two random samples from a population—one sample containing $n = 5$ observations and the second containing $n = 10$—and you want to compute $\bar{x}$ for each sample and use these statistics to estimate the population mean, μ. Intuitively, it would seem that the $\bar{x}$ based on the sample of ten measurements would contain more information about μ than the $\bar{x}$ based on five measurements. (After all, the sample of $n = 10$ may have cost twice as much to collect as the sample containing $n = 5$.) But how is this larger sample size reflected in the sampling distribution of a statistic?

For the statistics you will encounter in this text, the variance of the sampling distribution of a statistic will be inversely proportional to the sample size.* Or, you can say that the standard deviation of the sampling distribution is proportional to $1/\sqrt{n}$. (This relationship can be seen in the standard deviation of a sample mean, $\bar{x}$, that is equal to $\sigma/\sqrt{n}$.) So, to reduce the standard

---

* Note that this is not true of all statistics, but it is true for most.

deviation of the sampling distribution of a statistic by $\frac{1}{2}$, you will need 4 times as many observations in your sample ($1/\sqrt{n} = 1/\sqrt{4} = \frac{1}{2}$). Or to reduce the standard deviation to $\frac{1}{3}$ its original value, you will need 9 times as many observations.

The sampling distributions for the sample mean, $\bar{x}$, based on random samples from a normally distributed population, are shown in Figure 7.12 for $n = 1, 4,$ and 16 observations. The curve for $n = 1$ represents the probability distribution of the population. Those for $n = 4$ and $n = 16$ are sampling distributions of $\bar{x}$. Note how the distributions contract (variation decreases) for $n = 4$ and $n = 16$. The standard deviation of $\bar{x}$ based on $n = 16$ measurements is half the corresponding standard deviation of the distribution based on $n = 4$ measurements.

Figure 7.12 Three Sampling Distributions of $\bar{x}$

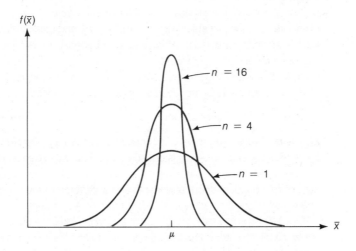

For most sampling distributions, the standard deviation of the distribution decreases as the sample size increases. We will use this result in Chapters 8 and 9 to help us determine the sample size needed to obtain a specified accuracy of estimation.

7.5
The Sampling Distribution of the Difference Between Two Statistics

Often, we will want to compare the proportion of people or objects in one population that possess a particular attribute with the proportion possessing that attribute in another. For example, we might want to compare the proportion of defective glass bottles that emerge from two glass-blowing processes, or we might want to compare the proportion of consumers who prefer product 1 with the proportion who prefer product 2. Or we might want to compare the means of two populations, say, the mean return from one type of investment with the mean return from another. All three of these problems will utilize a comparison of the corresponding sample statistics. For example, to estimate the difference in the means of two populations, we use the difference between the means, $\bar{x}_1$ and $\bar{x}_2$, of independent random samples selected from the two populations. How close will the difference in the sample means, $(\bar{x}_1 - \bar{x}_2)$, lie to the actual difference in the population means? To answer this question, we need to know something about the sampling distribution of the quantity $(\bar{x}_1 - \bar{x}_2)$.

We cannot completely specify the form of the sampling distribution of the difference between two statistics without considering particular cases, but we can say something about the mean, variance, and standard deviation of the sampling distribution.* We will give formulas for these quantities that will always apply and then demonstrate their use with an example.

Suppose you want to estimate the difference between two population parameters, θ_1 and θ_2. You have an unbiased statistic for estimating θ_1 (call it A) and another unbiased statistic for estimating θ_2 (call it B). Then, because these estimates are unbiased, it follows that $E(A) = \theta_1$ and $E(B) = \theta_2$ (i.e., the mean of the sampling distribution of A is θ_1 and the mean of the sampling distribution of B is θ_2). Further, assume that the variance of the sampling distribution of A is σ_A^2 and the variance of B is σ_B^2. Then it can be shown (the proof is omitted here) that the mean and variance of the sampling distribution of $(A - B)$, assuming A and B are independent, are

$$\mu_{(A-B)} = E(A - B) = \theta_1 - \theta_2 \qquad \sigma_{(A-B)}^2 = \sigma_A^2 + \sigma_B^2$$

We will use these results in Chapter 9 in making inferences about the difference between two population parameters.[†]

Example 7.4

Suppose you have two populations with means μ_1 and μ_2 and variances σ_1^2 and σ_2^2, respectively. Independent random samples of n_1 and n_2 observations are selected from the two populations: n_1 from population 1 and n_2 from population 2. The sample means, $\bar{x}_1$ and $\bar{x}_2$, are computed from the samples. Find the expected value and standard deviation of the sampling distribution of the difference between two sample means, $(\bar{x}_1 - \bar{x}_2)$.

Solution

Since we know from Section 7.3 that $E(\bar{x}_1) = \mu_1$ and $E(\bar{x}_2) = \mu_2$, it follows that the mean of the sampling distribution of $(\bar{x}_1 - \bar{x}_2)$ is

$$E(\bar{x}_1 - \bar{x}_2) = E(\bar{x}_1) - E(\bar{x}_2) = \mu_1 - \mu_2$$

The variance of the mean, $\bar{x}$, of a random sample of n observations is equal to the square of its standard deviation; i.e., $(\sigma/\sqrt{n})^2 = \sigma^2/n$ (where σ^2 is the variance of the sampled population). It follows that the variances of the sample means $\bar{x}_1$ and $\bar{x}_2$ are

$$\sigma_{\bar{x}_1}^2 = \frac{\sigma_1^2}{n_1} \qquad \text{and} \qquad \sigma_{\bar{x}_2}^2 = \frac{\sigma_2^2}{n_2}$$

---

* The theory of statistics provides information on the form of the sampling distribution for the following class of statistics: The sums or differences of any number of normally distributed random variables will have a sampling distribution that is normally distributed. The random variables need not be independent of each other.

† Although it is not relevant to our discussion, it also can be shown that the variance of the sum of two independent statistics A and B is $\sigma_{(A+B)}^2 = \sigma_A^2 + \sigma_B^2$.

Figure 7.13   Sampling
Distribution of $(\bar{x}_1 - \bar{x}_2)$

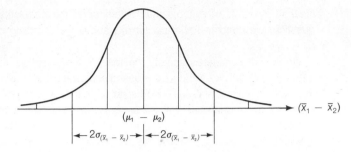

Then, using the formula for the variance of the difference of two independent statistics, we conclude

$$\sigma^2_{(\bar{x}_1 - \bar{x}_2)} = \sigma^2_{\bar{x}_1} + \sigma^2_{\bar{x}_2} = \frac{\sigma^2_1}{n_1} + \frac{\sigma^2_2}{n_2}$$

and the standard deviation of the sampling distribution of $(\bar{x}_1 - \bar{x}_2)$ is

$$\sigma_{(\bar{x}_1 - \bar{x}_2)} = \sqrt{\frac{\sigma^2_1}{n_1} + \frac{\sigma^2_2}{n_2}}$$

It can be shown that the sampling distribution of $(\bar{x}_1 - \bar{x}_2)$ will be approximately normal for sufficiently large values of n_1 and n_2. Therefore, for sufficiently large samples, the sampling distribution of $(\bar{x}_1 - \bar{x}_2)$ will appear as shown in Figure 7.13.   ■

Summary

Many practical business problems require that an inference be made about some population *parameter* (call it θ). If we want to make this inference on the basis of information in a sample, we need to compute a *sample statistic* that contains information about θ. The amount of information a sample statistic contains about θ is reflected by its *sampling distribution,* the probability distribution of the sample statistic. In particular, we want a sample statistic that is an *unbiased* estimator of θ and has a smaller variance than any other unbiased sample statistic.

When the population parameter of interest is the mean, μ, the sample mean, $\bar{x}$, provides an unbiased estimator with a standard deviation of $\sigma/\sqrt{n}$. In addition, the *Central Limit Theorem* assures us that the sampling distribution of the mean of a large sample will be approximately normally distributed, no matter what the shape of the relative frequency distribution of the sampled population.

The amount of information in a sample that is relevant to some population parameter is related to the sample size. For example, the standard deviation of the sampling distribution of the sample mean, $\bar{x}$, will be inversely proportional to the square root of the sample size (i.e., $1/\sqrt{n}$).

The sampling distributions for all the many statistics that can be computed from sample data could be discussed in detail, but this would delay discussion of the practical objective of this course — the role of statistical inference in business decision-making. Consequently, we will comment further on the sampling distributions of particular statistics when we use them as estimators or decision-makers in the following chapters.

Exercises 7.1–7.30

Learning the Mechanics

7.1 In each of the following cases, find the mean and standard deviation of the sampling distribution of the sample mean, $\bar{x}$, for a random sample of size n drawn from a population with mean μ and standard deviation σ:

a. $n = 10$, $\mu = 20$, $\sigma = 3$ **b.** $n = 40$, $\mu = 100$, $\sigma = 10$
c. $n = 12$, $\mu = 25$, $\sigma = 2$ **d.** $n = 100$, $\mu = 400$, $\sigma = 9$

7.2 A sample of $n = 25$ observations is drawn from a mound-shaped population with a mean equal to 15 and a standard deviation equal to 3.

a. Give the mean and standard deviation of the sampling distribution of the sample mean, $\bar{x}$.
b. Give the z-score corresponding to a value of $\bar{x}$ equal to 15.5.
c. Give the z-score corresponding to $\bar{x} = 14$.

7.3 Refer to Exercise 7.2. Find the probability that

a. $\bar{x}$ is larger than 16.   **b.** $\bar{x}$ is less than 16.
c. $\bar{x}$ is larger than 14.2.   **d.** $\bar{x}$ falls between 14 and 16.
e. $\bar{x}$ is less than 14.

7.4 The table contains fifty random samples of random digits, $x = 0, 1, 2, 3, \ldots, 9$, where $p(x) = \frac{1}{10}$. Each sample contains $n = 6$ measurements.

SAMPLE	SAMPLE	SAMPLE	SAMPLE
8,1,8,0,6,6	7,6,7,0,4,3	4,4,5,2,6,6	0,8,4,7,6,9
7,2,1,7,2,9	1,0,5,9,9,6	2,9,3,7,1,3	5,6,9,4,4,2
7,4,5,7,7,1	2,4,4,7,5,6	5,1,9,6,9,2	4,2,3,7,6,3
8,3,6,1,8,1	4,6,6,5,5,6	8,5,1,2,3,4	1,2,0,6,3,3
0,9,8,6,2,9	1,5,0,6,6,5	2,4,5,3,4,8	1,1,9,0,3,2
0,6,8,8,3,5	3,3,0,4,9,6	1,5,6,7,8,2	7,8,9,2,7,0
7,9,5,7,7,9	9,3,0,7,4,1	3,3,8,6,0,1	1,1,5,0,5,1
7,7,6,4,4,7	5,3,6,4,2,0	3,1,4,4,9,0	7,7,8,7,7,6
1,6,5,6,4,2	7,1,5,0,5,8	9,7,7,9,8,1	4,9,3,7,3,9
9,8,6,8,6,0	4,4,6,2,6,2	6,9,2,9,8,7	5,5,1,1,4,0
3,1,6,0,0,9	3,1,8,8,2,1	6,6,8,9,6,0	4,2,5,7,7,9
0,6,8,5,2,8	8,9,0,6,1,7	3,3,4,6,7,0	8,3,0,6,9,7
8,2,4,9,4,6	1,3,7,3,4,3		

a. Use the 300 random digits to construct a relative frequency histogram for the data. This relative frequency distribution should approximate $p(x)$.
b. Use the methods of Section 5.3 to show that $E(x) = \mu = 4.5$.
c. Use the methods of Section 5.3 to show that $\sigma^2 = E[(x - \mu)^2] = 8.25$.
d. Suppose you intend to make an inference about the mean, μ, using the median of a sample of $n = 6$ measurements. To see how well the sample median will estimate μ, calculate the median, m, for each of the fifty samples. Construct a relative frequency histogram for the sample medians to see how close they lie to $\mu = 4.5$. Calculate the mean and standard deviation of the fifty medians.

7.5 Calculate $\bar{x}$ for each of the fifty samples in Exercise 7.4.

a. Construct a relative frequency histogram for the sample means to see how close they lie to $\mu = 4.5$. This will be a rough approximation to the sampling distribution of $\bar{x}$ for $n = 6$ observations.

b. Use the results of parts b and c in Exercise 7.4 to find $\mu_{\bar{x}}$ and $\sigma_{\bar{x}}$. Do these numbers describe the location and spread of your histogram for the fifty sample means?

c. Compare your approximation of the sampling distribution of the sample mean in part a with the sampling distribution of the sample median in part d of Exercise 7.4. Do the sample means or the sample medians appear to fall closer to $\mu = 4.5$? Or is there very little difference for samples of $n = 6$ observations?

7.6 To see the effect of sample size on the standard deviation of the sampling distribution of a statistic, refer to Exercise 7.4 and combine pairs of samples (moving down the columns of the table) to obtain twenty-five samples of $n = 12$ measurements. Calculate the median for each sample.

a. Construct a relative frequency histogram for the twenty-five medians. Compare this with the histogram prepared for Exercise 7.4, part d, which is based on samples of $n = 6$ digits.

b. Calculate the mean and standard deviation of the twenty-five medians. Compare the standard deviation of this sampling distribution with the standard deviation of the sampling distribution in Exercise 7.4, part d. What relationship would you expect to exist between the two standard deviations?

7.7 Refer to Exercise 7.6. Repeat the exercise, but use the means of the samples rather than the medians, and compare the results to those obtained in Exercise 7.5.

7.8 Suppose a sample of $n = 50$ items is drawn from a population of manufactured products and the weight, x, of each item is recorded. Prior experience has shown that the weight has a probability distribution with $\mu = 6$ ounces and $\sigma = 2.5$ ounces. Then $\bar{x}$, the sample mean, will be approximately normally distributed (because of the Central Limit Theorem).

a. Calculate $\mu_{\bar{x}}$ and $\sigma_{\bar{x}}$.

b. What is the probability that the manufacturer's sample has a mean weight of between 5.75 and 6.25 ounces?

c. What is the probability that the manufacturer's sample has a mean weight of less than 5.5 ounces?

d. How would the sampling distribution of $\bar{x}$ change if the sample size, n, were increased from 50 to, say, 100?

7.9 Independent random samples of twenty-five observations each are chosen from two normal populations with the following means and standard deviations:

POPULATION 1	POPULATION 2
$\mu_1 = 12$	$\mu_2 = 10$
$\sigma_1 = 4$	$\sigma_2 = 3$

Let $\bar{x}_1$ and $\bar{x}_2$ denote the two sample means.

a. Give the mean and standard deviation of the sampling distribution of $\bar{x}_1$.
b. Give the mean and standard deviation of the sampling distribution of $\bar{x}_2$.
c. Suppose you were to calculate the difference $(\bar{x}_1 - \bar{x}_2)$ between the sample means. Find the mean and standard deviation of the sampling distribution of $(\bar{x}_1 - \bar{x}_2)$.
d. Will the sampling distribution of $(\bar{x}_1 - \bar{x}_2)$ be a normal distribution? Explain.

7.10 Refer to Exercise 7.9.

a. Give the z-score corresponding to $(\bar{x}_1 - \bar{x}_2) = 1.5$.
b. Find the probability that $(\bar{x}_1 - \bar{x}_2)$ is larger than 1.5.
c. Find the probability that $(\bar{x}_1 - \bar{x}_2)$ is less than 1.5.
d. Find the probability that $(\bar{x}_1 - \bar{x}_2)$ is larger than 1 or less than -1.

7.11 A population consists of four numbers, 1, 2, 2, and 3, marked on poker chips.

a. How many different samples of $n = 2$ chips could be selected (without replacement) from the population? List the possible samples.
b. Give the probability of selecting any one of these samples (assume that the sampling is random).
c. Calculate $\bar{x}$ for each of the samples in part b.
d. Calculate the probability associated with each of the possible values of $\bar{x}$.
e. Graph the population probability distribution and the sampling distribution of $\bar{x}$ (obtained in part d).

7.12 Suppose x equals the number of heads observed when a single coin is tossed (i.e., $x = 0$ or $x = 1$). The population corresponding to x is the set of 0's and 1's generated when the coin is tossed repeatedly a large number of times. Suppose we select $n = 2$ observations from this population (i.e., we toss the coin twice and observe two values of x).

a. List the three different samples (combinations of 0's and 1's) that could be obtained.
b. Calculate the value of $\bar{x}$ for each of the samples.
c. List the values that $\bar{x}$ can assume, and find the probabilities of observing these values.
d. Construct a graph of the sampling distribution of $\bar{x}$.

7.13 Suppose x equals the number of heads observed when a single coin is tossed (i.e., $x = 0$ or $x = 1$). The population corresponding to x is the set of 0's and 1's generated when the coin is tossed repeatedly a large number of times. Suppose we select $n = 3$ observations from this population (i.e., we toss the coin three times and observe the three values of x).

a. List the four different samples (combinations of 0's and 1's) that could be obtained.
b. Calculate the value of $\bar{x}$ for each of the samples.
c. List the values that $\bar{x}$ can assume, and find the probabilities of observing these values.
d. Construct a graph of the sampling distribution of $\bar{x}$.

7.14 A random sample of size n is to be drawn from a large population with mean 100 and standard deviation 10, and the sample mean, $\bar{x}$, is to be calculated. To see the effect of different sample sizes on the standard deviation of the sampling distribution of $\bar{x}$, plot $\sigma/\sqrt{n}$ against n for $n = 1, 5, 10, 20, 30, 40,$ and 50.

7.15 Refer to Exercise 7.14. If you increase the sample size from $n = 5$ to $n = 25$, does the information in the sample mean, $\bar{x}$, pertinent to μ increase by the same amount as it does for an increase in sample size from $n = 30$ to $n = 50$? How is this answer shown in the graph you constructed for Exercise 7.14?

Applying the Concepts

7.16 Marketing managers face many decision-making situations in which accurate information is needed about future sales; examples include setting quotas for sales representatives and assessing the need for advertising. In retail organizations, the organization's buyers provide marketing managers with information about future sales. Typically, buyers combine historical information on past sales with assessments of future consumer demand to make subjective 6-month forecasts of sales for specific products.

In a recent study, Steven Hartley (1983) conducted an experiment to evaluate the forecasting skills of 140 retail buyers of two large midwestern retail organizations. In one part of the experiment, sixty-one of the buyers were given historical sales data for the previous 30 months and asked to forecast sales 6 months from now. For each buyer, Hartley calculated the difference between the actual number of units sold 6 months later and the buyer's forecast. This difference is sometimes called *forecast error* and is denoted here as x. In order to characterize the accuracy of this group of sixty-one buyers, Hartley calculated $\bar{x}$, the mean forecast error for the sample.

a. Assume the sample of sixty-one buyers was randomly selected from a large population of buyers whose forecast errors have a distribution with mean 10 and standard deviation 16. Describe the sampling distribution of $\bar{x}$.

b. Hartley found $\bar{x} = 13.49$. Given the information in part a about the population of buyers, is this a likely result? Explain.

c. Suppose $\bar{x} = 0$ and $s^2 = 1$. What do these statistics tell you about the accuracy of the forecasts of the sixty-one buyers?

7.17 A local bank reported to the federal government that its 5,246 savings accounts have a mean balance of $1,000 and a standard deviation of $240. Government auditors have asked to randomly sample sixty-four of the bank's accounts in order to assess the reliability of the mean balance reported by the bank. The auditors say they will certify the bank's report only if the sample mean balance is within $60 of the reported mean balance. What is the probability that the auditors will *not* certify the bank's report, even if the mean balance really is $1,000? (Assume the standard deviation reported by the bank is accurate.)

7.18 Suppose a manufacturing process that produces floppy disks for microcomputers can be characterized by the probability distribution in the table.

a. Compute the mean and standard deviation of the number of flaws per disk.

b. Describe the approximate sampling distribution of the mean number of flaws per disk in a random sample of 400 disks selected from the production process.

c. Compute the mean and standard deviation of $\bar{x}$.

d. Find the probability that the mean number of flaws per disk in a random sample of 400 disks is less than .30.

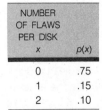

NUMBER OF FLAWS PER DISK	
x	$p(x)$
0	.75
1	.15
2	.10

7.19 The distribution of starting salaries of men who received college degrees last year had a mean equal to $15,000 and a standard deviation equal to $1,200. A random sample of thirty-six starting salaries of women who received college degrees last year had a sample mean equal to $15,600.

a. What is the probability that a random sample of thirty-six starting salaries of men who graduated last year would have a sample mean at least as large as $15,600?

b. Based on your answer to part a, does it appear that the starting salaries of women should be characterized by the same probability distribution that characterizes men's starting salaries? Explain.

7.20 To determine whether a metal lathe that produces machine bearings is properly adjusted, a random sample of thirty-six bearings is collected and the diameter of each is measured. If the standard deviation of the diameter of the machine bearings measured over a long period of time is 0.001 inch, what is the probability that the mean diameter x of the sample will lie within 0.0001 inch of the population mean diameter of the bearings?

7.21 Refer to Exercise 7.20. Suppose the mean diameter of the bearings produced by the machine is supposed to be 0.5 inch. The company decides to use the sample mean (from Exercise 7.20) to decide whether the process is in control — i.e., whether it is producing bearings with a mean diameter of 0.5 inch. The machine will be considered out of control if the mean of the sample of $n = 36$ diameters is less than 0.4994 inch or larger than 0.5006 inch. If the true mean diameter of the bearings produced by the machine is 0.501 inch, what is the probability that the test will fail to imply that the process is out of control?

7.22 Northern States Power (NSP), a private utility in Minnesota, is required by federal and state law to offer in-home energy audits to its customers. The purpose of the law is to encourage households to conserve energy. In early 1981, NSP mailed many of its customers an energy-audit offer, but only 3% of the households responded with an audit request. The State of Minnesota had expected a response rate of 30% – 50%. In an attempt to improve this response rate, Richard Weijo (1983) evaluated alternative means of making NSP customers aware of the audit program and of motivating them to make inexpensive energy-saving changes to their homes.

As part of the study, two independent random samples were selected from among the 9,900 households in St. Paul and its suburbs that were scheduled to receive energy-audit offers by NSP in April 1982. The 280 households in the first sample received an inexpensive waterflow controller along with their energy-audit offer. The 348 households in the second sample received only the energy-audit offer. Each household in both samples was contacted by telephone and questioned about the mailing it had received. Five questions were designed to measure how much the head of a household could recall about the information contained in the energy-audit offer. Each household received a score from 0 to 5, corresponding to the number of questions correctly answered. Let x denote the score received by a household whose mailing contained the waterflow controller and y denote the score received by a household whose mailing consisted only of the energy-audit offer. To compare the effectiveness of the two types of mailings with respect to information recall, Weijo calculated $\bar{x}$ and $\bar{y}$ for the two samples of households.

a. The scores received by the 280 households that were mailed the waterflow controller can be viewed as a sample from the population of scores that would exist if all 9,900 households had been sent the waterflow controller and then been interviewed. Suppose this hypothetical population of scores has standard deviation 1.2. Describe the sampling distribution of $\bar{x}$.

b. Suppose all 9,900 households had received only the energy-audit offer and were later scored with respect to their recall of information about the mailing. Assume the standard deviation of this population of scores is 1.0, and describe the sampling distribution of $\bar{y}$.

c. How large would the sample of households receiving the waterflow controller have to be in order to have $\sigma_{\bar{x}}^2 = \sigma_{\bar{y}}^2$?

7.23 In any production process, some variation in the quality of the product is unavoidable. Variation in product quality can be divided into two categories: variation due to *assignable causes* and *random variation*. The former includes variation due to causes over which the manufacturer has some degree of control, such as variation due to inferior quality raw materials or use of unskilled workers in the production process. The latter is "variation in quality which is the result of many complex causes, the result of each cause being slight; by and large nothing can be done about this source of variation except to modify the process" (Wetherill, 1977).

As part of a company's quality control program, it is a common practice to monitor the variation in the quality characteristics of a product over time. For example, the amount of alkali in soap might be monitored each hour by randomly selecting from the production process and measuring the quantity of alkali in $n = 5$ test specimens of soap. The mean, $\bar{x}$, of the sample alkaline measurements would be plotted against time, as shown on *control chart* (a). If the process is in control, the only source of quality variation is random variation. In that case, $\bar{x}$ should assume a distribution about the process mean, μ, with standard deviation, $\sigma_{\bar{x}}$. Control chart (b) shows a horizontal line to locate the process mean and two lines, called

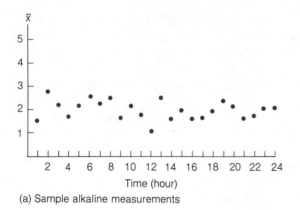

(a) Sample alkaline measurements

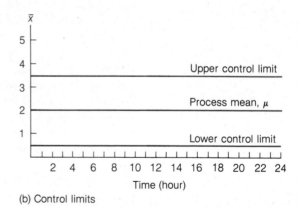

(b) Control limits

control limits, located $3\sigma_{\bar{x}}$ above and below μ. If $\bar{x}$ falls within the control limits, the process is deemed to be in control. If $\bar{x}$ is outside the limits, there is strong evidence that assignable causes of variation are present, and the process is deemed to be out of control. Suppose experience has shown that the percentage of alkali in a test specimen of soap follows approximately a normal distribution with $\mu = 2\%$ and $\sigma = 1\%$.

a. If $n = 5$, how far from μ should the upper and lower control limits be located?

b. If the process is in control, what is the probability that $\bar{x}$ will fall outside the control limits?

7.24 Refer to Exercise 7.23. The soap company has decided to set tighter control limits than the $3\sigma_{\bar{x}}$ limits described in Exercise 7.23. In particular, when the process is in control, the company is willing to risk a .10 probability that $\bar{x}$ falls outside the control limits.

a. The company still wants the control limits to be located at equal distances above and below the process mean and is still planning to use $n = 5$ measurements in each hourly sample. Where should the control limits be located?

b. Suppose the control limits developed in part a are implemented, but unknown to the company, μ is currently 3% (not 2%). What is the probability that $\bar{x}$ will fall outside the control limits if $n = 5$? If $n = 10$?

7.25 Refer to Exercise 7.23. In order to improve the sensitivity of control charts, *warning limits* are sometimes included on the chart along with the control limits. These limits are typically set at $\mu \pm 1.96\,\sigma_{\bar{x}}$. If two successive data points fall outside the warning limits, the process is deemed to be out of control (Wetherill, 1977).

a. If the soap process is in control (i.e., it follows a normal distribution with $\mu = 2\%$ and $\sigma = 1\%$), what is the probability that the next value of $\bar{x}$ will fall outside the warning limits?

b. If the soap process is in control, how many of the next forty values of $\bar{x}$ plotted on the control chart would be expected to fall above the upper warning limit?

c. If the soap process is in control, what is the probability that the next two values of $\bar{x}$ will fall below the lower warning limit?

7.26 A manufacturer of aluminum foil claims that its 75-foot roll has a mean length of 75.05 feet per roll and a standard deviation of 0.12 foot. To check this claim, a consumer group plans to randomly sample thirty-six of the company's 75-foot rolls, measure the length of each, and compute the sample mean length.

a. Assuming the manufacturer's claim is true, describe the sampling distribution of the sample mean.

b. Assuming the manufacturer's claim is true, what is the probability that the sample mean will be less than 75 feet?

c. Suppose the sample mean actually equals 74.97 feet. Can this evidence be used to refute the manufacturer's claim? Explain.

7.27 Suppose you are going to purchase a case of expensive wine. You plan to open two bottles for immediate use, and you will keep the remaining bottles if the two are acceptable. Suppose there are ten bottles in the case, and unknown to you, the condition of the wine in the bottles is as shown below (1 is good, 0 is bad):

BOTTLE	1	2	3	4	5	6	7	8	9	10
CONDITION	1	0	0	1	1	1	1	1	0	1

Since you are interested only in the ten bottles in the case, the collection of ten 0 or 1 responses is the population of interest to you.

a. If you randomly sample two bottles from the case, how many different samples (different pairs of bottles) could you select? List them.

b. Suppose you are going to accept the case only if both bottles in the sample are good. Identify all samples containing two good bottles. What is the probability that you will accept the case? [*Hint:* See the definition of a random sample in Section 4.6.]

c. Let x equal the number of good bottles in the sample of $n = 2$. Construct the sampling distribution of x.

7.28 In purchasing supplies for your manufacturing process, you can purchase a particular part from one of two suppliers, A or B. The parts are in short supply, but you think you can buy 20,000–25,000 from A and 40,000–50,000 from B. Given this information, within what range would you expect the total number of available parts to fall? [*Hint:* To solve this practical problem, you have to make some assumptions about the probability distributions of x_A and x_B, the numbers of parts you will be able to purchase from suppliers A and B. Suppose you interpret the statement that "you can buy 20,000–25,000 from A" to mean that the probability distribution of x_A appears as shown in Figure (a).

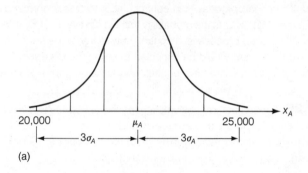

(a)

That is, assume μ_A falls in the middle of the interval $20,000 \le x_A \le 25,000$ and the interval spans $6\sigma_A$, where σ_A is the standard deviation of the probability distribution of x_A. Then $6\sigma_A = 5,000$ and $\sigma_A = 833.3$. Now, find σ_B, μ_A, μ_B, and the interval shown in Figure (b).

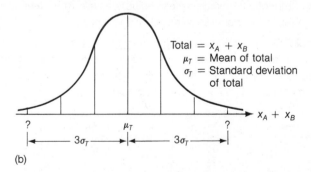

(b)

7.29 A building contractor has decided to purchase a load of factory-reject aluminum siding if the average number of flaws per piece of siding in a sample of size thirty-five from the factory's reject pile is 2.1 or less. Suppose the number of flaws per piece of siding in the factory's reject pile has a Poisson probability distribution with a mean of 2.5. Find the probability that the contractor will not purchase a load of siding. [*Hint:* If x is a Poisson random variable with mean λ, then the variance of the random variable x is also equal to λ.]

7.30 The distribution of the number of loaves of bread sold per day by a large bakery over the past 5 years has a mean of 250 and a standard deviation of 45 loaves.

a. Describe the sampling distribution of the total number of loaves of bread sold in 30 randomly selected days. [*Hint:* See the footnote in Section 7.3 that gives the application of the Central Limit Theorem to the sum of the measurements in a sample.]

b. What is the approximate probability that the total number of loaves sold in 30 randomly selected days is between 7,000 and 8,000?

c. What is the approximate probability that the total number of loaves sold in 30 randomly selected days is greater than 8,100 loaves?

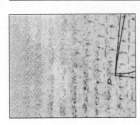

On Your Own . . .

To better understand the Central Limit Theorem and the notion of a sampling distribution, consider the following experiment: Toss four identical coins and record the number of heads observed. Repeat this experiment four more times, so that you generate a total of five observations for the random variable x, the number of heads when four coins are tossed.

Now, derive and graph the probability distribution for x, assuming the coins are balanced. Note that the mean of this distribution is $\mu = 2$ and the standard deviation is $\sigma = 1$. This probability distribution represents the one from which you are drawing a random sample of five measurements.

Next, calculate the mean, $\bar{x}$, of the five measurements; i.e., calculate the mean number of heads you observed in five repetitions of the experiment. Although you have repeated the basic experiment five times, you have only one observed value of $\bar{x}$. To derive the probability distribution or sampling distribution of $\bar{x}$ empirically, you have to repeat the entire process (of tossing four coins five times) many times. Do it 100 times.

The approximate sampling distribution of $\bar{x}$ can be derived theoretically by making use of the Central Limit Theorem. We expect at least an approximate normal probability distribution, with mean $\mu = 2$ and standard deviation

$$\sigma_{\bar{x}} = \frac{\sigma}{\sqrt{n}} = \frac{1}{\sqrt{5}} = .45$$

Count the number of your 100 values of $\bar{x}$ that fall in each of the following intervals:

Interval	Interval	Interval	Interval	Interval	Interval
←——— 1 ———→	←——— 2 ———→	←——— 3 ———→	←——— 4 ———→	←——— 5 ———→	←——— 6 ———→

$$\begin{array}{ccccc} 1.10 & 1.55 & 2 & 2.45 & 2.90 \\ \mu - 2\sigma_{\bar{x}} & \mu - \sigma_{\bar{x}} & \mu & \mu + \sigma_{\bar{x}} & \mu + 2\sigma_{\bar{x}} \end{array}$$

Use the normal probability distribution with $\mu = 2$ and $\sigma_{\bar{x}} = .45$ to calculate the expected number of the 100 values of $\bar{x}$ in each of the intervals. How closely does the theory describe your experimental results?

References

Blume, M. "On the assessment of risk." *Journal of Finance,* Mar. 1971, *26,* 1–10.

Elton, E. J., & Gruber, M. J. *Modern portfolio theory and investment analysis.* New York: Wiley, 1981.

Francis, J. C. *Investments: Analysis and management.* 3d ed. New York: McGraw-Hill, 1980. Chapter 14.

Hartley, S. W. *Judgmental sales forecasting: An experimental investigation of task structure and environmental complexity.* Unpublished Ph.D. dissertation, University of Minnesota, 1983.

Hogg, R. V., & Craig, A. T. *Introduction to mathematical statistics.* 4th ed. New York: Macmillan, 1978. Chapter 4.

Lindgren, B. W. *Statistical theory.* 3d ed. New York: Macmillan, 1976. Chapter 2.

Neter, J., Wasserman, W., & Whitmore, G. A. *Applied statistics.* 2d ed. Boston: Allyn & Bacon, 1983. Chapters 8 and 9.

Sharpe, W. F. *Investments.* 2d ed. Englewood Cliffs, N.J.: Prentice-Hall, 1981. Chapter 5.

Weijo, R. O. *Evaluating information, incentive, and door-to-door interventions for the MECS energy audit program: A theoretical application of the Petty and Cacippo elaboration likelihood model.* Unpublished Ph.D. dissertation, University of Minnesota, 1983.

Wetherill, G. B. *Sampling inspection and quality control.* 2d ed. New York: Chapman and Hall, 1977. Chapter 3.

Winkler, R. L., & Hays, W. *Statistics: Probability, inference, and decision.* 2d ed. New York: Holt, Rinehart and Winston, 1975. Chapter 5.

CHAPTER 8

Estimation and a Test of an Hypothesis: Single Sample

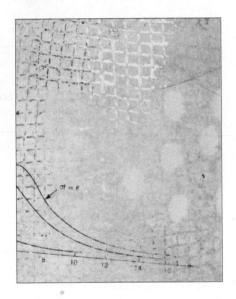

Where We've Been . . .

In the preceding chapters we learned that populations are characterized by numerical descriptive measures (called *parameters*), and that decisions about their values are based on sample statistics computed from sample data. Since statistics vary in a random manner from sample to sample, inferences based on them will be subject to uncertainty. This property is reflected in the sampling (probability) distribution of a statistic.

Where We're Going . . .

This chapter puts all the preceding material into practice; that is, we will estimate or make decisions about population means or proportions based on a single sample selected from a population. Most important, we will use the sampling distribution of a sample statistic to assess the uncertainty associated with an inference.

Contents

The estimation of the mean gas mileage for a new car model, the test of a claim that a certain brand of television tube has a mean life of 5 years, and the estimation of the mean yearly sales for companies in the steel industry are business problems with a common element. In each case, we are interested in making an inference about the mean of a population. This important problem constitutes the primary topic of this chapter.

We will concentrate on two types of inferences about a population parameter: *estimation of the parameter* and *tests of hypotheses, or claims, about the parameter.* You will see that different techniques are used for making inferences, depending on whether a sample contains a large or small number of measurements. Regardless, our objectives remain the same. We want to make the best use of the information in the sample to make an inference and to assess its reliability.

In Sections 8.1, 8.2, and 8.3 we consider large-sample methods for estimation and tests of hypotheses about population means. The small-sample analogs of these two topics are covered in Section 8.4. We consider large-sample inferences about a binomial proportion in Section 8.5. Finally, we show in Section 8.6 how to compute the sample size required to estimate a population parameter with a specified degree of reliability.

8.1 Large-Sample Estimation of a Population Mean

Suppose a large credit corporation wants to estimate the average amount of money owed by its delinquent debtors; i.e., debtors who are more than 2 months behind in payment. To accomplish this objective, the company plans to sample 100 of its delinquent accounts and to use the sample mean, $\bar{x}$, of the amounts overdue to estimate μ, the mean for *all* delinquent accounts. Further, it plans to use the sampling distribution of the sample mean to assess the accuracy of the estimate. How will this be accomplished?

Recall that for sufficiently large samples the sampling distribution of the sample mean is approximately normal, as shown in Figure 8.1. Now, suppose you plan to take a sample of $n = 100$ measurements and calculate the following interval:

$$\bar{x} \pm 2\sigma_{\bar{x}} = \bar{x} \pm \frac{2\sigma}{\sqrt{n}}$$

Figure 8.1 Sampling Distribution of $\bar{x}$

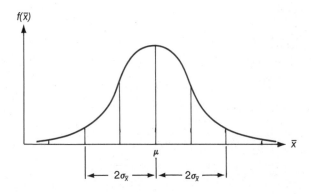

That is, you will form an interval 2 standard deviations around the sample mean. What is the chance, before we have drawn the sample, that this interval will enclose μ, the population mean?

To answer this question, refer to Figure 8.1. If the 100 measurements yield a value of $\bar{x}$ that falls between the two lines shown in color, i.e., within 2 standard deviations of μ, then the interval $\bar{x} \pm 2\sigma_{\bar{x}}$ will contain μ. If $\bar{x}$ falls outside either of these boundaries, then the interval $\bar{x} \pm 2\sigma_{\bar{x}}$ will not contain μ. Since the area under the normal curve (the sampling distribution of $\bar{x}$) between these boundaries is approximately .95 (more precisely, from Table IV of Appendix B, the area is .9544), we know that the interval $\bar{x} \pm 2\sigma_{\bar{x}}$ will contain μ with a probability approximately equal to .95.

To illustrate, suppose that the sum and the sum of squared deviations for the sample of debits of 100 delinquent accounts are

$$\sum_{i=1}^{n} x_i = \$23,300 \qquad \sum_{i=1}^{n} (x_i - \bar{x})^2 = 801,900$$

First calculate the sample statistics:

$$\bar{x} = \frac{\sum_{i=1}^{100} x_i}{n} = \frac{23,300}{100} = \$233 \qquad s = \sqrt{\frac{\sum_{i=1}^{100} (x_i - \bar{x})^2}{n-1}} = \sqrt{\frac{801,900}{99}} = \$90$$

Then, to form the interval of 2 standard deviations around $\bar{x}$, we calculate

$$\bar{x} \pm 2\sigma_{\bar{x}} = 233 \pm 2 \left(\frac{\sigma}{\sqrt{100}} \right)$$

But now we face a problem. You can see that without knowing the standard deviation, σ, of the original population—i.e., the standard deviation of the amounts of *all* delinquent accounts—we cannot calculate this interval. However, since we have a large sample ($n = 100$ measurements), we can approximate the interval by using the sample standard deviation, s, to approximate σ. Thus,

$$\bar{x} \pm 2 \left(\frac{\sigma}{\sqrt{100}} \right) \approx \bar{x} \pm 2 \left(\frac{s}{\sqrt{100}} \right)$$

$$= 233 \pm 2 \left(\frac{90}{10} \right) = 233 \pm 18$$

That is, we estimate the mean amount of delinquency for all accounts to fall within the interval ($215, $251).

Can we be sure that μ, the true mean amount due, is within the interval ($215, $251)? We cannot be certain, but we can be reasonably confident that it is. This confidence is derived from the knowledge that if we were to repeatedly draw samples of 100 accounts from this group of delinquent accounts and form an interval of 2 standard deviations around $\bar{x}$ each time, approximately 95% of the intervals would contain μ. We have no way of knowing (without looking at all the delinquent accounts) whether our sample interval is one of the 95% that contain μ or one of the 5% that do not, so we simply state that we are 95% confident our interval ($215, $251) contains μ. Thus, we have given an interval estimate of the mean delinquency per account and a measure of the reliability of the estimate.

The formula that tells us how to calculate an interval estimate based on sample data is called an *interval estimator.* The probability, .95, that measures the confidence that we can place in the interval estimate is called a *confidence coefficient.* The percentage, 95%, is called the *confidence level* for the interval estimate.

Definition 8.1

An *interval estimator* is a formula that tells us how to use sample data to calculate an interval that estimates a population parameter.

Definition 8.2

The *confidence coefficient* is the probability that an interval estimator encloses the population parameter if the estimator is used repeatedly a very large number of times. The *confidence level* is the confidence coefficient expressed as a percentage.

The foregoing is an example of how an interval can be used to estimate a population parameter. This is a common statistical practice because, when we use an interval estimator, we can usually assess the level of confidence we have that the interval actually contains the true value of the parameter. Figure 8.2 shows what happens when a number of samples are drawn from a population and a confidence interval for a parameter, say θ, is calculated from each. The location of θ is indicated by the vertical line in the figure. Ten confidence intervals, one based on each of ten samples, are shown as horizontal line segments. Note that the confidence intervals move from sample to sample — sometimes containing θ and other times missing θ. If our confidence level is 95%, then in the long-run, 95% of our sample confidence intervals will contain θ.

Suppose you wish to choose a *confidence coefficient* other than .95. Notice that in Figure 8.1 the confidence coefficient .95 is equal to the total area under the sampling distribution, less .05 of the area; this .05 is divided equally between the two tails. Using this idea, we can construct a confidence interval with any desired confidence coefficient by increasing or decreasing the area (call it α) assigned to the tails of the sampling distribution (see Figure

Figure 8.2   Interval Estimators for θ: Ten Samples

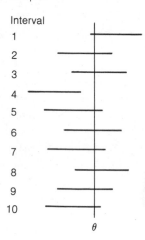

Figure 8.3   Locating $z_{\alpha/2}$ on the Standard Normal Curve

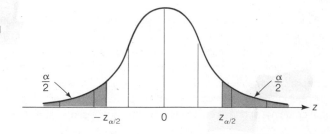

8.3). For example, if we place $\alpha/2$ in each tail and if $z_{\alpha/2}$ is the z value such that the area $\alpha/2$ will lie to its right, then the confidence interval with confidence coefficient $(1 - \alpha)$ is

$$\bar{x} \pm z_{\alpha/2}\sigma_{\bar{x}}$$

Large-Sample $100(1 - \alpha)$% Confidence Interval for μ

$$\bar{x} \pm z_{\alpha/2}\sigma_{\bar{x}} \qquad \sigma_{\bar{x}} = \sigma/\sqrt{n} \approx s/\sqrt{n} \quad \text{if } n > 30$$

where $z_{\alpha/2}$ is the z value with an area $\alpha/2$ to its right (see Figure 8.3) and $\sigma_{\bar{x}} = \sigma/\sqrt{n}$. The parameter σ is the standard deviation of the sampled population and n is the sample size. When σ is unknown and n is large (say $n \geq 30$), the value of σ can be approximated by the sample standard deviation, s.

To illustrate, for a confidence coefficient of .90, $(1 - \alpha) = .90$, $\alpha = .10$, $\alpha/2 = .05$, and $z_{.05}$ is the z value that locates .05 in one tail of the sampling distribution. Recall that Table IV of Appendix B gives the areas between the mean and a specified z value. Since the total area to the right of the mean is .50, $z_{.05}$ will be the z value corresponding to the tabulated area to the right of the mean equal to .450. This z value is $z_{.05} = 1.645$. Confidence coefficients used in practice (in reports and published articles) usually range from .90 to .99. The most common confidence coefficients with corresponding values of α and $z_{\alpha/2}$ are shown in Table 8.1.

Table 8.1

Commonly Used Values of $z_{\alpha/2}$

CONFIDENCE LEVEL $100(1 - \alpha)$	α	$\alpha/2$	$z_{\alpha/2}$	z_α
90%	.10	.05	1.645	1.281
95%	.05	.025	1.96	1.645
99%	.01	.005	2.575	2.327

2 TAILED TEST $\alpha/2$ & $z_{\alpha/2}$ 1 TAILED TEST

Example 8.1

Unoccupied seats on flights cause the airlines to lose revenue. Suppose a large airline wants to estimate its average number of unoccupied seats per flight over the past year. To accomplish this, the records of 225 flights are randomly selected from the files, and the number of unoccupied seats is noted for each of the sampled flights. The sample mean and standard deviation are

$$\bar{x} = 11.6 \text{ seats} \qquad s = 4.1 \text{ seats}$$

Estimate μ, the mean number of unoccupied seats per flight during the past year, using a 90% confidence interval.

Solution

The general form of the large-sample 90% confidence interval for a population mean is

$$\bar{x} \pm z_{\alpha/2}\sigma_{\bar{x}} = \bar{x} \pm z_{.05}\sigma_{\bar{x}}$$

$$= \bar{x} \pm 1.645 \left(\frac{\sigma}{\sqrt{n}} \right)$$

For the 225 records sampled, we have

$$11.6 \pm 1.645 \left(\frac{\sigma}{\sqrt{225}} \right)$$

Since we do not know the value of σ (the standard deviation of the number of unoccupied seats per flight for all flights of the year), we use our best approximation, the sample standard deviation, s. Then the 90% confidence interval is, approximately,

$$11.6 \pm 1.645 \left(\frac{4.1}{\sqrt{225}} \right) = 11.6 \pm 0.45$$

or, from 11.15 to 12.05. That is, the airline can be 90% confident that the mean number of unoccupied seats per flight was between 11.15 and 12.05 during the sampled year. ∎

Case Study 8.1

Dancing to the
Customer's Tune:
The Need to Assess
Customer
Preferences

The following quotations have been extracted from the Dec. 13, 1976, issue of *Business Week:*

"We're dancing to the tune of the customer as never before," says J. Janvier Wetzel, vice-president for sales promotion at Los Angeles–based Broadway Department Stores. "With population growth down to a trickle compared with its previous level, we're no longer spoiled with instant success every time we open a new store. Traditional department stores are locked in the biggest competitive battle in their history."

The nation's retailers are becoming uncomfortably aware that today's operating environment is vastly different from that of the 1960s. Population growth is slowing, a growing singles market is emerging, family formations are coming at later ages, and more women are embarking on careers. Of the 71 million households in the U.S. today, the dominant consumer buying segment is families headed by persons over 45. But by 1980 this group will have lost its majority status to the 25 to 40 year-old group. Merchants must now reposition their stores to attract these new customers.

To do so retailers are using market research to ferret out new purchasing attitudes and lifestyles and then translating this into customer buying segments. . . . department stores are taking a hard look at some of the basics of their business by . . . spending heavily for far more elaborate market research. Data on demographics, psychographics (measurement of attitudes), and lifestyles are being fed into retailers' computers so they can make marketing decisions based on actual spending patterns and estimate their inventory needs with less risk.

In order to stock their various departments with the type and style of goods that appeal to their potential group of customers, a downtown department store should be interested in estimating the average age of downtown shoppers, not shoppers in general. Suppose a downtown department store questions forty-nine downtown shoppers concerning their age (the offer of a small gift certificate may help convince shoppers to respond to such questions). The sample mean and standard deviation are found to be 40.1 and 8.6, respectively. The store could then estimate μ, the mean age of all downtown shoppers, with a 95% confidence interval as follows:

$$\bar{x} \pm 1.96 \left(\frac{s}{\sqrt{n}} \right) = 40.1 \pm 1.96 \left(\frac{8.6}{\sqrt{49}} \right)$$

$$= 40.1 \pm 2.4$$

Thus, the department store should gear its sales to the segment of consumers with average age between 37.7 and 42.5.

Exercises
8.1–8.13

Learning the Mechanics

8.1 A random sample of 100 observations from a population produced the following summary statistics:

$$\sum x = 500 \qquad \sum x^2 = 6{,}066$$

a. Find a 95% confidence interval for μ.
b. Interpret the confidence interval you found in part a.

8.2 A random sample of sixty-four observations from a population produced the following summary statistics:

$$\sum x = 200 \qquad \sum x^2 = 639$$

a. Find a 95% confidence interval for μ.
b. Interpret the confidence interval you found in part a.

8.3 A random sample of eighty observations from a normally distributed population produced a sample mean of 14.1 and a standard deviation of 2.6.

a. Find a 95% confidence interval for μ.
b. Find a 99% confidence interval for μ.
c. What happens to the width of a confidence interval as the sample size is held fixed and the value of the confidence coefficient is increased?
d. Would your confidence interval be valid if the distribution of the original population was not normal? Explain.

8.4 Refer to Exercise 8.3. Suppose the sample contained only thirty-two observations.

a. Recompute the 95% confidence interval for μ.
b. What is the effect on the width of a confidence interval of reducing the sample size as the confidence coefficient remains fixed? Of increasing the sample size as the confidence coefficient remains fixed?

8.5 Explain what is meant by the statement "We are 95% confident that our interval estimate contains μ."

8.6 Describe the relationship between the size of the confidence coefficient and the width of the confidence interval.

8.7 Describe the relationship between the sample size and the width of the confidence interval.

Applying the Concepts

8.8 A brief article in the *Wall Street Journal* (Mar. 1, 1984) states that of forty-eight sources surveyed, Prudential Bache Securities gave the lowest estimate (3%) of the rise in the

Consumer Price Index for 1984 and Prudential Insurance (Prudential Bache's owner) gave the highest (5.6%).

a. Find an approximate value for the sample standard deviation of the sample of forty-eight estimates. [*Hint:* Assume that the range is approximately equal to 4s.]

b. Assume that the forty-eight estimates represent a random sample of estimates from a large number of estimate sources. If the mean of the sample was 4.3%, find a 90% confidence interval for the mean estimated increase in the Consumer Price Index for this population of estimates.

8.9 At the end of 1978, 1979, and 1980, the average price of a share of stock traded on the New York Stock Exchange (NYSE) was $29.84, $31.99, and $36.87, respectively (*Statistical Abstract of the United States: 1981,* p. 525). To investigate the average share price at the end of 1982, a random sample of thirty-six NYSE stocks was drawn. Their closing prices on Dec. 31, 1982, are listed in the table.

Consumers Pwr Co	27\frac{5}{8}$	Western Pac Inds Del	55$\frac{5}{8}$
Sealed Air Corp	28$\frac{5}{8}$	Phillips Van Heusen Cp	19$\frac{1}{4}$
City Investing Co	46$\frac{1}{4}$	Handleman Co Del	19
Duquesne Lt Co	15	Dennys Inc	31$\frac{7}{8}$
Onicare Inc.	43$\frac{5}{8}$	House Fabrics Inc	28
Detroit Edison Co	24$\frac{1}{8}$	Commonwealth Edison Co	23$\frac{1}{8}$
Consumers Pwr Co	19$\frac{5}{8}$	Public Svc Co Ind Inc	28
Virginia Elec & Pwr Co	58	White Cons Inds Inc	36
Duke Power Co	21$\frac{5}{8}$	American Nat Res Co	33$\frac{1}{4}$
Fischbach Corp	48$\frac{5}{8}$	Boston Edison Co	26
Union Elec Co	35	Atlantic Met Corp	20$\frac{5}{8}$
L & N Hsg Corp	29$\frac{1}{4}$	Financial Corp Amer	25$\frac{7}{8}$
Barnett Banks Fla Inc	27	Superscope Inc	2$\frac{5}{8}$
Ahmanson H. F. & Co	27$\frac{5}{8}$	Cp Natl Corp	29$\frac{7}{8}$
Reynolds R. J. Inds Inc	51	Gleason Wks	10$\frac{1}{4}$
Woolworth F. W. Co	36	Great Lakes Intl Inc	23$\frac{5}{8}$
Penna Pwr & Lt	21	Evans Prods Co	8$\frac{3}{8}$
Honda Motor Ltd	43	Middle South Utils Inc	14$\frac{7}{8}$

a. Using an 80% confidence interval, estimate the average price of a share of stock at the end of 1982.

b. Use the latest edition of the *Statistical Abstract of the United States* to determine the actual average price of a stock on the NYSE at the end of 1982. Is this figure in agreement with your confidence interval? Explain. If not, provide a possible explanation for the disagreement.

8.10 Automotive engineers are continually improving their products. Suppose a new type of brake light has been developed by General Motors. As part of a product safety evaluation program, General Motors' engineers wish to estimate the mean driver response time to the new brake light. (Response time is the length of time from the point that the brake is applied until the driver in the following car takes some corrective action.) Fifty drivers are selected at random and the response time (in seconds) for each driver is recorded, yielding the following results: $\bar{x} = .72$, $s^2 = .0936$. Estimate the mean driver response time to the new brake light using a 99% confidence interval.

8.11 A new process that has recently been developed can transform ordinary iron into a kind of super-iron called metallic glass ("One Answer to Imports," 1981). Metallic glass is three to four times as strong as the toughest steel alloys and up to 100 times as resistant to corrosion as the best stainless steel. One of the problems with metallic glass, however, is its tendency to become brittle at very high temperatures. In order to estimate the mean temperature, μ, at which a particular type of metallic glass becomes brittle, thirty-six pieces of the metallic glass were randomly sampled from a recent production run. Each piece was independently subjected to higher and higher temperatures until it became brittle. The temperature at which brittleness was first noticed was recorded for each piece in the sample. The following results were obtained: $\bar{x} = 480°F$, $s = 11°F$. Use a 90% confidence interval to estimate μ. Interpret your confidence interval.

8.12 As an aid in the establishment of personnel requirements, the director of a hospital wishes to estimate the mean number of people who are admitted to the emergency room during a 24-hour period. The director randomly selects sixty-four different 24-hour periods and determines the number of admissions for each. For this sample, $\bar{x} = 19.8$ and $s = 5$. Estimate the mean number of admissions per 24-hour period with a 95% confidence interval. Interpret the result.

RANK	NUMBER OF SURVEY RESPONDENTS
1	24
2	101
3	430
4	355

8.13 [*Note:* This exercise requires the use of methods discussed in optional Section 3.8.] In an article in the *Harvard Business Review,* Rosen, Rynes, and Mahoney (1983) reported the results of a survey conducted to gather the views of managers on issues relating to the salary gap between males and females. A sample of 910 *Harvard Business Review* subscribers was polled. Eighty-three percent of the women surveyed believed that, among the factors that contribute to the salary gap, discrimination in setting wage rates (men earn more than women in similar jobs) was a very important factor. Only 40% of the men surveyed thought this was a very important factor. Concerning their power to influence compensation policy, the respondents were asked to rank each of the following groups from 1 to 4, with 1 indicating the group with the most clout: the federal government, organized labor, personnel administrators, and women's political groups. Suppose the rankings given in the table were obtained for women's political groups. The actual average (mean) rank for women's political groups obtained by the survey was 3.2, which is approximately the same as the average rank of the hypothetical data given in the table.

a. Use a 90% confidence interval to estimate the average rank for women's political groups that would be obtained if all *Harvard Business Review* subscribers responded to the survey questionnaire.

b. What assumptions had to be made when constructing the confidence interval?

c. In the context of this problem, carefully explain what it means to be 90% confident that your confidence interval includes the population mean.

8.2 Large-Sample Test of an Hypothesis about a Population Mean

Suppose building specifications in a certain city require that the average breaking strength of residential sewer pipe be more than 2,400 pounds per foot of length (that is, per lineal foot). Each manufacturer who wants to sell pipe in this city must demonstrate that its product meets the specification. Note that we are again interested in making an inference about the mean, μ, of a population. However, in this example, we are less interested in estimating the value of μ than we are in testing an *hypothesis* about its value. That is, we want to decide whether the mean breaking strength of the pipe exceeds 2,400 pounds per lineal foot.

The method used to reach a decision is based on the rare event concept explained in earlier chapters. We define two hypotheses, one the direct opposite of the other, and hope to show that one of the hypotheses, the one we wish to support, is true by showing that the sample data disagree with its direct opposite. The research hypothesis that the manufacturer wishes to establish ($\mu > 2,400$ pounds) is called in statistics the ***alternative hypothesis*** and is denoted by the symbol H_a. The direct opposite of the alternative hypothesis (that $\mu = 2,400$ pounds or less) is called the *null hypothesis* and is denoted by the symbol H_0. Consequently, the objective is to gain support for the alternative (research) hypothesis by showing that the sample data disagree with the null hypothesis; that is, we want to show that the observed sample could occur with only a very small probability (thus indicating a rare event) if, in fact, the null hypothesis is true. The null and alternative hypotheses chosen by the manufacturer are summarized as follows:

Null hypothesis (H_0): $\mu = 2,400$ (i.e., the manufacturer's pipe does not meet specifications)

Alternative (research) hypothesis (H_a): $\mu > 2,400$ (i.e., the manufacturer's pipe does meet specifications)

Next, we need a procedure for using the information in the sample to decide which hypothesis is true. Since we are testing hypotheses about a population mean, μ, it is reasonable to use the sample mean, $\bar{x}$, to decide between the two hypotheses. Specifically, we will reject the null hypothesis, H_0, in favor of the alternative hypothesis, H_a, when the sample mean, $\bar{x}$, strongly indicates that μ exceeds 2,400 pounds per lineal foot.

We would find it very difficult to believe that $\mu = 2,400$ pounds if, in fact, $\bar{x}$ is very large— i.e., much larger than 2,400. Such a rare event would lead us to reject the null hypothesis, H_0: $\mu = 2,400$, and conclude that the alternative hypothesis, $H_a : \mu > 2,400$, is true. A convenient measure of the distance between $\bar{x}$ and 2,400 is the z-score,

$$z = \frac{\bar{x} - 2,400}{\sigma_{\bar{x}}} = \frac{\bar{x} - 2,400}{\sigma/\sqrt{n}}$$

which expresses the distance in units of $\sigma_{\bar{x}}$. Thus if z were to equal 2, it would mean that $\bar{x}$ lies $2\sigma_{\bar{x}}$ above μ. If $z = -1.5$, it would mean that $\bar{x}$ lies $1.5\sigma_{\bar{x}}$ below μ.

How large a z-score will be required before you decide to reject the null hypothesis? If you examine Figure 8.4, you will note that the chance of observing a value of $\bar{x}$ more than 1.645 standard deviations above 2,400 is only .05, if in fact the true mean μ is 2,400. Thus, if the sample mean is more than 1.645 standard deviations above 2,400, either H_0 is true and a

Figure 8.4 The Sampling Distribution of $\bar{x}$, Assuming $\mu = 2,400$

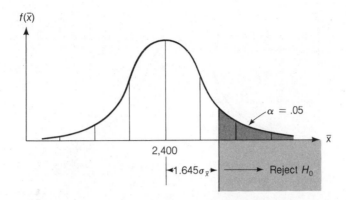

relatively rare event has occurred (probability .05 or less) or H_a is true and the population mean exceeds 2,400. Since we would most likely reject the notion that a rare event has occurred, we would reject the null hypothesis ($\mu = 2,400$) and conclude that the alternative hypothesis ($\mu > 2,400$) is true. What is the probability that this procedure will lead us to a wrong decision?

Deciding that the alternative hypothesis is true if it is false is called a *Type I error.* As indicated in Figure 8.4, the probability of making a Type I error—that is, deciding in favor of the alternative hypothesis if in fact the null hypothesis is true—is only $\alpha = .05$. That is,

$$\alpha = P(\text{Type I error})$$
$$= P(\text{Rejecting the null hypothesis if in fact the null hypothesis is true})$$

In our example,

$$\alpha = P(z > 1.645 \text{ if in fact } \mu = 2,400) = .05$$

Therefore, the test can be summarized as follows:

Null and alternative hypotheses: $H_0: \mu = 2,400$ $H_a: \mu > 2,400$

Test statistic: $z = \dfrac{\bar{x} - 2,400}{\sigma_{\bar{x}}}$

Rejection region: $z > 1.645$ for $\alpha = .05$

To illustrate the use of the test, suppose we tested fifty sections of sewer pipe and found the mean and standard deviation for these fifty measurements of breaking strength to be

$\bar{x} = 2,460$ pounds per lineal foot $s = 200$ pounds per lineal foot

As in the case of estimation, we can use s to approximate σ when s is calculated from a large set of sample measurements.

The test statistic is

$$z = \frac{\bar{x} - 2,400}{\sigma_{\bar{x}}} = \frac{\bar{x} - 2,400}{\sigma/\sqrt{n}} \approx \frac{\bar{x} - 2,400}{s/\sqrt{n}}$$

Figure 8.5 Location of the Test Statistic for a Test of the Hypothesis H_0: $\mu = 2,400$

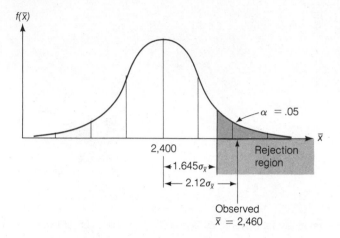

Substituting $\bar{x} = 2,460$, $n = 50$, and $s = 200$, we have

$$z \approx \frac{2,460 - 2,400}{200/\sqrt{50}} = \frac{60}{28.28} = 2.12$$

Therefore, the sample mean lies $2.12\sigma_{\bar{x}}$ above the hypothesized value of μ, 2,400, as shown in Figure 8.5. Since this value of z exceeds 1.645, it falls in the rejection region. That is, we reject the null hypothesis that $\mu = 2,400$ and accept the alternative hypothesis, $\mu > 2,400$. Thus, it appears that the company's pipe has a mean strength that exceeds 2,400 pounds per lineal foot.

How much faith can be placed in this conclusion? What is the probability that our statistical test could lead us to reject the null hypothesis (and conclude that the company's pipe met the city's specifications) if in fact the null hypothesis was true? The answer is "$\alpha = .05$." That is, we selected the level of risk, α, of making a Type I error when we constructed the test. Thus, the chance is only 1 in 20 that our test could lead us to conclude the manufacturer's pipe satisfied the city's specifications if in fact this conclusion was false.

Now suppose the sample data had not indicated that the sewer pipe met the city's specifications; i.e., what would we have concluded if $z \leq 1.645$? We would have stated that the evidence in the sample was not sufficient to support the alternative hypothesis at the $\alpha = .05$ *level of significance.* Note that we carefully avoid stating that the null hypothesis is true, for then we would be risking a second type of error—concluding the null hypothesis is true (the pipe fails to meet specifications) if in fact the alternative hypothesis is true (the pipe does meet specifications). We call this a *Type II error.* The probability of committing a Type II error is usually denoted by the symbol β (beta).

For example, if μ is really equal to 2,475 pounds per lineal foot instead of the hypothesized 2,400 pounds, the sample mean, $\bar{x}$, would fall in the nonrejection region approximately 16% of the time (see Figure 8.6). Therefore, the probability, β, of failing to reject the null hypothesis, if in fact it is false, is equal to .16. (We will show how this value is obtained in Example 8.3.) The risk of concluding that the pipe does not meet specifications, if it is really 75 pounds stronger

Figure 8.6 The Probability β of Failing to Reject H_0 if μ Really Equals 2,475 Pounds

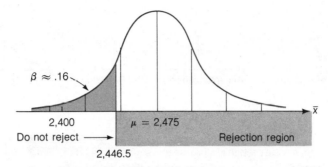

Figure 8.7 Values of β When $\mu = 2,425$, 2,450, and 2,475 Pounds per Lineal Foot

than the minimum 2,400 pounds per lineal foot, is rather large ($\beta = .16$). This risk increases (see Figure 8.7) as the actual value of μ decreases toward the hypothesized value of $\mu = 2,400$. The values of β, corresponding to the shaded areas in Figure 8.7, are given for $\mu = 2,425$, 2,450, and 2,475.

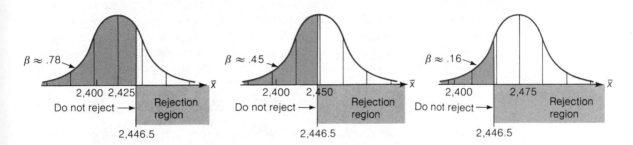

Table 8.2 summarizes the four possible situations that might arise when an hypothesis is tested. The two possible states of nature correspond to the two columns of the table; that is, either H_0 is true or H_a is true. The two rows of the table indicate the two possible decisions that can be reached: that either H_0 is true or H_a is true. The four consequences of the decisions are shown in the body of the table. Regardless of the hypothesis you accept, you are subject to one of two types of risk: the risk of making a Type I error, measured by α, or the risk of making a Type II error, measured by β. Note that a Type I error can be made *only* when the alternative hypothesis is accepted (which occurs when the null hypothesis is rejected) and a Type II error can be made *only* when the null hypothesis is accepted. Not too surprisingly, the measures of these two types of risk, α and β, are related.

Table 8.2

Decisions and Consequences for a Test of an Hypothesis

| | | TRUE STATE OF NATURE | |
		H_0 *true*	H_a *true*
DECISION	H_0 *true*	Correct decision	Type II error (probability β)
	H_a *true*	Type I error (probability α)	Correct decision

You can see in Figure 8.8 on the next page that α is decreased by moving the rejection region farther out into the tail of the sampling distribution. By doing so, the rejection region becomes smaller and the acceptance region becomes larger. What happens to β as the acceptance region becomes larger?

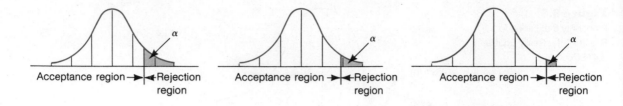

Figure 8.8 Reducing α Reduces the Rejection Region and Enlarges the Acceptance Region

Since β is the probability of accepting H_0 if in fact some alternative value of the parameter is true, β is the probability that the test statistic falls in the acceptance region. And the larger the acceptance region, the larger will be the value of β. So, the relationship between α and β is what you might expect intuitively: As you decrease one type of risk (say, the risk α of falsely accepting H_a), you increase the other (the risk β of falsely accepting H_0). Fortunately, we can reduce both types of risk by increasing the sample size. The more information you have in the sample, the greater will be the ability of the test statistic to reach the correct decision.

In theory, we could consider the probabilities of the two types of risk, α and β, and the possible financial losses attached to the Type I and II errors, and choose the rejection region to minimize the expected loss. In practice, β is difficult to calculate for many tests, and it is impossible to specify a meaningful alternative to the null hypothesis for others. In short, the theory does not always work. So, as an introduction to tests of hypotheses, we suggest the

---

Elements of a Test of an Hypothesis

1. *Null Hypothesis* (H_0): A theory that is phrased in terms of the values of one or more population parameters. The theory is usually one we wish to discredit.

2. *Alternative* (*Research*) *Hypothesis* (H_a): A theory that opposes the null hypothesis and that we wish to establish as true.

3. *Test Statistic:* A sample statistic used to decide whether to reject the null hypothesis.

4. *Rejection Region:* The numerical values of the test statistic for which the null hypothesis will be rejected. The rejection region is chosen so that the probability is α that it will contain the test statistic when the null hypothesis is true (thereby leading to an incorrect conclusion), where α is usually chosen to be small (for example, .01, .05, or .10).

5. *Experiment and Calculation of Test Statistic:* The sampling experiment is performed, and the numerical value of the test statistic is determined.

6. *Conclusion:*

   a. If the numerical value of the test statistic falls in the rejection region, we conclude that the alternative hypothesis is true (i.e., reject the null hypothesis), and we know that the test procedure will lead to this conclusion incorrectly only $100\alpha\%$ of the time it is used.

   b. If the test statistic does not fall in the rejection region, we reserve judgment about which hypothesis is true. We do not accept the null hypothesis because we do not (in general) know the probability β that our test procedure will lead us to falsely accept H_0.

following procedure: Select the null hypothesis as the opposite of the alternative hypothesis (the one you want to support). Then, if you reject the null hypothesis and accept the alternative hypothesis, you will know the probability of having made an incorrect decision. It will be α, and you can choose this value as large or small as you wish prior to the selection of your sample. If the test statistic does not fall in the rejection region, *do not* accept the null hypothesis unless you know β. Withhold judgment and seek a larger sample size to give you more information on which to base a decision. Or, estimate the parameter using a confidence interval. This will give an interval estimate of its true value and a measure of the reliability of your inference.

The elements of a test of an hypothesis are summarized in the previous box.

Example 8.2   Sewer pipe produced by another manufacturer was submitted to the city for testing. A sampling of the strengths of seventy sections of pipe gave

$$\bar{x} = 2,430 \qquad s = 190$$

Do these statistics, calculated from the sample data, present sufficient evidence to indicate that the manufacturer's pipe meets the city's specifications?

Solution   As in our earlier discussion, the elements of the test are

$$H_0: \mu = 2,400 \qquad H_a: \mu > 2,400 \quad \leftarrow \text{WANT TO PROVE } H_a \text{ is TRUE}$$

Test statistic: $z = \dfrac{\bar{x} - 2,400}{\sigma_{\bar{x}}} = \dfrac{\bar{x} - 2,400}{\sigma/\sqrt{n}} \approx \dfrac{\bar{x} - 2,400}{s/\sqrt{n}}$

Rejection region: $z > 1.645$ for $\alpha = .05$

Substituting $\bar{x}$ and s into the formula for the test statistic, we have

$$z \approx \frac{\bar{x} - 2,400}{s/\sqrt{n}} = \frac{2,430 - 2,400}{190/\sqrt{70}} = 1.32$$

In other words, the sample mean of 2,430, although greater than 2,400, is only $1.32\sigma_{\bar{x}}$ above that value (see Figure 8.9). Therefore, the sample does not provide sufficient evidence to conclude that the sewer pipe meets the city's strength specifications.

Figure 8.9 Location of the Test Statistic for Example 8.2

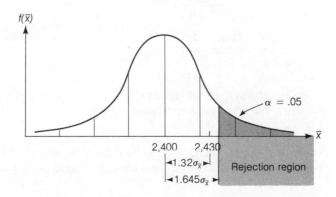

Although the value of the sample mean, $\bar{x}$, could be used as a test statistic to test an hypothesis about a population mean, μ, it is easier to use the z statistic. In fact, for the above examples, we based the decision to either reject or not reject the null hypothesis on the computed value of z. That is, saying you will reject H_0 in Example 8.2 if $\bar{x}$ lies more than $1.645\sigma_{\bar{x}}$ above $\mu = 2,400$ is the same as saying you will reject H_0 if $z > 1.645$.

Example 8.3

Calculate the probability, β, of a Type II error for the test described at the beginning of this section if μ actually equals 2,475 pounds per lineal foot. This is the probability of failing to conclude that the manufacturer's sewer pipe does meet specifications when the mean strength of the pipe exceeds the specified minimum strength by 75 pounds per lineal foot.

Solution

The rejection region for the test is $z > 1.645$ or, equivalently, values of $\bar{x}$ that lie more than $1.645\sigma_{\bar{x}}$ above the hypothesized mean, $\mu = 2,400$. Thus, the rejection region, expressed in terms of $\bar{x}$, is

$$\bar{x} > \mu + 1.645\sigma_{\bar{x}}$$

or

$$\bar{x} > 2,400 + 1.645(28.28)$$

or

$$\bar{x} > 2,446.5$$

This point is shown on the $\bar{x}$-axis in Figure 8.10.

Figure 8.10 Calculating β for Example 8.3 When $\mu = 2,475$

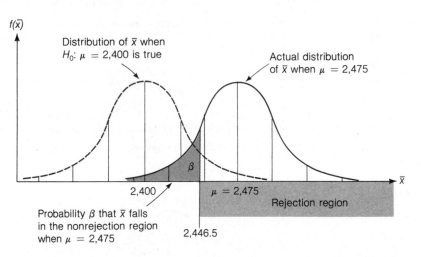

The probability, β, of not rejecting H_0: $\mu = 2,400$ when μ is really equal to 2,475 is the probability that $\bar{x}$ falls in the nonrejection region, i.e.,

$$\bar{x} < 2,446.5$$

This is the shaded area under the normal curve with mean $\mu = 2,475$ in Figure 8.10. To find this area, we need to find the z value corresponding to $\bar{x} = 2,446.5$ for $\mu = 2,475$; i.e.,

$$z = \frac{\bar{x} - \mu}{\sigma_{\bar{x}}} = \frac{2{,}446.5 - 2{,}475}{28.28} = -1.01$$

From Table IV in Appendix B, for $z = -1.01$, the tabulated value is .3438; this is the area between $\bar{x} = 2{,}446.5$ and $\mu = 2{,}475$. The area under the normal curve *below* $\bar{x} = 2{,}446.5$ is β, the probability that $\bar{x}$ will fall in the nonrejection region. Thus,

$$\beta = .5 - .3438 = .1562$$

Therefore, prior to conducting the test, the probability that it will fail to indicate that the manufacturer's pipe strength exceeds 2,400 pounds per lineal foot is approximately .16. ∎

The alternative hypothesis for Example 8.2, namely that $\mu > 2{,}400$ pounds per lineal foot, leads to a ***one-tailed*** (or ***one-sided***) statistical test because we rejected the null hypothesis only for large values of z (values in the upper tail of the z distribution). But some statistical investigations seek to show that μ is *either* larger or smaller than some specified value. This type of alternative (research) hypothesis — for example, $H_a: \mu > 2{,}400$ or $\mu < 2{,}400$ — will be supported for large positive or large negative values of z. Thus, the rejection region will be located in both tails of the z distribution, splitting α between the two tails (see Figure 8.11). Such a statistical test is said to be ***two-sided*** or ***two-tailed***. The value of z, denoted by the symbol $z_{\alpha/2}$, that places half of α in the upper tail of the z distribution, can be obtained from the table of areas under the normal curve (Table IV of Appendix B).

Figure 8.11 Rejection Region for a Two-Tailed Test of the Mean

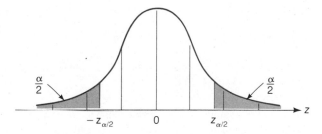

Notice that alternative hypotheses are always expressed as (strict) inequalities; i.e., you are always attempting to show that μ is larger than some value (upper one-tailed test), smaller than some value (lower one-tailed test), or not equal to some value (a two-tailed test). In contrast, the null hypothesis is always expressed as an equality, say $\mu = 2{,}400$, even though the opposite of $\mu > 2{,}400$ is $\mu \leq 2{,}400$. This is because we need to determine from the sampling distribution of $\bar{x}$ those values that contradict the null hypothesis and support the alternative hypothesis, $H_a: \mu > 2{,}400$. Any value of $\bar{x}$ that leads to rejection of $H_0: \mu = 2{,}400$ in favor of $H_a: \mu > 2{,}400$ would certainly also lead to rejection of any hypothesized value of μ less than 2,400. For this reason, the null hypothesis is given as the equality $H_0: \mu = 2{,}400$ rather than the inequality $\mu \leq 2{,}400$.

> ### Steps to Follow in Selecting the Null and Alternative Hypotheses
>
> **1.** Decide on the hypothesis you wish to support. Remember, this will give a range of possible values for the parameter being tested and will be expressed as an inequality in the alternative hypothesis H_a.
>
> Example: $H_a: \mu > 2,400$
>
> **2.** Define the opposite of the alternative hypothesis. This will be the set of all possible values of the parameter that are not contained in H_a.
>
> Example: $\mu \leq 2,400$
>
> For the null hypothesis, H_0, choose the value of the parameter that is nearest in value to those specified in H_a.
>
> Example: Of the values $\mu \leq 2,400$, the one nearest in value to those contained in $H_a: \mu > 2,400$ is $\mu = 2,400$. Thus the null hypothesis is $H_0: \mu = 2,400$.

Example 8.4   A manufacturer of cereal wants to test the hypothesis that a filling machine is set to load boxes with a mean load of $\mu = 12$ ounces per box. If the mean load either exceeds 12 ounces per box or is less than this amount, the manufacturer wants to detect the situation. Suppose that 100 boxes of cereal are filled and weighed and that $\bar{x}$ and s were calculated to be

$\bar{x} = 11.85$ ounces $s = 0.5$ ounce

Test to see whether the data indicate that the mean filling weight, μ, differs from 12 ounces. Use $\alpha = .05$.

Solution   Since we wish to determine whether the mean filling weight *differs* from 12 ounces, we wish to detect $\mu > 12$ or $\mu < 12$ if either of these situations exists. Therefore, we will wish to conduct a two-tailed statistical test. The elements of the test are

$H_0: \mu = 12$

$H_a: \mu \neq 12$ (i.e., $\mu > 12$ or $\mu < 12$)

Test statistic: $z = \dfrac{\bar{x} - 12}{\sigma_{\bar{x}}}$

Rejection region: $z > 1.96$ or $z < -1.96$ (see Figure 8.12)

Note that $z = 1.96$ was chosen for the boundary of the upper rejection region because $P(z > 1.96) = \alpha/2 = .025$. (This value is obtained from Table IV of Appendix B.) We now

Figure 8.12   Two-Tailed Rejection Region: $\alpha = .05$

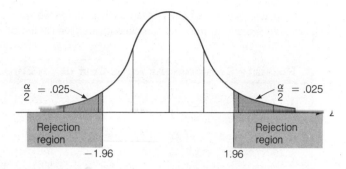

calculate

$$z = \frac{\bar{x} - 12}{\sigma_{\bar{x}}} = \frac{\bar{x} - 12}{\sigma/\sqrt{n}} = \frac{11.85 - 12}{\sigma/\sqrt{100}}$$

$$\approx \frac{11.85 - 12}{s/10} = \frac{-.15}{.5/10} = -3.0$$

You can see in Figure 8.12 that the calculated z value, -3.0, is well into the lower-tail rejection region and there is ample evidence to indicate that the mean filling level, μ, differs from 12 ounces. It appears that, on the average, the machine is under-filling the boxes. How reliable is this conclusion? We know that the test statistic will erroneously reject the null hypothesis only 5% of the time (because $\alpha = .05$). Therefore, we are reasonably confident that this statistical test has led us to a correct conclusion.   ∎

Large-Sample Test of an Hypothesis about μ

One-Tailed Test

$H_0: \mu = \mu_0$*

$H_a: \mu < \mu_0$

(or $H_a: \mu > \mu_0$)

Test statistic: $z = \dfrac{\bar{x} - \mu_0}{\sigma_{\bar{x}}}$

Rejection region: $z < -z_\alpha$

(or $z > z_\alpha$)

where α is chosen so that

$$P(z > z_\alpha) = \alpha$$

Two-Tailed Test

$H_0: \mu = \mu_0$*

$H_a: \mu \neq \mu_0$

Test statistic: $z = \dfrac{\bar{x} - \mu_0}{\sigma_{\bar{x}}}$

Rejection region: $z < -z_{\alpha/2}$

or $z > z_{\alpha/2}$

where $z_{\alpha/2}$ is chosen so that

$$P(z > z_{\alpha/2}) = \alpha/2$$

As we have indicated by the preceding examples, a large-sample statistical test of an hypothesis concerning a population mean can be either one-tailed or two-tailed, depending

* *Note:* μ_0 is the symbol for the numerical value assigned to μ under the null hypothesis.

FOR Z TAILED → CONFIDENCE INTERVAL =

$\bar{X} \pm Z_{\alpha/2} \; \sigma_{\bar{X}}$

WHERE $\sigma_{\bar{X}} = \frac{\sigma}{\sqrt{n}} \approx \frac{s}{\sqrt{n}}$ IF $n > 30$

on the nature of the alternative (research) hypothesis we wish to support. The two possible conclusions resulting from the sample data are given in the box.

Possible Conclusions for a Test of an Hypothesis

1. If the calculated z-score <u>falls in</u> the rejection region, conclude that the alternative hypothesis is true.

2. If the calculated z-score <u>does not fall in</u> the rejection region, state that the data do not provide evidence to support the alternative hypothesis. (The null hypothesis should not be accepted unless the probability β of a Type II error has been calculated. This is not easy to do for most sampling distributions.)

Case Study 8.2

Statistical Quality Control, Part 1

In Exercise 7.23 we described a graphical device, known as a control chart, that can be used in manufacturing operations to monitor the variation over time in the quality of products being produced. Although a relatively recent invention (the control chart was developed by Walter A. Shewhart of Bell Telephone Laboratories in 1924), this device has become a basic tool of quality control engineers and operations managers the world over. Japan's emergence as an industrial superpower is due in part to their early adoption and refinement of quality control techniques, such as the control chart, that were developed in the United States (Duncan, 1974). In this case study and Case Study 8.3 we expand the discussion of control charts and demonstrate that they are simply vehicles for conducting hypothesis tests.

Suppose it is desired to monitor the pitch diameter of the threads on a particular aircraft fitting. When the process is in control, the pitch diameters follow a normal distribution with mean μ_0 and standard deviation σ_0. Recall from Exercise 7.23 that such monitoring can be accomplished by (1) randomly sampling n items from the production process at regular time intervals, (2) measuring the pitch diameter of each item sampled, and (3) plotting the mean diameter of each sample, $\bar{x}$, on a control chart like that in Figure 8.13. Then if a value of $\bar{x}$ falls above the upper control limit or below the lower control limit, there is strong evidence that the

Figure 8.13

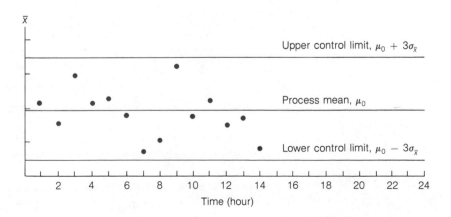

process is out of control — i.e., that the quality of the product being produced does not meet established standards. Otherwise, the process is deemed to be in control.

In the language of hypothesis testing, this decision process can be described as follows:

1. There are two hypotheses of interest:

H_0: Process is in control, $\mu = \mu_0$

H_a: Process is out of control, $\mu \neq \mu_0$

2. The test statistic used to investigate these hypotheses is $\bar{x}$.

3. The upper and lower control limits define the rejection region for the test.

4. Since the control limits are located at $\mu_0 \pm 3\sigma_{\bar{x}}$, the probability of committing a Type I error is $\alpha = .0026$. (Why?)

Thus, each time a quality control engineer plots a sample mean on a control chart and observes where it falls in relation to the control limits, the engineer is conducting a two-tailed hypothesis test.

Exercises 8.14–8.32

Learning the Mechanics

8.14 What is the difference between an alternative hypothesis and a null hypothesis?

8.15 Define each of the following:

a. Type I error   **b.** Type II error   **c.** α **d.** β

8.16 When do you risk making a Type I error? A Type II error?

8.17 In testing an hypothesis, who or what determines the size of the rejection region?

8.18 For each of the following rejection regions, sketch the sampling distribution of z and indicate the location of the rejection region:

a. $z > 1.96$ **b.** $z > 1.645$

c. $z > 2.575$ **d.** $z < -1.29$

e. $z < -1.645$ or $z > 1.645$ **f.** $z < -2.575$ or $z > 2.575$

8.19 If the rejection region is defined as in Exercise 8.18, what is the probability that a Type I error will be made in each case?

8.20 If you test an hypothesis and reject the null hypothesis in favor of your alternative hypothesis, does your test prove that the alternative hypothesis is correct? Explain.

8.21 A random sample of forty-nine observations produced the following sums:

$$\sum x = 20.7 \qquad \sum x^2 = 10.9$$

a. Test the null hypothesis that $\mu = .47$ against the alternative hypothesis that $\mu < .47$. Test using $\alpha = .10$. Interpret the results of the test.

b. Test the null hypothesis that $\mu = .47$ against the alternative hypothesis that $\mu \neq .47$. Test using $\alpha = .10$. Interpret the results.

8.22 Suppose you are interested in conducting the following statistical test:

$$H_0: \mu = 200 \qquad H_a: \mu > 200$$

and you have decided to use the following decision rule: "Reject H_0 if the sample mean of a random sample of 100 items is more than 212." Assume that the standard deviation of the population is 80.

a. Express the decision rule in terms of z.

b. Find α, the probability of making a Type I error, using this decision rule.

8.23 A random sample of sixty observations produced the following sums:

$$\sum x = 27.4 \qquad \sum x^2 = 14.3$$

a. Test the null hypothesis that $\mu = .40$ against the alternative hypothesis that $\mu > .40$. Test using $\alpha = .05$. Interpret the results.

b. Test the null hypothesis that $\mu = .40$ against the alternative hypothesis that $\mu \neq .40$. Test using $\alpha = .05$. Interpret the results.

Applying the Concepts

8.24 Small increases in the mean charge for monthly long-distance telephone calls produce substantial increases in the profits for telephone companies. A telephone company's records indicate that private customers pay an average of $17.10 per month for long-distance telephone calls; the standard deviation of the amounts paid for long-distance calls is $9.80.

a. If a random sample of fifty bills is taken, what is the probability that the sample mean is greater than $20?

b. If a random sample of 100 bills is taken, what is the probability that the sample mean is greater than $20?

c. Suppose a random sample of 100 customers' bills during a given month produced a sample mean of $21.25 expended for long-distance calls. Do these data indicate that the mean level of the amounts billed per month for long-distance telephone calls has increased from $17.10? Test using $\alpha = .05$.

8.25 The Environmental Protection Agency (EPA) estimated that the 1983 G-car obtains a mean of 35 miles per gallon on the highway, and the company that manufactures the car claims that it exceeds the EPA estimate in highway driving. To support its assertion, the company randomly selects thirty-six 1983 G-cars and records the mileage obtained for each car over a driving course similar to that used by the EPA. The following data resulted:

$$\bar{x} = 36.8 \text{ miles per gallon} \qquad s = 6.0 \text{ miles per gallon}$$

a. If the auto manufacturer wishes to show that the mean miles per gallon for 1983 G-cars is greater than 35 miles per gallon, what should it choose for the alternative hypothesis? The null hypothesis?

b. Do the data provide sufficient evidence to support the auto manufacturer's claim? Test using $\alpha = .05$.

8.26 In 1979, basic cable television service cost an average of $7.37 per month in the United States (*Statistical Abstract of the United States: 1981,* p. 565). In March 1983, the Federal Communications Commission (FCC) noted that the cost of basic cable service had risen only about 8% since 1979 and that it cost on average no more than $8.00 per month. Suppose a consumer advocacy group doubts the FCC's claim. In order to investigate the claim, the group randomly samples 33 of the more than 4,000 cable systems in the United States and asks each what its basic service charge was in early 1983. The following results are obtained:

$ 8.53	$8.41	$7.80	$8.20	$8.14	$7.89	$7.92
20.01	8.96	6.50	8.79	7.73	8.15	8.00
7.66	7.76	7.63	8.16	7.50	7.64	6.99
9.83	7.86	7.97	6.96	8.63	7.64	
8.13	8.35	7.83	7.88	7.65	7.75	

a. Specify the null and alternative hypotheses that should be used by the consumer advocacy group in investigating the FCC's claim.
b. With respect to the hypotheses you specified in part a, explain the practical implications of making a Type I error and a Type II error.
c. Conduct the hypothesis test you described in part a, and interpret the test's results in the context of this exercise. Use $\alpha = .10$.

8.27 A pain reliever currently being used in a hospital is known to bring relief to patients in a mean time of 3.5 minutes. To compare a new pain reliever with the one currently being used, the new drug is administered to a random sample of fifty patients. The mean time to relief for the sample of patients is 2.8 minutes, and the standard deviation is 1.1 minutes. Do the data provide sufficient evidence to conclude that the new drug was effective in reducing the mean time until a patient receives relief from pain? Test using $\alpha = .05$.

8.28 A manufacturer of fishing line claims that the mean breaking strength of a competitor's 20-pound line is really less than 20 pounds. A sample of forty pieces of the competitor's 20-pound line has been drawn and each piece tested. The following results were obtained:

$$\bar{x} = 19.6 \text{ pounds} \qquad s = 0.8 \text{ pound}$$

Does the evidence support the manufacturer's claim at $\alpha = .10$?

8.29 Refer to Exercise 8.9.

a. Do the data provide sufficient evidence to conclude that the average price of a share of stock at the end of 1982 is lower than it was in 1980? Test using $\alpha = .05$.
b. Use the latest edition of the *Statistical Abstract of the United States* to determine the actual average price of a stock on the New York Stock Exchange at the end of 1982. Is this figure in agreement with the results of your hypothesis test? Explain. If they are not in agreement, provide a possible explanation for the disagreement.

8.30 A machine is set to produce nails with a mean length of 1 inch. Nails that are too long or too short do not meet the customer's specifications and must be rejected. To avoid producing too many rejects, the nails produced by the machine are sampled from time to time and tested as a check to see whether the machine is still operating properly — i.e., producing nails with a mean length of 1 inch. Suppose fifty nails have been sampled, and $\bar{x} = 1.02$ inches and $s = 0.04$ inch. At $\alpha = .01$, does the sample evidence indicate that the machine is producing nails with a mean not equal to 1 inch; that is, is the production process out of control?

8.31 Refer to Example 8.3. Find the probability, β, of a Type II error when $\mu = 2,425$. Compare your answer with the one given on Figure 8.7.

8.32 Refer to Example 8.3. Find the probability, β, of a Type II error when $\mu = 2,450$. Compare your answer with the one given on Figure 8.7.

8.3
Observed
Significance
Levels:
p-Values

According to the statistical test procedure described in Section 8.2, the value of α and, correspondingly, the rejection region are selected prior to conducting the test, and the conclusion is stated in terms of rejecting or not rejecting the null hypothesis. A second method of presenting the results of a statistical test reports the extent to which the test statistic disagrees with the null hypothesis and leaves to the reader the task of deciding whether to reject the null hypothesis. This measure of disagreement is called the *observed significance level* (or *p-value*) for the test.

Definition 8.3

The *observed significance level,* or *p-value,* for a specific statistical test is the probability (assuming H_0 was true) of observing a value of the test statistic that is at least as contradictory to the null hypothesis, and as supportive of the alternative hypothesis, as the one computed from the sample data.

For example, the value of the test statistic computed for the sample of $n = 50$ sections of sewer pipe was $z = 2.12$. Since the test was one-tailed — i.e., $H_a: \mu > 2,400$ — values of the test statistic even more contradictory to H_0 than the one observed would be values larger than $z = 2.12$. Therefore, the observed significance level (*p*-value) for this test is

$$p = P(z \geq 2.12)$$

or, equivalently, the area under the standard normal curve to the right of $z = 2.12$ (see Figure 8.14).

The area A in Figure 8.14 is given in Table IV of Appendix B as .4830. Therefore, the upper-tail area corresponding to $z = 2.12$ is

$$p\text{-value} = .5 - .4830 = .0170$$

Consequently, we say these test results are highly significant; that is, they disagree rather strongly with the null hypothesis, $H_0: \mu = 2,400$, and favor $H_a: \mu > 2,400$. The probability of observing a z value at least as large as 2.12 is only .0170, if in fact H_0 is true.

Figure 8.14 Finding the *p*-Value for an Upper-Tail Test When $z = 2.12$

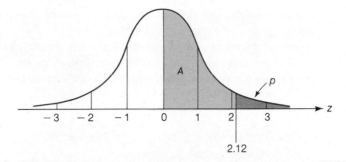

2.12

If you are inclined to select $\alpha = .05$ for this test, then you would reject the null hypothesis because the *p*-value for the test, .0170, is less than .05. In contrast, if you choose $\alpha = .01$, you would not reject the null hypothesis because the *p*-value for the test is larger than .01. Thus, the use of the observed significance level is identical to the test procedure described in the preceding sections except that the choice of α is left to the reader.

Example 8.5 Find the observed significance level for the test of the mean filling weight in Example 8.4.

Solution Example 8.4 presented a two-tailed test of the hypothesis,

$H_0: \mu = 12$ ounces

against the alternative hypothesis,

$H_a: \mu \neq 12$ ounces

The observed value of the test statistic in Example 8.4 was $z = -3.0$, and any value of z less than -3.0 or greater than $+3.0$ (because this is a two-tailed test) would be even more contradictory to H_0. Therefore, the observed significance level for the test is

p-value $= P(z < -3.0 \text{ or } z > +3.0)$

Consulting Table IV in Appendix B, we find that $P(z > 3.0) = .5 - .4987 = .0013$. Therefore, the *p*-value for the test is

$2(.0013) = .0026$

These test results would be called highly significant *in a statistical sense*. Whether the results are highly significant in a *practical* sense depends on how much the actual mean filling weight differs from the desired weight of 12 ounces—i.e., whether the difference is large enough to be significant from an economic point of view. ■

When publishing the results of a statistical test of hypothesis in journals, case studies, reports, etc., many researchers make use of *p*-values. Instead of selecting α a priori and then conducting a test as outlined in this chapter, the researcher will compute and report the value of the appropriate test statistic and its associated *p*-value. It is left to the reader of the report to judge the significance of the result—i.e., the reader must determine whether to reject the null hypothesis in favor of the alternative hypothesis, based on the reported *p*-value. This *p*-value is often referred to as the *attained significance level* of the test. Usually, the null hypothesis will be rejected if the observed significance level is *less* than the fixed significance level, α, chosen by the reader. The inherent advantages of reporting test results in this manner are twofold: (1) readers are able to draw their own conclusions about the reported hypothesis test by choosing α themselves and comparing it to the reported p-value and (2) a measure of the degree of significance of the test result (i.e., the p-value) is provided.

How to Decide Whether to Reject H_0 Using Reported p-Values

1. Choose the maximum value of α you are willing to tolerate.
2. If the observed significance level (p-value) of the test is less than the maximum value of α, then reject the null hypothesis.

Exercises 8.33–8.39

Learning the Mechanics

8.33 In a test of the hypothesis H_0: $\mu = 50$ versus H_a: $\mu > 50$, a sample of $n = 100$ observations possessed mean $\bar{x} = 50.5$ and standard deviation $s = 3.3$. Find and interpret the p-value for this test.

8.34 In a test of the hypothesis H_0: $\mu = 10$ versus H_a: $\mu \neq 10$, a sample of $n = 50$ observations possessed mean $\bar{x} = 9.5$ and standard deviation $s = 2.1$. Find and interpret the p-value for this test.

Applying the Concepts

8.35 *USA Today* (Aug. 17, 1983) reported that for the 1983–1984 academic year, 4-year private colleges charged students an average of $4,627 for tuition and fees, while at 4-year public colleges the average was $1,105. Suppose that for 1984–1985 a random sample of thirty private colleges yielded the following data on tuition and fees: $\bar{x} = \$5,000$ and $s = \$1,643$. Assume that $4,627 is the population mean for 1983–1984.

a. Specify the null and alternative hypotheses you would use to investigate whether the mean amount for tuition and fees in 1984–1985 was significantly larger (in the statistical sense) than it was in 1983–1984.
b. Calculate the p-value for the hypothesis test you described in part a, and explain what the p-value indicates about the statistical significance of the test results.
c. Explain the difference between statistical significance and practical significance in the context of this exercise.

8.36 Florida's housing market remains strong due to the steady stream of new residents fleeing harsh northern winters. This year, the state association of realtors claims that the mean cost of a new home in Florida is $78,380. One realtor who claims that this figure is too low obtained a random sample of thirty sale prices from a list of all homes sold in Florida during the last 6 months. The sample mean and standard deviation were:

$$\bar{x} = \$81,290$$

$$s = \$6,500$$

a. The realtor wishes to conduct an hypothesis test to substantiate her claim. Identify the null and alternative hypotheses of interest to her.

b. Find the observed significance level for this test, and interpret its value.

8.37 Refer to Exercise 8.25. Find the observed significance level for the test, and interpret its value.

8.38 Refer to the test of the pain-relieving drug in Exercise 8.27. Comment on the observed significance level for this test.

8.39 Refer to Exercise 8.30. Find the observed significance level for the test and interpret its value.

8.4 Small-Sample Inferences about a Population Mean

One of the items of interest to an investor in the stock market is the amount a company's annual earnings per share will increase or decrease over the next year. Recall that earnings per share is computed by dividing the total annual earnings of the company by the total number of shares of stock outstanding. One way of trying to project the change in earnings per share is to ask the opinion of several experts, thus obtaining a sample of projections for the particular company. Then, this sample of opinions can be used to make an inference about the mean projected earnings per share, μ, of all stock analysts. However, time and cost restrictions would probably limit the sample of opinions to a small number, and thus the large-sample inferential techniques of Sections 8.1 and 8.2 may not be applicable.

Many inferences in business must be made on the basis of very limited information—i.e., *small samples.* When making an inference about a population mean, μ, small samples have two immediate problematic effects:

Problem 1 The shape of the sampling distribution of the sample mean $\bar{x}$ now depends on the shape of the population that is sampled. Because the Central Limit Theorem applies only to large samples, we can no longer assume that the sampling distribution of $\bar{x}$ is approximately normal.

Problem 2 Although it is still true that $\sigma_{\bar{x}} = \sigma/\sqrt{n}$, the sample standard deviation s may provide a poor approximation of the population standard deviation σ when the sample size is small.

Solution to Problem 1 According to Theorem 7.1, the sampling distribution of $\bar{x}$ will be normal (approximately normal) even for small samples *if the population being sampled is normal (approximately normal).*

Solution to Problem 2   Instead of using the statistic

$$z = \frac{\bar{x} - \mu}{\sigma_{\bar{x}}} = \frac{\bar{x} - \mu}{\sigma/\sqrt{n}}$$

which requires knowledge of, or a good approximation to, σ, we use the statistic

$$t = \frac{\bar{x} - \mu}{s/\sqrt{n}}$$

which replaces the population standard deviation, σ, by the sample standard deviation, s.

The distribution of the *t statistic* in repeated sampling was discovered by W. S. Gosset, a scientist in the Guinness brewery, who published his discovery in 1908 under the pen name of Student. The main result of Gosset's work is that if we are sampling from a normal distribution, the t statistic will have a sampling distribution very much like that of the z statistic: mound-shaped, symmetric, and with mean zero. The primary difference between the sampling distributions of t and z is that the t distribution is more variable than the z, which follows intuitively when you realize that t contains two random quantities ($\bar{x}$ and s), while z contains only one ($\bar{x}$).

The actual increase in variability in the sampling distribution of t depends on the sample size, n. In particular, the smaller the value of n, the more variable will be the sampling distribution of t. A convenient way of expressing this dependence is to say that the t statistic has $(n - 1)$ *degrees of freedom* (df). Recall that the quantity $(n - 1)$ is the divisor that appears in the formula for s^2. This number plays a key role in the sampling distribution of s^2 and will appear in discussions of other statistics in later chapters.

In Figure 8.15, we show both the sampling distribution of z and the sampling distribution of a t statistic with 4 degrees of freedom (df). You can see that the increased variability of the t statistic means that the t value, t_α, that locates an area α in the upper tail of the t distribution will be larger than the corresponding value z_α. Values of t that will be used in forming small-sample confidence intervals for μ and rejection regions for small-sample tests of hypotheses about μ are given in Table V of Appendix B. A partial reproduction of this table is shown in Figure 8.16. Note that t_α values are listed for degrees of freedom from 1 to 29, where α refers to the tail area to the right of t_α. For example, if we want the t value with an area of .025 to its right and 4 df, we look in the table under the column $t_{.025}$ for the entry in the row corresponding to 4 df. This entry is $t_{.025} = 2.776$, as shown in Figure 8.17. The corresponding standard normal z-score is $z_{.025} = 1.96$.

Figure 8.15   Standard Normal (z) Distribution and t Distribution with 4 df

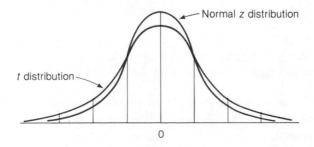

Normal z distribution

t distribution

0

Figure 8.16 Repro-
duction of Part of Table V,
Appendix B

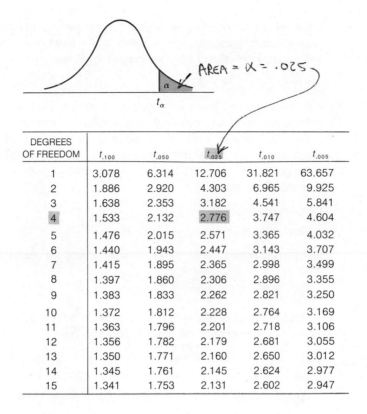

Note that the last row of Table V, where df = infinity, contains the standard normal z values. This follows from the fact that as the sample size n grows very large, s becomes closer to σ, and thus t becomes closer in distribution to z. In fact, when df = 29, there is little difference between corresponding tabulated values of z and t. Thus, we choose the arbitrary cutoff of $n = 30$ (df = 29) to distinguish between the large- and small-sample inferential techniques.

Figure 8.17 The $t_{.025}$
Value in a t Distribution with
4 df and the Corresponding
$z_{.025}$ Value

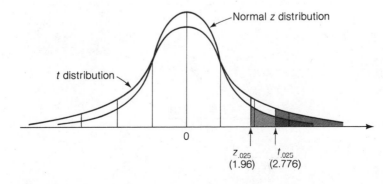

Returning to the projected earnings per share example, suppose we can get a sample of five expert opinions about next year's earnings per share for a stock. We calculate the mean and standard deviation of these five projections to be

$$\bar{x} = \$2.63 \qquad s = \$0.72$$

If we know that last year's earnings were $2.01 per share, is there enough evidence to indicate that the mean expert projection, μ, exceeds last year's figure?

The type of inference desired is a test of an hypothesis. Since we want to show that the mean expert projection for this year exceeds last year's earnings per share, we will test the null hypothesis that $\mu = \$2.01$ against the alternative hypothesis that $\mu > \$2.01$. Thus, the elements of the test are

Null hypothesis H_0: $\mu = \$2.01$

Alternative hypothesis H_a: $\mu > \$2.01$

Since σ is unknown and the sample is small ($n = 5$), we use the t statistic:

Test statistic: $t = \dfrac{\bar{x} - \mu_0}{s/\sqrt{n}} = \dfrac{\bar{x} - 2.01}{s/\sqrt{n}}$

Assumption: The relative frequency distribution of the population of projected earnings per share is approximately normal.

Note that we must assume the normality of our population in order to use the t statistic. If we want to test at the $\alpha = .05$ level, the rejection region will be

Rejection region: $t > t_{.05} = 2.132$ where df $= n - 1 = 4$

This rejection region is shown in Figure 8.18.

Figure 8.18 Rejection Region for Projected Earnings per Share Test

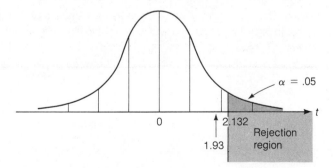

We now calculate

$$t = \frac{\bar{x} - 2.01}{s/\sqrt{n}} = \frac{2.63 - 2.01}{.72/\sqrt{5}}$$

$$= \frac{.62}{.72/2.24} = 1.93$$

Since the value of t, 1.93, calculated from the sample data does not exceed the tabulated value of 2.132, we cannot conclude that the mean projection of all experts exceeds last year's earnings of $2.01.

We summarize the technique for conducting a small-sample test of an hypothesis about a population mean in the box.

Small-Sample Test of an Hypothesis about μ

One-Tailed Test

$H_0: \mu = \mu_0$

$H_a: \mu < \mu_0$

   (or $H_a: \mu > \mu_0$)

Test statistic: $t = \dfrac{\bar{x} - \mu_0}{s/\sqrt{n}}$

Rejection region: $t < -t_\alpha$

   (or $t > t_\alpha$

   when $H_a: \mu > \mu_0$)

Two-Tailed Test

$H_0: \mu = \mu_0$

$H_a: \mu \neq \mu_0$

Test statistic: $t = \dfrac{\bar{x} - \mu_0}{s/\sqrt{n}}$

Rejection region: $t < -t_{\alpha/2}$

   or $t > t_{\alpha/2}$

where t_α and $t_{\alpha/2}$ are based on $(n - 1)$ degrees of freedom.

Assumption: A random sample is selected from a population with a relative frequency distribution that is approximately normal.

Remember, the basic assumption necessary for the use of the t statistic is that the sampled population possesses a relative frequency distribution that is approximately normal. What can be done if you know that your population relative frequency distribution is decidedly nonnormal, say highly skewed?

What Can Be Done if the Population Relative Frequency Distribution Departs Greatly from Normal?

Answer: Use the nonparametric statistical methods of Chapter 16.

Example 8.6

A major car manufacturer wants to test a new engine to see whether it meets new air pollution standards. The mean emission, μ, of all engines of this type must be less than 20 parts per million of carbon. Ten engines are manufactured for testing purposes, and the mean and standard deviation of the emissions for this sample of engines are determined to be

   $\bar{x} = 17.1$ parts per million $s = 3.0$ parts per million

Do the data supply sufficient evidence to allow the manufacturer to conclude that this type of engine meets the pollution standard? Assume that the manufacturer is willing to risk a Type I error with probability equal to $\alpha = .01$.

Solution   The manufacturer wants to establish the alternative hypothesis that the mean emission level, μ, for all engines of this type is less than 20 parts per million. The elements of this small-sample one-tailed test are

$$H_0: \mu = 20 \qquad H_a: \mu < 20$$

Test statistic: $t = \dfrac{\bar{x} - 20}{s/\sqrt{n}}$

Assumption: The relative frequency distribution of the population of emission levels for all engines of this type is approximately normal.

Rejection region: For $\alpha = .01$ and df $= n - 1 = 9$, the one-tailed rejection region (see Figure 8.19) is $t < -t_{.01} = -2.821$

Figure 8.19 Rejection Region for Example 8.6

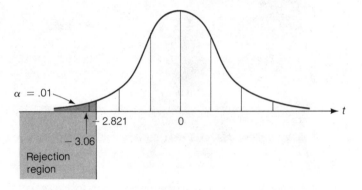

We now calculate the test statistic:

$$t = \frac{\bar{x} - 20}{s/\sqrt{n}} = \frac{17.1 - 20}{3.0/\sqrt{10}} = -3.06$$

Since the calculated t falls in the rejection region (see Figure 8.19), the manufacturer concludes that $\mu < 20$ parts per million and the new engine type meets the pollution standard. Are you satisfied with the reliability associated with this inference? The probability is only $\alpha = .01$ that the test would support the alternative hypothesis if in fact it was false. ∎

Example 8.7 Find the observed significance level for the test in Example 8.6.

Solution   The test performed in Example 8.6 was a one-tailed test, in which $H_0: \mu = 20$ would be rejected in favor of $H_a: \mu < 20$ for values of t in the lower tail of the t distribution. Since the value of t computed from the sample data was $t = -3.06$, the observed significance level (or p-value) for the test is equal to the probability that t would assume a value less than or equal to -3.06, if in fact H_0 was true. This is equal to the area in the lower tail of the t distribution (shaded in Figure 8.20). To find this area—i.e., the p-value for the test—we consult the t table in Table V of Appendix B. Unlike the table of areas under the normal curve, Table V gives only the t values corresponding to the areas .100, .050, .025, .010, and .005. Therefore, we

Figure 8.20 The Observed Significance Level for the Test in Example 8.6

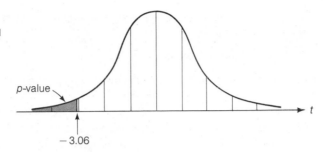

p-value

-3.06

t

can only approximate the p-value for the test. Since the observed t value was based on 9 degrees of freedom, we use the df $= 9$ row in Table V and move across the row until we reach the t value that is closest to the observed $t = -3.06$. [*Note:* We ignore the minus sign.] The t values corresponding to p-values of .010 and .005 are 2.821 and 3.250, respectively. Since the observed t value falls between $t_{.010}$ and $t_{.005}$, the p-value for the test lies between .010 and .005. We could interpolate to more accurately locate the p-value for the test, but it is easier and adequate for our purposes to choose the larger area as the p-value and thus report it as .010. ∎

We may also use the t distribution to form a small-sample confidence interval for a population mean μ, *if the population is approximately normally distributed.* Recall that the large-sample confidence interval for μ is

$$\bar{x} \pm z_{\alpha/2}\sigma_{\bar{x}} = \bar{x} \pm z_{\alpha/2}\left(\frac{\sigma}{\sqrt{n}}\right)$$

where $100(1 - \alpha)\%$ is the desired confidence level. To form the small-sample confidence interval, replace σ by s and $z_{\alpha/2}$ by $t_{\alpha/2}$ (remember, the degrees of freedom must be specified for the tabulated t value).

Small-Sample Confidence Interval for μ

$$\bar{x} \pm t_{\alpha/2}\left(\frac{s}{\sqrt{n}}\right)$$

where $t_{\alpha/2}$ is based on $(n - 1)$ degrees of freedom.

Assumption: The relative frequency distribution of the sampled population is approximately normal.

Example 8.8   When food prices began their rapid increase in the early 1970's, some of the major television networks began periodically to purchase a grocery basket full of food at supermarkets around the country. They always bought the same items at each store so they could compare food prices. Suppose you want to estimate the mean price for a grocery basket in a specific geographic region of the country. You purchase the specified items at a random sample of twenty supermarkets in the region. The mean and standard deviation of the costs at the twenty supermarkets are

$$\bar{x} = \$56.84 \qquad s = \$8.63$$

Form a 95% confidence interval for the mean cost, μ, of a grocery basket for this region.

Solution   If we assume that the distribution of costs for the grocery basket at all supermarkets in the region is approximately normal, we can use the t statistic to form the confidence interval. For a confidence level of 95%, we need the tabulated value of t with df $= n - 1 = 19$:

$$t_{\alpha/2} = t_{.025} = 2.093$$

Then the confidence interval is

$$\bar{x} \pm t_{.025} \left(\frac{s}{\sqrt{n}} \right) = 56.84 \pm 2.093 \left(\frac{8.63}{\sqrt{20}} \right)$$

$$= 56.84 \pm 4.04 = (52.80, 60.88)$$

Thus, we are reasonably confident that the interval from $52.80 to $60.88 contains the true mean cost, μ, of the grocery basket. This is because, if we were to use our interval estimator on repeated occasions, 95% of the intervals constructed would contain μ. ∎

We have emphasized throughout this section that the assumption of a normally distributed population is necessary for making small-sample inferences about μ when using the t statistic. While many business phenomena do have approximately normal distributions, it is also true that many business phenomena have distributions that are not normal or even mound-shaped. Empirical evidence acquired over the years has shown that the t distribution is rather insensitive to moderate departures from normality. That is, the use of the t statistic when sampling from mound-shaped populations generally produces credible results; however, for cases in which the distribution is distinctly nonnormal, *nonparametric methods* should be used. Nonparametric statistics are the subject of Chapter 16.

Exercises 8.40–8.59

Learning the Mechanics

8.40 In what ways are the distributions of the z statistic and t statistic alike? How do they differ?

8.41 Under what circumstances should you use the t distribution in testing an hypothesis about a population mean?

8.42 Let t_0 be a particular value of t. Use Table V of Appendix B to find t_0 values such that the following statements are true:

a. $P(t \geq t_0) = .025$ where df $= 8$ **b.** $P(t \geq t_0) = .01$ where df $= 10$

c. $P(t \leq t_0) = .005$ where df $= 17$ **d.** $P(t \leq t_0) = .05$ where df $= 14$

8.43 The following sample of five measurements was randomly selected from a normally distributed population: 4, 7, 3, 4, 6

a. Test the null hypothesis that the mean of the population is 6 against the alternative hypothesis, $\mu < 6$. Use $\alpha = .05$.

b. Test the null hypothesis that the mean of the population is 6 against the alternative hypothesis, $\mu \neq 6$. Use $\alpha = .05$.

8.44 Find the observed significance level for each test in Exercise 8.43.

8.45 Refer to Exercise 8.43.

a. Find a 95% confidence interval for μ.

b. Give the value of t that would be used to form a 90% confidence interval for μ.

c. Describe a practical situation that would motivate you to form a confidence interval for μ rather than testing an hypothesis about μ.

8.46 The following sample of six measurements was randomly selected from a normally distributed population: 1, 3, -1, 5, 1, 2

a. Test the null hypothesis that the mean of the population is 3 against the alternative hypothesis, $\mu < 3$. Use $\alpha = .05$.

b. Test the null hypothesis that the mean of the population is 3 against the alternative hypothesis, $\mu \neq 3$. Use $\alpha = .05$.

8.47 Find the observed significance level for each test in Exercise 8.46.

8.48 Refer to Exercise 8.46.

a. Find a 95% confidence interval for μ.

b. Give the value of t that would be used to form a 90% confidence interval for μ.

Applying the Concepts

8.49 In any bottling process, a manufacturer will lose money if the bottles contain either more or less than is claimed on the label. Accordingly, bottlers pay close attention to the amount of their product being dispensed by bottle-filling machines. Suppose a quality control inspector for a catsup company is interested in testing whether the mean number of ounces of catsup per family-size bottle differs from the labeled amount of 20 ounces. The inspector samples nine bottles, measures the weight of their contents, and finds that $\bar{x} = 19.7$ ounces and $s = 0.3$ ounce.

a. Does the sample evidence indicate that the catsup dispensing machine needs adjustment? Test at $\alpha = .05$.

b. What is the p-value for the hypothesis test you conducted in part a?

c. What assumptions are necessary so that the procedure used in part a is valid?

d. Find a 90% confidence interval for the mean number of ounces of catsup being dispensed.

8.50 What is an MBA degree really worth? *Forbes* (Dec. 19, 1983) gives the median starting salaries for MBA's from fourteen business schools for the spring of 1983. Five of these median salaries, randomly selected from the group, are shown in the table. Suppose the data could be viewed as a random sample of the median starting salaries in 1983 for all MBA programs. Estimate the mean of the population of median MBA starting salaries using a 95% confidence interval. Interpret the interval. List any assumptions you make.

SCHOOL	MEDIAN STARTING SALARY, SPRING 1983
Columbia	$34,534
Dartmouth	$35,000
Northwestern	$31,100*
NYU	$30,600
Virginia	$33,000

* Estimate

8.51 In an article entitled "Huge Phone Bills Look Like Mobster Fraud," the *Orlando Sentinel* (Mar. 15, 1984) comments on the rash of huge telephone bills received by some AT&T customers in early 1984. Unexplained huge bills received during this brief period of time (often by private individuals) possessed the following dollar values: $109,500, $61,180, $125,883, $35,236, $26,337, $93,315, and $36,063. Suppose these bills represent a random sample of the sizes of the thefts of telephone services that AT&T might expect in the future. Use the data to obtain an estimate of the mean size of a theft in the future. Use a 90% confidence interval. List any assumptions you make.

8.52 A company purchases large quantities of naphtha in 50-gallon drums. Because the purchases are on-going, small shortages in the drums can represent a sizable loss to the company. The weights of the drums vary slightly from drum to drum, so the weight of the naphtha is measured after removing it from the drums. Suppose the company samples the contents of twenty drums, measures the naphtha in each, and calculates $\bar{x} = 49.70$ gallons and $s = 0.32$ gallon. Do the sample statistics provide sufficient evidence to indicate that the mean fill per 50-gallon drum is less than 50 gallons? Use $\alpha = .10$. List your assumptions.

8.53 A cigarette manufacturer advertises that its new low-tar cigarette "contains on average no more than 4 milligrams of tar." You have been asked to test the claim using the following sample information: $n = 25$, $\bar{x} = 4.16$ milligrams, $s = 0.30$ milligram. Does the sample information disagree with the manufacturer's claim? Test using $\alpha = .05$. List any assumptions you make.

8.54 In an effort to offset Russia's growing armored force, the U.S. Defense Department has selected a new Army tank designed by Chrysler Corp. The tank, called M-1, can reach an average top speed of 45 miles per hour, a speed the Defense Department believes is faster than the Soviets' fastest and most powerful tank, the T-72. To estimate the mean top speed of the T-72, suppose the Defense Department gained access to data on three of Russia's tanks and found the top speed for the three tanks had an average of 43.5 miles per hour and a standard deviation of 2.5 miles per hour. Find a 95% confidence interval for the mean top speed of the T-72 tanks. What assumptions must you make to form this confidence interval? Interpret the interval estimate.

8.55 According to the Internal Revenue Service Code, interest payments are a deductible expense. That is, persons who itemize their tax deductions (as opposed to taking the standard deduction) may reduce their taxable income by the amount of interest they paid (e.g., mortgage interest and finance charges) during the year. The average interest deduction claimed in 1980 by taxpayers of various income levels is shown in the table.

ADJUSTED GROSS INCOME ($ thousands)	AVERAGE INTEREST DEDUCTION ($)
15–20	2,604
20–25	2,792
25–30	3,011
30–50	3,527
50–100	5,626
100–200	10,384
200–500	20,815

Source: *Wall Street Journal*, Dec. 8, 1982, p. 1.

Suppose twelve tax returns are randomly sampled by the Internal Revenue Service from the population of 1984 tax returns with adjusted gross incomes between $25,000 and $30,000. The interest deduction claimed on each return is listed below:

$3,050	$3,101	$3,415
2,910	3,333	3,002
3,872	3,102	3,222
2,806	2,851	2,999

a. Assume the population of interest deductions from which the sample was drawn is approximately normally distributed. Do the sample data provide sufficient evidence to conclude that in 1984 the average interest deduction claimed by taxpayers in the $25,000–$30,000 adjusted gross income bracket is significantly greater than in 1980? Use $\alpha = .05$.

b. Find and interpret the p-value for the test.

8.56 In a recent nationwide survey of 1,000 men and women conducted by Caldwell Davis Partners (an advertising agency), it was found that two-thirds of the people surveyed perceived themselves as younger than their actual chronological age. These findings may help explain the recent failures of a line of food advertised as being for senior citizens and a shampoo directed at "hair over 40." The survey also indicated that, on average, men and women perceived themselves to be 6 years younger and 7 years younger, respectively, than their actual ages. However, men and women under 30 generally perceived themselves as older than their actual age (Nemy, 1982). A researcher randomly sampled ten college students under the age of 30 and asked them how old they were and how old they perceived themselves to be. The results are shown in the table at the top of the next page.

CHRONOLOGICAL AGE	PERCEIVED AGE
20	22
19	21
25	30
22	25
26	22
19	19
18	20
20	18
20	21
21	21

a. Do the sample data support the survey's findings with respect to the perceptions of men and women under 30? Test using $\alpha = .10$.

b. What assumption must hold in order for the procedure you used in part a to be valid?

8.57 One of the most feared predators in the ocean is the great white shark. Although it is known that the white shark grows to a mean length of 21 feet, a marine biologist believes that the great white sharks off the Bermuda coast grow much longer due to unusual feeding habits. To test this claim, a number of full-grown great white sharks are captured off the Bermuda coast, measured, and then set free. However, because the capture of sharks is difficult, costly, and very dangerous, only three are sampled. Their lengths are 24, 20, and 22 feet. Do the data provide sufficient evidence to support the marine biologist's claim? Find the observed significance level for the test. What assumptions must be made in order to carry out the test? Do you think these assumptions are likely to be satisfied in this particular sampling situation?

8.58 Suppose you want to estimate the mean percentage of gain in per share value for growth-type mutual funds over a specific 2-year period. Ten mutual funds are randomly selected from the population of all the commonly listed funds. The percentage gain figures are shown below (negative values indicate losses):

11.2   4.8   −2.6   16.8   −1.9

10.1   9.6   14.9   10.1   11.2

Find a 90% confidence interval for the mean percentage of gain for the population of funds. Assume that the population of percentage gains for growth-type mutual funds can be adequately approximated by a normal distribution.

8.59 The Occupational Safety and Health Act of 1970 (OSHA) allows issuance of engineering standards to assure safe workplaces for all Americans. In 1975, the standards for exposure to arsenic in smelters, herbicide production facilities, and other places where arsenic is used were reviewed, and the previous maximum allowable level of 0.5 milligram per cubic meter of air was reduced to 0.004. Suppose smelters at two plants are being investigated to determine whether they are meeting OSHA standards. Two analyses of the air are made at each plant, and the results (in milligrams per cubic meter of air) are shown in the table.

PLANT 1		PLANT 2	
Observation	Arsenic level	Observation	Arsenic level
1	0.01	1	0.05
2	0.005	2	0.09

a. Do the data provide sufficient evidence to indicate that plant 1 fails to meet the OSHA standard? Specify the null and alternative hypotheses. Then conduct the test using $\alpha = .05$. Interpret your results.

b. Repeat the instructions of part a for plant 2.

c. Find the p-values for the tests in parts a and b and interpret them.

8.5 Large-Sample Inferences about a Binomial Probability

Many market studies are conducted by companies with the objective of determining the fraction of buyers of a particular product that prefer the company's brand. For example, a tobacco company may conduct a market study by sampling and interviewing 1,000 smokers to determine their brand preference. The objective of the survey is to estimate the proportion of all smokers who smoke the company's brand. The number, x, of the 1,000 sampled who smoke the company's brand is a binomial random variable (see Section 5.4 for a description of the binomial experiment). The probability, p, that a smoker prefers the company's brand is the parameter to be estimated.

How would you estimate the probability, p, of success in a binomial experiment? One logical answer is to use the proportion of successes in the sample. That is, we can estimate p by calculating

$$\hat{p} \text{ (read ''p hat'')} = \frac{\text{Number of successes in the sample}}{\text{Number of trials}} = \frac{x}{n}$$

Thus, if 313 of the 1,000 smokers were found to smoke the company's brand, we would estimate the proportion p of all smokers who prefer the brand to be

$$\hat{p} = \frac{x}{n} = \frac{313}{1,000} = .313$$

To determine the reliability of the estimator $\hat{p}$, we need to know its sampling distribution. That is, if we were to draw samples of 1,000 smokers over and over again, each time calculating a new estimate $\hat{p}$, what would be the frequency distribution of all the $\hat{p}$ values? The answer lies in viewing $\hat{p}$ as the average or mean number of successes per trial over the n trials. Thus, if each success in the sample is assigned a value equal to 1 and each failure is assigned a 0, then the sum of all n sample observations is x, the total number of successes; and $\hat{p} = x/n$ is the average or mean number of successes per trial in the n trials. The Central Limit Theorem tells us that the relative frequency distribution of the sample mean for any population is approximately normal for sufficiently large samples. Therefore, the sampling distribution of $\hat{p}$ has the characteristics indicated in Figure 8.21 and listed in the box on the next page.

Figure 8.21   Sampling
Distribution of $\hat{p}$

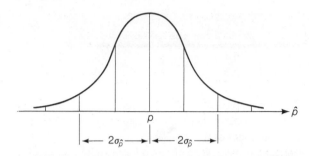

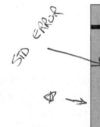

Sampling Distribution of $\hat{p}$

1. The mean of the sampling distribution of $\hat{p}$ is p; i.e., $\hat{p}$ is an unbiased estimator of p.
2. The standard deviation of the sampling distribution of $\hat{p}$ is $\sqrt{pq/n}$; i.e., $\sigma_{\hat{p}} = \sqrt{pq/n}$, where $q = 1 - p$.
3. For large samples, the sampling distribution of $\hat{p}$ is approximately normal. A sample size will be considered large if the interval $\hat{p} \pm 3\sigma_{\hat{p}}$ does not include 0 or 1. [*Note:* p will usually be unknown. You will have to guess or approximate its value to apply this criterion.]

The fact that the sampling distribution of $\hat{p}$ is approximately normal for sufficiently large samples allows us to form confidence intervals and test hypotheses about p in a manner that is completely analogous to that used for large-sample inferences about μ:

Large-Sample Confidence Interval for p

$$\hat{p} \pm z_{\alpha/2}\sigma_{\hat{p}} = \hat{p} \pm z_{\alpha/2}\sqrt{pq/n} \approx \hat{p} \pm z_{\alpha/2}\sqrt{\hat{p}\hat{q}/n} \qquad \text{where } \hat{p} = \frac{x}{n} \text{ and } \hat{q} = 1 - \hat{p}$$

[*Note:*   When n is large, we can use $\hat{p}$ to approximate the value of p in the formula for $\sigma_{\hat{p}}$.]

Thus, if 313 of 1,000 smokers smoke the company's brand, a 95% confidence interval for the proportion of all smokers who prefer the company's brand is

Table 8.3

Values of pq
for Several
Different
p Values

p	pq
.5	.25
.6 or .4	.24
.7 or .3	.21
.8 or .2	.16
.9 or .1	.09

$$\hat{p} \pm z_{\alpha/2}\sigma_{\hat{p}} = .313 \pm 1.96\sqrt{pq/1{,}000}$$

where $q = 1 - p$. Just as we needed an approximator for σ in calculating a large-sample confidence interval for μ, we now need an approximation for p. As Table 8.3 shows, the approximation for p need not be especially accurate, because the value of pq needed for the confidence interval is relatively insensitive to changes in p. Therefore, we can use $\hat{p}$ to approximate p. Keeping in mind that $\hat{q} = 1 - \hat{p}$, we substitute these values into the formula for the confidence interval:

$$\hat{p} \pm 1.96\sqrt{pq/1{,}000} \approx \hat{p} \pm 1.96\sqrt{\hat{p}\hat{q}/1{,}000}$$
$$= .313 \pm 1.96\sqrt{(.313)(.687)/1{,}000} = .313 \pm .029$$
$$= (.284, .342)$$

The company can be 95% confident that the interval from 28.4% to 34.2% contains the true percentage of all smokers who prefer its brand. That is, in repeated construction of confidence intervals, approximately 95% of all samples would produce confidence intervals that enclose p.

Tests of hypotheses concerning p are also analogous to those for population means (large samples).

Large-Sample Test of an Hypothesis about p

One-Tailed Test

$H_0: p = p_0$
(p_0 — hypothesized value of p)

$H_a: p < p_0$
(or $H_a: p > p_0$)

Test statistic: $z = \dfrac{\hat{p} - p_0}{\sigma_{\hat{p}}}$

where $\sigma_{\hat{p}} = \sqrt{[p_0(1 - p_0)]/n}$, assuming H_0 is true

Rejection region: $z < -z_\alpha$
(or $z > z_\alpha$
when $H_a: p > p_0$)

Two-Tailed Test

$H_0: p = p_0$
$H_a: p \neq p_0$

Test statistic: $z = \dfrac{\hat{p} - p_0}{\sigma_{\hat{p}}}$

Rejection region: $z < -z_{\alpha/2}$
or $z > z_{\alpha/2}$

Example 8.9

The reputations (and hence, sales) of many businesses can be severely damaged by shipments of manufactured items that contain an unusually large percentage of defectives. For example, a manufacturer of flashbulbs for cameras may want to be reasonably certain that less than 5% of the bulbs are defective. Suppose 300 bulbs are randomly selected from a very large shipment, each is tested, and 10 defective bulbs are found. Does this provide sufficient evidence for the manufacturer to conclude that the fraction defective in the entire shipment is less than .05? Use $\alpha = .01$.

Solution

The objective of the sampling is to determine whether there is sufficient evidence to indicate that p is less than .05. Consequently, we will test the null hypothesis that $p = .05$ against the alternative hypothesis that $p < .05$. The elements of the test are

$H_0: p = .05 \qquad H_a: p < .05$

Test statistic: $z = \dfrac{\hat{p} - .05}{\sigma_{\hat{p}}}$

Rejection region: $z < -z_{.01} = -2.33$ (see Figure 8.22 on the next page)

We now calculate the test statistic:

$$z = \frac{\hat{p} - .05}{\sigma_{\hat{p}}} = \frac{(10/300) - .05}{\sqrt{p_0 q_0/n}} = \frac{.033 - .05}{\sqrt{p_0 q_0/300}}$$

Figure 8.22 Rejection Region for Example 8.9

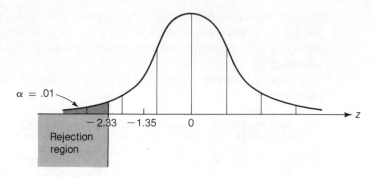

Notice that we use p_0 to calculate $\sigma_{\hat{p}}$ because the test statistic is computed on the assumption that the null hypothesis is true; i.e., $p = p_0$. Therefore, substituting the values for p_0 and q_0 into the z statistic, we obtain

$$z \approx \frac{-.017}{\sqrt{(.05)(.95)/300}} = \frac{-.017}{.0126} = -1.35$$

As shown in Figure 8.22, the calculated z value does not fall in the rejection region. Therefore, based on this test, there is insufficient evidence to indicate that the shipment contains fewer than 5% defective bulbs. ∎

Example 8.10 In Example 8.9, we found that we did not have sufficient evidence, at the $\alpha = .01$ level of significance, to indicate that the fraction defective, p, of flashbulbs was less than $p = .05$. How strong was the weight of evidence favoring the alternative hypothesis ($H_a: p < .05$)? Find the observed significance level for the test.

Solution The computed value of the test statistic was $z = -1.35$. Therefore, for this one-tailed test,

Observed significance level $= P(z \le -1.35)$

This lower-tail area is shown in Figure 8.23. The area A between $z = 0$ and $z = 1.35$ is given in Table IV, Appendix B, as .4115. Therefore, the observed significance level is $.5 - .4115 = .0885$. Note that this probability is quite small. We may not have rejected H_0: $p = .05$ for $\alpha = .01$, but the probability of observing a z value as small or smaller than -1.35 is only .0885. Therefore, we would reject H_0 if we choose $\alpha = .10$ (since the p-value is less than .10), or we would not reject H_0 (the conclusion of Example 8.9) if we choose $\alpha = .05$.

Figure 8.23 The Observed Significance Level for Example 8.9

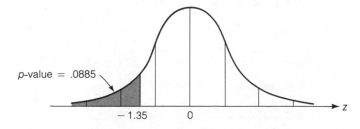

∎

The confidence interval and test of an hypothesis for p in previous examples are based on the assumption that the sample size n is large enough so that $\hat{p}$ will have an approximately normal sampling distribution. As a rule of thumb, this condition will be satisfied if the interval $\hat{p} \pm 3\sigma_{\hat{p}}$ does not contain 0 or 1.*

Small-sample estimators and test procedures are also available for p. These are omitted from our discussion because most surveys conducted in business use samples that are large enough to employ the large-sample estimators and tests presented in this section.

Case Study 8.3
Statistical Quality
Control, Part 2

In complicated assembly operations (such as railway car assembly), many quality variables could be measured (e.g., strength of welds, degree of corrosion, and number of paint flaws), and in principle, each could be monitored over time using control charts, as described in Case Study 8.2. In some situations, however, an alternative, simpler procedure may be more appropriate. For example, n finished products could be randomly sampled at regular time intervals, inspected for defects, and simply classified as being defective or nondefective products. Then $\hat{p}$, the proportion of defectives in each sample, could be determined and plotted on a control chart like the one in Figure 8.24. In this way, the proportion of defective products produced and, therefore, product quality and the current capability of the production process could be monitored over time (Wetherill, 1977).

Figure 8.24 Control
Chart for Proportion Defective

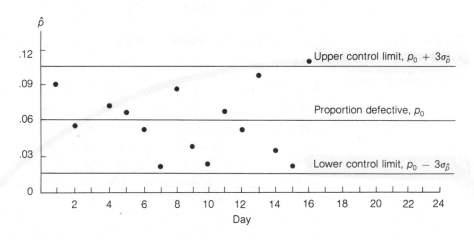

In order to construct the control chart shown in Figure 8.24, it is necessary to know (i.e., have a good estimate for) p_0, the proportion of defectives produced when the process is operating "normally" (i.e., in control). Then, assuming n is large enough to use the normal distribution to approximate the sampling distribution of $\hat{p}$, the control limits are located $3\sigma_{\hat{p}}$ above and below p_0. If a value of $\hat{p}$ falls above the upper limit, it is a signal that the process is turning out more defectives than usual and may be out of control. But what is the significance

---

* This requirement is equivalent to that given in Section 6.5 for a normal distribution to provide an adequate approximation to a binomial distribution, although the requirement was stated in terms of the binomial random variable, x, rather than the sample fraction of successes, $\hat{p}$.

of the lower control limit? Why should the manufacturer be concerned if fewer defectives than usual are being produced? Two important reasons follow (Caplen, 1970):

1. It may be an indication that the inspector is not performing his or her job carefully and may be missing defectives that normally would be identified. As a result, defective products may be sold to customers.

2. If the inspector is performing adequately, it may be an indication that the production process really is temporarily better. If so, the low $\hat{p}$ value signals management to begin a search for the causes for the improvement. If found, it may be possible to improve the production process permanently.

As in Case Study 8.2, this control chart procedure for monitoring the proportion of defective products is nothing more than a two-tailed hypothesis test with the following elements:

1. H_0: Process is in control, $p = p_0$
   H_a: Process is out of control, $p \neq p_0$
2. The test statistic is $\hat{p}$.
3. The rejection region is defined by the upper and lower control limits.
4. Since the control limits are located at $p_0 \pm 3\sigma_{\hat{p}}$, the probability of committing a Type I error is approximately $\alpha = .0026$. (Why?)

Z of $3 = .4987$

Exercises 8.60–8.74

Learning the Mechanics

8.60 Explain the meaning of the phrase "$\hat{p}$ is an unbiased estimator of p."

8.61 Given $\hat{p} = .42$ and $n = 400$, construct a 95% confidence interval for p.

8.62 Given $\hat{p} = .76$ and $n = 144$, construct a 90% confidence interval for p.

8.63 Suppose a random sample of 100 observations from a binomial population gave a value of $\hat{p} = .63$ and you wish to test the null hypothesis that the population parameter p is equal to .70 against the alternative hypothesis, $p < .70$.

a. Noting that $\hat{p} = .63$, what does your intuition tell you? Does the value of $\hat{p}$ appear to contradict the null hypothesis?

b. Use the large-sample z test to test H_0: $p = .70$ against the alternative hypothesis, H_a: $p < .70$. How do the test results compare with your intuitive decision from part a?

c. Find and interpret the p-value for the hypothesis test you conducted in part b.

8.64 Suppose the sample in Exercise 8.63 has produced $\hat{p} = .83$ and we wish to test H_0: $p = .9$ against the alternative hypothesis, H_a: $p < .9$.

a. Calculate the value of the z statistic for this test.

b. Note that $\hat{p} - p_0 = .83 - .9 = -.07$ is the same as for Exercise 8.63. Considering this, why is the absolute value of z for this exercise larger than that calculated in Exercise 8.63?

c. Complete the test and interpret your results.

d. Find the observed significance level for your hypothesis test, and interpret its value.

Applying the Concepts

8.65 According to a spokesperson for General Mills, the company's "cents-off" coupon offers are designed to get people to buy their products and their refund offers (money returned with proof of repeated purchases) are designed to encourage people to continue buying their products. In a national survey conducted by the Nielsen Clearing House in 1975, 65% of the respondents indicated that they used cents-off coupons when grocery shopping. In a 1980 survey, the Nielsen organization found that 76% of those surveyed used cents-off coupons ("A Penny Refunded is a Penny Earned," *Minneapolis Star,* Nov. 29, 1981, p. 7F).

a. Suppose the 1980 survey consisted of a random sample of 100 shoppers of whom 76 indicated that they used cents-off coupons. Use this information to determine whether the percentage of shoppers using coupons in 1980 is significantly greater than 65%. Test using $\alpha = .05$.

b. Find the observed significance level for the test you conducted in part a, and interpret its value.

8.66 Standard Oil of California used a sample survey to determine whether people's attitudes toward Standard's corporate image tended to be favorable or unfavorable. The sample results indicated that, for the first time in thirty years, more people had unfavorable than favorable attitudes. Standard Oil responded by initiating an institutional advertising campaign to help improve its image (*Marketing News,* 1976). Suppose another large oil corporation conducted a similar survey with the following results:

Unfavorable opinions	3,465
Favorable opinions	2,502
No opinions	821

a. Examine the data. Based on your intuition, does it appear that more than 50% of the general public possess an unfavorable attitude toward the company?

b. Do the sample data support the hypothesis that more than 50% of the general public hold unfavorable opinions about the company? Test at $\alpha = .05$.

c. Construct a 90% confidence interval for the proportion of individuals with no opinion.

d. List any assumptions that you made in answering parts b and c.

8.67 Refer to Exercise 8.66. Find the observed significance level for the test you conducted in part b and interpret its value.

8.68 Following the examination of 209 fish that were randomly selected from the five Great Lakes, the Michigan Department of Agriculture reported that contamination of Great Lakes fish with toxic DDT, dieldrin, and PCB's is at its lowest level in years. Descriptions of the contaminated fish that were examined are given in the table on the next page. Even though contaminant levels are down, Michigan's Public Health Department still advises against eating more than one meal of Great Lakes fish a week — and none at all for pregnant women ("Level of Tainted Fish Falls in Great Lakes," *Minneapolis Tribune,* Oct. 24, 1982, p. 15C).

TYPE OF FISH	NUMBER	LAKE	CONTAMINANT
Lake trout	1	Superior	DDT
Lake trout	3	Michigan	PCB's
Lake trout	7	Michigan	Dieldrin
Lake trout	1	Huron	Dieldrin
Whitefish	4	Michigan	Dieldrin
Chub	9	Michigan	Dieldrin

a. Is the sample of fish large enough to use the normal distribution to approximate the sampling distribution of $\hat{p}$, the proportion of contaminated fish in the sample? Explain.

b. Estimate the proportion of contaminated fish in the Great Lakes using an 80% confidence interval.

8.69 Marketing research has been defined by the American Marketing Association as the "systematic gathering, recording, and analyzing of data about problems relating to the marketing of goods and services" (American Marketing Association, 1961). Companies may have their own marketing research departments, or they may contract the services of a marketing research firm. The marketing research department of a large West Coast manufacturer of facial tissue paper was charged with the responsibility of determining consumer preferences regarding the softness of their newly developed product (brand A) relative to the industry leader (brand B). A random sample of 205 consumers was selected and asked to rank the softness of brands A and B. In the results, 119 ranked brand A as softer, and 86 ranked brand B as softer.

a. Do the data indicate that brand A is perceived by consumers as being superior to brand B in terms of softness? Test using $\alpha = .05$.

b. Find the p-value for the test and interpret its value.

8.70 Shoplifting is an escalating problem for retailers. According to *U.S. News and World Report* (Feb. 21, 1977), one New York City store randomly selected 500 shoppers and observed them while they were in the store. One in twelve was seen stealing. How accurate is this estimate? To help you answer this question, construct a 95% confidence interval for p, the proportion of all the store's customers who are shoplifters.

8.71 Interested in how well their new computer billing operation is working, a company statistician samples 400 bills that are ready for mailing and checks them for errors. Twenty-four are found to contain at least one error. Find a 90% confidence interval for p, the true proportion of bills that contain errors.

8.72 A producer of frozen orange juice claims that 20% of all orange juice drinkers prefer its product. To test the validity of this claim, a competitor samples 200 orange juice drinkers and finds that only 33 prefer the producer's brand.

a. Does the sample evidence indicate that the proportion of orange juice drinkers who prefer the producer's brand is significantly less than .20? Test at $\alpha = .10$.

b. Find the p-value of the hypothesis test you conducted in part a. Interpret its value.

8.73 In an article titled "Searching for a Forever Home," *Time* (May 2, 1983) reports on how television programs aid in the adoption of "forgotten" children — orphans who have physical or mental handicaps. One method of stimulating the adoption program is to present television profiles of the children. The article documents the success of these programs, noting that Oklahoma City's station KOCO helped to place 92 of the 119 it profiled, New York's WCBS placed 21 of 35, and Atlanta's WXIA placed 79 out of 177. How effective were these three television stations in promoting the adoption of the forgotten children?

a. Find a 95% confidence interval for each television station's placement success rate.

b. Suppose that the 331 children profiled by the three stations could be regarded as a random sample from the population of all similar profiles that might be presented by television stations throughout the country. Do the data provide sufficient evidence to indicate that the national placement success rate exceeds .5? Test using $\alpha = .05$.

8.74 The following is a very useful result concerning the mean and variance of some sampling distributions: Suppose that c is a constant and x is a statistic with mean μ and variance σ^2. Then it can be shown (the proof is omitted here) that the mean and variance of cx are

$$E(cx) = cE(x) = c\mu \qquad \sigma_{cx}^2 = c^2\sigma^2$$

Application: If you draw a random sample of n people from a large population of consumers and x is the number in the sample who favor some proposal (favor a particular product, etc.), then x is a binomial random variable with mean $\mu = np$ and variance $\sigma^2 = npq$ (from Chapter 5). The proportion of people in the sample who favor the proposal, x/n, is used to estimate the population proportion, p.

a. Use the information above to show that the sampling distribution of the sample proportion, x/n, has a mean equal to p and a standard deviation equal to $\sqrt{p(1-p)/n}$.

b. Let each person in the population who favors the proposal be represented by a 1 and each person who does not by a 0. Then the entire population of consumers can be viewed as a collection of 1's and 0's; x will equal the sum of the 1's and 0's in the sample of n, and x/n will be the sample average. What will be the approximate form of the sampling distribution of the sample proportion when the sample size n is large? Why?

c. Suppose you select a random sample of 1,600 consumers from a large population that (unknown to you) contains 20% ($p = .2$) who favor the proposal. What is the probability that your sample proportion will differ from the population proportion ($p = .2$) by more than .01?

8.6
Determining
the Sample
Size

When an experiment is planned with the purpose of estimating a population parameter — say, a mean, μ, or a binomial probability, p — the required reliability of the estimate and the number of measurements to be included in the sample must be determined. How can this sample size be selected?

To answer this question, we use the knowledge acquired in Section 7.4 about the relation between the sample size and the variance of the sampling distribution of a statistic. Since the variance is inversely proportional to the sample size, we can force the statistic to fall (with a specified probability) as close to the population parameter as we please by choosing a sufficiently large value for the sample size. For example, since the standard deviation of the sampling distribution of $\bar{x}$ (see Figure 8.25) is $\sigma_{\bar{x}} = \sigma/\sqrt{n}$, we can make $\sigma_{\bar{x}}$ as small as we please by choosing a sufficiently large value for the sample size n.

Figure 8.25   Sampling Distribution of $\bar{x}$

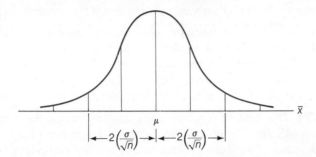

Recall that in Section 8.1 we estimated the mean overdue amount for all delinquent accounts in a large credit corporation. A sample of 100 delinquent accounts produced an estimate $\bar{x}$ that was within \$18 of the true mean amount due, μ, for all delinquent accounts with a probability approximately equal to .95. Suppose the corporation wanted μ estimated to within \$5 with 95% confidence. How large a sample would be required?

For the sample size $n = 100$, we found an approximate 95% confidence interval to be

$$\bar{x} \pm 2\sigma_{\bar{x}} \approx \$233 \pm \$18$$

If we now want our estimator $\bar{x}$ to be within \$5 of μ, we must have

$$2\sigma_{\bar{x}} = 5$$

or

$$\frac{2\sigma}{\sqrt{n}} = 5$$

The necessary sample size is found by solving the above equation for n. To do this, we need an approximation for σ. For our example, the appropriate approximation is the standard deviation of the 100 accounts, $s = 90$. Thus,

$$\frac{2\sigma}{\sqrt{n}} \approx \frac{2s}{\sqrt{n}}$$

$$= \frac{2(90)}{\sqrt{n}} = 5$$

$$\sqrt{n} = \frac{2(90)}{5} = 36$$

$$n = (36)^2 = 1{,}296$$

The company will have to sample approximately 1,300 delinquent accounts to estimate the mean overdue amount μ to within \$5 with about 95% confidence. [*Note:*   This could include the 100 contained in the pilot sample.]

A similar argument follows if we want to determine the sample size necessary for estimating a binomial probability to within a given bound B with a specified confidence level. The general equations for determining the sample size to estimate both μ and p are given in the box.

Sample Size Determination with $100(1 - \alpha)\%$ Confidence

For estimating μ to within a bound B with probability $(1 - \alpha)$, the required sample size is found by solving the following equation for n:

$$z_{\alpha/2}\left(\frac{\sigma}{\sqrt{n}}\right) = B$$

The solution is

$$n = \frac{z_{\alpha/2}^2 \sigma^2}{B^2}$$

B IS A TOLER-ANCE VALUE (ie 10% = .10) OR PLUG IN VALUE GIVEN IF UNITS MATCH

The value of σ is estimated by the standard deviation s obtained from a prior sample (pilot study, etc.). Alternatively, we may approximate the range R of observations in the population and use $\sigma \approx R/4$.

- -

For estimating p to within a bound B with probability $(1 - \alpha)$, the required sample size is found by solving the following equation for n:

$$z_{\alpha/2}\sqrt{pq/n} = B$$

The solution is

$$n = \frac{z_{\alpha/2}^2 pq}{B^2}$$

The value of p substituted into these expressions is obtained from an estimate based on a prior sample, from prior information, or most conservatively, is chosen equal to .5. (The value $p = .5$ gives the largest value for $\sigma_{\hat{p}}$ and, consequently, results in a solution that is as large as or larger than the required sample size.)

Example 8.11   Refer to Example 8.9 in which a flashbulb manufacturer was making an inference about the fraction defective in a shipment. Suppose the manufacturer wants to estimate the true fraction p to within 1% (i.e., $B = .01$) with 90% confidence. How large a sample would be needed (assume the true p value is near .05)?

Solution   Since we want the error of estimation to be less than $B = .01$ with probability .90, we must have $\alpha = 1 - .90 = .10$. Then $z_{\alpha/2} = z_{.05} = 1.645$. Substituting these values into the formula for n, we obtain

$$n = \frac{z_{\alpha/2}^2 pq}{B^2} = \frac{(1.645)^2(.05)(.95)}{(.01)^2} = 1{,}285.4 \approx 1{,}286$$

Thus, a large sample — about 1,286 bulbs — must be tested if the manufacturer wants to be 90% sure the estimate of the fraction defective will fall within 1% of the true value of p. (A cost-benefit analysis would be required before we could know whether such accuracy is worth the cost of the sampling.)   ∎

Exercises 8.75 – 8.86

Learning the Mechanics

8.75 If you wish to estimate a population mean correct to within .2 with probability .95 and you know, from prior sampling, that σ^2 is approximately equal to 6.1, how many observations would have to be included in your sample?

8.76 Suppose you wish to estimate the mean of a normal population using a 95% confidence interval and you know from prior information that $\sigma^2 \approx 1$.

a. To see the effect of the sample size on the width of the confidence interval, calculate the width of the confidence interval for $n = 16, 25, 49, 100, 400$.

b. Plot the widths as a function of sample size n on graph paper. Connect the points by a smooth curve and note how the width decreases as n increases.

8.77 Suppose you wish to estimate a population mean correct to within .15 with probability equal to .90. You do not know σ^2, but you know that the observations will range in value between 24 and 27. Find the approximate sample size that will produce the desired accuracy of the estimate.

a. You wish to be conservative to ensure that the sample size will be ample to achieve the desired accuracy of the estimate. [*Hint:* Using your knowledge of data variation from Section 3.7, assume that the range of the observations will equal 4σ.]

b. Calculate the approximate sample size assuming the range of the observations is equal to 6σ.

8.78 Find the approximate sample size necessary to estimate a binomial proportion p correct to within .02 with probability equal to .90.

a. Assume you know p is near .8.

b. Assume you have no knowledge of the value of p, but you wish to be certain that your sample is large enough to achieve the specified accuracy for the estimate.

Applying the Concepts

8.79 According to the *Minneapolis Star* ("Monitor: Vehicle speeds," 1980), the federal government requires states to certify that they are enforcing the 55-miles-per-hour speed limit and that motorists are driving at that speed. A state is in jeopardy of losing millions of dollars in federal road funds if more than 60% of its vehicles on 55-miles-per-hour highways are exceeding the speed limit. The Minnesota Highway Patrol conducts seventy radar surveys each year at a total of fifty sites to estimate the proportion p of vehicles exceeding 55 miles per hour. Each sample survey involves at least 400 vehicles.

a. How large a sample should be selected at site # 42 on Interstate 35W to estimate p to within 3% with 90% confidence? Last year approximately 60% of all vehicles exceeded 55 miles per hour.

b. The highway patrol also estimates μ, the average speed of vehicles on state highways. Accordingly, it wants to know whether the sample size determined in part a is large enough to also estimate μ to within .25 mile per hour with 90% confidence. Assume that the standard deviation of vehicle speeds is approximately 2 miles per hour. How large a sample should be taken at site # 42 to estimate μ with the desired reliability?

8.80 The EPA standards on the amount of suspended solids that can be discharged into rivers and streams is a maximum of 60 milligrams per liter daily, with a maximum monthly average of 30 milligrams per liter. Suppose you want to test a randomly selected sample of n water specimens and to estimate the mean daily rate of pollution produced by a mining operation. If you want your estimate correct to within 1 milligram with probability equal to .95, how many water specimens would you have to include in your sample? Assume prior knowledge indicates that pollution readings in water samples taken during a day are approximately normally distributed with a standard deviation equal to 5 milligrams.

8.81 Suppose a department store wants to estimate μ, the average age of the customer in its contemporary apparel department, correct to within 2 years with probability equal to .95. Approximately how large a sample would be required? [*Note:* The management does not know σ but guesses that the age of its customers ranges from 15 to 45. If you take this range to equal 4σ, you will have a conservative approximation to σ that can be used to calculate n.]

8.82 A marketing research organization wishes to estimate the proportion of television viewers who watch a particular prime-time situation comedy on May 24. The proportion is expected to be approximately .30. At a minimum, how many viewers should be randomly selected to ensure that a 95% confidence interval for the true proportion of viewers will have a width of .01 or less?

8.83 Before a bill to increase federal price supports for farmers comes before the U.S. Congress, a Congressman would like to know how nonfarmers feel about the issue. Approximately how many nonfarmers should the Congressman survey in order to estimate the true proportion favoring this bill to within .05 with probability equal to .98? [*Hint:* Since you do not have prior knowledge about p, substitute $p = .5$ into the formula to find the sample size. This will give a value for n that is at least as large as required.]

8.84 According to a Food and Drug Administration (FDA) study, the average cup of coffee contains an average of 115 milligrams of caffeine, with the amount per cup ranging from 60 to 180 milligrams. In contrast, sugar-free Mr. Pibb tested at 58.8 milligrams caffeine per 12-ounce serving, Coca-Cola and Diet Coke at 45.6 milligrams, and Pepsi at 38.4 milligrams. Suppose you want to repeat the FDA experiment to obtain an estimate of the mean caffeine content in a cup of coffee correct to within 5 milligrams per cup with 95% confidence. How many cups of coffee would have to be included in your sample?

8.85 Suppose you are a retailer and you want to estimate the proportion of your customers who are shoplifters. You decide to select a random sample of shoppers and check closely to determine whether they steal any merchandise while in the store. Suppose experience suggests that the percentage of shoplifters is near 5%. How many customers should you include in your sample if you want to estimate the proportion of shoplifters in your store correct to within .02 with probability equal to .90?

8.86 A market researcher wants to select one sample to estimate both μ, the average age of people living within 5 miles of a proposed shopping mall site, and p, the proportion of people within that 5-mile radius who are between 20 and 40 years of age. He wants to estimate μ with a 95% confidence interval that is no more than 6 years wide and p with a 90% confidence interval of width no greater than .1. It is known from previous studies of this population that the standard deviation of the ages in the population is 10 years, and it is believed that p is near .4. How large a sample does the researcher need to draw in order to construct confidence intervals for both μ and p that satisfy the above specifications?

Summary

The objective of statistics is to make inferences about a population based on information in a sample. In this chapter, we have presented several methods for accomplishing this objective.

The inference-making techniques we discussed are *estimation* and *hypothesis testing.* Estimation of a population parameter is accomplished by using an interval estimate with a probability of coverage (*confidence coefficient*) that is fixed by the researcher at a high level (usually .90, .95, or .99). On the other hand, when a specific *alternative (research) hypothesis* about a parameter is tested, the probability α of falsely rejecting the *null hypothesis* and accepting the alternative hypothesis is chosen to be small. Thus, we try to minimize the chance of error in both of these inference-making procedures.

One of the most important parameters about which inferences are made is the population mean, μ. The sample mean, $\bar{x}$, is used for making the inference, but the inferential procedure depends on the *sample size.* When the sample size is large (we have specified $n > 30$ as large), the *standard normal z statistic* is used. The *t statistic* is used when σ is unknown and a small sample is drawn from a normally (or approximately normally) distributed population.

Supplementary Exercises 8.87–8.107

8.87 Let t_0 be a particular value of t. Use Table V of Appendix B to find the values such that the following statements are true:

a. $P(t \le t_0) = .05$ where df $= 20$ **b.** $P(t \ge t_0) = .005$ where df $= 9$
c. $P(t \le -t_0 \text{ or } t \ge t_0) = .10$ where df $= 8$
d. $P(t \le -t_0 \text{ or } t \ge t_0) = .01$ where df $= 17$

8.88 This exercise is designed to give you practice computing p-values. Find approximate values for each of the following:

a. For df $= 10$, find $P(t \ge 1.95)$.   **b.** For df $= 25$, find $P(t \le -2.60)$.
c. For df $= 15$, find $P(t \le -1.45 \text{ or } t \ge 1.45)$.
d. For df $= 7$, find $P(t \le -3.33 \text{ or } t \ge 3.33)$.

8.89 If the rejection of the null hypothesis of a particular test would cause your firm to go out of business, would you want α to be small or large? Explain.

8.90 A large New York City bank is interested in estimating (1) the proportion of weeks in which it processes more than 100,000 checks and (2) the average number of checks it processes per week. The bank maintains records of x, the number of checks processed each week. Suppose the bank records the number of checks, x, processed per week for 50 weeks randomly sampled from among the past 6 years. Define *in the context of the problem* each of the following:

a. $\bar{x}$. **b.** $\hat{p}$ **c.** σ_x **d.** μ_x **e.** n **f.** $\sigma_{\bar{x}}$ **g.** p **h.** s_x

8.91 A firm's president, vice-presidents, department managers, and others use financial data generated by the firm's accounting system to help them make decisions regarding such things as pricing, budgeting, and plant expansion. To provide reasonable certainty that the system provides reliable data, internal auditors periodically perform various checks of the system (Taylor & Glezen, 1979). Suppose an internal auditor is interested in determining the proportion of sales invoices in a population of 5,000 sales invoices for which the "total sales" figure is in error. She plans to estimate the true proportion of invoices in error based on a random sample of size 100.

a. Assume that the population of invoices is numbered from 1 to 5,000 and that every invoice ending with a 0 is in error (i.e., 10% are in error). Use the random number table (Table I in Appendix B) to draw a random sample of 100 invoices from the population of 5,000 invoices. For example, random number 456 stands for invoice number 456. List the invoice numbers in your sample and indicate which of your sampled invoices are in error (i.e., those ending in a 0).

b. Use the results of your sample of part a to construct a 90% confidence interval for the true proportion of invoices in error.

c. Recall that the true population proportion of invoices in error is equal to .1. Compare the true proportion with the estimate of the true proportion you developed in part b. Does your confidence interval include the true proportion?

8.92 A company is interested in estimating μ, the mean number of days of sick leave taken by all its employees. The firm's statistician selects at random 100 personnel files and notes the number of sick days taken by each employee. The following sample statistics are computed:

$\bar{x} = 12.2$ days $s = 10$ days

a. Estimate μ using a 90% confidence interval.

b. How many personnel files would the statistician have to select in order to estimate μ to within 2 days with 99% confidence?

c. Do the data support the alternative hypothesis that μ, the mean number of sick days taken by the employees, is greater than 10.9 days? Test at $\alpha = .05$. Report the observed significance level of the test.

8.93 A sample of 300 transistors are tested and 12 are found to be defective. Find a 95% confidence interval for p, the true fraction defective.

8.94 Refer to Exercise 8.93. Approximately how many transistors would need to be sampled in order to estimate p to within .01 with probability equal to .95?

8.95 In checking the reliability of a bank's records, auditing firms sometimes ask a sample of the bank's customers to confirm the accuracy of their savings account balances as reported by the bank. Suppose an auditing firm is interested in estimating the proportion of a bank's savings accounts on whose balances the bank and the customer disagree. Of 200 savings account customers questioned by the auditors, fifteen said their balance disagreed with that reported by the bank.

a. Estimate the actual proportion of the bank's savings accounts on whose balances the bank and customer disagree using a 95% confidence level.

b. The bank claims that the true fraction of accounts on which there is disagreement is no more than .05. You, as an auditor, doubt this claim. Does the sample provide evidence that the true fraction of accounts subject to disagreement exceeds .05? Use $\alpha = .10$ to perform the test.

8.96 Find and interpret the p-value for the test in part b of Exercise 8.95.

8.97 Refer to Exercise 8.95. How many savings account customers should the auditors question if they want to estimate p to within .02 with probability equal to .95?

8.98 The EPA sets a limit of 5 parts per million on PCB (a dangerous substance) in water. A major manufacturing firm producing PCB for electrical insulation discharges small amounts from the plant. The company management, attempting to control the amount of PCB in its discharge, has given instructions to halt production if the mean amount of PCB in the effluent exceeds 3 parts per million. A random sampling of fifty water specimens produced the following statistics: $\bar{x} = 3.1$ parts per million, $s = 0.5$ part per million.

a. Do these statistics provide sufficient evidence to halt the production process? Use $\alpha = .01$.

b. If you were the plant manager, would you want to use a large or a small value for α for the test in part a? Explain.

c. Find the p-value for the test and interpret its value.

8.99 A large mail-order company has placed an order for 5,000 electric can openers with a supplier on condition that no more than 2% of the can openers will be defective. To check the shipment, the company tests a random sample of 400 of the can openers and finds eleven are defective. Does this provide sufficient evidence to indicate that the proportion of defective can openers in the shipment exceeds 2%? Test using $\alpha = .05$.

8.100 Find and interpret the observed significance level for the hypothesis test you conducted in Exercise 8.99.

8.101 Refer to Exercise 8.99. Suppose the company wants to estimate the proportion, p, of defective can openers in the shipment correct to within .04 with probability equal to .95. Approximately how large a sample would be required?

8.102 The Internal Revenue Service is conducting an audit of the 10,000 outlets of a large fast-food chain. They are interested in determining the average error in reported income last year for all outlets in the chain. The size of the chain precludes a census (an audit of all 10,000 outlets), so 100 outlets are randomly selected and audited. Let x = Error in reported income = (Actual income − Reported income) for a given firm. The audits yielded the following statistics:

$$\bar{x} = \$12,522 \qquad s = \$4,000$$

a. Construct a 95% confidence interval for the mean error in reported income per outlet.
b. What does the confidence interval from part a reflect regarding the chain's income-reporting behavior last year?

8.103 Many people think that a national lobby's successful fight against gun control legislation is reflecting the will of a small minority of Americans. A random sample of 4,000 citizens yielded 2,250 who are in favor of gun control legislation. Use a 95% confidence interval to estimate the true proportion of Americans who favor gun control legislation. Interpret the result.

8.104 In the past, a chemical company produced 880 pounds of a certain type of plastic per day. Now, using a newly developed and less expensive process, the mean daily yield of plastic for the first 50 days of production was 871 pounds; the standard deviation was 21 pounds.

a. Do the data provide sufficient evidence to indicate that the mean daily yield for the new process is less than for the old procedure? (Test using $\alpha = .01$.)
b. What assumptions must you make in order to use the statistical test you employed?

8.105 Refer to Exercise 8.104. Find and interpret the p-value for the test conducted.

8.106 A discount store claims that its steel-belted radial tires are more resistant to wear than those of a major tire company. The following experiment was performed to test this claim. On each of forty cars, one discount tire and one rubber company tire were mounted on the rear axle. After each car was driven 8,000 miles, the tires were inspected for wear. Suppose the tires of the discount store show less wear on thirty-two of the cars. What would you conclude about the discount store's claim? Why?

8.107 [*Note:* This exercise uses material discussed in optional Section 5.5.] A survey of 2,000 Americans reported in the *Gainesville Sun* (Mar. 19, 1984) contains both good and bad news for the nation's pharmacists and physicians. The good news is that there is plenty of business. Americans have a minor physical ailment once every 3 days, on the average. The bad news is that the respondents handle 90% of the problems themselves by treating themselves with over-the-counter drugs, home remedies, or simply ignoring their ailments. The estimate of the time between ailments is based on the reported number, x, of ailments a respondent might expect to encounter in a typical 2-week period. The average for the survey of 2,000 respondents was 4.5. How accurate is this sample estimate of the mean number, μ, of ailments per person per 2-week period for the population of all adult Americans? To answer this question, find a 99% confidence interval for μ and interpret your results. [*Hint:* The probability distribution of the number of ailments per person in a 2-week period can be approximated by a Poisson probability distribution. For a Poisson random variable, $\sigma^2 = \mu$ and, therefore, an estimate of σ^2 is provided by the sample mean $\bar{x}$.]

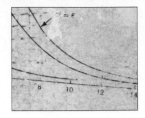

On Your Own . . .

Choose a population pertinent to your major area of interest that has an unknown mean (or, if the population is binomial, that has an unknown proportion of success). For example, a marketing major may be interested in the proportion of consumers who prefer a particular product. An advertising major might want to estimate the proportion of the television viewing audience who regularly watch a particular program. An economics major may want to estimate the mean monthly expenditure of college students on food.

Define the parameter you want to estimate and conduct a *pilot study* to obtain an initial estimate of the parameter of interest and, more important, an estimate of the variability associated with the estimator. A pilot study is a small experiment (perhaps twenty to thirty observations) used to gain some information about the population of interest. The purpose is to help plan more elaborate future experiments. Based on the results of your pilot study, determine the sample size necessary to estimate the parameter to within a reasonable bound (of your choice) with a 95% confidence interval.

References

"A penny refunded is a penny earned." *Minneapolis Star,* Nov. 29, 1981, 7F.

"Advertising deters but doesn't end hostility." *Marketing News,* Feb. 13, 1976, 5.

Caplen, R. *A practical approach to quality control.* London: Business Books, 1970. Chapter 15.

Conway, J. J. "Business energy audit and control practices." *Business Economics,* Mar. 1980, *15,* 21–22.

Duncan, A. J. *Quality control and industrial statistics.* 4th ed. Homewood, Ill.: Richard D. Irwin, 1974. Chapter 1.

Environmental Protection Agency. *Environment midwest,* Sept.–Oct. 1976, Region V. Washington, D.C.: U.S. Government Printing Office.

"Level of tainted fish falls in Great Lakes." *Minneapolis Tribune,* Oct. 24, 1983, 15C.

"McDonald's blends new products with savvy merchandising." *Business Week,* July 11, 1977, 59.

Mendenhall, W., & Reinmuth, J. E. *Statistics for management and economics.* 4th ed. Boston: Duxbury, 1982. Chapters 8 and 9.

"Monitor: Vehicle speeds." *Minneapolis Star,* May 2, 1980, 11A.

Nemy, E. "Survey says two-thirds of Americans see themselves as younger than they are." *Minneapolis Tribune,* Dec. 19, 1982, 2F.

"One answer to imports: Wonder-iron." *Fortune,* Feb. 9, 1981, 71.

Report of definitions committee of the American Marketing Association. Chicago: American Marketing Association, 1961.

Rosen, B., Rynes, S., & Mahoney, T. A. "Compensation, jobs, and gender." *Harvard Business Review,* July–Aug. 1983, 170–190.

Taylor, D. H., & Glezen, G. W. *"Auditing, integrated concepts and procedures."* New York: Wiley, 1979. P. 3.

U.S. Bureau of the Census. *Statistical abstract of the United States: 1981.* 102d ed. Washington, D.C.: U.S. Government Printing Office, 1981.

Wetherill, G. B. *Sampling, inspection, and quality control.* 2d ed., London: Chapman and Hall, 1977. Chapter 3.

Willis, R. E., & Chervany, N. L. *Statistical analysis and modeling for management decision-making.* Belmont, Calif.: Wadsworth, 1974. Chapters 8 and 11.

CHAPTER 9

Two Samples: Estimation and Tests of Hypotheses

Where We've Been . . .

The two methods for making statistical inferences, estimation and tests of hypotheses, were presented in Chapter 8. Confidence intervals and tests of hypotheses based on single samples were used to make inferences about sampled populations. We gave confidence intervals and tests of hypotheses concerning a population mean, μ, and a binomial proportion, p, and learned how to select the sample size necessary to obtain a specified amount of information concerning a parameter.

Where We're Going . . .

Now that we have learned to make inferences about a single population, it is natural that we would want to compare two populations. We may want to compare the mean costs per pound in the manufacture of two drugs or the mean lives of two industrial products. We may also wish to compare two population proportions, say the proportions of consumers who prefer a product before and after an advertising campaign. How to decide whether differences exist in population means or proportions and how to estimate these differences will be the subject of this chapter.

Contents

333

9.1 Large-Sample Inferences about the Difference Between Two Population Means: Independent Sampling

Suppose a chain of department stores is considering two suburbs of a large city as alternatives for locating a new store. The final decision about which location to choose is to be based on a comparison of the mean incomes of families living in the two suburbs.* The store is to be located in the suburb that has the higher mean income per household.

Let μ_1 represent the mean income of families in suburb 1 and μ_2 represent the mean income of families in suburb 2. Then our objective is to make an inference about $(\mu_1 - \mu_2)$, the difference between the mean incomes for the two suburbs.

Suppose independent samples of 100 households are randomly selected from each suburb, and the mean incomes, $\bar{x}_1$ and $\bar{x}_2$, are calculated for the two samples. An intuitively appealing estimator for $(\mu_1 - \mu_2)$ is the difference between the sample means, $(\bar{x}_1 - \bar{x}_2)$. The performance of this estimator in repeated sampling is summarized by the properties of its sampling distribution (see Figure 9.1).[†]

Figure 9.1 Sampling Distribution of $(\bar{x}_1 - \bar{x}_2)$

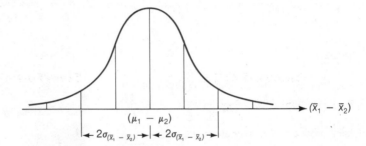

Properties of the Sampling Distribution of $(\bar{x}_1 - \bar{x}_2)$

1. The sampling distribution of $(\bar{x}_1 - \bar{x}_2)$ is approximately normal for *large* samples.
2. The mean of the sampling distribution of $(\bar{x}_1 - \bar{x}_2)$ is $(\mu_1 - \mu_2)$.
3. If the two samples are independent, the standard deviation of the sampling distribution is

$$\sigma_{(\bar{x}_1 - \bar{x}_2)} = \sqrt{\frac{\sigma_1^2}{n_1} + \frac{\sigma_2^2}{n_2}}$$

where σ_1^2 and σ_2^2 are the variances of the two populations being sampled, and n_1 and n_2 are the respective sample sizes.

Since the shape of the sampling distribution is approximately normal for large samples, we can use the z statistic to make inferences about $(\mu_1 - \mu_2)$, just as we did for a single mean.

---

* Assume the incomes within a suburb are moderately homogeneous and hence the distributions are not heavily skewed. For this case, the mean would be a satisfactory measure of central tendency for the data.

† The sampling distribution of $(\bar{x}_1 - \bar{x}_2)$ for large samples was discussed in Section 7.5.

The procedures for forming confidence intervals and testing hypotheses are summarized in the boxes. Note the similarity of these procedures to their counterparts for a single mean (Sections 8.1 and 8.2).

Large-Sample Confidence Interval for $(\mu_1 - \mu_2)$

$$(\bar{x}_1 - \bar{x}_2) \pm z_{\alpha/2}\sigma_{(\bar{x}_1 - \bar{x}_2)} = (\bar{x}_1 - \bar{x}_2) \pm z_{\alpha/2}\sqrt{\frac{\sigma_1^2}{n_1} + \frac{\sigma_2^2}{n_2}}$$

Assumptions: The two samples are randomly selected in an independent manner from the two populations. The sample sizes, n_1 and n_2, are large enough so that $\bar{x}_1$ and $\bar{x}_2$ each have approximately normal sampling distributions and so that s_1^2 and s_2^2 provide good approximations to σ_1^2 and σ_2^2. This will be true if $n_1 \geq 30$ and $n_2 \geq 30$.

Large-Sample Test of an Hypothesis for $(\mu_1 - \mu_2)$

One-Tailed Test

H_0: $(\mu_1 - \mu_2) = D_0$

H_a: $(\mu_1 - \mu_2) < D_0$
  [or H_a: $(\mu_1 - \mu_2) > D_0$]

Two-Tailed Test

H_0: $(\mu_1 - \mu_2) = D_0$

H_a: $(\mu_1 - \mu_2) \neq D_0$

where D_0 = Hypothesized difference between the means (this is often zero) *D₀ OFTEN =0*

Test statistic: $z = \dfrac{(\bar{x}_1 - \bar{x}_2) - D_0}{\sigma_{(\bar{x}_1 - \bar{x}_2)}}$

Test statistic: $z = \dfrac{(\bar{x}_1 - \bar{x}_2) - D_0}{\sigma_{(\bar{x}_1 - \bar{x}_2)}}$

where $\sigma_{(\bar{x}_1 - \bar{x}_2)} = \sqrt{\dfrac{\sigma_1^2}{n_1} + \dfrac{\sigma_2^2}{n_2}}$

Rejection region: $z < -z_\alpha$
  [or $z > z_\alpha$ when
  H_a: $(\mu_1 - \mu_2) > D_0$]

Rejection region: $z < -z_{\alpha/2}$
  or $z > z_{\alpha/2}$

Assumptions: Same as for the large-sample confidence interval above.

For example, suppose the means and standard deviations of the incomes of the sampled households from the two suburbs are as follows:

SUBURB 1	SUBURB 2
$\bar{x}_1 = \$18{,}750$	$\bar{x}_2 = \$15{,}150$
$s_1 = \$3{,}200$	$s_2 = \$2{,}700$
$n_1 = 100$	$n_2 = 100$

Then to form a 95% confidence interval for the difference $(\mu_1 - \mu_2)$ between the true mean suburban incomes, we calculate

$$(\bar{x}_1 - \bar{x}_2) \pm 1.96\sqrt{\frac{\sigma_1^2}{n_1} + \frac{\sigma_2^2}{n_2}} = (18{,}750 - 15{,}150) \pm 1.96\sqrt{\frac{\sigma_1^2}{100} + \frac{\sigma_2^2}{100}}$$

To complete the calculations for this confidence interval, we must estimate σ_1^2 and σ_2^2. Since the samples are both relatively large, the sample variances s_1^2 and s_2^2 will provide reasonable approximations. Thus, our interval is approximately

$$3{,}600 \pm 1.96\sqrt{\frac{(3{,}200)^2}{100} + \frac{(2{,}700)^2}{100}} = 3{,}600 \pm 821 = (2{,}779,\ 4{,}421)$$

Using this estimation procedure, confidence intervals of this type will enclose the difference in population means, $(\mu_1 - \mu_2)$, 95% of the time. Therefore, we are reasonably confident that the mean income of households in suburb 1 is between $2,779 and $4,421 higher than the mean income of households in suburb 2. Based on this information, the department store chain should build the new store in suburb 1.

Example 9.1   The management of a restaurant wants to determine whether a new advertising campaign has increased its mean daily income (gross). The daily incomes for 50 business days prior to the campaign's beginning were recorded. After conducting the advertising campaign and allowing a 20-day period for the advertising to take effect, the restaurant management recorded the income for 30 business days. These two samples will allow the management to make an inference about the effect of the advertising campaign on the restaurant's daily income. A summary of the results of the two samples is shown below:

BEFORE CAMPAIGN	AFTER CAMPAIGN
$n_1 = 50$	$n_2 = 30$
$\bar{x}_1 = \$1{,}255$	$\bar{x}_2 = \$1{,}330$
$s_1 = \$215$	$s_2 = \$238$

Do these samples provide sufficient evidence for the management to conclude that the mean income has been increased by the advertising campaign? Test using $\alpha = .05$.

Solution   We can best answer this question by performing a test of an hypothesis. Defining μ_1 as the mean daily income before the campaign and μ_2 as the mean daily income after the campaign, we will attempt to support the alternative (research) hypothesis that $\mu_2 > \mu_1$ [i.e., that $(\mu_1 - \mu_2) < 0$]. Thus, we will test the null hypothesis, $(\mu_1 - \mu_2) = 0$, rejecting this hypothesis if $(\bar{x}_1 - \bar{x}_2)$ equals a large negative value. The elements of the test are as follows:

H_0: $(\mu_1 - \mu_2) = 0$ (i.e., $\mu_1 = \mu_2$; note that $D_0 = 0$ for this hypothesis test)

H_a: $(\mu_1 - \mu_2) < 0$ (i.e., $\mu_1 < \mu_2$)

Test statistic: $z = \dfrac{(\bar{x}_1 - \bar{x}_2) - D_0}{\sigma_{(\bar{x}_1 - \bar{x}_2)}} = \dfrac{(\bar{x}_1 - \bar{x}_2) - 0}{\sigma_{(\bar{x}_1 - \bar{x}_2)}}$

Rejection region: $z < -z_\alpha = -1.645$ (see Figure 9.2)

Figure 9.2 Rejection Region for Advertising Campaign Example

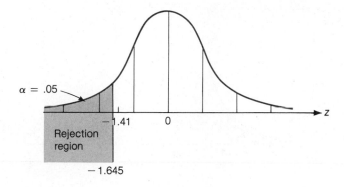

We now calculate

$$z = \frac{(\bar{x}_1 - \bar{x}_2) - 0}{\sigma_{(\bar{x}_1 - \bar{x}_2)}} = \frac{(1{,}255 - 1{,}330)}{\sqrt{\dfrac{\sigma_1^2}{n_1} + \dfrac{\sigma_2^2}{n_2}}}$$

$$\approx \frac{-75}{\sqrt{\dfrac{s_1^2}{n_1} + \dfrac{s_2^2}{n_2}}} = \frac{-75}{\sqrt{\dfrac{(215)^2}{50} + \dfrac{(238)^2}{30}}} = \frac{-75}{53.03} = -1.41$$

As you can see in Figure 9.2, the calculated z value does not fall in the rejection region. The samples do not provide sufficient evidence, at $\alpha = .05$, for the restaurant management to conclude that the advertising campaign has increased the mean daily income. ■

Example 9.2 Find the observed significance level for the test from Example 9.1.

Solution The alternative hypothesis in Example 9.1, $H_a : (\mu_1 - \mu_2) < 0$, required a lower one-tailed test using

$$z = \frac{\bar{x}_1 - \bar{x}_2}{\sigma_{(\bar{x}_1 - \bar{x}_2)}}$$

as a test statistic. Since the value of z calculated from the sample data was -1.41, the observed significance level (p-value) for the test is the probability of observing a value of z at least as contradictory to the null hypothesis as $z = -1.41$; i.e.,

$$p\text{-value} = P(z \le -1.41)$$

This probability is computed assuming H_0 is true and is equal to the shaded area shown in Figure 9.3.

The tabulated area corresponding to $z = 1.41$ in Table IV, Appendix B, is .4207. Therefore, the observed significance level for the test is

$$p\text{-value} = .5 - .4207 = .0793$$

Figure 9.3   The Observed Significance Level for Example 9.1

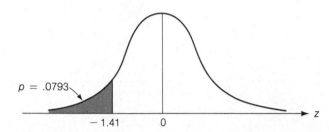

$p = .0793$

-1.41 0 z

You will recall that in Example 9.1, we chose $\alpha = .05$ as the probability of a Type I error and consequently did not reject H_0; that is, we did not find sufficient evidence to indicate that $(\mu_1 - \mu_2) < 0$. If the results of the test had been presented in terms of an observed significance level and left for us to interpret, we might not have reached such an inflexible conclusion. Observing a value of z as small as $z = -1.41$ is an improbable event (rare event) if, in fact, $\mu_1 = \mu_2$. Since the probability is fairly small (.0793) — in fact, quite close to .05 — we would conclude that there is some evidence to suggest that $\mu_1 < \mu_2$. Naturally, we would be more certain of this conclusion if the observed significance level were smaller, say .05, .01, or, better yet, .001. However, the practical question to be answered is not whether the test results are statistically significant but whether the difference between μ_1 and μ_2 is large enough to have a practical business significance. To shed light on this question, we will wish to estimate the difference, $(\mu_1 - \mu_2)$.

Example 9.3   Find a 95% confidence interval for the difference in mean daily incomes before and after the advertising campaign of Example 9.1 and discuss the implications of the confidence interval.

Solution   The 95% confidence interval for $(\mu_1 - \mu_2)$ is

$$(\bar{x}_1 - \bar{x}_2) \pm z_{\alpha/2}\sqrt{\frac{\sigma_1^2}{n_1} + \frac{\sigma_2^2}{n_2}}$$

Once again, we will substitute s_1^2 and s_2^2 for σ_1^2 and σ_2^2 because these quantities will provide good approximations to σ_1^2 and σ_2^2 for samples as large as $n_1 = 50$ and $n_2 = 30$. Then, the 95% confidence interval for $(\mu_1 - \mu_2)$ is

$$(1{,}255 - 1{,}330) \pm 1.96\sqrt{\frac{(215)^2}{50} + \frac{(238)^2}{30}} = -75 \pm 103.94$$

Thus, we estimate the difference in mean daily income to fall in the interval $-\$178.94$ to $\$28.94$. In other words, we estimate that μ_2, the mean daily income *after* the advertising campaign, could be larger than μ_1, the mean daily income *before* the campaign, by as much as \$178.94 per day, or it could be less than μ_1 by \$28.94 per day.

Now what should the restaurant management do? You can see that the sample sizes collected in the experiment were not large enough to detect a difference between μ_1 and μ_2. To be able to detect a difference (if in fact a difference exists), the management will have to repeat the experiment and increase the sample sizes. This will reduce the width of the confidence interval for $(\mu_1 - \mu_2)$. The restaurant management's best estimate of $(\mu_1 - \mu_2)$ is the point estimate $(\bar{x}_1 - \bar{x}_2) = -\$75$. Thus, the management must decide whether the cost of conducting the advertising campaign is overshadowed by a possible gain in mean daily income estimated at \$75 (but which might be as large as \$178.94 or could be as low as $-\$28.94$). Based on this analysis, the management will decide whether to continue the experiment or reject the new advertising program as a poor investment. ■

Exercises 9.1–9.14

Learning the Mechanics

9.1 Suppose you select two independent random samples, forty observations from population 1 and fifty from population 2. The sample means and variances are shown in the table.

SAMPLE 1	SAMPLE 2
$n_1 = 40$	$n_2 = 50$
$\bar{x}_1 = 3.6$	$\bar{x}_2 = 4.2$
$s_1^2 = .32$	$s_2^2 = .25$

a. Find the approximate value of $\sigma_{(\bar{x}_1 - \bar{x}_2)}$ by using s_1^2 and s_2^2 to approximate the values of σ_1^2 and σ_2^2.

b. Use the approximate value of $\sigma_{(\bar{x}_1 - \bar{x}_2)}$ found in part a to sketch the approximate sampling distribution of $(\bar{x}_1 - \bar{x}_2)$ assuming $\mu_1 = \mu_2$.

c. Locate the observed value of $(\bar{x}_1 - \bar{x}_2)$ on the graph you drew in part b. Does it appear that this value contradicts the null hypothesis $\mu_1 = \mu_2$?

d. Use Table IV in Appendix B to locate the rejection region for the z test of the null hypothesis $\mu_1 = \mu_2$. Assume that the alternative hypothesis is $\mu_1 \neq \mu_2$ and that $\alpha = .05$.

e. Calculate the value of the z statistic, and complete the test in part d. Interpret the results.

f. What is the *p*-value for this hypothesis test?

9.2 Explain how the alternative hypothesis for a statistical test is selected. For example, refer to Exercise 9.1 and explain the conditions (in a practical situation) that would imply an alternative hypothesis of the form $H_a: \mu_1 < \mu_2$.

9.3 Refer to Exercise 9.1. Find a 90% confidence interval for $(\mu_1 - \mu_2)$. Interpret the interval.

9.4 Two independent random samples have been selected: 100 from population 1 and 100 from population 2. The sample means and variances are shown in the table.

SAMPLE 1	SAMPLE 2
$n_1 = 100$	$n_2 = 100$
$\bar{x}_1 = 55.2$	$\bar{x}_2 = 50.1$
$s_1^2 = 144$	$s_2^2 = 169$

a. Find the approximate value of $\sigma_{(\bar{x}_1 - \bar{x}_2)}$ by using s_1^2 and s_2^2 to approximate the values of σ_1^2 and σ_2^2.

b. Describe the approximate sampling distribution of $(\bar{x}_1 - \bar{x}_2)$ if in fact $(\mu_1 - \mu_2) = 15$.

c. Use Table IV in Appendix B to determine the rejection region for the z test of the null hypothesis $\mu_1 = \mu_2$ versus the alternative hypothesis $\mu_1 > \mu_2$. Use $\alpha = .10$.

d. Use the data given in the table to conduct the hypothesis test described in part c. Interpret the results.

e. Report the observed significance level for the hypothesis test and explain its meaning.

9.5 Refer to Exercise 9.4. Find a 98% confidence interval for $(\mu_1 - \mu_2)$. Interpret the result.

Applying the Concepts

9.6 A paper company conducted an experiment to compare the mean time to unload shipments of logs for two different unloading procedures. Random samples of fifty trucks each were unloaded using a new method and the company's current method. The objective of the experiment is to determine whether the new method will reduce the mean unloading time. The sample means and standard deviations are shown in the table.

NEW METHOD	CURRENT METHOD
$n_1 = 50$	$n_2 = 50$
$\bar{x}_1 = 25.4$ minutes	$\bar{x}_2 = 27.3$ minutes
$s_1 = 3.1$ minutes	$s_2 = 3.7$ minutes

a. Do the data provide sufficient evidence to indicate that the mean unloading time for the new method is less than the mean unloading time for the method currently in use? Test using $\alpha = .05$.

b. Give the observed significance level for the test.

9.7 Refer to Exercise 9.6. Find a 90% confidence interval for the difference in mean unloading times between the two methods.

9.8 Tennant Co., a Minnesota manufacturer of industrial floor-cleaning machines, recently began using "quality circles" to help improve the quality of their product. The term *quality circles* describes a process in which groups comprised of both white-collar and blue-collar employees attempt to solve quality, productivity, and/or work environment problems. According to a recent survey of 6,800 companies by the New York Stock Exchange's Office of Economic Research, 74% had quality circle programs.

In 1979, at the time Tennant began its quality circles program, a sample of finished machines was found to have an average of 4.2 defects per machine. Because of such defects, the company had to pay its employees $16.6 million for the 39,600 hours of labor required to rework the defective machines. In 1982, a sample of machines revealed a substantial improvement in quality. The mean number of defectives was reduced to 1.3 flaws per machine, and rework was down to 3,500 hours of labor (Marcotty, 1983a, 1983b). Assume that each sample of machines was randomly selected and was of size 100. Further, assume that the sample standard deviations for 1979 and 1982 were 2.0 and 1.1, respectively.

a. While the decline in the average number of defects per machine between 1979 and 1982 appears to be significant from a managerial perspective, is it statistically significant? To answer this question, conduct the appropriate hypothesis test and report and interpret the observed significance level of the test.

b. In the context of the problem, describe the Type I and Type II errors associated with your hypothesis test of part a.

9.9 Thirty-six stocks were randomly selected from those listed on the New York Stock Exchange (NYSE), and thirty stocks were randomly selected from those listed on the American Stock Exchange (ASE). The closing prices of all sixty-six stocks on Dec. 31, 1982, are listed in the table.

NYSE		ASE	
Firm	Closing price	Firm	Closing price
Consumers Pwr Co	$27\frac{5}{8}$	American Maize Prods	$10\frac{6}{8}$
Sealed Air Corp	$28\frac{2}{8}$	Aloha Airls Inc	$8\frac{5}{8}$
City Investing Co	$46\frac{4}{8}$	Lloyd S. Electrs Inc	$2\frac{3}{8}$
Duquesne Lt Co	15	Mite Corp	27
Onicare Inc	$43\frac{5}{8}$	Vintage Enterprises	$5\frac{5}{8}$
Detroit Edison Co	$24\frac{4}{8}$	Caressa Inc	14
Consumers Pwr Co	$19\frac{5}{8}$	Pneumatic Scale Corp	16
Virginia Elec & Pwr Co	58	Wards Inc	$16\frac{2}{8}$
Duke Power Co	$21\frac{6}{8}$	Avondale Mls	24
Fischbach Corp	$48\frac{5}{8}$	Electro Audio Dynamics	$3\frac{1}{8}$
Union Elec Co	35	Martin Processing Inc	$3\frac{4}{8}$
L & N Hsg Corp	$29\frac{4}{8}$	Raymond Inds Inc	$19\frac{5}{8}$
Barnett Banks Fla Inc	27	Pizza Inn Inc	$6\frac{3}{8}$
Ahmanson H. F. & Co	$27\frac{6}{8}$	Telesciences Inc	24
Reynolds R. J. Inds Inc	51	Enerserv Prods Inc	$3\frac{3}{8}$
Woolworth F. W. Co	36	Starrett Hsg Corp	$4\frac{6}{8}$
Penna Pwr & Lt	21	Eastern Co	$11\frac{2}{8}$
Honda Motor Ltd	43	Blocker Energy Corp	$3\frac{1}{8}$
Western Pac Inds Del	$55\frac{2}{8}$	Laneco Inc	27
Phillips Van Heusen Cp	$19\frac{4}{8}$	Berry Inds Corp	3
Handleman Co Del	19	EAC Inds Inc	$8\frac{3}{8}$
Dennys Inc	$31\frac{7}{8}$	Chilton Corp	$12\frac{1}{8}$
House Fabrics Inc	28	Scope Inds	31
Commonwealth Edison Co	$23\frac{1}{8}$	Forest City Enterprise	$18\frac{2}{8}$
Public Svc Co Ind Inc	28	Transcontntl Energy Del	$4\frac{6}{8}$
White Cons Inds Inc	36	Ultimate Corp	$13\frac{4}{8}$
American Nat Res Co	$33\frac{4}{8}$	Royal Palm Bch Colony	$2\frac{4}{8}$
Boston Edison Co	26	Noel Inds Inc	$3\frac{2}{8}$
Atlantic Met Corp	$20\frac{6}{8}$	TIE/Communications Inc	38
Financial Corp Amer	$25\frac{7}{8}$	Asamera Inc	$13\frac{2}{8}$
Superscope Inc	$2\frac{5}{8}$		
Cp Natl Corp	$29\frac{7}{8}$		
Gleason Wks	$10\frac{4}{8}$		
Great Lakes Intl Inc	$23\frac{6}{8}$		
Evans Prods Co	$8\frac{3}{8}$		
Middle South Utils Inc	$14\frac{7}{8}$		

a. Use a 95% confidence interval to estimate the difference between the mean price of a share of stock traded on the NYSE and the mean price of a share of stock traded on the ASE. Interpret your result.

b. Carefully define the populations about which you can make inferences using the confidence interval you constructed in part a.

c. Suppose ten more stocks were randomly selected from each stock exchange. If the confidence interval of part a were recalculated using $n_1 = 46$ and $n_2 = 40$, would the width of the resulting confidence interval necessarily be narrower? Explain.

9.10 As part of a study in participative management, George H. Hines (1974) sampled workers from two types of New Zealand sociocultural backgrounds: those who believed in the existence of a class system and those who believed that they lived and worked in a classless society. Each worker in the sampling was selected from a work environment with a high degree of participatory management. Do workers who consider themselves to be social equals with their management superiors possess different levels of job satisfaction than those workers who see themselves as socially different from management? Each worker in the independent random samples was asked to answer this question by rating his or her job satisfaction on a scale of 1 (poor) to 7 (excellent). Based on the results of this study (shown in the table), what can you say about differences in job satisfaction for the two different sociocultural types of workers? Use $\alpha = .10$.

	BELIEF IN EXISTENCE OF A CLASS SYSTEM	
	Yes	No
SAMPLE SIZE	175	277
MEAN	5.42	5.19
STANDARD DEVIATION	1.24	1.17

9.11 An experiment has been conducted to compare the productivity of two machines. Machine 1 produced an average of 51.4 items per hour and a standard deviation of $s_1 = 2.1$ for 35 randomly selected hours during the past 2 weeks. Machine 2 produced an average of 49.5 items per hour and a standard deviation of $s_2 = 1.8$ for 45 randomly selected hours during the past 2 weeks.

a. Describe the populations being compared.

b. Do the samples provide sufficient evidence at $\alpha = .10$ to conclude that machine 1 produces more items per hour, on the average, than machine 2?

c. Report the p-value for the test you conducted in part b.

9.12 Refer to Exercise 9.11. Construct a 95% confidence interval for $(\mu_1 - \mu_2)$. Would a 99% confidence interval be narrower or wider than the one you constructed? Why?

9.13 Two manufacturers of corrugated fiberboard each claim that the strength of their product tests at more than 360 pounds per square inch on the average. As a result of consumer complaints, a consumer products testing firm believes that firm A's product is stronger than firm B's. To test its belief, 100 fiberboards were chosen randomly from firm A's inventory and 100 were chosen from firm B's inventory. The strength of each fiberboard was tested and the results (in pounds per square inch) are summarized in the table.

a. Does the sample information support the consumer products testing firm's belief? Test at $\alpha = .05$.

b. What assumptions did you make in conducting the test in part a? Do you think such assumptions could comfortably be made in practice? Why or why not?

A	B
$\bar{x}_1 = 365$	$\bar{x}_2 = 352$
$s_1 = 23$	$s_2 = 41$

9.14 Refer to Exercise 9.13. Does the sample information support firm A's claim that the mean strength of its corrugated fiberboard is more than 360 pounds per square inch? Test at $\alpha = .10$.

9.2
Small-Sample Inferences about the Difference Between Two Population Means: Independent Sampling

Suppose a television network wanted to determine whether major sports events or first-run movies attract more viewers in the prime-time hours. It selected twenty-eight prime-time evenings; of these, thirteen had programs devoted to major sports events, and the remaining fifteen had first-run movies. The number of viewers (estimated by a television viewer rating firm) was recorded for each program. If μ_1 is the mean number of sports viewers per evening of sports programming and μ_2 is the mean number of movie viewers per evening, we want to detect a difference between μ_1 and μ_2—if such a difference exists. Therefore, we want to test the null hypothesis

$$H_0: (\mu_1 - \mu_2) = 0$$

against the alternative hypothesis

$$H_a: (\mu_1 - \mu_2) \neq 0 \quad \text{(i.e., either } \mu_1 > \mu_2 \text{ or } \mu_2 > \mu_1)$$

Since the sample sizes are small, s_1^2 and s_2^2 will be unreliable estimates of σ_1^2 and σ_2^2 and the z test statistic will be inappropriate for the test. But, as in the case of a single mean (Section 8.4), we can construct a Student's t statistic. This statistic (formula to be given subsequently) has the familiar t distribution described in Chapter 8. *To use the t statistic, both sampled populations must be approximately normally distributed with equal population variances, and the random samples must be selected independently of each other.* The normality and equal variances assumptions would imply relative frequency distributions for the populations that would appear as shown in Figure 9.4. We will assume that the distributions of the two populations of numbers of television viewers will approximately satisfy these assumptions.

Figure 9.4 Assumptions for the Two-Sample t:
(1) Normal Populations
(2) Equal Variances

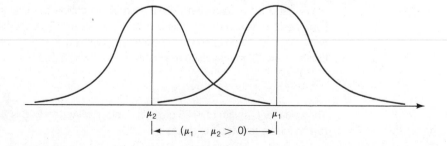

Since we assume the two populations have equal variances ($\sigma_1^2 = \sigma_2^2 = \sigma^2$), it is reasonable to combine the sum of squares of deviations from the two samples to construct a pooled sample estimator of σ^2 for use in the t statistic. Thus, if s_1^2 and s_2^2 are the two sample variances (both estimating the variance σ^2 common to both populations), the pooled estimator of σ^2, denoted as s_p^2, is

$$s_p^2 = \frac{\overbrace{\sum_{i=1}^{n_1}(x_i - \bar{x}_1)^2}^{\substack{\text{From}\\\text{sample 1}}} + \overbrace{\sum_{i=1}^{n_2}(x_i - \bar{x}_2)^2}^{\substack{\text{From}\\\text{sample 2}}}}{n_1 + n_2 - 2}$$

or

$$s_p^2 = \frac{(n_1 - 1)s_1^2 + (n_2 - 1)s_2^2}{(n_1 - 1) + (n_2 - 1)}$$

$$= \frac{(n_1 - 1)s_1^2 + (n_2 - 1)s_2^2}{n_1 + n_2 - 2}$$

where x_1 represents a measurement from sample 1 and x_2 represents a measurement from sample 2. Recall that the term *degrees of freedom* was defined in Section 8.4 as 1 less than the sample size for each sample—i.e., $(n_1 - 1)$ for sample 1 and $(n_2 - 1)$ for sample 2. Since we are pooling the information on σ^2 obtained from both samples, the degrees of freedom associated with the pooled variance s_p^2 is equal to the sum of the degrees of freedom for the two samples, namely, the denominator of s_p^2—i.e., $(n_1 - 1) + (n_2 - 1) = n_1 + n_2 - 2$.

To obtain the small-sample test statistic for testing $H_0: (\mu_1 - \mu_2) = D_0$, substitute the pooled estimate of σ^2 into the formula for the two-sample z statistic (Section 9.1) to obtain

$$t = \frac{(\bar{x}_1 - \bar{x}_2) - D_0}{\sqrt{s_p^2\left(\dfrac{1}{n_1} + \dfrac{1}{n_2}\right)}}$$

It can be shown that this statistic, like the t statistic of Chapter 8, has a t distribution with $(n_1 + n_2 - 2)$ degrees of freedom.

We will use the television viewer example to outline the final steps for this t test: The hypothesized difference in mean number of viewers is $D_0 = 0$. The rejection region will be two-tailed and will be based on a t distribution with $(n_1 + n_2 - 2)$ or $(13 + 15 - 2) = 26$ df. Letting $\alpha = .05$, the rejection region for the test would be

$$t < -t_{\alpha/2} \quad \text{or} \quad t > t_{\alpha/2}$$

The value for $t_{.025}$ with df $= 26$ given in Table V of Appendix B is 2.056. Thus, the rejection region for the television example is

$$t < -2.056 \quad \text{or} \quad t > 2.056$$

This rejection region is shown in Figure 9.5.

Figure 9.5 Rejection Region for a Two-Tailed t Test: $\alpha = .05$, df $= 26$

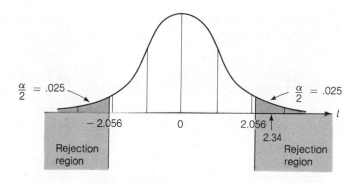

Now, suppose the television network's samples produce the results shown in the table:

SPORTS	MOVIE
$n_1 = 13$	$n_2 = 15$
$\bar{x}_1 = 6.8$ million	$\bar{x}_2 = 5.3$ million
$s_1 = 1.8$ million	$s_2 = 1.6$ million

[*Note:* Although the sample estimates of variance are not equal, the assumption that the population variances are equal may still be valid. We will present a method for checking this assumption statistically in Section 9.3.]

We first calculate

$$s_p^2 = \frac{(n_1 - 1)s_1^2 + (n_2 - 1)s_2^2}{n_1 + n_2 - 2} = \frac{(13 - 1)(1.8)^2 + (15 - 1)(1.6)^2}{13 + 15 - 2}$$

$$= \frac{74.72}{26} = 2.87$$

Then,

$$t = \frac{(\bar{x}_1 - \bar{x}_2) - D_0}{\sqrt{s_p^2\left(\frac{1}{n_1} + \frac{1}{n_2}\right)}} = \frac{(6.8 - 5.3) - 0}{\sqrt{2.87\left(\frac{1}{13} + \frac{1}{15}\right)}}$$

$$= \frac{1.5}{.64} = 2.34$$

Since the observed value of t, $t = 2.34$, falls in the rejection region (see Figure 9.5), the samples provide sufficient evidence to indicate that the mean numbers of viewers differ for major sports events and first-run movies shown in prime time. Or, we say that the test results are statistically significant at the $\alpha = .05$ level of significance. Because the rejection was in the positive or upper tail of the t distribution, the indication is that the mean number of viewers for sports events exceeds that for movies.

The t statistic can also be used to construct confidence intervals for the difference between population means. Both the confidence interval and the test of hypothesis procedures are summarized in the boxes.

Small-Sample Confidence Interval for $(\mu_1 - \mu_2)$

$$(\bar{x}_1 - \bar{x}_2) \pm t_{\alpha/2} \sqrt{s_p^2 \left(\frac{1}{n_1} + \frac{1}{n_2} \right)}$$

where

$$s_p^2 = \frac{(n_1 - 1)s_1^2 + (n_2 - 1)s_2^2}{n_1 + n_2 - 2}$$

and $t_{\alpha/2}$ is based on $(n_1 + n_2 - 2)$ df.

Assumptions: 1. Both sampled populations have relative frequency distributions that are approximately normal.
2. The population variances are equal.
3. The samples are randomly and independently selected from the populations.

Small-Sample Test of an Hypothesis for $(\mu_1 - \mu_2)$ (Independent Samples)

One-Tailed Test

H_0: $(\mu_1 - \mu_2) = D_0$

H_a: $(\mu_1 - \mu_2) < D_0$
    [or H_a: $(\mu_1 - \mu_2) > D_0$]

Test statistic:

$$t = \frac{(\bar{x}_1 - \bar{x}_2) - D_0}{\sqrt{s_p^2 \left(\frac{1}{n_1} + \frac{1}{n_2} \right)}}$$

Rejection region:

$t < -t_\alpha$

[or $t > t_\alpha$ when

H_a: $(\mu_1 - \mu_2) > D_0$]

where t_α is based on $(n_1 + n_2 - 2)$ df.

Two-Tailed Test

H_0: $(\mu_1 - \mu_2) = D_0$

H_a: $(\mu_1 - \mu_2) \neq D_0$

Test statistic:

$$t = \frac{(\bar{x}_1 - \bar{x}_2) - D_0}{\sqrt{s_p^2 \left(\frac{1}{n_1} + \frac{1}{n_2} \right)}}$$

Rejection region:

$t < -t_{\alpha/2}$

or $t > t_{\alpha/2}$

where $t_{\alpha/2}$ is based on $(n_1 + n_2 - 2)$ df.

Assumptions: Same as for the small-sample confidence interval for $(\mu_1 - \mu_2)$ above.

Example 9.4

Suppose you want to estimate the difference in annual operating costs for automobiles with rotary engines and those with standard engines. You find eight owners of cars with rotary engines and twelve owners of cars with standard engines who have purchased their cars within the last 2 years and are willing to participate in the experiment. Each of the twenty owners keeps accurate records of the amount spent on operating his or her car (including gasoline, oil, repairs, etc.) for a 12-month period. All costs are recorded on a per-thousand-mile basis to adjust for differences in mileage driven during the 12-month period. The results are summarized in the table. Estimate the true difference $(\mu_1 - \mu_2)$ in the mean operating costs per thousand miles between cars with rotary and cars with standard engines. Use a 90% confidence interval.

ROTARY	STANDARD
$n_1 = 8$	$n_2 = 12$
$\bar{x}_1 = \$56.96$	$\bar{x}_2 = \$52.73$
$s_1 = \$4.85$	$s_2 = \$6.35$

Solution

The objective of this experiment is to obtain a 90% confidence interval for $(\mu_1 - \mu_2)$. To use the small-sample confidence interval for $(\mu_1 - \mu_2)$, the following assumptions must be satisfied:

1. The operating cost per thousand miles is normally distributed for cars with both rotary and standard engines. Since these costs are averages (because we observe them on a per-thousand-mile basis), the Central Limit Theorem lends credence to this assumption.

2. The variance in cost is the same for the two types of cars. Under these circumstances, we might expect the variation in costs from automobile to automobile to be about the same for both types of engines.

3. The samples are randomly and independently selected from the two populations. We have randomly chosen twenty different owners for the two samples in such a way that the cost measurement for one owner is not dependent on the cost measurement for any other owner. Therefore, this assumption would be valid.

The first step in performing the test is to calculate the pooled estimate of variance:

$$s_p^2 = \frac{(n_1 - 1)s_1^2 + (n_2 - 1)s_2^2}{n_1 + n_2 - 2}$$

$$= \frac{(8 - 1)(4.85)^2 + (12 - 1)(6.35)^2}{8 + 12 - 2}$$

$$= 33.7892$$

where s_p^2 possesses $(n_1 + n_2 - 2) = (8 + 12 - 2) = 18$ df. Then, the 90% confidence interval for $(\mu_1 - \mu_2)$, the difference in mean operating costs for the two types of automobiles, is

$$(\bar{x}_1 - \bar{x}_2) \pm t_{\alpha/2}\sqrt{s_p^2\left(\frac{1}{n_1} + \frac{1}{n_2}\right)} = (56.96 - 52.73) \pm t_{.05}\sqrt{33.7892\left(\frac{1}{8} + \frac{1}{12}\right)}$$

$$= 4.23 \pm 1.734(2.653) = 4.23 \pm 4.60$$

$$= (-0.37, 8.83)$$

This means that, with 90% confidence, we estimate the difference in mean operating costs per thousand miles between cars with rotary engines and those with standard engines to fall in the interval from $-\$0.37$ to $\$8.83$. In other words, we estimate the mean operating costs for rotary engines to be anywhere from $0.37 less than to $8.83 more than the operating costs per thousand miles for standard engines. Although the sample means seem to suggest that rotary cars cost more to operate, there is insufficient evidence to indicate that $(\mu_1 - \mu_2)$ differs from zero because the interval includes zero as a possible value for $(\mu_1 - \mu_2)$. To show a difference in mean operating costs (if it exists), it would be necessary to increase the sample sizes and thereby narrow the width of the confidence interval for $(\mu_1 - \mu_2)$. ■

The two-sample t statistic is a powerful tool for comparing population means when the assumptions are satisfied. It has also been shown to retain its usefulness when the sampled populations are only approximately normally distributed. And when the sample sizes are equal, the assumption of equal population variances can be relaxed. That is, when $n_1 = n_2$, σ_1^2 and σ_2^2 can be quite different and the test statistic will still have (approximately) a Student's t distribution. When the experimental situation does not satisfy the assumptions, other statistical tests are available. These nonparametric statistical tests are described in Chapter 16.

What Can Be Done if the Assumptions Are Not Satisfied?

Answer: If you are concerned that your assumptions are not satisfied, use the Wilcoxon rank sum test for independent samples to test for a shift in population distributions. (See Chapter 16.)

Exercises 9.15–9.29

Learning the Mechanics

9.15 To use the t statistic to test for differences in the means of two populations, what assumptions must be made about the two populations? About the two samples?

9.16 In the t tests of this section, σ_1^2 and σ_2^2 are assumed to be equal. Thus, we say $\sigma_1^2 = \sigma_2^2 = \sigma^2$. Why is a pooled estimator of σ^2 used instead of either s_1^2 or s_2^2?

9.17 Independent random samples from normal populations produced the results shown in the table.

SAMPLE 1	SAMPLE 2
2.1	3.4
3.6	3.0
1.4	4.1
3.0	3.9
2.9	3.5
3.2	

a. Calculate the pooled estimate of σ^2.
b. Do the data provide sufficient evidence to indicate that $\mu_2 > \mu_1$? Test using $\alpha = .10$.
c. Find the approximate observed significance level for the test, and interpret its value.

9.18 Refer to Exercise 9.17. Find a 90% confidence interval for $(\mu_1 - \mu_2)$. Interpret the confidence interval.

9.19 Independent random samples from two normal populations produced the results shown in the table.

SAMPLE 1	SAMPLE 2
$n_1 = 12$	$n_2 = 16$
$\bar{x}_1 = 35$	$\bar{x}_2 = 43$
$s_1 = 4.2$	$s_2 = 3.7$

a. Calculate the pooled estimate of σ^2.
b. Do these data provide sufficient evidence to indicate that $\mu_1 \neq \mu_2$? Test using $\alpha = .05$.
c. Find the approximate p-value for the test, and interpret its value.

9.20 Refer to Exercise 9.19. Find a 95% confidence interval for $(\mu_1 - \mu_2)$. Interpret the confidence interval.

9.21 In Section 9.1, a z statistic was used to test hypotheses about the difference between two population means. In this section, we are also concerned with testing hypotheses about the difference between two population means, but we do so with a t statistic. Explain.

Applying the Concepts

9.22 An industrial plant wants to determine which of two types of fuel — gas or electric — will produce more useful energy at the lower cost. One measure of economical energy production, called the *plant investment per delivered quad,* is calculated by taking the amount of money (in dollars) invested in the particular utility by the plant and dividing by the delivered amount of energy (in quadrillion British thermal units). The smaller this ratio, the less an industrial plant pays for its delivered energy.

Random samples of eleven plants using electrical utilities and sixteen plants using gas utilities were taken, and the plant investment per quad was calculated for each. The data produced the results shown in the table.

	ELECTRIC	GAS
SAMPLE SIZE	11	16
MEAN INVESTMENT/QUAD (BILLIONS)	$22.5	$17.5
VARIANCE	17.5	15

a. Do these data provide sufficient evidence at $\alpha = .05$ to indicate a difference in the average investment per quad between the plants using gas and those using electrical utilities?

b. Find a 90% confidence interval for $(\mu_1 - \mu_2)$. Give a practical interpretation of this interval.

9.23 A manufacturing company is interested in determining whether there is a significant difference between the average number of units produced per day by two different machine operators. A random sample of ten daily outputs was selected for each operator from the outputs over the past year. The data on number of items produced per day are summarized in the table.

OPERATOR 1	OPERATOR 2
$n_1 = 10$	$n_2 = 10$
$\bar{x}_1 = 35$	$\bar{x}_2 = 31$
$s_1^2 = 17.2$	$s_2^2 = 19.1$

a. Do the samples provide sufficient evidence at $\alpha = .05$ to conclude that a difference does exist between the mean daily outputs of the machine operators?

b. What assumptions must you make so that this test will be valid?

c. Find a 90% confidence interval for $(\mu_1 - \mu_2)$. Explain clearly the meaning of your confidence interval.

9.24 One way corporations raise money for expansion is to issue *bonds,* which are loan agreements to repay the purchaser a specified amount of money with a fixed rate of interest paid periodically over the life of the bond. The sale of the bonds is usually handled by an underwriting firm. In a study described in the *Harvard Business Review* (July–Aug. 1979), D. Logue and R. Rogalski ask the question, "Does It Pay to Shop for Your Bond Underwriter?" The reason for the question is that the price of a bond may rise or fall after its issuance. Therefore, whether a corporation receives the market price for a bond depends upon the skill of the underwriter. The mean change in the prices of twenty-seven bonds handled over a 12-month period by one underwriter and in the prices of twenty-three bonds handled by another are given in the table.

	UNDERWRITER 1	UNDERWRITER 2
SAMPLE SIZE	27	23
SAMPLE MEAN	−.0491	−.0307
SAMPLE VARIANCE	.009800	.002465

a. Do the data provide sufficient evidence to indicate a difference in the mean change in bond prices handled by the two underwriters? Test using $\alpha = .05$.

b. Find a 95% confidence interval for the mean difference for the two underwriters, and interpret it.

9.25 Marketing strategists would like to be able to predict consumer response to new products and their accompanying promotional schemes. To this end, studies that examine the differences between buyers and nonbuyers of a product are of interest. One such study conducted by Shuchman and Riesz (1975) was aimed at characterizing the purchasers and nonpurchasers of Crest toothpaste. Purchasers were defined as households that converted to Crest following its endorsement by the Council on Dental Therapeutics of the American Dental Association on August 1, 1960, and remained "loyal" to Crest until at least April 1963. Nonpurchasers were defined as households that did not convert to Crest during the same time period. Using demographic data collected from a sample of 499 purchasers and 499 nonpurchasers, Shuchman and Riesz demonstrated that both the mean household size (number of persons) and mean household income were significantly larger for purchasers than for nonpurchasers. A similar study utilized random samples of size 20 and yielded the data in the table on the age of the householder primarily responsible for making toothpaste purchases.

PURCHASERS				NONPURCHASERS			
34	35	23	44	28	22	44	33
52	46	28	48	55	63	45	31
28	34	33	52	60	54	53	58
41	32	34	49	52	52	66	35
50	45	29	59	25	48	59	61

a. Do the data present sufficient evidence to conclude there is a difference in the mean age of purchasers and nonpurchasers? Use $\alpha = .10$.

b. What assumptions are necessary in order to answer part a?

c. Give the observed significance level for the test, and interpret its value.

d. Find a 90% confidence interval for the difference between the mean ages of purchasers and nonpurchasers.

9.26 With the emergence of Japan as an industrial superpower, U.S. businesses have begun taking a close look at Japanese management styles and philosophies. Some of the credit for the high quality of Japanese products has been attributed to the Japanese system of permanent employment for their workers. In the United States, high job turnover rates are common in many industries and are associated with high product defect rates. High turnover rates mean U.S. plants are more highly populated with inexperienced workers who are unfamiliar with the company's product lines than is the case in Japan. In a recent study of the air-conditioner industry in Japan and the United States, David Garvin (1983) reported that the difference in the average annual turnover rate of workers between U.S. plants and Japanese plants was 3.1%. In another study, five Japanese and five U.S. plants that manufacture air-conditioners were randomly sampled, and their turnover rates were found to be those listed in the table.

U.S. PLANTS	JAPANESE PLANTS
7.11%	3.52%
6.06%	2.02%
8.00%	4.91%
6.87%	3.22%
4.77%	1.92%

a. Do the data provide sufficient evidence to indicate that the mean annual percentage turnover for U.S. plants exceeds the corresponding mean percentage for Japanese plants? Test using $\alpha = .05$.

b. Report the observed significance level of the test you conducted in part a.

c. List any assumptions you made in conducting the hypothesis test of part a.

9.27 Sales quotas are sales volume objectives assigned to specific sales units, such as regions, districts, or salespersons' territories. They are usually expressed in terms of dollar sales volume. Sometimes, in order to achieve manufacturing efficiency or long-term goals, sales managers set quotas for specific products at challenging levels. The underlying idea is that, by setting challenging quotas and attaching significant rewards to their achievement, it is possible to direct salespersons' efforts along desired paths (Winer, 1973). The Universal Products Company (real company, fictitious name) manufactures and markets electronic and electromechanical industrial equipment. It has a sales force of over 1,000 salespersons, organized in ten districts and 135 branch offices. Salespersons have sales quotas on two specific products, Dataprinters and Micromagnetics, as well as an overall sales volume quota. Many salespersons have complained that having to make the existing quota on Dataprinters takes an inordinate amount of time and keeps them from generating a higher overall sales volume. In order to determine how a relaxation of the Dataprinter quota would affect total sales volume, Winer compared the sales volumes of a sample of branch offices whose salespersons all worked under the standard quota with the sales volumes of a sample of branch offices whose salespersons all were given a lower Dataprinter quota. Data were collected for a 7-month period and are reported in the table at the top of page 352 in terms of total sales per worker-month (in thousands of dollars).

a. Do the data present sufficient evidence to indicate a difference between mean sales per worker-month for the two types of sales quotas? Use $\alpha = .10$.

b. What assumptions, if any, was it necessary to make in order to carry out the hypothesis test required in part a?

c. Summarize the results of this study in words that a manager who is not familiar with the language of statistics could understand.

BRANCH	LOWER QUOTA	STANDARD QUOTA
1		17.7
2	15.6	
3		15.1
4	14.0	
5		12.3
6		12.0
7	11.2	
8	11.0	
9		10.5
10	10.3	
11		10.0
12	9.4	

9.28 Suppose you are personnel manager for a company, and you suspect a difference in the mean length of work time lost due to sickness for two types of employees: those who work at night versus those who work during the day. Particularly, you suspect that the mean time lost for the night shift exceeds the mean for the day shift. To check your theory, you randomly sample the records for ten employees for each shift category and record the number of days lost due to sickness within the past year. The data are shown in the table.

NIGHT SHIFT, 1		DAY SHIFT, 2	
21	2	13	18
10	19	5	17
14	6	16	3
33	4	0	24
7	12	7	1

$$\bar{x}_1 = 12.8 \qquad\qquad \bar{x}_2 = 10.4$$

$$\sum_{i=1}^{n} x_i^2 = 2{,}436 \qquad\qquad \sum_{i=1}^{n} x_i^2 = 1{,}698$$

a. Calculate s_1^2 and s_2^2.

b. Show that the pooled estimate of the common population standard deviation, σ, is 8.86. Look at the range of the observations within each of the two samples. Does it appear that the estimate, 8.86, is a reasonable value for σ?

c. If μ_1 and μ_2 represent the mean number of days per year lost due to sickness for the night and day shifts, respectively, test the null hypothesis $H_0: \mu_1 = \mu_2$ against the alternative $H_a: \mu_1 > \mu_2$. Use $\alpha = .05$. Do the data provide sufficient evidence to indicate that $\mu_1 > \mu_2$?

d. What assumptions must be satisfied so that the t test from part c is valid?

e. Suppose you were concerned that the assumptions of part d might not be satisfied. What alternative to a Student's t test do you have?

9.29 Many armchair quarterbacks try to figure out which makes a good football team—

offense or defense. Some even think one conference is better than another. Some data from the 1982 season, from the Sept. 1, 1983, issue of *Sports Illustrated,* are shown in the table.

AFC	YARDS PER GAME RUSHING	NFC	YARDS PER GAME RUSHING
Bills	152	Cowboys	146
Patriots	150	Saints	140
Dolphins	149	Cardinals	134
Jets	146	Falcons	131
Steelers	132	Redskins	127
Chargers	125	Packers	120
Raiders	120	Rams	114
Colts	116	Lions	114
Broncos	113	Bears	110
Bengals	105	Bucs	106
Chiefs	105	Vikings	101
Browns	97	Giants	94
Oilers	89	Eagles	92
Seahawks	88	49ers	82

a. Find the mean and variance of yards per game rushing for each of the two conferences.

b. Do the data provide sufficient evidence to indicate that the mean yards per game rushing differ for the two conferences? Test using $\alpha = .05$.

9.3 Comparing Two Population Variances: Independent Random Samples

Suppose you want to use the two-sample t statistic to compare the mean productivity of two paper mills. However, you are concerned that the assumption of equal variances of the productivity for the two plants may be unrealistic. It would be helpful to have a statistical procedure to check the validity of this assumption.

The common statistical procedure for comparing population variances σ_1^2 and σ_2^2 makes an inference about the ratio, σ_1^2/σ_2^2, based on the ratio of the sample variances, s_1^2/s_2^2. Thus, we will attempt to support the alternative hypothesis that the ratio σ_1^2/σ_2^2 differs from 1 (i.e., the variances are unequal) by testing the null hypothesis that the ratio equals 1 (i.e., the variances are equal).

$$H_0: \frac{\sigma_1^2}{\sigma_2^2} = 1 \quad (\sigma_1^2 = \sigma_2^2) \qquad H_a: \frac{\sigma_1^2}{\sigma_2^2} \neq 1 \quad (\sigma_1^2 \neq \sigma_2^2)$$

We will use the test statistic $F = s_1^2/s_2^2$.

To establish a rejection region for the test statistic, we need to know how s_1^2/s_2^2 is distributed in repeated samples. That is, we need to know the sampling distribution of s_1^2/s_2^2. As you will subsequently see, the sampling distribution of s_1^2/s_2^2 is based on two of the assumptions already required for the t test, namely:

1. The two sampled populations are normally distributed.

2. The samples are randomly and independently selected from their respective populations.

When these assumptions are satisfied and when the null hypothesis is true (i.e., $\sigma_1^2 = \sigma_2^2$), the sampling distribution of $F = s_1^2/s_2^2$ is the **F distribution** with $\nu_1 = (n_1 - 1)$ numerator degrees of freedom and $\nu_2 = (n_2 - 1)$ denominator degrees of freedom. The shape of the F distribution will depend on the degrees of freedom associated with s_1^2 and s_2^2—i.e., $(n_1 - 1)$ and $(n_2 - 1)$. An F distribution with $\nu_1 = 7$ and $\nu_2 = 9$ df is shown in Figure 9.6. As you can see, the distribution is skewed to the right.

Figure 9.6   An F
Distribution with 7 and 9 df

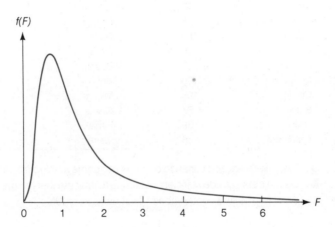

We need to be able to find F values corresponding to the tail areas of this distribution in order to establish the rejection region for our test of hypothesis because, when the population variances are unequal, we expect the ratio F of the sample variances to be either very large or very small. The upper-tail F values can be found in Tables VI, VII, VIII, and IX of Appendix B. Table VII is partially reproduced in Figure 9.7. It gives F values that correspond to $\alpha = .05$ upper-tail areas for different degrees of freedom. The columns of Tables VI, VII, VIII, and IX correspond to various degrees of freedom for the numerator sample variance, s_1^2, while the rows correspond to the degrees of freedom for the denominator sample variance, s_2^2. Thus, if the numerator degrees of freedom is 7 and the denominator degrees of freedom is 9, we look in the seventh column and ninth row of Table VII to find $F_{.05} = 3.29$. As shown in Figure 9.8, $\alpha = .05$ is the tail area to the right of 3.29 in the F distribution with 7 and 9 df. That is, if $\sigma_1^2 = \sigma_2^2$, the probability that the F statistic will exceed 3.29 is $\alpha = .05$.

Suppose we want to compare the variability in production for two paper mills and we have obtained the results shown in the table.

SAMPLE 1	SAMPLE 2
$n_1 = 13$ days	$n_2 = 18$ days
$\bar{x}_1 = 26.3$ production units	$\bar{x}_2 = 19.7$ production units
$s_1 = 8.2$ production units	$s_2 = 4.7$ production units

Figure 9.7   Reproduction of Part of Table VII, Appendix B: $\alpha = .05$

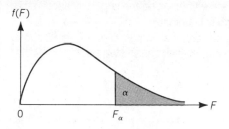

		NUMERATOR DEGREES OF FREEDOM							
ν_1 / ν_2	1	2	3	4	5	6	7	8	9
1	161.4	199.5	215.7	224.6	230.2	234.0	236.8	238.9	240.5
2	18.51	19.00	19.16	19.25	19.30	19.33	19.35	19.37	19.38
3	10.13	9.55	9.28	9.12	9.01	8.94	8.89	8.85	8.81
4	7.71	6.94	6.59	6.39	6.26	6.16	6.09	6.04	6.00
5	6.61	5.79	5.41	5.19	5.05	4.95	4.88	4.82	4.77
6	5.99	5.14	4.76	4.53	4.39	4.28	4.21	4.15	4.10
7	5.59	4.74	4.35	4.12	3.97	3.87	3.79	3.73	3.68
8	5.32	4.46	4.07	3.84	3.69	3.58	3.50	3.44	3.39
9	5.12	4.26	3.86	3.63	3.48	3.37	3.29	3.23	3.18
10	4.96	4.10	3.71	3.48	3.33	3.22	3.14	3.07	3.02
11	4.84	3.98	3.59	3.36	3.20	3.09	3.01	2.95	2.90
12	4.75	3.89	3.49	3.25	3.11	3.00	2.91	2.85	2.80
13	4.67	3.81	3.41	3.18	3.03	2.92	2.83	2.77	2.71
14	4.60	3.74	3.34	3.11	2.96	2.85	2.76	2.70	2.65

DENOMINATOR DEGREES OF FREEDOM

To form the rejection region for a two-tailed F test we want to make certain that the upper tail is used because only the upper-tail values of F are shown in Tables VI, VII, VIII, and IX. To accomplish this, *we will always place the larger sample variance in the numerator of the F test statistic.* This has the effect of doubling the tabulated value for α, since we double the

Figure 9.8   An F
Distribution for 7 and 9 df:
$\alpha = .05$

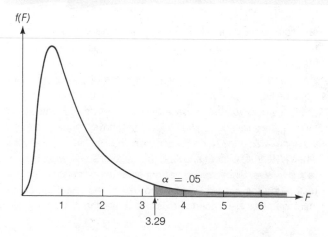

probability that the F ratio will fall in the upper tail by always placing the larger sample variance in the numerator. That is, we make the test two-tailed by putting the larger variance in the numerator rather than establishing rejection regions in both tails.

Thus, for our production example, we have a numerator s_1^2 with $v_1 = n_1 - 1 = 12$ and a denominator of s_2^2 with $v_2 = n_2 - 1 = 17$. Therefore, the test statistic will be

$$F = \frac{\text{Larger sample variance}}{\text{Smaller sample variance}} = \frac{s_1^2}{s_2^2}$$

and we will reject H_0: $\sigma_1^2 = \sigma_2^2$ for $\alpha = .10$ when the calculated value of F exceeds the tabulated value:

$$F_{.05} = 2.38 \text{ (see Figure 9.9)}$$

Figure 9.9   Rejection Region for Production Example: F Distribution

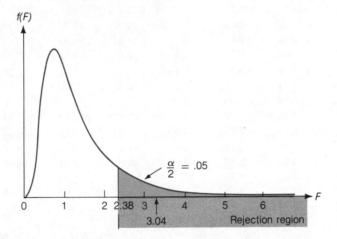

Now, what do the data tell us? We calculate

$$F = \frac{s_1^2}{s_2^2} = \frac{(8.2)^2}{(4.7)^2} = 3.04$$

and compare it to the rejection region shown in Figure 9.9. You can see that the F value 3.04 falls in the rejection region, and therefore, the data provide sufficient evidence to indicate that the population variances differ. Consequently, we would be reluctant to use the two-sample t statistic to compare the population means because the assumption of equal population variances is questionable.

What would you have concluded if the value of F calculated from the samples had not fallen in the rejection region? Would you have concluded that the null hypothesis of equal variances was true? No, because then you risk the possibility of a Type II error (accepting H_0 when H_a is true) without knowing the value of β, the probability of accepting H_0: $\sigma_1^2 = \sigma_2^2$ if in fact it is false. Since we will not consider the calculation of β for specific alternatives in this text, when the F statistic does not fall in the rejection region, we simply conclude that insufficient sample evidence exists to refute the null hypothesis that $\sigma_1^2 = \sigma_2^2$.

The F test for equal population variances is summarized in the box.

F Test for Equal Population Variances

One-Tailed Test

$H_0: \sigma_1^2 = \sigma_2^2$

$H_a: \sigma_1^2 < \sigma_2^2$
  (or $H_a: \sigma_1^2 > \sigma_2^2$)

Test statistic:

$$F = \frac{s_2^2}{s_1^2} \text{ when } H_a: \sigma_1^2 < \sigma_2^2$$

$$\left(\text{or } F = \frac{s_1^2}{s_2^2} \text{ when } H_a: \sigma_1^2 > \sigma_2^2 \right)$$

Rejection region:

$F > F_\alpha$

where F_α is based on $v_1 = n_2 - 1$ and
$v_2 = n_1 - 1$ df

(or $F > F_\alpha$ when $H_a: \sigma_1^2 > \sigma_2^2$,
where F_α is based on $v_1 = n_1 - 1$ and
$v_2 = n_2 - 1$ df

Two-Tailed Test

$H_0: \sigma_1^2 = \sigma_2^2$

$H_a: \sigma_1^2 \neq \sigma_2^2$

Test statistic:

$$F = \frac{\text{Larger sample variance}}{\text{Smaller sample variance}}$$

$$= \frac{s_1^2}{s_2^2} \text{ when } s_1^2 > s_2^2$$

$$\left(\text{or } F = \frac{s_2^2}{s_1^2} \text{ when } s_2^2 > s_1^2 \right)$$

Rejection region:

$F > F_{\alpha/2}$ when $s_1^2 > s_2^2$

where $F_{\alpha/2}$ is based on $v_1 = n_1 - 1$
and $v_2 = n_2 - 1$ df

(or $F > F_{\alpha/2}$ when $s_2^2 > s_1^2$,
where $F_{\alpha/2}$ is based on $v_1 = n_2 - 1$
and $v_2 = n_1 - 1$ df

Assumptions: 1. Both sampled populations are normally distributed.
              2. The samples are random and independent.

Example 9.5

Refer to Example 9.4, in which we used the two-sample t statistic to compare the mean operating costs of cars with rotary and standard engines. Use the F test to check the assumption that the population variances are equal. Use $\alpha = .10$.

Solution The elements of the test are as follows:

$$H_0: \frac{\sigma_1^2}{\sigma_2^2} = 1 \qquad H_a: \frac{\sigma_1^2}{\sigma_2^2} \neq 1$$

Test statistic: $F = \dfrac{\text{Larger sample variance}}{\text{Smaller sample variance}} = \dfrac{s_2^2}{s_1^2}$

To find the rejection region, we proceed as follows: The numerator degrees of freedom is $v_1 = n_2 - 1 = 11$; the denominator degrees of freedom is $v_2 = n_1 - 1 = 7$. Thus, from Table VII of Appendix B we find the rejection region:

$$F > F_{\alpha/2} = F_{.05} \approx 3.60$$

(Since no tabled value is given for $v_1 = 11$, we average the entries at 10 and 12 to obtain $F_{.05} \approx 3.60$.)

We now calculate

$$F = \frac{s_2^2}{s_1^2} = \frac{(6.35)^2}{(4.85)^2} = 1.71$$

This F value is not in the rejection region. Therefore, there is insufficient evidence at the $\alpha = .10$ level to refute the assumption of equal population variances. ■

The following example shows that the F statistic is sometimes used to compare population variances in their own right rather than just to check the validity of an assumption.

Example 9.6

STOCK 1	STOCK 2
$n_1 = 25$	$n_2 = 25$
$\bar{x}_1 = .250$	$\bar{x}_2 = .125$
$s_1 = .76$	$s_2 = .46$

Suppose an investor wants to compare the risks associated with two different stocks, where the risk of a given stock is measured by the variation in daily price changes. Suppose we obtain a random sample of twenty-five daily price changes for stock 1 and twenty-five for stock 2. The sample results are summarized in the table. Compare the risks associated with the two stocks by testing the null hypothesis that the variances of the price changes for the stocks are equal. Use $\alpha = .10$.

Solution

Since we wish to detect a difference in population variances, we will want to detect either $\sigma_1^2 > \sigma_2^2$ or $\sigma_2^2 > \sigma_1^2$. Therefore, we choose as the alternative (research) hypothesis, H_a: $\sigma_1^2 \neq \sigma_2^2$, and will conduct the following two-tailed test:

$$H_0: \frac{\sigma_1^2}{\sigma_2^2} = 1 \qquad H_a: \frac{\sigma_1^2}{\sigma_2^2} \neq 1$$

Test statistic: $F = \dfrac{\text{Larger sample variance}}{\text{Smaller sample variance}} = \dfrac{s_1^2}{s_2^2}$

Assumptions: 1. The changes in daily prices for each stock have relative frequency distributions that are approximately normal.
2. The samples are randomly and independently selected from a set of daily stock reports.

Rejection region: $F > F_{\alpha/2} = F_{.05} = 1.98$
where $F_{.05}$ possesses $v_1 = n_1 - 1 = 24$ and $v_2 = n_2 - 1 = 24$ df.

We calculate

$$F = \frac{s_1^2}{s_2^2} = \frac{(.76)^2}{(.46)^2} = 2.73$$

The calculated F exceeds the rejection value of 1.98. Therefore, we conclude that the variances of daily price changes differ for the two stocks. It appears that the risk, as measured by the variance of daily price changes, is greater for stock 1 than for stock 2. How much reliability can we place in this inference? Only one time in ten (since $\alpha = .10$), on the average, would this statistical test lead us to conclude erroneously that σ_1^2 and σ_2^2 were different when in fact they were equal. ■

Example 9.7

Find the approximate observed significance level for the F test in Example 9.6.

Solution

Since the observed value of the F statistic in Example 9.6 was 2.73, the observed significance level for the test would equal the probability of observing a value of F at least as contradictory to $H_0: \sigma_1^2 = \sigma_2^2$ as $F = 2.73$, if in fact H_0 was true. Since we give the F tables in Appendix B only for values of α equal to .10, .05, .025, and .01, we can only approximate the observed significance level. Checking Tables VI, VII, VIII, and IX, we find $F_{.05} = 1.98$, $F_{.025} = 2.27$, and $F_{.01} = 2.66$. Since the observed value of $F = 2.73$ slightly exceeds $F_{.01}$, the observed significance level for the test will be slightly less than

Approximate p-value $= 2(.01) = .02$

Note that we doubled the α value shown in Table IX because this was a two-tailed test.

■

We have presented the F test as a test of an hypothesis of equality of variances—i.e., $\sigma_1^2 = \sigma_2^2$. Although this is the most common application of the test, it can also be used to test an hypothesis that the ratio of the population variances is equal to some specified value, H_0: $\sigma_1^2/\sigma_2^2 = k$. The test would be conducted exactly the same way as a test of an hypothesis concerning the equality of variances except that we would use the test statistic

$$F = \frac{s_1^2}{s_2^2}\left(\frac{1}{k}\right)$$

What Do You Do if the Assumption of Normal Population Distributions Is Not Satisfied?

Answer: The F test is much more sensitive to departures from normality than the t test for comparing population means discussed in Section 9.2. If you have doubts about the normality of the population frequency distributions, you can use a nonparametric method for comparing the two population variances. A method can be found in the references listed at the end of this chapter.

Exercises
9.30–9.39

Learning the Mechanics

9.30 Under what conditions is the sampling distribution of s_1^2/s_2^2 an F distribution?

9.31 Use Tables VI, VII, VIII, and IX of Appendix B to find each of the following F values:

a. $F_{.05}$ where $\nu_1 = 9$ and $\nu_2 = 6$ **b.** $F_{.01}$ where $\nu_1 = 18$ and $\nu_2 = 14$
c. $F_{.025}$ where $\nu_1 = 11$ and $\nu_2 = 4$ **d.** $F_{.10}$ where $\nu_1 = 20$ and $\nu_2 = 5$

9.32 Given ν_1 and ν_2, find the following probabilities:

a. $\nu_1 = 2$, $\nu_2 = 30$, $P(F \geq 5.39)$ **b.** $\nu_1 = 24$, $\nu_2 = 10$, $P(F < 2.74)$
c. $\nu_1 = 7$, $\nu_2 = 1$, $P(F \leq 236.8)$ **d.** $\nu_1 = 40$, $\nu_2 = 40$, $P(F > 2.11)$

SAMPLE 1	SAMPLE 2
$n_1 = 12$	$n_2 = 27$
$\bar{x}_1 = 31.7$	$\bar{x}_2 = 37.4$
$s_1^2 = 3.87$	$s_2^2 = 8.75$

SAMPLE 1	SAMPLE 2
3.1	2.3
4.4	1.4
1.2	3.7
1.7	8.9
0.7	5.5
3.4	

9.33 Independent random samples were selected from each of two normally distributed populations, $n_1 = 12$ from population 1 and $n_2 = 27$ from population 2. The means and variances for the two samples are shown in the table.

a. Do the data provide sufficient evidence to indicate a difference between the population variances? Test using $\alpha = .10$.

b. Find and interpret the approximate p-value for the test.

9.34 Independent random samples were selected from each of two normally distributed populations, $n_1 = 6$ from population 1 and $n_2 = 5$ from population 2. The data are shown in the table.

a. Do these data provide sufficient evidence to indicate a difference between the population variances? Use $\alpha = .05$.

b. Find and interpret the approximate observed significance level for the test.

Applying the Concepts

9.35 Suppose your firm has been experimenting with two different physical arrangements of its assembly line. It has been determined that both arrangements yield approximately the same average number of finished units per day. To obtain an arrangement that produces greater process control you suggest that the arrangement with the smaller variance in the number of finished units produced per day be permanently adopted. Two independent random samples yield the results shown in the table. Do the samples provide sufficient evidence at $\alpha = .10$ to conclude that the variances of the number of units produced per day differ for the two arrangements? If so, which arrangement would you choose? If not, what would you suggest the firm do?

ASSEMBLY LINE 1	ASSEMBLY LINE 2
$n_1 = 21$ days	$n_2 = 21$ days
$s_1^2 = 1,432$	$s_2^2 = 3,761$

9.36 The quality control department of a paper company measures the brightness (a measure of reflectance) of finished paper on a periodic basis throughout the day. Two instruments that are available to measure the paper specimens are subject to error, but they can be adjusted so the mean readings for a control paper specimen are the same for both instruments. Suppose you are concerned about the precision of the two instruments— namely, that instrument 2 is less precise than instrument 1. To check this theory, five measurements of a single paper sample are made on both instruments. The data are shown in the table. Do the data provide sufficient evidence to indicate that instrument 2 is less precise than instrument 1? Test using $\alpha = .05$.

INSTRUMENT 1	INSTRUMENT 2
29	26
28	34
30	30
28	32
30	28

9.37 Refer to Exercise 9.27 in Section 9.2, in which a t test was used to determine whether sales volume was affected by the type of sales quota assigned to salespersons. In conducting the t test, it was assumed that the variance of total sales per worker-month was the same for both populations being studied. Do the data provide sufficient evidence to indicate that this assumption may be violated? Test using $\alpha = .05$.

9.38 Recent technological advances have turned the telephone operator's workplace into what some experts call "the office of the future." For example, directory-assistance operators use computers to look up telephone numbers, and then by flicking a key have a recorded voice give the number to the customer. The computerization of the operator's workplace has significantly shortened the time necessary to service a customer. Thus, while the number of telephone calls made in this country per year increased from 67 billion in 1950 to 310 billion in 1980, the number of telephone operators decreased from 244,000 to 128,000. However, the computer not only speeds the operator's work, it monitors the operator's work as well — somewhat like a foreman. This monitoring has led some telephone company offices to issue a guideline of 30 seconds as the maximum amount of time an operator should spend completing operator-assisted calls (Serrin, 1983). To study the effect of this guideline on the mean time to complete a call, a researcher planned to estimate the difference in the mean time between offices that do and offices that do not issue the guideline to its operators. The completion times shown in the table were sampled from the computer-collected data that results from monitoring the operators.

TIME GUIDELINE ISSUED (Seconds)		TIME GUIDELINE NOT ISSUED (Seconds)	
31.2	26.3	30.0	21.4
33.5	27.3	22.6	39.8
27.2	25.9	35.9	45.3
23.5	20.3	41.3	37.1
28.8	26.8	28.9	25.6

a. The researcher knows that in order to be able to use the two-sample t statistic in constructing a confidence interval, the assumption of equal population variances should first be examined. Test the equality of the population variances using $\alpha = .05$. What does your test indicate about the appropriateness of using the two-sample t in this situation?

b. List any assumptions you made in conducting the hypothesis test of part a.

c. In the context of this problem, describe the Type I and Type II errors associated with your hypothesis test of part a.

d. What is the approximate p-value of the test you conducted in part a?

9.39 In Exercise 9.23 a manufacturing company was interested in determining whether a significant difference existed between the mean number of units produced per day by two different machine operators. Two independent random samples yielded the data shown in the table.

OPERATOR 1	OPERATOR 2
$n_1 = 10$	$n_2 = 10$
$\bar{x}_1 = 35$ units	$\bar{x}_2 = 31$ units
$s_1^2 = 17.2$	$s_2^2 = 19.1$

a. In order to conduct the hypothesis test required in Exercise 9.23 you had to assume $\sigma_1^2 = \sigma_2^2$. Use an F test with $\alpha = .10$ to determine whether the data violate this assumption. Explain the significance of your result.

b. If your conclusion in part a were incorrect, would you have committed a Type I error or a Type II error? Explain.

9.4
Inferences about the Difference Between Two Population Means: Paired Difference Experiments

Suppose you want to compare the mean daily sales of two restaurants located in the same city. If you were to record the restaurants' total sales for each of 12 days (2 work weeks), the results might appear as shown in Table 9.1.

Table 9.1 Daily Sales for Two Restaurants

DAY	RESTAURANT 1	RESTAURANT 2
1 (Monday)	$ 759	$ 678
2 (Tuesday)	981	933
3 (Wednesday)	1,005	918
4 (Thursday)	1,449	1,302
5 (Friday)	1,905	1,782
6 (Saturday)	2,073	1,971
7 (Monday)	693	639
8 (Tuesday)	873	825
9 (Wednesday)	1,074	999
10 (Thursday)	1,338	1,281
11 (Friday)	1,932	1,827
12 (Saturday)	2,106	2,049
	$\bar{x}_1 = \$1,349.00$	$\bar{x}_2 = \$1,267.00$
	$s_1 = \$530.07$	$s_2 = \$516.03$

Test the null hypothesis that the mean daily sales, μ_1 and μ_2, for the two restaurants are equal against the alternative hypothesis that they differ; i.e.,

$$H_0: (\mu_1 - \mu_2) = 0 \qquad H_a: (\mu_1 - \mu_2) \neq 0$$

Using the two-sample t statistic (Section 9.2) we would calculate

$$s_p^2 = \frac{(n_1 - 1)s_1^2 + (n_2 - 1)s_2^2}{n_1 + n_2 - 2}$$

$$= \frac{(12 - 1)(530.07)^2 + (12 - 1)(516.03)^2}{12 + 12 - 2}$$

$$= 273,630.6$$

and

$$t = \frac{(\bar{x}_1 - \bar{x}_2) - 0}{\sqrt{s_p^2\left(\dfrac{1}{n_1} + \dfrac{1}{n_2}\right)}} = \frac{(1,349.00 - 1,267.00}{\sqrt{273,630.6\left(\dfrac{1}{12} + \dfrac{1}{12}\right)}}$$

$$= \frac{82.0}{213.54} = .38$$

This small t value will not lead to rejection of H_0 when compared to the t distribution with $n_1 + n_2 - 2 = 22$ df, even if α were chosen as large as .20 ($t_{\alpha/2} = t_{.10} = 1.321$). Thus, we might conclude that insufficient evidence exists to infer that there is a difference in mean daily sales for the two restaurants.

However, if you examine the data in Table 9.1 more closely, you will find this conclusion difficult to accept. The sales of restaurant 1 exceed those of restaurant 2 *for every one of the 12 days*. This, in itself, is strong evidence to indicate that μ_1 differs from μ_2, and we will subsequently confirm this fact. Why, then, was the t test unable to detect this difference?

The cause of this apparent inconsistency with the test result is that the two-sample t is inappropriate, because the assumption of independent samples is invalid. If you examine the pairs of daily sales, you will note that the sales of the two restaurants tend to rise and fall together over the days of the week. This pattern suggests a very strong daily dependence between the two samples and a violation of the assumption of independence required for the two-sample t test of Section 9.2. In this particular situation, note the *large variation within samples* (reflected by the large value of s_p^2) in comparison to the *small difference between the sample means.* Because s_p^2 was so large, the t test was unable to detect a possible difference between μ_1 and μ_2.

Table 9.2

Daily Sales and Differences for Two Restaurants

DAY	RESTAURANT 1	RESTAURANT 2	(RESTAURANT 1 − RESTAURANT 2)
1 (Monday)	$ 759	$ 678	$ 81
2 (Tuesday)	981	933	48
3 (Wednesday)	1,005	918	87
4 (Thursday)	1,449	1,302	147
5 (Friday)	1,905	1,782	123
6 (Saturday	2,073	1,971	102
7 (Monday)	693	639	54
8 (Tuesday)	873	825	48
9 (Wednesday)	1,074	999	75
10 (Thursday)	1,338	1,281	57
11 (Friday)	1,932	1,827	105
12 (Saturday)	2,106	2,049	57

$$\bar{x}_D = \$82.00$$
$$s_D = \$32.00$$

Now, consider a valid method to analyze the data of Table 9.1. We add to this table a column of differences between the daily sales of the restaurants, and thus form Table 9.2. We can regard these daily differences in sales as a random sample of all daily differences, past and present. Then we can use this sample to make inferences about the mean, μ_D, of the population of differences, *which is equal to the difference* ($\mu_1 - \mu_2$): i.e., the mean of the population (sample) of differences equals the difference between the population (sample) means. Thus, our test becomes

$$H_0: \mu_D = 0 \quad \text{(i.e., } \mu_1 - \mu_2 = 0) \qquad H_a: \mu_D \neq 0 \quad \text{(i.e., } \mu_1 - \mu_2 \neq 0)$$

The test statistic is a one-sample t since we are now analyzing a single sample of differences:

Test statistic: $\quad t = \dfrac{\bar{x}_D - 0}{s_D / \sqrt{n_D}}$

where

$\bar{x}_D$ = Sample mean of differences

s_D = Sample standard deviation of differences

n_D = Number of differences

Assumptions: 1. The population of differences in daily sales is approximately normally distributed.

2. The sample differences are randomly selected from a population of differences.

To find the rejection region, we first choose $\alpha = .05$. Then we will reject H_0 if

$$t < -t_{.025} \quad \text{or} \quad t > t_{.025}$$

where $t_{.025}$ is based on $(n_D - 1)$ degrees of freedom.

Referring to Table V of Appendix B, we find the t value corresponding to $\alpha/2 = .025$ and $n_D - 1 = 12 - 1 = 11$ df to be $t_{.025} = 2.201$. Thus, the null hypothesis will be rejected if $t < -2.201$ or $t > 2.201$. Note that the number of degrees of freedom has decreased from $n_1 + n_2 - 2 = 22$ to 11 by using the *paired difference experiment* rather than the two independent random samples design.

Now calculate

$$t = \frac{\bar{x}_D - 0}{s_D/\sqrt{n_D}} = \frac{82.00}{32.00/\sqrt{12}} = 8.88$$

Because this value of t falls in the rejection region, we conclude that the difference in mean daily sales for the two restaurants differs from zero. The fact that $\bar{x}_1 - \bar{x}_2 = \bar{x}_D = \$82.00$ strongly suggests that the mean daily sales for restaurant 1 exceeds the mean daily sales for restaurant 2.

This kind of experiment, in which observations are paired and the differences analyzed, is called a *paired difference experiment.* In many cases a paired difference experiment can provide more information about the difference between population means than an independent samples experiment. The differencing removes the variability due to the dimension on which the observations are paired. For instance, in the restaurant example, the day-to-day variability in daily sales is removed by analyzing the differences between the restaurants' daily sales. The removal of the variability due to this extra dimension is called *blocking,* and the paired difference experiment is a simple example of a *randomized block experiment.* In our example, the days represent the blocks. [*Note:* Randomized block experiments are discussed in greater detail in Chapter 15.]

Some other examples for which the paired difference experiment might be appropriate are the following:

1. To compare the performance of two automobile salespeople, we might test an hypothesis about the difference $(\mu_1 - \mu_2)$ in their respective mean monthly sales. If we randomly choose n_1 months of salesperson 1's sales and independently choose n_2 months of salesperson 2's sales, the month-to-month variability caused by the seasonal nature of new car sales might inflate s_p^2 and prevent the two-sample t statistic from detecting a difference between μ_1 and μ_2, if such a difference actually exists. However, by taking the difference in monthly sales for the two salespeople for each of n months, the month-to-month variability (seasonal variation) in sales can be eliminated and the probability of detecting a difference between μ_1 and μ_2, if a difference exists, is increased.

2. Suppose you want to estimate the difference $(\mu_1 - \mu_2)$ in mean price between two major brands of premium gasoline. If you were to choose two independent random samples of stations for each brand, the variability in price due to geographic location may be large. To eliminate this source of variability, you could choose pairs of stations, one station for each brand, in close geographic proximity and use the sample of differences between the prices of the brands to make an inference about $(\mu_1 - \mu_2)$.

3. Suppose a college placement center wants to estimate the difference $(\mu_1 - \mu_2)$ in mean starting salaries for men and women graduates who seek jobs through the center. If it independently samples men and women, the starting salaries may vary due to their different college majors and differences in grade-point averages. To eliminate these sources of variability, the placement center could match male and female job-seekers according to their majors and grade-point averages. Then the differences between the starting salaries of each pair in the sample could be used to make an inference about $(\mu_1 - \mu_2)$.

The hypothesis-testing and confidence interval procedures based on a paired difference experiment are summarized in the next two boxes.

Paired Difference Test of an Hypothesis

One-Tailed Test

H_0: $(\mu_1 - \mu_2) = D_0$,
  i.e., $(\mu_D = D_0)$

H_a: $(\mu_1 - \mu_2) < D_0$,
  i.e., $(\mu_D < D_0)$

  [or H_a: $(\mu_1 - \mu_2) > D_0$,
  i.e., $(\mu_D > D_0)$]

Test statistic: $t = \dfrac{\bar{x}_D - D_0}{s_D/\sqrt{n_D}}$

Rejection region:

  $t < -t_\alpha$

  [or $t > t_\alpha$
  when H_a: $(\mu_1 - \mu_2) > D_0$]

where t_α has $(n_D - 1)$ df.

Two-Tailed Test

H_0: $(\mu_1 - \mu_2) = D_0$,
  i.e., $(\mu_D = D_0)$

H_a: $(\mu_1 - \mu_2) \neq D_0$,
  i.e., $(\mu_D \neq D_0)$

Test statistic: $t = \dfrac{\bar{x}_D - D_0}{s_D/\sqrt{n_D}}$

Rejection region:

  $t < -t_{\alpha/2}$

  or $t > t_{\alpha/2}$

where $t_{\alpha/2}$ has $(n_D - 1)$ df.

Assumptions: 1. The relative frequency distribution of the population of differences is normal.
2. The differences are randomly selected from the population of differences.

> ## Paired Difference Confidence Interval
>
> $$\bar{x}_D \pm t_{\alpha/2} \frac{s_D}{\sqrt{n_D}}$$
>
> where $t_{\alpha/2}$ has $(n_D - 1)$ df.
>
> Assumption:　Same as for the paired difference test (previous box).

Example 9.8　　A paired difference experiment is conducted to compare the starting salaries of male and female college graduates who find jobs. Pairs are formed by choosing a male and a female with the same major and similar grade-point averages. Suppose a random sample of ten pairs is formed in this manner, and the starting annual salary of each person is recorded. The results are shown in Table 9.3. Test to see whether there is evidence that the mean starting salary, μ_1, for males exceeds the mean starting salary, μ_2, for females. Use $\alpha = .05$.

Table 9.3

PAIR	MALE	FEMALE	DIFFERENCE (MALE − FEMALE)
1	$14,300	$13,800	$ 500
2	16,500	16,600	−100
3	15,400	14,800	600
4	13,500	13,500	0
5	18,500	17,600	900
6	12,800	13,000	−200
7	14,500	14,200	300
8	16,200	15,100	1,100
9	13,400	13,200	200
10	14,200	13,500	700

Solution　　Since we are interested in determining whether the data indicate that μ_1 exceeds μ_2—i.e., whether the mean starting salary for men exceeds the mean starting salary for women—we will choose a one-sided alternative (research) hypothesis. Then the elements of the paired difference test are

$$H_0: \mu_D = 0 \quad (\mu_1 - \mu_2 = 0) \qquad H_a: \mu_D > 0 \quad (\mu_1 - \mu_2 > 0)$$

Test statistic:　$t = \dfrac{\bar{x}_D - 0}{s_D/\sqrt{n_D}}$

Assumption:　The relative frequency distribution for the population of differences is normal.

Since the test is upper-tailed, we will reject H_0 if

$$t > t_\alpha = t_{.05} = 1.833$$

where t_α is based on $n_D - 1 = 9$ df. The rejection region is shown in Figure 9.10.

Figure 9.10 Rejection
Region for Example 9.8

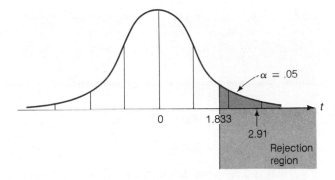

Using x_{Di} to represent the ith difference measurement, we now calculate

$$\sum_{i=1}^{10} x_{Di} = 500 + (-100) + \cdots + 700 = 4,000$$

and

$$\sum_{i=1}^{10} x_{Di}^2 = 3,300,000$$

Then,

$$\bar{x}_D = \frac{\sum_{i=1}^{10} x_{Di}}{10} = \frac{4,000}{10} = 400$$

$$s_D^2 = \frac{\sum_{i=1}^{n_D} (x_{Di} - \bar{x}_D)^2}{n_D - 1} = \frac{\sum_{i=1}^{10} x_{Di}^2 - \left(\sum_{i=1}^{10} x_{Di}\right)^2 / 10}{9}$$

$$= \frac{3,300,000 - (4,000)^2/10}{9} = 188,888.89$$

$$s_D = \sqrt{s_D^2} = 434.61$$

Substituting these values into the formula for the test statistic, we find that

$$t = \frac{\bar{x}_D - 0}{s_D/\sqrt{n_D}} = \frac{400}{434.61/\sqrt{10}} = \frac{400}{137.44} = 2.91$$

As you can see in Figure 9.10, the calculated t falls in the rejection region. Thus, we conclude at $\alpha = .05$ that the mean starting salary for males exceeds the mean starting salary for females.   ■

One measure of the amount of information about $(\mu_1 - \mu_2)$ gained by using a paired difference experiment rather than an independent samples experiment in Example 9.8 is the relative widths of the confidence intervals obtained by the two methods. A 95% confidence interval for $(\mu_1 - \mu_2)$ using the paired difference experiment is

$$\bar{x}_D \pm t_{\alpha/2}\frac{s_D}{\sqrt{n_D}}$$

where t_α has $n_D - 1 = 9$ df. Substituting into this formula, we obtain

$$400 \pm t_{.025}\frac{434.61}{\sqrt{10}} = 400 \pm 2.262\frac{434.61}{\sqrt{10}}$$

$$= 400 \pm 310.88 \approx 400 \pm 311 = (\$89, \$711)$$

If we analyzed the same data as though they were from an independent samples experiment,* we would first calculate the following quantities:

MALES	FEMALES
$\bar{x}_1 = \$14,930$	$\bar{x}_2 = \$14,530$
$s_1^2 = 3,009,000$	$s_2^2 = 2,331,222.22$

Then

$$s_p^2 = \frac{(n_1 - 1)s_1^2 + (n_2 - 1)s_2^2}{n_1 + n_2 - 2} = \frac{9(3,009,000) + 9(2,331,222.22)}{18}$$

$$= 2,670,111.11$$

where s_p^2 is based on $(n_1 + n_2 - 2) = (10 + 10 - 2) = 18$ df.

The 95% confidence interval is

$$(\bar{x}_1 - \bar{x}_2) \pm t_{\alpha/2}\sqrt{s_p^2\left(\frac{1}{n_1} + \frac{1}{n_2}\right)} = 400 \pm t_{.025}\sqrt{2,670,111.11\left(\frac{1}{10} + \frac{1}{10}\right)}$$

$$= 400 \pm 2.101\sqrt{2,670,111.11\left(\frac{1}{10} + \frac{1}{10}\right)}$$

$$= 400 \pm 1,535.35$$

$$\approx 400 \pm 1,535 = (-\$1,135, \$1,935)$$

The confidence interval for the independent sampling experiment is about five times wider than for the corresponding paired difference confidence interval. Blocking out the variability due to differences in majors and grade-point averages significantly increases the information about the difference in mean male and female starting salaries by providing a much more accurate (smaller confidence interval for the same confidence coefficient) estimate of $(\mu_1 - \mu_2)$.

You may wonder whether a paired difference experiment is always superior to an independent samples experiment. The answer is: Most of the time, but not always. We sacrifice half the degrees of freedom in the t statistic when a paired difference design is used instead of an

---

* This is done only to provide a measure of the increase in the amount of information obtained by a paired design in comparison to an unpaired design. Actually, if an experiment is designed using pairing, an unpaired analysis would be invalid because the assumption of independent samples would not be satisfied.

independent samples design. This is a *loss* of information, and unless this loss is more than compensated for by the reduction in variability obtained by blocking (pairing), the paired difference experiment will result in a net loss of information about $(\mu_1 - \mu_2)$. Thus, we should be convinced that the pairing will significantly reduce variability before performing the paired difference experiment. Most of the time this will happen.

One final note: The pairing of the observations is determined *before* the experiment is performed (that is, by the *design* of the experiment). *A paired difference experiment is never obtained by pairing the sample observations after the measurements have been acquired.* Such is the stuff of which statistical lies are made!

What Do You Do When the Assumption of a Normal Distribution for the Population of Differences Is Not Satisfied?

Answer: Use the Wilcoxon signed rank test for the paired difference design. (See Chapter 16.)

Case Study 9.1
Comparing Salaries for Equivalent Work

Procedures to maintain comparable salaries between federal white-collar workers and those in the private sector are mandated by federal law. William M. Smith (1976) has discussed one statistical mechanism used in complying with this law. An annual survey, the *National Survey for Professional, Administrative, Technical, and Clerical Pay,* is conducted by the Bureau of Labor Statistics. Salary information is collected for approximately eighty-five work-level categories ranging from clerical to administrative positions in twenty occupations.

The design of the survey resembles a paired difference design because the occupation and experience of employees in the private and government sectors are matched as closely as possible before a comparison is made. Test statistics like the paired difference t can be used to compare the mean salaries for the two sectors. Then, if the data indicate that the mean salaries differ for certain levels, the need for an adjustment is indicated.

Smith points out that presidential or legislative intervention often prevents the adjustments indicated by the data from being enacted. However, the results of the survey are valuable as a salary guide for the private sector and to those performing general economic analyses.

Exercises 9.40–9.51

Learning the Mechanics

9.40 A paired difference experiment yielded the data shown in the table.

PERSON	BEFORE x_1	AFTER x_2
1	83	92
2	60	71
3	55	56
4	99	104
5	77	89

a. Compute $\bar{x}_D$ and s_D.

b. Demonstrate that $\bar{x}_D = \bar{x}_1 - \bar{x}_2$.

c. Is there sufficient evidence to conclude that $\mu_1 \neq \mu_2$? Test using $\alpha = .05$.

d. Find and interpret the approximate p-value for the paired difference test.

e. What assumptions are necessary so the paired difference test will be valid?

9.41 Refer to Exercise 9.40. Construct a 95% confidence interval for μ_D.

9.42 A paired difference experiment produced the following data:

$$n_D = 18 \qquad \bar{x}_1 = 92 \qquad \bar{x}_2 = 95.5 \qquad \bar{x}_D = -3.5 \qquad s_D^2 = 21$$

a. Determine the values of t for which the null hypothesis, $\mu_1 - \mu_2 = 0$, would be rejected in favor of the alternative hypothesis $\mu_1 - \mu_2 < 0$. Use $\alpha = .10$.

b. Conduct the paired difference test described in part a. Draw the appropriate conclusions.

c. What assumptions are necessary so that the paired difference test will be valid?

9.43 Refer to Exercise 9.42. Construct a 90% confidence interval for μ_D.

9.44 Frequently, a paired difference experiment provides more information about the difference between two population means than an independent random samples experiment. Explain. Also explain when it may not.

Applying the Concepts

9.45 A large corporation is considering hiring a consultant to conduct a yearly in-house assertiveness training course for its incoming group of management trainees. Before signing a contract with the consultant, the corporation wishes to assess the effectiveness of the course. Ten trainees were randomly selected to participate in the course and each was given tests designed to measure assertiveness before the course and after the course was completed. Higher scores on the test indicate higher levels of assertiveness. The test scores are shown in the table.

TRAINEE	BEFORE	AFTER	TRAINEE	BEFORE	AFTER
1	50	62	6	56	65
2	61	63	7	47	42
3	51	49	8	66	69
4	43	44	9	42	35
5	52	48	10	50	43

a. Do the data provide sufficient evidence to conclude that the trainees are more assertive after taking the course? Test using $\alpha = .05$.

b. Report the approximate p-value for the test and interpret its value.

c. Based on the results of the test, would you recommend that the corporation hire the consultant? Explain.

d. What assumptions must you make so that the paired *t* test will be valid?

9.46 *Time* (Dec. 7, 1981) reports that a growing number of corporations are encouraging their employees to "get things off their chests" by communicating directly to management on hot-line phones, through the mail, or in face-to-face meetings. For example, American Express Corp. has instituted a mail program that guarantees their employees anonymity (if desired) and an answer from the responsible person (including the company chairperson) within 10 days. A similar program at IBM generates an average of 13,000 letters a year from IBM's 195,000 U.S. employees. Such programs reflect a growing concern on the part of American business for ways to improve worker productivity.

Before instituting an employee complaint/suggestion program in its manufacturing plant, a company randomly sampled eight workers and measured their productivity in terms of the number of items produced per day. A year after the start of the complaint program the productivity of seven of these workers was reevaluated. (The eighth had been promoted in the interim.) The productivity data are shown in the table.

EMPLOYEE ID NUMBER	AUGUST 1983	AUGUST 1984
1011	10	9
0033	9	11
0998	12	14
0006	8	9
1802	10	9
0246	11	14
0777	14	—
1112	11	13

a. Do the data provide evidence that the complaint/suggestion program has helped to increase worker productivity? Test using $\alpha = .10$, and clearly state any assumptions you make in conducting the test.

b. Discuss how the 1-year gap between productivity evaluations could weaken the results of the study.

9.47 A pupillometer is a device used to observe changes in an individual's pupil dilations as he or she is exposed to different visual stimuli. Since there is a direct correlation between the amount an individual's pupil dilates and his or her interest in the stimuli, marketing organizations sometimes use pupillometers to help them evaluate potential consumer interest in new products, alternative package designs, and other factors. The Design and Market Research Laboratories of the Container Corporation of America used a pupillometer to evaluate consumer reaction to different silverware patterns for one of its clients (McGuire, 1973). Suppose fifteen consumers were chosen at random, and each was shown two different silverware patterns. The pupillometer readings for each consumer are shown in the table (in millimeters).

CONSUMER	PATTERN 1	PATTERN 2	CONSUMER	PATTERN 1	PATTERN 2
1	1.00	0.80	9	0.98	0.91
2	0.97	0.66	10	1.46	1.10
3	1.45	1.22	11	1.85	1.60
4	1.21	1.00	12	0.33	0.21
5	0.77	0.81	13	1.77	1.50
6	1.32	1.11	14	0.85	0.65
7	1.81	1.30	15	0.15	0.05
8	0.91	0.32			

a. Use a 90% confidence interval to estimate the difference in the mean amount of pupil dilation per consumer for silverware patterns 1 and 2.

b. Give a practical interpretation of the interval.

9.48 Among the better known and most frequently enforced antitrust laws are those against price fixing (Sherman Act, Section One) and monopolization or attempt to monopolize (Sherman Act, Section Two). Other antitrust violations include price discrimination, retail price maintenance, and tying the sale of a product to the purchase of another product. Alan R. Beckenstein, H. Landis Gabel, and Karlene Roberts (1983) surveyed 188 *Fortune 500* industrial companies and found that, on average (without adjusting for inflation), these companies "spent $3\frac{1}{2}$ times the amount on antitrust investigations, legal fees, fines, damages, court costs, and out-of-court settlements in the 1970's as they did in the 1960's." Further, they claim that, on average, these companies faced 3.22 more antitrust litigations in the 1970's than in the 1960's. As a result, Beckenstein, Gabel, and Roberts argue that companies need to give more attention to the possible legal consequences of their actions than they have in the past. They conclude that today's legal risks make it imperative that managers at all levels in the organization be involved with designing and implementing strategies to comply with the antitrust laws. Another survey of ten *Fortune 500* companies yielded the data in the table about the number of litigations faced by the firms in the 1960's and 1970's.

FIRM	1960's	1970's
1	10	10
2	8	12
3	9	8
4	7	16
5	8	14
6	7	6
7	6	11
8	9	12
9	8	11
10	7	12

a. Do the data provide sufficient evidence to reject Beckenstein, Gabel, and Roberts' claim? Conduct an hypothesis test and use the *p*-value of your test to help you answer this question.

b. Use a 90% confidence interval to estimate the difference in the mean number of antitrust litigations per firm in the 1970's and the 1960's. Compare your results to Beckenstein, Gabel, and Roberts' result.

9.49 A manufacturer of automobile shock absorbers was interested in comparing the durability of its shocks with that of the shocks produced by its biggest competitor. To make the comparison, one of the manufacturer's and one of the competitor's shocks were randomly selected and installed on the rear wheels of each of six cars. After the cars had been driven 20,000 miles, the strength of each test shock was measured, coded, and recorded. Results of the examination are shown in the table.

CAR NUMBER	MANUFACTURER'S SHOCK	COMPETITOR'S SHOCK
1	8.8	8.4
2	10.5	10.1
3	12.5	12.0
4	9.7	9.3
5	9.6	9.0
6	13.2	13.0

a. Do the data present sufficient evidence to conclude that there is a difference in the mean strength of the two types of shocks after 20,000 miles of use? Use $\alpha = .05$.

b. Find the approximate observed significance level for the test, and interpret its value.

c. What assumptions are necessary to apply a paired difference analysis to the data?

d. Construct a 95% confidence interval for $(\mu_1 - \mu_2)$. Interpret the confidence interval.

9.50 Suppose the data in Exercise 9.49 are based on independent random samples.

a. Do the data provide sufficient evidence to indicate a difference between the mean strengths for the two types of shocks? Use $\alpha = .05$.

b. Construct a 95% confidence interval for $(\mu_1 - \mu_2)$. Interpret your result.

c. Compare the confidence intervals you obtained in Exercise 9.49 and in part b of this exercise. Which is wider? To what do you attribute the difference in width? Assuming in each case that the appropriate assumptions are satisfied, which interval provides you with more information about $(\mu_1 - \mu_2)$? Explain.

d. Are the results of an unpaired analysis valid when the data have been collected from a paired experiment?

9.51 In Case Study 9.1 we discussed the *National Survey for Professional, Administrative, Technical, and Clerical Pay,* which is conducted annually to determine whether federal pay scales are commensurate with private sector salaries. Recall that the government and private workers in the study are matched as closely as possible before the salaries are compared. Suppose that the table shows the annual salaries for twelve pairs of individuals in the sample, matched on job level and experience.

PAIR	PRIVATE	GOVERNMENT	PAIR	PRIVATE	GOVERNMENT
1	$12,500	$11,750	7	$15,800	$14,500
2	22,300	20,900	8	17,500	17,900
3	14,500	14,800	9	23,300	21,400
4	32,300	29,900	10	42,100	43,200
5	20,800	21,500	11	16,800	15,200
6	19,200	18,400	12	14,500	14,200

a. Use these data to construct a 99% confidence interval for the difference between the mean salaries of the private and government sectors.

b. What assumptions are necessary for the validity of the procedure you used in part a?

9.5 Inferences about the Difference Between Population Proportions: Independent Binomial Experiments

Suppose that a manufacturer of campers wants to compare the potential market for its products in the northeastern United States to the market in the southeastern Unites States. Such a comparison would help the manufacturer decide where to concentrate sales efforts. The company randomly chooses 1,000 households in the northeastern United States (NE) and 1,000 households in the southeastern United States (SE) and determines whether each household plans to buy a camper within the next 5 years. The objective is to use this sample information to make an inference about the difference $(p_1 - p_2)$ between the proportion p_1 of *all* households in the NE and the proportion p_2 of *all* households in the SE that plan to purchase a camper within 5 years.

The two samples represent independent binomial experiments (see Section 5.4 for the characteristics of binomial experiments), with the binomial random variables x_1 and x_2 being the numbers of the 1,000 sampled households in each area that indicate they will purchase a camper within 5 years. The results of the sampling can be summarized as follows:

NE	SE
$n_1 = 1,000$	$n_2 = 1,000$
$x_1 = 42$	$x_2 = 24$

We can now calculate the *sample* proportions $\hat{p}_1$ and $\hat{p}_2$ of the households in the NE and SE, respectively, that are prospective buyers:

$$\hat{p}_1 = \frac{x_1}{n_1} = \frac{42}{1,000} = .042 \qquad \hat{p}_2 = \frac{x_2}{n_2} = \frac{24}{1,000} = .024$$

The difference between the sample proportions, $(\hat{p}_1 - \hat{p}_2)$, is an intuitively appealing estimator of the difference between the population parameters, $(p_1 - p_2)$. For our example, the estimate is

$$(\hat{p}_1 - \hat{p}_2) = .042 - .024 = .018$$

To judge the reliability of the estimator $(\hat{p}_1 - \hat{p}_2)$, we must observe its performance in repeated sampling from the two populations. That is, we need to know the sampling distribution of $(\hat{p}_1 - \hat{p}_2)$. Properties of the sampling distribution are given in the box at the top of the next page. Remember that $\hat{p}_1$ and $\hat{p}_2$ can be viewed as means of the number of successes in the respective samples so that the Central Limit Theorem will apply when the sample sizes are large.

Since the distribution of $(\hat{p}_1 - \hat{p}_2)$ in repeated sampling is approximately normal, we can use the z statistic to derive confidence intervals for $(p_1 - p_2)$ or to test an hypothesis about $(p_1 - p_2)$. For the camper example, a 95% confidence interval for the difference $(p_1 - p_2)$ is

$$(\hat{p}_1 - \hat{p}_2) \pm 1.96\sigma_{(\hat{p}_1 - \hat{p}_2)} = (\hat{p}_1 - \hat{p}_2) \pm 1.96\sqrt{\frac{p_1 q_1}{n_1} + \frac{p_2 q_2}{n_2}}$$

The quantities $p_1 q_1$ and $p_2 q_2$ must be estimated in order to complete the calculation of the standard deviation, $\sigma_{(\hat{p}_1 - \hat{p}_2)}$, and hence of the confidence interval. In Section 8.5, we showed

---

Properties of the Sampling Distribution of $(\hat{p}_1 - \hat{p}_2)$

1. If the sample sizes n_1 and n_2 are large (see Section 6.5 for a guideline), the sampling distribution of $(\hat{p}_1 - \hat{p}_2)$ is approximately normal.

2. The mean of the sampling distribution of $(\hat{p}_1 - \hat{p}_2)$ is $(p_1 - p_2)$;* i.e.,

$$E(\hat{p}_1 - \hat{p}_2) = p_1 - p_2$$

Thus, $(\hat{p}_1 - \hat{p}_2)$ is an unbiased estimator of $(p_1 - p_2)$.

3. The standard deviation of the sampling distribution of $(\hat{p}_1 - \hat{p}_2)$* is

$$\sigma_{(\hat{p}_1 - \hat{p}_2)} = \sqrt{\frac{p_1 q_1}{n_1} + \frac{p_2 q_2}{n_2}}$$

---

that the value of pq is relatively insensitive to the value chosen to approximate p. Therefore, $\hat{p}_1 \hat{q}_1$ and $\hat{p}_2 \hat{q}_2$ will provide satisfactory estimates of $p_1 q_1$ and $p_2 q_2$, respectively. Then

$$(\hat{p}_1 - \hat{p}_2) \pm 1.96 \sqrt{\frac{p_1 q_1}{n_1} + \frac{p_2 q_2}{n_2}} \approx (\hat{p}_1 - \hat{p}_2) \pm 1.96 \sqrt{\frac{\hat{p}_1 \hat{q}_1}{n_1} + \frac{\hat{p}_2 \hat{q}_2}{n_2}}$$

$$= (.042 - .024) \pm 1.96 \sqrt{\frac{(.042)(.958)}{1,000} + \frac{(.024)(.976)}{1,000}}$$

$$= .018 \pm .016 = (.002, .034)$$

Thus, we estimate the difference $(p_1 - p_2)$ to fall in the interval $(.002, .034)$. It appears that there are between 0.2% and 3.4% more households in the NE than in the SE that plan to purchase campers in the next 5 years. The confidence coefficient associated with our interval estimate is .95.

Large-Sample $100(1 - \alpha)\%$ Confidence Interval for $(p_1 - p_2)$

$$(\hat{p}_1 - \hat{p}_2) \pm z_{\alpha/2} \sigma_{(\hat{p}_1 - \hat{p}_2)} = (\hat{p}_1 - \hat{p}_2) \pm z_{\alpha/2} \sqrt{\frac{p_1 q_1}{n_1} + \frac{p_2 q_2}{n_2}}$$

$$\approx (\hat{p}_1 - \hat{p}_2) \pm z_{\alpha/2} \sqrt{\frac{\hat{p}_1 \hat{q}_1}{n_1} + \frac{\hat{p}_2 \hat{q}_2}{n_2}}$$

The z statistic,

$$z = \frac{(\hat{p}_1 - \hat{p}_2) - (p_1 - p_2)}{\sigma_{(\hat{p}_1 - \hat{p}_2)}}$$

is used to test the null hypothesis that $(p_1 - p_2)$ equals some specified difference — say D_0.

---

* The mean and variance of the sampling distribution of $(\hat{p}_1 - \hat{p}_2)$ can be derived using the formulas given in Section 7.5.

For the special case where $D_0 = 0$ —i.e., where we want to test the null hypothesis that $(p_1 - p_2) = 0$ (or, equivalently, that $p_1 = p_2$) —the best estimate of $p_1 = p_2 = p$ is obtained by dividing the total number of successes $(x_1 + x_2)$ for the two samples by the total number of observations $(n_1 + n_2)$; i.e.,

$$\hat{p} = \frac{x_1 + x_2}{n_1 + n_2}$$

Then the best estimate of $\sigma_{(\hat{p}_1 - \hat{p}_2)}$ is

$$\sigma_{(\hat{p}_1 - \hat{p}_2)} = \sqrt{\frac{p_1 q_1}{n_1} + \frac{p_2 q_2}{n_2}} \approx \sqrt{\frac{\hat{p}\hat{q}}{n_1} + \frac{\hat{p}\hat{q}}{n_2}} = \sqrt{\hat{p}\hat{q}\left(\frac{1}{n_1} + \frac{1}{n_2}\right)}$$

The test is summarized in the box.

Large-Sample Test of an Hypothesis about $(p_1 - p_2)$

One-Tailed Test

H_0: $(p_1 - p_2) = D_0$

H_a: $(p_1 - p_2) < D_0$
   [or H_a: $(p_1 - p_2) > D_0$]

Two-Tailed Test

H_0: $(p_1 - p_2) = D_0$

H_a: $(p_1 - p_2) \neq D_0$

where $D_0 =$ Hypothesized value of $(p_1 - p_2)$

Test statistic: $z = \dfrac{(\hat{p}_1 - \hat{p}_2) - D_0}{\sigma_{(\hat{p}_1 - \hat{p}_2)}}$

Test statistic: $z = \dfrac{(\hat{p}_1 - \hat{p}_2) - D_0}{\sigma_{(\hat{p}_1 - \hat{p}_2)}}$

Rejection region: $z < -z_\alpha$
     [or $z > z_\alpha$ when
     H_a: $(p_1 - p_2) > D_0$]

Rejection region: $z < -z_{\alpha/2}$
     or $z > z_{\alpha/2}$

Note: $\sigma_{(\hat{p}_1 - \hat{p}_2)} = \sqrt{\dfrac{p_1 q_1}{n_1} + \dfrac{p_2 q_2}{n_2}}$

To calculate $\sigma_{(\hat{p}_1 - \hat{p}_2)}$, approximate p_1 and p_2 using $\hat{p}_1$ and $\hat{p}_2$ except for the special case where $D_0 = p_1 - p_2 = 0$. Then use

$$\hat{p}_1 = \hat{p}_2 = \hat{p} = \frac{x_1 + x_2}{n_1 + n_2} \quad\text{and}\quad \sigma_{(\hat{p}_1 - \hat{p}_2)} \approx \sqrt{\hat{p}\hat{q}\left(\frac{1}{n_1} + \frac{1}{n_2}\right)}$$

Example 9.9   A consumer agency wants to determine whether there is a difference between the proportions of the two leading automobile models that need major repairs (more than $300) within 2 years of their purchase. A sample of 400 2-year owners of model 1 are contacted, and a sample of 500 2-year owners of model 2 are contacted. The numbers x_1 and x_2 of owners who report that their cars needed major repairs within the first 2 years are 53 and 78, respectively. Test the null hypothesis that no difference exists between the proportions in populations 1 and 2 needing major repairs against the alternative that a difference does exist. Use $\alpha = .10$.

Solution   If we define p_1 and p_2 as the true proportions of model 1 and model 2 owners, respectively, whose cars need major repairs within 2 years, the elements of the test are

$$H_0: (p_1 - p_2) = 0 \qquad H_a: (p_1 - p_2) \neq 0$$

Test statistic: $z = \dfrac{(\hat{p}_1 - \hat{p}_2) - 0}{\sigma_{(\hat{p}_1 - \hat{p}_2)}}$

Rejection region ($\alpha = .10$): $z > z_{\alpha/2} = z_{.05} = 1.645$

or $z < -z_{\alpha/2} = -z_{.05} = -1.645$ (see Figure 9.11)

Figure 9.11   Rejection Region for Example 9.9

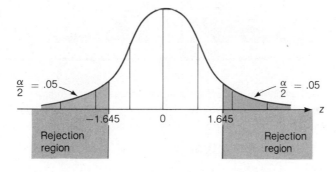

We now calculate

$$z = \frac{(\hat{p}_1 - \hat{p}_2) - 0}{\sigma_{(\hat{p}_1 - \hat{p}_2)}} = \frac{(\hat{p}_1 - \hat{p}_2)}{\sqrt{\dfrac{p_1 q_1}{n_1} + \dfrac{p_2 q_2}{n_2}}}$$

$$\approx \frac{(\hat{p}_1 - \hat{p}_2)}{\sqrt{\hat{p}\hat{q}\left(\dfrac{1}{n_1} + \dfrac{1}{n_2}\right)}}$$

where $\hat{p} = \dfrac{x_1 + x_2}{n_1 + n_2} = \dfrac{53 + 78}{400 + 500} = .1456$

$$= \frac{(53/400 - 78/500)}{\sqrt{(.1456)(.8544)\left(\dfrac{1}{400} + \dfrac{1}{500}\right)}} = \frac{-.0235}{.0237} = -.99$$

The samples provide insufficient evidence at $\alpha = .10$ to detect a difference between the proportions of the two models that need repairs within 2 years. Even though 2.35% more sampled owners of model 2 found major repairs, this difference is only .99 standard deviation ($z = -.99$) from the hypothesized difference of zero between the true proportions.   ∎

Example 9.10   Find the observed significance level for the test in Example 9.9.

Solution   The observed value of z for this two-tailed test was $z = -.99$. Therefore, the observed significance level is

$$p\text{-value} = P(z < -.99 \text{ or } z > .99)$$

Figure 9.12   The Observed Significance Level for the Test of Example 9.9

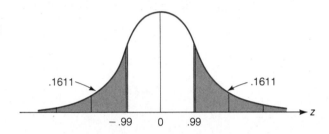

This probability is equal to the shaded area shown in Figure 9.12. The area corresponding to $z = .99$ is given in Table IV of Appendix B as .3389. Therefore, the p-value for the test, the sum of the two shaded tail areas under the standard normal curve, is

$$p\text{-value} = 2(.5 - .3389)$$
$$= .3222$$

The probability of observing a z as large as .99 or less than $-.99$ if in fact $p_1 = p_2$ is .3222. This large p-value indicates that there is little or no evidence of a difference between p_1 and p_2.   ■

Case Study 9.2
Hotel Room
Interviewing —
Anxiety and
Suspicion

Writing in the *Sloan Management Review,* Lois Kaufman and John Wolf (1982) describe the typical approach used by sales managers for attracting and interviewing prospective sales representatives:

To maintain product distribution and enhance customer service, corporate sales personnel are typically assigned to a district sales office that is tied to a regional office by telephone or telex. The managers who are responsible for staffing sales territories usually operate with considerable autonomy. When hiring sales representatives, they usually advertise for these positions in local newspapers, and traditionally invite applicants to interviews which are held in hotel rooms.

The purpose of the article was to examine the effects of the hotel interview site on prospective sales representatives, and on women in particular.

As part of their study, Kaufman and Wolf asked a sample of seventy-four* female college students from Rutgers University, Montclair State College, and Union College whether they would agree to a job interview in a room at a local hotel. Sixty-two percent said they would. A sample of seventy-four college women were asked whether they would agree to a job interview in a room of a local office building. Ninety-eight percent said they would. The authors

---

* Sample sizes were obtained via personal communication from Professor Kaufman.

used a one-tailed hypothesis test to examine the following hypotheses:

$$H_0: p_1 - p_2 = 0 \qquad H_a: p_1 - p_2 > 0$$

where

p_1 = Proportion of female college students who, if offered a job interview in a room of a local office building, would say they would attend the interview

p_2 = Proportion of female college students who, if offered a job interview in a room of a local hotel, would say they would attend the interview

They obtained an observed significance level of less than .05 for their z statistic and concluded that the proportion of women who would agree to an interview in an office building is significantly greater than the proportion willing to interview in a hotel room.

A similar but less extreme result was obtained when college men were asked the same questions. For the women $\hat{p}_1 - \hat{p}_2 = .36$, while for the men $\hat{p}_1 - \hat{p}_2 = .09$. Based on these results and other information supplied by the men and women who participated in their study, Kaufman and Wolf explained the study's findings as follows:

> Both men and women find hotel rooms more stressful than offices, but women are even more anxious than men about the prospect of interviewing in hotels. Most respondents said they would take precautions if they interviewed in hotels. Hotel room hiring was described with such words as "shady," "suspicious," "secretive," and "fishy."

Kaufman and Wolf summarized the implications of their findings by saying:

> We believe that companies should reexamine their hiring practices and recognize that hotel room interviewing may not be the best approach to recruiting and hiring talented employees. Companies should consider using college campuses, local placement agencies, civic centers, libraries, or government buildings as possible interview sites. Although companies may not intend to discourage applicants when they interview in hotels, our survey showed that many women as well as some men will not attend an interview held in a hotel.

Exercises 9.52–9.69

Learning the Mechanics

9.52 What are the characteristics of a binomial experiment?

9.53 The quantities $\hat{p}_1$ and $\hat{p}_2$ have been defined to be x_1/n_1 and x_2/n_2, respectively. What assumptions do we make about x_1 and x_2?

9.54 Random samples of $n_1 = 200$ and $n_2 = 220$ from two binomial populations, 1 and 2, produced $x_1 = 38$ and $x_2 = 71$ successes, respectively.

a. Compute the sample proportions, $\hat{p}_1$ and $\hat{p}_2$.

b. Find the values of z for which the null hypothesis $H_0: (p_1 - p_2) = 0$ would be rejected in favor of the alternative hypothesis $H_a: (p_1 - p_2) \neq 0$. Use $\alpha = .10$.

c. Test the hypotheses described in part b. Interpret your results.

d. Find and interpret the p-value for the test.

e. What assumptions must be satisfied so the test will be valid?

9.55 Refer to Exercise 9.54. Construct a 98% confidence interval for $(p_1 - p_2)$. Interpret your confidence interval.

9.56 A random sample of size $n_1 = 500$ from population 1 and a random sample of size $n_2 = 500$ from population 2 yielded $x_1 = 140$ and $x_2 = 192$ successes, respectively.

a. Given

$$H_0: (p_1 - p_2) = 0 \qquad H_a: (p_1 - p_2) < 0$$

find the values of z for which the null hypothesis would be rejected in favor of the alternative hypothesis. Use $\alpha = .025$.

b. Conduct the test described above. Interpret the results.

c. Find the observed significance level of the hypothesis test, and interpret its value.

d. What assumptions must be satisfied so the test will be valid?

9.57 Refer to Exercise 9.56. Construct an 80% confidence interval for $(p_1 - p_2)$. Interpret your confidence interval.

9.58 Explain how the Central Limit Theorem is used in finding an approximate sampling distribution for $(\hat{p}_1 - \hat{p}_2)$.

9.59 Explain how knowing the sampling distribution of $(\hat{p}_1 - \hat{p}_2)$ can help measure the reliability of the estimator $(\hat{p}_1 - \hat{p}_2)$.

Applying the Concepts

9.60 The Business Economics Division of Dun & Bradstreet regularly surveys business executives to determine their expectations for business in the coming months. The results are distributed to companies and investors in a quarterly newsletter. During the time period Aug. 11–25, 1983, interviews were conducted with 402 wholesalers and 450 retailers. Twenty-three percent of the wholesalers and 34% of the retailers expected their inventories to be higher at the end of the fourth quarter than at the beginning. Thirty-one percent of the wholesalers and 23% of the retailers expected inventories to decrease (Dun & Bradstreet, 1982).

a. Do the data provide sufficient evidence to indicate a difference in the proportions of wholesalers and retailers who expect no change in the level of inventories? Test using $\alpha = .10$.

b. Use a 90% confidence interval to estimate the difference in the proportions of wholesalers and retailers who expect no change in the level of inventories. List any assumptions you make in constructing the confidence interval.

9.61 To aid in the development of new products and/or to guide their marketing programs, producers of food products attempt to identify the taste preferences of various segments of the population. Accordingly, a recent study by Professor Susan Schiffman of the Duke University Center for the Study of Aging and Human Development should be of interest to the food industry. Professor Schiffman conducted an experiment that showed that a person's ability to identify food by smell and taste decreases with increasing age. As a result, she recommends adding simulated odors to the food of older people to improve its flavor. Part of Professor Schiffman's experiment involved asking a random sample of older persons and a random sample of college students to smell, taste, and identify a variety of foods that had been blended to prevent identification by "feel." Subjects were blindfolded during the experiment (Meier, 1980). Suppose that blended apple was correctly identified by 81 of 100 students and by 51 of 100 older people.

a. Would these data support Professor Schiffman's conclusion that the ability to identify food decreases with age? Test using $\alpha = .05$.

b. Report the p-value of the hypothesis test, and interpret its value.

c. What assumption must be satisfied so the hypothesis test of part a will be valid? Why was this assumption necessary?

9.62 Suppose a firm switches its table salt container from a cylinder (expensive) to a rectangular box (inexpensive). The firm samples 1,000 households nationwide, both before and after the switch, to estimate the percentage of households that purchase its brand of salt. The results obtained are shown in the table.

	BEFORE	AFTER
Sample size	1,000	1,000
Number of households using firm's brand	475	305

a. Estimate the true difference in the percentage of households that use the firm's salt before and after the packaging switch. Use a 90% confidence interval.

b. Interpret the confidence interval of part a. Express clearly the reliability of the interval.

9.63 Refer to Exercise 9.62. The firm's vice-president in charge of sales claims the switch to the box has seriously hurt the firm's market share. Does the sample evidence support this claim at the .05 significance level?

9.64 Exercise 8.73 discusses the efforts of three television stations using profiles to promote the adoption of "forgotten" children — orphans who have physical or mental handicaps. Oklahoma City's station KOCO helped to place 92 out of 119 children it profiled in comparison with New York's WCBS, which placed 21 out of 35 (*Time*, May 2, 1983). Because the techniques employed in presenting the profiles likely differ for the two television stations, we might wish to compare their rates of success in placing the children for adoption.

a. Do the data provide sufficient evidence to indicate a difference in placement success rates between stations KOCO and WCBS? Test using $\alpha = .05$.

b. Find a 95% confidence interval for the difference in the two success rates.

9.65 Moving companies (home movers, etc.) are required by the government to publish a Carrier Performance Report each year. One of the descriptive statistics they must include in this report is the percentage of shipments on which a $50 or greater claim for loss or damage was filed in the previous year. Suppose company A and company B each decide to estimate this figure by sampling their records, and they obtain the data shown in the table on the next page.

	COMPANY A	COMPANY B
Total shipments delivered	9,542	6,631
Number of shipments on which a claim of $50 or greater was filed	1,653	501

a. Estimate the true proportion of shipments on which a claim of $50 or greater was made against company A. Use an estimate that reflects its reliability.

b. Repeat part a for company B.

c. Use a 95% confidence interval to estimate the true difference in the proportions of shipments that result in claims being made against company A and company B.

9.66 Refer to Exercise 9.65. Test the null hypothesis that no difference exists between the true percentage of shipments resulting in claims made against company A and company B against the alternative hypothesis that a difference does exist. Use $\alpha = .05$. Do your test results indicate that one carrier is superior to the other? If so, which one? Explain how you arrived at your conclusion.

9.67 If α were set at .01 in Exercise 9.66, would you be less likely or more likely to reject the null hypothesis if in fact it is true? Explain.

9.68 The Reserve Mining Company of Minnesota commissioned a team of physicians to study the breathing patterns of its miners who were exposed to taconite dust. The physicians compared the breathing of 307 miners who had been employed in Reserve's Babbit, Minnesota, mine for more than 20 years with that of 35 Duluth area men with no history of exposure to taconite dust. The physicians concluded that "there is no significant difference in respiratory symptoms or breathing ability between the group of men who have worked in the taconite industry for more than 20 years and a group of men of similar smoking habits but without exposure to taconite dust" (*Minneapolis Tribune,* Feb. 20, 1977). Using the statistical procedures you have learned in this chapter, design an hypothesis test (give H_0, H_a, test statistic, etc.) that would have been appropriate for use in the physicians' study.

9.69 Refer to Exercise 9.68. Suppose the physicians determined that 61 of the 307 miners had breathing irregularities and that 5 of the 35 Duluth men had breathing irregularities. Test to determine whether the data indicate that a higher proportion of breathing irregularities exists among those who have been exposed to taconite dust than among those who have not been exposed.

9.6 Determining the Sample Size

You can find the appropriate sample size to estimate the difference between two population parameters with a specified degree of reliability by using the method described in Section 8.6. That is, to estimate the difference between two parameters correct to within B units with probability $(1 - \alpha)$, set $z_{\alpha/2}$ standard deviations of the sampling distribution of the estimator equal to B. Then solve for the sample size. To do this, you have to specify a particular ratio between n_1 and n_2. Most often, you will want to have equal sample sizes — i.e., $n_1 = n_2 = n$. We will illustrate the procedure with two examples.

See p. 323

Example 9.11 The sales manager for a chain of supermarkets wants to determine whether store location, management, and other factors produce a difference in the mean meat purchase per customer (zero purchases to be excluded) at two different stores. The estimate of the difference in mean meat purchase per customer is to be correct to within $2.00 with probability equal to .95. If the two sample sizes are to be equal, find $n_1 = n_2 = n$, the number of customer meat sales to be randomly selected from each store.

Solution To solve the problem, you have to know something about the variation in the dollar amount of meat sales per customer. Suppose you know that the sales have a range of approximately $30 at each store. Then you could approximate $\sigma_1 = \sigma_2 = \sigma$ by letting the range equal 4σ, and

$$4\sigma \approx \$30$$
$$\sigma \approx \$7.50$$

The next step is to solve the equation

$$z_{\alpha/2}\sqrt{\frac{\sigma_1^2}{n_1} + \frac{\sigma_2^2}{n_2}} = B$$

for n, where $n = n_1 = n_2$. Since we want the estimate to lie within $B = \$2.00$ of $(\mu_1 - \mu_2)$ with probability equal to .95, $z_{\alpha/2} = z_{.025} = 1.96$. Then, letting $\sigma_1 = \sigma_2 = 7.5$ and solving for n, we have

$$1.96\sqrt{\frac{(7.5)^2}{n} + \frac{(7.5)^2}{n}} = 2.00$$

$$1.96\sqrt{\frac{2(7.5)^2}{n}} = 2.00$$

$$n = 108.05 \approx 108$$

Consequently, you will have to randomly sample 108 meat sales per store to estimate the difference in mean meat sales per customer correct to within $2.00 with probability approximately equal to .95. ∎

Example 9.12 A production supervisor suspects a difference exists between the proportions of defective items produced by two different machines. Experience has shown that the proportion defective for the two machines is in the neighborhood of .03. If the supervisor wants to estimate the difference in the proportions correct to within .005 with probability .95, how many items must be randomly sampled from the production of each machine? (Assume that you want $n_1 = n_2 = n$.)

Binomial

Solution For the specified level of reliability, $z_{\alpha/2} = z_{.025} = 1.96$. Then, letting $p_1 = p_2 = .03$ and $n_1 = n_2 = n$, we find the required sample size per machine by solving the following equation for n:

$$z_{\alpha/2}\sqrt{\frac{p_1 q_1}{n_1} + \frac{p_2 q_2}{n_2}} = B$$

$$1.96\sqrt{\frac{(.03)(.97)}{n} + \frac{(.03)(.97)}{n}} = .005$$

$$1.96\sqrt{\frac{2(.03)(.97)}{n}} = .005$$

$$n = 8{,}943.2$$

You can see that this may be a tedious sampling procedure. If the supervisor insists on estimating $(p_1 - p_2)$ correct to within .005 with probability equal to .95, approximately 9,000 items will have to be inspected for each machine.   ■

You can see from the calculations in Example 9.12 that $\sigma_{(\hat{p}_1 - \hat{p}_2)}$ (and hence the solution, $n_1 = n_2 = n$) depends on the actual (but unknown) values of p_1 and p_2. In fact, the solution for $n_1 = n_2 = n$ is largest when $p_1 = p_2 = .5$. Therefore, if we have no prior information on the approximate values of p_1 and p_2, we use $p_1 = p_2 = .5$ in the formula for $\sigma_{(\hat{p}_1 - \hat{p}_2)}$. If p_1 and p_2 really are close to .5, then the values of n_1 and n_2 that you have calculated will be appropriate. If p_1 and p_2 differ substantially from .5, then your solutions for n_1 and n_2 will be larger than needed. Consequently, using $p_1 = p_2 = .5$ when solving for n_1 and n_2 is a conservative procedure because the sample sizes n_1 and n_2 will be at least as large as (and probably larger than) needed.

Exercises 9.70–9.78

Learning the Mechanics

9.70 Suppose you want to estimate the difference between two population means correct to within 1.5 with probability .95. If prior information suggests that the population variances are approximately equal to

$$\sigma_1^2 = \sigma_2^2 = 12$$

and you want to select independent random samples of equal size from the populations, how large should the sample sizes, μ_1 and μ_2, be?

9.71 An experimenter wants to estimate the difference between two population proportions correct to within .06 with confidence coefficient .90. Suppose the experimenter has no prior information about the values of p_1 and p_2. If the sample sizes are to be equal, how large should they be?

9.72 Suppose you want to estimate the difference between two population proportions correct to within .04 with confidence coefficient equal to .90. Also suppose you think both p_1 and p_2 are near .4 and you want to select samples of equal size from the two populations. Find the required sample sizes, n_1 and n_2.

Applying the Concepts

9.73 In Exercise 9.38 you should have rejected the hypothesis that $\sigma_1^2 = \sigma_2^2$ and concluded that it is inappropriate to use the two-sample t statistic in making inferences about $(\mu_1 - \mu_2)$. In such cases, inferences about $(\mu_1 - \mu_2)$ can still be made if data are plentiful enough so that large-sample procedures such as those in Section 9.1 can be used. Accordingly, how many additional completion times should be sampled in order that the difference in the mean completion times for operators working with and without the 30-second guideline can be estimated to within 2 seconds with probability .80? Assume equal sample sizes are desired.

9.74 Rat damage creates a large financial loss in the production of sugarcane. One aspect of the problem that has been investigated by the U.S. Department of Agriculture concerns the optimal place to locate rat poison. To be most effective in reducing rat damage, should the poison be located in the middle of the field or on the outer perimeter? One way to answer this question is to determine where the greater amount of damage occurs. If damage is measured by the proportion of cane stalks that have been damaged by rats, how many stalks from each section of the field should be sampled in order to estimate the true difference between the proportions of stalks damaged in the two sections to within .02 with probability .95?

9.75 Refer to Exercise 9.61 in Section 9.5 and the experiment conducted to investigate whether a person's ability to identify food by smell and taste decreases with increasing age. How large should Professor Schiffman's samples be if she wishes to estimate the difference in the proportion of students and the proportion of older people who are able to identify blended apple to within .05 with probability .90?

9.76 An article in the *Wall Street Journal* (June 6, 1977) stated that soaring prices of new cars have created a swing toward automobile loans in excess of 36 months. In fact, several automobile finance companies indicate the percentage of long-term loans (in excess of 36 months, with most at 48 months) increased from less than 10% in 1976 to somewhere near 50% in 1977. Suppose you plan to survey potential buyers in your sales region to estimate the proportion of buyers in the over 40 age group who favor 48-month automobile loans and the proportion in the 40 and under age group who favor the 48-month automobile loans. You intend to select random samples of the same size from each of these two groups.

a. Approximately how many potential automobile buyers should be included in your samples to estimate the difference in proportions correct to within .05 with probability equal to .95?

b. Suppose you want to obtain individual estimates for the proportions in the two age groups. Will the sample size found in part a be large enough to provide estimates of each proportion correct to within .05 with probability equal to .95?

9.77 Suppose you are interested in the growth rate of dividends. Consider investing $1,000 in a stock, and suppose you want to estimate the dividend rate on your $1,000 investment at the end of 5 years. Particularly, you want to compare two types of stocks, electrical utilities and oil companies. To conduct your study, you plan to randomly select n oil stocks and n electrical utility stocks. For each stock, you will check the records, calculate the number of shares of stock you could have purchased 5 years ago for $1,000, and then calculate the dividend rate (in percent) that the stock would be paying today on your $1,000 investment. Suppose you think the dividend rates will vary over a range of roughly 25%. To obtain an approximate value for σ_1 and σ_2, let $\sigma_1 = \sigma_2 = \sigma$ and let the range be 4σ. Then the range is $25 \approx 4\sigma$ and $\sigma \approx 6.25$. How large should n be if you want to estimate the difference in the mean rates of dividend return correct to within 3% with 95% confidence?

9.78 A television manufacturer wants to compare the proportions of its sets that need repair within 1 year with the proportion of a competitor's sets that need repair within 1 year. If it is desired to estimate the difference in proportions to within .05 with 90% confidence, and if the manufacturer plans to sample twice as many buyers of its sets as buyers of the competitor's sets, how many buyers of each brand must be sampled? Assume the proportion of sets that need repair will be about .2 for both brands.

Summary

We have presented various techniques for using the information in two samples to make inferences about the difference between population parameters. As you would expect, we are able to make reliable inferences with fewer assumptions about the sampled populations when the sample sizes are large. When we cannot take large samples from the populations, the *two-sample t statistic* permits us to use the limited sample information to make inferences about the *difference between means* when the assumptions of normality and equal population variances are at least approximately true. The *paired difference experiment* offers the possibility of increasing the information about $(\mu_1 - \mu_2)$ by pairing similar observational units to control variability. In designing a paired difference experiment, we expect that the reduction in variability will more than compensate for the loss in degrees of freedom.

Two other inferential procedures for making comparisons between population parameters were presented in this chapter. The *F test* was used to compare two population variances, σ_1^2 and σ_2^2. This test is useful in checking the assumption of equal population variances, an assumption that is essential to the independent samples t test (and confidence interval) for a comparison of two population means. The F test can also be used to compare the variances of two populations when these variances assume practical importance as a measure of risk, error, etc.

This chapter concluded with a comparison of two binomial parameters, p_1 and p_2. Practical examples of such comparisons are numerous; they frequently appear in the analysis of business surveys. A company might want to compare the proportion of consumers who prefer a new product A to a new (or old) product B. Or, the comparison might occur in a production setting when a manufacturer wants to compare the fractions of defectives that emerge from two production lines.

Supplementary Exercises 9.79–9.102

[*Note:* In each problem, state the assumptions necessary for the procedure to be valid.]

9.79 To market a new cigarette, a tobacco company decides to use two different advertising agencies, one operating in the East and one in the West. After the cigarette has been on the market for 6 months, random samples of smokers are taken from each of the two regions and questioned concerning their cigarette preference. The numbers in the samples favoring the new brand are shown in the table. Do the data provide sufficient evidence to indicate a difference in the proportions preferring the new brand between the two regions? Use $\alpha = .05$. Based on your test, what inference can be made about the difference in the effectiveness of the two advertising agencies?

	SAMPLE SIZE	NUMBER PREFERRING NEW BRAND
EAST	500	12
WEST	450	15

9.80 When new instruments are developed to perform chemical analyses of products (food, medicine, etc.), they are usually evaluated with respect to two criteria: accuracy and precision. *Accuracy* refers to the ability of the instrument to identify correctly the nature and amounts of a product's components. *Precision* refers to the consistency with which the instrument will identify the components of the same material in repeated analyses. Thus, a large variability in the identification of the components of a single sample of a product indicates a lack of precision. Suppose a pharmaceutical firm is considering two brands of an instrument designed to identify the components of certain drugs. As part of a comparison of precision, ten test-tube samples of a well-mixed batch of a drug are selected and then five are analyzed by instrument A and five by instrument B. The data shown in the table are the percentages of the primary component of the drug given by the instruments. Do these data provide evidence of a difference in the precision of the two machines? Use $\alpha = .10$.

A	B
43	46
48	49
37	43
52	41
45	48

9.81 The procedure outlined in this exercise was developed by Tele-Research, Inc., for evaluating the effectiveness of newly developed television commercials prior to their release. The exercise describes part of an actual study in which the procedure was used (Jenssen, 1966). Three hundred ninety-two shoppers were randomly selected as they entered a large Los Angeles supermarket and were asked to describe their preferences for several product brands. One of these was a brand, XYZ, whose new television commercial was the object of the study. Ostensibly in exchange for their time, the shoppers were given a packet of ten different cents-off coupons for products sold in the supermarket. Included were coupons for XYZ. The coupons could be used only in that particular store and only on that particular day. A second sample of 387 shoppers was given the same interview, but was also asked to watch four television commercials in a trailer parked outside the supermarket. One of the commercials was a newly developed ad for XYZ. Following the viewing, the shoppers were asked for their reactions to the commercials. The shoppers were then given the same packet of coupons. Of the 392 shoppers not exposed to the television commercials, 57 redeemed the coupon for XYZ. Of the 387 shoppers who were exposed to XYZ's commercials, 84 redeemed the XYZ coupon.

a. Do the sample data provide sufficient evidence to conclude that the new XYZ commercial motivates shoppers to purchase the XYZ brand? Use $\alpha = .05$.

b. Find and interpret the observed significance level for the test.

9.82 List the assumptions necessary for each of the following inferential techniques:

a. Large-sample inferences about the difference $(\mu_1 - \mu_2)$ between population means using a two-sample z-statistic.

b. Small-sample inferences about $(\mu_1 - \mu_2)$ using an independent samples design and a two-sample t statistic.

c. Small-sample inferences about $(\mu_1 - \mu_2)$ using a paired difference design and a single-sample t statistic to analyze the differences.

d. Large-sample inferences about the difference $(p_1 - p_2)$ between binomial proportions using a two-sample z statistic.

9.83 Advertising companies often try to characterize the average user of a client's product so advertisements can be targeted at particular segments of the buying community. Suppose a new movie is about to be released and an advertising company wants to determine whether to aim the advertisements at people under 25 years old or those over 25. They plan to arrange an advance showing of the movie to a number of individuals from each group and then to obtain an opinion about the movie from each individual. How many individuals should be included in each sample if the advertising company wants to estimate the difference in the proportions of viewers in each age group who will like the movie to within .05 with 90% confidence? Assume the sample size for each group will be the same and about half of each group will like the movie.

9.84 To compare the rate of return an investor can expect on tax-free municipal bonds with the rate of return on taxable bonds, an investment advisory firm randomly samples ten bonds of each type and computes the annual rate of return over the past 3 years for each bond. The rate of return is then adjusted for taxes, assuming the investor is in a 30% tax bracket. The means and standard deviations for the adjusted returns are shown in the table.

TAX-FREE BONDS	TAXABLE BONDS
$\bar{x}_1 = 7.8\%$	$\bar{x}_2 = 7.3\%$
$s_1 = 1.1\%$	$s_2 = 1.0\%$

a. Test to determine whether there is a difference in the mean rates of return between tax-free and taxable bonds for investors in the 30% tax bracket. Use $\alpha = .05$.

b. Find the approximate observed significance level for the test of part a, and interpret its value.

c. What assumptions were necessary for the validity of the testing procedure you used in part a?

9.85 Refer to Exercise 9.84. Do the sample data cast doubt on the assumption of equal population variances? Use $\alpha = .10$.

9.86 A major interface between consumers and retailers occurs when the consumer is dissatisfied with the product purchased and returns to the retailer to obtain satisfaction. The actions taken by retailers in such situations, however, may not conform to the expectations of consumers. The resulting frustration and ill will benefit neither the consumer nor the retailer. Ronald Dornoff and Clint Tankersley (1975) conducted a study to test the hypothesis that differences exist between retailers' and consumers' perceptions regarding actions taken by retailers in market transactions. A random sample of 300 consumers was selected from the Cincinnati Metropolitan Area Telephone Directory and asked via mail questionnaire to react to scenarios like the following:

A customer calls the retailer to report that her refrigerator purchased two weeks ago is not cooling properly and that all the food has spoiled.

Action that should be taken by the retailer: The customer should be reimbursed for the value of the spoiled food.

One hundred usable questionnaires were returned. The same questionnaire was presented in person to 100 managers and assistant managers of a random sample of 40 retail establishments drawn from the yellow pages of the Cincinnati Telephone Directory. For the above scenario, eighty-nine consumers agreed with the action prescribed for the retailer, three disagreed, and eight had no opinion. Thirty-seven retailers (managers and/or assistant managers) agreed with the prescribed action, fifty-four disagreed, and nine had no opinion.

a. Use a 95% confidence interval to estimate the difference in the proportions of consumers and retailers who agree with the action prescribed in the scenario. Draw appropriate conclusions regarding the hypothesis of interest to Dornoff and Tankersley.

b. What assumption(s), if any, must be made in constructing the confidence interval?

c. Discuss the implications of the composition of the sample of retailers for the validity of the conclusions you made in part a. How would you improve the sampling procedure?

9.87 An automobile manufacturer wants to estimate the difference in the mean miles per gallon rating for two models it produces. If the range of ratings is expected to be about 6 miles per gallon for each model, how many cars of each type must be tested in order to estimate the difference in means to within 0.5 mile per gallon with 90% confidence?

9.88 A consumer protection agency wants to compare the work of two electrical contractors in order to evaluate their safety records. The agency plans to inspect residences in which each of these contractors has done the wiring to estimate the difference in the proportions of residences that are electrically deficient. Suppose the proportions of deficient work are expected to be about .10 for both contractors. How many homes should be inspected to estimate the difference in proportions to within .05 with 90% confidence?

9.89 Management training programs are often instituted to teach supervisory skills and thereby increase productivity. Suppose a company psychologist administers a set of examinations to each of ten supervisors before such a training program begins and then administers similar examinations at the end of the program. The examinations are designed to measure supervisory skills, with higher scores indicating increased skill. The results of the tests are shown in the table.

SUPERVISOR	BEFORE TRAINING PROGRAM	AFTER TRAINING PROGRAM
1	63	78
2	93	92
3	84	91
4	72	80
5	65	69
6	72	85
7	91	99
8	84	82
9	71	81
10	80	87

a. Do the data provide evidence that the training program is effective in increasing supervisory skills, as measured by the examination scores? Use $\alpha = .10$.

b. Find and interpret the approximate p-value for the test.

9.90 Two banks, bank 1 and bank 2, independently sampled forty and fifty of their business accounts, respectively, and determined the number of the bank's services (loans, checking, savings, investment counseling, etc.) each sampled business was using. Both banks offer the same services. A summary of the data supplied by the samples is listed in the table. Do the samples provide sufficient evidence to conclude that the average number of services used by bank 1's business customers is significantly greater (at $\alpha = .10$) than the average number of services used by bank 2's business customers?

BANK 1	BANK 2
$\bar{x}_1 = 2.2$	$\bar{x}_2 = 1.8$
$s_1 = 1.15$	$s_2 = 1.10$

9.91 Find a 99% confidence interval for $(\mu_1 - \mu_2)$ in Exercise 9.90. Does the interval include zero? Interpret the confidence interval.

9.92 Radio stations sometimes conduct prize giveaways in an attempt to increase their share of the listening audience. Suppose a station manager calls 300 randomly selected households in a city, and finds that sixty-five have members who regularly listen to the station. The station then conducts a 2-month promotional contest and follows it with a survey of 500 randomly chosen households. The survey shows that 154 households have members who regularly listen to the station.

a. Use a 90% confidence interval to estimate the difference between the proportions of those who regularly listen to the station before and after the promotional contest.

b. Construct a 95% confidence interval for the proportion of those who listen to the station after the promotion is over.

9.93 Suppose you have been offered similar jobs in two different locales. To help in deciding which job to accept, you would like to compare the cost of living in the two cities. One of your primary concerns is the cost of housing, so you obtain a copy of a newspaper from each locale and begin to study the housing prices in the classified advertisements. One convenient method for getting a general idea of prices is to compute the prices on a per-square-foot basis. This is done by dividing the price of the house by the heated area (in square feet) of the house. Random samples of sixty-three advertisements in locale 1 and seventy-eight in locale 2 produce the results shown in the table. Is there evidence that the mean housing price per square foot differs in the two locales? Use $\alpha = .01$.

LOCALE 1	LOCALE 2
$\bar{x}_1 = \$50.40$ per square foot	$\bar{x}_2 = \$53.70$ per square foot
$s_1 = \$4.50$ per square foot	$s_2 = \$5.30$ per square foot

9.94 Some power plants are located near rivers or oceans so the water can be used for cooling their condensers. As part of an environmental impact study, suppose a power company wants to estimate the mean difference in water temperature between the discharge of its plant and the off-shore waters. How many sample measurements must be taken at each site to estimate the true mean difference to within 0.2°C with 95% confidence? Assume the range in readings will be about 4°C at each site and the same number of readings will be taken at each site.

9.95 The use of preservatives by food processors has become a controversial issue. Suppose two preservatives are extensively tested and determined safe for use in meats. A processor wants to compare the preservatives for their effects on retarding spoilage. Suppose fifteen cuts of fresh meat are treated with preservative A and fifteen with B, and the number of hours until spoilage begins is recorded for each of the thirty cuts of meat. The results are summarized in the table.

PRESERVATIVE A	PRESERVATIVE B
$\bar{x}_1 = 106.4$ hours	$\bar{x}_2 = 96.5$ hours
$s_1 = 10.3$ hours	$s_2 = 13.4$ hours

a. Is there evidence of a difference in the mean time until spoilage begins for the two preservatives at $\alpha = .05$?

b. Can you recommend an experimental design that the processor could have used to reduce the variability in the data?

9.96 Refer to Exercise 9.95. Construct a 95% confidence interval for the difference between the mean times until spoilage for the two preservatives.

9.97 An economist wants to investigate the difference in unemployment rates between an urban industrial community and a university community in the same state. She interviews 525 potential members of the work force in the industrial community and 375 in the university community. Of these, 47 and 22, respectively, are unemployed. Use a 95% confidence interval to estimate the difference in unemployment rates in the two communities.

9.98 Careful auditing is essential to all businesses, large and small. Suppose a firm wants to compare the performance of two auditors it employs. One measure of auditing performance is error rate, so the firm decides to sample 200 pages at random from the work of each auditor and carefully examine each page for errors. Suppose the number of pages on which at least one error is found is 17 for auditor A and 25 for auditor B.

a. Do the data provide evidence of a difference between the true error rates for the two auditors? Use $\alpha = .01$.

b. Find the p-value for the test and interpret its value.

9.99 A large department store plans to renovate one of its floors, with one of the results being an increase in floor space for one department. The management has narrowed the decision about which department to enlarge to two departments: men's clothing and sporting goods. The final decision will be based on mean sales, with the department having the greater mean to be enlarged. The last 12 months' sales data are shown in the table at the top of the next page.

MONTH	MEN'S CLOTHING	SPORTING GOODS
1	$15,726	$17,533
2	11,243	10,895
3	22,325	19,449
4	23,494	21,500
5	12,676	18,925
6	13,492	21,426
7	15,525	16,774
8	15,799	16,223
9	16,449	16,135
10	16,993	17,834
11	19,832	18,429
12	32,434	34,565

a. Use these data to form a 95% confidence interval for the mean difference in monthly sales for the two departments.

b. On the basis of the confidence interval formed in part a, can you make a recommendation to the store management as to which department should be enlarged?

c. What assumptions are necessary to make valid the procedure you used in part a?

9.100 Smoke detectors are highly recommended safety devices for early fire detection in homes and businesses. It is extremely important that the devices are not defective. Suppose that 100 brand A smoke detectors are tested and 12 fail to emit a warning signal. Subjected to the same test, 15 out of 90 brand B detectors fail to operate. Form a 90% confidence interval to estimate the difference in the fractions of defective smoke detectors produced by the two companies. Interpret this confidence interval.

9.101 The federal government is interested in determining whether salary discrimination exists between men and women in the private sector. Suppose random samples of fifteen women and twenty-two men are drawn from the population of first-level managers in the private sector. The information on their annual salaries is summarized in the table.

WOMEN	MEN
$\bar{x}_1 = \$23,400$	$\bar{x}_2 = \$24,700$
$s_1 = \$2,300$	$s_2 = \$3,100$
$n_1 = 15$	$n_2 = 22$

a. Do the data provide sufficient evidence at $\alpha = .05$ to indicate that the mean salary of male first-level managers exceeds the mean salary of females in that position?

b. What assumptions are necessary for the validity of the test used in part a?

9.102 Refer to Exercise 9.101. Conduct a test to determine whether the data indicate that the assumption of equal salary variances is false. Use $\alpha = .10$.

On Your Own . . .

Many stock market indexes, like the Dow Jones Average, act both as indicators of stock market trends and as economic indicators. One way of comparing economic conditions at the end of two consecutive years would be to estimate the difference in the mean closing prices of all stocks on the New York Stock Exchange. Below, we have outlined two methods of sampling to estimate the difference in mean closing prices on the last day of market operations for two consecutive years, say 1983 and 1984.

Method 1
Two Independent
Samples

Step 1 Obtain lists of the closing prices of all stocks on the New York Stock Exchange for the last operating days of 1983 and 1984. (Any library will have these available.)

Step 2 Using a table of random numbers, randomly choose fifteen stocks from the 1983 list and record the closing price of each.

Step 3 Again refer to a table of random numbers and choose a second (independent) sample of fifteen closing prices from the 1984 list.

Step 4 Using the two samples of closing prices, form a 95% confidence interval for the true difference in mean closing prices for the two years.

Method 2
Paired Samples

Step 1 Same as for method 1.

Step 2 Same as for method 1.

Step 3 Obtain the 1984 closing prices for the *same stocks as those used in 1983.*

Step 4 Using this set of paired observations, form a 95% confidence interval for the true mean difference in closing prices for the two years.

Before actually collecting any data, state which method you think will provide more information (and why). Then, to compare the two methods, first perform the entire experiment outlined in method 1. After you have completed this, obtain the 1984 closing prices for the *same* stocks as the 1983 stocks analyzed and complete step 4 of method 2.

Which method provided a narrower confidence interval and thus more information on this performance of the experiment? Does this agree with your preliminary answer?

References

Beckenstein, A. R., Gabel, H. L., & Roberts, K. "An executive's guide to antitrust compliance." *Harvard Business Review,* Sept.–Oct. 1983, 94–102.

Dornoff, R. J., & Tankersley, C. B. "Perceptual differences in market transactions: A source of customer frustration." *Journal of Consumer Affairs,* Summer 1975, *9,* 97–103.

Dun & Bradstreet. *Business Expectations,* Oct. 28, 1982, *23*(4).

Garvin, D. A. "Quality on the line." *Harvard Business Review,* Sept.–Oct. 1983, 65–75.

Gibbons, J. D. *Nonparametric statistical inference.* New York: McGraw-Hill, 1971.

Hines, G. H. "Sociocultural influences on employee expectancy and participative management." *Academy of Management Journal,* 1974, *17*(2).

Hollander, M., & Wolfe, D. A. *Nonparametric statistical methods.* New York: Wiley, 1973.

Jenssen, W. J. "Sales effects of TV, radio, and print advertising." *Journal of Advertising Research,* June 1966, *6,* 2–7.

Kaufman, L., & Wolf, J. "Hotel room interviewing — anxiety and suspicion." *Sloan Management Review,* Spring 1982, *23*(3).

"Lending an ear." *Time,* Dec. 7, 1981, 62.

Marcotty, J. "Quantity of quality circles proves they're no fad." *Minneapolis Tribune,* Nov. 20, 1983a, 1D.

Marcotty, J. "Tennant tightens up loose screws." *Minneapolis Tribune,* Nov. 20, 1983b, 1D.

McGuire, E. P. *Evaluating new product proposals.* New York: National Industrial Conference Board, 1973. Pp. 54–55.

Meier, P. "Taste: It's in the buds — and they don't improve with age." *Minneapolis Tribune,* June 8, 1980.

Mendenhall, W. *Introduction to probability and statistics.* 6th ed. Boston: Duxbury, 1983. Chapter 8.

Neter, J., Wasserman, W., & Whitmore, G. A. *Applied statistics.* 2d ed. Boston: Allyn & Bacon, 1982. Chapter 13.

Serrin, W. "Technology takes toll on operators." *Minneapolis Tribune,* Nov. 27, 1983, 1D.

Shuchman, A., & Riesz, P. C. "Correlates of persuasibility: The Crest case." *Journal of Marketing Research,* Feb. 1975, *12, 7*–11.

Siegel, S. *Nonparametric statistics for the behavioral sciences.* New York: McGraw-Hill, 1956.

Smith, W. M. "Federal pay procedures and the comparability survey." *Monthly Labor Review,* Aug. 1976, 27–31.

Winer, L. "The effect of product sales quotas on sales force productivity." *Journal of Marketing Research,* May 1973, *10,* 180.

Winkler, R. L., & Hays, W. L. *Statistics: Probability, inference, and decision.* 2d ed., New York: Holt, Rinehart and Winston, 1975. Chapter 6.

CHAPTER 10

Simple Linear Regression

Where We've Been . . .

The answers to many questions that arise in business require knowledge about the mean of a population or about the difference between two population means. Estimating and testing hypotheses about means, or the difference between two means, were the subjects of Chapters 8 and 9.

Where We're Going . . .

Suppose you want to predict the assessed value of a house in a particular community. Using the methods of Chapter 8, you could select a random sample of houses from the community and use the mean of their assessed values to predict the assessed value of the house of interest to you. But using this procedure would ignore the information contained in easily observed variables that are related to assessed house value—namely, the square feet of floor space, number of bathrooms, age of the house, etc. In this chapter we will consider the problem of relating the mean value of a single dependent variable y (for example, assessed house value) to a single independent variable x (say, square feet of floor space) using a linear relationship. The more complex problem of relating y to many independent variables will be the topic of Chapter 11.

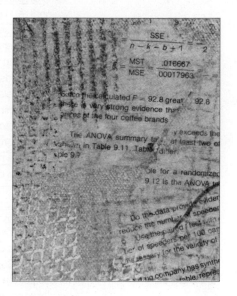

Contents

Much business research is devoted to the topic of *modeling* — i.e., trying to describe how variables are related. For example, an econometrician might be interested in modeling the relationship between the level of consumption expenditure and disposable personal income. An advertising agency might want to know the relationship between a firm's sales revenue and the amount spent on advertising. And an investment firm may be interested in relating the performance of the stock market to the current discount rate of the Federal Reserve Board.

The simplest graphical model for relating a variable *y* to a single independent variable *x* is a straight line. In this chapter we discuss *simple linear (straight-line) models* and show how to fit them to a set of data points using the *method of least squares.* We then show how to judge whether a relationship exists between *y* and *x*, and how to use the model to estimate *E(y)*, the mean value of *y*, and to predict a future value of *y* for a given value of *x*. The totality of these methods is called a *simple linear regression analysis.*

Most models for business variables are much more complicated than implied by a straight-line relationship. Nevertheless, the methods of this chapter are very useful, and they set the stage for the formulation and fitting of more complex models in succeeding chapters. Thus, this chapter provides an intuitive justification for the techniques used in a regression analysis and identifies most of the types of inferences we will want to make using a *multiple linear regression analysis* later in this book.

10.1
Probabilistic
Models

An important consideration in merchandising a product is the amount of money spent on advertising. Suppose you want to model the monthly sales revenue of an appliance store as a function of the monthly advertising expenditure. The first question to be answered is this: Do you think an exact relationship exists between these two variables? That is, can the exact value of sales revenue be predicted if the advertising expenditure is specified? We think you will agree this is not possible for several reasons. Sales depend on many variables other than advertising expenditure — for example, time of year, state of the general economy, inventory, and price structure. However, even if many variables are included in the model (the topic of Chapter 11), it is still unlikely that we can predict the monthly sales *exactly*. There will almost certainly be some variation in sales due strictly to *random phenomena* that cannot be modeled or explained. We will refer to all unexplained variations in sales — caused by important but unincluded variables or by unexplainable random phenomena — as *random error.*

If we construct a model that hypothesizes an exact relationship between variables, it is called a *deterministic model.* For example, if we believe that monthly sales revenue *y* will be exactly ten times the monthly advertising expenditure *x*, we write

$$y = 10x$$

This represents a *deterministic* relationship between the variables *y* and *x*.

On the other hand, if we believe that the model should be constructed to allow for random error, then we hypothesize a *probabilistic model.* This includes both a deterministic component and a random error component. For example, if we hypothesize that the sales *y* is related to advertising *x* by

$$y = 10x + \text{Random error}$$

we are hypothesizing a *probabilistic* relationship between y and x. Note that the deterministic component of this probabilistic model is $10x$.

General Form of a Probabilistic Model

y = Deterministic component + Random error

where y is the variable to be predicted.

As you will see, the random error plays an important role in testing hypotheses and finding confidence intervals for the deterministic portion of the model and enables us to estimate the magnitude of the error of prediction when the model is used to predict some value of y to be observed in the future.

We begin with the simplest of probabilistic models—*a first-order linear model,* which graphs as a straight line. The elements of the straight-line model are summarized in the box.

A First-Order (Straight-Line) Model

$y = \beta_0 + \beta_1 x + \varepsilon$

where

y = *Dependent* or *response* variable (variable to be modeled)

x = *Independent** or *predictor* variable (variable used as a predictor of y)

ε (epsilon) = Random error component

β_0 (beta zero) = y-intercept of the line—i.e., point at which the line intercepts or cuts through the y-axis (see Figure 10.1)

β_1 (beta one) = Slope of the line—i.e., amount of increase (or decrease) in the deterministic component of y for every 1-unit increase in x (see Figure 10.1)

Figure 10.1 The Straight-Line Model

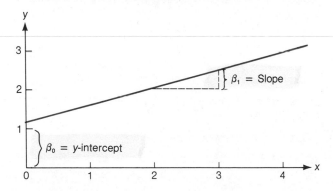

* The word *independent* should not be interpreted in a probabilistic sense. The phrase *independent variable* is used in regression analysis to refer to a predictor variable for the response y.

Note that we use Greek symbols β_0 and β_1 to represent the y-intercept and slope of the model. They are population parameters with numerical values that will be known only if we have access to the entire population of (x, y) measurements.

It is helpful to think of regression modeling as a five-step procedure.

Step 1 Hypothesize the deterministic component of the probabilistic model.

Step 2 Use sample data to estimate unknown parameters in the model.

Step 3 Specify the probability distribution of the random error term, and estimate any unknown parameters of this distribution.

Step 4 Statistically check the usefulness of the model.

Step 5 When satisfied that the model is useful, use it for prediction, estimation, and other purposes.

In this chapter we will skip step 1 and deal with steps 2–5 for only the straight-line model. Chapters 11 and 12 will discuss how to build more complex models.

Exercises 10.1–10.5

Learning the Mechanics

10.1 In each case graph the line that passes through the points.

a. (1, 0) and (2, 4)
b. (0, 3) and (3, 7)
c. (−1, −2) and (3, 1)
d. (2, 3) and (4, −5)

10.2 The equation for a straight line (deterministic) is

$$y = \beta_0 + \beta_1 x$$

If the line passes through the point $(-1, 3)$, then $x = -1$, $y = 3$ must satisfy the equation; i.e.,

$$3 = \beta_0 + \beta_1(-1)$$

Similarly, if the line passes through the point $(3, 4)$, then $x = 3$, $y = 4$ must satisfy the equation; i.e.,

$$4 = \beta_0 + \beta_1(3)$$

Use these two equations to solve for β_0 and β_1, and find the equation of the line that passes through the points $(-1, 3)$ and $(3, 4)$.

10.3 Refer to Exercise 10.2. Find the equations of the lines that pass through the points listed in Exercise 10.1.

10.4 Plot the following lines:

a. $y = 1 + 3x$ **b.** $y = 2 - x$ **c.** $y = 1 + 2x$
d. $y = 3x$ **e.** $y = -3 + 2x$ **f.** $y = -x$

10.5 Give the slope and y-intercept for each of the lines defined in Exercise 10.4.

10.2
Fitting the
Model: The
Method of
Least Squares

Suppose an appliance store conducts a 5-month experiment to determine the effect of advertising on sales revenue. The results are shown in Table 10.1. (The number of measurements is small, and the measurements themselves are unrealistically simple to avoid arithmetic confusion in this initial example.) The relationship between sales revenue, y, and advertising expenditure, x, is hypothesized to follow a first-order linear model, that is,

$$y = \beta_0 + \beta_1 x + \varepsilon$$

The question is this: How can we best use the information in the sample of five observations in Table 10.1 to estimate the unknown y-intercept β_0 and slope β_1?

Table 10.1

Advertising–Sales Data

MONTH	ADVERTISING EXPENDITURE x ($ hundreds)	SALES REVENUE y ($ thousands)
1	1	1
2	2	1
3	3	2
4	4	2
5	5	4

To gain information on the approximate values of these parameters, it is helpful to plot the sample data. Such a plot, called a *scattergram,* locates each of the five data points on a graph, as in Figure 10.2. Note that the scattergram suggests a general tendency for y to increase as x increases. If you place a ruler on the scattergram, you will see that a line may be drawn through three of the five points, as shown in Figure 10.3. To obtain the equation of this visually fitted line, note that the line intersects the y-axis at $y = -1$, so the y-intercept is -1. Also, y increases exactly 1 unit for every 1-unit increase in x, indicating that the slope is $+1$. Therefore, the equation is

$$\tilde{y} = -1 + 1(x) = -1 + x$$

where $\tilde{y}$ is used to denote the value of y predicted from the visually fitted model.

Figure 10.2 Scattergram for Data in Table 10.1

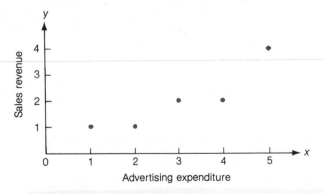

One way to decide quantitatively how well a straight line fits a set of data is to note the extent to which the data points deviate from the line. For example, to evaluate the visual

Figure 10.3   Visual
Straight-line Fit to the Data

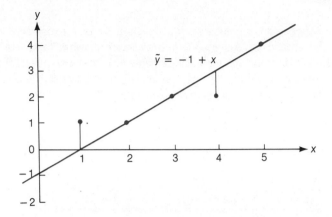

model in Figure 10.3 we calculate the **deviations** — i.e., the differences between the observed and the predicted values of y. These deviations, or **errors,** are the vertical distances between observed and predicted values (see Figure 10.3). The observed and predicted values of y, their differences, and their squared differences are shown in Table 10.2. Note that the **sum of errors** equals 0 and the **sum of squares of the errors (SSE)** is equal to 2.

Table 10.2

Comparing Observed and
Predicted Values for the
Visual Model

x	y	$\hat{y} = -1 + x$	$(y - \hat{y})$	$(y - \hat{y})^2$
1	1	0	$(1 - 0) =$ 1	1
2	1	1	$(1 - 1) =$ 0	0
3	2	2	$(2 - 2) =$ 0	0
4	2	3	$(2 - 3) = -1$	1
5	4	4	$(4 - 4) =$ 0	0
			Sum of errors = 0	Sum of squared errors (SSE) = 2

You can see by shifting the ruler around the graph that it is possible to find many lines for which the sum of the errors is equal to 0, but it can be shown that there is one (and only one) line for which the *SSE is a minimum.* This line is called the **least squares line,** the **regression line,** the **least squares prediction equation,** or the **fitted line.**

To find the least squares line for a set of data, assume that we have a sample of n data points that can be identified by corresponding values of x and y, say $(x_1, y_1), (x_2, y_2), \ldots, (x_n, y_n)$. For example, the $n = 5$ data points shown in Table 10.2 are (1, 1), (2, 1), (3, 2), (4, 2), and (5, 4). The straight-line model for the response, y, in terms of x is

$$y = \beta_0 + \beta_1 x + \varepsilon$$

The equation of the line that relates the mean value $E(y)$ to x (called the **line of means**) is

$$E(y) = \beta_0 + \beta_1 x$$

The fitted line, which we will calculate using the five data points, is represented as

$$\hat{y} = \hat{\beta}_0 + \hat{\beta}_1 x$$

The "hats" can be read as "estimator of." Thus, $\hat{y}$ is an estimator of the mean value of y, $E(y)$, and a predictor of some future value of y; and $\hat{\beta}_0$ and $\hat{\beta}_1$ are estimators of β_0 and β_1, respectively.

For a given data point, say the point (x_i, y_i), the observed value of y is y_i and the predicted value of y would be obtained by substituting x_i into the prediction equation:

$$\hat{y}_i = \hat{\beta}_0 + \hat{\beta}_1 x_i$$

And the deviation of the ith value of y from its predicted value is

$$y_i - \hat{y}_i = y_i - (\hat{\beta}_0 + \hat{\beta}_1 x_i)$$

Then the sum of squares of the deviations of the y values about their predicted values for all the n data points is

$$SSE = \sum_{i=1}^{n} [y_i - (\hat{\beta}_0 + \hat{\beta}_1 x_i)]^2 \qquad SSE = \sum (Y_i - \hat{Y}_i)^2$$

The quantities $\hat{\beta}_0$ and $\hat{\beta}_1$ that make the SSE a minimum are called the *least squares estimates* of the population parameters β_0 and β_1, and the prediction equation $\hat{y} = \hat{\beta}_0 + \hat{\beta}_1 x$ is called the *least squares line*.

Definition 10.1

The *least squares line* is one that has a smaller SSE than any other straight-line model.

The values of $\hat{\beta}_0$ and $\hat{\beta}_1$ that minimize the SSE are (proof omitted) given by the formulas in the following box:*

Formulas for the Least Squares Estimates

Slope: $\quad \hat{\beta}_1 = \dfrac{SS_{xy}}{SS_{xx}}$

y-intercept: $\quad \hat{\beta}_0 = \bar{y} - \hat{\beta}_1 \bar{x}$

where

$$SS_{xy} = \sum_{i=1}^{n} x_i y_i - \frac{\left(\sum_{i=1}^{n} x_i\right)\left(\sum_{i=1}^{n} y_i\right)}{n} = \sum_{i=1}^{n} (X_i - \bar{X})(Y_i - \bar{Y})$$

$$SS_{xx} = \sum_{i=1}^{n} x_i^2 - \frac{\left(\sum_{i=1}^{n} x_i\right)^2}{n} = \sum_{i=1}^{n} (X_i - \bar{X})^2$$

n = Sample size

---

* Students who are familiar with the calculus should note that the values of $\hat{\beta}_0$ and $\hat{\beta}_1$ that minimize SSE $= \sum_{i=1}^{n} (y_i - \hat{y}_i)^2$ are obtained by setting the two partial derivatives $\partial SSE/\partial \beta_0$ and $\partial SSE/\partial \beta_1$ equal to zero. Furthermore, we denote the *sample* solutions to the equations by $\hat{\beta}_0$ and $\hat{\beta}_1$, where the ^ (hat) denotes that these are sample estimates of the true population intercept β_0 and slope β_1. The solutions to these two equations yield the formulas shown in the box.

Table 10.3

Preliminary Computations for the Advertising–Sales Example

x_i	y_i	x_i^2	x_iy_i
1	1	1	1
2	1	4	2
3	2	9	6
4	2	16	8
5	4	25	20
Totals $\Sigma x_i = 15$	$\Sigma y_i = 10$	$\Sigma x_i^2 = 55$	$\Sigma x_iy_i = 37$

Preliminary computations for finding the least squares line for the advertising–sales example are contained in Table 10.3. We can now calculate*

$$SS_{xy} = \sum x_iy_i - \frac{\left(\sum x_i\right)\left(\sum y_i\right)}{5} = 37 - \frac{(15)(10)}{5}$$

$$= 37 - 30 = 7$$

$$SS_{xx} = \sum x_i^2 - \frac{\left(\sum x_i\right)^2}{5} = 55 - \frac{(15)^2}{5}$$

$$= 55 - 45 = 10$$

Then, the slope of the least squares line is

$$\hat{\beta}_1 = \frac{SS_{xy}}{SS_{xx}} = \frac{7}{10} = .7$$

and the y-intercept is

$$\hat{\beta}_0 = \bar{y} - \hat{\beta}_1\bar{x} = \frac{\sum y_i}{5} - \hat{\beta}_1\frac{\left(\sum x_i\right)}{5}$$

$$= \frac{10}{5} - (.7)\frac{15}{5} = 2 - (.7)(3) = 2 - 2.1 = -.1$$

The least squares line is thus

$$\hat{y} = \hat{\beta}_0 + \hat{\beta}_1x = -.1 + .7x$$

The graph of this line is shown in Figure 10.4.

The observed and predicted values of y, the deviations of the y values about their predicted values, and the squares of these deviations are shown in Table 10.4. Note that the sum of squares of the deviations (SSE) is 1.10, and (as we would expect) this is less than the SSE = 2.0 obtained in Table 10.2 for the visually fitted line.

* Since summations are used extensively from this point on, we will omit the limits on Σ when the summation includes all the measurements in the sample, i.e., when the symbol is $\sum_{i=1}^{n}$, we will write Σ.

Figure 10.4 The Line
$\hat{y} = -.1 + .7x$
Fit to the Data

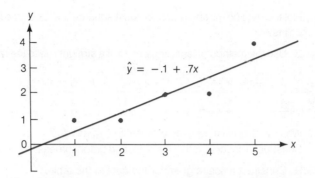

Table 10.4
Comparing Observed and
Predicted Values for the
Least Squares Model

x	y	$\hat{y} = -.1 + .7x$	$(y - \hat{y})$	$(y - \hat{y})^2$
1	1	.6	$(1 - .6) = \quad .4$	0.16
2	1	1.3	$(1 - 1.3) = -.3$	0.09
3	2	2.0	$(2 - 2.0) = \quad 0$	0.00
4	2	2.7	$(2 - 2.7) = -.7$	0.49
5	4	3.4	$(4 - 3.4) = \quad .6$	0.36
			Sum of errors $= \quad 0$	SSE $= 1.10$

To summarize, we have defined the best-fitting straight line to be the one that satisfies the least squares criterion; that is, the sum of the squared errors will be smaller than for any other straight-line model.

**Exercises
10.6 – 10.14**

Learning the Mechanics

10.6 Use the method of least squares to fit a straight line to the seven data points in the table.

x	2	3	4	5	6	7	8
y	2	3	3	4	5	7	8

a. What are the least squares estimates of β_0 and β_1?
b. Plot the data points and graph the least squares line. Does the line pass through the data points?

10.7 Use the method of least squares to fit a straight line to the five data points in the table.

x	-3	-1	0	1	3
y	0	2	3	6	9

a. What are the least squares estimates of β_0 and β_1?

b. Plot the data points and graph the least squares line. Does the line pass through the data points?

10.8 Use the method of least squares to fit a straight line to the ten data points in the table.

x	1	−1	2	0	4	−2	4	−2	5	1
y	−1	−5	1	−3	6	−6	4	−5	4	0

a. What are the least squares estimates of β_0 and β_1?
b. Construct a scattergram of the data, and graph the least squares line on the scattergram.

10.9 Construct a scattergram for the data in the table.

x	.5	1	1.5
y	2	1	3

a. Plot the following two lines on your scattergram:

$$y = 3 - x$$
$$y = 1 + x$$

b. Which of these lines would you choose to characterize the relationship between x and y? Explain.
c. Show that the sum of errors for both of these lines equals zero.
d. Which of these lines has the smaller SSE?
e. Find the least squares line for the data, and compare it to the two lines described above.

Applying the Concepts

10.10 Due primarily to the price controls of the Organization of Petroleum Exporting Countries (OPEC), a cartel of crude oil suppliers, the price of crude oil has risen dramatically since the early 1970's. As a result, motorists have been confronted with a similar upward spiral of gasoline prices. The data in the table are typical prices for a gallon of regular leaded gasoline and a barrel of crude oil (refiner acquisition cost) for the indicated years.

YEAR	GASOLINE y (¢/gal)	CRUDE OIL x ($/bbl)
1973	38.8	4.15
1975	56.7	10.38
1976	59.0	10.89
1977	62.2	11.96
1978	62.6	12.46
1979	85.7	17.72
1980	119.1	28.07
1981	133.3	36.11

Source: *Statistical Abstract of the United States: 1981*, p. 476.

a. Use the data to calculate the least squares line that describes the relationship between the price of a gallon of gasoline and the price of a barrel of crude oil.

b. Plot your least squares line on a scattergram of the data. Does your least squares line appear to be an appropriate characterization of the relationship between y and x? Explain.

c. If the price of crude oil fell to $20 per barrel, to what level (approximately) would the price of regular gasoline fall? Justify your response.

10.11 A company that developed a new type of fertilizer is interested in investigating the relationship between the yield of potatoes, y, and the amount of the new fertilizer that is applied to the potato plants, x. An agronomist divided a field into eight plots of equal size and applied differing amounts of fertilizer to each. The yield of potatoes (in pounds) and the fertilizer application (in pounds) were recorded for each plot. The data are shown in the table.

x	1	1.5	2	2.5	3	3.5	4	4.5
y	25	31	27	28	36	35	32	34

a. Construct a scattergram for the data.

b. Find the least squares estimates of β_0 and β_1.

c. According to your least squares line, approximately how many pounds of potatoes would you expect from a plot to which 3.75 pounds of fertilizer had been applied? [*Note:* A measure of the reliability of these predictions will be discussed in Section 10.8.]

10.12 A car dealer is interested in modeling the relationship between the number of cars sold by the firm each week and the number of salespeople who work on the showroom floor. The dealer believes the relationship between the two variables can best be described by a straight line. The sample data shown in the table were supplied by the car dealer.

WEEK OF	NUMBER OF CARS SOLD y	NUMBER OF SALESPEOPLE ON DUTY x
January 30	20	6
June 29	18	6
March 2	10	4
October 26	6	2
February 7	11	3

a. Construct a scattergram for the data.

b. Assuming the relationship between the variables is best described by a straight line, use the method of least squares to estimate the y-intercept and the slope of the line.

c. Plot the least squares line on your scattergram.

d. According to your least squares line, approximately how many cars should the dealer expect to sell in a week if five salespeople are kept on the showroom floor each day? [*Note:* A measure of the reliability of these predictions will be discussed in Section 10.8.]

10.13 Is the percentage of games won by a major league baseball team related to the team's batting average? The accompanying table shows the percentage of games won and the batting averages for the fourteen teams in the American League at one point during the 1983 season.

PERCENTAGE OF GAMES WON y	TEAM BATTING AVERAGE x	PERCENTAGE OF GAMES WON y	TEAM BATTING AVERAGE x
56.5	.261	53.0	.271
50.0	.273	41.6	.263
51.7	.264	54.1	.273
51.2	.256	48.3	.259
41.8	.262	39.3	.237
56.0	.271	52.9	.262
49.4	.271	60.0	.275

a. If you were to model the relationship between a major league team's percentage of games won, y, and the team's batting average, x, using a straight line, would you expect the slope of the line to be positive or negative? Explain.

b. Fit a simple linear regression model to the data.

c. Construct a scattergram for the data, and graph the least squares line. Does the slope of the least squares line seem to agree with the points on your scattergram?

d. Can you explain why the percentage of games won does not appear to be strongly related to a team's batting average?

10.14 An appliance company is interested in relating the sales rate of 17-inch color television sets to the price per set. To do this, the company randomly selected 15 weeks in the past year and recorded the number of sets sold each week and the price at which the sets were being sold during that week. The data are shown in the table.

WEEK	NUMBER OF 17-INCH COLOR TELEVISION SETS SOLD PER WEEK y	PRICE x ($)	WEEK	NUMBER OF 17-INCH COLOR TELEVISION SETS SOLD PER WEEK y	PRICE x ($)
1	55	350	9	20	400
2	54	360	10	45	340
3	25	385	11	50	350
4	18	400	12	35	335
5	51	370	13	30	330
6	20	390	14	30	325
7	45	375	15	53	365
8	19	390			

a. Find the least squares line relating y to x.

b. Plot the data and graph the least squares line as a check on your calculations.

10.3
Model
Assumptions

In Section 10.2, we assumed that the probabilistic model relating the firm's sales revenue y to advertising dollars x is

$$y = \beta_0 + \beta_1 x + \varepsilon$$

and recall that the least squares estimate of the deterministic component of the model $\beta_0 + \beta_1 x$ is

$$\hat{y} = \hat{\beta}_0 + \hat{\beta}_1 x = -.1 + .7x$$

Now we turn our attention to the random component ε of the probabilistic model and its relation to the errors in estimating β_0 and β_1. In particular, we will see how the probability distribution of ε determines how well the model describes the true relationship between the dependent variable y and the independent variable x.

We make four basic assumptions about the general form of the probability distribution of ε:

Assumption 1   The mean of the probability distribution of ε is zero. That is, the average of the errors over an infinitely long series of experiments is zero for each setting of the independent variable x. This assumption implies that the mean value of y, $E(y)$, for a given value of x is $E(y) = \beta_0 + \beta_1 x$.

Assumption 2   The variance of the probability distribution of ε is constant for all values of the independent variable, x. For our straight-line model, this assumption means that the variance of ε is equal to a constant, say σ^2, for all values of x.

Assumption 3   The probability distribution of ε is normal.

Assumption 4   The errors associated with any two different observations are independent. That is, the error associated with one value of y has no effect on the errors associated with other y values.

The implications of the first three assumptions can be seen in Figure 10.5, which shows distributions of errors for three particular values of x—namely, x_1, x_2, and x_3. Note that the relative frequency distributions of the errors are normal, with a mean of zero and a constant variance σ^2 (all the distributions shown have the same amount of spread or variability). The

Figure 10.5   The Probability Distribution of ε

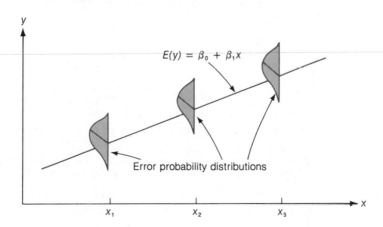

straight line shown in Figure 10.5 plots the mean value $E(y)$ for a given value of x. Then, the line of means is given by the equation

$$E(y) = \beta_0 + \beta_1 x$$

Various techniques exist for checking the validity of these assumptions, and there are remedies to be applied when they appear to be invalid. These topics, which are beyond the scope of this text, are discussed in some of the references at the end of the chapter.

In actual practice, the assumptions need not hold exactly in order for least squares estimators and test statistics (to be described subsequently) to possess the measures of reliability that we would expect from a regression analysis. The assumptions will be satisfied adequately for many applications encountered in business.

10.4 An Estimator of σ^2

It seems reasonable to assume that the greater the variability of the random error ε (which is measured by its variance σ^2), the greater will be the errors in the estimation of the model parameters β_0 and β_1 and in the error of prediction when $\hat{y}$ is used to predict y for some value of x. Consequently, you should not be surprised, as we proceed through this chapter, to find that σ^2 appears in the formulas for all confidence intervals and test statistics that we use.

In most practical situations, σ^2 will be unknown, and we must use our data to estimate its value. The best (proof omitted) estimate, s^2, of σ^2 is obtained by dividing the sum of squares of deviations,

$$SSE = \sum (y_i - \hat{y}_i)^2$$

by the number of degrees of freedom (df) associated with this quantity. We use 2 df to estimate the y-intercept and slope in the straight-line model, leaving $(n - 2)$ df for the error variance estimation (see the formulas in the box).

Estimation of σ^2

$$s^2 = \frac{SSE}{\text{Degrees of freedom for error}} = \frac{SSE}{n - 2}$$

where

$$SSE = \sum (y_i - \hat{y}_i)^2 = SS_{yy} - \hat{\beta}_1 SS_{xy}$$

$$SS_{yy} = \sum (y_i - \bar{y})^2 = \sum y_i^2 - \frac{\left(\sum y_i \right)^2}{n}$$

Warning: When performing these calculations, you may be tempted to round the calculated values of SS_{yy}, $\hat{\beta}_1$, and SS_{xy}. Be certain to carry at least six significant figures for each of these quantities to avoid substantial errors in the calculation of SSE.

In the advertising – sales example, we previously calculated $SSE = 1.10$ for the least squares line $\hat{y} = -.1 + .7x$. Recalling that there were $n = 5$ data points, we have

$n - 2 = 5 - 2 = 3$ df for estimating σ^2. Thus,

$$s^2 = \frac{SSE}{n - 2} = \frac{1.10}{3} = .367$$

is the estimated variance, and

$$s = \sqrt{.367} = .61$$

is the estimated standard deviation of ε.

You may be able to obtain an intuitive feeling for s by recalling the interpretation given to a standard deviation in Chapter 3 and remembering that the least squares line estimates the mean value of y for a given value of x. Since s measures the spread of the distribution of y values about the least squares line, we should not be surprised to find that most of the observations lie within $2s$ or $2(.61) = 1.22$ of the least squares line. For this simple example (only five data points), all five data points fall within $2s$ of the least squares line. In Section 10.8, we will use s to evaluate the error of prediction when the least squares line is used to predict a value of y to be observed for a given value of x.

Exercises 10.15–10.22

Learning the Mechanics

10.15 Suppose you fit a least squares line to twelve data points and calculate $SSE = .507$. Find s^2, the estimator of σ^2, the variance of the random error term ε.

10.16 Calculate SSE and s^2 for each of the following cases:

a. $n = 18$, $SS_{yy} = 95$, $SS_{xy} = 50$, $\hat{\beta}_1 = .75$
b. $n = 35$, $\Sigma y^2 = 860$, $\Sigma y = 50$, $SS_{xy} = 2,700$, $\hat{\beta}_1 = .2$
c. $n = 20$, $\Sigma(y_i - \bar{y})^2 = 58$, $SS_{xy} = 91$, $SS_{xx} = 170$

10.17 Calculate SSE and s^2 for the least squares lines obtained in Exercises 10.6–10.13.

Applying the Concepts

10.18 In Exercise 10.10, the price of a gallon of gasoline, y, was modeled as a function of the price of a barrel of crude oil, x, using the following equation: $y = \beta_0 + \beta_1 x + \varepsilon$. Estimates of β_0 and β_1 were found to be 25.883 and 3.115, respectively.

a. Estimate the variance and standard deviation of ε.
b. Suppose the price of a barrel of crude oil is $15. Estimate the mean and standard deviation of the price of a gallon of gasoline under these circumstances.
c. Repeat part b for a crude oil price of $30 per barrel.
d. What assumptions about ε did you make in answering parts b and c?

10.19 Although the cable-television industry could provide viewers with 100 or more channels, a study by the A. C. Nielsen Co. suggests that that may be many more than viewers want or will ever watch. The Nielsen survey indicates that as the number of television channels increases, the percentage of channels viewed for 10 minutes a week or more declines (Landro & Mayer, 1982). In a similar study, twenty households were sampled, and the number of channels available to each household was recorded. In addition, each household was asked to monitor its television viewing for a week and report the number of channels watched for 10 minutes or more. The results appear in the table.

HOUSEHOLD	NUMBER OF CHANNELS AVAILABLE x	NUMBER OF CHANNELS WATCHED FOR 10 MINUTES y	HOUSEHOLD	NUMBER OF CHANNELS AVAILABLE x	NUMBER OF CHANNELS WATCHED FOR 10 MINUTES y
1	12	6	11	25	10
2	29	10	12	8	6
3	4	3	13	5	4
4	20	8	14	10	4
5	40	12	15	16	9
6	5	3	16	4	4
7	6	5	17	5	1
8	4	4	18	45	13
9	14	8	19	35	5
10	20	6	20	50	10

a. The least squares line for this data set is $\hat{y} = 3.3267 + .1806x$. Plot this line on a scattergram of the data.

b. Calculate SSE and s^2.

c. Does the least squares line tend to support the Nielsen findings? [*Note:* We present a statistical test to detect a relationship between y and x in Section 10.5.]

10.20 A breeder of thoroughbred horses wishes to model the relationship between the gestation period and the length of life of a horse. The breeder believes that the two variables may follow a linear trend. The information in the table was supplied to the breeder from various thoroughbred stables across the state.

HORSE	GESTATION PERIOD x (days)	LIFE LENGTH y (years)
1	416	24
2	279	25.5
3	298	20
4	307	21.5
5	356	22
6	403	23.5
7	265	21

a. Fit a least squares line to the data. Plot the data points and graph the least squares line as a check on your calculations.

b. According to your least squares line, approximately how long would you expect a horse to live whose gestation period was 400 days?

c. Calculate SSE and s^2.

d. What is the interpretation of s^2?

10.21 An electronics dealer believes that sales of quadraphonic systems increase as the number of hours of quadraphonic programming on a city's FM stations increases. Records for the dealer's sales during the last 6 months and the amount of quadraphonic programming for the corresponding months are given in the table.

MONTH	AMOUNT OF QUADRAPHONIC PROGRAMMING x (hours)	NUMBER OF QUADRAPHONIC SYSTEMS SOLD y
1	33.6	7
2	36.3	10
3	38.7	13
4	36.6	11
5	39.0	14
6	38.4	18

a. Fit a least squares line to the data.
b. Plot the data, and graph the least squares line as a check on your calculations.
c. Calculate SSE and s^2.

10.22 A company keeps extensive records on its new salespeople on the premise that sales should increase with experience. A random sample of seven new salespeople produced the data on experience and sales shown in the table.

MONTHS ON JOB x	MONTHLY SALES y ($ thousands)
2	2.4
4	7.0
8	11.3
12	15.0
1	0.8
5	3.7
9	12.0

a. Fit a least squares line to the data.
b. Plot the data and graph the least squares line.
c. Predict the sales that a new salesperson would be expected to generate after 6 months on the job. After 9 months. [*Note:* A measure of reliability for these predictions will be discussed in Section 10.8.]
d. Calculate SSE and s^2.

10.5
Assessing the Utility of the Model: Making Inferences about the Slope β_1

Refer again to the data of Table 10.1 and suppose that the appliance store's sales revenue is *completely unrelated* to the advertising expenditure. What could be said about the values of β_0 and β_1 in the hypothesized probabilistic model

$$y = \beta_0 + \beta_1 x + \varepsilon$$

if x contributes no information for the prediction of y? The implication is that the mean of y—i.e., the deterministic part of the model $E(y) = \beta_0 + \beta_1 x$—does not change as x changes. Regardless of the value of x, you always predict the same value of y. In the straight-line model, this means that the true slope, β_1, is equal to zero. Therefore, to test the null hypothesis that x contributes no information for the prediction of y against the alternative hypothesis that these variables are linearly related with a slope differing from zero, we test

$$H_0: \beta_1 - 0 \qquad H_a: \beta_1 \neq 0$$

If the data support the alternative hypothesis, we conclude that x does contribute information for the prediction of y using the straight-line model [although the true relationship between $E(y)$ and x could be more complex than a straight line]. Thus, to some extent, this is a test of the utility of the hypothesized model.

The appropriate test statistic is found by considering the sampling distribution of $\hat{\beta}_1$, the least squares estimator of the slope β_1.

Sampling Distribution of $\hat{\beta}_1$

If the four assumptions about ε (see Section 10.3) are satisfied, then the sampling distribution of $\hat{\beta}_1$, the least squares estimator of slope, will be normal, with mean β_1 (the true slope) and standard deviation

$$\sigma_{\hat{\beta}_1} = \frac{\sigma}{\sqrt{SS_{xx}}} \qquad \text{(see Figure 10.6)}$$

Figure 10.6 Sampling Distribution of $\hat{\beta}_1$

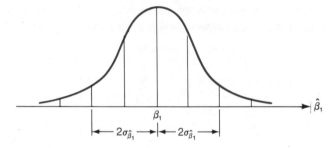

Since σ will usually be unknown, the appropriate test statistic will generally be a Student's t statistic formed as follows:

$$t = \frac{\hat{\beta}_1 - \text{Hypothesized value of } \beta_1}{s_{\hat{\beta}_1}} \qquad \text{where} \quad s_{\hat{\beta}_1} = \frac{s}{\sqrt{SS_{xx}}}$$

$$= \frac{\hat{\beta}_1 - 0}{s/\sqrt{SS_{xx}}}$$

Note that we have substituted the estimator s for σ, and then formed $s_{\hat{\beta}_1}$ by dividing s by $\sqrt{SS_{xx}}$. The number of degrees of freedom associated with this t statistic is the same as the number of degrees of freedom associated with s. Recall that this will be $(n-2)$ df when the hypothesized model is a straight line (see Section 10.4).

The setup of our test of the utility of the model is summarized in the box:

A Test of Model Utility

One-Tailed Test

$H_0: \beta_1 = 0$

$H_a: \beta_1 < 0$
  (or $H_a: \beta_1 > 0$)

Test statistic: $t = \dfrac{\hat{\beta}_1}{s_{\hat{\beta}_1}} = \dfrac{\hat{\beta}_1}{s/\sqrt{SS_{xx}}}$

Rejection region: $t < -t_\alpha$
                 (or $t > t_\alpha$)

where t_α is based on $(n-2)$ df.

Two-Tailed Test

$H_0: \beta_1 = 0$

$H_a: \beta_1 \neq 0$

Test statistic: $t = \dfrac{\hat{\beta}_1}{s_{\hat{\beta}_1}} = \dfrac{\hat{\beta}_1}{s/\sqrt{SS_{xx}}}$

Rejection region: $t < -t_{\alpha/2}$
                 or $t > t_{\alpha/2}$

where $t_{\alpha/2}$ is based on $(n-2)$ df.

Assumptions: The four assumptions about ε listed in Section 10.3. PG 407

For the advertising–sales example, we will choose $\alpha = .05$ and, since $n = 5$, df $= (n-2) = 5 - 2 = 3$. Then the rejection region for the two-tailed test is

$$t < -t_{.025} = -3.182 \qquad t > t_{.025} = 3.182$$

We previously calculated $\hat{\beta}_1 = .7$, $s = .61$, and $SS_{xx} = 10$. Thus,

$$t = \frac{\hat{\beta}_1}{s/\sqrt{SS_{xx}}} = \frac{.7}{.61/\sqrt{10}} = \frac{.7}{.19} = 3.7$$

Since this calculated t value falls in the upper-tail rejection region (see Figure 10.7), we reject the null hypothesis and conclude that the slope β_1 is not zero. The sample evidence indicates that x contributes information for the prediction of y using a linear model for the relationship between sales revenue and advertising.

What conclusion can be drawn if the calculated t value does not fall in the rejection region? We know from previous discussions of the philosophy of hypothesis-testing that such a t

Figure 10.7 Rejection
Region and Calculated t
Value for Testing Whether
the Slope $\beta_1 = 0$

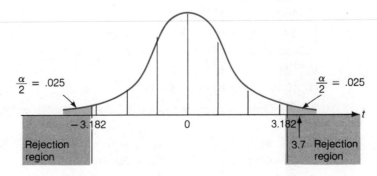

value does *not* lead us to accept the null hypothesis. That is, we do not conclude that $\beta_1 = 0$. Additional data might indicate that β_1 differs from zero, or a more complex relationship may exist between y and x, requiring the fitting of a model other than the straight-line model. We will discuss several such models in Chapter 11.

Another way to make inferences about the slope β_1 is to estimate it using a confidence interval. This interval is formed as shown in the box.

A 100(1 − α)% Confidence Interval for the Slope β_1

$$\hat{\beta}_1 \pm t_{\alpha/2} s_{\hat{\beta}_1} \qquad \text{where} \quad s_{\hat{\beta}_1} = \frac{s}{\sqrt{SS_{xx}}}$$

and $t_{\alpha/2}$ is based on $(n-2)$ df.

For the advertising–sales example, a 95% confidence interval for the slope β_1 is

$$\hat{\beta}_1 \pm t_{.025} s_{\hat{\beta}_1} = .7 \pm 3.182 \left(\frac{s}{\sqrt{SS_{xx}}} \right) = .7 \pm 3.182 \left(\frac{.61}{\sqrt{10}} \right) = .7 \pm .61$$

Thus, we estimate with 95% confidence that the interval from .09 to 1.31 includes the slope parameter β_1.

Since all the values in this interval are positive, it appears that β_1 is positive and that the mean of y, $E(y)$, increases as x increases. However, the rather large width of the confidence interval reflects the small number of data points (and, consequently, a lack of information) in the experiment. We would expect a narrower interval if the sample size were increased.

Exercises 10.23–10.35

Learning the Mechanics

10.23 How many degrees of freedom are associated with the values of s^2 computed for the least squares lines of the following exercises?

a. 10.6   **b.** 10.7   **c.** 10.8
d. 10.18   **e.** 10.19   **f.** 10.22

10.24 Do the data provide sufficient evidence to indicate that β_1 differs from zero for the least squares lines of the following exercises? (Test using $\alpha = .05$.)

a. 10.6   **b.** 10.7   **c.** 10.8
d. 10.18   **e.** 10.19   **f.** 10.22

10.25 Construct both a 95% and a 90% confidence interval for β_1 for each of the following cases:

a. $\hat{\beta}_1 = 31$, $s = 3$, $SS_{xx} = 35$, $n = 10$
b. $\hat{\beta}_1 = 64$, $SSE = 1{,}960$, $SS_{xx} = 30$, $n = 14$
c. $\hat{\beta}_1 = -8.4$, $SSE = 146$, $SS_{xx} = 64$, $n = 20$

Applying the Concepts

10.26 The expenses involved in a manufacturing operation may be categorized as being for *raw materials, direct labor,* and *overhead*. The term *direct labor* refers to the persons employed to transform the raw materials into the finished product. *Overhead* refers to all expenses other than those for raw materials and direct labor that are involved with running the factory (e.g., supervisory labor, maintenance of equipment, and office supplies) (Gray & Johnston, 1977). A manufacturer of ten-speed racing bicycles is interested in estimating the relationship between its monthly factory overhead and the total number of bicycles produced per month. The estimate will be used to help develop the manufacturing budget for next year. The data in the table have been collected for the previous 12 months.

MONTH	PRODUCTION LEVEL (Thousands of units)	OVERHEAD ($ thousands)	MONTH	PRODUCTION LEVEL (Thousands of units)	OVERHEAD ($ thousands)
1	16.9	41.4	7	16.3	37.5
2	15.6	35.0	8	15.5	37.0
3	17.4	38.3	9	23.4	47.9
4	11.6	29.5	10	28.4	55.6
5	17.7	39.6	11	27.1	53.1
6	17.6	37.4	12	19.2	40.6

a. Find the least squares prediction equation relating monthly overhead y to monthly production level x.

b. Test to determine whether the straight-line model contributes information for the prediction of overhead costs. Use $\alpha = .05$.

c. Which of the four assumptions we make about ε may be inappropriate in this problem? Explain.

10.27 During June, July, and early August of 1981, a total of ten bids were made by DuPont, Seagram, and Mobil to take over Conoco. Finally, on August 5, DuPont announced that it had succeeded. The total value of the offer accepted by Conoco was $7.54 billion, making it the largest takeover in the history of American business. As part of an analysis of the Conoco takeover, Richard S. Ruback (1982) used regression analysis to examine whether movements in the rate of return of each of the above-mentioned companies' common stock could be explained by movements in the rate of return of the stock market as a whole. He used the following model: $y = \beta_0 + \beta_1 x + \varepsilon$, where y is the daily rate of return of a stock, x is the daily rate of return of the stock market as a whole as measured by the daily rate of return of Standard & Poor's 500 Composite Index, and ε is believed to satisfy the assumptions of Section 10.3. (This model is known in the finance literature as the *market model*. Note that the parameter β_1 reflects the sensitivity of the stock's rate of return to movements in the stock market as a whole.) Using daily data from the beginning of 1979 through the end of 1980 ($n = 504$), Ruback obtained the least squares lines shown in the table at the top of the next page for the four firms in question. The t statistics associated with values of $\hat{\beta}_1$ are shown to the right of each least squares prediction equation.

FIRM	ESTIMATED MARKET MODEL	
Conoco	$\hat{y} = .0010 + 1.40x$	$(t = 21.93)$
DuPont	$\hat{y} = -.0005 + 1.21x$	$(t = 18.76)$
Mobil	$\hat{y} = .0010 + 1.62x$	$(t = 16.21)$
Seagram	$\hat{y} = .0013 + .76x$	$(t = 6.05)$

a. For each of the models, test $H_0: \beta_1 = 0$ versus $H_a: \beta_1 \neq 0$. Use $\alpha = .01$. Draw the appropriate conclusion regarding the usefulness of the market model in each case.

b. If the rate of return of Standard & Poor's 500 Composite Index increased by .10, how much change would occur in the mean rate of return of Conoco's common stock? How much change would occur in the mean rate of return of Seagram's common stock?

c. Which of the two stocks, Conoco or Seagram, appears to be more responsive to changes in the market as a whole? Explain.

10.28 In Exercise 10.10 the following least squares line was developed to describe the relationship between the price of a gallon of regular gasoline, y, and the price of a barrel of crude oil, x:

$$\hat{y} = 25.883 + 3.115x$$

Construct a 90% confidence interval to estimate the mean increase in the price of gasoline (in cents) per $1.00 increase per barrel in the price of crude oil.

10.29 Refer to the cable television study described in Exercise 10.19. Do the data provide sufficient evidence to indicate that the number of available channels provides information for the prediction of the number of channels watched for 10 minutes? Test using $\alpha = .10$.

10.30 A large car rental agency sells its cars after using them for a year. Among the records kept for each car are mileage and maintenance costs for the year. To evaluate the performance of a particular car model in terms of maintenance costs, the agency wants to use a 95% confidence interval to estimate the mean increase in maintenance costs for each additional 1,000 miles driven. Assume the relationship between maintenance cost and miles driven is linear. Use the data in the table to accomplish the objective of the rental agency.

CAR	MILES DRIVEN x (thousands)	MAINTENANCE COST y (dollars)
1	54	326
2	27	159
3	29	202
4	32	200
5	28	181
6	36	217

10.31 Buyers are often influenced by bulk advertising of a particular product. For example, suppose you have a product that sells for 25¢. If it is advertised at 2/50¢, 3/75¢, or 4/$1, some people may think they are getting a bargain. To test this theory, a store manager advertised an item for equal periods of time at five different bulk rates and observed the data listed in the table. Do the data provide sufficient evidence to indicate that sales increase as the number in the bulk increases?

ADVERTISED NUMBER IN BULK SALE x	VOLUME SOLD y
1	27
2	36
3	34
4	63
5	52

10.32 The precision of $\hat{\beta}_1$ as an estimator of β_1 is generally measured by its standard deviation $\sigma_{\hat{\beta}_1}$. In general, the larger the value of $\sigma_{\hat{\beta}_1}$, the wider (less precise) are confidence intervals for β_1; the smaller the value of $\sigma_{\hat{\beta}_1}$, the narrower (more precise) are confidence intervals for β_1.

a. Examine the formula for $\sigma_{\hat{\beta}_1}$ and explain how the observed values of the independent variable influence the size of $\sigma_{\hat{\beta}_1}$.

b. Sometimes it is possible to obtain data for a regression study by setting the independent variable, x, at different levels and observing the resulting values of the dependent variable, y. For example, suppose a supermarket chain was interested in studying the relationship between the sales of a product and the number of square feet of display space devoted to the product. Data for such a study would be generated by utilizing display areas of different sizes in different stores and observing the resulting sales. If you were designing such a study, how would your answer to part a influence the choice of display area sizes?

10.33 Do the data in Exercise 10.21 provide sufficient evidence to indicate that sales, y, tend to increase as the number of hours of programming, x, increases (i.e., that $\beta_1 > 0$)? Test using $\alpha = .10$.

10.34 Do the data in Exercise 10.22 support the theory that sales increase as the experience of a salesperson increases? Test using $\alpha = .05$.

10.35 Will the national 55-mile-per-hour highway speed limit provide a substantial savings in fuel? To investigate the relationship between automobile gasoline consumption and driving speed, a small economy car was driven twice over the same stretch of an interstate freeway at each of six different speeds. The numbers of miles per gallon measured for each of the twelve trips are shown in the table.

MILES PER HOUR	50	55	60	65	70	75
MILES PER GALLON	34.8, 33.6	34.6, 34.1	32.8, 31.9	32.6, 30.0	31.6, 31.8	30.9, 31.7

a. Fit a least squares line to the data.

b. Is there sufficient evidence to conclude that a straight-line model provides useful information about the relationship between gasoline consumption and speed? Test using $\alpha = .05$.

c. Construct a 90% confidence interval for β_1 and interpret it.

10.6 Correlation: Another Measure of the Utility of the Model

The claim is often made that the crime rate and the unemployment rate are "highly correlated." Another popular belief is that the Gross National Product (GNP) and the rate of inflation are "correlated." Some people even believe that the Dow Jones Industrial Average and the lengths of fashionable skirts are "correlated." Thus, the term *correlation* implies a relationship between two variables.

The *Pearson product moment correlation coefficient r,* defined in the box, provides a quantitative measure of the strength of the linear relationship between x and y, just as does the least squares slope $\hat{\beta}_1$. However, unlike the slope, the correlation coefficient r is *scaleless.* The value of r is always between −1 and +1, no matter what the units of x and y are.

> ### Definition 10.2
>
> The *Pearson product moment coefficient of correlation r* is a measure of the strength of the linear relationship between two variables x and y. It is computed (for a sample of n measurements on x and y) as follows:
>
> $$r = \frac{SS_{xy}}{\sqrt{SS_{xx}SS_{yy}}}$$

Note that r is computed from the same quantities used in fitting the least squares line. Since both r and $\hat{\beta}_1$ provide information about the utility of the model, it is not surprising that there is a similarity in their computational formulas. In particular, note that SS_{xy} appears in the numerators of both expressions and, since both denominators are always positive, r and $\hat{\beta}_1$ will always be of the same sign (either both positive or both negative). A value of r near or equal to zero implies little or no linear relationship between the values of y and x that were observed in the sample. In contrast, the closer r is to 1 or −1, the stronger the linear relationship between

Figure 10.8 Values of r and Their Implications

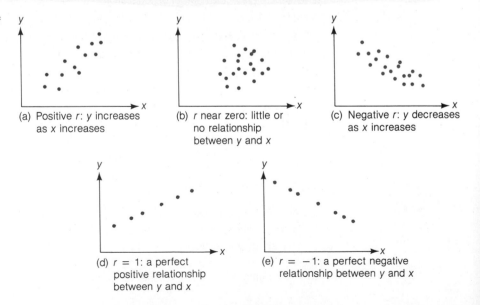

(a) Positive r: y increases as x increases

(b) r near zero: little or no relationship between y and x

(c) Negative r: y decreases as x increases

(d) r = 1: a perfect positive relationship between y and x

(e) r = −1: a perfect negative relationship between y and x

MINITAB:
CORR
COMMAND →
= r

y and x. And, if $r = 1$ or $r = -1$, all the points fall exactly on the least squares line. Positive values of r imply that y increases as x increases; negative values imply that y decreases as x increases. Each of these situations is portrayed in Figure 10.8.

Example 10.1

A firm wants to know the correlation between the size of its sales force and its yearly sales revenue. The records for the past 10 years are examined, and the results listed in Table 10.5 are obtained. Calculate the coefficient of correlation r for the data.

Table 10.5

Sales Force–Revenue Data, Example 10.1

YEAR	NUMBER OF SALESPEOPLE x	SALES y ($ hundred thousands)	YEAR	NUMBER OF SALESPEOPLE x	SALES y ($ hundred thousands)
1975	15	1.35	1980	29	2.93
1976	18	1.63	1981	30	3.41
1977	24	2.33	1982	32	3.26
1978	22	2.41	1983	35	3.63
1979	25	2.63	1984	38	4.15

Solution

We need to calculate SS_{xy}, SS_{xx}, and SS_{yy}:

$$SS_{xy} = \sum x_i y_i - \frac{\left(\sum x_i\right)\left(\sum y_i\right)}{10} = 800.62 - \frac{(268)(27.73)}{10} = 57.456$$

$$SS_{xx} = \sum x_i^2 - \frac{\left(\sum x_i\right)^2}{10} = 7{,}668 - \frac{(268)^2}{10} = 485.6$$

$$SS_{yy} = \sum y_i^2 - \frac{\left(\sum y_i\right)^2}{10} = 83.8733 - \frac{(27.73)^2}{10} = 6.97801$$

Then, the coefficient of correlation is

$$r = \frac{SS_{xy}}{\sqrt{SS_{xx} SS_{yy}}} = \frac{57.456}{\sqrt{(485.6)(6.97801)}} = \frac{57.456}{58.211} = .99$$

Thus, the size of the sales force and sales revenue are very highly correlated—at least over the past 10 years. The implication is that a strong positive linear relationship exists between these variables (see Figure 10.9 on page 420). We must be careful, however, not to jump to any unwarranted conclusions. For instance, the firm may be tempted to conclude that the best thing it can do to increase sales is to hire a large number of new salespeople. The implication of such a conclusion is that there is a *causal* relationship between the two variables. However, **high correlation does not imply causality.** The fact is that many things have probably contributed both to the increase in the size of the sales force and to the increase in sales revenue. The firm's expertise has undoubtedly grown, the rate of inflation has increased (so that 1984 dollars are not worth as much as 1975 dollars), and perhaps the scope of products and services sold by the firm has widened. We must be careful not to infer a causal relationship on the basis of high sample correlation. The only safe conclusion when a high correlation is observed in the sample data is that a linear trend may exist between x and y. ∎

Figure 10.9 Scatter-gram for Example 10.1

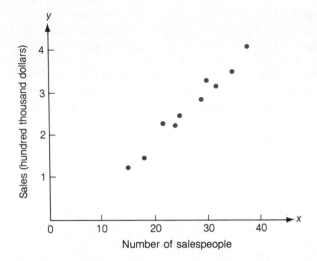

Keep in mind that the correlation coefficient r measures the correlation between x values and y values in the sample, and that a similar linear coefficient of correlation exists for the population from which the data points were selected. The **population correlation coefficient** is denoted by the symbol ρ (rho). As you might expect, ρ is estimated by the corresponding sample statistic, r. Or, rather than estimating ρ, we might want to test the hypothesis H_0: $\rho = 0$ against H_a: $\rho \neq 0$—i.e., test the hypothesis that x contributes no information for the prediction of y using the straight-line model against the alternative that the two variables are at least linearly related. However, we have already performed this identical test in Section 10.5 when we tested H_0: $\beta_1 = 0$ against H_a: $\beta_1 \neq 0$. That is, the null hypothesis H_0: $\rho = 0$ is equivalent to the hypothesis H_0: $\beta_1 = 0$. When we tested the null hypothesis H_0: $\beta_1 = 0$ in connection with the advertising – sales example, the data led to a rejection of the hypothesis for $\alpha = .05$. This implies that the null hypothesis of a zero linear correlation between the two variables (advertising and sales) can also be rejected at $\alpha = .05$. The only real difference between the least squares slope $\hat{\beta}_1$ and the coefficient of correlation r is the measurement scale. Therefore, the information they provide about the utility of the least squares model is to some extent redundant. For this reason, we will use the slope to make inferences about the existence of a positive or negative linear relationship between two variables.

10.7
The
Coefficient of
Determination

Another way to measure the contribution of x in predicting y is to consider how much the errors of prediction of y were reduced by using the information provided by x. To illustrate, suppose a sample of data has the scattergram shown in Figure 10.10(a). If we assume that x contributes no information for the prediction of y, the best prediction for a value of y is the sample mean $\bar{y}$, which is shown as the horizontal line in Figure 10.10(b). The vertical line segments in Figure 10.10(b) are the deviations of the points about the mean $\bar{y}$. Note that the sum of squares of deviations for the model $\hat{y} = \bar{y}$ is

$$SS_{yy} = \sum (y_i - \bar{y})^2$$

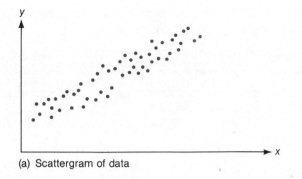

(a) Scattergram of data

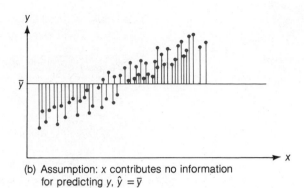

(b) Assumption: x contributes no information for predicting y, $\hat{y} = \bar{y}$

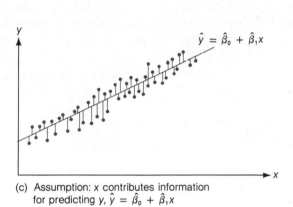

(c) Assumption: x contributes information for predicting y, $\hat{y} = \hat{\beta}_0 + \hat{\beta}_1 x$

Figure 10.10 A Comparison of the Sum of Squares of Deviations for Two Models

Now suppose you fit a least squares line to the same set of data and locate the deviations of the points about the line as shown in Figure 10.10(c). Compare the deviations about the prediction lines in parts (b) and (c) of Figure 10.10. You can see that:

1. If x contributes little or no information for the prediction of y, the sums of squares of deviations for the two lines,

$$SS_{yy} = \sum (y_i - \bar{y})^2 \quad \text{and} \quad SSE = \sum (y_i - \hat{y}_i)^2$$

will be nearly equal.

2. If x does contribute information for the prediction of y, the SSE will be smaller than SS_{yy}. In fact, if all the points fall on the least squares line, then SSE = 0.

Then, the reduction in the sum of squares of deviations that can be attributed to x, expressed as a proportion of SS_{yy}, is

$$\frac{SS_{yy} - SSE}{SS_{yy}}$$

It can be shown that this quantity is equal to the square of the simple linear coefficient of correlation r (the Pearson product moment coefficient of correlation).

Definition 10.3

The *coefficient of determination* is the square of the coefficient of correlation. It represents the proportion of the sum of squares of deviations of the y values about their predicted values that can be attributed to a linear relation between y and x.

$$r^2 = \frac{SS_{yy} - SSE}{SS_{yy}} = 1 - \frac{SSE}{SS_{yy}}$$

Note that r^2 is always between 0 and 1, because r is between -1 and $+1$. Thus, an r^2 of .60 means that the sum of squares of deviations of the y values about their predicted values has been reduced 60% by the use of the least squares equation $\hat{y}$, instead of $\bar{y}$, to predict y.

Example 10.2   Calculate the coefficient of determination for the advertising–sales example. The data are repeated in Table 10.6.

Table 10.6

ADVERTISING EXPENDITURE x ($ hundreds)	SALES REVENUE y ($ thousands)
1	1
2	1
3	2
4	2
5	4

Solution   We first calculate

$$SS_{yy} = \sum y_i^2 - \frac{\left(\sum y_i\right)^2}{5} = 26 - \frac{(10)^2}{5} = 26 - 20 = 6$$

From previous calculations,

$$SSE = \sum (y_i - \hat{y}_i)^2 = 1.10$$

Then, the coefficient of determination is given by

$$r^2 = \frac{SS_{yy} - SSE}{SS_{yy}} = \frac{6.0 - 1.1}{6.0} = \frac{4.9}{6.0} = .82$$

So we know that by using the advertising expenditure x to predict y with the least squares line

$$\hat{y} = -.1 + .7x$$

the total sum of squares of deviations of the five sample y values about their predicted values has been reduced 82% by the use of $\hat{y}$, instead of $\bar{y}$, to predict y.   ■

Case Study 10.1

Estimating the Cost of a Construction Project

As evidenced by the cost overruns of public building projects, the initial estimate of the ultimate cost of a structure is often rather poor. These estimates usually rely on a precise definition of the proposed building in terms of working drawings and specifications. However, cost estimators do not take random error into account, so no measure of reliability is possible for their deterministic estimates. Crandall and Cedercreutz (1976) propose the use of a probabilistic model to make cost estimates. They use regression models to relate cost to independent variables like volume, amount of glass, and floor area. Crandall and Cedercreutz's rationale for choosing this approach is that "one of the principal merits of the least squares regression model, for the purpose of preliminary cost estimating, is the method of dealing with anticipated error." They go on to point out that when random error is anticipated, "statistical methods, such as regression analysis, attack the problem head on."

Crandall and Cedercreutz initially focused on the cost of mechanical work (heating, ventilating, and plumbing), since this part of the total cost is generally difficult to predict. Conventional cost estimates rely heavily on the amount of ductwork and piping used in construction, but this information is not precisely known until too late to be of use to the cost estimator. One of several models discussed was a simple linear model relating mechanical cost to floor area. Based on the data associated with twenty-six factory and warehouse buildings, the least squares prediction equation given in Figure 10.11 was found. It was concluded that floor area and mechanical cost are linearly related, since the t statistic (for testing $H_0: \beta_1 = 0$) was found to equal 3.61, which is significant with an α as small as .002. Thus, floor area should be useful when predicting the mechanical cost of a factory or warehouse. In addition, the regression model enables the reliability of the predicted cost to be assessed.

The value of the coefficient of determination r^2 was found to be .35. This tells us that only 35% of the variation among mechanical costs is accounted for by the differences in floor areas. Since there is only one independent variable in the model, this relatively small value of r^2 should not be too surprising. If other variables related to mechanical cost were included in

Figure 10.11 Simple Linear Model Relating Cost to Floor Area

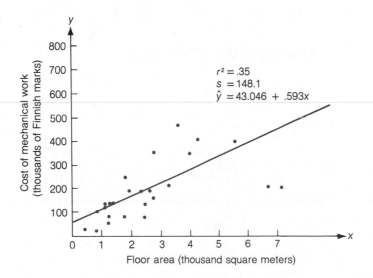

$$r^2 = .35$$
$$s = 148.1$$
$$\hat{y} = 43.046 + .593x$$

the model, they would probably account for a significant portion of the remaining 65% of the variation in mechanical cost not explained by floor area. In the next chapter, we discuss this important aspect of relating a response to more than one independent variable.

Learning the Mechanics

10.36 Construct a scattergram for the data sets shown in parts a and b. Then calculate r and r^2 for each data set. Interpret their values.

a.

x	-2	-1	0	1	2
y	-3	1	2	5	6

b.

x	-2	-1	0	1	2
y	7	6	3	2	0

10.37 Explain what each of the following sample correlation coefficients tells you about the relationship between the x and y values in the sample:

a. $r = 1$ **b.** $r = 0$ **c.** $r = -1$
d. $r = .05$ **e.** $r = .85$ **f.** $r = -.91$

10.38 Construct a scattergram for the data sets shown in parts a and b. Then calculate r and r^2 for each data set. Interpret their values.

a.

x	1	4	2	4	6
y	0	2	1	3	6

b.

x	-2	1	1	0	4
y	10	4	3	5	0

10.39 Calculate r^2 for the least squares lines in each of the following exercises:

a. 10.6   **b.** 10.7   **c.** 10.8

10.40 Describe the slope of the least squares line if:

a. $r = .5$ **b.** $r = -.9$ **c.** $r = .84$ **d.** $r = 0$

Applying the Concepts

10.41 Data on monthly sales, y, price per unit during the month, x_1, and amount spent on advertising, x_2, for a product are shown for a 5-month period in the table. Based on this sample, which variable — price or advertising expenditure — appears to provide more information about sales? Explain.

MONTH	TOTAL MONTHLY SALES y (thousands)	PRICE PER UNIT x_1	AMOUNT SPENT ON ALL FORMS OF ADVERTISING x_2 (hundreds)
June	$40	$0.85	$6.0
July	50	0.76	5.0
August	55	0.75	8.0
September	30	1.00	7.5
October	45	0.80	5.5

10.42 In Exercise 10.13, we gave the percentage, y, of games won and the batting average, x, for fourteen major league baseball teams at a point midway into the 1983 season. They are repeated here in the table.

PERCENTAGE OF GAMES WON y	TEAM BATTING AVERAGE x	PERCENTAGE OF GAMES WON y	TEAM BATTING AVERAGE x
56.5	.261	53.0	.271
50.0	.273	41.6	.263
51.7	.264	54.1	.273
51.2	.256	48.3	.259
41.8	.262	39.3	.237
56.0	.271	52.9	.262
49.4	.271	60.0	.275

a. Calculate the correlation coefficient, r, and the coefficient of determination, r^2, for the data. Interpret their values.

b. Do the data provide sufficient evidence to conclude that a correlation exists between a team's percentage of wins and its batting average? Test using $\alpha = .05$. [*Hint:* See the last paragraph of Section 10.6.]

10.43 A *negotiable certificate of deposit* is a marketable receipt for funds deposited in a bank for a specified period of time at a specified rate of interest (Cook, 1983). The accompanying table lists the end-of-quarter interest rate for 3-month certificates of deposit during the period January 1979 through September 1983. The table also lists end-of-quarter values of

YEAR	QUARTER	INTEREST RATE	S&P 500
1979	I	10.13	101.59
	II	9.95	102.91
	III	11.89	109.32
	IV	13.43	107.94
1980	I	17.57	104.69
	II	8.49	114.24
	III	11.29	125.46
	IV	18.65	135.76
1981	I	14.43	136.00
	II	16.90	131.21
	III	16.84	116.18
	IV	12.49	122.55
1982	I	14.21	111.96
	II	14.46	109.61
	III	10.66	120.42
	IV	8.66	135.28
1983	I	8.69	152.96
	II	9.20	168.11
	III	9.39	164.40

Source: *Standard & Poor's Trade and Securities Statistics, 1983,* Standard & Poor's Corporation.

Standard & Poor's 500 Stock Composite Average (an indicator of stock market activity) for the same time period. Find the coefficient of determination and the correlation coefficient for the data, and interpret your results.

10.44 In the summer of 1981, the Minnesota Department of Transportation installed a state-of-the-art weigh-in-motion scale in the concrete surface of the eastbound lanes of Interstate 494 in Bloomington, Minnesota. The system is computerized and monitors traffic continuously. It is capable of distinguishing among thirteen different types of vehicles (car, five-axle semi, five-axle twin trailer, etc.). The primary purpose of the system is to provide traffic counts and weights for use in the planning and design of future roadways. After installation, a study was undertaken to determine whether the scale's readings correspond with the static weights of the vehicles being monitored. (Studies of this type are known as *calibration studies.*) After some preliminary comparisons using a two-axle-six-tire truck carrying different loads (see table), calibration adjustments were made in the software of the weigh-in-motion system and the scales were reevaluated (Wright, Owen, & Pena, 1983).

TRIAL NUMBER	STATIC WEIGHT OF TRUCK x (thousand pounds)	WEIGH-IN-MOTION READING PRIOR TO CALIBRATION ADJUSTMENT y_1 (thousand pounds)	WEIGH-IN-MOTION READING AFTER CALIBRATION ADJUSTMENT y_2 (thousand pounds)
1	27.9	26.0	27.8
2	29.1	29.9	29.1
3	38.0	39.5	37.8
4	27.0	25.1	27.1
5	30.3	31.6	30.6
6	34.5	36.2	34.3
7	27.8	25.1	26.9
8	29.6	31.0	29.6
9	33.1	35.6	33.0
10	35.5	40.2	35.0

Source: Adapted from data in Wright, Owen, and Pena (1983).

a. Construct two scattergrams, one of y_1 versus x and the other of y_2 versus x.
b. Use the scattergrams of part a to evaluate the performance of the weigh-in-motion scale both before and after the calibration adjustment.
c. Calculate the correlation coefficient for both sets of data, and interpret their values. Explain how these correlation coefficients can be used to evaluate the weigh-in-motion scale.
d. Suppose the sample correlation coefficient for y_2 and x were 1. Could this happen if the static weights and the weigh-in-motion readings disagreed? Explain.

10.45 A problem of economic and social concern in the United States is the importation and sale of illicit drugs. The data shown in the table are part of a larger body of data collected by the Florida attorney general's office in an attempt to relate the incidence of drug seizures and drug arrests to the characteristics of the Florida counties. Given are the number, y, of drug arrests per county in 1982, the density, x_1, of the county (population per square mile), and the number, x_2, of law enforcement employees. In order to simplify the calculations, we show data for only ten counties.

		COUNTY									
		1	2	3	4	5	6	7	8	9	10
POPULATION DENSITY, x_1		169	68	278	842	18	42	112	529	276	613
NUMBER OF LAW ENFORCEMENT EMPLOYEES, x_2		498	35	772	5,788	18	57	300	1,762	416	520
NUMBER OF ARRESTS IN 1982, y		370	44	716	7,416	25	50	189	1,097	256	432

a. Fit a least squares line to relate the number, y, of drug arrests per county in 1982 to the county population density, x_1.

b. We might expect the mean number of arrests to increase as the population density increases. Do the data support this theory? Test using $\alpha = .05$.

c. Calculate the coefficient of determination for this regression analysis and interpret its value.

10.46 Repeat the instructions of Exercise 10.45 using the number, x_2, of county law enforcement employees as the independent variable.

10.47 Refer to Exercise 10.45.

a. Calculate the correlation coefficient, r, between the county population density, x_1, and the number of law enforcement employees, x_2.

b. Does the correlation between x_1 and x_2 differ significantly from zero? Test using $\alpha = .05$.

10.48 A firm's *demand curve* describes the quantity of its product that can be sold at different possible prices, other things being equal (Leftwich, 1973). Over the period of a year, a tire company varied the price of one of its radial tires in order to estimate the demand curve for the tire. They observed that when the price was set very low or very high, they sold few tires. The latter result they understood; the former they determined was due to consumer misperception that the tire's low price must be linked to poor quality. The data in the table describe the tire's sales over the experimental period.

TIRE PRICE x ($)	NUMBER SOLD y (hundreds)
20	13
35	57
45	85
60	43
70	17

a. Calculate a least squares line to approximate the firm's demand curve.

b. Construct a scattergram and plot your least squares line as a check on your calculations.

c. Test $H_0: \beta_1 = 0$ using a two-tailed test and $\alpha = .05$. Draw the appropriate conclusion in the context of the problem.

d. Does the nonrejection of H_0 in part c imply that no relationship exists between tire price and sales volume? Explain.

e. Calculate the coefficient of determination for the least squares line of part a and interpret its value in the context of the problem.

10.8 Using the Model for Estimation and Prediction

If we are satisfied that a useful model has been found to describe the relationship between sales revenue and advertising, we are ready to accomplish the original objectives for building the model: using it to estimate or to predict sales on the basis of advertising dollars spent.

The most common uses of a probabilistic model can be divided into two categories. The first is the use of the model for estimating the mean value of y, $E(y)$, for a specific value of x.

For our example, we may want to estimate the mean sales revenue for *all* months during which $400 ($x = 4$) is expended on advertising.

The second use of the model entails predicting a particular y value for a given x.

That is, if we decide to expend $400 next month, we want to predict the firm's sales revenue for that month.

In the case of estimating a mean value of y, we are attempting to estimate the mean result of a very large number of experiments at the given x value. In the second case, we are trying to predict the outcome of a single experiment at the given x value.

In which of these model uses do you expect to have more success; i.e., which value — the mean or individual value of y — can we estimate (or predict) with more accuracy?

Before answering this question, we first consider the problem of choosing an estimator (or predictor) of the mean (or individual) y value. We will use the least squares model

$$\hat{y} = \hat{\beta}_0 + \hat{\beta}_1 x$$

both to estimate the mean value of y and to predict a particular value of y for a given value of x. For our example, we found

$$\hat{y} = -.1 + .7x$$

so that the estimated mean value of sales revenue for all months when $x = 4$ (advertising = $400) is

$$\hat{y} = -.1 + .7(4)$$
$$= 2.7$$

or $2,700 (the units of y are thousands of dollars). The identical value is used to predict the y value when $x = 4$. That is, both the estimated mean value and the predicted value of y equal $\hat{y} = 2.7$ when $x = 4$, as shown in Figure 10.12.

The difference in these two model uses lies in the relative accuracy of the estimate and the prediction. These accuracies are best measured by the repeated sampling errors of the least

Figure 10.12　Estimated Mean Value and Predicted Individual Value of Sales Revenue y for $x = 4$

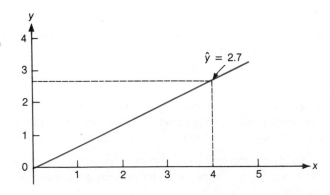

squares line when it is used as an estimator and as a predictor, respectively. These errors are given in the box.

Handwritten note: SE = STD ERROR

Sampling Errors for the Estimator of the Mean of y and the Predictor of an Individual y

1. The standard deviation of the sampling distribution of the estimator $\hat{y}$ of the mean value of y at a particular value of x, say x_p, is

$$\sigma_{\hat{y}} = \sigma\sqrt{\frac{1}{n} + \frac{(x_p - \bar{x})^2}{SS_{xx}}}$$

where σ is the standard deviation of the random error ε.

2. The standard deviation of the prediction error for the predictor $\hat{y}$ of an individual y value for $x = x_p$ is

$$\sigma_{(y-\hat{y})} = \sigma\sqrt{1 + \frac{1}{n} + \frac{(x_p - \bar{x})^2}{SS_{xx}}}$$

where σ is the standard deviation of the random error ε.

Handwritten note: $Ci = \hat{y} \pm t \times SE$

Handwritten note: TO FIND AVERAGE Y VALUE FOR A SIMPLE RANDOM SAMPLE SIZE = M WITH A GIVEN X:

The true value of σ will rarely be known. Thus, we estimate σ by s and calculate the estimation and prediction intervals as shown in the following boxes.

Handwritten note: $SE = S\sqrt{\frac{1}{n} + \frac{1}{M} + \frac{(x-\bar{x})^2}{Sxx}}$

A 100(1 − α)% Confidence Interval for the Mean Value of y for x = x_p

Handwritten note: MEAN VALUE OF Y GIVEN X

$\hat{y} \pm t_{\alpha/2}$(Estimated standard deviation of $\hat{y}$)

or

$$\hat{y} \pm t_{\alpha/2}s\sqrt{\frac{1}{n} + \frac{(x_p - \bar{x})^2}{SS_{xx}}}$$

where $t_{\alpha/2}$ is based on $(n-2)$ df.

Handwritten note: ← M = ∞ $\frac{1}{M} = ≈0$

A 100(1 − α)% Prediction Interval for an Individual y for x = x_p

Handwritten note: INDIVIDUAL VALUE OF Y FOR A GIVEN X

$\hat{y} \pm t_{\alpha/2}$ [Estimated standard deviation of $(y - \hat{y})$]

or

$$\hat{y} \pm t_{\alpha/2}s\sqrt{1 + \frac{1}{n} + \frac{(x_p - \bar{x})^2}{SS_{xx}}}$$

where $t_{\alpha/2}$ is based on $(n-2)$ df.

Handwritten note: ← M = 1 $\frac{1}{M} = 1$

Handwritten note: $SS_{xx} = (n-1)(STD\ DEV.\ OF\ x)^2$

Example 10.3   Find a 95% confidence interval for mean monthly sales when the appliance store spends $400 on advertising.

Solution   For a $400 advertising expenditure, $x_p = 4$ and, since $n = 5$, df $= n - 2 = 3$. Then the confidence interval for the mean value of y is

$$\hat{y} \pm t_{\alpha/2} s \sqrt{\frac{1}{n} + \frac{(x_p - \bar{x})^2}{SS_{xx}}}$$

or

$$\hat{y} \pm t_{.025} s \sqrt{\frac{1}{5} + \frac{(4 - \bar{x})^2}{SS_{xx}}}$$

Recall that $\hat{y} = 2.7$, $s = .61$, $\bar{x} = 3$, and $SS_{xx} = 10$. From Table V in Appendix B, $t_{.025} = 3.182$. Thus, we have

$$2.7 \pm (3.182)(.61) \sqrt{\frac{1}{5} + \frac{(4 - 3)^2}{10}} = 2.7 \pm (3.182)(.61)(.55)$$

$$= 2.7 \pm 1.1 \text{ or } (1.6, 3.8)$$

We estimate that the interval from $1,600 to $3,800 encloses the mean sales revenue when the store expends $400 a month on advertising. Note that we used a small amount of data for purposes of illustration in fitting the least squares line and that the width of the interval could be decreased by using a larger number of data points. ■

Example 10.4   Predict the monthly sales for next month if a $400 expenditure is to be made on advertising. Use a 95% prediction interval.

Solution   To predict the sales for a particular month for which $x_p = 4$, we calculate the 95% prediction interval as

$$\hat{y} \pm t_{\alpha/2} s \sqrt{1 + \frac{1}{n} + \frac{(x_p - \bar{x})^2}{SS_{xx}}} = 2.7 \pm (3.182)(.61) \sqrt{1 + \frac{1}{5} + \frac{(4 - 3)^2}{10}}$$

$$= 2.7 \pm (3.182)(.61)(1.14)$$

$$= 2.7 \pm 2.2 \text{ or } (.5, 4.9)$$

Therefore, we predict that the sales next month will fall in the interval from $500 to $4,900. ■

As in the case for the confidence interval for the mean value of y, the prediction interval for y is quite large. This is because we have chosen a small number of data points to fit the least squares line. The width of the prediction interval could be reduced by using a larger number of data points.

A comparison of the confidence interval for the mean value of y and the prediction interval for some future value of y for a $400 advertising expenditure ($x = 4$) is illustrated in Figure

Figure 10.13 A 95%
Confidence Interval for Mean
Sales and a Prediction
Interval for Sales When $x = 4$

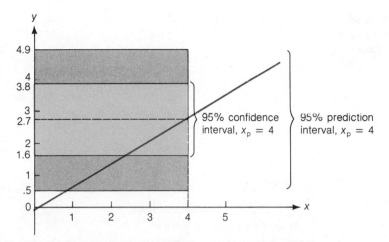

10.13. It is important to note that the prediction interval for an individual value of y will always
be wider than the confidence interval for a mean value of y. You can see this by examining the
formulas for the two intervals and you can see it in Figure 10.13.

The error in estimating the mean value of y, $E(y)$, for a given value of x, say x_p, is the
distance between the least squares line and the true line of means, $E(y) = \beta_0 + \beta_1 x$. This
error, $[\hat{y} - E(y)]$, is shown in Figure 10.14. In contrast, *the error $(y_p - \hat{y})$ in predicting some
future value of y is the sum of two errors* —the error of estimating the mean of y, $E(y)$,
shown in Figure 10.14, plus the random error that is a component of the value of y to be
predicted (see Figure 10.15). Consequently, the error of predicting a particular value of y will
be larger than the error of estimating the mean value of y for a particular value of x. Note from
their formulas that both the error of estimation and the error of prediction take their smallest
values when $x_p = \bar{x}$. The farther x_p lies from $\bar{x}$, the larger will be the errors of estimation and

Figure 10.14 Error of
Estimating the Mean Value
of y for a Given Value of x

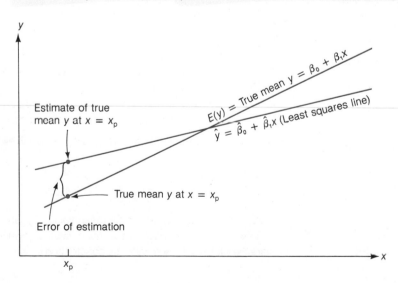

Figure 10.15 Error of Predicting a Future Value of y for a Given Value of x

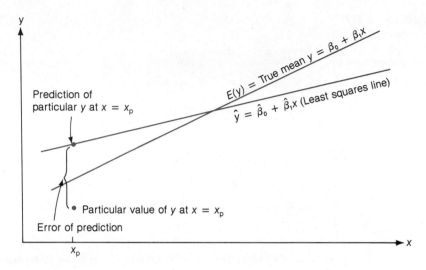

Prediction of particular y at $x = x_p$

$E(y) =$ True mean $y = \beta_0 + \beta_1 x$

$\hat{y} = \hat{\beta}_0 + \hat{\beta}_1 x$ (Least squares line)

Particular value of y at $x = x_p$

Error of prediction

x_p

prediction. You can see why this is true by noting the deviations for different values of x_p between the line of means $E(y) = \beta_0 + \beta_1 x$ and the predicted line of means $\hat{y} = \hat{\beta}_0 + \hat{\beta}_1 x$ shown in Figure 10.15. The deviation is larger at the extremities of the interval where the largest and smallest values of x in the data set occur.

Exercises 10.49–10.59

Learning the Mechanics

10.49 The data from Exercise 10.7 are repeated in the table.

x	−3	−1	0	1	3
y	0	2	3	6	9

a. Find a 90% confidence interval for the mean value of y when $x_p = -1$.
b. Find a 90% prediction interval for y when $x_p = -1$.
c. Compare the widths of the intervals you constructed in parts a and b. Which is wider and why? [*Note:* Both intervals are wide because of the small number of data points.]

10.50 The data from Exercise 10.8 are repeated in the table.

x	1	−1	2	0	4	−2	4	−2	5	1
y	−1	−5	1	−3	6	−6	4	−5	4	0

a. Find a 95% confidence interval for the mean value of y when $x_p = 5$.
b. Find a 95% confidence interval for the mean value of y when $x_p = 1$.
c. Compare the widths of the intervals you constructed in parts a and b. Which is wider and why?

10.51 In fitting a least squares line to $n = 12$ data points, the following quantities were computed:

$$SS_{xx} = 25 \qquad \bar{x} = 2 \qquad SS_{yy} = 17 \qquad \bar{y} = 3 \qquad SS_{xy} = 20$$

a. Find the least squares line.　**b.** Graph the least squares line.
c. Calculate SSE.　**d.** Calculate s^2.
e. Find a 95% confidence interval for the mean value of y when $x_p = 1$.
f. Find a 95% prediction interval for y when $x_p = 1.5$.

Applying the Concepts

10.52 In planning for an initial orientation meeting with new accounting majors, the chairman of the Accounting Department wants to emphasize the importance of doing well in the major courses to get better-paying jobs after graduation. To support this point, the chairman plans to show that there is a strong positive correlation between starting salaries for recent accounting graduates and their grade-point averages in the major courses. Records for seven of last year's accounting graduates are selected at random and given in the table.

GRADE-POINT AVERAGE IN MAJOR COURSES x	STARTING SALARY y ($ thousands)
2.58	16.5
3.27	18.8
3.85	19.5
3.50	19.2
3.33	18.5
2.89	16.6
2.23	15.6

a. Find the least squares prediction equation.
b. Plot the data, and graph the line as a check on your calculations.
c. Do the data provide sufficient evidence that grade-point average contributes useful information for predicting starting salary?
d. Find a 95% prediction interval for the starting salary of a graduate whose grade-point average is 3.2.
e. What is the mean starting salary for graduates with grade-point averages equal to 3.0? Use a 95% confidence interval.

10.53 Refer to Exercise 10.10. Find a 95% confidence interval for the mean price of a gallon of gasoline when crude oil costs $30 per barrel.

10.54 Managers are an important part of any organization's resource base. Accordingly, the organization should be just as concerned about forecasting its future managerial needs as it is with forecasting its needs for, say, the natural resources used in its production processes. According to William F. Glueck (1977), one commonly used procedure for forecasting the demand for managers is to model the relationship between sales and the number of managers needed. The theory is that "the demand for managers is the result of the increases and decreases in the demand for products and services that an enterprise offers its customers and clients'' (p. 274). In order to develop this relationship, data such as those shown in the table can be collected from a firm's records.

DATE	MONTHLY SALES x (units)	NUMBER OF MANAGERS y	DATE	MONTHLY SALES x (units)	NUMBER OF MANAGERS y
3/80	5	10	9/82	30	22
6/80	4	11	12/82	31	25
9/80	8	10	3/83	36	30
12/80	7	10	6/83	38	30
3/81	9	9	9/83	40	31
6/81	15	10	12/83	41	31
9/81	20	11	3/84	51	32
12/81	21	17	6/84	40	30
3/82	25	19	9/84	48	32
6/82	24	21	12/84	47	32

a. Use simple linear regression to model the relationship between the number of managers and the number of units sold.

b. Plot your least squares line on a scattergram of the data. Does it appear that the relationship between y and x is linear? If not, does it appear that your least squares model will provide a useful approximation to the relationship? Explain.

c. Test the usefulness of your model. Use $\alpha = .05$. State your conclusion in the context of the problem.

d. The company projects that next May it will sell thirty-nine units. Use your least squares model to construct (1) a 90% confidence interval for the mean number of managers needed when the sales level is 39 and (2) a 90% prediction interval for the number of managers needed next May.

e. Compare the widths and interpret the two intervals you constructed in part d.

10.55 Refer to Exercise 10.45. Find a 90% confidence interval for the mean number of arrests in a county that has a population density, x, equal to 300 people per square mile.

10.56 Refer to Exercise 10.55. Find a 90% prediction interval for the number of drug arrests next year for a county with a population density of 300 people per square mile. Compare your answer with the answer to Exercise 10.55 and explain the reason for the difference in the interval widths.

10.57 Explain why the confidence interval for the mean value of y for $x = x_p$ gets wider the farther x_p is from $\bar{x}$. What are the implications of this phenomenon for estimation and prediction?

10.58 Explain why for a given x value, the prediction interval for an individual y value will always be wider than the confidence interval for the mean value of y.

10.59 Many variables affect the total dollar expenditure by quarter for tourists visiting the state of Florida. One of these is the average number of nights stayed in Florida. Shown in the

TOTAL EXPENDITURES y ($ billions)	AVERAGE NIGHTS x
2.03	18.6
1.50	17.6
.88	8.3
1.03	9.2
2.48	19.4
3.34	28.9
2.50	18.0
3.52	27.8
1.67	12.1
2.88	20.8

table are the total expenditures, y, per quarter and the average number of nights stayed in Florida for 10 quarters.

a. Plot the data points on graph paper.

b. Find the least squares line relating y to x_1. As a check on your calculations, graph the line in your plot from part a to see if the line appears to model the relationship between y and x.

c. Do the data provide sufficient evidence to indicate that the number of nights stayed in Florida contributes information for the prediction of total quarterly tourist expenditures? Test using $\alpha = .05$.

d. Calculate r and r^2, and interpret their values.

e. Find a 90% confidence interval for the mean quarterly tourist expenditures if the average number of nights stayed in Florida is 15.

f. Find a 90% prediction interval for the mean quarterly tourist expenditures if the average number of nights stayed in Florida is 15.

g. Explain the difference in the widths of the intervals found in parts e and f.

10.9 Simple Linear Regression: An Example

In the previous sections we have presented the basic elements necessary to fit and use a straight-line regression model. In this final section we assemble these elements by applying them in an example.

Suppose a fire insurance company wants to relate the amount of fire damage in major residential fires to the distance between the residence and the nearest fire station. The study is to be conducted in a large suburb of a major city; a sample of fifteen recent fires in this suburb is selected. The amount of damage, y, and the distance, x, between the fire and the nearest fire station are recorded for each fire. The results are given in Table 10.7.

Table 10.7
Fire Damage Data

DISTANCE FROM FIRE STATION x (miles)	FIRE DAMAGE y ($ thousands)	DISTANCE FROM FIRE STATION x (miles)	FIRE DAMAGE y ($ thousands)
3.4	26.2	2.6	19.6
1.8	17.8	4.3	31.3
4.6	31.3	2.1	24.0
2.3	23.1	1.1	17.3
3.1	27.5	6.1	43.2
5.5	36.0	4.8	36.4
0.7	14.1	3.8	26.1
3.0	22.3		

Step 1 First, we hypothesize a model to relate fire damage, y, to the distance, x, from the nearest fire station. We will hypothesize a straight-line probabilistic model:

$$y = \beta_0 + \beta_1 x + \varepsilon$$

Step 2 Next, we use the data to estimate the unknown parameters in the deterministic component of the hypothesized model. We make some preliminary calculations:

$$SS_{xx} = \sum x_i^2 - \frac{\left(\sum x_i\right)^2}{15} = 196.16 - \frac{(49.2)^2}{15}$$

$$= 196.160 - 161.376 = 34.784$$

$$SS_{yy} = \sum y_i^2 - \frac{\left(\sum y_i\right)^2}{15} = 11{,}376.48 - \frac{(396.2)^2}{15}$$

$$= 11{,}376.480 - 10{,}464.963 = 911.517$$

$$SS_{xy} = \sum x_iy_i - \frac{\left(\sum x_i\right)\left(\sum y_i\right)}{15} = 1{,}470.65 - \frac{(49.2)(396.2)}{15}$$

$$= 1{,}470.650 - 1{,}299.536 = 171.114$$

Then the least squares estimates of the slope β_1 and intercept β_0 are

$$\hat{\beta}_1 = \frac{SS_{xy}}{SS_{xx}} = \frac{171.114}{34.784} = 4.919$$

$$\hat{\beta}_0 = \bar{y} - \hat{\beta}_1\bar{x} = \frac{396.2}{15} - 4.919\left(\frac{49.2}{15}\right)$$

$$= 26.413 - (4.919)(3.28) = 26.413 - 16.134$$
$$= 10.279$$

And the least squares equation is

$$\hat{y} = 10.279 + 4.919x$$

This prediction equation is graphed in Figure 10.16, along with a plot of the data points.

Figure 10.16 Least Squares Model for the Fire Damage Data

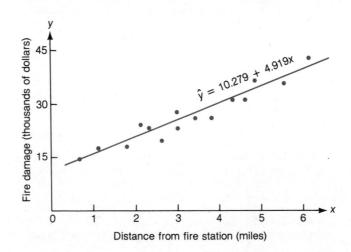

Step 3 Now, we specify the probability distribution of the random error component, ε. The assumptions about the distribution will be identical to those listed in Section 10.3. Although we know that these assumptions are not completely satisfied (they rarely are for any practical problem), we are willing to assume they are approximately satisfied for this example. We have to estimate the variance σ^2 of ε, so we calculate

$$SSE = \sum (y_i - \hat{y}_i)^2 = SS_{yy} - \hat{\beta}_1 SS_{xy}$$

where the last expression represents a shortcut formula for SSE. Thus,

$$SSE = 911.517 - (4.919)(171.114)$$
$$= 911.517 - 841.709766 = 69.807234^*$$

To estimate σ^2, we divide SSE by the degrees of freedom available for error, $n - 2$. Thus,

$$s^2 = \frac{SSE}{n-2} = \frac{69.807234}{15-2} = 5.3698$$
$$s = \sqrt{5.3698} = 2.32$$

Step 4 We can now check the utility of the hypothesized model — that is, whether x really contributes information for the prediction of y using the straight-line model. First test the null hypothesis that the slope β_1 is zero — i.e., that there is no linear relationship between fire damage and the distance from the nearest fire station — against the alternative that the slope β_1 differs from zero. We test

$$H_0: \beta_1 = 0 \qquad H_a: \beta_1 \neq 0$$

Test statistic: $\quad t = \dfrac{\hat{\beta}_1 - 0}{s_{\hat{\beta}_1}} = \dfrac{\hat{\beta}_1}{s/\sqrt{SS_{xx}}}$

Assumptions: Those made about ε in Section 10.3.

For $\alpha = .05$, we will reject H_0 if

$$t > t_{\alpha/2} \qquad \text{or} \qquad t < -t_{\alpha/2}$$

where for $n = 15$, df $= n - 2 = 15 - 2 = 13$ and $t_{.025} = 2.160$. We then calculate the t statistic:

$$t = \frac{\hat{\beta}_1}{s_{\hat{\beta}_1}} = \frac{\hat{\beta}_1}{s/\sqrt{SS_{xx}}}$$
$$= \frac{4.919}{2.32/\sqrt{34.784}} = \frac{4.919}{.393} = 12.5$$

This large t value leaves little doubt that the distance between the fire and the fire station contributes information for the prediction of fire damage. Particularly, it appears (as we might suspect) that fire damage increases as the distance increases.

---

* The values for SS_{yy}, $\hat{\beta}_1$, and SS_{xy} used to calculate SSE are exact for this example. For other problems where rounding is necessary, at least six significant figures should be carried for these quantities. Otherwise, the calculated value of SSE may be substantially in error.

We gain additional information about the relationship by forming a confidence interval for the slope β_1. A 95% confidence interval is

$$\hat{\beta}_1 \pm t_{.025} s_{\hat{\beta}_1} = 4.919 \pm (2.160)(.393)$$
$$= 4.919 \pm .849 = (4.070, 5.768)$$

We estimate that the interval from \$4,070 to \$5,768 encloses the mean increase (β_1) in fire damage per additional mile distance from the fire station.

Another measure of the utility of the model is the coefficient of correlation r:

$$r = \frac{SS_{xy}}{\sqrt{SS_{xx} SS_{yy}}}$$

$$= \frac{171.114}{\sqrt{(34.784)(911.517)}} = \frac{171.114}{178.062} = .96$$

The high correlation provides further support for our conclusion that β_1 differs from zero; it appears that fire damage and distance from the fire station are highly correlated.

The coefficient of determination is

$$r^2 = (.96)^2 = .92$$

which implies that 92% of the sum of squares of deviations of the y values about $\bar{y}$ is explained by the distance, x, between the fire and the fire station. All signs point to a strong linear relationship between y and x.

Step 5 We are now prepared to use the least squares model. Suppose the insurance company wants to predict the fire damage if a major residential fire were to occur 3.5 miles from the nearest fire station; i.e., $x_p = 3.5$. The predicted value is

$$\hat{y} = \hat{\beta}_0 + \hat{\beta}_1 x_p$$
$$= 10.279 + (4.919)(3.5)$$
$$= 10.279 + 17.216 = 27.5$$

(we round to the nearest tenth to be consistent with the units of the original data in Table 10.7). If we want a 95% prediction interval, we calculate

$$\hat{y} \pm t_{.025} s \sqrt{1 + \frac{1}{n} + \frac{(x_p - \bar{x})^2}{SS_{xx}}} = 27.5 \pm (2.16)(2.32) \sqrt{1 + \frac{1}{15} + \frac{(3.5 - 3.28)^2}{34.784}}$$

$$= 27.5 \pm (2.16)(2.32)\sqrt{1.0681}$$
$$= 27.5 \pm 5.2 = (22.3, 32.7)$$

The model yields a 95% prediction interval for fire damage in a major residential fire 3.5 miles from the nearest station of \$22,300 to \$32,700.

One caution before closing: We would not use this prediction model to make predictions for homes less than 0.7 mile or more than 6.1 miles from the nearest fire station. A look at the data in Table 10.7 reveals that all the x values fall between 0.7 and 6.1. It is dangerous to use the model to make predictions outside the region in which the sample data fall. A straight line might not provide a good model for the relationship between the mean value of y and x for values of x beyond the range of the sample data.

Summary

We have introduced an extremely useful tool in this chapter — *the method of least squares* for fitting a prediction equation to a set of data. The application of this methodology, along with the associated inferential procedures, is referred to as *regression analysis.* In five steps we showed how to use sample data to build a model relating a dependent variable y to a single independent variable x.

1. The first step is to hypothesize a *probabilistic model.* In this chapter, we confined our attention to the *first-order (straight-line) model,* $y = \beta_0 + \beta_1 x + \varepsilon$.

2. The second step is to use the method of least squares to estimate the unknown parameters in the *deterministic component,* $\beta_0 + \beta_1 x$. The least squares estimates yield a model $\hat{y} = \hat{\beta}_0 + \hat{\beta}_1 x$ with a *sum of squared errors (SSE)* that is smaller than the SSE for any other straight-line model.

3. The third step is to specify the probability distribution of the *random error component, ε.*

4. The fourth step is to assess the utility of the hypothesized model. Included here are making inferences about the *slope, β_1*; calculating the *coefficient of correlation, r*; and calculating the *coefficient of determination, r^2.*

5. Finally, if we are satisfied with the model, we can use it to *estimate the mean y value, E(y),* for a given x value and/or to *predict an individual y value* for a specific value of x.

The following chapter develops more fully the concepts introduced in this chapter.

Supplementary Exercises 10.60–10.72

10.60 In fitting a least squares line to $n = 15$ data points, the following quantities were computed:

$$SS_{xx} = 50 \qquad SS_{yy} = 25 \qquad SS_{xy} = -30$$

$$\bar{x} = 1.3 \qquad \bar{y} = 27$$

a. Find the least squares line.
b. Graph the least squares line.
c. Calculate SSE.
d. Calculate s^2.
e. Find a 90% confidence interval for β_1. Interpret this interval.
f. Find a 90% confidence interval for the mean value of y when $x_p = 1.8$.
g. Find a 90% prediction interval for y when $x_p = 1.8$.

10.61 Spiraling energy costs have generated interest in energy conservation in businesses of all sizes. Consequently, firms planning to build new plants or make additions to existing facilities have become very conscious of the energy efficiency of proposed new structures. As a result, such firms are interested in knowing the relationship between a building's yearly energy consumption and the factors that influence heat loss. Some of these factors are the number of building stories above and below ground, the materials used in the construction of the building shell, the number of square feet of building shell, and climatic conditions (ASHRAE, 1968). The table lists the energy consumption in British thermal units (a

BTU is the amount of heat required to raise 1 pound of water 1°Fahrenheit) for 1984 for twenty-two buildings that were all subjected to the same climatic conditions.

BTU/YEAR (Thousands)	SHELL AREA (Square feet)	BTU/YEAR (Thousands)	SHELL AREA (Square feet)
1,371,000	13,530	337,500	5,650
2,422,000	26,060	567,500	8,001
672,200	6,355	555,300	6,147
233,100	4,576	239,400	2,660
218,900	24,680	2,629,000	19,240
354,000	2,621	1,102,000	10,700
12,220,000	59,660	2,680,000	23,680
3,135,000	23,350	423,500	9,125
1,470,000	18,770	423,500	6,510
1,408,000	12,220	1,691,000	13,530
2,201,000	25,490	1,870,000	18,860

a. Use the method of least squares to estimate the relationship between BTU consumption per year, y, and building shell area, x.

b. Investigate the usefulness of the model you developed in part a. Does building shell area, x, contribute information for the prediction of y? Test using $\alpha = .10$.

c. Give the approximate observed significance level for the test in part b, and interpret its value.

d. Calculate r^2, and interpret its value.

e. A company wishes to build a new warehouse that will contain 8,000 square feet of shell area. Predict the energy consumption for this building using a 90% prediction interval.

f. The application of the model you developed in part a to the warehouse problem of part e is appropriate only if certain assumptions can be made about the new warehouse. What are these assumptions?

10.62 The data in the table give the market share for a product as a function of television advertising expenditures.

MONTH	MARKET SHARE y (percent)	TELEVISION ADVERTISING EXPENDITURE x ($ thousands)
January	15	23
March	17	25
May	13	21
July	14	24
September	16	26

a. Use the methods of this chapter to find the least squares line relating market share to television advertising expenditure. Plot the data, and graph the least squares line as a check on your calculations.

b. Do the data provide sufficient evidence to indicate that x contributes information for the prediction of y? Test using $\alpha = .10$.

c. Find a 95% confidence interval for β_1, and interpret your result.

d. Find a 90% confidence interval for the expected market share when $25,000 is spent on television advertising.

e. Find a 95% prediction interval for the market share that will be obtained when $23,000 is spent in television advertising.

10.63 The table shows the number of passengers carried by scheduled airlines and railroads in the United States over the period from 1950 to 1980.

YEAR	PASSENGERS CARRIED BY SCHEDULED AIR CARRIERS IN THE UNITED STATES y (millions)	PASSENGERS CARRIED BY RAILROADS IN THE UNITED STATES x (millions)
1950	19	488
1955	42	433
1960	62	327
1965	103	306
1970	169	289
1974	208	275
1975	205	270
1976	223	272
1977	240	276
1978	275	262
1979	317	274
1980	297	281

Source: U.S. Bureau of the Census, *Statistical Abstract of the United States: 1982*.

a. Find the correlation coefficient and the coefficient of determination for the data in the table and interpret their values.

b. Do the data provide sufficient evidence to indicate that x and y are correlated?

10.64 A large supermarket chain has its own store brand for many grocery items. These tend to be priced lower than other brands. For a particular item, the chain wants to study the effect of varying the price for the major competing brand on the sales of the store brand item, while the prices for the store brand and all other brands are held fixed. The experiment is conducted at one of the chain's stores over a 7-week period and the results are shown in the table.

WEEK	MAJOR COMPETITOR'S PRICE x	STORE BRAND SALES y
1	37¢	122
2	32	107
3	29	99
4	35	110
5	33	113
6	31	104
7	35	116

a. Find the least squares line relating store brand sales, y, to major competitor's price, x.
b. Plot the data and graph the line as a check on your calculations.
c. Does x contribute information for the prediction of y?
d. Calculate r and r^2 and interpret their values.
e. Find a 90% confidence interval for mean store brand sales when the competitor's price is 33¢.
f. Suppose you were to set the competitor's price at 33¢. Find a 90% prediction interval for next week's sales.

10.65 Sometimes it is known from theoretical considerations that the straight-line relationship between two variables, x and y, passes through the origin of the xy-plane. Consider the relationship between the total weight of a shipment of 50-pound bags of flour, y, and the number of bags in the shipment, x. Since a shipment containing $x = 0$ bags (i.e., no shipment at all) has a total weight of $y = 0$, a straight-line model of the relationship between x and y should pass through the point $x = 0$, $y = 0$. In such a case you could assume $\beta_0 = 0$ and characterize the relationship between x and y with the following model:

$$y = \beta_1 x + \varepsilon$$

The least squares estimate of β_1 for this model is:

$$\hat{\beta}_1 = \frac{\sum x_i y_i}{\sum x_i^2}$$

From the records of past flour shipments, fifteen shipments were randomly chosen and the data shown in the table were recorded.

WEIGHT OF SHIPMENT	NUMBER OF 50-POUND BAGS IN SHIPMENT	WEIGHT OF SHIPMENT	NUMBER OF 50-POUND BAGS IN SHIPMENT
5,050	100	7,162	150
10,249	205	24,000	500
20,000	450	4,900	100
7,420	150	14,501	300
24,685	500	28,000	600
10,206	200	17,002	400
7,325	150	16,100	400
4,958	100		

a. Find the least squares line for the given data under the assumption that $\beta_0 = 0$. Plot the least squares line on a scattergram of the data.
b. Find the least squares line for the given data using the model

$$y = \beta_0 + \beta_1 x + \varepsilon$$

(i.e., do not restrict β_0 to equal 0). Plot this line on the same scatterplot you constructed in part a.
c. Refer to part b. Why might $\hat{\beta}_0$ be different from zero even though the true value of β_0 is known to be zero?

d. The estimated standard error of $\hat{\beta}_0$ is equal to

$$s\sqrt{\frac{1}{n} + \frac{\bar{x}^2}{SS_{xx}}}$$

Use the t statistic,

$$t = \frac{\hat{\beta}_0 - 0}{s\sqrt{(1/n) + (\bar{x}^2/SS_{xx})}}$$

to test the null hypothesis $H_0: \beta_0 = 0$ against the alternative $H_a: \beta_0 \neq 0$. Use $\alpha = .10$. Should you include β_0 in your model?

10.66 As a result of the increase in the number of suburban shopping centers, many center-city stores are suffering financially. A downtown department store thinks that increased advertising might help lure more shoppers into the area. To study the effect of advertising on sales, records were obtained for several mid-year months during which the store varied advertising expenditures. Those records are shown in the table.

ADVERTISING EXPENSE x ($ thousands)	SALES y ($ thousands)
0.9	30
1.1	34
0.8	32
1.2	37
0.7	31

a. Estimate the coefficient of correlation between sales and advertising expenditures.
b. Do the data provide sufficient evidence to indicate a nonzero correlation between sales, y, and advertising expense, x?

10.67 A certain manufacturer evaluates the sales potential for a product in a new marketing area by selecting several stores within the area to sell the product on a trial basis for a 1-month period. The sales figures for the trial period are then used to project sales for the entire area. [*Note:* The same number of trial stores is used each time.]

TOTAL SALES DURING TRIAL PERIOD x ($ hundreds)	TOTAL SALES FOR FIRST MONTH FOR THE ENTIRE AREA y ($ hundreds)
16.8	48.2
14.0	46.8
18.3	54.3
22.1	59.7
14.9	48.3
23.2	67.5

a. Use the data in the table to develop a simple linear model for predicting first-month sales for the entire area based on sales during the trial period.

b. Plot the data, and graph the line as a check on your calculations.

c. Do the data provide sufficient evidence to indicate that total sales during the trial period contribute information for predicting total sales during the first month? Test using $\alpha = .10$.

d. Find the approximate p-value for the test in part c, and interpret its value.

e. Use a 90% prediction interval to predict total sales for the first month for the entire area if the trial sales are $2,000.

10.68 Although the income tax system is structured so people with higher incomes should pay in taxes a higher percentage of their incomes, there are many loopholes and tax shelters available for individuals with higher incomes. A sample of seven individual 1984 tax returns gave the data listed in the table on income and percent taxes paid.

INDIVIDUAL	GROSS INCOME x ($ thousands)	TAXES PAID y (percentage of total income)
1	35.8	16.7
2	80.2	21.4
3	14.9	15.2
4	7.3	10.1
5	9.1	12.2
6	150.7	19.6
7	25.9	17.3

a. Fit a least squares line to the data.

b. Plot the data, and graph the line as a check on your calculations.

c. Calculate r and r^2, and interpret them.

d. Find a 90% confidence interval for the mean percent taxes paid in 1984 by individuals with gross incomes of $70,000.

10.69 As part of the first-year evaluation for new salespeople, a large food-processing firm projects the second-year sales for each salesperson based on his or her sales for the first year.

FIRST-YEAR SALES x ($ thousands)	SECOND-YEAR SALES y ($ thousands)
75.2	99.3
91.7	125.7
100.3	136.1
64.2	108.6
81.8	102.0
110.2	153.7
77.3	108.8
80.1	105.4

a. Use the data in the table on eight salespeople for this firm to fit a simple linear prediction model for second-year sales based on the first year's sales. Assume the data have been adjusted in terms of a base year to discount inflation effects.

b. Plot the data, and graph the line as a check on your calculations.

c. Do the data provide sufficient information to indicate that x contributes information for the prediction of y?

d. Find the approximate p-value for the test in part c, and interpret its value.

e. Calculate r^2, and interpret its value.

f. If a salesperson has first-year sales of $90,000, find a 90% prediction interval for next year's sales.

10.70 The rate of increase in prices of single-family homes in the United States has been rising faster than the rate of inflation in recent years. As a result, many investors have directed their funds to the housing market as a hedge against inflation. One way an investor can assess the value of a specific house is to compare it to the sale prices of similar homes that have recently been sold. Another popular approach, according to Cho and Reichert (1980), involves the use of regression analysis to model the relationship between price and the variables that influence price. Independent variables that could be utilized are total living area, number of rooms, number of baths, age of property, etc. Of these factors, Cho and Reichert indicate that total living area provides the most information for determining the worth of a house. The table lists the final selling price and total living area for a sample of twenty-four homes in the same geographic area that were sold during the last 6 months.

AREA (Square feet)	PRICE ($)	AREA (Square feet)	PRICE ($)	AREA (Square feet)	PRICE ($)
1,100	40,000	1,570	51,300	1,150	40,500
1,455	48,700	1,400	48,400	1,705	56,100
1,630	53,800	1,380	46,000	1,890	62,300
1,490	50,300	1,310	44,500	1,920	63,300
1,210	41,900	1,535	50,800	1,800	59,600
1,857	61,100	1,620	53,600	1,820	60,000
1,835	60,300	1,350	46,200	1,970	66,800
2,200	75,100	1,275	45,000	2,010	67,100

a. Find the least squares line for the data.

b. Plot the least squares line on a scattergram of the data. Compute r^2 to obtain a measure of how well the line fits the data points.

c. Define β_0 and β_1 in the context of this problem.

d. Do the data provide evidence that living area contributes information for predicting the price of a home? Use $\alpha = .05$.

e. Find a 95% confidence interval for β_1. Does your confidence interval support the conclusion you reached in part d? Explain.

f. Find the approximate observed significance level for the test in part d, and interpret its value.

g. Estimate the mean selling price for homes with a total living area of 1,900 square feet. Use a 90% confidence interval.

10.71 A box plot (see Section 3.10) can be used to analyze the deviations between the observed values of y and the predicted values. The objective is to determine whether any of these deviations (called *residuals*) may be outliers. The presence of outliers might indicate a faulty observation or a departure from the assumptions of Section 10.3. To perform such an analysis, calculate the values of the residuals and treat the resulting data set in the manner described in Section 3.10.

a. Compute the set of residuals for the least squares line you developed in Exercise 10.61.
b. Construct a box plot for these residuals.
c. Does the box plot suggest that it may be inappropriate to characterize ε as being normally distributed? Explain.

10.72 When a sample is drawn from a population with correlation coefficient, ρ, equal to zero, the sample correlation may still turn out to be significantly different from zero. In such cases the correlation is said to be *spurious* or irrelevant. As more measurements are included in the sample, the spurious correlation will shrink toward zero. Calculate the sample correlation coefficient for the data in the table and comment on whether you believe the correlation is spurious.

DATE	PRIME INTEREST RATE	RATE OF GROWTH IN MONEY SUPPLY (M1)*	DATE	PRIME INTEREST RATE	RATE OF GROWTH IN MONEY SUPPLY (M1)*
2/81	20.00	.36%	2/82	17.00	−.29
3/81	19.00	1.19	3/82	16.50	.22
4/81	18.00	2.09	4/82	16.50	.91
5/81	20.50	−.95	5/82	16.50	−.20
6/81	20.50	−.19	6/82	16.50	−.02
7/81	20.50	.23	7/82	16.50	−.02
8/81	20.50	.40	8/82	15.50	.86
9/81	20.50	.02	9/82	13.50	1.16
10/81	19.50	.39	10/82	13.50	1.72
11/81	18.00	.81	11/82	12.00	1.41
12/81	15.75	1.03	12/82	11.50	.74
1/82	15.75	1.75			

* M1 = Currency + Demand deposits + Travelers' checks + Other checkable deposits
Source: *Economic Report of the President,* 1983, pp. 233, 240.

10.73 In Exercise 10.72 you considered the correlation between the prime interest rate and the rate of growth of the money supply for the years 1981–1982.

a. Do the data of Exercise 10.72 indicate that the population correlation coefficient, ρ, is greater than zero? Test using $\alpha = .05$ and report the p-value of your test.
b. What do the results of your hypothesis test suggest about the form of the relationship between the prime interest rate and the rate of growth of the money supply?
c. Construct a scattergram of the data in Exercise 10.72. Does the pattern of points in your scattergram support the conclusion you made in part a? Explain.

On Your Own . . .

The Gross National Product (GNP) is one of the nation's best-known economic indicators. Many economists have developed models to forecast future values of the GNP. There is surely a large number of variables that should be included if an accurate prediction is to be made. For the moment, however, consider the simple case of choosing one important variable to include in a simple straight-line model for GNP.

First, list three independent variables (x_1, x_2, and x_3) that you think might be (individually) strongly related to the GNP. Next, obtain ten yearly values (preferably for the last 10 years) of the three independent variables and the GNP.*

a. Use the least squares formulas given in this chapter to fit three straight-line models — one for each independent variable — for predicting the GNP.

b. Interpret the sign of the estimated slope coefficient, $\hat{\beta}_1$, in each case, and test the utility of the model by testing $H_0: \beta_1 = 0$ against $H_a: \beta_1 \neq 0$.

c. Calculate the coefficient of determination r^2 for each model. Which of the independent variables predicts the GNP best over the 10 sample years when a straight-line model is used? Is this variable necessarily best in general (i.e., for all years)? Explain.

References   *ASHRAE guide and data book: Applications.* New York: American Society of Heating, Refrigerating, and Air-Conditioning Engineers, Inc., 1968. Section IV.

Cho, C. C., & Reichert, A. "An application of multiple regression analysis for appraising single-family housing values." *Business Economics,* Jan. 1980, *15,* 47–52.

Cook, T. Q. (ed.) *Instruments of the money market.* 4th ed. Richmond, Va.: Federal Reserve Bank of Richmond, 1977.

Crandall, J. S., & Cedercreutz, M. "Preliminary cost estimates for mechanical work." *Building Systems Design,* Oct.–Nov., *73,* 35–51.

Draper, N., & Smith, H. *Applied regression analysis.* 2d ed. New York: Wiley, 1981.

Glueck, W. F. *Management.* Hinsdale, Ill.: Dryden Press, 1977.

Gray, J., & Johnston, K. S. *Accounting and management action.* 2d ed. New York: McGraw-Hill, 1977. Pp. 267–268.

Hartwig, F., & Dearing, B. E. *Exploratory data analysis.* Beverly Hills, Calif.: Sage, 1979. Pp. 23–24.

Landro, L., & Mayer, J. "Cable-TV viewing study dims prospect of large increase in number of channels." *Wall Street Journal,* Nov. 16, 1982, 10.

Leftwich, R. H. *The price system and resource allocation.* 5th ed. Hinsdale, Ill.: Dryden Press, 1973. P. 123.

Mansfield, E. *Economics.* 3d ed. New York: Norton, 1980. P. 166.

Mendenhall, W., & McClave, J. T. *A second course in business statistics: Regression analysis.* San Francisco: Dellen, 1981.

Miller, R. B., & Wichern, D. W. *Intermediate business statistics: Analysis of variance, regression, and time series.* New York: Holt, Rinehart and Winston, 1977. Chapter 5.

* The assumption that the random errors are independent is debatable for time series data. For the purposes of illustration, we assume they are approximately independent. The problem of dependent errors is discussed in Chapter 14.

Neter, J., Wasserman, W., & Kutner, M. H. *Applied linear regression models.* Homewood, Ill.: Richard D. Irwin, 1983.

Ruback, R. S. "The Conoco takeover and stockholder returns." *Sloan Management Review,* Winter 1982, *23,* 13–33.

Tukey, J. W. *Exploratory data analysis.* Reading, Mass.: Addison-Wesley, 1977. Chapter 2.

Weisberg, S. *Applied linear regression.* New York: Wiley, 1980.

Wright, J. L., Owen, F., & Pena, D. "Status of MN/DOT's weigh-in-motion program," St. Paul: Minnesota Department of Transportation, Jan. 1983.

Younger, M. S. *A handbook for linear regression.* North Scituate, Mass.: Duxbury, 1979.

CHAPTER 11

Multiple Regression

Where We've Been . . .

In Chapter 10 we demonstrated how to model the relationship between a dependent variable, y, and an independent variable, x, using a straight line. We fit the straight line to the data points, used r and r^2 to measure the strength of the relationship between y and x, and used the resulting prediction equation to estimate the mean value of y or to predict some future value of y for a given value of x.

Where We're Going . . .

This chapter converts the basic concept of Chapter 10 into a powerful estimation and prediction device by modeling the mean value of y as a function of two or more independent variables. This will enable you to model a response, y (say, the assessed value of a house), as a function of quantitative variables (such as floor space and age of the house) or as a function of qualitative variables (such as type of construction and location). As in the case of simple linear regression, multiple regression analysis includes fitting the model to a data set, testing the utility of the model, and using it for the estimation of the mean value of y for given values of the independent variables. We also use the model to predict some particular value of y to be observed in the future.

Contents

11.1
A Multiple
Regression
Analysis: The
Model and the
Procedure

Most practical applications of regression use models that are more complex than the first-order (straight-line) model. For example, a realistic probabilistic model for monthly sales revenue would include more than just the advertising expenditure discussed in Chapter 10 in order to provide a good predictive model for sales. Factors such as season, inventory on hand, sales force, and price are a few of the many variables that might influence sales. Thus, we would want to incorporate these and other potentially important independent variables into the model if we need to make accurate predictions.

Probabilistic models that include terms involving x^2, x^3 (or higher-order terms), or more than one independent variable are called *multiple regression models.* The general form of these models is

$$y = \beta_0 + \beta_1 x_1 + \beta_2 x_2 + \cdots + \beta_k x_k + \varepsilon$$

The dependent variable, y, is now written as a function of k independent variables, x_1, x_2, . . . , x_k. The random error term is added to make the model probabilistic rather than deterministic. The value of the coefficient β_i determines the contribution of the independent variable x_i, given that the other x variables are held constant, and β_0 is the y-intercept. The coefficients β_0, β_1, . . . , β_k will usually be unknown, because they represent population parameters.

At first glance it might appear that the regression model shown above would not allow for anything other than straight-line relationships between y and the independent variables, but this is not true. Actually, x_1, x_2, . . . , x_k can be functions of variables as long as the functions do not contain unknown parameters. For example, the dollar sales, y, of new housing in a region could be a function of the independent variables

x_1 = Mortgage interest rate

x_2 = (Mortgage interest rate)^2 = x_1^2

x_3 = Unemployment rate in the region

and so on. You could even insert a cyclical term (if it would be useful) of the form $x_4 = \sin t$, where t is a time variable. The multiple regression model is quite versatile and can be made to model many different types of response variables.

The same steps we followed in developing a straight-line model are applicable to the multiple regression model.

Step 1 Hypothesize the form of the model. This involves the choice of the independent variables to be included in the model.

Step 2 Estimate the unknown parameters β_0, β_1, . . . , β_k.

Step 3 Specify the probability distribution of the random error component ε and estimate its variance, σ^2.

Step 4 Check the utility of the model.

Step 5 Use the fitted model to estimate the mean value of y or to predict a particular value of y for given values of the independent variables.

The initial step—hypothesizing the form of the model—is the subject of Chapter 12. In this chapter we assume that the form of the model is known, and we will discuss steps 2–5 for a given model.

Case Study 11.1
Predicting Corporate Executive Compensation

Towers, Perrin, Forster & Crosby (TPF&C), an international management consulting firm, has developed a unique and interesting application of multiple regression analysis. Many firms are interested in evaluating their management salary structure, and TPF&C uses multiple regression models to accomplish this salary evaluation. The Compensation Management Service, as TPF&C calls it, measures both the internal and external consistency of a company's pay policies to determine whether they reflect management's intent.

The dependent variable, y, used to represent executive compensation is annual salary. The independent variables used to explain salary structure include the executive's age, education, rank, and bonus eligibility; number of employees under the executive's direct supervision; as well as variables that describe the company for which the executive works, such as annual sales, profit, and total assets.

The initial step in developing models for executive compensation is to obtain a sample of executives from various client firms, which TPF&C calls the Compensation Data Bank. The data for these executives are used to estimate the model coefficients (the β parameters), and these estimates are then substituted into the linear model to form a prediction equation. To predict a particular executive's compensation, TPF&C substitutes into the prediction equation the values of the independent variables that pertain to the executive (the executive's age, rank, etc.). This application of multiple regression analysis is developed more fully in Section 11.8.

11.2 Model Assumptions

We noted in Section 11.1 that the multiple regression model is of the form

$$y = \beta_0 + \beta_1 x_1 + \beta_2 x_2 + \cdots + \beta_k x_k + \varepsilon$$

where y is the response variable that you wish to predict; $\beta_0, \beta_1, \ldots, \beta_k$ are parameters with unknown values; $x_1, x_2, \ldots, x_k$ are information-contributing variables that are measured without error; and ε is a random error component. Since $\beta_0, \beta_1, \ldots, \beta_k$ and $x_1, x_2, \ldots, x_k$ are nonrandom, the quantity

$$\beta_0 + \beta_1 x_1 + \beta_2 x_2 + \cdots + \beta_k x_k$$

represents the deterministic portion of the model. Therefore, y is composed of two components—one fixed and one random—and, consequently, y is a random variable.

$$y = \underbrace{\beta_0 + \beta_1 x_1 + \cdots + \beta_k x_k}_{\substack{\text{Deterministic} \\ \text{portion of model}}} + \underbrace{\varepsilon}_{\substack{\text{Random} \\ \text{error}}}$$

We will assume (as in Chapter 10) that the random error can be positive or negative and that for any setting of the x values, $x_1, x_2, \ldots, x_k$, the random error ε has a normal probability distribution with mean equal to zero and variance equal to σ^2. Further, we assume that the random errors associated with any (and every) pair of y values are probabilistically independent. That is, the error, ε, associated with any one y value is independent of the error associated with any other y value. These assumptions are summarized as follows:

Assumptions for Random Error ε

1. For any given set of values of $x_1, x_2, \ldots, x_k$, the random error ε has a normal probability distribution with mean equal to zero and variance equal to σ^2.

2. The random errors are independent (in a probabilistic sense).

The assumptions that we have described for a multiple regression model imply that the mean value, $E(y)$, for a given set of values of $x_1, x_2, \ldots, x_k$ is equal to

$$E(y) = \beta_0 + \beta_1 x_1 + \beta_2 x_2 + \cdots + \beta_k x_k$$

Models of this type are called *linear* statistical models because $E(y)$ is a *linear function* of the unknown parameters $\beta_0, \beta_1, \ldots, \beta_k$.

All the estimation and statistical test procedures described in this chapter depend on the data satisfying the assumptions described in this section. Since we will rarely, if ever, know for certain whether this occurs, we will want to know how well a regression analysis works and how much faith we can place in our inferences when certain assumptions are not satisfied. We will have more to say on this topic after we discuss the methods of a regression analysis more thoroughly and have shown how they are used in a practical situation.

11.3 Fitting the Model: The Method of Least Squares

The method of fitting multiple regression models is identical to that of fitting the first-order (straight-line) model — namely, the method of least squares. That is, we choose the estimated model

$$\hat{y} = \hat{\beta}_0 + \hat{\beta}_1 x_1 + \cdots + \hat{\beta}_k x_k$$

that minimizes

$$\text{SSE} = \sum (y_i - \hat{y}_i)^2$$

As in the case of the straight-line model, the sample estimates $\hat{\beta}_0, \hat{\beta}_1, \ldots, \hat{\beta}_k$ will be obtained as solutions to a set of simultaneous linear equations.*

The primary difference between fitting the simple and multiple regression models is computational difficulty. The $(k + 1)$ simultaneous linear equations that must be solved to find the $(k + 1)$ estimated coefficients $\hat{\beta}_0, \hat{\beta}_1, \ldots, \hat{\beta}_k$ are often difficult (sometimes impossible) to solve with a pocket or desk calculator. Consequently, we resort to the use of computers.

---

* Students who are familiar with calculus should note that $\hat{\beta}_0, \hat{\beta}_1, \ldots, \hat{\beta}_k$ are the solutions to the set of equations $\partial\text{SSE}/\partial\hat{\beta}_0 = 0$, $\partial\text{SSE}/\partial\hat{\beta}_1 = 0$, $\ldots$, $\partial\text{SSE}/\partial\hat{\beta}_k = 0$. The solution, given in matrix notation, is presented in Mendenhall and McClave (1981) as well as other texts listed in the references at the end of the chapter.

Many computer packages have been developed to fit a multiple regression model by the method of least squares. We will present output from several of the more popular computer packages, commencing, in our first example, with the computer output from the SAS System.* Since the SAS regression output is similar to that of most other package regression programs, you should have little trouble interpreting regression output from other packages as you encounter them in future examples and exercises, at your computer center, or in using a microcomputer.

To illustrate, suppose we theorize that monthly electrical usage, y, in all-electric homes is related to the size, x, of the home by the model $y = \beta_0 + \beta_1 x + \beta_2 x^2 + \varepsilon$. To estimate the unknown parameters β_0, β_1, and β_2, values of y and x were collected for each of ten homes during a particular month. The data are shown in Table 11.1.

Table 11.1

SIZE OF HOME x (square feet)	MONTHLY USAGE y (kilowatt-hours)	SIZE OF HOME x (square feet)	MONTHLY USAGE y (kilowatt-hours)
1,290	1,182	1,840	1,711
1,350	1,172	1,980	1,804
1,470	1,264	2,230	1,840
1,600	1,493	2,400	1,956
1,710	1,571	2,930	1,954

Notice that we include a term involving x^2 in the model above because we expect curvature in the graph of the response model relating y to x. The term involving x^2 is called a **second-order,** or **quadratic,** term. Figure 11.1 illustrates that the electrical usage appears to increase in a curvilinear manner with the size of the home. This provides some support for the inclusion of the second-order term, x^2, in the model.

Figure 11.1 Scatter-gram of the Home Size–Electrical Usage Data

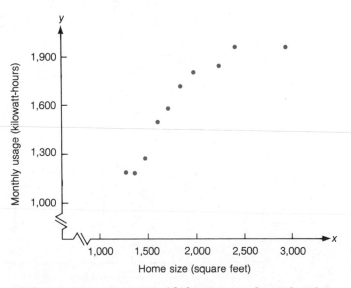

Home size (square feet)

* SAS is the registered trademark of SAS Institute Inc., Cary, N.C., U.S.A.

Figure 11.2 SAS Computer Printout for the Home Size–Electrical Usage Data

SOURCE	DF	SUM OF SQUARES	MEAN SQUARE	F VALUE	PR > F
MODEL	2	831069.54637065	415534.77318533	189.71	0.0001
ERROR	7	15332.55362935	2190.36480419		ROOT MSE
CORRECTED TOTAL	9	846402.10000000		R-SQUARE	46.8013333
				0.981885	

PARAMETER	ESTIMATE	T FOR H0: PARAMETER = 0	PR > |T|	STD ERROR OF ESTIMATE
INTERCEPT	-1216.14388700	-5.01	0.0016	242.80636850
X	2.39893018	9.76	0.0001	0.24583560
X*X	-0.00045004	-7.62	0.0001	0.00005908

Part of the output from the SAS multiple regression routine for the data in Table 11.1 is reproduced in Figure 11.2. The least squares estimates of the β parameters appear in the column labeled ESTIMATE. You can see that $\hat{\beta}_0 = -1,216.1$, $\hat{\beta}_1 = 2.3989$, and $\hat{\beta}_2 = -.00045$. Therefore, the equation that minimizes the SSE for the data is

$$\hat{y} = -1,216.1 + 2.3989x - .00045x^2$$

The minimum value of SSE, 15,332.6, also appears in the printout. [*Note:* Much detail on the printout has not yet been discussed. We will continue throughout this chapter to shade the aspects of the printout that are under discussion.]

Note that the graph of the multiple regression model (Figure 11.3, a response curve) provides a good fit to the data of Table 11.1. Furthermore, the small value of $\hat{\beta}_2$ does *not* imply that the curvature is insignificant, since the numerical value of $\hat{\beta}_2$ is dependent on the scale of the measurements. We will test the contribution of the second-order coefficient β_2 in Section 11.5.

Figure 11.3 Least Squares Model for the Home Size–Electrical Usage Data

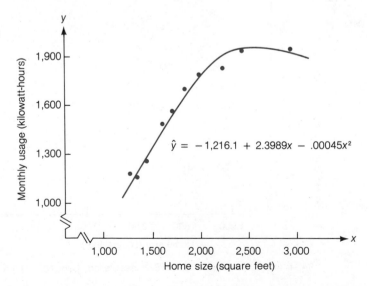

$$\hat{y} = -1,216.1 + 2.3989x - .00045x^2$$

The ultimate goal of this multiple regression analysis is to use the fitted model to predict electrical usage, y, for a home of a specific size (area), x. And, of course, we will want to give a prediction interval for y so we will know how much faith we can place in the prediction. That is, if the prediction model is used to predict electrical usage, y, for a given size of home, x, what will be the error of prediction? To answer this question, we need to estimate σ^2, the variance of ε.

11.4 Estimation of σ^2, the Variance of ε

You will recall that σ^2 is the variance of the random error, ε. If $\sigma^2 = 0$, all the random errors will equal zero and the predicted values, $\hat{y}$, will be identical to $E(y)$; that is, $E(y)$ will be estimated without error. In contrast, a large value of σ^2 implies large (absolute) values of ε and larger deviations between the predicted values, $\hat{y}$, and the mean value, $E(y)$. Consequently, the larger the value of σ^2, the greater will be the error in estimating the model parameters β_0, $\beta_1, \ldots, \beta_k$ and the error in predicting a value of y for a specific set of values of x_1, $x_2, \ldots, x_k$. Thus, σ^2 plays a major role in making inferences about $\beta_0, \beta_1, \ldots, \beta_k$, in estimating $E(y)$, and in predicting y for specific values of $x_1, x_2, \ldots, x_k$.

Since the variance, σ^2, of the random error, ε, will rarely be known, we must use the results of the regression analysis to estimate its value. You will recall that σ^2 is the variance of the probability distribution of the random error, ε, for a given set of values for $x_1, x_2, \ldots, x_k$, and hence that it is the mean value of the squares of the deviations of the y values (for given values of $x_1, x_2, \ldots, x_k$) about the mean value $E(y)$.* Since the predicted value, $\hat{y}$, estimates $E(y)$ for each of the data points, it seems natural to use

$$SSE = \sum (y_i - \hat{y}_i)^2$$

to construct an estimator of σ^2.

For example, in the second-order model describing electrical usage as a function of home size, we found that $SSE = 15{,}332.6$. We now want to use this quantity to estimate the variance of ε. Recall that the estimator for the straight-line model was $s^2 = SSE/(n - 2)$ and note that the denominator is ($n -$ Number of estimated β parameters), which is ($n - 2$) in the first-order (straight-line) model. Since we must estimate one more parameter, β_2, for the second-order model, the estimator of σ^2 is

$$s^2 = \frac{SSE}{n - 3}$$

That is, the denominator becomes ($n - 3$) because there are now three β parameters in the model. The numerical estimate for this example is

$$s^2 = \frac{SSE}{10 - 3} = \frac{15{,}332.6}{7} = 2{,}190.36$$

---

* Remember, we stated in Section 11.2 that $y = E(y) + \varepsilon$. Therefore, ε is equal to the deviation $y - E(y)$. Also, by definition, the variance of a random variable is the expected value of the square of the deviation of the random variable from its mean. According to our model, $E(\varepsilon) = 0$. Therefore, $\sigma^2 = E(\varepsilon^2)$.

In many computer printouts and textbooks, s^2 is called the *mean square for error (MSE)*. This estimate of σ^2 is shown in the column titled MEAN SQUARE in the SAS printout in Figure 11.2.

For the general multiple regression model

$$y = \beta_0 + \beta_1 x_1 + \beta_2 x_2 + \cdots + \beta_k x_k + \varepsilon$$

we must estimate the $(k + 1)$ parameters $\beta_0, \beta_1, \beta_2, \ldots, \beta_k$. Thus, the estimator of σ^2 is SSE divided by the quantity $(n - \text{Number of estimated } \beta \text{ parameters})$.

We will use the estimator of σ^2 both to check the utility of the model (Sections 11.5 and 11.6) and to provide a measure of reliability of predictions and estimates when the model is used for those purposes (Section 11.7). Thus, you can see that the estimation of σ^2 plays an important part in the development of a regression model.

Estimator of σ^2 for Multiple Regression Model with k Independent Variables

$$\text{MSE} = \frac{\text{SSE}}{n - \text{Number of estimated } \beta \text{ parameters}}$$

$$= \frac{\text{SSE}}{n - (k + 1)}$$

11.5 Estimating and Testing Hypotheses about the β Parameters

Sometimes the individual β parameters in a model have particular practical significance, and we want to estimate their values or test hypotheses about them. For example, if electrical usage, y, is related to home size, x, by the straight-line relationship

$$y = \beta_0 + \beta_1 x_1 + \varepsilon$$

then β_1 has a very practical interpretation. That is, you saw in Chapter 10 that β_1 is the mean increase in kilowatt-hours of electrical usage, y, for a square foot increase in home size, x.

As proposed in the preceding sections, suppose that the electrical usage, y, is related to home size, x, by the quadratic model

$$y = \beta_0 + \beta_1 x + \beta_2 x^2 + \varepsilon$$

Then the mean value of y for a given value of x is

$$E(y) = \beta_0 + \beta_1 x + \beta_2 x^2$$

What is the practical interpretation of β_2? As noted earlier, the parameter β_2 measures the curvature of the response curve shown in Figure 11.3. If $\beta_2 > 0$, the slope of the curve will increase as x increases, as shown in Figure 11.4(a). If $\beta_2 < 0$, the slope of the curve will decrease as x increases, as shown in Figure 11.4(b).

Figure 11.4 The Interpretation of β_2 for a Second-Order Model

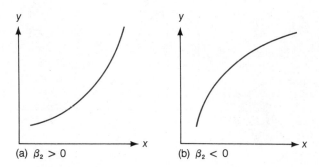

(a) $\beta_2 > 0$ (b) $\beta_2 < 0$

Intuitively, we would expect the electrical usage, y, to rise almost proportionally to home size, x. Then, eventually, as the size of the home increases, the increase in electrical usage for a 1-unit increase in home size might begin to decrease. Thus, a forecaster of electrical usage would want to determine whether this type of curvature actually was present in the response curve, or, equivalently, the forecaster would want to test the null hypothesis

$$H_0: \beta_2 = 0 \qquad \text{(No curvature in the response curve)}$$

against the alternative hypothesis

$$H_a: \beta_2 < 0 \qquad \text{(Downward curvature exists in the response curve)}$$

A test of this hypothesis can be performed using a Student's t test.

The t test utilizes a test statistic analogous to that used to make inferences about the slope of the straight-line model (Section 10.5). The t statistic is formed by dividing the sample estimate, $\hat{\beta}_2$, of the parameter, β_2, by the estimated standard deviation of the sampling distribution of $\hat{\beta}_2$:

$$\text{Test statistic:} \quad t = \frac{\hat{\beta}_2}{s_{\hat{\beta}_2}}$$

We use the symbol $s_{\hat{\beta}_2}$ to represent the estimated standard deviation of $\hat{\beta}_2$. The formula for computing $s_{\hat{\beta}_2}$ is very complex, but its computation is performed automatically as part of most standard multiple regression computer analyses. Thus, most computer packages list the estimated standard deviation $s_{\hat{\beta}_i}$ for each estimated model coefficient $\hat{\beta}_i$. In addition, they usually give the calculated t values for testing $H_0: \beta_i = 0$ for each coefficient in the model.

The rejection region for the test is found in exactly the same way as the rejection regions for the t tests in Chapters 8 and 9. That is, we consult Table V in Appendix B to obtain an upper-tail value of t. This is a value, t_α, such that $P(t > t_\alpha) = \alpha$. We can then use this value to construct rejection regions for either one- or two-tailed tests. To illustrate, in the electrical usage example, the error degrees of freedom is $(n - 3) = 7$, the denominator of the estimate of σ^2. Then the rejection region for a one-tailed test with $\alpha = .05$ is

$$\text{Rejection region:} \quad t < -t_\alpha; \quad \alpha = .05, \quad \text{df} = 7$$

$$t < -1.895 \qquad \text{(see Figure 11.5 on the next page)}$$

Figure 11.5 Rejection Region for Test of β_2

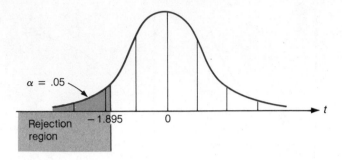

In Figure 11.6 we again show a portion of the SAS printout for the electrical usage example. The following quantities are shaded:

1. The estimated coefficients, $\hat{\beta}_0$, $\hat{\beta}_1$, and $\hat{\beta}_2$
2. The SSE
3. The MSE (estimate of σ^2, the variance of ε)

The estimated standard deviations for the estimated model coefficients appear under the column labeled STD ERROR OF ESTIMATE. The t statistics for testing the null hypotheses that the coefficients β_0, β_1, . . . , β_k individually equal zero appear under the column headed T FOR H0: PARAMETER = 0. The t value corresponding to the test of the null hypothesis H_0: $\beta_2 = 0$ is the last one in the column; i.e., $t = -7.62$. Since this value falls in the rejection region (i.e., it is less than -1.895), we conclude that the second-order term $\beta_2 x^2$ makes an important contribution to the prediction model of electrical usage.

Figure 11.6 SAS Output for the Home Size–Electrical Usage Data

SOURCE	DF	SUM OF SQUARES	MEAN SQUARE	F VALUE	PR > F
MODEL	2	831069.54637065	415534.77318533	189.71	0.0001
ERROR	7	15332.55362935	2190.36480419		ROOT MSE
CORRECTED TOTAL	9	846402.10000000		R-SQUARE	46.8013333
				0.981885	

PARAMETER	ESTIMATE	T FOR H0: PARAMETER = 0	PR > |T|	STD ERROR OF ESTIMATE
INTERCEPT	-1216.14388700	-5.01	0.0016	242.80636850
X	2.39893018	9.76	0.0001	0.24583560
X*X	-0.00045004	-7.62	0.0001	0.00005908

The SAS printout shown in Figure 11.6 also lists the two-tailed observed significance levels (or p-values) for each t value. These values appear under the column headed PR > |T|. The observed significance level .0001 corresponds to the quadratic term, and this implies that we would reject H_0: $\beta_2 = 0$ in favor of H_a: $\beta_2 \neq 0$ at any α level larger than .0001. Since our alternative hypothesis was one-sided, H_a: $\beta_2 < 0$, the observed significance level is half that given in the printout; i.e., $\frac{1}{2}(.0001) = .00005$. Thus, there is very strong evidence that the mean electrical usage increases more slowly per square foot for large houses than for small houses.

We can also form a 95% confidence interval for the parameter β_2 as follows:

$$\hat{\beta}_2 \pm t_{\alpha/2} s_{\hat{\beta}_2} = -.000450 \pm (2.365)(.0000591)$$

or $(-.000590, -.000310)$. Note that the t value 2.365 corresponds to $\alpha/2 = .025$ and $(n - 3) = 7$ df. This interval constitutes a 95% confidence interval for β_2, the rate of change in curvature in mean electrical usage as home size is increased. Note that all values in the interval are negative, providing strong support for the conclusion of our test.

Testing an hypothesis about a single β parameter that appears in any multiple regression model is accomplished in exactly the same manner as described for the second-order electrical usage model. The form of the t test is shown in the box.

Test of an Individual Parameter Coefficient in the Multiple Regression Model

$$y = \beta_0 + \beta_1 x_1 + \beta_2 x_2 + \cdots + \beta_k x_k + \varepsilon$$

One-Tailed Test

$H_0: \beta_i = 0$*

$H_a: \beta_i > 0$
   (or $\beta_i < 0$)

Test statistic: $t = \dfrac{\hat{\beta}_i}{s_{\hat{\beta}_i}}$

Rejection region: $t > t_\alpha$
   (or $t < -t_\alpha$)

Two-Tailed Test

$H_0: \beta_i = 0$*

$H_a: \beta_i \neq 0$

Test statistic: $t = \dfrac{\hat{\beta}_i}{s_{\hat{\beta}_i}}$

Rejection region: $t > t_{\alpha/2}$
   or $t < -t_{\alpha/2}$

where

  n = Number of observations

  k = Number of independent variables in the model

and $t_{\alpha/2}$ is based on $[n - (k + 1)]$ df.

Assumptions: See Section 11.2 for the assumptions about the probability distribution of the random error component ε.

Example 11.1

A collector of antique grandfather clocks believes that the price received for the clocks at an antique auction increases with the age of the clocks and with the number of bidders. Thus, the following model is hypothesized:

$$y = \beta_0 + \beta_1 x_1 + \beta_2 x_2 + \varepsilon$$

---

* To test the null hypothesis that a parameter, β_i, equals some value other than zero, say $H_0: \beta_i = \beta_{i0}$, use the test statistic $t = (\hat{\beta}_i - \beta_{i0})/s_{\hat{\beta}_i}$. All other aspects of the test will be as described in the box.

where

y = Auction price

x_1 = Age of clock (years) x_2 = Number of bidders

A sample of thirty-two auction prices of grandfather clocks, along with their age and the number of bidders, is given in Table 11.2. The model $y = \beta_0 + \beta_1 x_1 + \beta_2 x_2 + \varepsilon$ is fit to the data, and a portion of the SAS printout is shown in Figure 11.7. Test the hypothesis that the auction price increases as the number of bidders increases (and age is held constant), i.e., $\beta_2 > 0$. Use $\alpha = .05$.

Table 11.2
Auction Price Data

AGE x_1	NUMBER OF BIDDERS x_2	AUCTION PRICE y	AGE x_1	NUMBER OF BIDDERS x_2	AUCTION PRICE y
127	13	$1,235	170	14	$2,131
115	12	1,080	182	8	1,550
127	7	845	162	11	1,884
150	9	1,522	184	10	2,041
156	6	1,047	143	6	854
182	11	1,979	159	9	1,483
156	12	1,822	108	14	1,055
132	10	1,253	175	8	1,545
137	9	1,297	108	6	729
113	9	946	179	9	1,792
137	15	1,713	111	15	1,175
117	11	1,024	187	8	1,593
137	8	1,147	111	7	785
153	6	1,092	115	7	744
117	13	1,152	194	5	1,356
126	10	1,336	168	7	1,262

Figure 11.7 SAS Printout for Example 11.1

SOURCE	DF	SUM OF SQUARES	MEAN SQUARE	F VALUE	PR > F
MODEL	2	4277159.70340504	2138579.85170252	120.65	0.0001
ERROR	29	514034.51534496	17725.32811534		ROOT MSE
CORRECTED TOTAL	31	4791194.21875000	R-SQUARE		133.13650181
			0.892713		

PARAMETER	ESTIMATE	T FOR H0: PARAMETER = 0	PR > |T|	STD ERROR OF ESTIMATE
INTERCEPT	-1336.72205214	-7.71	0.0001	173.35612607
X1	12.73619884	14.11	0.0001	0.90238049
X2	85.81513260	9.86	0.0001	8.70575681

Solution The hypothesis of interest concerns the parameter β_2. Specifically,

$H_0: \beta_2 = 0 \qquad H_a: \beta_2 > 0$

Test statistic: $\quad t = \dfrac{\hat{\beta}_2}{s_{\hat{\beta}_2}}$

Rejection region: For $\alpha = .05$, $t > t_{.05}$

where df $= n - (k + 1) = 32 - 3 = 29$

or $t > 1.699$ (see Figure 11.8)

Figure 11.8 Rejection Region for $H_0: \beta_2 = 0$

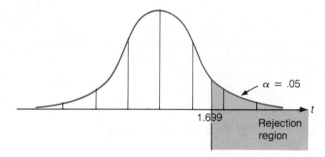

The calculated t value, $t = 9.86$, is indicated in Figure 11.7. This value exceeds 1.699 and therefore falls in the rejection region. Thus, the collector can conclude that the mean auction price of the clocks increases as the number of bidders increases, when age is held constant.

Note that the values $\hat{\beta}_1 = 12.74$ and $\hat{\beta}_2 = 85.82$ (shaded in Figure 11.7) are easily interpreted. We estimate that the mean auction price increases \$12.74 per year of age of the clock, and the mean price increases by \$85.82 per additional bidder. ∎

Be careful not to try to interpret the estimated intercept $\hat{\beta}_0 = -1,336.72$ in the same way as we interpreted $\hat{\beta}_1$ and $\hat{\beta}_2$. You might think that this implies a negative price for clocks 0 years of age with 0 bidders. However, these zeros are meaningless numbers in this example, since the ages range from 108 to 194 and the number of bidders ranges from 5 to 15. Keep in mind that we are modeling y within the range of values observed for the predictor variables and that interpretations of the models for values of the independent variables outside their sampled ranges can be very misleading.

Some computer programs use an F test to test hypotheses concerning the individual β parameters. If you conduct a two-tailed t test and reject the hypothesis if $t > t_{\alpha/2}$ or $t < -t_{\alpha/2}$, then the corresponding F test will imply rejection if the computed value of F (which is equal to the square of the computed t statistic) is larger than F_α, because the square of the Student's t with ν degrees of freedom is equal to an F statistic with 1 df in the numerator and ν df in the denominator. Thus, $t_{\alpha/2}^2 = F_\alpha$, where t is based on ν df and F has 1 numerator and ν denominator degrees of freedom, respectively. As an example, when we tested the curvature parameter β_2 in the second-order model relating electrical usage to home size, the computed t value was -7.62 (see Figure 11.6). The equivalent F statistic yields

$$F = t^2 = (-7.62)^2 = 58.06$$

Suppose we wanted to conduct a two-tailed statistical test of $H_0: \beta_2 = 0$ against $H_a: \beta_2 \neq 0$. The upper-tail rejection region for a two-tailed test with $\alpha = .05$ is

$$F > F_{.05} \qquad \text{where } F_{.05} \text{ is based on } v_1 = 1 \text{ df, } v_2 = 7 \text{ df}$$

or

$$F > 5.59$$

Note that the F value, 5.59, is equal to the square of 2.365, the value of t that corresponds to $t_{.025}$ with 7 df. In other words, you can conduct a two-tailed test of the null hypothesis $H_0: \beta_i = 0$ using either a two-tailed t test or a one-tailed F test. If you want to conduct a one-tailed test to detect $H_a: \beta_i > 0$ (or $H_a: \beta_i < 0$), the F test is not appropriate. You will have to conduct the test using a t statistic.

Exercises 11.1–11.9

Learning the Mechanics

11.1 Suppose you fit the multiple regression model

$$y = \beta_0 + \beta_1 x_1 + \beta_2 x_2 + \beta_3 x_3 + \varepsilon$$

to $n = 30$ data points and obtained the following result:

$$\hat{y} = 3.4 - 4.6x_1 + 2.7x_2 + .93x_3$$

The estimated standard errors of $\hat{\beta}_2$ and $\hat{\beta}_3$ are 1.86 and .29, respectively.

a. Test the null hypothesis $H_0: \beta_2 = 0$ against the alternative hypothesis $H_a: \beta_2 \neq 0$. Use $\alpha = .05$.

b. Test the null hypothesis $H_0: \beta_3 = 0$ against the alternative hypothesis $H_a: \beta_3 \neq 0$. Use $\alpha = .05$.

c. The null hypothesis $H_0: \beta_2 = 0$ is not rejected. In contrast, the null hypothesis $H_0: \beta_3 = 0$ is rejected. Explain how this can happen even though $\hat{\beta}_2 > \hat{\beta}_3$.

11.2 Suppose you fit the second-order model,

$$y = \beta_0 + \beta_1 x + \beta_2 x^2 + \varepsilon$$

to $n = 25$ data points. Your estimate of β_2 is $\hat{\beta}_2 = .47$, and the estimated standard error of the estimate is $s_{\hat{\beta}_2} = .15$.

a. Test the null hypothesis that the mean value of y is related to x by the (*first-order*) linear model

$$E(y) = \beta_0 + \beta_1 x$$

($H_0: \beta_2 = 0$) against the alternative hypothesis that the true relationship is given by the quadratic model (a *second-order* linear model),

$$E(y) = \beta_0 + \beta_1 x + \beta_2 x^2$$
$$(H_a: \beta_2 \neq 0). \text{ Use } \alpha = .05.$$

b. Suppose you wanted to determine only whether the quadratic curve opens upward; i.e., as x increases, the slope of the curve increases. Give the test statistic and the rejection region for the test for $\alpha = .05$. Do the data support the theory that the slope of the curve increases as x increases? Explain.

c. What is the value of the F statistic for testing the null hypothesis $H_0: \beta_2 = 0$ against H_a: $\beta_2 \neq 0$?

d. Could the F statistic in part c be used to conduct the test in part b? Explain.

11.3 How is the number of degrees of freedom available for estimating σ^2, the variance of ε, related to the number of variables in a regression model?

Applying the Concepts

11.4 Economists have two major types of data available to them: *time series data* and *cross-sectional data*. For example, an economist estimating a consumption function, say, household food consumption as a function of household income and household size, might measure the variables of interest for a particular sample of households at a particular point in time. In this case, the economist is using *cross-sectional data*. If instead, the economist is interested in how total consumption in the United States is related to national income, the economist probably would track these variables over time. In this case, the economist is using *time series data* (Wonnacott & Wonnacott, 1979). The cross-sectional data in the table have been collected for a random sample of twenty-five households in Washington, D.C.

HOUSEHOLD	FOOD CONSUMPTION DURING 1984 ($ thousands)	1984 HOUSEHOLD INCOME ($ thousands)	NUMBER OF PERSONS IN HOUSEHOLD AT END OF 1984	HOUSEHOLD	FOOD CONSUMPTION DURING 1984 ($ thousands)	1984 HOUSEHOLD INCOME ($ thousands)	NUMBER OF PERSONS IN HOUSEHOLD AT END OF 1984
1	3.2	31.1	4	14	3.1	85.2	2
2	2.4	20.5	2	15	4.5	35.6	9
3	3.8	42.3	4	16	3.5	68.5	3
4	1.9	18.9	1	17	4.0	10.5	5
5	2.5	26.5	2	18	3.5	21.6	4
6	3.0	29.8	4	19	1.8	29.9	1
7	2.6	24.3	3	20	2.9	28.6	3
8	3.2	38.1	4	21	2.6	20.2	2
9	3.9	52.0	5	22	3.6	38.7	5
10	1.7	16.0	1	23	2.8	11.2	3
11	2.9	41.9	3	24	4.5	14.3	7
12	1.7	9.9	1	25	3.5	16.9	5
13	4.5	33.1	7				

a. It has been hypothesized that household food consumption, y, is related to household income, x_1, and to the size of the household, x_2, as follows:

$$y = \beta_0 + \beta_1 x_1 + \beta_2 x_2 + \varepsilon$$

The SAS computer printout for fitting the model to the data is shown here. Give the least squares prediction equation.

SAS Printout for Exercise 11.4

```
DEPENDENT VARIABLE: FOOD

SOURCE                      DF    SUM OF SQUARES    MEAN SQUARE    F VALUE
MODEL                        2      15.46228509     7.73114255     100.80
ERROR                       22       1.68731491     0.07669613
CORRECTED TOTAL             24      17.14960000                    PR > F

                                                                   0.0001
R-SQUARE              C.V.            ROOT MSE       FOOD MEAN

0.901612             8.9221          0.27694067      3.10400000

                     T FOR HO:     PR > !T!    STD ERROR OF
PARAMETER    ESTIMATE    PARAMETER=0              ESTIMATE

INTERCEPT    1.43260377      9.76      0.0001     0.14673751
INCOME       0.00999062      3.15      0.0046     0.00316806
SIZE         0.37928986     13.68      0.0001     0.02772472
```

b. Do the data provide sufficient evidence to conclude that food consumption increases with household income? Test using $\alpha = .01$.

c. As a check on your conclusion of part b, construct a scattergram of household food consumption versus household income. Does the plot support your conclusion in part b? Explain.

d. In Chapter 10, we used the method of least squares to fit a straight line to a set of data points that were plotted in two dimensions. In this exercise, we are fitting a plane to a set of points plotted in three dimensions. We are attempting to determine the plane, $\hat{y} = \hat{\beta}_0 + \hat{\beta}_1 x_1 + \hat{\beta}_2 x_2$, that, according to the principle of least squares, best fits the data points. Sketch the least squares plane you developed in part a. Be sure to label all three axes of your graph.

e. Find the value of MSE for the least squares model. Explain what it is used for.

11.5 Henry and Haynes (1978) report that in the middle 1970's Data Resources, Inc. (DRI), a firm that supplies economic information analyses and advice to government, industry, and financial institutions, used multiple regression to develop a model that characterized a particular bank's demand for mortgage loans. Working with quarterly time series data on the variables described here, DRI obtained the following least squares model:

$$\hat{y} = 37,350.40 + 0.61x_1 - 155.74x_2 + 19,934.7x_3 - 5,354.9x_4 + 5,317.61x_5$$
$$(3.5) \qquad (5.5) \qquad (-2.8) \qquad (4.5) \qquad (-3.9) \qquad (2.7)$$

where

y = Mortgage loan demand (in dollars)

x_1 = Seasonally adjusted mortgage loans outstanding during previous period

x_2 = Deposits at mutual savings banks and savings and loan associations

x_3 = Average number of housing starts per month

x_4 = State's rate of unemployment

x_5 = Conventional mortgage loan interest rate

The numbers in parentheses are the t statistics associated with the estimates of the model coefficients above them. Assume $n = 28$. The above model, along with one for the demand for commercial loans and another for the demand for installment loans, became the heart of the bank's loan-demand forecasting system.

a. Find the estimated standard deviation of $\hat{\beta}_2$.

b. Prior to fitting the model, DRI hypothesized that β_2 should be negative because x_2 represents an alternative source of mortgage money available to the consumer. Do the data support this hypothesis? Test using $\alpha = .01$. State your conclusion in the context of the problem.

c. Report the approximate p-value of your test.

d. Provide an economic explanation for why it is reasonable to expect β_4 to be negative.

11.6 To run a manufacturing operation efficiently, it is necessary to know how long it takes employees to manufacture the product. Without such information, the cost of making the product cannot be determined. Furthermore, management would not be able to establish an effective incentive plan for its employees because it would not know how to set work standards (Chase & Aquilano, 1979). Estimates of production time are frequently obtained using time studies. The data in the table were obtained from a recent time study of a sample of fifteen employees on an automobile assembly line.

TIME TO COMPLETE TASK y (minutes)	MONTHS OF EXPERIENCE x	TIME TO COMPLETE TASK y (minutes)	MONTHS OF EXPERIENCE x
10	24	17	3
20	1	18	1
15	10	16	7
11	15	16	9
11	17	17	7
19	3	18	5
11	20	10	20
13	9		

a. The SAS computer printout for fitting the model, $y = \beta_0 + \beta_1 x + \beta_2 x^2 + \varepsilon$, is shown at the top of the next page. Find the least squares prediction equation.

```
┌─────────────────────────────────────────────────────────────────────────┐
│ DEPENDENT VARIABLE: Y                                                     │
│                                                                           │
│ SOURCE                       DF    SUM OF SQUARES   MEAN SQUARE   F VALUE │
│ MODEL                         2     156.11947722    78.05973861     65.59 │
│ ERROR                        12      14.28052278     1.19004356    PR > F │
│ CORRECTED TOTAL              14     170.40000000                   0.0001 │
│                                                                           │
│ R-SQUARE              C.V.            ROOT MSE       Y MEAN              │
│ 0.916194            7.3709          1.09089118    14.80000000            │
│                                                                           │
│                          T FOR H0:   PR > !T!   STD ERROR OF            │
│ PARAMETER      ESTIMATE   PARAMETER=0              ESTIMATE              │
│ INTERCEPT   20.09110757      27.72     0.0001     0.72470507            │
│ X           -0.67052219      -4.33     0.0010     0.15470634            │
│ X*X          0.00953474       1.51     0.1576     0.00632580            │
└─────────────────────────────────────────────────────────────────────────┘
```

b. Plot the fitted equation on a scattergram of the data. Is there sufficient evidence to support the inclusion of the quadratic term in the model? Explain.

c. Test the null hypothesis that $\beta_2 = 0$ against the alternative that $\beta_2 \neq 0$. Use $\alpha = .01$. Does the quadratic term make an important contribution to the model?

d. Your conclusion in part c should have been to drop the quadratic term from the model. Do so and fit the "reduced model," $y = \beta_0 + \beta_1 x + \varepsilon$, to the data.

e. Define β_1 in the context of this exercise. Find a 90% confidence interval for β_1 in the reduced model of part d.

11.7 A researcher wished to investigate the effects of several factors on production line supervisors' attitudes toward handicapped workers. A study was conducted involving forty randomly selected supervisors. The response y, a supervisor's attitude toward handicapped workers, was measured with a standardized attitude scale. Independent variables used in the study were

$$x_1 = \begin{cases} 1 & \text{if the supervisor is female} \\ 0 & \text{if the supervisor is male} \end{cases}$$

$x_2 = $ Number of years of experience in a supervisory job

The researcher fit the model

$$y = \beta_0 + \beta_1 x_1 + \beta_2 x_2 + \beta_3 x_2^2 + \varepsilon$$

to the data with the following results:

$$\hat{y} = 50 + 5x_1 + 5x_2 - .1x_2^2 \qquad s_{\hat{\beta}_3} = .03$$

a. Is there sufficient evidence to indicate that the quadratic term in years of experience, x_2^2, is useful for predicting attitude score? Use $\alpha = .05$.

b. Sketch the predicted attitude score, $\hat{y}$, as a function of the number of years of experience, x_2, for male supervisors ($x_1 = 0$). Next, substitute x_1 into the least squares equation and thereby obtain a plot of the prediction equation for female supervisors. [*Note:* For both males and females, plotting $\hat{y}$ for $x_2 = 0, 2, 4, 6, 8,$ and 10 will produce a good picture of the prediction equations. The vertical distance between the males' and females' prediction curves is the same for all values of x_2.]

11.8 An employer has found that factory workers who are with the company longer tend to invest more in a company investment program per year than workers with less time in the company. The following model is believed to be adequate in modeling the relationship of annual amount invested, y, to years working for the company, x:

$$y = \beta_0 + \beta_1 x + \beta_2 x^2 + \varepsilon$$

The employer checks the records for a sample of fifty factory employees for a previous year, and fits the above model to get $\hat{\beta}_2 = .0015$ and $s_{\hat{\beta}_2} = .000712$. Test to determine whether the employer can conclude that $\beta_2 > 0$. Use $\alpha = .05$.

11.9 To project personnel needs for the Christmas shopping season, a department store wants to project sales for the season. The sales for the previous Christmas season are an indication of what to expect for the current season. However, the projection should also reflect the current economic environment by taking into consideration sales for a more recent period. The following model might be appropriate:

$$y = \beta_0 + \beta_1 x_1 + \beta_2 x_2 + \varepsilon$$

where

$x_1 = $ Previous Christmas sales

$x_2 = $ Sales for August of current year

$y = $ Sales for upcoming Christmas

Data for 10 previous years were used to fit the prediction equation, and the following were calculated (all units are in thousands of dollars):

$$\hat{\beta}_1 = .62 \qquad s_{\hat{\beta}_1} = .273$$
$$\hat{\beta}_2 = .55 \qquad s_{\hat{\beta}_2} = .181$$

Use these results to determine whether there is evidence to indicate that August sales contribute information for predicting Christmas sales.

11.6
Checking the Utility of a Model: R^2 and the Analysis of Variance F Test

Conducting t tests on each β parameter in a model is not a good way to determine whether a model is contributing information for the prediction of y. If we were to conduct a series of t tests to determine whether the independent variables are contributing to the predictive relationship, it is very likely that we would make one or more errors in deciding which terms to retain in the model and which to exclude. For example, suppose that all the β parameters (except β_0) are in fact equal to zero. Although the probability of concluding that any *single* β parameter differs from zero is only α, the probability of rejecting *at least one* of a set of null hypotheses when each is true is much higher. You can see why this is true by considering the following analogy. The probability of observing a head on a single toss of a coin is .5, but the probability of observing *at least one* head in five tosses of a coin is .97. Thus, in multiple regression models for which a large number of independent variables are being considered, conducting a series of t tests may include a large number of insignificant variables and exclude some useful ones. If we want to test the utility of a multiple regression model, we will need a global test (one that encompasses all the β parameters). We would also like to find some statistical quantity that measures how well the model fits the data.

We commence with the easier problem — finding a measure of how well a linear model fits a set of data. For this we use the multiple regression equivalent of r^2, the coefficient of determination for the straight-line model (Chapter 10). Thus, we define the *sample multiple coefficient of determination, R^2*, as

$$R^2 = 1 - \frac{\sum (y_i - \hat{y}_i)^2}{\sum (y_i - \bar{y})^2} = 1 - \frac{SSE}{SS_{yy}}$$

where $\hat{y}_i$ is the predicted value of y_i for the model. Just as for the simple linear model, R^2 is a sample statistic that represents the fraction of the sample variation of the y values (measured by SS_{yy}) that is attributable to the regression model. Thus, $R^2 = 0$ implies a complete lack of fit of the model to the data, and $R^2 = 1$ implies a perfect fit, with the model passing through every sample data point. In general, the larger the value of R^2, the better the model fits the data.

To illustrate, the value $R^2 = .982$ for the electrical usage example is indicated in Figure 11.9. This very high value of R^2 implies that 98.2% of the sample variation in electrical usage is attributable to, or explained by, the independent variable (home size) x. Thus, R^2 is a sample statistic that tells how well the model fits the data, and thereby represents a measure of the utility of the model.

Figure 11.9   SAS Printout for Electrical Usage Example

```
SOURCE            DF     SUM OF SQUARES        MEAN SQUARE      F VALUE       PR > F
MODEL              2     831069.54637065   415534.77318533      189.71       0.0001

ERROR              7      15332.55362935     2190.36480419                 ROOT MSE
CORRECTED TOTAL    9     846402.10000000                      R-SQUARE    46.8013333
                                                              0.981885


                                  T FOR H0:     PR > !T!    STD ERROR OF
PARAMETER          ESTIMATE     PARAMETER = 0                ESTIMATE
INTERCEPT     -1216.14388700          -5.01      0.0016    242.80636850
X                2.39893018           9.76      0.0001      0.24583560
X*X             -0.00045004          -7.62      0.0001      0.00005908
```

The fact that R^2 is a sample statistic implies that it can be used to make inferences about the utility of the model for predicting y values for specific settings of the independent variables. In particular, for the electrical usage data, the test

H_0: $\beta_1 = \beta_2 = 0$

H_a: At least one of the parameters β_1 and β_2 is nonzero

would formally test the global utility of the model. The test statistic used to test this null hypothesis is

Test statistic: $F = \dfrac{R^2/k}{(1 - R^2)/[n - (k + 1)]}$

where n is the number of data points and k is the number of parameters in the model, not including β_0. Then, when H_0 is true, this F test statistic will have an F probability distribution with k df in the numerator and $[n - (k + 1)]$ df in the denominator. The upper-tail values of the F distribution are given in Tables VI, VII, VIII, and IX of Appendix B.

The F test statistic becomes large as the coefficient of determination R^2 becomes large. To determine how large F must be before we can conclude at a given value of α that the model is useful for predicting y, we set up the rejection region as follows:

Rejection region: $\quad F > F_\alpha \quad$ where $\quad v_1 = k$ df, $\quad v_2 = n - (k + 1)$ df

For the electrical usage example, $n = 10$, $k = 2$, $n - (k + 1) = 7$, and $\alpha = .05$. Consequently, we will reject H_0: $\beta_1 = \beta_2 = 0$ if

$$F > F_{.05} \quad \text{where} \quad v_1 = 2, \quad v_2 = 7$$

or

$$F > 4.74 \quad \text{(see Figure 11.10)}$$

From the computer printout (Figure 11.9), we find that the computed F is 189.71. Since this value greatly exceeds the tabulated value of 4.74, we conclude that at least one of the model coefficients β_1 and β_2 is nonzero. Therefore, this global F test indicates that the second-order model $y = \beta_0 + \beta_1 x + \beta_2 x^2 + \varepsilon$ is useful for predicting electrical usage.

Figure 11.10 Rejection Region for the F Statistic with $v_1 = 2$, $v_2 = 7$, and $\alpha = .05$

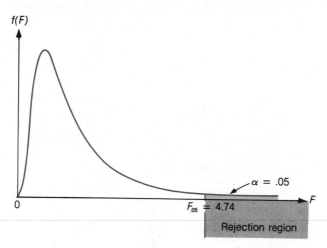

Example 11.2

Refer to Example 11.1, in which an antique collector modeled the auction price, y, of grandfather clocks as a function of the age of the clock, x_1, and the number of bidders, x_2. The hypothesized model was

$$y = \beta_0 + \beta_1 x_1 + \beta_2 x_2 + \varepsilon$$

A sample of thirty-two observations was obtained, with the results summarized in the SAS printout repeated in Figure 11.11. Discuss the coefficient of determination R^2 for this example and then conduct the global F test of model utility using $\alpha = .05$.

Figure 11.11 SAS Printout for Example 11.2

SOURCE	DF	SUM OF SQUARES	MEAN SQUARE	F VALUE	PR > F
MODEL	2	4277159.70340504	2138579.85170252	120.65	0.0001
ERROR	29	514034.51534496	17725.32811534		ROOT MSE
CORRECTED TOTAL	31	4791194.21875000	R-SQUARE 0.892713		133.13650181

PARAMETER	ESTIMATE	T FOR H0: PARAMETER = 0	PR > |T|	STD ERROR OF ESTIMATE
INTERCEPT	-1336.72205214	-7.71	0.0001	173.35612607
X1	12.73619884	14.11	0.0001	0.90238049
X2	85.81513260	9.86	0.0001	8.70575681

Solution The R^2 value is .89 (see Figure 11.11). This implies that 89% of the variation of the sample y values (the auction prices) about their mean can be explained by the least squares model. We now test:

H_0: $\beta_1 = \beta_2 = 0$ [*Note:* $k = 2$]

H_a: At least one of the two model coefficients is nonzero

Test statistic: $F = \dfrac{R^2/k}{(1 - R^2)/[n - (k + 1)]}$

Rejection region: $F > F_\alpha$ where $v_1 = k$ df, $v_2 = n - (k + 1)$ df

For this example, $n = 32$, $k = 2$, and $n - (k + 1) = 32 - 3 = 29$. Then, for $\alpha = .05$, we will reject H_0: $\beta_1 = \beta_2 = 0$ if $F > F_{.05}$ — i.e., if $F > 3.33$ (obtained from Table VII in Appendix B). The computed value of the F test statistic is 120.65 (see Figure 11.11). Since this value of F falls in the rejection region ($F = 120.65$ greatly exceeds $F_{.05} = 3.33$), the data provide strong evidence that at least one of the model coefficients is nonzero. The model appears to be useful for predicting auction prices. ■

Can we be sure that the best prediction model has been found if the global F test indicates that a model is useful? Unfortunately, we cannot. There is no way of knowing whether the addition of other independent variables will further improve the utility of the model, as Example 11.3 indicates.

Example 11.3 Refer to Examples 11.1 and 11.2. Suppose the collector, having observed many auctions, believes that the *rate of increase* of the auction price with age will be driven upward by a large number of bidders. Thus, instead of a relationship like that shown in Figure 11.12(a), in which the rate of increase in price with age is the same for any number of bidders, the collector believes the relationship is like that shown in Figure 11.12(b). Note that as the number of bidders increases from five to fifteen, the slope of the price versus age line increases. When the slope of the relationship between y and one independent variable (x_1) depends on the

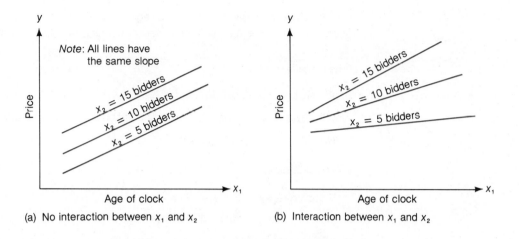

(a) No interaction between x_1 and x_2 (b) Interaction between x_1 and x_2

Figure 11.12 Examples of No Interaction and Interaction Models

value of a second independent variable (x_2), as is the case here, we say that x_1 and x_2 *interact.** A model that accounts for this type of interaction is written

$$y = \beta_0 + \beta_1 x_1 + \beta_2 x_2 + \beta_3 x_1 x_2 + \varepsilon$$

Note that the increase in the mean price, $E(y)$, for each 1-year increase in age, x_1, is no longer given by the constant β_1, but is now $\beta_1 + \beta_3 x_2$. That is, the amount $E(y)$ increases for each 1-unit increase in x_1 is *dependent on the number of bidders, x_2.* Thus, the two variables x_1 and x_2 interact to affect y.

The thirty-two data points listed in Table 11.2 were used to fit the first-order model with interaction. A portion of the SAS printout is shown in Figure 11.13.

Figure 11.13 Portion of the SAS Printout for the Model with Interaction

SOURCE	DF	SUM OF SQUARES	MEAN SQUARE	F VALUE	PR > F
MODEL	3	4572547.98717668	1524182.66239223	195.19	0.0001
ERROR	28	218646.23157332	7808.79398476		ROOT MSE
CORRECTED TOTAL	31	4791194.21875000		R-SQUARE	88.36738077
				0.954365	

PARAMETER	ESTIMATE	T FOR H0: PARAMETER = 0	PR > |T|	STD ERROR OF ESTIMATE
INTERCEPT	322.75435309	1.10	0.2806	293.32514660
X1	0.87328775	0.43	0.6688	2.01965115
X2	-93.40991991	-3.14	0.0039	29.70767946
X1*X2	1.29789828	6.15	0.0001	0.21102602

* Further discussion of interaction is given in Chapter 12.

Test the hypothesis that the price–age slope increases as the number of bidders increases — i.e., that age, x_1, and number of bidders, x_2, interact positively.

Solution   The model is

$$y = \beta_0 + \beta_1 x_1 + \beta_2 x_2 + \beta_3 x_1 x_2 + \varepsilon$$

and the hypothesis of interest to the collector concerns the parameter β_3. Specifically,

H_0: $\beta_3 = 0$ H_a: $\beta_3 > 0$

Test statistic: $t = \dfrac{\hat{\beta}_3}{s_{\hat{\beta}_3}}$

Rejection region: For $\alpha = .05$, $t > t_{.05}$

where df $= n - (k + 1)$

In this example, $n = 32$, $k = 3$, df $= n - (k + 1) = 32 - 4 = 28$, and thus, $t_{.05} = 1.701$.

The t value corresponding to $\hat{\beta}_3$ is indicated in Figure 11.13. The value, $t = 6.15$, exceeds 1.701, and therefore falls in the rejection region. Thus, the collector can conclude that the rate of change of the mean price of the clocks with age increases as the number of bidders increases — i.e., x_1 and x_2 interact positively. Thus, it appears that the interaction term should be included in the model.   ■

One note of caution: Although the coefficient of x_2 is negative ($\hat{\beta}_2 = -93.41$), this does *not* imply that the auction price decreases as the number of bidders increases. Since interaction is present, the rate of change (slope) of mean auction price with the number of bidders *depends on* x_1, the age of the clock. Thus, for example, the estimated rate of change of y with x_2 for a 150-year-old clock is

Estimated x_2 slope $= \hat{\beta}_2 + \hat{\beta}_3 x_1$
$$= -93.41 + 1.30(150) = 101.60$$

In other words, we estimate that the auction price of a 150-year-old clock will *increase* by $101.60 for every additional bidder. Although this rate of increase will vary as x_1 is changed, it will remain positive for the range of values of x_1 included in the sample. Extreme care is needed in interpreting the signs and sizes of coefficients in a multiple regression model.

To summarize the discussion in this section, the value of R^2 is an indicator of how well the prediction equation fits the data. More important, it can be used (in the F statistic) to determine whether the data provide sufficient evidence to indicate that the model contributes information for the prediction of y. Intuitive evaluations of the contribution of the model based on the computed value of R^2 must be examined with care. The value of R^2 will increase as more and more variables are added to the model. Consequently, you could force R^2 to take a value very close to 1 even though the model contributes no information for the prediction of y. In fact, R^2 will equal 1 when the number of terms in the model equals the number of data points. Therefore, you should not rely solely on the value of R^2 to tell you whether the model is useful for predicting y. Use the F test.

**Exercises
11.10–11.19**

Learning the Mechanics

11.10 Suppose you fit the model

$$y = \beta_0 + \beta_1 x_1 + \beta_2 x_2 + \beta_3 x_1 x_2 + \beta_4 x_1^2 + \beta_5 x_2^2 + \varepsilon$$

to $n = 30$ data points and you obtain

   SSE $= .42$ $R^2 = .91$

a. Do the values of SSE and R^2 suggest that the model provides a good fit to the data? Explain.

b. Is the model of any use in predicting y? Test the null hypothesis that $E(y) = \beta_0$, i.e.,

   H_0: $\beta_1 = \beta_2 = \cdots = \beta_5 = 0$

against the alternative hypothesis

   H_a: At least one of the parameters $\beta_1, \beta_2, \ldots, \beta_5$ is nonzero

Use $\alpha = .05$.

11.11 Suppose you fit the model

$$y = \beta_0 + \beta_1 x_1 + \beta_2 x_2 + \varepsilon$$

to $n = 20$ data points and obtain

$$\sum (y_i - \hat{y}_i)^2 = 1.47 \qquad \sum (y_i - \bar{y})^2 = 2.73$$

a. Find R^2. Does the value of R^2 suggest that the model provides a good fit to the data? Explain.

b. Test the null hypothesis that $\beta_1 = \beta_2 = 0$ against the alternative hypothesis that at least one of the parameters, β_1 and β_2, differs from zero. Use $\alpha = .05$. Does the model contribute information for the prediction of y?

Applying the Concepts

[*Note: Starred (*) exercises require the use of a computer.*]

11.12 If producers (providers) of goods (services) are able to reduce the unit cost of their goods by increasing the scale of their operation, they are the beneficiaries of an economic force known as *economies of scale*. Economies of scale cause a firm's long-run average costs to decline (Ferguson & Maurice, 1970). The question of whether economies of scale, diseconomies of scale, or neither (i.e., constant economies of scale) exist in the U.S. motor freight, common carrier industry has been debated for years. In an effort to settle the debate within a specific subsection of the trucking industry, Sugrue, Ledford, and Glaskowsky (1982) used regression analysis to model the relationship between each of a number of profitability/cost measures and the size of the operation. In one case, they modeled expense per vehicle-mile, y_1, as a function of the firm's total revenue, x. In another case, they modeled expense per ton-mile, y_2, as a function of x. Data were collected from 264 firms and the least squares results obtained are shown in the table.

DEPENDENT VARIABLE	$\hat{\beta}_0$	$\hat{\beta}_1$	r	F
Expense per vehicle-mile	2.279	−.00000069	−.0783	1.616
Expense per ton-mile	.1680	−.000000066	−.0902	2.148

a. Investigate the usefulness of the two models estimated by Sugrue, Ledford, and Glaskowsky. Use $\alpha = .05$. Draw appropriate conclusions in the context of the problem.

b. Are the p-values of the hypothesis tests you conducted in part a greater than .10 or less than .10? Explain.

c. What do your hypothesis tests of part a suggest about economies of scale in the subsection of the trucking industry investigated by Sugrue, Ledford, and Glaskowsky — the long-haul, heavy-load, intercity-general-freight common carrier sector? Explain.

11.13 In hopes of increasing the company's share of the fine food market, researchers for a meat-processing firm that prepares meats for exclusive restaurants are working to improve the quality of its hickory-smoked hams. One of their studies concerns the effect of time spent in the smokehouse on the flavor of the ham. Hams that were in the smokehouse for varying amounts of time were each subjected to a taste test by a panel of ten food experts. The following model was thought to be appropriate by the researchers:

$$y = \beta_0 + \beta_1 t + \beta_2 t^2 + \varepsilon$$

where

$y =$ Mean of the taste scores for the ten experts

$t =$ Time in the smokehouse (hours)

Assume the least squares model estimated using a sample of twenty hams is

$$\hat{y} = 20.3 + 5.2t - .0025t^2$$

and that $s_{\hat{\beta}_2} = .0011$. The coefficient of determination is $R^2 = .79$.

a. Is there evidence to indicate that the overall model is useful? Test at $\alpha = .05$.

b. Is there evidence to indicate that the quadratic term is important in this model? Test at $\alpha = .05$.

11.14 Writing in *Accounting Review,* Benston (1966) describes how multiple regression can be used by accountants in cost analysis. He points out that multiple regression models can be used to shed light on "the factors that cause costs to be incurred and the magnitudes of their effects" (p. 658). The independent variables of such a regression model are the factors believed to be related to cost, the dependent variable. The estimates of the coefficients of the regression model provide measures of the magnitude of the factors' effects on cost. In some instances, however, Benston notes that it may be desirable to use physical units instead of cost as the dependent variable in a cost analysis. Such would be the case if most of the cost associated with the activity of interest is a function of some physical unit, such as hours of labor. The advantage of this approach is that the regression model will provide estimates of the number of labor hours required under different circumstances, and these hours can then be costed at the current labor rate.

The sample data shown in the table have been collected from a firm's accounting and production records to provide cost information about the firm's shipping department. The variables for which data were collected were suggested by Benston.

WEEK	HOURS OF LABOR y	THOUSANDS OF POUNDS SHIPPED x_1	PERCENTAGE OF UNITS SHIPPED BY TRUCK x_2	AVERAGE NUMBER OF POUNDS PER SHIPMENT x_3
1	100	5.1	90	20
2	85	3.8	99	22
3	108	5.3	58	19
4	116	7.5	16	15
5	92	4.5	54	20
6	63	3.3	42	26
7	79	5.3	12	25
8	101	5.9	32	21
9	88	4.0	56	24
10	71	4.2	64	29
11	122	6.8	78	10
12	85	3.9	90	30
13	50	3.8	74	28
14	114	7.5	89	14
15	104	4.5	90	21
16	111	6.0	40	20
17	110	8.1	55	16
18	100	2.9	64	19
19	82	4.0	35	23
20	85	4.8	58	25

The SAS computer printout for fitting the model $y = \beta_0 + \beta_1 x_1 + \beta_2 x_2 + \beta_3 x_3 + \varepsilon$ to the data is shown here.

SAS Printout for Exercise 11.14

```
DEPENDENT VARIABLE: LABOR

SOURCE                        DF    SUM OF SQUARES     MEAN SQUARE    F VALUE

MODEL                          3     5158.31382780    1719.43794260     17.87
ERROR                         16     1539.88617220      96.24288576     PR > F
CORRECTED TOTAL               19     6698.20000000                      0.0001

R-SQUARE                 C.V.            ROOT MSE         LABOR MEAN

0.770104               10.5148          9.81034585       93.30000000

                         T FOR H0:     PR > !T!    STD ERROR OF
PARAMETER      ESTIMATE   PARAMETER=0               ESTIMATE

INTERCEPT    131.92425208      5.13      0.0001     25.69321439
WEIGHT         2.72608977      1.20      0.2483      2.27500488
TRUCK          0.04721841      0.51      0.6199      0.09334856
AVGSHIP       -2.58744391     -4.03      0.0010      0.64281819
```

a. Find the least squares prediction equation.

b. Use an F test to investigate the usefulness of the model specified in part b. Use $\alpha = .01$, and state your conclusion in the context of the problem.

c. Test $H_0: \beta_2 = 0$ versus $H_a: \beta_2 \neq 0$ using $\alpha = .05$. What do the results of your test suggest about the magnitude of the effects of x_2 on labor costs?

d. Find R^2, and interpret its value in the context of the problem.

e. If shipping department employees are paid $7.50 per hour, how much less, on average, will it cost the company per week if the average number of pounds per shipment increases from a level of 20 to 21? Assume x_1 and x_2 remain unchanged. Your answer to this question is an estimate of what is known in economics as the *expected marginal cost* associated with a 1-pound increase in x_3.

11.15 Because the coefficient of determination R^2 always increases when a new independent variable is added to the model, it may be tempting to include many variables in a model to force R^2 to be near 1. However, doing so reduces the degrees of freedom available for estimating σ^2, which adversely affects our ability to make reliable inferences. As an example, suppose you want to use eighteen economic indicators to predict next year's GNP. You fit the model

$$y = \beta_0 + \beta_1 x_1 + \beta_2 x_2 + \cdots + \beta_{17} x_{17} + \beta_{18} x_{18} + \varepsilon$$

where $y = $ GNP and $x_1, x_2, \ldots, x_{18}$ are indicators. Only 20 years of data ($n = 20$) are used to fit the model, and you obtain $R^2 = .95$. Test to determine whether this impressive looking R^2 is large enough to infer that the model is useful — i.e., that at least one term in the model is important for predicting GNP. Use $\alpha = .05$.

11.16 A utility company of a major city gave the average utility bills listed in the table for a standard-sized home during the last year.

MONTH	AVERAGE MONTHLY TEMPERATURE x (°F)	AVERAGE UTILITY BILL y	MONTH	AVERAGE MONTHLY TEMPERATURE x (°F)	AVERAGE UTILITY BILL y
January	38	$99	July	84	$80
February	45	91	August	89	95
March	49	78	September	79	65
April	57	61	October	64	56
May	69	55	November	54	74
June	78	63	December	41	93

a. Plot the points in a scattergram.

b. Use the methods of Chapter 10 to fit the model

$$y = \beta_0 + \beta_1 x + \varepsilon$$

★c. What do you conclude about the utility of this model? Hypothesize another model that might better describe the relationship between the average utility bill and average temperature. If you have access to a computer package, fit the model and test its utility.

11.17 Refer to Exercise 11.7. Recall that the dependent variable being modeled was production line supervisors' scores on a test designed to measure attitudes toward handicapped workers. The independent variables were the sex of the supervisor ($x_1 = 1$ if female, 0 if male) and the supervisor's years of experience (x_2). Suppose the same model is proposed as in Exercise 11.7, with the addition of an interaction between x_1 and x_2; i.e.,

$$y = \beta_0 + \beta_1 x_1 + \beta_2 x_2 + \beta_3 x_2^2 + \beta_4 x_1 x_2 + \varepsilon$$

This model is fit to the same data (consisting of forty observations) as in Exercise 11.7 with the result

$$\hat{y} = 50 + 5x_1 + 6x_2 - .2x_2^2 - x_1 x_2$$

and

$$s_{\hat{\beta}_4} = .02 \qquad R^2 = .87$$

a. Interpret the value of R^2.
b. Is there sufficient evidence to indicate that this model is useful for predicting attitude score? Test H_0: $\beta_1 = \beta_2 = \beta_3 = \beta_4 = 0$ using $\alpha = .05$.
c. Is there evidence that the interaction between sex and years of experience is useful in the prediction model?
d. Sketch the predicted attitude score, $\hat{y}$, as a function of the number of years of experience, x_2, for males ($x_1 = 0$). Next, substitute $x_1 = 1$ into the least squares equation and thereby obtain a plot of the prediction equation for females. Compare these sketches with those obtained when the model without interaction was fit in Exercise 11.7. [*Note:* For both males and females, plotting $\hat{y}$ for $x_2 = 0, 2, 4, 6, 8,$ and 10 will produce a good picture of the prediction equations. The interaction term allows the vertical distance between the males' and females' prediction curves to change as x_2 changes.]

*11.18 A company that services microcomputers is interested in developing a regression model that will assist them in their manpower planning. In particular, they want a model that describes the relationship between the time a service person spends on a preventive maintenance service call to a customer, y, and two independent variables: the number of microcomputers to be serviced, x_1, and the service person's number of months of experience in preventive maintenance, x_2. Company records were sampled and the data in the table were obtained.

MAINTENANCE TIME (Hours)	NUMBER OF MICROCOMPUTERS	EXPERIENCE (Months)
1.0	1	12
3.1	3	8
17.0	10	5
14.0	8	2
6.0	5	10
1.8	1	1
11.5	10	10
9.3	5	2
6.0	4	6
12.2	10	8

a. Fit the model $y = \beta_0 + \beta_1 x_1 + \beta_2 x_2 + \varepsilon$ to the data.

b. Investigate whether the overall model is useful. Test using $\alpha = .10$.

c. Find R^2 for the fitted model. Interpret your result.

d. Fit the model $y = \beta_0 + \beta_1 x_1 + \beta_2 x_2 + \beta_3 x_1 x_2 + \varepsilon$ to the data.

e. Find R^2 for the model of part d.

f. Explain why you should not rely solely on a comparison of the two R^2 values for drawing conclusions about which model is more useful for predicting y.

g. Do the data provide sufficient evidence to indicate that the interaction term, $x_1 x_2$, contributes information for the prediction of y? [*Hint:* Test H_0: $\beta_3 = 0$.]

h. Can you be certain that the model you selected in part f is the best model to use in predicting maintenance time? Explain.

*11.19 Regression analysis can be used to model the relationship between the selling price of a house and its total living area (for more details, see Exercise 10.70). The table contains the final selling prices and total living areas for a sample of twenty-six houses in the same geographic area that were sold during the last 6 months.

AREA (Square feet)	PRICE	AREA (Square feet)	PRICE
1,100	$41,900	1,620	$53,600
1,480	48,700	1,380	46,500
1,630	54,500	1,275	45,000
1,490	50,300	1,150	39,000
1,210	40,900	1,750	56,100
1,857	61,100	1,890	63,300
1,835	58,700	2,060	73,000
2,150	77,200	1,870	65,000
1,570	49,300	1,920	63,300
1,430	48,400	1,800	59,200
1,410	44,000	1,820	60,000
1,310	44,500	1,970	66,800
1,535	52,000	1,960	67,100

a. Construct a scattergram for the data. Is there evidence to suggest that it would be inappropriate to represent the relationship between price and area with a straight line? Explain.

b. Fit the following model to the data:

$$y = \beta_0 + \beta_1 x + \beta_2 x^2 + \varepsilon$$

where y = Price and x = Area. Plot the fitted equation on the scattergram of part a.

c. Find R^2 for the least squares equation of part b. Interpret your result.

d. Use the F test statistic to investigate whether the overall model is useful for predicting y. Test using $\alpha = .05$.

e. Do the data provide sufficient evidence to indicate that the second-order term (x^2) contributes information for the prediction of y? Test using $\alpha = .05$.

11.7 Using the Model for Estimation and Prediction

In Section 10.8 we discussed the use of the least squares line for estimating the mean value of y, $E(y)$, for some value of x, say $x = x_p$. We also showed how to use the same fitted model to predict, when $x = x_p$, some value of y to be observed in the future. Recall that the least squares line yielded the same value for both the estimate of $E(y)$ and the prediction of some future value of y. That is, both are the result of substituting x_p into the prediction equation, $\hat{y} = \hat{\beta}_0 + \hat{\beta}_1 x$, and calculating $\hat{y}$. There the equivalence ends. The confidence interval for the mean, $E(y)$, was narrower than the prediction interval for y because of the additional uncertainty attributable to the random error, ε, when predicting some future value of y.

These same concepts carry over to the multiple regression model. For example, suppose we want to estimate the mean electrical usage for a given home size, say $x_p = 1{,}500$ square feet. Assuming the quadratic model represents the true relationship between electrical usage and home size, we want to estimate

$$E(y) = \beta_0 + \beta_1 x_p + \beta_2 x_p^2 = \beta_0 + \beta_1(1{,}500) + \beta_2(1{,}500)^2$$

Substituting into the least squares prediction equation yields the following estimate of $E(y)$:

$$\hat{y} = \hat{\beta}_0 + \hat{\beta}_1(1{,}500) + \hat{\beta}_2(1{,}500)^2$$
$$= -1{,}216.144 + 2.3989(1{,}500) - .00045004(1{,}500)^2 = 1{,}369.7$$

To form a confidence interval for the mean, we need to know the standard deviation of the sampling distribution for the estimator $\hat{y}$. For multiple regression models, the form of this standard deviation is rather complex. However, some regression packages allow us to obtain

Figure 11.14 SAS Printout for Estimated Mean Value and Corresponding Confidence Interval for $x_p = 1{,}500$

X	PREDICTED VALUE	LOWER 95% CL FOR MEAN	UPPER 95% CL FOR MEAN
1500	1369.66088739	1324.98831001	1414.33346477

Figure 11.15 Confidence Interval for Mean Electrical Usage

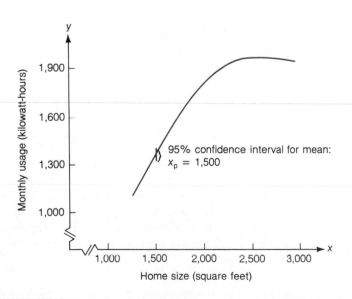

the confidence intervals for mean values of y at any given setting of the independent variables. A portion of the SAS output for the electrical usage example is shown in Figure 11.14. The mean value and corresponding 95% confidence interval for $x_p = 1,500$ are shown in the columns labeled PREDICTED VALUE, LOWER 95% CL FOR MEAN, and UPPER 95% CL FOR MEAN. Note that

$$\hat{y} = 1,369.7$$

which agrees with our earlier calculation. The 95% confidence interval for the true mean of y is shown to be 1,325.0 to 1,414.3 (see Figure 11.15).

If we were interested in predicting the electrical usage for a particular 1,500 square foot home, $\hat{y} = 1,369.7$ would be used as the predicted value. However, the prediction interval for a particular value of y will be wider than the confidence interval for the mean value. This is reflected by the printout shown in Figure 11.16, which gives the predicted value of y and corresponding 95% prediction interval for $x_p = 1,500$. This prediction interval, which extends from 1,250.3 to 1,489.0, is shown in Figure 11.17.

Figure 11.16 SAS Printout for Predicted Value and Corresponding Prediction Interval for $x_p = 1,500$

```
                 PREDICTED       LOWER 95% CL      UPPER 95% CL
        X          VALUE          INDIVIDUAL        INDIVIDUAL
      1500     1369.66088739    1250.31627944     1489.00549533
```

Figure 11.17 Prediction Interval for Electrical Usage

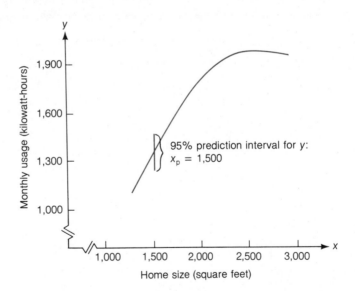

Unfortunately, not all computer packages have the capability to produce confidence intervals for means and prediction intervals for particular y values. This is a rather serious oversight since the estimation of mean values and the prediction of particular values represent the culmination of our model building efforts: using the model to make inferences about the dependent variable y.

Case Study 11.2
Predicting the Sales of Crest Toothpaste

Knowing the determinants of demand for its product would assist a company in focusing its marketing efforts on the appropriate market segments (e.g., middle-income families with school-age children). In addition, knowing the relationship between those determinants and product sales would assist the company in predicting sales and, therefore, in its planning endeavors throughout the organization. Using a model developed by Roger D. Carlson (1981) as her starting point, Carolyn I. Allmon (1982) employed multiple regression analysis to investigate the determinants of demand for Crest toothpaste and to predict Crest's sales.

Allmon modeled sales of Crest as a function of advertising expenditures, personal disposable income, and the ratio of Crest's advertising budget to that for Colgate toothpaste, Crest's closest competitor. More specifically, Allmon hypothesized the following model:

$$y = \beta_0 + \beta_1 x_1 + \beta_2 x_2 + \beta_3 x_3 + \varepsilon$$

where

y = Sales of Crest toothpaste in the current year, computed by multiplying Crest's market share by the total market (thousands of dollars)

x_1 = Advertising budget for Crest in the current year (thousands of dollars)

x_2 = U.S. personal disposable income in the current year (billions of dollars)

x_3 = Ratio of Crest's advertising budget to Colgate's advertising budget in current year (rounded to nearest hundredth)

Allmon hypothesized that the effect of each independent variable on sales is positive — i.e., that β_1, β_2, and β_3 have positive signs. Her belief that β_1 is positive follows from the fact that Procter and Gamble, the firm that manufactures Crest, has continued to advertise Crest heavily over many years. It is unlikely they would do this if advertising did not positively affect sales. That β_2 should be positive follows from a study of toothbrushing frequency in which it was shown that as family income increased, family members brushed their teeth more frequently. Allmon argues that since Colgate and Crest are competitors, sales of Colgate should affect sales of Crest and vice versa. Therefore, the larger is x_3, the higher y should be. Accordingly, β_3 should be positive.

The model was estimated using the method of least squares on data collected for the years 1967–1979. The following results were obtained:

$$\hat{y} = \begin{array}{cccc} 30,626 & + 3.8932x_1 & + 86.519x_2 & - 29,607x_3 \\ (19,808) & (2.0812) & (18.693) & (23,822) \\ 1.5461 & 1.8706 & 4.6283 & -1.2429 \end{array}$$

$$R^2 = .9575 \qquad F = 67.595$$

where the numbers in parentheses are the standard errors of the coefficient estimates and the numbers below them are the associated t statistics.

Since $F = 67.595 > F_{.01} = 6.99$ (with $v_1 = 3$, $v_2 = 9$), Allmon concluded that at least one of the model coefficients is nonzero and that the model is useful for predicting sales. Next, she conducted one-sided, upper-tailed hypothesis tests to determine whether the data support her expectations about the positive influence of each of the independent variables on sales. Comparing $t_{.05} = 1.833$ (df $= 9$) to the t statistics given, it can be seen that the data support her hypotheses with respect to β_1 and β_2, but that the null hypothesis $H_0: \beta_3 = 0$ cannot be rejected. Thus, she concluded,

> my model indicates that income is a significant determinant of sales as is advertising expenditure in the current year. The competition of Colgate dental cream via its advertising expenditure appears not to affect Crest sales significantly. This information could be used by Procter and Gamble in the formulation of their advertising policy, for example, in determining the segment of the market to which most advertising should be directed.

Allmon's primary purpose for developing the model was prediction. As part of her test of the predictive power of the model, Allmon substituted the values for x_1, x_2, and x_3 in 1980 (which were known at the time) into the fitted model and calculated $\hat{y}$. Her model predicted sales of \$251,060,340 and actual sales were \$245,000,000. Allmon's model did substantially better than Carlson's model, the model she had set out to refine. Carlson's model predicted sales of \$275,447,450.

In concluding the report of her findings, Allmon pointed out several limitations of the model. Among them were the following:

1. It was developed from annual data. Accordingly, the results should be viewed cautiously, since evidence exists that suggests the cumulative effect of advertising on sales lasts less than a year.
2. The sample is quite small. Accordingly, even one more data point may substantially change the coefficient estimates and overall model fit.
3. None of the data were obtained from primary sources (such as Procter and Gamble). All data except disposable income were collected from the publication *Advertising Age,* a secondary data source.

11.8 Multiple Regression: An Example

Let us return to the executive compensation example introduced in Case Study 11.1. Recall that the management consultant firm of Towers, Perrin, Forster & Crosby (TPF&C) uses a multiple regression model to project executive salaries. Suppose the list of independent variables given in Table 11.3 is to be used to build a model for the salaries of corporate executives.

Table 11.3

List of Independent Variables for Executive Compensation Example

INDEPENDENT VARIABLE	DESCRIPTION
x_1	Years of experience
x_2	Years of education
x_3	1 if male; 0 if female
x_4	Number of employees supervised
x_5	Corporate assets (\$ millions)
x_6	x_1^2
x_7	$x_3 x_4$

Step 1 The first step is to hypothesize a model relating executive salary to the independent variables listed in Table 11.3. TPF&C have found that executive compensation models that use the logarithm of salary as the dependent variable are better predictive models than those using the salary as the dependent variable. This is probably because salaries tend to be incremented in *percentages* rather than dollar values. When a dependent variable undergoes percentage changes as the independent variables are varied, the logarithm of the dependent variable will be more suitable as a dependent variable. The model we propose is

$$y = \beta_0 + \beta_1 x_1 + \beta_2 x_2 + \beta_3 x_3 + \beta_4 x_4 + \beta_5 x_5 + \beta_6 x_6 + \beta_7 x_7 + \varepsilon$$

where $y = \log(\text{Executive salary})$, $x_6 = x_1^2$ (second-order term in years of experience), and $x_7 = x_3 x_4$ (cross product or interaction term between sex and number of employees supervised). The variable x_3 is a *dummy* variable; it is used to describe an independent variable that is not measured on a numerical scale, but instead is *qualitative (categorical)* in nature. Sex is such a variable, since its values, male and female, are categories rather than numbers. Thus, we assign the value $x_3 = 1$ if the executive is male, $x_3 = 0$ if the executive is female. (For more detail on the use and interpretation of dummy variables, see Chapter 12.) The interaction term, $x_3 x_4$, allows for the possibility that the relationship between the number of employees supervised, x_4, and corporate salary is dependent on sex, x_3. For example, as the number of supervised employees increases, with all other factors being equal, a woman's salary might rise more rapidly than a man's. (The concept of interaction is also explained in more detail in Chapter 12.)

Step 2 Now, we estimate the model coefficients $\beta_0, \beta_1, \ldots, \beta_7$. Suppose that a sample of 100 executives is selected, and the variables y and $x_1, x_2, \ldots, x_7$ are recorded (or, in the case of x_6 and x_7, calculated). The sample is then used as input for a computer regression routine; the SAS output is shown in Figure 11.18. The least squares model is

$$\hat{y} = 8.88 + .045x_1 + .033x_2 + .119x_3 + .00033x_4 + .0020x_5 - .00072x_6 + .00031x_7$$

Figure 11.18 SAS Printout for Executive Compensation Example

SOURCE	DF	SUM OF SQUARES	MEAN SQUARE	F VALUE	PR > F
MODEL	7	27.06425564	3.86632223	1819.30	0.0001
ERROR	92	0.19551523	0.00212517	R-SQUARE	ROOT MSE
CORRECTED TOTAL	99	27.25977087		0.992828	0.0460995

PARAMETER	ESTIMATE	T FOR H0: PARAMETER = 0	PR > |T|	STD ERROR OF ESTIMATE
INTERCEPT	8.87878688	192.49	0.0001	0.04612667
X1 (EXPERIENCE)	0.04460301	26.83	0.0001	0.00166257
X2 (EDUCATION)	0.03326230	12.31	0.0001	0.00270306
X3 (SEX)	0.11892473	6.89	0.0001	0.01724977
X4 (EMPLOYEES SUPERVISED)	0.00033216	19.97	0.0001	0.00001664
X5 (ASSETS)	0.00201021	73.25	0.0001	0.00002744
X6 (= X1*X1)	-0.00071702	-15.11	0.0001	0.00004746
X7 (= X3*X4)	0.00031244	16.16	0.0001	0.00001933

Step 3 The next step is to specify the probability distribution of ε, the random error component. We assume that ε is normally distributed, with a mean of zero and a constant variance σ^2. Furthermore, we assume that the errors are independent. The estimate of the variance, σ^2, is given in the SAS printout as

$$s^2 = \text{MSE} = \frac{\text{SSE}}{n - (k + 1)} = \frac{\text{SSE}}{100 - (7 + 1)} = 0.0021$$

Step 4 We now want to see how well the model predicts salaries. First, note that $R^2 = .993$. This implies that 99.3% of the variation in y (logarithm of salaries) for these 100 sampled executives is accounted for by the model. The significance of this can be tested:

H_0: $\beta_1 = \beta_2 = \cdots = \beta_7 = 0$

H_a: At least one of the model coefficients is nonzero

Test statistic: $F = \dfrac{R^2/k}{(1 - R^2)/[n - (k + 1)]}$

Rejection region: For $\alpha = .05$, $F > F_{.05}$

where $\nu_1 = k = 7$ df, $\nu_2 = n - (k + 1) = 92$ df

where from Table VII in Appendix B, $F_{.05} \approx 2.1$. The test statistic is given on the SAS printout. Since $F = 1{,}819.3$ exceeds the tabulated value of F, we conclude that the model does contribute information for predicting executive salaries. It appears that at least one of the β parameters in the model differs from zero.

We may be particularly interested in whether the data provide evidence that the mean salary of executives increases as the asset value of the company increases, when all other variables (experience, education, etc.) are held constant. In other words, we may want to know whether the data provide sufficient evidence to show that $\beta_5 > 0$. We use the following test:

H_0: $\beta_5 = 0$ H_a: $\beta_5 > 0$

Test statistic: $t = \dfrac{\hat{\beta}_5}{s_{\hat{\beta}_5}}$

For $\alpha = .05$, $n = 100$, $k = 7$, and df $= n - (k + 1) = 92$, we will reject H_0 if $t > t_{.05}$, where (because the degrees of freedom of t are so large) $t_{.05} \approx z_{.05} = 1.645$. Thus, we reject H_0 if

$t > 1.645$

The computed t value corresponding to the independent variable, x_5, is 73.25 (see Figure 11.18). Since this value exceeds 1.645, we find evidence that the mean salary of executives does increase as the company assets increase, when all other variables are held constant.

Step 5 The culmination of the modeling effort is to use the model for estimation and prediction. Suppose a firm is trying to determine fair compensation for an executive with the characteristics shown in Table 11.4. The least squares model can be used to obtain a predicted value for the logarithm of salary. That is,

$$\hat{y} = \hat{\beta}_0 + \hat{\beta}_1(12) + \hat{\beta}_2(16) + \hat{\beta}_3(0) + \hat{\beta}_4(400) + \hat{\beta}_5(160.1) + \hat{\beta}_6(144) + \hat{\beta}_7(0)$$

Table 11.4

Values of Independent
Variables for a Particular
Executive

$x_1 = 12$ years of experience
$x_2 = 16$ years of education
$x_3 = 0$ (female)
$x_4 = 400$ employees supervised
$x_5 = $ \$160.1 million (the firm's asset value)
$x_6 = x_1^2 = 144$
$x_7 = x_3x_4 = 0$

This predicted value is given in Figure 11.19, a partial reproduction of the SAS regression printout for this problem: $\hat{y} = 10.298$. The 95% prediction interval is also given: from 10.203 to 10.392. To predict the salary of an executive with these characteristics we take the antilogarithm of these values. That is, the predicted salary is $e^{10.298} = $ \$29,700 (rounded to the nearest hundred) and the 95% prediction interval is from $e^{10.203}$ to $e^{10.392}$ (or from \$27,000 to \$32,600). Thus, an executive with the characteristics given in Table 11.4 should be paid between \$27,000 and \$32,600 to be consistent with the sample data.

Figure 11.19 SAS Printout for Executive Compensation Problem

X1	X2	X3	X4	X5	X6	X7	PREDICTED VALUE	LOWER 95% CL INDIVIDUAL	UPPER 95% CL INDIVIDUAL
12	16	0	400	160.1	144	0	10.29766682	10.20298295	10.39235070

11.9
Statistical
Computer
Programs

There are a number of different statistical program packages; some of the most popular are BMDP, Minitab, SAS, and SPSS (see the references at the end of the chapter). You may have access to one or more of these packages at your computer center.

The multiple regression programs for these packages may differ in what they are programmed to do, how they do it, and the appearance of their computer printouts, but all of them print the basic outputs needed for a regression analysis. For example, some will compute confidence intervals for $E(y)$ and prediction intervals for y. Others will not. Some test the null hypotheses that the individual β parameters equal to zero using Student's t tests, while others use F tests.* But all give the least squares estimates, the values of SSE, s^2, etc.

To illustrate, the Minitab, SAS, and SPSS regression analysis computer printouts for Example 11.3 are shown in Figure 11.20 (page 486). For that example, we fit the model

$$y = \beta_0 + \beta_1 x_1 + \beta_2 x_2 + \beta_3 x_1 x_2 + \varepsilon$$

to $n = 32$ data points. The variables in the model were

$y = $ Auction price

$x_1 = $ Age of clock (years) $x_2 = $ Number of bidders

---

* A two-tailed Student's t test based on ν df is equivalent to an F test where the F statistic has 1 df in the numerator and ν df in the denominator. See Section 11.5.

Figure 11.20 Computer Printouts for Example 11.3

(a) Minitab Regression Printout

```
THE REGRESSION EQUATION IS
Y = 323. + 0.873 X1 - 93.4 X2
    + 1.30 X3

                          ST. DEV.    T-RATIO =
    COLUMN  COEFFICIENT   OF COEF.    COEF/S.D.
    --         323.         293.        1.10
X1  C1         0.87         2.02        0.43
X2  C2        -93.4         29.7       -3.14
X3  C4         1.298        0.211       6.15

THE ST. DEV. OF Y ABOUT REGRESSION LINE IS
S =    88.4
WITH ( 32- 4) =  28 DEGREES OF FREEDOM

R-SQUARED = 95.4 PERCENT
R-SQUARED = 94.9 PERCENT, ADJUSTED FOR D.F.

ANALYSIS OF VARIANCE

DUE TO       DF      SS        MS=SS/DF
REGRESSION    3   4572524.     1524174.
RESIDUAL     28    218645.       7809.
TOTAL        31   4791168.
```

(b) SAS Regression Printout

```
DEPENDENT VARIABLE: Y          AUCTION PRICE

SOURCE          DF    SUM OF SQUARES    MEAN SQUARE     F VALUE    PR > F    R-SQUARE
MODEL            3    4572547.98717668  1524182.66239223  195.19    0.0001    0.954365
ERROR           28    218646.23157332   7808.79398476              ROOT MSE    Y MEAN
CORRECTED TOTAL 31    4791194.21875000                            88.36738077  1327.15625000
                                                                             C.V.
                                                                           6.6584

                           T FOR HO:
PARAMETER      ESTIMATE    PARAMETER=0   PR > !T!    STD ERROR OF
                                                      ESTIMATE
INTERCEPT   322.75435309      1.10        0.2806   293.32514660
X1            0.87328775      0.43        0.6688     2.01965115
X2          -93.40991991     -3.14        0.0039    29.70767946
X1*X2         1.29789828      6.15        0.0001     0.21102602
```

(c) SPSS Regression Printout

```
DEPENDENT VARIABLE..   Y       AUCTION PRICE

VARIABLE(S) ENTERED ON STEP NUMBER   1...   X1   AGE
                                            X2   NUMBER OF BIDDERS
                                            X3   AGE*BIDDERS

MULTIPLE R         0.97692     ANALYSIS OF VARIANCE
R SQUARE           0.95436                    DF    SUM OF SQUARES    MEAN SQUARE        F
ADJUSTED R SQUARE  0.94948     REGRESSION      3.   4572547.98718   1524182.66239   195.18797
STANDARD ERROR    88.36738     RESIDUAL       28.    218646.23157     7808.79398

---------- VARIABLES IN THE EQUATION ----------
VARIABLE        B         BETA      STD ERROR B        F
X1          0.8732878   0.06085      2.01965        0.187
X2        -93.40992    -0.67471     29.70768        9.887
X3          1.297898    1.37032      0.21103       37.828
(CONSTANT) 322.7544
```

Notice that the Minitab printout gives the prediction equation at the top of the printout. The independent variables, shown in the prediction equation and listed at the left side of the printout, are x_1, x_2, and x_3. Thus, Minitab treats the product $x_1 x_2$ as a third independent variable, x_3, which must be computed before the fitting begins. For this reason, the Minitab prediction equation will always appear on the printout as first-order even though some of the independent variables shown in the prediction equation may actually be the squares or cross products of other independent variables. The inclusion of the squares or cross products of independent variables is treated in the same manner in the SPSS program shown in Figure 11.20. The SAS program is the only one of these three that can be automatically instructed to include these terms, and they appear in the printout with an asterisk (*) that indicates multiplication. Thus, in the SAS printout, $x_1 x_2$ is printed as X1*X2.

The estimates of the regression coefficients appear opposite the identifying variable in the Minitab column titled COEFFICIENT, in the SAS column titled ESTIMATE, and in the SPSS column titled B. Compare the estimates given in these three columns. Note that the Minitab printout gives the estimates with a much lesser degree of accuracy (fewer decimal places) than the SAS and SPSS printouts. (Ignore the column titled BETA in the SPSS printout. These are standardized estimates and will not be discussed in this text.)

The estimated standard errors of the estimates are given in the Minitab column titled ST. DEV. OF COEF., in the SAS column titled STD ERROR OF ESTIMATE, and in the SPSS column titled STD ERROR B.

The values of the test statistics for testing H_0: $\beta_i = 0$, where $i = 1, 2, 3$, are shown in the Minitab column titled T-RATIO = COEF/S.D. and in the SAS column titled T FOR H0: PARAMETER = 0. Note that the computed t values shown in the Minitab and SAS columns are identical (except for the number of decimal places) and that Minitab does not give the observed significance level of the test. Consequently, to draw conclusions from the Minitab printout, you must compare the computed values of t with the critical values given in a t table (Table V in Appendix B). In contrast, the SAS printout gives the observed significance level for each t test in the column titled PR > |T|. Note that these observed significance levels have been computed assuming that the tests are two-tailed. The observed significance levels for one-tailed tests would equal half of these values.

The SPSS program conducts tests of H_0: $\beta_i = 0$, where $i = 1, 2, 3$, using the F statistic. The computed F values, which are appropriate only for two-tailed tests of the null hypothesis H_0: $\beta_i = 0$ against H_a: $\beta_i \neq 0$, are shown in the SPSS printout in the column titled F. The observed significance level is not given, so you must compare these values with those shown in the F table for numerator degrees of freedom $\nu_1 = 1$ and denominator degrees of freedom equal to the number ν_2 that is associated with the SSE. For this example, $\nu_2 = 28$.

The Minitab printout gives the value SSE $= 218645$ under the ANALYSIS OF VARIANCE column headed SS and in the row identified as RESIDUAL. The value of $s^2 = 7809$ is shown in the same row under the column headed MS = SS/DF, and the degrees of freedom, DF, appears in the same row as 28. The corresponding values are shown at the top of the SAS printout in the row labeled ERROR and in the columns designated as SUM OF SQUARES, MEAN SQUARE, and DF, respectively. These quantities appear with similar headings in the SPSS printout.

The value of R^2, as defined in Section 11.6, is given in the Minitab printout as 95.4 PERCENT (we defined this quantity as a ratio where $0 \leq R^2 \leq 1$). It is given in the top right corner of the SAS printout as 0.954365, and it is shown in the left column of the SPSS printout as 0.95436. (Ignore the quantities shown in the Minitab printout as R^2 ADJUSTED FOR D.F. and in the SPSS printout as ADJUSTED R SQUARE. These quantities are adjusted for the degrees of freedom associated with the total SS and SSE and are not used or discussed in this text.)

The F statistic for testing the utility of the model (Section 11.6)—i.e., testing the null hypothesis that all model parameters (except β_0) equal zero— is shown under the title F VALUE as 195.19 in the top center of the SAS printout. In addition, the SAS printout gives the observed significance level of this F test under PR > F as 0.0001. This F value, 195.18797, is also printed at the right side of the SPSS printout, but no observed significance level is given. Thus, if you are using the SPSS regression analysis package, you must compare the printed F value with those tabulated in F tables (Tables VI, VII, VIII, and IX in Appendix B). The F statistic for testing the utility of the model is not given in the Minitab printout. If you are using Minitab and wish to obtain the value of this statistic, you must compute it using the formula given in Section 11.6:

$$F = \frac{R^2/k}{(1 - R^2)/[n - (k + 1)]}$$

(The value of R^2 is given in the Minitab printout; $n = 32$ and $k = 3$.) You can also compute the value of the F statistic directly from the mean square entries given in the ANALYSIS OF VARIANCE table. Thus, it can be shown (proof omitted) that the F statistic for testing

$$H_0: \beta_1 = \beta_2 = \cdots = \beta_k = 0$$

is

$$F = \frac{\text{Mean square for regression}}{\text{Mean square for error (or residuals)}} = \frac{\text{Mean square for regression}}{s^2}$$

These quantities are given in the Minitab printout under the column marked MS = SS/DF. Thus,

$$F = \frac{1,524,174}{7,809} = 195.18$$

a value that agrees with the values given in the SAS and SPSS printouts. The logic behind this test and other tests of hypotheses concerning sets of the β parameters will be presented in Section 12.4.

We will not comment on the merits or demerits of the various packages because you will have to use and become familiar with the output of the package(s) available at your computer center. Most of the computer printouts are similar, and it is relatively easy to learn how to read one output after you have become familiar with another. We have used different packages in the solution of the examples to help you with this problem.

11.10 Some Comments on the Assumptions

When we apply a regression analysis to a set of data, we never know for certain that the assumptions of Section 11.2 are satisfied. How far can we deviate from the assumptions and still expect a multiple regression analysis to yield results that will have the reliability stated in this chapter? How can we detect departures (if they exist) from the assumptions of Section 11.2 and what can we do about them? We provide some partial answers to these questions in this section and will direct you to further discussion in succeeding chapters.

Remember from Section 11.2 that

$$y = E(y) + \varepsilon$$

where the expected value $E(y)$ of y for a given set of values of $x_1, x_2, \ldots, x_k$ is

$$E(y) = \beta_0 + \beta_1 x_1 + \beta_2 x_2 + \cdots + \beta_k x_k$$

and ε is a random error. The first assumption we made was that the mean value of the random error for *any* given set of values of $x_1, x_2, \ldots, x_k$ is $E(\varepsilon) = 0$. One consequence of this assumption is that the mean $E(y)$ for a specific set of values of $x_1, x_2, \ldots, x_k$ is

$$E(y) = \beta_0 + \beta_1 x_1 + \beta_2 x_2 + \cdots + \beta_k x_k$$

That is,

$$
\underbrace{y}_{} = \underbrace{E(y)}_{\substack{\text{Mean value of } y \\ \text{for specific values} \\ \text{of } x_1, x_2, \ldots, x_k}} + \underbrace{\varepsilon}_{\substack{\text{Random} \\ \text{error}}}
$$

The second consequence of the assumption is that the least squares estimators of the model parameters, $\beta_0, \beta_1, \beta_2, \ldots, \beta_k$, will be unbiased regardless of the remaining assumptions that we attribute to the random errors and their probability distributions.

The properties of the sampling distributions of the parameter estimators $\hat{\beta}_0, \hat{\beta}_1, \ldots, \hat{\beta}_k$ will depend on the remaining assumptions that we specify concerning the probability distributions of the random errors. Recall that we assumed that for any given set of values of $x_1, x_2, \ldots, x_k$, ε has a normal probability distribution with mean equal to zero and variance equal to σ^2. Also, we assumed that the random errors are probabilistically independent.

It is unlikely that the assumptions stated above are satisfied exactly for many practical situations. If departures from the assumptions are not too great, experience has shown that a least squares regression analysis produces estimates — predictions and statistical test results — that possess, for all practical purposes, the properties specified in this chapter. If the observations are likely to be correlated (as in the case of data collected over time), we must check for correlation between the random errors and may have to modify our methodology if correlation exists. A test for correlation of the random errors, along with methods for coping with correlated errors, can be found in Chapter 14. If the variance of the random error, ε, changes from one setting of the independent variables to another, we can sometimes transform the data so that the standard least squares methodology will be appropriate.

Techniques for detecting nonhomogeneous variances of the random errors (a condition called *heteroscedasticity*) and some methods for treating this type of data are discussed in Mendenhall and McClave (1981).

Frequently, the data $(y, x_1, x_2, \ldots, x_k)$ are ***observational;*** i.e., we just observe an experimental unit and record values for $y, x_1, x_2, \ldots, x_k$. Do such data violate the assumption that $x_1, x_2, \ldots, x_k$ are fixed? For this particular case, if we can assume that $x_1, x_2, \ldots, x_k$ are *measured without error,* then the mean value $E(y)$ can be viewed as a conditional mean. That is, $E(y)$ is the mean value of y, *given* that the x variables assume a specific set of values. With this modification in our thinking, the least squares regression analysis is applicable to observational data.

To conclude, remember that when you perform a regression analysis the reliability you can place in your inferences is dependent on the satisfaction of the assumptions discussed in Section 11.2. Although the random errors will rarely satisfy these assumptions exactly, the reliability specified by a regression analysis will hold approximately for many types of data encountered in business.

11.11 Some Pitfalls: Estimability, Multicollinearity, and Extrapolation

There are several problems you should be aware of when constructing a prediction model for some response, y. A few of the most important are discussed in this section.

Problem 1
Parameter Estimability

Suppose you want to fit a model relating a firm's monthly profit, y, to the advertising expenditure, x. We propose the first-order model $E(y) = \beta_0 + \beta_1 x$. Now, suppose we have 3 months of data, and the firm spent \$1,000 on advertising during each month. The data are shown in Figure 11.21. You can see the problem: The parameters of the line cannot be estimated when all the data are concentrated at a single x value. Recall that it takes two points (x values) to fit a straight line. Thus, the parameters are not estimable when only one x value is observed.

Figure 11.21 Profit and Advertising Expenditure Data: 3 Months

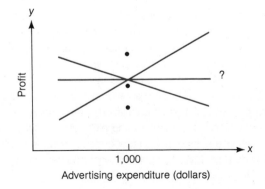

Advertising expenditure (dollars)

A similar problem would occur if we attempted to fit the second-order model

$$E(y) = \beta_0 + \beta_1 x + \beta_2 x^2$$

to a set of data for which only one *or two* different x values were observed (see Figure 11.22). At least three different x values must be observed before a second-order model can be fit to a set of data (that is, before all three parameters are estimable). In general, the number of levels of x must be at least one more than the order of the polynomial in x that you want to fit.

Figure 11.22 Only Two x Values Observed — the Second-Order Model Is Not Estimable

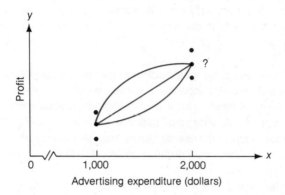

Since most business variables are not controlled by the researcher, the independent variables will almost always be observed at a sufficient number of levels to permit estimation of the model parameters. However, when the computer program you use suddenly refuses to fit a model, the problem is probably inestimable parameters.

Problem 2

Multicollinearity

Often, two or more of the independent variables used in the model for $E(y)$ will contribute redundant information. That is, the independent variables will be correlated with each other. For example, suppose we want to construct a model to predict the gasoline mileage rating of a truck as a function of its load, x_1, and the horsepower, x_2, of its engine. In general, you would expect heavy loads to require greater horsepower and to result in lower mileage ratings. Thus, although both x_1 and x_2 contribute information for the prediction of mileage rating, some of the information is overlapping because x_1 and x_2 are correlated.

If the model

$$E(y) = \beta_0 + \beta_1 x_1 + \beta_2 x_2$$

were fit to a set of data, we might find that the t values for both $\hat{\beta}_1$ and $\hat{\beta}_2$ (the least squares estimates) are nonsignificant. However, the F test for $H_0: \beta_1 = \beta_2 = 0$ would probably be highly significant. The tests may seem to be contradictory, but really they are not. The t tests indicate that the contribution of one variable, say $x_1 = $ Load, is not significant after the effect of $x_2 = $ Horsepower has been discounted (because x_2 is also in the model). The significant F test, on the other hand, tells us that at least one of the two variables is making a contribution to the prediction of y (i.e., β_1, β_2, or both differ from zero). In fact, both are probably contributing, but the contribution of one overlaps with that of the other.

When highly correlated independent variables are present in a regression model, the results may be confusing. The researcher may want to include only one of the variables in the final model. One way of deciding which variable to include is by using *stepwise regression,* a topic discussed in Chapter 12. Generally, only one (or a small number) of a set of multicollinear independent variables will be included in the regression model by a stepwise regression procedure. This procedure tests the parameter associated with each variable in the presence of all the variables already in the model. For example, if at one step, the variable Truck load is included as a significant variable in the prediction of the mileage rating, then the variable Horsepower will probably never be added in a future step. Thus, if a set of independent variables is thought to be multicollinear, some screening by stepwise regression may be helpful.

Problem 3

Prediction Outside
the Experimental
Region

By the late 1960's, many research economists had developed highly technical models to relate the state of the economy to various economic indexes and other independent variables. Many of these models were multiple regression models, where, for example, the dependent variable y might be next year's growth in GNP and the independent variables might include this year's rate of inflation, this year's Consumer Price Index, and other factors. In other words, the model might be constructed to predict next year's economy using this year's knowledge.

Unfortunately, these models were almost unanimously unsuccessful in predicting the recession in the early 1970's. What went wrong? One of the problems was that the regression models were used to predict y for values of the independent variables that were outside the region in which the model was developed. For example, the inflation rate in the late 1960's, when the models were developed, ranged from 6% to 8%. When the double-digit inflation of the early 1970's became a reality, some researchers attempted to use the same models to predict future growth in GNP. As you can see in Figure 11.23, the model may be very accurate for predicting y when x is in the range of experimentation, but the use of the model outside that range is a dangerous practice.

Figure 11.23   Using a
Regression Model Outside
the Experimental Region

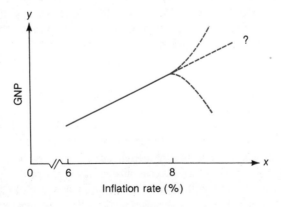

Problem 4

Correlated Errors

Another problem associated with using a regression model to predict an economic variable y based on independent variables $x_1, x_2, \ldots, x_k$ arises from the fact that the data are frequently time series. That is, the values of both the dependent and independent variables are observed sequentially over a period of time. The observations tend to be correlated over time, which in turn often causes the prediction errors of the regression model to be correlated. Thus, the assumption of independent errors is violated, and the model tests and prediction intervals are no longer valid. One solution to this problem is to construct a time series model; this will be the subject of Chapter 14.

Summary

We have discussed some of the methodology of *multiple regression analysis,* a technique for modeling a dependent variable y as a function of several independent variables x_1, $x_2, \ldots, x_k$. The steps we follow in constructing and using multiple regression models are much the same as those for the simple straight-line models:

1. The form of the probabilistic model is hypothesized.
2. The model coefficients are estimated using the method of least squares.
3. The probability distribution of ε is specified and σ^2 is estimated.
4. The utility of the model is checked.
5. If the model is deemed useful, it may be used to make estimates and to predict values of y to be observed in the future.

We have covered steps 2–5 in this chapter, assuming that the model was specified. The most important topic, model building—step 1, is discussed in Chapter 12. Additional material on these topics can be found in the references at the end of the chapter.

Supplementary Exercises 11.20–11.46

[*Note:* Starred (*) exercises require the use of a computer.]

11.20 Suppose you used Minitab to fit the model

$$y = \beta_0 + \beta_1 x_1 + \beta_2 x_2 + \varepsilon$$

to $n = 15$ data points and you obtained the printout shown here.

```
THE REGRESSION EQUATION IS
Y =     90.1 -  1.84 X1 +  .285 X2

                                ST. DEV.   T-RATIO =
          COLUMN   COEFFICIENT  OF COEF.   COEF/S.D.

            --           90.1      23.1        3.90
X1   C2              -1.836       .367       -5.01
X2   C3                .285       .231        1.24

THE ST. DEV. OF Y ABOUT REGRESSION LINE IS
S =       10.7
WITH (  15- 3) =  12 DEGREES OF FREEDOM

R-SQUARED = 91.6 PERCENT
R-SQUARED = 90.2 PERCENT, ADJUSTED FOR D.F.

ANALYSIS OF VARIANCE

  DUE TO      DF      SS     MS=SS/DF

REGRESSION    2    14801.     7400.
RESIDUAL     12     1364.      114.
TOTAL        14    16165.
```

a. What is the least squares prediction equation?

b. Find R^2 and interpret its value.

c. Is there sufficient evidence to indicate that the model is useful for predicting y? Conduct an F test using $\alpha = .05$.

d. Test the null hypothesis $H_0: \beta_1 = 0$ against the alternative hypothesis $H_a: \beta_1 \neq 0$. Test using $\alpha = .05$. Draw the appropriate conclusions.

11.21 Several states now require all high school seniors to pass an achievement test before they can graduate. On the test, the seniors must demonstrate their familiarity with basic verbal and mathematical skills. Suppose the educational testing company that creates and administers these exams wants to model the score, y, on one of its exams as a function of the student's IQ, x_1, and socioeconomic status (SES). The SES is a categorical (or *qualitative*) variable with three levels: low, medium, and high. As we will demonstrate in Chapter 12, two *dummy (indicator)* variables are needed to describe a qualitative independent variable with three levels. Thus, we define

$$x_2 = \begin{cases} 1 & \text{if SES is medium} \\ 0 & \text{if SES is low or high} \end{cases} \qquad x_3 = \begin{cases} 1 & \text{If SES is high} \\ 0 & \text{if SES is low or medium} \end{cases}$$

Data were collected for a random sample of sixty seniors who have taken the test, and the model

$$E(y) = \beta_0 + \beta_1 x_1 + \beta_2 x_2 + \beta_3 x_3$$

was fit to the data, with the results shown in the SAS printout.

SOURCE	DF	SUM OF SQUARES	MEAN SQUARE	F VALUE	PR > F
MODEL	3	12268.56439492	4089.52146497	188.33	0.0001
ERROR	56	1216.01893841	21.71462390		
CORRECTED TOTAL	59	13484.58333333		R-SQUARE	ROOT MSE
				0.909822	4.65989527

PARAMETER	ESTIMATE	T FOR H0: PARAMETER=0	PR > |T|	STD ERROR OF ESTIMATE
INTERCEPT	-13.06166081	-3.21	0.0022	4.07101383
X1	0.74193946	17.56	0.0001	0.04224805
X2	18.60320572	12.49	0.0001	1.48895324
X3	13.40965415	8.97	0.0001	1.49417069

a. Identify the least squares equation.

b. Interpret the value of R^2 and test to determine whether the data provide sufficient evidence to indicate that this model is useful for predicting achievement test scores.

c. Sketch the relationship between predicted achievement test score and IQ for the three levels of SES. [*Note:* Three graphs of $\hat{y}$ versus x_1 must be drawn: the first for the low SES model ($x_2 = x_3 = 0$), the second for the medium SES model ($x_2 = 1$, $x_3 = 0$), and the third for the high SES model ($x_2 = 0$, $x_3 = 1$). The increase in predicted achievement test score per unit increase in IQ is the same for all three levels of SES; i.e., all three lines are parallel.]

11.22 Refer to Exercise 11.21. We now use the same data to fit the model

$$E(y) = \beta_0 + \beta_1 x_1 + \beta_2 x_2 + \beta_3 x_3 + \beta_4 x_1 x_2 + \beta_5 x_1 x_3$$

Thus, we now add the interaction between IQ and SES to the model. The SAS printout for this model is shown here.

SOURCE	DF	SUM OF SQUARES	MEAN SQUARE	F VALUE	PR > F
MODEL	5	12515.10021009	2503.02004202	139.42	0.0001
ERROR	54	969.48312324	17.95339117		
CORRECTED TOTAL	59	13484.58333333		R-SQUARE	ROOT MSE
				0.928104	4.23714422

PARAMETER	ESTIMATE	T FOR H0: PARAMETER = 0	PR > |T|	STD ERROR OF ESTIMATE
INTERCEPT	0.60129643	0.11	0.9096	5.26818519
X1	0.59526252	10.70	0.0001	0.05563379
X2	-3.72536406	-0.37	0.7115	10.01967496
X3	-16.23196444	-1.90	0.0631	8.55429931
X1*X2	0.23492147	2.29	0.0260	0.10263908
X1*X3	0.30807756	3.53	0.0009	0.08739554

a. Identify the least squares prediction equation.

b. Interpret the value of R^2 and test to determine whether the data provide sufficient evidence to indicate that this model is useful for predicting achievement test scores.

c. Sketch the relationship between predicted achievement test score and IQ for the three levels of SES. [*Note:* The interaction terms in the model allow nonparallelism among the three SES models; i.e., the mean increase in achievement test score per unit increase in IQ differs for the three levels of SES. To determine whether the interaction between IQ and SES is contributing to the prediction of achievement test score, we must test the null hypothesis H_0: $\beta_4 = \beta_5 = 0$ against the alternative that at least one of the coefficients of the interaction terms is nonzero. The method for testing portions of a regression model involving more than one β parameter (but less than all of them) will be discussed in Chapter 12.]

11.23 The recent expansion of U.S. grain exports has intensified the importance of the linkage between the domestic grain transportation system and international transportation. As a first step in evaluating the economics of this interface, Martin and Clement (1982) used multiple regression to estimate ocean transport rates for grain shipped from the lower Columbia River international ports. These ports include Portland, Oregon, and Vancouver, Longview, and Kalama, Washington. Rates per long ton, y, were modeled as a function of the following independent variables:

x_1 = Shipment size (long tons)

x_2 = Distance to destination port (miles)

x_3 = Bunker fuel price ($ per barrel)

$x_4 = \begin{cases} 1 & \text{if American flagship} \\ 0 & \text{if foreign flagship} \end{cases}$

x_5 = Size of port as measured by U.S. Defense Mapping Agency standards

x_6 = Quantity of grain exported from region during year of interest

The method of least squares was used to fit the model to 140 observations from the period 1978–1980. The following results were obtained:

$$\hat{y} = -18.469 - .367x_1 + 6.434x_2 - .2692x_2^2 + 1.7992x_3 + 50.292x_4 + 2.275x_5 - .018x_6$$
$$(-2.76)\quad(-5.62)\quad(3.64)\quad(-2.25)\quad(12.96)\quad(19.14)\quad(1.71)\quad(-2.69)$$

$$R^2 = .8979$$

The numbers in parentheses are the t statistics associated with the $\hat{\beta}$ values above them.

a. Test H_0: $\beta_1 = \beta_2 = \beta_3 = \beta_4 = \beta_5 = \beta_6 = \beta_7 = 0$. Use $\alpha = .01$. Interpret the results of your test in the context of the problem.

b. Binkley and Harrer (1979) estimated a similar rate function using multiple regression but used different independent variables. The coefficient of determination for their model was .46. Compare the explanatory power of the Binkley and Harrer model with that of Martin and Clement.

c. According to the least squares model, do transport rates increase with distance? Do they increase at an increasing rate? Explain.

11.24 Suppose you have developed a regression model to explain the relationship between y and x_1, x_2, and x_3. The ranges of the variables you used to develop your model are as follows: $10 \le y \le 100$, $5 \le x_1 \le 55$, $.5 \le x_2 \le 1$, and $1,000 \le x_3 \le 2,000$. Explain why you would have more confidence using your prediction equation to predict y when $x_1 = 30$, $x_2 = .6$, and $x_3 = 1,300$ than when $x_1 = 60$, $x_2 = .4$, and $x_3 = 900$.

11.25 Plastics made under different environmental conditions are known to have differing strengths. A scientist would like to know which combination of temperature and pressure yields a plastic with a high breaking strength. A small preliminary experiment was conducted at two pressure levels and two temperature levels. The following model was proposed:

$$E(y) = \beta_0 + \beta_1 x_1 + \beta_2 x_2 + \beta_3 x_1 x_2$$

where

y = Breaking strength (pounds)

x_1 = Temperature (°F) x_2 = Pressure (pounds per square inch)

A sample of $n = 16$ observations yielded

$$\hat{y} = 226.8 + 4.9x_1 + 1.2x_2 - .7x_1 x_2$$

with

$$s_{\hat{\beta}_1} = 1.11 \qquad s_{\hat{\beta}_2} = .27 \qquad s_{\hat{\beta}_3} = .34$$

Do the data indicate there is an interaction between temperature and pressure? Test using $\alpha = .05$.

11.26 A large government agency would like to predict the number of people it will hire within the next year to fill the thirty positions that are currently open. Historically, the agency has been unable to fill all its job openings. It has been decided to model the number of positions filled in a year, y, as a function of the number of positions open, x_1, and the recruiting budget for the year in dollars, x_2 (e.g., for advertising the positions, paying travel expenses, etc.). A random sample of 10 years of recruiting records was drawn from the agency's 30 years of records. The model

$$E(y) = \beta_0 + \beta_1 x_1 + \beta_2 x_2$$

was fit to the data using the Minitab regression computer program package. The results shown in the printout were obtained.

```
THE REGRESSION EQUATION IS
Y =    .0562 +   .273 X1 +  .0006 X2

                              ST. DEV.   T-RATIO =
        COLUMN   COEFFICIENT  OF COEF.   COEF/S.D.

        --            .056       .902        .06
X1      C2           .2733      .0971       2.81
X2      C3          .000560    .000129      4.34

THE ST. DEV. OF Y ABOUT REGRESSION LINE IS
S =      1.33
WITH (  10- 3) =    7 DEGREES OF FREEDOM

R-SQUARED = 97.9 PERCENT
R-SQUARED = 97.3 PERCENT, ADJUSTED FOR D.F.

ANALYSIS OF VARIANCE

  DUE TO      DF      SS     MS=SS/DF

REGRESSION    2    583.18     291.59
RESIDUAL      7     12.42       1.77
TOTAL         9    595.60
```

a. Identify the least squares prediction equation.
b. Is there sufficient evidence to indicate that the model contributes information for predicting the number, y, of positions that will be filled? Conduct an F test using $\alpha = .05$.
c. Test the null hypothesis $H_0: \beta_2 = 0$ against the alternative hypothesis $H_a: \beta_2 \neq 0$ using $\alpha = .05$. Interpret the results of your test in the context of the problem.
d. Use the least squares prediction equation to predict how many of the thirty positions the agency will fill next year if the recruiting budget is $10,000.
e. Which (if any) of the assumptions we make about ε in a regression analysis are likely to be violated in this problem? Explain.

11.27 After a regression model is fit to a set of data, a confidence interval for the mean value of y at a given setting of the independent variables will *always* be narrower than the corresponding prediction interval for a particular value of y at the same setting of the independent variables. Why?

*11.28 A florist is interested in how sunlight and misting affect the thickness of the leaves on a new variety of ivy. Sixteen ivy plants of the same age and appearance were randomly divided into four groups of four plants each. One group received no misting and indirect sunlight; one, misting and indirect sunlight; one, no misting and direct sunlight; and the last, misting and direct sunlight. After 3 months, the thickness of a center leaf from each plant was measured, with the results listed in the table on page 498 (measurements in millimeters).

		SUNLIGHT	
		Direct	Indirect
MISTING	No mist	0.64, 0.63, 0.61, 0.62	0.60, 0.61, 0.58, 0.59
	Mist	0.65, 0.63, 0.64, 0.64	0.62, 0.61, 0.60, 0.60

a. Fit the model $y = \beta_0 + \beta_1 x_1 + \beta_2 x_2 + \beta_3 x_1 x_2 + \varepsilon$ to the data, where

$$x_1 = \begin{cases} 1 & \text{if mist was present} \\ 0 & \text{if no mist} \end{cases} \qquad x_2 = \begin{cases} 1 & \text{if direct sunlight} \\ 0 & \text{if indirect sunlight} \end{cases}$$

b. Is there sufficient evidence to conclude that the model is useful in predicting the thickness of leaves on this variety of ivy?

c. Is there evidence of an interaction between sunlight condition and misting condition? Test using $\alpha = .05$.

11.29 Recent increases in gasoline prices have increased interest in modes of transportation other than the automobile. A metropolitan bus company wants to know whether changes in numbers of bus riders are related to changes in gasoline prices. By using information in the company files and gasoline price information obtained from fuel distributors, the company planned to fit the following model:

$$y = \beta_0 + \beta_1 x_1 + \beta_2 x_2 + \beta_3 x_1 x_2 + \varepsilon$$

where

$x_1 =$ Average wholesale price for regular gasoline in a given month

$$x_2 = \begin{cases} 1 & \text{if the bus travels a city route only} \\ 0 & \text{if the bus travels a suburb–city route} \end{cases}$$

$y =$ Total number of riders in a bus over the month

a. For the above model, how would you test to determine whether the relationship between the mean number of riders and gasoline price is different for the two different types of bus routes?

b. Suppose 12 months of data are kept, and the least squares model is

$$\hat{y} = 500 + 50x_1 + 5x_2 - 10x_1 x_2$$

Graph the predicted relationship between number of riders and gasoline price for city buses and for suburb–city buses. Compare the slopes.

c. If $s_{\hat{\beta}_3} = 3.0$, do the data indicate that gasoline price affects the number of riders differently for city and suburb–city buses? Use $\alpha = .05$.

11.30 During the winter months a sample of 100 homes is taken to obtain information concerning the relationship between kilowatt usage, y, and total window and glass area, x (measured as a percentage of the total wall area). A second-order model, $y = \beta_0 + \beta_1 x + \beta_2 x^2 + \varepsilon$, was used to model this relationship. The multiple coefficient of determination for the data was .24. Test whether the data indicate that the model contributes information for the prediction of y. Use $\alpha = .05$. [*Hint:* Use the methods of Section 11.6.]

*11.31 Refer to Exercise 10.20. The breeder of thoroughbred horses has been advised that the prediction model could probably be improved if a quadratic term were added. The following model is therefore proposed:

$$y = \beta_0 + \beta_1 x + \beta_2 x^2 + \varepsilon$$

where, as before

y = Lifetime of horse (years)

x = Gestation period of horse (days)

a. Find the least squares prediction equation and test its adequacy.

b. Has the addition of the quadratic term contributed significant information for the prediction of a thoroughbred horse's lifetime? Test H_0: $\beta_2 = 0$ against the alternative H_a: $\beta_2 \neq 0$ using $\alpha = .05$.

11.32 Most companies institute rigorous safety programs to assure employee safety. Suppose accident reports over the last year at a company are sampled, and the number of hours the employee had worked before the accident occurred, x, and the amount of time the employee lost from work, y, are recorded. A quadratic model is proposed to investigate a fatigue hypothesis that more serious accidents occur near the end of workdays than near the beginning. Thus, the proposed model is

$$E(y) = \beta_0 + \beta_1 x + \beta_2 x^2$$

A total of sixty accident reports are examined and part of the computer printout appears as shown:

SOURCE	DF	SUM OF SQUARES	MEAN SQUARE	F VALUE
MODEL	2	112.110	56.055	1.28
ERROR	57	2496.201	43.793	R-SQUARE
TOTAL	59	2608.311		.0430

a. Do the data support the fatigue hypothesis? Use $\alpha = .05$ to test whether the proposed model is useful in predicting the lost work time, y.

b. Does the result of the test in part a necessarily mean that no fatigue factor exists? Explain.

11.33 Refer to Exercise 11.32. Suppose the company persists in using the quadratic model despite its apparent lack of utility. The fitted model is

$$\hat{y} = 12.3 + 0.25x - .0033x^2$$

where $\hat{y}$ is the predicted time lost (days) and x is the number of hours worked prior to an accident.

a. Use the model to predict the number of days missed by an employee who has an accident after 6 hours of work.

b. Suppose the 95% prediction interval for the predicted value in part a is determined to be (1.35, 26.01). Interpret this interval. Does this interval support your conclusion about this model in Exercise 11.32?

11.34 *Operations management* is concerned with planning and controlling those organizational functions and systems that produce goods and services (Schroeder, 1981). One concern of the operations manager of a production process is the level of productivity of the process. An operations manager at a large manufacturing plant is interested in predicting the level of productivity of assembly line A next year (i.e., the number of units that will be produced by the assembly line next year). To do so, she has decided to use regression analysis to model the level of productivity, y, as a function of time, x. The number of units produced by assembly line A was determined for each of the past 15 years ($x = 1, 2, \ldots, 15$). The model

$$E(y) = \beta_0 + \beta_1 x + \beta_2 x^2$$

was fit to the data using Minitab. The results shown in the printout were obtained.

```
THE REGRESSION EQUATION IS
Y = - 1187. - 1333. X1 -  45.6 X2

                               ST. DEV.    T-RATIO =
        COLUMN    COEFFICIENT  OF COEF.    COEF/S.D.

          --         -1187.      446.        -2.66
  X1    C2            1333.      128.        10.38
  X2    C3           -45.59      7.80        -5.84

THE ST. DEV. OF Y ABOUT REGRESSION LINE IS
S =        501.
WITH (   15- 3) =   12 DEGREES OF FREEDOM

R-SQUARED = 97.3 PERCENT
R-SQUARED = 96.9 PERCENT, ADJUSTED FOR D.F.

ANALYSIS OF VARIANCE

  DUE TO        DF           SS         MS=SS/DF

REGRESSION     2      110578719.     55289359.
RESIDUAL      12        3013365.       251114.
TOTAL         14      113592083.
```

a. Identify the least squares prediction equation.

b. Find R^2 and interpret its value in the context of this problem.

c. Is there sufficient evidence to indicate that the model is useful for predicting the productivity of assembly line A? Test using $\alpha = .05$.

d. Test the null hypothesis $H_0: \beta_2 = 0$ against the alternative hypothesis $H_a: \beta_2 \neq 0$ using $\alpha = .05$. Interpret the results of your test in the context of this problem.

e. Which (if any) of the assumptions we make about ε in a regression analysis are likely to be violated in this problem? Explain.

[*Note:* In this exercise time series data were used to obtain the least squares prediction equation. We will discuss time series data and time series models in Chapters 13 and 14.]

11.35 To increase the motivation and productivity of workers, an electronics manufacturer decides to experiment with a new pay incentive structure at one of two plants. The experimental plan will be tried at plant A for 6 months, while workers at plant B will remain on the original pay plan. To evaluate the effectiveness of the new plan, the average assembly time for part of an electronic system was measured for employees at both plants at the beginning and end of the 6-month period. Suppose the following model was proposed:

$$y = \beta_0 + \beta_1 x_1 + \beta_2 x_2 + \varepsilon$$

where

y = Assembly time (hours) at end of 6-month period

x_1 = Assembly time (hours) at beginning of 6-month period

$$x_2 = \begin{cases} 1 & \text{if plant A} \\ 0 & \text{if plant B} \end{cases} \quad \text{(dummy variable)}$$

A sample of $n = 42$ observations yielded

$$\hat{y} = 0.11 + 0.98x_1 - 0.53x_2$$

where

$$s_{\hat{\beta}_1} = .231 \qquad s_{\hat{\beta}_2} = .48$$

Test to see whether, after allowing for the effect of initial assembly time, plant A had a lower mean assembly time than plant B. Use $\alpha = .01$. [*Note:* When the {0, 1} coding is used to define a dummy variable, the coefficient of the variable represents the difference between the mean response at the two levels represented by the variable. Thus, the coefficient β_2 is the difference in mean assembly time between plant A and plant B at the end of the 6-month period, and $\hat{\beta}_2$ is the sample estimator of that difference.]

11.36 A company that relies on door-to-door sales wants to determine the relationship, if any, between the proportion of customers who buy its product, y, and two independent variables: price, x_1, and years of experience of the salesperson, x_2. Twenty salespeople employed by the company are randomly assigned to sell the products, five to each of four prices, ranging from $1.98 to $5.98. Each salesperson makes a sales presentation to thirty prospects, and the percentage of sales is recorded. The twenty observations are used to fit the model

$$y = \beta_0 + \beta_1 x_1 + \beta_2 x_2 + \varepsilon$$

The least squares model is

$$\hat{y} = -.30 - .010x_1 + .10x_2$$

with $s_{\hat{\beta}_1} = .0030$, $s_{\hat{\beta}_2} = .025$, and $R^2 = .86$.

a. Interpret the values of $\hat{\beta}_1$ and $\hat{\beta}_2$.

b. Is there sufficient evidence to conclude that the overall model is useful for predicting y? Use $\alpha = .05$.

c. Do the data support the hypothesis that as the price of the product is increased the mean proportion of buyers will decrease?

d. Is there evidence that as the experience of the salesperson increases the mean proportion of buyers increases?

11.37 Refer to Exercise 11.36. Suppose it is claimed that the least squares model cannot be correct, since $\hat{\beta}_0 = -.30$, and a negative proportion of buyers is clearly impossible. How do you refute this argument?

11.38 The Environmental Protection Agency (EPA) wants to model the gas mileage ratings, y, of automobiles as a function of their engine size, x. A second -order model,

$$E(y) = \beta_0 + \beta_1 x + \beta_2 x^2$$

is proposed. A sample of fifty engines of varying sizes is selected, and the miles per gallon rating of each is determined. The least squares model is

$$\hat{y} = 51.3 - 10.1x + 0.15x^2$$

The size, x, of the engine is measured in hundreds of cubic inches. Also, $s_{\hat{\beta}_2} = .0037$ and $R^2 = .93$.

a. Sketch the predicted relationship between y and x for values of x between $x = 1$ and $x = 4$.

b. Is there evidence that the quadratic term in the model is contributing to the prediction of the miles per gallon rating, y? Use $\alpha = .05$.

c. Use the model to estimate the mean miles per gallon rating for all cars with 350-cubic-inch engines ($x = 3.5$).

d. Suppose a 95% confidence interval for the quantity estimated in part c is determined to be (17.2, 18.4). Interpret this interval.

e. Suppose you purchase an automobile with a 350-cubic-inch engine and determine that the miles per gallon rating is 14.7. Is it surprising that this value lies outside the confidence interval given in part d? Explain.

11.39 To determine whether extra personnel are needed for the day, the owners of a water adventure park would like to find a model that would allow them to predict the day's attendance each morning based on the day of the week and weather conditions. The model is of the form

$$E(y) = \beta_0 + \beta_1 x_1 + \beta_2 x_2 + \beta_3 x_3$$

where

$y = $ Daily attendance

$x_1 = \begin{cases} 1 & \text{if weekend} \\ 0 & \text{otherwise} \end{cases}$ (dummy variable)

$x_2 = \begin{cases} 1 & \text{if sunny} \\ 0 & \text{if overcast} \end{cases}$ (dummy variable)

$x_3 = $ Predicted daily high temperature (°F)

After taking 30 days of data, the owners obtained the following least squares model:

$$\hat{y} = -105 + 25x_1 + 100x_2 + 10x_3$$

with $s_{\hat{\beta}_1} = 10$, $s_{\hat{\beta}_2} = 30$, and $s_{\hat{\beta}_3} = 4$. Also, $R^2 = .65$.

a. Interpret the estimated model coefficients.

b. Is there sufficient evidence to conclude that this model is useful in the prediction of daily attendance? Use $\alpha = .05$.

c. Is there sufficient evidence to conclude that mean attendance increases on weekends? Use $\alpha = .10$.

d. Use the model to predict the attendance on a sunny weekday with a predicted high temperature of 95°F.

e. Suppose the 90% prediction interval for part d is (645, 1,245). Interpret this interval.

11.40 Refer to Exercise 11.39. The owners of the water adventure park are advised that the prediction model could probably be improved if interaction terms were added. In particular, it is thought that the *rate* of increase in mean attendance with increases in predicted high temperature will be greater on weekends than on weekdays. The following model is therefore proposed:

$$E(y) = \beta_0 + \beta_1 x_1 + \beta_2 x_2 + \beta_3 x_3 + \beta_4 x_1 x_3$$

The same 30 days of data as were used in Exercise 11.39 are used to obtain the least squares model

$$\hat{y} = 250 - 700 x_1 + 100 x_2 + 5 x_3 + 15 x_1 x_3$$

with $s_{\hat{\beta}_4} = 3.0$ and $R^2 = .96$.

a. Graph the predicted day's attendance, y, against the day's predicted high temperature, x_3, for a sunny weekday and for a sunny weekend day. Graph both on the same graph for x_3 between 70°F and 100°F. Note that the slope for the weekend day is greater.

b. Do the data indicate that the interaction term is a useful addition to the model? Use $\alpha = .05$.

c. Use this model to predict the attendance for a sunny weekday with a predicted high temperature of 95°F.

d. Suppose the 90% prediction interval for part c is (800, 850). Compare this with the prediction interval for the model without interaction in Exercise 11.39, part e. Do the relative widths of the prediction intervals support or refute your conclusion about the utility of the interaction term (part b)?

11.41 Refer to Exercise 11.40. The owners, noting that $\hat{\beta}_1 = -700$, conclude the model is ridiculous because it seems to imply that the mean attendance will be 700 less on weekends than on weekdays. Refute their argument.

11.42 Many students must work part-time to help finance their college education. A survey of 100 students was completed at a university to determine whether the number of hours worked per week, x, was affecting their grade-point averages, y. A quadratic model was proposed:

$$y = \beta_0 + \beta_1 x + \beta_2 x^2 + \varepsilon$$

The 100 observations yielded the least squares model

$$\hat{y} = 2.8 - .005x - .0002x^2$$

with $R^2 = .12$.

a. Do these statistics indicate that the model is useful in explaining grade-point averages? Use $\alpha = .05$.

b. Interpret the value $R^2 = .12$. Do you think the relationship between y and x is strong? Would you expect to be able to predict grade-point averages precisely (narrow prediction interval) if you knew how many hours students work per week?

*11.43 A company that services two brands of microcomputers would like to be able to predict the amount of time it takes to perform preventive maintenance on each brand. They believe the following predictive model is appropriate:

$$y = \beta_0 + \beta_1 x_1 + \beta_2 x_2 + \varepsilon$$

where

$y =$ Maintenance time

$$x_1 = \begin{cases} 1 & \text{if brand A} \\ 0 & \text{if brand B} \end{cases}$$

$x_2 =$ Service person's number of months of experience in preventive maintenance

Ten service people were randomly selected, and each was randomly assigned to perform preventive maintenance on either a brand A or brand B microcomputer. The following data were obtained.

MAINTENANCE TIME (Hours)	BRAND	EXPERIENCE (Months)	MAINTENANCE TIME (Hours)	BRAND	EXPERIENCE (Months)
2.0	1	2	1.5	0	2
1.8	1	4	1.7	1	6
0.8	0	12	1.2	0	5
1.1	1	12	1.4	1	9
1.0	0	8	1.2	0	7

a. Fit the model to the data.

b. Investigate whether the overall model is useful. Test using $\alpha = .05$.

c. Find R^2 for the fitted model. Does the value of R^2 support your findings in part b? Explain.

d. Find a 90% confidence interval for β_2. Interpret your result in the context of the exercise.

e. Use the fitted model to predict how long it will take a person with 6 months of experience to service a brand B microcomputer.

f. How long would it take the person referred to in part e to service ten brand B microcomputers? List any assumptions you made in reaching your prediction.

g. Find a 95% prediction interval for the time required to perform preventive maintenance on a brand A microcomputer by a person with 4 months of experience.

*11.44 Many colleges and universities develop regression models for predicting the grade-point average (GPA) of incoming freshmen. This predicted GPA can then be used to make admission decisions. Although most models use many independent variables to predict GPA, we will illustrate by choosing two variables:

$x_1 =$ Verbal score on college entrance examination (percentile)

$x_2 =$ Mathematics score on college entrance examination (percentile)

The data in the table are obtained for a random sample of forty freshmen at one college.

VERBAL x_1	MATHEMATICS x_2	GPA y	VERBAL x_1	MATHEMATICS x_2	GPA y
81	87	3.49	79	75	3.45
68	99	2.89	81	62	2.76
57	86	2.73	50	69	1.90
100	49	1.54	72	70	3.01
54	83	2.56	54	52	1.48
82	86	3.43	65	79	2.98
75	74	3.59	56	78	2.58
58	98	2.86	98	67	2.73
55	54	1.46	97	80	3.27
49	81	2.11	77	90	3.47
64	76	2.69	49	54	1.30
66	59	2.16	39	81	1.22
80	61	2.60	87	69	3.23
100	85	3.30	70	95	3.82
83	76	3.75	57	89	2.93
64	66	2.70	74	67	2.83
83	72	3.15	87	93	3.84
93	54	2.28	90	65	3.01
74	59	2.92	81	76	3.33
51	75	2.48	84	69	3.06

a. Fit the first-order model (no quadratic and no interaction terms)

$$y = \beta_0 + \beta_1 x_1 + \beta_2 x_2 + \varepsilon$$

Interpret the value of R^2, and test whether the data indicate that the terms in the model are useful for predicting freshman GPA. Use $\alpha = .05$.

b. Sketch the relationship between predicted GPA, $\hat{y}$, and verbal score, x_1, for the following mathematics scores: $x_2 = 60$, 75, and 90.

*11.45 Refer to Exercise 11.44. Now fit the following second-order model to the data:

$$y = \beta_0 + \beta_1 x_1 + \beta_2 x_2 + \beta_3 x_1^2 + \beta_4 x_2^2 + \beta_5 x_1 x_2 + \varepsilon$$

a. Interpret the value of R^2, and test whether the data indicate that this model is useful for predicting freshman GPA. Use $\alpha = .05$.

b. Sketch the relationship between predicted GPA, $\hat{y}$, and the verbal score, x_1, for the following mathematics scores: $x_2 = 60$, 75, and 90. Compare these graphs with those for the first-order model in Exercise 11.44.

c. Test whether the interaction term, $\beta_5 x_1 x_2$, is important for the prediction of GPA. Use $\alpha = .10$. Note that this term permits the distance between three mathematics score curves for GPA versus verbal score to change as the verbal score changes.

*11.46 An economist is interested in estimating the demand function for passenger car motor fuel in the United States. While demand is clearly a function of many variables, the economist initially wants to model demand as a function of consumer income and the price of gasoline and plans to estimate the model using yearly time series data over the period 1965–1980. As a measure of income, it was decided to use the average gross weekly earnings for each year for production or nonsupervisory workers on private nonagricultural payrolls. These data are available from the Bureau of Labor Statistics (BLS). However, since both earnings and the cost of living increased over this period, the BLS earnings data do not reflect actual purchasing power. Accordingly, the earnings data—originally expressed in *current dollars* (i.e., the number of dollars actually earned)—were converted to 1967 dollars. This was accomplished by dividing each figure by the Consumer Price Index (CPI) for that year and multiplying the result by 100. (This procedure is described in detail in Chapter 13.) The resulting earnings data—called *real earnings*—are the number of dollars that would have to have been earned in 1967 to equal the purchasing power of current year weekly earnings. These data appear in the table at the top of the next page.

Data on the actual price of gasoline and the relative price of gasoline (computed by dividing the CPI for gasoline by the CPI for all items) were also collected and appear in the table. The relative price data reflect the price of gasoline relative to the prices of other consumer goods. The economist believes the relative price may have a substantial influence on demand. For example, even though actual gasoline prices increase, consumers may actually increase their demand for gasoline if the relative price decreases.

Finally, data have been collected on motor fuel consumed per year and the population of the United States. The population data have been included so that the effects of the growing U.S. population on demand for motor fuel could be removed if desired. This can be accomplished by dividing the total motor fuel consumed in a year by the population that year. The result is called *per capita* motor fuel consumption. By using per capita consumption as the measure of demand, the economist can distinguish the effects on demand of factors such as price and income from the effects of population growth (Blair & Kenny, 1982).

a. Explain what is being measured by the yearly per capita motor fuel consumption variable.

b. Initially, the economist hypothesizes that per capita motor fuel consumption is a linear function of the relative price of gasoline. Use the method of least squares to estimate this model.

c. Investigate the usefulness of this preliminary model. Use $\alpha = .05$. Also, find R^2.

d. Next, the economist would like to expand the model described in part b to include a second independent variable, average gross real weekly earnings. Use the method of least squares to fit this expanded model.

e. Investigate the usefulness of the expanded model of part d. Use $\alpha = .05$. Also, find R^2.

f. From an economic (or intuitive) perspective, do the signs of the estimated coefficients of the expanded model seem to be appropriate? Explain. [*Note:* The model will be modified in part b of Exercise 12.63 to resolve this problem.]

g. Using the expanded model, estimate the mean per capita demand for motor fuel when average gross weekly earnings are $110.36 and the relative price of a gallon of gasoline is 1.521. What reservations (if any) do you have about the goodness of your estimate?

YEAR	MOTOR FUEL CONSUMED BY CARS (Billion gallons)	POPULATION OF UNITED STATES (Millions)	AVERAGE GROSS REAL WEEKLY EARNINGS (1967 $)	PRICE OF GALLON OF REGULAR GASOLINE ($)	RELATIVE PRICE OF GALLON OF GASOLINE
1965	50.3	194.3	101.01	.32	1.004
1966	53.31	196.6	101.67	.33	.998
1967	55.11	198.7	101.84	.34	1.000
1968	58.52	200.7	103.39	.34	.973
1969	62.45	202.7	104.38	.36	.954
1970	65.8	205.1	103.04	.36	.908
1971	69.51	207.1	104.96	.36	.876
1972	73.5	209.9	109.26	.37	.859
1973	78.0	211.9	109.23	.40	.887
1974	74.2	213.9	104.78	.53	1.083
1975	76.5	216.0	101.45	.57	1.060
1976	78.8	218.0	102.90	.59	1.043
1977	80.7	220.2	104.13	.62	1.037
1978	83.8	222.6	104.30	.63	1.005
1979	80.2	225.1	101.02	.86	1.222
1980	73.7	227.7	95.18	1.19	1.496

Source: All data from *Statistical Abstract of the United States,* various years; except average gross real weekly earnings, which are from *Employment and Earnings,* U.S. Department of Labor, Bureau of Labor Statistics, Oct. 1983, p. 109.

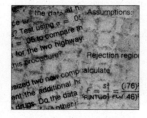

On Your Own . . .

This is a continuation of the "On Your Own" presented in Chapter 10, in which you selected three independent variables as predictors of the Gross National Product and obtained 10 years of data for each. Now fit the multiple regression model (use an available computer package, if possible)

$$y = \beta_0 + \beta_1 x_1 + \beta_2 x_2 + \beta_3 x_3 + \varepsilon$$

where

y = Gross National Product

x_1 = First variable you chose

x_2 = Second variable you chose

x_3 = Third variable you chose

a. Compare the coefficients $\hat{\beta}_1$, $\hat{\beta}_2$, and $\hat{\beta}_3$ to their corresponding slope coefficients in the Chapter 10 "On Your Own," where you fit three separate straight-line models. How do you account for the differences?

b. Calculate the coefficient of determination R^2, and conduct the F test of the null hypothesis H_0: $\beta_1 = \beta_2 = \beta_3 = 0$. What is your conclusion?

If the independent variables you chose are themselves highly correlated, you may encounter some results that are difficult to explain. For example, the coefficients $\hat{\beta}_1$, $\hat{\beta}_2$, and $\hat{\beta}_3$ may assume signs that are the opposite of what you expected. Or you may get a highly significant F value in part b, but the individual t statistics for x_1, x_2, and x_3 may all be nonsignificant. This phenomenon — a high correlation between the independent variables in a regression model — is *multicollinearity.* This topic was discussed in Section 11.11.

References

Allmon, C. I. "Advertising and sales relationships for toothpaste: Another look." *Business Economics,* Sept. 1982, *17,* 55–61.

Benston, G. J. "Multiple regression analysis of cost behavior." *Accounting Review,* Oct. 1966, *41,* 657–672.

Binkley, J. K., & Harrer, B. "Major determinants of ocean freight rates for grains: An econometric analysis." *American Journal of Agricultural Economics,* Feb. 1981, *63,* 47–57.

Blair, R. D., & Kenny, L. W. *Microeconomics for managerial decision making.* New York: McGraw-Hill, 1982. Chapter 3.

Carlson, R. D. "Advertising and sales relationships for toothpaste." *Business Economics,* Sept. 1981, *16,* 36–39.

Chase, R. B., & Aquilano, N. J. *Production and operations management.* Rev. ed. Homewood, Ill.: Richard D. Irwin, 1979. Chapter 11.

Chatterjee, S., & Price, B. *Regression analysis by example.* New York: Wiley, 1977.

Dixon, W. J., Brown, M. B., Engelman, L., Frane, J. W., Hill, M. A., Jennrich, R. I., & Toporek, J. D. *BMDP statistical software.* Berkeley: University of California Press, 1983.

Draper, N. R., & Smith, H. *Applied regression analysis.* 2d ed. New York: Wiley, 1981.

Ferguson, C. E., & Maurice, S. C. *Economics analysis.* Homewood, Ill.: Richard D. Irwin, 1970. Chapter 6.

Henry, W. R., & Haynes, W. W. *Managerial economics: Analysis and cases.* 4th ed. Dallas: Business Publications, 1978. Chapter 5.

Martin, M. V., & Clement, D. A. "An analysis of port-specific international grain freight rates: The case of the lower Columbia River port area." *Transportation Journal,* Fall 1982, *22,* 18–26.

Mendenhall, W., & McClave, J. T. *A second course in business statistics: Regression analysis.* San Francisco: Dellen, 1981.

Miller, R. B., & Wichern, D. W. *Intermediate business statistics: Analysis of variance, regression, and time series.* New York: Holt, Rinehart and Winston, 1977. Chapters 6–8.

Neter, J., Wasserman, W., & Kutner, M. *Applied linear regression models.* Homewood, Ill.: Richard D. Irwin, 1983.

Nie, N., Hull, C. H., Jenkins, J. G., Steinbrenner, K., & Bent, D. H. *Statistical package for the social sciences.* 2d ed. New York: McGraw-Hill, 1975.

Ryan, T. A., Joiner, B. L., & Ryan, B. F. *Minitab student handbook.* North Scituate, Mass.: Duxbury, 1976.

SAS user's guide: Statistics. 1982 ed. Ray, A. A., ed. SAS Institute Inc. Box 8000, Cary, N.C. 27511.

Schroeder, R. G. *Operations management: Decision making in the operations function.* New York: McGraw-Hill, 1981.

Sugrue, P. K., Ledford, M. H., & Glaskowsky, N. A., Jr. "Operating economies of scale in the U.S. long-haul common carrier, motor freight industry." *Transportation Journal,* Fall 1982, *22,* 27–41.

Weisberg, S. *Applied linear regression.* New York: Wiley, 1980.

Winkler, R. L., & Hays, W. L. *Statistics: Probability, inference, and decision.* 2d ed. New York: Holt, Rinehart and Winston, 1975. Chapter 10.

Wonnacott, R. J., & Wonnacott, T. H. *Econometrics.* 2d ed. New York: Wiley, 1979. Chapter 6.

Younger, M. S. *A handbook for linear regression.* North Scituate, Mass.: Duxbury, 1979.

CHAPTER 12

Introduction to Model Building

Where We've Been . . .

One of the most important topics in applied statistics, regression analysis, was presented in Chapters 10 and 11. Simple linear regression, using a straight line to model the relationship between a dependent variable y and a single independent variable x, was the topic of Chapter 10. Multiple regression, relating a dependent variable to any number of independent variables, was the topic of Chapter 11. In both chapters, we learned how to fit regression models to a set of data and how to use the model to estimate the mean value of y or to predict a future value of y for a given value of x.

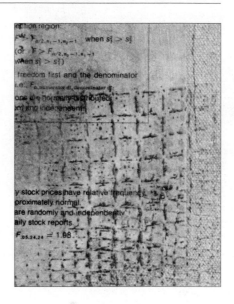

Where We're Going . . .

In Chapters 10 and 11, an important problem was circumvented—the selection of a model that is appropriate for the given data. No matter how much you know about regression analysis, or how well you can fit a model to a set of data and interpret the results, the information will be of little value if you choose an ill-fitting model to relate the mean value of y to the independent variables. The process of choosing a reasonable model and using the data to modify and improve it, is called *model building.* We introduce you to this topic in Chapter 12.

Contents

We have indicated in Chapters 10 and 11 that the first step in the construction of a regression model is to hypothesize the form of the deterministic portion of the probabilistic model. This *model building,* or model construction, stage is the key to the success (or failure) of the regression analysis. If the hypothesized model does not reflect, at least approximately, the true nature of the relationship between the mean response $E(y)$ and the independent variables $x_1, x_2, \ldots, x_k$, the modeling effort will usually be unrewarded.

By *model building,* we mean developing a model that will provide a good fit to a set of data and that will give good estimates of the mean value of y and good predictions of future values of y for given values of the independent variables. To illustrate, suppose you wish to relate the demand, y, for a given product to advertising expenditure, x, and (unknown to you) the second-order model

$$E(y) = \beta_0 + \beta_1 x + \beta_2 x^2$$

would permit you to predict y with a very small error of prediction [see Figure 12.1(a)]. Unfortunately, you have erroneously chosen the first-order model

$$E(y) = \beta_0 + \beta_1 x$$

to explain the relationship between y and x [see Figure 12.1(b)].

Figure 12.1 Two Models for Relating Demand y to Advertising Expenditure x

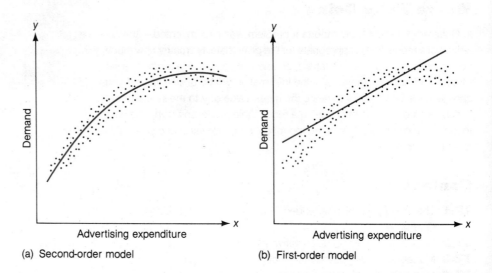

(a) Second-order model   (b) First-order model

The consequence of choosing the wrong model is clearly demonstrated by comparing Figures 12.1(a) and (b). The errors of prediction for the second-order model are relatively small in comparison to those for the first-order model. The lesson to be learned from this simple example is clear. Choosing a good set of independent (predictor) variables, $x_1, x_2, \ldots, x_k$, will not guarantee a good prediction equation. In addition to selecting independent variables that contain information about y, you must specify an equation relating y to $x_1, x_2, \ldots, x_k$ that will provide a good fit to your data.

In the following sections, we will present some useful models for relating a response y to one or more predictor variables.

12.1 The Two Types of Independent Variables: Quantitative and Qualitative

In Chapter 2, we defined two types of variables that may arise in business applications: quantitative and qualitative. In regression analysis, the dependent variable will always be quantitative, but the independent variables may be either quantitative or qualitative. As you will see, the way an independent variable enters the model depends on its type.

Definition 12.1

A *quantitative* independent variable is one that assumes numerical values corresponding to the points on a line. An independent variable that is not quantitative is called *qualitative.*

The Gross National Product, prime interest rate, number of defects in a product, and kilowatt-hours of electricity used per day are all examples of quantitative independent variables. On the other hand, suppose three different styles of packaging, A, B, and C, are used by a manufacturer. This independent variable is qualitative, since it is not measured on a numerical scale. Certainly, the style of packaging is an independent variable that may affect the sales of a product, and we would want to include it in a model describing the product's sales, *y.*

Definition 12.2

The *levels* of an independent variable are its different intensity settings.

For a quantitative independent variable, the levels correspond to the numerical values it assumes. For example, if the number of defects in a product ranges from 0 to 3, the independent variable has four levels: 0, 1, 2, and 3.

The levels of a qualitative variable are not numerical. They can be defined only by describing them. For example, the independent variable for the style of packaging was observed at three levels: A, B, and C.

Example 12.1

In Chapter 11 we considered the problem of predicting executive salaries as a function of several independent variables. Consider the following four independent variables that may affect executive salaries:

a. Number of years of experience
b. Sex of the employee
c. Firm's net asset value
d. Rank of the employee

For each of these independent variables, give its type and describe the levels you would expect to observe.

Solution   **a.** The independent variable for the number of years of experience is quantitative because its values are numerical. We would expect to observe levels ranging from 0 to 40 (approximately) years.

b. The independent variable for sex is qualitative because its levels can be described only by the nonnumerical labels "female" and "male."

c. The independent variable for the firm's net asset value is quantitative, with a large number of possible levels corresponding to the range of dollar values representing various firms' net asset values.

d. Suppose the independent variable for the rank of the employee is observed at three levels: supervisor, assistant vice-president, and vice-president. Since we cannot assign a realistic numerical measure of relative importance to each position, rank is a qualitative independent variable. ■

Quantitative independent variables are treated differently from qualitative variables in regression modeling. In the next section, we will begin our discussion of how quantitative variables are used in the modeling effort.

Exercises 12.1–12.4

Applying the Concepts

12.1 The marketing department of a large consumer food products company conducted a study to investigate the effect of the following independent variables on the total number of units sold per month of one of the company's new products:

a. Monthly advertising expenditure   **b.** Type of container
c. Color of container   **d.** Medium used for advertising
e. Net weight of the product

Classify each of the variables as quantitative or qualitative and describe the levels that the variables may assume.

12.2 Companies keep personnel files on their employees that contain important information on each individual's background. The data could be used, for example, to predict employee performance ratings. Identify the independent variables listed below as qualitative or quantitative. For qualitative variables, suggest several levels that might be observed. For quantitative variables, give a range of values (levels) for which the variable might be observed.

a. Age   **b.** Years of experience with the company
c. Highest educational degree   **d.** Job classification
e. Marital status   **f.** Religious preference
g. Salary   **h.** Sex

12.3 Which of the assumptions about ε (Section 10.3) prohibit the use of a qualitative variable as a dependent variable?

12.4 Exercise 11.23 described the least squares model developed by Martin and Clement to estimate ocean transport rates for grain shipped from the lower Columbia River international ports. Classify y, x_1, x_2, and x_4 as quantitative or qualitative variables and describe the levels that each variable may assume.

12.2
Models with a Single Quantitative Independent Variable

The most common linear models relating y to a single quantitative independent variable x are those derived from a polynomial expression of the type shown in the box. Specific models, obtained by assigning particular values to p, are listed below.

Formula for a pth-Order Polynomial with One Quantitative Independent Variable

$$E(y) = \beta_0 + \beta_1 x + \beta_2 x^2 + \beta_3 x^3 + \cdots + \beta_p x^p$$

where p is an integer and $\beta_0, \beta_1, \ldots, \beta_p$ are unknown parameters that must be estimated.

---

1. First-Order Model

$$E(y) = \beta_0 + \beta_1 x$$

Comments on Model Parameters:

β_0: y-intercept $\qquad$ β_1: Slope of the line

General Comments: The first-order model is used when you expect the rate of change in y per unit change in x to remain fairly stable over the range of values of x for which you wish to predict y (see Figure 12.2). Most relationships between $E(y)$ and x are curvilinear, but the curvature over the range of values of x for which you wish to predict y may be very slight. When this occurs, a first-order (straight-line) model should provide a good fit to your data.

Figure 12.2 Graph of a First-Order Model

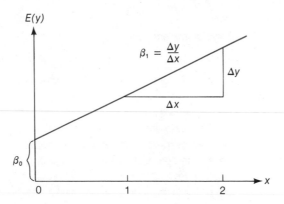

2. Second-Order Model

$$E(y) = \beta_0 + \beta_1 x + \beta_2 x^2$$

Comments on Model Parameters:

β_0: *y*-intercept

β_1: Changing the value of β_1 shifts the parabola to the right or left; increasing the value of β_1 causes the parabola to shift to the left

β_2: Rate of curvature

General Comments: A second-order model traces a parabola, one that opens either downward ($\beta_2 < 0$) or upward ($\beta_2 > 0$), as shown in Figure 12.3. Since most relationships will possess some curvature, a second-order model will often be a good choice to relate *y* to *x*.

Figure 12.3 Graphs of Two Second-Order Models

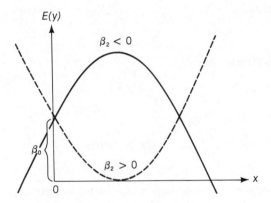

3. Third-Order Model

$$E(y) = \beta_0 + \beta_1 x + \beta_2 x^2 + \beta_3 x^3$$

Comments on Model Parameters:

β_0: *y*-intercept

β_3: The magnitude of β_3 controls the rate of reversal of curvature for the curve

General Comments: Reversals in curvature are not common, but such relationships can be modeled by third- and higher-order polynomials. As can be seen in Figure 12.3, a second-order model contains no reversals in curvature. The slope continues to either increase or decrease as *x* increases and produces either a trough or a peak. A third-order model (see Figure 12.4) contains one reversal in curvature and produces one peak and one trough. In general, a graph of a *p*th-order polynomial will contain a total of ($p - 1$) peaks and troughs.

Most functional relationships in nature seem to be smooth (except for random error), that is, they are not subject to rapid and irregular reversals in direction. Consequently, the second-order polynomial model is perhaps the most useful of those described above. To develop a better understanding of how this model is used, consider Example 12.2.

Figure 12.4 Graphs of Two Third-Order Models

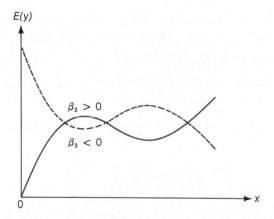

Example 12.2

Power companies must be able to predict the peak power load at their various stations in order to operate effectively. The *peak power load* is the maximum amount of power that must be generated each day to meet demand.

Suppose a power company located in the southern part of the United States decides to model daily peak power load, y, as a function of the daily high temperature, x, and the model is to be constructed for the summer months when demand is greatest. Although we would expect the peak power load to increase as the high temperature increases, the *rate* of increase in $E(y)$ might also increase as x increases. That is, a 1-unit increase in high temperature from 100 to 101°F might result in a larger increase in power demand than would a 1-unit increase from 80 to 81°F. Therefore, we postulate the second-order model

$$E(y) = \beta_0 + \beta_1 x + \beta_2 x^2$$

and we expect β_2 to be positive.

A random sample of 25 summer days is selected, and the data are shown in Table 12.1. Fit a second-order model using these data, and test the hypothesis that the power load increases at an increasing *rate* with temperature—i.e., that $\beta_2 > 0$.

Table 12.1
Power Load Data

TEMPERATURE (°F)	PEAK LOAD (Megawatts)	TEMPERATURE (°F)	PEAK LOAD (Megawatts)	TEMPERATURE (°F)	PEAK LOAD (Megawatts)
94	136.0	106	178.2	76	100.9
96	131.7	67	101.6	68	96.3
95	140.7	71	92.5	92	135.1
108	189.3	100	151.9	100	143.6
67	96.5	79	106.2	85	111.4
88	116.4	97	153.2	89	116.5
89	118.5	98	150.1	74	103.9
84	113.4	87	114.7	86	105.1
90	132.0				

Solution   The SAS printout shown in Figure 12.5 gives the least squares fit of the second-order model using the data in Table 12.1. The prediction equation is

$$\hat{y} = 385.048 - 8.293x + .05982x^2$$

A plot of this equation and the observed values is given in Figure 12.6.

Figure 12.5   Portion of the SAS Printout for the Second-Order Model of Example 12.2

SOURCE	DF	SUM OF SQUARES	MEAN SQUARE	F VALUE	PR > F
MODEL	2	15011.77199776	7505.88599888	259.69	0.0001
ERROR	22	635.87840224	28.90356374	R-SQUARE	ROOT MSE
CORRECTED TOTAL	24	15647.65040000			5.37620347
				0.959363	

PARAMETER	ESTIMATE	T FOR H0: PARAMETER = 0	PR > |T|	STD ERROR OF ESTIMATE
INTERCEPT	385.04809323	6.98	0.0001	55.17243578
TEMP	-8.29252680	-6.38	0.0001	1.29904502
TEMP*TEMP	0.05982337	7.93	0.0001	0.00754855

Figure 12.6   Plot of the Observations and the Second-Order Least Squares Fit

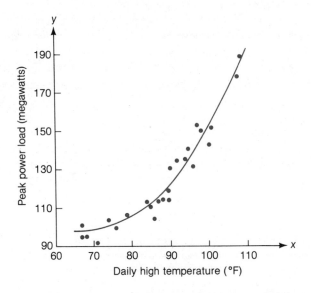

We now test whether the sample value $\hat{\beta}_2 = .05982$ is large enough to conclude *in general* that the power load increases at an increasing rate with temperature:

$$H_0: \quad \beta_2 = 0 \qquad H_a: \quad \beta_2 > 0$$

Test statistic: $t = \dfrac{\hat{\beta}_2}{s_{\hat{\beta}_2}}$

For $\alpha = .05$, $n = 25$, and $k = 2$, we reject H_0 if

$$t > t_{.05}$$

where $t_{.05} = 1.717$ (from Table V of Appendix B) is based on $n - (k + 1) = 22$ degrees of freedom. From Figure 12.5, the calculated value of t is 7.93. Since this value exceeds $t_{.05} = 1.717$, we reject H_0 at $\alpha = .05$ and conclude that the mean power load increases at an increasing rate with temperature. ∎

**Exercises
12.5–12.18**

Learning the Mechanics

12.5 The graphs depict pth-order polynomials with one independent variable. For each graph, identify the order of the polynomial. Find the value of β_0 and β_1 for each.

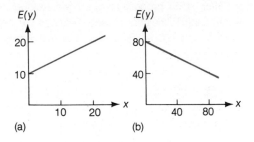

(a)   (b)

12.6 The graphs depict pth-order polynomials for one independent variable. For each graph, identify the order of the polynomial, the value of β_0, and the sign of β_2.

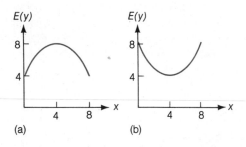

(a)   (b)

12.7 Graph the following polynomials and identify the order of each on your graph:

a. $E(y) = 2 + 3x$ **b.** $E(y) = 2 + 3x^2$
c. $E(y) = 1 + 2x + 2x^2 + x^3$ **d.** $E(y) = 2x + 2x^2 + x^3$
e. $E(y) = 2 - 3x^2$ **f.** $E(y) = -2 + 3x$

12.8 How do you decide the order of the polynomial you should use to model a response that is a function of one quantitative independent variable?

12.9 Suppose $E(y)$ can best be modeled by a second-order polynomial in x, where x is a quantitative variable. Write the probabilistic model for y.

Applying the Concepts

[*Note: Starred (*) exercises require the use of a computer.*]

12.10 A company that sells and services copy machines conducted a study to relate the number of service calls per month required for a particular brand of table-top copier to the age of the copier (in months). All copiers used in the study were utilized by their owners to produce between 10,000 and 12,000 copies per month. The company suspects that new and old copiers require more service calls than those of middle age.

a. Based on this information, propose an appropriate model relating the mean number of service calls per month to the copier's age. Define all variables in your proposed model.
b. Indicate whether you think β_0 and β_2 assume positive or negative values, and explain the reasons for your decisions.

12.11 Suppose you want to model the appraised value of a house, y, as a function of the number, x, of square feet of living space it contains. Regardless of how the appraisal is to be used, we would expect y to increase as x increases. In some instances, particularly if the appraisal is for tax purposes, the rate of increase in y decreases as x increases.

a. Write a suitable linear model to relate y and x.
b. Specify the signs of the coefficients in your model so they agree with the given verbal explanation of the relationship between y and x. Sketch the relationship on graph paper.

12.12 The strength of a certain plastic is thought to be related to the amount of pressure used to produce the plastic. Researchers believe that, as pressure is increased, the strength of the plastic increases until, at some point, increases in pressure have a detrimental effect on strength. Write a model to relate the strength, y, of the plastic to pressure, x, that would reflect the above beliefs. Sketch the model.

12.13 An economist has proposed the following model to describe the relationship between the number of items produced per day (output) and the number of hours of labor expended per day (input) in a particular production process:

$$y = \beta_0 + \beta_1 x + \beta_2 x^2 + \varepsilon$$

where

$y = $ Number of items produced per day

$x = $ Number of hours of labor per day

A portion of the Minitab computer printout that results from fitting this model to a sample of 25 weeks of production data is shown at the top of the next page. Do the data provide sufficient

```
THE REGRESSION EQUATION IS
Y = - 6.17 + 2.04 X1 - .0323 X2

                                ST. DEV.    T-RATIO =
          COLUMN    COEFFICIENT  OF COEF.   COEF/S.D.

          --           -6.173      1.666      -3.71
X1   C2                 2.036       .185      11.02
X2   C3                -.03231      .00489     -6.60

THE ST. DEV. OF Y ABOUT REGRESSION LINE IS
S =       1.243
WITH (  25- 3) =   22 DEGREES OF FREEDOM

R-SQUARED = 95.5 PERCENT
R-SQUARED = 95.1 PERCENT, ADJUSTED FOR D.F.

ANALYSIS OF VARIANCE

  DUE TO      DF      SS      MS=SS/DF

REGRESSION    2    718.168   359.084
RESIDUAL     22     33.992     1.545
TOTAL        24    752.160
```

evidence to indicate that the *rate* of increase in output per unit increase of input decreases as the input increases? Test using $\alpha = .05$.

12.14 A company is considering having the employees on its assembly line work 4 days per week for 10 hours each instead of 5 days for 8 hours. Management is concerned that the effect of fatigue due to longer afternoons of work might increase assembly times to an unsatisfactory level. An experiment with the 4-day week is planned in which time studies will be conducted on some of the workers during the afternoons. It is believed that an adequate model of the relationship between assembly time, y, and time since lunch, x, should allow for the average assembly time to decrease for a while after lunch (as workers get back in the groove) before it starts to increase as the workers become tired.

a. Propose a model to relate $E(y)$ and x that would reflect management's belief. Define all terms in your model.

b. Sketch the shape of the function described by your hypothesized model.

12.15 Underinflated or overinflated tires can affect gas mileage. A new brand of tire was tested for its effect on mileage at different pressures with the results shown in the table.

a. Plot the data on a scattergram.

b. If you were given only the information for $x = 30, 31, 32, 33$, what kind of model would you suggest? For $x = 33, 34, 35, 36$? For all the data?

*12.16 A veterinarian who works for a large midwestern pig cooperative believes that she has developed a daily vitamin pellet that will substantially increase the weight of mature pigs within 1 month. However, she is uncertain of the relationship between the daily dose (amount of the vitamin) and the percentage gain in weight after 1 month. To better understand this relationship, she randomly selects sixteen pigs of the same age and weight and feeds them different doses for a 1-month trial period. The data given in the table on page 520 resulted.

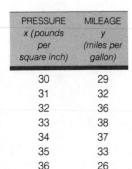

PRESSURE x (pounds per square inch)	MILEAGE y (miles per gallon)
30	29
31	32
32	36
33	38
34	37
35	33
36	26

WEIGHT GAIN (% original weight)	DAILY PELLET DOSE	WEIGHT GAIN (% original weight)	DAILY PELLET DOSE
82	0	90	4
78	0	95	4
80	1	89	5
87	1	93	5
87	2	90	6
95	2	85	6
97	3	84	7
90	3	90	7

a. Plot the data on a scattergram.

b. Fit the model $E(y) = \beta_0 + \beta_1 x + \beta_2 x^2$ to the data.

c. Is there evidence to support the inclusion of the second-order term in the model of part b? Test using $\alpha = .05$.

d. Plot the fitted model of part b on the scattergram of part a.

*12.17 The Federal Reserve System (FRS) was established in 1913 to provide central banking facilities for the United States. It is often referred to as the "banker's bank." One of its major responsibilities is to control the flow of the nation's money supply in order to facilitate orderly economic growth. One of the ways this is accomplished is through the buying and selling of government securities. The sale of securities to the public draws money from the commercial banking system; the purchase of securities by the FRS from the public increases the money in the commercial banking system. The resulting ebb and flow of the money supply affects the level of interest rates (the prices paid for borrowed money) in the economy (*Federal Reserve System*, 1963). In Exercise 10.72, we investigated the correlation between the rate of growth of the money supply and the prime interest rate. The data used in that exercise are repeated in the table.

DATE	PRIME INTEREST RATE	RATE OF GROWTH IN MONEY SUPPLY (M1*)	DATE	PRIME INTEREST RATE	RATE OF GROWTH IN MONEY SUPPLY (M1*)
2/81	20.00%	.36%	2/82	17.00%	−.29%
3/81	19.00	1.19	3/82	16.50	.22
4/81	18.00	2.09	4/82	16.50	.91
5/81	20.50	−.95	5/82	16.50	−.20
6/81	20.50	−.19	6/82	16.50	−.02
7/81	20.50	.23	7/82	16.50	−.02
8/81	20.50	.40	8/82	15.50	.86
9/81	20.50	.02	9/82	13.50	1.16
10/81	19.50	.39	10/82	13.50	1.72
11/81	18.00	.81	11/82	12.00	1.41
12/81	15.75	1.03	12/82	11.50	.74
1/82	15.75	1.75			

*M1 = Currency + Demand deposits + Travelers checks + Other checkable deposits

Source: *Economic Report of the President*, 1983, pp. 233, 240.

a. Fit a straight line to the data using the prime interest rate as the dependent variable, y. Compute R^2.

b. Based on the results of part a, describe in words the apparent relationship between interest rates and M1 growth.

c. Plot the least squares line on a scattergram of the data. Does it appear that a second-order model might better explain the variation in interest rates?

d. Fit a second-order model to the data and compute R^2.

e. Plot the prediction equation you developed in part d on a scattergram of the data.

f. Do the data provide sufficient evidence to conclude that $\beta_2 \neq 0$? Test using $\alpha = .05$. Draw the appropriate conclusions regarding the usefulness of the second-order model relative to the first-order model of part a for explaining the variation in interest rates.

12.18 Automobile accidents result in a tragic loss of life, and in addition, they represent a serious dollar loss to the nation's economy. Shown in the table are the number of highway deaths (to the nearest hundred) and the number of licensed vehicles (in hundreds of thousands) for the years 1950–1979. (The years are coded 1–30 for convenience.) During the years 1974–1979 (years 25–30 in the table), the nationwide 55-mile-per-hour speed limit was in effect.

YEAR	DEATHS y	NUMBER OF VEHICLES x_1	YEAR	DEATHS y	NUMBER OF VEHICLES x_1
1	34.8	49.2	16	49.1	91.8
2	37.0	51.9	17	53.0	95.9
3	37.8	53.3	18	52.9	98.9
4	38.0	56.3	19	54.9	103.1
5	35.6	58.6	20	55.8	107.4
6	38.4	62.8	21	54.6	111.2
7	39.6	65.2	22	54.3	116.3
8	38.7	67.6	23	56.3	122.3
9	37.0	68.8	24	55.5	129.8
10	37.9	72.1	25	46.4	134.9
11	38.1	74.5	26	45.9	137.9
12	38.1	76.4	27	47.0	143.5
13	40.8	79.7	28	49.5	148.8
14	43.6	83.5	29	51.5	153.6
15	47.7	87.3	30	51.9	159.4

a. Write a second-order model relating the number, y, of highway deaths for a year to the number, x_1, of licensed vehicles.

b. The SAS computer printout for fitting the model to the data is shown at the top of the next page. Is there sufficient evidence to indicate that the model provides information for the prediction of the number of annual highway deaths? Test using $\alpha = .05$.

SAS Printout for Exercise 12.18

```
DEPENDENT VARIABLE: DEATHS

SOURCE                        DF    SUM OF SQUARES    MEAN SQUARE    F VALUE
MODEL                          2      1222.15591739   611.07795869     44.50
ERROR                         27       370.79108261    13.73300306    PR > F
CORRECTED TOTAL               29      1592.94700000                    0.0001

R-SQUARE              C.V.          ROOT MSE      DEATHS MEAN
0.767229             8.1644        3.70580667     45.39000000

                                T FOR H0:     PR > ITI    STD ERROR OF
PARAMETER            ESTIMATE    PARAMETER=0               ESTIMATE
INTERCEPT          -1.40844827      -0.20      0.8397      6.89488584
VEHICLES            0.84549914       5.78      0.0001      0.14618237
VEHICLES*VEHICLES  -0.00332195      -4.68      0.0001      0.00070933
```

c. Give the p-value for the test of part b, and interpret it.

d. Does the second-order term contribute information for the prediction of y? Test using $\alpha = .05$.

e. Give the p-value for the test of part d, and interpret it.

12.3 Models with Two Quantitative Independent Variables

1. First-Order Model

$$E(y) = \beta_0 + \beta_1 x_1 + \beta_2 x_2$$

Comments on Model Parameters:

β_0: y-intercept, the value of $E(y)$ when $x_1 = x_2 = 0$

β_1: Change in $E(y)$ for a 1-unit increase in x_1, when x_2 is held fixed

β_2: Change in $E(y)$ for a 1-unit increase in x_2, when x_1 is held fixed

General Comments: The graph in Figure 12.7 traces a *response surface* (in contrast to the *response curve* used to relate $E(y)$ to a *single* quantitative variable). Particularly, a first-order model relating $E(y)$ to two independent quantitative variables, x_1 and x_2, graphs as a plane in three-dimensional space. The plane traces the value of $E(y)$ for every combination of values (x_1, x_2) that correspond to points in the x_1, x_2 plane. Most response surfaces in the real world are well behaved (smooth), and they have curvature. Consequently, a first-order model is appropriate only if the response surface is fairly flat over the x_1, x_2 region that is of interest to you.

The assumption that a first-order model will adequately characterize the relationship between $E(y)$ and the variables x_1 and x_2 is equivalent to assuming that x_1 and x_2 do not interact; that is, you assume that the effect on $E(y)$ of a change in x_1 (for a fixed value of x_2) is the same regardless of the value of x_2 (and vice versa). Thus, no interaction implies that the effect of

Figure 12.7 Computer-Generated Graph of a First-Order Model

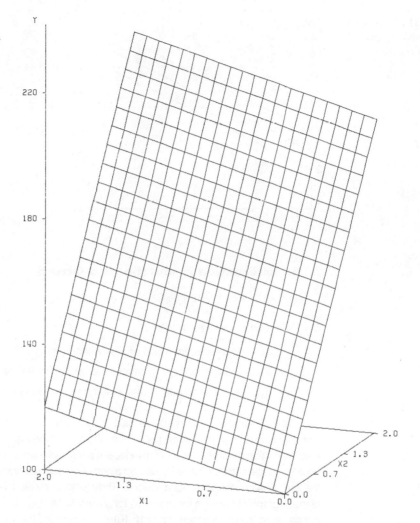

changes in one variable (say x_1) on $E(y)$ is *independent* of the value of the second variable (say x_2). For example, if we assign values to x_2 in a first-order model, the graph of $E(y)$ as a function of x_1 would produce parallel lines as shown in Figure 12.8 (next page). These lines, called **contour lines,** show the contours of the surface when it is sliced by three planes, each of which is parallel to the $E(y)$, x_1 plane, at distances $x_2 = 1$, 2, and 3 from the origin.

Definition 12.3

Two variables x_1 and x_2 are said to *interact* if the change in $E(y)$ for a 1-unit change in x_1 (when x_2 is held fixed) is dependent on the value of x_2.

Figure 12.8 A Graph Indicating No Interaction Between x_1 and x_2

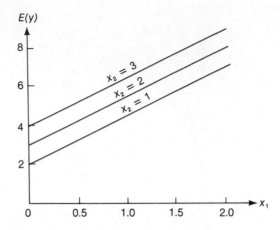

2. An Interaction Model (Second-Order)

$$E(y) = \beta_0 + \beta_1 x_1 + \beta_2 x_2 + \beta_3 x_1 x_2$$

Comments on Model Parameters:

β_0: y-intercept, the value of $E(y)$ when $x_1 = x_2 = 0$

β_1 and β_2: Changing β_1 and β_2 causes the surface to shift along the x_1- and x_2-axes

β_3: Controls the rate of twist in the ruled surface (see Figure 12.9)

General Comments: This model is said to be second-order because the order of the highest-order term $(x_1 x_2)$ in x_1 and x_2 is 2; i.e., the sum of the exponents of x_1 and x_2 equals 2. This interaction model traces a ruled surface in a three-dimensional space (Figure 12.9). You could produce such a surface by placing a pencil perpendicular to a line and moving it along the line, while rotating it around the line. The resulting surface would appear as a twisted plane. A graph of $E(y)$ as a function of x_1 for given values of x_2 (say $x_2 = 1, 2$, and 3) produces nonparallel contour lines (see Figure 12.10), thus indicating that the change in $E(y)$ for a given change in x_1 is dependent on the value of x_2 and, therefore, that x_1 and x_2 interact. Interaction is an extremely important concept because it is easy to get in the habit of fitting first-order models and individually examining the relationships between $E(y)$ and each of a set of independent variables, $x_1, x_2, \ldots, x_k$. Such a procedure is meaningless when interaction exists (which is, at least to some extent, almost always the case), and it can lead to gross errors in interpretation. For example, suppose the relationship between $E(y)$ and x_1 and x_2 is as shown in Figure 12.10 and that you have observed y for each of the $n = 9$ combinations of values of x_1 and x_2 ($x_1 = 1, 2, 3$ and $x_2 = 1, 2, 3$). If you fit a first-order model in x_1 and x_2 to the data, the fitted plane would be (except for random error) approximately parallel to the x_1, x_2 plane, thus suggesting that x_1 and x_2 contribute very little information about $E(y)$. That this is not the case is clearly indicated by the figure. Fitting a first-order model to the data would not allow for the twist in the true surface and would therefore give a false impression of the

Figure 12.9 Computer-Generated Graph for an Interaction Model (Second-Order)

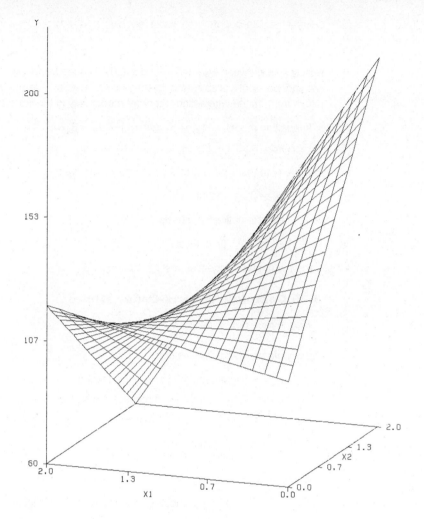

Figure 12.10 A Graph Indicating Interaction Between x_1 and x_2

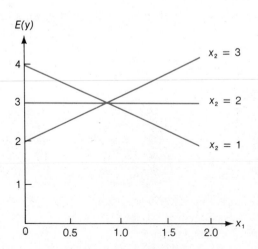

relationship between $E(y)$ and x_1 and x_2. The procedure for detecting interaction between two independent variables can be seen by examining the model. The interaction model differs from the noninteraction first-order model only in the inclusion of the $\beta_3 x_1 x_2$ term:

Interaction model: $E(y) = \beta_0 + \beta_1 x_1 + \beta_2 x_2 + \beta_3 x_1 x_2$

First-order model: $E(y) = \beta_0 + \beta_1 x_1 + \beta_2 x_2$

Therefore, to test for the presence of interaction, we test

$H_0:\quad \beta_3 = 0$ (no interaction)

against the alternative hypothesis

$H_a:\quad \beta_3 \neq 0$.   (interaction)

using the familiar Student's t test of Section 11.5.

3. A Complete Second-Order Model

$$E(y) = \beta_0 + \beta_1 x_1 + \beta_2 x_2 + \beta_3 x_1 x_2 + \beta_4 x_1^2 + \beta_5 x_2^2$$

Comments on Model Parameters:

β_0: y-intercept, the value of $E(y)$ when $x_1 = x_2 = 0$

β_1 and β_2:   Changing β_1 and β_2 causes the surface to shift along the x_1- and x_2-axes

β_3:   The value of β_3 controls the rotation of the surface

β_4 and β_5:   Signs and values of these parameters control the type of surface and the rates of curvature

The following three types of surfaces may be produced by a second-order model:

β_4 and β_5 positive: A paraboloid that opens upward [Figure 12.11(a)]

β_4 and β_5 negative: A paraboloid that opens downward [Figure 12.11(b)]

β_4 and β_5 differ in sign: A saddle-shaped surface [Figure 12.11(c)]

Figure 12.11 Graphs of Three Second-Order Surfaces

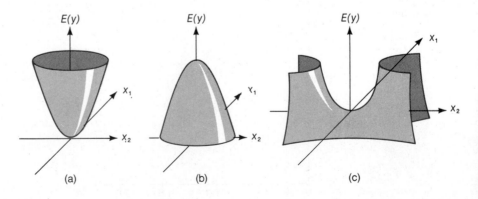

General Comments: A complete second-order model is the three-dimensional equivalent of a second-order model with a single quantitative variable. Instead of tracing parabolas, it traces paraboloids and saddle surfaces. Since you fit only a portion of the complete surface to the data, a complete second-order model provides a large variety of gently curving surfaces. It is a good choice for a model if you expect curvature in the response surface relating $E(y)$ to x_1 and x_2.

**Exercises
12.19–12.29**

Learning the Mechanics

12.19 Write a first-order model relating $E(y)$ to two independent quantitative variables, x_1 and x_2.

12.20 Modify the model you constructed in Exercise 12.19 to include an interaction term.

12.21 Modify the model you constructed in Exercise 12.20 to make it a complete second-order model.

12.22 Suppose the true relationship between $E(y)$ and the quantitative independent variables x_1 and x_2 is described by the first-order model

$$E(y) = 4 - x_1 + 2x_2$$

a. Describe the corresponding response surface.
b. Plot the contour lines of the response surface for $x_1 = 2, 3, 4$, where $0 \leq x_2 \leq 5$.
c. Plot the contour lines of the response surface for $x_2 = 2, 3, 4$, where $0 \leq x_1 \leq 5$.
d. Use the contour lines you plotted in parts b and c to explain how changes in the settings of x_1 and x_2 affect $E(y)$.
e. Use your graph from part b to determine how much $E(y)$ changes when x_1 is changed from 4 to 2 and, simultaneously, x_2 is changed from 1 to 2.

12.23 Suppose the true relationship between $E(y)$ and the quantitative independent variables x_1 and x_2 is

$$E(y) = 4 - x_1 + 2x_2 + x_1 x_2$$

a. Identify the order of the model.
b. Describe the corresponding response surface.
c. Plot the contour lines of the response surface for $x_1 = 0, 1, 2$, where $0 \leq x_2 \leq 5$.
d. Explain why the contour lines you plotted in part c are not parallel.
e. Use the contour lines you plotted in part c to explain how changes in the settings of x_1 and x_2 affect $E(y)$.
f. Use your graph from part c to determine how much $E(y)$ changes when x_1 is changed from 2 to 0 and, simultaneously, x_2 is changed from 4 to 5.

12.24 What does it mean to say that two variables affect the mean response, $E(y)$, independently of each other?

Applying the Concepts

12.25 The Department of Energy wants to develop a regression model to help forecast annual gasoline consumption in the United States, y. They have decided to model $E(y)$ as a function of two independent variables:

x_1 = Number of cars (millions) in use during year

x_2 = Number of trucks (millions) in use during year

a. Identify the independent variables as quantitative or qualitative.
b. Write the first-order model for $E(y)$.
c. Write the complete second-order model for $E(y)$.
d. With respect to the model of part c, specify the null and alternative hypotheses you would use in testing for the presence of interaction between x_1 and x_2.

12.26 The dissolved oxygen content, y, in rivers and streams is related to the amount, x_1, of nitrogen compounds per liter of water and the temperature, x_2, of the water. Write the complete second-order model relating $E(y)$ to x_1 and x_2.

12.27 Some corporations, instead of owning a fleet of cars, rent cars from a rental agency. A corporation may do this because it is sometimes more economical to rent new cars for a year than to buy new cars each year. A major rental agency wants to develop a model that will allow it to estimate the average annual cost to the prospective customer of renting cars, y, as a function of two independent variables:

x_1 = Number of cars rented

x_2 = Average number of miles driven per car during year (in thousands)

a. Identify the independent variables as quantitative or qualitative.
b. Write the first-order model for $E(y)$.
c. Write a model for $E(y)$ that contains all first-order and interaction terms. Sketch typical response curves showing the mean cost, $E(y)$, versus the average mileage driven, x_2, for different values of x_1. (Assume that x_1 and x_2 interact.)
d. Write the complete second-order model for $E(y)$.

12.28 Refer to Exercise 12.27. Suppose the model from part c is fit, with the following result:

$$\hat{y} = 1 + .05x_1 + x_2 + .05x_1x_2$$

(The units of $\hat{y}$ are thousands of dollars.) Graph the estimated cost $\hat{y}$ as a function of the average number of miles driven, x_2, over the range $x_2 = 10$ to $x_2 = 50$ (10,000–50,000 miles) for $x_1 = 1$, 5, and 10. Do these functions agree (approximately) with the graphs you drew for Exercise 12.27, part c?

12.29 An economist is interested in modeling the relationship between quarterly sales of central air-conditioning systems (in thousands) for single-family homes in the United States and two quantitative independent variables, housing starts in the previous quarter (in thousands) and the gross national product (in billions of 1972 dollars). Data were collected, and a model was fit. The displayed portion of the resulting Minitab printout describes the least squares prediction equation. In the prediction equation, $x_3 = x_1^2$ and $x_4 = x_2^2$.

```
THE REGRESSION EQUATION IS
Y =    149. + .472 X1 - .0993 X2
      - .0005 X3 + .0000 X4

                              ST. DEV.   T-RATIO =
          COLUMN   COEFFICIENT  OF COEF.   COEF/S.D.

          --        148.5      224.5        .66
X1   C2.            .472        .126       3.74
X2   C3            -.099        .162        -.61
X3   C12         -.000535      .000359     -1.49
X4   C13          .0000153     .0000294     .52

THE ST. DEV. OF Y ABOUT REGRESSION LINE IS
S =      6.884
WITH (  16-5) = 11 DEGREES OF FREEDOM

R-SQUARED = 92.0 PERCENT
R-SQUARED = 89.1 PERCENT, ADJUSTED FOR D.F.

ANALYSIS OF VARIANCE

  DUE TO       DF        SS    MS=SS/DF

REGRESSION     4     6002.08   1500.52
RESIDUAL      11      521.36     47.40
TOTAL         15     6523.44
```

a. Write the prediction equation for the response surface.

b. Describe the geometric form of the response surface of part a.

c. Do the data provide sufficient evidence to conclude that the model hypothesized by the economist is useful for predicting quarterly sales of central air-conditioning systems? Test using $\alpha = .01$.

d. Does it appear that the variation in air conditioner sales could be adequately explained by a less complex regression model? Explain. [*Note:* In the next section we discuss a formal procedure for making this inference.]

12.4 Model Building: Testing Portions of a Model

The presentation of models with one and with two quantitative independent variables raises a very general question. Do certain terms in the model contribute more information than others for the prediction of y?

To illustrate, suppose you have collected data on a response, y, and two quantitative independent variables, x_1 and x_2, and you are considering the use of either a first-order or a second-order model to relate $E(y)$ to x_1 and x_2. Will the second-order model provide better predictions of y than the first-order model? To answer this question, examine the two models and note that the second-order model contains all the terms contained in the first-order model plus three additional terms, those involving β_3, β_4, and β_5.

First-order model: $E(y) = \beta_0 + \beta_1 x_1 + \beta_2 x_2$

$$\overbrace{}^{\text{Second-order terms}}$$

Second-order model: $E(y) = \beta_0 + \beta_1 x_1 + \beta_2 x_2 + \beta_3 x_1 x_2 + \beta_4 x_1^2 + \beta_5 x_2^2$

Therefore, asking whether the second-order model contributes more information for the prediction of y than the first-order model is equivalent to asking whether at least one of the parameters, β_3, β_4, or β_5, differs from zero—i.e., whether the terms involving β_3, β_4, and β_5 should be retained in the model. Therefore, to test whether the second-order terms should be included in the model, we test the null hypothesis

$$H_0: \quad \beta_3 = \beta_4 = \beta_5 = 0$$

(i.e., the second-order terms do not contribute information for the prediction of y) against the alternative hypothesis

$$H_a: \quad \text{At least one of the parameters, } \beta_3, \beta_4, \text{ or } \beta_5, \text{ differs from zero}$$

(i.e., at least one of the second-order terms contributes information for the prediction of y).

The procedure for conducting this test is intuitive: First, we use the method of least squares to fit the first-order model and calculate the corresponding sum of squares for error, SSE_1 (the sum of squares of the deviations between observed and predicted y values). Next, we fit the second-order model and calculate its sum of squares for error, SSE_2. Then, we compare SSE_1 to SSE_2 by calculating $SSE_1 - SSE_2$. If the second-order terms contribute to the model, then SSE_2 should be much smaller than SSE_1, and the difference $(SSE_1 - SSE_2)$ will be large. The larger the difference, the greater the weight of evidence that the second-order model provides better predictions of y than does the first-order model.

The sum of squares for error will always decrease when new terms are added to the model. The question is whether this decrease is large enough to conclude that it is due to more than just an increase in the number of model terms and to chance. To test the null hypothesis that the parameters of the second-order terms β_3, β_4, and β_5 simultaneously equal zero, we use an F statistic calculated as follows:

$$F = \frac{\text{Drop in SSE/Number of } \beta \text{ parameters being tested}}{s^2 \text{ for the complete second-order model}} = \frac{(SSE_1 - SSE_2)/3}{SSE_2/[n - (5 + 1)]}$$

When the assumptions listed in Section 11.2 about the error term, ε, are satisfied and the β parameters for the second-order terms are all zero (H_0 is true), this F statistic has an F distribution with $v_1 = 3$ and $v_2 = n - 6$ degrees of freedom. Note that v_1 is the number of β parameters being tested and v_2 is the number of degrees of freedom associated with s^2 in the complete model.

If the second-order terms *do* contribute to the model (H_a is true), we expect the F statistic to be large. Thus, we use a one-tailed test and reject H_0 when F exceeds some critical value, F_α, as shown in Figure 12.12. A summary of the steps used in testing the null hypothesis that a set of model parameters are all equal to zero is shown in the next box.

Figure 12.12 Rejection Region for the F Test of H_0: $\beta_3 = \beta_4 = \beta_5 = 0$

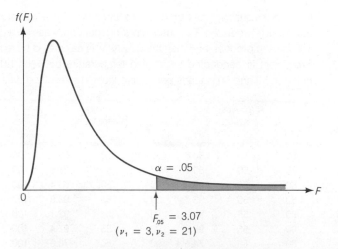

$f(F)$

$\alpha = .05$

0

$F_{.05} = 3.07$
$(\nu_1 = 3, \nu_2 = 21)$

F Test for Testing the Null Hypothesis: Set of β Parameters Equal Zero

Reduced model: $E(y) = \beta_0 + \beta_1 x_1 + \cdots + \beta_g x_g$

Complete model: $E(y) = \beta_0 + \beta_1 x_1 + \cdots + \beta_g x_g + \beta_{g+1} x_{g+1} + \cdots + \beta_k x_k$

H_0: $\beta_{g+1} = \beta_{g+2} = \cdots = \beta_k = 0$

H_a: At least one of the β parameters under test is nonzero

Test statistic: $F = \dfrac{(\text{SSE}_1 - \text{SSE}_2)/(k - g)}{\text{SSE}_2/[n - (k + 1)]}$

where

$\text{SSE}_1 = $ Sum of squared errors for the reduced model

$\text{SSE}_2 = $ Sum of squared errors for the complete model

$k - g = $ Number of β parameters specified in H_0

$k + 1 = $ Number of β parameters in the complete model

$n = $ Sample size

Rejection region: $F > F_\alpha$

where

$\nu_1 = k - g = $ Degrees of freedom for the numerator

$\nu_2 = n - (k + 1) = $ Degrees of freedom for the denominator

---

Example 12.3

Many companies manufacture products (e.g., steel, paint, gasoline) that are at least partially chemically produced. In many instances, the quality of the finished product is a function of the temperature and pressure at which the chemical reactions take place. Suppose you wanted to model the quality, y, of a product as a function of the temperature, x_1, and the pressure, x_2, at which it is produced. Four inspectors independently assign a quality score between 0 and 100 to each product, and then the quality, y, is calculated by averaging the four scores. An experiment is conducted by varying temperature between 80 and 100°F and pressure between 50 and 60 pounds per square inch. The resulting data are given in Table 12.2.

Table 12.2

Temperature, Pressure, and Quality of the Finished Product

x_1 (°F)	x_2 (pounds per square inch)	y	x_1 (°F)	x_2 (pounds per square inch)	y	x_1 (°F)	x_2 (pounds per square inch)	y
80	50	50.8	90	50	63.4	100	50	46.6
80	50	50.7	90	50	61.6	100	50	49.1
80	50	49.4	90	50	63.4	100	50	46.4
80	55	93.7	90	55	93.8	100	55	69.8
80	55	90.9	90	55	92.1	100	55	72.5
80	55	90.9	90	55	97.4	100	55	73.2
80	60	74.5	90	60	70.9	100	60	38.7
80	60	73.0	90	60	68.8	100	60	42.5
80	60	71.2	90	60	71.3	100	60	41.4

a. Fit a second-order model to the data.
b. Sketch the response surface.
c. Do the data provide sufficient evidence to indicate that the second-order terms contribute information for the prediction of y?

Solution   **a.** The complete second-order model is

$$E(y) = \beta_0 + \beta_1 x_1 + \beta_2 x_2 + \beta_3 x_1 x_2 + \beta_4 x_1^2 + \beta_5 x_2^2$$

The data in Table 12.2 were used to fit this model, and a portion of the SAS output is shown in Figure 12.13. The least squares prediction equation is

$$\hat{y} = -5{,}127.90 + 31.10x_1 + 139.75x_2 - .146x_1 x_2 - .133x_1^2 - 1.14x_2^2$$

Figure 12.13   Portion of the SAS Printout for Example 12.3

SOURCE	DF	SUM OF SQUARES	MEAN SQUARE	F VALUE	PR > F
MODEL	5	8402.26453714	1680.45290743	596.32	0.0001
ERROR	21	59.17842582	2.81802028	R-SQUARE	ROOT MSE
CORRECTED TOTAL	26	8461.44296296		0.993006	1.67869601

PARAMETER	ESTIMATE	T FOR H0: PARAMETER = 0	PR > !T!	STD ERROR OF ESTIMATE
INTERCEPT	-5127.89907417	-46.49	0.0001	110.29601483
X1	31.09638889	23.13	0.0001	1.34441322
X2	139.74722222	44.50	0.0001	3.14005411
X1*X2	-0.14550000	-15.01	0.0001	0.00969196
X1*X1	-0.13338889	-19.46	0.0001	0.00685325
X2*X2	-1.14422222	-41.74	0.0001	0.02741299

Figure 12.14 Plot of Second-Order Least Squares Model for Example 12.3

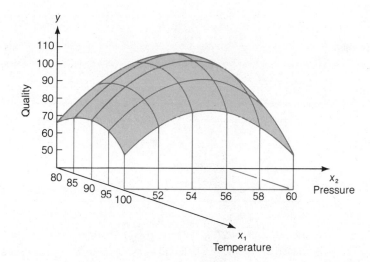

b. A three-dimensional graph of this prediction model is shown in Figure 12.14. Note that the mean quality seems to be greatest for temperatures of about 85–90°F and for pressures of about 55–57 pounds per square inch.* Further experimentation in these ranges might lead to a more precise determination of the optimal temperature–pressure combination.

c. To determine whether the data provide sufficient evidence to indicate that the second-order terms contribute information for the prediction of y, we test

$$H_0: \quad \beta_3 = \beta_4 = \beta_5 = 0$$

against the alternative hypothesis

$$H_0: \quad \text{At least one of the parameters, } \beta_3, \beta_4, \text{ or } \beta_5, \text{ differs from zero}$$

The first step in conducting the test is to drop the second-order terms out of the complete (second-order) model and fit the reduced model

$$E(y) = \beta_0 + \beta_1 x_1 + \beta_2 x_2$$

to the data. The SAS computer printout for this procedure is shown in Figure 12.15 (next page). You can see that the sums of squares for error, given in Figures 12.13 and 12.15 for the complete and reduced models, respectively, are

$$SSE_2 = 59.17842582 \qquad SSE_1 = 6{,}671.50851852$$

and that s^2 for the complete model is

$$s_2^2 = 2.81802028$$

---

* Students with knowledge of calculus should note that we can solve for the exact temperature and pressure that maximize quality in the least squares model by solving $\partial\hat{y}/\partial x_1 = 0$ and $\partial\hat{y}/\partial x_2 = 0$ for x_1 and x_2. These estimated optimal values are $x_1 = 86.25°F$ and $x_2 = 55.58$ pounds per square inch. Remember, however, that these represent only sample estimates of the coordinates for the optimal value.

Figure 12.15 SAS Computer Printout for the Reduced (First-Order) Model in Example 12.3

```
DEPENDENT VARIABLE: Y

SOURCE                       DF    SUM OF SQUARES    MEAN SQUARE    F VALUE

MODEL                         2     1789.93444444    894.96722222      3.22
ERROR                        24     6671.50851852    277.97952160    PR > F
CORRECTED TOTAL              26     8461.44296296                     0.0577

R-SQUARE              C.V.              ROOT MSE         Y MEAN

0.211540            24.8984           16.67271788    66.96296296

                              T FOR H0:     PR > !T!    STD ERROR OF
PARAMETER        ESTIMATE     PARAMETER=0                  ESTIMATE

INTERCEPT      106.08518519          1.90     0.0700     55.94500427
X1              -0.91611111         -2.33     0.0285      0.39297973
X2               0.78777778          1.00     0.3262      0.78595946
```

Recall that $n = 27$, $k = 5$, and $g = 2$. Therefore, the calculated value of the F statistic, based on $v_1 = k - g = 3$ and $v_2 = n - (k + 1) = 21$ degrees of freedom is

$$F = \frac{(\text{SSE}_1 - \text{SSE}_2)/(k - g)}{\text{SSE}_2/[n - (k + 1)]} = \frac{(\text{SSE}_1 - \text{SSE}_2)/(k - g)}{s_2^2}$$

where $v_1 = k - g$ is equal to the number of parameters involved in H_0 and s_2^2 is the value of s^2 for the complete model. Therefore,

$$F = \frac{(6{,}671.50851852 - 59.17842582)/3}{2.81802028}$$

$$= 782.1$$

The final step in the test is to compare this computed value of F with the tabulated value based on $v_1 = 3$ and $v_2 = 21$ degrees of freedom. If we choose $\alpha = .05$, $F_{.05} = 3.07$. Since the computed value of F falls in the rejection region (see Figure 12.12) — i.e., it exceeds $F_{.05} = 3.07$ — we reject H_0 and conclude that at least one of the second-order terms contributes information for the prediction of y. In other words, the data support the contention that the curvature we see in the response surface is not due simply to random variation in the data. The second-order model does appear to provide better predictions of y than a first-order model. ∎

Example 12.3 demonstrates the motivation for testing an hypothesis that each one of a set of β parameters equals zero, and it also demonstrates the procedure. Other applications of this test appear in the following sections.

Exercises 12.30 – 12.38

Learning the Mechanics

12.30 Suppose you fit the regression model

$$y = \beta_0 + \beta_1 x_1 + \beta_2 x_2 + \beta_3 x_1 x_2 + \beta_4 x_1^2 + \beta_5 x_2^2 + \varepsilon$$

to $n = 30$ data points and you wish to test the null hypothesis $H_0: \beta_3 = \beta_4 = \beta_5 = 0$.

a. What would the alternative hypothesis be?

b. Explain in detail how you would find the quantities necessary to compute the F statistic for your hypothesis test.

c. How many numerator and denominator degrees of freedom are associated with your F statistic?

12.31 Refer to Exercise 12.30. Suppose you fit the complete and reduced models for the hypothesis test described in Exercise 12.30 and obtained $SSE_1 = 246.1$ and $SSE_2 = 215.2$. Conduct the hypothesis test and interpret the results of your test. Use $\alpha = .05$.

12.32 Explain why the F test used to compare complete and reduced models is a one-tailed, upper-tailed test.

Applying the Concepts

[*Note: Starred (*) exercises require the use of a computer.*]

12.33 A large research and development company rates the performance of each of the members of its technical staff once a year. Each person is rated on a scale of 0 to 100 by his or her immediate supervisor, and this merit rating is used to help determine the size of the person's pay raise for the coming year. The company's personnel department is interested in developing a regression model to help them forecast the merit rating that an applicant for a technical position will receive after he or she has been with the company 3 years. The company proposes to use the following model to forecast the merit ratings of applicants who have just completed their graduate studies and have no prior related job experience:

$$E(y) = \beta_0 + \beta_1 x_1 + \beta_2 x_2 + \beta_3 x_1 x_2 + \beta_4 x_1^2 + \beta_5 x_2^2$$

where

$y =$ Applicant's merit rating after 3 years

$x_1 =$ Applicant's grade-point average (GPA) in graduate school

$x_2 =$ Applicant's verbal score on the Graduate Record Examination (percentile)

A random sample of $n = 40$ employees who have been with the company more than 3 years was selected. Each employee's merit rating after 3 years, his or her graduate school GPA, and the percentile in which the verbal Graduate Record Exam score fell were recorded. The above model was fit to these data. The following is a portion of the resulting computer printout:

```
SOURCE    DF   SUM OF SQUARES   MEAN SQUARE

MODEL     5        4911.56         982.31
ERROR     34       1830.44          53.84
TOTAL     39       6742.00        R-SQUARE
                                    0.729
```

The reduced model, $E(y) = \beta_0 + \beta_1 x_1 + \beta_2 x_2$, was fit to the same data and the resulting computer printout is partially reproduced at the top of the next page.

```
SOURCE    DF    SUM OF SQUARES    MEAN SQUARE

MODEL     2         3544.84        1772.42
ERROR     37        3197.16          86.41
TOTAL     39        6742.00       R-SQUARE
                                     0.526
```

a. Identify the null and alternative hypotheses for a test to determine whether the complete model contributes information for the prediction of y.

b. Identify the null and alternative hypotheses for a test to determine whether a second-order model contributes more information than a first-order model for the prediction of y.

c. Conduct the hypothesis test you described in part a. Test using $\alpha = .05$. Draw the appropriate conclusions in the context of the problem.

d. Conduct the hypothesis test you described in part b. Test using $\alpha = .05$. Draw the appropriate conclusions in the context of the problem.

*12.34 A firm would like to be able to forecast its yearly sales in each of its sales regions. The firm has decided to base its forecasts on regional population size and its yearly regional advertising expenditures. The population data in the table were obtained from the Bureau of the Census, and the advertising and sales data were obtained from the firm's internal records.

SALES REGION	SALES (Thousands of units)	POPULATION OF REGION (Thousands)	ADVERTISING EXPENDITURES ($ thousands)
1	65	200	8
2	80	210	10
3	85	205	9
4	100	300	8.5
5	108	320	12
6	114	290	10
7	40	90	6
8	45	85	8
9	150	450	9
10	42	87	9
11	220	480	13
12	200	500	15

a. Fit a complete second-order model to the data.

b. Is the complete second-order model useful for forecasting sales? Test using $\alpha = .05$.

c. The firm is planning to market its product in a new sales region next year. The region has a population of 400,000, and the firm plans to spend $12,000 on advertising. Use the fitted model you obtained in part a to forecast next year's sales in this new region. [*Note:* We would want to express this estimate as a prediction interval, but its computation is beyond the scope of this text. The procedure is described in the references at the end of the chapter. You may also find that it can be obtained using your statistical computer package.]

12.35 Refer to Exercise 12.34, in which a firm would like to develop a regression model to forecast its yearly sales in each of its sales regions. The model under consideration is a complete second-order model:

$$E(y) = \beta_0 + \beta_1 x_1 + \beta_2 x_2 + \beta_3 x_1 x_2 + \beta_4 x_1^2 + \beta_5 x_2^2$$

where

y = Yearly regional sales

x_1 = Population of sales region

x_2 = Yearly regional advertising expenditures

The following is a portion of the computer printout that results from fitting this model to the $n = 12$ data points given in Exercise 12.34:

```
SOURCE    DF   SUM OF SQUARES   MEAN SQUARE

MODEL     5        38638.97        7727.79
ERROR     6          159.94          26.66
TOTAL    11        38798.91       R-SQUARE
                                     0.996
```

The reduced first-order model, $E(y) = \beta_0 + \beta_1 x_1 + \beta_2 x_2$, was fit to the same data and the resulting computer printout is partially reproduced here:

```
SOURCE    DF   SUM OF SQUARES   MEAN SQUARE

MODEL     2         36704.5        18352.2
ERROR     9          2094.4          232.7
TOTAL    11         38798.9       R-SQUARE
                                     0.946
```

Is there sufficient evidence to conclude that a second-order model contributes more information for the prediction of y than a first-order model? Test using $\alpha = .05$.

12.36 Refer to Exercise 12.25, in which the Department of Energy wants to develop a regression model to help forecast annual gasoline consumption in the United States. The complete and reduced models for the test that you described in part d of Exercise 12.25 were fit to $n = 25$ data points. The resulting values for SSE_1 and SSE_2 were 1,065.9 and 400.6, respectively.

a. Conduct the test to determine whether the data present sufficient evidence to indicate interaction between x_1 and x_2. Test using $\alpha = .05$.

b. Find the approximate observed significance level for the test in part a.

*12.37 In Exercise 11.4, we found that a first-order model was useful for characterizing the relationship between household food consumption and the two independent variables, household income and size of the household. The sample data are repeated in the table on page 538 and the accompanying SAS printout summarizes the results of fitting a first-order model to the data.

538

HOUSEHOLD	FOOD CONSUMPTION DURING 1984 y ($ thousands)	1984 HOUSEHOLD INCOME x_1 ($ thousands)	NUMBER OF PERSONS IN HOUSEHOLD AT END OF 1984 x_2	HOUSEHOLD	FOOD CONSUMPTION DURING 1984 y ($ thousands)	1984 HOUSEHOLD INCOME x_1 ($ thousands)	NUMBER OF PERSONS IN HOUSEHOLD AT END OF 1984 x_2
1	3.2	31.1	4	14	3.1	85.2	2
2	2.4	20.5	2	15	4.5	35.6	9
3	3.8	42.3	4	16	3.5	68.5	3
4	1.9	18.9	1	17	4.0	10.5	5
5	2.5	26.5	2	18	3.5	21.6	4
6	3.0	29.8	4	19	1.8	29.9	1
7	2.6	24.3	3	20	2.9	28.6	3
8	3.2	38.1	4	21	2.6	20.2	2
9	3.9	52.0	5	22	3.6	38.7	5
10	1.7	16.0	1	23	2.8	11.2	3
11	2.9	41.9	3	24	4.5	14.3	7
12	1.7	9.9	1	25	3.5	16.9	5
13	4.5	33.1	7				

SAS Printout for Exercise 12.37

```
DEPENDENT VARIABLE: FOOD

SOURCE                        DF    SUM OF SQUARES    MEAN SQUARE    F VALUE

MODEL                          2      15.46228509      7.73114255     100.80
ERROR                         22       1.68731491      0.07669613     PR > F
CORRECTED TOTAL               24      17.14960000                     0.0001

R-SQUARE              C.V.            ROOT MSE        FOOD MEAN

0.901612             8.9221          0.27694067      3.10400000

                            T FOR H0:    PR > !T!    STD ERROR OF
PARAMETER      ESTIMATE    PARAMETER=0               ESTIMATE

INTERCEPT     1.43260377      9.76       0.0001      0.14673751
INCOME        0.00999062      3.15       0.0046      0.00316806
SIZE          0.37928986     13.68       0.0001      0.02772472
```

a. Fit a complete second-order model to the data.

b. Is the complete second-order model useful for explaining the variation in household food consumption? Test using $\alpha = .05$.

c. Is there sufficient evidence to conclude that at least one of the β parameters associated with the second-order terms differs from zero? Test using $\alpha = .05$.

d. Do the data provide sufficient evidence to conclude that household income and household size interact? Test using $\alpha = .05$.

e. Describe the danger involved in conducting a series of hypothesis tests (such as in parts b, c, and d) for determining which terms to retain in a regression model and which to exclude.

12.38 In Exercise 11.14, we found that a first-order model was useful for explaining the variation in the number of hours worked per week in the shipping department of a particular firm. The data used to fit the model are repeated in the accompanying table.

WEEK	HOURS OF LABOR y	THOUSANDS OF POUNDS SHIPPED x_1	PERCENTAGE OF UNITS SHIPPED BY TRUCK x_2	AVERAGE NUMBER OF POUNDS PER SHIPMENT x_3
1	100	5.1	90	20
2	85	3.8	99	22
3	108	5.3	58	19
4	116	7.5	16	15
5	92	4.5	54	20
6	63	3.3	42	26
7	79	5.3	12	25
8	101	5.9	32	21
9	88	4.0	56	24
10	71	4.2	64	29
11	122	6.8	78	10
12	85	3.9	90	30
13	50	3.8	74	28
14	114	7.5	89	14
15	104	4.5	90	21
16	111	6.0	40	20
17	110	8.1	55	16
18	100	2.9	64	19
19	82	4.0	35	23
20	85	4.8	58	25

a. Write a complete second-order model for the data.

b. The SAS computer printout for fitting the second-order model of part a is shown here. Find the prediction equation.

SAS Printout for Exercise 12.38

```
DEPENDENT VARIABLE: LABOR

SOURCE                       DF    SUM OF SQUARES    MEAN SQUARE     F VALUE

MODEL                         9    6043.40529897    671.48947766      10.25
ERROR                        10     654.79470103     65.47947010      PR > F
CORRECTED TOTAL              19    6698.20000000                      0.0006

R-SQUARE                 C.V.           ROOT MSE      LABOR MEAN

0.902243              8.6730         8.09193859     93.30000000

                                   T FOR H0:     PR > !T!    STD ERROR OF
PARAMETER            ESTIMATE     PARAMETER=0               ESTIMATE

INTERCEPT         655.80722615          2.90      0.0159    226.28033719
WEIGHT            -57.32665806         -1.73      0.1138     33.08376144
TRUCK              -3.38961628         -1.77      0.1079      1.91983172
AVGSHIP           -28.27072935         -2.66      0.0238     10.61901566
WEIGHT*TRUCK         0.22403392          1.52      0.1583      0.14691511
WEIGHT*AVGSHIP       2.20142243          2.44      0.0348      0.90189596
TRUCK*AVGSHIP        0.08858647          2.23      0.0496      0.03966598
WEIGHT*WEIGHT        0.45327631          0.34      0.7414      1.33580032
TRUCK*TRUCK          0.00371216          0.92      0.3800      0.00404162
AVGSHIP*AVGSHIP      0.20833049          1.64      0.1315      0.12683455
```

   c. Do the data provide sufficient evidence to indicate that the model is useful for predicting y? Test using $\alpha = .05$.

   d. Is there sufficient evidence to indicate that the second-order terms are useful for predicting y? Test using $\alpha = .05$.

12.5
Models with One Qualitative Independent Variable

Suppose we want to write a model for the mean profit, $E(y)$, per sales dollar of a construction company as a function of the sales engineer who estimates and bids on a job. (For the purpose of explanation, we will ignore other independent variables that might affect the response.) Further, suppose there are three sales engineers, Adams, Brown, and Clark. Then Sales engineer is a single qualitative variable set at three levels corresponding to Adams, Brown, and Clark. Note that with a qualitative independent variable, we cannot attach a quantitative meaning to a given level. All we can do is describe it.

To simplify our notation, let μ_A be the mean profit per sales dollar for Adams, and let μ_B and μ_C be the corresponding mean profits for Brown and Clark. Our objective is to write a single prediction equation that will give the mean value of y for the three sales engineers. This can be done as follows:

$$E(y) = \beta_0 + \beta_1 x_1 + \beta_2 x_2$$

where

$$x_1 = \begin{cases} 1 & \text{if Brown is the sales engineer} \\ 0 & \text{if Brown is not the sales engineer} \end{cases}$$

$$x_2 = \begin{cases} 1 & \text{if Clark is the sales engineer} \\ 0 & \text{if Clark is not the sales engineer} \end{cases}$$

The variables x_1 and x_2 are not meaningful independent variables as for the case of the models with quantitative independent variables. Instead, they are *dummy* (or *indicator*) *variables* that make the model function. To see how they work, let $x_1 = 0$ and $x_2 = 0$. This condition will apply when we are seeking the mean response for Adams (neither Brown nor Clark will be the sales engineer; hence, it must be Adams). Then the mean value of y when Adams is the sales engineer is

$$\mu_A = E(y) = \beta_0 + \beta_1(0) + \beta_2(0) = \beta_0$$

This tells us that the mean profit per sales dollar for Adams is β_0. Or, it means that $\beta_0 = \mu_A$.

Now suppose we want to represent the mean response, $E(y)$, when Brown is the sales engineer. Checking the dummy variable definitions, we see that we should let $x_1 = 1$ and $x_2 = 0$:

$$\mu_B = E(y) = \beta_0 + \beta_1 x_1 + \beta_2 x_2 = \beta_0 + \beta_1(1) + \beta_2(0) = \beta_0 + \beta_1$$

or, since $\beta_0 = \mu_A$,

$$\mu_B = \mu_A + \beta_1$$

Then it follows that the interpretation of β_1 is

$$\beta_1 = \mu_B - \mu_A$$

which is the difference in the mean profit per sales dollar between Brown and Adams.

Finally, if we want the mean value of y when Clark is the sales engineer, we let $x_1 = 0$ and $x_2 = 1$:

$$\mu_C = E(y) = \beta_0 + \beta_1(0) + \beta_2(1) = \beta_0 + \beta_2$$

or, since $\beta_0 = \mu_A$,

$$\mu_C = \mu_A + \beta_2$$

Then it follows that the interpretation of β_2 is

$$\beta_2 = \mu_C - \mu_A$$

Note that we were able to describe *three levels* of the qualitative variable with only *two dummy variables*. This is because the mean of the base level (Adams, in this case) is accounted for by the intercept β_0.

Since Sales engineer is a qualitative variable, we will use a bar graph to show the value of mean profit $E(y)$ for the three levels of Sales engineer (see Figure 12.16). Particularly, note that the height of the bar, $E(y)$, for each level of Sales engineer is equal to the sum of the model parameters shown in the preceding equations. You can see that the height of the bar corresponding to Adams is β_0; i.e., $E(y) = \beta_0$. Similarly, the heights of the bars corresponding to Brown and Clark are $E(y) = \beta_0 + \beta_1$ and $E(y) = \beta_0 + \beta_2$, respectively.*

Now, carefully examine the model with a single qualitative independent variable at three levels, because we will use exactly the same pattern for any number of levels. Also, the interpretation of the parameters will always be the same.

Figure 12.16 Bar Chart Comparing $E(y)$ for Three Sales Engineers

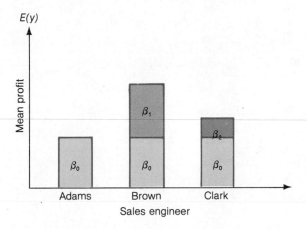

* Either β_1 or β_2, or both, could be negative. If, for example, β_1 were negative, the height of the bar corresponding to Brown would be *reduced* (rather than increased) from the height of the bar for Adams by the amount β_1. Figure 12.16 is constructed assuming β_1 and β_2 are positive quantities.

One level is selected as the base level (we used Adams as level A). Then for the one–zero system of coding* for the dummy variables,

$$\mu_A = \beta_0$$

The coding for all dummy variables is as follows: To represent the mean value of y for a particular level, let that dummy variable equal 1; otherwise, the dummy variable is set equal to 0. Using this system of coding, we have

$$\mu_B = \beta_0 + \beta_1$$
$$\mu_C = \beta_0 + \beta_2$$
$$\vdots$$

Because $\mu_A = \beta_0$, any other model parameter will represent the difference in means between that level and the base level:

$$\beta_1 = \mu_B - \mu_A$$
$$\beta_2 = \mu_C - \mu_A$$
$$\vdots$$

Procedure for Writing a Model with One Qualitative Independent Variable at k Levels

$$E(y) = \beta_0 + \beta_1 x_1 + \beta_2 x_2 + \cdots + \beta_{k-1} x_{k-1}$$

where x_i is the dummy variable for level i and

$$x_i = \begin{cases} 1 & \text{if } E(y) \text{ is the mean for level } i \\ 0 & \text{otherwise} \end{cases}$$

Then, for this system of coding

$$\mu_A = \beta_0 \qquad \text{and} \qquad \beta_1 = \mu_B - \mu_A$$
$$\mu_B = \beta_0 + \beta_1 \qquad\qquad\qquad \beta_2 = \mu_C - \mu_A$$
$$\mu_C = \beta_0 + \beta_2 \qquad\qquad\qquad \beta_3 = \mu_D - \mu_A$$
$$\mu_D = \beta_0 + \beta_3 \qquad\qquad\qquad \vdots$$
$$\vdots$$

---

* We do not have to use a one–zero system of coding for the dummy variables. Any two-value system will work, but the interpretation given to the model parameters will depend on the code. Using the one–zero system makes the model parameters easy to interpret.

Example 12.4 Suppose a large chain of department stores wants to compare the mean dollar amounts owed by its delinquent credit card customers in three different annual income groups: under $12,000, $12,000–$25,000, and over $25,000. A sample of ten customers with delinquent accounts is selected from each group and the amount owed by each is recorded, as shown in Table 12.3. Do the data provide sufficient evidence to indicate that the mean dollar amounts owed by customers differ for the three income groups?

Table 12.3

Income Class: Dollars Owed

	CATEGORY		
	1 *Under $12,000*	2 *$12,000–$25,000*	3 *Over $25,000*
	$148	$513	$335
	76	264	643
	393	433	216
	520	94	536
	236	535	128
	134	327	723
	55	214	258
	166	135	380
	415	280	594
	153	304	465
TOTALS	$2,296	$3,099	$4,278

Solution The model relating $E(y)$ to the single qualitative variable, Income level, is

$$E(y) = \beta_0 + \beta_1 x_1 + \beta_2 x_2$$

where

$$x_1 = \begin{cases} 1 & \text{if income level 2} \\ 0 & \text{if not} \end{cases} \qquad x_2 = \begin{cases} 1 & \text{if income level 3} \\ 0 & \text{if not} \end{cases}$$

and

$$\beta_1 = \mu_2 - \mu_1 \qquad \beta_2 = \mu_3 - \mu_1$$

where μ_1, μ_2, and μ_3 are the mean responses for income categories 1, 2, and 3, respectively. Testing the null hypothesis that the means for the three income levels are equal, i.e., $\mu_1 = \mu_2 = \mu_3$, is equivalent to testing

$$H_0: \quad \beta_1 = \beta_2 = 0$$

because if $\beta_1 = \mu_2 - \mu_1 = 0$ and $\beta_2 = \mu_3 - \mu_1 = 0$, then μ_1, μ_2, and μ_3 must be equal. The alternative hypothesis is

$$H_a: \quad \text{At least one of the parameters, } \beta_1 \text{ or } \beta_2, \text{ differs from zero}$$

There are two ways to conduct this test. We can fit the complete model shown above and the reduced model (deleting the terms involving β_1 and β_2),

$$E(y) = \beta_0$$

and conduct the F test described in the preceding section (we leave this as an exercise for you). Or, we can use the F test of the complete model (Section 11.6), which tests the null hypothesis that all parameters in the model, with the exception of β_0, equal zero. Either way you conduct the test, you will obtain the same computed value of F, the value shown on the SAS printout for a test of the complete model. The SAS printout for fitting the complete model,

$$E(y) = \beta_0 + \beta_1 x_1 + \beta_2 x_2$$

is shown in Figure 12.17 and the value of the F statistic for testing the complete model, $F = 3.48$, is shaded. We will wish to compare this value with the tabulated value of F based on $v_1 = 2$ and $v_2 = 27$ degrees of freedom. If we choose $\alpha = .05$, we will reject $H_0: \beta_1 = \beta_2 = 0$ if the computed value of F exceeds $F_{.05} = 3.35$. Since the computed value of F, $F = 3.48$, exceeds $F_{.05} = 3.35$, we reject H_0 and conclude that at least one of the parameters, β_1 or β_2, differs from zero. Or, equivalently, we conclude that the data provide sufficient evidence to indicate that the mean indebtedness does vary from one income group to another. ∎

Figure 12.17 SAS Computer Printout for Example 12.4

```
DEPENDENT VARIABLE: Y

SOURCE                      DF    SUM OF SQUARES        MEAN SQUARE      F VALUE
MODEL                        2    198772.46666667    99386.23333333        3.48

ERROR                       27    770670.90000000    28543.36666667      PR > F
CORRECTED TOTAL             29    969443.36666667                         0.0452

R-SQUARE              C.V.              ROOT MSE            Y MEAN
0.205038           52.3978         168.94782232       322.43333333

                               T FOR HO :    PR > !T!   STD ERROR OF
PARAMETER        ESTIMATE    PARAMETER=0                  ESTIMATE
INTERCEPT     229.60000000          4.30     0.0002     53.42599243
X1             80.30000000          1.06     0.2973     75.55576307
X2            198.20000000          2.62     0.0141     75.55576307
```

We need to make two additional comments about Example 12.4. First, regression analysis is not the only way to analyze these data. Another procedure for calculating the value of the F statistic, known as an *analysis of variance,* is described in Chapter 15; this example is reworked, using that procedure, in Example 15.2. Second, if you choose to analyze the data by fitting complete and reduced models (Section 12.4), you will find that the least squares estimate of β_0 in the reduced model,

$$E(y) = \beta_0$$

is $\bar{y}$, the mean of all $n = 30$ observations, and the sum of squares for error for the reduced model is

$$\text{SSE}_1 = \sum (y_i - \hat{y}_i)^2 = \sum (y_i - \bar{y})^2 = 969{,}443.367$$

This value is shown in the SAS printout in Figure 12.17 as SUM OF SQUARES corresponding to CORRECTED TOTAL. We leave the remaining steps, calculating the drop in SSE and the resulting F statistic, to you. You will find that the value you obtain will be the same as the value of F shown in the SAS printout in Figure 12.17.

Learning the Mechanics

12.39 Write a regression model relating the mean value of y to a qualitative independent variable that can assume two levels. Interpret all the terms in the model.

12.40 Write a regression model relating $E(y)$ to a qualitative independent variable that can assume three levels. Interpret all the terms in the model.

12.41 The following model was used to relate $E(y)$ to a single qualitative variable with four levels:

$$E(y) = \beta_0 + \beta_1 x_1 + \beta_2 x_2 + \beta_3 x_3$$

where

$$x_1 = \begin{cases} 1 & \text{if level 2} \\ 0 & \text{if not} \end{cases} \qquad x_2 = \begin{cases} 1 & \text{if level 3} \\ 0 & \text{if not} \end{cases} \qquad x_3 = \begin{cases} 1 & \text{if level 4} \\ 0 & \text{if not} \end{cases}$$

This model was fit to $n = 30$ data points and the following result was obtained:

$$\hat{y} = 10.2 - 4x_1 + 12x_2 + 2x_3$$

Find estimates for $E(y)$ when the qualitative independent variable is set at each of the following levels:

a. Level 1   **b.** Level 2   **c.** Level 3   **d.** Level 4

12.42 Refer to Exercise 12.41. Specify the null and alternative hypotheses you would use to test whether $E(y)$ is the same for all four levels of the independent variable.

Applying the Concepts

[*Note: Starred (*) exercises require the use of a computer.*]

12.43 In 1983, 4-year private colleges charged an average of $4,627 for tuition and fees for the year; 4-year public colleges charged $1,105 (*USA Today*, Aug. 17, 1983, p. 1). In order to estimate the difference in the mean amounts charged for the 1985–1986 academic year, random samples of forty private colleges and forty public colleges were contacted and questioned about their tuition structures.

a. Which of the procedures described in Chapter 9 could be used to estimate the difference in mean charges between private and public colleges?

b. Propose a regression model involving the qualitative independent variable — type of college — that could be used to investigate the difference between the means. Be sure to specify the coding scheme for the dummy variable in the model.

c. Explain how the regression model you developed in part b could be used to estimate the difference between the population means.

12.44 An independent testing laboratory has been hired to compare the lifelength (in months) of four different brands of color television picture tubes, A, B, C, and D. Life data have been obtained on ten randomly selected picture tubes of each brand. Propose a regression model involving the qualitative independent variable, Brand of color tube, to estimate the mean lifelength of a tube. Interpret each term in your model.

12.45 The director of marketing of a company that sells business machines is interested in modeling mean monthly sales (in thousands of dollars) per salesperson, $E(y)$, as a function of the type of sales incentive plan that is in effect: commission only, straight salary, or salary plus commission on each sale. The director has proposed the following model:

$$E(y) = \beta_0 + \beta_1 x_1 + \beta_2 x_2$$

where

$$x_1 = \begin{cases} 1 & \text{if salesperson is paid a straight salary} \\ 0 & \text{otherwise} \end{cases}$$

$$x_2 = \begin{cases} 1 & \text{if salesperson is paid a salary plus commission} \\ 0 & \text{otherwise} \end{cases}$$

A portion of the computer printout that results from using Minitab to fit this model to the sales data collected from a sample of fifteen salespersons (five from each incentive plan) is shown here.

```
THE REGRESSION EQUATION IS
Y =    20.0 -  8.60 X1 +  3.80 X2

                              ST. DEV.   T-RATIO =
        COLUMN    COEFFICIENT  OF COEF.   COEF/S.D.

          --         20.000     2.898       6.90
X1    C21            -8.60      4.10       -2.10
X2    C22             3.80      4.10        .93

THE ST. DEV. OF Y ABOUT REGRESSION LINE IS
S =      6.481
WITH ( 15- 3) =   12 DEGREES OF FREEDOM

R-SQUARED = 44.5 PERCENT
R-SQUARED = 35.2 PERCENT, ADJUSTED FOR D.F.

ANALYSIS OF VARIANCE

 DUE TO       DF      SS     MS=SS/DF

REGRESSION     2    403.60    201.80
RESIDUAL      12    504.00     42.00
TOTAL         14    907.60
```

a. Do the data provide sufficient evidence to conclude that there is a difference in mean monthly sales among the three incentive plans? Test using $\alpha = .05$.

b. Use the least squares prediction equation to estimate the mean sales for salespersons working on a straight salary basis.

c. Use the least squares prediction equation to estimate the mean sales for salespersons working on a commission only basis.

[*Note:* We would prefer to use confidence intervals for the estimates in parts b and c, but their calculation is beyond the scope of this text. This procedure can be found in the references at the end of the chapter.]

12.46 Refer to Exercise 12.45. Find a 90% confidence interval for the difference between the mean monthly sales for salespersons on salary plus commission versus those on commission only.

12.47 The manager of a supermarket wants to model the total weekly sales of beer, y, as a function of brand. This model will enable the manager to plan the store's inventory. The market carries three brands, B_1, B_2, and B_3.

a. What type of independent variable is Brand of beer?
b. Write the model relating mean weekly beer sales, $E(y)$, as a function of brand of beer. Be sure to explain any dummy variables you use.
c. Interpret the β parameters of your model in part b.
d. In terms of the model parameters, what is the mean weekly sales for brand B_3?

12.48 Refer to Exercise 12.47. Suppose the manager uses brand B_1 as the base level and obtains the prediction equation

$$\hat{y} = 450 + 60x_1 - 30x_2$$

where

$$x_1 = \begin{cases} 1 & \text{if brand } B_2 \\ 0 & \text{otherwise} \end{cases} \qquad x_2 = \begin{cases} 1 & \text{if brand } B_3 \\ 0 & \text{otherwise} \end{cases}$$

a. What is the difference between the estimated mean weekly sales for brands B_2 and B_1?
b. What is the estimated mean weekly sales for brand B_2?

[*Note:* We would generally form confidence intervals for the true means in order to assess the reliability of these estimates. Our objective in these exercises is to develop the ability to use the models to obtain the estimates.]

*__12.49__ Five varieties of peas are currently being tested by a large agribusiness cooperative in Ohio to determine which is best suited for production in that state. A field was divided into twenty plots, with each variety of peas planted in four plots. The yields in bushels of peas produced from each plot are shown in the table.

VARIETY OF PEAS				
A	B	C	D	E
26.2	29.2	29.1	21.3	20.1
24.3	28.1	30.8	22.4	19.3
21.8	27.3	33.9	24.3	19.9
28.1	31.2	32.8	21.8	22.1

a. Write a model for the data to reflect the yield in bushels as a function of pea variety and interpret all parameters in the model.

b. Fit the data to the proposed model.

c. Do the data provide sufficient evidence to indicate the model is useful for predicting harvest yield? Use $\alpha = .05$.

*12.50 A firm's *debt-to-equity ratio* is a measure of the extent to which management is using borrowed funds. It is a measure of considerable importance to individuals and organizations that are potential lenders to the firm. A high debt-to-equity ratio signals that in case of default, the lender will likely not recover outstanding loans to the firm since insufficient equity exists to cover all the firm's obligations. In addition, the higher the debt, the more funds that are required to service the debt. As a result, if business turns downward, the firm may not have sufficient operating funds to meet debt service payments (Spiro, 1982). The debt-to-equity ratios for firms in four different industries are given in the table for the fiscal year that ended during 1983.

INSURANCE		PUBLISHING		ELECTRIC UTILITIES		BANKING	
Firm	*Debt-to-equity*	*Firm*	*Debt-to-equity*	*Firm*	*Debt-to-equity*	*Firm*	*Debt-to-equity*
Chubb	0.1	Deluxe		Pacific Power		U.S. Bancorp	0.5
Kemper	0.0	Check	0.0	& Light	1.1	Sun Banks	0.2
St. Paul Cos.	0.1	New York		Houston Ind.	0.8	Mellon	
Lincoln		Times	0.4	Florida Power		National	0.5
National	0.2	A. C. Nielsen	0.1	& Light	0.8	Michigan	
USF & G	0.0	Dow Jones	0.1	Penn Power		National	0.3
Aetna	0.1	Gannett	0.3	& Light	0.9	Southeast	
				North States		Banking	0.4
				Pur.	0.7		
				Ohio Edison	1.2		
				Orange and			
				Rockland	0.6		

Source: *Forbes,* ''36th Annual Report on American Industry,'' Jan. 2, 1984.

a. Propose a regression model involving the qualitative independent variable Industry that could be used to investigate whether the mean debt-to-equity ratio varies among the four industries. Be sure to specify the coding scheme for the dummy variables in your model.

b. Test the null hypothesis that the mean debt-to-equity ratios are equal in the four industries. Use $\alpha = .05$.

c. Do the data provide sufficient evidence to conclude that the mean debt-to-equity ratios of the electric utilities industry and the insurance industry differ? Test using $\alpha = .10$.

12.6 Comparing the Slopes of Two or More Lines

Suppose you wish to relate the mean monthly sales, $E(y)$, of a company to monthly advertising expenditure, x, for three different advertising media — say, newspaper, radio, and television — and you wish to use first-order (straight-line) models to model the responses for all three media. Graphs of these three relationships might appear as shown in Figure 12.18.

Since the lines in Figure 12.18 are hypothetical, a number of practical business questions arise. Is one advertising medium as effective as any other; that is, do the three mean sales

Figure 12.18 Graphs of the Relationship Between Mean Sales, $E(y)$, and Advertising Expenditure, x

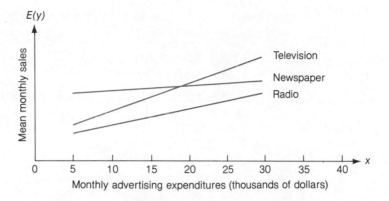

lines differ for the three advertising media? Do the increases in mean sales per dollar increase in advertising differ for the three advertising media; that is, do the slopes of the three lines differ? Note that each of the two practical business questions has been rephrased into a question about the parameters that define the three lines of Figure 12.18. To answer them, we must write a single linear statistical model that will characterize the three lines of Figure 12.18. Then the practical business questions can be answered by testing hypotheses about the model parameters.

In the preceding example, the response (monthly sales) is a function of *two* independent variables, one quantitative (advertising expenditure, x) and one qualitative (type of medium). We will examine the different models that can be constructed relating $E(y)$ to these two independent variables.

1. The straight-line relationship between mean sales, $E(y)$, and advertising expenditure is the same for all three media; that is, a single line will describe the relationship between $E(y)$ and advertising expenditure, x_1, for all the media (see Figure 12.19).

$$E(y) = \beta_0 + \beta_1 x_1 \qquad x_1 = \text{Advertising expenditure}$$

Figure 12.19 The Relationship Between $E(y)$ and x_1 Is the Same for All Media

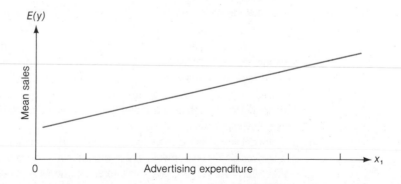

2. The straight lines relating mean sales, $E(y)$, to advertising expenditure, x_1, differ from one medium to another, but the increase in mean sales per unit increase in dollar advertising

expenditure, x_1, is the same for all media. That is, the lines are parallel but have different y-intercepts (see Figure 12.20).

$$E(y) = \beta_0 + \beta_1 x_1 + \beta_2 x_2 + \beta_3 x_3$$

$x_1 =$ Advertising expenditure

$$x_2 = \begin{cases} 1 & \text{if radio medium} \\ 0 & \text{if not} \end{cases} \qquad x_3 = \begin{cases} 1 & \text{if television medium} \\ 0 & \text{if not} \end{cases}$$

Figure 12.20   Parallel Response Lines for the Three Media

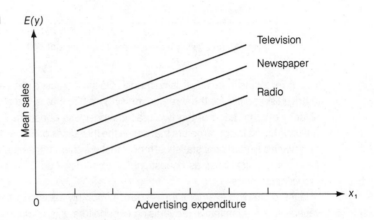

Notice that this model is essentially a combination of a first-order model with a single quantitative variable and the model with a single qualitative variable:

First-order model with a single
   quantitative variable: $E(y) = \beta_0 +$ $\boxed{\beta_1 x_1}$

Model with a single
   qualitative variable
   at three levels: $E(y) = \beta_0 +$ $\boxed{\beta_2 x_2 + \beta_3 x_3}$

where x_1, x_2, and x_3 are defined as above. The model described implies no interaction between the two independent variables, advertising expenditure x_1 and the qualitative variable Type of advertising medium. The change in $E(y)$ for a 1-unit increase in x_1 is identical (i.e., the slopes of the lines are equal) for all three advertising media. The terms corresponding to each of the independent variables are called ***main effect*** terms because they imply no interaction.

3. The straight lines relating mean sales, $E(y)$, to advertising expenditure, x_1, differ for the three advertising media; that is, the intercepts and slopes differ for the three lines (see Figure 12.21). As you will see, this interaction model is obtained by adding interaction terms (those involving the cross product terms, one each from each of the two independent variables).

Main effect,
advertising   Main effect,
expenditure   type of medium   Interaction

$$E(y) = \beta_0 + \overbrace{\beta_1 x_1} + \overbrace{\beta_2 x_2 + \beta_3 x_3} + \overbrace{\beta_4 x_1 x_2 + \beta_5 x_1 x_3}$$

Note that each of the preceding models is obtained by adding terms to model 1, the single first-order model used to model the responses for all three media. Model 2 is obtained by adding the main effect terms for the qualitative variable, Type of medium; and model 3 is obtained by adding the interaction terms to model 2.

Figure 12.21 Different Response Lines for the Three Media

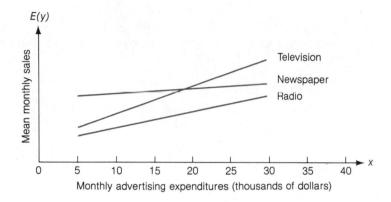

Will a single line (Figure 12.19) characterize the responses for all three media or do the three response lines differ as shown in Figure 12.21? A test of the null hypothesis that a single first-order model adequately describes the relationship between $E(y)$ and advertising expenditure x_1 for all three media is a test of the null hypothesis that the parameters of model 3, β_2, β_3, β_4, and β_5, equal zero; i.e.,

$$H_0: \quad \beta_2 = \beta_3 = \beta_4 = \beta_5 = 0$$

This hypothesis can be tested by fitting the complete model (model 3) and the reduced model (model 1) and conducting an F test, as described in Section 12.4.

Suppose we assume that the response lines for the three media will differ but wonder whether the data present sufficient evidence to indicate differences in the slopes of the lines. To test the null hypothesis that model 2 adequately describes the relationship between $E(y)$ and advertising expenditure x_1, we wish to test

$$H_0: \quad \beta_4 = \beta_5 = 0$$

that is, that the two independent variables, advertising expenditure x_1 and the qualitative variable, Type of medium, do not interact. This test can be conducted by fitting the complete model (model 3) and the reduced model (model 2), calculating the drop in the sum of squares for error, and conducting an F test.

Example 12.5   Substitute the appropriate values of the dummy variables in model 3 to obtain the equations of the three response lines in Figure 12.21.

Solution   The complete model that characterizes the three lines in Figure 12.21 is

$$E(y) = \beta_0 + \beta_1 x_1 + \beta_2 x_2 + \beta_3 x_3 + \beta_4 x_1 x_2 + \beta_5 x_1 x_3$$

where

$x_1 = $ Advertising expenditure

$$x_2 = \begin{cases} 1 & \text{if radio medium} \\ 0 & \text{if not} \end{cases} \qquad x_3 = \begin{cases} 1 & \text{if television medium} \\ 0 & \text{if not} \end{cases}$$

Examining the coding, you can see that $x_2 = x_3 = 0$ when the advertising medium is newspaper. Substituting these values into the expression for $E(y)$, we obtain the newspaper medium line.

Newspaper Medium Line:

$$\begin{aligned} E(y) &= \beta_0 + \beta_1 x_1 + \beta_2(0) + \beta_3(0) + \beta_4 x_1(0) + \beta_5 x_1(0) \\ &= \beta_0 + \beta_1 x_1 \end{aligned}$$

Similarly, we substitute the appropriate values of x_2 and x_3 into the expression for $E(y)$ to obtain the radio medium line and the television medium line.

Radio Medium Line:

$$E(y) = \beta_0 + \beta_1 x_1 + \beta_2(1) + \beta_3(0) + \beta_4 x_1(1) + \beta_5 x_1(0)$$

$$= \overbrace{\beta_0 + \beta_2}^{y\text{-intercept}} + \overbrace{(\beta_1 + \beta_4)x_1}^{\text{Slope}}$$

Television Medium Line:

$$E(y) = \beta_0 + \beta_1 x_1 + \beta_2(0) + \beta_3(1) + \beta_4 x_1(0) + \beta_5 x_1(1)$$

$$= \overbrace{\beta_0 + \beta_3}^{y\text{-intercept}} + \overbrace{(\beta_1 + \beta_5)x_1}^{\text{Slope}} \qquad\blacksquare$$

If you were to fit model 3, obtain estimates of $\beta_0, \beta_1, \beta_2, \ldots, \beta_5$, and substitute them into the equations for the three media lines shown in Example 12.5, you would obtain exactly the same prediction equations as you would obtain if you fit three separate straight lines, one to each of the three sets of media data. You may ask why we would not fit the three lines separately. Why fit a model (model 3) that combines all three lines into the same equation? The answer is that you need to use this procedure if you wish to use statistical tests to compare the three media lines. We need to be able to express a practical question about the lines in terms of an hypothesis that a set of parameters in the model equal zero. You could not do this if you were to perform three separate regression analyses and fit a line to each set of media data.

Example 12.6 An industrial psychologist conducted an experiment to investigate the relationship between worker productivity and a measure of salary incentive for two manufacturing plants, one, A, with union representation and the other, B, with nonunion representation. The productivity, y, per worker was measured by recording the number of machined castings that a worker could produce in a 4-week, 40-hour-per-week period. The incentive was the amount, x_1, of bonus (in cents per casting) paid for all castings produced in excess of 1,000 per worker for the 4-week period. Nine workers were selected from each plant and three from each group of nine were assigned to receive a 20¢ bonus per casting, three a 30¢ bonus, and three a 40¢ bonus per casting. The productivity data for the eighteen workers, three for each plant type and incentive combination, are shown in the table.

| | INCENTIVE | | | | | | | | |
	20¢/casting			30¢/casting			40¢/casting		
UNION PLANT	1,435	1,512	1,491	1,583	1,529	1,610	1,601	1,574	1,636
NONUNION PLANT	1,575	1,512	1,488	1,635	1,589	1,661	1,645	1,616	1,689

a. Plot the data points, and graph the prediction equations for the two productivity lines. Assume that the relationship between mean productivity and incentive is first-order.

b. Do the data provide sufficient evidence to indicate a difference in worker response to incentives between the two plants?

Solution If we assume that a first-order model* is adequate to detect a change in mean productivity, $E(y)$, as a function of incentive, x_1, then the model that produces two productivity lines, one for each plant, is

$$E(y) = \beta_0 + \beta_1 x_1 + \beta_2 x_2 + \beta_3 x_1 x_2$$

where

$$x_1 = \text{Incentive} \qquad x_2 = \begin{cases} 1 & \text{if nonunion plant} \\ 0 & \text{if union plant} \end{cases}$$

a. The SAS printout for the regression analysis is shown in Figure 12.22 (next page). The prediction equation obtained by reading the parameter estimates from the printout is

$$\hat{y} = 1{,}365.833 + 6.217x_1 + 47.778x_2 + .033x_1 x_2$$

The prediction equation for the union plant can be obtained by substituting $x_2 = 0$ into the general prediction equation. Then

$$\begin{aligned} \hat{y} &= \hat{\beta}_0 + \hat{\beta}_1 x_1 + \hat{\beta}_2(0) + \hat{\beta}_3 x_1(0) \\ &= \hat{\beta}_0 + \hat{\beta}_1 x_1 \\ &= 1{,}365.833 + 6.217x_1 \end{aligned}$$

---

* Although the model contains a term involving $x_1 x_2$, it is first-order (that is, it graphs as a straight line) in the quantitative variable x_1. The variable x_2 is a dummy variable that introduces or deletes terms in the model. The order of a term is determined only by the quantitative variables that appear in the term.

Figure 12.22   SAS Computer Printout for the Complete Model of Example 12.6

```
DEPENDENT VARIABLE: Y

SOURCE                          DF   SUM OF SQUARES      MEAN SQUARE    F VALUE
MODEL                            3   57332.38888889   19110.79629630     11.46
ERROR                           14   23349.22222223    1667.80158730    PR > F
CORRECTED TOTAL                 17   80681.61111112                     0.0005

R-SQUARE              C.V.              ROOT MSE          Y MEAN
0.710600            2.5901            40.83872656    1576.72222222

                                 T FOR HO:     PR > !T!    STD ERROR OF
PARAMETER           ESTIMATE    PARAMETER=0                  ESTIMATE
INTERCEPT       1365.83333333         26.35      0.0001     51.83641257
X1                 6.21666667          3.73      0.0022      1.66723403
X2                47.77777778          0.65      0.5251     73.30775769
X1*X2              0.03333333          0.01      0.9889      2.35782498
```

Similarly, the prediction equation for the nonunion plant is obtained by substituting $x_2 = 1$ into the general prediction equation. Then,

$$\hat{y} = \hat{\beta}_0 + \hat{\beta}_1 x_1 + \hat{\beta}_2 x_2 + \hat{\beta}_3 x_1 x_2$$
$$= \hat{\beta}_0 + \hat{\beta}_1 x_1 + \hat{\beta}_2(1) + \hat{\beta}_3 x_1(1)$$

$$= \overbrace{(\hat{\beta}_0 + \hat{\beta}_2)}^{y\text{-intercept}} + \overbrace{(\hat{\beta}_1 + \hat{\beta}_3)}^{\text{Slope}} x_1$$
$$= (1{,}365.833 + 47.778) + (6.217 + .033)x_1$$
$$= 1{,}413.611 + 6.250x_1$$

The graphs of these prediction equations are shown in Figure 12.23.

Figure 12.23   Graphs of the Prediction Equations for the Two Productivity Lines of Example 12.6

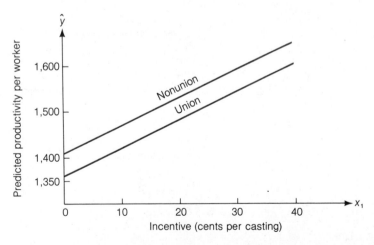

b. To determine whether the data provide sufficient evidence to indicate a difference in worker response to incentives for the two plants, we test the null hypothesis that a *single* line characterizes the relationship between productivity per worker and the amount of incentive, x_1, against the alternative hypothesis that we need two separate lines to characterize the relationship, one for each plant. If there is no difference in mean response $E(y)$ to x_1 between the two plants, then we do not need Type of plant in the model; i.e., we do not need the terms involving x_2. Therefore, we wish to test

$$H_0: \quad \beta_2 = \beta_3 = 0$$

against the alternative hypothesis

H_a: At least one of the two parameters, β_2 or β_3, differs from zero

The SAS computer printout for fitting the reduced model,

$$E(y) = \beta_0 + \beta_1 x_1$$

to the data is shown in Figure 12.24. Reading SSE_2 and SSE_1 from Figures 12.22 and 12.24, respectively, we obtain

Complete model: $SSE_2 = 23{,}349.22$

Reduced model: $SSE_1 = 34{,}056.28$

Drop in SSE $= SSE_1 - SSE_2 = 10{,}707.06$

Figure 12.24   SAS Computer Printout for the Reduced Model of Example 12.6

```
DEPENDENT VARIABLE: Y

SOURCE                       DF    SUM OF SQUARES      MEAN SQUARE    F VALUE

MODEL                         1    46625.33333333    46625.33333333    21.91
ERROR                        16    34056.27777778     2128.51736111    PR > F
CORRECTED TOTAL              17    80681.61111112                      0.0003

R-SQUARE              C.V.              ROOT MSE            Y MEAN

0.577893            2.9261           46.13585765        1576.72222222

                            T FOR H0:    PR > :T:    STD ERROR OF
PARAMETER       ESTIMATE    PARAMETER=0              ESTIMATE

INTERCEPT     1389.72222222      33.56      0.0001    41.40819949
X1               6.23333333       4.68      0.0003     1.33182749
```

The value of s^2 for the complete model is obtained from Figure 12.22:

$$s^2 = 1{,}667.80$$

Substituting these values, along with $k = 3$ and $g = 1$, into the formula for the F statistic yields

$$F = \frac{(SSE_1 - SSE_2)/(k - g)}{s^2}$$

$$= \frac{10{,}707.06/2}{1{,}667.80} = 3.21$$

The numerator degrees of freedom (the number of parameters involved in H_0) is 2 and the denominator degrees of freedom (the number associated with s^2 in the complete model) is 14. If we choose $\alpha = .05$, the tabulated value of $F_{.05}$, given in Table VII of Appendix B, is 3.74. Since the computed value, $F = 3.21$, is less than the tabulated value, $F_{.05} = 3.74$, there is insufficient evidence (at $\alpha = .05$) to indicate a difference in worker response to incentives between the two plants. Therefore, there is no evidence to indicate that two different lines, one for each plant, are needed to describe the relationship between the mean productivity per worker, $E(y)$, and the amount of incentive, x_1.

∎

Example 12.7   Refer to Example 12.6 and explain how you would determine whether the data provide sufficient evidence to indicate that the incentive, x_1, affects mean productivity.

Solution   If incentive did *not* affect mean productivity, we would not need terms involving x_1 in the model. Therefore, we would test the null hypothesis

$$H_0: \quad \beta_1 = \beta_3 = 0$$

against the alternative hypothesis

$$H_a: \quad \text{At least one of the parameters, } \beta_1 \text{ or } \beta_3, \text{ differs from zero}$$

We would fit the reduced model,

$$E(y) = \beta_0 + \beta_2 x_2$$

to the data and find SSE_1. The values of SSE_2 and s^2 for the complete model would be the same as those used in Example 12.6. Finally, you would calculate the value of the F statistic and compare it with a tabulated value of F based on $v_1 = 2$ and $v_2 = 14$ degrees of freedom. If the test leads to rejection of H_0, you have evidence to indicate that the increase in mean productivity that appears to be present in the graphs in Figure 12.23 is not due to random variation in the data.

∎

Exercises 12.51 – 12.63

Learning the Mechanics

12.51 Write a first-order model that relates $E(y)$ to one quantitative independent variable.

12.52 Add the main effect terms for one qualitative independent variable at three levels to the model of Exercise 12.51.

12.53 Add terms to the model of Exercise 12.52 to allow for interaction between the quantitative and qualitative independent variables.

12.54 Under what circumstances will the response lines of the model in Exercise 12.53 be parallel?

12.55 Under what circumstances will the model of Exercise 12.53 have only one response line?

Applying the Concepts

[*Note: Starred (*) exercises require the use of a computer.*]

12.56 The Florida Citrus Commission is interested in evaluating the performance of two orange juice extractors, brand A and brand B. It is believed that the size of the fruit used in the test may influence the juice yield (amount of juice per pound of oranges) obtained by the extractors. The commission wants to develop a regression model relating the mean juice yield, $E(y)$, to the type of orange juice extractor (brand A or brand B) and the size of orange (diameter), x_1.

a. Identify the independent variables as qualitative or quantitative.
b. Write a model that describes the relationship between $E(y)$ and size of orange as two parallel lines, one for each brand of extractor.
c. Modify the model of part b to permit the slopes of the two lines to differ.
d. Sketch typical response lines for the model of part b. Do the same for the model of part c. Carefully label your graphs.
e. Specify the null and alternative hypotheses you would use to determine whether the model in part c provides more information for predicting yield than does the model in part b.
f. Explain how you would obtain the quantities necessary to compute the F statistic that would be used in testing the hypotheses you described in part e.

12.57 An economist is interested in modeling the mean monthly demand $E(y)$ (in thousands of units) for a particular product as a function of the product's price (in dollars) and the season of the year. The following model has been proposed:

$$E(y) = \beta_0 + \beta_1 x_1 + \beta_2 x_2 + \beta_3 x_3 + \beta_4 x_4$$

where

$x_1 = $ Price

$$x_2 = \begin{cases} 1 & \text{if spring} \\ 0 & \text{otherwise} \end{cases} \qquad x_3 = \begin{cases} 1 & \text{if summer} \\ 0 & \text{otherwise} \end{cases} \qquad x_4 = \begin{cases} 1 & \text{if fall} \\ 0 & \text{otherwise} \end{cases}$$

A portion of the Minitab computer printout that results from fitting this model to a sample of 16 months of sales data selected from the last 2 years is shown at the top of the next page.

```
THE REGRESSION EQUATION IS
Y =    12.1 -   1.11 X1 +  3.94 X2
     +  7.17 X3 +  3.72 X4

                                ST. DEV.   T-RATIO =
         COLUMN   COEFFICIENT   OF COEF.   COEF/S.D.

          --        12.067       1.473       8.19
   X1    C2         -1.113        .187      -5.93
   X2    C3          3.942        .858       4.59
   X3    C4          7.166        .815       8.80
   X4    C5          3.724        .819       4.55

THE ST. DEV. OF Y ABOUT REGRESSION LINE IS
S =     1.135
WITH (  16- 5) =   11 DEGREES OF FREEDOM

R-SQUARED = 93.1 PERCENT
R-SQUARED = 90.6 PERCENT, ADJUSTED FOR D.F.

ANALYSIS OF VARIANCE

  DUE TO      DF        SS      MS=SS/DF

REGRESSION    4     191.590     47.897
RESIDUAL     11      14.160      1.287
TOTAL        15     205.750
```

The reduced model, $E(y) = \beta_0 + \beta_1 x_1$, was also fit to the same data, and the resulting computer printout is partially reproduced here:

```
THE REGRESSION EQUATION IS
Y =   . 17.4 -   1.35 X1

                                ST. DEV.   T-RATIO =
         COLUMN   COEFFICIENT   OF COEF.   COEF/S.D.

          --        17.394       2.863       6.08
   X1    C2         -1.348        .403      -3.34

THE ST. DEV. OF Y ABOUT REGRESSION LINE IS
S =     2.859
WITH (  16- 2) =   14 DEGREES OF FREEDOM

R-SQUARED = 44.4 PERCENT
R-SQUARED = 40.4 PERCENT, ADJUSTED FOR D.F.

ANALYSIS OF VARIANCE

  DUE TO      DF        SS      MS=SS/DF

REGRESSION    1      91.345     91.345
RESIDUAL     14     114.405      8.172
TOTAL        15     205.750
```

a. Is there sufficient evidence to conclude that mean monthly demand depends on the season of the year? Test using $\alpha = .05$.

b. Find an estimate for $E(y)$ when the price is $8.00 and it is summer. Interpret your result.

[*Note:* We prefer to use a confidence interval for the estimate of part b but its calculation is beyond the scope of this text. This procedure can be found in the references at the end of the chapter.]

*12.58 A consumer advocacy organization conducted an experiment to compare the effectiveness of three commercially available weight-reducing diets. Ten people were assigned to each of the three diets for a 1-month period of time. Their weights (in pounds) were recorded at the beginning of the month and again at the end of the month. The results obtained are shown in the table.

DIET A		DIET B		DIET C	
x_1, weight before	y, weight loss	x_1, weight before	y, weight loss	x_1, weight before	y, weight loss
227	14	255	19	206	7
286	16	193	8	222	9
180	−2	186	4	168	2
176	8	145	15	132	0
204	15	219	16	173	−3
155	5	273	19	210	8
303	17	289	25	269	10
146	7	168	6	275	15
215	15	194	12	241	8
187	6	248	21	219	5

a. Construct a first-order regression model to relate weight loss, y, to weight before the program, x_1, and the type of diet. Be sure to specify the dummy variable coding scheme you use.
b. Suppose the effect of initial weight on weight loss varies from diet to diet. Write the appropriate regression model for this case. Sketch typical response curves depicting this situation.
c. Fit the models in parts a and b to the data given in the table.
d. Do the data provide sufficient evidence to indicate an interaction between initial weight and type of diet? That is, is the model of part b preferable to the model of part a? Test using $\alpha = .05$.
e. With respect to the model of part b, specify the null and alternative hypotheses you would use to test whether a difference exists among the mean weight losses for the three weight-reducing programs.
f. Conduct the test of part e using $\alpha = .05$.

12.59 Researchers for a dog food company have developed a new puppy food they hope will compete with the major brands. One premarketing test involved comparing the new food with two competitors in terms of weight gain. Fifteen 8-week-old German shepherd puppies, each from a different litter, were divided into three groups of five puppies each. Each group was fed one of the three brands of food.

a. Set up a model that assumes the initial weight, x_1, is linearly related to final weight, y, but does not allow for differences among the three brands; i.e., assume the response curve is the same for the three brands of dog food. Sketch the response curve as it might appear.

b. Set up a model that assumes the effect of initial weight is linearly related to final weight, and allows the intercepts of the lines to differ for the three brands. In other words, assume the initial weight and brand both affect final weight, but in an independent fashion. Sketch typical response curves.

c. Now write the main effects plus interaction model. For this model we assume the initial weight is linearly related to final weight, but both the slope and the intercept of the line depend on the brand. Sketch typical response curves.

12.60 A company is studying three different safety programs, A, B, and C, in an attempt to reduce the number of work-hours lost due to accidents. Each program is to be tried at three of the company's nine factories, and the plan is to monitor the lost work-hours, y, for a 1-year period beginning 6 months after the new safety program is instituted.

a. Write a main effects model relating $E(y)$ to the lost work-hours, x_1, the year before the plan is instituted and to the type of program that is instituted.

b. In terms of the model parameters from part a, what hypothesis would you test to determine whether the mean work-hours lost differ for the three safety programs?

12.61 Refer to Exercise 12.60. After the three safety programs have been in effect for 18 months, the complete main effects model is fit to the $n = 9$ data points. With safety program A as the base level, the following results were obtained:

$$\hat{y} = -2.1 + .88x_1 - 150x_2 + 35x_3 \qquad SSE = 1,527.27$$

Then the reduced model $E(y) = \beta_0 + \beta_1 x_1$ is fit, with the result

$$\hat{y} = 15.3 + .84x_1 \qquad SSE = 3,113.14$$

Test whether the mean work-hours lost differ for the three programs. Use $\alpha = .05$.

12.62 An insurance company is experimenting with three different training programs, A, B, and C, for its salespeople. The following main effects model is proposed:

$$E(y) = \beta_0 + \beta_1 x_1 + \beta_2 x_2 + \beta_3 x_3$$

where

$y = $ Monthly sales (in thousands of dollars)

$x_1 = $ Number of months experience

$x_2 = \begin{cases} 1 & \text{if training program B used} \\ 0 & \text{otherwise} \end{cases}$ $\qquad x_3 = \begin{cases} 1 & \text{if training program C used} \\ 0 & \text{otherwise} \end{cases}$

Training program A is the base level.

a. What hypothesis would you test to determine whether the mean monthly sales differ for salespeople trained by the three programs?

b. After experimenting with fifty salespeople over a 5-year period, the complete model is fit, with the result

$$\hat{y} = 10 + .5x_1 + 1.2x_2 - .4x_3 \qquad SSE = 140.5$$

Then the reduced model $E(y) = \beta_0 + \beta_1 x_1$ is fit to the same data, with the result

$$\hat{y} = 11.4 + .4x_1 \qquad SSE = 183.2$$

Test the hypothesis you formulated in part a. Use $\alpha = .05$.

*12.63 In Exercise 11.46, an economist modeled the per capita demand for passenger car motor fuel in the United States as a function of two quantitative independent variables, personal income and the relative price of a gallon of gasoline. In this exercise we explore the relationship between per capita demand for motor fuel, y, and only one of those variables, the relative price of a gallon of gasoline, x. The data are repeated in the table.

YEAR	MOTOR FUEL CONSUMED BY CARS (Billion gallons)	POPULATION OF UNITED STATES (Millions)	RELATIVE PRICE OF GALLON OF GASOLINE
1965	50.3	194.3	1.004
1966	53.31	196.6	.998
1967	55.11	198.7	1.000
1968	58.52	200.7	.973
1969	62.45	202.7	.954
1970	65.8	205.1	.908
1971	69.51	207.1	.876
1972	73.5	209.9	.859
1973	78.0	211.9	.887
1974	74.2	213.9	1.083
1975	76.5	216.0	1.060
1976	78.8	218.0	1.043
1977	80.7	220.2	1.037
1978	83.8	222.6	1.005
1979	80.2	225.1	1.222
1980	73.7	227.7	1.496

Source: *Statistical Abstract of the United States,* various years.

a. Construct a scattergram of the data.
b. In 1973, the Organization of Petroleum Exporting Countries (OPEC) began manipulating the supply of oil — and therefore gasoline — which subsequently caused prices to climb to record heights. This accounts for the unusual pattern you should have observed in the scattergram. Propose a first-order regression model that allows for differences in the relationship between y and x before and after OPEC began manipulating oil prices. [*Note:* Allow for differences in the slopes of the two regression lines.]
c. Fit your proposed model to the data.

d. Plot the two prediction equations associated with the least squares model obtained in part c on the scattergram of the data constructed in part a. Interpret these equations in the context of the problem.

e. Do the data provide sufficient evidence to conclude that the relationship between demand for motor fuel and the relative price of gasoline changed after 1973? Test using $\alpha = .05$.

f. Is there sufficient evidence to conclude that the slopes of the demand functions prior to 1973 and after 1973 differ? Test using $\alpha = .05$.

12.7 Comparing Two or More Response Curves

Suppose we think that the relationship between mean monthly sales, $E(y)$, and advertising expenditure, x_1 (Section 12.6), is second-order. The scenario for writing the models for this situation is as follows.

1. The mean sales curves are identical for all three advertising media; that is, a single second-order curve will suffice to describe the relationship between $E(y)$ and x_1 for all the media (see Figure 12.25).

$$E(y) = \beta_0 + \beta_1 x_1 + \beta_2 x_1^2 \qquad x_1 = \text{Advertising expenditure}$$

Figure 12.25 The Relationship Between $E(y)$ and x_1 Is the Same for All Media

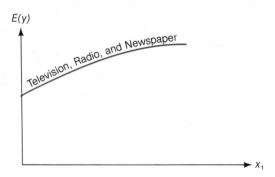

2. The response curves have the same shapes but different y-intercepts (see Figure 12.26).

$$E(y) = \beta_0 + \beta_1 x_1 + \beta_2 x_1^2 + \beta_3 x_2 + \beta_4 x_3$$

$x_1 = \text{Advertising expenditure}$

$$x_2 = \begin{cases} 1 & \text{if radio medium} \\ 0 & \text{if not} \end{cases} \qquad x_3 = \begin{cases} 1 & \text{if television medium} \\ 0 & \text{if not} \end{cases}$$

3. The response curves for the three advertising media are different—i.e., Advertising expenditure and Type of medium interact (see Figure 12.27).

$$E(y) = \beta_0 + \beta_1 x_1 + \beta_2 x_1^2 + \beta_3 x_2 + \beta_4 x_3 + \beta_5 x_1 x_2 + \beta_6 x_1 x_3 + \beta_7 x_1^2 x_2 + \beta_8 x_1^2 x_3$$

Figure 12.26 The Response Curves Have the Same Shapes but Different y-Intercepts

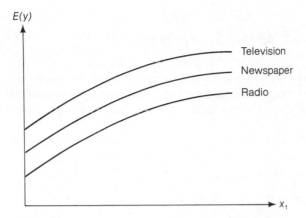

Figure 12.27 The Response Curves Differ for the Three Media

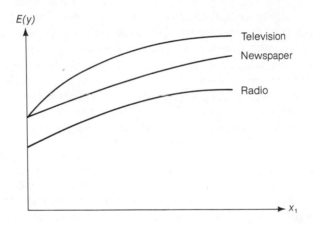

Example 12.8 Give the equation of the second-order model for the radio advertising medium.

Solution   Model 3 characterizes the relationship between $E(y)$ and x_1 for the radio advertising medium (see the coding) when $x_2 = 1$ and $x_3 = 0$. Substituting these values into model 3, we obtain

$$\begin{aligned}
E(y) &= \beta_0 + \beta_1 x_1 + \beta_2 x_1^2 + \beta_3 x_2 + \beta_4 x_3 + \beta_5 x_1 x_2 + \beta_6 x_1 x_3 + \beta_7 x_1^2 x_2 + \beta_8 x_1^2 x_3 \\
&= \beta_0 + \beta_1 x_1 + \beta_2 x_1^2 + \beta_3(1) + \beta_4(0) + \beta_5 x_1(1) + \beta_6 x_1(0) + \beta_7 x_1^2(1) + \beta_8 x_1^2(0) \\
&= (\beta_0 + \beta_3) + (\beta_1 + \beta_5)x_1 + (\beta_2 + \beta_7)x_1^2
\end{aligned}$$

■

Example 12.9 What null hypothesis about the parameters of model 3 would you test if you wished to determine whether the second-order curves for the three media are identical?

Solution   If the curves were identical, we would not need the independent variable Type of medium in the model; that is, we would delete all terms involving x_2 and x_3. This would produce model 1,

$$E(y) = \beta_0 + \beta_1 x_1 + \beta_2 x_1^2$$

and the null hypothesis would be

$$H_0: \quad \beta_3 = \beta_4 = \beta_5 = \beta_6 = \beta_7 = \beta_8 = 0$$ ■

Example 12.10   Suppose we assume that the response curves for the three media differ but we want to know whether the second-order terms contribute information for the prediction of y. Or, equivalently, will a second-order model give better predictions than a first-order model?

Solution   The only difference between model 3 and a first-order model are those terms involving x_1^2. Therefore, the null hypothesis, "the second-order terms contribute no information for the prediction of y," is equivalent to

$$H_0: \quad \beta_2 = \beta_7 = \beta_8 = 0$$ ■

Examples 12.9 and 12.10 identify two tests that answer practical questions concerning a collection of second-order models. Other comparisons among the curves can be made by testing appropriate sets of model parameters (see the exercises).

The models described in the preceding sections provide only an introduction to statistical modeling. Models can be constructed to relate $E(y)$ to any number of quantitative and/or qualitative independent variables. You can compare response curves and surfaces for different levels of a qualitative variable or for different combinations of levels of two or more qualitative independent variables. A general explanation of how to write linear statistical models can be found in Chapter 6 of Mendenhall and McClave (1981).

Case Study 12.1
Forecasting Peak-Hour Traffic Volume*

In designing future metropolitan roadways or redesigning existing roads, highway engineers rely heavily on traffic volume forecasts. Should the road have two, three, or four lanes in each direction? How should the on- and off-ramps be configured? Should the on-ramps be metered? Should one or more lanes be reversible to accommodate rush hour traffic? Should one or more lanes be restricted to carpools? The answers to such questions depend primarily on the traffic volumes the road must be able to handle during the peak travel times of the day—morning and evening rush hours.

Traffic forecasters at the Minnesota Department of Transportation use regression analysis to estimate weekday peak-hour traffic volumes on existing and proposed roadways. In particular, they model the traffic volume for the hour with the highest volume (this is the peak hour, typically 7–8 A.M.), y, as a function of the road's total traffic volume for the day, x_1. The model is developed using traffic data from existing roadways. Upon obtaining a forecast for the total weekday traffic volume for the road in question, the forecasters use the regression model to estimate (forecast) the mean peak-hour volume for the road.

For a recent project involving the redesign of a section of Interstate 494 in Bloomington, Minnesota, the forecasters collected data on peak-hour traffic volumes and weekday traffic

---

* Personal communications from John Sem, Director; Allan E. Pint, State Traffic Forecast Engineer; and James Page, Sr., Transportation Planner, Traffic and Commodities Studies Section, Minnesota Department of Transportation, St. Paul, Minnesota.

Figure 12.28 Scattergram: Peak-Hour Traffic Volume versus Total Traffic Volume for the Day

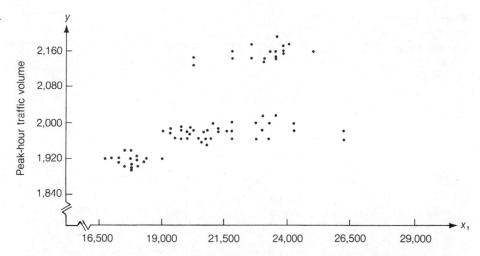

volumes (using electronic sensors that count vehicles) at eight locations in the Minneapolis area believed to be similar to the one being redesigned. One of the characteristics that was common to the Interstate 494 site and the eight other locations was that the peak-hour volume at each was nearing its theoretical upper bound. A sample of $n = 72$ measurements was obtained and a scattergram of the data was constructed (see Figure 12.28).

The traffic forecasters were surprised to see the isolated group of observations at the top of the scattergram. They investigated and found that all these data points were collected on Interstate 35W at the intersection of 46th Street, on the south side of Minneapolis. It turned out that, while all locations in the sample were three-lane highways (including this location), this location was unique because the highway widens to four lanes just a short distance north of the electronic sensor. Accordingly, this location was *not* similar to the section of Interstate 494 being redesigned, as was originally thought. It was decided that the eighteen measurements collected at this location should be kept in the sample (in order to maintain a large sample size for the estimation of σ^2), but that a separate peak-hour-volume response curve should be estimated for this location through the use of a dummy variable in the regression model.

Knowing that peak-hour traffic volumes have a theoretical upper bound and that the locations sampled were nearing their bounds, the forecasters hypothesized that a second-order model should be used to explain the variation in peak-hour volume. Since this hypothesis was also supported by the scattergram, they fit the following model to the $n = 72$ data points:

$$E(y) = \beta_0 + \beta_1 x_1 + \beta_2 x_1^2 + \beta_3 x_2 + \beta_4 x_1 x_2$$

where

$$x_2 = \begin{cases} 1 & \text{if Interstate 35W and 46th Street} \\ 0 & \text{otherwise} \end{cases}$$

The results are shown in the Minitab printout in Figure 12.29. In order to formally investigate whether the relationship between peak-hour volume and total traffic volume for the day at the

Figure 12.29 Peak-Hour Traffic Volume: Complete Model

```
THE REGRESSION EQUATION IS
Y =     779. +  .104 X1 -  .0000 X2
     +  98.0 X3 +  .0029 X4

                                 ST. DEV.    T-RATIO=
          COLUMN    COEFFICIENT   OF COEF.   COEF/S.D.

          --            779.0      141.8      5.49
     X1   C2            .1039      .0136      7.63
     X2   C3       -.000002220  .000000324   -6.84
     X3   C4             98.0      75.6       1.30
     X4   C5            .00291     .00332      .88

THE ST. DEV. OF Y ABOUT REGRESSION LINE IS
S =      15.47
WITH (  72- 5) =   67 DEGREES OF FREEDOM


R-SQUARED = 97.2 PERCENT
R-SQUARED = 97.0 PERCENT, ADJUSTED FOR D.F.


ANALYSIS OF VARIANCE

  DUE TO      DF         SS     MS=SS/DF

REGRESSION     4    555747.6    138936.9
RESIDUAL      67     16031.3       239.3
TOTAL         71    571778.9
```

Interstate 35W location is different from that at the other locations, they eliminated the terms $\beta_3 x_2$ and $\beta_4 x_1 x_2$ from the model and fit the resulting reduced model to the same data, with the results shown in Figure 12.30. From the information contained on the two printouts, the forecasters calculated:

$$F = \frac{(295{,}602 - 16{,}031.3)/2}{16{,}031.3/67} = 584.2$$

Figure 12.30 Peak-Hour Traffic Volume: Reduced Model

```
THE REGRESSION EQUATION IS
Y =     197. +  .149 X1 -  .0000 X2

                                 ST. DEV.    T-RATIO =
          COLUMN    COEFFICIENT   OF COEF.   COEF/S.D.

          --            197.4      578.9       .34
     X1   C2            .1492      .0555      2.69
     X2   C3       -.00000295    .00000132   -2.24

THE ST. DEV. OF Y ABOUT REGRESSION LINE IS
S =      65.45
WITH (  72- 3) = 69 DEGREES OF FREEDOM


R-SQUARED = 48.3 PERCENT
R-SQUARED = 46.8 PERCENT, ADJUSTED FOR D.F.


ANALYSIS OF VARIANCE

  DUE TO      DF        SS     MS=SS/DF

REGRESSION     2    276177     138088
RESIDUAL      69    295602       4284
TOTAL         71    571779
```

and compared it to $F_{.01} \approx 4.96$, where $v_1 = 2$ and $v_2 = 67$. They concluded that the two response curves were different. In addition, the forecasters noted that β_1 was significantly greater than zero and that β_2 was significantly less than zero—as would be expected, since peak-hour volume has an upper bound. Accordingly, for estimating and predicting peak-hour volumes at the Interstate 494 site, the forecasters chose the following prediction equation:

$$\hat{y} = 779 + .1039x_1 - .00000222x_1^2$$

Exercises 12.64–12.77

Learning the Mechanics

12.64 Write a complete second-order model that relates $E(y)$ to one independent quantitative variable.

12.65 Add the main effect terms for one qualitative variable at three levels to the model of Exercise 12.64.

12.66 Add terms to the model of Exercise 12.65 to allow for interaction between the quantitative and qualitative independent variables.

12.67 Under what circumstances will the response curves of the model in Exercise 12.66 have the same shape but different y-intercepts?

12.68 Under what circumstances will the response curves of the model in Exercise 12.66 be parallel lines?

12.69 Under what circumstances will the response curves of the model in Exercise 12.66 be identical?

12.70 Write a model for $E(y)$ in which there are two independent variables, one quantitative and one qualitative with four levels. Construct the model so the associated response curves are second-order and the independent variables do not interact.

Applying the Concepts

[*Note: Starred (*) exercises require the use of a computer.*]

12.71 A pharmaceutical company wants to develop a regression model that will predict the mean time to relief after the administration of a new pain-killing drug. Two variables that are believed to be good predictors of relief time are the age of the patient and the method of drug administration. There are three methods of administration:

1. Orally in liquid form
2. Orally in pill form
3. Intravenously

The following model was proposed by the pharmaceutical company:

$$E(y) = \beta_0 + \beta_1 x_1 + \beta_2 x_2 + \beta_3 x_3 + \beta_4 x_1 x_2 + \beta_5 x_1 x_3$$

where

y = Time to relief (in minutes)

x_1 = Age of patient (in years)

$x_2 = \begin{cases} 1 & \text{if drug administered orally in pill form} \\ 0 & \text{if not} \end{cases}$

$x_3 = \begin{cases} 1 & \text{if drug administered intravenously} \\ 0 & \text{if not} \end{cases}$

The data in the table, obtained on twelve patients, were used to fit the above model.

METHOD 1		METHOD 2		METHOD 3	
Age	Time to relief	Age	Time to relief	Age	Time to relief
51	22	46	28	37	19
36	25	40	24	60	17
31	20	26	23	25	21
20	25	32	25	38	20

a. Multiple regression analysis produced the following results:

```
SOURCE              DF    SUM OF SQUARES    MEAN SQUARE      F    PR > F    R-SQUARE

MODEL               5          87.473         17.495       4.90   0.0394    0.803120
ERROR               6          21.443          3.574
CORRECTED TOTAL    11         108.916
```

Test whether the model is useful in predicting mean time to relief. Use α = .05.

b. What hypothesis would you use to test whether the age–administration method interaction terms contribute to the prediction of mean time to relief?

c. The reduced model

$$E(y) = \beta_0 + \beta_1 x_1 + \beta_2 x_2 + \beta_3 x_3$$

was fit to the data and produced SSE = 38.289. Does this provide sufficient evidence at α = .05 to indicate that the interaction terms should be kept in the model?

12.72 An operations manager is interested in modeling $E(y)$, the expected length of time per month (in hours) that a machine will be shut down for repairs as a function of the type of machine (001 or 002) and the age of the machine (in years). He has proposed the following model:

$$E(y) = \beta_0 + \beta_1 x_1 + \beta_2 x_1^2 + \beta_3 x_2$$

where

x_1 = Age of machine $\qquad x_2 = \begin{cases} 1 & \text{if machine type 001} \\ 0 & \text{if machine type 002} \end{cases}$

Data were obtained on $n = 20$ machine breakdowns and were used to estimate the parameters of the above model. A portion of the regression analysis computer printout is shown here:

```
SOURCE    DF    SUM OF SQUARES    MEAN SQUARE

MODEL     3        2396.364          798.788
ERROR     16        128.586            8.037
TOTAL     19       2524.950       R-SQUARE
                                     0.949
```

The reduced model, $E(y) = \beta_0 + \beta_1 x_1 + \beta_2 x_2$, was fit to the same data. The regression analysis computer printout is partially reproduced here:

```
SOURCE    DF    SUM OF SQUARES    MEAN SQUARE

MODEL     2        2342.42          1171.21
ERROR     17        182.53            10.74
TOTAL     19       2524.95       R-SQUARE
                                     0.928
```

Is there sufficient evidence to conclude that the second-order (x_1^2) term in the model proposed by the operations manager is necessary? Test using $\alpha = .05$.

*12.73 Refer to Exercise 12.72. The data that were used to fit the operations manager's complete and reduced models are displayed in the table.

DOWN TIME PER MONTH (Hours)	MACHINE TYPE	MACHINE AGE (Years)	DOWN TIME PER MONTH (Hours)	MACHINE TYPE	MACHINE AGE (Years)
10	001	1.0	10	002	2.0
20	001	2.0	20	002	4.0
30	001	2.7	30	002	5.0
40	001	4.1	44	002	8.0
9	001	1.2	9	002	2.4
25	001	2.5	25	002	5.1
19	001	1.9	20	002	3.5
41	001	5.0	42	002	7.0
22	001	2.1	20	002	4.0
12	001	1.1	13	002	2.1

a. Use the data to test the null hypothesis that $\beta_1 = \beta_2 = 0$. Test using $\alpha = .10$.
b. Carefully interpret the results of the test in the context of the problem.

12.74 An equal rights group has charged that women are being discriminated against in terms of the salary structure in a state university system. It is thought that a complete second-order model will be adequate to describe the relationship between salary and years of experience for both groups. A sample is to be taken from the records for faculty members (all of equal status) within the system and the following model is to be fit:

$$E(y) = \beta_0 + \beta_1 x_1 + \beta_2 x_1^2 + \beta_3 x_2 + \beta_4 x_1 x_2 + \beta_5 x_1^2 x_2$$

where

$y = $ Annual salary (in thousands of dollars)

$x_1 = $ Experience (years) $x_2 = \begin{cases} 1 & \text{if female} \\ 0 & \text{if male} \end{cases}$

a. What hypothesis would you test to determine whether the *rate* of increase of mean salary with experience is different for males and females?

b. What hypothesis would you test to determine whether there are differences in mean salaries that are attributable to sex?

[*Note:*   In practice, we would include other variables in the model. We include only two here to simplify the exercise.

12.75 Refer to Exercise 12.18, where we presented data on the number of highway deaths and the number of licensed vehicles on the road for the years 1950–1979. We mentioned that the number of deaths, y, may also have been affected by the existence of the national 55-mile-per-hour speed limit during the years 1974–1979 (i.e., years 25–30). Define the dummy variable

$x_2 = \begin{cases} 1 & \text{if 55-mile-per-hour speed limit was in effect} \\ 0 & \text{if not} \end{cases}$

a. Introduce the variable x_2 into the second-order model of Exercise 12.18 to account for the presence or absence of the 55-mile-per-hour speed limit in a given year. Include terms involving the interaction between x_2 and x_1.

b. Refer to your model for part a. Sketch on a single piece of graph paper your visualization of the two response curves, the second-order curves relating y to x_1 before and after the imposition of the 55-mile-per-hour speed limit.

c. Suppose that x_1 and x_2 do not interact. How would that affect the graphs of the two response curves of part b?

d. Refer to part c. Suppose that x_1 and x_2 do interact. How would this affect the graphs of the two response curves?

12.76 In Exercise 12.18, we fit a second-order model to data relating the number, y, of U.S. highway deaths per year to the number, x_1, of licensed vehicles on the road. In Exercise 12.75 we added a qualitative variable, x_2, to account for the presence or absence of the 55-mile-per-hour national speed limit. The accompanying SAS computer printout gives the results of fitting the model

$$E(y) = \beta_0 + \beta_1 x_1 + \beta_2 x_1^2 + \beta_3 x_2 + \beta_4 x_1 x_2 + \beta_5 x_1^2 x_2$$

to the data. Use this printout and the printout for Exercise 12.18 to determine whether the data provide sufficient evidence to indicate that the qualitative variable (speed limit) contributes information for the prediction of the annual number of highway deaths. Test using $\alpha = .05$. Discuss the practical implications of your test results.

SAS Printout for Exercise 12.76

```
DEPENDENT VARIABLE: DEATHS

SOURCE                         DF    SUM OF SQUARES    MEAN SQUARE    F VALUE

MODEL                           5    1428.02852498    285.60570500      41.56
ERROR                          24     164.91847502      6.87160313     PR > F
CORRECTED TOTAL                29    1592.94700000                     0.0001

R-SQUARE                     C.V.        ROOT MSE    DEATHS MEAN

0.896470                   5.7752       2.62137428    45.39000000

                                       T FOR H0:    PR > !T!   STD ERROR OF
PARAMETER               ESTIMATE      PARAMETER=0                 ESTIMATE

INTERCEPT             16.94054815           2.21      0.0372      7.68054270
VEHICLES              0.34942808            1.89      0.0715      0.18528901
VEHICLES*VEHICLES    -0.00017135           -0.16      0.8724      0.00105538
LIMIT                41.38712279            0.11      0.9155    385.80676597
VEHICLES*LIMIT       -0.75118159           -0.14      0.8878      5.26806364
VEHICLE*VEHICL*LIMIT  0.00245917            0.14      0.8921      0.01794470
```

*12.77 *Productivity* has been defined as the relationship between inputs and outputs of a productive system. In order to manage a system's productivity, it is necessary to measure it. Productivity is typically measured by dividing a measure of system output by a measure of the inputs to the system. Some examples of productivity measures are Sales/Salesperson, (Yards of carpet laid)/(Number of carpet layers), Shipments/[(Direct labor) + (Indirect labor) + (Materials)]. Notice that productivity can be improved by producing greater output with the same inputs or by producing the same output with fewer inputs. In manufacturing operations, productivity ratios like the shipments example just cited generally vary with the volume of output produced (Schroeder, 1981). The production data in the table have been collected for a random sample of months for the three regional plants of a particular manufacturing firm. Each plant manufactures the same product.

NORTH PLANT		SOUTH PLANT		WEST PLANT	
Productivity ratio	Number of units produced	Productivity ratio	Number of units produced	Productivity ratio	Number of units produced
1.30	1,000	1.43	1,015	1.61	501
.90	400	1.50	925	.74	140
1.21	650	.91	150	1.19	303
.75	200	.99	222	1.88	930
1.32	850	1.33	545	1.72	776
1.29	600	1.15	402	1.39	400
1.18	756	1.51	709	1.86	810
1.10	500	1.01	176	.99	220
1.26	925	1.24	392	.79	160
.93	300	1.49	699	1.59	626
.81	258	1.37	800	1.82	640
1.12	590	1.39	660	.91	190

a. Construct a scattergram for the data. Plot the data from the north plant using dots, from the south plant using small circles, and from the west plant using small triangles.

b. Visually fit each plant's response curve to the scattergram.

c. Based on the results of part b, propose a second-order regression model that could be used to estimate the relationship between productivity and volume for the three plants.

d. Fit the model you proposed in part c to the data.

e. Is there sufficient evidence to conclude that the productivity response curves for the three plants differ? Test using $\alpha = .05$.

f. Do the data provide sufficient evidence to conclude that the second-order model contributes more information for the prediction of productivity than a first-order model? Test using $\alpha = .05$.

g. Next month, 890 units are scheduled to be produced at the west plant. Use the model you developed in part d to predict next month's productivity ratio at the west plant.

12.8 Model Building: Stepwise Regression

The problem of predicting executive salaries was discussed in Chapter 11. Perhaps the biggest problem in building a model to describe executive salaries is choosing the important independent variables to be included in the model. The list of potentially important independent variables is extremely long, and we need some objective method of screening out those that are not important.

The problem of deciding which of a large set of independent variables to include in a model is common. Trying to determine which variables influence the profit of a firm, affect product quality, or are related to the state of the economy are only a few examples.

A systematic approach to building a model with a large number of independent variables is difficult because the interpretation of multivariable interactions and higher-order polynomials is tedious. We therefore turn to a screening procedure known as *stepwise regression.*

The most commonly used stepwise regression procedure, available in most popular computer packages, works as follows: The user first identifies the response, y, and the set of potentially important independent variables, $x_1, x_2, \ldots, x_k$, where k will generally be large. (Note that this set of variables could represent both first- and higher-order terms, as well as any interaction terms that might be important information contributors.) The response and independent variables are then entered into the computer, and the stepwise procedure begins.

Step 1 The computer fits all possible one-variable models of the form

$$E(y) = \beta_0 + \beta_1 x_i$$

to the data. For each model, the test of the null hypothesis

$$H_0: \quad \beta_1 = 0$$

against the alternative hypothesis

$$H_a: \quad \beta_1 \neq 0$$

is conducted using the t (or the equivalent F) test for a single β parameter. The independent variable that produces the largest (absolute) t value is declared the best one-variable predictor of y. Call this independent variable x_1.

Step 2 The stepwise program now begins to search through the remaining $(k-1)$ independent variables for the best two-variable model of the form

$$E(y) = \beta_0 + \beta_1 x_1 + \beta_2 x_i$$

This is done by fitting all two-variable models containing x_1 and each of the other $(k-1)$ options for the second variable x_i. The t values for the test $H_0: \beta_2 = 0$ are computed for each of the $(k-1)$ models (corresponding to the remaining independent variables x_i, $i = 2$, $3, \ldots, k$), and the variable having the largest t is retained. Call this variable x_2.

At this point, some computer packages diverge in methodology. The better packages now go back and check the t value of $\hat{\beta}_1$ *after* $\hat{\beta}_2 x_2$ *has been added to the model.* If the t value has become nonsignificant at some specified α level (say $\alpha = .10$), the variable x_1 is removed and a search is made for the independent variable with a β parameter that will yield the most significant t value in the presence of $\hat{\beta}_2 x_2$. Other packages do not recheck $\hat{\beta}_1$, but proceed directly to step 3.

The best-fitting plane may yield a different value for $\hat{\beta}_1$ than that obtained in step 1, because $\hat{\beta}_1$ and $\hat{\beta}_2$ may be correlated. Thus, both the value of $\hat{\beta}_1$ and, therefore, its significance will usually change from step 1 to step 2. For this reason, the computer packages that recheck the t values at each step are preferred.

Step 3 The stepwise procedure now checks for a third independent variable to include in the model with x_1 and x_2. That is, we seek the best model of the form

$$E(y) = \beta_0 + \beta_1 x_1 + \beta_2 x_2 + \beta_3 x_i$$

To do this, we fit all the $(k-2)$ models using x_1, x_2, and each of the $(k-2)$ remaining variables, x_i, as a possible x_3. The criterion is again to include the independent variable with the largest t value. Call this best third variable x_3.

The better programs now recheck the t values corresponding to the x_1 and x_2 coefficients, replacing the variables with t values that have become nonsignificant. This procedure is continued until no additional independent variables can be found that yield significant t values (at the specified α level) in the presence of the variables already in the model.

The result of the stepwise procedure is a model containing only those terms with t values that are significant at the specified α level. Thus, in most practical situations, only several of the large number of independent variables will remain. However, it is very important *not* to jump to the conclusion that all the independent variables important for predicting y have been identified or that the unimportant independent variables have been eliminated. Remember, the stepwise procedure is using only *sample estimates* of the true model coefficients (β's) to select the important variables. An extremely large number of single β parameter t tests have been conducted, and the probability is very high that one or more errors have been made in including or excluding variables. That is, we have very probably included some unimportant independent variables in the model (Type I errors) and eliminated some important ones (Type II errors).

There is a second reason why we might not have arrived at a good model. When we choose the variables to be included in the stepwise regression, we may often omit high-order terms (to keep the number of variables manageable). Consequently, we may have initially omitted several important terms from the model. Thus, we should recognize stepwise regression for what it is: an objective screening procedure.

Now, we will consider interactions and quadratic terms (for quantitative variables) among variables screened by the stepwise procedure. It would be best to develop this response surface model with a second set of data independent of that used for the screening, so the results of the stepwise procedure can be partially verified with new data. However, this is not always possible because in many business modeling situations only a small amount of data is available.

Remember, do not be deceived by the impressive looking t values that result from the stepwise procedure — it has retained only the independent variables with the largest t values. Also, if you have used a main effects model for your stepwise procedure, remember that it may be greatly improved by the addition of interaction and quadratic terms.

Example 12.11   In Section 11.8, we fit a multiple regression model for executive salaries as a function of experience, education, sex, and other factors. A preliminary step in the construction of this model was the determination of the most important independent variables. Ten independent variables were considered, as shown in Table 12.4. It would be very difficult to construct a second-order model with ten independent variables. Therefore, use the sample of 100 executives from Section 11.8 to decide which of the ten variables should be included in the construction of the final model for executive salaries.

Table 12.4
Independent Variables in the Executive Salary Example

INDEPENDENT VARIABLE	DESCRIPTION
x_1	Experience (years) — quantitative
x_2	Education (years) — quantitative
x_3	Sex (1 if male, 0 if female) — qualitative
x_4	Number of employees supervised — quantitative
x_5	Corporate assets (millions of dollars) — quantitative
x_6	Board member (1 if yes, 0 if no) — qualitative
x_7	Age (years) — quantitative
x_8	Company profits (past 12 months, millions of dollars) — quantitative
x_9	Has international responsibility (1 if yes, 0 if no) — qualitative
x_{10}	Company's total sales (past 12 months, millions of dollars) — quantitative

Solution   We will use stepwise regression with the main effects of the ten independent variables to identify the most important variables. The dependent variable, y, is the natural logarithm of the executive salaries. The SAS stepwise regression printout is shown in Figure 12.31. Note that the first variable included in the model is x_4, Number of employees supervised. At the second step, x_5, Corporate assets, enters the model. At the sixth step, x_6, a dummy variable for the qualitative variable Board member or not, is brought into the model. However, because the significance (.2295) of the F statistic (SAS uses the $F = t^2$ statistic in the stepwise procedure

Figure 12.31 SAS Stepwise Regression Computer Printout for Exercise 11.4

STEP 1 VARIABLE X4 ENTERED   R-SQUARE = 0.42071677

	DF	SUM OF SQUARES	MEAN SQUARE	F	PROB>F
REGRESSION	1	11.46854285	11.46864285	71.17	0.0001
ERROR	98	15.79112802	0.16113396		
TOTAL	99	27.25977087			

	B VALUE	STD ERROR	F	PROB>F
INTERCEPT	10.20077500			
X4 (EMPLOYEES SUPERVISED)	0.00057284	0.00006790	71.17	0.0001

STEP 2 VARIABLE X5 ENTERED   R-SQUARE = 0.78299675

	DF	SUM OF SQUARES	MEAN SQUARE	F	PROB>F
REGRESSION	2	21.34431198	10.67215599	175.00	0.0001
ERROR	97	5.91545889	0.06098411		
TOTAL	99	27.25977087			

	B VALUE	STD ERROR	F	PROB>F
INTERCEPT	9.87702903			
X4 (EMPLOYEES SUPERVISED)	0.00058353	0.00004178	:95.06	0.0001
X5 (ASSETS)	0.00183730	0.00014438	:61.94	0.0001

STEP 3 VARIABLE X1 ENTERED   R-SQUARE = 0.89667614

	DF	SUM OF SQUARES	MEAN SQUARE	F	PROB>F
REGRESSION	3	24.44318616	8 14772872	277.71	0.0001
ERROR	96	2.81658471	0 02933942		
TOTAL	99	27.25977087			

	B VALUE	STD ERROR	F	PROB>F
INTERCEPT	9.66449288			
X1 (EXPERIENCE)	0.01870784	0.00182032	105.62	0.0001
X4 (EMPLOYEES SUPERVISED)	0.0005525:	0.00002914	359.59	0.0001
X5 (ASSETS)	0.00191195	0.00010041	362.60	0.0001

(continued)

Figure 12.31 (continued)

STEP 4
VARIABLE X3 ENTERED   R-SQUARE = 0.94815717

	DF	SUM OF SQUARES	MEAN SQUARE	F	PROB>F
REGRESSION	4	25.84654710	6.46163678	434.37	0.0001
ERROR	95	1.41322377	0.01487604		
TOTAL	99	27.25977087			

	B VALUE	STD ERROR	F	PROB>F
INTERCEPT	9.40077349			
X1 (EXPERIENCE)	0.02074868	0.00131310	249.68	0.0001
X3 (SEX)	0.30011726	0.03089939	94.34	0.0001
X4 (EMPLOYEES SUPERVISED)	0.00055288	0.00002075	710.15	0.0001
X5 (ASSETS)	0.00190876	0.00007150	712.74	0.0001

STEP 5
VARIABLE X2 ENTERED   R-SQUARE = 0.96039323

	DF	SUM OF SQUARES	MEAN SQUARE	F	PROB>F
REGRESSION	5	26.18009940	5.23601988	455.87	0.0001
ERROR	94	1.07967147	0.01148587		
TOTAL	99	27.25977087			

	B VALUE	STD ERROR	F	PROB>F
INTERCEPT	8.85387930			
X1 (EXPERIENCE)	0.02141724	0.00116047	340.61	0.0001
X2 (EDUCATION)	0.03315807	0.00615303	29.04	0.0001
X3 (SEX)	0.31927842	0.02738298	135.95	0.0001
X4 (EMPLOYEES SUPERVISED)	0.00056061	0.00001829	939.84	0.0001
X5 (ASSETS)	0.00193684	0.00006304	943.98	0.0001

STEP 6
VARIABLE X6 ENTERED   R-SQUARE = 0.96100666

	DF	SUM OF SQUARES	MEAN SQUARE	F	PROB>F
REGRESSION	6	26.19682148	4.36613691	382.00	0.0001
ERROR	93	1.06294939	0.01142956		
TOTAL	99	27.25977087			

	B VALUE	STD ERROR	F	PROB>F
INTERCEPT	8.87509152			
X1 (EXPERIENCE)	0.02133460	0.00115963	338.48	0.0001
X2 (EDUCATION)	0.03272195	0.00614851	28.32	0.0001
X3 (SEX)	0.31093801	0.02817264	121.81	0.0001
X4 (EMPLOYEES SUPERVISED)	0.00055820	0.00001835	925.32	0.0001
X5 (ASSETS)	0.00193764	0.00006289	949.31	0.0001
X6 (BOARD)	0.03866226	0.03196369	1.46	0.2295

STEP 7
VARIABLE X6 REMOVED   R-SQUARE = 0.96039323

	DF	SUM OF SQUARES	MEAN SQUARE	F	PROB>F
REGRESSION	5	26.18009940	5.23601988	455.87	0.0001
ERROR	94	1.07967147	0.01148587		
TOTAL	99	27.25977087			

	B VALUE	STD ERROR	F	PROB>F
INTERCEPT	8.85387930			
X1 (EXPERIENCE)	0.02141724	0.00116047	340.61	0.0001
X2 (EDUCATION)	0.03331807	0.00615303	29.04	0.0001
X3 (SEX)	0.31927842	0.02738298	135.95	0.0001
X4 (EMPLOYEES SUPERVISED)	0.00056061	0.00001829	939.84	0.0001
X5 (ASSETS)	0.00193684	0.00006304	943.98	0.0001

rather than the t statistic) for x_6 is greater than the preassigned $\alpha = .10$, x_6 is removed from the model. Thus, at step 7 the procedure indicates that the five-variable model including x_1, x_2, x_3, x_4, and x_5 is best. That is, none of the other independent variables can meet the $\alpha = .10$ criterion for admission to the model.

Thus, in our final modeling effort (Section 11.8) we concentrated on these five independent variables, and determined that several second-order terms were important in the prediction of executive salaries. ■

Case Study 12.2

A Statistical Model for Land Appraisal

New factors and a lack of knowledge about the importance of factors that affect value continue to complicate the job of the rural appraiser. In order to provide knowledge on the subject, this article reports on and evaluates a study in which multiple linear regression equations were used to evaluate and quantify factors affecting value. . . . It is believed that the findings obtained with these equations, and the relationships they indicate, will be of value to the appraiser.

The authors of this statement, James O. Wise and H. Jackson Dover (1974), use stepwise regression to identify a number of important factors (variables) that can be used to predict rural property values. They obtained their results by analyzing a sample of 105 cases from seven counties in Georgia. Part of their findings are duplicated in Table 12.5. The variable names are listed in the order in which the stepwise regression procedure identified their importance, and the t values found at each step are given for each variable. Note that both qualitative and quantitative variables have been included. Since each qualitative variable is at two levels, only one main effect term could be included in the model for each factor.

Since there were 105 cases used in the study, a large number of degrees of freedom are associated with each t statistic (first 103, then 102, etc.). Thus, we should compare the value of the test statistic to a corresponding z value (1.645 for $\alpha = .10$ and the two-sided alternative hypothesis $H_a: \beta_i \neq 0$) when we judge the importance of each variable. Although Wise and Dover imply that the variable Size is important, we might not include it, since the t value is only 1.142.

Table 12.5

Stepwise Regression Analysis of Price per Acre

VARIABLE NAME	t VALUE
Residential land (yes–no)	10.466
Seedlings and saplings (number)	6.692
Percent ponds (percent)	4.141
Distance to state park (miles)	3.985
Branches or springs (yes–no)	3.855
Site index (ratio)	3.160
Size (acres)	1.142
Farmland (yes–no)	2.288

Summary

Although this chapter provides only an introduction to the very important topic of *model building,* it enables you to construct many interesting and useful models for business phenomena. You can build on this foundation and, with experience, develop competence in this fascinating area of statistics. Successful model building requires a delicate blend of knowledge of the process being modeled, geometry, and formal statistical testing.

The first step in model building is to identify the response variable, y, and a set of independent variables. Each independent variable is then classified as either *quantitative* or *qualitative,* and *dummy variables* are defined to represent the qualitative independent variables. If the total number of independent variables is large, you may want to use *stepwise regression* to screen out those that do not seem important for the prediction of y.

When the number of independent variables is manageable, the model builder is ready to begin a systematic effort. At least *second-order models,* those containing *two-way interactions* and *quadratic terms* in the quantitative variables, should be considered. Remember that a model with no interaction terms implies that each of the independent variables affects the response independently of the other independent variables. Quadratic terms add curvature to the contour curves when $E(y)$ is plotted as a function of the independent variable. The F test for testing a set of β parameters aids in deciding the final form of the prediction model.

Many problems can arise in regression modeling, and the intermediate steps are often tedious and frustrating. However, the end result of a careful and determined modeling effort is very rewarding — you will have a better understanding of the process generating the dependent variable y and a predictive model for y.

Supplementary Exercises 12.78 – 12.96

[*Note:* Starred (*****) *exercises require the use of a computer.*]

12.78 Why is the model building step "the key to the success or failure of a regression analysis"?

12.79 Investors are interested in knowing the relationship between the behavior of a mutual fund and the behavior of the stock market as a whole. Researchers in finance have hypothesized that the model that appropriately characterizes this relationship is

$$E(y) = \beta_0 + \beta_1 x$$

where

$y =$ Monthly rate of return of a mutual fund

$x =$ Monthly rate of return of the stock market as a whole as measured by the monthly rate of return to a market index such as Standard & Poor's 500 Composite Index

The value of β_1 in the above model is referred to as the mutual fund's *beta coefficient.* Assuming the above model is true, investors can predict how the returns of an individual mutual fund will react to changes in the behavior of the market. For example, if $\beta_1 > 1$, the implication is that the return to the mutual fund will be greatly influenced by the behavior of the market and will move in the same direction as the change in the market return. If $0 \le \beta_1 < 1$, the return to the mutual fund will be less sensitive to changes in market behavior but will also move in the same direction as the change in the market return.

In a recent study, Alexander and Stover (1980) included a dummy variable in the above model to determine whether the beta coefficient for an individual mutual fund depends on whether the market is moving generally upward (a *bull market*) or generally downward (a *bear market*).

a. Modify the above regression model (as Alexander and Stover did) to reflect the possibility that $E(y)$ may depend on whether the market is bullish or bearish. Include an interaction term in your model and carefully define the dummy variable coding scheme you use.

b. Using the model you developed in part a, describe the differences that may exist between the response curves of $E(y)$ under bull and bear markets.

c. Specify the hypothesis you would test to determine whether a mutual fund's beta coefficient is different during bull and bear markets.

d. Specify the hypothesis you would test to determine whether $E(y)$ should be characterized as $E(y) = \beta_0 + \beta_1 x$ or as in the modified model you developed in part a.

12.80 The audience for a product's advertising can be divided into four segments according to the degree of exposure received as a result of the advertising. These segments are groups of consumers who receive very high (VH), high (H), medium (M), or low (L) exposure to the advertising. A company is interested in exploring whether its advertising effort affects its product's market share. Accordingly, the company identifies twenty-four sample groups of consumers who have been exposed to its advertising, six groups at each exposure level. Then, the company determines its product's market share within each group.

a. Write a regression model that expresses the company's market share as a function of advertising exposure level. Define all terms in your model, and list any assumptions you make about them.

b. Did you include interaction terms in your model? Why or why not?

c. How many degrees of freedom are associated with the F test you would use to test the overall usefulness of the model you constructed in part a?

12.81 One of the distinguishing features of banks as compared with other financial service institutions is their well-developed system for permitting convenient, personal access to the services they offer. One indication of the demand for these services is the number of trips individuals make to their bank each year. Murphy and Stock (1983) employed multiple regression analysis to investigate the determinants of household trips to the bank in the state of Oklahoma. In the summer of 1979, personal interviews were conducted with a random sample of 597 residents of Oklahoma. The interviewees were asked questions about their yearly banking activities, including number of trips to the bank per year and number of miles to the bank. At the same time, data were collected on other variables, such as number of cars in the household, kind of work (if any) done by the interviewee, etc. The method of least squares was used to develop the following model:

$$\hat{y} = 18.40 + 2.02x_1 - .254x_2 + 1.65x_3 + 1.124x_4 - .06x_5 + .00017x_6 - 8.679x_7 - 3.21x_8 - 1.29x_9 - 11.59x_{10} + .092x_{11}$$
$$(3.696) \ (-3.788) \ (1.637) \ \ (1.138) \ \ (-.63) \ \ \ (2.15) \ \ \ (-3.052) \ (-.958) \ (-.407) \ \ (-2.705) \ (3.239)$$
$$R^2 = .1836$$
$$F = 11.96$$

where

y = Number of trips to the bank per year

x_1 = Number of people in household

x_2 = Miles to bank

x_3 = Number of cars in household

x_4 = Years of education

x_5 = Miles to work

x_6 = Total family income

$$x_7 = \begin{cases} 1 & \text{if not employed} \\ 0 & \text{otherwise} \end{cases} \qquad x_8 = \begin{cases} 1 & \text{if white-collar job} \\ 0 & \text{otherwise} \end{cases}$$

$$x_9 = \begin{cases} 1 & \text{if blue-collar job} \\ 0 & \text{otherwise} \end{cases} \qquad x_{10} = \begin{cases} 1 & \text{if farm-related job} \\ 0 & \text{otherwise} \end{cases}$$

x_{11} = Number of shopping trips per year for purposes other than banking

The numbers in parentheses are the t statistics associated with the coefficient estimates above them.

a. Identify which independent variables in Murphy and Stock's model are qualitative and which are quantitative.

b. Murphy and Stock use four dummy variables to describe the kind of work done by the sample of Oklahomans. How many different levels can the variable, kind of work, assume? List them.

c. Interpret the value of R^2 in the context of the problem.

d. Test the usefulness of Murphy and Stock's model for explaining the variation in y. Use $\alpha = .01$.

e. Specify the null and alternative hypotheses you would use to test whether the trips-to-the-bank response surface is the same regardless of the kind of work done by the interviewee.

12.82 A fast-food restaurant chain is interested in modeling the mean weekly sales of a restaurant, $E(y)$, as a function of the weekly traffic flow on the street where the restaurant is located and the city in which the restaurant is located. The table at the top of the next page contains data that were collected on twenty-four restaurants in four cities. The model that has been proposed is

$$E(y) = \beta_0 + \beta_1 x_1 + \beta_2 x_2 + \beta_3 x_3 + \beta_4 x_4$$

where

x_1 = Traffic flow

$$x_2 = \begin{cases} 1 & \text{if city 1} \\ 0 & \text{otherwise} \end{cases} \qquad x_3 = \begin{cases} 1 & \text{if city 2} \\ 0 & \text{otherwise} \end{cases} \qquad x_4 = \begin{cases} 1 & \text{if city 3} \\ 0 & \text{otherwise} \end{cases}$$

CITY	TRAFFIC FLOW (Thousands of cars)	WEEKLY SALES y ($ thousands)	CITY	TRAFFIC FLOW (Thousands of cars)	WEEKLY SALES y ($ thousands)
1	59.3	6.3	3	75.8	8.2
1	60.3	6.6	3	48.3	5.0
1	82.1	7.6	3	41.4	3.9
1	32.3	3.0	3	52.5	5.4
1	98.0	9.5	3	41.0	4.1
1	54.1	5.9	3	29.6	3.1
1	54.4	6.1	3	49.5	5.4
1	51.3	5.0	4	73.1	8.4
1	36.7	3.6	4	81.3	9.5
2	23.6	2.8	4	72.4	8.7
2	57.6	6.7	4	88.4	10.6
2	44.6	5.2	4	23.2	3.3

Below is a portion of the computer printout that results from fitting the model to the data in the table:

```
SOURCE            DF    SUM OF SQUARES    MEAN SQUARE

MODEL             4         116.6555        29.1639
ERROR            19           2.4941         0.1313
CORRECTED TOTAL  23         119.1496        R-SQUARE
                                             0.979
```

The reduced model, $E(y) = \beta_0 + \beta_1 x_1$, was also fit to the same data and the resulting computer printout is partially reproduced below:

```
SOURCE            DF    SUM OF SQUARES    MEAN SQUARE

MODEL             1         111.3423       111.3423
ERROR            22           7.8073         0.3549
CORRECTED TOTAL  23         119.1496        R-SQUARE
                                             0.934
```

a. Test the null hypothesis that $\beta_1 = \beta_2 = \beta_3 = \beta_4 = 0$ using $\alpha = .05$. Interpret the results of your test.

b. Is mean weekly sales, $E(y)$, dependent on the city where a restaurant is located? Test using $\alpha = .05$. Interpret the results of your test.

c. Describe the nature of the response lines that the complete model, $E(y) = \beta_0 + \beta_1 x_1 + \beta_2 x_2 + \beta_3 x_3 + \beta_4 x_4$, would generate. Does the model imply interaction between city and traffic flow?

d. Use the prediction equation based on the complete model to graph the response lines that relate predicted weekly sales, $\hat{y}$, to traffic flow, x_1 (for each of the four cities). Do the graphed response lines suggest an interaction between city and traffic flow?

e. Write a model that includes interaction between city and traffic flow.

* **f.** Fit the model of part e to the data.

*g. Do the data provide sufficient evidence to indicate that the slopes of the lines differ for at least two of the four cities? Test using $\alpha = .05$.

12.83 One factor that must be considered in developing a shipping system that is beneficial to both the customer and the seller is time of delivery. A manufacturer of farm equipment can ship its products by either rail or truck. Quadratic models are thought to be adequate in relating time of delivery to distance traveled for both modes of transportation. Consequently, it has been suggested that the following model be fit:

$$E(y) = \beta_0 + \beta_1 x_1 + \beta_2 x_1^2 + \beta_3 x_2 + \beta_4 x_1 x_2 + \beta_5 x_1^2 x_2$$

where

$y =$ Shipping time

$x_1 =$ Distance to be shipped $\qquad x_2 = \begin{cases} 1 & \text{if rail} \\ 0 & \text{if truck} \end{cases}$

a. What hypothesis would you test to determine whether the data indicate that the quadratic distance terms are useful in the model—i.e., whether curvature is present in the relationship between mean delivery time and distance?

b. What hypothesis would you test to determine whether there is a difference in mean delivery time by rail and by truck?

12.84 Refer to Exercise 12.83. Suppose the model is fit to a total of fifty observations on delivery time. The sum of squared errors is SSE $= 226.12$. Then, the reduced model

$$E(y) = \beta_0 + \beta_1 x_1 + \beta_2 x_1^2$$

is fit to the same data, and SSE $= 259.34$. Test whether the data indicate that the mean delivery time differs for rail and truck deliveries. Use $\alpha = .05$.

*12.85 In Exercise 12.80, a company was concerned about the relationship between its market share and its advertising effort. The data in the table were obtained by the company.

MARKET SHARE WITHIN SAMPLE GROUP	ADVERTISING EXPOSURE LEVEL	MARKET SHARE WITHIN SAMPLE GROUP	ADVERTISING EXPOSURE LEVEL	MARKET SHARE WITHIN SAMPLE GROUP	ADVERTISING EXPOSURE LEVEL
10.1	L	11.2	M	11.9	H
10.3	L	10.9	M	12.9	H
10.0	L	10.8	M	10.7	VH
10.3	L	11.0	M	10.8	VH
10.2	L	12.2	H	11.0	VH
10.5	L	12.1	H	10.5	VH
10.6	M	11.8	H	10.8	VH
11.0	M	12.6	H	10.6	VH

a. Fit the model you constructed in part a of Exercise 12.80 to the data.

b. Is there evidence to suggest that the firm's expected market share differs for different levels of advertising exposure? Test using $\alpha = .05$.

12.86 To make a product more appealing to the consumer, an automobile manufacturer is experimenting with a new type of paint that is supposed to help the car maintain its new-car look. The durability of this paint depends on the length of time the car body is in the oven after it has been painted. In the initial experiment, three groups of ten car bodies each were baked for three different lengths of time — 12, 24, and 36 hours — at the standard temperature setting. Then, the paint finish of each of the thirty cars was analyzed to determine a durability rating, y.

a. Write a second-order model relating the mean durability, $E(y)$, to the length of baking.

b. Could a third-order model be fit to the data? Explain.

12.87 Refer to Exercise 12.86. Suppose the Research and Development Department develops three new types of paint to be tested. Thus, ninety cars are to be tested — thirty for each type of paint — in the manner described in Exercise 12.86. Write a model that describes $E(y)$ as a function of the type of paint and bake time. Assume the independent variables interact.

*****12.88** In Exercise 12.79, we discussed the relationship between the behavior of an individual mutual fund and the behavior of the stock market as a whole. The table lists the monthly rates of return for the Dreyfus Fund (a mutual fund) and the monthly rates of return for Standard & Poor's 500 Composite Index (S&P) for the period January 1966 to December 1971. The bear market periods were from January 1966 through September 1966 and from December 1968 through May 1970. The bull market periods were from October 1966 through November 1968 and from June 1970 through December 1971 (Alexander & Stover, 1980).

Data for Exercise 12.88

TIME PERIOD	RETURNS Dreyfus	S&P	TIME PERIOD	RETURNS Dreyfus	S&P	TIME PERIOD	RETURNS Dreyfus	S&P	TIME PERIOD	RETURNS Dreyfus	S&P
1/66	0.008	0.006	7/67	0.073	0.047	1/69	−0.001	−0.007	7/70	0.051	0.075
2/66	0.067	−0.013	8/67	−0.019	−0.007	2/69	−0.070	−0.043	8/70	0.051	0.051
3/66	−0.008	−0.021	9/67	0.010	0.034	3/69	0.015	0.036	9/70	0.047	0.035
4/66	0.021	0.022	10/67	−0.029	−0.028	4/69	0.014	0.023	10/70	−0.026	−0.010
5/66	−0.074	−0.049	11/67	0.011	0.007	5/69	−0.003	0.003	11/70	0.040	0.054
6/66	0.024	−0.015	12/67	0.025	0.028	6/69	−0.066	−0.054	12/70	0.046	0.058
7/66	−0.011	−0.012	1/68	−0.063	−0.043	7/69	−0.059	−0.059	1/71	0.044	0.042
8/66	0.099	−0.073	2/68	−0.042	−0.026	8/69	0.057	0.045	2/71	0.025	0.014
9/66	−0.011	−0.005	3/68	0.022	0.011	9/69	−0.001	−0.024	3/71	0.031	0.038
10/66	0.015	0.049	4/68	0.100	0.083	10/69	0.050	0.046	4/71	0.035	0.038
11/66	0.079	0.010	5/68	0.021	0.016	11/69	−0.027	−0.030	5/71	−0.034	−0.037
12/66	0.008	0.000	6/68	0.001	0.011	12/69	−0.027	−0.018	6/71	−0.008	0.002
1/67	0.086	0.080	7/68	−0.038	−0.017	1/70	−0.083	−0.074	7/71	−0.926	−0.040
2/67	0.010	0.007	8/68	0.021	0.016	2/70	−0.044	0.059	8/71	0.045	0.041
3/67	0.041	0.041	9/68	0.056	0.040	3/70	−0.007	0.003	9/71	−0.028	−0.006
4/67	0.048	0.044	10/68	0.010	0.009	4/70	−0.110	−0.089	10/71	−0.039	−0.040
5/67	−0.039	−0.048	11/68	0.062	0.053	5/70	−0.060	−0.055	11/71	0.019	0.003
6/67	0.027	0.019	12/68	−0.025	−0.040	6/70	−0.042	−0.048	12/71	0.075	0.090

Sources: Standard & Poor's Composite Index returns from Ibbotson, R. G., and Singuefield, R. A., *Stocks, Bonds, Bills, and Inflation: The Past (1926–1976) and the Future (1977–2000)*, Financial Analysts Research Foundation, 1977; and Dreyfus returns from *The Wall Street Journal*.

a. Fit the model you developed in part a of Exercise 12.79 to the data shown in the table.

b. Using the fitted model, estimate the Dreyfus Fund's beta coefficient for bull markets. Estimate the corresponding parameter for bear markets. Describe the relative responsiveness of the mutual fund to the market during bullish and bearish periods.

c. Test the hypothesis you specified in part c of Exercise 12.79. Draw the appropriate conclusions. Test using $\alpha = .05$.

d. Test the hypothesis you specified in part d of Exercise 12.79. Draw the appropriate conclusions. Test using $\alpha = .05$.

12.89 To model the relationship between y, a dependent variable, and x, an independent variable, a researcher has taken one measurement on y at each of five different x values. Drawing on his mathematical expertise, the researcher realizes that he can fit the fourth-order polynomial model

$$E(y) = \beta_0 + \beta_1 x + \beta_2 x^2 + \beta_3 x^3 + \beta_4 x^4$$

and it will pass exactly through all five points, yielding SSE $= 0$. The researcher, delighted with the "excellent" fit of the model, eagerly sets out to use it to make inferences. What problems will he encounter in attempting to make inferences?

12.90 Due to an increase in gasoline prices, many service stations are offering self-service gasoline at reduced prices. Suppose an oil company wants to model the mean monthly gasoline sales, $E(y)$, of its affiliated stations as a function of the type of service they offer: self-service, full service, or both.

a. How many dummy variables will be needed to describe the qualitative independent variable Type of service?

b. Write the main effects model relating $E(y)$ to the type of service. Describe the coding of the dummy variables.

*12.91 In Case Study 11.2, we described the first-order regression model developed by Carolyn I. Allmon for predicting the sales of Crest toothpaste. The data she used to estimate the model are presented in the table. Using these data and the procedures you learned in this chapter, attempt to develop a second-order model that, according to the appropriate F test, explains more of the variation in sales than Allmon's model. Describe each step of your model building process.

YEAR	CREST SALES ($ thousand)	ADVERTISING BUDGET ($ thousand)	ADVERTISING RATIO	INCOME ($ billion)	YEAR	CREST SALES ($ thousand)	ADVERTISING BUDGET ($ thousand)	ADVERTISING RATIO	INCOME ($ billion)
1966	86,250	—	—	—	1974	126,000	18,250	1.27	998.3
1967	105,000	16,300	1.25	547.9	1975	162,000	17,300	1.07	1,096.1
1968	105,000	15,800	1.34	593.4	1976	191,625	23,000	1.17	1,194.4
1969	121,600	16,000	1.22	638.9	1977	189,000	19,300	1.07	1,311.5
1970	113,750	14,200	1.00	695.3	1978	210,000	23,056	1.54	1,462.9
1971	113,750	15,000	1.15	751.8	1979	224,250	26,000	1.59	1,641.7
1972	128,925	14,000	1.13	810.3	1980	245,000	28,000	1.56	1,821.7
1973	142,500	15,400	1.05	914.5					

Source: Allmon (1982).

12.92 Many companies must accurately estimate their costs before a job is begun in order to acquire a contract and make a profit. A heating and plumbing contractor, for example, may base cost estimates for new homes on the total area of the house and whether central air conditioning is to be installed.

a. Write a main effects model relating the mean cost of material and labor, $E(y)$, to the area and central air conditioning variables.

b. Write a complete second-order model for the mean cost as a function of the same two variables.

c. What hypothesis would you test to determine whether the second-order terms are useful for predicting mean cost?

d. Explain how you would compute the F statistic needed to test the hypothesis of part c.

12.93 Refer to Exercise 12.92. The contractor samples twenty-five recent jobs and fits both the complete second-order model (part b) and the reduced main effects model (part a), so that a test can be conducted to determine whether the additional complexity of the second-order model is necessary. The resulting SSE and R^2 values are shown in the table.

	SSE	R^2
Main effects	8.548	.950
Second-order	6.133	.964

a. Is there sufficient evidence to conclude that the second-order terms are important for predicting the mean cost? Use $\alpha = .05$.

b. Suppose the contractor decides to use the main effects model to predict costs. Use the global F test (Section 11.6) to determine whether the main effects model is useful for predicting costs.

*12.94 A firm has developed a new type of light bulb and is interested in evaluating its performance in order to help decide whether to market the bulb. It is known that the level of light output of the bulb depends on the cleanliness of its surface area and the length of time the bulb has been in operation (i.e., the number of hours the bulb has been turned on). The data in the table have been obtained. Use these data and the procedures you learned in this chapter to build a regression model that relates Drop in light output to Bulb surface cleanliness and Length of operation.

DROP IN LIGHT OUTPUT (% original output)	BULB SURFACE (C = Clean, D = Dirty)	LENGTH OF OPERATION (Hours)	DROP IN LIGHT OUTPUT (% original output)	BULB SURFACE (C = Clean, D = Dirty)	LENGTH OF OPERATION (Hours)
0	C	0	0	D	0
16	C	400	4	D	400
22	C	800	6	D	800
27	C	1,200	8	D	1,200
32	C	1,600	9	D	1,600
36	C	2,000	11	D	2,000
38	C	2,400	12	D	2,400

*12.95 In Exercises 11.46 and 12.63, models for characterizing the demand for passenger car motor fuel were investigated. The data used in those exercises are repeated in the table. Using the procedures you learned in this chapter, build a regression model that includes both qualitative and quantitative independent variables and provides a better explanation of the variation in motor fuel demand than either of the models developed in Exercises 11.46 and 12.63. Use the appropriate F tests to establish your model's superiority.

YEAR	MOTOR FUEL CONSUMED BY CARS (Billion gallons)	POPULATION OF UNITED STATES (Millions)	AVERAGE GROSS REAL WEEKLY EARNINGS (1967 $)	RELATIVE PRICE OF GALLON OF GASOLINE
1965	50.3	194.3	101.01	1.004
1966	53.31	196.6	101.67	.998
1967	55.11	198.7	101.84	1.000
1968	58.52	200.7	103.39	.973
1969	62.45	202.7	104.38	.954
1970	65.8	205.1	103.04	.908
1971	69.51	207.1	104.96	.876
1972	73.5	209.9	109.26	.859
1973	78.0	211.9	109.23	.887
1974	74.2	213.9	104.78	1.083
1975	76.5	216.0	101.45	1.060
1976	78.8	218.0	102.90	1.043
1977	80.7	220.2	104.13	1.037
1978	83.8	222.6	104.30	1.005
1979	80.2	225.1	101.02	1.222
1980	73.7	227.7	95.18	1.496

Source: All data from *Statistical Abstract of the United States*, various years; except average gross real weekly earnings, which are from *Employment and Earnings*, U.S. Department of Labor, Bureau of Labor Statistics, Oct. 1983, p. 109.

*12.96 The table lists the $n = 72$ observations used by the Minnesota Department of Transportation to develop the peak-hour traffic volume model described in Case Study 12.1. Observations 55–72 are from Interstate 35W at 46th Street.

a. Use the data to replicate the model building process described in Case Study 12.1.
b. Compare your results of part a with those presented in Figures 12.28–12.30.
c. Compute the set of residuals for the final model of part a. [*Hint:* Refer to Exercise 10.71.]
d. Construct a box plot for the residuals.
e. Does the box plot constructed in part d suggest the existence of outliers in the set of residuals?
f. Does the box plot suggest that it may be inappropriate to characterize ε as being normally distributed? Explain.

OBSERVATION NUMBER	PEAK-HOUR VOLUME	24-HOUR VOLUME	OBSERVATION NUMBER	PEAK-HOUR VOLUME	24-HOUR VOLUME	OBSERVATION NUMBER	PEAK-HOUR VOLUME	24-HOUR VOLUME
1	1,990.94	20,070	25	1,923.87	18,184	49	1,978.72	24,249
2	1,989.63	21,234	26	1,922.79	16,926	50	1,975.29	23,321
3	1,986.96	20,633	27	1,917.64	19,062	51	1,973.55	22,842
4	1,986.96	20,676	28	1,916.17	18,043	52	1,973.91	20,626
5	1,983.78	19,818	29	1,916.17	18,043	53	1,972.92	26,166
6	1,983.13	19,931	30	1,916.13	16,691	54	1,966.65	21,755
7	1,982.47	19,266	31	1,912.49	17,339	55	2,120.00	20,250
8	1,981.53	19,658	32	1,912.49	17,339	56	2,140.00	20,251
9	1,979.83	19,203	33	1,909.98	17,867	57	2,160.00	21,852
10	1,979.83	19,958	34	1,907.04	17,773	58	2,186.52	23,511
11	1,978.40	19,152	35	1,907.46	17,678	59	2,180.29	22,431
12	1,978.90	21,651	36	1,905.14	18,024	60	2,174.03	23,734
13	1,977.38	20,198	37	1,902.37	17,405	61	2,174.03	23,734
14	1,972.87	20,508	38	2,017.76	23,517	62	2,167.97	23,387
15	1,964.45	19,783	39	2,009.38	23,017	63	2,160.02	24,885
16	1,962.85	20,815	40	2,007.10	22,808	64	2,160.54	23,332
17	1,964.26	20,105	41	2,007.28	23,152	65	2,159.72	23,838
18	1,961.85	20,500	42	2,004.17	24,352	66	2,155.61	23,662
19	1,961.26	19,593	43	1,997.58	20,939	67	2,147.93	22,948
20	1,958.97	20,818	44	1,994.53	21,822	68	2,147.93	22,948
21	1,943.78	17,480	45	1,984.70	22,918	69	2,147.85	23,551
22	1,927.83	17,768	46	1,984.01	21,129	70	2,144.23	21,637
23	1,928.36	17,659	47	1,983.17	21,674	71	2,142.41	23,543
24	1,925.65	18,357	48	1,982.02	26,148	72	2,137.39	22,594

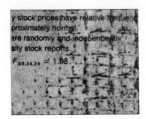

On Your Own . . .

We continue our "On Your Own" theme from Chapters 10 and 11. Remember that you selected three independent variables related to the annual GNP. Now, increase your list of three variables to include approximately ten that you feel would be useful in predicting the GNP. Obtain data for as many years as possible for the new list of variables and the GNP. With the aid of a computer analysis package, use a stepwise regression program to choose the important variables among those you have listed. To test your intuition, list the variables in the order you think they will be selected before you conduct the analysis. How does your list compare with the stepwise regression results?

After the group of ten variables has been narrowed to a smaller group of variables by the stepwise analysis, try to improve the model by including interactions and quadratic terms. Be sure to consider the meaning of each interaction or quadratic term before adding it to the model — a quick sketch can be very helpful. See if you can systematically construct a useful model for predicting the GNP. You might want to hold out the last several years of data to test the predictive ability of your model after it is constructed. (As noted in Section 12.8, using the same data to construct *and* to evaluate predictive ability can lead to invalid statistical tests and a false sense of security.)

References

Alexander, G. J., & Stover, R. D. "Consistency of mutual fund performance during varying market conditions." *Journal of Economics and Business,* Spring 1980, *32,* 219–226.

Allmon, C. I. "Advertising and sales relationships for toothpaste: Another look." *Business Economics,* Sept. 1982, *17,* 58.

Chatterjee, S., & Price, B. *Regression analysis by example.* New York: Wiley, 1977.

Draper, N., & Smith, H. *Applied regression analysis.* 2d ed., New York: Wiley, 1981.

Federal Reserve System: Purpose and functions. Washington, D.C.: Board of Governors of the Federal Reserve System, 1963.

Graybill, F. A. *Theory and application of the linear model.* North Scituate, Mass.: Duxbury, 1976.

Mendenhall, W. *Introduction to linear models and the design and analysis of experiments.* Belmont, Calif.: Wadsworth, 1968.

Mendenhall, W., & McClave, J. T. *A second course in business statistics: Regression analysis.* San Francisco: Dellen, 1981.

Miller, R. B., & Wichern, D. W. *Intermediate business statistics: Analysis of variance, regression, and time series.* New York: Holt, Rinehart and Winston, 1977. Chapters 6–8.

Murphy, N. B., & Stock, D. R. "Determinants of the use of banking facilities: Trips to the bank in Oklahoma." *Review of Regional Economics and Business,* Oct. 1983, *8,* 33–35.

Neter, J., Wasserman, W., & Kutner, M. *Applied linear regression models.* Homewood, Ill.: Richard D. Irwin, 1983.

Schroeder, R. G. *Operations management: Decision making in the operations function.* New York: McGraw-Hill, 1981. Chapter 18.

Spiro, H. T. *Finance for the non-financial manager.* 2d ed. New York: Wiley, 1982. Chapter 16.

Weisberg, S. *Applied linear regression.* New York: Wiley, 1980.

Winkler, R. L., & Hays, W. L. *Statistics: Probability, inference and decision.* 2d ed. New York: Holt, Rinehart and Winston, 1975. Chapter 10.

Wise, J. O., & Dover, H. J. "An evaluation of a statistical method of appraising rural property." *Appraisal Journal,* Jan. 1974, *42,* 103–113.

Younger, M. S. *A handbook for linear regression.* North Scituate, Mass.: Duxbury, 1979.

CHAPTER 13

Time Series: Index Numbers and Descriptive Analyses

Where We've Been . . .

In Chapters 10, 11, and 12, we discussed the construction, estimation, and use of regression models. We saw that regression models provide very powerful tools for analyzing and exploiting the relationships among variables. However, when the data are collected sequentially over time, the assumption of independent random errors (essential for the valid use of regression models) is probably not satisfied.

Where We're Going . . .

In this chapter, we consider data that are collected sequentially over time, i.e., time series data. We begin with a type of time series data often used to characterize some aspect of the economy—namely, index numbers. The remainder of the chapter is devoted to a study of analytical and graphical methods that help us understand the behavior of time series data. Methods for forecasting future values of a time series will be discussed in Chapter 14.

Contents

If you turn to the financial section of a newspaper, you are very likely to see a graph of the Dow Jones Average* over the past several months or years. The Dow Jones Average is a number based on the daily stock prices of thirty large corporations listed on the New York Stock Exchange and is calculated at the close of each day's trading. Many people believe the Dow Jones Average characterizes the present status of the stock market, which explains the predisposition of the news media to report it and graph its values. Numerical variables, such as the Dow Jones Average, that are calculated, measured, or observed sequentially on a regular chronological basis are called *time series.* The rate of inflation, Consumer Price Index, balance of trade, Producer Price Index, and annual profit of a firm are other examples of business and economic time series.

Time series data, like other types of data we have discussed in previous chapters, are subjected to two kinds of analyses: *descriptive* and *inferential.* Descriptive analyses, the topic of this chapter, use graphical and numerical techniques to provide a clear understanding of the time series. After graphing the data, you will often want to use it to make inferences about the future values of the time series; i.e., you will want to *forecast* future values. For example, once you understand the past and present trends of the Dow Jones Average, you would probably want to forecast its future trend before making decisions about buying and selling stocks. Since significant amounts of money may be riding on the accuracy of your forecasts, you would be interested in measures of their reliability. Forecasts and their measures of reliability are examples of *inferential techniques* in time series analysis. Inferential techniques will be the topic of Chapter 14.

13.1 Index Numbers: An Introduction

The most common technique for characterizing a business or economic time series is to compute *index numbers.* Index numbers measure how a time series changes over time. Change is measured relative to a preselected time period, called the *base period.*

Definition 13.1

An *index number* is a number that measures the change in a variable over time relative to the value of the variable during a specific *base period.*

Two types of indexes dominate business and economic applications: *price* and *quantity indexes.* Price indexes measure changes in the price of a commodity or group of commodities over time. The CPI is a price index because it measures price changes of a group of commodities that are intended to reflect typical purchases of American consumers. On the other hand, an index constructed to measure the change in the total number of automobiles produced annually by American manufacturers would be an example of a quantity index.

---

* We are referring to the Dow Jones Industrial Average.

Methods of calculating index numbers range from very simple to extremely complex, depending on the numbers and types of commodities represented by the index. The next two sections provide details on the calculation and interpretation of several important types of index numbers.

13.2 Simple Index Numbers

When an index number is based on the price or quantity of a single commodity, it is called a *simple index number.*

Definition 13.2

A *simple index number* is based on the relative changes (over time) in the price or quantity of a single commodity.

Table 13.1

Silver Prices, 1970–1982

YEAR	PRICE ($/ounce)
1970	1.771
1971	1.546
1972	1.684
1973	2.558
1974	4.708
1975	4.419
1976	4.353
1977	4.620
1978	5.440
1979	11.090
1980	20.633
1981	10.481
1982	7.950

For example, consider the price of silver between 1970 and 1982, shown in Table 13.1. To construct a simple index to describe the relative changes in silver prices, we must first choose a *base period.* The choice is important because the price for all other periods will be compared with the price during the base period. We will select 1972 as the base period, a time just preceding the period of rapid economic inflation associated with dramatic oil price increases.

To calculate the simple index number for a particular year, we divide that year's price by the price during the base year and multiply the result by 100. Thus, for the 1975 silver price index number, we calculate

$$1975 \text{ index number} = \left(\frac{1975 \text{ silver price}}{1972 \text{ silver price}}\right)100 = \left(\frac{4.419}{1.684}\right)100$$

$$= 262.4$$

Similarly, the index number for 1982 is

$$1982 \text{ index number} = \left(\frac{1982 \text{ silver price}}{1972 \text{ silver price}}\right)100 = \left(\frac{7.950}{1.684}\right)100$$

$$= 472.09$$

The index number for the base period is always 100. In our example, we have

$$1972 \text{ index number} = \left(\frac{1972 \text{ silver price}}{1972 \text{ silver price}}\right)100 = 100$$

Thus, the silver price had risen by 162.4% (the difference between the 1975 and 1972 index numbers) between 1972 and 1975, and by 372.09% between 1972 and 1982. The simple index numbers for silver between 1970 and 1982 are given in Table 13.2 (page 594), and are portrayed graphically in Figure 13.1. The steps for calculating simple index numbers are summarized in the next box.

Figure 13.1   Graph of Silver Price Index, 1970–1982

Table 13.2

Simple Index Numbers for Silver Prices (Base 1972)

YEAR	INDEX
1970	105.17
1971	91.81
1972	100.00
1973	151.90
1974	279.57
1975	262.41
1976	258.49
1977	274.35
1978	323.04
1979	658.55
1980	1,225.24
1981	622.39
1982	472.09

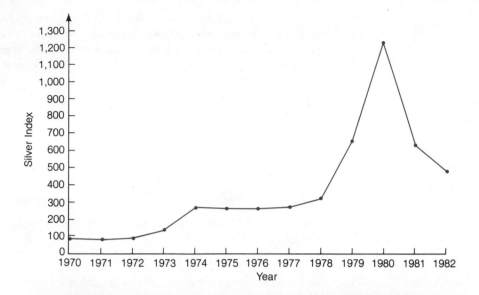

Steps for Calculating a Simple Index Number

1. Obtain the prices or quantities for the commodity over the time period of interest.
2. Select a base period.
3. Calculate the index number for each period according to the formula:

$$\text{Index number at time } t = \left(\frac{\text{Time series value at time } t}{\text{Time series value at base period}} \right) 100$$

Symbolically,

$$I_t = \left(\frac{Y_t}{Y_0} \right) 100$$

where I_t is the index number at time t, Y_t is the time series value at time t, and Y_0 is the time series value at the base period.

Example 13.1   Foreign crude oil prices between 1970 and 1982 are shown in Table 13.3. Construct a simple index for foreign crude oil prices using 1972 as the base period and portray the index on the same graph as the silver price index (Table 13.2).

Table 13.3

Foreign Crude Oil Prices, 1970–1982

YEAR	PRICE ($/barrel)	YEAR	PRICE ($/barrel)	YEAR	PRICE ($/barrel)
1970	1.80	1975	11.51	1979	18.00
1971	2.18	1976	11.51	1980	28.00
1972	2.48	1977	12.70	1981	32.00
1973	5.18	1978	15.40	1982	34.00
1974	10.46				

Solution　Represent the foreign crude oil price at time t by Y_t, the price during the base period (1972) by Y_0, and the simple index number at time t by I_t. Then

$$I_t = \left(\frac{Y_t}{Y_0}\right)100$$

For example, the index number for 1975 is

$$I_{1975} = \left(\frac{Y_{1975}}{Y_0}\right)100 = \left(\frac{11.51}{2.48}\right)100$$

$$= 464.11$$

The interpretation is that crude oil prices increased by 364.11% between 1972 and 1975. All the index numbers for foreign crude oil prices are similarly calculated and are given in Table 13.4. The graphs of the silver and crude oil price indexes are combined in Figure 13.2. Since the same base period was used for both simple indexes, the two graphs intersect at the 1972 base period, where both indexes have a value of 100. ■

Figure 13.2　Simple Indexes for Silver and Crude Oil Prices (Base 1972)

Table 13.4
Simple Index Numbers for Crude Oil Prices (Base 1972)

YEAR	INDEX
1970	72.58
1971	87.90
1972	100.00
1973	208.87
1974	421.77
1975	464.11
1976	464.11
1977	512.10
1978	620.97
1979	725.81
1980	1,129.03
1981	1,290.32
1982	1,370.97

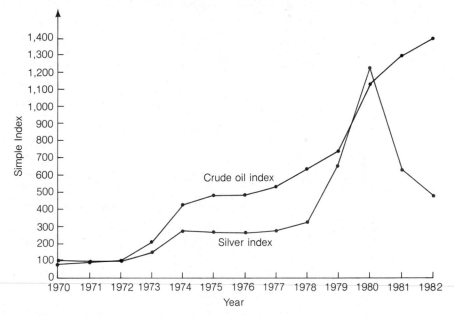

Portraying two indexes on the same graph (as we did in Example 13.1) indicates another reason indexes are calculated: Two or more commodities' relative price (or quantity) changes can be compared, even though the units of measurement are different (dollars per ounce and dollars per barrel, in our examples). In other words, apples and oranges *can* be compared, so long as you use index numbers to represent them. Figure 13.2 reveals that, during the period 1972–1978, the price of crude oil escalated more rapidly than that of silver, relative to the 1972 price. Also, the very high silver prices in 1980 are obvious on the graph. Of course, these index numbers provide only a *descriptive* comparison of the two time series. Any inferential implications of such a comparison will require a blend of inferential statistical analysis and economic theory.

Learning the Mechanics

13.1 Explain in words how to construct a simple index.

13.2 The table describes beer production in the United States for the period 1970 – 1982. Use 1977 as the base period to compute the simple index for this time series.

13.3 Refer to Exercise 13.2. Is this an example of a quantity index or a price index? Explain.

13.4 Refer to Exercise 13.2. Recompute the simple index using 1980 as the base period. Plot the two indexes on the same graph.

YEAR	U.S. BEER PRODUCTION (Million barrels)	YEAR	U.S. BEER PRODUCTION (Million barrels)
1970	133.1	1977	170.5
1971	137.4	1978	179.1
1972	141.3	1979	184.2
1973	148.6	1980	194.1
1974	156.2	1981	193.7
1975	160.6	1982	196.2
1976	163.7		

Source: *Standard & Poor's Statistical Service*, annual, Standard & Poor's Corporation.

Applying the Concepts

13.5 A stock you are interested in buying has had the yearly closing prices shown in the table.

a. Using 1972 as the base period, calculate the simple index for this stock's yearly closing price between 1970 and 1983.

b. By what percentage did the stock price increase or decrease between 1972 and 1983? Between 1980 and 1983?

13.6 The table at the top of the next page lists the average retail prices (in cents per gallon, excluding taxes) of gasoline for a sample of fifty-five cities in the United States on the first day of each month during the period January 1973 through December 1981.

YEAR	CLOSING PRICE
1970	$30.125
1971	25.500
1972	32.000
1973	38.375
1974	42.500
1975	47.125
1976	49.125
1977	38.750
1978	22.250
1979	28.750
1980	43.000
1981	52.875
1982	45.250
1983	59.750

	JAN.	FEB.	MAR.	APR.	MAY	JUNE	JULY	AUG.	SEPT.	OCT.	NOV.	DEC.
1973	25.31	24.81	25.94	26.32	26.49	26.78	26.82	26.81	26.74	27.69	28.56	30.30
1974	32.85	36.07	38.10	39.50	41.69	43.59	43.61	43.73	43.04	40.87	40.67	41.16
1975	42.29	42.23	42.27	42.79	43.84	45.20	47.37	48.03	48.03	48.07	47.55	47.55
1976	46.80	46.22	45.57	45.90	46.11	47.89	48.54	48.68	48.72	48.72	48.56	48.32
1977	48.35	48.85	49.58	50.28	51.00	51.74	51.70	51.71	51.48	51.33	51.26	51.12
1978	51.15	51.06	51.02	51.22	51.74	52.44	53.30	53.30	54.53	54.69	55.38	56.37
1979	68.42	70.05	73.25	77.25	81.41	87.82	93.09	96.84	99.03	99.77	101.10	107.00
1980	112.70	119.10	122.60	122.90	123.40	123.60	123.50	123.30	122.06	121.69	122.51	123.26
1981	132.71	142.13	143.45	142.79	140.01	139.67	138.25	137.67	139.62	137.11	136.90	136.56

Source: *Standard & Poor's Trade and Securities Statistics,* annual, Standard & Poor's Corporation.

a. Using January 1973 as the base period, calculate and plot the simple index for monthly retail gasoline prices between January 1973 and December 1981.

b. Interpret the value of the index you obtained for October 1973 and for August 1980.

c. Use the simple index to interpret the change in the price of gasoline between January 1980 and December 1981.

d. Is this a price or quantity index? Explain.

13.7 Civilian employment is broadly classified by the federal government into one of two categories—agricultural and nonagricultural. The nonagricultural employment category is further subclassified into white-collar, blue-collar, service, and other. Employment figures (in millions of workers) for three of the classes are given in the table for the 1972–1982 period.

YEAR	WHITE-COLLAR	BLUE-COLLAR	SERVICE	YEAR	WHITE-COLLAR	BLUE-COLLAR	SERVICE
1972	39.33	28.72	11.03	1978	48.09	32.07	13.06
1973	40.73	30.08	11.21	1979	50.33	32.67	13.08
1974	42.19	30.05	11.49	1980	51.88	31.45	13.23
1975	42.79	28.30	11.80	1981	52.95	31.26	13.44
1976	44.37	29.36	12.17	1982	53.47	29.60	13.74
1977	45.96	30.68	12.59				

a. Compute simple indexes for each of the three time series using 1977 as the base period.

b. Which segments have shown the highest and the lowest growth in employment in 1982 as compared to 1972?

c. Are these indexes price or quantity indexes? Explain.

13.3 Composite Index Numbers

A *composite index number* represents combinations of the prices or quantities of several commodities. For example, suppose you want to construct an index for the total number of sales of the three major automobile manufacturers in the United States. The first step is to collect data on the sales of each manufacturer during the period in which you are interested. The total sales of automobiles by each manufacturer between 1972 and 1982 are shown in

Table 13.5. To summarize the information from all three time series in a single index, we add the sales of each manufacturer for each year. That is, we form a new time series consisting of the total number of automobiles sold by the three manufacturers.

Table 13.5   Sales of Automobiles by Three Manufacturers (Thousands)

YEAR	GENERAL MOTORS	FORD	CHRYSLER	YEAR	GENERAL MOTORS	FORD	CHRYSLER
1972	7,790.52	5,593.04	2,192.00	1978	9,482.00	6,462.06	2,212.00
1973	8,683.80	5,871.00	2,423.00	1979	8,993.00	5,810.30	1,796.00
1974	6,690.00	5,258.93	2,015.00	1980	7,101.00	4,328.45	1,225.00
1975	6,629.00	4,577.77	1,773.00	1981	6,762.00	4,313.18	1,283.00
1976	8,568.00	5,304.44	2,371.00	1982	6,244.00	4,254.90	1,182.00
1977	9,068.00	6,422.30	2,328.00				

Source: *Moody's Industrial Manual.*

We now construct a simple index for the *total* of the three series. Selecting 1977 as the base year, we divide each total by the 1977 total sales. The resulting *simple composite index* is shown in Table 13.6.

Table 13.6

Simple Composite Index for Total Automobiles Sold by Three Manufacturers

YEAR	INDEX	YEAR	INDEX
1972	87.41	1978	101.90
1973	95.28	1979	93.16
1974	78.37	1980	71.02
1975	72.85	1981	69.36
1976	91.16	1982	65.56
1977	100.00		

Definition 13.3

A *simple composite index* is a simple index for a time series consisting of the total price or total quantity of two or more commodities.

Example 13.2

One of the primary uses of index numbers is to characterize changes in stock prices over time. Stock market indexes have been constructed for many different types of companies and industries, and several composite indexes have been developed to characterize all stocks. These indexes are reported on a daily basis in the news media (e.g., Standard and Poor's 500 Stocks Index and Dow Jones 65 Stocks Index).

Consider the monthly prices given in Table 13.7 for four high-technology company stocks listed on the New York Stock Exchange between 1981 and 1983. To see how this type of stock fared as the recession of the early 1980's ended and the market began to rally in 1982, construct a simple composite index using January 1981 as the base period. Graph the index, and comment on its implications.

Table 13.7

Monthly Prices of Four High-Technology Company Stocks

	AT&T	DIGITAL EQUIPMENT	HARRIS	IBM	TOTAL
1981					
Jan.	$51.500	$ 88.250	$47.125	$ 65.500	$252.375
Feb.	52.125	87.625	45.750	64.500	250.000
Mar.	51.625	93.000	55.250	62.125	262.000
Apr.	52.125	87.625	48.750	64.875	253.375
May	57.875	113.125	51.500	58.500	281.000
June	57.500	101.625	45.250	59.125	263.500
July	56.125	95.750	45.750	56.375	254.000
Aug.	56.875	92.500	42.125	55.375	246.875
Sept.	58.125	89.625	39.875	54.875	242.500
Oct.	58.375	96.375	39.125	49.625	243.500
Nov.	60.375	92.250	40.125	54.500	247.250
Dec.	58.750	86.750	40.000	57.625	243.125
1982					
Jan.	60.125	90.250	35.500	64.625	250.500
Feb.	54.625	84.625	32.750	61.750	233.750
Mar.	56.625	76.750	29.500	60.500	223.375
Apr.	31.000	80.375	30.500	64.625	206.500
May	32.125	76.500	26.000	62.125	196.750
June	30.500	71.250	25.000	61.375	188.125
July	52.500	66.625	26.500	66.250	211.875
Aug.	56.625	84.625	28.000	71.000	240.250
Sept.	57.000	80.625	34.000	74.750	246.375
Oct.	59.500	90.500	35.500	80.375	265.875
Nov.	60.125	105.000	37.250	86.375	288.750
Dec.	60.000	100.500	37.250	97.125	294.875
1983					
Jan.	69.250	121.750	40.500	98.750	330.250
Feb.	68.250	123.000	49.250	100.375	340.875
Mar.	65.625	128.625	45.625	104.750	344.625
Apr.	68.000	117.375	43.000	117.500	345.875
May	66.375	112.250	44.000	112.750	335.375
June	63.625	120.250	46.375	121.000	351.250
July	64.250	102.625	41.250	122.000	330.125
Aug.	68.375	104.250	35.750	119.375	327.750
Sept.	67.750	104.375	38.500	128.125	338.750
Oct.	62.000	65.375	34.375	126.750	288.500
Nov.	64.000	69.625	40.750	117.375	291.750
Dec.	61.500	72.000	40.125	122.000	295.625

Solution First, we calculate the total of the four stock prices each month. These totals are shown in Table 13.7. Then the simple composite index is calculated by dividing each monthly total by the January 1981 total. The index values are given in Table 13.8, and a graph of the simple composite index is shown in Figure 13.3.

Table 13.8
Simple Composite Index of
Stock Prices

1981	INDEX	1982	INDEX	1983	INDEX
Jan.	100.00	Jan.	99.26	Jan.	130.86
Feb.	99.06	Feb.	92.62	Feb.	135.07
Mar.	103.81	Mar.	88.51	Mar.	136.55
Apr.	100.40	Apr.	81.82	Apr.	137.05
May	111.34	May	77.96	May	132.89
June	104.41	June	74.54	June	139.18
July	100.64	July	83.95	July	130.81
Aug.	97.82	Aug.	95.20	Aug.	129.87
Sept.	96.09	Sept.	97.62	Sept.	134.22
Oct.	96.48	Oct.	105.35	Oct.	114.31
Nov.	97.97	Nov.	114.41	Nov.	115.60
Dec.	96.33	Dec.	116.84	Dec.	117.14

Figure 13.3 Graph of
Simple Composite Index of
Four Stocks

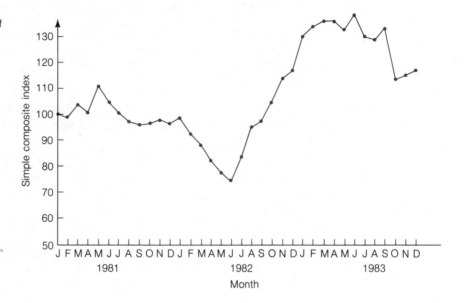

The effect of the recession on these stocks is apparent. Note the dip in prices in late 1981 and early 1982, with the index reaching its lowest point of 74.54 in June 1982. The 1983 recovery is also shown, with the December 1983 index indicating an increase of 17.14% over the January 1981 composite price. However, note that the drop in the Digital Equipment Corporation stock in October 1983 has a dramatic effect, since the index had increased by 34.22% between January 1981 and September 1983. This illustrates why most popular stock indexes are composites of more than four stocks — so that a significant change in one stock will not have such a profound effect on the index. ■

A simple composite price index has a major drawback: The quantity of the commodity that is purchased during each period is not taken into account when only the price totals are used to calculate the index. We can remedy this situation by constructing a *weighted composite price index.*

Definition 13.4

A *weighted composite price index* weights the prices by quantities purchased prior to calculating totals for each time period. The weighted totals are then used to compute the index in the same way that the unweighted totals are used for simple composite indexes.

Since the quantities purchased change from time period to time period, the choice of which time period quantities to use as the basis for the weighted composite index is an important one. A *Laspeyres index* uses the base period quantities as weights. The rationale is that the prices at each time period should be compared as if the same quantities were purchased each period as were purchased during the base period. This method measures price inflation (or deflation) by fixing the purchase quantities at their base period values. The method for calculating a Laspeyres index is given in the box.

Steps for Calculating a Laspeyres Index

1. Collect price information for each of the k price series to be used in the composite index. Denote these series by $P_{1t}, P_{2t}, \ldots, P_{kt}$.

2. Select a base period. Call this time period t_0.

3. Collect purchase quantity information for the base period. Denote the k quantities by $Q_{1t_0}, Q_{2t_0}, \ldots, Q_{kt_0}$.

4. Calculate the weighted totals for each time period according to the formula

$$\sum_{i=1}^{k} Q_{it_0} P_{it}$$

5. Calculate the Laspeyres index, I_t, at time t by taking the ratio of the weighted total at time t to the base period weighted total and multiplying by 100. That is,

$$I_t = \frac{\sum_{i=1}^{k} Q_{it_0} P_{it}}{\sum_{i=1}^{k} Q_{it_0} P_{it_0}} \times 100$$

Example 13.3

The January prices for the four high-technology company stocks are given in Table 13.9 (next page). Suppose that, in January 1981, an investor purchased the quantities shown in the table. [*Note:* Only January prices and quantities are used to simplify the example. The same methods can be applied to calculate the index for other months.] Calculate the Laspeyres index for the investor's portfolio of high-technology stocks using January 1981 as the base period.

Table 13.9
January Prices of High-Technology Stocks with Quantities Purchased

	AT&T	DIGITAL EQUIPMENT	HARRIS	IBM
SHARES PURCHASED	500	100	100	1,000
JANUARY 1981 PRICE	$51.500	$88.250	$47.125	$65.500
JANUARY 1982 PRICE	$60.125	$90.250	$35.500	$64.625
JANUARY 1983 PRICE	$69.250	$121.750	$40.500	$98.750

Solution First, we calculate the weighted price totals for each time period, using the January 1981 quantities as weights. Thus,

$$\text{January 1981 weighted total} = \sum_{i=1}^{4} Q_{i,1981} P_{i,1981}$$

$$= 500(51.500) + 100(88.250) + 100(47.125) + 1{,}000(65.500)$$

$$= 104{,}787.50$$

$$\text{January 1982 weighted total} = \sum_{i=1}^{4} Q_{i,1981} P_{i,1982}$$

$$= 500(60.125) + 100(90.250) + 100(35.500) + 1{,}000(64.625)$$

$$= 107{,}262.50$$

$$\text{January 1983 weighted total} = \sum_{i=1}^{4} Q_{i,1981} P_{i,1983}$$

$$= 500(69.250) + 100(121.750) + 100(40.500) + 1{,}000(98.750)$$

$$= 149{,}600.00$$

Then the Laspeyres index is calculated by multiplying the ratio of each weighted total to the base period weighted total by 100. Thus,

$$I_{1981} = \frac{\sum_{i=1}^{4} Q_{i,1981} P_{i,1981}}{\sum_{i=1}^{4} Q_{i,1981} P_{i,1981}} \times 100 = 100$$

$$I_{1982} = \frac{\sum_{i=1}^{4} Q_{i,1981} P_{i,1982}}{\sum_{i=1}^{4} Q_{i,1981} P_{i,1981}} \times 100 = \frac{107{,}262.50}{104{,}787.50} = 102.36$$

$$I_{1983} = \frac{\sum_{i=1}^{4} Q_{i,1981} P_{i,1983}}{\sum_{i=1}^{4} Q_{i,1981} P_{i,1981}} \times 100 = \frac{149{,}600.00}{104{,}787.50} = 142.77$$

The implication is that these stocks were worth 2.36% more to the investor in January 1982 than in January 1981 and 42.77% more in January 1983. ∎

The Laspeyres index is appropriate when the base period quantities are reasonable weights to apply to all time periods. This is the case in applications such as that described in Example 13.3, where the base period quantities represent actual quantities of stock purchased and held for some period of time. Laspeyres indexes are also appropriate when the base period quantities remain reasonable approximations of purchase quantities in subsequent periods. However, it can be misleading when the relative purchase quantities change significantly from those in the base period.

Probably the best-known Laspeyres index is the all-items Consumer Price Index (CPI). This monthly composite index is made up of hundreds of item prices, and the U.S. Bureau of Labor Statistics (BLS) sampled over 40,000 families' purchases in 1972–1973 to determine the base period quantities. Thus, the all-items CPI published each month reflects quantities purchased in 1972–1973 by a sample of families across the United States. However, as prices increase for some commodities more quickly than for others, consumers tend to substitute less expensive commodities where possible. For example, as automobile and gasoline prices rapidly inflated in the mid-1970's, consumers began to purchase smaller cars. The net effect of using the base period quantities for the CPI is to overestimate the effect of inflation on consumers, because the quantities are fixed at levels that will actually change in response to price changes.

There are several solutions to the problem of purchase quantities that change relative to those of the base period. One is to change the base period regularly, so that the quantities are regularly updated. A second solution is to compute the index at each time period by using the purchase quantities of that period, rather than those of the base period. A *Paasche* index is calculated by using price totals weighted by the purchase quantities of the period the index value represents. The steps for calculating a Paasche index are given in the box.

Steps for Calculating a Paasche Index

1. Collect price information for each of the k price series to be used in the composite index. Denote these series by $P_{1t}, P_{2t}, \ldots, P_{kt}$.

2. Select a base period. Call this time period t_0.

3. Collect purchase quantity information for every period. Denote the k quantities for period t by $Q_{1t}, Q_{2t}, \ldots, Q_{kt}$.

4. Calculate the Paasche index for time t by multiplying the ratio of the weighted total at time t to the weighted total at time t_0 (base period) by 100, where the weights used are the purchase quantities for time period t. Thus,

$$I_t = \frac{\sum_{i=1}^{k} Q_{it} P_{it}}{\sum_{i=1}^{k} Q_{it} P_{it_0}} \times 100$$

Example 13.4 The January prices and volumes (actual quantities purchased) in thousands of shares for the four high-technology company stocks are shown for 1981, 1982, and 1983 in Table 13.10. Calculate and interpret the Paasche index, using January 1981 as the base period.

Table 13.10 January Prices and Volumes of High-Technology Company Stocks

	AT&T		DIGITAL EQUIPMENT		HARRIS		IBM	
	Price	Volume	Price	Volume	Price	Volume	Price	Volume
JANUARY 1981	$51.500	20,730	$ 88.250	11,260	$47.125	3,300	$65.500	36,730
JANUARY 1982	60.125	13,056	90.250	5,015	35.500	1,559	64.625	18,600
JANUARY 1983	69.250	30,213	121.750	10,996	40.500	1,390	98.750	20,807

Solution   The key to calculating a Paasche index is to remember that the weights (purchase quantities) change for each time period. Thus,

$$I_{1981} = \frac{\sum_{i=1}^{4} Q_{i,1981} P_{i,1981}}{\sum_{i=1}^{4} Q_{i,1981} P_{i,1981}} \times 100 = 100$$

$$I_{1982} = \frac{\sum_{i=1}^{4} Q_{i,1982} P_{i,1982}}{\sum_{i=1}^{4} Q_{i,1982} P_{i,1981}} \times 100 = \frac{2,494,965}{2,406,726} \times 100 = 103.67$$

$$I_{1983} = \frac{\sum_{i=1}^{4} Q_{i,1983} P_{i,1983}}{\sum_{i=1}^{4} Q_{i,1983} P_{i,1981}} \times 100 = \frac{5,542,000}{3,954,729} \times 100 = 140.14$$

The implication is that 1982 prices represent a 3.67% increase over 1981 prices, assuming the purchase quantities were at January 1982 levels for *both* periods. Similarly, the 1983 index value of 140.14 implies a 40.14% increase when purchase quantities are at the January 1983 level. ■

The Paasche index is most appropriate when you want to compare current prices to base period prices at *current* purchase levels. However, there are several major problems associated with the Paasche index. First, it requires that purchase quantities be known for every time period. This rules out a Paasche index for applications such as the CPI because the time and monetary resource expenditures required to collect quantity information are considerable. (Recall that more than 40,000 families were sampled to estimate purchase quantities in

1972–1973.) A second problem is that, although each period is compared to the base period, it is difficult to compare the index at two other periods because the quantities used are different for each period. For example, for the four high-technology stocks in Example 13.4, we calculated index values of 103.67 in 1982 and 140.14 in 1983. Although this apparently represents an increase of 36.47 from 1982 to 1983, these two index values are determined using different quantities, and therefore, the change in the index is affected by changes in both prices *and* quantities. This fact makes it difficult to interpret the change in a Paasche index between periods when neither is the base period.

Although there are other types of indexes that use different weighting factors, the Laspeyres and Paasche indexes are the most popular composite indexes. Depending on the primary objectives in constructing an index, one of them will probably be suitable for most purposes.

Case Study 13.1

The Consumer Price Index: CPI-U and CPI-W

The Consumer Price Index (CPI), first published by the U.S. Bureau of Labor Statistics (BLS) in 1919, is the country's principal measure of price changes. One major use of the CPI is as an indicator of inflation, through which the success or failure of government economic policies can be monitored. A second major use of the CPI is to escalate income payments. Millions of workers have escalator clauses in their collective bargaining contracts that call for increases in wage rates based on increases in the CPI. In addition, the incomes of Social Security beneficiaries and retired military and federal civil service employees are tied to the CPI. It has been estimated that a 1% increase in the CPI can trigger an increase of over $1 billion in income payments.

Since 1978, the BLS has published two national, all-items indexes: the new CPI-U and the traditional CPI-W. The CPI-U measures the price change of a constant market basket of goods and services that are representative of the purchases of all urban residents — approximately 80% of the U.S. population. The CPI-W measures the price change of a constant market basket of goods and services that are representative of the purchases of urban wage earners and clerical workers — approximately 50% of all urban residents. The base period for both indexes is 1967. The CPI-U is the index typically reported by the press and broadcast media. The CPI-W is the index used in the escalator clauses of most labor contracts and government benefit programs. In addition to these two national indexes, the BLS publishes CPI-U and CPI-W indexes for each of twenty-eight metropolitan areas. The national indexes and the metropolitan indexes are reported monthly (or bimonthly in the case of twenty-three metropolitan indexes) in the BLS's *CPI Detailed Report*.

The market basket of goods priced by both the CPI-U and the CPI-W includes a homeownership component. Accounting for over 20% of the overall weight of the indexes, the homeownership component influences the indexes more than food, energy, or medical care. This component includes the costs associated with purchasing a home (the price of the home and mortgage interest), as well as the cost of property taxes, property insurance, and maintenance and repairs. During the 1970's and early 1980's, the use of these quantities to measure the cost of homeownership met with much criticism. The following two arguments were made by critics:

1. Since the CPI is used to measure the change in purchasing power for the purpose of escalating income or determining the rate of inflation, it "should not include the impact of rising prices on the value of assets such as houses. Just as the CPI excludes changes in the value of stocks and bonds, . . . the change in the asset value of the house (appreciation or depreciation) and the cost of equity in holding that asset should be distinguished from the change in the cost of the shelter provided by the house. It is the cost of consuming the shelter provided by the house—not the investment aspects of homeownership—which should be reflected in an index used to keep real income constant" (*CPI Issues,* p. 2).

2. The CPI overstates the rate of inflation because "it uses *current* house prices and *current* mortgage interest rates . . . the CPI should not measure the costs of purchasing the base period houses in today's prices and today's mortgage interest rates, but rather the CPI should measure what people are actually paying for housing" (*CPI Issues,* p. 2).

In response to these criticisms, the BLS developed and experimented with an entirely new approach to measuring the cost of housing. As a result, instead of explicitly including in the market basket the homeownership costs described above, the BLS now recommends that a *rental equivalency* component be included. This approach assumes that a household's cost of consuming the flow of services from the housing unit can be represented by the income that the household could receive by renting the home to someone else. This rental equivalency approach to measuring homeownership costs was implemented in an experimental version of the CPI-U called the CPI-U-X1.

Figure 13.4 shows the movement that the CPI-U and CPI-U-X1 would have displayed over the period 1970–1981. Notice that the two indexes generally move together, but that the

Figure 13.4 Changes in the Consumer Price Index for All Urban Consumers: Official (CPI-U) and Experimental Rental Equivalence (CPI-U-X1) Measures [*Note:* Percent changes are calculated using 12 months of unadjusted data.] Source: Gillingham and Lane, 1982, p. 13.

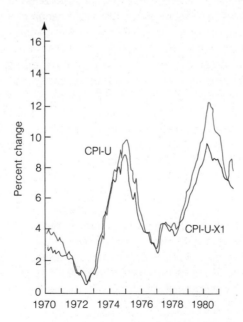

CPI-U-X1 tends to stay below the CPI-U, particularly during the periods of high mortgage interest rates in 1970, 1974–1975, and 1978–1981. If, as some critics charge, the CPI-U overstates inflation during periods of high mortgage interest rates, it appears that the experimental CPI-U-X1 should provide a better measure of inflation. In January 1983, the BLS changed the official CPI-U to include the rental equivalency approach to measuring home-ownership costs and was planning to make a similar change in the CPI-W in 1985.

Exercises 13.8–13.16

Learning the Mechanics

13.8 Explain in words how to calculate the following types of indexes:

a. Simple composite index

b. Weighted composite index

c. Laspeyres index

d. Paasche index

13.9 Using May 1980 as the base period, compute the simple composite index for commodities in the table:

DATE 1980	PRICE OF COFFEE ($ per pound)	PRICE OF GASOLINE ($ per gallon)	PRICE OF SUGAR ($ per pound)
Jan.	1.87	1.13	0.27
Feb.	1.84	1.19	0.35
Mar.	2.06	1.23	0.31
Apr.	1.94	1.23	0.32
May	2.02	1.23	0.42
June	2.02	1.24	0.44
July	1.81	1.24	0.40
Aug.	1.78	1.23	0.44
Sept.	1.88	1.22	0.47
Oct.	1.90	1.22	0.55

Source: *Standard & Poor's Trade and Securities Statistics*, Standard & Poor's Corporation, Jan. 1981.

13.10 Explain in words the difference between Laspeyres and Paasche indexes.

Applying the Concepts

13.11 The gross national product (GNP) is used as an indicator of the health of the U.S. economy. The GNP is the sum of several components. One of these is personal consumption expenditures, which is itself the sum of expenditures for durable goods, nondurable goods, and services. Consider the personal consumption expenditures data listed in the table at the top of the next page.

YEAR	DURABLE GOODS ($ billion)	NONDURABLE GOODS ($ billion)	SERVICES ($ billion)
1961	41.6	155.3	138.1
1962	46.7	161.6	147.0
1963	51.4	167.1	156.1
1964	56.3	176.9	167.1
1965	62.8	188.6	178.7
1966	67.7	204.7	192.4
1967	69.6	212.6	208.1
1968	80.0	230.4	225.6
1969	85.5	247.0	247.2
1970	84.9	264.7	269.1
1971	97.1	277.7	293.4
1972	111.2	299.3	322.4
1973	122.9	334.4	351.3
1974	121.9	375.7	388.3
1975	131.7	409.1	432.4
1976	156.5	440.4	482.8
1977	178.8	481.2	549.8
1978	200.3	530.6	619.8
1979	212.3	602.2	696.3
1980	211.6	674.3	785.3
1981	234.6	734.5	874.1
1982	242.7	762.0	966.3

a. Using these three component values for the years 1961–1982, construct a simple composite index for personal consumption, using 1967 as the base year.

b. Suppose we want to update the index by making 1974 the base year. Update the index, using only the index values you calculated in part a, without referring to the original data.

13.12 Refer to Exercise 13.11, in which a personal consumption expenditure index was constructed. Graph the personal consumption expenditure index for the years 1961–1982, first using 1967 as the base year and then 1974 as the base year. What effect does changing the base year have on the graph of this index?

13.13 Refer to Exercise 13.11. Suppose the output quantities in 1967, measured in billions of units purchased, are as follows:

Durable goods: 8.5

Nondurable goods: 120.1

Services: 30.7

Use the outputs to calculate the Laspeyres index from 1961 to 1982 with 1967 as the base period.

13.14 Refer to Exercises 13.11 and 13.13. Plot the simple composite index and Laspeyres index on the same graph. Comment on the differences between the two indexes.

13.15 The level of price and production of metals in the United States is one measure of the strength of the industrial economy. The table lists the 1982 prices (in dollars per ton) and production (in tons) for three metals important to U.S. industry.

MONTH	IRON		ALUMINUM		LEAD	
	Price	Production	Price	Production	Price	Production
Jan.	213	4,489	1,683	350.5	652.5	44.6
Feb.	213	4,169	1,683	311.4	635.4	44.8
Mar.	213	4,622	1,683	336.3	643.9	45.3
Apr.	213	3,967	1,683	318.6	615.6	45.9
May	213	3,909	1,683	320.9	602.7	46.4
June	213	3,516	1,683	299.9	562.4	46.9
July	213	3,595	1,683	296.9	604.2	40.8
Aug.	213	3,277	1,683	287.1	575.3	47.3
Sept.	213	3,160	1,683	271.1	571.1	46.0
Oct.	213	3,077	1,672	275.3	556.7	49.6
Nov.	213	2,648	1,672	266.3	537.9	46.4
Dec.	213	2,712	1,672	275.1	526.1	50.0

Source: *Standard & Poor's Statistical Service.*

a. Compute simple composite price and quantity indexes for the 12-month period, using January as the base period.

b. Compute the Laspeyres price index for the 12-month period using January as the base period.

c. Plot the simple composite and Laspeyres indexes on the same graph. Comment on the differences.

13.16 Refer to Exercise 13.15.

a. Compute the Paasche price index for metals for the 12-month period using January as the base period.

b. Plot the Laspeyres and Paasche indexes on the same graph. Comment on the differences.

c. Compare the Laspeyres and Paasche index values for September and December. Which index is more appropriate for describing the change in this 4-month period? Explain.

13.4 Smoothing with Moving Averages

As you have seen in the previous sections, index numbers are useful for describing trends and changes in time series. However, time series often have such irregular fluctuations that trends are difficult to describe. Index numbers can be misleading in such cases because the series is changing so rapidly. Methods for removing the rapid fluctuations in a time series so the general trend can be seen are called *smoothing* techniques.

Probably the simplest smoothing technique is the *moving average method.* The *N-point moving average* of a time series is the average of the time series values at *N* adjacent time periods. For example, consider the time series consisting of the annual closing-day Dow Jones Average (DJA) from 1961 to 1983 (see Table 13.11). As shown in Figure 13.5, there are time periods during which the DJA oscillates rather rapidly.

Table 13.11

Dow Jones Average and 7-Point Moving Average

YEAR	DJA	7-POINT MOVING AVERAGE	YEAR	DJA	7-POINT MOVING AVERAGE
1961	731.14	—	1973	923.88	876.44
1962	652.10	—	1974	759.37	875.90
1963	762.95	—	1975	802.49	864.50
1964	874.13	811.48	1976	974.92	848.51
1965	969.26	841.86	1977	835.15	854.24
1966	785.69	863.04	1978	805.01	874.19
1967	905.11	873.89	1979	838.74	909.05
1968	943.75	875.41	1980	963.99	949.58
1969	800.36	872.76	1981	899.01	—
1970	838.92	892.50	1982	1,046.54	—
1971	884.76	871.68	1983	1,258.64	—
1972	950.71	851.50			

Figure 13.5 Dow Jones Average, 1961–1983

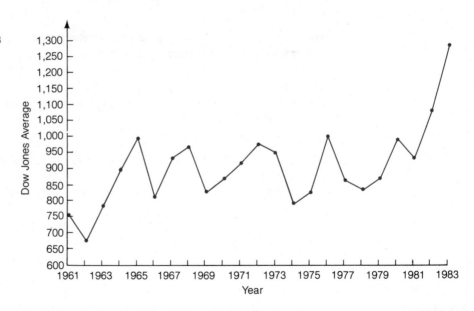

To smooth the DJA series, we will use a 7-point moving average. The value of the 7-point moving average for a particular year is the mean of the DJA for seven periods: the three previous time periods, the time period of interest, and the three subsequent time periods. Denoting the DJA time series by Y_t and the 7-point moving average by M_t, we can write the calculation formula for M_t as

$$M_t = \frac{Y_{t-3} + Y_{t-2} + Y_{t-1} + Y_t + Y_{t+1} + Y_{t+2} + Y_{t+3}}{7}$$

For example,

$$M_{1964} = \frac{Y_{1961} + Y_{1962} + Y_{1963} + Y_{1964} + Y_{1965} + Y_{1966} + Y_{1967}}{7}$$

$$= \frac{731.14 + 652.10 + 762.95 + 874.13 + 969.26 + 785.69 + 905.11}{7}$$

$$= 811.48$$

The complete 7-point moving average is given in Table 13.11. Note that the first three and last three values for Y_t have no corresponding moving average, M_t, because each 7-point moving average calculation requires values for Y_t for three preceding and three subsequent time periods. The 7-point moving average is plotted along with the DJA values in Figure 13.6.

Figure 13.6 Moving Average for the Dow Jones Average

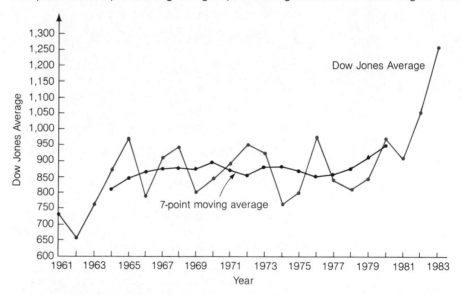

Note that the trend of the DJA is easier to follow with the moving average than with the series itself. The 7-point moving average removes most of the short-term fluctuation, making it possible to see the long-term trend. The main disadvantage of the 7-point moving average is the loss of three data points at each end of the series.

The choice of N in calculating an N-point moving average is an important one. Large values of N produce a smoother moving average, but more points on each end of the series are lost and the moving average may wind up so smooth that important changes in the time series are lost. Small values of N retain more points on each end of the series, but do not yield the same degree of smoothing. We usually try several values of N to determine one that yields a smooth series without missing important changes or losing too many points at the beginning and end of the series.

To see the effect of changing N, we will consider a 4-point moving average for the DJA series. The selection of an even value of N produces a special problem: The average of an even number of points is not "centered" at any specific time period. For example, the average of four time period values is centered between the second and third time periods. Thus, for the DJA data (Table 13.11), the first 4-point moving average is

Table 13.12

Uncentered 4-Point Moving Average for DJA Series

YEAR	UNCENTERED 4-POINT MOVING AVERAGE
1961	
1962	755.08
1963	814.61
1964	848.01
1965	883.55
1966	900.95
1967	858.73
1968	872.04
1969	866.95
1970	868.69
1971	899.57
1972	879.68
1973	859.11
1974	865.17
1975	842.98
1976	854.39
1977	863.46
1978	860.72
1979	876.69
1980	937.07
1981	1,042.05
1982	
1983	

$$M_{1962.5} = \frac{Y_{1961} + Y_{1962} + Y_{1963} + Y_{1964}}{4}$$

$$= \frac{731.14 + 652.10 + 762.95 + 874.13}{4}$$

$$= 755.08$$

The complete uncentered 4-point moving average for the DJA series is given in Table 13.12.

It is often inconvenient to use an uncentered moving average because its time periods do not correspond to the time periods of the original time series. For this reason a *centered* moving average is defined, for even N-point moving averages, as the mean of each consecutive pair of uncentered moving average values. For example, the first value of the centered 4-point moving average for the DJA series is

$$M_{1963} = \frac{M_{1962.5} + M_{1963.5}}{2}$$

$$= \frac{755.08 + 814.61}{2}$$

$$= 784.85$$

The general formula for the centered moving average for an even value of N is

$$M_t = \frac{M_{t-.5} + M_{t+.5}}{2}$$

The centered 4-point moving average for the DJA series is given in Table 13.13, and shown graphically with the 7-point moving average in Figure 13.7. Note that the 4-point moving average is not as smooth as the 7-point moving average, but it more quickly reflects changes in the series. Also, only two points are lost on each end of the centered 4-point moving average. The method for constructing moving averages is summarized in the box.

Figure 13.7 4-Point and 7-Point Moving Averages for Dow Jones Average Time Series

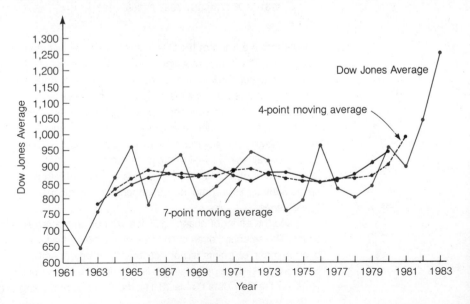

Table 13.13

Centered 4-Point Moving Average

YEAR	CENTERED 4-POINT MOVING AVERAGE
1961	—
1962	—
1963	784.85
1964	831.31
1965	865.78
1966	892.25
1967	879.84
1968	865.39
1969	869.50
1970	867.82
1971	884.13
1972	889.63
1973	869.40
1974	862.14
1975	854.08
1976	848.69
1977	858.92
1978	862.09
1979	868.71
1980	906.88
1981	989.56
1982	—
1983	—

Steps for Constructing a Moving Average

1. Select N, the number of consecutive time series values that will be averaged to form the N-point moving average. Remember that the larger is the value of N, the smoother is the moving average, and the more points that are lost on each end of the series. Usually you will need to try several values of N before deciding which is most appropriate.

2. If N is odd, the N-point moving average is the mean of N consecutive values of the time series:

$$M_t = \frac{Y_{t-(N-1)/2} + \cdots + Y_t + \cdots + Y_{t+(N-1)/2}}{N}$$

Note that $(N-1)/2$ points are lost on each end of the series.

3. If N is even, first calculate the uncentered moving average as the mean of N consecutive values of the time series:

$$M_{t-.5} = \frac{Y_{t-N/2} + \cdots + Y_t + \cdots + Y_{t+N/2-1}}{N}$$

and

$$M_{t+.5} = \frac{Y_{t-N/2+1} + \cdots + Y_t + \cdots + Y_{t+N/2}}{N}$$

Then calculate the centered moving average by computing the mean of each adjacent pair of uncentered values:

$$M_t = \frac{M_{t-.5} + M_{t+.5}}{2}$$

Note that $N/2$ values are lost at each end of the series.

You may have noticed that the N-point moving average for an odd value of N assigns equal weight to each of the N values of the time series. Thus, for a 3-point moving average,

$$M_t = \frac{Y_{t-1} + Y_t + Y_{t+1}}{3}$$

$$= \tfrac{1}{3}Y_{t-1} + \tfrac{1}{3}Y_t + \tfrac{1}{3}Y_{t+1}$$

Every value used to calculate M_t is given an equal weight of $\tfrac{1}{3}$. On the other hand, the centered 4-point moving average is

$$M_t = \frac{M_{t-.5} + M_{t+.5}}{2}$$

$$= \frac{\dfrac{Y_{t-2} + Y_{t-1} + Y_t + Y_{t+1}}{4} + \dfrac{Y_{t-1} + Y_t + Y_{t+1} + Y_{t+2}}{4}}{2}$$

$$= \tfrac{1}{8}Y_{t-2} + \tfrac{1}{4}Y_{t-1} + \tfrac{1}{4}Y_t + \tfrac{1}{4}Y_{t+1} + \tfrac{1}{8}Y_{t+2}$$

Thus, for N, even, the centered N-point moving average assigns one-half the weight to the first and last time periods as to the middle time periods used in the calculation of M_t.

Both are specific examples of *weighted moving averages,* where M_t is defined as the weighted average of T values of the time series; i.e.,

$$M_t = \sum_{k=1}^{T} W_k Y_k$$

with the sum of the weights equal to 1:

$$\sum_{k=1}^{T} W_k = 1$$

Many other types of moving averages have been developed, using a variety of different weighting schemes to accomplish specific objectives. A scheme that has received much attention is one that assigns positive weight to current and past values of the time series, and zero weight to future values. This application of a weighted moving average is called *exponential smoothing,* and is the topic of Section 13.5.

Exercises 13.17–13.25

Learning the Mechanics

13.17 Which will produce a smoother description of the trend of a time series, a 3- or 7-point moving average? Why?

13.18 Compute the missing values in the 3- and 5-point moving average columns of the table.

YEAR	PRICE OF GOLD Y_t ($ per troy ounce)	3-POINT MOVING AVERAGE OF GOLD PRICES	5-POINT MOVING AVERAGE OF GOLD PRICES
1970	36.41		
1971	41.25	45.42	
1972	58.61		
1973	97.81		
1974	159.70	139.64	
1975	161.40	148.63	
1976	124.80		
1977	148.30		
1978	193.50		276.08
1979	307.80	369.10	
1980	606.01		

Source: *Standard & Poor's Trade and Securities Statistics,* annual, Standard & Poor's Corporation.

13.19 Plot the gold-price time series and the 3-point moving average of Exercise 13.18 on a graph. Examine the differences between the time series and its 3-point moving average [i.e., examine the distances $(Y_t - M_t)$]. Can you identify any cyclical patterns in the time series?

13.20 Refer to Exercise 13.2. Calculate a 3-point and a 5-point moving average for U.S. beer production between 1970 and 1982.

13.21 Consider the quarterly housing starts given in the table.

YEAR	QUARTER	HOUSING STARTS Y_t (thousands of dwellings)	UNCENTERED 4-POINT MOVING AVERAGE	CENTERED 4-POINT MOVING AVERAGE M_t
1977	I	367.40		
	II	581.10		
	III	561.50	496.78	487.39
	IV	477.10	477.99	
1978	I	292.25	460.54	
	II	511.30	435.11	
	III	459.80	412.59	
	IV	387.00	413.78	
1979	I	297.00		413.60
	II	523.20	410.45	
	III	434.60	401.48	
	IV	351.10		
1980	I	218.70	323.88	
	II	291.10		

Source: *Standard & Poor's Trade and Securities Statistics*, annual, Standard & Poor's Corporation.

a. Compute the missing values for the uncentered and centered 4-point moving average columns of the table.

b. Plot the time series, Y_t, and the centered 4-point moving average on a graph. Comment on the smoothing achieved by the moving average.

Applying the Concepts

13.22 A composite index incorporating twelve leading indicators of the state of the economy is given in the table. Using the values of this index for 1967 to 1982, calculate moving averages for $N = 3$, 5, and 7, and graph them. Which moving average series most clearly depicts the long-term trend of the index?

YEAR	COMPOSITE INDEX	YEAR	COMPOSITE INDEX
1967	104.6	1975	119.6
1968	112.1	1976	127.7
1969	108.2	1977	140.2
1970	109.0	1978	143.0
1971	117.9	1979	135.5
1972	132.1	1980	137.3
1973	129.3	1981	127.1
1974	109.8	1982	132.8

13.23 The table lists the monthly commercial failures of new ventures in the United States for the years 1981 and 1982.

	JAN.	FEB.	MAR.	APR.	MAY	JUNE	JULY	AUG.	SEPT.	OCT.	NOV.	DEC.
1981	1,282	1,161	1,191	1,640	1,470	1,373	1,511	1,318	1,347	1,999	1,331	1,594
1982	1,582	1,942	1,733	1,894	1,910	1,917	2,129	2,837	2,180	2,336	2,105	2,240

a. Plot the time series.

b. Calculate moving averages for $N = 3, 5,$ and 7. Plot each moving average series on the same graph. Which moving average series best characterizes the long-run trend? Explain.

13.24 Refer to Exercise 13.6, where the average first-of-the-month retail prices of gasoline for fifty-five U.S. cities are given from January 1973 through December 1981. To see the trend in gasoline prices, compute the 5-point moving average for the series, and then plot the retail prices and the moving average on a graph.

13.25 The table shows the quarterly sales index of a particular brand of calculator at a campus bookstore. The quarters are based on an academic year, so the first quarter represents fall; the second, winter; the third, spring; and the fourth, summer.

YEAR	FIRST QUARTER	SECOND QUARTER	THIRD QUARTER	FOURTH QUARTER
1979	438	398	252	160
1980	464	429	376	216
1981	523	496	425	318
1982	593	576	456	398
1983	636	640	526	498

a. Construct a 4-point moving average; then plot the time series and moving average on a graph.

b. Note the seasonal pattern of the time series, i.e., the regularity with which the fall quarter sales are higher than the moving average trend and the summer quarter sales are lower. Compute the ratio of each time series value, Y_t, to the moving average value at the same time, M_t, and multiply by 100. The result is called a *seasonal index* because it measures the percentage deviation of each quarter's value from the moving average trend.

c. Calculate the average of the four seasonal percentages you computed for the first quarter index values. Repeat for each of the other quarters. This will yield four averages that represent the average percentage deviation of each quarter from the trend. This is called the *ratio-to-moving average method* of measuring seasonal variation.

13.5 Exponential Smoothing

As we saw in Section 13.4, moving averages smooth time series data by creating a weighted average of past, current, and future values of the series. However, the objective of smoothing is often to provide a means for forecasting future values of the time series. Moving averages are not useful for forecasting because their calculation requires the use of future values. (Recall that values at the end of the series are lost because the future values are unavailable.)

To be useful for forecasting, a weighted moving average that assigns no weight to future values must be defined.

Exponential smoothing is one type of weighted average that assigns positive weights to past and current values only. A single weight, w, called the *exponential smoothing constant,* is selected so that w is between 0 and 1. Then the exponentially smoothed series, E_t, is calculated as follows:

$$E_1 = Y_1$$
$$E_2 = wY_2 + (1 - w)E_1$$
$$E_3 = wY_3 + (1 - w)E_2$$
$$\vdots$$
$$E_t = wY_t + (1 - w)E_{t-1}$$

Thus, the exponentially smoothed value at time t assigns the weight w to the current series value and the weight $(1 - w)$ to the previous smoothed value.

For example, consider the Dow Jones Average time series in Table 13.11. Suppose we want to calculate the exponentially smoothed series using a smoothing constant of $w = .3$. The calculations proceed as follows:

$$E_{1961} = Y_{1961} = 731.14$$
$$E_{1962} = .3Y_{1962} + (1 - .3)E_{1961}$$
$$= .3(652.10) + .7(731.14) = 707.43$$
$$E_{1963} = .3Y_{1963} + (1 - .3)E_{1962}$$
$$= .3(762.95) + .7(707.43) = 724.09$$
$$\vdots$$

All the exponentially smoothed values corresponding to $w = .3$ are given in Table 13.14. Note that no values are lost at the beginning or end of the exponentially smoothed series.

Table 13.14

Dow Jones Average with Exponential Smoothing (1961–1983)

YEAR	DJA	EXPONENTIALLY SMOOTHED DJA $(w = .3)$	YEAR	DJA	EXPONENTIALLY SMOOTHED DJA $(w = .3)$
1961	731.14	731.14	1973	923.88	897.59
1962	652.10	707.43	1974	759.37	856.12
1963	762.95	724.09	1975	802.49	840.03
1964	874.13	769.10	1976	974.92	880.50
1965	969.26	829.15	1977	835.15	866.90
1966	785.69	816.11	1978	805.01	848.33
1967	905.11	842.81	1979	838.74	845.45
1968	943.75	873.09	1980	963.99	881.01
1969	800.36	851.27	1981	899.01	886.41
1970	838.92	847.57	1982	1,046.54	934.45
1971	884.76	858.73	1983	1,258.64	1,031.71
1972	950.71	886.32			

The DJA and exponentially smoothed DJA are graphed in Figure 13.8. Like many averages, the exponentially smoothed series changes less rapidly than the time series itself. The choice of w affects the smoothness of E_t. The smaller (closer to 0) is the value of w, the smoother is E_t. Since small values of w give more weight to the past values of the time series, the smoothed series is not as affected by rapid changes in the current values and, therefore, appears smoother than the original series. Conversely, choosing w near 1 yields an exponentially smoothed series that is much like the original series. That is, large values of w give more weight to the current value of the time series so the smoothed series looks like the original series. This concept is illustrated in Figure 13.9. The steps for calculating an exponentially smoothed series are given in the next box.

Figure 13.8 Exponentially Smoothed Values ($w = .3$) for the Dow Jones Average

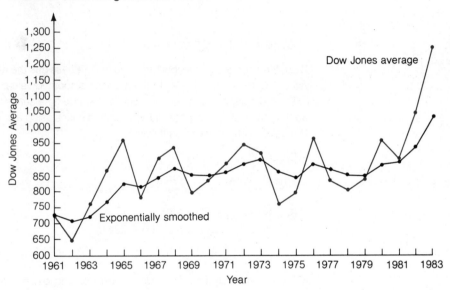

Figure 13.9 Exponentially Smoothed Values ($w = .3$ and $w = .7$) for the Dow Jones Average

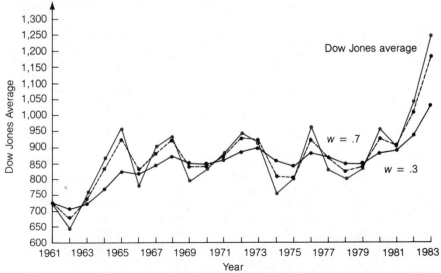

Steps for Calculating an Exponentially Smoothed Series

1. Select an exponential smoothing constant, w, between 0 and 1. Remember that small values of w give less weight to the current value of the series and yield a smoother series. Larger choices of w assign more weight to the current value of the series and yield a more variable series.

2. Calculate the exponentially smoothed series E_t from the original time series Y_t as follows:

$$E_1 = Y_1$$
$$E_2 = wY_2 + (1 - w)E_1$$
$$E_3 = wY_3 + (1 - w)E_2$$
$$\vdots$$
$$E_t = wY_t + (1 - w)E_{t-1}$$

Example 13.5 Consider the IBM common stock price from January 1981 to December 1983, shown in Table 13.15. Create the exponentially smoothed series using $w = .5$, and plot both series.

Table 13.15 IBM Stock Price and Exponentially Smoothed Series ($w = .5$)

1981	IBM STOCK PRICE	EXPONENTIALLY SMOOTHED STOCK PRICE ($w = .5$)	1982	IBM STOCK PRICE	EXPONENTIALLY SMOOTHED STOCK PRICE ($w = .5$)	1983	IBM STOCK PRICE	EXPONENTIALLY SMOOTHED STOCK PRICE ($w = .5$)
Jan.	$65.500	$65.500	Jan.	$64.625	$60.124	Jan.	$ 98.750	$ 93.923
Feb.	64.500	65.000	Feb.	61.750	60.937	Feb.	100.375	97.149
Mar.	62.125	63.563	Mar.	60.500	60.719	Mar.	104.750	100.950
Apr.	64.875	64.219	Apr.	64.625	62.672	Apr.	117.500	109.225
May	58.500	61.360	May	62.125	62.399	May	112.750	110.988
June	59.125	60.243	June	61.375	61.887	June	121.000	115.994
July	56.375	58.309	July	66.250	64.069	July	122.000	118.997
Aug.	55.375	56.842	Aug.	71.000	67.535	Aug.	119.375	119.186
Sept.	54.875	55.859	Sept.	74.750	71.143	Sept.	128.125	123.656
Oct.	49.625	52.742	Oct.	80.375	75.759	Oct.	126.750	125.203
Nov.	54.500	53.621	Nov.	86.375	81.067	Nov.	117.375	121.289
Dec.	57.625	55.623	Dec.	97.125	89.096	Dec.	122.000	121.644

Solution To create the exponentially smoothed series with $w = .5$, we calculate

$$E_1 = Y_1 = 65.500$$
$$E_2 = wY_2 + (1 - w)E_1$$
$$= .5(64.500) + .5(65.500) = 65.000$$
$$\vdots$$
$$E_{36} = wY_{36} + (1 - w)E_{35}$$
$$= .5(122.000) + .5(121.289) = 121.645$$

The plot of the original and exponentially smoothed series is shown in Figure 13.10.

Figure 13.10 IBM Stock Price and Exponentially Smoothed Price ($w = .5$)

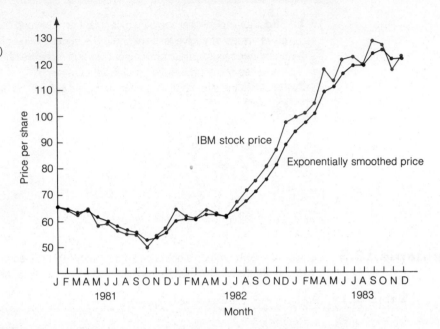

The smoothed series provides a good picture of the general trend of the original series. Notice, however, that the exponentially smoothed series and the original price series are very similar in appearance. This is because the IBM price series is itself relatively smooth over this time period. Nevertheless, the exponentially smoothed series will be less sensitive to any short-term deviations of the prices from the trend and therefore, may be useful even for relatively smooth series. ∎

One of the primary uses of exponential smoothing is for forecasting future values of a time series. Because only current and past values of the time series are used in exponential smoothing, it is easily adapted to forecasting. We will demonstrate this application of exponentially smoothed series in Chapter 15.

Exercises 13.26 – 13.31

Learning the Mechanics

13.26 Describe the effect of selecting an exponential constant of $w = .2$. Of $w = .8$. Which will produce a smoother trend?

13.27 Refer to Exercise 13.21.

a. Calculate the exponentially smoothed series for housing starts using a smoothing constant of $w = .5$.

b. Plot on a graph both the centered 4-point moving average from Exercise 13.21 and the exponentially smoothed series calculated in part a of this exercise. Comment on the differences between the two smoothed series.

13.28 Refer to Exercise 13.2.

a. Calculate the exponentially smoothed series for U.S. beer production for the period 1970–1982 using $w = .2$.

b. Calculate the exponentially smoothed series using $w = .8$.

c. Plot the two exponentially smoothed series ($w = .2$ and $w = .8$) on a graph.

Applying the Concepts

13.29 Standard & Poor's 500 Stock Composite Average (S&P 500) is a stock market index. Like the Dow Jones Average, it is an indicator of stock market activity. The table contains end-of-quarter values of the S&P 500 for the years 1971–1983.

YEAR	QUARTER	S&P 500	YEAR	QUARTER	S&P 500	YEAR	QUARTER	S&P 500
1971	I	100.31	1976	I	102.77	1980	I	105.36
	II	99.20		II	104.28		II	113.72
	III	98.34		III	105.24		III	127.14
	IV	102.09		IV	107.46		IV	131.44
1972	I	107.20	1977	I	98.42	1981	I	134.94
	II	107.14		II	100.48		II	129.06
	III	110.55		III	96.53		III	118.77
	IV	118.06		IV	95.10		IV	119.13
1973	I	111.52	1978	I	89.21	1982	I	117.09
	II	104.26		II	95.53		II	109.82
	III	108.43		III	102.54		III	121.79
	IV	97.55		IV	96.11		IV	138.91
1974	I	93.98	1979	I	101.59	1983	I	151.07
	II	86.00		II	102.91		II	165.11
	III	63.54		III	109.32		III	168.66
	IV	68.56		IV	107.94		IV	164.12
1975	I	83.36						
	II	95.19						
	III	83.87						
	IV	98.19						

Source: *Standard & Poor's Trade and Securities Statistics,* annual, Standard & Poor's Corporation.

a. Compute an exponentially smoothed series for the S&P 500 data using a smoothing coefficient of $w = .7$.

b. Plot the original time series and the exponentially smoothed series on a graph.

13.30 Refer to Exercise 13.18. Use the exponential smoothing constant $w = .5$ to smooth the gold price series between 1970 and 1980.

13.31 Refer to Exercise 13.7. Using $w = .4$, compute an exponentially smoothed series for each of the three time series: white-collar, blue-collar, and service employment. Plot the three smoothed series on the same graph.

13.32 There was phenomenal growth in the transportation sector of the economy during the 1960's and 1970's. The personal consumption expenditure figures are given in the table.

YEAR	PERSONAL CONSUMPTION EXPENDITURE ON TRANSPORTATION ($ billions)	YEAR	PERSONAL CONSUMPTION EXPENDITURE ON TRANSPORTATION ($ billions)
1960	42.4	1972	105.4
1961	44.8	1973	114.6
1962	47.4	1974	117.9
1963	49.5	1975	129.4
1964	54.3	1976	155.2
1965	58.4	1977	179.3
1966	60.4	1978	198.1
1967	63.3	1979	219.4
1968	69.3	1980	239.5
1969	75.7	1981	260.8
1970	80.6	1982	269.9
1971	92.3		

a. Compute exponentially smoothed values of this personal consumption time series using the smoothing constants $w = .2$ and $w = .8$.

b. Plot the actual series and the two smoothed series on the same graph. Comment on the trend in personal consumption expenditure on transportation in the 1970's as compared to the 1960's.

Summary

Time series are observations made sequentially over time. *Index numbers* measure the changes in a time series or group of time series. *Simple* index numbers are based on a single series, while *composite* index numbers measure changes in several series simultaneously. Price indexes that are weighted by purchase quantities are *weighted* composite indexes. *Laspeyres indexes* use weights that are base period purchase quantities, while *Paasche* indexes use the current period purchase quantities as weights.

Smoothing techniques are used to make it easier to discern trends in time series. *Moving averages* combine past, current, and future values of the time series. *Exponential smoothing* combines past and current values of the series.

Supplementary Exercises 13.33 – 13.44

13.33 The U.S. steel industry was the object of much economic attention in the 1970's and early 1980's due to the increasing market share of imported steel, the effects of several recessions, and other economic woes. Prices of different varieties of U.S. steel are given in the table for the period 1971 – 1982.

YEAR	COLD ROLLED STEEL (¢/pound)	HOT ROLLED STEEL (¢/pound)	GALVANIZED STEEL (¢/pound)	YEAR	COLD ROLLED STEEL (¢/pound)	HOT ROLLED STEEL (¢/pound)	GALVANIZED STEEL (¢/pound)
1971	10.00	7.48	9.61	1977	20.39	13.79	18.10
1972	10.77	8.40	10.88	1978	23.11	15.53	20.47
1973	11.08	8.40	10.59	1979	25.55	17.05	22.32
1974	12.78	9.10	12.39	1980	26.50	18.46	23.88
1975	16.03	11.13	14.80	1981	31.50	20.15	26.88
1976	18.16	12.20	16.07	1982	33.25	20.80	26.75

a. Compute 3-point moving averages for each of the three price series.

b. Plot the three price series and their smoothed 3-point moving averages on the same graph.

13.34 Refer to Exercise 13.33.

a. Compute the exponentially smoothed series corresponding to each of the price series using the smoothing constant $w = .5$.

b. Plot the prices and their exponentially smoothed series on the same graph.

c. What is the main advantage associated with using exponential smoothing instead of moving averages for relatively short series like these?

13.35 Refer to Exercise 13.33.

a. Calculate a simple composite index for the three steel price series using 1977 as the base period.

b. Is the index a price index or a quantity index?

c. What information would you need in order to calculate a Laspeyres index with a base period of 1977? A Paasche index with a base period of 1977?

13.36 Foreign exchange rates, the values of foreign currency in U.S. dollars, are important to investors and international travelers. The table lists the monthly foreign exchange rates of the British pound in 1981 and 1982.

MONTH	1981 ($/£)	1982 ($/£)	MONTH	1981 ($/£)	1982 ($/£)
Jan.	2.411	1.885	July	1.876	1.732
Feb.	2.296	1.847	Aug.	1.828	1.728
Mar.	2.236	1.807	Sept.	1.821	1.714
Apr.	2.088	1.774	Oct.	1.846	1.695
May	2.187	1.811	Nov.	1.894	1.635
June	1.985	1.758	Dec.	1.911	1.616

a. Calculate a simple index for the foreign exchange rate series using January 1981 as the base period.

b. Plot the index, and use the plot to identify the best time for a U.S. traveler to visit Britain during this period.

13.37 Refer to Exercise 13.32. Using 1975 as the base period, compute a simple index for the personal consumption series.

13.38 A major portion of total consumer credit is extended in the categories of automobile loans, mobile home loans, and revolving credit. Figures for the period 1972–1982 are given in the table.

Amounts Outstanding
(Thousands of Dollars)

YEAR	AUTOMOBILE	MOBILE HOME	REVOLVING CREDIT
1972	126,759	9,495	7,183
1973	148,177	13,552	9,092
1974	164,594	14,642	13,681
1975	172,353	14,434	15,019
1976	193,992	14,573	17,189
1977	230,564	14,945	39,274
1978	273,645	15,235	48,309
1979	312,024	16,838	56,937
1980	313,472	17,322	58,352
1981	333,375	18,486	63,049
1982	352,246	18,942	68,286

a. Calculate a simple composite index using 1972 as the base period.
b. Compute a simple composite index for the series using 1980 as the base period.
c. Are the indexes constructed in parts a and b price or quantity indexes?
d. Compute a simple index for automobile loans using 1980 as the base. Plot the simple index and the composite index from part b on the same graph.

13.39 Refer to Exercise 13.38.

a. Calculate a 3-point moving average of the simple composite index generated in part b of that exercise.
b. Using a smoothing constant of $w = .3$, calculate an exponentially smoothed series corresponding to the simple composite index.
c. Plot the simple composite index, the 3-point moving average, and the exponentially smoothed series on the same graph. Comment on the relative smoothness of the three series.

13.40 Refer to Exercise 13.38. Assume that in 1980 the number of outstanding loans of each type are as follows:

Automobile: 40,000

Mobile home: 10,000

Revolving credit: 100,000

a. Calculate a Laspeyres index for 1980–1982 using 1980 as a base and the quantities given above.
b. Which category of credit is given most weight in the calculation of the Laspeyres index?

13.41 Refer to Exercise 13.38. Suppose the numbers of outstanding loans in each category from 1980 to 1982 are as shown in the table at the top of the next page.

YEAR	AUTOMOBILE	MOBILE HOME	REVOLVING CREDIT
1980	40,000	10,000	100,000
1981	45,000	11,000	90,000
1982	50,000	15,000	80,000

a. Calculate the Paasche index for 1980–1982 using 1980 as a base and the quantities given in the table.

b. Compare the simple composite index (from Exercise 13.38), the Laspeyres index (from Exercise 13.40), and the Paasche index. Explain why the 1982 values are different for each index, and interpret each.

13.42 Three of the many indicators used for measuring the level of economic activity are the index of net business formation, the index of new private housing units authorized by local building permits, and the index of stock prices. End-of-year values of these indicators for the period 1967–1981 are given in the table.

YEAR	INDEX OF NET BUSINESS FORMATION	INDEX OF NEW PRIVATE HOUSING UNITS AUTHORIZED	INDEX OF STOCK PRICES
1967	105.9	115.2	103.7
1968	116.9	121.8	115.8
1969	114.9	101.3	99.1
1970	105.3	154.9	98.0
1971	115.2	186.9	107.9
1972	119.8	208.5	127.8
1973	114.0	111.0	103.1
1974	106.3	74.9	73.0
1975	116.0	94.0	96.5
1976	121.0	130.2	113.8
1977	134.8	151.2	102.1
1978	133.8	146.8	104.5
1979	133.9	101.3	107.8
1980	121.3	100.9	133.4
1981	106.2	84.4	123.8

a. Calculate a simple composite index for the three indicator series, using 1970 as the base period.

b. Compute the simple index for each of the three indicator series, using a base period of 1970 for each. Plot the three simple indexes and the simple composite index on the same graph.

13.43 Refer to Exercise 13.42.

a. Calculate an exponentially smoothed series corresponding to the index of stock prices using $w = .2$. Using $w = .8$.

b. Plot on a graph both the index of stock prices and the two exponentially smoothed series from part a. Which exponential smoothing constant yields a smoother series? Explain.

YEAR	CPI
1970	116.3
1971	121.3
1972	125.3
1973	133.1
1974	147.7
1975	161.2
1976	170.5
1977	181.5
1978	195.4
1979	217.4
1980	246.8

13.44 The number of dollars a person receives in a year is referred to as his or her *monetary* (or *money*) *income.* This figure can be adjusted to reflect the purchasing power of the dollars received relative to the purchasing power of dollars in some base period. The result is called a person's *real income.* Monetary income and real income can be compared to determine, for example, whether an increase in a person's monetary income truly reflects an increase in his or her purchasing power. The Consumer Price Index (CPI) can be used to adjust monetary income to obtain real income (in terms of 1967 dollars). To compute your real income for a specific year, simply divide your monetary income for the year by that year's CPI and multiply by 100. The table lists the CPI for each year during the period 1970–1980.

a. Suppose your monetary income increased from $20,000 in 1970 to $35,000 in 1980. What were your real incomes in 1970 and 1980? Were you able to buy more goods and services in 1970 or in 1980? Explain.

b. What monetary income would have been required in 1980 to provide equivalent purchasing power to a 1970 monetary income of $20,000?

References

Gillingham, R., & Lane, W., "Changing the treatment of shelter costs for homeowners in the CPI." *Monthly Labor Review,* June 1982, 9–14.

U.S. Department of Labor, *BLS handbook of methods.* Vol. II. "The Consumer Price Index." Bureau of Labor Statistics, Bulletin 2134-2, Apr. 1984.

U.S. Department of Labor, *The Consumer Price Index: Concepts and content over the years.* Bureau of Labor Statistics, Report 517, May 1978.

U.S. Department of Labor, *CPI issues.* Bureau of Labor Statistics, Report S93, Feb. 1980.

CHAPTER 14

Time Series: Models and Forecasting

Where We've Been . . .

In Chapter 13 we discussed methods for describing time series. Index numbers were used to describe changes in a time series; moving averages and exponential smoothing were introduced to describe trends.

Where We're Going . . .

In Chapter 14 we use mathematical models (like the regression models of Chapters 10–12) to describe time series. These models range in complexity from the relatively simple exponential smoothing model to time series models that account for correlation between values observed at different points in time. The primary objective of constructing these models is to use them for forecasting future values of the time series.

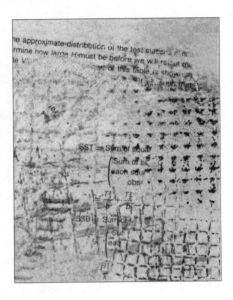

Contents

14.1
Time Series
Components

Before forecasts of future values of a time series can be made, some type of model that can be projected into the future must be used to describe the series. Time series models range in complexity from *descriptive models,* such as the simple moving averages and exponential smoothing models discussed in Chapter 13, to *inferential models,* such as the combinations of regression and specialized time series models to be discussed in this chapter. Whether the model is simple or complex, the objective is the same: to produce accurate forecasts of future values of the time series.

Many different algebraic representations of time series models have been proposed. One of the most widely used is an *additive model** of the form

$$Y_t = T_t + C_t + S_t + R_t$$

Table 14.1

Dow Jones Average, 1961–1983

YEAR	DJA
1961	731.14
1962	652.10
1963	762.95
1964	874.13
1965	969.26
1966	785.69
1967	905.11
1968	943.75
1969	800.36
1970	838.92
1971	884.76
1972	950.71
1973	923.88
1974	759.37
1975	802.49
1976	974.92
1977	835.15
1978	805.01
1979	838.74
1980	936.99
1981	899.01
1982	1,046.54
1983	1,258.64

The *secular trend, T_t,* also known as the *long-term trend,* is a time series that describes the long-term movements of Y_t. For example, if you want to characterize the secular trend of the production of automobiles since 1930, you would show T_t as an upward moving time series over the period from 1930 to the present. This does not imply that the automobile production series has always moved upward from month to month and from year to year, but it does mean the long-term trend has been an increasing one over that period of time.

The *cyclical effect, C_t,* generally describes fluctuations of the time series about the secular trend that are attributable to business and economic conditions at the time. For example, the closing Dow Jones Average for the last business day of the year for the years 1961–1983 is given in Table 14.1. You can see in Figure 14.1[†] that it has a generally increasing secular trend. However, during periods of recession, the Dow Jones Average tends to lie below the secular trend, while in times of general economic expansion, it lies above the long-term trend line.

The *seasonal effect, S_t,* describes the fluctuations in the time series that recur during specific time periods. For example, quarterly power loads for a utility company tend to be highest in the summer months (quarter III), with another smaller peak in the winter months (quarter I). The spring and fall (quarters II and IV) seasonal effects are negative, meaning that the series tends to lie below the long-term trend line during those quarters.

The *residual effect, R_t,* is what remains of Y_t after the secular, cyclical, and seasonal components have been removed. Part of the residual effect may be attributable to unpredictable rare events (earthquake, presidential assassination, people landing on the moon, etc.) and part to the randomness of human actions. In any case, the presence of the residual component makes it impossible to forecast the future values of a time series without error. Thus, the presence of the residual effect emphasizes a point we first made in Chapter 10 in connection with regression models: No business phenomena should be described by deterministic models. All realistic business models, time series or otherwise, should include a residual component.

---

* Another useful form of the model is *multiplicative:* $Y_t = T_t C_t S_t R_t$. This can be changed to an additive form by taking natural logarithms, i.e., $\ln Y_t = \ln T_t + \ln C_t + \ln S_t + \ln R_t$.

[†] The secular trend shown in Figure 14.1 is a 7-point moving average.

Figure 14.1 Secular Trend for the Dow Jones Average

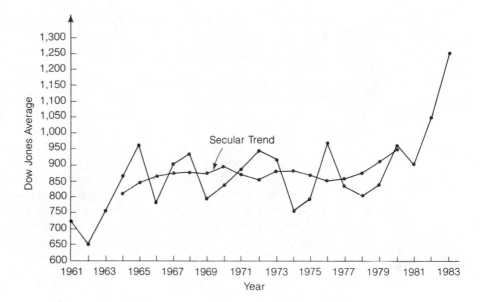

Each of the four components contributes to the determination of the value of Y_t at each time period. Although it will not always be possible to characterize each component separately, the component model provides a useful theoretical formulation that helps the time series analyst achieve a better understanding of the phenomena affecting the path followed by the time series.

14.2 Forecasting: Exponential Smoothing

In Chapter 13, we discussed exponential smoothing as a method for describing a time series by removing the irregular fluctuations. In terms of the time series components discussed in the previous section, exponential smoothing tends to deemphasize (or ''smooth'') most of the residual effects. This, coupled with the fact that exponential smoothing uses only past values of the series, makes it a useful tool for forecasting time series.

Recall that the formula for exponential smoothing is

$$E_t = wY_t + (1 - w)E_{t-1}$$

where w, the **exponential smoothing constant,** ranges from 0 to 1. The selection of w controls the smoothness of E_t. A choice near 0 places more emphasis (weight) on *past* values of the time series and, therefore, yields a smoother series. On the other hand, a choice near 1 gives more weight to *current* values of the series.

Suppose the objective is to forecast the next value of the time series, Y_{t+1}. The **exponential smoothing forecast** is defined as a weighted average of the previous (most recent) value of the time series, Y_t, and the exponentially smoothed value at time t, E_t. That is,

$$F_{t+1} = wY_t + (1 - w)E_t$$

where F_{t+1} is the *forecast* of Y_{t+1}. It is instructive to rearrange the terms in the equation so that

$$F_{t+1} = E_t + w(Y_t - E_t)$$

Thus, the forecast of Y_{t+1} is equal to the exponentially smoothed value at time *t*, plus an *adjustment* for the difference, or error, between the observed and smoothed values at time *t*. This adjustment shows why the exponentially smoothed forecast is an example of an *adaptive forecast* — it explicitly adapts to the error made at time *t*.

Because exponential smoothing consists of averaging past and present values, the smoothed values will tend to lag behind the series when a long-term trend exists. In addition, the averaging tends to smooth any seasonal component. Therefore, exponentially smoothed forecasts are appropriate only when the trend and seasonal components are relatively insignificant. Since the exponential smoothing model assumes that the time series has little or no trend or seasonal component, the forecast F_{t+1} is used to forecast not only Y_{t+1}, but also *all* future values of Y_t. That is, the forecast for two time periods ahead is

$$F_{t+2} = F_{t+1}$$

and for three time periods ahead is

$$F_{t+3} = F_{t+2} = F_{t+1}$$

The exponential smoothing forecasting technique is summarized in the box.

Calculation of Exponentially Smoothed Forecasts

1. Given the observed time series, $Y_1, Y_2, \ldots, Y_t$, first calculate the exponentially smoothed values $E_1, E_2, \ldots, E_t$ using

$$E_1 = Y_1$$
$$E_2 = wY_2 + (1 - w)E_1$$
$$\vdots$$
$$E_t = wY_t + (1 - w)E_{t-1}$$

2. Calculate the forecast, F_{t+1}, for Y_{t+1} as follows:

$$F_{t+1} = wY_t + (1 - w)E_t$$

3. Assuming that Y_t is relatively free of trend and seasonal components, use the same forecast for all future values of Y_t:

$$F_{t+2} = F_{t+1}$$
$$F_{t+3} = F_{t+1}$$
$$\vdots$$

Two important points must be made about exponentially smoothed forecasts:

1. The choice of *w* is critical. If you decide that *w* will be small (near 0), you will obtain a smooth, slowly changing series of forecasts. On the other hand, the selection of a large value of *w* (near 1) will yield more rapidly changing forecasts that depend mostly on the current values of the series. In general, several values of *w* should be tried to determine how sensitive the forecast series is to the choice of *w*. Forecasting experience will provide the best basis for the choice of *w* for a particular application.

2. The further into the future you forecast, the less certain you can be of the accuracy of your forecast. Since the exponentially smoothed forecast is constant for all future values, any changes in trend and/or seasonality are not taken into account. However, the uncertainty associated with future forecasts applies not only to exponentially smoothed forecasts, but also to all methods of forecasting. In general, time series forecasting should be confined to the short term.

Example 14.1

The annual Dow Jones Averages from 1961 to 1980 are given in Table 14.2, along with the exponentially smoothed values using $w = .3$ and $w = .7$. Use the exponential smoothing technique to forecast the values from 1981 to 1983 using both $w = .3$ and $w = .7$.

Table 14.2

Dow Jones Average (1961–1980) with Exponentially Smoothed Values

YEAR	DJA	EXPONENTIALLY SMOOTHED ($w = .3$)	($w = .7$)	YEAR	DJA	EXPONENTIALLY SMOOTHED ($w = .3$)	($w = .7$)
1961	731.14	731.14	731.14	1971	884.76	858.73	870.91
1962	652.10	707.43	675.81	1972	950.71	886.32	926.77
1963	762.95	724.09	736.81	1973	923.88	897.59	924.75
1964	874.13	769.10	832.93	1974	759.37	856.12	808.98
1965	969.26	829.15	928.36	1975	802.49	840.03	804.44
1966	785.69	816.11	828.49	1976	974.92	880.50	923.78
1967	905.11	842.81	882.12	1977	835.15	866.90	861.74
1968	943.75	873.09	925.26	1978	805.01	848.33	822.03
1969	800.36	851.27	837.83	1979	838.74	845.45	833.73
1970	838.92	847.57	838.59	1980	963.99	881.01	924.91

Solution

First, we calculate the exponentially smoothed forecasts using $w = .3$. Following the steps outlined in the box, we find:

$$F_{1981} = wY_{1980} + (1 - w)E_{1980}$$
$$= .3(963.99) + .7(881.01) = 905.90$$

$$F_{1982} = F_{1981} = 905.90$$

$$F_{1983} = F_{1982} = F_{1981} = 905.90$$

The same steps are repeated using $w = .7$, and both sets of forecasts are shown in Table 14.3. Also shown are the actual Dow Jones Averages from 1981 to 1983. The *forecast error,* defined as the actual value minus the forecast value, is given for each exponentially smoothed forecast.

Table 14.3

Dow Jones Forecasts,
1981–1983

YEAR	ACTUAL DJA	FORECAST $(w = .3)$	FORECAST ERROR	FORECAST $(w = .7)$	FORECAST ERROR
1981	899.01	905.90	−6.89	952.27	−53.26
1982	1,046.54	905.90	140.64	952.27	94.27
1983	1,258.64	905.90	352.74	952.27	306.37

Notice that the one-step-ahead forecasts for 1981 have considerably smaller forecast errors than the two- and three-step-ahead forecasts for 1982 and 1983. Neither the $w = .3$ nor the $w = .7$ forecast projects the 1982–1983 upturn in the DJA, because exponentially smoothed forecasts implicitly assume no trend exists in the time series. This example dramatically illustrates the risk associated with anything other than very short-term forecasting. ■

Many time series have long-term, or secular, trends. For such series the exponentially smoothed forecast is inappropriate for all but the very short term. In the next section we present an extension of the exponentially smoothed forecast — the *Holt–Winters forecast* — that allows for secular trend in the forecasts.

14.3 Forecasting Trends: The Holt–Winters Forecasting Model

In this section we present an extension of the exponential smoothing method of forecasting that explicitly recognizes the trend in a time series. The *Holt–Winters forecasting model* consists of both an exponentially smoothed component (E_t) and a trend component (T_t). The trend component is used in the calculation of the exponentially smoothed value. The following equations show that both E_t and T_t are weighted averages:

$$E_t = wY_t + (1 - w)(E_{t-1} + T_{t-1})$$
$$T_t = v(E_t - E_{t-1}) + (1 - v)T_{t-1}$$

Note that the equations require *two* smoothing constants, w and v, each of which is between 0 and 1. As before, w controls the smoothness of E_t; a choice near 0 places more emphasis on past values of the time series, while a value of w near 1 gives more weight to current values of the series, and deemphasizes the past.

The trend component of the series is estimated *adaptively,* using a weighted average of the most recent change in the level and the trend estimate from the previous period. A choice of the weight v near 0 places more emphasis on the past estimates of trend (represented by T_{t-1}), while a choice of v near 1 gives more weight to the current change in level [represented by $(E_t - E_{t-1})$].

The calculation of the Holt–Winters components, which proceeds much like the exponential smoothing calculations, is summarized in the box.

Steps for Calculating Components of Holt–Winters Model

1. Select an exponential smoothing constant w between 0 and 1. Small values of w give less weight to the current values of the time series, and more weight to the past. Larger choices assign more weight to the current value of the series.

2. Select a trend smoothing constant v between 0 and 1. Small values of v give less weight to the current changes in the level of the series, and more weight to the past trend. Larger values assign more weight to the most recent trend of the series and less to past trends.

3. Calculate the two components, E_t and T_t, from the time series Y_t beginning at time $t = 2$ as follows:

$$E_2 = Y_2$$
$$T_2 = Y_2 - Y_1$$
$$E_3 = wY_3 + (1 - w)(E_2 + T_2)$$
$$T_3 = v(E_3 - E_2) + (1 - v)T_2$$
$$\vdots$$
$$E_t = wY_t + (1 - w)(E_{t-1} + T_{t-1})$$
$$T_t = v(E_t - E_{t-1}) + (1 - v)T_{t-1}$$

[*Note:* E_1 and T_1 are not defined.]

Example 14.2

The yearly sales data for a firm's first 35 years of operation are given in Table 14.4. Calculate the Holt–Winters exponential smoothing and trend components for this time series using $w = .7$ and $v = .5$. Show the data and the exponential smoothing component, E_t, on the same graph.

Table 14.4

A Firm's Yearly Sales Revenue (Thousands of Dollars)

t	Y_t	t	Y_t	t	Y_t
1	4.8	13	48.4	25	100.3
2	4.0	14	61.6	26	111.7
3	5.5	15	65.6	27	108.2
4	15.6	16	71.4	28	115.5
5	23.1	17	83.4	29	119.2
6	23.3	18	93.6	30	125.2
7	31.4	19	94.2	31	136.3
8	46.0	20	85.4	32	146.8
9	46.1	21	86.2	33	146.1
10	41.9	22	89.9	34	151.4
11	45.5	23	89.2	35	150.9
12	53.5	24	99.1		

Solution   Following the formulas for the Holt–Winters components given in the box, we calculate:

$$E_2 = Y_2 = 4.0$$

$$T_2 = Y_2 - Y_1 = 4.0 - 4.8 = -0.8$$

$$\begin{aligned} E_3 &= .7Y_3 + (1 - .7)(E_2 + T_2) \\ &= .7(5.5) + .3(4.0 - 0.8) \\ &= 4.8 \end{aligned}$$

$$\begin{aligned} T_3 &= .5(E_3 - E_2) + (1 - .5)T_2 \\ &= .5(4.8 - 4.0) + .5(-0.8) \\ &= 0 \end{aligned}$$

$$\vdots$$

All the E_t and T_t values are given in Table 14.5, and a graph of Y_t and E_t is shown in Figure 14.2. Note that the trend component, T_t, measures the general upward trend in Y_t. The choice of $v = .5$ gives equal weight to the most recent trend and to past trends in the sales of the firm. The result is that the exponential smoothing component, E_t, provides a smooth, upward-trending description of the firm's sales. ∎

Table 14.5   Holt–Winters Components for Sales Data

MONTH	SALES Y_t	E_t (w = .7)	T_t (v = .5)	MONTH	SALES Y_t	E_t (w = .7)	T_t (v = .5)	MONTH	SALES Y_t	E_t (w = .7)	T_t (v = .5)
1	4.8	—	—	13	48.4	50.5	1.1	25	100.3	100.1	3.8
2	4.0	4.0	−0.8	14	61.6	58.6	4.6	26	111.7	109.4	6.5
3	5.5	4.8	.0	15	65.6	64.9	5.4	27	108.2	110.5	3.8
4	15.6	12.4	3.8	16	71.4	71.1	5.8	28	115.5	115.1	4.2
5	23.1	21.0	6.2	17	83.4	81.5	8.1	29	119.2	119.3	4.2
6	23.3	24.5	4.8	18	93.6	92.4	9.5	30	125.2	124.7	4.8
7	31.4	30.8	5.6	19	94.2	96.5	6.8	31	136.3	134.2	7.2
8	46.0	43.1	8.9	20	85.4	90.8	0.5	32	146.8	145.2	9.1
9	46.1	47.9	6.9	21	86.2	87.7	−1.2	33	146.1	148.5	6.2
10	41.9	45.8	2.4	22	89.9	88.9	−0.1	34	151.4	152.4	5.0
11	45.5	46.3	1.4	23	89.2	89.1	0.1	35	150.9	152.9	2.7
12	53.5	51.8	3.5	24	99.1	96.1	3.6				

Our objective is to use the Holt–Winters exponentially smoothed series to forecast future values of the time series. For the one-step-ahead forecast, this is accomplished by adding the most recent exponentially smoothed component to the most recent trend component. That is, the forecast at time $(t + 1)$, given observed values up to time t, is

$$F_{t+1} = E_t + T_t$$

The idea is that we are constructing the forecast by combining the most recent smoothed estimate, E_t, with the estimate of the expected increase (or decrease) attributable to trend, T_t.

The forecast for two steps ahead is similar, except that we add estimated trend for *two* periods:

$$F_{t+2} = E_t + 2T_t$$

Figure 14.2 Sales
Data and Holt–Winters
Exponentially Smoothed
Series

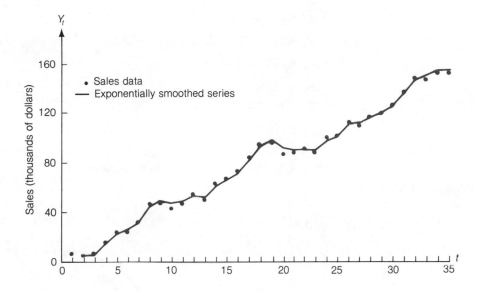

Similarly, for the k-step-ahead forecast, we add the estimated increase (or decrease) in trend over k periods:

$$F_{t+k} = E_t + kT_t$$

The Holt–Winters forecasting methodology is summarized in the box.

Holt–Winters Forecasting

1. Calculate the exponentially smoothed and trend components, E_t and T_t, for each observed value of Y_t $(t \geq 2)$ using the formulas given in the previous box.

2. Calculate the one-step-ahead forecast using

$$F_{t+1} = E_t + T_t$$

3. Calculate the k-step-ahead forecast using

$$F_{t+k} = E_t + kT_t$$

Example 14.3   Refer to Example 14.2 and Table 14.5, where we listed the firm's 35 yearly sales figures, along with the Holt–Winters components using $w = .7$ and $v = .5$. Use the Holt–Winters forecasting technique to forecast the firm's annual sales in years 36–40.

Solution   For year 36 we calculate

$$F_{36} = E_{35} + T_{35}$$
$$= 152.9 + 2.7 = 155.6$$

The forecast 2 years ahead is

$$F_{37} = E_{35} + 2T_{35} = 152.9 + 2(2.7) = 158.3$$

For years 38–40 we find

$$F_{38} = 152.9 + 3(2.7) = 161.0$$
$$F_{39} = 152.9 + 4(2.7) = 163.7$$
$$F_{40} = 152.9 + 5(2.7) = 166.4$$

These forecasts are displayed in Figure 14.3. Note that the upward trend in the forecast is a result of the Holt–Winters estimated trend component. ■

Figure 14.3 Holt–Winters Sales Forecasts, Years 36–40

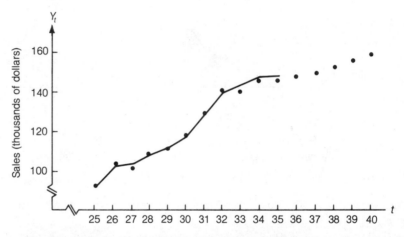

The selection of $w = .7$ and $v = .5$ as the smoothing and trend weights for the sales forecasts in Example 14.3 was based on the objectives of assigning more weight to recent series values in the exponentially smoothed component, and of assigning equal weights to the recent and past trend estimates. However, you may want to try several different combinations of weights when using the Holt–Winters forecasting model so that you can assess the sensitivity of the forecasts to the choice of weights. Experience with the particular time series and Holt–Winters forecasts will help in the selection of w and v in a practical application.

Although the forecast errors can be used to measure forecast accuracy *after* the future values of the time series have been observed, we prefer to have some measure of forecast error *before* the actual values are observed. This is a disadvantage associated with exponentially smoothed forecasts (both the simple and Holt–Winters models): No measure of forecast error (i.e., reliability) is known. However, by using exponentially smoothed forecasts and calculating the forecast errors, a distribution of errors can be generated and used to measure the reliability of the forecasting procedure. Nevertheless, exponential smoothing is more descriptive than inferential, and only inferential models (e.g., regression models) are accompanied by measures of the **standard error of forecast.** Of course, this does not mean that exponential smoothing forecasts will necessarily be outperformed by inferential models—only that the inferential models include a measure of forecast error, while descriptive models, such as the exponential smoothing forecast models, have no such measures. We will discuss an inferential model in the next section.

Exercises
14.1 – 14.6

YEAR	BEER PRODUCTION (Million barrels)
1970	133.1
1971	137.4
1972	141.3
1973	148.6
1974	156.2
1975	160.6
1976	163.7
1977	170.5
1978	179.1
1979	184.2
1980	194.1
1981	193.7
1982	196.2

Learning the Mechanics

14.1 How is the reliability of an exponential smoothing forecast measured?

14.2 The U.S. beer production for the years 1970–1982 is given in the table.

a. Use the 1970–1981 values to forecast the 1982 production using simple exponential smoothing with $w = .3$. With $w = .7$. Calculate the forecast errors associated with each.

b. Use the Holt–Winters model with $w = .7$ and $v = .3$ to forecast the 1982 production. Repeat with $w = .3$ and $v = .7$. Calculate the forecast errors associated with each.

c. Compare the simple exponential smoothing forecasts to the Holt–Winters forecasts. Does there appear to be a trend in the beer production time series? Which forecasting technique is likely to be more appropriate?

14.3 Refer to part a of Exercise 14.2. Use the 1970–1982 values to forecast the 1983 production, using exponential smoothing with $w = .3$. With $w = .7$. Can the errors be measured or estimated for these 1983 forecasts? Explain.

Applying the Concepts

14.4 Standard & Poor's 500 Stock Composite Average (S&P 500) is a stock market index. Like the Dow Jones Industrial Average, it is an indicator of stock market activity. The table contains end-of-quarter values of the S&P 500 for the years 1971–1983.

YEAR	QUARTER	S&P 500	YEAR	QUARTER	S&P 500	YEAR	QUARTER	S&P 500
1971	I	100.31	1976	I	102.77	1980	I	105.36
	II	99.20		II	104.28		II	113.72
	III	98.34		III	105.24		III	127.14
	IV	102.09		IV	107.46		IV	131.44
1972	I	107.20	1977	I	98.42	1981	I	134.94
	II	107.14		II	100.48		II	129.06
	III	110.55		III	96.53		III	118.77
	IV	118.06		IV	95.10		IV	119.13
1973	I	111.52	1978	I	89.21	1982	I	117.09
	II	104.26		II	95.53		II	109.82
	III	108.43		III	102.54		III	121.79
	IV	97.55		IV	96.11		IV	138.91
1974	I	93.98	1979	I	101.59	1983	I	151.07
	II	86.00		II	102.91		II	165.11
	III	63.54		III	109.32		III	168.66
	IV	68.56		IV	107.94		IV	164.12
1975	I	83.36						
	II	95.19						
	III	83.87						
	IV	98.19						

Source: *Standard & Poor's Trade and Securities Statistics*, annual, Standard & Poor's Corporation.

a. Use $w = .7$ to smooth the series between 1971 and 1982. Then forecast the four quarterly values in 1983 using *only* the information through the fourth quarter of 1982.

b. Compute the forecast errors for the 1983 forecasts.

c. Repeat parts a and b using $w = .3$.

d. Use the Holt–Winters methodology with $w = .7$ and $v = .5$ to forecast the 1983 quarterly values. Repeat with $w = .3$ and $v = .5$.

14.5 Refer to Exercise 14.4.

a. Use the 1971–1983 values to forecast the quarterly 1984 values using simple exponential smoothing with $w = .3$ and $w = .7$.

b. Calculate the forecasts using the Holt–Winters model with $w = .3$ and $v = .5$. Repeat with $w = .7$ and $v = .5$.

c. Is there any way to know which of the four sets of forecasts from parts a and b is best? Explain.

14.6 Gold and other precious metals became attractive investments during the inflationary period of the late 1970's and early 1980's. The table shows monthly gold prices from January 1979 to December 1983.

	1979	1980	1981	1982	1983
Jan.	233.7	691.0	523.5	378.0	479.9
Feb.	251.3	636.0	500.5	353.7	490.4
Mar.	239.7	500.5	513.7	320.0	419.7
Apr.	246.3	518.0	477.2	354.5	432.0
May	270.2	526.5	475.5	318.7	437.7
June	283.5	661.5	422.0	317.5	412.8
July	290.1	629.0	401.5	346.2	423.4
Aug.	315.2	636.7	430.0	405.2	416.4
Sept.	402.0	682.0	428.7	409.7	411.5
Oct.	382.0	644.0	430.8	427.7	393.9
Nov.	411.2	627.2	406.7	414.2	382.7
Dec.	559.5	589.7	397.5	444.7	388.0

Source: *Standard & Poor's Statistical Service,* Standard & Poor's Corporation.

a. Use exponential smoothing with $w = .5$ to calculate monthly smoothed values from January 1979 to December 1982. Then forecast the twelve 1983 monthly gold prices.

b. Calculate the forecast errors for 1983. What is the trend in errors as the time distance increases?

c. Calculate twelve one-step-ahead forecasts for 1983 by updating the exponentially smoothed values with each month's actual value, and then forecasting the next month's value.

d. Calculate each month's one-step-ahead forecast error, and compare them with the forecast errors in part b. What does the comparison indicate about the difference between short-term and long-term forecasting?

e. Repeat parts a–d using the Holt–Winters technique with $w = .5$ and $v = .5$.

14.4 Forecasting Trends: Simple Linear Regression

Perhaps the simplest *inferential* forecasting model is one with which you are familiar: the simple linear regression model. A straight-line model is fit relating the time series, Y_t, to the time, t, and the least squares line is used to forecast future values of Y_t.

Suppose a firm is interested in forecasting its sales revenues for each of the next 5 years. To make such forecasts and assess their reliability, a time series model must be constructed. Refer again to the yearly sales data for a firm's 35 years of operation, given in Table 14.4. A plot of the data (Figure 14.4) reveals a linearly increasing trend, so that the model

$$E(Y_t) = \beta_0 + \beta_1 t$$

seems plausible for the secular trend. Fitting the model by least squares (see Section 10.2), we find the least squares model

$$\hat{Y}_t = \hat{\beta}_0 + \hat{\beta}_1 t = .4015 + 4.2956t$$

with

$$SSE = 1,345.45$$

Figure 14.4 Plot of Sales Data

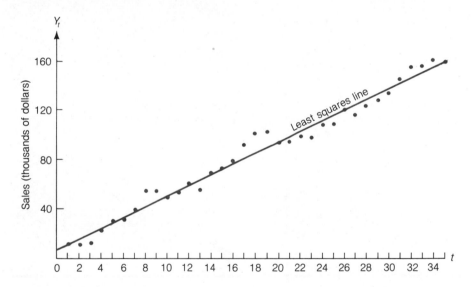

This least squares line is shown in Figure 14.4, and the SAS printout is given in Figure 14.5 on the next page. We can now forecast sales for years 36–40. The forecasts of sales and the corresponding 95% prediction intervals are shown in the printout. For example, for $t = 36$, we have

$$\hat{Y}_{36} = 155.0$$

with the 95% prediction interval (141.3, 168.8). Similarly, we can obtain the forecasts and prediction intervals for years 37–40. The observed sales, forecast sales, and prediction intervals are shown in Figure 14.6. Although it is not easily perceptible in the figure, the

Figure 14.5   SAS Printout for Least Squares Fit (Straight Line) to Y_t = Sales

SOURCE	DF	SUM OF SQUARES	MEAN SQUARE	F VALUE	PR > F
MODEL	1	65875.20816807	65875.20816807	1615.72	0.0001
ERROR	33	1345.45354622	40.77131958		ROOT MSE
CORRECTED TOTAL	34	67220.66171429		R-SQUARE	6.38524233
				0.979985	

PARAMETER	ESTIMATE	T FOR H0: PARAMETER = 0	PR > |T|	STD ERROR OF ESTIMATE
INTERCEPT	0.40151261	0.18	0.8567	2.20570829
T	4.29563025	40.20	0.0001	0.10686692

T	PREDICTED VALUE	LOWER 95% CL INDIVIDUAL	UPPER 95% CL INDIVIDUAL
36	155.04420168	141.30017574	168.78822762
37	159.33983193	145.53232286	173.14734101
38	163.63546218	149.76135290	177.50957147
39	167.93109244	153.98731054	181.87487434
40	172.22672269	158.21024159	186.24320379

Figure 14.6   Observed (Years 1–35) and Forecast (Years 36–40) Sales Using the Straight-Line Model

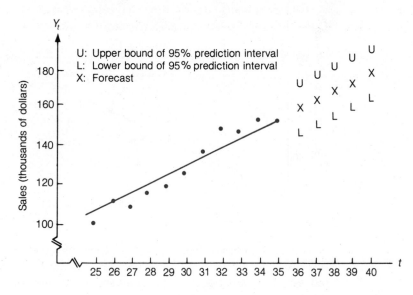

prediction intervals widen as we attempt to forecast further into the future (see the printout in Figure 14.5). This agrees with the intuitive notion that short-term forecasts should be more reliable than long-term forecasts.

There are two problems associated with forecasting time series using a least squares model.

Problem 1   We are using the least squares model to forecast values outside the region of observation of the independent variable, t. That is, we are forecasting for values of t between 36 and 40, but the observed sales are for t values between 1 and 35. As we noted in Chapters 10–12, it is extremely risky to use a least squares regression model for prediction outside the experimental region.

Problem 1 obviously cannot be avoided. Since forecasting always involves predictions about the future values of a time series, some or all of the independent variables will probably be outside the region of observation on which the model was developed. It is important that the forecaster recognize the dangers of this type of prediction. If underlying conditions change drastically after the model is estimated (e.g., if federal price controls are imposed on the firm's products during the 36th year of operation), the forecasts and their confidence intervals are probably useless.

Problem 2   Although the straight-line model may adequately describe the secular trend of the sales, we have not attempted to build any cyclical effects into the model. Thus, the effect of inflationary and recessionary periods will be to increase the error of the forecasts because the model does not anticipate such periods.

Fortunately, the forecaster often has some degree of control over problem 2, as we will demonstrate in the remainder of the chapter.

In forming the prediction intervals for the forecasts, we made the standard regression assumptions (Chapters 10 and 11) about the random error component of the model. We assume the errors have zero mean, constant variance, normal probability distributions, and are *independent*. The latter assumption is dubious in time series models, especially in the presence of short-term trends. Often, if a year's value lies above the secular trend line, the next year's value has a tendency to be above the line also. That is, the errors tend to be correlated (see Figure14.4).

We will discuss how to deal with correlated errors in Sections 14.6 and 14.7. For now, we can characterize the simple linear regression forecasting method as simple and useful for discerning secular trends, but probably too simplistic for most time series. And, as with all forecasting methods, the simple linear regression forecasts should be applied only over the short term.

Case Study 14.1

Forecasting the Demand for Emergency Room Services

In Case Study 6.2, we described how queueing theory was used to model the emergency room of the Richmond Memorial Hospital in Richmond, Virginia. In this case study, we describe how a regression model was used to forecast the demand for emergency room services. In particular, we describe the procedure used by the hospital to forecast the average number of emergency room visits per day during the month of August 1970.

Data were collected on the emergency room's operations since its opening in October 1955 (month 1) through January 1970 (month 124). The data on patient visits for each August since the emergency room opened are shown in Table 14.6 (next page). A straight-line regression model was used to model the trend in Y_t, the average number of visits per day during August. Using time, t (measured in months), as the independent variable, the following least squares model was obtained:

$$\hat{Y}_t = 38.788 + .60990t$$

Table 14.6

Emergency Room Data
for the Month of August:
1959–1969

MONTH t	NUMBER OF VISITS	AVERAGE NUMBER OF VISITS PER DAY Y_t	MONTH t	NUMBER OF VISITS	AVERAGE NUMBER OF VISITS PER DAY Y_t
11	1,367	44.09	71	3,019	97.38
23	1,642	52.96	83	2,794	90.12
35	1,780	57.41	95	2,846	91.80
47	2,060	66.45	107	3,001	96.80
59	2,257	72.80	119	3,548	114.45

This least squares line is plotted on a scattergram of the data in Figure 14.7. The plot reveals an upward trend in emergency room visits. Although some seasonal variation was present, a similar upward trend was observed for the other 11 months of the year. It was determined that the increase in the demand for emergency room services was greater than the rise in the Richmond area population. This finding substantiated management's belief that the emergency room was increasingly serving as a replacement for the family physician.

Figure 14.7 Least
Squares Trend Line for
Average Number of Visits
per Day During August

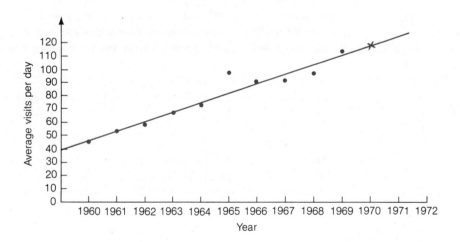

For August 1970, the model yielded a point forecast of $\hat{Y}_{131} = 38.788 + .60990(131) = 118.68$ for the average number of visits per day. The associated 95% prediction interval was (100.20, 137.16). The actual demand in August turned out to be 119.20 and is indicated by a cross (×) in the plot of Figure 14.7. Thus, the actual demand fell close to the least squares trend line and well within the bounds of the prediction interval.

Even for projections 18 months into the future, the hospital found this least squares prediction procedure to be superior to previous methods employed by the hospital. As a result, it was adopted for regular use in budgeting for the emergency room and associated services (Bolling, 1972).

14.5 Seasonal Regression Models

Many time series have distinct seasonal patterns. Retail sales are usually highest around Christmas, spring, and fall, with lulls in the winter and summer periods. Energy usage is highest in summer and winter, and lowest in spring and fall. Teenage unemployment rises in summer months when schools are not in session, and falls near Christmas when many businesses hire part-time help.

Multiple regression models can be used to forecast future values of a time series with strong seasonal components. To accomplish this, the mean value of the time series, $E(Y_t)$, is given a mathematical form that describes both the secular trend and seasonal components of the time series. Although the seasonal model can assume a wide variety of mathematical forms, the use of dummy variables to describe seasonal differences is common.

For example, consider the power load data for a southern utility company shown in Table 14.7. Data have been obtained on a quarterly basis from 1971 to 1982. A model that combines the expected growth in usage and the seasonal component is

$$E(Y_t) = \beta_0 + \beta_1 t + \beta_2 Q_1 + \beta_3 Q_2 + \beta_4 Q_3$$

Table 14.7

Quarterly Power Loads for a Southern Utility Company, 1971–1982

YEAR	QUARTER	POWER LOAD (Megawatts)	YEAR	QUARTER	POWER LOAD (Megawatts)
1971	1	68.8	1977	1	130.6
	2	65.0		2	116.8
	3	88.4		3	144.2
	4	69.0		4	123.3
1972	1	83.6	1978	1	142.3
	2	69.7		2	124.0
	3	90.2		3	146.1
	4	72.5		4	135.5
1973	1	106.8	1979	1	147.1
	2	89.2		2	119.3
	3	110.7		3	138.2
	4	91.7		4	127.6
1974	1	108.6	1980	1	143.4
	2	98.9		2	134.0
	3	120.1		3	159.6
	4	102.1		4	135.1
1975	1	113.1	1981	1	149.5
	2	94.2		2	123.3
	3	120.5		3	154.4
	4	107.4		4	139.4
1976	1	116.2	1982	1	151.6
	2	104.4		2	133.7
	3	131.7		3	154.5
	4	117.9		4	135.1

where

t = Time period, ranging from $t = 1$ for quarter 1, 1971, to $t = 48$ for quarter 4, 1982

$$Q_1 = \begin{cases} 1 & \text{if quarter 1} \\ 0 & \text{if quarter 2, 3, or 4} \end{cases}$$

$$Q_2 = \begin{cases} 1 & \text{if quarter 2} \\ 0 & \text{if quarter 1, 3, or 4} \end{cases}$$

$$Q_3 = \begin{cases} 1 & \text{if quarter 3} \\ 0 & \text{if quarter 1, 2, or 4} \end{cases}$$

The printout in Figure 14.8 shows the least squares fit of this model to the data in Table 14.7.

Figure 14.8
SAS Printout of Least Squares Fit to Power Load Time Series

```
DEPENDENT VARIABLE: POWER LOAD

SOURCE                    DF    SUM OF SQUARES      MEAN SQUARE     F VALUE

MODEL                      4    28374.99250583    7093.74812646     114.88
ERROR                     43     2655.13561917      61.74733998     PR > F
CORRECTED TOTAL           47    31030.12812500                      0.0001

R-SQUARE          C.V.           ROOT MSE          Y3 MEAN

0.914434          6.6766         7.85794757        117.69375000

                                 T FOR H0:      PR > !T!    STD ERROR OR
PARAMETER          ESTIMATE      PARAMETER=0                  ESTIMATE

INTERCEPT        70.50852273 B      22.63        0.0001       3.11552479
T                 1.63621066        19.92        0.0001       0.08213932
QUARTER    1     13.65863199 B       4.25        0.0001       3.21744388
           2     -3.73591200 B      -1.16        0.2512       3.21219719
           3     18.46954400 B       5.76        0.0001       3.20904506
           4      0.00000000 B
```

Note that the model appears to fit well, with $R^2 = .91$, indicating that the model accounts for 91% of the sample variability in power loads over the 12-year period. The global $F = 114.88$ strongly supports the hypothesis that the model has predictive utility. The standard deviation (ROOT MSE) of 7.86 indicates that the model predictions will usually be accurate to within approximately $\pm 2(7.86)$, or about ± 16 megawatts. Furthermore, $\hat{\beta}_1 = 1.64$ indicates an estimated average growth in load of 1.64 megawatts per quarter. Finally, the seasonal dummy variables have the following interpretations (refer to Chapter 12):

$\hat{\beta}_2 = 13.66$ Quarter 1 loads average 13.66 megawatts more than quarter 4 loads.

$\hat{\beta}_3 = -3.74$ Quarter 2 loads average 3.74 megawatts less than quarter 4 loads.

$\hat{\beta}_4 = 18.47$ Quarter 3 loads average 18.47 megawatts more than quarter 4 loads.

Thus, as expected, winter and summer loads exceed spring and fall loads, with the peak occurring during the summer months.

In order to forecast the 1983 power loads, we calculate the predicted value $\hat{Y}$ for $k = 49$, 50, 51, and 52, at the same time substituting the dummy variable appropriate for each quarter. Thus, for 1983,

$$\hat{Y}_{\text{Quarter 1}} = \hat{\beta}_0 + \hat{\beta}_1(49) + \hat{\beta}_2 = 70.51 + 1.636(49) + 13.66 = 164.3$$

$$\hat{Y}_{\text{Quarter 2}} = \hat{\beta}_0 + \hat{\beta}_1(50) + \hat{\beta}_3 = 148.6$$

$$\hat{Y}_{\text{Quarter 3}} = \hat{\beta}_0 + \hat{\beta}_1(51) + \hat{\beta}_4 = 172.4$$

$$\hat{Y}_{\text{Quarter 4}} = \hat{\beta}_0 + \hat{\beta}_1(52) = 155.6$$

The predicted values and 95% prediction intervals are given in Table 14.8; the data and least squares predicted values are graphed in Figure 14.9. The color line on the graph connects the predicted values. Also shown in Table 14.8 and Figure 14.9 are the actual 1983 quarterly power loads. Notice that all 1983 power loads fall inside the forecast intervals.

Table 14.8

Predicted Power Loads, Confidence Intervals, and Actual Power Loads (Megawatts) for 1983

QUARTER	PREDICTED LOAD	LOWER 95% CONFIDENCE LIMIT	UPPER 95% CONFIDENCE LIMIT	ACTUAL LOAD
1	164.3	147.3	181.4	151.3
2	148.6	131.5	165.6	132.9
3	172.4	155.4	189.5	160.5
4	155.6	138.5	172.6	161.0

Figure 14.9 Regression Forecasting Model for a Southern Utility Company

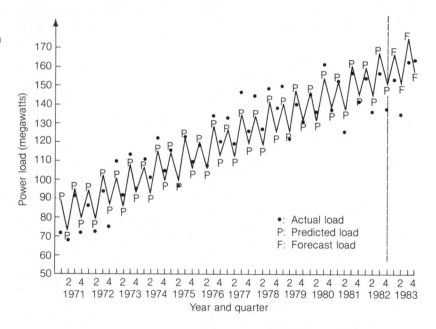

The seasonal model used to forecast the power loads is an *additive model* because the secular trend component ($\beta_1 t$) is added to the seasonal component ($\beta_2 Q_1 + \beta_3 Q_2 + \beta_4 Q_3$) to form the model. A *multiplicative model* would have the same form, except that the dependent variable would be the natural logarithm of power load; i.e.,

$$\ln Y_t = \beta_0 + \beta_1 t + \beta_2 Q_1 + \beta_3 Q_2 + \beta_4 Q_3 + \varepsilon$$

To see the multiplicative nature of this model, we take the antilogarithm of both sides of the equation to get

$$Y_t = \exp\{\beta_0 + \beta_1 t + \beta_2 Q_1 + \beta_3 Q_2 + \beta_4 Q_3 + \varepsilon\}$$
$$= \underbrace{\exp\{\beta_0\}}_{\text{Constant}} \underbrace{\exp\{\beta_1 t\}}_{\substack{\text{Secular} \\ \text{trend}}} \underbrace{\exp\{\beta_2 Q_1 + \beta_3 Q_2 + \beta_4 Q_3\}}_{\substack{\text{Seasonal} \\ \text{component}}} \underbrace{\exp\{\varepsilon\}}_{\substack{\text{Residual} \\ \text{component}}}$$

The multiplicative model often provides a better forecasting model when the time series is changing at an increasing rate over time.

If the time series data are observed monthly, a regression forecasting model would have to use eleven dummy variables to describe monthly seasonality, or three dummy variables could be used (as in the previous models) if the seasonal changes are hypothesized to occur quarterly. In general, this approach to seasonal modeling requires one dummy variable less than the number of seasonal changes expected to occur.

There are approaches in addition to the regression dummy variable method for forecasting seasonal time series. Trigonometric (sine and cosine) terms can be used in regression models to model periodicity. Other time series models (the Holt–Winters exponential smoothing model, for example) do not make use of the regression approach at all, and there are various methods for adding seasonal components to these models. We have chosen to discuss the regression approach because it makes use of the important modeling concepts covered in Chapters 11 and 12, and because the regression forecasts are accompanied by prediction intervals that provide some measure of the forecast reliability. While most other methods do not have explicit measures of reliability, many have proved their merit by providing good forecasts for particular applications. Consult the references at the end of this chapter for details of other seasonal models.

Exercises 14.7–14.12

Learning the Mechanics

[*Note:*　*Starred (*) exercises require the use of a computer.*]

14.7 What is the advantage of regression forecasts as compared with exponentially smoothed forecasts? Does this advantage assure that regression forecasts will prove to be more accurate?

14.8 The annual price of galvanized steel (in cents per pound) from 1971 to 1982 is shown in the table. Use simple linear regression to forecast the 1983 and 1984 prices. Calculate the 95% forecast intervals for each.

YEAR	PRICE	YEAR	PRICE
1971	9.61	1977	18.10
1972	10.88	1978	20.47
1973	10.59	1979	22.32
1974	12.39	1980	23.88
1975	14.80	1981	26.88
1976	16.07	1982	26.75

*14.9 Quarterly retail sales over a 10-year period for a department store are shown (in hundred thousand dollars) in the table.

| YEAR | QUARTER | | | |
	1	2	3	4
1	8.3	10.3	8.7	13.5
2	9.8	12.1	10.1	15.4
3	12.1	14.5	12.7	17.1
4	13.7	16.0	14.2	19.2
5	17.4	19.7	18.0	23.1
6	18.2	20.5	18.6	24.0
7	20.0	22.2	20.5	25.1
8	22.3	25.1	22.9	27.7
9	24.7	26.9	25.1	29.8
10	25.8	28.7	26.0	32.2

a. Write a regression model that contains trend and seasonal components to describe the sales data.

b. Use a least squares regression program to fit the model. Evaluate the fit of the model and interpret the coefficients.

c. Use the regression model to forecast the quarterly sales during the 11th year. Give 95% confidence intervals for the forecasts.

Applying the Concepts

14.10 There was phenomenal growth in the transportation sector of the U.S. economy during the 1960's and 1970's. The personal consumption expenditure figures (in billion dollars) for this sector are given in the table.

YEAR	EXPENDITURE	YEAR	EXPENDITURE
1960	42.4	1972	105.4
1961	44.8	1973	114.6
1962	47.4	1974	117.9
1963	49.5	1975	129.4
1964	54.3	1976	155.2
1965	58.4	1977	179.3
1966	60.4	1978	198.1
1967	63.3	1979	219.4
1968	69.3	1980	239.5
1969	75.7	1981	260.8
1970	80.6	1982	269.9
1971	92.3		

a. Fit the simple regression model

$$E(Y_t) = \beta_0 + \beta_1 t$$

where t is the number of years since 1960 (i.e., $t = 0, 1, \ldots, 22$).

b. Forecast the personal consumption expenditure from 1983 to 1985. Calculate 95% confidence intervals for these forecasts.

*14.11 The table presents the quarterly sales index for a particular brand of calculator at a campus bookstore. The quarters are based on an academic year, so the first quarter represents fall; the second, winter; the third, spring; and the fourth, summer.

YEAR	FIRST QUARTER	SECOND QUARTER	THIRD QUARTER	FOURTH QUARTER
1979	438	398	252	160
1980	464	429	376	216
1981	523	496	425	318
1982	593	576	456	398
1983	636	640	526	498

a. Fit the model

$$E(Y_t) = \beta_0 + \beta_1 t + \beta_2 Q_1 + \beta_3 Q_2 + \beta_4 Q_3$$

where

$$Q_1 = \begin{cases} 1 & \text{if quarter 1} \\ 0 & \text{otherwise} \end{cases} \qquad Q_2 = \begin{cases} 1 & \text{if quarter 2} \\ 0 & \text{otherwise} \end{cases} \qquad Q_3 = \begin{cases} 1 & \text{if quarter 3} \\ 0 & \text{otherwise} \end{cases}$$

Evaluate the fit and interpret the model estimates.

b. Use the model to forecast the quarterly 1984 sales. Place 95% confidence intervals on the forecasts.

14.12 A composite index incorporating twelve leading indicators of the state of the economy is given in the table.

YEAR	COMPOSITE INDEX	YEAR	COMPOSITE INDEX
1967	104.6	1975	119.6
1968	112.1	1976	127.7
1969	108.2	1977	140.2
1970	109.0	1978	143.0
1971	117.9	1979	135.5
1972	132.1	1980	137.3
1973	129.3	1981	127.1
1974	109.8	1982	132.8

a. Use the method of least squares to fit a simple regression model to the index.

b. Forecast the 1983 and 1984 index values, and calculate 95% confidence intervals for the forecasts.

14.6 Autocorrelation and the Durbin–Watson Test

Recall that one of the assumptions we make when using a regression model to make predictions is that the errors are independent. However, with time series data, this assumption is questionable. The cyclical component of a time series may result in deviations from the secular trend that tend to cluster alternately on the positive and negative sides of the trend, as shown in Figure 14.10.

The observed errors between the time series and the regression model for the secular trend (and seasonal component, if present) are called *time series residuals.* Thus, if the time series Y_t has an estimated trend of $\hat{Y}_t$, then the time series residual is

$$\hat{R}_t = Y_t - \hat{Y}_t$$

Figure 14.10 Illustration of Cyclical Errors

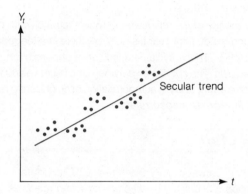

For example, consider the sales forecasting data in Table 14.4 (page 633), to which we fit a simple straight-line regression model. The plot of the data and model is repeated in Figure 14.11, and a plot of the time series residuals is shown in Figure 14.12 (page 650).

Figure 14.11 Plot of Sales Data

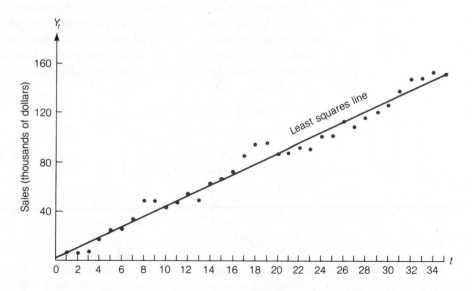

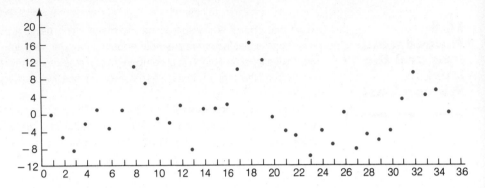

Notice the tendency of the residuals to group alternately into positive and negative clusters. That is, if the residual for year t is positive, there is a tendency for the residual for year $(t + 1)$ to be positive. These cycles are indicative of possible positive correlation between neighboring residuals. The correlation between time series residuals at different points in time is called *autocorrelation,* and the autocorrelation of neighboring residuals (time periods t and $t + 1$) is called *first-order autocorrelation.*

Definition 14.1

The correlation between time series residuals at different points in time is called *autocorrelation.* Correlation between neighboring residuals (at times t and $t + 1$) is called *first-order autocorrelation.* In general, correlation between residuals at times t and $t + d$ is called dth order autocorrelation.

Rather than speculate about the presence of autocorrelation among time series residuals, we prefer to test for it. For most business economic time series, the relevant test is for first-order autocorrelation. Other higher-order autocorrelations may indicate seasonality, e.g., fourth-order autocorrelation in a quarterly time series. However, when we use the term *autocorrelation* in this text we are referring to first-order autocorrelation unless otherwise specified. So, we test

H_0: No first-order autocorrelation of residuals

H_a: Positive first-order autocorrelation of residuals

The *Durbin–Watson d statistic* is used to test for the presence of first-order autocorrelation. The statistic is given by the formula

$$d = \frac{\sum_{t=2}^{n} (\hat{R}_t - \hat{R}_{t-1})^2}{\sum_{t=1}^{n} \hat{R}_t^2}$$

where n is the number of observations (time periods) and $(\hat{R}_t - \hat{R}_{t-1})$ represents the difference between a pair of successive time series residuals. The value of d always falls in the interval from 0 to 4. The interpretations of the values of d are given in the box. Most statistical software packages include a routine that calculates d for time series residuals.

Interpretation of Durbin–Watson d Statistic

$$d = \frac{\sum_{t=2}^{n} (\hat{R}_t - \hat{R}_{t-1})^2}{\sum_{t=1}^{n} \hat{R}_t^2}$$

Range of d: $0 \le d \le 4$

1. If the residuals are uncorrelated, then $d \approx 2$.
2. If the residuals are positively autocorrelated, then $d < 2$, and if the autocorrelation is very strong, $d \approx 0$.
3. If the residuals are negatively autocorrelated, then $d > 2$, and if the autocorrelation is very strong, $d \approx 4$.

Durbin and Watson (1951) give tables for the lower-tail values of the d statistic, which we show in Tables XV ($\alpha = .05$) and XVI ($\alpha = .01$) of Appendix B. Part of Table XV is reproduced in Table 14.9 (page 652). For the sales example, we have $k = 1$ independent variable and $n = 35$ observations. Using $\alpha = .05$ for the one-tailed test for positive autocorrelation, we obtain the tabled values $d_L = 1.40$ and $d_U = 1.52$. The meaning of these values is illustrated in Figure 14.13. Because of the complexity of the sampling distribution of d, it is not possible to specify a single point that acts as a boundary between the rejection and nonrejection regions, as we did for the z, t, F, and other test statistics. Instead, an upper (d_U) and lower (d_L) bound are specified so that a d value less than d_L *does* provide strong evidence of positive autocorrelation at $\alpha = .05$ (recall that small d values indicate positive autocorrelation), a d value greater than d_U *does not* provide evidence of positive autocorrelation at $\alpha = .05$, and a value of d between d_L and d_U might or might not be significant at the $\alpha = .05$ level. If $d_L < d < d_U$, more information is needed before we can reach any conclusion about the presence of autocorrelation.

Figure 14.13 Rejection Region for the Durbin–Watson d Test: Sales Example

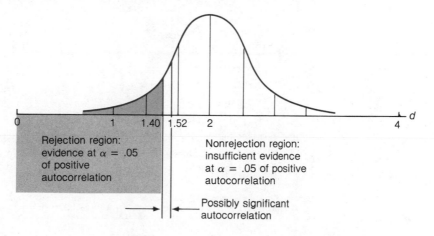

Rejection region: evidence at $\alpha = .05$ of positive autocorrelation

Nonrejection region: insufficient evidence at $\alpha = .05$ of positive autocorrelation

Possibly significant autocorrelation

Table 14.9

Reproduction of Part of
Table XV, Appendix B
($\alpha = .05$)

n	$k = 1$		$k = 2$		$k = 3$		$k = 4$		$k = 5$	
	d_L	d_U	d_L	d_U	d_L	d_U	d_L	d_U	d_L	d_U
31	1.36	1.50	1.30	1.57	1.23	1.65	1.16	1.74	1.09	1.83
32	1.37	1.50	1.31	1.57	1.24	1.65	1.18	1.73	1.11	1.82
33	1.38	1.51	1.32	1.58	1.26	1.65	1.19	1.73	1.13	1.81
34	1.39	1.51	1.33	1.58	1.27	1.65	1.21	1.73	1.15	1.81
35	1.40	1.52	1.34	1.58	1.28	1.65	1.22	1.73	1.16	1.80
36	1.41	1.52	1.35	1.59	1.29	1.65	1.24	1.73	1.18	1.80
37	1.42	1.53	1.36	1.59	1.31	1.66	1.25	1.72	1.19	1.80
38	1.43	1.54	1.37	1.59	1.32	1.66	1.26	1.72	1.21	1.79
39	1.43	1.54	1.38	1.60	1.33	1.66	1.27	1.72	1.22	1.79
40	1.44	1.54	1.39	1.60	1.34	1.66	1.29	1.72	1.23	1.79

Tests for negative autocorrelation and two-tailed tests can be conducted by making use of the symmetry of the sampling distribution of the d statistic about its mean, 2 (see Figure 14.13). The test procedure is summarized in the accompanying box.

Durbin–Watson d Test

One-Tailed Test

H_0: No first-order autocorrelation

H_a: Positive first-order autocorrelation
(or H_a: Negative first-order auto-correlation)

Test statistic:

$$d = \frac{\sum_{t=2}^{n} (\hat{R}_t - \hat{R}_{t-1})^2}{\sum_{t=1}^{n} \hat{R}_t^2}$$

Rejection region: $d < d_{L,\alpha}$
[or $(4 - d) < d_{L,\alpha}$ if
H_a: Negative first-order autocorrelation]

where $d_{L,\alpha}$ is the lower tabled value corresponding to k independent variables and n observations. The corresponding upper value, $d_{U,\alpha}$, defines a "possibly significant" region between $d_{L,\alpha}$ and $d_{U,\alpha}$ (see Figure 14.13).

Two-Tailed Test

H_0: No first-order autocorrelation

H_a: Positive or negative first-order autocorrelation

Test statistic:

$$d = \frac{\sum_{t=2}^{n} (\hat{R}_t - \hat{R}_{t-1})^2}{\sum_{t=1}^{n} \hat{R}_t^2}$$

Rejection region: $d < d_{L,\alpha/2}$
or $(4 - d) < d_{L,\alpha/2}$

where $d_{L,\alpha/2}$ is the lower tabled value corresponding to k independent variables and n observations. The corresponding upper value, $d_{U,\alpha/2}$, defines a "possibly significant" region between $d_{L,\alpha/2}$ and $d_{U,\alpha/2}$ (see Figure 14.13).

Assumption: The residuals are normally distributed.

The SAS printout for the sales example is presented in Figure 14.14. It shows that the computed value of d is .82, which is less than the tabulated value of $d_L = 1.40$. Thus, we conclude that the residuals of the straight-line model for sales are positively autocorrelated.

Figure 14.14

SAS Printout for the Regression Analysis: Annual Sales Data

```
DEPENDENT VARIABLE: Y     SALES (THOUSANDS OF DOLLARS)

SOURCE                DF      SUM OF SQUARES      MEAN SQUARE     F VALUE

MODEL                  1      65875.20816807   65875.20816807    1615.72
ERROR                 33       1345.45354622      40.77131958     PR > F
CORRECTED TOTAL       34      67220.66171429                      0.0001


R-SQUARE           C.V.            ROOT MSE           Y MEAN

0.979985         8.2154          6.38524233        77.72285714


                            T FOR H0:    PR > ITI   STD ERROR OF
PARAMETER     ESTIMATE     PARAMETER=0             ESTIMATE

INTERCEPT   0.40151261          0.18      0.8567    2.20570829
T           4.29563025         40.20      0.0001    0.10686692


OBSERVATION     OBSERVED VALUE    PREDICTED VALUE        RESIDUAL

     1            4.80000000         4.69714286       0.10285714
     2            4.00000000         8.99277311      -4.99277311
     3            5.50000000        13.28840336      -7.78840336
     4           15.60000000        17.58403361      -1.98403361
     5           23.10000000        21.87966387       1.22033613
     6           23.30000000        26.17529412      -2.87529412
     7           31.40000000        30.47092437       0.92907563
     8           46.00000000        34.76655462      11.23344538
     9           46.10000000        39.06218487       7.03781513
    10           41.90000000        43.35781513      -1.45781513
    11           45.50000000        47.65344538      -2.15344538
    12           53.50000000        51.94907563       1.55092437
    13           48.40000000        56.24470588      -7.84470588
    14           61.60000000        60.54033613       1.05966387
    15           65.60000000        64.83596639       0.76403361
    16           71.40000000        69.13159664       2.26840336
    17           83.40000000        73.42722689       9.97277311
    18           93.60000000        77.72285714      15.87714286
    19           94.20000000        82.01848739      12.18151261
    20           85.40000000        86.31411765      -0.91411765
    21           86.20000000        90.60974790      -4.40974790
    22           89.90000000        94.90537815      -5.00537815
    23           89.20000000        99.20100840     -10.00100840
    24           99.10000000       103.49663866      -4.39663866
    25          100.30000000       107.79226891      -7.49226891
    26          111.70000000       112.08789916      -0.38789916
    27          108.20000000       116.38352941      -8.18352941
    28          115.50000000       120.67915966      -5.17915966
    29          119.20000000       124.97478992      -5.77478992
    30          125.20000000       129.27042017      -4.07042017
    31          136.30000000       133.56605042       2.73394958
    32          146.80000000       137.86168067       8.93831933
    33          146.10000000       142.15731092       3.94268908
    34          151.40000000       146.45294118       4.94705882
    35          150.90000000       150.74857143       0.15142857
  SUM OF RESIDUALS                                    0.00000000
  SUM OF SQUARED RESIDUALS                          1345.45354622
  SUM OF SQUARED RESIDUALS - ERROR SS               -0.00000000
  FIRST ORDER AUTOCORRELATION                        0.58962415
  DURBIN-WATSON D                                    0.82072679
```

Once strong evidence of first-order autocorrelation has been established, as in the case of the sales example, doubt is cast on the least squares results and any inferences drawn from them. In the next section, we will present a time series model that accounts for the autocorrelation of the random errors. The residual correlation can be taken into account in a time series model and thereby used to improve both the fit of the model and the reliability of model inferences and forecasts.

Exercises 14.13–14.16

Learning the Mechanics

14.13 Define autocorrelation. Explain why it is important in time series modeling and forecasting.

14.14 Suppose you fit the seasonal model

$$E(Y_t) = \beta_0 + \beta_1 t + \beta_2 Q_1 + \beta_3 Q_2 + \beta_4 Q_3$$

to quarterly time series data collected over a 10-year period.

a. Set up the test of hypothesis for positively correlated residuals. Specify H_0, H_a, the test statistic, and the rejection region.

b. Suppose the Durbin–Watson d statistic is calculated to be 1.14. What is the appropriate conclusion?

Applying the Concepts

14.15 The decrease in the value of the dollar from 1964 to 1979 is illustrated by the data in the table. The buying power of the dollar (compared with 1967) is listed for each year. The first-order model

$$Y_t = \beta_0 + \beta_1 t + \varepsilon$$

was fit to the data using the method of least squares. The following least squares estimates of β_0 and β_1 were calculated:

$$\hat{\beta}_0 = 85.092 \quad \text{and} \quad \hat{\beta}_1 = -.0427$$

YEAR t	VALUE Y_t	YEAR t	VALUE Y_t
1964	1.076	1972	.799
1965	1.058	1973	.755
1966	1.029	1974	.680
1967	1.000	1975	.621
1968	.960	1976	.587
1969	.911	1977	.551
1970	.860	1978	.512
1971	.824	1979	.467

Source: *Statistical Abstract of the United States: 1980.*

a. Calculate and plot the regression residuals against t. Is there a tendency for the residuals to have long positive and negative runs? To what do you attribute this phenomenon?

b. Calculate the Durbin–Watson d statistic, and test the null hypothesis that the time series residuals are uncorrelated. Use $\alpha = .05$.

c. What assumption(s) must be satisfied in order for the test of part b to be valid?

14.16 The table gives the factory sales of passenger cars in the United States for the years 1975 and 1976.

MONTH	TIME t	1975 SALES Y_t (thousands)	TIME t	1976 SALES Y_t (thousands)
Jan.	1	391.4	13	647.4
Feb.	2	410.5	14	682.0
Mar.	3	492.6	15	834.5
Apr.	4	586.2	16	789.0
May	5	612.6	17	775.6
June	6	632.1	18	850.1
July	7	504.5	19	558.8
Aug.	8	484.6	20	518.4
Sept.	9	667.5	21	652.1
Oct.	10	745.6	22	690.8
Nov.	11	605.9	23	766.1
Dec.	12	579.5	24	732.7

Source: *Business and Statistical Abstracts, 1977.*

a. Fit the first-order time series model

$$Y_t = \beta_0 + \beta_1 t + \varepsilon$$

to the data using the method of least squares.

b. Is there evidence at the $\alpha = .10$ level of significance that the residuals are autocorrelated?

14.7 Forecasting with Autoregressive Models

The Durbin–Watson d test can be used to test for the presence of first-order autocorrelation. After we are convinced that the time series residuals are autocorrelated, we will want to take advantage of this autocorrelation to obtain better forecasts.

We can take advantage of autocorrelated residuals by modeling the residual component of the time series. A useful model for autocorrelated time series residuals is the *first-order autoregressive model* for the residual component R_t:*

$$R_t = \phi R_{t-1} + \varepsilon_t$$

where ϕ (the Greek letter phi) is a constant coefficient between -1 and 1, and ε_t is a normally distributed and *independent* time series (called *white noise* by time series analysts) with a

---

* We use R_t to denote the true residual, $Y_t - E(Y_t)$, and $\hat{R}_t$ to denote the estimated residual, $Y_t - \hat{Y}_t$.

mean of 0 and a constant variance. This model implies that values of R_t are autocorrelated. The first-order autocorrelation of R_t and R_{t-1} is equal to ϕ, and the dth-order autocorrelation between residuals d time periods apart, R_t and R_{t-d}, is equal to ϕ^d. The autocorrelations corresponding to first-order autoregressive models are shown for several values of ϕ in Figure 14.15.

Note that the first-order autocorrelation is largest, and the autocorrelations diminish rapidly

Figure 14.15 Auto-correlation Functions for Several First-Order Autoregressive Models: $R_t = \phi R_{t-1} + \varepsilon_t$

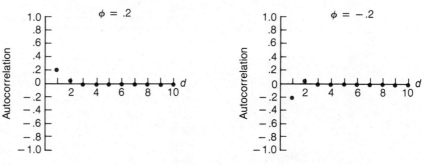

(a) Weak autocorrelation

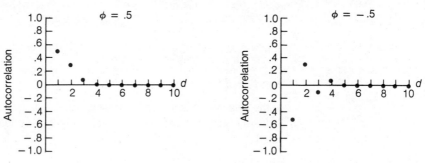

(b) Moderate autocorrelation

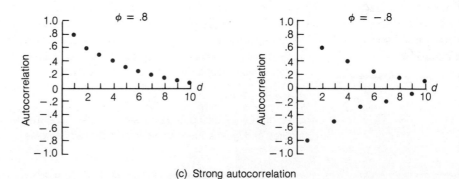

(c) Strong autocorrelation

as the order d (distance between time periods) increases* because positive values of ϕ imply positive autocorrelations for all orders d. Since positive autocorrelations generate cyclic behavior in the time series residuals, first-order autoregressive models used for business and economic time series have positive values for ϕ.

In summary, the pair of models

$$Y_t = \beta_0 + \beta_1 t + R_t$$
$$R_t = \phi R_{t-1} + \varepsilon_t$$

provides a description of the yearly sales of the firm that makes use of the autocorrelation of the time series residuals and therefore provides a more realistic description. In order to estimate the parameters of this pair of models (β_0, β_1, and ϕ), a modification of least squares is used. Although the details of this technique are beyond the scope of this text, several statistical software packages include the technique that provides estimates of these parameters. For example, the SAS printout that results from using this modified least squares technique to fit the pair of models to the sales revenue data of Table 14.4 is shown in Figure 14.16. [*Caution:* The SAS time series model is defined so that ϕ has the opposite sign from the value contained in our model. Consequently, you must multiply the estimate of ϕ shown in the portion of the SAS printout titled ESTIMATES OF THE AUTOREGRESSIVE PARAMETERS (beneath the heading COEFFICIENT) by -1 to obtain the estimate of ϕ for our model.] The fitted models are

$$\hat{Y}_t = .4058 + 4.2959t + \hat{R}_t$$
$$\hat{R}_t = .5896\hat{R}_{t-1}$$

with

$$SSE = 877.69$$

Figure 14.16 SAS Printout for Straight-Line Autoregressive Model Fit to Sales Data

	DF	SUM OF SQUARES	MEAN SQUARE	F RATIO	APPROX PROB
REGRESS	1	14046.52	14046.52	528.13	.0001
ERROR	33	877.6854	26.5965		
TOTAL	34	14924.21		R-SQUARE = .9412	

VARIABLE	B VALUE	STD DEVIATION	T RATIO	APPROX PROB
INTERCEPT	0.40575698772	3.93594906111	0.103	0.9185
T	4.29593038119	0.18693269351	22.981	0.0001

ESTIMATES OF THE AUTOREGRESSIVE PARAMETERS

LAG	COEFFICIENT	STD DEVIATION	T RATIO
1	-0.58962415	0.136522	-4.318880

* The autoregressive model is called a *stationary model* because the autocorrelations depend only on the distance, d, between residuals, and not on the time, t. Most time series models postulate a stationary residual component.

Note that the SSE has been reduced from 1,345.45 for the least squares fit to 877.69 for the pair of models just shown.* Thus, we expect our forecasts to be more reliable for the straight-line autoregressive models.

To obtain forecasts for years 36–40, we find

$$\hat{R}_{35} = Y_{35} - [.4058 + 4.2959(35)] = 150.9 - 150.7623 = .1377$$

We use the estimated value of $\hat{R}_{35} = .1377$ to obtain

$$\hat{R}_{36} = \hat{\phi}\hat{R}_{35} = (.5896)(.1377) = .0812$$

and then

$$\hat{Y}_{36} = \hat{\beta}_0 + \hat{\beta}_1(36) + \hat{R}_{36}$$
$$= .4058 + (4.2959)(36) + .0812 = 155.14$$

Approximate 95% prediction limits (not shown on the SAS printout) are (144.8, 165.5). Note that this interval is narrower than the interval we obtained for the same forecast using the least squares model, (141.3, 168.8). The procedure for forecasting $Y_{37}-Y_{40}$ is similar, and the entire set of forecasts and approximate prediction limits are shown in Figure 14.17.

Figure 14.17 Forecasts and Prediction Intervals for Years 36–40 Using Straight-Line Autoregressive Models

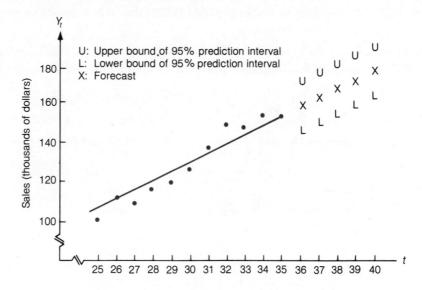

A comparison of Figures 14.6 and 14.17 reveals that the prediction intervals are somewhat narrower when the autoregressive model is used for the random component. It appears that the autoregressive model for R_t helps identify the short-term cyclical effects on sales, thereby making the forecasts more reliable.

---

* The value of R^2 in the SAS printout resulting from the modified least squares technique is not comparable to the R^2 value obtained from the ordinary least squares fit. To compare the adequacy of the fitted time series (straight-line autoregressive) models with that of the simple straight-line model, compare the respective values of SSE.

The type of modeling exemplified by the combination of regressive–autoregressive models for the sales data is useful for many business time series. First, a regressive model is postulated for the deterministic component to describe the secular trend and, if appropriate, the seasonal effect. Then, the random component is modeled to describe the cyclical and residual effects. The autoregressive model is useful for this random component; it has the general form

$$R_t = \phi_1 R_{t-1} + \phi_2 R_{t-2} + \cdots + \phi_p R_{t-p} + \varepsilon_t$$

and is called an **autoregressive model of order p.** The name *autoregressive* comes from the fact that R_t is regressed on its own past values. As the order, p, is increased, more complex

Forecasting with Regression Models with First-Order Autoregressive Residuals

1. Postulate a regression model for Y_t as a function of the predictor time series x_{1t}, $x_{2t}, \ldots, x_{kt}$ (e.g., time t, seasonal dummy variables, and so on):

$$Y_t = \beta_0 + \beta_1 x_{1t} + \beta_2 x_{2t} + \cdots + \beta_k x_{kt} + R_t$$

2. Use the method of least squares to fit the regression model and calculate the Durbin–Watson d statistic for the time series residuals.

3. Assuming the Durbin–Watson test reveals autocorrelation, model the time series residual, R_t, using the first-order autoregressive model

$$R_t = \phi R_{t-1} + \varepsilon_t$$

4. Use a statistical software package to obtain estimates of the parameters β_0, $\beta_1, \ldots, \beta_k$, and ϕ.

5. To forecast the value for Y_{t+1}, first compute

$$\hat{R}_t = Y_t - (\hat{\beta}_0 + \hat{\beta}_1 x_{1t} + \cdots + \hat{\beta}_k x_{kt})$$
$$\hat{R}_{t+1} = \hat{\phi} \hat{R}_t$$
$$\hat{Y}_{t+1} = \hat{\beta}_0 + \hat{\beta}_1 x_{1,t+1} + \cdots + \hat{\beta}_k x_{k,t+1} + \hat{R}_{t+1}$$

6. Approximate 95% prediction limits for the forecast are given by

$$\hat{Y}_{t+1} \pm 2\sqrt{MSE}$$

7. Future forecasts can be calculated recursively, first calculating the residual

$$\hat{R}_{t+2} = \hat{\phi} \hat{R}_{t+1}$$

and then

$$\hat{Y}_{t+2} = \hat{\beta}_0 + \hat{\beta}_1 x_{1,t+2} + \cdots + \hat{\beta}_k x_{k,t+2} + \hat{R}_{t+2}$$

and so forth.

8. An approximate 95% prediction interval for the m-step-ahead forecast is

$$\hat{Y}_{t+m} \pm 2\sqrt{MSE(1 + \hat{\phi}^2 + \cdots + \hat{\phi}^{2(m-1)})}$$

autocorrelation functions can be modeled. An even more flexible model is the *autoregressive–moving average (ARMA) model:*

$$R_t = \phi_1 R_{t-1} + \cdots + \phi_p R_{t-p} + \varepsilon_t + \theta_1 \varepsilon_{t-1} + \cdots + \theta_q \varepsilon_{t-q}$$

The ARMA model relates the current time series residuals to a linear function of the last p residuals and a linear function of the current and last q white noise errors. Of course, as the ARMA model becomes more complex, there are more parameters to estimate, and the techniques for identifying the model, for estimating the parameters, and for forecasting become more complex. We will leave the details of the general ARMA approach to the references at the end of this chapter. The forecasting technique for the first-order autoregressive model is summarized in the preceding box.

Example 14.4

Consider the power load data for a southern utility company given in Table 14.7. In Section 14.5, we fit the model

$$E(Y_t) = \beta_0 + \beta_1 t + \beta_2 Q_1 + \beta_3 Q_2 + \beta_4 Q_3$$

using the method of least squares. The least squares fit for this model is shown in Figure 14.18. Note that the Durbin–Watson d statistic is small ($d = .50$), indicating positively correlated residuals. (Note that $d < d_L \approx 1.37$ from Table XV, using $\alpha = .05$, $k = 4$, and $n = 48$.)

Figure 14.18 Least Squares Model for Power Load Data

```
DEPENDENT VARIABLE: POWER LOAD

SOURCE                      DF    SUM OF SQUARES     MEAN SQUARE     F VALUE

MODEL                        4    28374.99250583    7093.74812646    114.88
ERROR                       43     2655.13561917      61.74733998    PR > F
CORRECTED TOTAL             47    31030.12812500                     0.0001


R-SQUARE              C.V.             ROOT MSE          Y3 MEAN

0.914434             6.6766          7.85794757       117.69375000


                                     T FOR H0:      PR > :T:    STD ERROR OF
PARAMETER            ESTIMATE      PARAMETER=0                   ESTIMATE

INTERCEPT          70.50852273           22.63      0.0001       3.11552479
T                   1.63621066           19.92      0.0001       0.08213932
QUARTER      1     13.65863199            4.25      0.0001       3.21744388
             2     -3.73591200           -1.16      0.2512       3.21219719
             3     18.46954400            5.76      0.0001       3.20904506
             4      0.00000000

         SUM OF RESIDUALS                          0.00000000
         SUM OF SQUARED RESIDUALS               2655.13561917
         SUM OF SQUARED RESIDUALS - ERROR SS      -0.00000000
         PRESS STATISTIC                        3363.53250809
         FIRST ORDER AUTOCORRELATION               0.65704967
         DURBIN-WATSON D                           0.50375439
```

Fit the regression–autoregression pair of models given by

$$Y_t = \beta_0 + \beta_1 t + \beta_2 Q_1 + \beta_3 Q_2 + \beta_4 Q_3 + R_t$$
$$R_t = \phi R_{t-1} + \varepsilon_t$$

and use these models to forecast the 1983 quarterly power loads. Give approximate prediction intervals for each forecast.

Solution   Using SAS PROC AUTOREG yields the printout shown in Figure 14.19. The fitted models are

$$\hat{Y}_t = 68.84 + 1.65t + 13.82Q_1 - 3.44Q_2 + 18.71Q_3$$
$$\hat{R}_t = 0.657\hat{R}_{t-1}$$

Figure 14.19   First-Order Autoregressive Model for Power Load Data

```
                    DEPENDENT VARIABLE = POWER LOAD

                    ORDINARY LEAST SQUARES ESTIMATES

                    VARIABLE   DF    B VALUE

                    INTERCPT    1    70.50852
                    T           1     1.636211
                    Q1          1    13.65863
                    Q2          1    -3.73591
                    Q3          1    18.46954

                  ESTIMATES OF AUTOCORRELATIONS

LAG    COVARIANCE    CORRELATION   -1 9 8 7 6 5 4 3 2 1 0 1 2 3 4 5 6 7 8 9 1

  0     55.3153       1.000000     |                     |********************|
  1     36.3449       0.657050     |                     |*************        |

                    PRELIMINARY MSE=     31.43491

              ESTIMATES OF THE AUTOREGRESSIVE PARAMETERS

           LAG      COEFFICIENT    STD DEVIATION      T RATIO

             1      -0.65704967      0.108808       -6.038589
          SSE             1290.97
          DFE                  42
          MSE             30.73737
          ROOT MSE         5.54413
          R-SQUARE         0.9170

VARIABLE   DF      B VALUE       STD DEVIATION    T RATIO    APPROX PROB

INTERCPT    1   68.8433211783   4.49089157821     15.330       0.0001
T           1    1.6505670318   0.15051366875     10.966       0.0001
Q1          1   13.8245278433   1.69507481390      8.156       0.0001
Q2          1   -3.439641       1.90614907401     -1.804       0.0783
Q3          1   18.7128217554   1.65184459851     11.328       0.0001
```

A comparison of Figures 14.18 and 14.19 is instructive. First, note that the coefficient estimates change when the autoregressive residual model is added, but only slightly. The average increase in load per quarter is now estimated to be $\hat{\beta}_1 = 1.65$ (compared to 1.64), and the seasonal dummy variable estimates also change slightly, but their interpretations remain the same: Peak loads occur in the summer and winter quarters. Of special significance is the change in standard deviation (ROOT MSE) from 7.86 for the regression model to 5.54 for the regression–autoregression pair. Thus, we expect the prediction error associated with the pair of models to be approximately ±2(5.54), or about 11 megawatts. This represents a reduction of about 30% when compared with the error associated with the regression model. In other words, accounting for the autocorrelation between residuals in this case has reduced estimated prediction (and forecasting) error by about 30%.

The forecasting process begins with the calculation of the residual for the last observation, quarter 4 of 1982 ($t = 48$):

$$\hat{R}_{48} = Y_{48} - [\hat{\beta}_0 + \hat{\beta}_1(48)]$$
$$= 135.1 - [68.84 + 1.65(48)] = -12.94$$
$$\hat{R}_{49} = \hat{\phi}\hat{R}_{48} = (.657)(-12.94) = -8.50$$
$$\hat{Y}_{49} = \hat{\beta}_0 + \hat{\beta}_1(49) + \hat{\beta}_2 + \hat{R}_{49}$$
$$= 68.84 + 1.65(49) + 13.82 - 8.50 = 155.01$$

For quarter 2 of 1984, we forecast

$$\hat{R}_{50} = \hat{\phi}\hat{R}_{49} = (.657)(-8.50) = -5.58$$
$$\hat{Y}_{50} = \hat{\beta}_0 + \hat{\beta}_1(50) + \hat{\beta}_3 + \hat{R}_{50}$$
$$= 68.84 + 1.65(50) - 3.44 - 5.58 = 142.3$$

Similar computations give the forecasts for the last two quarters of 1983. The forecasts are shown in Table 14.10. Also shown are approximate 95% forecast intervals, which are computed using

$$\hat{Y}_{49} \pm 2\sqrt{MSE} = 155.01 \pm 2\sqrt{30.74}$$
$$= (143.9,\ 166.1)$$

$$\hat{Y}_{50} \pm 2\sqrt{MSE(1 + \hat{\phi}^2)} = 142.3 \pm 2\sqrt{30.74[1 + (.657)^2]}$$
$$= (129.0,\ 155.6)$$

and so forth. Note that the forecast intervals are narrower than those given for the regression model alone (Table 14.8). This reflects the advantage of using the regression–autoregression pair when the residuals are autocorrelated: Forecast accuracy will usually be increased. ∎

Table 14.10
1983 Power Load Forecasts (Megawatts) Using the Regression–Autoregression Models

QUARTER	FORECAST	LOWER 95% FORECAST BOUND	UPPER 95% FORECAST BOUND	ACTUAL LOAD
1	155.0	143.9	166.1	151.3
2	142.3	129.0	155.6	132.9
3	168.0	152.7	183.3	160.5
4	152.2	136.1	168.3	161.0

Regression and ARMA models represent an extremely powerful combination for forecasting business and economic time series. All components of the time series — secular, seasonal, cyclical, and residual — can be modeled by the combination. However, the successful and skillful application of this approach requires considerable practice and expertise. Additionally, once the parameters are estimated, the model is relatively inflexible. Unlike the exponential smoothing model, which is adaptive to changes in the time series, the regression–ARMA parameters do not change with time unless the parameters are periodically reestimated. Nevertheless, the regression–ARMA pair is widely applied by forecasters.

Exercises
14.17–14.21

Learning the Mechanics

14.17 Write the regression–autoregression pair of models that would be fit to annual data if only a secular trend were being postulated in the regression model. Explain the role of each of the parameters in the models.

14.18 Repeat Exercise 14.17 assuming that the data are quarterly and that seasonal dummy variables are to be added to the regression model.

Applying the Concepts

14.19 The Dow Jones Industrial Average (DJA) is the most widely followed stock market indicator. The values of the DJA from 1961 to 1980 are given in the table. The results of using SAS PROC AUTOREG to fit the regression–autoregression pair

$$Y_t = \beta_0 + \beta_1 t + R_t$$
$$R_t = \phi R_{t-1} + \varepsilon_t$$

where t is the number of years since 1960 (i.e., $t = 1, 2, \ldots, 20$) are given in the computer printout shown here. Evaluate the fit of the model, and interpret the estimated coefficients.

YEAR	DJA
1961	731.14
1962	652.10
1963	762.95
1964	874.13
1965	969.26
1966	785.69
1967	905.11
1968	943.75
1969	800.36
1970	838.92
1971	884.76
1972	950.71
1973	923.88
1974	759.37
1975	802.49
1976	974.92
1977	835.15
1978	805.01
1979	838.74
1980	963.99

Regression–Autoregression Pair for Exercise 14.19

```
                      DEPENDENT VARIABLE = DOW JONES

                   ORDINARY LEAST SQUARES ESTIMATES

                       VARIABLE   DF    B VALUE

                       INTERCPT    1    753.4038
                       T           1    10.42875

                   ESTIMATES OF AUTOCORRELATIONS

LAG    COVARIANCE    CORRELATION   -1 9 8 7 6 5 4 3 2 1 0 1 2 3 4 5 6 7 8 9 1
  0      10073.1      1.000000     |                   |********************|
  1      2499.24      0.248110     |                   |*****               |

                   PRELIMINARY MSE=      9453.007

               ESTIMATES OF THE AUTOREGRESSIVE PARAMETERS

             LAG       COEFFICIENT   STD DEVIATION     T RATIO

              1       -0.24811023       0201995      -1.228302
         SSE         212122.4
         DFE              20
         MSE         10606.12
         ROOT MSE     102.986
         R-SQUARE       0.2807

     VARIABLE    DF      B VALUE    STD DEVIATION   T RATIO   APPROX PROB

     INTERCPT     1   743.437200831  56.9693090830   13.050     0.0001
     T            1    11.529723866   4.1269552249    2.794     0.0112
```

14.20 Refer to Exercise 14.19. Use the estimated models to forecast the Dow Jones Industrial Average from 1981 to 1983, and complete the table given at the top of the next page. Compare these forecasts to the exponentially smoothed forecasts in Table 14.3.

YEAR	ACTUAL DJA	FORECAST	FORECAST ERROR
1981	899.01		
1982	1,046.54		
1983	1,258.64		

14.21 Refer to Exercises 14.19 and 14.20. Calculate approximate 95% forecast bounds. Do these bounds contain the actual DJA values?

Summary

Time series are often modeled as a combination of four components: *secular, seasonal, cyclical,* and *residual. Exponential smoothing* is an adaptive method for forecasting time series with little or no secular or seasonal trends. The *Holt–Winters model* provides an adaptive forecasting technique for a time series with a significant trend (secular) component. Simple linear regression can be used to forecast long-term trends of time series, and also allows the computation of prediction intervals to evaluate the forecast's reliability. Multiple regression models can be used to describe both long-term and seasonal components.

Since many business and economic time series models exhibit cyclical behavior, the *Durbin–Watson d statistic* is important for testing *residual autocorrelation.* When autocorrelation is present, the combination of regression and autoregression models represents a useful forecasting tool. This pair of models is capable of describing all components of the time series, and of providing forecasts with prediction intervals.

Forecasting is an especially difficult aspect of statistical inference, because, by definition, we are extrapolating out of the range of the time period containing the data. Forecasts should be confined to the short term and, when possible, some measure of forecast reliability should be calculated. However, probably the best measure of a forecasting technique's usefulness is the comparison of the forecasts against the future realization of the time series values.

Supplementary Exercises 14.22 – 14.35

[*Note:* Starred (*) exercises require the use of a computer.]

14.22 Civilian employment is broadly classified by the federal government into one of two categories—agricultural and nonagricultural. The nonagricultural employment category is further subclassified into white-collar, blue-collar, service, and other. Employment figures (in millions of workers) for three of the classes are given in the table for the 1972–1982 period.

YEAR	WHITE-COLLAR	BLUE-COLLAR	SERVICE	YEAR	WHITE-COLLAR	BLUE-COLLAR	SERVICE
1972	39.33	28.72	11.03	1978	48.09	32.07	13.06
1973	40.73	30.08	11.21	1979	50.33	32.67	13.08
1974	42.19	30.05	11.49	1980	51.88	31.45	13.23
1975	42.79	28.30	11.80	1981	52.95	31.26	13.44
1976	44.37	29.36	12.17	1982	53.47	29.60	13.74
1977	45.96	30.68	12.59				

a. Use $w = .5$ to compute exponential smoothing forecasts for each of the three series for 1983.

b. Use the Holt–Winters model with $w = .5$ and $v = .5$ to compute 1983 forecasts for each of the three series.

14.23 Refer to Exercise 14.10. Use $w = .3$ and $v = .7$ to compute the Holt–Winters forecasts from 1983 to 1985. Compare these to the linear regression forecasts of Exercise 14.10.

14.24 A stock you are interested in buying has had the yearly closing prices shown in the table for the years 1970–1983.

a. Use exponential smoothing with $w = .8$ to forecast the 1984 and 1985 closing prices. If you buy at the end of 1983 and sell at the end of 1985, what is your expected gain (loss)?
b. Repeat part a using the Holt–Winters model with $w = .8$ and $v = .5$.
c. In which forecast do you have more confidence? Explain.

14.25 Refer to Exercise 14.24.

a. Fit a simple linear regression model to the stock price.
b. Forecast the 1984 and 1985 closing prices using the regression model, and place 95% confidence bounds on each forecast.

14.26 Refer to Exercise 14.25. Calculate the time series residuals for the simple linear model, and use the Durbin–Watson d statistic to test for the presence of autocorrelation.

14.27 The Gross National Product (GNP) is a measure of total U.S. output, and is therefore an important indicator of the U.S. economy. The quarterly GNP values (in billions of dollars) from 1971 to 1982 are given in the table below:

YEAR	STOCK PRICE
1970	$30.125
1971	25.500
1972	32.000
1973	38.375
1974	42.500
1975	47.125
1976	49.125
1977	38.750
1978	22.250
1979	28.750
1980	43.000
1981	52.875
1982	45.250
1983	59.750

YEAR	QUARTER 1	2	3	4
1971	1,049.3	1,068.9	1,086.6	1,105.8
1972	1,142.4	1,171.7	1,196.1	1,233.5
1973	1,283.5	1,307.6	1,337.7	1,376.7
1974	1,387.7	1,423.8	1,451.6	1,473.8
1975	1,479.8	1,516.7	1,578.5	1,621.8
1976	1,672.0	1,698.6	1,729.0	1,772.5
1977	1,834.8	1,895.1	1,954.4	1,988.9
1978	2,031.7	2,139.5	2,202.5	2,281.6
1979	2,335.5	2,377.9	2,454.8	2,502.9
1980	2,572.9	2,578.8	2,639.1	2,736.0
1981	2,866.6	2,912.5	3,004.9	3,032.2
1982	3,021.4	3,070.2	3,090.7	3,109.6

Use $w = .5$ and $v = .5$ to calculate Holt–Winters forecasts for 1983. Then complete the following table:

QUARTER	ACTUAL GNP	FORECAST	FORECAST ERROR
1	3,171.5		
2	3,272.0		
3	3,362.2		
4	3,432.0		

*14.28 Refer to Exercise 14.27.

a. Use the simple linear regression model to forecast the 1983 quarterly GNP. Place 95% confidence limits on the forecasts.

b. The GNP values given are *seasonally adjusted,* which means that an attempt to remove seasonality has been made prior to reporting the figures. Add quarterly dummy variables to the model. Use the partial F test (discussed in Section 12.4) to determine whether the data indicate the significance of the seasonal component. Does the test support the assertion that the GNP figures are seasonally adjusted?

c. Use the seasonal model to forecast the 1983 quarterly GNP values.

*14.29 Refer to Exercise 14.28.

a. Calculate the time series residuals for the seasonal model, and use the Durbin–Watson test to determine whether the residuals are autocorrelated. Use $\alpha = .05$.

b. Use SAS PROC AUTOREG, or a similar procedure, to fit the seasonal regression–autoregression pair of models. Forecast the 1983 quarterly GNP, and calculate approximate 95% forecast bounds. Do these bounds contain the actual GNP values? (See Exercise 14.27 for the actual values.)

*14.30 Refer to Exercises 14.27–14.29. A multiplicative model for GNP can be formed by using the natural logarithm of GNP as the dependent variable in the regression models.

a. Fit the simple linear regression and seasonal regression models using ln(GNP) as the dependent variable.

b. Compute the forecasts and forecast bounds for the quarterly 1983 GNP using the models in part a. Take the antilogarithm of the regression forecasts and bounds to express them in the original units (billions of dollars).

14.31 A major portion of total consumer credit is extended in the categories of automobile loans, mobile home loans, and revolving credit. Amounts outstanding (in thousands of dollars) for the period 1972–1982 are given in the table.

YEAR	AUTOMOBILE	MOBILE HOME	REVOLVING CREDIT
1972	126,759	9,495	7,183
1973	148,177	13,552	9,092
1974	164,594	14,642	13,681
1975	172,353	14,434	15,019
1976	193,992	14,573	17,189
1977	230,564	14,945	39,274
1978	273,645	15,235	48,309
1979	312,024	16,838	56,937
1980	313,472	17,322	58,352
1981	333,375	18,486	63,049
1982	352,246	18,942	68,286

a. Use simple linear regression models for each credit category to forecast the 1983 and 1984 values. Place 95% confidence bounds on each forecast.

b. Calculate the Holt–Winters forecasts for 1983 and 1984 using $w = .7$ and $v = .7$. Compare the results with the simple linear regression forecasts of part a.

14.32 Consider the monthly IBM stock prices from January 1981 to December 1983 shown in the table. Also shown are the exponentially smoothed values for $w = .5$. Use the exponentially smoothed series to forecast the monthly values of the IBM stock price from January 1984 to March 1984.

1981	IBM STOCK PRICE	EXPONENTIALLY SMOOTHED STOCK PRICE ($w = .5$)	1982	IBM STOCK PRICE	EXPONENTIALLY SMOOTHED STOCK PRICE ($w = .5$)	1983	IBM STOCK PRICE	EXPONENTIALLY SMOOTHED STOCK PRICE ($w = .5$)
Jan.	$65.500	$65.500	Jan.	$64.625	$60.124	Jan.	$ 98.750	$ 93.923
Feb.	64.500	65.000	Feb.	61.750	60.937	Feb.	100.375	97.149
Mar.	62.125	63.563	Mar.	60.500	60.719	Mar.	104.750	100.950
Apr.	64.875	64.219	Apr.	64.625	62.672	Apr.	117.500	109.225
May	58.500	61.360	May	62.125	62.399	May	112.750	110.988
June	59.125	60.243	June	61.375	61.887	June	121.000	115.994
July	56.375	58.309	July	66.250	64.069	July	122.000	118.997
Aug.	55.375	56.842	Aug.	71.000	67.535	Aug.	119.375	119.186
Sept.	54.875	55.859	Sept.	74.750	71.143	Sept.	128.125	123.656
Oct.	49.625	52.742	Oct.	80.375	75.759	Oct.	126.750	125.203
Nov.	54.500	53.621	Nov.	86.375	81.067	Nov.	117.375	121.289
Dec.	57.625	55.623	Dec.	97.125	89.096	Dec.	122.000	121.644

14.33 Refer to Exercise 14.32. Use a simple linear regression model to forecast the January–March 1984 prices. Place 95% confidence bounds on the forecasts.

*14.34 Refer to Exercises 14.32 and 14.33.

a. Calculate the time series residuals and use the Durbin–Watson d statistic to test for autocorrelation.

b. Use SAS PROC AUTOREG, or a similar procedure, to fit the simple linear regression with autoregressive residuals. Forecast the January–March 1984 prices, and place approximate 95% confidence bounds on each.

*14.35 Refer to Exercises 14.32–14.34. Another method often employed when forecasting economic time series is *first differencing*. This method models the differences between successive values of a time series, $Y_t - Y_{t-1}$. For example, the pair of models

$$Y_t - Y_{t-1} = R_t$$
$$R_t = \phi R_{t-1} + \varepsilon_t$$

is the first difference–autoregressive pair.

a. Fit this pair of models to the IBM price data given in Exercise 14.32. To accomplish this, first compute the differences (there will be thirty-five differences), and then use SAS PROC AUTOREG or a similar procedure to fit the autoregressive model.

b. Use the estimated models to forecast the January–March 1984 prices. To accomplish this, use

$$\hat{R}_{36} = Y_{36} - Y_{35}$$
$$\hat{R}_{37} = \hat{\phi}\hat{R}_{36}$$
$$\hat{Y}_{37} = Y_{36} + \hat{R}_{37}$$
$$\vdots$$

References

Anderson, T. W. *The statistical analysis of time series.* New York: Wiley, 1971.

Bolling, W. B. "Queuing model of a hospital emergency room." *Industrial Engineering,* Sept. 1972, 26–31.

Box, G. E. P., & Jenkins, G. M. *Time series analysis: Forecasting and control.* 2d ed. San Francisco: Holden-Day, 1977.

Durbin, J., & Watson, G. S. "Testing for serial correlation in least squares regression, I." *Biometrika,* 1950, *37,* 409–428.

Durbin, J., & Watson, G. S. "Testing for serial correlation in least squares regression, II." *Biometrika,* 1951, *38,* 159–178.

Durbin, J., & Watson, G. S. "Testing for serial correlation in least squares regression, III." *Biometrika,* 1971, *58,* 1–19.

Fuller, W. A. *Introduction to statistical time series.* New York: Wiley, 1976.

Granger, C. W. J., & Newbold, P. *Forecasting economic time series.* New York: Academic Press, 1977.

Mendenhall, W., & McClave, J. T. *A second course in business statistics: Regression analysis.* San Francisco: Dellen, 1981.

Nelson, C. R. *Applied time series analysis for managerial forecasting.* San Francisco: Holden-Day, 1973.

CHAPTER 15

Analysis of Variance

Where We've Been . . .

As we have seen in preceding chapters, the solutions of many business problems are based on inferences about population means. Methods for estimating and testing hypotheses about a single mean and the comparison of two means were presented in Chapters 8 and 9. Chapters 10–12 dealt with linear models for estimating the mean value of a response using regression models, and Chapters 13 and 14 treated the special case where the response measurements represent a time series.

Where We're Going . . .

This chapter extends the methods of Chapters 8–12 to the comparison of more than two means. We will use sampling procedures that are analogous to the independent sampling and paired difference designs of Chapter 9. Then we will investigate the effect of two independent variables on a response using data collected via a factorial experiment.

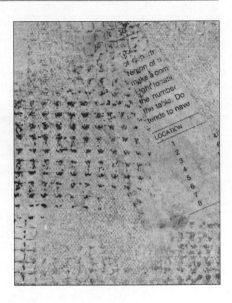

Contents

In Chapter 9, we learned how to compare the means of two populations using independent random samples (Section 9.2) and the paired difference design (Section 9.4). But most experiments tend to be more complex, often involving the comparison of more than two populations using a variety of sampling schemes called *experimental designs*. Therefore, this chapter presents an extension of the methodology of Chapter 9 to the comparison of two or more population means using the *completely randomized design* and a design analogous to the paired difference design.*

Recall that a *completely randomized sampling design* for comparing the means of 3, 4, or, in general, *k* populations is one in which you select independent random samples from each of the *k* populations.

Definition 15.1

A *completely randomized design* (often called an *independent sampling design*) is one in which independent random samples are drawn from each of the populations of interest.

To illustrate, suppose a consumer group wants to compare the mean gas mileage for four different compact car models using a completely randomized design. The experimental units are cars and the measurements are the miles-per-gallon ratings for cars driven over a 1,000-mile course. Each car is assigned a different driver, and the contribution of the driver to a car's rating is inseparable from the contribution of the car. Consequently, the *variability* in the miles-per-gallon rating due to the driver contributes to the experimental error.

A particular car model is associated with one of the four populations of measurements that is of interest to the consumer group. For example, suppose four models are identified as A, B, C, and D, and one of the models, call it model A, is an Oldsmobile Omega. The consumer group might define the population of measurements for population A as the miles-per-gallon ratings for every Oldsmobile Omega manufactured in 1984, and the populations associated with models B, C, and D can be defined in a similar manner. If a random sample of cars (say fifteen) is randomly and independently selected from each population, then the consumer group is using a *completely randomized design*.

As noted in Chapter 9, a paired difference design for comparing two population means often provides more information because it makes a comparison of observations from two populations (call them A and B) between pairs of matched (or similar) experimental units. For example, if you were comparing the miles-per-gallon ratings for two car models, measurements would vary substantially for the same model because of the difference in the driving habits of the drivers. To remove this source of variation, you could pair an A and a B car and assign both cars to a *single* driver. The driver would drive both cars and obtain the ratings for

---

* The different populations can be viewed as the levels of one qualitative independent variable or the combination of levels of two or more qualitative independent variables. Therefore, all the data described in this chapter could be analyzed using a multiple regression analysis (see Exercise 15.67). The advantages of using the analysis of variance procedure described here are: (1) it is easier to understand and (2) the computations are relatively simple and can be performed on a hand calculator.

each. *By taking the difference between these measurements for all driver pairs, you would cancel out the variation among drivers.*

The extension of the paired difference design to a combination of more than two means implies that larger groups of experimental units are matched. To compare the means for the four car models, you would use matched groups of four experimental units. You could have each driver drive four cars, one of each model type. The group of four experimental units (matched on drivers) is called a *block* and the resulting design, using a number of blocks, is called a *randomized block design.* For example, a randomized block design using five blocks (drivers) to compare the four car models (A, B, C, and D) is shown in Figure 15.1. The word *randomized* in the phrase *randomized block design* implies that the cars should be driven by each driver in a random sequence. This is done to eliminate any bias that might result from a particular position in the block. For example, driver 1 would drive the four car models in the sequence B, A, C, D.

Figure 15.1 A
Randomized Block Design
for Comparing Four Car
Models

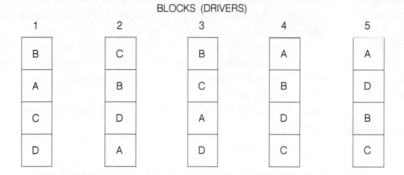

BLOCKS (DRIVERS)

Because the design of experiments first achieved importance in agricultural experimentation, the terminology of the subject has an agricultural flavor. Most agricultural experiments involve the *treatment* of experimental units in two or more different ways and then a comparison of the means of the populations of measurements corresponding to the different treatments. For example, they might compare the yield of plots of corn treated with four different types of fertilizer, say A, B, C, and D. The four fertilizer types would be called *treatments.* Similarly, they might compare the gain in the weight of pigs fed on four different diets, A, B, C, and D. Again, the diets are called *treatments,* and the objective of the experiment is to compare the means of the populations of measurements corresponding to the four treatments. As you will subsequently see, the design of an experiment involves both selecting the treatments to be included in an experiment and deciding how to apply the treatments to the experimental units.

Definition 15.2

A *randomized block design* is a design devised to compare the means for *k treatments* utilizing *matched blocks* of *k experimental units.* Each treatment appears once in every block.

The advantages obtained by selecting data according to a designed experiment are twofold. First, you can often acquire more information than could be obtained from the same amount of data collected in an undesigned manner. Second, the data can be analyzed using a simple procedure called an *analysis of variance.* In the sections that follow, we will show you how to compare two or more treatment means based on the completely randomized and the randomized block designs. We will then use an analysis of variance to analyze the data from designed two-variable experiments.

15.1 Comparing More Than Two Population Means: The Completely Randomized Design

The *completely randomized design* makes use of independent random samples to compare more than two population means. If we assume there are k population means to be compared, the notation for the completely randomized design would appear as shown in Table 15.1.

To decide whether a difference exists among the treatment means $\mu_1, \mu_2, \ldots, \mu_k$, we examine the *spread* (or *variation*) among the sample means. The greater the variation, the greater will be the evidence to indicate differences among $\mu_1, \mu_2, \ldots, \mu_k$. This variation, measured by a weighted sum of squares of deviations of the sample means $\bar{x}_1, \bar{x}_2, \ldots, \bar{x}_k$ about the overall mean $\bar{\bar{x}}$, is called the *sum of squares for treatments* and is given by the expression

$$SST = \sum n_i(\bar{x}_i - \bar{\bar{x}})^2$$

Note that each squared distance between the sample mean and the overall mean is multiplied by a weight, the sample size n_i. Also, note that the SST is large when the sample means are very different.

Table 15.1

Summary Notation for a Completely Randomized Design

	POPULATIONS (TREATMENTS)			
	1	2	3 . . .	k
Mean	μ_1	μ_2	μ_3 . . .	μ_k
Variance	σ_1^2	σ_2^2	σ_3^2 . . .	σ_k^2
	INDEPENDENT RANDOM SAMPLES			
	1	2	3 . . .	k
Sample size	n_1	n_2	n_3 . . .	n_k
Sample totals	T_1	T_2	T_3 . . .	T_k
Sample means	$\bar{x}_1$	$\bar{x}_2$	$\bar{x}_3$ . . .	$\bar{x}_k$

Total number of measurements $= n = n_1 + n_2 + n_3 + \cdots + n_k$
Sum of all n measurements $= \sum x_i$
Mean of all n measurements $= \bar{\bar{x}}$
Sum of squares of all n measurements $= \sum x_i^2$

Now, suppose we want to test the null hypothesis that the k treatment means are equal; i.e.,

$$H_0: \quad \mu_1 = \mu_2 = \cdots = \mu_k$$

versus the alternative hypothesis

$$H_a: \quad \text{At least two of the treatment means differ}$$

Large values of SST will show support for the alternative hypothesis. That is, if the sum of squared differences between the sample means and the overall mean is large, we will tend to believe that the population means differ.

How large must the SST be before we reject H_0 and accept H_a? We will compare this measure of variability among sample means to a measure of the variability of the experimental units themselves—i.e., the within-sample variability.

You can see how this principle works by comparing the dot diagrams for two samples as shown in Figure 15.2. Five observations for sample 1 and five for sample 2 are shown. The locations of the sample means are indicated by the two arrows. Do you think the data provide sufficient evidence to indicate a difference in the corresponding population means μ_1 and μ_2? In our opinion, the difference between $\bar{x}_1$ and $\bar{x}_2$ is not large enough to indicate a difference between μ_1 and μ_2. This is because the *difference between sample means is small in relation to the variability within the sample observations.*

Figure 15.2 Dot Diagrams for Two Samples (No Evidence of a Difference Between Population Means)

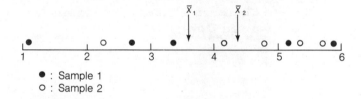

● : Sample 1
○ : Sample 2

Now look at two more samples of $n_1 = n_2 = 5$ measurements, as shown in Figure 15.3. The data appear to give clear evidence of a difference between μ_1 and μ_2 because the difference between the sample means, $\bar{x}_1$ and $\bar{x}_2$, is large in comparison with the variability within the sample observations.

Figure 15.3 Dot Diagrams for Two Samples (Evidence of a Difference Between Population Means)

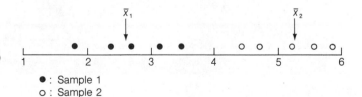

● : Sample 1
○ : Sample 2

To measure the within-sample variability, we pool the within-sample sum of squared deviations about the mean:

$$SSE = \sum_{i=1}^{n_1} (x_{1i} - \bar{x}_1)^2 + \sum_{i=1}^{n_2} (x_{2i} - \bar{x}_2)^2 + \cdots + \sum_{i=1}^{n_k} (x_{ki} - \bar{x}_k)^2$$

where x_{1i} is the ith measurement in sample 1, x_{2i} is the ith measurement in sample 2, etc. We use **SSE** to denote the **sum of squared errors;** this is the same concept used in the least squares approach to fitting models (Chapters 10 and 11). As with regression models, the SSE measures unexplained variability. But in this case, it measures variability unexplained by the differences among the sample means. That is, the SSE is a pooled measure of the variability within the k samples.*

We now want to compare the variability between treatment means (SST) to the within-sample variability (SSE). The first step is to divide each sum of squares by its degrees of freedom, to obtain **mean squares.** We have $(k - 1)$ degrees of freedom for treatments — one for each of the k treatment means minus one for the estimation of the overall mean. Thus, we calculate

$$\text{MST} = \frac{\text{SSE}}{k - 1}$$

where MST denotes **mean square for treatments.**

The degrees of freedom for error equals $(n - k)$, one for each of the n measurements minus one for each of the k treatment means being estimated. Thus, we calculate

$$\text{MSE} = \frac{\text{SSE}}{n - k}$$

where MSE denotes **mean square for error.**

Test to Compare k Treatment Means for a Completely Randomized Design

H_0: $\mu_1 = \mu_2 = \cdots = \mu_k$

H_a: At least two treatment means differ

Test statistic: $F = \dfrac{\text{MST}}{\text{MSE}}$

Assumptions: 1. All k population probability distributions are normal.
2. The k population variances are equal.
3. Samples are selected randomly and independently from the respective populations.

Rejection region: $F > F_\alpha$ where F_α is based on $(k - 1)$ numerator degrees of freedom (associated with the MST) and $(n - k)$ denominator degrees of freedom (associated with the MSE).

---

* This is an extension of the pooled estimator of σ^2 discussed in Chapter 9. For the two-sample case,

$$s_p^2 = \frac{\sum_{i=1}^{n_1} (x_{1i} - \bar{x}_1)^2 + \sum_{i=1}^{n_2} (x_{2i} - \bar{x}_2)^2}{n_1 + n_2 - 2}$$

The numerator of s_p^2 is the SSE.

We now compare the two sources of variability — the source due to differences among the sample (treatment) means and the source due to within-sample differences among experimental units — by forming an F statistic:

$$F = \frac{MST}{MSE}$$

Large values of the F statistic indicate that the differences among the sample means are large, and therefore support the alternative hypothesis that the population means differ. The test, with necessary assumptions, is summarized in the preceding box. Because the F statistic involves a comparison of two sources of variation, this procedure for comparing two or more population means is usually referred to as an *analysis of variance,* or *ANOVA.*

Example 15.1

Suppose a large chain of department stores wants to compare the mean dollar amounts owed by its delinquent credit card customers in three different annual income groups: under $12,000, $12,000–$25,000, and over $25,000. A sample of ten customers with delinquent accounts is to be selected from each group and the amount owed by each recorded.

Set up the test to compare the population mean amounts owed by the three groups. (We will give the data and perform the test in a later example.)

Solution

We will test the null hypothesis that the mean amount owed by each income group is the same. Denoting the mean amounts owed by the low-, middle-, and high-income groups by μ_1, μ_2, and μ_3, respectively, we will test

H_0: $\mu_1 = \mu_2 = \mu_3$

H_a: At least two of the mean amounts differ

The test statistic compares the variability among the sample mean amounts due to the within-sample variability; i.e.,

Test statistic: $F = \dfrac{MST}{MSE}$

Assumptions: 1. The amounts due for each of the three income groups have (at least approximately) normal distributions.
2. The variances of the distributions of amounts due are the same for the three income groups.
3. Samples were randomly and independently selected from the three populations.

Rejection region: There are three treatments (the income groups) being compared, so the treatment degrees of freedom is $(k - 1) = (3 - 1) = 2$. There are $n = 30$ measurements in the combined samples, so the error degrees of freedom is $(n - k) = (30 - 3) = 27$. Using $\alpha = .05$, we will reject the null hypothesis that the true means are the same if

$F > F_{.05}$

where (from Table VII in Appendix B) $F_{.05} = 3.35$. This rejection region is shown in Figure 15.4. Once the test is set up, we are prepared to collect samples, perform the calculations, and state conclusions.   ■

Figure 15.4   Rejection Region for Example 15.1: Numerator df = 2, Denominator df = 27

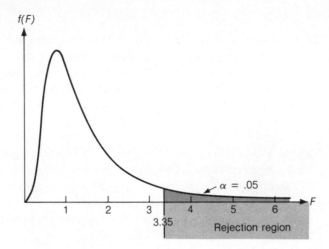

Although the sums of squares, SST and SSE, can be calculated by the formulas given earlier in this section, simpler computing formulas are available. Much of the theory and computation of analysis of variance rests on the concept of *partitioning the sum of squares of deviations* of all the x values about the overall mean:

$$SS(\text{Total}) = \sum (x_i - \bar{\bar{x}})^2$$

This is called the *total sum of squares.* The partitioning is diagrammed in Figure 15.5.

Figure 15.5   Partitioning of the Total Sum of Squares for the Completely Randomized Design

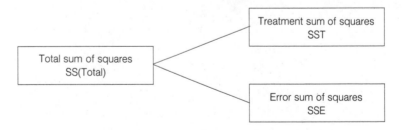

The computational simplification offered by the partitioning is that the SSE can be computed by subtraction; i.e.,

$$SSE = SS(\text{Total}) - SST$$

We present the computational formulas that lead to the calculation of the *F* statistic in the box.

Formulas for the Calculations in the Completely Randomized Design

CM = Correction for mean

$$= \frac{(\text{Total of all observations})^2}{\text{Total number of observations}} = \frac{\left(\sum x_i\right)^2}{n}$$

SS(Total) = Total sum of squares

$$= (\text{Sum of squares of all observations}) - \text{CM} = \sum x_i^2 - \text{CM}$$

SST = Sum of squares for treatments

$$= \left(\begin{array}{c} \text{Sum of squares of treatment totals with} \\ \text{each square divided by the number of} \\ \text{observations for that treatment} \end{array}\right) - \text{CM} = \frac{T_1^2}{n_1} + \frac{T_2^2}{n_2} + \cdots + \frac{T_k^2}{n_k} - \text{CM}$$

SSE = Sum of squares for error = SS(Total) − SST

$$\text{MST} = \text{Mean square for treatments} = \frac{\text{SST}}{k-1}$$

$$\text{MSE} = \text{Mean square for error} = \frac{\text{SSE}}{n-k}$$

$$F = \text{Test statistic} = \frac{\text{MST}}{\text{MSE}}$$

where

n = Total number of observations

k = Number of treatments

Example 15.2 Refer to Example 15.1, in which we set up a test to compare the mean indebtedness of delinquent credit card holders in three different income classes. The data for this experiment are given in Table 15.2. Perform the calculations required to obtain the F statistic and state a conclusion.

Table 15.2

Income Class: Dollars Owed

	UNDER $12,000	$12,000–$25,000	OVER $25,000
	$148	$513	$335
	76	264	643
	393	433	216
	520	94	536
	236	535	128
	134	327	723
	55	214	258
	166	135	380
	415	280	594
	153	304	465
TOTALS	$2,296	$3,099	$4,278

Solution   From the table, the totals for the three samples are $T_1 = \$2,296$, $T_2 = \$3,099$, and $T_3 = \$4,278$, so

$$\sum x_i = T_1 + T_2 + T_3 = 9,673$$
$$\sum x_i^2 = (148)^2 + (76)^2 + \cdots + (465)^2 = 4,088,341$$

Then, following the order of calculations listed earlier, we find

$$CM = \frac{\left(\sum x_i\right)^2}{n} = \frac{(9,673)^2}{30} = 3,118,897.633$$

$$SS(\text{Total}) = \sum x_i^2 - CM$$
$$= 4,088,341 - 3,118,897.633 = 969,443.367$$

$$SST = \frac{T_1^2}{n_1} + \frac{T_2^2}{n_2} + \frac{T_3^2}{n_3} - CM$$

$$= \frac{(2,296)^2}{10} + \frac{(3,099)^2}{10} + \frac{(4,278)^2}{10} - 3,118,897.633$$

$$= 3,317,670.1 - 3,118,897.633 = 198,772.467$$

$$SSE = SS(\text{Total}) - SST$$
$$= 969,443.367 - 198,772.467 = 770,670.9$$

$$MST = \frac{SST}{k-1} = \frac{198,772.467}{2} = 99,386.234$$

$$MSE = \frac{SSE}{n-k} = \frac{770,670.9}{27} = 28,543.367$$

Finally, the F statistic is

$$F = \frac{MST}{MSE} = \frac{99,386.234}{28,543.367} = 3.48$$

This calculated F exceeds the tabulated value (the value that locates the rejection region; see Example 15.1) $F_{.05} = 3.35$. Therefore, we conclude at $\alpha = .05$ that the mean indebtedness of the delinquent credit card holders differs for at least two of the three income groups. ∎

The results of an analysis of variance are often summarized in tabular form. The general form of an *ANOVA table* for a completely randomized design is shown in Table 15.3. *Source* refers to the source of variation, and for each source, *df* refers to the degrees of freedom, *SS* to the sum of squares, *MS* to the mean square, and *F* to the *F* statistic comparing the treatment mean square to the error mean square. Table 15.4 is the ANOVA summary table corresponding to the analysis of variance data for Examples 15.1 and 15.2.

Because the completely randomized design involves the selection of independent random samples, we can find a confidence interval for a single treatment mean by using the method of Section 8.4 or for the difference between two treatment means by using the methods of

Table 15.3

ANOVA Summary Table for
a Completely Randomized
Design

SOURCE	df	SS	MS	F
Treatments	$k-1$	SST	MST	MST/MSE
Error	$n-k$	SSE	MSE	
Total	$n-1$	SS(Total)		

Table 15.4

ANOVA Summary Table for
Examples 15.1 and 15.2

SOURCE	df	SS	MS	F
Income group	2	198,772.467	99,386.234	3.48
Error	27	770,670.900	28,543.367	
Total	29	969,443.367		

Section 9.2. The estimate of σ^2 will be based on the pooled sum of squares within all k samples, that is,

$$MSE = s^2 = \frac{SSE}{n-k}$$

This is the same quantity that is used as the denominator for the analysis of variance F test. The formulas for the confidence intervals of Chapters 8 and 9 are reproduced in the box.

Confidence Intervals for Means

Single treatment mean (say, treatment i): $\bar{x}_i \pm t_{\alpha/2} \dfrac{s}{\sqrt{n_i}}$

Difference between two treatment means (say, treatments i and j):

$$(\bar{x}_i - \bar{x}_j) \pm t_{\alpha/2} s \sqrt{\frac{1}{n_i} + \frac{1}{n_j}}$$

where $s = \sqrt{MSE}$ and $t_{\alpha/2}$ is the tabulated value of t (Table V, Appendix B) that locates $\alpha/2$ in the upper tail of the t distribution and has $(n-k)$ degrees of freedom (the degrees of freedom associated with error in the ANOVA).

Example 15.3   Refer to Example 15.2, and find a 95% confidence interval for the mean indebtedness of people with incomes less than $12,000 per year.

Solution   From Table 15.4, MSE $= 28,543.367$. Then,

$$s = \sqrt{MSE} = \sqrt{28,543.367} = 168.9$$

The sample mean indebtedness for those with income levels under $12,000 is

$$\bar{x}_1 = \frac{T_1}{n_1} = \frac{2,296}{10} = 229.6$$

The tabulated value, $t_{.025}$, for 27 df (the same as for MSE) is 2.052. So, a 95% confidence interval for μ_1, the mean indebtedness of people with incomes less than $12,000, is

$$\bar{x}_1 \pm t_{\alpha/2} \frac{s}{\sqrt{n_1}} = 229.6 \pm 2.052 \left(\frac{168.9}{\sqrt{10}} \right) = 229.6 \pm 109.6$$

or (120.0, 339.2).

Note that this confidence interval is quite wide—probably too wide to be of any practical value. The reason the interval is so wide can be seen in the large amount of variation within each income class. For example, the indebtedness for people with incomes under $12,000 varies from $55 to $520. Consequently, if you want to obtain a more accurate estimate of treatment means with a narrower confidence interval, you will have to select larger samples of people from within each income class. ∎

Example 15.4

Find a 95% confidence interval for the difference in mean indebtedness between people with incomes under $12,000 and those with incomes over $25,000.

Solution

The mean of the sample for people with incomes over $25,000 is

$$\bar{x}_3 = \frac{T_3}{n_3} = \frac{4,278}{10} = 427.8$$

and, from Example 15.3, $\bar{x}_1 = 229.6$. The tabulated value, $t_{.025}$, is the same as for Example 15.3—namely, 2.052. Then, the 95% confidence interval for $(\mu_3 - \mu_1)$, the difference in mean indebtedness between the two groups, is

$$(\bar{x}_3 - \bar{x}_1) \pm t_{.025} s \sqrt{\frac{1}{n_3} + \frac{1}{n_1}} = (427.8 - 229.6) \pm (2.052)(168.9) \sqrt{\frac{1}{10} + \frac{1}{10}}$$

$$= 198.2 \pm 155.0$$

or (43.2, 353.2).

As for the confidence interval for a single mean, the confidence interval for the difference $(\mu_3 - \mu_1)$ is very wide. This is due to the excessive within-sample variation. To obtain a narrower confidence interval, the sample sizes for the three income groups must be increased. However, the fact that the interval contains only positive numbers allows us to conclude, with 95% confidence, that the mean indebtedness of those with incomes over $25,000 exceeds the mean indebtedness of those with incomes less than $12,000. ∎

Case Study 15.1

Measuring a Manager's Knowledge of Computers

In the past 10 years computers and computer training have become integral parts of the curricula of secondary schools and universities. As a result, younger business professionals tend to be more comfortable with computers than their more senior counterparts.

'The older the person is, the worse it is,' said Arnold S. Kahn of the American Psychological Association. 'The older they are and the longer they wait before learning, the more dissatisfied they will become.' The computer's unrelenting march into offices and factories is often cited as a chief cause of work-related stress. As computers and robots come into the workplace, many workers fear they'll never master the new skills required (Aplin-Brownlee, 1984).

In 1984, Gary W. Dickson,* Professor of Management Information Systems at the Univer-

* Personal communication from Gary W. Dickson, Jan. 1984.

sity of Minnesota, investigated the computer literacy of middle managers with 10 years or more management experience. As part of his study, Dickson designed a questionnaire to measure a manager's technical knowledge of computers. If the questionnaire were properly designed, the scores received by managers could be used as predictors of their knowledge of computers, with higher scores indicating greater knowledge. To check the design of the questionnaire (i.e., its validity), nineteen middle managers from the Minneapolis–St. Paul metropolitan area were randomly sampled and asked to complete the questionnaire. Their scores appear in Table 15.5. (The highest possible score on the questionnaire was 169.)

Table 15.5

Questionnaire Scores of Middle Managers

MANAGER	LEVEL OF TECHNICAL EXPERTISE	SCORE	MANAGER	LEVEL OF TECHNICAL EXPERTISE	SCORE
1	1	82	11	1	80
2	1	114	12	1	105
3	1	90	13	2	110
4	1	80	14	2	133
5	2	128	15	3	128
6	2	90	16	2	130
7	3	156	17	2	104
8	1	88	18	3	151
9	1	93	19	3	140
10	2	130			

Prior to completing the questionnaire, the managers were asked to describe their knowledge of and experience with computers. This information was used to classify the managers as possessing a high (3), medium (2), or low (1) level of technical computer expertise. These data also appear in Table 15.5.

In order to evaluate the questionnaire's design, Dickson used analysis of variance to compare the mean scores of each of the three groups of managers. If the questionnaire were properly designed, the mean scores should differ. In particular, the mean score of managers with a high level of expertise should be greater than the mean score of managers with a medium level of expertise, etc. Dickson used Minitab to obtain the ANOVA table displayed in Figure 15.6.

Figure 15.6 ANOVA Table for Managers' Scores

```
ANALYSIS OF VARIANCE

DUE TO    DF      SS     MS=SS/DF   F-RATIO

FACTOR     2    7634.      3817.      19.19
ERROR     16    3182.       199.
TOTAL     18   10815.

LEVEL     N     MEAN    ST. DEV.

1         8     91.5      12.3
2         7    117.9      16.6
3         4    143.8      12.4

POOLED ST. DEV.=          14.1
```

Since $F = 19.19$ is greater than $F_{.01} = 6.23$ ($v_1 = 2$, $v_2 = 16$), Dickson concluded that the mean scores differ for at least two of the three groups of managers. However, this result could be obtained even with a poorly designed questionnaire. For example, a significant F statistic could result even if the mean for the high group were lower than the mean for the low group. Accordingly, Dickson used confidence intervals to examine the differences between individual group means. Using the information on the Minitab printout along with the appropriate t value, he developed the following 95% confidence intervals:

$$7.15 \le \mu_3 - \mu_2 \le 44.65$$
$$10.92 \le \mu_2 - \mu_1 \le 41.88$$

Since these confidence intervals indicate that $\mu_3 > \mu_2 > \mu_1$, Dickson concluded that the questionnaire could be used as a predictor of managers' technical knowledge of computers.

**Exercises
15.1 – 15.15**

Learning the Mechanics

15.1 Use Tables VI, VII, VIII, and IX of Appendix B to find each of the following F values:

a. $F_{.05}$, $v_1 = 2$, $v_2 = 2$ **b.** $F_{.01}$, $v_1 = 2$, $v_2 = 2$
c. $F_{.10}$, $v_1 = 20$, $v_2 = 40$ **d.** $F_{.025}$, $v_1 = 12$, $v_2 = 9$

15.2 Find the following probabilities:

a. $P(F \le 2.88)$ for $v_1 = 20$, $v_2 = 21$
b. $P(F > 3.52)$ for $v_1 = 15$, $v_2 = 15$
c. $P(F > 2.40)$ for $v_1 = 15$, $v_2 = 15$
d. $P(F \le 1.69)$ for $v_1 = 40$, $v_2 = 40$

15.3 Independent random samples were selected from three normally distributed populations with common (but unknown) variance, σ^2. The data are shown in the table.

SAMPLE 1	SAMPLE 2	SAMPLE 3
3.8	5.4	1.3
1.2	2.0	.7
2.9		3.1
3.3		

a. Compute the appropriate sums of squares and mean squares and fill in the appropriate entries in the analysis of variance table:

SOURCE	df	SS	MS	F
Treatments				
Error				
Total				

b. Test the hypothesis that the population means are equal (i.e., $\mu_1 = \mu_2 = \mu_3$) against the alternative hypothesis that at least one mean is different from the other two. Test using $\alpha = .05$.

c. Find a 90% confidence interval for $(\mu_2 - \mu_3)$. Interpret the interval.

d. What would happen to the width of the confidence interval in part c if you quadrupled the number of observations in the two samples?

e. Find a 95% confidence interval for μ_2.

f. Approximately how many observations would be required if you wished to be able to estimate a population mean correct to within .4 with probability equal to .95?

15.4 A partially completed ANOVA summary for a completely randomized design is shown in the table.

SOURCE	df	SS	MS	F
Treatments	6	16.9		
Error				
Total	41	45.2		

a. Complete the ANOVA table.

b. How many treatments are involved in the experiment?

c. Do the data provide sufficient evidence to indicate a difference among the population means? Test using $\alpha = .10$.

d. Find the approximate observed significance level for the test in part c, and interpret it.

e. Suppose that $\bar{x}_1 = 3.7$ and $\bar{x}_2 = 4.1$. Do the data provide sufficient evidence to indicate a difference between μ_1 and μ_2? Assume that there are seven observations for each treatment. Test using $\alpha = .10$.

f. Refer to part e. Find a 90% confidence interval for $(\mu_1 - \mu_2)$.

g. Refer to part e. Find a 90% confidence interval for μ_1.

15.5 Describe in words the type of variability being measured by each of the following sums of squares:

a. SSE   **b.** SST   **c.** SS(Total)

15.6 Explain why the F test used in the analysis of variance to test the null hypothesis H_0: $\mu_1 = \mu_2 = \cdots = \mu_k$ is a one-tailed, upper-tailed test.

15.7 What assumptions are necessary for the validity of the F test in a completely randomized design?

Applying the Concepts

15.8 An accounting firm that specializes in auditing the financial records of large corporations is interested in evaluating the appropriateness of the fees it charges for its services. As part of its evaluation it wants to compare the costs it incurs in auditing corporations of different sizes. The accounting firm decided to measure the size of its client corporations in terms of their yearly sales. Accordingly, its population of client corporations was divided into three subpopulations:

A: Those with sales over $250 million

B: Those with sales between $100 million and $250 million

C: Those with sales under $100 million

The firm chose random samples of ten corporations from each of the subpopulations and determined the costs (in thousands of dollars) given in the table from its records.

a. Construct a dot diagram (refer to Figures 15.2 and 15.3) for the sample data using different types of dots for each of the three samples. Indicate the location of each of the sample means. Based on the information reflected in your dot diagram, do you believe that a significant difference exists among the subpopulation means? Explain.

b. Use an analysis of variance to determine whether there is a significant difference among the average audit costs of the three subpopulations of firms. Test using $\alpha = .05$.

c. Find the approximate observed significance level for the test in part b, and interpret it.

d. Construct a 95% confidence interval for $(\mu_A - \mu_B)$.

e. What assumptions must be satisfied so that the inferences in parts b and d will be valid?

15.9 The application of *management by objectives* (MBO), a method of performance appraisal, is the object of a study by Y. K. Shetty and H. M. Carlisle of Utah State University ("Organizational Correlates of a Management by Objectives Program," *Academy of Management Journal,* 1974, *17*). The study dealt with the reactions of a university faculty to an MBO program. One hundred nine faculty members were asked to comment on whether they thought the MBO program was successful in improving their performance within their respective departments and the university. Each response was assigned a score from 1 (significant improvement) to 5 (significant decrease). The table shows the sample sizes, sample totals, mean scores, and sum of squares of deviations *within* each sample for samples of scores corresponding to the four academic ranks. Assume that the four samples in the table can be viewed as independent random samples of scores selected from among the four academic ranks.

COSTS INCURRED IN AUDITS		
A	*B*	*C*
250	100	80
150	150	125
275	75	20
100	200	186
475	55	52
600	80	92
150	110	88
800	160	141
325	132	76
230	233	200

		ACADEMIC RANK		
	Instructor	Assistant professor	Associate professor	Professor
SAMPLE SIZE	15	41	29	24
SAMPLE TOTAL	42.960	145.222	92.249	73.224
SAMPLE MEAN	2.864	3.542	3.181	3.051
WITHIN-SAMPLE SUM OF SQUARED DEVIATIONS	2.0859	14.0186	7.9247	5.6812

a. Perform an analysis of variance for the data.

b. Arrange the results in an analysis of variance table.

c. Do the data provide sufficient evidence to conclude there is a difference in mean scores among the four academic ranks? Test using $\alpha = .05$.

d. Find a 95% confidence interval for the difference in mean scores between instructors and professors.

e. Do the data provide sufficient evidence to indicate a difference in mean scores between nontenured faculty members (instructors and assistant professors) and tenured faculty members (associate and full professors)? Test using $\alpha = .05$.

15.10 Most new products are test marketed in several locations, frequently using different advertising techniques.* Suppose the table represents the number of sales for a new product at each of three locations during each of the last 4 months.

LOCATION		
I	*II*	*III*
456	441	501
421	419	467
397	415	520
419	420	493

a. Treat this as a completely randomized design, and test to determine whether there is a difference among the mean sales at the three locations. Use $\alpha = .05$.

b. Estimate the difference in the mean sales between locations I and III using a 90% confidence interval.

15.11 In Exercise 12.50, regression analysis was applied to the data in the table to investigate whether the mean debt-to-equity ratio varies among the insurance, publishing, electric utilities, and banking industries. In this exercise, we will use analysis of variance to perform the same investigation.

INSURANCE		PUBLISHING		ELECTRIC UTILITIES		BANKING	
Firm	*Debt-to-equity*	*Firm*	*Debt-to-equity*	*Firm*	*Debt-to-equity*	*Firm*	*Debt-to-equity*
Chubb	0.1	Deluxe		Pacific Power		U.S. Bancorp	0.5
Kemper	0.0	Check	0.0	& Light	1.1	Sun Banks	0.2
St. Paul Cos.	0.1	New York		Houston Ind.	0.8	Mellon	
Lincoln		Times	0.4	Florida Power		National	0.5
National	0.2	A. C. Nielsen	0.1	& Light	0.8	Michigan	
USF & G	0.0	Dow Jones	0.1	Penn Power		National	0.3
Aetna	0.1	Gannett	0.3	& Light	0.9	Southeast	
				North States		Banking	0.4
				Pur.	0.7		
				Ohio Edison	1.2		
				Orange and			
				Rockland	0.6		

Source: *Forbes*, "36th Annual Report on American Industry," Jan. 2, 1984.

a. Construct a dot diagram of the type shown in Figure 15.2 for each of the four sets of sample data. Indicate the location of each sample mean. Based on the information reflected in your dot diagram, do you believe that a difference exists among the industry means? Explain.

b. Conduct an analysis of variance for the data. Is there sufficient evidence to indicate that the mean debt-to-equity ratio varies among the four industries? Test using $\alpha = .01$.

15.12 A company that employs a large number of salespeople is interested in learning which of the salespeople sell the most: those strictly on commission, those with a fixed salary, or those with a reduced fixed salary plus a commission. The previous month's records for a sample of salespeople are inspected and the amount of sales (in dollars) is recorded for each, as shown in the table at the top of the next page.

* For an example of test marketing, see Klompmaker et al. (1976).

COMMISSIONED	FIXED SALARY	COMMISSION PLUS SALARY
$425	$420	$430
507	448	492
450	437	470
483	432	501
466	444	
492		

a. Do the data provide sufficient evidence to indicate a difference among the mean sales for the three types of compensation? Use $\alpha = .05$.

b. Use a 90% confidence interval to estimate the mean sales for salespeople who receive a commission plus salary.

c. Use a 90% confidence interval to estimate the difference in mean sales between salespeople on commission plus salary and those on fixed salary.

15.13 How does flexitime, which allows workers to set their individual work schedules, affect worker job satisfaction? Researchers recently conducted a study to compare a measure of job satisfaction for workers using three types of work scheduling: flexitime, staggered starting hours, and fixed hours. Workers in each group worked according to their specified work scheduling system for 4 months. Although each worker filled out job satisfaction questionnaires both before and after the 4-month test period, we will examine only the post-test-period scores. The sample sizes, means, and standard deviations of the scores for the three groups are shown in the table.

| | GROUP | | |
	Flexitime	Staggered	Fixed
SAMPLE SIZE	27	59	24
MEAN	35.22	31.05	28.71
STANDARD DEVIATION	10.22	7.22	9.28

a. Assume that the data were collected according to a completely randomized design. Use the information in the table to calculate the treatment totals, CM, and SST.

b. Use the values of the sample standard deviations to calculate the sum of squares of deviations *within* each of the three samples. Then calculate SSE, the sum of these quantities.

c. Construct an analysis of variance table for the data.

d. Do the data provide sufficient evidence to indicate differences in mean job satisfaction scores among the three groups? Test using $\alpha = .05$.

e. Find a 90% confidence interval for the difference in mean job satisfaction scores between workers on flexitime and those on fixed schedules.

f. Do the data provide sufficient evidence to indicate a difference in mean scores between workers on flexitime and those using staggered starting hours? Test using $\alpha = .05$.

15.14 In Exercise 9.24, we compared the mean bond price changes over a 12-month period for two underwriters. Similar data providing a comparison of five underwriting firms were extracted from the paper by D. Logue and R. Rogalski *(Harvard Business Review,* July–Aug. 1979) and are shown in the table. Suppose the data represent independent random samples from the five populations.

| | UNDERWRITER | | | | |
	1	2	3	4	5
Sample size	27	20	23	11	15
Sample mean	−.0491	−.0479	−.0307	−.0438	−.0051
Sample variance	.009800	.006459	.002465	.001462	.002834

a. Use the sample means and sample sizes to calculate the sample totals.

b. Use the sample variances and the sample sizes to calculate the sum of squares of deviations within each of the samples. Then calculate SSE, the sum of these five quantities.

c. Perform an analysis of variance and display the results in an ANOVA table.

d. Do the data provide sufficient evidence to indicate differences among the mean bond price changes over the 12-month period for the five underwriters? Test using $\alpha = .05$.

e. Find a 95% confidence interval for the difference in the means of the bond price changes between underwriters 4 and 5.

15.15 Auditors may be called upon to perform compilations, reviews, or audits for their nonpublic clients. To do compilations and reviews of financial statements requires auditors an average of 25% and 50% fewer hours, respectively, than to perform an annual audit. Both auditors and clients fear that users of compilations and reviews — both of which are new forms of auditor association with a firm's financial reports — might not recognize the limited nature of these reports and might assume that the auditor was accepting the same degree of responsibility for them as for audited annual financial statements. To investigate these fears, Johnson, Pany, and White (1983) conducted an experiment designed to measure bankers' reactions to these three alternative forms of auditors' reports. Ninety-eight loan officers responded to a questionnaire in which they were asked to review a financial statement and background information for a commercial loan applicant. Thirty-one of the officers received a compilation, twenty-five received a review, twenty-seven an audit, and fifteen received a financial statement with no auditor association. One of the questions dealt with the loan officers' level of confidence about the financial statement's conformance to generally accepted accounting principles (GAAP). They were asked to indicate their level of confidence on a scale from 0 to 10 (no confidence to extreme confidence). Johnson, Pany, and White hypothesized that the mean level of confidence would not be the same for all four types of financial statements. Further, they hypothesized that the mean level of confidence associated with the audit would be greater than with the next highest form of auditor association, the review. Some of the data obtained from their experiment are summarized in the tables at the top of the next page.

SOURCE	df	SS
Type of report	3	273
Error	94	494
Total	97	767

	TREATMENT MEANS
No auditor association	3.9
Compilation	5.5
Review	6.1
Audit	8.8

a. Do the data provide sufficient evidence to conclude that the mean level of confidence differs among the four forms of auditor association? Test using $\alpha = .05$.

b. Report the approximate p-value of your test.

c. Do the data provide sufficient evidence to conclude that the mean level of confidence associated with the audit is significantly higher than the mean for the review? Test using $\alpha = .05$.

d. Use a 95% confidence interval to estimate the difference between the mean confidence levels of the compilation and the review.

e. Relate your findings for parts a, c, and d to the expressed fear that users of financial reports might assume auditors were accepting the same degree of responsibility for each form of financial report.

15.2 Randomized Block Design

The *randomized block design* uses groups of *homogeneous experimental units* (matched as closely as possible) to compare the means of the populations associated with k treatments. Suppose there are b blocks of relatively homogeneous experimental units. Since each treatment must be represented in each block, the blocks will each contain k experimental units, which will be randomly assigned to the k treatments. The general format of the randomized block design is shown in Figure 15.7. Although we show the treatments in order within the blocks, in practice they would be assigned to the experimental units in a random order (thus the name *randomized block design*). The notation for the results of a randomized block experiment is summarized in Table 15.6.

Figure 15.7 General Form of the Randomized Block Design (Treatment i is Denoted by T_i)

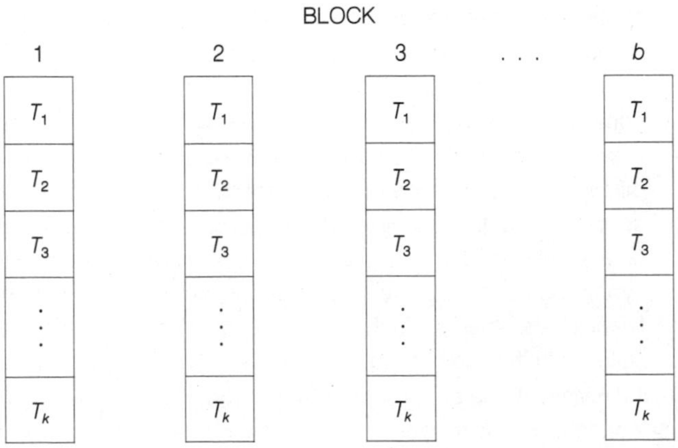

Table 15.6

Notation for the Results of a Randomized Block Experiment

	TREATMENT 1	TREATMENT 2 . . .	TREATMENT k
Sample size	b	b . . .	b
Sample totals	T_1	T_2 . . .	T_k
	BLOCK 1	BLOCK 2 . . .	BLOCK b
Sample size	k	k . . .	k
Sample totals	B_1	B_2 . . .	B_b

Total number of observations $= bk = n$

Sum of all observations $= \sum x_i$

Sum of squares of all observations $= \sum x_i^2$

We are interested in using the randomized block design to test the same null and alternative hypotheses we tested using the completely randomized design; i.e.,

H_0: $\mu_1 = \mu_2 = \cdots = \mu_k$

H_a: At least two treatment means differ

The test statistic is also identical to that used for the completely randomized design:

Test statistic: $F = \dfrac{\text{MST}}{\text{MSE}}$

The numerator of the F statistic, MST (mean square for treatments), is computed exactly as it was for the completely randomized design. However, the denominator, MSE (mean square for error), is computed differently. This is most easily seen from Figure 15.8, which illustrates the partitioning of SS(Total), the total sum of squares about the overall mean. Note that the SS(Total) is now partitioned into three parts. The SSE for the completely randomized experiment has been further subdivided into two parts—the sum of squares for blocks, SSB, and

Figure 15.8 Partitioning of the Total Sum of Squares for the Randomized Block Design

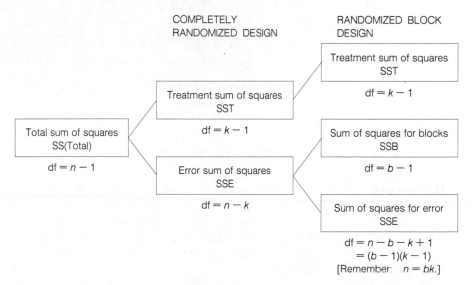

the sum of squares for error, the SSE for the randomized block design. (We use the same symbol, SSE, for the sum of squares for error in both designs, although their computational formulas differ.)

Figure 15.8 may help you understand how a randomized block design works. Since

$$SS(Total) = SSB + SST + SSE$$

it follows that the SSE for this design is

$$SSE = SS(Total) - SST - SSB$$

In other words, the SSE will equal the sum of squares for error for the completely randomized design [SS(Total) − SST] *minus* SSB. Thus, the randomized block design permits us to remove the variation between blocks from within-sample variation and, hopefully, will decrease the MSE. Remember, the smaller the value of the MSE (which appears in the denominator of the F statistic), the more likely it is that we will detect a difference among the treatment means, if such a difference exists.

The test for treatment differences using the randomized block design is summarized in the box.

Test to Compare k Treatment Means: Randomized Block Design

H_0: $\mu_1 = \mu_2 = \cdots = \mu_k$

H_a: At least two treatment means differ

Test statistic: $F = \dfrac{MST}{MSE}$

Assumptions: 1.   The probability distributions of observations corresponding to all the block–treatment combinations are normal.
2.   The variances of all the probability distributions are equal.

Rejection region: $F > F_\alpha$ where F_α is based on $(k - 1)$ numerator degrees of freedom and $(n - b - k + 1)$ denominator degrees of freedom.

The formulas needed for the analysis of a randomized block design are presented in the box at the top of the next page.

Example 15.5   A study was conducted in a large city following the dramatic increase in coffee prices during the final quarter of 1976. The objective was to compare the mean supermarket prices of the four leading brands at the end of the year. Ten supermarkets in the city were selected, and the price per pound was recorded for each brand. Set up the test of the null hypothesis that the mean prices of the four brands sold in the city were the same at the end of the year. Use $\alpha = .05$.

Formulas for the Calculations in the Randomized Block Design

CM = Correction for mean

$$= \frac{(\text{Total of all observations})^2}{\text{Total number of observations}} = \frac{\left(\sum x_i\right)^2}{n}$$

$SS(\text{Total})$ = Total sum of squares

$$= (\text{Sum of squares of all observations}) - CM = \sum x_i^2 - CM$$

SST = Sum of squares for treatments

$$= \begin{pmatrix} \text{Sum of squares of treatment totals with} \\ \text{each square divided by } b, \text{ the number of} \\ \text{observations for that treatment} \end{pmatrix} - CM = \frac{T_1^2}{b} + \frac{T_2^2}{b} + \cdots + \frac{T_k^2}{b} - CM$$

SSB = Sum of squares for blocks

$$= \begin{pmatrix} \text{Sum of squares of block totals with} \\ \text{each square divided by } k, \text{ the number} \\ \text{of observations in that block} \end{pmatrix} - CM = \frac{B_1^2}{k} + \frac{B_2^2}{k} + \cdots + \frac{B_b^2}{k} - CM$$

SSE = Sum of squares for error = $SS(\text{Total}) - SST - SSB$

MST = Mean square for treatments = $\dfrac{SST}{k-1}$

MSB = Mean square for blocks = $\dfrac{SSB}{b-1}$

MSE = Mean square for error = $\dfrac{SSE}{n-k-b+1}$

F = Test statistic = $\dfrac{MST}{MSE}$

where

n = Total number of observations

b = Number of blocks

k = Number of treatments

Solution   We would expect coffee prices to be more homogeneous within a store than between stores. In other words, the experimental units—the 1-pound cans of coffee—will be more homogeneous (with respect to price) within stores. The stores, then, act as blocks and the coffee brands act as treatments.

Denote the true mean prices of the four brands as μ_1, μ_2, μ_3, and μ_4. Then the elements of the test are

H_0: $\mu_1 = \mu_2 = \mu_3 = \mu_4$

H_a: At least two brands have different mean prices

Test statistic: $\dfrac{\text{MST}}{\text{MSE}}$

Assumptions:
1. The probability distributions of coffee prices corresponding to all the supermarket–brand combinations are normal.
2. The variances of the probability distributions are equal.

Rejection region: Since we have $k = 4$ treatments (brands) and $b = 10$ blocks (stores), we use a tabulated F value with $k - 1 = 4 - 1 = 3$ df in the numerator, and $n - b - k + 1 = (4)(10) - 10 - 4 + 1 = 27$ df in the denominator. Then, for $\alpha = .05$, we will reject H_0 if $F > F_{.05}$ where (from Table VII, Appendix B) $F_{.05} = 2.96$. ■

Example 15.6

The data (and totals) for the coffee price study described in Example 15.5 are given in Table 15.7. Calculate the F statistic. Do the data provide sufficient evidence to indicate a difference among the mean prices for the four brands of coffee?

Table 15.7
Price per Pound of Coffee

SUPERMARKET	BRAND A	B	C	D	TOTALS
1	$2.43	$2.47	$2.47	$2.41	9.78
2	2.48	2.52	2.53	2.48	10.01
3	2.38	2.44	2.42	2.35	9.59
4	2.40	2.47	2.46	2.39	9.72
5	2.35	2.42	2.44	2.32	9.53
6	2.43	2.49	2.47	2.42	9.81
7	2.55	2.62	2.64	2.56	10.37
8	2.41	2.49	2.47	2.39	9.76
9	2.53	2.60	2.59	2.49	10.21
10	2.35	2.43	2.44	2.36	9.58
TOTALS	24.31	24.95	24.93	24.17	98.36

Solution

Following the order of calculations listed in the box, we have

$$\sum x_i^2 = (2.43)^2 + (2.48)^2 + \cdots + (2.36)^2 = 242.0966$$

$$CM = \frac{\left(\sum x_i\right)^2}{n} = \frac{(98.36)^2}{40} = 241.86724$$

$$SS(\text{Total}) = \sum_i^2 - CM = 242.0966 - 241.86724 = .22936$$

$$SST = \frac{T_1^2}{10} + \frac{T_2^2}{10} + \frac{T_3^2}{10} + \frac{T_4^2}{10} - CM$$

$$= \frac{(24.31)^2}{10} + \frac{(24.95)^2}{10} + \frac{(24.93)^2}{10} + \frac{(24.17)^2}{10} - 241.86724$$

$$= 241.91724 - 241.86724 = .05000$$

$$SSB = \frac{B_1^2}{4} + \frac{B_2^2}{4} + \cdots + \frac{B_{10}^2}{4} - CM$$

$$= \frac{(9.78)^2}{4} + \frac{(10.01)^2}{4} + \cdots + \frac{(9.58)^2}{4} - 241.86724$$

$$= 242.04175 - 241.86724 = .17451$$

$$\text{SSE} = \text{SS(Total)} - \text{SST} - \text{SSB}$$

$$= .22936 - .05 - .17451 = .00485$$

$$\text{MST} = \frac{\text{SST}}{k-1} = \frac{.05}{3} = .016667$$

$$\text{MSB} = \frac{\text{SSB}}{b-1} = \frac{.17451}{9} = .019390$$

$$\text{MSE} = \frac{\text{SSE}}{n-k-b+1} = \frac{.00485}{27} = .00017963$$

$$F = \frac{\text{MST}}{\text{MSE}} = \frac{.016667}{.00017963} = 92.8$$

Since the calculated $F = 92.8$ greatly exceeds the tabulated value of $F_{.05} = 2.96$, there is very strong evidence that at least two of the means for the populations of prices of the four coffee brands differ. ∎

The ANOVA summary table for a randomized block analysis would appear as shown in Table 15.8. Table 15.9 is the ANOVA for the data analysis in Example 15.6.

Table 15.8
ANOVA Summary Table for a Randomized Block Design

SOURCE	df	SS	MS	F
Treatment	$k-1$	SST	MST	MST/MSE
Block	$b-1$	SSB	MSB	
Error	$n-k-b+1$	SSE	MSE	
Total	$n-1$	SS(Total)		

Table 15.9
ANOVA Table for Example 15.6

SOURCE	df	SS	MS	F
Treatment	3	.05000	.016667	92.8
Block	9	.17451	.019390	
Error	27	.00485	.00017963	
Total	39	.22936		

The formula for the confidence interval for the difference between a pair of treatment means is identical to the formula presented in Section 9.2 except for the estimate of σ^2, which is now

$$s^2 = \text{MSE} = \frac{\text{SSE}}{n-k-b+1}$$

This quantity appears in the ANOVA table. The formula for the confidence interval is shown in the box at the top of the next page.

> ### 100(1 − α)% Confidence Interval for the Difference in a Pair of Treatment Means (Say, $\mu_i - \mu_j$)
>
> $$(\bar{x}_i - \bar{x}_j) \pm t_{\alpha/2} s \sqrt{\frac{1}{b} + \frac{1}{b}} \quad \text{or} \quad (\bar{x}_i - \bar{x}_j) \pm t_{\alpha/2} s \sqrt{\frac{2}{b}}$$
>
> where b is the number of blocks and $t_{\alpha/2}$ is the tabulated value of t (Table V, Appendix B) that locates $\alpha/2$ in the upper tail of the t distribution with $(n - k - b + 1)$ df.

Example 15.7

Refer to the coffee brand price data in Example 15.6, and find a 90% confidence interval for the difference in the mean price of brand A versus brand B.

Solution

From Example 15.6, the sample means for brands A and B (identified as 1 and 2, respectively) are

$$\bar{x}_1 = \frac{T_1}{b} = \frac{24.31}{10} = \$2.431 \qquad \bar{x}_2 = \frac{T_2}{b} = \frac{24.95}{10} = \$2.495$$

From Table V in Appendix B, $t_{.05} = 1.703$ (where t is based on 27 df), and from Table 15.9, we have

$$s^2 = \text{MSE} = .00017963$$

Thus, $s = .0134$ and the 90% confidence interval for $(\mu_1 - \mu_2)$ is

$$(\bar{x}_1 - \bar{x}_2) \pm t_{.05} s \sqrt{\frac{2}{b}}$$

Substituting into the formula, we get

$$(2.431 - 2.495) \pm (1.703)(.0134) \sqrt{\frac{2}{10}}$$

or $(-.074, -.054)$. Thus, we estimate the mean price of brand B to exceed the mean price for A by as little as $0.054 or as much as $0.074. ∎

We can also conduct a test of an hypothesis to determine whether differences exist among block means. This test will help to decide whether blocking was successful in reducing the experimental error. That is, if the block means differ, we know the experimental units are indeed more homogeneous within blocks than between blocks, and the use of the randomized block experiment is justified. Such information is useful if similar experiments are to be conducted.

The test procedure for block means is very similar to that for treatment means. We compare the variation among blocks, as measured by the mean square for blocks (MSB), to the variation due to error, as measured by the mean square for error (MSE). The test is summarized in the box.

> ## Test to Compare b Block Means: Randomized Block Design
>
> H_0:   The b block means are equal
>
> H_a: At least two block means differ
>
> Test statistic: $F = \dfrac{MSB}{MSE}$
>
> Assumptions: Same as for the test of treatment means.
>
> Rejection region: We will reject H_0 if $F > F_\alpha$ where F_α is based on $\nu_1 = (b - 1)$, the number of blocks minus 1, and $\nu_2 = (n - k - b + 1)$ degrees of freedom.

Example 15.8

Refer to Examples 15.5 and 15.6, in which we used a randomized block design to compare the mean prices of four brands of coffee. The blocks were supermarkets in a large city. Test the null hypothesis that the block means are the same — i.e., that the average price of coffee is the same for the ten supermarkets. Use $\alpha = .05$.

Solution   The test for comparing the block means is

H_0:   Mean coffee prices are the same for all ten supermarkets

H_a: Mean coffee prices differ for at least two supermarkets

Test statistic: $F = \dfrac{MSB}{MSE}$

Assumptions: Same as for the test comparing the mean prices of the four coffee brands (Example 15.5).

Rejection region: The numerator and denominator degrees of freedom for the F statistic are $b - 1 = 10 - 1 = 9$ and $n - k - b + 1 = 27$, respectively. Then the rejection region is $F > F_{.05}$ where (from Table VII, Appendix B) $F_{.05} = 2.25$.

We calculated MSB and MSE in Example 15.6. Substituting these values into the F statistic, we have

$$F = \frac{MSB}{MSE} = \frac{.019390}{.00017963} = 107.9$$

Since the calculated F value greatly exceeds the tabulated F value, the data provide sufficient evidence to indicate that the means of coffee prices differ among the ten supermarkets. The decision to use a randomized block design was wise. Blocking had the effect of reducing the SSE and increasing the amount of information in the experiment. Future price comparison studies might benefit from this information. Table 15.10 (page 696) is the complete ANOVA summary table for this experiment.   ∎

Table 15.10

Complete ANOVA Summary
Table for Example 15.8

SOURCE	df	SS	MS	F
Treatment	3	.05000	.016667	92.8
Block	9	.17451	.019390	107.9
Error	27	.00485	.00017963	
Total	39	.22936		

We conclude this section with a caution: The result of the test for the equality of block means must be interpreted with care, especially when the calculated value of the F test statistic does not fall in the rejection region. This does not necessarily imply that the block means are the same — i.e., that blocking is unimportant. Reaching this conclusion would be equivalent to accepting the null hypothesis, a practice we have carefully avoided due to the unknown probability of committing a Type II error (that is, of accepting H_0 when H_a is true). In other words, even when a test for block differences is inconclusive, we may still want to use the randomized block design in similar future experiments. If the experimenter believes the experimental units are more homogeneous within blocks than among blocks, he or she should use the randomized block design regardless of whether the test comparing the block means shows them to be different.

**Exercises
15.16 – 15.27**

Learning the Mechanics

15.16 A randomized block design was conducted to compare the mean responses for three treatments, A, B, and C, in four blocks. The data are shown in the table.

TREATMENT	BLOCK			
	1	2	3	4
A	3	6	1	2
B	5	7	4	6
C	2	3	2	2

a. Compute the appropriate sums of squares and mean squares and fill in the entries in the analysis of variance table.

SOURCE	df	SS	MS	F
Treatment				
Block				
Error				
Total				

b. Do the data provide sufficient evidence to indicate a difference among treatment means? Test using $\alpha = .05$.

c. Do the data provide sufficient evidence to indicate that blocking was effective in reducing the experimental error? Test using $\alpha = .05$.

d. Find the approximate observed significance level for the test in part c, and interpret it.

e. Find a 90% confidence interval for $(\mu_A - \mu_B)$.

f. What assumptions are required to make the F tests in parts b and c valid?

15.17 The analysis of variance for a randomized block design produced the ANOVA table shown here.

SOURCE	df	SS	MS	F
Treatment	3	28.2		
Block	5		13.80	
Error		34.1		
Total				

a. Complete the ANOVA table.

b. Do the data provide sufficient evidence to indicate a difference among the treatment means? Test using $\alpha = .01$.

c. Do the data provide sufficient evidence to indicate that blocking was a useful design strategy for this experiment? Explain.

d. If the sample means for treatments A and B are $\bar{x}_A = 9.7$ and $\bar{x}_B = 12.1$, respectively, find a 90% confidence interval for $(\mu_A - \mu_B)$. Interpret the interval.

15.18 Explain the difference between a completely randomized design and a randomized block design.

15.19 Explain why the following statement is true: The smaller the value of MSE in relation to the value of MST, the more likely it is that we will detect a difference among the treatment means, if such a difference exists.

15.20 What assumptions are necessary for the validity of the F test in a randomized block design?

Applying the Concepts

15.21 A large clothing manufacturer conducted an experiment to study the effect on productivity of increases in its employees' hourly wages. Four treatments were used in the experiment:

Treatment 1: No increase in hourly wage

Treatment 2: Increase hourly wage by $0.50

Treatment 3: Increase hourly wage by $1.00

Treatment 4: Increase hourly wage by $1.50

Twelve employees were selected and grouped into three blocks of size four according to the length of time they had been with the company. The four treatments were randomly assigned to the four employees in each block. The employees were observed for 3 weeks, and their productivity was measured as the average number of nondefective garments each produced per hour. The resulting productivity measures appear in the table at the top of the next page.

	TREATMENT			
	1	2	3	4
Group 1 (less than 1 year)	2.4	3.0	3.1	3.2
Group 2 (1 – 5 years)	4.8	6.1	5.9	5.7
Group 3 (over 5 years)	5.1	7.0	7.2	7.3

a. Use an analysis of variance to determine whether there is evidence of a difference among the mean productivity levels under the four different pay programs. Use $\alpha = .05$. Construct the ANOVA summary table.

b. Find the approximate observed significance level for the test and interpret it.

c. Why was blocking utilized in this experiment?

d. Use a 95% confidence interval to estimate the difference in mean productivity for treatments 1 and 3.

15.22 A power plant that uses water from the surrounding bay for cooling its condensers is required by the Environmental Protection Agency (EPA) to determine whether discharging its heated water into the bay has a detrimental effect on the flora (plant life) in the water. The EPA requests that the power plant make its investigation at three strategically chosen locations, called *stations*. Stations 1 and 2 are located near the plant's discharge tubes, while station 3 is farther out in the bay. During one randomly selected day in each of 4 months, a diver descends to each of the stations, randomly samples a square meter area of the bottom, and counts the number of blades of the different types of grasses present. The results for one important grass type are shown in the table.

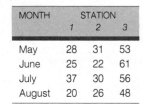

MONTH	STATION		
	1	2	3
May	28	31	53
June	25	22	61
July	37	30	56
August	20	26	48

a. Is there sufficient evidence to indicate a difference among the mean numbers of blades found per square meter per month for the three stations? Use $\alpha = .05$.

b. Is there sufficient evidence to indicate a difference among the mean numbers of blades found per square meter for the 4 months? Use $\alpha = .05$.

c. Place a 90% confidence interval on the difference in means between stations 1 and 3.

15.23 A food chain sells a particular item at all its stores. Each store carries three brands, two of which are economy brands. The management decides to discontinue selling one of the economy brands. It has decided to look at the *turn time* of each brand—i.e., the average time between successive purchases of the same brand. Five of the stores in the chain are selected, and an employee in each store reports the turn time (in minutes) for each brand.

STORE	ECONOMY BRAND	
	1	2
1	4.1	3.9
2	5.2	5.1
3	5.0	5.0
4	4.9	4.7
5	6.1	5.9

a. Is there a difference in the mean turn times for the two economy brands? Use $\alpha = .05$.

b. What is the purpose of the blocks in this experiment? Why is the mean square for blocks so large?

c. Recall that a randomized block design with $k = 2$ treatments is a paired difference experiment (Chapter 9). Analyze the data as a paired difference experiment using a t test to compare the treatment means. Test using $\alpha = .05$.

d. Compare the computed F and t values from parts a and c, and verify that $F = t^2$. Also verify that for the rejection region values of F and t, $F_\alpha = t_{\alpha/2}^2$ and, hence, the F test (of the randomized block analysis) and the t test (of the paired difference analysis) are equivalent for $k = 2$ treatments.

15.24 The Bell Telephone Company's long-distance phone charges may appear to be exorbitant when compared with some of its competitors, but this is because a comparison of charges between competing companies is often analogous to comparing apples and eggs. Bell's charges for individuals are on a per-call basis. In contrast, its competitors often charge a monthly minimum long-distance fee, reduce the charges as the usage rises, or both. Shown in the table is a sampling of long-distance charges from Orlando, Florida, to twelve cities for three non-Bell companies offering long-distance service. The data were contained in an advertisement in the *Orlando Sentinel,* Mar. 19, 1984. A note in fine print below the advertisement states that the rates are based on "30 hours of usage" for each of the servicing companies.

The data in the table are pertinent for companies making phone calls to large cities. Therefore, assume that the cities receiving the calls were randomly selected from among all large cities in the United States.

FROM ORLANDO TO:	TIME	LENGTH OF CALL (Minutes)	COMPANY 1	2	3
New York	Day	2	$ .77	$ .79	$ .66
Chicago	Evening	3	.69	.71	.59
Los Angeles	Day	2	.87	.88	.66
Atlanta	Evening	1	.22	.23	.20
Boston	Day	3	1.15	1.19	.99
Phoenix	Day	5	1.92	1.98	1.65
West Palm Beach	Evening	2	.49	.42	.40
Miami	Day	3	1.12	1.05	.99
Denver	Day	10	3.85	3.96	3.30
Houston	Evening	1	.22	.23	.20
Tampa	Day	3	1.06	1.00	.99
Jacksonville	Day	3	1.06	1.00	.99

a. What type of design was used for the data collection?

b. Perform an analysis of variance for the data. Present the results in an ANOVA table.

c. Do the data provide sufficient evidence to indicate differences in mean charges among the three companies? Test using $\alpha = .05$.

d. Company 3 placed the advertisement, so it might be more relevant to compare the charges for companies 1 and 2. Do the data provide sufficient evidence to indicate a difference in mean charges for these two companies? Test using $\alpha = .05$.

15.25 A construction firm employs three cost estimators. Usually only one estimator works on each potential job, but it is advantageous to the company if the estimators are consistent enough that it does not matter which of the three estimators is assigned to a particular job. To check on the consistency of the estimators, several jobs are selected and all three estimators are asked to make estimates. The estimates (in thousands of dollars) for each job by each estimator are given in the table at the top of the next page.

JOB	ESTIMATOR		
	A	B	C
1	27.3	26.5	28.2
2	66.7	67.3	65.9
3	104.8	102.1	100.8
4	87.6	85.6	86.5
5	54.5	55.6	55.9
6	58.7	59.2	60.1

a. Do these estimates provide sufficient evidence that the means for at least two of the estimators differ? Use $\alpha = .05$.

b. Find the approximate observed significance level for the test, and interpret it.

c. Present the complete ANOVA summary table for this experiment.

d. Use a 90% confidence interval to estimate the difference between the mean responses given by estimators B and C.

15.26 The table lists the number of strikes that occurred per year in five U.S. manufacturing industries over the period from 1976 to 1981. Only work stoppages that continued for at least 1 day and involved six or more workers were counted.

YEAR	FOOD AND KINDRED PRODUCTS	PRIMARY METAL INDUSTRY	ELECTRICAL EQUIPMENT AND SUPPLIES	FABRICATED METAL PRODUCTS	CHEMICALS AND ALLIED PRODUCTS
1976	227	197	204	309	129
1977	221	239	199	354	111
1978	171	187	190	360	113
1979	178	202	195	352	143
1980	155	175	140	280	89
1981	109	114	106	203	60

Source: *Statistical Abstract of the United States.*

a. Perform an analysis of variance and determine whether there is sufficient evidence to conclude that the mean number of strikes per year differs among the five industries. Test using $\alpha = .05$.

b. Construct the appropriate ANOVA table.

15.27 According to an advertisement in the *Gainesville Sun* (Mar. 18, 1984), shopping at local supermarket A can save you up to 21%. As proof of the statement, the advertising supermarket gives the results of a survey taken February 29, 1984, of the prices of forty-nine grocery items at supermarket A and at three of its competitors. Ten of these price comparisons are shown in the table. The data for a particular item represent a matched set of four observations, one for each of the supermarkets. As a result, the data in the table can be viewed as having been collected according to a randomized block design.

ITEM	SUPERMARKET			
	A	B	C	D
Hi C fruit drink	$ .59	$ .63	$ .79	$ .63
Cheerios cereal	1.10	1.18	1.39	1.18
Hunt's tomato paste	.31	.33	.43	.33
Del Monte green beans	.35	.40	.57	.38
Dole pineapple	.36	.39	.39	.39
Muellers spaghetti	.31	.33	.41	.33
Charmin	1.20	1.12	1.29	1.23
Duncan Hines cake mix	.77	.85	1.12	.77
Dial soap	.52	.60	.63	.55
Heinz ketchup	1.12	1.24	1.39	1.15

a. Construct an analysis of variance table for the data.

b. Although you can see in the table that supermarket A's prices are as low as or lower than its competitors on nine of the ten items, test to determine if there is sufficient evidence to indicate that the mean prices of items differ among the four supermarkets. Test using $\alpha = .05$.

c. Supermarket D is supposed to be a low-cost, no-frills supermarket. Do the data provide evidence of a difference in mean prices per item between supermarkets A and D? Test using $\alpha = .05$.

d. Do the results of supermarket A's survey convince you that you can save money by shopping at supermarket A? Explain.

15.3
The Analysis of Variance for a Two-Way Classification of Data: Factorial Experiments

A randomized block design is often called a *two-way classification of data* because:

1. It involves two independent variables: one factor and one direction of blocking.

2. Each level of one independent variable occurs with every level of the other independent variable.

A two-way classification of data always permits the display of the data in a two-way table, a table containing r rows and c columns. For example, the data for the randomized block design of Example 15.6 are displayed in Table 15.7, which contains $r = 10$ rows and $c = 4$ columns. Each of the $rc = (10)(4) = 40$ cells of the two-way table contains one observation.

The treatment selection for a two-factor experiment may also yield a two-way classification of data. For example, suppose you want to relate the mean number of defects on a finished item (say, a new desk top) to two factors: type of nozzle for the varnish spray gun and length of spraying time. Three types of nozzle (three levels) and two lengths of spraying time (two levels) are to be used in the experiment. If we choose the treatments for the experiment to include all combinations of the three levels of nozzle type with the two levels of spraying time, we will obtain a two-way classification of data. This selection of treatments is called *complete 3 × 2 factorial experiment.*

> ### Definition 15.3
>
> A *factorial experiment* is a method for selecting the treatments (i.e., the factor level combinations) to be included in an experiment. A *complete factorial experiment* is one in which observations are made for every combination of the factor levels.

If we included a third factor — say, paint type — at three levels in the experiment, then a complete factorial experiment would include all of the $3 \times 2 \times 3 = 18$ combinations of nozzle type, spraying time, and paint type. The resulting collection of data would be called a three-way classification of data.

Factorial experiments are useful methods for selecting treatments because they permit the estimation of and testing of hypotheses about factor interactions. In this section we show how to perform an analysis of variance for a two-way classification of data. In the process, you will learn that the computational procedure is the same for both the randomized block design and the two-factor factorial experiment because both involve a two-way classification of data. You will also learn why the analysis of variance F tests differ and the practical interpretations that can be derived from them.

Suppose a two-way classification represents a two-factor factorial experiment with factor A at a levels and factor B at b levels. Further assume that the ab treatments of the factorial experiment are replicated r times so that there are r observations for each of the ab treatment combinations (i.e., there are r observations in each of the ab cells of the two-way table). Then the total number n of observations is $n = abr$ and the total sum of squares, SS(Total), can be partitioned into four parts, SS(A), SS(B), SS(AB), and SSE. The sources of variation and their respective degrees of freedom are shown in Figure 15.9.

When the number of observations per cell for a two-way factorial experiment is the same for every cell (r observations per cell), the degrees of freedom and sums of squares for the analysis of variance are additive; i.e.,

Sums of squares: $\text{SS(Total)} = \text{SS}(A) + \text{SS}(B) + \text{SS}(AB) + \text{SSE}$

Degrees of freedom: $n - 1 = abr - 1$
$$= (a - 1) + (b - 1) + (a - 1)(b - 1) + ab(r - 1)$$

and the analysis of variance table would appear as shown in Table 15.11. Note that for a factorial experiment, the number, r, of observations per factor level combination must always be two or more (i.e., $r \geq 2$). Otherwise, you will not have any degrees of freedom for SSE.

Table 15.11

ANOVA Table for a Two-Way Classification of Data with r Observations per Cell

SOURCE	df	SS	MS
Main effects A	$(a - 1)$	SS(A)	SS(A)/$(a - 1)$
Main effects B	$(b - 1)$	SS(B)	SS(B)/$(b - 1)$
AB interaction	$(a - 1)(b - 1)$	SS(AB)	SS(AB)/$[(a - 1)(b - 1)]$
Error	$ab(r - 1)$	SSE	SSE/$[ab(r - 1)]$
Total	$abr - 1$	SS(Total)	

The notation and the formulas for calculating the sums of squares and mean squares for Table 15.11 are similar to those encountered in the analysis of variance for the completely

Figure 15.9 Partitioning of the Total Sum of Squares for a Two-Factor Factorial Experiment

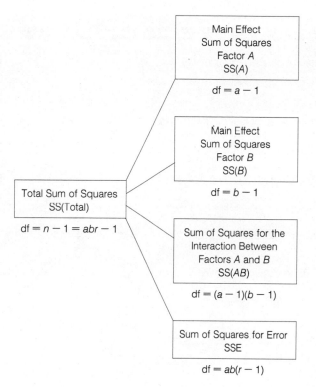

Main Effect
Sum of Squares
Factor A
SS(A)

df $= a - 1$

Main Effect
Sum of Squares
Factor B
SS(B)

df $= b - 1$

Total Sum of Squares
SS(Total)

df $= n - 1 = abr - 1$

Sum of Squares for the
Interaction Between
Factors A and B
SS(AB)

df $= (a - 1)(b - 1)$

Sum of Squares for Error
SSE

df $= ab(r - 1)$

randomized and the randomized block designs. They are shown in the boxes on pages 704–705. Then, before we actually work through an example, we need to know what we are going to do with these mean squares. Particularly, we need to know something about their practical significance.

To understand the practical significance of the four sources of variation in the analysis of variance table (Table 15.11), visualize the data in the two-way table (Table 15.12). The ab cells of the two-way table correspond to the ab treatments in a completely randomized design. For each of the ab treatments, we have a random sample of r observations. Therefore, as in the case of the completely randomized design of Section 15.1, SSE is the pooled sum of squares *within* the ab samples and MSE is its corresponding mean square.

Table 15.12
Two-Way Table for a Two-Factor Factorial Experiment

r observations in each cell

	LEVEL	FACTOR B AT b LEVELS 1	2	3	$\cdots$	b	LEVEL MEANS FOR FACTOR A
	1						$\bar{A}_1$
FACTOR A AT a LEVELS	2						$\bar{A}_2$
	3						$\bar{A}_3$
	$\vdots$						$\vdots$
	a						$\bar{A}_a$
LEVEL MEANS FOR FACTOR B		$\bar{B}_1$	$\bar{B}_2$	$\bar{B}_3$	$\cdots$	$\bar{B}_b$	

Notation for the Analysis of Variance for a Two-Way Classification of Data

a = Number of levels of independent variable 1

b = Number of levels of independent variable 2

r = Number of measurements in any pair of levels of independent variables 1 and 2

A_i = Total of all measurements of independent variable 1 at level i ($i = 1, 2, \ldots, a$)

$\bar{A}_i$ = Mean of all measurements of independent variable 1 at level i ($i = 1, 2, \ldots, a$) $= \dfrac{A_i}{br}$

B_j = Total of all measurements of independent variable 2 at level j ($j = 1, 2, \ldots, b$)

$\bar{B}_j$ = Mean of all measurements of independent variable 2 at level j ($j = 1, 2, \ldots, b$) $= \dfrac{B_j}{ar}$

AB_{ij} = Total of all measurements at the ith level of independent variable 1 and at the jth level of independent variable 2 ($i = 1, 2, \ldots, a; j = 1, 2, \ldots, b$)

n = Total number of measurements $= abr$

$\displaystyle\sum_{i=1}^{n} x_i^2$ = Sum of squares of all n measurements

$$CM = \frac{(\text{Total of all } n \text{ measurements})^2}{n} = \frac{\left(\displaystyle\sum_{i=1}^{n} x_i\right)^2}{n}$$

Now, suppose we have calculated the row, column, and cell means in a table for a two-factor factorial experiment and the means appear as shown in Table 15.13. Notice that the difference in the means for levels 1 and 2 for factor A is $\bar{A}_1 - \bar{A}_2 = 4 - 7 = -3$. Now check the difference in the cell means for levels 1 and 2 of factor A when factor B is at level 1. This also is $7 - 10 = -3$. In fact, if you look at any level of factor B, the difference in the cell means for levels 1 and 2 of factor A is the same as the overall difference in the level means, $\bar{A}_1 - \bar{A}_2 = -3$. Similarly, if you compare the means of any pair of factor B levels, say levels 2 and 3, for a given level of factor A, the difference is constant and equal to the overall difference in B levels, $\bar{B}_2 - \bar{B}_3 = 2.33 - 3.33 = -1$. Of course, the numbers in Table 15.13 are fictitious, but they illustrate a situation in which the effect of one factor on the response is independent of the effect of the level of the other factor. When this situation exists, we say that factors A and B *do not interact*.

Table 15.13

Cell, Row, and Column Means for a Fictitious 3×3 Factorial Experiment When No Interaction Is Present

	LEVEL	FACTOR B 1	FACTOR B 2	FACTOR B 3	MEANS
FACTOR A	1	7	2	3	$\bar{A}_1 = 4$
	2	10	5	6	$\bar{A}_2 = 7$
	3	5	0	1	$\bar{A}_3 = 2$
MEANS		$\bar{B}_1 = 7.33$	$\bar{B}_2 = 2.33$	$\bar{B}_3 = 3.33$	

Formulas for the Calculations for a Two-Way Classification of Data

$CM =$ Correction for the mean

$$= \frac{(\text{Total of all } n \text{ measurements})^2}{n} = \frac{\left(\sum\limits_{i=1}^{n} x_i\right)^2}{n}$$

$SS(\text{Total}) =$ Total sum of squares

$$= \text{Sum of squares of all } n \text{ measurements} - CM = \sum_{i=1}^{n} x_i^2 - CM$$

$SS(A) =$ Sum of squares for main effects, independent variable 1

$$= \left(\begin{array}{c}\text{Sum of squares of the totals } A_1, A_2, \ldots, A_a \\ \text{divided by the number of measurements} \\ \text{in a single total, namely } br\end{array}\right) - CM = \frac{\sum\limits_{i=1}^{a} A_i^2}{br} - CM$$

$SS(B) =$ Sum of squares for main effects, independent variable 2

$$= \left(\begin{array}{c}\text{Sum of squares of the totals } B_1, B_2, \ldots, B_b \\ \text{divided by the number of measurements} \\ \text{in a single total, namely } ar\end{array}\right) - CM = \frac{\sum\limits_{j=1}^{b} B_j^2}{ar} - CM$$

$SS(AB) =$ Sum of squares for AB interaction

$$= \left(\begin{array}{c}\text{Sum of squares of the cell} \\ \text{totals } AB_{11}, AB_{12}, \ldots, AB_{ab}, \\ \text{divided by the number of} \\ \text{measurements in a single} \\ \text{total, namely } r\end{array}\right) - SS(A) - SS(B) - CM = \frac{\sum\limits_{j=1}^{b}\sum\limits_{i=1}^{a} AB_{ij}^2}{r} - SS(A) - SS(B) - CM$$

In contrast to Table 15.13, suppose that the cell means appear as shown in Table 15.14. Examining Table 15.14, you can see that the means of the observations for the different levels of factor A, 7.33, 6.33, and 6.66, differ very little, but the cell means for given levels of factor B differ greatly. They even reverse themselves in sign. For example, the difference in the cell means for levels 1 and 2 of factor A for level 1 of factor B is $15 - 4 = 11$. The corresponding difference for level 2 of factor B is $5 - 10 = -5$. Clearly, the overall difference in the observation means for levels 1 and 2 of factor A, $\bar{A}_1 - \bar{A}_2 = 7.33 - 6.33 = 1$, tells us very little about the difference in a pair of cell means for any specific level of factor B. Table 15.14 illustrates a situation in which the mean response *depends* upon the particular combination of levels of factors A and B. When this situation occurs, we say that factors A and B *interact*.

Table 15.14

Cell, Row, and Column Means for a Fictitious 3×3 Factorial Experiment When Interaction Is Present

	LEVEL	FACTOR B 1	2	3	MEANS
	1	15	5	2	$\bar{A}_1 = 7.33$
FACTOR A	2	4	10	5	$\bar{A}_2 = 6.33$
	3	1	6	13	$\bar{A}_3 = 6.66$
MEANS		$\bar{B}_1 = 6.66$	$\bar{B}_2 = 7$	$\bar{B}_3 = 6.66$	

The interaction sum of squares, SS(*AB*), and its respective mean square,

$$MS(AB) = \frac{SS(AB)}{(a-1)(b-1)}$$

provide a measure of the interaction between factors *A* and *B*. If MS(*AB*) is substantially larger than the mean square for error, MSE, we have evidence of factor interaction. To test the null hypothesis that there is *no interaction* between factors *A* and *B*, we use the familiar test statistic

$$F = \frac{MS(AB)}{MSE}$$

and reject H_0 if $F \geq F_\alpha$ where F_α is based on $\nu_1 = (a-1)(b-1)$ and $\nu_2 = ab(r-1)$ degrees of freedom.

The sum of squares SS(*A*), called the main effect sum of squares for factor *A*, measures the variation of the factor *A* level means, $\overline{A}_1, \overline{A}_2, \ldots, \overline{A}_a$, about the mean of all *abr* observations. To test the null hypothesis that there are no differences among the mean values of the response for the levels of factor *A*, we compute the mean square for *A*,

$$MS(A) = \frac{SS(A)}{a-1}$$

Test Statistics and Rejection Regions for a Two-Factor Factorial Experiment

For Factor Interaction

Test statistic: $F = \dfrac{MS(AB)}{MSE}$

Rejection region: $F \geq F_\alpha$, where F_α is based on $\nu_1 = (a-1)(b-1)$ and $\nu_2 = ab(r-1)$ degrees of freedom

For Main Effects for Factor A

Test statistic: $F = \dfrac{MS(A)}{MSE}$

Rejection region: $F \geq F_\alpha$, where F_α is based on $\nu_1 = a-1$ and $\nu_2 = ab(r-1)$ degrees of freedom

For Main Effects for Factor B

Test statistic: $F = \dfrac{MS(B)}{MSE}$

Rejection region: $F \geq F_\alpha$, where F_α is based on $\nu_1 = b-1$ and $\nu_2 = ab(r-1)$ degrees of freedom and use the test statistic

$$F = \frac{MS(A)}{MSE}$$

We will reject H_0 if $F \geq F_\alpha$ where F_α is based on $v_1 = a - 1$ and $v_2 = ab(r - 1)$ degrees of freedom. A similar test for evidence of the main effects for factor B uses the F statistic

$$F = \frac{MS(B)}{MSE}$$

and rejects H_0 if $F \geq F_\alpha$ where F_α is based on $v_1 = b - 1$ and $v_2 = ab(r - 1)$ degrees of freedom.

Tests for main effects are important when no interaction exists between factors A and B. If the test for factor interaction is statistically significant (i.e., if there is evidence of factor interaction), then we will want to focus attention on the individual cell (treatment) means, perhaps locating the one that is the largest or the smallest. Formulas for confidence intervals for a single cell mean and the difference between a pair of cell means are shown in the boxes.

100(1 − α)% Confidence Interval for the Mean of a Single Cell of the Two-Way Table

$$\bar{x}_{ij} \pm t_{\alpha/2} \frac{s}{\sqrt{r}}$$

where $\bar{x}_{ij}$ is the cell mean for the cell in the ith row, jth column,

r = Number of measurements per cell

$s = \sqrt{MSE}$

and $t_{\alpha/2}$ is based upon $ab(r - 1)$ df.

100(1 − α)% Confidence Interval for the Difference in a Pair of Cell Means

Let

$\bar{x}_1$ = Sample mean of the r measurements in the first cell

$\bar{x}_2$ = Sample mean of the r measurements in the second cell

Then, the 100(1 − α)% confidence interval for the difference between the cell means is

$$(\bar{x}_1 - \bar{x}_2) \pm t_{\alpha/2} s \sqrt{\frac{2}{r}}$$

where $s = \sqrt{MSE}$ and $t_{\alpha/2}$ is based upon $ab(r - 1)$ df.

A method for making pairwise comparisons of some or all of the cell means will be presented in Section 15.4.

Example 15.9

A manufacturer whose daily supply of raw materials is variable and limited, can use the material to produce two different products in various proportions. The profit per unit of raw material obtained by producing each of the two products depends on the length of a product's manufacturing run and hence on the amount of raw material assigned to it. Other factors, such as worker productivity, machine breakdown, etc., affect the profit per unit as well, but their net effect on profit is random and uncontrollable. The manufacturer has conducted an experiment to investigate the effect of the level of Supply of raw materials, S, and the Ratio of its assignment, R,* to the two product manufacturing lines on the profit per unit of raw material. The ultimate goal would be to be able to choose the best ratio to match each day's supply of raw materials. The levels of Supply of raw material chosen for the experiment were 15, 18, and 21 tons; the levels of the Ratio of allocation to the two product lines were $\frac{1}{2}$, 1, and 2. The response was the profit (in cents) per unit of raw material supply obtained from a single day's production. Three replications of a complete 3×3 factorial experiment were conducted in a random sequence (i.e., a completely randomized design). The data for the 27 days are shown in Table 15.15.

Table 15.15

| | | RAW MATERIAL SUPPLY, S (TONS) | | |
		15	18	21
RATIO OF RAW MATERIAL ALLOCATION, R	$\frac{1}{2}$	23, 20, 21	22, 19, 20	19, 18, 21
	1	22, 20, 19	24, 25, 22	20, 19, 22
	2	18, 18, 16	21, 23, 20	20, 22, 24

  a. Calculate the appropriate sums of squares, and construct an ANOVA table.
  b. Do the data present sufficient evidence to indicate a Supply S–Ratio R interaction?
  c. Find a 95% confidence interval to estimate the mean profit per unit of raw materials when $S = 18$ tons and the ratio of allocation is $R = 1$.
  d. Find a 95% confidence interval to estimate the difference in mean profit per unit of raw materials between $S = 18$, $R = \frac{1}{2}$ and $S = 18$, $R = 1$.

Solution **a.** The sums of squares for the ANOVA table are calculated as follows:

$$CM = \frac{(\text{Total of all } n \text{ measurements})^2}{n} = \frac{(558)^2}{27} = 11{,}532$$

$$SS(\text{Total}) = \sum_{i=1}^{n} x_i^2 - CM = 11{,}650 - 11{,}532 = 118$$

---

* The letter R has been used in this example to denote Ratio of raw material allocation. Although this is the same symbol that appears in R^2, the coefficient of determination for a multiple regression analysis, the context should make the meaning clear.

The next step is to construct a table showing the totals of x values for each combination of levels of Supply, S, and Ratio, R, and then the totals for each level of S and for each level of R. These totals, computed from the raw data table, are shown in Table 15.16.

Table 15.16

		RAW MATERIAL SUPPLY, S (TONS)			TOTALS
		15	18	21	
RATIO OF RAW MATERIAL ALLOCATION, R	$\frac{1}{2}$	64	61	58	$R_1 = 183$
	1	61	71	61	$R_2 = 193$
	2	52	64	66	$R_3 = 182$
TOTALS		$S_1 = 177$	$S_2 = 196$	$S_3 = 185$	Total $= 558$

Then,

$$SS(\text{Supply}) = \frac{\sum_{j=1}^{3} S_j^2}{9} - CM = \frac{(177)^2 + (196)^2 + (185)^2}{9} - CM$$

$$= \frac{103,970}{9} - 11,532 = 20.22$$

$$SS(\text{Ratio}) = \frac{\sum_{i=1}^{3} R_i^2}{9} - CM = \frac{(183)^2 + (193)^2 + (182)^2}{9} - CM$$

$$= \frac{103,862}{9} - 11,532 = 8.22$$

$$SS(SR) = \sum_{j=1}^{3} \sum_{i=1}^{3} \frac{SR_{ij}^2}{3} - SS(\text{Supply}) - SS(\text{Ratio}) - CM$$

$$= \frac{(64)^2 + (61)^2 + (58)^2 + \cdots + (66)^2}{3} - 20.22 - 8.22 - 11,532$$

$$= \frac{34,820}{3} - 20.22 - 8.22 - 11,532 = 46.23$$

$$SSE = SS(\text{Total}) - SS(\text{Supply}) - SS(\text{Ratio}) - SS(SR)$$
$$= 118.00 - 20.22 - 8.22 - 46.23 = 43.33$$

The ANOVA table is given in Table 15.17.

Table 15.17

SOURCE	df	SS	MS
Supply	2	20.22	10.11
Ratio	2	8.22	4.11
Supply–Ratio interaction	4	46.23	11.56
Error	18	43.33	2.41
Total	26	118.00	

b. To test the null hypothesis that Supply and Ratio do not interact, we use the test statistic

$$F = \frac{MS(SR)}{MSE} = \frac{11.56}{2.41} = 4.80$$

The degrees of freedom associated with MS(SR) and s^2 are 4 and 18, respectively (given in Table 15.17). Therefore, we reject H_0 if $F \geq F_{.05}$, where $v_1 = 4$, $v_2 = 18$, and $F_{.05} = 2.93$. Since the computed value of F (4.80) exceeds $F_{.05}$, we reject H_0 and conclude that Supply and Ratio interact. The presence of interaction tells you that the mean profit depends on the particular combination of levels of Supply, S, and Ratio, R. Consequently, there is little point in checking to determine whether the means differ for the three levels of Supply or whether they differ for the three levels of Ratio. For example, the Supply level that gave the highest mean profit (over all levels of R) might not be the same Supply–Ratio level combination that produces the largest mean profit per unit of raw material.

c. A 95% confidence interval for the mean $E(x)$ when Supply $S = 18$ and Ratio $R = 1$ is

$$\bar{x}_{18,1} \pm t_{.025}\left(\frac{s}{\sqrt{r}}\right)$$

where $\bar{x}_{18,1}$ is the mean of the $r = 3$ values of x obtained for $S = 18$ and $R = 1$, $s = \sqrt{MSE} = \sqrt{2.41} = 1.55$, and $t_{.025} = 2.101$ is based on 18 df. Substituting, we obtain

$$\frac{71}{3} \pm 2.101\left(\frac{1.55}{\sqrt{3}}\right)$$

$$23.67 \pm 1.88$$

Therefore, our interval estimate for the mean profit per unit of raw material when $S = 18$ and $R = 1$ is $21.79 to $25.55.

d. A 95% confidence interval for the difference in mean profit per unit of raw material for two different combinations of levels of S and R is

$$(\bar{x}_1 - \bar{x}_2) \pm t_{.025}s\sqrt{\frac{2}{r}}$$

where $\bar{x}_1$ and $\bar{x}_2$ represent the means of the $r = 3$ replications for the factor level combinations $S = 18$, $R = \frac{1}{2}$ and $S = 18$, $R = 1$, respectively. Substituting, we obtain

$$\left(\frac{61}{3} - \frac{71}{3}\right) \pm (2.101)(1.55)\sqrt{\frac{2}{3}}$$

$$-3.33 \pm 2.66$$

Therefore, the interval estimate for the difference in mean profit per unit of raw material for the two factor level combinations is $(-\$5.99, -\$0.67)$. The negative values indicate that we estimate the mean for $S = 18$, $R = \frac{1}{2}$ to be less than the mean for $S = 18$, $R = 1$ by between $0.67 and $5.99. ■

The techniques illustrated in the solution of Example 15.9 would answer most of the practical questions you might have about profit per unit of Supply of raw materials if the two independent variables affecting the response were qualitative. But since both independent variables are quantitative, we can obtain much more information about their effect on response by performing a multiple regression analysis on the data. For example, the analysis of variance in Example 15.9 enables us to estimate the mean profit per unit of Supply for *only* the nine combinations of Supply – Ratio levels used in the factorial experiment. It will not permit us to estimate the mean response for any other combination of levels of the independent variables. For example, the prediction equation obtained from a regression analysis would enable us to estimate the mean profit per unit of Supply when $S = 17$, $R = 1$. We could not obtain this estimate from the analysis of variance in Example 15.9.

Exercises 15.28 – 15.34

Learning the Mechanics

15.28 The partially completed ANOVA table for a 3×4 factorial experiment with two observations for each factor level combination is shown here.

SOURCE	df	SS	MS	F
A		.8		
B		5.3		
AB		9.6		
Error				
Total		17.0		

a. Describe the experiment completely, giving the number of factors, levels, and so forth.
b. Complete the analysis of variance table.
c. What is meant by factor interaction, and what is the practical implication if it exists?
d. Do the data provide sufficient evidence to indicate an interaction between factors A and B? Test using $\alpha = .05$.
e. What are the practical implications of your test results for part d?

15.29 The partially completed ANOVA table given here is for a two-factor factorial experiment.

SOURCE	df	SS	MS	F
A	3		.75	
B	1	.95		
AB			.30	
Error				
Total	23	6.5		

a. Give the number of levels for each factor.

b. How many observations were collected for each factor level combination?

c. Complete the analysis of variance table.

d. Test for factor interaction and factor main effects using $\alpha = .05$.

e. What are the practical implications of your tests of part d?

15.30 The two-way table gives data for a 2×3 factorial experiment with two observations for each factor level combination.

		FACTOR B		
	LEVEL	*1*	*2*	*3*
FACTOR A	*1*	3.1, 4.0	4.6, 4.2	6.4, 7.1
	2	5.9, 5.3	2.9, 2.2	3.3, 2.5

a. Perform an analysis of variance for the data, and display the results in an analysis of variance table.

b. Do the data provide evidence of factor interaction? Test using $\alpha = .05$.

c. What are the practical implications of the test results of part b?

d. Find a 90% confidence interval for the difference between the mean responses for factor level combinations $A(1)$, $B(1)$ and $A(2)$, $B(1)$.

15.31 The accompanying two-way table gives data for a 2×2 factorial experiment with two observations per factor level combination.

		FACTOR B	
	LEVEL	*1*	*2*
FACTOR A	*1*	29.6	47.3
		35.2	42.1
	2	12.9	28.4
		17.6	22.7

a. Perform an analysis of variance for the data, and display the results in an analysis of variance table.

b. Do the data provide evidence of factor interaction? Test using $\alpha = .05$.

c. Do the data provide sufficient evidence to indicate a main effect due to factor A? Test using $\alpha = .05$. What is the practical implication of this test result?

d. Do the data provide sufficient evidence to indicate a main effect due to factor B? Test using $\alpha = .05$. What is the practical implication of this test result?

e. Find a 95% confidence interval for the difference in mean response between levels 1 and 2 of factor B.

Applying the Concepts

15.32 A beverage distributor wanted to determine the combination of advertising agency (two levels) and advertising medium (three levels) that would produce the largest increase in sales per advertising dollar. Each of the advertising agencies prepared copy or film, as required for each of the media — newspaper, radio, and television. Twelve small towns of roughly the same size were selected for the experiment and two each were assigned to receive an advertisement prepared and transmitted by each of the six agency–medium combinations. The dollar increases in sales per advertising dollar, based on a 1-month sales period, are shown in the table.

| | | ADVERTISING MEDIUM | | |
		Newspaper	Radio	Television
AGENCY	1	15.3	20.1	12.7
		12.7	17.4	16.2
	2	18.9	24.3	12.5
		22.4	28.8	9.4

a. Perform an analysis of variance for the data and display your results in an analysis of variance table.

b. Do the data provide sufficient information to indicate an agency–medium interaction? Test using $\alpha = .05$.

c. What are the practical implications of the test of part b?

15.33 How do women compare with men in their ability to perform laborious tasks that require strength? Some information on this question is provided in a study, by M. D. Phillips and R. L. Pepper, of the firefighting ability of men and women ("Shipboard Fire-Fighting Performance of Females and Males," *Human Factors,* 1982, *24*). Phillips and Pepper conducted a 2 × 2 factorial experiment to investigate the effect of the factor Sex (male or female) and the factor Weight (light or heavy) on the length of time required for a person to perform a particular firefighting task. Eight persons were selected for each of the 2 × 2 = 4 Sex–Weight categories of the 2 × 2 factorial experiment and the length of time needed to complete the task was recorded for each of the thirty-two persons. The means and standard deviations of the four samples are shown in the table.

| | LIGHT | | HEAVY | |
	Mean	Standard deviation	Mean	Standard deviation
FEMALE	18.30	6.81	14.50	2.93
MALE	13.00	5.04	12.25	5.70

a. Calculate the total of the $n = 8$ time measurements for each of the four categories of the 2 × 2 factorial experiment.

b. Calculate CM.

c. Use the results of parts a and b to calculate the sums of squares for Sex, Weight, and for the Sex–Weight interaction.

d. Calculate each sample variance. Then calculate the sum of squares of deviations *within* each sample for each of the four samples.

e. Calculate SSE. [*Hint:*   SSE is the pooled sum of squares of the deviations calculated in part d.]

f. Now that you know SS(Sex), SS(Weight), SS(Sex – Weight), and SSE, find SS(Total).

g. Summarize the calculations in an analysis of variance table.

h. Explain the practical significance of the presence (or absence) of Sex – Weight interaction. Do the data provide evidence of a Sex – Weight interaction?

i. Do the data provide sufficient evidence to indicate a difference in time required to complete the task between light men and women? Test using $\alpha = .05$.

j. Do the data provide sufficient evidence to indicate a difference in time to complete the task between heavy men and women? Test using $\alpha = .05$.

15.34 Refer to Exercise 15.33. Phillips and Pepper (1982) give data on another 2×2 factorial experiment utilizing twenty males and twenty females. The experiment involved the same treatments with ten persons assigned to each Sex – Weight category. The response measured for each person was the pulling force the person was able to exert on the starter cord of a P-250 fire pump. The means and standard deviations of the four samples (corresponding to the $2 \times 2 = 4$ categories of the experiment) are shown in the table.

| | LIGHT | | HEAVY | |
	Mean	Standard deviation	Mean	Standard deviation
FEMALES	46.26	14.23	62.72	13.97
MALES	88.07	8.32	86.29	12.45

a. Use the procedures outlined in Exercise 15.33 to perform an analysis of variance for the experiment. Display your results in an analysis of variance table.

b. Explain the practical significance of the presence (or absence) of Sex – Weight interaction. Do the data provide sufficient evidence of a Sex – Weight interaction?

c. Do the data provide sufficient evidence to indicate a difference in force exerted between light men and women? Test using $\alpha = .05$.

d. Do the data provide sufficient evidence to indicate a difference in force exerted between heavy men and women? Test using $\alpha = .05$.

15.4
A Procedure for Making Multiple Comparisons

Many experiments are conducted to determine the largest (or the smallest) mean in a set. For example, suppose a supermarket manager has developed five different formats, A, B, C, D, and E, for the supermarket's weekly advertisement. The manager would then want to determine whether the different formats affect the store's sales and, if they do, which format produces the largest mean sales. Similarly, a production engineer might wish to determine which among six machines or which among three foremen achieve the highest mean productivity per hour. An investment banker might wish to choose one from among five investment strategies that will produce the greatest investment gain over a fixed period of time.

Choosing the treatment with the largest mean from among five treatments might seem to be a simple matter. All we need to do is to make, say $n_1 = n_2 = \cdots = n_5 = 10$ observations on each treatment, obtain the sample means, $\bar{x}_A, \bar{x}_B, \ldots, \bar{x}_E$, and compare them using Student's t tests to determine whether differences exist among the pairs of means. The problem with this procedure is that a Student's t test with its associated value of α is valid only when the two treatments to be compared are selected *prior to* experimentation. After you have looked at the data, you cannot use a Student's t statistic to compare the treatments corresponding to the largest and smallest sample means because they will always be farther apart, on the average, than the means for any pair of treatments selected at random. And, if you conduct a series of t tests — each with a chance, α, of indicating a difference between a pair of means when, in fact, no difference exists — then the risk of making at least one Type I error in a series of t tests will be larger than the value of α specified for a single t test.

There are a number of procedures for comparing and ranking a group of treatment means. The one we present, known as *Tukey's method for multiple comparisons,* utilizes the Studentized range,

$$q = \frac{\bar{x}_{max} - \bar{x}_{min}}{s/\sqrt{n}}$$

(where $\bar{x}_{max}$ and $\bar{x}_{min}$ are the largest and smallest sample means, respectively), to determine whether the difference in any pair of sample means implies a difference in the corresponding treatment means. The logic behind this multiple comparisons procedure is that, if we determine a critical value for the difference between the largest and smallest sample means, $|\bar{x}_{max} - \bar{x}_{min}|$, one that implies a difference in their respective treatment means, then any other pair of sample means that differ by as much as or more than this critical value would also imply a difference in corresponding treatment means. Tukey's procedure selects this critical distance, ω, so that the probability of making one or more Type I errors (concluding that a difference exists between a pair of treatment means when, in fact, they are identical) is α. Therefore, the risk of making a Type I error applies to the whole procedure, i.e., to all the comparisons of means, rather than to a single comparison.

Tukey's procedure assumes that the k sample means are based on independent random samples, each containing the same number, n_t, of observations. If $s = \sqrt{MSE}$ is the computed standard deviation for the analysis, then the distance ω is

$$\omega = q_\alpha(k, v)\frac{s}{\sqrt{n_t}}$$

The tabulated statistic, $q_\alpha(k, v)$, is the critical value of the Studentized range, the value that locates α in the upper tail of the q distribution. This critical value depends on α, the number of treatment means involved in the comparison, and v (the number of degrees of freedom associated with MSE). Values of $q_\alpha(k, v)$ for $\alpha = .05$ and $\alpha = .01$ are given in Tables XIII and XIV, respectively, in Appendix B. A portion of Table XIII, Appendix B, is shown in Table 15.18 (page 716). If, for example, you wish to make pairwise comparisons among $k = 5$ sample means and if MSE is based on $v = 12$ df, then for $\alpha = .05$, $q_\alpha(5, 12) = 4.51$.

Table 15.18 A Portion of Table XIII, Appendix B:
Tabulated Values of the Studentized Range, $q(k, \nu)$, Upper 5%

ν \ k	2	3	4	5	6	7	8	9	10	11	12	13	14
5	3.64	4.60	5.22	5.67	6.03	6.33	6.58	6.80	6.99	7.17	7.32	7.47	7.60
6	3.46	4.34	4.90	5.30	5.63	5.90	6.12	6.32	6.49	6.65	6.79	6.92	7.03
7	3.34	4.16	4.68	5.06	5.36	5.61	5.82	6.00	6.16	6.30	6.43	6.55	6.66
8	3.26	4.04	4.53	4.89	5.17	5.40	5.60	5.77	5.92	6.05	6.18	6.29	6.39
9	3.20	3.95	4.41	4.76	5.02	5.24	5.43	5.59	5.74	5.87	5.98	6.09	6.19
10	3.15	3.88	4.33	4.65	4.91	5.12	5.30	5.46	5.60	5.72	5.83	5.93	6.03
11	3.11	3.82	4.26	4.57	4.82	5.03	5.20	5.35	5.49	5.61	5.71	5.81	5.90
12	3.08	3.77	4.20	4.51	4.75	4.95	5.12	5.27	5.39	5.51	5.61	5.71	5.80
13	3.06	3.73	4.15	4.45	4.69	4.88	5.05	5.19	5.32	5.43	5.53	5.63	5.71
14	3.03	3.70	4.11	4.41	4.64	4.83	4.99	5.13	5.25	5.36	5.46	5.55	5.64

Tukey's Multiple Comparisons Procedure

1. Calculate $\omega = q_\alpha(k, \nu)\dfrac{s}{\sqrt{n_t}}$

where

k = Number of sample means

$s = \sqrt{\text{MSE}}$

ν = Number of degrees of freedom associated with MSE

n_t = Number of observations in each of the k samples

$q_\alpha(k, \nu)$ = Critical value of the Studentized range (Tables XIII and XIV of Appendix B)

2. Rank the k sample means. Any pair of sample means differing by more than ω will imply a difference in the corresponding population means.

Assumptions: Samples were randomly and independently selected from normal populations with means $\mu_1, \mu_2, \ldots, \mu_k$ and common variance σ^2.

Example 15.10 Refer to the study of the effect of raw material supply and ratio of material allocation on a manufacturer's profit in Example 15.9. Since we found evidence to indicate factor interaction, we now want to examine the means of the nine treatments corresponding to the nine combinations of levels of raw material supply, S, and ratio of raw material allocation, R. Use Tukey's multiple comparisons procedure with $\alpha = .05$ to rank the treatment means and to determine which of the means can be judged to be different.

Solution   The sample means for the nine factor level combinations are shown in Table 15.19.

Table 15.19

Sample Means for the $k = 9$ Treatments, Example 15.9

		RAW MATERIAL SUPPLY, S (TONS)		
		15	18	21
RATIO OF RAW MATERIAL ALLOCATION, R	$\frac{1}{2}$	21.33	20.33	19.33
	1	20.33	23.67	20.33
	2	17.33	21.33	22.00

Since the sample means in Table 15.19 are the mean profits per unit of raw material supply for a day's production, we would want to find the raw material supply, S, and ratio of allocation, R, that produces the maximum profit. The first step in the ranking procedure is to calculate ω for $k = 9$ treatment means, $n_t = 3$ observations per treatment, $\alpha = .05$, and $s = 1.55$ (calculated in part c of Example 15.9). Since MSE is based on $v = 18$ df, the value of $q_{.05}(k, v)$ given in Table XIII of Appendix B is

$$q_{.05}(9, 18) = 4.96$$

and then

$$\omega = q_{.05}(9, 18)\frac{s}{\sqrt{n_t}} = 4.96\left(\frac{1.55}{\sqrt{3}}\right) = 4.44$$

Therefore, population means corresponding to pairs of sample means that differ by more than $\omega = 4.44$ will be judged to be different. The sample means for the nine Supply–Ratio combinations are ranked and displayed below.

17.33 $\overline{19.33, \quad 20.33, \quad 20.33, \quad 20.33, \quad 21.33, \quad 21.33, \quad 22.00, \quad 23.67}$

Using $\omega = 4.44$ as a yardstick to determine differences between pairs of treatments, you can see that there is no evidence to indicate a difference between any pairs of treatments that are adjacent in the ranking. There is evidence to indicate that the treatment means corresponding to sample means 22.00 and 23.67 cents are different from the treatment mean with sample mean equal to 17.33. There is no evidence to indicate a difference in the treatments corresponding to the eight largest sample means, 19.33 to 23.67 (indicated by the overbar). Further experimentation would be required to determine whether the observed differences among the eight largest sample means really imply differences among the corresponding population means. ∎

Exercises 15.35 – 15.42

Learning the Mechanics

15.35 Give the values of $q_\alpha(k, v)$ for the values of k, v, and α shown here.

a. $k = 3$, $v = 9$, $\alpha = .05$ **b.** $k = 5$, $v = 15$, $\alpha = .01$
c. $k = 4$, $v = 8$, $\alpha = .01$ **d.** $k = 4$, $v = 12$, $\alpha = .05$

15.36 Independent random samples of four observations per sample were collected from five populations. The value of SSE for this completely randomized design was .72 and the sample means were $\bar{x}_1 = 4.3$, $\bar{x}_2 = 4.9$, $\bar{x}_3 = 3.9$, $\bar{x}_4 = 3.7$, and $\bar{x}_5 = 4.4$.

a. How many degrees of freedom are associated with SSE?
b. Calculate s^2.
c. Find ω for $\alpha = .05$, and explain what it is.
d. Rank the sample means, and determine which pairs (if any) appear to differ. Use $\alpha = .05$.

15.37 If you were to compare the means of two populations based on independent samples of equal size, you would test for a difference using the Student's t statistic of Section 9.2:

$$t = \frac{\bar{x}_1 - \bar{x}_2}{s\sqrt{\dfrac{1}{n_1} + \dfrac{1}{n_2}}} = \frac{\bar{x}_1 - \bar{x}_2}{s\sqrt{\dfrac{2}{n_1}}} \qquad \text{when } n_1 = n_2$$

For $\alpha = .05$, the rejection region is $t \geq t_{.025}$ or $t \leq -t_{.025}$. Suppose that $n_1 = n_2 = 4$ and $s^2 = 9$.

a. How many degrees of freedom would be associated with s^2?
b. How large could the difference between $\bar{x}_1$ and $\bar{x}_2$ (either positive or negative) be before you rejected the null hypothesis, $H_0: \mu_1 = \mu_2$?
c. Find the value of ω for $k = 2$, $\nu = 6$, and compare it with your answer to part b.
d. Use the results of part b to explain the meaning of ω.

Applying the Concepts

15.38 Refer to Exercise 15.8. Use Tukey's multiple comparisons procedure to determine which, if any, of the mean audit costs differ for the three classifications of corporation size. Use $\alpha = .05$, and interpret your results.

15.39 Refer to Exercise 15.10. Use Tukey's multiple comparisons procedure to rank the mean sales for the three locations, and interpret your results.

15.40 Refer to the 2×3 factorial experiment of Exercise 15.30. Use Tukey's multiple comparisons procedure to determine which, if any, pairs of population means differ. Use $\alpha = .05$, and interpret your results.

15.41 Refer to the 2×2 factorial experiment of Exercise 15.31. Use Tukey's multiple comparisons procedure to determine which, if any, pairs of population means differ. Use $\alpha = .05$, and interpret your results.

15.42 In Exercise 15.32, a beverage distributor was seeking the combination of advertising agency and medium that would produce the largest increase in sales per dollar expended. Use Tukey's multiple comparisons procedure to rank the means, and explain how your results relate to the distributor's objective. Use $\alpha = .05$.

Summary

This chapter presents an extension of the independent sampling and paired difference experiments to allow for the comparison of two or more means. The *completely randomized design* (or *independent sampling design*) uses independent samples from each of k populations to compare their means. The *randomized block design,* like the paired difference design, uses relatively *homogeneous blocks of experimental units,* with each *treatment* randomly assigned to one experimental unit in each block to compare the treatment means.

For both designs, the comparison of population (or treatment) means is made by comparing the sample *variation* among the treatment means, as measured by the *mean square for treatments (MST),* to the variation attributable to differences among experimental units, as measured by the *mean square for error (MSE).* If the ratio of MST to MSE is large, we conclude that a difference exists between the means of at least two of the k populations.

The analysis of variance, used to analyze data from the completely randomized and randomized block designs, is also used to analyze data obtained from a two-factor *factorial experiment.* In order to use an analysis of variance for this experiment, we must take an equal number, r ($r \geq 2$), of observations for all factor level combinations. The most important information to be derived from the analysis of variance for a factorial experiment is whether the factors appear to interact. If *interaction* is present, we know we cannot examine the effects of the factors on the response independently of each other. Rather, we must focus attention on the means for the factor level combinations. The ranking and comparison of a group of treatment means can be accomplished by using *Tukey's multiple comparisons procedure.*

Unfortunately, much of the data of interest in business research cannot be collected according to a preconceived statistical design. However, in cases where you can design your experiment, knowledge of the principles exemplified by the completely randomized, randomized block, and factorial designs should prove to be helpful. If you would like to study other types of experimental designs, consult the references at the end of this chapter.

Supplementary Exercises 15.43–15.72

15.43 The set of activities and decisions through which a firm moves from its initial awareness of an innovative industrial procedure to its final adoption or rejection of the innovation is referred to as the *industrial adoption process.* The process can be described as having five stages: (1) awareness, (2) interest (additional information requested), (3) evaluation (advantages and disadvantages compared), (4) trial (innovation is tested), and (5) adoption. As part of a study of the industrial adoption process, Ozanne and Churchill (1971) hypothesized that firms use a greater number of informational inputs to the process (e.g., visits by salespersons) in the later stages than in the earlier stages. In particular, they tested the hypotheses that a greater number of informational inputs are used in the interest stage than in the awareness stage, and that a greater number are used in the evaluation stage than in the interest stage. Ozanne and Churchill collected the information given in the table (page 720) on the number of informational inputs used by a sample of thirty-seven industrial firms that recently adopted a particular new automatic machine tool.

COMPANY	NUMBER OF INFORMATIONAL SOURCES USED			COMPANY	NUMBER OF INFORMATIONAL SOURCES USED		
	Awareness stage	Interest stage	Evaluation stage		Awareness stage	Interest stage	Evaluation stage
1	2	2	3	20	1	1	1
2	1	1	2	21	1	2	1
3	3	2	3	22	1	4	3
4	2	1	2	23	2	3	3
5	3	2	4	24	1	1	1
6	3	4	6	25	3	1	4
7	1	1	2	26	1	1	5
8	1	3	4	27	1	3	1
9	2	3	3	28	1	1	1
10	3	2	4	29	3	2	2
11	1	2	4	30	4	2	3
12	3	3	3	31	1	2	3
13	4	4	4	32	1	3	2
14	4	2	7	33	1	2	2
15	3	2	2	34	2	3	2
16	4	5	4	35	1	2	4
17	2	1	1	36	2	2	3
18	1	1	3	37	2	3	2
19	1	3	2				

a. Do the data provide sufficient evidence to indicate that differences exist in the mean number of informational inputs of the three stages of the industrial adoption process studied by Ozanne and Churchill? Test using $\alpha = .05$.

b. Find a 90% confidence interval for the difference in the mean number of informational inputs between the evaluation and awareness stages.

15.44 Advertising agencies are continually faced with the problem of creating attractive gimmicks to use in advertising campaigns. One agency recently decided to run an experiment to compare the preferences of financial analysts for three different brands of financial calculators, including its client's brand (brand A). It hoped to show that (1) financial analysts were not indifferent toward the three brands of calculators and (2) its client's brand was preferred to the industry leader, brand C. Three financial analysts were selected to perform an identical series of calculations on each of the three brands of calculators, A, B, and C. To avoid the possibility of fatigue, a suitable time period separated each set of calculations, and the calculators were used in random order by each analyst. A preference rating, based on a 0–100 scale, was recorded for each machine–analyst combination. These data are shown in the table.

ANALYST	BRAND		
	A	B	C
1	85	90	95
2	70	70	75
3	65	60	80

a. Do the data provide sufficient evidence to indicate a difference among the financial analysts' preferences for the three brands? Use $\alpha = .05$.

b. Construct a 95% confidence interval for the difference in the mean preference scores for brands A and C.

c. Do you think the advertising agency will elect to use the results of this experiment in its advertising campaign for brand A? Explain.

d. Why did the experimenter employed by the advertising agency have each analyst test all three calculators instead of assigning three different analysts to each calculator?

15.45 It has been hypothesized that treatment, after casting, of a plastic used in optic lenses will improve wear. Four different treatments are to be tested. To determine whether any differences in mean wear exist among treatments, twenty-eight castings from a single formulation of the plastic were made, and seven castings were randomly assigned to each of the treatments. Wear was determined by measuring the increase in "haze" after 200 cycles of abrasion (better wear being indicated by small increases). The results are given in the table.

| TREATMENT | | | |
A	B	C	D
9.16	11.95	11.47	11.35
13.29	15.15	9.54	8.73
12.07	14.75	11.26	10.00
11.97	14.79	13.66	9.75
13.31	15.48	11.18	11.71
12.32	13.47	15.03	12.45
11.78	13.06	14.86	12.38

a. Is there evidence of a difference in mean wear among the four treatments? Use $\alpha = .05$.

b. Find the approximate observed significance level for the test, and interpret its value.

c. Estimate the mean difference in haze increase between treatments B and C using a 99% confidence interval.

d. Find a 90% confidence interval for the mean wear for lenses receiving treatment A.

e. Use Tukey's multiple comparisons procedure to determine which, if any, pairs of means differ. Use $\alpha = .05$, and interpret your results.

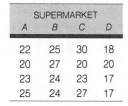

| SUPERMARKET | | | |
A	B	C	D
22	25	30	18
20	27	20	20
23	24	23	17
25	24	27	17

15.46 Higher wholesale beef prices over the past few years have resulted in the sale of ground beef with higher fat content in an attempt to keep retail prices down. Four different supermarket chains were chosen, and four 1-pound packages of ground beef were randomly selected from each. The percentage of fat content was measured for each package, with the results shown in the table.

a. What type of experimental design does this represent?

b. Do the data provide evidence at the $\alpha = .05$ level that the mean percentage of fat content differs for at least two of the four supermarket chains?

c. Use a 90% confidence interval to estimate the mean percentage of fat content per pound at supermarket C.

d. Use Tukey's multiple comparisons procedure to determine which, if any, pairs of means differ. Use $\alpha = .05$, and interpret your results.

15.47 A company is planning to market a new cereal, with one of three possible package designs. To determine which has the most appeal, five stores are supplied with all three package designs. All packages are priced the same, so if any design outsells the others, it will be due primarily to visual attractiveness. The cereal is on the market for several months, and the number of sales for each design at each store is recorded in the table.

STORE	DESIGN		
	A	B	C
1	101	111	100
2	98	102	105
3	121	120	114
4	132	140	127
5	95	98	94

a. Test to determine whether there are differences among the mean numbers of sales for the three designs. Use $\alpha = .01$.

b. Give statistical justification as to why blocking was (or was not) necessary in this experiment.

c. What assumptions were necessary for the validity of the test you conducted in part a?

15.48 Explain the differences between a paired difference design (Chapter 9) and a randomized block design.

15.49 Several companies are experimenting with the concept of paying production workers (generally paid by the hour) on a salary basis. It is believed that absenteeism and tardiness will increase under this plan, yet some companies feel that the working environment and overall productivity will improve. Fifty production workers under the salary plan are monitored at company A, and fifty under the hourly plan are monitored at company B. The number of work-hours missed due to tardiness or absenteeism over a 1-year period is recorded for each worker. The results are partially summarized in the table.

SOURCE	df	SS	MS	F
Company		3,237.2		
Error		16,167.7		
Total	99			

a. Fill in the information missing from the table.

b. Is there evidence at $\alpha = .05$ that the mean number of hours missed differs for employees of the two companies?

c. Is there sufficient information given to form a confidence interval for the difference between the mean number of hours missed at the two companies?

15.50 A large citrus products company is interested in purchasing several new orange juice extractors. To help them with their purchase decision, six different manufacturers of juice extractors have agreed to let the company conduct an experiment to compare the yields of juices for the six different brands of extractors. Because of the possibility of a variation in the amount of juice per orange from one truckload of oranges to another, equal weights of oranges from a single truckload were assigned to each extractor, and this process was repeated for fifteen loads. The amount of juice recorded for each extractor for each truckload produced the sums of squares shown in the table.

SOURCE	df	SS	MS	F
Extractor		84.71		
Truckload		159.29		
Error		95.33		
Total		339.33		

a. Complete the ANOVA table.

b. Do the data provide sufficient evidence to indicate a difference among the mean amounts of juice extracted by the six extractors? Use $\alpha = .05$.

15.51 The table shows the partially completed analysis of variance for a two-factor factorial experiment.

SOURCE	df	SS	MS	F
A	3	2.6		
B	5	9.2		
AB			3.1	
Error		18.7		
Total	47			

a. Complete the analysis of variance table.

b. Give the number of levels for each factor and the number of observations per factor level combination.

c. Do the data provide sufficient evidence to indicate an interaction between the factors? Test using $\alpha = .05$.

d. State the practical implications of your test result in part c.

15.52 The data shown in the table are for a 4×3 factorial experiment with two observations per factor level combination.

		LEVEL OF B		
		1	2	3
LEVEL OF A	1	2 4	5 6	1 3
	2	5 4	2 2	10 9
	3	7 10	1 0	5 3
	4	8 7	12 11	7 4

a. Perform an analysis of variance for the data and display the results in an analysis of variance table.

b. Do the data provide sufficient information to indicate an interaction between the factors? Test using $\alpha = .05$.

c. Suppose the objective of the experiment is to select the factor level combination with the largest mean. Based on the data and Tukey's multiple comparisons procedure with $\alpha = .05$, which pairs of means appear to differ?

15.53 Sixteen workers were randomly selected to participate in an experiment to determine the effects of work scheduling and method of payment on attitude toward the job. Two types of scheduling were employed, the standard 8–5 workday and a modification whereby the worker was permitted to start the day at either 7 or 8 A.M. and to vary the starting time as desired; in addition, the worker was allowed to choose, on a daily basis, either a $\frac{1}{2}$-hour or 1-hour lunch period. The two methods of payment were a standard hourly rate and a reduced hourly rate with an added piece rate based on the worker's production. Four workers were randomly assigned to each of the four scheduling–payment combinations, and each completed an attitude test after 1 month on the job. The test scores are shown in the table.

		PAYMENT	
		Hourly rate	Hourly and piece rate
SCHEDULING	8–5	54, 68 55, 63	89, 75 71, 83
	Worker-modified schedule	79, 65 62, 74	83, 94 91, 86

a. Construct an analysis of variance table for the data.

b. Do the data provide sufficient information to indicate a factor interaction? Test using $\alpha = .05$. Explain the practical implications of your test.

c. Do the data indicate that any of the scheduling–payment combinations produce a mean attitude score that is clearly higher than the other three? Test using $\alpha = .05$, and interpret your results.

15.54 Due to increased energy shortages and costs, utility companies are stressing ways in which home and apartment utility bills can be cut. One utility company reached an agreement with the owner of a new apartment complex to conduct a test of energy-saving plans for apartments. The tests were to be conducted before the apartments were rented. Four apartments were chosen that were identical in size, amount of shade, and direction faced. Four plans were to be tested, one on each apartment. The thermostat was set at 75°F in each apartment, and the monthly utility bill was recorded for each of the 3 summer months. The results are listed in the table.

MONTH	TREATMENT			
	1	2	3	4
June	$74.44	$68.75	$71.34	$65.47
July	86.96	73.47	83.62	72.33
August	82.00	71.23	79.98	70.87

Treatment 1:   No insulation in walls or ceilings

Treatment 2:   Insulation in walls and ceilings

Treatment 3:   Awning for windows, but no insulation in walls or ceilings

Treatment 4:   Insulation in walls and ceilings and awnings for windows

a. Is there evidence that the mean monthly utility bills differ for at least two of the four treatments? Use $\alpha = .01$.

b. Is there evidence that blocking is important — i.e., that the mean bills differ for at least two of the three months? Use $\alpha = .05$.

c. To determine whether awnings on the windows help reduce costs, place a 95% confidence interval on the difference in the mean monthly utility bills for treatments 2 and 4.

15.55 From time to time, one branch office of a company must make shipments to a certain branch office in another state. There are three package delivery services between the two cities where the branch offices are located. Since the price structures for the three delivery services are quite similar, the company wants to compare the delivery times. The company plans to make several different types of shipments to its branch office. To compare the carriers, each shipment will be sent in triplicate, one with each carrier. The results listed in the table are the delivery times in hours.

SHIPMENT	CARRIER		
	I	II	III
1	15.2	16.9	17.1
2	14.3	16.4	16.1
3	14.7	15.9	15.7
4	15.1	16.7	17.0
5	14.0	15.6	15.5

a. Is there evidence of a difference in the mean delivery times among the three companies? Use $\alpha = .05$.

b. Use a 99% confidence interval to estimate the difference between the mean delivery times for carriers I and II.

c. What assumptions are necessary for the validity of the procedures you used in parts a and b?

15.56 A fast-food chain expects mean gross sales of $800,000 per year per franchise. A random sampling of the chain's stores was selected in Los Angeles, Miami, and Chicago, and the results (in units of $100,000) are given in the table.

MIAMI	LOS ANGELES	CHICAGO
8.7	8.7	7.8
7.4	8.0	7.6
7.9	9.0	6.9
8.0	8.3	5.7
8.5	9.0	
7.9		

a. Is there evidence of a difference in the mean gross sales among the chain's stores in these three cities? Use $\alpha = .01$.

b. Form a 90% confidence interval for the mean gross sales of the Miami stores in this fast-food chain.

15.57 A corporation manages a very large number of stores that it classifies into three geographic divisions. Three stores are randomly selected from each division and a study is made to determine the mean inflation rate for the items in inventory. The inflation rate is recorded in the table as a percentage change in price over a year's time.

DIVISION		
1	2	3
1.1	1.4	0.4
0.9	1.6	0.3
0.8	1.0	0.5

a. Is there sufficient evidence to indicate a difference in the mean inflation rates among the stores in different divisions?

b. In division 1, the numbers 1.1, 0.9, and 0.8 represent a random sample from what population?

15.58 One indicator of employee morale is the length of time employees stay with a company. A large corporation has three factories located in similar areas of the country. Although the corporation management attempts to maintain uniformity in management, working conditions, and employee relations at its various factories, it realizes that differences may exist among the various factories. To study this phenomenon, employee records are randomly selected at each of the three factories, and the length of employee service with the company is recorded. A summary of the data is in the table. Is there evidence of a difference in mean length of service among the three factories? Use $\alpha = .05$.

FACTORY	1	2	3
NUMBER IN SAMPLE	15	21	17
SST = 421.74	SSE = 3574.06		

15.59 England has experimented with different 40-hour work weeks to maximize production and minimize expenses. A factory tested a 5-day week (8 hours per day), a 4-day week (10 hours per day), and a $3\frac{1}{3}$-day week (12 hours per day), with the weekly production results shown in the table (in thousands of dollars worth of items produced).

8-HOUR DAY	10-HOUR DAY	12-HOUR DAY
87	75	95
96	82	76
75	90	87
90	80	82
72	73	65
86		

a. What type of experimental design was used here?

b. Construct an ANOVA summary table for this experiment.

c. Is there evidence of a difference among the mean productivity levels for the three lengths of workday?

15.60 Refer to Exercise 15.59. Form a 90% confidence interval for the mean weekly productivity when 12-hour workdays are used.

15.61 Mileage tests were performed to compare three different brands of regular gas. Four different automobiles were used in the experiment, and each brand of gas was used in each car until the mileage was determined. The results in miles per gallon are shown in the table.

BRAND	AUTOMOBILE			
	1	2	3	4
A	20.2	18.7	19.7	17.9
B	19.7	19.0	20.3	19.0
C	18.3	18.5	17.9	21.1

a. Is there evidence of a difference in the mean mileage rating among the three brands of gasoline? Use $\alpha = .05$.

b. Construct the ANOVA summary table for this experiment.

c. Is there evidence of a difference in the mean mileage among the four models; i.e., is blocking important in this type of experiment? Use $\alpha = .05$.

15.62 Refer to Exercise 15.61. Form a 99% confidence interval for the difference between the mean mileage ratings of brands B and C.

15.63 To reduce the time spent in transferring materials from one location to another, three methods have been devised. With no previous information available on the effectiveness of these three approaches, a study is performed. Each approach is tried several times, and the amount of time to completion (in hours) is recorded in the table.

a. What type of experimental design was used?

b. Is there evidence that the mean time to completion of the task differs for at least two of the three methods? Use $\alpha = .01$.

c. Form a 95% confidence interval for the mean time to completion for method B.

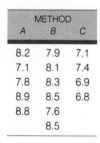

METHOD		
A	B	C
8.2	7.9	7.1
7.1	8.1	7.4
7.8	8.3	6.9
8.9	8.5	6.8
8.8	7.6	
	8.5	

15.64 Methods of displaying goods can have an effect on their sales. The manager of a large produce market would like to try three different display types for a certain fruit. The locations for the three displays are chosen in a way that the manager thinks each display type will be equally accessible to the customers. The three displays will be set up for five 1-week periods. Between each of these periods will be a 2-week period when a standard display is used. For each of the 5 experimental weeks, the sales (in dollars) of fruit from each display is determined, with the results shown in the table.

PERIOD	DISPLAY		
	A	B	C
1	$125	$153	$108
2	137	135	113
3	110	122	105
4	119	133	112
5	141	144	136

a. Is there evidence of a difference among mean sales for the three types of display? Use $\alpha = .05$.

b. Do the data indicate that the use of weeks as blocks was necessary? Test at $\alpha = .05$.

c. Construct the ANOVA summary table for this experiment.

15.65 Refer to Exercise 15.64. Use a 95% confidence interval to estimate the difference between the mean sales for displays A and C.

15.66 In hopes of attracting more riders, a city transit company plans to have express bus service from a suburban terminal to the downtown business district. These buses will travel along a major city street where there are numerous traffic lights that will affect travel time. The city decides to perform a study of the effect of four different plans (a special bus lane, traffic signal progression, etc.) on the travel times for the buses. Travel times (in minutes) are measured for several weekdays during a morning rush-hour trip while each plan was in effect. The results are recorded in the table.

a. What type of experimental design was used?

b. Is there evidence of a difference among the mean travel times for the four plans? Use $\alpha = .01$.

c. Form a 95% confidence interval for the difference between the mean travel times using plan 1 (express lane) and plan 3 (a control — no special travel arrangements).

PLAN			
1	2	3	4
27	25	34	30
25	28	29	33
29	30	32	31
26	27	31	
	24	36	

15.67 To be able to provide its clients with comparative information on two large suburban residential communities, a realtor wants to know the average home value in each community. Eight homes are selected at random within each community and are appraised by the realtor. The appraisals are given in the table (in thousands of dollars). Can you conclude that the average home value is different in the two communities? You have three ways of analyzing this problem.

a. Use the two-sample t statistic (Section 9.2) to test $H_0: \mu_A = \mu_B$.

b. Consider the regression model

$$y = \beta_0 + \beta_1 x + \varepsilon$$

where

$$x = \begin{cases} 1 & \text{if community B} \\ 0 & \text{if community A} \end{cases} \qquad y = \text{Appraised price}$$

Since $\beta_1 = \mu_B - \mu_A$, testing $H_0: \beta_1 = 0$ is equivalent to testing $H_0: \mu_A = \mu_B$. Use the partial reproduction of the SAS printout shown here to test $H_0: \beta_1 = 0$. Use $\alpha = .05$.

COMMUNITY	
A	B
43.5	73.5
49.5	62.0
38.0	47.5
66.5	36.5
57.5	44.5
32.0	56.0
67.5	68.0
71.5	63.5

SOURCE	DF	SUM OF SQUARES	MEAN SQUARE	F VALUE	PR > F
MODEL	1	40.64062500	40.64062500	0.21	0.6501
ERROR	14	2648.71875000	189.19419643		ROOT MSE
CORRECTED TOTAL	15	2689.35937500		R-SQUARE	13.75478813
				0.015112	

PARAMETER	ESTIMATE	T FOR H0: PARAMETER = 0	PR > ITI	STD ERROR OF ESTIMATE
INTERCEPT	53.25000000	10.95	0.0001	4.86305198
X	3.18750000	0.46	0.6501	6.87739406

c. Use the ANOVA method to test $H_0: \mu_A = \mu_B$. Use $\alpha = .05$.

d. Using the results of the three tests in parts a–c, verify that the tests are the equivalent (for this special case, $k = 2$) of the completely randomized design in terms of the test statistic value and rejection region. For the three methods used, what are the advantages and disadvantages (limitations) of using each in analyzing results for this type of experimental design?

15.68 An *analytical review* is a procedure used by auditors to identify the areas within a firm's financial records that have the highest potential for material misstatement (error). Analytical review procedures consist of analyses of expected relationships among the firm's operating and financial data, using trends, ratios, reasonableness tests, and other procedures. The diversity in the practice of analytical reviews both among and within CPA firms motivated Blocher, Esposito, and Willingham (1983) to examine the effects of certain situational variables on auditor judgments about the proper nature and extent of analytical review procedures in the payroll audit area. As part of their study, they investigated how explicit guidance to the auditor in the form of a checklist of suggested analytical review procedures influenced the auditor's planning for the extent of the analytical review work. They hypothesized that the checklist would cause the auditor to plan for more hours of analytical review work than if no checklist were used. Forty-four auditors from a large audit firm participated in their experiment. Each auditor was given detailed information about a particular (hypothetical) firm and asked to estimate the total number of hours needed for an analytical review of the firm's payroll expense. Twenty-two of the forty-four auditors were given a checklist to use in preparing their estimate. The auditors' responses are given in the table.

AUDITOR	CHECKLIST?	ANALYTICAL REVIEW HOURS	AUDITOR	CHECKLIST?	ANALYTICAL REVIEW HOURS	AUDITOR	CHECKLIST?	ANALYTICAL REVIEW HOURS
1	YES	4	16	NO	10	31	YES	10
2	YES	16	17	NO	6	32	YES	6
3	YES	8	18	NO	5	33	YES	12
4	YES	18	19	NO	13	34	NO	8
5	YES	18	20	NO	20	35	NO	10
6	YES	30	21	NO	8	36	NO	8
7	YES	4	22	NO	6	37	NO	8
8	YES	8	23	YES	16	38	NO	4
9	YES	21	24	YES	4	39	NO	8
10	YES	24	25	YES	8	40	NO	20
11	YES	10	26	YES	10	41	NO	2
12	NO	4	27	YES	10	42	NO	8
13	NO	4	28	YES	6	43	NO	3
14	NO	4	29	YES	10	44	NO	12
15	NO	25	30	YES	14			

Source: Blocher, Esposito, and Willingham (1983).

a. Blocher, Esposito, and Willingham used an analysis of variance to show that the difference between the mean number of hours for analytical review specified by the auditors using a checklist and those not using a checklist is "weakly significant (p-value $= .095$)."

Check their result by constructing the appropriate ANOVA table, conducting an F test, and finding the approximate observed significance level of your F test.

b. In the context of the problem, specify the Type I and Type II errors associated with your F test of part a.

c. Use a two-sample t statistic to conduct the hypothesis test of part a.

15.69 Thirty-six stocks were randomly selected from those listed on the New York Stock Exchange (NYSE), thirty stocks were randomly selected from those listed on the American Stock Exchange (ASE), and fifteen stocks were randomly selected from those traded over-

NYSE Firm	Closing Price	ASE Firm	Closing Price	OTC Firm	Closing Price
Consumers Pwr Co	$27\frac{5}{8}$	American Maize Prods	$10\frac{5}{8}$	Lyon Metal Prods	$19\frac{7}{8}$
Sealed Air Corp	$28\frac{3}{8}$	Aloha Airls Inc	$8\frac{5}{8}$	Cochrane Furniture	7
City Investing Co	$46\frac{1}{4}$	Lloyd S Electrs Inc	$2\frac{3}{4}$	King Kullen Grocery	$22\frac{5}{8}$
Duquesne Lt Co	15	Laneco Inc	27	Am Surgery Ctrs	$3\frac{1}{8}$
Onicare Inc	$43\frac{5}{8}$	Vintage Enterprises	$5\frac{5}{8}$	Dart Drug Corp	31
Detroit Edison Co	$24\frac{3}{8}$	Caressa Inc	14	Uniflex Inc	$1\frac{1}{8}$
Consumers Pwr Co	$19\frac{5}{8}$	Pneumatic Scale Corp	16	La Z Boy Chair Co	$20\frac{5}{8}$
Virginia Elec & Pwr Co	58	Wards Inc	$16\frac{5}{8}$	Team Inc	$3\frac{5}{8}$
Duke Power Co	$21\frac{1}{8}$	Avondale Mls	24	Cutler Fed Inc	$2\frac{5}{8}$
Fischbach Corp	$48\frac{5}{8}$	Electro Audio Dynamics	$3\frac{1}{4}$	Tinsley Labs Inc	$7\frac{7}{8}$
Union Elec Co	35	Martin Processing Inc	$3\frac{3}{4}$	Atwood Oceanics Inc	21
L & N Hsg Corp	$29\frac{1}{4}$	Raymond Inds Inc	$19\frac{5}{8}$	Northwestern Pub Svc	$17\frac{5}{8}$
Barnett Banks Fla Inc	27	Pizza Inn Inc	$6\frac{3}{4}$	Flahs Inc	$1\frac{1}{8}$
Ahmanson H.F. & Co	$27\frac{7}{8}$	Telesciences Inc	24	Am Diagnostics	$6\frac{5}{8}$
Reynolds R.J. Inds Inc	51	Enerserve Prods Inc	$3\frac{3}{8}$	ADI Electrs Inc	$2\frac{5}{8}$
Woolworth F.W. Co	36	Starrett Hsg Corp	$4\frac{5}{8}$		
Penna Pwr & Lt	21	Eastern Co	$11\frac{7}{8}$		
Honda Motor Ltd	43	Blocker Energy Corp	$3\frac{1}{4}$		
Western Pac Inds Del	$55\frac{5}{8}$	Mite Corp	27		
Phillips Van Heusen Cp	$19\frac{1}{4}$	Berry Inds Corp	3		
Handleman Co Del	19	EAC Inds Inc	$8\frac{3}{8}$		
Dennys Inc	$31\frac{7}{8}$	Chilton Corp	$12\frac{1}{4}$		
House Fabrics Inc	28	Scope Inds	31		
Commonwealth Edison Co	$23\frac{1}{8}$	Forest City Enterprise	$18\frac{5}{8}$		
Public Svc Co Ind Inc	28	Transcontntl Energy Del	$4\frac{5}{8}$		
White Cons Inds Inc	36	Ultimate Corp	$13\frac{1}{4}$		
American Nat Res Co	$33\frac{1}{4}$	Royal Palm Bch Colony	$2\frac{1}{4}$		
Boston Edison Co	26	Noel Inds Inc	$3\frac{3}{8}$		
Atlantic Met Corp	$20\frac{5}{8}$	TIE/Communications Inc	38		
Financial Corp Amer	$25\frac{7}{8}$	Asamera Inc	$13\frac{3}{8}$		
Superscope Inc	$2\frac{5}{8}$				
Cp Natl Corp	$29\frac{7}{8}$				
Gleason Wks	$10\frac{1}{4}$				
Great Lakes Intl Inc	$23\frac{5}{8}$				
Evans Prods Co	$8\frac{3}{8}$				
Middle South Utils Inc	$14\frac{7}{8}$				

the-counter (OTC). The closing prices of all eighty-one stocks on December 31, 1982, are listed in the accompanying table.

a. Do the data provide sufficient evidence to conclude that the mean closing price differed among the three markets on December 31, 1982? Base your conclusion on the p-value of your test statistic.

b. Using 90% confidence intervals, investigate the differences between the mean closing prices of the three markets. Interpret your results in the context of the problem.

15.70 In Case Study 15.1, Dickson used an analysis of variance to evaluate a questionnaire that he had designed to measure the computer expertise of middle managers. The data he employed in the analysis are displayed in Table 15.5. Use the data to replicate the analysis performed by Dickson — including the confidence intervals. Compare your results with those presented in Figure 15.6.

15.71 In Example 12.4, we compared the mean dollar amounts owed for delinquent credit card customers using a multiple regression analysis. The data are reproduced in the table. The purpose of this exercise is to demonstrate that the multiple regression analysis of Example 12.4 yields the same information as an analysis of variance.

	CATEGORY 1 *Under $12,000*	CATEGORY 2 *$12,000–$25,000*	CATEGORY 3 *Over $25,000*
	$148	$513	$335
	76	264	643
	393	433	216
	520	94	536
	236	535	128
	134	327	723
	55	214	258
	166	135	380
	415	280	594
	153	304	465
Totals	$2,296	$3,099	$4,278

a. Perform an analysis of variance for the data, and display the results in an ANOVA table.

b. Compare your analysis of variance table with the one shown at the top of the multiple regression computer printout in Figure 12.17. Except for rounding errors, the two tables should be identical.

c. Do the data present sufficient evidence to indicate differences among the three population means? Find the approximate p-value for the test, and compare your computed F statistic value and p-value with those shown on the multiple regression computer printout in Figure 12.17. They should be identical except for rounding errors. Interpret the results of your test.

15.72 In Example 12.6, we used a multiple regression analysis to analyze data for a 2×3 factorial experiment. The experiment measured worker productivity for each of two types of manufacturing plant (union and nonunion) and for each of three levels of bonus compensation. Three workers were randomly assigned to each of the six plant type–incentive factor level combinations. The objective of the experiment was to examine the relationship between worker productivity, y, and incentive level, x, for the two types of plants. Since the data in the table are the results of a 2×3 factorial experiment with the same number of observations per factor level combination, we can analyze the data using an analysis of variance.

| TYPE OF PLANT | INCENTIVE | | |
	20¢/casting	30¢/casting	40¢/casting
Union	1,435, 1,512, 1,491	1,583, 1,529, 1,610	1,601, 1,574, 1,636
Nonunion	1,575, 1,512, 1,488	1,635, 1,589, 1,661	1,645, 1,616, 1,689

a. Construct an analysis of variance table for the data.

b. Do the data provide sufficient evidence to indicate an interaction between incentive level and type of plant? Test using $\alpha = .05$.

c. What are the practical implications of the test results of part b?

d. Compare your SSE with the one obtained in the multiple regression analysis, Figure 12.22. Why do they differ?

e. Compare the results of the analysis of Example 12.6 with those of your analysis of variance. Then consider the following: If one (or both) of the factors in a two-factor factorial experiment is a quantitative independent variable, a multiple regression analysis provides more practical information than an analysis of variance. Why? [*Note:* If both factors are qualitative variables, the two methods of analysis yield the same results.]

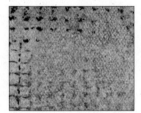

On Your Own . . .

Due to ever-increasing food costs, consumers are becoming more discerning in their choice of supermarkets. It usually is more convenient to shop at only one market, as opposed to buying different items at different markets. Thus, it would be useful to compare the mean food expenditure for a market basket of food items from store to store. Since there is a great deal of variability in the prices of products sold at any supermarket, we will consider an experiment that blocks on products.

Choose three (or more) supermarkets in your area that you want to compare; then choose approximately ten (or more) food products you typically purchase. For each food item, record the price each store charges in the following manner:

FOOD ITEM 1	FOOD ITEM 2 . . .	FOOD ITEM 10
Price store 1	Price store 1 . . .	Price store 1
Price store 2	Price store 2 . . .	Price store 2
Price store 3	Price store 3 . . .	Price store 3

Use the data you obtain to test

H_0:   Mean expenditures at the stores are the same

H_a: Mean expenditures for at least two of the stores are different

Also, test to determine whether blocking on food items is advisable in this kind of experiment. Fully interpret the results of your analysis.

References

Aplin-Brownlee, V. "Many workers facing terror of 'technophobia'." *Minneapolis Star and Tribune,* Jan. 10, 1984, 1C.

Blocher, E., Esposito, R. S., & Willingham, J. J. "Auditors' analytical review judgments for payroll expense." *Auditing, A Journal of Practice and Theory,* Fall 1983, *3,* 75–91.

Dawson, L. M. "Campus attitudes toward business." *Business Topics,* Summer 1969, *17,* 36–46.

Johnson, D. A., Pany, K., & White, R. "Audit reports and the loan decision: Actions and perceptions." *Auditing: A Journal of Practice and Theory,* Spring 1983, *2,* 38–51.

Klompmaker, J. E., Hughes, G. D., & Haley, R. I. "Test marketing in new products development." *Harvard Business Review,* May–June 1976, 128.

Logue, D., & Rogalski, R. *Harvard Business Review,* July–Aug. 1979.

Mendenhall, W. *Introduction to linear models and the design and analysis of experiments.* Belmont, Calif.: Wadsworth, 1968. Chapter 8.

Mendenhall, W., & McClave, J. T. *A second course in business statistics: Regression analysis.* San Francisco: Dellen, 1981.

Miller, R. B., & Wichern, D. W. *Intermediate business statistics: Analysis of variance, regression, and time series.* New York: Holt, Rinehart and Winston, 1977. Chapter 4.

Neter, J., & Wasserman, W. *Applied linear statistical models.* Homewood, Ill.: Richard D. Irwin, 1974.

Ozanne, U. B., & Churchill, G. A. "Adoption research: Information sources in the industrial purchasing decision." In R. L. Day & T. E. Ness, eds., *Marketing models, behavioral science applications.* Scranton, Pa.: Intext Educational Publishers, 1971. Pp. 249–265.

Phillips, M. D., & Pepper, R. L. "Shipboard fire-fighting performance of females and males." *Human Factors,* 1982, *24*(3).

Scheffé, H. *The analysis of variance.* New York: Wiley, 1959.

Shetty, Y. K., & Carlisle, H. M. "Organizational correlates of a management by objectives program." *Academy of Management Journal, 1974, 17*(1).

CHAPTER 16

Nonparametric Statistics

Where We've Been . . .

Chapters 8, 9, and 15 presented techniques for making inferences about the mean of a single population and for comparing the means of two or more populations. Chapters 10–12 treated simple and multiple regression — the problem of relating the mean of a population of y values to a set of independent variables $x_1, x_2, \ldots, x_k$. Most of the techniques discussed in Chapters 8–12 and 15 are based on the assumption that the sampled populations have probability distributions that are approximately normal with equal variances. But how can you analyze data from populations that do not satisfy these assumptions? Or, how can you make comparisons between populations when you cannot assign specific numerical values to your observations?

Where We're Going . . .

In this chapter, we present statistical techniques for comparing two or more populations that are based on an ordering of the sample measurements according to their relative magnitudes. These techniques, which require fewer or less stringent assumptions concerning the nature of the probability distributions of the populations, are called *nonparametric statistical methods.* We will present nonparametric statistical techniques for comparing two or more populations using two of the experimental designs described in Chapter 15 — the completely randomized and the randomized block designs.

Contents

The t and F tests for comparing two or more populations (Chapters 9 and 15) are unsuitable for some types of business data. These data fall into two categories: The first are data sets that do not satisfy the assumptions upon which the t and F tests are based. For both tests, we assume that the random variables being measured have normal probability distributions with equal variances. Yet in practice, the observations from one population may exhibit much greater variability than those from another, or the probability distributions may be decidedly nonnormal. For example, the distribution might be very flat, peaked, or strongly skewed to the right or left. When any of the assumptions required for the t and F tests are seriously violated, the computed t and F statistics may not follow the standard t and F distributions. If this is true, the tabulated values of t and F (Tables V–IX, Appendix B) are not applicable, the correct value of α for the test is unknown, and the t and F tests are of dubious value.

The second type of data for which t and F tests are inappropriate are responses that are not susceptible to measurement but that can be *ranked in order of magnitude*. For example, if we want to compare the managerial ability of two executives based on subjective evaluations of trained observers, despite the fact that we cannot give an exact value to the managerial ability of a single executive, we may be able to decide that executive A has more ability than executive B. If executives A and B are evaluated by each of ten observers, we have the standard problem of comparing the probability distributions for two populations of ratings, one for executive A and one for B. But the t test of Chapter 9 would be inappropriate because the only data that can be recorded are preferences; i.e., each observer decides either that A is better than B or vice versa.

Consider another example of this type of data. Most firms that plan to market a new product nationally first test the product in a few cities or regions to determine its acceptability. For a food product this may entail taste tests in which consumers rank the new product in order of preference with respect to one or more currently popular brands. A consumer probably has a preference for each product, but the strength of the preference is difficult, if not impossible, to measure. Consequently, the best we can do is have each consumer examine the new product along with a few established products, and rank them according to preference: 1 for the most preferred, 2 for second, etc.

The *nonparametric* counterparts of the t and F tests compare the probability distributions of the sampled populations, rather than specific parameters of these populations (such as the means or variances). For example, nonparametric tests can be used to compare the probability distribution of the strengths of preferences for a new product to the probability distributions of the strengths of preferences for the currently popular brands. If it can be inferred that the distribution for the new product lies above (to the right of) the others (see Figure 16.1), the

Figure 16.1 Probability Distributions of Strengths of Preference Measurements (New Product Is Preferred)

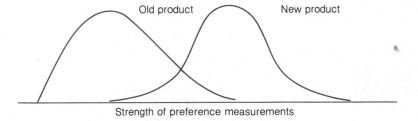

Old product   New product

Strength of preference measurements

implication is that the new product tends to be more preferred than the currently popular products. Such an inference might lead to a decision to market the product nationally.

Many nonparametric methods use the *relative ranks* of the sample observations rather than their actual numerical values. These tests are particularly valuable when we are unable to obtain numerical measurements of some phenomena but are able to rank them in comparison to each other. Statistics based on ranks of measurements are called *rank statistics.* In Sections 16.1 and 16.3, we present rank statistics for comparing two probability distributions using independent samples. In Sections 16.2 and 16.4, the matched pairs and randomized block designs are used to make nonparametric comparisons of populations. Finally, in Section 16.5 we present a nonparametric measure of correlation between two variables — *Spearman's rank correlation coefficient.* For a more complete discussion of tests based on rank statistics, see Lehmann (1975).

16.1 Comparing Two Populations: Wilcoxon Rank Sum Test for Independent Samples

Suppose two independent random samples are to be used to compare two populations, and the t test of Chapter 9 is inappropriate for making the comparison. Either we are unwilling to make assumptions about the form of the underlying probability distributions, or we are unable to obtain exact values of the sample measurements but can rank them in order of magnitude. For either of these situations, if the data can be ordered, the *Wilcoxon rank sum test* (developed by Frank Wilcoxon) can be used to test an hypothesis that the probability distributions associated with the two populations are equivalent.

For example, suppose six economists who work for the federal government and seven university economists are randomly selected, and each is asked to predict next year's percentage change in cost of living as compared with this year's figure. The objective of the study is to compare the government economists' predictions to those of the university economists. The data are shown in Table 16.1.

Table 16.1
Percentage Cost of Living Change, as Predicted by Government and University Economists

GOVERNMENT ECONOMIST		UNIVERSITY ECONOMIST	
Prediction	*Rank*	*Prediction*	*Rank*
3.1	4	4.4	6
4.8	7	5.8	9
2.3	2	3.9	5
5.6	8	8.7	11
0.0	1	6.3	10
2.9	3	10.5	12
		10.8	13

The two populations of predictions are those that would be obtained from *all* government and *all* university economists if they could all be questioned. To compare their probability distributions, we first *rank the sample observations as though they were all drawn from the same population.* That is, we pool the measurements from both samples and then rank the measurements from the smallest (a rank of 1) to the largest (a rank of 13). The ranks of the economists' predictions are indicated in Table 16.1.

The test statistic for the Wilcoxon test is based on the totals of the ranks for each of the two samples — that is, on the *rank sums.* If the two rank sums are nearly equal, the implication is that there is no evidence that the probability distributions from which the samples were drawn are different. On the other hand, if the two rank sums are very different, the implication is that the two samples may have come from different populations.

In the economists' predictions example, we arbitrarily denote the rank sum for government economists by T_A and that for university economists by T_B. Then

$$T_A = 4 + 7 + 2 + 8 + 1 + 3 = 25$$
$$T_B = 6 + 9 + 5 + 11 + 10 + 12 + 13 = 66$$

The sum of T_A and T_B will always equal $n(n + 1)/2$, where $n = n_1 + n_2$. So, for this example, $n_1 = 6$, $n_2 = 7$, and

$$T_A + T_B = \frac{13(13 + 1)}{2} = 91$$

Since $T_A + T_B$ is fixed, a small value for T_A implies a large value for T_B (and vice versa) and a large difference between T_A and T_B. Therefore, the smaller the value of one of the rank sums, the greater is the evidence to indicate that the samples were selected from different populations.

Figure 16.2 Reproduction of Part of Table X, Appendix B

a. $\alpha = .025$ one-tailed; $\alpha = .05$ two-tailed

n_2 \ n_1	3		4		5		6		7		8		9		10	
	T_L	T_U	T_L	T_U	T_L	T_U	T_L	T_U	T_L	T_U	T_L	T_U	T_L	T_U	T_L	T_U
3	5	16	6	18	6	21	7	23	7	26	8	28	8	31	9	33
4	6	18	11	25	12	28	12	32	13	35	14	38	15	41	16	44
5	6	21	12	28	18	37	19	41	20	45	21	49	22	53	24	56
6	7	23	12	32	19	41	26	52	28	56	29	61	31	65	32	70
7	7	26	13	35	20	45	28	56	37	68	39	73	41	78	43	83
8	8	28	14	38	21	49	29	61	39	73	49	87	51	93	54	98
9	8	31	15	41	22	53	31	65	41	78	51	93	63	108	66	114
10	9	33	16	44	24	56	32	70	43	83	54	98	66	114	79	131

Values that locate the rejection region for the rank sum associated with the smaller sample are given in Table X of Appendix B. A partial reproduction of this table is shown in Figure 16.2. The columns of the table represent n_1, the first sample size, and the rows represent n_2, the second sample size. *The T_L and T_U entries in the table are the boundaries of the lower and upper regions, respectively, for the rank sum associated with the sample that has fewer measurements.* If the sample sizes n_1 and n_2 are the same, either rank sum may be used as the test statistic. To illustrate, suppose $n_1 = 8$ and $n_2 = 10$. For a two-tailed test with $\alpha = .05$, we consult part a of the table and find that the null hypothesis will be rejected if the rank sum of sample 1 (the sample with fewer measurements), T, is less than or equal to $T_L = 54$ *or* greater than or equal to $T_U = 98$. The two-tailed Wilcoxon rank sum test is summarized in the box.

Wilcoxon Rank Sum Test: Independent Samples*

One-Tailed Test

H_0: Two sampled populations have identical probability distributions

H_a: The probability distribution for population A is shifted to the right of that for B

Test statistic: The rank sum, T, associated with the sample with fewer measurements (if sample sizes are equal, either rank sum can be used)

Rejection region: Assuming the smaller sample size is associated with distribution A (or, if sample sizes are equal, we use the rank sum T_A), we reject H_0 if $T_A \geq T_U$, where T_U is the upper value given by Table X in Appendix B for the chosen *one-tailed* α value.

Two-Tailed Test

H_0: Two sampled populations have identical probability distributions

H_a: The probability distribution for population A is shifted to the left *or* to the right of that for B

Test statistic: The rank sum, T, associated with the sample with fewer measurements (if the sample sizes are equal, either rank sum can be used)

Rejection region: $T \leq T_L$ or $T \geq T_U$, where T_L is the lower value given by Table X in Appendix B for the chosen *two-tailed* α value, and T_U is the upper value from Table X.

[*Note:* If the one-sided alternative is that the probability distribution for A is shifted to the *left* of B (and T_A is the test statistic), we reject H_0 if $T_A \leq T_L$.]

Assumptions: 1. The two samples are random and independent.
2. The observations obtained can be ranked in order of magnitude. [*Note:* No assumptions have to be made about the shape of the population probability distributions.]

Example 16.1 Test the hypothesis that the university economists' predictions of next year's percentage change in cost of living tend to be higher than the government economists'. Conduct the test using the data in Table 16.1 and $\alpha = .05$.

Solution H_0: The probability distributions corresponding to the government and university economists' predictions of inflation rate are identical

H_a: The probability distribution for the university economists' predictions lies above (to the right of) that for the government economists' predictions

Test statistic: Since fewer government economists ($n_1 = 6$) than university economists ($n_2 = 7$) were sampled, the test statistic is T_A, the rank sum of the government economists' predictions.

Rejection region: Since the test is one-sided, we consult part b of Table X for the rejection region corresponding to $\alpha = .05$. We will reject H_0 only for $T_A \leq T_L$, the lower value from Table X, since we are specifically testing that the distribution of the government economists' predictions lies *below* the distribution of university economists' predictions, as shown in Figure 16.3 (next page). Thus, we will reject H_0 if $T_A \leq 30$.

* Another statistic used for comparing two populations based on independent random samples is the *Mann–Whitney U statistic*. The U statistic is a simple function of the rank sums. It can be shown that the Wilcoxon rank sum test and the Mann–Whitney U test are equivalent.

Figure 16.3 Alternative Hypothesis and Rejection Region for Example 16.1

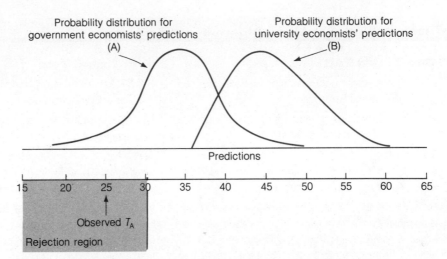

Since T_A, the rank sum of the government economists' predictions in Table 16.1, is 25, it is in the rejection region (see Figure 16.3). Therefore, we can conclude that the university economists' predictions tend, in general, to exceed the government economists' predictions. ∎

Occasionally some measurements in the two samples will be tied (i.e., have equal values). When this occurs, we assign the average of the ranks that would be assigned to the measurements if they were unequal but occurred in successive order. For example, if the third- and fourth-ranked measurements were equal, both would receive a rank of 3.5.

Wilcoxon Rank Sum Test: Large Independent Samples

One-Tailed Test

H_0: Two sampled populations have identical probability distributions

H_a: The probability distribution for population A is shifted to the right of that for B

Test statistic:

$$z = \frac{T_A - \dfrac{n_1(n_1 + n_2 + 1)}{2}}{\sqrt{\dfrac{n_1 n_2(n_1 + n_2 + 1)}{12}}}$$

Rejection region: $z > z_\alpha$

Two-Tailed Test

H_0: Two sampled populations have identical probability distributions

H_a: The probability distribution for population A is shifted to the left *or* to the right of that for B

Test statistic:

$$z = \frac{T_A - \dfrac{n_1(n_1 + n_2 + 1)}{2}}{\sqrt{\dfrac{n_1 n_2(n_1 + n_2 + 1)}{12}}}$$

Rejection region: $z < -z_{\alpha/2}$
                     or $z > z_{\alpha/2}$

Assumptions: $n_1 \geq 10$ and $n_2 \geq 10$

Table X of Appendix B gives values of T_L and T_U for sample sizes n_1 and n_2 less than or equal to 10. When both sample sizes are 10 or larger, the sampling distribution of T_A can be approximated by a normal distribution with mean and variance

$$E(T_A) = \frac{n_1(n_1 + n_2 + 1)}{2} \quad \text{and} \quad \sigma^2_{T_A} = \frac{n_1 n_2(n_1 + n_2 + 1)}{12}$$

Therefore, for $n_1 \geq 10$ and $n_2 \geq 10$, we can conduct the Wilcoxon rank sum test using the familiar z test of Chapters 8 and 9. The large-sample test is summarized in the preceding box.

Exercises 16.1 – 16.13

Learning the Mechanics

16.1 Specify the test statistic and the rejection region for the Wilcoxon rank sum test for independent samples in each of the following situations:

a. H_0: Two probability distributions, A and B, are identical

H_a: Probability distribution for population A is shifted to the right or left of the probability distribution for population B

$n_A = 8$, $n_B = 6$, $\alpha = .10$

b. H_0: Two probability distributions, A and B, are identical

H_a: Probability distribution for population A is shifted to the right of the probability distribution for population B

$n_A = 5$, $n_B = 6$, $\alpha = .05$

c. H_0: Two probability distributions, A and B, are identical

H_a: Probability distribution for population A is shifted to the left of the probability distribution for population B

$n_A = 10$, $n_B = 8$, $\alpha = .025$

16.2 Suppose you want to compare two treatments, A and B. In particular, you wish to determine whether the distribution for population B is shifted to the right of the distribution for population A. You plan to use the Wilcoxon rank sum test to help you with your decision.

a. Specify the null and alternative hypotheses you would test.

b. If $n_A = 9$, $n_B = 4$, and $\alpha = .05$, specify the rejection region for the test.

16.3 Refer to Exercise 16.2. Suppose you obtained the following independent random samples of observations on experimental units subjected to two treatments, treatment A and treatment B:

A: 36, 39, 33, 29, 42, 33, 35, 28, 34

B: 35, 48, 52, 66

Conduct a test of the hypotheses described in Exercise 16.2. Test using $\alpha = .05$.

16.4 Explain the difference between the one- and two-tailed versions of the Wilcoxon rank sum test for independent random samples.

Applying the Concepts

U.S. PLANTS	JAPANESE PLANTS
7.11%	3.52%
6.06	2.02
8.00	4.91
6.87	3.22
4.77	1.92

16.5 Recall that the variance of a binomial sample proportion, $\hat{p}$, depends on the value of the population parameter, p. As a consequence, the variance of a sample percentage, $(100\hat{p})\%$, will also depend on p. The relevance of this fact is that if you conduct an unpaired t test (Section 9.2) to compare the means of two populations of percentages, you may be violating the assumption that $\sigma_1^2 = \sigma_2^2$, upon which the t test is based. If the disparity in the variances is large, you will obtain more reliable test results using the Wilcoxon rank sum test for independent samples. In Exercise 9.26, we used a Student's t test to compare the mean annual percentages of labor turnover between U.S. and Japanese manufacturers of air conditioners. The annual percentage turnover rates for five U.S. and five Japanese plants are shown in the table. Do the data provide sufficient evidence to indicate that the mean annual percentage turnover for American plants exceeds the corresponding mean for Japanese plants? Test using the Wilcoxon rank sum test with $\alpha = .05$. Do your test conclusions agree with those of the t test in Exercise 9.26?

DAMAGE PER ACCIDENT	
Before right-turn law	After right-turn law
$150	$ 145
500	390
250	680
301	560
242	899
435	1,250
100	290
402	963

16.6 A state highway department has decided to investigate the increased severity of automobile accidents occurring at a particular urban intersection since the adoption of the right-turn-on-red law. From police records, they chose a random sample of eight accidents that occurred at the intersection before the law was enacted and a random sample of eight accidents that occurred after the law was enacted. They used the total damage estimate for each accident as a measure of the accident's severity. The damage estimates are recorded in the table. Use the Wilcoxon rank sum test to determine whether the damages tended to increase after the enactment of the law. Test using $\alpha = .05$. Draw appropriate conclusions.

SCORES	
Younger age group	Older age group
4	1
3	5
4	4
2	3
3	3
5	4
4	3

16.7 Seven people between the ages of 15 and 25 and seven people between the ages of 45 and 60 were randomly selected to help determine the preferences of the two age groups for a newly developed snack food. Each person was asked to taste the product and evaluate it on a scale of 1 to 5, with higher scores indicating a greater likelihood of purchasing the product regularly. The results of the taste test appear in the table. The vice-president of the company's consumer foods division believes the new product will be more of a hit with consumers between 15 and 25 years of age than with older consumers, and plans to design the product's advertising campaign accordingly. Do the taste test data support the vice-president's belief? Test using $\alpha = .05$. Carefully interpret the results and implications of the test in the context of this problem.

TWIN BLADES		SINGLE BLADES	
8	15	10	13
17	10	6	14
9	6	3	5
11	12	7	7

16.8 A major razor blade manufacturer advertises that its twin-blade disposable razor will "get you a lot more shaves" than any single-blade disposable razor on the market. A rival blade company that has been very successful in selling single-blade razors wishes to test this claim. Independent random samples of eight single-blade shavers and eight twin-blade shavers are taken, and the number of shaves that each gets before indicating a preference to change blades is recorded. The results are shown in the table.

a. Do the data support the twin-blade manufacturer's claim? Use $\alpha = .05$.

b. Do you think this experiment was designed in the best possible way? If not, what design might have been better?

PREVIOUS MANAGER	PRESENT MANAGER
9	8
12	11
10	7
14	5
15	13

SUBDIVISION			
A		B	
43	39	57	88
48	47	39	46
42		55	41
60		52	64

16.9 The owner of a restaurant recently fired the restaurant manager and hired a new one because of the number of customer complaints that were made. The owner decided to wait 3 months before evaluating the new manager. Then, the number of complaints for each of the next 5 weeks was recorded and compared with the number of complaints per week for the last 5 weeks that the previous manager had worked. The results are given in the table. Have things improved under the new manager?

16.10 A realtor wants to determine whether a difference exists between home prices in two subdivisions. Six homes from subdivision A and eight homes from subdivision B are sampled, and the prices (in thousands of dollars) are recorded in the table.

a. Use the two-sample t test to compare the population mean prices per house in the two subdivisions. What assumptions are necessary for the validity of this procedure? Do you think they are reasonable in this case?

b. Use the Wilcoxon rank sum test to determine whether there is a shift in the locations of the probability distributions of house prices in the two subdivisions.

16.11 An educational psychologist claims that the order in which test questions are asked affects a student's ability to answer correctly. To investigate this assertion, a professor randomly divides a class of thirteen students into two groups — seven in one group and six in the other. The professor prepares one set of test questions but arranges the questions in two different orders. On test A, the questions are arranged in order of increasing difficulty (that is, from easiest to most difficult), while on test B, the order is reversed. One group of students is given test A, the other test B, and the test score is recorded for each student. The results are as follows:

Test A: 90, 71, 83, 82, 75, 91, 65

Test B: 66, 78, 50, 68, 80, 60

Do the data provide sufficient evidence to indicate a difference between the two tests in a student's ability to answer the questions? Test using $\alpha = .05$.

16.12 Thirty-six stocks were randomly selected from those listed on the New York Stock Exchange (NYSE), and thirty stocks were randomly selected from those listed on the American Stock Exchange (ASE). The closing prices of all sixty-six stocks on December 31, 1982 are listed in the table on page 744.

a. Use the two-sided Wilcoxon rank sum test (the large-sample procedure) to determine whether the data provide sufficient evidence to indicate a shift in the locations of the distributions of closing prices for the two stock exchanges. Specify your null and alternative hypotheses and interpret the result of your test in the context of the problem. Use $\alpha = .05$.

b. In the context of the problem, specify the Type I and Type II errors associated with the test of part a.

c. Using the testing procedure of part a, what is the probability of committing a Type I error?

NYSE		ASE	
Firm	*Closing Price*	*Firm*	*Closing Price*
Consumers Pwr Co	$27\frac{5}{8}$	American Maize Prods	$10\frac{5}{8}$
Sealed Air Corp	$28\frac{5}{8}$	Aloha Airls Inc	$8\frac{5}{8}$
City Investing Co	$46\frac{1}{4}$	Lloyd S Electrs Inc	$2\frac{3}{8}$
Duquesne Lt Co	15	Laneco Inc	27
Onicare Inc	$43\frac{5}{8}$	Vintage Enterprises	$5\frac{5}{8}$
Detroit Edison Co	$24\frac{1}{4}$	Caressa Inc	14
Consumers Pwr Co	$19\frac{5}{8}$	Pneumatic Scale Corp	16
Virginia Elec & Pwr Co	58	Wards Inc	$16\frac{5}{8}$
Duke Power Co	$21\frac{5}{8}$	Avondale Mls	24
Fischbach Corp	$48\frac{5}{8}$	Electro Audio Dynamics	$3\frac{1}{8}$
Union Elec Co	35	Martin Processing Inc	$3\frac{4}{8}$
L & N Hsg Corp	$29\frac{4}{8}$	Raymond Inds Inc	$19\frac{5}{8}$
Barnett Banks Fla Inc	27	Pizza Inn Inc	$6\frac{3}{8}$
Ahmanson H. F. & Co	$27\frac{5}{8}$	Telesciences Inc	24
Reynolds R. J. Inds Inc	51	Enerserve Prods Inc	$3\frac{3}{8}$
Woolworth F. W. Co	36	Starrett Hsg Corp	$4\frac{4}{8}$
Penna Pwr & Lt	21	Eastern Co	$11\frac{5}{8}$
Honda Motor Ltd	43	Blocker Energy Corp	$3\frac{1}{8}$
Western Pac Inds Del	$55\frac{5}{8}$	Mite Corp	27
Phillips Van Heusen Cp	$19\frac{4}{8}$	Berry Inds Corp	3
Handleman Co Del	19	EAC Inds Inc	$8\frac{3}{8}$
Dennys Inc	$31\frac{7}{8}$	Chilton Corp	$12\frac{1}{8}$
House Fabrics Inc	28	Scope Inds	31
Commonwealth Edison Co	$23\frac{1}{8}$	Forest City Enterprise	$18\frac{5}{8}$
Public Svc Co Ind Inc	28	Transcontntl Energy Del	$4\frac{5}{8}$
White Cons Inds Inc	36	Ultimate Corp	$13\frac{4}{8}$
American Nat Res Co	$33\frac{4}{8}$	Royal Palm Bch Colony	$2\frac{4}{8}$
Boston Edison Co	26	Noel Inds Inc	$3\frac{5}{8}$
Atlantic Met Corp	$20\frac{5}{8}$	TIE/Communications Inc	38
Financial Corp Amer	$25\frac{7}{8}$	Asamera Inc	$13\frac{5}{8}$
Superscope Inc	$2\frac{5}{8}$		
Cp Natl Corp	$29\frac{7}{8}$		
Gleason Wks	$10\frac{1}{4}$		
Great Lakes Intl Inc	$23\frac{5}{8}$		
Evans Prods Co	$8\frac{3}{8}$		
Middle South Utils Inc	$14\frac{7}{8}$		

16.13 A *management information system* (MIS) is a computer-based information-processing system designed to support the operations, management, and decision functions of an organization. The development of an MIS involves three stages: definition of the system, physical design of the system, and implementation of the system (Davis, 1974). Steven Alter and Michael Ginzberg (1978) have shown that the successful implementation of an MIS is related to the quality of the entire development process. The implementation of an MIS could fail due to inadequate planning by and negotiating between the designers and the future users of the system prior to the construction of the system. Or, it could fail simply because members of the organization were improperly trained to use the system effectively.

Thirty firms that recently implemented an MIS were surveyed; sixteen were satisfied with the implementation results, fourteen were not. Each firm was asked to rate the quality of the planning and negotiation stages of the development process. Quality was to be rated on a scale of 0 to 100, with higher numbers indicating better quality. In particular, a score of 100 indicates that all the problems that occurred in the planning and negotiation stages appear to have been successfully resolved, while a score of 0 indicates that none of the problems appear to have been resolved. The results obtained are shown in the table.

FIRMS WITH SUCCESSFUL MIS		FIRMS WITH UNSUCCESSFUL MIS	
52	90	60	65
70	75	50	55
40	80	55	70
80	95	70	90
82	90	41	85
65	86	40	80
59	95	55	90
60	93		

Source: Based on Alter and Ginzberg (1978).

a. Ginzberg used the Mann–Whitney U test (a procedure equivalent to the Wilcoxon rank sum test) on similar data to investigate differences in the quality of the development processes of successfully and unsuccessfully implemented MIS's. Use the large-sample Wilcoxon rank sum test to determine whether the distribution of quality scores for successfully implemented systems lies above the distribution of scores for unsuccessfully implemented systems. Test using $\alpha = .05$.

b. Under what circumstances could you use the two-sample t test of Chapter 9 to conduct the same test?

16.2
Comparing
Two
Populations:
Wilcoxon
Signed Rank
Test for the
Paired
Difference
Experiment

Nonparametric techniques can also be used to compare two probability distributions when a paired difference design is used. For example, for some paper products, softness of the paper is an important consideration in determining consumer acceptance. One method of determining softness is to have judges give a sample of the products a softness rating. Suppose each of ten judges is given a sample of two products that a company wants to compare. Each judge rates the softness of each product on a scale from 1 to 10, with higher ratings implying a softer product. The results are shown in Table 16.2 (next page).

Since this is a paired difference experiment, we analyze the differences between the measurements (see Section 9.4). However, the nonparametric approach requires that we calculate the ranks of the absolute values of the differences between the measurements — i.e., the ranks of the differences after removing any minus signs. Note that tied absolute differences are assigned the average of the ranks they would receive if they were unequal but successive measurements. After the absolute differences are ranked, the sum of the ranks of

Table 16.2

Paper Softness Ratings

JUDGE	PRODUCT A	B	DIFFERENCE (A − B)	ABSOLUTE VALUE OF DIFFERENCE	RANK OF ABSOLUTE VALUE
1	6	4	2	2	5
2	8	5	3	3	7.5
3	4	5	−1	1	2
4	9	8	1	1	2
5	4	1	3	3	7.5
6	7	9	−2	2	5
7	6	2	4	4	9
8	5	3	2	2	5
9	6	7	−1	1	2
10	8	2	6	6	10

$$T_+ = \text{Sum of positive ranks} = 46$$

$$T_- = \text{Sum of negative ranks} = 9$$

the positive differences, T_+, and the sum of the ranks of the negative differences, T_-, are computed.

We are now prepared to test the nonparametric hypotheses:

H_0: The probability distributions of the ratings for products A and B are identical

H_a: The probability distribution for product A is shifted to the right or left of the probability distribution of the ratings for product B

Test statistic: $T =$ Smaller of the positive and negative rank sums T_+ and T_-

The smaller the value of T, the greater will be the evidence to indicate that the two probability distributions differ in location. The rejection region for T can be determined by consulting Table XI of Appendix B. A portion of that table is shown in Figure 16.4. This table gives a value, T_0, for each value of n, the number of matched pairs. The values of T_0 are tabulated for both a one- and a two-tailed test. For a two-tailed test with $\alpha = .05$, we will reject H_0 if $T \le T_0$. The T_0 value that locates the rejection region for the judges' ratings in Table 16.2 is the value indicated for $n = 10$ pairs of observations. This value of T_0 is 8. Therefore, the rejection region for the test (see Figure 16.5) is

Rejection region: $T \le 8$ for $\alpha = .05$

Figure 16.5 Rejection Region for Paired Difference Experiment

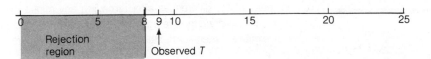

Figure 16.4 Reproduction of Part of Table XI of Appendix B

ONE-TAILED	TWO-TAILED	n = 5	n = 6	n = 7	n = 8	n = 9	n = 10
$\alpha = .05$	$\alpha = .10$	1	2	4	6	8	11
$\alpha = .025$	$\alpha = .05$		1	2	4	6	8
$\alpha = .01$	$\alpha = .02$			0	2	3	5
$\alpha = .005$	$\alpha = .01$				0	2	3
		n = 11	n = 12	n = 13	n = 14	n = 15	n = 16
$\alpha = .05$	$\alpha = .10$	14	17	21	26	30	36
$\alpha = .025$	$\alpha = .05$	11	14	17	21	25	30
$\alpha = .01$	$\alpha = .02$	7	10	13	16	20	24
$\alpha = .005$	$\alpha = .01$	5	7	10	13	16	19
		n = 17	n = 18	n = 19	n = 20	n = 21	n = 22
$\alpha = .05$	$\alpha = .10$	41	47	54	60	68	75
$\alpha = .025$	$\alpha = .05$	35	40	46	52	59	66
$\alpha = .01$	$\alpha = .02$	28	33	38	43	49	56
$\alpha = .005$	$\alpha = .01$	23	28	32	37	43	49
		n = 23	n − 24	n = 25	n = 26	n = 27	n = 28
$\alpha = .05$	$\alpha = .10$	83	92	101	110	120	130
$\alpha = .025$	$\alpha = .05$	73	81	90	98	107	117
$\alpha = .01$	$\alpha = .02$	62	69	77	85	93	102
$\alpha = .005$	$\alpha = .01$	55	61	68	76	84	92

Since the smaller rank sum for the paper data, $T = T_- = 9$, does not fall within the rejection region, the experiment has not provided sufficient evidence to indicate that the two paper products differ with respect to their softness ratings at $\alpha = .05$.

Note that, if a significance level of $\alpha = .10$ had been used, the rejection region would have been $T \le 11$, and we would have rejected H_0. In other words, the samples do provide evidence that the probability distributions of the softness ratings differ at $\alpha = .10$.

Example 16.2 Suppose the U.S. Consumer Product Safety Commission (CPSC) wants to test the hypothesis that New York City electrical contractors are more likely to install unsafe electrical outlets in urban homes than in suburban homes. A pair of homes, one urban and one suburban and both serviced by the same electrical contractor, is chosen for each of ten randomly selected electrical contractors. A commission inspector assigns each of the twenty homes a safety rating between 1 and 10, with higher numbers implying safer electrical conditions. The results are shown in Table 16.3. Use the Wilcoxon signed rank test to determine whether the CPSC hypothesis is supported at the $\alpha = .05$ level.

Table 16.3 Electrical Safety Ratings for Ten Pairs of New York City Homes

ELECTRICAL CONTRACTOR	URBAN HOME	SUBURBAN HOME	ELECTRICAL CONTRACTOR	URBAN HOME	SUBURBAN HOME
1	7	9	6	6	10
2	4	5	7	8	9
3	8	8	8	10	8
4	9	8	9	9	4
5	3	6	10	5	9

Wilcoxon Signed Rank Test for a Paired Difference Experiment

One-Tailed Test

H_0: Two sampled populations have identical probability distributions

H_a: The probability distribution for population A is shifted to the right of that for population B

Test statistic: T_-, the negative rank sum (we assume the differences are computed by subtracting each paired B measurement from the corresponding A measurement)

Rejection region: $T_- \leq T_0$, where T_0 is found in Table XI in Appendix B for the one-tailed significance level α and the number of untied pairs, n.

Two-Tailed Test

H_0: Two sampled populations have identical probability distributions

H_a: The probability distribution for population A is shifted to the right or to the left of that for population B

Test statistic: T, the smaller of the positive and negative rank sums, T_+ and T_-

Rejection region: $T \leq T_0$, where T_0 is found in Table XI in Appendix B for the two-tailed significance level α and the number of untied pairs, n.

[*Note:* If the alternative hypothesis is that the probability distribution for A is shifted to the left of B, we use T_+ as the test statistic and reject H_0 if $T_+ \leq T_0$.]

Assumptions: 1. A random sample of pairs of observations has been taken.
2. The absolute differences in the paired observations can be ranked. [*Note:* No assumptions have to be made about the form of the population probability distributions.]

Solution The null and alternative hypotheses are

H_0: The probability distributions of home electrical ratings are identical for urban and suburban homes

H_a: The electrical ratings for suburban homes tend to exceed the electrical ratings for urban homes

These hypotheses can be tested for the data in Table 16.3 using the Wilcoxon signed rank test. Since a paired difference design was used (the homes were selected in urban–suburban pairs so that the electrical contractor was the same for both), we first calculate the difference between the ratings for each pair of homes, and then rank the absolute values of the differences (see Table 16.4). Note that one pair of ratings were the same (both 8), and the resulting zero difference contributes to neither the positive nor the negative rank sum. Thus, we eliminate this pair from the calculation of the test statistic.

Test statistic: T_+, the positive rank sum

Table 16.4

Differences in Ratings and the Ranks of Their Absolute Values

RATING		DIFFERENCE	RANK OF ABSOLUTE DIFFERENCE
Urban	Suburban	(Urban − Suburban)	
7	9	−2	4.5
4	5	−1	2
8	8	0	(Eliminated)
9	8	1	2
3	6	−3	6
6	10	−4	7.5
8	9	−1	2
10	8	2	4.5
9	4	5	9
5	9	−4	7.5
		Positive rank sum = T_+ = 15.5	

In Table 16.4, we compute the urban minus suburban rating differences, and if the alternative hypothesis is true, we would expect most of these differences to be negative. Or, in other words, we would expect the *positive* rank sum T_+ to be small if the alternative hypothesis is true (see Figure 16.6).

Figure 16.6 The Alternative Hypothesis for Example 16.2; We Expect T_+ to Be Small

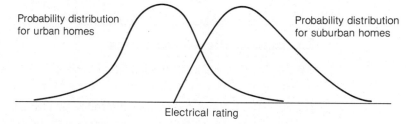

Probability distribution for urban homes

Probability distribution for suburban homes

Electrical rating

Rejection region: For $\alpha = .05$, from Table XI of Appendix B, we use $n = 9$ (remember, one pair of observations was eliminated) to find the rejection region for this one-tailed test:

$$T_+ \leq 8$$

Since the computed value $T_+ = 15.5$ exceeds the critical value of 8, we conclude that this sample provides insufficient evidence at $\alpha = .05$ to support the alternative hypothesis. We *cannot* conclude on the basis of this sample information that suburban homes have safer electrical outlets than urban homes. ∎

As is the case for the rank sum test for independent samples, the sampling distribution of the signed rank statistic can be approximated by a normal distribution when the number n of paired observations is large (say $n \geq 25$). The large-sample z test is summarized in the box at the top of the next page.

Wilcoxon Signed Rank Test for a Paired Difference Experiment: Large Sample

One-Tailed Test

H_0: Two sampled populations have identical probability distributions

H_a: The probability distribution for population A is shifted to the right of that for population B

Test statistic:

$$z = \frac{T_+ - \dfrac{n(n+1)}{4}}{\sqrt{\dfrac{n(n+1)(2n+1)}{24}}}$$

Rejection region: $z > z_\alpha$

Assumptions: $n \geq 25$

Two-Tailed Test

H_0: Two sampled populations have identical probability distributions

H_a: The probability distribution for population A is shifted to the right or to the left of that for population B

Test statistic:

$$z = \frac{T_+ - \dfrac{n(n+1)}{4}}{\sqrt{\dfrac{n(n+1)(2n+1)}{24}}}$$

Rejection region: $z < -z_{\alpha/2}$
or $z > z_{\alpha/2}$

Exercises 16.14 – 16.24

Learning the Mechanics

16.14 Specify the test statistic and the rejection region for the Wilcoxon signed rank test for the paired difference design in each of the following situations:

a. H_0: Two probability distributions, A and B, are identical
   H_a: Probability distribution for population A is shifted to the right or left of the probability distribution for population B
   $n = 25$, $\alpha = .10$

b. H_0: Two probability distributions, A and B, are identical
   H_a: Probability distribution for population A is shifted to the right of the probability distribution for population B
   $n = 41$, $\alpha = .05$

c. H_0: Two probability distributions, A and B, are identical
   H_a: Probability distribution for population A is shifted to the left of the probability distribution for population B
   $n = 8$, $\alpha = .005$

16.15 Suppose you want to test an hypothesis that two treatments, A and B, are equivalent against the alternative hypothesis that the responses for A tend to be larger than those for B. You plan to use a paired difference experiment and to analyze the resulting data using the Wilcoxon signed rank test.

a. Specify the null and alternative hypotheses you would test.

b. If $n = 10$ and $\alpha = .025$, specify the rejection region for the test.

16.16 Refer to Exercise 16.15. Suppose the paired difference experiment yielded the data in the table. Conduct the test indicated by your answers to Exercise 16.15. Test using $\alpha = .025$.

PAIR OF EXPERIMENTAL UNITS	TREATMENT A	B
1	56	42
2	62	45
3	98	87
4	45	31
5	82	71
6	76	75
7	74	63
8	29	30
9	63	59
10	80	82

16.17 Explain the difference between the one- and two-tailed versions of the Wilcoxon signed rank test for the paired difference experiment.

Applying the Concepts

16.18 According to the American Bar Association, in 1981 there were 498,249 lawyers in the United States. About 73% of these lawyers were in private practice; about 15% worked in government as judges, prosecutors, legislators, etc.; and about 10% worked for businesses. Because of mushrooming government regulation, high outside legal fees, and complex litigation, the number of corporate lawyers has been growing at a rapid pace. The data shown in the table are the average salaries for lawyers with 8 years experience for a sample of ten U.S. cities.

CITY	CORPORATE LAWYERS	LAWYERS WITH LAW FIRMS
Atlanta	$35,000	$34,000
Boston	32,500	35,500
Cincinnati	34,000	30,500
Des Moines	32,000	39,000
Houston	36,000	35,500
Los Angeles	45,000	45,500
Milwaukee	36,500	37,000
New York	42,000	50,000
Pittsburgh	34,500	34,000
San Francisco	31,500	35,500

Source: *The American Almanac of Jobs and Salaries*, 1982, pp. 379–389.

a. Use the Wilcoxon signed rank test to determine whether the data provide sufficient evidence to conclude that the salaries of corporate lawyers differ from those of lawyers working for law firms. Test using $\alpha = .05$.

b. Under what circumstances would it be appropriate to conduct the test in part a using the paired difference t test described in Chapter 9?

16.19 Traditionally, jobs in the United States have required employees to perform their work during a fixed 8-hour workday. A recent job-scheduling innovation that is helping managers to overcome the motivation and absenteeism problems associated with the fixed workday is a concept called *flexitime*. Flexitime is a flexible working hours program that permits employees to design their own 40-hour work week (Certo, 1980). The management of a large manufacturing firm is considering adopting a flexitime program for its hourly employees and has decided to base the decision on the success or failure of a pilot flexitime program. Ten employees were randomly selected and given a questionnaire designed to measure their attitude toward their job. These same people were then permitted to design and follow a flexitime workday. After 6 months, attitudes toward their jobs were again measured. The resulting attitude scores are displayed in the table. The higher the score, the more favorable is the employee's attitude toward his or her work. Use a nonparametric test procedure to evaluate the success of the pilot flexitime program. Test using $\alpha = .05$.

EMPLOYEE	BEFORE FLEXITIME	AFTER FLEXITIME
1	54	68
2	25	42
3	80	80
4	76	91
5	63	70
6	82	88
7	94	90
8	72	81
9	33	39
10	90	93

WEEK	1983	1984
2	6	8
8	3	5
22	2	2
35	1	0
48	4	7
51	7	10

16.20 Refer to Exercise 16.6, in which a state highway department was interested in investigating the effects of the right-turn-on-red law at a particular urban intersection. The severity of the accidents that occur at the intersection was examined in Exercise 16.6. The highway department also wants to compare the probability distribution of the number of accidents that occurred per week before the law with the probability distribution of the number of accidents per week after the law. They randomly selected 6 weeks of the year and looked up the number of accidents that occurred in each of those weeks in the year preceding the adoption of the law (1983) and in the year following the adoption of the law (1984). The data are displayed in the table.

a. Use the Wilcoxon signed rank test for a paired difference experiment to investigate whether the probability distribution of the number of accidents per week after the law is located above (i.e., to the right of) the probability distribution of the number of accidents before the law.

b. Explain why a paired difference design was utilized in this study.

16.21 In Exercise 9.48, a paired difference test was used to compare the mean number of antitrust litigations per firm in the 1960's with the mean number per firm in the 1970's. The data are repeated in the table. Beckenstein, Gabel, and Roberts (1983) claim that, on average, companies faced more antitrust litigations in the 1970's than in the 1960's. Do the data support their claim? Test using the Wilcoxon signed rank test with $\alpha = .05$. Be sure to specify your null and alternative hypotheses.

	NUMBER OF LITIGATIONS			NUMBER OF LITIGATIONS	
FIRM	1960's	1970's	FIRM	1960's	1970's
1	10	10	6	7	6
2	8	12	7	6	11
3	9	8	8	9	12
4	7	16	9	8	11
5	8	14	10	7	12

16.22 A manufacturer of household appliances is considering one of two chains of department stores to be the sales merchandiser for its product in a particular region of the United States. Before choosing one chain, the manufacturer wants to make a comparison of the product exposure that might be expected for the two chains. Eight locations are selected where both chains have stores, and on a specific day, the number of shoppers entering each store is recorded. The data are shown in the table. Is there sufficient evidence to indicate that one of the chains tends to have more customers per day than the other? Test using $\alpha = .05$.

LOCATION	A	B
1	879	1,085
2	445	325
3	692	848
4	1,565	1,421
5	2,326	2,778
6	857	992
7	1,250	1,303
8	773	1,215

WEEK	MACHINE TYPE	
	A	B
1	14	12
2	17	13
3	10	14
4	15	12
5	14	9
6	9	11
7	12	11

16.23 A food vending company currently uses vending machines made by two different manufacturers. Before purchasing new machines, the company wants to compare the two types in terms of reliability. Records for 7 weeks are given in the table; the data indicate the number of breakdowns per week for each type of machine. The company has the same number of machines of each type. Is the probability distribution of the number of breakdowns for machine A shifted to the left or to the right of the probability distribution of the number of breakdowns for machine B? Use $\alpha = .05$.

16.24 Economic indexes provide measures of economic change. The January 23, 1984, issue of *U.S. News & World Report* listed the indexes in the table for the first week of January

1984 and the first week of January 1983. By comparing these two sets of indexes, you can obtain information regarding changes in the economy that occurred during 1983.

	JANUARY 1984	JANUARY 1983
Steel production	66.3	47.2
Automobile production	107.8	66.4
Crude petroleum production	97.8	98.3
Lumber production	59.7	91.4
Freight car loadings	57.2	50.8
Electric power production	217.1	190.8

a. Conduct a paired difference t test to compare the mean values of these indexes for January 1983 and January 1984. Use $\alpha = .05$. What assumptions are necessary for the validity of this procedure? Why might these assumptions be doubtful?

b. Use the Wilcoxon signed rank test to determine whether the data provide evidence that the probability distribution of the economic indexes has changed. Use $\alpha = .05$.

16.3 Kruskal–Wallis H Test for a Completely Randomized Design

Recall that a completely randomized design is one in which *independent* random samples are selected from each of k populations to be compared (Section 15.1). In Chapter 15, we used an analysis of variance and the F test to compare the means of the k populations (assuming the populations have normal probability distributions with equal variances). We now present a nonparametric technique that requires no assumptions concerning the population probability distributions to compare the k populations.

For example, suppose you want to compare the numbers of employees in companies representing each of three different business classifications: agriculture, manufacturing, and service. You sample ten companies from each type and record the number of employees in each sampled business (see Table 16.5). You can see that the assumptions necessary for a parametric comparison of the means are doubtful for these data; the probability distributions are very likely to be skewed to the right, as indicated by the presence of some extremely large values. In addition, the variability in number of employees may not be constant for the different classifications. We therefore base our comparison on the rank sums for the classifications. The ranks are computed for each observation according to the relative magnitude of the measurements *when all k samples are combined* (see Table 16.5). Note that ties are handled in the usual manner, by assigning the average value of the ranks to each of the tied observations.

We test

H_0: All three populations have identical probability distributions

H_a: At least two of the three population probability distributions differ in location

If we denote the three sample rank sums by R_1, R_2, and R_3, the **test statistic** is given by

$$H = \frac{12}{n(n+1)} \sum_{j=1}^{k} \frac{R_j^2}{n_j} - 3(n+1)$$

Table 16.5

Number of Employees in Thirty Different Companies

AGRICULTURE	Rank	MANUFACTURING	Rank	SERVICE	Rank
10	5	244	25	17	9.5
350	27	93	19	249	26
4	2	3,532	30	38	15
26	13	17	9.5	5	3
15	8	526	29	101	20
106	21	133	22	1	1
18	11	14	7	12	6
23	12	192	23	233	24
62	17	443	28	31	14
8	4	69	18	39	16
$R_1 = 120$		$R_2 = 210.5$		$R_3 = 134.5$	

where n_j is the number of measurements in the *j*th sample and n is the ***total sample size*** $(n = n_1 + n_2 + \cdots + n_k)$. For the data in Table 16.5, we have $n_1 = n_2 = n_3 = 10$, and $n = 30$. The rank sums are $R_1 = 120$, $R_2 = 210.5$, and $R_3 = 134.5$. Thus,

$$H = \frac{12}{30(31)}\left[\frac{(120)^2}{10} + \frac{(210.5)^2}{10} + \frac{(134.5)^2}{10}\right] - 3(31)$$

$$= 99.097 - 93 = 6.097$$

If the null hypothesis is true, the distribution of *H* in repeated sampling is approximately a χ^2 ***(chi square) distribution.*** This approximation for the sampling distribution of *H* is adequate as long as each of the *k* sample sizes exceeds five (see the references for more detail). The χ^2 probability distribution is characterized by a single parameter, called the ***degrees of freedom associated with the distribution.*** Several χ^2 probability distributions with different degrees of freedom are shown in Figure 16.7. The degrees of freedom corresponding to the approximate sampling distribution of *H* will always be $(k - 1)$, one less than the number of probability

Figure 16.7 Several χ^2 Probability Distributions

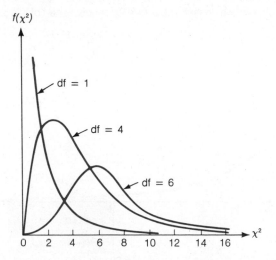

Figure 16.8 Reproduction of Part of Table XII of Appendix B

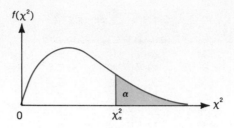

DEGREES OF FREEDOM	$\chi^2_{.100}$	$\chi^2_{.050}$	$\chi^2_{.025}$	$\chi^2_{.010}$	$\chi^2_{.005}$
1	2.70554	3.84146	5.02389	6.63490	7.87944
2	4.60517	5.99147	7.37776	9.21034	10.5966
3	6.25139	7.81473	9.34840	11.3449	12.8381
4	7.77944	9.48773	11.1433	13.2767	14.8602
5	9.23635	11.0705	12.8325	15.0863	16.7496
6	10.6446	12.5916	14.4494	16.8119	18.5476
7	12.0170	14.0671	16.0128	18.4753	20.2777
8	13.3616	15.5073	17.5346	20.0902	21.9550
9	14.6837	16.9190	19.0228	21.6660	23.5893
10	15.9871	18.3070	20.4831	23.2093	25.1882
11	17.2750	19.6751	21.9200	24.7250	26.7569

distributions being compared. Because large values of H support the alternative hypothesis that at least two of the $(k - 1)$ population probability distributions differ in location, the rejection region for the test will be located in the upper tail of the χ^2 distribution, as shown in Figure 16.8.

For the data of Table 16.5, the approximate distribution of the test statistic H is a χ^2 distribution with $(k - 1) = 2$ df. To determine how large H must be before we will reject the null hypothesis, we consult Table XII in Appendix B; part of this table is shown in Figure 16.8.

Figure 16.9 Rejection Region for the Comparison of Three Probability Distributions

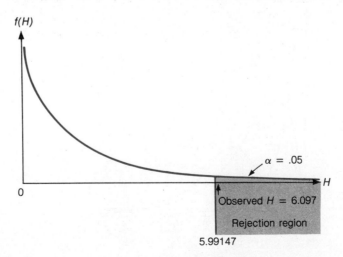

Entries in the table give an upper-tail value of χ^2, call it χ^2_α, such that $P(\chi^2 > \chi^2_\alpha) = \alpha$. The columns of the table identify the value of α associated with the tabulated value of χ^2_α, and the rows correspond to the degrees of freedom. Thus, for $\alpha = .05$ and df $= 2$, we can reject the null hypothesis that the three probability distributions are the same if

$$H > \chi^2_{.05} \quad \text{where} \quad \chi^2_{.05} = 5.99147$$

The rejection region is pictured in Figure 16.9. Since the calculated $H = 6.097$ exceeds the critical value of 5.99147, we conclude that at least two of the three probability distributions describing the number of employees for the three sampled business types differ in location.

The Kruskal–Wallis H test for comparing more than two probability distributions is summarized in the box. Note that we can use the Wilcoxon rank sum test to compare the separate pairs of populations if the Kruskal–Wallis H test supports the alternative hypothesis that at least two of the probability distributions differ.

Kruskal–Wallis H Test for Comparing k Probability Distributions

H_0: The k probability distributions are identical

H_a: At least two of the k probability distributions differ in location

Test statistic: $H = \dfrac{12}{n(n + 1)} \sum_{j=1}^{k} \dfrac{R_j^2}{n_j} - 3(n + 1)$

where

n_j = Number of measurements in sample j

R_j = Rank sum for sample j, where the rank of each measurement is computed according to its relative magnitude in the totality of data for the k samples

n = Total sample size $= n_1 + n_2 + \cdots + n_k$

Rejection region: $H > \chi^2_\alpha$ with $(k - 1)$ df

Assumptions: 1. The k samples are random and independent.
2. There are five or more measurements in each sample.
3. The observations can be ranked.

[*Note:* No assumptions have to be made about the shape of the population probability distributions.]

Exercises 16.25–16.36

Learning the Mechanics

16.25 Use Table XII in Appendix B to find each of the following χ^2 values:

a. $\chi^2_{.05}$, df $= 20$ **b.** $\chi^2_{.025}$, df $= 15$ **c.** $\chi^2_{.01}$, df $= 36$
d. $\chi^2_{.10}$, df $= 80$ **e.** $\chi^2_{.05}$, df $= 2$ **f.** $\chi^2_{.005}$, df $= 10$

16.26 Use Table XII in Appendix B to find each of the following probabilities:

a. $P(\chi^2 \geq 3.07382)$ where df $= 12$
b. $P(\chi^2 \leq 24.4331)$ where df $= 40$
c. $P(\chi^2 \geq 14.6837)$ where df $= 9$
d. $P(\chi^2 < 34.1696)$ where df $= 20$
e. $P(\chi^2 < 6.26214)$ where df $= 15$
f. $P(\chi^2 \leq .584375)$ where df $= 3$

16.27 Suppose you want to use the Kruskal–Wallis H test to compare the probability distributions of three populations. The following are independent random samples selected from the three populations:

I:	66	33	55	88	58	62	69	49
II:	22	31	16	25	30	33	40	
III:	75	96	102	75	88	78		

a. What type of experimental design was used?
b. Specify the null and alternative hypotheses you would test.
c. Specify the rejection region that would be used for your hypothesis test at $\alpha = .01$.

16.28 Refer to Exercise 16.27. Conduct the test at $\alpha = .01$.

16.29 Under what circumstances does the χ^2 distribution provide an appropriate characterization of the sampling distribution of the Kruskal–Wallis H statistic?

Applying the Concepts

16.30 A random sample of six senior computer systems analysts was selected from each of three industries: banking, federal government, and retail sales. Their salaries were determined and are recorded in the table. You have been hired to determine whether differences exist among the salary distributions for senior systems analysts in the three industries.

BANKING	FEDERAL GOVERNMENT	RETAIL SALES
$30,000	$28,000	$20,100
24,500	34,000	19,200
27,100	39,000	20,500
26,000	35,000	20,600
23,800	34,100	21,100
25,800	36,200	19,300

Source: Based on *The American Almanac of Jobs and Salaries*, 1982, p. 420.

a. Under what circumstances would it be appropriate to use the F test for a completely randomized design to perform the required analysis?
b. Which assumptions required by the F test are likely to be violated in this problem? Explain.

c. Use the Kruskal–Wallis *H* test to determine whether the salary distributions differ among the three industries. Specify your null and alternative hypotheses, and state your conclusions in the context of the problem. Use $\alpha = .05$.

16.31 CRS, a national car rental company, was interested in comparing the quality of service at its three largest airport locations. Six business travelers who frequently rent from a competitor were randomly selected at each airport and asked to use (free of charge) a CRS car the next time they rented a car at that airport. The travelers were asked to rate the service they received in four categories: (1) timeliness of service, (2) friendliness of employees, (3) cleanliness of the car, and (4) mechanical performance of the car. They were to use a rating scale of 1 to 10 for each category, with higher numbers indicating better service. An average score was computed for each traveler. These averages are reported in the table.

NEW YORK Kennedy	CHICAGO O'Hare	DALLAS Dallas–Fort Worth
7.50	7.25	9.25
6.25	6.75	8.75
7.50	5.75	9.00
4.75	8.00	9.25
6.25	5.75	8.75
7.00	6.00	8.75

a. Use the Kruskal–Wallis *H* test to determine whether the level of service ratings differ among the three car rental outlets. Use $\alpha = .10$.
b. What experimental design was used by CRS?

16.32 The Environmental Protection Agency wants to determine whether temperature changes in the ocean's water caused by a nuclear power plant will have a significant effect on the animal life in the region. Recently hatched specimens of a certain species of fish are randomly divided into four groups. The groups are placed in separate simulated ocean environments that are identical in every way except for water temperature. Six months later, the specimens are weighed. The results (in ounces) are given in the table. Do the data provide sufficient evidence to indicate that one (or more) of the temperatures tend(s) to produce larger weight increases than the other temperatures? Test using $\alpha = .10$.

38°F	42°F	46°F	50°F
22	15	14	17
24	21	28	18
16	26	21	13
18	16	19	20
19	25	24	21
	17	23	

16.33 An economist is interested in knowing whether property tax rates differ among three types of school districts — urban, suburban, and rural. A random sample of several districts of each type produced the data in the table (rate is in mills, where 1 mill = $1/1,000). Do the data indicate a difference in the level of property taxes among the three types of school districts? Use $\alpha = .05$.

URBAN	SUBURBAN	RURAL
4.3	5.9	5.1
5.2	6.7	4.8
6.2	7.6	3.9
5.6	4.9	6.2
3.8	5.2	4.2
5.8	6.8	4.3
4.7		

16.34 A large charitable fund-raising organization attempts to use civic pride to increase contributions during its annual drive. Contribution records are selected randomly at the organization offices in each of four cities within the same state. The amount (in dollars) of each contribution for those selected is given in the table. Is there evidence that at least two of the probability distributions of the amounts contributed differ in location? Use $\alpha = .10$.

CITY 1	CITY 2	CITY 3	CITY 4
75	65	15	45
20	30	25	30
30	45	10	25
45	50	35	60
25	35	5	55
	70		

	BRAND	
A	B	C
36	49	71
48	33	31
5	60	140
67	2	59
53	55	42

16.35 Three different brands of magnetron tubes (the key components in microwave ovens) were subjected to stressful testing, and the number of hours each operated without repair was recorded. Although these times do not represent typical lifetimes, they do indicate how well the tubes can withstand extreme stress.

a. Use the F test for a completely randomized design (Chapter 15) to test the hypothesis that the mean length of life under stress is the same for the three brands. Use $\alpha = .05$. What assumptions are necessary for the validity of this procedure? Is there any reason to doubt these assumptions?

b. Use the Kruskal–Wallis H test to determine whether evidence exists to conclude that at least two of the probability distributions of length of life under stress differ in location. Use $\alpha = .05$.

16.36 In Exercise 12.50, regression analysis was applied to the data repeated here in the table to investigate whether the mean debt-to-equity ratio varies among the insurance, publishing, electric utility, and banking industries. In Exercise 15.11, an analysis of variance F test was used to perform the same investigation. Suppose that the assumptions required by regression analysis and the F test are not satisfied.

INSURANCE		PUBLISHING		ELECTRIC UTILITIES		BANKING	
Firm	Debt-to-equity	Firm	Debt-to-equity	Firm	Debt-to-equity	Firm	Debt-to-equity
Chubb	0.1	Deluxe		Pacific Power		U.S. Bancorp	0.5
Kemper	0.0	Check	0.0	& Light	1.1	Sun Banks	0.2
St. Paul Cos.	0.1	New York		Houston Ind.	0.8	Mellon	
Lincoln		Times	0.4	Florida Power		National	0.5
National	0.2	A. C. Nielsen	0.1	& Light	0.8	Michigan	
USF & G	0.0	Dow Jones	0.1	Penn Power		National	0.3
Aetna	0.1	Gannett	0.3	& Light	0.9	Southeast	
				North States		Banking	0.4
				Pur.	0.7		
				Ohio Edison	1.2		
				Orange and			
				Rockland	0.6		

Source: *Forbes*, "36th Annual Report on American Industry," Jan. 2, 1984.

a. Compare the assumptions required by the analysis of variance F test and the Kruskal–Wallis H test. Which procedure can be more widely applied? Explain.

b. Use the Kruskal–Wallis H test to investigate whether debt-to-equity ratios differ among the four industries. Be sure to specify your null and alternative hypotheses and to state your conclusion in the context of the problem. Use $\alpha = .05$.

c. Assuming the Kruskal–Wallis H test indicates that differences exist among the four industries, which nonparametric procedure could be employed to compare the distributions of debt-to-equity ratios for the electric utility and banking industries?

16.4
The Friedman F_r Test for a Randomized Block Design

In Section 15.2, we used relatively homogeneous blocks of experimental units to compare k population means, based on a randomized block design. However, it was necessary to assume that the k populations had normal probability distributions and that their variances were equal. No assumptions are required for the nonparametric counterpart, the *Friedman F_r test,* to compare the k probability distributions.

For example, suppose a marketing firm wants to compare the relative effectiveness of three different modes of advertising: direct-mail, newspaper ads, and magazine ads. For fifteen clients, all three modes are used over a 1-year period, and the marketing firm records the year's percentage response to each type of advertising. That is, the firm divides the number of responses to a particular type of advertising by the total number of potential customers reached by the advertisements of that type. The results are shown in Table 16.6 on the next page.

The fifteen companies act as blocks in this experiment because we would expect the percentage responses to depend on the nature of the products of the company, its size, etc. Thus, we *rank the observations within each company (block)* and then *compute the rank sums for each of the three types of advertising (treatments).*

Table 16.6

Percentage Response to
Three Types of Advertising
for Fifteen Different
Companies

COMPANY	DIRECT-MAIL	RANK	NEWSPAPER	RANK	MAGAZINE	RANK
1	7.3	1	15.7	3	10.1	2
2	9.4	2	18.3	3	8.2	1
3	4.3	1	11.2	3	5.1	2
4	11.3	2	19.1	3	6.5	1
5	3.3	1	9.2	3	8.7	2
6	4.2	1	10.5	3	6.0	2
7	5.9	1	8.7	2	12.3	3
8	6.2	1	14.3	3	11.1	2
9	4.3	2	3.1	1	6.0	3
10	10.0	1	18.8	3	12.1	2
11	2.2	1	5.7	2	6.3	3
12	6.3	2	20.2	3	4.3	1
13	8.0	1	14.1	3	9.1	2
14	7.4	2	6.2	1	18.1	3
15	3.2	1	8.9	3	5.0	2
		$R_1 = 20$		$R_2 = 39$		$R_3 = 31$

The null and alternative hypotheses are

H_0:   The probability distributions of the response rates are identical for the three modes of advertising

H_a: At least two of the three probability distributions differ in location

The Friedman F_r **test statistic** is based on the rank sums

$$F_r = \frac{12}{bk(k+1)} \sum_{j=1}^{k} R_j^2 - 3b(k+1)$$

where b is the number of blocks, k is the number of treatments, and R_j is the jth rank sum. For the data in Table 16.6,

$$F_r = \frac{12}{(15)(3)(4)} (R_1^2 + R_2^2 + R_3^2) - (3)(15)(4)$$

$$= \frac{12}{(15)(3)(4)} [(20)^2 + (39)^2 + (31)^2] - (3)(15)(4)$$

$$= 192.13 - 180 = 12.13$$

As for the Kruskal–Wallis H statistic, the χ^2 distribution with $(k-1)$ degrees of freedom provides an approximation to the sampling distribution of F_r. We assume the approximation is adequate if either b (the number of blocks) or k (the number of treatments) exceeds five. Then, for the advertising example, we use $\alpha = .10$ to form the rejection region:

Rejection region: $F_r > \chi^2_{.10}$ with $k - 1 = 2$ df

Consulting Table XII in Appendix B, we find that $\chi^2_{.10}$ based on 2 df is 4.60517. Consequently, we will reject H_0 if $F_r > 4.60517$ (see Figure 16.10). Since the calculated $F_r = 12.13$ exceeds

Figure 16.10
Rejection Region for
the Advertising Example

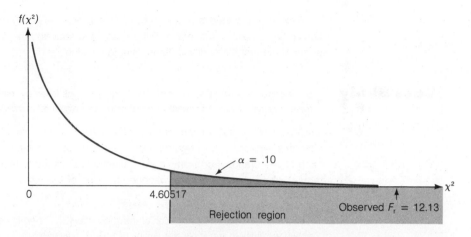

the critical value of 4.60517, we conclude that at least two of the response rate probability distributions for the three modes of advertising differ in location.

The Friedman F_r test for a randomized block design is summarized in the box.

Friedman F_r Test for a Randomized Block Design

H_0: The probability distributions for the k treatments are identical

H_a: At least two of the probability distributions differ in location

Test statistic: $F_r = \dfrac{12}{bk(k+1)} \displaystyle\sum_{j=1}^{k} R_j^2 - 3b(k+1)$

where

b = Number of blocks

k = Number of treatments

R_j = Rank sum of the jth treatment, where the rank of each measurement is computed relative to its position *within its own block*

Rejection region: $F_r > \chi_\alpha^2$ with $(k-1)$ df

Assumptions: 1. The treatments are randomly assigned to experimental units within the blocks.
2. The measurements can be ranked within blocks.
3. Either the number of blocks (b) or the number of treatments (k) should exceed five for the χ^2 approximation to be adequate.

[*Note:* No assumptions have to be made about the shape of the population probability distributions.]

Tied observations within blocks are handled in the usual manner by assigning the average value of the rank to each of the tied observations.

The Wilcoxon signed rank test for paired difference designs (Section 16.2) can be used to compare the pairs of treatments if the F_r statistic supports the alternative hypothesis that some of the probability distributions differ in location.

Case Study 16.1

Consumer Rankings of Products

Since consumers' images reflect to some extent actions taken by marketers in dealing with many marketing variables, it is frequently desirable to determine if these images have patterns.

McClure (1971) studied the pattern of consumers' images of three appliances. Five attributes—price, looks, need for repair, ease of use, and familiarity—were examined for each of two brands. For example, a consumer was asked to rank brand A's refrigerators, ranges, and automatic clothes washers in terms of the attribute ''ease of use.'' McClure states:

> Conceptually, it was an investigation of the ''halo effect'' . . . which refers to the individual's supposed tendency to imbue his evaluations of specific characteristics of an appliance with the same direction of general feeling expressed about the brand. The halo effect would be considered operative to the extent that the individual's general image of Brand X influences his rating of an individual appliance of that brand when asked to evaluate it.

Responses of 282 female heads of households were obtained in a large midwestern city. For each of the ten responses (five attributes for two brands) a Friedman F_r test was conducted. The three types of appliances represented the treatments, and the 282 consumers represented the blocks. A significant value of the test statistic F_r would indicate consistent ranking of the three appliances by the 282 subjects for the attribute—i.e., that the probability distributions of ranks given the three appliances differ. A small value of F_r would lend credence to the hypothesis that the rankings are randomly performed—i.e., that they have approximately the same probability distributions. McClure found that the rank probability distributions differ for all attributes except ''price'' for brand A (at the $\alpha = .10$ level); brand A refrigerators consistently tend to obtain the highest ranking. However, brand B has no such clear pattern, with only the ''familiarity'' rankings showing significant differences. The subjects seemed to be most familiar with the brand B clothes washer but could not agree on the ranking of the other attributes.

McClure concluded his article:

> Many marketing researchers have not been aware of the Friedman two-way analysis of variance by ranks. However, it has potential for use in situations common to many consumer surveys in which sets of ordinal [rank] data are generated by each respondent.

Exercises 16.37–16.45
───────

Learning the Mechanics

16.37 Suppose you have used a randomized block design to help you compare the effectiveness of three different treatments, A, B, and C. You obtained the data given in the table and plan to conduct a Friedman F_r test.

BLOCK	A	B	C
1	9	11	18
2	13	13	13
3	11	12	12
4	10	15	16
5	9	8	10
6	14	12	16
7	10	12	15

a. Specify the null and alternative hypotheses you would test.

b. Specify the rejection region for the test, using $\alpha = .10$.

16.38 Refer to Exercise 16.37. Conduct the test that you described using $\alpha = .10$.

Applying the Concepts

16.39 An *optical mark reader* (OMR) is a machine that is able to "read" pencil marks that have been entered on a scannable form. When connected to a computer, such systems are able to read and analyze data in one step. As a result, the keypunching of data into a machine-readable code can be eliminated. Eliminating this step reduces the possibility that the data will be contaminated by human error. OMR's are used by schools to grade exams and by survey research organizations to compile data from questionnaires (Oas, 1980). A manufacturer of OMR's believes its product can operate equally well in a variety of temperature and humidity environments. To determine whether operating data contradict this belief, the manufacturer asks a well-known industrial testing laboratory to test its product. Five recently produced OMR's were randomly selected and each was operated in five different environments. The number of forms each was able to process in an hour was recorded and used as a measure of the OMR's operating efficiency. These data appear in the table. Use the Friedman F_r test to determine whether evidence exists to indicate that the probability distributions for the number of forms processed per hour differ in location for at least two of the environments. Test using $\alpha = .10$.

MACHINE NUMBER	ENVIRONMENT				
	1	2	3	4	5
1	8,001	8,025	8,100	8,055	7,991
2	7,910	7,932	7,900	7,990	7,892
3	8,111	8,101	8,201	8,175	8,102
4	7,802	7,820	7,904	7,850	7,819
5	7,500	7,601	7,702	7,633	7,600

16.40 In Exercise 15.26, the data on the number of strikes per year in five U.S. manufacturing industries were treated as if they were generated by a randomized block design, with years used as the blocking variable. An analysis of variance F test was used to investigate whether the mean number of strikes per year differed among industries. The results are repeated in the table.

YEAR	FOOD AND KINDRED PRODUCTS	PRIMARY METAL INDUSTRY	ELECTRICAL EQUIPMENT AND SUPPLIES	FABRICATED METAL PRODUCTS	CHEMICALS AND ALLIED PRODUCTS
1976	227	197	204	309	129
1977	221	239	199	354	111
1978	171	187	190	360	113
1979	178	202	195	352	143
1980	155	175	140	280	89
1981	109	114	106	203	60

Source: *Statistical Abstract of the United States.*

a. What can be learned about the five industries by conducting a Friedman F_r test?

b. Conduct a Friedman F_r test using $\alpha = .05$. Specify the null and alternative hypotheses and state your conclusion in the context of the problem.

c. Find the approximate p-value for the test of part b, and interpret its value.

16.41 As part of the process of choosing a script for a television commercial, an advertising agency asks a panel of six executives to rate the scripts. The panel members are asked to use a rating scale of 1 to 10, with higher ratings indicating greater potential impact on the viewing audience. The ratings obtained are shown in the table.

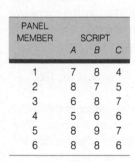

PANEL MEMBER	SCRIPT A	B	C
1	7	8	4
2	8	7	5
3	6	8	7
4	5	6	6
5	8	9	7
6	8	8	6

a. Use the Friedman F_r test to determine whether evidence exists to indicate that the levels at which the executives rate the scripts differ. Test using $\alpha = .10$.

b. Use the appropriate Wilcoxon signed rank test to determine whether script B's probability distribution of ratings lies significantly above script C's. Test using $\alpha = .10$.

16.42 Corrosion of different metals is a problem in many mechanical devices. Three sealers used to help retard the corrosion of metals were tested to see whether there were any differences among them. Samples of ten different metal compositions were treated with each of the three sealers, and the amount of corrosion was measured after exposure to the same environmental conditions for 1 month. The data are given in the table. Is there any evidence of a difference in the abilities of the sealers to prevent corrosion? Test using $\alpha = .05$.

METAL	SEALER 1	2	3
1	4.6	4.2	4.9
2	7.2	6.4	7.0
3	3.4	3.5	3.4
4	6.2	5.3	5.9
5	8.4	6.8	7.8
6	5.6	4.8	5.7
7	3.7	3.7	4.1
8	6.1	6.2	6.4
9	4.9	4.1	4.2
10	5.2	5.0	5.1

16.43 In recent years, domestic car manufacturers have devoted more attention to the small-car market. To compare the popularity of four domestic small cars within a city, a local trade organization obtained the information given in the table from four car dealers—one dealer for each of the four car makes. Is there evidence of differences in location among the probability distributions of the number of cars sold for each type? Use $\alpha = .10$.

Number of Small Cars Sold

| MONTH | MAKE OF CAR | | | |
	A	B	C	D
1	9	17	14	8
2	10	20	16	9
3	13	15	19	12
4	11	12	19	11
5	7	18	13	8

| EAR | SPRAY | | |
	A	B	C
1	21	23	15
2	29	30	21
3	16	19	18
4	20	19	18
5	13	10	14
6	5	12	6
7	18	18	12
8	26	32	21
9	17	20	9
10	4	10	2

16.44 A serious drought-related problem for farmers is the spread of aflatoxin, a highly toxic substance caused by mold, which contaminates field corn. In higher levels of contamination, aflatoxin is potentially hazardous to animal and possibly human health. (Officials of the Food and Drug Administration have set a maximum limit of 20 parts per billion aflatoxin as safe for interstate marketing.) Three sprays, A, B, and C, have been developed to control aflatoxin in field corn. To determine whether differences exist among the sprays, ten ears of corn are randomly chosen from a contaminated corn field and each is divided into three pieces of equal size. The sprays are then randomly assigned to the pieces for each ear of corn, thus setting up a randomized block design. The table gives the amount (in parts per billion) of aflatoxin present in the corn samples after spraying. Use the Friedman F_r test to determine whether there is evidence that the distributions of the levels of aflatoxin in corn differ for at least two of the three sprays. Test at $\alpha = .05$.

16.45 A randomized block design was used to collect the data in the table.

| BLOCK | TREATMENT | | | |
	W	X	Y	Z
1	21	30	28	25
2	30	45	36	29
3	29	38	30	31
4	48	60	52	47
5	66	75	51	70
6	15	25	20	21

a. Do the data provide sufficient evidence to conclude that at least two of the probability distributions associated with the treatments differ in location? Test using $\alpha = .05$.
b. Describe the Type I and Type II errors associated with the test you conducted in part a.
c. Find the approximate p-value of the hypothesis test you conducted in part a.

16.5
Spearman's
Rank
Correlation
Coefficient

When economic conditions are favorable, many banks advertise special loan rates for new cars, appliances, and other items to attract customers. Suppose a bank wants to determine whether to aim its advertising at a broad spectrum of potential borrowers or to concentrate on a specific income group. It randomly samples ten noncommercial customers from recent files and ascertains the present income of each and the total amount each has borrowed over the past 3 years (excluding mortgages and business loans). The data are shown in Table 16.7.

Table 16.7
Income–Amount Borrowed Data

CUSTOMER	INCOME	RANK	TOTAL BORROWED	RANK
1	$14,800	5	$4,300	7
2	8,900	1	4,800	8
3	83,600	10	500	2
4	22,100	8	3,300	5
5	18,200	7	5,500	9
6	13,700	4	3,700	6
7	41,800	9	0	1
8	9,300	2	3,200	4
9	12,700	3	6,100	10
10	16,100	6	1,800	3

One method of determining whether a correlation exists between income and amount borrowed is to calculate the Pearson product moment correlation, r (Section 10.6). However, to make an inference about the population correlation ρ (Greek rho), we must assume that the two random variables, income and amount borrowed, are normally distributed. This assumption is usually inappropriate for incomes because they tend to have a relative frequency distribution that is heavily skewed to the right (Figure 16.11). Although the modal income (that with the largest relative frequency) may be relatively low, there are typically enough individuals with high incomes to make income distributions asymmetric.

Figure 16.11 Typical Relative Frequency Distribution of Incomes

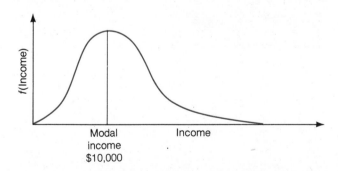

Thus, we turn to a nonparametric approach to correlation, which does not require underlying normal distributions. This nonparametric method, like those in the previous sections of this chapter, uses the ranks of the measurements to determine a measure of correlation. It is shown in the box.

Spearman's Rank Correlation Coefficient

$$r_S = \frac{SS_{uv}}{\sqrt{SS_{uu}SS_{vv}}}$$

where

$$SS_{uv} = \sum (u_i - \bar{u})(v_i - \bar{v}) = \sum u_i v_i - \frac{\left(\sum u_i\right)\left(\sum v_i\right)}{n}$$

$$SS_{uu} = \sum (u_i - \bar{u})^2 = \sum u_i^2 - \frac{\left(\sum u_i\right)^2}{n}$$

$$SS_{vv} = \sum (v_i - \bar{v})^2 = \sum v_i^2 - \frac{\left(\sum v_i\right)^2}{n}$$

u_i = Rank of the ith measurement in sample 1

v_i = Rank of the ith measurement in sample 2

n = Number of pairs of measurements (number of measurements in each sample)

Note that the definition of Spearman's rank correlation coefficient is identical to the definition of Pearson's r (see page 418), except that Spearman's r_S uses ranks. You can use the shortcut formula shown in the box for calculating r_S if there are no ties. The shortcut formula will also provide a satisfactory approximation to r_S when the number of ties is small relative to the number of pairs.

Shortcut Formula for r_S

$$r_S = 1 - \frac{6 \sum d_i^2}{n(n^2 - 1)}$$

where

$d_i = u_i - v_i$ (difference in the ranks of the ith measurement for sample 1 and sample 2)

Example 16.3   Calculate Spearman's rank correlation coefficient, r_S, for the bank customer data given in Table 16.7.

Solution   The ranks are reproduced in Table 16.8 (next page), along with the difference, d_i, for each pair of measurements. Then,

$$r_S = 1 - \frac{6 \sum d_i^2}{n(n^2 - 1)} = 1 - \frac{6(260)}{10(100 - 1)} = 1 - 1.576 \doteq -.576$$

The sign of r_S indicates the nature of the relationship between the two variables. Positive values indicate a tendency for the variables to increase together, and negative values indicate a tendency for one variable to increase while the other decreases.

Table 16.8

Calculation of Spearman's Rank Correlation Coefficient

CUSTOMER	INCOME RANK u_i	TOTAL BORROWED RANK v_i	DIFFERENCE $d_i = u_i - v_i$	DIFFERENCE SQUARED d_i^2
1	5	7	-2	4
2	1	8	-7	49
3	10	2	8	64
4	8	5	3	9
5	7	9	-2	4
6	4	6	-2	4
7	9	1	8	64
8	2	4	-2	4
9	3	10	-7	49
10	6	3	3	9
				Total $= 260$

■

The strength of the relationship between the ranks is indicated by the numerical size of r_S. Since r_S is really a Pearson product moment correlation of the ranks, it must lie between -1 and $+1$. Recall that a correlation of 0 implies no linear relationship, while correlations of -1 and $+1$ imply perfect negative and positive relationships, respectively. In Example 16.3, we obtained $r_S = -.576$. Is this different enough from 0 to conclude that the variables are related in the population?

If we define ρ_S as the population Spearman rank correlation coefficient, this question can be answered by conducting the test

H_0: $\rho_S = 0$ (There is no population correlation between ranks)

H_a: $\rho_S \neq 0$ (There is a population correlation between ranks)

Test statistic: r_S, the sample Spearman rank correlation coefficient

To determine a rejection region, we consult Table XVII in Appendix B, which is partially reproduced in Figure 16.12. Note that the left-hand column gives values of n, the number of pairs of measurements. The entries in the table are values for an upper-tail rejection region, since only positive values are given. Thus, for $n = 10$ and $\alpha = .05$, the value .564 is the boundary of the upper-tailed rejection region, so that $P(r_S > .564) = .05$ if in fact H_0 is true. That is, we would expect to see r_S exceed .564 only 5% of the time if in fact there is no relationship between the variables. The two-tailed rejection region is $r_S > .564$ or $r_S < -.564$, and the α value is therefore double the table value: $\alpha = 2(.05) = .10$. Thus, we have

Rejection region: $r_S < -.564$ or $r_S > .564$ for $\alpha = .10$

Since the calculated value from Example 16.3 is $r_S = -.576$, which is less than $-.564$, we reject H_0 at $\alpha = .10$ and conclude that the population rank correlation coefficient, ρ_S, differs from 0. In fact, it appears that bank customers at lower income levels tend to borrow more

Figure 16.12 Reproduction of Part of Table XVII of Appendix B

n	$\alpha = .05$	$\alpha = .025$	$\alpha = .01$	$\alpha = .005$
5	.900	—	—	—
6	.829	.886	.943	—
7	.714	.786	.893	—
8	.643	.738	.833	.881
9	.600	.683	.783	.833
10	.564	.648	.745	.794
11	.523	.623	.736	.818
12	.497	.591	.703	.780
13	.475	.566	.673	.745
14	.457	.545	.646	.716
15	.441	.525	.623	.689
16	.425	.507	.601	.666
17	.412	.490	.582	.645
18	.399	.476	.564	.625
19	.388	.462	.549	.608
20	.377	.450	.534	.591

than those at higher income levels. Therefore, the bank would be wise to aim its loan advertising at those in the middle- and lower-income groups, unless it wants to attempt to entice those who rarely borrow to become customers, in which case higher-income groups should be the target.

A summary of Spearman's nonparametric test for correlation is shown in the box.

Spearman's Nonparametric Test for Rank Correlation

One-Tailed Test

H_0: $\rho_S = 0$

H_a: $\rho_S > 0$
 (or H_a: $\rho_S < 0$)

Test statistic: r_S, the sample rank correlation (formulas for calculating r_S are given on page 769)

Rejection region:

$r_S > r_{S,\alpha}$

 (or $r_S < -r_{S,\alpha}$ when

H_a: $\rho_S < 0$)

where $r_{S,\alpha}$ is the value from Table XVII corresponding to the upper-tail area α and n pairs of observations

Two-Tailed Test

H_0: $\rho_S = 0$

H_a: $\rho_S \neq 0$

Test statistic: r_S, the sample rank correlation (formulas for calculating r_S are given on page 769)

Rejection region:

$r_{S,\alpha} < -r_{S,\alpha/2}$

 or $r_S > r_{S,\alpha/2}$

where $r_{S,\alpha/2}$ is the value from Table XVII corresponding to the upper-tail area $\alpha/2$ and n pairs of observations

Example 16.4   Manufacturers of perishable foods often use preservatives to retard spoilage. One concern is that using too much preservative will change the flavor of the food. Suppose an experiment is conducted using samples of a food product with varying amounts of preservative added. Both length of time until the food shows signs of spoiling and a taste rating are recorded for each sample. The taste rating is the average rating for three tasters, each of whom rates each sample on a scale from 1 (good) to 5 (bad). Twelve sample measurements are shown in Table 16.9. Use a nonparametric test to find out whether the spoilage times and taste ratings are negatively correlated. Use $\alpha = .05$.

Table 16.9
Data for Example 16.4

SAMPLE	TIME UNTIL SPOILAGE Days	RANK	TASTE RATING	RANK
1	30	2	4.3	11
2	47	5	3.6	7.5
3	26	1	4.5	12
4	94	11	2.8	3
5	67	7	3.3	6
6	83	10	2.7	2
7	36	3	4.2	10
8	77	9	3.9	9
9	43	4	3.6	7.5
10	109	12	2.2	1
11	56	6	3.1	5
12	70	8	2.9	4

[*Note:* Tied measurements are assigned the average of the ranks that would be given the measurements if they were different but consecutive.]

Solution   The test is one-tailed, with

$$H_0:\ \rho_S = 0 \qquad H_a:\ \rho_S < 0$$

Test statistic:* $r_S = 1 - \dfrac{6 \sum d_i^2}{n(n^2 - 1)}$

Rejection region: Reject H_0 if $r_S < -r_{S,.05}$, where from Table XVII, for $\alpha = .05$ and $n = 12$, $-r_{S,.05} = -.497$. [*Note:* The value of α need not be doubled since the test is one-tailed.]

The first step in the computation of r_S is to sum the squares of the differences between ranks:

$$\sum d_i^2 = (2 - 11)^2 + (5 - 7.5)^2 + \cdots + (8 - 4)^2 = 536.5$$

Then

$$r_S = 1 - \frac{6(536.5)}{12(144 - 1)} = -.876$$

_____
* The shortcut formula is not exact when there are tied measurements, but it is a good approximation when the total number of ties is not large relative to n.

Since $-.876 < -.497$, we reject H_0 and conclude that the preservative does affect the taste of this food adversely. ■

Case Study 16.2

The Problem of Nonresponse Bias in Mail Surveys

Researchers who collect their sample data via mail questionnaires often run the risk that their respondents will not be a representative sample of the entire population. The reason for this, according to Rosenthal and Rosnow (1975), is the tendency for respondents to be (1) better educated, (2) of higher social-class status, (3) more intelligent, (4) in need of social approval, (5) more social, and (6) more interested in the research topic than nonrespondents.

Researchers sometimes attempt to verify the representativeness of their sample by obtaining information about the demographic characteristics of the nonrespondents and comparing them to those of the sample of respondents. Finding similarities gives researchers confidence in the representativeness of their sample. Another approach is to contact a small sample of the nonrespondents and obtain responses to the questionnaire. These responses can be compared with those of the original respondents; the more similar the patterns of responses, the more confident the researcher can be that the original sample of returned questionnaires is representative of the population from which the sample came.

In a recent marketing research study by David W. Finn, Chih-Kang Wang, and Charles W. Lamb (1983), a random sample of twenty nonrespondents to their mail questionnaire were contacted by telephone and asked to respond to the following question on the questionnaire: "In general, what is your willingness to buy products made in each of the following countries?" They were asked to indicate their willingness by responding on a 5-point scale that ranged from "extremely willing" to "extremely unwilling." The mean willingness score was computed for each country and the countries were ranked accordingly. Similarly, a rank ordering was developed for the 273 respondents to their mail questionnaire. Both sets of rankings are displayed in Table 16.10.

Table 16.10

Ranking of Consumer Willingness to Buy Products Made in Indicated Countries

COUNTRY	RANK ORDER* Respondent	Nonrespondent
United Kingdom	1	1
Japan	2	3
France	3	2
Taiwan	4	4
Brazil	5	5
India	6	6
Iran	7	7
Angola	8	8
USSR	9	9
Cuba	10	10

* Data were collected in Spring 1977.

Finn, Wang, and Lamb compared the rank orderings for the respondents and nonrespondents using Spearman's rank correlation coefficient. They obtained $r_s = .9879$ (p-value $<$ 0.01) and concluded that "respondents and nonrespondents in this study did not differ attitudinally." Further, they noted that even if respondents and nonrespondents to a mail survey differ demographically, as was the case in their study, the Spearman rank correlation result indicates that such differences should not automatically be interpreted as signalling the existence of nonresponse bias. The sample of opinions obtained from the respondents may, in fact, be representative of the population of opinions even though respondents and nonrespondents differ demographically.

Exercises
16.46 – 16.55

Learning the Mechanics

16.46 Specify the rejection region for Spearman's nonparametric test for rank correlation in each of the following situations:

a. H_0: $\rho_S = 0$,　H_a: $\rho_S \neq 0$,　$n = 9$,　$\alpha = .05$
b. H_0: $\rho_S = 0$,　H_a: $\rho_S > 0$,　$n = 25$,　$\alpha = .025$
c. H_0: $\rho_S = 0$,　H_a: $\rho_S < 0$,　$n = 30$,　$\alpha = .005$

16.47 Compute Spearman's rank correlation coefficient for each of the following pairs of sample observations:

a.

x	y
30	26
55	36
60	65
19	25
40	35

b.

x	y
90	81
100	95
120	75
137	52
41	136

c.

x	y
1	11
15	26
4	15
10	21

d.

x	y
5	80
20	83
15	91
10	82
3	87

16.48 Explain the significance of the sign of Spearman's rank correlation coefficient.

Applying the Concepts

16.49 The table reports the 1950 and 1980 sales (in millions of dollars) of a sample of thirty major U.S. corporations.

CORPORATION	1950 SALES	1980 SALES	CORPORATION	1950 SALES	1980 SALES
Abbott Laboratories	74	2,038	General Electric Corp.	2,233	24,959
Allis-Chalmers Corp.	344	2,064	Gillette Co.	99	2,315
American Cyanamid Co.	322	3,454	Gulf Oil Corp.	1,150	26,483
Armstrong World Industries	187	1,323	IBM Corp.	215	26,213
Boeing Co.	307	9,426	International Paper Co.	498	5,043
Borg-Warner Corp.	331	2,673	PepsiCo., Inc.	40	5,975
Bristol-Myers Co.	52	3,158	Philip Morris, Inc.	306	7,328
Caterpillar Tractor Co.	337	8,598	Phillips Petroleum Co.	533	13,377
Celanese Corp.	233	3,348	RCA Corp.	584	8,011
Coca-Cola Co.	215	5,913	R. J. Reynolds Industries, Inc.	758	8,449
Continental Group, Inc.	398	5,119	Standard Brands, Inc.	301	3,018
Corning Glass Works	117	1,530	Sterling Drug, Inc.	139	1,701
Curtiss-Wright Corp.	136	228	The Timken Co.	144	1,338
Eaton Corp.	148	3,176	Union Carbide Corp.	758	9,994
Fruehauf Corp.	128	2,082	Westinghouse Electric Corp.	1,020	8,514

Source: Dharan (1983), p. 262.

a. Calculate Spearman's rank correlation coefficient for these data, and interpret its value in the context of the problem.

b. Test $H_0: \rho_s = 0$ against $H_a: \rho_s > 0$ using $\alpha = .05$. Interpret the null and alternative hypotheses in the context of the problem.

c. Explain why Spearman's rank correlation coefficient can be more widely applied to make inferences about the correlation between two variables than Pearson's product moment correlation coefficient.

16.50 A *negotiable certificate of deposit* is a marketable receipt for funds deposited in a bank for a specified period of time at a specified rate of interest (Cook, 1977). The table lists the end-of-the-quarter interest rate for 3-month certificates of deposit during the period January 1976 through September 1983. The table also lists end-of-the-quarter values of Standard & Poor's 500 Stock Composite Average, an indicator of stock market activity, for the same time period.

YEAR	QUARTER	INTEREST RATE	S&P 500	YEAR	QUARTER	INTEREST RATE	S&P 500
1976	I	5.35	102.77	1980	I	17.57	104.69
	II	5.88	104.28		II	8.49	114.55
	III	5.32	105.24		III	11.29	126.51
	IV	4.68	107.46		IV	18.65	95.10
1977	I	4.83	98.42	1981	I	14.43	136.00
	II	5.42	100.48		II	16.90	131.21
	III	6.18	96.53		III	16.84	116.18
	IV	6.72	95.10		IV	12.49	122.55
1978	I	6.85	89.21	1982	I	14.21	111.96
	II	7.82	95.53		II	14.46	109.61
	III	8.61	102.54		III	10.66	120.42
	IV	10.72	96.11		IV	8.66	135.28
1979	I	10.13	101.59	1983	I	8.69	152.96
	II	9.95	102.91		II	9.20	168.11
	III	11.89	109.32		III	9.39	164.40
	IV	13.43	107.94				

Source: *Standard & Poor's Trade and Securities Statistics,* annual, Standard & Poor's Corporation.

a. Compute Spearman's rank correlation coefficient to measure the strength of the relationship between the interest rate on certificates of deposit and the S&P 500.

b. Test the null hypothesis that the interest rate on certificates of deposit and the S&P 500 are not correlated against the alternative hypothesis that these variables are correlated. Use $\alpha = .10$.

c. Repeat parts a and b using monthly data instead of quarterly data. These can be obtained at your library in *Standard & Poor's Trade and Securities Statistics.* Compare the results you obtained for monthly data with those you obtained using the quarterly data.

16.51 It has been conjectured that income is one of the primary determinants of an individual's satisfaction with his or her job. To investigate this theory, fifteen employees of a particular firm are chosen at random and their gross salaries are noted. Each of the employees is then asked to complete a questionnaire designed to measure job satisfaction. The resulting scores (higher scores correspond to greater satisfaction) and gross incomes are given in the table.

EMPLOYEE	JOB SATISFACTION SCORE	INCOME ($ thousand)	EMPLOYEE	JOB SATISFACTION SCORE	INCOME ($ thousand)
1	92	29.9	9	45	16.0
2	51	18.7	10	72	25.0
3	88	32.0	11	53	17.2
4	65	15.0	12	43	9.7
5	80	26.0	13	87	20.1
6	31	9.0	14	30	15.5
7	38	11.3	15	74	16.5
8	75	22.1			

a. Compute Spearman's rank correlation coefficient for these data.

b. Is there evidence that job satisfaction and income are positively correlated? Use $\alpha = .05$.

16.52 Many large businesses send representatives to college campuses to conduct job interviews. To aid the interviewer, one company decides to study the correlation between the strength of an applicant's references (the company requires three references) and the performance of the applicant on the job. Eight recently hired employees are sampled, and independent evaluations of both references and job performance are made on a scale from 1 to 20. The scores are given in the table.

EMPLOYEE	REFERENCES	JOB PERFORMANCE
1	18	20
2	14	13
3	19	16
4	13	9
5	16	14
6	11	18
7	20	15
8	9	12

a. Compute Spearman's rank correlation coefficient for these data.

b. Is there evidence that strength of references and job performance are positively correlated? Use $\alpha = .05$.

16.53 The decision to build a new plant or to move an existing plant to a new location involves long-term commitment of both human and monetary resources. Accordingly, such decisions should be made only after carefully considering the relevant factors associated with numerous alternative plant sites. G. Michael Epping (1982) examined the relationship between the location factors deemed important by businesses that located in Arkansas and those that considered Arkansas but located elsewhere. A questionnaire that asked manufacturers to rate the importance of thirteen general location factors on a 9-point scale was completed by 118 firms that had moved a plant to Arkansas in the period 1955 to 1977 and by 73 firms that had recently considered Arkansas but located elsewhere. Epping averaged the importance ratings and arrived at the rankings shown in the table. Calculate Spearman's rank correlation coefficient for these data and carefully interpret its value in the context of the problem.

FACTOR	MANUFACTURERS LOCATING IN ARKANSAS Rank	MANUFACTURERS NOT LOCATING IN ARKANSAS Rank
Labor	1	1
Taxes	2	2
Industrial site	3	4
Information sources and special inducements	4	5
Legislative laws and structure	5	3
Utilities and resources	6	7
Transportation facilities	7	8
Raw material supplies	8	10
Community	9	6
Industrial financing	10	9
Markets	11	12
Business services	12	11
Personal preferences	13	13

16.54 A large manufacturing firm wants to determine whether a relationship exists between the number of work-hours an employee misses per year and the employee's annual wages. A sample of fifteen employees produced the data in the table. Do these data provide evidence that the number of work-hours missed is related to annual wages? Use $\alpha = .05$.

EMPLOYEE	WORK-HOURS MISSED	ANNUAL WAGES ($ thousand)	EMPLOYEE	WORK-HOURS MISSED	ANNUAL WAGES ($ thousand)
1	49	12.8	9	191	7.8
2	36	14.5	10	6	15.8
3	127	8.3	11	63	10.8
4	91	10.2	12	79	9.7
5	72	10.0	13	43	12.1
6	34	11.5	14	57	21.2
7	155	8.8	15	82	10.9
8	11	17.2			

16.55 Two expert wine tasters were asked to rank six brands of wine. Their rankings are shown in the table at the top of the next page. Do the data present sufficient evidence to indicate a positive correlation in the rankings of the two experts? Use $\alpha = .05$.

BRAND	EXPERT 1	EXPERT 2
A	6	5
B	5	6
C	1	2
D	3	1
E	2	4
F	4	3

Summary

We have presented several useful *nonparametric techniques* for comparing two or more populations. Nonparametric techniques are useful when the underlying assumptions for their parametric counterparts are not justified or when it is impossible to assign specific values to the observations. Nonparametric methods provide more general comparisons of populations than parametric methods because they compare the probability distributions of the populations rather than specific parameters.

Rank sums are the primary tools of nonparametric statistics. The *Wilcoxon rank sum statistic* can be used to compare two populations based on an independent sampling experiment, and the *Wilcoxon signed rank test* can be used for a *paired difference experiment*. The *Kruskal–Wallis H test* is applied when comparing k populations using a *completely randomized design*. The *Friedman F_r test* is used to compare k populations when a *randomized block design* is used.

The strength of nonparametric statistics lies in their general applicability. Few restrictive assumptions are required, and they may be used for observations that can be ranked but not measured exactly. Therefore, nonparametric methods provide useful alternatives to the parametric tests of Chapters 8, 9, and 15.

Supplementary Exercises 16.56–16.82

BEFORE	AFTER
12	4
5	2
10	7
9	3
14	8
6	

16.56 When is it inappropriate to use the t and F tests of Chapters 9 and 15 for comparing two or more population means?

16.57 A study was conducted to determine whether the installation of a traffic light was effective in reducing the number of accidents at a busy intersection. Samples of 6 months prior to installation and 5 months after installation of the light yielded the numbers of accidents per month listed in the table.

a. Is there sufficient evidence to conclude that the traffic light aided in reducing the number of accidents? Test using $\alpha = .025$.

b. Explain why this type of data might or might not be suitable for analysis using the t test of Chapter 9.

16.58 In Exercise 10.44, a calibration study undertaken by the Minnesota Department of Transportation to evaluate its newly installed weigh-in-motion scale was described. Pearson's product moment correlation coefficient was used to measure the strength of the relationship between the static weight of a truck and the truck's weight as measured by the weigh-in-motion equipment. The data are repeated in the table.

TRUCK NUMBER	STATIC WEIGHT OF TRUCK x *(thousand pounds)*	WEIGH-IN-MOTION READING PRIOR TO CALIBRATION ADJUSTMENT y_1 *(thousand pounds)*	WEIGH-IN-MOTION READING AFTER CALIBRATION ADJUSTMENT y_2 *(thousand pounds)*
1	27.9	26.0	27.8
2	29.1	29.9	29.1
3	38.0	39.5	37.8
4	27.0	25.1	27.1
5	30.3	31.6	30.6
6	34.5	36.2	34.3
7	27.8	25.1	26.9
8	29.6	31.0	29.6
9	33.1	35.6	33.0
10	35.5	40.2	35.0

Source: Adapted from data in Wright, Owen, and Pena (1983).

a. Calculate Spearman's rank correlation coefficient for x and y_1 and for x and y_2. Interpret, in the context of the problem, the values you obtain. Compare your results with those of Exercise 10.44, part c.

b. In the context of this problem, describe the circumstances that would result in Spearman's rank correlation coefficient being exactly 1. Being exactly 0.

16.59 An experiment was conducted to compare two print types, A and B, to determine whether type A is easier to read. Ten subjects were randomly divided into two groups of five. Each subject was given the same material to read, one group receiving the material printed with type A, the other group receiving print type B. The time necessary for each subject to read the material (in seconds) is shown below:

Type A: 95, 122, 101, 99, 108

Type B: 110, 102, 115, 112, 120

Do the data provide sufficient evidence to indicate that print type A is easier to read? Test using $\alpha = .05$.

16.60 A national clothing store franchise operates two stores in one city—one urban and one suburban. To stock the stores with clothing suited to the customers' needs, a survey is conducted to determine the incomes of the customers. Ten customers in each store are offered significant discounts if they will reveal the annual income of their household. The results are listed in the table (in thousands of dollars). Is there evidence that the probability distributions of the customers' incomes differ in location for the two stores? Use $\alpha = .05$.

STORE 1		STORE 2	
18.8	29.5	12.3	10.3
27.9	16.3	19.2	15.6
12.2	22.1	6.3	9.8
85.3	15.7	24.5	8.6
13.1	24.0	11.0	19.3

SUPERVISOR			
1	*2*	*3*	*4*
20	17	16	8
19	11	15	12
20	13	13	10
18	15	18	14
17	14	11	9
	16		10

16.61 Suppose a company wants to study how personality relates to leadership. Four supervisors with different types of personalities are selected. Several employees are then selected from the group supervised by each, and these employees are asked to rate the leader of their group on a scale from 1 to 20 (20 signifies highly favorable). The resulting data are shown in the table. Is there evidence to indicate that the probability distributions of ratings differ in location for at least two of the four supervisors? Use $\alpha = .05$.

16.62 Refer to Exercise 16.61. Suppose the company is particularly interested in comparing the ratings of the personality types represented by supervisors 1 and 3. Make this comparison using $\alpha = .05$.

16.63 The length of time required for a human to respond to a new pain killer was tested in the following manner: Seven randomly selected subjects were assigned to receive both aspirin and the new drug. The two treatments were spaced in time and assigned in random order. The length of time (in minutes) required for a subject to indicate that he or she could physically feel pain relief was recorded for both the aspirin and the drug. The data are shown in the table. Do the data provide sufficient evidence to indicate the new drug is more effective than aspirin in reducing pain? Test using $\alpha = .05$.

SUBJECT	1	2	3	4	5	6	7
ASPIRIN	15	20	12	20	17	14	17
DRUG	7	14	13	11	10	16	11

16.64 A union wants to determine the preferences of its members before negotiating with management. Ten union members are randomly selected, and an extensive questionnaire is completed by each member. The responses to the various aspects of the questionnaire will enable the union to rank in order of importance the items to be negotiated. The rankings are shown in the table. Is there evidence that the distributions of preferences differ in location for at least two of the four items? Use $\alpha = .05$.

PERSON	MORE PAY	JOB STABILITY	FRINGE BENEFITS	SHORTER HOURS
1	2	1	3	4
2	1	2	3	4
3	4	3	2	1
4	1	4	2	3
5	1	2	3	4
6	1	3	4	2
7	2.5	1	2.5	4
8	3	1	4	2
9	1.5	1.5	3	4
10	2	3	1	4

16.65 An insurance company wants to determine whether a relationship exists between the number of claims filed by owners of family policies and the annual incomes of the families. A random sample of ten policies was selected for the study. The data are shown in the table. Do the data on claims and annual income provide sufficient evidence to conclude that a correlation exists between the number of claims per policy and the annual income of the policyholder? Use $\alpha = .10$.

FAMILY	CLAIMS 3-year period	ANNUAL INCOME Averaged over 3 years ($ thousand)
1	5	14.5
2	1	9.6
3	9	62.5
4	0	22.5
5	4	10.3
6	7	16.2
7	0	8.1
8	2	21.2
9	6	17.1
10	3	12.3

16.66 A state highway patrol was interested in knowing whether frequent patrolling of highways substantially reduced the number of speeders. Two similar interstate highways were selected for the study—one very heavily patrolled and the other only occasionally patrolled. After 1 month, random samples of 100 cars were chosen on each highway and the number of cars exceeding the speed limit was recorded. This process was repeated on 5 randomly selected days. The data are shown in the table.

DAY	HIGHWAY 1 Heavily patrolled	HIGHWAY 2 Occasionally patrolled
1	35	60
2	40	36
3	25	48
4	38	54
5	47	63

a. Use the paired t test with $\alpha = .05$ to compare the population mean number of speeders per 100 cars for the two highways. What assumptions are necessary for the validity of this procedure? Do you think the assumptions are reasonable in this situation?

b. Use a nonparametric procedure to determine whether the data provide evidence to indicate that heavy patrolling tends to reduce the number of speeders. Test using $\alpha = .05$.

16.67 In recent years, many magazines have been forced to raise their prices because of increased postage, printing, and paper costs. Because magazines are now more expensive, some households may be subscribing to fewer magazines than they did 3 years ago. Ten households were selected at random, and the numbers of magazines subscribed to 3 years ago and now were determined. The results are listed in the table. Does this sample provide sufficient evidence to indicate that households tend to subscribe to fewer magazines now than they did 3 years ago? Use $\alpha = .05$.

HOUSEHOLD	3 YEARS AGO	NOW	HOUSEHOLD	3 YEARS AGO	NOW
1	8	4	6	6	5
2	3	5	7	4	3
3	6	4	8	2	2
4	3	3	9	9	6
5	10	5	10	8	2

16.68 Two fluoride toothpastes (A and B) and one nonfluoride toothpaste were compared for their effectiveness in preventing cavities. Three randomly selected groups of subjects used the toothpastes for 6 months, and each subject was examined before and after the study to determine the number of new cavities that developed. The data are shown in the table. Do the data provide sufficient evidence to indicate that the use of one of the toothpastes tends to be more effective in reducing the number of new cavities?

A		B		NONFLUORIDE	
0	0	2	0	4	4
1	1	0	1	3	3
3	3	3	2	5	4
1	2	3	1	4	5
2	2				

16.69 A hotel had a problem with people reserving rooms for a weekend and then not honoring their reservations (no-shows). As a result, the hotel developed a new reservation and deposit plan that it hoped would reduce the number of no-shows. One year after the policy was initiated, the management evaluated its effect in comparison with the old policy. Compare the records given in the table for the ten nonholiday weekends preceding the institution of the new policy and the ten nonholiday weekends preceding the evaluation time. Has the situation improved under the new policy? Test at $\alpha = .05$.

Number of No-Shows

BEFORE		AFTER	
10	11	4	4
5	8	3	2
3	9	8	5
6	6	5	7
7	5	6	1

16.70 A clothing manufacturer employs five inspectors who provide quality control of workmanship. Every item of clothing produced carries with it the number of the inspector who checked it. Thus, the company can evaluate an inspector by keeping records of the number of complaints received about products bearing his or her inspection number. The numbers of returns for 6 months are given in the table. Do the data provide sufficient evidence to indicate that the probability distributions of the number of complaints differ in location for at least two of the five inspectors? Use $\alpha = .10$.

MONTH	INSPECTOR				
	1	2	3	4	5
1	8	10	7	6	9
2	5	7	4	12	12
3	5	8	6	10	6
4	9	6	8	10	13
5	4	13	3	7	15
6	4	8	2	6	9

16.71 Refer to Exercise 16.70. Use the Wilcoxon signed rank test to determine whether evidence exists to indicate that the probability distributions of the number of complaints of inspectors 1 and 4 differ in location. Use $\alpha = .05$.

16.72 A savings and loan association is considering three locations in a large city as potential office sites. The company has hired a marketing firm to compare the incomes of people living in the area surrounding each site. The market researchers interview ten households chosen at random in each area to determine the type of job, length of employment, etc., of those in the households who work. This information will enable them to estimate the annual income of each household. The results in the table are obtained. Is there evidence of differences in location in the income distributions for the three sites? Use $\alpha = .05$.

Estimated Annual Income
(Thousands of Dollars)

SITE 1		SITE 2		SITE 3	
14.3	16.2	19.3	22.2	14.5	18.3
15.5	23.5	25.5	83.5	9.3	23.3
12.1	14.7	30.2	27.9	17.2	16.7
8.3	18.0	52.1	21.2	13.2	20.0
20.5	15.1	28.6	24.0	12.6	15.2

16.73 Refer to Exercise 16.72. Use the Wilcoxon rank sum test to compare the locations of the probability distributions of incomes in sites 1 and 2. Use $\alpha = .05$.

16.74 A manufacturer wants to determine whether the number of defectives produced by its employees tends to increase as the day progresses. Unknown to the employees, a complete inspection is made of every item that was produced on one day, and the hourly fraction defective is recorded. The resulting data are given in the table. Is there evidence that the fraction defective increases as the day progresses? Test at $\alpha = .05$.

HOUR	FRACTION DEFECTIVE
1	0.02
2	0.05
3	0.03
4	0.08
5	0.06
6	0.09
7	0.11
8	0.10

16.75 A businesswoman who is looking for a new investment considers a certain suburban community to be a good location for a new restaurant. She decides to survey some residents in the area to see what type of restaurant would be preferred. Ten people are chosen at random, and each is asked to estimate how many times in the past 6 months he or she has eaten in each of three types of restaurants — fast-food, family menu, and smorgasbord. The businesswoman then ranks the numbers for each person to obtain a preference ranking. The results are shown in the table. Is there evidence of differences in the locations of the probability distributions of preferences for the three restaurant types? Use $\alpha = .05$.

PERSON	PREFERENCE RANKING OF RESTAURANT TYPE		
	Fast-food	Family menu	Smorgasbord
1	1	2.5	2.5
2	2	1	3
3	3	2	1
4	3	1	2
5	3	1	2
6	2	3	1
7	1.5	1.5	3
8	1	2	3
9	3	1	2
10	3	2	1

16.76 Twelve samples of variously priced carpeting were selected and tested for wearability. The cost per square yard and the number of months of wear for each of the twelve samples of carpeting are listed in the table. Do the data provide sufficient evidence to indicate that wearability increases as the price increases? Test using $\alpha = .05$.

COST	MONTHS OF WEAR	COST	MONTHS OF WEAR
$ 6.95	32.5	$ 8.45	25.2
4.25	24.8	17.95	35.3
10.85	25.6	12.95	34.6
7.99	18.4	9.99	29.7
15.25	28.3	14.85	29.9
20.50	20.4	6.25	26.3

16.77 For many years, the Girl Scouts of America have sold cookies using various sales techniques. One troop experimented with several techniques, and reported the number of sales per scout listed in the table. Is there evidence that the probability distributions of number of sales differ in location for at least two of the four techniques? Use $\alpha = .10$.

DOOR-TO-DOOR	TELEPHONE	GROCERY STORE STAND	DEPARTMENT STORE STAND
47	63	113	25
93	19	50	36
58	29	68	21
37	24	37	27
62	33	39	18
		77	31

16.78 Refer to Exercise 16.77. Compare the locations of the probability distributions of the number of sales for the door-to-door and grocery store stand techniques. Use $\alpha = .05$.

16.79 Suppose the personnel director of a company interviewed six potential job applicants without knowing anything about their backgrounds and then rated them on a scale from 1 to 10. Independently, the director's supervisor made an evaluation of the background qualifications of each candidate on the same scale. The results are shown in the table. Is there evidence that candidates' qualification scores are related to their interview performance? Use $\alpha = .10$.

CANDIDATE	QUALIFICATIONS	INTERVIEW PERFORMANCE
1	10	8
2	8	9
3	9	10
4	4	5
5	5	3
6	6	6

16.80 A taste test conducted to compare three brands of beer utilized ten randomly selected beer drinkers. Each person was given three unmarked glasses of beer — one containing each brand — and was asked to rate each on a scale from 1 to 10 (a higher score indicates a better taste). Do the data given in the table indicate that one (or more) of the brands of beer is preferred to the others? Test using $\alpha = .05$.

PERSON	A	B	C	PERSON	A	B	C
1	5	7	3	6	10	9	8
2	8	8	5	7	6	8	7
3	6	7	7	8	5	5	4
4	9	6	7	9	6	8	5
5	9	8	5	10	7	6	4

16.81 Two car-rental companies have long waged an advertising war. An independent testing agency is hired to compare the number of rentals at one major airport. After 10 days, the agency has the data listed in the table. At this point, can either car-rental company claim to be number one at this airport? Use $\alpha = .05$.

DAY	RENTAL COMPANY A	RENTAL COMPANY B	DAY	RENTAL COMPANY A	RENTAL COMPANY B
1	29	22	6	16	20
2	26	29	7	35	30
3	19	30	8	43	45
4	28	25	9	29	38
5	27	26	10	32	40

16.82 David K. Campbell, James Gaertner, and Robert P. Vecchio (1983) investigated the perceptions of accounting professors with respect to the present and desired importance of various factors considered in promotion and tenure decisions at major universities. One hundred fifteen professors at universities with accredited doctoral programs responded to a mailed questionnaire. The questionnaire asked the professors to rate (1) the *current* importance placed on twenty factors in the promotion and tenure decisions at their universities and

(2) how they believe the factors *should* be weighted. Responses were obtained on a 5-point scale ranging from "no importance" to "extreme importance." The resulting ratings were averaged and converted to the rankings shown in the table. Calculate Spearman's rank correlation coefficient for the data and carefully interpret its value in the context of the problem.

FACTOR	CURRENT IMPORTANCE	IDEAL IMPORTANCE
I. Teaching (and related items):		
Teaching performance	6	1
Advising and counseling students	19	15
Students' complaints/praise	14	17
II. Research:		
Number of journal articles	1	6.5
Quality of journal articles	4	2
Refereed publications:		
a. Applied studies	5	4
b. Theoretical empirical studies	2	3
c. Educationally oriented	11	8
Papers at professional meetings	10	12
Journal editor or reviewer	9	10
Other (textbooks, etc.)	7.5	11
III. Service and professional interaction:		
Service to profession	15	9
Professional/academic awards	7.5	6.5
Community service	18	19
University service	16	16
Collegiality/cooperativeness	12	13
IV. Other		
Academic degrees attained	3	5
Professional certification	17	14
Consulting activities	20	20
Grantsmanship	13	18

On Your Own . . .

In Chapters 15 and 16 we have discussed two methods of analyzing a randomized block design. When the populations have normal probability distributions and their variances are equal, we can use the analysis of variance described in Chapter 15. Otherwise, we can use the Friedman F_r test.

In the "On Your Own" section of Chapter 15, we asked you to conduct a randomized block design to compare supermarket prices, and to use an analysis of variance to interpret the data. Now use the Friedman F_r test to compare the supermarket prices.

How do the results of the two analyses compare? Explain the similarity (or lack of similarity) between the two results.

References

Alter, S., & Ginzberg, M. "Managing uncertainty in MIS implementation." *Sloan Management Review,* Fall 1978, *20,* 23–31.

Beckenstein, A. R., Gabel, H. L., & Roberts, K. "An executive's guide to antitrust compliance." *Harvard Business Review,* Sept.–Oct. 1983, 94–102.

Campbell, D. K., Gaertner, J., & Vecchio, R. P. "Perceptions of promotion and tenure criteria: A survey of accounting educators." *Journal of Accounting Education,* Spring 1983, *1,* 83–92.

Certo, S. C. *Principles of modern management.* Dubuque, Iowa: Wm. C. Brown, 1980. Chapter 14.

Conover, W. J. *Practical nonparametric statistics.* New York: Wiley, 1971.

Cook, T. Q., ed. *Instruments of the money market.* 4th ed. Richmond, Va.: Federal Reserve Bank of Richmond, 1977.

Davis, G. B. *Management information systems.* New York: McGraw-Hill, 1974.

Dharan, B. G. "Empirical identification procedures for earnings models." *Journal of Accounting Education,* Spring 1983, *21,* 256–270.

Epping, G. M. "Importance factors in plant location in 1980." *Growth and Change,* Apr. 1982, *13,* 47–51.

Finn, D. W., Wang, C.-K., & Lamb, C. W. "An examination of the effects of sample composition bias in a mail survey." *Journal of the Market Research Society,* Oct. 1983, *25,* 331–338.

Garvin, D. A. "Quality on the line." *Harvard Business Review,* Sept.–Oct. 1983, 65–75.

Gibbons, J. D. *Nonparametric statistical inference.* New York: McGraw-Hill, 1971.

Hollander, M., & Wolfe, D. A. *Nonparametric statistical methods.* New York: Wiley, 1973.

Lehmann, E. L. *Nonparametrics: Statistical methods based on ranks.* San Francisco: Holden-Day, 1975.

McClure, P. "Analyzing consumer image data using the Friedman two-way analysis of variance by ranks." *Journal of Marketing Research,* Aug. 1971, *8,* 370–371.

Oas, J. A. "Processing, collection of primary data simplified by optimal mark reading." *Marketing News,* Dec. 12, 1980, 24.

Rosenthal, R., & Rosnow, R. L. *The volunteer subject.* New York: Wiley, 1975.

Siegel, S. *Nonparametric statistics for the behavioral sciences.* New York: McGraw-Hill, 1956.

Winkler, R. L., & Hays, W. L. *Statistics: Probability, inference, and decision.* 2d ed. New York: Holt, Rinehart and Winston, 1975. Chapter 12.

Wright, J. L., Owen, F., & Pena, D. "Status of MN/DOT's weigh-in-motion program." St. Paul: Minnesota Department of Transportation, Jan. 1983.

CHAPTER 17

The Chi Square Test and the Analysis of Contingency Tables

Where We've Been . . .

The preceding chapters have presented statistical methods for analyzing many types of business data. Chapters 8–12 and 15 were appropriate for populations of data generated by quantitative random variables that were independent and had (at least approximately) normal probability distributions with a common variance. Nonparametric statistical procedures were presented in Chapter 16 to compare two or more populations when the assumptions of normality or common variance were likely to be violated or when the responses could be ranked only according to their relative magnitudes.

Where We're Going . . .

The methods of this chapter are appropriate for a type of data known as *count* or *classificatory data.* For example, a brokerage company might want to investigate the relationship between its customers' investment preferences (stocks, bonds, mutual funds, etc.) and its customers' occupations. To do this, the company would sample its customers and count the number in each preference–occupation category. Then, this data would be used to make inferences about the actual proportions of their population of customers in each category. Problems of this type, as well as others that involve count data, are the topic of Chapter 17.

Contents

Many business experiments consist of enumerating the number of occurrences of some event. For example, we may count the number of defectives during a particular shift at a manufacturing plant, or the number of consumers who choose each of three brands of coffee, or the number of sales made by each of five automobile salespeople during the month of June.

In some instances, the objective of collecting the count data is to analyze the distribution of the counts in the various *classes* or *cells.* For example, we may want to estimate the proportion of smokers who prefer each of three different brands of cigarettes by counting the number in a sample of smokers who buy each brand. We will say that count data classified on a single scale has a *one-dimensional classification.* The analysis of one-dimensional count data is discussed in Section 17.1.

In many instances the objective of collecting the count data is to determine the relationship between two different methods of classifying the data. For example, we may be interested in knowing whether the size and model of the automobile purchased by new car buyers are related. Or the relationship between the shift and the number of defectives produced in a plant could be of interest. When count data are classified in a *two-dimensional* table, we call the result a *contingency table.* The analysis of general contingency tables is discussed in Section 17.2. In Section 17.3 we consider some special cases of contingency table analyses.

17.1 One-Dimensional Count Data: Multinomial Distribution

Table 17.1

Consumer Preference Survey

A	B	STORE BRAND
61	53	36

Consumer preference surveys can be valuable aids in making marketing decisions. Suppose a large supermarket chain conducts a consumer preference survey by recording the brand of bread purchased by customers in its stores. Assume the chain carries three brands of bread — two major brands (A and B) and its own store brand. The brand preferences of a random sample of 150 buyers are observed, and the resulting count data appear in Table 17.1. Do these data indicate that a preference exists for any of the brands?

To answer this question, we have to know the underlying probability distribution of these count data. This distribution, called the *multinomial probability distribution,* is an extension of the binomial distribution (Section 5.4). The properties of the multinomial distribution are shown in the box.

Properties of the Multinomial Probability Distribution

1. The experiment consists of n identical trials.

2. There are k possible outcomes to each trial.

3. The probabilities of the k outcomes, denoted by $p_1, p_2, \ldots, p_k$, remain the same from trial to trial, where $p_1 + p_2 + \cdots + p_k = 1$.

4. The trials are independent.

5. The random variables of interest are the counts $n_1, n_2, \ldots, n_k$ in each of the k cells.

You can see that the properties of the multinomial experiment closely resemble those of the binomial experiment and that, in fact, a binomial experiment is a multinomial experiment for the special case where $k = 2$.

In most practical applications involving a multinomial experiment, the true values of the k outcome probabilities, $p_1, p_2, \ldots, p_k$, will be unknown. The objective is therefore to make inferences about these probabilities.

Note that the consumer preference survey given in Table 17.1 satisfies the multinomial conditions. Suppose we want to test the null hypothesis that there is no preference for any of the three brands versus the alternative hypothesis that a preference exists for one or more of the brands. Then, letting

p_1 = Proportion of all customers who prefer brand name A

p_2 = Proportion of all customers who prefer brand name B

p_3 = Proportion of all customers who prefer the store brand

we want to test

H_0: $p_1 = p_2 = p_3 = \frac{1}{3}$ (No preference)

H_a: At least one of the proportions exceeds $\frac{1}{3}$ (A preference exists)

If the null hypothesis is true (i.e., if $p_1 = p_2 = p_3 = \frac{1}{3}$), then we would expect to see approximately $\frac{1}{3}$ of the customers in the sample purchase each brand. Or, more formally, the expected value (mean value) of the number of customers purchasing brand name A is given by

$$E(n_1) = np_1$$
$$= n(\tfrac{1}{3}) = 150(\tfrac{1}{3}) = 50$$

Similarly, $E(n_2) = E(n_3) = 50$ if no preference exists.

The following test statistic measures the degree of disagreement between the data and the null hypothesis:

$$X^2 = \frac{[n_1 - E(n_1)]^2}{E(n_1)} + \frac{[n_2 - E(n_2)]^2}{E(n_2)} + \frac{[n_3 - E(n_3)]^2}{E(n_3)}$$
$$= \frac{(n_1 - 50)^2}{50} + \frac{(n_2 - 50)^2}{50} + \frac{(n_3 - 50)^2}{50}$$

Note that the farther the observed numbers n_1, n_2, and n_3 are from their expected value (50), the larger X^2 will become. That is, large values of X^2 cast doubt on the null hypothesis and suggest that it is false.

We have to know the distribution of X^2 in repeated sampling before we can decide whether the data indicate that a preference exists. If in fact H_0 is true, X^2 can be shown to have approximately a χ^2 distribution with $(k-1)$ degrees of freedom.* The χ^2 distribution was first introduced in Section 16.3, and the critical values are given in Table XII of Appendix B. For the consumer preference survey in Table 17.1, with $\alpha = .05$ and $k - 1 = 3 - 1 = 2$ df, we will reject H_0 if

$$X^2 > \chi^2_{.05}$$

* The derivation of the degrees of freedom for X^2 involves the number of linear restrictions imposed on the count data. We will simply give the degrees of freedom for each usage of X^2 and refer the interested reader to the references at the end of the chapter for more detail.

This value of χ^2 (found in Table XII) is 5.99147 (see Figure 17.1). The computed value of the test statistic is

$$X^2 = \frac{(n_1 - 50)^2}{50} + \frac{(n_2 - 50)^2}{50} + \frac{(n_3 - 50)^2}{50}$$

$$= \frac{(61 - 50)^2}{50} + \frac{(53 - 50)^2}{50} + \frac{(36 - 50)^2}{50} = 6.52$$

Since the computed $X^2 = 6.52$ exceeds the critical value of 5.99147, we conclude at $\alpha = .05$ that there is a customer preference for one or more of the brands of bread.

Figure 17.1 Rejection Region for Consumer Preference Survey

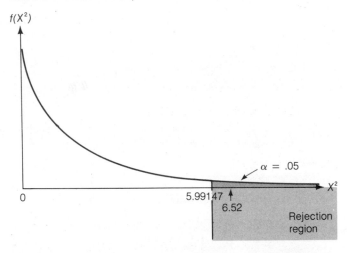

The general form for a test of an hypothesis concerning multinomial probabilities is shown in the box.

A Test of an Hypothesis about Multinomial Probabilities

H_0: $p_1 = p_{1,0}$, $p_2 = p_{2,0}$, . . . , $p_k = p_{k,0}$, where $p_{1,0}$, $p_{2,0}$, . . . , $p_{k,0}$ represent the hypothesized values of the multinomial probabilities

H_a: At least one of the multinomial probabilities does not equal its hypothesized value

Test statistic: $X^2 = \sum_{i=1}^{k} \frac{[n_i - E(n_i)]^2}{E(n_i)}$ $\frac{(ACTUAL - EXPECTED)^2}{EXPECTED}$

where $E(n_i) = np_{i,0}$, the expected number of outcomes of type i assuming H_0 is true. The total sample size is n.

Rejection region: $X^2 > \chi_\alpha^2$ where $df = k - 1$

Assumptions: The sample size n will be large enough so that, for every cell, the expected cell count, $E(n_i)$, will be equal to five or more.

Example 17.1   A large firm has established what it hopes is an objective system of deciding on annual pay increases for its employees. The system is based on a series of evaluation scores determined by the supervisors of each employee. Employees with scores above 80 receive a merit pay increase, those with scores between 50 and 80 receive the standard increase, while those below 50 receive no increase. The firm designed the plan with the objective that, on the average, 25% of its employees would receive merit increases, 65% would receive standard increases, and 10% would receive no increase.

After 1 year of operation using the new plan, the distribution of pay increases for the 600 company employees was as shown in Table 17.2. Test at the $\alpha = .01$ level to determine whether these data indicate that the distribution of pay increases differs significantly from the proportions established by the firm.

Table 17.2
Distribution of Pay Increases

NO INCREASE	STANDARD INCREASE	MERIT INCREASE
42	365	193

Solution   Define

p_1 = Proportion of employees who receive no pay increase

p_2 = Proportion of employees who receive a standard increase

p_3 = Proportion of employees who receive a merit increase

Then the null hypothesis representing the firm's design is

H_0: $p_1 = .10$, $p_2 = .65$, $p_3 = .25$

and the alternative hypothesis is

H_a: At least two of the proportions differ from the firm's proposed plan

Test statistic: $X^2 = \sum \dfrac{[n_i - E(n_i)]^2}{E(n_i)}$

where

$E(n_1) = np_{1,0} = 600(.10) = 60$

$E(n_2) = np_{2,0} = 600(.65) = 390$

$E(n_3) = np_{3,0} = 600(.25) = 150$

Rejection region: For $\alpha = .01$ and df $= k - 1 = 2$, reject H_0 if $X^2 > \chi^2_{.01}$, where (from Table XII, Appendix B) $\chi^2_{.01} = 9.21034$. We now calculate the test statistic:

$$X^2 = \frac{(42 - 60)^2}{60} + \frac{(365 - 390)^2}{390} + \frac{(193 - 150)^2}{150} = 19.33$$

Since this value exceeds the table value of χ^2 (9.21034), the data provide strong evidence ($\alpha = .01$) that the company's pay plan is not working as planned. ∎

By focusing on one particular outcome of a multinomial experiment, we can use the methods developed in Section 8.5 for a binomial proportion to establish a confidence interval for any one of the multinomial probabilities.* For example, if we want a 95% confidence interval for the proportion of the company's employees who will receive merit increases under the new system, we calculate

$$\hat{p}_3 \pm 1.96\sigma_{\hat{p}_3} \approx \hat{p}_3 \pm 1.96 \sqrt{\frac{\hat{p}_3(1-\hat{p}_3)}{n}} \quad \text{where} \quad \hat{p}_3 = \frac{n_3}{n} = \frac{193}{600} = .32$$

$$= .32 \pm 1.96 \sqrt{\frac{(.32)(1-.32)}{600}} = .32 \pm .04$$

Thus, we estimate that between 28% and 36% of the firm's employees will qualify for merit increases under the new plan. It appears that the firm will have to raise the requirements for merit increases in order to achieve the stated goal of a 25% employee qualification rate.

Case Study 17.1

Investigating Response Bias in a Diary Survey

Marketing researchers sometimes collect data from consumers by asking them to keep diaries of their purchases or product usage. Such diary methods generally provide more accurate data than collection methods (such as the telephone interview) that require the consumer to recall from memory the details of his or her purchases and activities. However, diary methods are not problem-free. Frequently, response rates by consumers to requests for diary data are lower than for other types of market research surveys such as mailed questionnaires. In addition, recording biases (such as the nonrecording of events that occurred or the recording of inappropriate events) may be present in diary data (McKenzie, 1983).

John McKenzie (1983) recently studied the accuracy of telephone-call data collected by diary methods in Great Britain. As part of his study, he compared the demographic profile of a sample of 1,802 telephone users who responded to a request for diary data to the demographic profile of the population from which the sample of all those who were asked to keep diaries was selected. The population data were available from telephone company records. The particular population used in this study consisted of 29,507 households.

Table 17.3 shows the education profiles of the population and the sample. These data can be used to determine if the distribution of terminal education ages for the sample differs significantly from the distribution for the population. If a significant difference exists, then it can be inferred that the sample is not representative of the population and that the survey results have been affected by *response bias.*

Table 17.3

Terminal Education Age of Head of Household

	POPULATION		SAMPLE	
	Frequency	Relative frequency	Frequency	Relative frequency
Up to 15	13,137	$p_1 = .445$	791	.439
16–18	7,021	$p_2 = .238$	531	.295
19+	3,074	$p_3 = .104$	202	.112
Not known	6,275	$p_4 = .213$	278	.154

* Note that focusing on one outcome has the effect of combining the other $(k-1)$ outcomes into a single group. Thus, we obtain, in effect, two outcomes — or a binomial experiment.

The sample data should lead to rejection of the following null hypothesis if the population and sample profiles differ:

H_0: $p_1 = .445$, $p_2 = .238$, $p_3 = .104$, $p_4 = .213$

H_a: At least one of the relative frequencies differs from its hypothesized value

The sample data yield

$$X^2 = \frac{(791 - 801.89)^2}{801.89} + \frac{(531 - 428.88)^2}{428.88} + \frac{(202 - 187.41)^2}{187.41} + \frac{(278 - 383.83)^2}{383.83} = 54.78$$

Since $X^2 = 54.78 > \chi^2_{.005} = 12.8381$ (df $= 3$), the null hypothesis is rejected and the existence of response bias is confirmed. McKenzie found similar discrepancies between the population and sample with respect to the age, sex, and social class of the head of household.

When response biases such as these can be identified or are suspected, they can generally be overcome by increasing the response rates of the survey. For a discussion of ways to increase response rates, see Sudman and Ferber (1971, 1974).

Exercises 17.1–17.13

Learning the Mechanics

17.1 Use Table XII of Appendix B to find each of the following χ^2 values:

a. $\chi^2_{.05}$ for df $= 15$ **b.** $\chi^2_{.990}$ for df $= 100$

c. $\chi^2_{.10}$ for df $= 12$ **d.** $\chi^2_{.005}$ for df $= 2$

17.2 Find the following probabilities:

a. $P(\chi^2 \leq .872085)$ for df $= 6$ **b.** $P(\chi^2 > 30.5779)$ for df $= 15$

c. $P(\chi^2 \geq 82.3581)$ for df $= 100$ **d.** $P(\chi^2 < 13.7867)$ for df $= 30$

17.3 Find the rejection region for a one-dimensional χ^2 test of a null hypothesis concerning $p_1, p_2, \ldots, p_k$ if:

a. $k = 3$ and $\alpha = .10$ **b.** $k = 5$ and $\alpha = .01$ **c.** $k = 4$ and $\alpha = .05$

17.4 What conditions must n satisfy to make the χ^2 test valid?

17.5 A multinomial experiment with $k = 5$ cells and $n = 300$ produced the data shown in the table.

CELL	n_i
1	48
2	69
3	83
4	61
5	39

a. Do these data provide sufficient evidence to contradict the null hypothesis that $p_1 = .15$, $p_2 = .25$, $p_3 = .30$, $p_4 = .20$, and $p_5 = .10$? Test using $\alpha = .05$.

b. Find the approximate observed significance level for the test in part a.

Applying the Concepts

17.6 Overweight trucks are responsible for much of the damage sustained by our local, state, and federal highway systems. Although illegal, overweight trucks proliferate. Truckers have learned to avoid weigh stations run by enforcement officers by taking back roads when weigh stations are open and/or by traveling during periods of the week when weigh stations are likely to be closed. A state highway planning agency recently monitored the movements of overweight trucks on a particular interstate highway using an unmanned, computerized scale that is built into the highway. Unknown to the truckers, the scale weighs their vehicles as they pass over it. For a particular week, each day's proportion of the week's total truck traffic (5-axle tractor truck semitrailers) was as shown in the table:

MONDAY	TUESDAY	WEDNESDAY	THURSDAY	FRIDAY	SATURDAY	SUNDAY
.191	.198	.187	.180	.155	.043	.046

Source: Dahlin and Owen (1984).

During the same week, the number of overweight trucks per day was as follows:

MONDAY	TUESDAY	WEDNESDAY	THURSDAY	FRIDAY	SATURDAY	SUNDAY
90	82	72	70	51	18	31

Source: Dahlin and Owen (1984).

a. The planning agency would like to know whether the number of overweight trucks per week is distributed over the 7 days of the week in direct proportion to the volume of truck traffic. Test using $\alpha = .05$.

b. Find the approximate p-value for the test of part a.

17.7 In 1960 there were 72,142,000 people in the U.S. labor force (including the armed services), of whom 23,272,000 were women. The table describes the age distribution of those women.

AGE (Years)	RELATIVE FREQUENCY IN 1960
16–19	.089
20–24	.111
25–34	.178
35–44	.228
45–54	.227
55–64	.128
65 and over	.039

Source: *Statistical Abstract of the United States: 1982–1983,* p. 377.

In 1981, there were 110,812,000 people in the labor force, of whom 46,873,000 were women. A random sample of 500 working women in 1981 yielded the age distribution shown in the next table.

AGE (Years)	FREQUENCY IN 1981
16–19	45
20–24	81
25–34	139
35–44	96
45–54	76
55–64	51
65 and over	12

Source: Based on the relative frequencies for 1981 cited in *Statistical Abstract of the United States: 1982–1983*, p. 377.

a. Do the sample data provide sufficient evidence to conclude that the 1981 age distribution of the female work force differs from the 1960 age distribution? Test using $\alpha = .05$.
b. In the context of the problem, specify the Type I and Type II errors associated with the hypothesis test of part a.
c. Find the approximate p-value for the test in part a.
d. Use 95% confidence intervals to estimate the proportion of women between the ages of 25 and 34 (inclusive) in the 1981 labor force and the proportion between 20 and 44 (inclusive).

17.8 A local manufacturing company utilizes a computerized sales invoice printing system. Each distinct bit of information on the invoices (e.g., sold-to address, ship-to address, sales tax, total sale) is referred to as a *field*. From a handwritten copy of each invoice, a keypunch operator transcribes the field data onto computer cards so that computer-printed invoices can be produced. The manager of data processing believes that the distribution of the number of errors per invoice appearing on printed invoices has changed dramatically since the physical arrangement of the fields on the invoices was changed 6 months ago. The table describes the distribution of the number of errors per invoice when the previous format was used:

ERRORS PER INVOICE	0	1	2	3	4	More than 4
PROPORTION OF FINISHED INVOICES	0.90	0.04	0.03	0.02	0.005	0.005

A random sample of 300 printed invoices was selected from those that were printed during the past week. Each invoice was examined for errors. The following data resulted:

ERRORS PER INVOICE	0	1	2	3	4	More than 4
NUMBER OF INVOICES	150	120	15	7	4	4

a. Do the data provide sufficient evidence to indicate that the proportions of printed invoices in the six error categories differ from the proportions using the previous format?
b. Find the approximate observed significance level for the test in part a.

17.9 A company that manufactures dice for gambling casinos in Nevada and New Jersey regularly inspects its product to be sure that only "fair" (i.e., balanced) dice are supplied to the casinos. One die was randomly chosen from a production lot and rolled 120 times. Counts of the numbers showing face up are recorded in the table. Do the data provide sufficient evidence to indicate that the die is unbalanced? Test using $\alpha = .10$.

NUMBERS FACE UP	1	2	3	4	5	6
FREQUENCY	28	27	20	18	15	12

17.10 Four inferential techniques, A, B, C, and D, are currently used by businesses to forecast demand for their product or service. To find out whether one technique is preferred to any other, a random sample of 200 businesses were asked which technique they preferred. A summary of their responses is shown in the table. Is there sufficient evidence to indicate that there are differences in the proportions of businesses preferring each technique? Test using $\alpha = .05$.

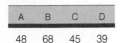

A	B	C	D
48	68	45	39

17.11 After purchasing a policy from one life insurance company, a person has a certain period of time in which the policy can be cancelled without financial obligation. The insurance company is interested in seeing whether those who cancel a policy during this time period are as likely to be in one policy-size category as another. Records for 250 people who cancelled policies during this period were selected at random from company files and the size of the policy was noted, with the results shown in the table. Is there sufficient evidence to conclude that the cancelled policies are not distributed equally among the five policy-size categories? Use $\alpha = .05$.

Number of People Cancelling per Policy-Size Category

SIZE OF POLICY ($ THOUSAND)				
10	15	20	25	30
31	39	67	54	59

17.12 Supermarket chains often carry products with their own brand labels and usually price them lower than the nationally known brands. A supermarket conducted a taste test to determine whether there was a difference in taste among the four brands of ice cream it carries: a local brand (A) and three national brands (B, C, D). A sample of 200 people participated, and they indicated the preferences shown in the table. Is there evidence of a difference in preference for the four brands? Test at $\alpha = .05$.

BRAND			
A	B	C	D
39	57	55	49

17.13 Most companies target their advertising at specific income groups. To provide information to advertisers about its readers' incomes, a magazine decides to conduct a survey. A previous survey had indicated that 25% of the readers earned less than $15,000 per year, 60% earned from $15,000 to $25,000 per year, and 15% earned more than $25,000 per year. The income category breakdown for the 6,478 people who responded to the latest survey is shown in the table. Do these new survey results indicate that the proportions of the readership in the three categories have changed since the previous survey?

	INCOME CATEGORY		
	Less than $15,000	$15,000–25,000	More than $25,000
NUMBER OF RESPONDENTS	1,653	3,946	879

17.2 Contingency Tables

The energy shortage has made many consumers more aware of the size of the automobiles they purchase. Suppose an automobile manufacturer who is interested in determining the relationship between the size and manufacturer of newly purchased automobiles randomly samples 1,000 recent buyers of American-made cars. The manufacturer classifies each purchase with respect to the size and manufacturer of the purchased automobile. The data are shown in Table 17.4, which is an example of a *contingency table.* Contingency tables consist of *multinomial count data classified on two scales, or dimensions.*

Table 17.4

Contingency Table for Automobile Size Example

| | MANUFACTURER | | | | TOTALS |
	A	B	C	D	
SMALL	157	65	181	10	413
INTERMEDIATE	126	82	142	46	396
LARGE	58	45	60	28	191
TOTALS	341	192	383	84	1,000

Let the probabilities for the multinomial experiment in Table 17.4 be those shown in Table 17.5. Thus, p_{11} is the probability that a new-car buyer purchases a small car of manufacturer A. Note the probability totals, called *marginal probabilities,* for each row and column. The marginal probability p_1 is the probability that a small car is purchased, and the marginal probability p_A is the probability that a car of manufacturer A is purchased.

Table 17.5

Probabilities for Contingency Table 17.4

| | MANUFACTURER | | | | TOTALS |
	A	B	C	D	
SMALL	p_{11}	p_{12}	p_{13}	p_{14}	p_1
INTERMEDIATE	p_{21}	p_{22}	p_{23}	p_{24}	p_2
LARGE	p_{31}	p_{32}	p_{33}	p_{34}	p_3
TOTALS	p_A	p_B	p_C	p_D	1

Suppose we want to know whether the two classifications, manufacturer and size, are dependent. That is, if we know which size car a buyer will choose, does that information give us a clue about the manufacturer of the car the buyer will choose? In a probabilistic sense we know (Chapter 4) that independence of events A and B implies that $P(A \cap B) = P(A)P(B)$. Similarly, in the contingency table analysis, if the two classifications are independent, the probability that an item is classified in any particular cell of the table is the product of the corresponding marginal probabilities. Thus, under the hypothesis of independence, in Table 17.5 we must have

$$p_{11} = p_1 p_A \qquad p_{12} = p_1 p_B$$

and so forth.

To test the hypothesis of independence, we use the same reasoning employed in the one-dimensional tests of Section 17.1. First, we calculate the expected (or mean) count in each cell assuming the null hypothesis of independence is true. We do this by noting that the expected count in the upper left-hand corner of the table, for example, is just the total number of multinomial trials, n, times the probability, p_{11}. Then

$$E(n_{11}) = np_{11}$$

and, if the classifications are independent,

$$E(n_{11}) = np_1 p_A$$

We can estimate p_1 and p_A by the sample proportions $\hat{p}_1 = n_1/n$ and $\hat{p}_A = n_A/n$. Thus, the estimate of the expected value $E(n_{11})$ is

$$\hat{E}(n_{11}) = n\left(\frac{n_1}{n}\right)\left(\frac{n_A}{n}\right) = \frac{n_1 n_A}{n}$$

Similarly,

$$\hat{E}(n_{12}) = \frac{n_1 n_B}{n}$$

$$\vdots$$

$$\hat{E}(n_{34}) = \frac{n_3 n_D}{n}$$

Using the data in Table 17.4, we find

$$\hat{E}(n_{11}) = \frac{n_1 n_A}{n} = \frac{(413)(341)}{1,000} = 140.833$$

$$\hat{E}(n_{12}) = \frac{n_1 n_B}{n} = \frac{(413)(192)}{1,000} = 79.296$$

$$\vdots$$

$$\hat{E}(n_{34}) = \frac{n_3 n_D}{n} = \frac{(191)(84)}{1,000} = 16.044$$

The observed data and the estimated expected values are shown in Table 17.6.

Table 17.6

Observed and Estimated Expected (in Parentheses) Counts

| | MANUFACTURER | | | |
	A	B	C	D
SMALL	157 (140.833)	65 (79.296)	181 (158.179)	10 (34.692)
INTERMEDIATE	126 (135.036)	82 (76.032)	142 (151.668)	46 (33.264)
LARGE	58 (65.131)	45 (36.672)	60 (73.153)	28 (16.044)

We now use the X^2 statistic to compare the observed and expected (estimated) counts in each cell of the contingency table:

$$X^2 = \frac{[n_{11} - \hat{E}(n_{11})]^2}{\hat{E}(n_{11})} + \frac{[n_{12} - \hat{E}(n_{12})]^2}{\hat{E}(n_{12})} + \cdots + \frac{[n_{34} - \hat{E}(n_{34})]^2}{\hat{E}(n_{34})}$$

$$= \sum_{i=1}^{3} \sum_{j=1}^{4} \frac{[n_{ij} - \hat{E}(n_{ij})]^2}{\hat{E}(n_{ij})}$$

Substituting the data of Table 17.6 into this expression yields

$$X^2 = \frac{(157 - 140.833)^2}{140.833} + \frac{(65 - 79.296)^2}{79.296} + \cdots + \frac{(28 - 16.044)^2}{16.044} = 45.81$$

Large values of X^2 imply that the observed and expected counts do not closely agree and therefore that the hypothesis of independence is false. To determine how large X^2 must be before it is too large to be attributed to chance, we make use of the fact that the sampling distribution of X^2 is approximately a χ^2 probability distribution when the classifications are independent. The number of degrees of freedom for the approximating χ^2 distribution will be $(r - 1)(c - 1)$, where r is the number of rows and c is the number of columns in the table.

For the size and manufacturer of automobiles example, the degrees of freedom for χ^2 is $(r - 1)(c - 1) = (3 - 1)(4 - 1) = 6$. Then, for $\alpha = .05$, we reject the hypothesis of independence if

$$X^2 > \chi^2_{.05} = 12.5916$$

Since the computed $X^2 = 45.81$ exceeds the value 12.5916, we conclude that the size and manufacturer of a car selected by a purchaser are dependent events.

The general form of a contingency table is shown in Table 17.7 (page 802). Note that the observed count in the cell located in the ith row and the jth column is denoted by n_{ij}, the ith row total is r_i, the jth column total is c_j, and the total sample size is n. Using this notation, we give the general form of the contingency table test for independent classifications in the box.

**General Form of a Contingency Table Analysis:
A Test for Independence**

H_0:   The two classifications are independent

H_a: The two classifications are dependent

SEE TABLE 17.7
PG 802

Test statistic: $X^2 = \sum_{i=1}^{r} \sum_{j=1}^{c} \frac{[n_{ij} - \hat{E}(n_{ij})]^2}{\hat{E}(n_{ij})}$

where

$$\hat{E}(n_{ij}) = \frac{r_i c_j}{n}$$

Rejection region: $X^2 > \chi^2_\alpha$, where χ^2_α is based on $(r - 1)(c - 1)$ df

Assumption: The sample size, n, will be large enough so that, for every cell, the expected cell count, $E(n_{ij})$, will be equal to five or more.

Table 17.7

General $r \times c$ Contingency Table

		COLUMN			ROW TOTALS
		1	*2*	$\cdots$	c	
	1	n_{11}	n_{12}	$\cdots$	n_{1c}	r_1
	2	n_{21}	n_{22}	$\cdots$	n_{2c}	r_2
ROW	$\vdots$	$\vdots$	$\vdots$		$\vdots$	$\vdots$
	r	n_{r1}	n_{r2}	$\cdots$	n_{rc}	r_r
COLUMN TOTALS		c_1	c_2	$\cdots$	c_c	n

Example 17.2

A large brokerage firm wants to determine whether the service it provides to affluent customers differs from the service it provides to lower-income customers. A sample of 500 customers is selected, and each customer is asked to rate his or her broker. The results are shown in Table 17.8. Test to determine whether there is evidence that broker rating and customer income are dependent. Use $\alpha = .10$.

Table 17.8

Observed and Estimated Expected (in Parentheses) Counts for Example 17.2

		CUSTOMER'S INCOME			TOTALS
		Under $20,000	*$20,000–$50,000*	*Over $50,000*	
	Outstanding	48	64	41	153
		(53.856)	(66.402)	(32.742)	
BROKER RATING	*Average*	98	120	50	268
		(94.336)	(116.312)	(57.352)	
	Poor	30	33	16	79
		(27.808)	(34.286)	(16.906)	
TOTALS		176	217	107	500

Solution

The first step is to calculate estimated expected cell frequencies under the assumption that the classifications are independent. Thus,

$$\hat{E}(n_{11}) = \frac{r_1 c_1}{n} = \frac{(153)(176)}{500} = 53.856$$

$$\hat{E}(n_{12}) = \frac{r_1 c_2}{n} = \frac{(153)(217)}{500} = 66.402$$

and so forth. All the estimated expected counts are shown in Table 17.8.

We are now ready to conduct the test for independence:

H_0:   The rating a customer gives his or her broker is independent of the customer's income

H_a: Broker rating and customer income are dependent

Test statistic: $X^2 = \sum\limits_{i=1}^{3} \sum\limits_{j=1}^{3} \dfrac{[n_{ij} - \hat{E}(n_{ij})]^2}{\hat{E}(n_{ij})}$

Rejection region: For $\alpha = .10$ and $(r - 1)(c - 1) = (2)(2) = 4$ df, reject H_0 if

$$X^2 > \chi^2_{.10}$$

where $\chi^2_{.10} = 7.77944$.

The calculated value of X^2 is

$$X^2 = \frac{(48 - 53.856)^2}{53.856} + \frac{(64 - 66.402)^2}{66.402} + \cdots + \frac{(16 - 16.906)^2}{16.906}$$

$$= 4.28$$

Since $X^2 = 4.28$ does not exceed the critical value, 7.77944, there is insufficient evidence at $\alpha = .10$ to conclude that broker rating and customer income are dependent. This survey does not support the firm's alternative hypothesis that affluent customers get different broker service than lower-income customers. ■

Case Study 17.2

Deceived Survey Respondents: Once Bitten, Twice Shy

In their article "Deceived Respondents: Once Bitten, Twice Shy," Sheets et al. (1974) explore a situation sometimes encountered by marketing research personnel:

> For some time, people engaged in marketing and other field-based research have had to contend with the consequences of a fairly widely used ploy in the direct selling field: gaining a potential customer's attention and interest by requesting cooperation in some sort of false survey. Despite the efforts of the American Association for Public Opinion Research, the American Marketing Association, and other groups, and regardless of Federal Trade Commission orders, this gambit is still in use, although perhaps somewhat modified.

The authors hypothesized that a previous exposure to a false survey will increase the probability that a person will refuse to respond in a legitimate survey. They conducted an experiment in which 104 individuals were asked to cooperate in a marketing research study. The fifty-four people who agreed to participate were then given a low-key sales presentation for a fictitious encyclopedia. Between 2 and 4 days later, forty-nine of the original fifty-four participants (five were not available) and seventy completely new individuals (the control group) were interviewed. Each group was asked the same opening question. The results of this survey are presented in Table 17.9.

Table 17.9

Experimental and Control Group Willingness to Participate in True Market Research

	EXPERIMENTAL	CONTROL	TOTALS
CONSENTED	12	36	48
REFUSED	37	34	71
TOTALS	49	70	119

A χ^2 test was used to analyze these count data. The χ^2 test statistic is found to be 8.691, significant at $\alpha = .005$. This indicates dependence of the refusal rate on previous exposure to false surveys. The interpretation given to these data by Sheets et al. (1974) is:

> The findings indicate support for the hypothesis: false market surveys have a deleterious effect upon respondent willingness to cooperate in subsequent market research studies. By inference, households that have been previously exposed to false research are half again as likely to refuse to cooperate in legitimate field research as those who have not. The implication for field researchers is either to stay away from areas that have had recent, heavy, direct, sales efforts or to plan for higher refusal rates in such areas.

Exercises 17.14–17.24

	B		
	B_1	B_2	B_3
A_1	39	75	42
A A_2	63	51	70
A_3	30	38	29

Learning the Mechanics

17.14 Find the rejection region for a test of independence of two classifications if the contingency table contains r rows and c columns and

a. $r = 5$, $c = 5$, $\alpha = .05$ **b.** $r = 3$, $c = 6$, $\alpha = .10$
c. $r = 2$, $c = 3$, $\alpha = .01$

17.15 Test the null hypothesis of independence of the two classifications, A and B, of the 3×3 (i.e., $r = 3$ and $c = 3$) contingency table shown in the margin. Test using $\alpha = .05$.

17.16 Test the null hypothesis of independence of the two classifications, A and B, of the 3×4 contingency table shown below. Test using $\alpha = .05$.

	B			
	B_1	B_2	B_3	B_4
A_1	22	38	29	51
A A_2	42	27	68	53
A_3	26	85	102	68

17.17 In a contingency table test for independence, explain why the null hypothesis is independence and the alternative hypothesis is dependence (instead of vice versa).

Applying the Concepts

17.18 Over the years, pollsters have found that the public's confidence in big business has been closely tied to the economic climate of the country. When businesses are growing and employment is increasing, public confidence is high. When the opposite occurs, public confidence is low. Harvey Kahalas (1981) explored the relationship between confidence in business and job satisfaction. He hypothesized that there is a relationship between level of confidence and job satisfaction, and that this is true for both union and nonunion workers. To test his hypothesis he used the sample data given in the tables (data were collected by the National Opinion Research Center).

I. Union members

		JOB SATISFACTION			
		Very satisfied	Moderately satisfied	Little dissatisfied	Very dissatisfied
CONFIDENCE IN MAJOR CORPORATIONS	A great deal	26	15	2	1
	Only some	95	73	16	5
	Hardly any	34	28	10	9

II. Nonunion Workers

		JOB SATISFACTION			
		Very satisfied	Moderately satisfied	Little dissatisfied	Very dissatisfied
CONFIDENCE IN MAJOR CORPORATIONS	A great deal	111	52	13	4
	Only some	246	142	37	18
	Hardly any	73	51	19	9

a. Kahalas concluded that his hypothesis was not supported by the data. Do you agree? Conduct the appropriate tests using $\alpha = .05$. Be sure to specify the null and alternative hypotheses of your tests.

b. Find and interpret the approximate p-values of the tests you conducted in part a.

17.19 In 1952, the National Broadcasting Company (NBC) conducted a study to determine the effects of television viewing on the purchase of products advertised on television. A sample of 2,452 women from the Davenport, Iowa, metropolitan area were interviewed, first in February and then again in May. Each time, the women were asked whether they watch a specific program and whether they purchase the product advertised during the program. Their responses are categorized in the table.

		BUYING, FEB./MAY				TOTALS
		Yes/Yes	Yes/No	No/Yes	No/No	
	Yes/Yes	460	173	191	351	1,175
VIEWING	Yes/No	76	59	44	113	292
FEB./MAY	No/Yes	86	27	53	80	246
	No/No	175	104	113	347	739
TOTALS		797	363	401	891	2,452

Source: *Journal of Marketing Research,* Feb. 1966, pp. 13–24.

a. If a χ^2 test of independence were conducted for the table, what would be the null and alternative hypotheses?

b. Conduct the test referred to in part a. Test using $\alpha = .05$.

c. What assumptions must you make so that the χ^2 test in part b will be valid?

17.20 In recent years, corporate boards of directors have been pressed to improve their monitoring of corporate economic performance and to become more careful overseers of the activities of management. In addition, boards are being asked to guide the long-term responsiveness of their respective organizations to the prevailing economic and social climate. These pressures have forced many boards of directors to become more articulate in defining the mission and strategies of their firms. To study the extent and nature of strategic planning being undertaken by boards of directors, Ahmed Tashakori and William Boulton (1983) questioned a sample of 119 chief executive officers of major U.S. corporations. One of the objectives of the study was to determine if a relationship exists between the composition of a board—where boards are classified as consisting of a majority of outside directors or a majority of inside directors—and its level of participation in the strategic planning process. To this end, the questionnaire data were used to classify the responding corporations according to the level of their board's participation in the strategic planning process:

Level 1: Board participates in formulation or implementation or evaluation of strategy

Level 2: Board participates in formulation and implementation, formulation and evaluation, or implementation and evaluation of strategy

Level 3: Board participates in formulation, implementation, and evaluation of strategy

The following results were obtained:

LEVEL	1	2	3
NUMBER OF FIRMS	22	37	60

Of these 119 firms, 100 had boards where outside directors constitute a majority. Their levels of participation in strategic planning were as follows:

LEVEL	1	2	3
NUMBER OF FIRMS	20	27	53

a. Tashakori and Boulton concluded that a relationship exists between a board's level of participation in the strategic planning process and the composition of the board. Do you agree? Construct the appropriate contingency table, and test using $\alpha = .10$.

b. In the context of the problem, specify the Type I and Type II errors associated with the test of part a.

c. Find the approximate p-value for the test in part a. Based on the p-value, would the null hypothesis have been rejected at $\alpha = .05$? Explain.

17.21 An insurance company that sells hospitalization policies wants to know whether there is a relationship between the amount of hospitalization coverage a person has and the length of stay in the hospital. Records are selected at random at a large hospital by hospital personnel, and the information on length of stay and hospitalization coverage is given to the insurance company. The results are summarized in the table. Can you conclude that there is a relationship between length of stay and hospitalization coverage? Use $\alpha = .01$.

		LENGTH OF STAY (DAYS)			
		5 or under	6–10	11–15	Over 15
	Under 25%	26	30	6	5
HOSPITALIZATION	25–50%	21	30	11	7
COVERAGE OF	51–75%	25	25	45	9
COSTS	Over 75%	11	32	17	11

17.22 In late 1977, many farmers across the United States went on strike, protesting that the prices of farm products, chiefly grains, were less than the cost of production. Although the main strike goal was to receive 100% of parity prices for all farm products, a second controversial strike goal was to induce farmers to reduce production, thereby reducing surpluses and boosting prices. A sample survey of 100 farmers was conducted to determine whether a relationship exists between a farmer's decision to participate in the strike and the farmer's opinion concerning the necessity for a cutback in production. The results are shown in the table. Is there evidence of a relationship between a farmer's strike position and the stand on a cutback in production? Use $\alpha = .05$.

		ON STRIKE	
		Yes	No
50% CUTBACK IN PRODUCTION	Favor	21	7
	Undecided	37	2
	Opposed	22	11

17.23 A study was conducted to help determine who takes advantage of sales and specials at food stores that advertise in newspapers. Shoppers were asked whether they usually check the advertisements before shopping and which of the following income brackets they fit into: annual income below $5,000, between $5,000 and $9,999, between $10,000 and $14,999, between $15,000 and $19,999, and $20,000 or more. Test to see whether the proportion of shoppers who watch the advertisements depends on income level. Use $\alpha = .10$.

	INCOME (DOLLARS)				
	Less than 5,000	5,000–9,999	10,000–14,999	15,000–19,999	20,000 or more
NUMBER OF YES RESPONSES	33	62	31	14	6
NUMBER OF NO RESPONSES	3	8	19	15	14

17.24 One criterion used to evaluate employees in the assembly section of a large factory is the number of defective pieces per 1,000 parts produced. The quality control department wants to find out whether there is a relationship between years of experience and defect rate. Since the job is repetitious, after the initial training period, any improvement due to a learning effect might be offset by a decrease in the motivation of a worker. A defect rate is calculated for each worker for a yearly evaluation. The results for 100 workers are given in the table.

		YEARS OF EXPERIENCE (AFTER TRAINING PERIOD)		
		<1*	$1 < 5$	$5 < 10$
DEFECT RATE	High	6	9	9
	Average	9	19	23
	Low	7	8	10

* The symbol "$<$" is read "less than," so "<1" is read "less than 1" and "$1 < 5$" is read "1 to less than 5."

a. Is there evidence of a relationship between defect rate and years of experience? Use $\alpha = .05$.

b. Find the approximate observed significance level for the test in part a.

17.3 Contingency Tables with Fixed Marginal Totals

Suppose a national college placement firm wants to determine whether the job performance of college graduates is related to the region of the country in which the graduate attended college. The firm randomly selects 800 of last year's graduates who are currently employed, 200 from each of four regions: northeast (NE), southeast (SE), northwest (NW), southwest (SW). Then the employer of each graduate is contacted, and a rating of the employee's job performance is obtained. The results are shown in Table 17.10. The only difference between this contingency table and those in the previous section is that the row totals in Table 17.10 are all determined before the experiment is conducted, whereas in Section 17.2, the marginal totals were not known until after the experiment was run. Fortunately, this fact does not affect the analysis. Thus, to test for dependence between job performance of college graduates and the region in which they attended college, we proceed as follows:

H_0: Job performance and region are independent

H_a: Job performance and region are dependent

Test statistic: $X^2 = \sum\limits_{i=1}^{4} \sum\limits_{j=1}^{3} \dfrac{[n_{ij} - \hat{E}(n_{ij})]^2}{\hat{E}(n_{ij})}$

Rejection region: For $\alpha = .05$ and $(r-1)(c-1) = 6$ df, we will reject H_0 if
$$X^2 > \chi^2_{.05} = 12.5916$$

Table 17.10

Results of Job Performance by Region

		JOB PERFORMANCE RATING			TOTALS
		Unsatisfactory	Satisfactory	Outstanding	
	NE	21 (16.75)	121 (134.75)	58 (48.5)	200
	NW	18 (16.75)	133 (134.75)	49 (48.5)	200
REGION	SE	10 (16.75)	147 (134.75)	43 (48.5)	200
	SW	18 (16.75)	138 (134.75)	44 (48.5)	200
TOTALS		67	539	194	800

We calculate the estimated expected counts exactly as in Section 17.2:

$$\hat{E}(n_{11}) = \frac{r_1 c_1}{n} = \frac{(200)(67)}{800} = 16.75$$

$$\hat{E}(n_{12}) = \frac{r_1 c_2}{n} = \frac{(200)(539)}{800} = 134.75$$

and so forth. The estimated expected counts are shown in parentheses in Table 17.10. Then,

$$X^2 = \frac{(21 - 16.75)^2}{16.75} + \frac{(121 - 134.75)^2}{134.75} + \cdots + \frac{(44 - 48.5)^2}{48.5}$$

$$= 9.51$$

Since $X^2 = 9.51$ does not exceed the critical value of 12.5916, the placement firm cannot conclude at the $\alpha = .05$ level that job performance rating and region of college training are dependent.

17.4
Caution

Because the X^2 statistic for testing hypotheses about multinomial probabilities is one of the most widely applied statistical tools, it is also one of the most abused statistical procedures. The user should always be certain that the experiment satisfies the properties of the multinomial experiment given in Section 17.1. Furthermore, the user should be certain that the sample is drawn from the correct population — that is, from the population about which the inference is to be made. If in Section 17.3 the placement firm had chosen 200 graduates from one college in each region, no valid inference could be made about the entire region. We would obtain a comparison of four colleges, not four regions.

The use of the χ^2 probability distribution as an approximation to the sampling distribution for X^2 should be avoided when the expected counts are very small. The approximation can become very poor when these expected counts are small, and thus the actual value of α may be very different from the tabled value. As a rule of thumb, an expected cell count of at least five will mean that the χ^2 probability distribution can be used to determine an approximate critical value.

Finally, if the X^2 value does not exceed the established critical value of χ^2, *do not accept the hypothesis of independence.* You would be risking a Type II error (accepting H_0 if in fact it is false), and the probability, β, of committing such an error is unknown. The usual alternative hypothesis is that the classifications are dependent. Because there is literally an infinite number of ways two classifications can be dependent, it is difficult to calculate one or even several values of β to represent such a broad alternative hypothesis. Therefore, we avoid concluding that two classifications are independent, even when X^2 is small.

Summary

The use of **count data** to test hypotheses about **multinomial probabilities** represents a very useful statistical technique. In a **one-dimensional table** we can use count data to test the hypothesis that the multinomial probabilities are equal to specified values. In a **two-dimensional contingency table,** we can test the independence of the two classifications. And these by no means exhaust the uses of the X^2 statistic. Many other applications can be found in the references at the end of this chapter.

Caution should be exercised to avoid misuse of the χ^2 procedure. The experiment must be multinomial,* and the expected counts should not be too small so that the χ^2 critical value may be used. Also, the X^2 statistic should not always be viewed as the final answer. If two classifications are found to be dependent, many measures of association exist for quantifying the nature and strength of their dependence (see the references).

---

* When the row (or column) totals are fixed, each row (or column) represents a separate multinomial experiment.

Supplementary Exercises 17.25 – 17.54

17.25 Consumers have traditionally viewed products with warranties more favorably than products without warranties. In fact, several studies have demonstrated that, when given the choice between two similar products, one of which is warranted, consumers prefer the warranted product, even at a higher price. Thus, consumers generally perceive warranties as a kind of "value" added to the product. However, a substantial number of firms have been found to perceive their warranties primarily as legal disclaimers of responsibility and nothing more. As a result of the differences in perceptions by consumers and businesses, Congress passed the Magnuson–Moss Warranty Act, which took effect in 1977. Its purpose was to reform consumer product warranty practices. According to this act, all warranties must be designated as "full" or "limited" and must be clearly written in readily understood language. Further, it specified what was to be contained in warranties (McDaniel & Rao, 1982).

Recently, McDaniel and Rao (1982) undertook a study to investigate consumer satisfaction with warranty practices since the advent of the Magnuson–Moss Warranty Act. Using a mailed questionnaire, they sampled 237 midwestern consumers who had purchased a major appliance within the past 6 to 18 months. One of the questions they asked the consumers was, "Do most retailers and dealers make a conscientious effort to satisfy their customers' warranty claims?" One hundred fifty-six answered yes, 61 were uncertain, and 20 said no.

The population of consumers from which this sample was drawn had also been investigated 2 years prior to the Magnuson–Moss Warranty Act. At that time, 37.0% of the population answered yes to the same question, 53.3% were uncertain, and 9.7% said no.

a. As reflected in the answers to the above question, have consumer attitudes toward warranties changed since the pre-Magnuson–Moss Act study? Test using $\alpha = .05$.

b. Compare the pre- and post-Magnuson–Moss Warranty Act responses, and describe the changes that have occurred.

17.26 The U.S. Postal Service is investigating the effect of alternative mail-sorting procedures on the percentage of sorting errors. A sorting error occurs when a piece of mail is placed into an incorrect zip code category. The three alternatives to be evaluated are:

1. All manual (i.e., mail clerks sort all mail)

2. Mixed manual–automated (i.e., mail clerks sort handwritten addresses and optical scanning machines sort typewritten addresses)

3. All automated (i.e., optical scanning machines sort all mail)

To evaluate these three alternatives, the Postal Service randomly selects 1,500 pieces of mail from the main post office in Washington, D.C. Five hundred pieces of mail are randomly assigned to each of the three sorting procedures. The experiment produced these error rates for the three sorting procedures:

All manual:	19%
Mixed manual–automated:	17%
All automated:	24%

a. Based on these sample data, would you conclude that the error rates differ among the mail sorting procedures? Test using $\alpha = .05$.

b. Find the approximate observed significance level for the test.

17.27 When a buyer charges a purchase, the seller records the sale in his or her record books under a category called *accounts receivable*. Some retailers monitor the status of their accounts receivable by regularly classifying each as being in one of the following categories: current, 1–30 days late, 31–60 days late, over 60 days late, or uncollectable. Historical data indicate that the status of a particular retailer's accounts receivable can be described as follows:

Current:	65%
1–30 days late:	15%
31–60 days late:	10%
Over 60 days late:	7%
Uncollectable:	3%

Six months after the interest rate charged to late accounts was increased, the status of the retailer's 200 accounts receivable was as follows:

Current:	78%
1–30 days late:	12%
31–60 days late:	5%
Over 60 days late:	2%
Uncollectable:	3%

a. Is there evidence to indicate that the increase in interest rates affected the timing of buyers' payments? Test using $\alpha = .10$.

b. Find the approximate observed significance level for the test.

17.28 In Case Study 9.2, we described part of the statistical analysis used by Kaufman and Wolf (1982) to examine the preferences and anxieties of men and women with respect to attending job interviews in hotel rooms. In this exercise, we supply you with additional data from their study and ask you to analyze it. A random sample of 302 students (95 men and 207 women) were asked whether they would be anxious or uncomfortable about interviewing in a hotel room. The responses are shown in the table. Do these data provide sufficient evidence to conclude that anxiety over hotel room interviewing is related to the interviewee's sex? Test using $\alpha = .05$.

	YES	NO
MEN	63.16%	36.84%
WOMEN	77.29%	22.71%

Source: Kaufman and Wolf (1982) and personal comunication from Lois Kaufman.

17.29 Organizations that loan money to businesses are in effect gambling that the business will become (or remain) successful long enough so that the loan will not be defaulted. Loan applicants are carefully screened to weed out those firms with a high probability of defaulting. Characteristics of an applicant firm that might be examined by a loan officer include such things as the firm's age and legal structure. The loan officer's evaluation will also consider the amount of the requested loan, the length of the loan, and the type of the loan (e.g., for existing business, to buy existing business, or to start a new business).

Albert L. Page et al. (1977) conducted an empirical investigation of the past loan performance of the Greater Cleveland Growth Corporation, an affiliate of the Office of Minority Business Enterprise. Part of the study involved identifying demographic and firm characteristic variables that are related to the status of loans made by the Growth Corporation. Loans are classified as paid off, current, or defaulted. Loans that are either paid off or current are regarded as good loans.

Page et al. examined a sample of sixty-four loan histories and observed the frequencies for the six loan status and legal structure categories as shown in the table.

LOAN STATUS	FIRM'S LEGAL STRUCTURE	FREQUENCY
Defaulted	Sole proprietorship	14
Paid off or current	Sole proprietorship	13
Defaulted	Partnership	10
Paid off or current	Partnership	1
Defaulted	Corporation	12
Paid off or current	Corporation	14

a. After applying a contingency table analysis to the data, Page et al. concluded that a relationship exists between the legal structure of an applicant firm and the success or failure of the loan. Test their conclusion using $\alpha = .05$.

b. Find the approximate observed significance level for the test in part a.

c. What assumptions must you make so that the test conclusions in part a will be valid?

d. Use a 95% confidence interval to estimate the proportion of loans made by the Growth Corporation that will be defaulted.

17.30 An experiment was conducted to compare two methods for operating a group family medical practice. Four hundred patients were randomly assigned to two groups: one group received the conventional direct contact with physicians, while the other group made first contact with a nurse practitioner and were then referred to a physician if a physician's services were deemed necessary. At the conclusion of the experiment the quality of each person's medical care was rated as satisfactory or unsatisfactory by an impartial medical observer in consultation with the patient. The results of the experiment are shown in the table. Do the data present sufficient evidence to indicate that quality ratings are dependent on the method of patient care? Test using $\alpha = .05$.

	CONVENTIONAL	NURSE PRACTITIONER	TOTALS
SATISFACTORY	148	161	309
UNSATISFACTORY	52	39	91
TOTALS	200	200	400

17.31 Along with the technological age comes the problem of workers being replaced by machines. A labor management organization wants to study the problem of workers displaced by automation in three industries. Case reports for 100 workers whose loss of job is directly attributable to technological advances are selected within each industry. For each worker selected, it is determined whether he or she was given another job within the same company, found a job with another company in the same industry, found a job in a new industry, or has been unemployed for longer than 6 months. The results are given in the table. Does the plight of automation-displaced workers depend on the industry? Use $\alpha = .01$.

		SAME COMPANY	NEW COMPANY (Same industry)	NEW INDUSTRY	UNEMPLOYED
	A	62	11	20	7
INDUSTRY	B	45	8	38	9
	C	68	19	8	5

17.32 Refer to Exercise 17.31. Estimate the difference between the proportions of displaced workers who find work in another industry for industries A and C. Use a 95% confidence interval.

17.33 A computer used by a 24-hour banking service is supposed to randomly assign each transaction to one of five memory locations. A check at the end of a day's transactions gave the following counts to each of the five memory locations:

MEMORY LOCATION	1	2	3	4	5
NUMBER OF TRANSACTIONS	90	78	100	72	85

Is there evidence to indicate a difference in the proportions of transactions assigned to the five memory locations? Test using $\alpha = .025$.

17.34 Refer to Case Study 17.2.

a. Verify that the value of the test statistic is 8.691.
b. Conduct the χ^2 test described in the case study.
c. Is the p-value of the test you conducted in part b less than or greater than .005? Explain.
d. In the context of the problem, describe the Type I and Type II errors associated with the test of part b.

17.35 A restaurateur who owns restaurants in four cities is considering the possibility of building separate dining rooms for nonsmokers to accommodate customers who wish to dine in a smoke-free environment. Since this would involve significant expense, the restaurateur plans to survey the customers at each restaurant and ask them the following question: "Would you be more comfortable dining here if there were a separate dining room for nonsmokers only?" Suppose seventy-five people were randomly selected and surveyed at each restaurant with the results shown in the table. Is there sufficient evidence to indicate that

		ANSWER TO QUESTION		
		Yes	No	It makes no difference
	1	38	32	5
RESTAURANT	2	42	26	7
	3	35	34	6
	4	37	30	8

customer preferences are different for the four restaurants (i.e., that customer preference and restaurant are dependent)? Use $\alpha = .10$.

17.36 It is commonly assumed that the more experience a job applicant has, the better that person will perform the necessary duties. Other factors, such as whether the person has a college degree or is male or female, also may be indicative of future performance. H. M. Greenberg and J. Greenberg (1980) argue that for sales jobs, the most important factor is the matching of the particular job requirement with an applicant's personal characteristics. This, they claim, will result in better retention of employees and produce higher levels of job performance. To validate this claim they studied two groups of recently hired sales personnel. In the first group, which numbered 1,980, all were job-matched; the 3,961 members of the second group were not. After 6 months they were evaluated, and the aggregate data are shown in the table, where 1 represents the highest level of performance and 4 represents the lowest. The tabulated values are the percentages of total sales personnel contained in the respective samples.

	PERFORMANCE					TOTALS
	1	*2*	*3*	*4*	*Quit or fired*	
JOB-MATCHED	9%	40%	32%	14%	5%	100%
NOT JOB-MATCHED	2%	17%	25%	31%	25%	100%

a. Use both the percentages given in the table and the sample sizes to construct a contingency table that shows the numbers of sales personnel falling in each category of the table.

b. Do the data provide sufficient evidence to indicate that the proportions of sales personnel falling in the performance categories depend on whether the people are job-matched? Test using $\alpha = .05$.

c. Do the data provide sufficient evidence to indicate that the proportion of sales personnel receiving the highest rating (1) is larger if job-matched than if not? Test using $\alpha = .05$. [*Note:* This will require a one-sided test.]

17.37 An economist wanted to determine whether there is a relationship between a person's income and his or her political affiliation. The economist randomly sampled 265 registered voters and determined the income and political affiliation of each. A summary of the data is shown in the table. Do the data provide sufficient evidence to indicate a relationship between political affiliation and annual income? Test using $\alpha = .10$.

	ANNUAL INCOME ($ THOUSAND)			
	20 or over	*14 < 20*	*8 < 14*	*Below 8*
REPUBLICAN	50	28	20	12
DEMOCRAT	14	35	35	41
OTHER	6	7	10	7

17.38 Despite a good winning percentage, a certain major league baseball team has not drawn as many fans as one would expect. In hopes of finding ways to increase attendance, management plans to interview fans who come to the games to find out why they come. One thing management might want to know is whether there are differences in support for the team among various age groups. Suppose the information in the table was collected during interviews with fans selected at random. Can you conclude that there is a relationship between age and number of games attended per year? Use $\alpha = .05$.

	NUMBER OF GAMES ATTENDED PER YEAR		
	1 or 2	3–5	Over 5
Under 20	78	107	17
AGE OF FAN 21–30	147	87	13
31–40	129	86	19
41–55	55	103	40
Over 55	23	74	22

17.39 If a company can identify times of day when accidents are most likely to occur, extra precautions can be instituted during those times. A random sampling of the accident report records over the last year at a plant gives the frequency of occurrence of accidents during the different hours of the workday. Can it be concluded from the data in the table that the proportions of accidents are different for the four time periods?

HOURS	1–2	3–4	5–6	7–8
NUMBER OF ACCIDENTS	31	28	45	47

SHIFT	NUMBER OF DEFECTIVES PRODUCED
First	25
Second	35
Third	80

17.40 *Product* or *service quality* is generally defined as fitness for use. This means the product or service meets the customer's needs. Generally speaking, fitness for use is based on five quality characteristics: technological (e.g., strength, hardness), psychological (taste, beauty), time-oriented (reliability), contractual (guarantee provisions), and ethical (courtesy, honesty). The quality of a service may involve all these characteristics, while the quality of a manufactured product generally depends on technological and time-oriented characteristics (Schroeder, 1981). Following a barrage of customer complaints about the quality of its product, a manufacturer of gasoline filters for automobiles had its quality inspectors sample 600 filters — 200 for each work shift — and check them for defects. The data in the table resulted.

a. Do the data indicate that the quality of the filters being produced may be related to the shift producing the filter? Test using $\alpha = .05$.

b. Estimate the proportion of defective filters produced by the first shift. Use a 95% confidence interval.

17.41 A national survey was conducted to determine the general public's view of the federal government's involvement in the regulation of private enterprise. Two hundred people from each of three income levels were asked if they thought the government was too involved, not involved enough, or involved just enough. A summary of their responses is shown in the table. Do the data provide sufficient information to indicate a relationship between income and view on government regulation of private enterprise? Test using $\alpha = .05$.

		INVOLVEMENT			TOTALS
		Too little	Just enough	Too much	
	Low	125	48	27	200
INCOME	Medium	103	58	39	200
	High	72	69	59	200
TOTALS		300	175	125	600

17.42 An appliance store is having a sale and wants to determine which modes of advertising are effective. A random sample of customers who learned about the sale indicated their source of information. A summary of the responses is given below:

Television: 53   Radio: 32   Newspaper: 36   Word of mouth: 48

Is there evidence that the proportions of customers who learned about the sale differ for the four modes of advertising? Use $\alpha = .05$.

17.43 Refer to Exercise 17.42. Estimate the proportion who learn about the sale by word of mouth. Use a 90% confidence interval.

17.44 Suppose an industrial security firm wants to conduct a study of criminal cases involving stolen company money in which employees have been found guilty. Among the data they record are the employee's salary (wages) and the amount of money stolen from the company for 400 recent cases. Does this information provide evidence of a relationship between employee income and amount stolen? Use $\alpha = .05$.

		AMOUNT STOLEN ($)			
		Under 5,000	5,000–9,999	10,000–19,999	20,000 or more
INCOME OF EMPLOYEE ($ THOUSAND)	Under 15	46	39	17	5
	15–25	78	79	61	19
	Over 25	5	14	25	12

17.45 A local bank plans to offer a special service to its young customers. To determine their economic interests, a survey of 100 people under 30 years of age is conducted. Each person is asked to identify his or her top two financial priorities from the six choices shown in the table. Use the χ^2 test to determine whether the proportions of responses differ for the six pairs of priorities. Test at $\alpha = .10$.

FIRST PRIORITY	SECOND PRIORITY	NUMBER OF RESPONSES
Buy a car	Go on a trip	15
Car	Save money	14
Save	Car	22
Save	Trip	23
Trip	Car	10
Trip	Save	16

17.46 A corporation owns several convenience stores that are open 24 hours a day. It is interested in knowing whether there is a relationship between the time of day and the size of purchase. One of its stores is selected at random to be involved in a study. Store records are collected over a period of several weeks and then 300 purchases are randomly selected. Since the register also prints the time of the purchase, this random selection procedure yields both amount and time of purchase. The information is summarized in the table. Is there a relationship between time and size of purchase? Use $\alpha = .05$.

		SIZE OF PURCHASE		
		$2 or less	$2.01–$7	Over $7
	8 A.M.–3:59 P.M.	65	38	14
TIME OF PURCHASE	4 P.M.–11:59 P.M.	61	49	10
	12 midnight–7:59 A.M.	29	27	7

17.47 Refer to Exercise 17.46. Use a 90% confidence interval to estimate the difference between the proportions of customers who spend $2 or less for the periods 8 A.M.–3:59 P.M. and 12 midnight–7:59 A.M.

17.48 Five candidates have just entered the race for mayor of a large city. To determine whether any of the candidates has an early lead in popularity, 2,000 voters were polled and each was asked to indicate the candidate he or she preferred. A summary of their responses is shown in the table.

CANDIDATE	I	II	III	IV	V
VOTERS WHO PREFER CANDIDATE	385	493	628	235	259

a. Do the data provide sufficient evidence to indicate a difference in preference for the five candidates? Test using $\alpha = .01$.

b. Find the approximate observed significance level for the test in part a.

17.49 A city has three television stations. Each station has its own evening news program from 6:00 to 6:30 P.M. every weekday. An advertising firm wants to know whether there is an unequal breakdown of the evening news audience among the three stations. One hundred people are selected at random from those who watch the evening news on one of these three stations. Each is asked to specify which news program he or she watches. Do the results in the table provide sufficient evidence to indicate that the three stations do not have equal shares of the evening news audience? Use $\alpha = .05$.

STATION	1	2	3
NUMBER OF VIEWERS	35	43	22

17.50 Several life insurance firms have policies geared to college students. To get more information about this group, a major insurance firm interviewed college students to find out the type of life insurance they preferred, if any. The table shown at the top of the next page was produced after surveying 1,600 students.

	PREFERRED A TERM POLICY	PREFERRED A WHOLE-LIFE POLICY	NO PREFERENCE
FEMALES	116	27	676
MALES	215	33	533

a. Is there evidence that the life insurance preference of students depends on their sex?

b. Find the approximate observed significance level for the test in part a.

17.51 Refer to Exercise 17.50. Estimate the difference in the proportions of female and male college students who have no preference about life insurance.

17.52 A statistical analysis is to be done on a set of data consisting of 1,000 monthly salaries. The analysis requires the assumption that the sample was drawn from a normal distribution. A preliminary test, called the χ^2 *goodness of fit test,* can be used to help determine whether it is reasonable to assume that the sample is from a normal distribution. Suppose the mean and standard deviation of the 1,000 salaries are hypothesized to be $900 and $50, respectively. Using the standard normal table, we can approximate the probability of a salary being in the intervals listed in the table. The third column represents the expected number of the 1,000 salaries to be found in each interval if the sample was drawn from a normal distribution with $\mu = 900$ and $\sigma = 50$. Suppose the last column contains the actual observed frequencies in the sample. Large differences between the observed and expected frequencies cast doubt on the normality assumption.

INTERVAL	PROBABILITY	EXPECTED FREQUENCY	OBSERVED FREQUENCY
Less than $800	.023	23	26
$800 < $850	.136	136	146
$850 < $900	.341	341	361
$900 < $950	.341	341	311
$950 < $1,000	.136	136	143
$1,000 or above	.023	23	13

a. Compute the X^2 statistic based on the observed and expected frequencies — just as you did in Section 17.1.

b. Find the tabulated χ^2 value when $\alpha = .05$ and there are 5 df (there are $k - 1 = 5$ df associated with this X^2 statistic).

c. Based on the X^2 statistic and the tabulated χ^2 value, is there evidence that the salary distribution is nonnormal?*

d. Find the approximate observed significance level for the test in part c.

17.53 Suppose a random variable is hypothesized to be normally distributed with mean 0 and standard deviation 1. A random sample of 200 observations on the variable yields

---

* If we want to test the null hypothesis that a population's relative frequency distribution is normal with unspecified mean and variance, we will need to estimate μ and σ in order to estimate the k cell probabilities. We lose 2 df corresponding to these estimates, so that the χ^2 rejection region will be based on $(k - 3)$ df.

frequencies in the listed intervals as shown in the table. Do the data provide sufficient evidence to contradict the hypothesis that x is normally distributed with $\mu = 0$ and $\sigma = 1$? Use the technique developed in Exercise 17.52.

INTERVAL	$x < -2$	$-2 \le x < -1$	$-1 \le x < 0$	$0 \le x < 1$	$1 \le x < 2$	$x \ge 2$
FREQUENCY	7	20	61	77	26	9

17.54 Refer to Exercise 9.86. Use contingency table analysis to test the hypothesis of interest to Dornoff and Tankersley. Use $\alpha = .01$. List the assumptions you made in conducting your hypothesis test, and comment on their appropriateness.

On Your Own . . .

Market researchers rely on surveys to estimate the proportions of the consumer market that prefer various brands of a product. Choose a product with which you are familiar, and *guesstimate* the proportion of consumers you think favor the major brands of the product. (Choose a product for which there are at least three major brands sold in the same store.)

Now go to a store that carries these brands, and observe how many consumers purchase each brand. Be sure to observe long enough so that at least five (and preferably at least ten) purchases of each brand have been made. Also, quit sampling after a predetermined length of time or after a predetermined number of total purchases, rather than at some arbitrary time, which could bias your results.

Use the count data to test the null hypothesis that the true proportions of consumers who favor each brand equal your presampling guesstimates of the proportions. Would failure to reject this null hypothesis imply that your guesstimates are correct?

References   Conover, W. J. *Practical nonparametric statistics*. New York: Wiley, 1971.

Dahlin, C., & Owen, F. *An analysis of data collected at the I-494 weighing-in-motion site.* St. Paul: Minnesota Department of Transportation, 1984.

Greenberg, H. M., & Greenberg, J. "Job-matching for better sales performance." *Harvard Business Review,* Sept. – Oct. 1980.

Hollander, M., & Wolfe, D. A. *Nonparametric statistical methods*. New York: Wiley, 1973.

Kahalas, H. "The relationship between confidence in business and job satisfaction for union and nonunion members." *Baylor Business Studies,* Feb. – Apr. 1981, *127,* 45 – 53.

Kaufman, L., & Wolf, J. "Hotel room interviewing — Anxiety and suspicion." *Sloan Management Review,* Spring 1982, *23,* 57 – 64.

McDaniel, S. W., & Rao, C. P. "Consumer attitudes toward and satisfaction with warranties and warranty performance — Before and after Magnuson – Moss." *Baylor Business Studies,* Nov. – Dec. 1982, *130,* 47 – 61.

McKenzie, J. "The accuracy of telephone call data collected by diary methods." *Journal of Marketing Research,* Nov. 1983, *20,* 417 – 427.

Neter, J., Wasserman, W., & Whitmore, G. A. *Applied statistics*. 2d ed. Boston: Allyn & Bacon, 1982. Chapter 17.

Page, A. L., Trombetta, W. L., Werner, C., & Kulifay, M. "Identifying successful versus unsuccessful loans held by the minority small business clients of an OMBE affiliate." *Journal of Business Research,* June 1977, *5,* 139–153.

Schroeder, R. G. *Operations management.* New York: McGraw-Hill, 1981. Chapter 19.

Sheets, T., Radlinski, A., Kohne, J., & Brunner, G. A. "Deceived respondents: Once bitten, twice shy." *Public Opinion Quarterly,* 1974, *18,* 261–263.

Siegel, S. *Nonparametric statistics for the behavioral sciences.* New York: McGraw-Hill, 1956. Chapter 9.

Sudman, S., & Ferber, R. "A comparison of alternative procedures for collecting consumer expenditure data for frequently purchased products." *Journal of Marketing Research,* May 1974, *11,* 128–135.

Sudman, S., & Ferber, R. "Experiments in obtaining consumer expenditures by diary methods." *Journal of the American Statistical Association,* Dec. 1971, *66,* 725–735.

Tashakori, A., & Boulton, W. "A look at the board's role in planning." *Journal of Business Strategy,* Winter 1983, *3,* 64–70.

Winkler, R. L., & Hays, W. L. *Statistics: Probability, inference and decision.* 2d ed. New York: Holt, Rinehart and Winston, 1975. Chapter 12.

CHAPTER 18

Decision Analysis Using Prior Information

Where We've Been . . .

In previous chapters we used a decision procedure to test hypotheses about population parameters. Using sample information, we decided to reject or accept the null hypothesis based on the calculated probabilities of making incorrect decisions — namely, the probability (α) of rejecting the null hypothesis if it was in fact true, and the probability (β) of accepting the null hypothesis if it was actually false. In this simplistic process, we assumed that a manager would be able to assess the gains or losses associated with each type of error and choose a test with acceptable values of α and β.

Where We're Going . . .

In Chapters 18 and 19, we present the basic concepts of a general theory for making decisions that explicitly accounts for the gains or losses associated with alternative decisions and the probabilities of the occurrence of these gains or losses. Chapter 18 is concerned with how to handle decision problems using only information that is currently available about the problem. In Chapter 19, we extend the analysis to include the case in which additional information can be obtained by sampling.

Contents

Suppose you have been given the responsibility of determining whether your firm should expand its sales region to include the southwestern part of the United States. Before making your decision, you would probably want answers to many questions. How large would the yearly demand for the product be? How many salespeople would be assigned to the new territory? How much and what types of advertising would be used? Are adequate warehousing facilities available? Who would the company's principal competitors be, and how would they react to new competition? Even if it were possible to obtain accurate answers *(perfect information)* to these and other pertinent questions, your decision problem would be extremely complex. Realistically, however, you cannot expect to receive perfect information. Thus, in making your decision, you will face the more complex problem of having to deal with answers about which you are uncertain.

How would you tackle such a decision problem? The most natural first step — and one that is used by most decision analysts — is to reduce the problem to a manageable size by considering only questions that bear significantly on the objective of your decision. In this case, your objective may be to increase corporate profit. It may turn out that the profitability of the decision to expand the sales region depends primarily on the extent of the demand for the product in the new territory during the first year after it has been introduced. However, since this demand is unknown, even with this simplified decision problem, you still must make your decision in the face of uncertainty. Given your uncertainty about the demand, how much information about demand in the new region would you want prior to making your decision, and how would you process such information? Answers to these questions are provided by the methodology referred to as *decision analysis,* which is the subject of this chapter and Chapter 19.

Decision analysis is a systematic approach to solving decision problems optimally under conditions of uncertainty. It *does not describe how or why* an individual makes a decision; rather, it *prescribes* a decision for the individual that is *consistent with his or her preferences and attitudes toward risk.* You might be asking yourself: "Why do I need to study decision-making as though it were a science, when I know most decisions (business or otherwise) are made on an intuitive level?" The answer is fourfold:

1. Yes, the vast majority of decisions made in business do not require, and are made without, formal analysis. But for that one crucial decision upon which "everything depends," it is very helpful to have a systematic, logical decision procedure to follow.

2. Most of us have had little experience intuitively processing the probabilistic and sample information that may confront us in a complex decision-making problem. Consequently, it is frequently more profitable to rely on the mechanically generated information of decision analysis to guide decision-making than on the less reliable information-processing capabilities of our intuition.

3. To use decision analysis, we are forced to consider carefully and logically all possible courses of action and the outcomes that could result from each. By so doing, we may see a side of the problem not seen before, or we may even discover that we have been addressing the wrong problem. Thus, the information obtained from decision analysis may more than compensate for the effort expended in the analysis.

4. Another reason business and economics majors should study decision analysis is that

many firms and government agencies use it on a regular basis. Consequently, you may very well be required to use decision analysis in your future employment.

One of the alternatives we face in making a decision is whether the decision should be made *now* — utilizing information we currently possess about the problem (we will refer to this as *prior information*) — or *postponed* until we have gathered additional information. In this chapter we study decision-making under uncertainty and assume that only prior information is available. In the next chapter, we will expand our study of decision-making to include situations in which additional information is available. We will discuss how to determine the value of additional information as well as when and how to use additional information in decision-making.

18.1 Three Types of Decision Problems

Although all decision problems involve the selection of a course of action from among two or more alternatives, we can classify them into one of three categories:

1. Decision-making under certainty
2. Decision-making under uncertainty
3. Decision-making under conflict

Decision-making under certainty entails the selection of a course of action when we *know* the result each alternative action will yield. If the number of alternatives being considered is small, such decisions may be easy to make. However, if the number of alternatives is large, the optimal decision may be difficult — if not impossible — to obtain. It may take too much time and/or be too costly to evaluate all the many alternatives individually and select the one with the most favorable results. Decision problems of this type are not addressed in this text, but here is a simple example of this type of problem:

> A furniture company constructs and finishes tables and chairs. Each table produced by the company nets a profit of $100 and each chair a profit of $60. During 1 week the company has 305 work-hours available for assembly operations and 355 work-hours available for finishing. From past experience it is known that each chair requires 3 hours to be assembled and $1\frac{1}{2}$ hours of finishing, while each table requires 4 hours for assembly and 2 hours for finishing. How many tables and how many chairs should the company produce over the week in order to maximize profits?

Note that a unique solution to this problem exists that will maximize the firm's profit. Many problems involving decision-making under certainty, including this one, are solved using a technique known as *linear programming.*

Decision-making under uncertainty* entails the selection of a course of action when we do *not know* with certainty the results that each alternative action will yield. Furthermore, we assume that the outcome of whatever course of action we select is affected only by chance and not by an opponent or competitor. We discuss decision-making under uncertainty in detail in this chapter and Chapter 19. Our introductory example concerning the decision of

---

* Some texts distinguish between "decision-making under risk" and "decision-making under uncertainty" according to whether probabilities are available to describe the degree of uncertainty confronted by the decision-maker. We make no such distinction.

whether to expand the sales region to the southwestern United States demonstrates decision-making under uncertainty.

Decision-making under conflict is similar to decision-making under uncertainty in that we do not know with certainty the result each available alternative course of action will yield. However, the reason for this uncertainty is different in the case of decision-making under conflict. In such cases, we are in effect "playing against" one or more opponents or competitors. The outcome of our chosen course of action depends on decisions made by our competitors. Decision problems of this type fall under the discipline known as *game theory*. Game theory is not discussed in this text; however, an example of this type of decision problem follows:

> A local businessman is interested in purchasing real estate somewhere in the Dallas area for the purpose of building a fast-food restaurant. He has narrowed his alternatives to five suburban neighborhoods. He is certain his venture will be profitable as long as none of the major fast-food chains decides to locate near his restaurant. Thus, the businessman's decision problem involves choosing a parcel of land while knowing that the results of his decision depend on the expansion plans of his potential competitors in the fast-food industry. Furthermore, the location decision facing other fast-food chains interested in the Dallas area depends to some extent on the decision of the Dallas businessman. They, too, would prefer not to locate near another restaurant of the same type.

Since our objective throughout this text has been to make inferences when we have only partial (or *imperfect*) information, we concentrate on decision-making under uncertainty in the remaining sections.

Exercises 18.1 – 18.4

Applying the Concepts

18.1 Compare and contrast decision-making under certainty, uncertainty, and conflict.

18.2 Describe two decision problems that you face every day. Categorize each as being a problem requiring a decision made under certainty, uncertainty, or conflict. Justify your categorization.

18.3 Categorize the following decision problems as decision-making under certainty, uncertainty, or conflict. Justify your categorization.

a. The management of a bank is considering an application for a commercial loan. If they decide to make the loan but the customer defaults, the bank will lose the amount of the loan plus the lost profits. On the other hand, if the bank fails to grant the loan and the customer would have repaid it, the bank will lose the interest on the loan.

b. A manufacturer is currently facing a decision about the price for an electric lawn mower it makes. If the company sets the price too high, potential customers will purchase competitors' mowers. If, on the other hand, the price is set too low, the competitors will also drop their prices, thereby reducing everyone's profits.

c. A computer hardware company has two contracts for producing electronic components for the space program. Since the contracts are for a fixed number of components at a fixed price, the decision problem involves how to allocate fixed production resources to maximize profit.

18.4 Categorize the following decision problems as decision-making under certainty, uncertainty, or conflict. Justify your categorization.

a. A plant manager wants to replace an obsolete piece of machinery with a new model. There are two brands on the market from which to choose. Both brands are of equal quality, have the same guarantee, and produce the same number of items per hour. However, brand B is $500 cheaper than brand A.

b. A company is faced with the decision of whether or not to increase its production capacity by adding a new building to the existing facilities. If the company decides not to expand, they expect to make a profit of $550,000 for each of the next 3 years regardless of the state of the economy. If they build the addition and the economy continues to expand, the addition is expected to increase company profits to at least $650,000 a year for the next 3 years. If they build the addition and the economy remains stable or experiences a downward trend over the next 3 years, the company would incur a reduction in profits to $475,000 or less per year for the next 3 years.

18.2
Decision-Making Under Uncertainty: Basic Concepts

We will use the following example to introduce some basic concepts: A profit-motivated entrepreneur is committed to producing a concert that will feature a current rock star sometime during the latter part of June next year. The promoter has been unable to finalize plans, however, due to indecision over whether to take a chance on rain and hold the concert in Memorial Stadium (40,000 seats outdoors) or play it safe and hold the concert in the Civic Center (15,000 seats indoors). A sellout is expected at least a month in advance, whichever facility is chosen. If the stadium is chosen and the weather cooperates, the promoter will make a net profit of about $350,000 (ticket proceeds less costs, taxes, and other expenses). If it is raining at concert time, the rock star may choose not to perform (according to the contract) and the promoter will lose about $40,000 (stadium rental, commitment to the rock star, administrative costs, salaries of security personnel, advertising). However, if the Civic Center is chosen, the entrepreneur would make a net profit of about $150,000 regardless of the weather. Which option would you choose? We will use decision analysis to make our selection later in the chapter.

We can identify three specific elements of this decision problem: First, a choice must be made between two possible courses of action — rent the stadium or rent the Civic Center. We refer to these alternatives as **actions.** Second, it is uncertain which event will occur — Rain or No rain. We refer to these events as **states of nature.** Third, depending on which action is chosen and which state of nature occurs on the evening of the concert, the decision-maker* will receive either a financial reward or a penalty for the chosen action. The consequences of the decision problem are referred to as **outcomes;** these may be either positive or negative. For example, if the action chosen by the promoter is Rent the stadium and the state of nature that occurs is Rain, the outcome that results is — $40,000. That is, the action/state of nature combination Rent the stadium/Rain will *cost* the promoter $40,000. The

---

* The term *decision-maker* is used to refer not only to an individual, but also to a corporation, a community, or in general, any entity faced with a decision problem.

combination Rent the stadium/No rain will yield a *profit* of $350,000. The reward (or penalty) corresponding to each action/state of nature combination is called the ***outcome*** or ***payoff***.

We can conveniently summarize all three elements of a decision problem in a ***payoff table*** (Table 18.1). Each of the set of possible actions the decision-maker has chosen to consider is associated with a row of the *payoff table*. Each state of nature is associated with a column. The numbers in the table are the outcomes of the decision problem. For example, $350,000 is the outcome that would result from the implementation of the action associated with the top row of the table (Rent stadium) and the occurrence of the state of nature associated with the right-hand column of the table (No rain).

Table 18.1

Payoff Table for the Rock Concert Decision Problem

| | | STATE OF NATURE | |
		Rain	No rain
ACTION	Rent stadium	−$40,000	$350,000
	Rent Civic Center	$150,000	$150,000

A decision problem can also be illustrated by a ***decision tree***. A payoff table and a decision tree may display the same information, but as we will see in the next chapter, it is sometimes more convenient to use a decision tree. The decision tree in Figure 18.1 corresponds to Table 18.1. Conceptually, the promoter's movement through time toward the outcome of the decision problem is represented by movement from left to right through the decision tree. The ■ denotes a ***decision fork*** and signals that a decision must be made. At this position on the tree, the decision-maker must choose between the two actions, Rent stadium and Rent Civic Center. If Rent stadium is chosen, then from the decision fork we move along the upper branch of the tree. The ● denotes a ***chance fork*** and signals that the next branch of the tree the promoter will follow will be determined by the chance occurrence of a state of nature. If the decision-maker is positioned at the upper chance fork of Figure 18.1 and it rains on the day of the concert, then the upper branch of the chance fork (labeled Rain) will lead the promoter to the consequence (−$40,000) of the action/state combination Rent stadium/Rain.

Both the selection of actions to be considered in a decision problem and the choice of an action to implement are under the control of the decision-maker, but the state of nature is not.

Figure 18.1   Decision Tree for the Rock Concert Decision Problem

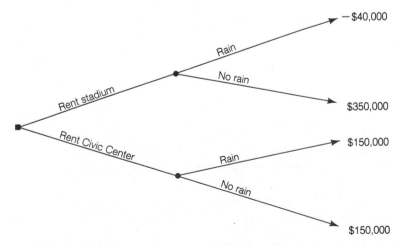

The decision-maker must choose a course of action *prior* to knowing which state of nature will occur and *without* being able to influence the random process generating the states of nature. *Note also that the states of nature considered in any decision problem must be mutually exclusive and collectively exhaustive.* That is, the state of nature that occurs must be clearly identifiable as one and only one of the listed states, and the list of states considered must include all possible states that can occur. The former constraint precludes any overlapping of, or vagueness in, state definitions; the latter precludes the possibility of any state occurrence not anticipated by the decision-maker. For practical purposes, the states of nature in the above example are mutually exclusive and collectively exhaustive. They are mutually exclusive because the weather on a June evening can be classified as either rainy or not rainy, but not both. They are collectively exhaustive because the list of possible weather patterns can be narrowed to include only rainy or not rainy.

All outcomes in a decision problem should be stated in terms of the same numerical quantity, and that quantity should be chosen to rank the outcomes relative to the decision-maker's overall objective. We refer to this measure of the outcomes of a decision problem as the *objective variable.* In the preceding example, the promoter's motive — or objective — for producing the rock concert was net profit. Accordingly, the decision outcomes are expressed in terms of net profit (dollars). If the objective had been to give as many people as possible an opportunity to see a live performance by the rock star, we would measure the outcomes of potential actions in terms of the number of people attending the concert.

We conclude by summarizing the concept of decision-making under uncertainty, the four elements common to this type of decision problem, and the methods for displaying these elements.

Decision-Making Under Uncertainty

If a decision-maker is faced with choosing one action from among two or more alternative actions, and each of these has possible outcomes that depend on the chance occurrence of one of a set of mutually exclusive and collectively exhaustive states of nature, the decision-maker is said to be faced with *decision-making under uncertainty.*

Four Elements Common to Decision Problems Involving Uncertainty

1. *Actions:* The set of two or more alternatives the decision-maker has chosen to consider. The decision-maker's problem is to choose one action from this set.
2. *States of nature:* The set of two or more mutually exclusive and collectively exhaustive chance events upon which the outcome of the decision-maker's chosen action depends.
3. *Outcomes:* The set of consequences resulting from all possible action/state of nature combinations.
4. *Objective variable:* The quantity used to measure and express the outcomes of a decision problem.

Table 18.2 and Figure 18.2 depict the general format for the payoff table and the decision tree, respectively. If the ith action is denoted by a_i and the jth state of nature by S_j, then the outcome resulting from the combination of the ith action with the jth state of nature is O_{ij}.

Table 18.2

General Form of a Payoff Table

		STATE OF NATURE			
		S_1	S_2	$\cdots$	S_m
	a_1	O_{11}	O_{12}	$\cdots$	O_{1m}
	a_2	O_{21}	O_{22}	$\cdots$	O_{2m}
ACTION	.	.	.		.
	.	.	.		.
	a_n	O_{n1}	O_{n2}	$\cdots$	O_{nm}

Figure 18.2   General Form of a Decision Tree

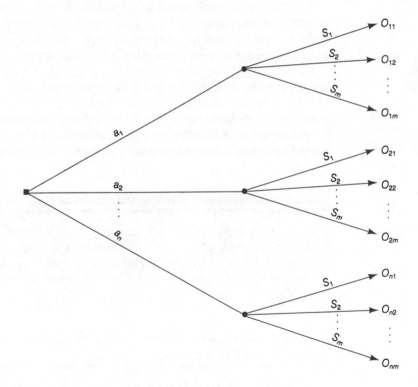

Exercises 18.5 – 18.10

Applying the Concepts

18.5 List and define the four primary elements of a decision problem under uncertainty.

18.6 The states of nature that are defined in a decision problem must be mutually exclusive and collectively exhaustive. In this context, what is meant by the phrase *mutually exclusive and collectively exhaustive*?

18.7 Describe a decision you make every day that is done in the face of uncertainty. Identify the actions and states of nature of your decision problem. Construct a decision tree to illustrate your decision problem.

18.8 For each of these decision problems, identify the actions, states of nature, outcomes, and objective variable:

a. A winery is considering introducing a new low-cost dinner wine. The introduction of the wine will cost $3 million in promotional and fixed costs per year. Each bottle sold will contribute $0.30 to profits. The management believes that sales could range from 5 to 25 million bottles per year.

b. An administrator in the Environmental Protection Agency is trying to determine how much to fine companies that discharge a particular type of effluent into the waterways of the United States. If the fine is set too low, all companies will simply pay the fine because it will be less costly than installing pollution-control equipment. On the other hand, if the fine is set too high, small companies may be driven out of business because they cannot afford the capital expenditures necessary to meet the new EPA standards. Thus, the problem of the EPA administrator is to set the fine to minimize the total social cost — that is, the cost to society of (1) firms being driven out of business and (2) waterways being polluted.

18.9 Refer to part b of Exercise 18.4, in which a company was faced with the decision of whether to increase its production capacity. For this decision problem, identify the actions, states of nature, outcomes, and the objective variable.

18.10 A company that manufactures a well-known line of designer jeans is contemplating whether to increase its advertising budget by $1 million for next year. If the expanded advertising campaign is successful, the company expects sales to increase by $1.6 million next year. If the advertising campaign fails, the company expects sales to increase by only $400,000 next year. If the company decides not to increase its advertising expenditures, it expects sales to increase by $200,000 next year.

a. Identify the actions, states of nature, outcomes, and the objective variable for this decision problem.

b. Construct a decision tree that illustrates the jeans manufacturer's decision problem.

18.3
Two Ways of Expressing Outcomes: Payoffs and Opportunity Losses

The outcomes of the rock concert example discussed in the previous section were in terms of the net profit that would be realized by the promoter depending on the decision (action) concerning the location of the concert and on the weather (state of nature) on the day of the concert. That is, net profit was the objective variable. Recall that the objective variable can assume both positive and negative values. In general, we refer to outcomes that reflect the *actual* reward to the decision-maker in terms of the objective variable as *payoffs.*

Alternatively, outcomes can be expressed in terms of *opportunities* for higher profits that the decision-maker has *lost* as a result of the action selected. For example, in the rock concert example, if the weather is not rainy, a decision to hold the concert in the Civic Center will bring in a profit of $150,000 and a decision to use the stadium will bring in a profit of $350,000. If, in fact, the Civic Center was chosen, then by not choosing to rent the stadium, the promoter will have *lost the opportunity* to net an additional $200,000. We refer to this $200,000 as the *opportunity loss** associated with the action/state combination Rent Civic Center/No rain. An opportunity loss may be determined in a similar fashion for each action/state combination of a decision problem, and an *opportunity loss table* may be constructed, as in Table 18.3. Notice that none of the opportunity losses of Table 18.3 is less than 0. A little thought should convince you that this is true in general for any opportunity loss. In Section 18.5, we will show that decision problems may be solved using outcomes expressed either as payoffs or as opportunity losses.

Table 18.3

Opportunity Loss Table for the Rock Concert Decision Problem

| | | STATE OF NATURE | |
		Rain	No rain
ACTION	Rent stadium	$190,000	0
	Rent Civic Center	0	$200,000

Definition 18.1

The *opportunity loss* is the difference between the payoff a decision-maker receives for a chosen action and the maximum that the decision-maker could have received for choosing the action yielding the highest payoff for the state of nature that occurred.

Opportunity Loss Determination

Repeat the following procedure for each state of nature in a decision problem — i.e., each column of a payoff table:

1. Find the maximum payoff in a column. The opportunity loss associated with this payoff is 0.
2. The opportunity loss associated with any other payoff in this column is found by subtracting that payoff from the maximum payoff in the column.

Example 18.1

A beer producer with breweries located in the western part of the United States and a distribution network that extends only as far east as the Mississippi River is considering expanding its sales region to include the northeastern part of the country. To do so, the producer must build a new brewery in the Northeast in order to overcome refrigeration problems that would arise from having to transport its beer. The problem is to determine how large a brewery to construct. It has been decided that the size should be based on the projected gross profits (profit before taxes) for the fifth year of operation for each of the four sizes of breweries under consideration. The firm's marketing department recognizes that the company cannot possibly obtain more than a 15% market share during the fifth year of operation and has put together a payoff table for the firm's planning committee (Table 18.4). Find the corresponding opportunity loss table.

* Sometimes called the *regret*.

Table 18.4

Payoff Table for the
Brewer's Decision Problem

		STATE OF NATURE Market share during fifth year of operation		
	Brewery size	S_1: 0% < 5%	S_2: 5% < 10%	S_3: 10%–15%
ACTION	a_1: Small	$300,000	$350,000	$450,000
	a_2: Medium	$250,000	$700,000	$800,000
	a_3: Large	$200,000	$600,000	$1,000,000
	a_4: Very large	−$100,000	$100,000	$500,000

Solution For each column of the payoff table (Table 18.4) find the maximum payoff:

Column 1   Column 2   Column 3

Maximum payoff: $300,000 $700,000 $1,000,000

The opportunity loss associated with each column maximum is 0. The opportunity loss associated with, for example, any other payoff in column 1 is found by subtracting that payoff from the column's maximum payoff, $300,000, as shown in Table 18.5. The resulting opportunity loss table is shown in Table 18.6.

Table 18.5   Calculation of Opportunity Losses for Example 18.1

		STATE OF NATURE		
	Brewery size	S_1: 0% < 5%	S_2: 5% < 10%	S_3: 10%–15%
ACTION	a_1: Small	0	$700,000 − $350,000 = $350,000	$1,000,000 − $450,000 = $550,000
	a_2: Medium	$300,000 − $250,000 = $50,000	0	$1,000,000 − $800,000 = $200,000
	a_3: Large	$300,000 − $200,000 = $100,000	$700,000 − $600,000 = $100,000	0
	a_4: Very large	$300,000 − (−$100,000) = $400,000	$700,000 − $100,000 = $600,000	$1,000,000 − $500,000 = $500,000

Table 18.6

Opportunity Loss Table for
the Brewer's Decision
Problem

		STATE OF NATURE Market share during fifth year of operation		
	Brewery size	S_1: 0% < 5%	S_2: 5% < 10%	S_3: 10%–15%
ACTION	a_1: Small	0	$350,000	$550,000
	a_2: Medium	$50,000	0	$200,000
	a_3: Large	$100,000	$100,000	0
	a_4: Very large	$400,000	$600,000	$500,000

After formulating and displaying a decision problem as just described, it may happen that an action has been included that should never be selected *no matter which state of nature occurs*. In Example 18.1, a_4 is such an action. Inspection of the payoff table (Table 18.4) or the opportunity loss table (Table 18.6) reveals that both actions a_2 and a_3 result in higher payoffs (and lower opportunity losses) than a_4 for each possible state of nature. Thus, a_4 is said to be *dominated* by both actions a_2 and a_3 and should never be chosen by the decision-maker. Accordingly, dominated actions should be dropped from consideration. Because dominated actions should not be admitted for consideration by the decision-maker, they are sometimes referred to as being *inadmissible actions.* We will see later that by eliminating inadmissible actions, we ease the computation burden necessary to solve a decision problem.

Definition 18.2

Action a_i is said to *dominate* action a_j, thereby making a_j *inadmissible,* if each of the following is true:

1. For each state of nature, the payoff for action a_i is greater than or equal to the payoff for a_j.
2. For at least one state of nature, the payoff for action a_i is greater than the payoff for a_j.

The decision-maker should eliminate dominated actions (inadmissible actions) from all decision problems.

To use decision analysis to prescribe a decision in the face of uncertainty, we must characterize our uncertainty concerning the states of nature of the problem with a probability distribution. We discuss the determination of such distributions in the next section.

Exercises
18.11 – 18.22

Learning the Mechanics

18.11 Explain the difference between payoffs and opportunity losses.

18.12 Why should a dominated action be eliminated from a decision problem?

18.13 Eliminate any inadmissible actions from the accompanying payoff table and convert it to an opportunity loss table.

		STATE OF NATURE			
		S_1	S_2	S_3	S_4
	a_1	-60	-5	0	45
ACTION	a_2	-65	-10	40	75
	a_3	-70	-15	40	70
	a_4	-80	-40	-10	80

18.14 Identify any inadmissible actions in the decision tree shown at the top of the next page, and redraw the tree without the inadmissible actions. The objective variable is total sales (in thousands of dollars).

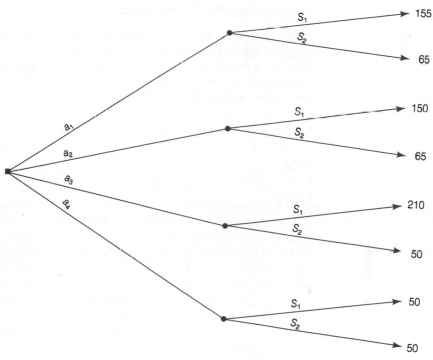

	S_1	S_2	S_3
a_1	15	40	0
a_2	10	10	8
a_3	43	0	15
a_4	20	20	10

18.15 Shown here is an opportunity loss table that has been derived from a payoff table.

a. Which action(s) in the table is (are) inadmissible? Justify your answer.

b. Why is it not possible to convert this opportunity loss table to the original payoff table?

18.16 The outcomes displayed on the decision tree below are in terms of payoffs. Convert the outcomes to opportunity losses.

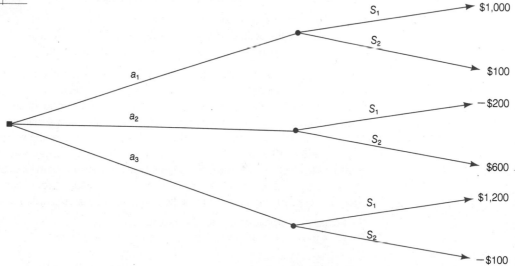

Applying the Concepts

18.17 A U.S. company that manufactures minicomputers is considering marketing its product in Europe. If it decides to do so, the company expects to attain a European market share of no more than 3% and no less than 1% over the next 3 years. The company's accounting department has determined that the payoff for this expansion should be an increase in total company profits for the next 3 years of $3 million if the product is able to attain a 3% market share, an increase of $1 million for a 2% market share, and a decrease of $1 million for a 1% market share. Total domestic profits for the next 3 years are expected to be $15 million regardless of whether or not the minicomputer is marketed in Europe.

a. Formulate the payoff table for this decision problem.
b. Convert the payoff table to an opportunity loss table.

18.18 A common problem in business is the management of perishable inventories — that is, items that lose the major portion of their economic value after a given date due to either obsolescence or spoilage. For example, if a corner newsstand orders too many papers and cannot sell them all, the excess papers have little value. Hence, these types of problems are called *newsboy problems*. Newsboy problems are common in retailing situations such as the following: A buyer for a large department store is trying to decide how many of a new style of dress to order. Because of rapid changes in fashion, she does not want to order too many dresses, but if she orders too few she will lose profits for her department. Each dress purchased will cost the store $30 and will sell for $50. Any dresses not sold at the end of the season will be sold at the annual half-price sale. The buyer believes the department will sell three, four, five, six, seven, or eight dozen dresses. Dresses must be purchased by the department store in lots of one dozen.

a. Formulate the payoff table for this decision problem.
b. Convert the payoff table to an opportunity loss table.

18.19 Refer to Exercise 18.10, in which a company that manufactures designer jeans must decide whether to increase its advertising budget for next year.

a. Formulate the payoff table for this decision problem.
b. Are either of the actions inadmissible? Explain.
c. Draw the decision tree that corresponds to your payoff table.

18.20 The purchasing agent for an automobile manufacturer is concluding a purchase agreement with a supplier of preformed body pieces. The pieces will be purchased in lots of 500, and the cost of a lot is $15,000. The body stamping has a frequent defect called a *burr*. If a piece is found to have a burr, it can be filed off by the automobile manufacturer at a cost of $10 per piece. Past experience with this supplier has shown that the proportion of defects tends to be 5%, 10%, or 50%. The supplier now offers a guarantee that it will assume the costs for all defective body moldings greater than 50 in a production lot of 500. This guarantee may be purchased for a cost of $1,000 before the lot begins production. The purchasing agent is interested in determining whether the guarantee should be purchased.

a. Formulate the payoff table for this problem.
b. Draw the decision tree that corresponds to your payoff table.

18.21 Computer products company A has sued computer products company B for patent infringements. The management of B is deciding whether they should settle the suit out of court. If they do so, the accounting and marketing departments calculate that company B would lose $50 million over the next 5 years in royalty payments. If they go to court and win, they will have $1 million in court costs. However, if they lose the suit, they will have to pay company A $100 million in royalty payments.

a. Formulate the payoff table for this decision problem.

b. Draw the decision tree that corresponds to your payoff table.

18.22 A winery can introduce a new low-cost dinner wine for $3 million in fixed and promotional costs per year. Each bottle sold will contribute $0.30 to profits. The management believes that sales will be 0.5 million, 10 million, 15 million, 20 million, or 25 million bottles per year.

a. Formulate the payoff table for this problem.

b. Construct the opportunity loss table.

18.4 Characterizing the Uncertainty in Decision Problems

In Chapter 4 we explained that probability distributions are used to characterize an individual's uncertainty about the outcomes of an experiment. In a decision problem, the observation of a state of nature associated with the problem may be regarded as an experiment and the various states of nature as experimental outcomes. Thus, it follows that a decision-maker can use a probability distribution to characterize the uncertainties associated with the states of nature that may occur in a decision problem. These probabilities measure the likelihood of the occurrence of the various states of nature and may be unknown. Consequently, we will assess these values using one of the following:

1. Information about the relative frequencies of the states

2. Judgmental (subjective) information about the states

3. A combination of relative frequency information and subjective information

In other words, we use any type of information that is available to assign probabilities to the states of nature.

For example, in the rock concert example of Section 18.2, the concert promoter could use historical weather data (relative frequency data) along with personal knowledge of the rock star's tendency to declare a day too rainy to perform (subjective information) to assess the probabilities of states for the decision problem. Or, if you wanted to decide whether to open your own business next year, you would be interested in knowing whether the economy would continue at a healthy pace for the next 3 years or whether it would fall into a recession. Since the observation of this experiment — observing the health of the economy over the next 3 years — can never be repeated, you must rely on your own experience or the advice of economic experts to assess the probabilities associated with these states of nature.

Caution: Great care must be taken in determining probabilities for the states of nature. Decision analyses based on poorly chosen probabilities may lead to inappropriate actions.

**Case Study
18.1**
Evaluating
Uncertainty in
Research and
Development

Although all management functions must cope with uncertainty, R&D [Research and Development] is generally agreed to be the function involving the largest number and the widest range of uncertainties. Thus, the R&D manager faces huge problems not only in selecting the most promising avenues for R&D effort and expenditure but also in attempting to insure a steady flow of technically successful projects.

In the above quote, Balthasar, Boschi, and Menke (1978) are describing how Sandoz, a Swiss pharmaceutical company, uses subjective probabilities as a basis for its research and development (R&D) planning and decisions. Twice a year a small group of experts is asked to assess the probability of technical success for each of Sandoz's R&D projects. The group of experts includes R&D line managers and other technical experts familiar with particular requirements for a project's success. When the program was begun, these probability assessments were obtained through interviews. Two basic methods of eliciting subjective probabilities were used—a direct method and an indirect method. A *direct method* is one that requires the expert to state the probability, or odds, of a project's success explicitly in numerical terms. An *indirect method* is one in which the expert's responses are not probabilities per se.

One indirect method used by Sandoz in the early stages of the program is the probability wheel. The wheel is a disk divided into two colored sections, one blue and one orange. The relative size of each section is adjustable. In the center of the disk is a pointer that can be spun and will stop in one of the two sections. The expert is asked which event is more likely: (1) the spinner will stop on the orange section, or (2) project A will succeed. If the answer is (1), the wheel is adjusted to decrease the relative size of the orange section. If the answer is (2), the wheel is adjusted to increase the relative size of the orange section. This procedure is repeated until the expert says the two events are equally likely. The relative size of the orange section is the expert's subjective probability of the success of project A.

Initially, all probabilities were elicited indirectly. As individual forecasters became more familiar with the process, probabilities were assigned directly to each project. When all the experts were sufficiently familiar with the technique, interviews were replaced by questionnaires. After individual probability assessments have been obtained from each expert, the entire group meets to discuss their assessments and arrive at one consensus probability for each R&D project. The advantage of the group assessment is that it brings together the opinions of individuals with different experience and information.

The consensus probabilities are then used in making decisions concerning R&D projects. There are many models and techniques for planning and controlling R&D that require input regarding the probability of a project's success. Obtaining subjective probability assessments allows management (as with Sandoz) to use these models as an aid in decision-making.

Sandoz is pleased with the results of using subjective probabilities in managing R&D. By comparing the experts' consensus success probabilities with the actual relative frequency of project successes over time, the researchers found that the probabilistic predictions are reliable estimates of future results. In line with their goal of "a steady flow of technically successful projects," Sandoz has found that decision-making based on subjective probabilities has reduced the variability in their expected success rate for projects in the early stage of development. The R&D managers at Sandoz conclude that explicit subjective probabilities are a useful input to assist in management planning and control in a highly uncertain environment.

18.5
Solving the Decision Problem Using the Expected Payoff Criterion

Now that we have shown you how to structure a decision problem by constructing a payoff table or an opportunity loss table and how to characterize the uncertainty associated with the states of nature in a decision problem, we have to choose a rule for reaching a decision. Numerous rules have been proposed, but the one most commonly used in decision analyses uses a payoff table and chooses the action that produces the *maximum expected payoff.* This is called the *expected payoff criterion.* Equivalently, you could use an opportunity loss table and choose the action that produces the *minimum expected opportunity loss.* This is called the *expected opportunity loss criterion.* It can be shown that both criteria lead to the same solution.

To understand how the expected payoff criterion is used to reach a decision, recall the definition of the expected value of a discrete random variable (Chapter 5). If x is a discrete random variable with probability distribution $p(x)$, then the expected (or mean) value of x is

$$E(x) = \sum_{\text{All } x} x p(x)$$

As we will illustrate, the random variable, x, in a decision problem is the payoff, and the probabilities associated with x are the same as those that describe the likelihood of occurrence of the states of nature.

For example, consider the brewery decision problem, Example 18.1 in Section 18.3. The payoff table is reproduced in Table 18.7. Note that we have eliminated the inadmissible action, a_4: Very large brewery.

Table 18.7
Payoff Table for the Brewery Example

		STATE OF NATURE		
		Market share during fifth year of operation		
	Brewery size	S_1: 0% < 5%	S_2: 5% < 10%	S_3: 10%–15%
	a_1: Small	$300,000	$350,000	$450,000
ACTION	a_2: Medium	$250,000	$700,000	$800,000
	a_3: Large	$200,000	$600,000	$1,000,000

Suppose the brewery had assessed the following probability distribution for the states of nature:

STATE	0% < 5%	5% < 10%	10%–15%
P(State will occur)	.4	.5	.1

Then if you choose action a_1 (see row 1 of Table 18.7), the payoffs can be $300,000, $350,000, or $450,000 with probabilities .4, .5, and .1, respectively. Thus, the probability distribution for the payoff, x, if you choose action a_1, is:

PAYOFF x	$300,000	$350,000	$450,000
$p(x)$	.4	.5	.1

The expected payoff of action a_1, denoted by the symbol $EP(a_1)$, is

$$EP(a_1) = \sum xp(x)$$
$$= (\$300,000)(.4) + (\$350,000)(.5) + (\$450,000)(.1)$$
$$= \$340,000$$

This tells us that, if we were faced with this decision problem a very large number of times and chose action a_1 each time, the mean or expected payoff would be $340,000 — assuming that the probabilities accurately reflect the likelihood of occurrence for the states of nature.

Similarly, we can write the probability distributions and expected payoffs for actions a_2 and a_3. For action a_2:

PAYOFF x	$250,000	$700,000	$800,000
$p(x)$	.4	.5	.1

$$EP(a_2) = \sum xp(x)$$
$$= (\$250,000)(.4) + (\$700,000)(.5) + (\$800,000)(.1)$$
$$= \$530,000$$

For action a_3:

PAYOFF x	$200,000	$600,000	$1,000,000
$p(x)$	.4	.5	.1

$$EP(a_3) = \sum xp(x)$$
$$= (\$200,000)(.4) + (\$600,000)(.5) + (\$1,000,000)(.1)$$
$$= \$480,000$$

Now examine the expected (mean) payoffs for each action, as summarized in Table 18.8. Which action would you choose? We think you would choose action a_2; i.e., you would recommend that the brewer construct a medium-sized brewery, because this strategy will produce the largest expected payoff — namely, $530,000.

Table 18.8

Expected Payoff Table for the Brewer's Decision Problem

ACTION a_i	EXPECTED PAYOFF FOR ACTION a_i $EP(a_i)$
a_1	$340,000
a_2	$530,000
a_3	$480,000

The Expected Payoff Criterion

Choose the action that produces the largest expected payoff.

As noted at the beginning of this section, we will arrive at the same solution to the brewer's decision problem if we use an opportunity loss table, find the expected opportunity loss for each action, and then choose the action that produces the minimum expected opportunity loss. The solution is again action a_2.

The Expected Opportunity Loss Criterion

Choose the action that produces the smallest expected opportunity loss. (This will always lead to the same decision as the expected payoff criterion.)

Example 18.2

A well-known cosmetics firm has been approached by a television producer to determine whether the firm would be interested in sponsoring a new television series next fall. The firm is faced with the choice of one of two actions. It can continue to sponsor a popular television show it has sponsored in the past, or it can shift to the producer's new prime-time show. The states of nature are the projected averages of the biweekly Nielsen ratings for the entire season. A Nielsen rating for a show is the percentage of homes in a sample taken by the A. C. Nielsen Co. that have watched the show for at least 6 minutes during the rating period. The objective variable is the firm's projected market share at the end of the television season next year. According to the expected payoff criterion, which show should the cosmetics firm sponsor? The firm's advertising agency and marketing department have come up with the representation of the firm's decision problem shown in the table.

| | | STATE OF NATURE Projected average Nielsen rating for the new show (probabilities in parentheses) | | | |
		S_1: Below 12 (.1)	S_2: 12–17 (.2)	S_3: 18–29 (.4)	S_4: 30 or more (.3)
ACTION	a_1: Sponsor old show	.12	.12	.12	.12
	a_2: Sponsor new show	.06	.10	.14	.17

Solution

Let x denote the payoff (market share) for a particular action and $p(x)$ its probability distribution. We now compute $E(x) = \sum_{\text{All } x} xp(x)$ for each action and choose the action that produces the larger expected payoff. Thus, for action a_1:

$$EP(a_1) = .12(.1) + .12(.2) + .12(.4) + .12(.3) = .12$$

and for action a_2:

$$EP(a_2) = .06(.1) + .10(.2) + .14(.4) + .17(.3) = .133$$

Since the expected payoff for action a_2 is larger than that for a_1, the firm should sponsor the new show rather than the old show. Notice that in this example the objective variable was market share and not profit. The expected payoff and expected opportunity loss criteria can be used, as stated above, for any objective variable we want to maximize. For some situations, however, we may want to minimize the expected value of the objective variable (or, equivalently, maximize the expected opportunity loss). For example, if an objective variable such as Time to process an order was used, we would prefer less time to more time. Then the expected payoff and expected opportunity loss criteria would have to be redefined, and we would seek the minimum expected payoff.   ∎

Case Study 18.2
Hurricanes: To Seed or Not to Seed?

The seeding of hurricanes as a means of lessening their destructive power was suggested by R. H. Simpson in the early 1960's. Even though the results of experimental hurricane seeding were encouraging, government policy through the early 1970's prohibited the seeding of hurricanes that threatened coastal areas. Howard, Matheson, and North (1972) analyzed the seeding of hurricanes using decision analysis to determine (1) whether existing government policy should be modified and (2) whether further experiments on hurricane seeding should be carried out. We will discuss the second question in Case Study 19.1.

   To answer the first question, Howard, Matheson, and North had to define the states of nature, assign probabilities to each of the possible states, and assess the consequences of each action/state combination. The actions specified were Seed a threatening hurricane and Don't seed a threatening hurricane. The states of nature were defined in terms of the percentage change in maximum wind speed over a 12-hour period. This measure was chosen because it is related to the primary cause of the destruction inflicted by most hurricanes, and it is this characteristic that seeding is expected to influence. Based on historical data, a probability distribution was assessed for changes in wind speed for a "representative hurricane" over a 12-hour period. Using Simpson's theoretical work on hurricane seeding and early experimental work on seeding, Howard, Matheson, and North also assessed a probability distribution for changes in wind speed of a seeded hurricane. These probability distributions are given in the table:

STATE *Change in wind speed*	STATE PROBABILITY *Unseeded hurricanes*	STATE PROBABILITY *Seeded hurricanes*
S_1: +25% or more	.054	.038
S_2: +10% to +25%	.206	.143
S_3: −10% to +10%	.480	.392
S_4: −25% to −10%	.206	.255
S_5: −25% or more	.054	.172

   The consequences of the action/state combinations considered were property damage resulting from the hurricane and government liability in the case of seeded hurricanes. Using a least squares regression analysis (see Chapter 10) and past records of hurricane damage, the authors modeled the relationship between changes in wind speed and property damage for a "representative hurricane." Results of their analysis appear in the next table.

CHANGE IN WIND SPEED	PREDICTED DAMAGE ($ million)
+25% or more	335.8
+10% to +25%	191.1
−10% to +10%	100.0
−25% to −10%	46.7
−25% or more	16.3

Howard, Matheson, and North assumed that if a hurricane did not "improve" after seeding, the government would bear increased legal and social costs. They used a percentage of the property damage resulting from the states S_1, S_2, and S_3 to estimate these costs. The total cost associated with a particular state was found by adding these government responsibility costs to the predicted property damages. Their estimates were 50% for S_1, 30% for S_2, and 5% for S_3. Thus, the outcomes for each state under the decision to seed would be (including the $0.25 million cost of seeding) as shown in the table. These quantities are expressed in terms of negative gains (losses).

STATE	OUTCOME ($ million)
S_1: +25% or more	−503.95
S_2: +10% to +25%	−248.65
S_3: −10% to +10%	−105.25
S_4: −25% to −10%	−46.95
S_5: −25% or more	−16.55

The expected payoff criterion can now be applied as usual. Based on the given probabilities and outcomes, the expected payoffs are

$$EP(\text{No seeding}) = -\$116.0 \text{ million} \qquad EP(\text{Seeding}) = -\$110.78 \text{ million}$$

As a result of their analysis, Howard, Matheson, and North recommended that the government change its policy and allow seeding of hurricanes that threaten coastal areas. They noted that the decision to seed a particular hurricane, however, should be based on a decision analysis that uses all the meteorological and geographic factors relevant to the particular case.

Exercises 18.23–18.33

Learning the Mechanics

18.23 Consider the payoff table shown here. Find the action that would be prescribed by the expected payoff criterion. Probabilities are in parentheses in the table.

		STATE OF NATURE			
		S_1 (.1)	S_2 (.3)	S_3 (.4)	S_4 (.2)
	a_1	−250	−400	0	300
ACTION	a_2	−300	−100	300	100
	a_3	−100	−40	−10	85

18.24 In the decision tree shown here, state probabilities are displayed in parentheses to the right of the state symbols, S_1 and S_2.

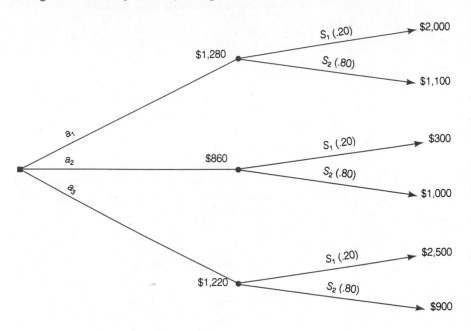

a. Identify any inadmissible actions, and explain why they are inadmissible.

b. The expected payoff for each action has been computed and appears to the left of the chance fork associated with each action in the decision tree. Verify that these expected payoffs are correct.

c. Identify the action that is prescribed by the expected payoff criterion.

18.25 Construct the decision tree for the decision problem described in Exercise 18.23. Include on your decision tree the state probabilities and the expected payoffs associated with each action. (For an example of such a tree, see Exercise 18.24.)

18.26 Consider the accompanying payoff table (probabilities are in parentheses).

| | STATE OF NATURE | | |
	S_1 (.20)	S_2 (.30)	S_3 (.50)
ACTION a_1	50	105	175
a_2	−20	0	300

a. Use the expected payoff criterion to select the better action.

b. Convert the payoff table to an opportunity loss table and use the expected opportunity loss criterion to select the better action.

18.27 In the decision tree shown here, state probabilities are displayed in parentheses to the right of the state symbols, S_1 and S_2. The outcomes on the decision tree are expressed in terms of opportunity losses. According to the expected opportunity loss criterion, which action should be selected?

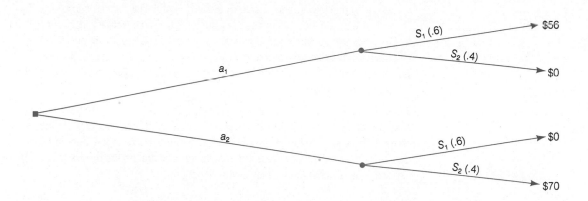

Applying the Concepts

18.28 *Materials Requirements Planning (MRP) systems* are computerized planning and control systems for manufacturing operations. They are used to manage raw materials and work-in-process inventories. Since their introduction in the mid-1960's, MRP systems have made it possible to simultaneously reduce inventories and improve customer service (Schroeder, 1981). The operations manager for a company that produces a defense product wishes to obtain an MRP system. He has narrowed his choices to three different MRP vendors, X, Y, and Z, whose systems cost $5,000, $4,000, and $3,000, respectively. In addition, each vendor charges a fee for implementing the system (e.g., adapting the system to fit the purchaser's needs, installing the system, and debugging the system); the size of the fee depends primarily on the extent to which the system must be modified to meet the purchaser's needs. Systems X, Y, and Z are similar and would require basically the same modifications, but the implementation fees charged by the vendors differ significantly. These fees are described in the table. The manager, in consultation with the vendors, has determined that the probability of a major modification being required is .3, the probability of a moderate modification is .5, and the probability of a minor modification is .2. This uncertainty concerning the extent of the modification required exists because the operations manager has not finalized the specifications of the system he desires and the vendors will not specify the extent of the modification required until after the specifications have been made.

EXTENT OF MODIFICATION	IMPLEMENTATION FEE		
	X	Y	Z
Major	$3,000	$4,000	$6,000
Moderate	1,000	1,400	2,000
Minor	200	400	500

a. The objective variable for this decision problem is the initial cost plus the implementation fee for a system. Since we want to minimize (rather than maximize) the value of this objective variable, we need to convert our problem to one of maximization. This can be done by multiplying each value of system cost (initial cost plus implementation fee) by -1. The action that maximizes the value of this new objective variable will be the one that minimizes the system cost. Eliminate any inadmissible actions, and formulate the payoff table for this decision problem.

b. According to the expected payoff criterion, which MRP system should the manager purchase? Explain.

18.29 A company that manufactures hair dryers would like you to help it choose the travel case design for its new portable model. It has constructed the accompanying payoff table to characterize the decision problem. The objective variable is the contribution to the company's profits over the next year that results from marketing the new portable dryer. Use the expected payoff criterion to answer the questions.

		STATE OF NATURE	
		S_1: Consumers like design	S_2: Consumers dislike design
ACTION	a_1: Design A	$500,000	$20,000
	a_2: Design B	$300,000	$50,000

a. If $P(S_1) = P(S_2) = .5$, which design should the company choose?

b. If $P(S_1) = \frac{2}{3}$ and $P(S_2) = \frac{1}{3}$, which design should it choose?

18.30 Reconsider Exercise 18.17, in which a minicomputer company is considering marketing its product in Europe. The company's marketing department has assessed the probability distribution in the table for the share of the European minicomputer market that the company will attain over the next 3 years. According to the expected payoff criterion, should the company enter the European market? Explain.

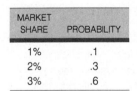

MARKET SHARE	PROBABILITY
1%	.1
2%	.3
3%	.6

18.31 Reconsider Exercise 18.20, which concerned the purchase of body pieces by an automobile manufacturer. A lot of 500 pieces is purchased for $15,000, and the proportion of defects in each lot is .05, .10, or .50. The supplier offers a guarantee that it will assume the costs for all defective body moldings greater than 50 in a production lot of 500. This guarantee may be purchased for a cost of $1,000 before the lot begins production. The data in the table have been gathered on 100 past production lots of preformed body pieces. Given only this information, should the guarantee be purchased? Explain. [*Hint:* Use the sample of 100 lots to estimate the probabilities of the states of nature.]

PROPORTION OF DEFECTS	NUMBER OF TIMES OBSERVED
0.05	55
0.10	24
0.50	21

SALES Dozen	PROBABILITY
3	.15
4	.25
5	.30
6	.15
7	.10
8	.05

18.32 Refer to the payoff table for the decision problem in Exercise 18.18. The dress buyer has assessed the probability distribution given in the table for the number of dresses she can sell. How many dozen dresses should the buyer order according to the expected payoff criterion?

18.33 Reconsider Exercises 18.10 and 18.19, in which a company that manufactures designer jeans is concerned about whether to increase its advertising budget for next year. The company has determined that, if the advertising budget is increased, the expanded advertising campaign will succeed with probability $\frac{2}{3}$ and will fail with probability $\frac{1}{3}$.

a. According to the expected payoff criterion, should the jeans manufacturer increase its advertising budget? Explain.
b. Convert the payoff table you developed in part a to an opportunity loss table.
c. According to the expected opportunity loss criterion, should the jeans manufacturer increase its advertising budget? Explain.

18.6
Two Non-probabilistic Decision-Making Criteria: Maximax and Maximin (Optional)

The expected payoff criterion is probabilistic because it requires that a probability distribution be assigned to the states of nature. There are several criteria that do not require the assignment of probabilities in order to reach a decision. Two common nonprobabilistic criteria are the *maximax* and *maximin decision rules.*

We will describe the maximax and maximin criteria by using the brewery decision problem first introduced in Example 18.1 (Section 18.3). The payoff table is reproduced in Table 18.9 (where the inadmissible action a_4 is omitted).

To use the *maximax rule,* we determine the maximum payoff associated with each action and choose the action that corresponds to the *maxi*mum of these *maxi*mum payoffs. Thus the name *maximax.* The easiest way to apply the maximax criterion is to find the maximum payoff in the entire table and choose the action corresponding to that payoff. Thus, the maximum payoff in Table 18.9 is $1,000,000, corresponding to action a_3: Large brewery. Therefore, the maximax criterion leads to the decision: Build a large brewery. Note that the maximax criterion ignores all information in the payoff table except the maximum value. That is, no state of nature except that associated with the maximum payoff is considered, and the size of the difference between the maximum payoff and the other payoffs is ignored. The maximax criterion is an optimistic one because it is based on the assumption (or hope) that the most favorable state of nature will occur.

Table 18.9

Payoff Table for the Brewer's Decision Problem

		STATE OF NATURE Market share during fifth year of operation		
	Brewery size	S_1: 0% < 5%	S_2: 5% < 10%	S_3: 10%–15%
	a_1: Small	$300,000	$350,000	$450,000
ACTION	a_2: Medium	$250,000	$700,000	$800,000
	a_3: Large	$200,000	$600,000	$1,000,000

ACTION	MINIMUM PAYOFF
a_1	$300,000
a_2	$250,000
a_3	$200,000

To use the *maximin criterion,* we determine the minimum payoff associated with each action and select the action that corresponds to the *maxi*mum of these *min*imum payoffs. In the brewery example, we find that the minimum payoffs are as indicated in the margin. Since the maximum of these minima is $300,000, corresponding to action a_1, the decision would be to build a small brewery if the maximin criterion was used. Note that the maximin criterion ignores all information except the minimum payoffs corresponding to each action. That is, no other states of nature except those corresponding to the minimum payoffs are considered. In the brewery example, all the minima are associated with the state of nature, less than 5%, so the other two states of nature are ignored by the maximin criterion. Furthermore, the size of the difference between the minimum payoffs and the other payoffs is given no weight in determining which action to take. The maximin criterion is pessimistic because it is based on the assumption that the least favorable state of nature will occur.

Since much information in the payoff table is ignored by the maximax and maximin decision criteria, it is not surprising that they often lead to decisions that are intuitively unappealing and even nonsensical. In the brewery example, the maximin criterion leads to the decision to build a small brewery. But the slight loss that would be sustained if a medium or large brewery were built and less than 5% of the market were obtained appears to be more than compensated for by the gain in profit if the market share were at least 5% and a medium or large brewery were built. Thus, most decision analysts prefer the expected payoff criterion to these nonprobabilistic criteria. The use of the nonprobabilistic criteria is generally confined to decision problems for which the decision-maker is not willing to assign probabilities to the states of nature.

Exercises 18.34 – 18.41

Learning the Mechanics

18.34 Consider the following payoff table:

		STATE OF NATURE		
		S_1	S_2	S_3
	a_1	75	105	60
	a_2	70	80	60
ACTION	a_3	-30	40	120
	a_4	105	90	200

a. Eliminate any inadmissible actions.
b. Find the action that would be prescribed by the maximax decision criterion.
c. Find the action that would be prescribed by the maximin decision criterion.

18.35 Consider the decision tree shown at the top of the next page.

a. Find the action that would be prescribed by the maximax criterion.
b. Find the action that would be prescribed by the maximin criterion.

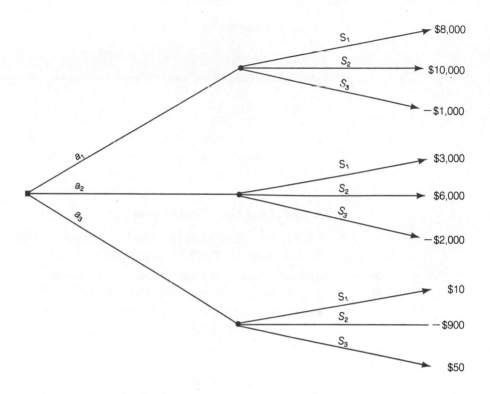

c. Explain why the action prescribed by the maximin criterion in part b is potentially unreasonable from a practical viewpoint.

18.36 Consider the decision tree shown here.

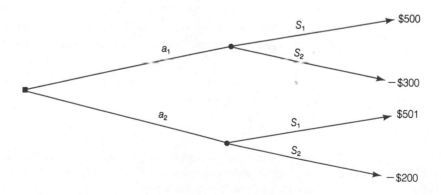

a. Find the action that would be prescribed by the maximax criterion.
b. Find the action that would be prescribed by the maximin criterion.

18.37 Consider the following payoff table:

		STATE OF NATURE						
		S_1	S_2	S_3	S_4	S_5	S_6	S_7
	a_1	50	35	10	0	−20	−80	−100
ACTION	a_2	100	30	20	10	−5	−40	−110
	a_3	105	0	−50	−100	−150	−300	−100

a. Find the action that would be prescribed by the maximax criterion.
b. Find the action that would be prescribed by the maximin criterion.

Applying the Concepts

18.38 Refer to Exercise 18.28, in which an operations manager is interested in purchasing an MRP system. Use the payoff table for the operations manager's decision problem to:

a. Find the action that would be prescribed by the maximax criterion.
b. Find the action that would be prescribed by the maximin criterion.

18.39 Refer to Exercise 18.17, in which a manufacturer of minicomputers is considering marketing its product in Europe. Use the payoff table for the company's marketing decision problem to:

a. Find the action that would be prescribed by the maximax criterion.
b. Find the action that would be prescribed by the maximin criterion.

18.40 Refer to Exercise 18.18, in which a buyer for a large department store is trying to decide how many of a new style of dress to order. Use the payoff table for the dress buyer's decision problem to:

a. Find the action that would be prescribed by the maximax criterion.
b. Find the action that would be prescribed by the maximin criterion.

18.41 Refer to Exercise 18.20, in which a purchasing agent for an automobile manufacturer is concluding a purchase agreement with a supplier of preformed body pieces. Use the payoff table for the purchasing agent's decision problem to:

a. Find the action that would be prescribed by the maximax criterion.
b. Find the action that would be prescribed by the maximin criterion.

18.7 The Expected Utility Criterion

The expected payoff (or opportunity loss) criterion sometimes fails to provide decisions that are consistent with the decision-maker's attitude toward risk. For example, suppose you were required to choose one of these two actions:

a_1: Deposit your $100,000 inheritance in the bank for 1 year at 7% interest.

a_2: Invest your $100,000 inheritance for 1 year with a .5 probability of having a total of $250,000 at the end of the year and a .5 probability of losing all your inheritance.

Which would you choose? Why? Most of us would probably choose action a_1, basing our decision on a "safety first" strategy. The usual argument goes, "Why pass up a chance for a sure $107,000 at the end of the year for a 50–50 chance to end up with nothing?" Notice that if you choose a_1, your decision is not in accord with the action prescribed by the expected payoff criterion, because

$$EP(a_1) = \$107,000(1) = \$107,000$$
$$EP(a_2) = \$250,000(.5) + 0(.5) = \$125,000$$

Thus, if we use the expected payoff criterion, we would select action a_2.

The expected payoff criterion can be adapted to reflect our attitude toward risk if we can express the outcomes of the decision problem in terms of an objective variable that better reflects the true relative values of outcomes. An objective variable that reflects the decision-maker's attitude toward risk is called a *utility function,* and the values assigned to the outcomes are referred to as *utility values,* or *utilities* (or sometimes *utiles*).

Definition 18.3

A *utility function* is a rule that assigns numerical values to the potential outcomes of a decision problem in such a way that

1. The values rank the outcomes in accordance with the decision-maker's preferences.
2. The function itself describes the decision-maker's attitude toward risk.

We now illustrate how to assign utility values to the monetary outcomes of the inheritance example. The payoff table for this example is shown in Table 18.10. As noted previously, many of us would be reluctant to gamble on the outcome of the investment if the chance of success were only .5, even though the expected payoff is higher for action a_2 ($125,000) than for action a_1 ($107,000). *The key to assigning utility values to the action/state of nature combinations is to answer the following question: What would the probability of success for the investment have to be for you to value actions a_1 and a_2 equally?* The answer to this question is a probability, p, such that if the probability of the investment's success exceeds p, you would prefer to invest the money (a_2), but if the success probability is less than p, you would prefer to deposit the money in the bank and take the safe return. The probability p is called the *utility of the outcome* $107,000, and we write $U(107,000) = p$. The minimum payoff ($0) and the maximum payoff ($250,000) are assigned utility values of 0 and 1, respectively, so that $U(0) = 0$, and $U(250,000) = 1$.

Table 18.10
Payoff Table for the
Inheritance Example

		STATE OF NATURE *Outcome of investment*	
		S_1: Failure	S_2: Success
ACTION	a_1: Deposit $100,000 in bank	$107,000	$107,000
	a_2: Invest $100,000	0	$250,000

Suppose you decide that the probability of the investment's success would have to be .7 before the two actions are equally appealing. Then the utility value assigned to $107,000 is .7, and the payoff table with the utility values as outcomes is shown in Table 18.11.

Table 18.11

Payoff Table for the Inheritance Example with Utility Values as Payoffs

		STATE OF NATURE (PROBABILITIES IN PARENTHESES) *Outcome of investment*	
		S_1: Failure (.5)	S_2: Success (.5)
ACTION	a_1: Deposit $100,000	.7	.7
	a_2: Invest $100,000	0	1

The general rule for assigning utility values to monetary outcomes* is given in the box.

Assigning Utility Values to Monetary Outcomes†

1. Identify the maximum and minimum payoffs in the decision table. Call them O_M and O_L, respectively.

2. Set $U(O_M) = 1$ and $U(O_L) = 0$, where $U(O)$ represents the utility value of outcome O.

3. To determine the utility value for any other outcome O_{ij} in the payoff table, determine the value of p that makes you have no preference between the following:

a. Receiving O_{ij} with certainty

b. Participating in a gamble in which you can win O_M with probability p or O_L with probability $(1 - p)$

Then, $U(O_{ij}) = p$.

We are now prepared to make a decision based on the *expected utility criterion*. We first find the expected utility for each action using the formula

$$EU(a_i) = \sum_{\substack{\text{All states} \\ \text{of nature}}} \begin{pmatrix} \text{Utility of the} \\ \text{action } a_i/\text{state of nature} \\ \text{combination} \end{pmatrix} \begin{pmatrix} \text{Probability} \\ \text{of the} \\ \text{state of nature} \end{pmatrix}$$

Thus, for the inheritance example,

$$EU(a_1) = .7(.5) + .7(.5) = .7$$
$$EU(a_2) = 0(.5) + 1(.5) = .5$$

---

* Utility functions may be assessed for the outcomes corresponding to any objective variable, but because the objective variable in business decision-making is typically monetary (or can be converted to a monetary equivalent), we have restricted our discussion to utility functions for money.

† The choice of 0 and 1 as the minimum and maximum utility values is arbitrary. The same result is obtained if the utility values are all multiplied by the same constant or if a constant is added to each of the values. However, in either case, utility values lose their probabilistic interpretation. For more detail on the choice of scale, its implications for interpersonal and intrapersonal comparisons of utility values, and other methods for assessing utility functions, see the references at the end of this chapter.

We now choose the action with the higher expected utility, which is action a_1. You can see that this decision differs from that yielded by the expected payoff criterion and that it more accurately reflects a safety-first attitude toward risk.

Expected Utility Criterion

Choose the action that has the greatest expected utility, where the expected utility of action a_i is given by

$$EU(a_i) = \sum_{\substack{\text{All states} \\ \text{of nature}}} \left(\begin{array}{c} \text{Utility of the} \\ \text{action } a_i/\text{state of nature} \\ \text{combination} \end{array} \right) \left(\begin{array}{c} \text{Probability} \\ \text{of the} \\ \text{state of nature} \end{array} \right)$$

Example 18.3

Recall the brewery size decision problem of Example 18.1. The payoff table is repeated in Table 18.12 (where the inadmissible action a_4 is left out). Suppose we assign the utility values shown in Table 18.13 to the monetary payoffs.

Table 18.12

Payoff Table for the Brewery Size Decision Problem

	Brewery size	STATE OF NATURE Market share during fifth year of operation		
		S_1: 0% < 5%	S_2: 5% < 10%	S_3: 10%–15%
	a_1: Small	$300,000	$350,000	$450,000
ACTION	a_2: Medium	$250,000	$700,000	$800,000
	a_3: Large	$200,000	$600,000	$1,000,000

Table 18.13

Utility Values for the Brewery Decision Problem

	Brewery size	STATE OF NATURE (PROBABILITIES IN PARENTHESES) Market share during fifth year of operation		
		S_1: 0% < 5% (.4)	S_2: 5% < 10% (.5)	S_3: 10%–15% (.1)
	a_1: Small	.35	.50	.65
ACTION	a_2: Medium	.20	.90	.95
	a_3: Large	0	.85	1.00

a. Interpret the utility value assigned to the $700,000 payoff, $U(700,000) = .9$.

b. Determine which action should be taken according to the expected utility criterion.

Solution · **a.** Referring to the rules for assigning utility values, we see that the utility value of .9 represents the probability that makes us have no preference between receiving $700,000 with certainty and participating in a gamble in which we can gain $1,000,000 (the maximum payoff) with probability .9 or $200,000 (the minimum payoff) with probability $(1 - .9) = .1$. You can see that we have again adopted a conservative strategy, because the expected payoff for the gamble is $1,000,000(.9) + 200,000(.1) = $920,000, which exceeds the fixed payoff of $700,000. In other words, the assignment of $U(700,000) = .9$ reflects our desire to receive the fixed payoff unless the odds are very high that we will win the gamble. The rest of the utility values can be similarly interpreted, and they all reflect this conservative attitude toward risk.

b. The expected utilities are calculated as follows:

$$EU(a_1) = .35(.4) + .50(.5) + .65(.1) = .455$$
$$EU(a_2) = .20(.4) + .90(.5) + .95(.1) = .625$$
$$EU(a_3) = 0(.4) + .85(.5) + 1.0(.1) = .525$$

Thus, according to our assignment of utility values to the monetary outcomes, the expected utility criterion indicates that we should select action a_2 and build a medium-sized brewery. ■

You can see that the assignment of utility values is personal and subjective. If careful thought is given to this task, the result will be a utility function that reflects your preferences for outcomes and your attitude toward risk. Applying the expected utility criterion will then yield a decision consistent with your preferences and risk attitude.

Exercises
18.42–18.48

Learning the Mechanics

18.42 Suppose you are indifferent (i.e., have no preference) between receiving $100 with certainty and participating in a gamble in which you have a probability of .2 of receiving $1,000 and a probability of .8 of receiving nothing. You are also indifferent between receiving $500 with certainty and participating in a gamble in which you have a probability of .7 of receiving $1,000 and a probability of .3 of receiving nothing. Finally, you are also indifferent between receiving $800 with certainty and participating in a gamble in which you have a probability of .95 of receiving $1,000 and a probability of .05 of receiving nothing.

a. Let $U(\$1,000) = 1$ and $U(\$0) = 0$. Find $U(\$100)$, $U(\$500)$, and $U(\$800)$.

b. Use these utility values to plot your utility function for money over the range from $0 to $1,000.

18.43 Consider the utility function* for money,

$$U(x) = x^2 \qquad 0 \le x \le 100$$

and the payoff table shown here (probabilities in parentheses).

		STATE OF NATURE		
		$S_1 (.25)$	$S_2 (.30)$	$S_3 (.45)$
ACTION	a_1	$75	$50	$30
	a_2	$60	$80	0

a. Use the utility function to convert the outcomes in the payoff table from monetary values to utility values (utiles).

b. Which action would be prescribed by the expected utility criterion?

---

* Notice that the minimum and maximum values of this utility function are not 0 and 1, respectively. Refer to the second footnote on page 850.

18.44 Consider the utility function for money,

$$U(x) = \frac{\ln(x + 51)}{5.525} \qquad -50 < x < 200$$

and the given payoff table (probabilities in parentheses).

		STATE OF NATURE		
		$S_1\,(.50)$	$S_2\,(.40)$	$S_3\,(.10)$
ACTION	a_1	$-\$10$	$\$50$	$\$90$
	a_2	0	$\$20$	$\$20$
	a_3	$-\$10$	$\$60$	$\$50$
	a_4	$-\$10$	$-\$50$	$\$200$

a. Eliminate any inadmissible actions.
b. Use the utility function to convert the outcomes in the payoff table from monetary values to utility values (utiles).
c. Which action is prescribed by the expected utility criterion?
d. Does this decision differ from the decision prescribed by the expected payoff criterion?

18.45 Consider the utility function for money,

$$U(x) = -1 + .01x \qquad 100 \le x \le 200$$

and the payoff table given here (probabilities are in parentheses).

		STATE OF NATURE			
		$S_1\,(.20)$	$S_2\,(.15)$	$S_3\,(.40)$	$S_4\,(.25)$
ACTION	a_1	$\$120$	$\$180$	$\$100$	$\$100$
	a_2	$\$105$	$\$165$	$\$190$	$\$150$
	a_3	$\$100$	$\$120$	$\$160$	$\$200$

a. Use the utility function to convert the outcomes in the payoff table from monetary values to utility values (utiles).
b. Which action is prescribed by the expected utility criterion?

Applying the Concepts

18.46 An investor is trying to decide whether to invest in a wildcat oil well. If the well is drilled and it is dry, she will lose $500,000. On the other hand, if the well is a gusher, she will make $1.5 million. It is also possible for the well to yield a lesser amount of oil than a gusher, in which case she will make $600,000.

a. A decision analyst asks her the following questions:

1. At what value of p would you be indifferent between the two situations: receive $600,000 with certainty, and receive $1.5 million with probability p or lose $500,000 with probability $(1 - p)$? She replies, at $p = .90$. What is the investor's utility value for $600,000?

2. At what value of p would you be indifferent between receiving $0 with certainty, and receiving $1.5 million with probability p or losing $500,000 with probability $(1 - p)$? She replies, at $p = .8$. Find her utility value for $0.

b. Graph the utility function for this investor for dollar values between $-$500,000 and $1,500,000.

18.47 Refer to Exercise 18.46. The investor now must decide whether to keep the $500,000 or invest it in the oil well. She assesses the probabilities of the states to be as follows:

$$P(\text{Dry well}) = .5$$

$$P(\text{Moderate success}) = .3$$

$$P(\text{Gusher}) = .2$$

a. Set up the payoff table for this decision problem.

b. Use the expected payoff criterion to determine which action the investor should select.

c. Substitute the utility values for the monetary outcomes in the payoff table of part a and use the expected utility criterion to select the action.

18.48 Refer to Exercise 18.32, in which you selected an action for the dress purchaser using the expected payoff criterion. Now suppose the buyer's utility function for money is

$$U(x) = \frac{\sqrt{x + 2,000}}{110} \qquad -2,000 \le x \le 10,000$$

How many dresses should she order? Should she be using her own utility function to make this decision? Why or why not?

18.8 Classifying Decision-Makers by Their Utility Functions

The attitude of a decision-maker toward risk may be characterized by the type of utility function he or she uses. Recall the inheritance decision problem of Section 18.7, with the payoff table given in Table 18.10 and a table of utility values given in Table 18.11. These tables are repeated here for convenience as Tables 18.14 and 18.15.

We know that these utility values reflect a conservative attitude toward risk, since the expected payoff of the investment must exceed $0(.3) + 250,000(.7) = \$175,000$ before the decision-maker prefers this gamble to the fixed $107,000 return. This attitude may be graphi-

Table 18.14

Payoff Table for the Inheritance Example

| | | STATE OF NATURE (PROBABILITIES IN PARENTHESES) | |
		Investment fails (.5)	Investment succeeds (.5)
ACTION	a_1: Deposit $100,000 in bank	$107,000	$107,000
	a_2: Invest $100,000	0	$250,000

Table 18.15

Utility Value Table for the Inheritance Example

| | | STATE OF NATURE (PROBABILITIES IN PARENTHESES) | |
		Investment fails (.5)	Investment succeeds (.5)
ACTION	a_1: Deposit $100,000	.7	.7
	a_2: Invest $100,000	0	1

cally portrayed by plotting the utility values on a vertical axis against the payoffs on a horizontal axis, as shown in Figure 18.3. The points are connected with a smooth curve. You can see that the shape of the utility function is *concave.* This shape is characteristic of a conservative attitude toward risk, and decision-makers whose utility functions are concave are called *risk-avoiders.*

Figure 18.3 Utility Function for the Inheritance Example; a Risk-Avoiding Attitude

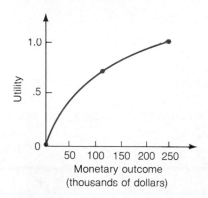

Now, suppose we decided to assign a utility value of .2 to the $107,000 payoff in Table 18.14. This value reflects a liberal, or gambling, attitude toward risk, since the interpretation is that we have no preference between a sure $107,000 and a .2 probability of receiving $250,000 (with a .8 probability of nothing). The expected payoff of the gamble is 0(.8) + $250,000(.2) = $50,000, which is less than the fixed payoff if we deposit the money in the bank. The graph of this utility function is shown in Figure 18.4. Note that the shape of this function is *convex,* which is the characteristic shape of utility functions of *risk-takers.*

Figure 18.4 Utility Function for the Inheritance Example; a Risk-Taking Attitude

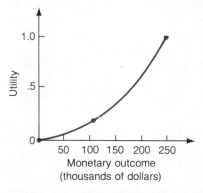

If the utility value of .428 is assigned to the $107,000 outcome, the implication is that we would have no preference between accepting $107,000 and gambling on receiving $250,000 with probability .428, a gamble that has an expected payoff of 0(.572) + 250,000(.428) = $107,000. The fact that both courses of action have the same expected payoff reflects a neutral attitude toward risk. The graph of the utility function in this case and, for *risk-neutral* decision-makers in general, is a straight line, as shown in Figure 18.5 (next page). Since the expected utility of action a_i is equal to the utility of the expected payoff for action a_i for straight-line utility functions, *the expected payoff criterion and the expected utility criterion are equivalent for the risk-neutral decision-makers.*

Figure 18.5   Utility
Function for the Inheritance
Example; a Risk-Neutral
Attitude

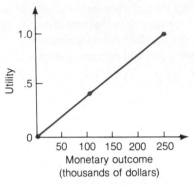

The three types of utility functions and the strategies they characterize are summarized in
the box.

Three Types of Utility Functions*

1. Risk-avoiding utility function   **2.** Risk-neutral utility function   **3.** Risk-taking utility function

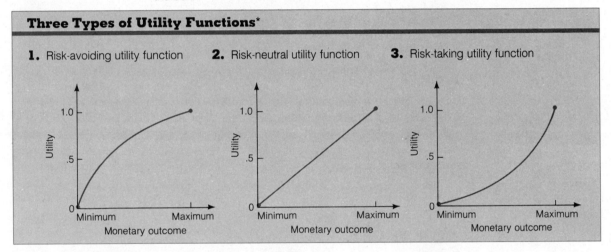

Example 18.4   For the brewery decision problem (Examples 18.1 and 18.3), consider the two utility functions
reflected in Table 18.16.

Table 18.16   Two Utility Functions for the Brewery Decision Problem

		SITUATION A			SITUATION B		
		STATE OF NATURE (PROBABILITIES IN PARENTHESES) *Market share during fifth year of operation*			STATE OF NATURE (PROBABILITIES IN PARENTHESES) *Market share during fifth year of operation*		
	Brewery size	S_1: 0% < 5% (.4)	S_2: 5% < 10% (.5)	S_3: 10%–15% (.1)	S_1: 0% < 5% (.4)	S_2: 5% < 10% (.5)	S_3: 10%–15% (.1)
	a_1: *Small*	.35	.50	.65	.04	.07	.11
ACTION	a_2: *Medium*	.20	.90	.95	.02	.30	.40
	a_3: *Large*	0	.85	1.00	0	.20	1.00

* Other types of utility functions may be obtained by combining these. For example, a decision-maker
may be risk-neutral for relatively small monetary outcomes and a risk-avoider for relatively large monetary
outcomes. Thus, the utility function might appear S-shaped.

α. Graph the utility functions, and identify the attitude toward risk that each characterizes.

b. Determine the action that should be taken in each situation.

Solution **α.** The utility functions are shown in Figure 18.6. Situation A is the same one we used and characterized as conservative in Example 18.3. You can see that the utility function in Figure 18.6(a) is *concave*, indicating a *risk-avoiding* attitude. However, the utility function corresponding to situation B is *convex*, which characterizes a *risk-taking* situation.

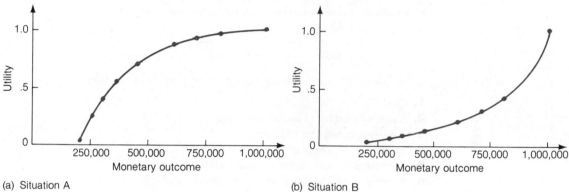

(a) Situation A

(b) Situation B

Figure 18.6 Utility Functions for the Brewery Decision Problem

b. We showed in Example 18.3 that for situation A,

$$EU(a_1) = .455 \qquad EU(a_2) = .625 \qquad EU(a_3) = .525$$

so the expected utility criterion selects action a_2: Build a medium-sized brewery. For situation B, we find

$$EU(a_1) = .04(.4) + .07(.5) + .11(.1) = .062$$
$$EU(a_2) = .02(.4) + .30(.5) + .40(.1) = .198$$
$$EU(a_3) = 0(.4) + .20(.5) + 1.00(.1) = .200$$

Thus, the expected utility criterion selects action a_3: Build a large brewery. Note that the risk-taking utility function leads to the selection of a riskier action, a_3, than the risk-avoiding and risk-neutral functions, which both select a_2 (see Section 18.5 for the risk-neutral — that is, expected payoff — solution). ■

Case Study 18.3
An Airport: To Expand or Not to Expand?

The Mexican government received two conflicting recommendations on airport development for Mexico City. One study recommended expanding the present airport at Texcoco, and the other suggested transferring all operations as soon as possible to a new airport to be built at Zumpango. As a result of this disagreement, the Mexican Ministry of Public Works employed Keeney, Raiffa, and de Neufville to evaluate alternatives for airport development and recommend the most effective strategy.

The basic decision problem, as described by Keeney (1973), involved the determination of which types of aircraft (international, I; domestic, D; general, G; and military, M) should operate at each of the two locations (Texcoco, T, and Zumpango, Z) over the next 30 years. To simplify the problem, Keeney, Raiffa, and de Neufville assumed that changes in operations from one site to another could occur at only three times: 1975, 1985, and 1995. Each airport development strategy (action) indicated which types of aircraft would operate at each location for each time period. Some examples of possible strategies are given in the table. Strategies 1 and 2 are the recommendations of the previous studies. Strategy 3 is one possible intermediate strategy. Keeney, Raiffa, and de Neufville evaluated 100 such strategies.

		1975		1985		1995	
		T	Z	T	Z	T	Z
	1	IDGM		IDGM		IDGM	
STRATEGY	2		IDGM		IDGM		IDGM
	3	DGM	I	MG	ID		IDGM

The outcome of each strategy was evaluated in terms of six attributes:

1. Cost
2. Capacity (number of aircraft operating)
3. Average access time to airport
4. Number of people killed or injured per aircraft accident
5. Number of people displaced by airport development
6. Number of people subjected to a high noise level

One step in the decision analysis was to evaluate utility functions for each of these attributes. The following description of the utility assessment for access time is representative of the other utility assessments. By questioning the clients, Keeney, Raiffa, and de Neufville determined that the bounds on average access time over all strategies were 12 minutes and 90 minutes. The best possible time, 12 minutes, was assigned a utility of 1; the worst possible time, 90 minutes, was assigned a utility of 0. The clients were then presented with a series of choices of the following type: 62 minutes access time for certain, or a lottery with p chance at 12 minutes and $(1 - p)$ chance at 90 minutes. The size of p was varied until the client indicated indifference between these two choices. In the case of 62 minutes, the client was indifferent for $p = .5$. Thus,

$$U(62 \text{ minutes}) = .5$$

Figure 18.7   Utility
Function for Case Study 18.3

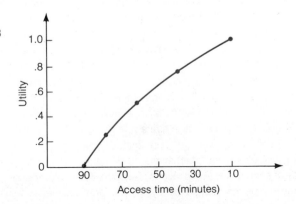

This process was repeated for several other access times, and the results were plotted as shown in Figure 18.7. You can see that the clients are risk-avoiders with respect to access time.

The results of the utility analysis for each attribute were combined to develop a set of utility functions. Probabilities for the various outcomes were also assessed. The utilities and probabilities were combined to determine an expected utility for each of the airport development strategies. The results of the decision analysis indicated that a strategy of gradual shift of operations from Texcoco to Zumpango over the next 30 years had the highest expected utility.

**Exercises
18.49 – 18.54**

Learning the Mechanics

18.49 Graph each of the following utility functions* for money and classify each as the utility function of a risk-avoiding, risk-taking, or risk-neutral decision-maker:

a. $U(x) = 2x^3$, $0 \le x \le 100$ **b.** $U(x) = \frac{1}{100}x$, $0 \le x \le 100$
c. $U(x) = \log(x + 100)$, $10 \le x \le 100$ **d.** $U(x) = -1 + .01x$, $100 \le x \le 200$

18.50 Consider the following utility function for money:

$$U(x) = (x + 1,000)^{1/2} \quad -1,000 \le x \le 1,000$$

a. Plot the function.
b. Is this the utility function of a risk-avoiding, risk-taking, or risk-neutral decision-maker?
c. Use this utility function and the expected utility criterion to identify the optimal action for the decision problem characterized by the payoff table shown here (probabilities in parentheses).

		STATE OF NATURE		
		S_1 (.2)	S_2 (.6)	S_3 (.2)
	a_1	−$500	$1,000	$250
ACTION	a_2	−750	900	810
	a_3	45	−100	650

18.51 Rework all parts of Exercise 18.50 using the utility function for money,

$$U(x) = (x + 1,000)^2 \quad -1,000 \le x \le 1,000$$

Is the action prescribed by the expected utility criterion the same as the action prescribed in Exercise 18.50? If not, explain the reason for this disagreement.

18.52 Consider the utility function for money,

$$U(x) = .001x \quad 0 \le x \le 1,000$$

and the payoff table given at the top of the next page (probabilities in parentheses).

---

* Notice that the minimum and maximum values of these utility functions are not 0 and 1, respectively. Refer to the second footnote on page 850.

| | | STATE OF NATURE | | | |
		S_1 (.10)	S_2 (.35)	S_3 (.35)	S_4 (.20)
	a_1	0	25	300	850
ACTION	a_2	1,000	500	200	80
	a_3	100	600	1,000	100

a. What does this utility function indicate about the decision-maker's attitude toward risk?

b. Which action is prescribed by the expected utility criterion? Should it differ from the action prescribed by the expected payoff criterion? Explain.

Applying the Concepts

18.53 Refer to Exercise 18.46, in which an investor is trying to decide whether to invest in a wildcat oil well.

a. Plot the utility function you constructed for the investor.

b. Categorize her as a risk-avoider, risk-taker, or risk-neutral.

18.54 Refer to Exercise 18.48, in which the dress purchaser used the utility function

$$U(x) = \frac{\sqrt{x + 2,000}}{110} \qquad -2,000 \le x \le 10,000$$

a. Plot the purchaser's utility function.

b. Is she a risk-taker, risk-avoider, or risk-neutral?

Summary

Decision analysis can be used to prescribe a course of action when the decision-maker is uncertain about the outcome that will result from a chosen action. For the prescribed action to fully reflect the decision-maker's preferences regarding the outcomes *and* his or her attitudes toward risk, the **expected utility criterion** should be used. In order to use this criterion, it is necessary for the decision-maker to assess a *utility function*. It is through a utility function that the decision-maker is able to quantify his or her preferences regarding the potential outcomes of the decision problem, as well as his or her attitudes toward risk. In fact, a decision-maker can be classified as a *risk-avoider, risk-taker,* or *risk-neutral* by examining the shape of his or her utility function.

If a decision-maker is risk-neutral, then both the expected utility criterion and the **expected payoff criterion** prescribe the same action. The expected payoff criterion has the advantage of not requiring the assessment of a utility function. Thus, many decision-makers assume risk-neutrality and use the expected payoff criterion as an approximation to the expected utility criterion.

To obtain meaningful results from decision analysis, the decision-maker must take great care in developing the inputs to the analysis. The *actions, states of nature, outcomes,* and *objective variable* must be properly defined. Much careful, logical through should go into the assessment of the utility function. The *probability distribution of the states of nature* should be assessed using as much information about the states of nature as it is possible to obtain. If conducted properly, decision analysis can provide valuable inputs to the decision-making process even if the decision it prescribes is not implemented. The detailed analysis and logical thinking it requires may uncover courses of action and/or states of nature not previously recognized. It may even be discovered that the wrong decision problem is being addressed.

Supplementary Exercises 18.55–18.69

[*Note: Starred (*) exercises refer to the optional section in this chapter.*]

18.55 A small company that produces auto parts for American-made cars expects to lose $1.5 million next year unless Congress passes a bill to limit the number of foreign-made cars that can be imported into the United States. If the bill passes, the company expects to make a profit of $2.5 million next year. The company's lobbyists in Washington believe that the probability that the bill will pass this year is .6. The auto parts company must decide whether to stay in business and risk a huge loss next year, or to lease its facility for a year to a Japanese firm for $500,000.

a. Identify the objective variable, actions, and states of nature of the auto parts company's decision problem.
b. Construct the payoff table for the decision problem.
c. Convert the payoff table to an opportunity loss table.
d. Verify that the expected payoff and expected opportunity loss criteria prescribe the same action.

18.56 Refer to Exercise 18.55. Assume that the auto parts manufacturer's utility function for money is as follows:

$$U(x) = .5 + .20x \qquad -2.5 \text{ million} \le x \le 2.5 \text{ million}$$

a. Plot the utility function.
b. Classify the utility function as being that of a risk-avoiding, risk-taking, or risk-neutral decision-maker.
c. According to the expected utility criterion, which action should the auto manufacturer select?

18.57 Consider the following payoff table, with state probabilities shown in parentheses:

	S_1 (.5)	S_2 (.3)	S_3 (.2)
a_1	12	77	-27
a_2	24	2	12
a_3	-20	41	80
a_4	25	5	70
a_5	40	50	10

a. Eliminate any inadmissible actions.

b. Construct an opportunity loss table for this decision problem.

c. Calculate both the expected payoffs and the expected opportunity losses for the actions, and verify that both criteria select the same action.

d. Construct a decision tree for this problem that includes both state probabilities and expected payoffs. (See Exercise 18.24 for a description of where to locate these quantities on your tree.)

18.58 Indicate what type of information (subjective, relative frequency, or both) you would use to assign probabilities to the events described here. Explain the reasoning behind your choice. How would you obtain the necessary information to assign the probabilities?

a. Your firm is in the automobile insurance business, and you want to assess a probability distribution to characterize the total dollar value of damage to a certain model car when an 18- to 21-year-old driver is in an accident.

b. Your company is introducing a new product, and you are assigned the task of assessing a probability distribution for the market share the product will obtain.

c. A drug company is attempting to develop a new type of birth control pill. The research is still in the early stages, and you want to assess the probability that the research will be successful.

d. You are a banker and are considering giving a 30-year mortgage of $75,000 to a family with a yearly income of $25,000. You want to assess the probability that the family will default on the loan.

18.59 A bank is trying to decide whether to make a 1-year commercial loan of $75,000 to an automobile repair shop. Past experience has shown that one of three outcomes will result if the loan is made:

Outcome 1: The customer will repay the loan plus the 10% interest with no complications.

Outcome 2: The customer will have difficulty repaying the loan. The loan will eventually be repaid with the 10% interest, but a $1,000 collection cost will have been incurred by the bank.

Outcome 3: The customer will declare bankruptcy, and the bank will recover only 60% of the amount loaned.

If the bank decides not to make the loan, the money will earn 8% for the year.

a. Construct the payoff table for this decision problem.

b. Convert the payoff table to an opportunity loss table.

c. Draw a decision tree for this problem.

18.60 Refer to Exercise 18.59. Suppose past records yield the frequency distribution for commercial loans shown in the table.

OUTCOME	FREQUENCY
1. Repaid	1,104
2. Repaid with difficulty	120
3. Defaulted	56

a. Use this information to assess the probabilities of the three outcomes.

b. Using the assessed probabilities and the expected payoff criterion, decide whether the bank should make the loan.

*18.61 Refer to Exercise 18.60. Suppose no probability estimates for the outcomes are available.

a. Use the maximax criterion to decide whether to make the loan.

b. Use the maximin criterion to make the decision.

c. Critique these two nonprobabilistic criteria for making this decision.

18.62 Refer to Exercises 18.59 and 18.60. Suppose the bank uses the following utility function for money:

$$U(x) = \frac{\sqrt{x + 100,000}}{1,000} \qquad -100,000 \le x \le 900,000$$

a. Graph this function over the given range of x, and classify the bank as risk-avoiding, risk-neutral, or risk-taking.

b. Use this function to assign utility values to the monetary payoffs in the decision table of Exercise 18.59. Based on the expected utility criterion, should the loan be made?

18.63 A hosiery company must make a pricing decision regarding its new line of stockings. Two economists have been hired to develop forecasting equations that relate the quantity demanded to the price of the stockings. The forecasting equations the economists derive are

Economist 1: $q = 10 - 2p$

Economist 2: $q = 16 - 4p$

where q is the quantity demanded in units of 100,000 and p is the price in dollars. Four prices are being considered: $0.99, $1.98, $2.75, and $3.50. Assume that one of the economists' forecasting equations will be correct, but you do not know which one.

a. Construct the payoff table for this problem.

b. Construct the opportunity loss table for this problem.

c. If the company believes the forecasting equations have an equal probability of being correct, which price should be charged according to the expected payoff criterion?

18.64 A medical doctor is involved in a $1 million malpractice suit. He can either settle out of court for $250,000 or go to court. If he goes to court and loses, he must pay the $925,000 plus $75,000 in court costs. If he wins in court, the plaintiffs pay the court costs.

a. Construct a payoff table for this decision problem.

b. Draw a decision tree for this problem.

c. The doctor's lawyer estimates the probability of winning to be .2. Use the expected payoff criterion to decide whether the doctor should settle or go to court. Enter the lawyer's assessed probabilities and the expected payoffs associated with each action on your decision tree. (See Exercise 18.24 for a description of where to locate these quantities.)

*18.65 Refer to Exercise 18.64. Suppose no estimate is available for the probability of winning the suit.

a. Use the maximax criterion to decide whether to settle or go to court.
b. Use the maximin criterion to make the decision.

18.66 Refer to Exercise 18.64. Suppose the doctor's utility function for money is given by

$$U(x) = \frac{\sqrt{1,000,000 + x}}{1,400} \qquad -1,000,000 \le x \le 1,000,000$$

a. Convert the payoffs in Exercise 18.64 to utility values.
b. Use the expected utility criterion to decide whether the doctor should settle or go to court.

18.67 A common problem with management information systems (MIS) is that managers fail to use them, even when they are installed and are technically sound. Suppose a large computer firm is considering an MIS that will cost $1,000,000 to build and operate over a 5-year period. If the company's managers use the system, a savings of $750,000 per year will be realized.

a. Construct the payoff table for this decision problem.
b. Convert the payoff table to an opportunity loss table.
c. Suppose the probability that the MIS will be used is assessed to be only .05. Use the expected opportunity loss criterion to decide whether to install the MIS.

18.68 Graph each of the following utility functions and classify the decision-maker's attitude toward risk:

a. $U(x) = \dfrac{100 + .5x}{250}, \quad -200 \le x \le 300$

b. $U(x) = \dfrac{\sqrt{x + 100}}{20}, \quad -100 \le x \le 300$

c. $U(x) = \dfrac{x^3 - 2x^2 - x + 10}{800}, \quad 0 \le x \le 10$

d. $U(x) = \dfrac{.1x^2 + 10x}{110}, \quad 0 \le x \le 10$

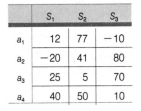

	S_1	S_2	S_3
a_1	12	77	-10
a_2	-20	41	80
a_3	25	5	70
a_4	40	50	10

18.69 Consider the accompanying payoff table. The decision-maker is indifferent between the following pairs of events:

1. Receive $0 with certainty, and win $80 with probability .15 or lose $20 with probability .85
2. Receive $20 with certainty, and win $80 with probability .3 or lose $20 with probability .7
3. Receive $40 with certainty, and win $80 with probability .55 or lose $20 with probability .45
4. Receive $60 with certainty, and win $80 with probability .8 or lose $20 with probability .2

a. Plot the utility values versus monetary values between −$20 and $80 (assign these endpoints utility values of 0 and 1, respectively).
b. Draw a smooth curve through the points in part a, and use this curve to assign utility values to all the payoffs in the table.

c. If the state probabilities are $P(S_1) = .4$, $P(S_2) = .35$, and $P(S_3) = .25$, which action should be selected according to the expected utility criterion? How does this compare with the action selected by the expected payoff criterion?

On Your Own . . .

Suppose you are trying to decide whether to promote an outdoor event scheduled for this spring. Choose an event that can be held only in good weather (concert, baseball game, famous speaker, etc.) and for which your city has an available facility. Based on the expected attendance and a reasonable ticket price, determine the payoff if the event is held. Remember to subtract your costs for advertising, facility rental, etc. These costs represent the (negative) payoff in case you decide to promote the event and it must be cancelled. Construct the payoff table corresponding to the two-action/two-state decision problem.

Now, based on *your own* knowledge of the climate in the area at the proposed time of the concert, assign probabilities to the states of nature: Rain and No rain. Based on these probabilities, which action (Promote or Don't promote) is selected by the expected payoff criterion?

References

Baird, B. F. *Introduction to decision analysis.* North Scituate, Mass.: Duxbury, 1978.

Balthasar, H. U., Boschi, R. A. A., & Menke, M. M. "Calling the shots in R & D." *Harvard Business Review,* May–June 1978, *56,* 151–160.

Brown, R. V., Kahr, A. S., & Peterson, C. *Decision analysis for the manager.* New York: Holt, Rinehart and Winston, 1974.

Bunn, D. *Applied decision analysis.* New York: McGraw-Hill, 1984.

Farquhar, P. H. Utility assessment methods. *Management Science,* Nov. 1984, *30*(11), 1283–1300.

Howard, R. A., Matheson, J. E., & North, D. W. "The decision to seed hurricanes." *Science,* June 1972, *176,* 1191–1202.

Keeney, R. L. "A decision analysis with multiple objectives: The Mexico City airport." *Bell Journal of Economics and Management,* 1973, *4,* 101–117.

Keeney, R. L., & Raiffa, H. *Decisions with multiple objectives: Preferences and value tradeoffs.* New York: Wiley, 1976.

Luce, R. D., & Raiffa, H. *Games and decisions.* New York: Wiley, 1957.

Raiffa, H. *Decision analysis. Introductory lectures on choices under uncertainty.* Reading, Mass.: Addison-Wesley, 1968.

Raiffa, H., & Schlaifer, R. *Applied statistical decision theory.* Cambridge, Mass.: MIT Press, 1961.

Schroeder, R. G. *Operations management decision making in the operations function.* New York: McGraw-Hill, 1981. Chapter 14.

Winkler, R. L. *An introduction to Bayesian inference and decision.* New York: Holt, Rinehart and Winston, 1972.

Winkler, R. L., & Hays, W. L. *Statistics: Probability, inference, and decision.* 2d ed. New York: Holt, Rinehart and Winston, 1975. Chapters 2 and 9.

CHAPTER 19

Decision Analysis Using Prior and Sample Information

Where We've Been . . .

In the previous chapter we discussed the use of the expected payoff and the expected utility criteria for making decisions in the presence of uncertainty, and we noted that such decisions are precarious when we have limited prior information about the states of nature.

Where We're Going . . .

In this chapter we show how to incorporate sample information into the decision-making process. The sample information is used to revise (and hopefully improve) the prior probabilities of the states of nature. The expected monetary value of sample information is considered, and we present an example of a more complex decision problem involving two actions and an infinite number of states of nature.

Contents

In Chapter 18, we presented solutions to decision problems using only currently available information. In this chapter we incorporate *sample information* into the decision process. In Section 19.1, we discuss the use of sample information to revise state of nature probabilities, and then in Section 19.2 we solve a decision problem using these revised probabilities and the expected payoff (or expected opportunity loss) criterion. The maximum expected worth of the sample information is calculated in Section 19.3, and then we compute the actual expected worth of this information in Section 19.4. Finally, an example of a decision problem involving two actions and an infinite number of states of nature is discussed in Section 19.5.

19.1
Revising State of Nature Probabilities: Bayes' Rule

Suppose you are trying to decide whether to purchase 100 shares of common stock in a particular company. You have decided that you want to make the purchase only if the probability is at least .75 that the stock's price will be higher a month from now. Based on your *prior information* about the company and stock market conditions, you assign a *prior probability* of only .6 to this event. Therefore, if you base your decision on your prior information, you will not buy the stock.

However, you may want to obtain *sample information* about the stock before making your decision. Your sample information might be an opinion from a reputable stock analyst whose predictions have the following reliability. Among the stocks that increase in price over a 1-month period, the analyst is able to predict the increase in 80% of the cases. But for stocks that will be stable or decrease in price, she predicts an increase in 40% of the cases. The analyst advises you that, in her opinion, the price of the stock in which you are interested will be higher 1 month from now. How should you revise your prior probability to incorporate this sample information?

Define the events

S_1: {Stock price will be higher 1 month from now}

S_2: {Stock price will be the same or lower 1 month from now}

I: {Analyst predicts the price will be higher 1 month from now}

We are interested in the conditional probability that the stock price will increase *given that* the analyst says it will increase — i.e., $P(S_1|I)$. Recall that the definition of conditional probability stipulates

$$P(S_1|I) = \frac{P(I \cap S_1)}{P(I)}$$

where $P(I \cap S_1)$ is the probability that the analyst says it will increase *and* it does in fact increase. We will find $P(S_1|I)$ in two steps.

Step 1   Find $P(I \cap S_1)$. Recall that $P(I \cap S_1) = P(I|S_1)P(S_1)$. We know that $P(I|S_1)$ — the probability that the analyst predicts a stock price will be higher in a month given that it will in fact be higher — is .8. Furthermore, $P(S_1)$ is the probability that the price will be higher a month from now, given no sample information; i.e., this is the prior probability of S_1, which we have assessed to be .6. Then

$$P(I \cap S_1) = P(I|S_1)P(S_1) = (.8)(.6) = .48$$

Step 2 Find $P(I)$. Note that $P(I)$ is the probability that the analyst predicts an increase in the stock's price. This will occur simultaneously with one of the two mutually exclusive, collectively exhaustive (i.e., no other states can occur) states of nature, S_1 and S_2. That is, either the stock will in fact be higher in price 1 month from now, or its price will be the same or lower. Thus,

$$P(I) = P(I \cap S_1) = P(I \cap S_2)$$

We have already found that $P(I \cap S_1) = .48$. In the same way,

$$P(I \cap S_2) = P(I|S_2)P(S_2)$$

We know that $P(I|S_2)$ — the probability that the analyst predicts a stock will increase in price when in fact it will not — is .4. Also,

$$P(S_2) = 1 - P(S_1) = 1 - .6 = .4$$

Then

$$P(I \cap S_2) = P(I|S_2)P(S_2) = (.4)(.4) = .16$$

and

$$P(I) = P(I \cap S_1) + P(I \cap S_2) = .48 + .16 = .64$$

Finally, we combine steps 1 and 2 to find

$$P(S_1|I) = \frac{P(I \cap S_1)}{P(I)} = \frac{.48}{.64} = .75$$

Thus, the probability that the stock will increase in price, given the sample information that the analyst predicts its rise, is .75. We refer to probabilities revised on the basis of sample information as *posterior probabilities*.* Since this posterior probability meets our previously established criterion that the probability of increase be at least .75, we now decide to purchase the stock.

Definition 19.1

A probability $P(S_i)$ of the state of nature S_i that does not incorporate sample information is called a *prior probability* of S_i.

A probability $P(S_i|I)$ of the state of nature S_i, given the sample information I, is called a *posterior probability* of S_i.

---

* We use the term *posterior* because the probabilities are determined *after* the sample information has been obtained, whereas *prior* probabilities are determined *before* sample information is obtained.

The process of revising prior probabilities to incorporate sample information is known as *Bayes' rule.* It is named for Thomas Bayes, an English Presbyterian minister and mathematician, who was one of the first to develop methods of calculating posterior probabilities. Bayes' rule for two states of nature and for k states of nature is given in the box. The states of nature are assumed to be mutually exclusive, collectively exhaustive events.

Bayes' Rule for Calculating Posterior Probabilities

Two states of nature: S_1 and S_2

$$P(S_1|I) = \frac{P(I \cap S_1)}{P(I)} = \frac{P(I|S_1)P(S_1)}{P(I|S_1)P(S_1) + P(I|S_2)P(S_2)}$$

where I is the sample information.

k states of nature: $S_1, S_2, \ldots, S_k$

$$P(S_i|I) = \frac{P(I \cap S_i)}{P(I)} = \frac{P(I|S_i)P(S_i)}{\sum_{j=1}^{k} P(I|S_j)P(S_j)}$$

A *probability revision table* organizes the calculation of posterior probabilities. In Table 19.1 we show the probability revision table for the stock price example, and the general form of the table is given in Table 19.2.

Table 19.1

Probability Revision Table for the Stock Price Example

(1) State of nature	(2) Prior probability	(3) Conditional probability of sample information	(4) Probability of intersection of state and sample information (2) × (3)	(5) Posterior probability (4) ÷ Total of (4)
S_1	.6	.8	.48	.75
S_2	.4	.4	.16	.25
Total:	1.0		.64	1.00

Table 19.2

Probability Revision Table (General)

(1) State of nature	(2) Prior probability	(3) Conditional probability of sample information	(4) Probability of intersection of state and sample information (2) × (3)	(5) Posterior probability (4) ÷ Total of (4)
S_1	$P(S_1)$	$P(I|S_1)$	$P(I \cap S_1)$	$P(S_1|I)$
S_2	$P(S_2)$	$P(I|S_2)$	$P(I \cap S_2)$	$P(S_2|I)$
$\vdots$	$\vdots$	$\vdots$	$\vdots$	$\vdots$
S_k	$P(S_k)$	$P(I|S_k)$	$P(I \cap S_k)$	$P(S_k|I)$
Total:	1		$P(I)$	1

In Example 19.1, we show how to apply Bayes' rule to a decision problem with monetary outcomes.

Example 19.1

A company has developed a home smoke detector that is considerably more reliable than those currently on the market, but it is also more expensive to produce. To market the detector competitively, the company will have to price it so low that the profit margin per unit will be quite small. Accordingly, the sales volume, and therefore the market share, will have to be high for the product to be worth marketing.

The company's accounting and marketing departments prepared Table 19.3 using the objective variable Net contribution to profit by the detector during its first 2 years on the market. The marketing department assessed the *prior state probabilities* (shown in parentheses in the table) using industry sales data for other detectors.

Table 19.3

Payoff Table for Example 19.1

| | | STATE OF NATURE (PRIOR PROBABILITIES IN PARENTHESES) *Market share after 2 years* | | | |
		S_1: .01 (.10)	S_2: .05 (.40)	S_3: .10 (.40)	S_4: .15 (.10)
ACTION	a_1: Market detector	−$1,500,000	−$200,000	$300,000	$1,000,000
	a_2: Do not market detector	0	0	0	0

Now suppose the company wants to incorporate *sample information* into the decision analysis. Twenty prospective detector purchasers are randomly sampled and asked their opinion of the new detector. Two of the twenty say they will purchase the detector if it is marketed. Use this sample information to *revise* the prior state probabilities by calculating the *posterior probabilities* associated with the states of nature.

Solution

This decision problem has four states of nature, and the prior probabilities are known (see Table 19.3). The next step is to calculate the probability of the sample information given each state of nature (column 3 of the probability revision table). Note that the sample consists of a consumer preference survey and that we can regard its outcome as a binomial random variable (see Section 5.4). The number of trials is $n = 20$, and the probability, p, represents the true market share the company will obtain upon marketing the detector. Thus, each state of nature represents a different value of p. The binomial random variable, x, is the number of the sampled consumers who will purchase the new smoke detector, and the survey result is $x = 2$. We now calculate the conditional probabilities of this sample result (using Table II in Appendix B):

$$P(I|S_1) = P(x = 2|p = .01) = \binom{20}{2}(.01)^2(.99)^{18} = .016$$

$$P(I|S_2) = P(x = 2|p = .05) = \binom{20}{2}(.05)^2(.95)^{18} = .189$$

$$P(I|S_3) = P(x = 2|p = .10) = \binom{20}{2}(.10)^2(.90)^{18} = .285$$

$$P(I|S_4) = P(x = 2|p = .15) = \binom{20}{2}(.15)^2(.85)^{18} = .229$$

We are now prepared to use the probability revision table to calculate the posterior probabilities for the states of nature. The calculations are shown in Table 19.4. Note that the sample information revised the probabilities of states S_3 and S_4 *upward* and the probabilities of states S_1 and S_2 *downward*. The posterior probabilities indicate that the company can be more optimistic about the market share of the smoke detector than it was prior to obtaining the sample information.

Table 19.4

Probability Revision Table for Example 19.1

(1)	(2)	(3)	(4)	(5)
		Conditional probability	Probability of intersection of state and sample	Posterior probability
State of nature	Prior probability	of sample information	information (2) × (3)	(4) ÷ Total of (4)
S_1: $p = .01$	.10	.016	.0016	.0075
S_2: $p = .05$	.40	.189	.0756	.3531
S_3: $p = .10$	.40	.285	.1140	.5325
S_4: $p = .15$	.10	.229	.0229	.1070
Total:	1.00		.2141	1.0001*

* Rounding error.   ■

The extent to which the prior probabilities are revised depends on the amount of information contained in the sample. For example, if 100 consumers had been surveyed in Example 19.1 and if the same *proportion* had responded favorably to the new smoke detector (i.e., $x = 10$), the four posterior state probabilities would be 0, .104, .826, and .069, respectively. Thus, the prior probability of state S_3: $p = .10$ is revised from .4 to .826. These probabilities are shown in Table 19.5 along with the posterior probabilities for a survey of $n = 20$ consumers (Example 19.1). As the sample size is increased, the weight given to the prior probabilities is diminished and more importance is attached to the sample information.

Table 19.5

Prior and Posterior Probabilities for the Smoke Detector Example: Two Different Sample Sizes

STATE	PRIOR PROBABILITY	POSTERIOR PROBABILITY $n = 20$ ($x = 2$)	$n = 100$ ($x = 10$)
S_1: $p = .01$	.10	.008	.000
S_2: $p = .05$	.40	.353	.104
S_3: $p = .10$	.40	.532	.826
S_4: $p = .15$	.10	.107	.069

Exercises 19.1 – 19.12

Learning the Mechanics

19.1 Give Bayes' rule for the case in which there are three states of nature, S_1, S_2, and S_3, and information I has been received by sampling.

19.2 Use the formula obtained in Exercise 19.1 to complete the following probability revision table:

(1) State of nature	(2) Prior probability	(3) Conditional probability of sample information	(4) (2) × (3)	(5) Posterior probability (4) ÷ Total of (4)
S_1	.25	60		
S_2	.40	.80		
S_3	.35	.10		
Total:	1.00			

19.3 Complete the following probability revision table:

(1) State of nature	(2) Prior probability	(3) Conditional probability of sample information	(4) (2) × (3)	(5) Posterior probability (4) ÷ Total of (4)
S_1	.35	.90		
S_2	.15	.10		
S_3	.30	.65		
S_4	.20	.30		
Total:	1.00			

19.4 Two coins are placed in a hat. One coin has two heads, while the other has a head and a tail. One of the coins is drawn at random. It is flipped and a head is observed. What is the posterior probability that the coin contains two heads? If a tail is observed, what is the posterior probability that the coin contains two heads?

19.5 What role does sampling play in decision analysis?

19.6 Compare and contrast prior and posterior information.

19.7 Consider this prior distribution for x:

x	5	10	15	20	25
$p(x)$	.2	.4	.2	.1	.1

The following conditional probabilities are associated with the sample information, I:

$P(I|x = 5) = .5$ $P(I|x = 10) = .8$ $P(I|x = 15) = .3$

$P(I|x = 20) = .2$ $P(I|x = 25) = .1$

a. Find the posterior probability distribution for x.
b. Find the mean and variance of the posterior probability distribution for x.

Applying the Concepts

19.8 A systems analyst is concerned about the proportion, p, of records that are in error in the inventory control system she designed. She assessed the probability distribution shown in the table at the top of the next page to characterize her beliefs regarding p.

PROPORTION OF ERRORS	PRIOR PROBABILITY
0.09	.40
0.10	.25
0.11	.15
0.12	.10
0.13	.10

a. Find the mean and variance of the analyst's prior probability distribution for p.

b. A random sample of twenty-five records yielded three incorrect records. Find the analyst's posterior probability distribution for p.

c. Find the mean and variance of the analyst's posterior probability distribution for p.

d. The posterior probability distribution you computed in part b combines the analyst's beliefs about p *and* the information about p contained in the sample. Using your results from parts a and c and graphs of the prior and posterior probability distributions, describe how the posterior distribution differs from the prior distribution. In so doing, you are explaining what the analyst learned about p by sampling.

19.9 A press produces masks for use in the manufacture of color television tubes. If the press is correctly adjusted, it will produce masks with a scrap rate of 5%. If it is not adjusted correctly, it will produce scrap at a 50% rate. From past company records, the machine is known to be correctly adjusted 90% of the time. A quality control inspector randomly selects one mask from those recently produced by the press and discovers it is defective. What is the probability that the machine is incorrectly adjusted?

19.10 Refer to Exercise 19.9. The quality control inspector observes a second mask and finds that it is also defective. Using the posterior probabilities from Exercise 19.8 as prior probabilities, calculate the posterior probability that the machine is incorrectly adjusted. What assumptions are required to make this calculation?

19.11 Suppose the proportion of defectives produced by a certain production process is 0.01, 0.05, or 0.10. The prior probability that it is 0.05 is twice the probability that it is 0.10. The prior probability that it is 0.01 is equal to the probability that it is 0.10.

a. Determine the prior probabilities associated with the proportion of defectives produced by the production process.

b. A sample of five units drawn at random yields three defectives. Revise the prior distribution you obtained in part a.

19.12 [*Note: This exercise refers to optional Section 5.5.*] A replacement parts inventory manager for a computer manufacturer believes the demand for a certain component is distributed as a Poisson random variable with a mean monthly demand of two, three, or four units. Suppose experience suggests that a mean monthly demand for three units is twice as likely as a mean monthly demand of two units, and that a mean monthly demand of two units is as likely as a mean monthly demand of four units.

a. If the demand for this component last month was four units, find the posterior distribution for the mean monthly demand for next month.

b. If the demand in the following month was two units, find the new posterior distribution for the mean monthly demand.

c. Comment on the ability of Bayes' rule to help a decision-maker "learn" about the shifting values of a parameter over time.

19.2
Solving
Decision
Problems
Using
Posterior
Probabilities

Recall that the expected payoff criterion (Section 18.5) selects the action with the highest expected payoff. The expected payoff for each action is computed using either the *prior probabilities* or the *posterior probabilities* of the states of nature, depending on whether sample information is available. For example, for the smoke detector decision problem (Example 19.1), the payoff table prior to obtaining sample information is given in Table 19.6. The expected payoffs for the two actions are

$$EP(a_1) = \sum_{\text{All states}} (\text{Payoff})(\text{Prior probability of state})$$

$$= (-1,500,000)(.10) + (-200,000)(.40) + (300,000)(.40) + (1,000,000)(.10)$$

$$= -\$10,000$$

$$EP(a_2) = 0(.10) + 0(.40) + 0(.40) + 0(.10) = 0$$

Thus, the expected payoff criterion, using prior probabilities, selects action a_2 and indicates that the firm should not market the new smoke detector.

Table 19.6

Payoff Table for the Smoke Detector Decision Problem

		STATE OF NATURE (PRIOR PROBABILITIES IN PARENTHESES)			
		$S_1: p = .01 (.10)$	$S_2: p = .05 (.40)$	$S_3: p = .10 (.40)$	$S_4: p = .15 (.10)$
ACTION	a_1: Market detector	−$1,500,000	−$200,000	$300,000	$1,000,000
	a_2: Do not market detector	0	0	0	0

In Example 19.1 we revised these prior probabilities based on the sample information that two out of twenty randomly sampled consumers would purchase the new detector if it were marketed. The payoff table with the posterior state probabilities is shown in Table 19.7.

Table 19.7 Payoff Table for the Smoke Detector Decision Problem

		STATE OF NATURE (PRIOR PROBABILITIES IN PARENTHESES)			
		$S_1: p = .01 (.008)$	$S_2: p = .05 (.353)$	$S_3: p = .10 (.532)$	$S_4: p = .15 (.107)$
ACTION	a_1: Market detector	−$1,500,000	−$200,000	$300,000	$1,000,000
	a_2: Do not market detector	0	0	0	0

The expected payoffs for the actions using the posterior probabilities are

$$EP(a_1) = \sum_{\text{All states}} (\text{Payoff})(\text{Posterior probability of state})$$

$$= (-1,500,000)(.008) + (-200,000)(.353) + (300,000)(.532) + (1,000,000)(.107) = -\$184,000$$

$$EP(a_2) = 0$$

Thus, the expected payoff criterion using posterior probabilities selects action a_1, indicating that the company should market the new detector. The sample information has altered the selection of the expected payoff criterion, changing it from a_2: Do not market to a_1: Market. Since the *posterior decision analysis* incorporates both prior and sample information, while the *prior decision analysis* incorporates only prior information, *we prefer the posterior decision to the prior decision.*

The expected payoff criterion using posterior probabilities is summarized in the box.

Expected Payoff Criterion Using Posterior Probabilities

Choose the action with the maximum expected payoff, where the expected payoffs are calculated using the posterior state probabilities.

$$EP(a_i) = \sum_{\text{All states}} \begin{pmatrix} \text{Payoff for} \\ \text{action } a_i/\text{state} \\ \text{combination} \end{pmatrix} \begin{pmatrix} \text{Posterior} \\ \text{probability} \\ \text{of state} \end{pmatrix}$$

Example 19.2   Suppose the company that is considering marketing the new smoke detector randomly samples 100 consumers and finds that 10 would purchase the new detector if it were marketed. The payoff table with the posterior probabilities is shown in Table 19.8. Which action should the company take if the expected payoff criterion is used?

Table 19.8   Payoff Table for the Smoke Detector Example

		STATE OF NATURE (PRIOR PROBABILITIES IN PARENTHESES)			
		$S_1: p = .01 \,(.000)$	$S_2: p = .05 \,(.104)$	$S_3: p = .10 \,(.826)$	$S_4: p = .15 \,(.069)$
ACTION	a_1: Market detector	$-\$1,500,000$	$-\$200,000$	$\$300,000$	$\$1,000,000$
	a_2: Do not market detector	0	0	0	0

Solution   We calculate the expected payoffs using the posterior probabilities. Thus,

$$EP(a_1) = \sum_{\text{All states}} \begin{pmatrix} \text{Payoff for} \\ \text{action } a_1/\text{state} \\ \text{combination} \end{pmatrix} \begin{pmatrix} \text{Posterior} \\ \text{probability} \\ \text{of state} \end{pmatrix}$$

$$= (-1,500,000)(.000) + (-200,000)(.104) + (300,000)(.826) + (1,000,000)(.069) = \$296,000$$

$$EP(a_2) = 0(.000) + 0(.104) + 0(.826) + 0(.069) = 0$$

The expected payoff criterion selects action a_1. This selection incorporates both prior information and the information contained in the sample of 100 consumers. ∎

The expected utility criterion presented in Section 18.7 may also be extended to incorporate sample information. Simply replace the prior probabilities by the posterior probabilities. This criterion will then prescribe an action that is consistent with the decision-maker's preferences for outcomes and risk attitude, as well as with the sample information. Thus, no matter which probabilistic criterion you use—expected payoff or expected utility—the incorporation of sample information requires only the substitution of posterior probabilities for prior probabilities.

**Exercises
19.13–19.17**

Learning the Mechanics

19.13 Use the posterior probabilities of Exercise 19.3 to select the action with the highest expected payoff in the following payoff table (outcomes are in thousands of dollars):

		STATE OF NATURE			
		S_1	S_2	S_3	S_4
	a_1	25	10	0	17
ACTION	a_2	30	10	2	0
	a_3	11	8	−16	21

19.14 Consider the payoff table given here (with prior probabilities in parentheses).

		STATE OF NATURE		
		$S_1 (.6)$	$S_2 (.1)$	$S_3 (.3)$
	a_1	10	20	−14
ACTION	a_2	−16	18	15
	a_3	21	12	9
	a_4	8	25	−20

a. Use the expected payoff criterion to choose an action.
b. Sampling information I has been obtained that suggests that S_1 is the true state of nature. The reliability of this information is reflected in the following probabilities:

$P(I|S_1) = .80 \qquad P(I|S_2) = .30 \qquad P(I|S_3) = .10$

Find the posterior state probabilities.
c. Compute the expected payoff for each action using the posterior probabilities.
d. Use your results of part c to determine which action is prescribed by the expected payoff criterion. Compare this action with the action selected in part a using prior probabilities.

19.15 Consider the accompanying payoff table.

		STATE OF NATURE		
		S_1 (.4)	S_2 (.3)	S_3 (.3)
ACTION	a_1	-160	200	100
	a_2	180	-172	90
	a_3	250	63	-80

a. Use the expected payoff criterion to choose an action.

b. Sampling information I has been obtained that suggests that S_2 is the true state of nature. The reliability of this information is reflected by the following probabilities:

$$P(I|S_1) = .20 \qquad P(I|S_2) = .60 \qquad P(I|S_3) = .20$$

Find the posterior state probabilities.

c. Given the sample information I described in part b, which action is implied by the expected payoff criterion?

Applying the Concepts

19.16 A large hospital is considering purchasing 100 new color television sets under one of two different purchase agreements. Under one agreement the TV sets would cost $460 each and all sets that are seriously defective would be replaced at no cost. Under the other agreement, the TV sets would cost $400 each and any seriously defective sets would have to be replaced by the hospital at $400 each. (Assume all replacement sets are nondefective.) The hospital's purchasing agent believes the probabilities shown in the table appropriately characterize the proportion of seriously defective sets in a shipment of 100 sets from the manufacturer.

PROPORTION DEFECTIVE	PROBABILITY
0.00	.4
0.05	.3
0.10	.1
0.15	.1
0.20	.1

a. Construct the payoff table for this decision problem. [*Note:* Costs represent negative payoffs.]

b. Use the expected payoff criterion to determine which purchase agreement the hospital should choose.

c. Suppose the hospital was able to randomly sample one TV set from the incoming shipment of 100 sets before deciding which purchase agreement to choose. According to the expected payoff criterion, which agreement should they select if the sampled set was defective? Nondefective?

19.17 A small company that produces auto parts for American-made cars expects to lose $1.5 million next year unless Congress passes a bill to limit the number of foreign-made cars that can be imported into the United States. If the bill passes, the company expects to make a profit of $2.5 million next year. The company's lobbyists in Washington have reported that the probability of the bill passing this year is .6. The auto parts company must decide whether to stay in business and risk a huge loss next year or to lease its facility for a year to a Japanese firm for $500,000. The company has just received new information from "a source close to the White House" that indicates Congress will pass the bill. The company assesses the reliability of the source as follows:

P(Source says bill will pass|Bill will pass) = .8

P(Source says bill will pass|Bill will not pass) = .1

a. Construct the payoff table for the company's decision problem. Include the company's prior state probabilities.
b. Compute the posterior state probabilities.
c. Describe the effect of the sample information on the company's prior beliefs regarding the passage of the bill by comparing the company's prior and posterior state probabilities.
d. Given the sample information, which action is prescribed by the expected payoff criterion?

19.3
The Expected Value of Perfect Information

Now that we know how to incorporate sample information into a decision analysis, we will consider the cost of obtaining this information. How much should we be willing to pay for sample information? In this section we will find the maximum expected worth of the sample information—*the expected value of perfect information.* In the next section we will calculate a reasonable price to pay for the sample information.

The calculation of the maximum expected worth of sample information is made easier by the use of the opportunity loss table. Recall (Section 18.3) that the opportunity loss values are determined for each action/state combination by subtracting the payoff for that combination from the maximum payoff for that state of nature. For example, consider the smoke detector example introduced in the previous two sections. The payoff table is shown in Table 19.9.

Table 19.9
Payoff Table for the Smoke Detector Example

| | | STATE OF NATURE (PRIOR PROBABILITIES IN PARENTHESES) | | | |
		$S_1: p = .01 (.10)$	$S_2: p = .05 (.40)$	$S_3: p = .10 (.40)$	$S_4: p = .15 (.10)$
ACTION	a_1: Market detector	−$1,500,000	−$200,000	$300,000	$1,000,000
	a_2: Do not market detector	0	0	0	0

To compute the opportunity losses, we subtract each entry in the payoff table from the maximum payoff in that column. Thus, for the state S_1, the maximum payoff is $0, and the opportunity loss (OL) for the (a_1, S_1) entry is

OL = 0 − (−1,500,000) = $1,500,000

That is, if the company chooses to market the detector (a_1) and the state of nature S_1 eventuates, the loss will be $1,500,000 compared with the outcome of not marketing the detector (a_2). The entire opportunity loss table is given in Table 19.10.

Table 19.10

Opportunity Loss Table for the Smoke Detector Example

| | | STATE OF NATURE (PRIOR PROBABILITIES IN PARENTHESES) | | | |
		$S_1: p = .01 (.10)$	$S_2: p = .05 (.40)$	$S_3: p = .10 (.40)$	$S_4: p = .15 (.10)$
ACTION	a_1: Market detector	$1,500,000	$200,000	0	0
	a_2: Do not market detector	0	0	$300,000	$1,000,000

The expected payoff criterion and its equivalent, the expected opportunity loss (EOL) criterion, select action a_2, since using the prior probabilities,

$EP(a_1) = -\$10,000$ $EOL(a_1) = \$230,000$

$EP(a_2) = 0$ $EOL(a_2) = \$220,000$

Recall that the expected opportunity loss criterion selects the action that *minimizes* the expected opportunity loss.

We can determine the maximum expected value of sample information by determining the expected value of perfect information. To calculate the expected value of perfect information, we compute the expected opportunity loss, assuming the sample information will tell us *with certainty* which state will occur, and subtract it from the expected opportunity loss for the action selected by prior decision analysis. That is,

$$\binom{\text{Expected value of perfect}}{\text{information (EVPI)}} = \text{EOL} \begin{pmatrix} \text{Action selected by} \\ \text{EOL criterion} \\ \text{using prior} \\ \text{probabilities} \end{pmatrix} - \text{EOL} \binom{\text{Action dictated by}}{\text{knowing state}}$$

But the expected opportunity loss for the action dictated by knowing which state will occur will always be 0, since in this case we will *always* select the correct action and therefore suffer *no loss*. Thus, EVPI is just the expected opportunity loss for the action selected by the EOL criterion based on prior probabilities.

In the smoke detector example, the EOL criterion selected action a_2, with $EOL(a_2) = \$220,000$. Thus, the expected value of perfect information is

$\text{EVPI} = EOL(a_2) = \$220,000$

The EVPI indicates that the maximum expected gain from sample information is $220,000. This will be the expected gain *only if* the sample information is perfect; i.e., if it tells us which state will occur. Unfortunately, this will rarely, if ever, be the case. Since, realistically, the sample cannot be expected to yield perfect information, EVPI can be viewed as an upper limit on the amount we should be willing to pay for sample information.

> ### Expected Value of Perfect Information
>
> $$EVPI = EOL(a')$$
>
> where a' is the action chosen by the expected opportunity loss criterion prior to obtaining sample information.

Example 19.3

A publisher of several different hobby-oriented magazines, airline magazines, and assorted newsletters is planning to computerize its warehouse. To do so will require extensive remodeling that, according to a consulting contractor, will take from 10 to 24 months to complete (depending on the availability of supplies and union labor). When asked to be more specific, the contractor gives the probability distribution shown in the table to characterize his uncertainty concerning how long the remodeling will take. While the remodeling is being completed, the publisher will have to rent temporary warehouse space. The owner of a vacant warehouse has presented four options concerning lease lengths and rent:

TIME	
t (months)	p (Time)
$t \le 12$	.2
$12 < t \le 18$	.5
$18 < t \le 24$	.3

1. 24 months @ $20,000, with the option to sign renewable 6-month leases @ $7,000 for as long as necessary
2. 18 months @ $16,000, with the same option as above
3. 12 months @ $11,000, with the same option as above
4. 6 months @ $7,000, renewable as often as necessary (assuming renewals would always be for periods of 6 months)

a. If the publisher's objective is to maximize its expected cash inflow, which rental plan should be chosen?

b. If the publisher were to hire another consulting contractor to reevaluate the length of time the remodeling would take, what is the maximum expected worth of the consultant's information?

Solution **a.** The actions among which the publisher must choose are the four rental plans. The random variable upon which the outcome of the publisher's chosen action depends is the length of time it takes to complete the remodeling. The possible realizations of this variable as specified by the contractor are the states of nature in the publisher's decision problem. Thus, the skeleton payoff table is shown in Table 19.11.

Table 19.11

Skeleton of Payoff Table for Example 19.3

		STATE OF NATURE (PRIOR PROBABILITIES IN PARENTHESES) Time (t) to complete remodeling (in months)		
		$t \le 12$ (.2)	$12 < t \le 18$ (.5)	$18 < t \le 24$ (.3)
ACTION	Rental plan 1			
	Rental plan 2			
	Rental plan 3			
	Rental plan 4			

Since the publisher's objective is to maximize cash inflow, the objective variable is Cash inflow. The possible values the objective variable can assume are determined by the various rental plans. Notice that, since rental payments are cash outflows, all the possible values the objective variable can assume in this problem are negative. Thus, if plan 3 is chosen and remodeling is completed in 12 months or less, the firm's rent payments will amount to $11,000, a cash inflow of $-$11,000. Accordingly, $O_{31} = -$11,000. If, however, the remodeling takes from 12 to 18 months, the cash inflow will be $-$18,000 $[-$11,000 + (-$7,000)]$, i.e., $O_{32} = -$18,000. The other outcomes can be determined similarly and are given in Table 19.12. Notice that plan 4 is an inadmissible action (why?) and can be eliminated from consideration.

Table 19.12

Payoff Table for Example 19.3

		STATE OF NATURE (PRIOR PROBABILITIES IN PARENTHESES)		
		$t \leq 12$ (.2)	$12 < t \leq 18$ (.5)	$18 < t \leq 24$ (.3)
ACTION	Plan 1	$-$20,000	$-$20,000	$-$20,000
	Plan 2	$-$16,000	$-$16,000	$-$23,000
	Plan 3	$-$11,000	$-$18,000	$-$25,000
	Plan 4	$-$14,000	$-$21,000	$-$28,000

The decision problem has now been completely formulated and is ready to be solved. First, it is necessary to determine the expected payoff for each action.

$$EP(\text{Plan 1}) = -20,000(.2) + (-20,000)(.5) + (-20,000)(.3) = -\$20,000$$

$$EP(\text{Plan 2}) = -16,000(.2) + (-16,000)(.5) + (-23,000)(.3) = -\$18,100$$

$$EP(\text{Plan 3}) = -11,000(.2) + (-18,000)(.5) + (-25,000)(.3) = -\$18,700$$

Since the expected payoff criterion selects the action with the maximum expected payoff (which in this case means the action with the *lowest expected cash outflow*), plan 2 should be chosen.

b. To determine the maximum expected worth of additional information, we compute the expected value of perfect information (EVPI). First, we convert the payoff table to an opportunity loss table (Table 19.13). Even though the values assumed by the objective variable in this problem are negative, the same rules apply for determining opportunity losses. For example, the opportunity loss associated with the action/state combination (plan 1, $t \leq 12$) was found by subtracting the payoff associated with (plan 1, $t \leq 12$) from the maximum payoff under the state ($t \leq 12$), which is $-$11,000.

Table 19.13 Opportunity Loss Table

		STATE OF NATURE		
		$t \leq 12$ (.2)	$12 < t \leq 18$ (.5)	$18 < t \leq 24$ (.3)
ACTION	Plan 1	$-$11,000 $- (-$20,000)$ $= $9,000	$-$16,000 $- (-$20,000)$ $= $4,000	$-$20,000 $- (-$20,000)$ $= 0$
	Plan 2	$-$11,000 $- (-$16,000)$ $= $5,000	$-$16,000 $- (-$16,000)$ $= 0$	$-$20,000 $- (-$23,000)$ $= $3,000
	Plan 3	$-$11,000 $- (-$11,000)$ $= 0$	$-$16,000 $- (-$18,000)$ $= $2,000	$-$20,000 $- (-$25,000)$ $= $5,000

The EVPI is the expected opportunity loss of the action that was chosen by the expected payoff (or EOL) criterion — i.e., EOL(Plan 2).

$$\text{EVPI} = \text{EOL(Plan 2)} = 5,000(.2) + 0(.5) + 3,000(.3) = \$1,900$$

Thus, even if the consulting contractor could tell the publishing company *with certainty* which state will occur, the expected value of this information is only $1,900. In other words, the publishing company cannot expect to gain more than $1,900 from the consultant's information and realistically can expect to gain less.   ■

In the next section we will discuss how to assign a more realistic value to the worth of sample information.

Exercises 19.18–19.24

Learning the Mechanics

19.18 Consider the following payoff table (prior probabilities in parentheses):

		STATE OF NATURE		
		S_1 (.65)	S_2 (.20)	S_3 (.15)
	a_1	$50	−$100	$200
ACTION	a_2	−$25	$150	$75
	a_3	$90	−$60	$180

a. Convert the payoff table to an opportunity loss table.
b. Find the expected value of perfect information and interpret your result.

19.19 Consider the decision tree shown here, with outcomes expressed as payoffs and prior probabilities in parentheses.

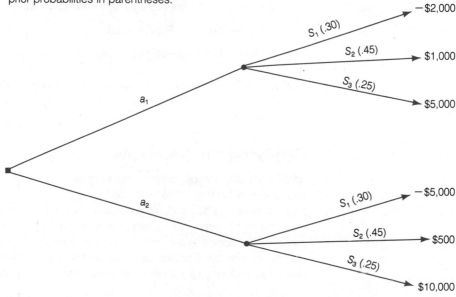

a. Convert the payoffs to opportunity losses.

b. Find the expected value of perfect information and interpret your result.

c. Suppose sample information I is obtained, and that the conditional probabilities associated with I are

$$P(I|S_1) = .10 \qquad P(I|S_2) = .95 \qquad P(I|S_3) = .15$$

Which state of nature does the sample information suggest is the true state of nature? Justify your response.

d. Using the sample information of part c, find the posterior probabilities for S_1, S_2, and S_3.

e. Using the results of part d, recalculate the expected value of perfect information. Explain why your result differs from the result you obtained in part b.

19.20 Consider the following payoff table (with prior probabilities in parentheses):

		STATE OF NATURE	
		S_1 (.15)	S_2 (.85)
ACTION	a_1	$6,000	−$3,000
	a_2	−$6,000	$20,000

a. Find the expected value of perfect information.

b. Sample information is obtained that suggests that S_1 is the true state of nature. The conditional probabilities of the sample information are

$$P(I_1|S_1) = .7 \qquad P(I_1|S_2) = .2$$

Using this sample information, calculate the revised EVPI. Does the EVPI increase or decrease? Why?

c. Suppose sample information had suggested that S_2 was the true state of nature. The conditional probabilities of the sample information are

$$P(I_2|S_1) = .30 \qquad P(I_2|S_2) = .80$$

Find the EVPI after receiving this sample result. Does the EVPI increase or decrease? Why?

d. Explain the difference in the changes in the EVPI for parts b and c. In general, under what conditions will the EVPI decrease after obtaining sample information? When will it increase?

Applying the Concepts

19.21 A petrochemical company has a distillation unit that occasionally goes out of control and produces batches of contaminated product. The cost of scrapping a contaminated batch of product is $25,000. If the contamination is only partial, then some of the finished product can be recovered by further processing at a cost of $15,000. Two actions are possible. The company can operate the unit under existing conditions, or it can perform maintenance on the distillation unit prior to each batch at a cost of $8,000 per batch. The maintenance procedure will ensure that each batch is acceptable. The probability that the distillation unit will be out of control is .05, and the probability that it will be partially out of control is .10.

a. Should management decide to install prebatch maintenance?

b. How much should the company be willing to pay for perfect knowledge about the state of the distillation unit for the next run?

19.22 Certified Public Accounting (CPA) firms are hired by private corporations to audit or certify their accounting records. In so doing, auditors check two main problem areas — possible fraud by company employees and acceptability of record-keeping practices. Upon completing its audit, the CPA firm either will certify that the client firm's records and financial statements are in order or will fail to certify them and will report on existing irregularities. If the auditor certifies the records when in fact errors and/or irregularities exist, the CPA firm may be sued by the client firm's stockholders for malpractice. If the CPA firm refuses to certify the records when in fact the records contain no errors or irregularities, it may be sued by the client.

Suppose you have audited a company's financial records, and you are faced with a certification decision. In your judgment, you have assessed the following costs for each: If you report incorrectly that the books are not certifiable when in fact they are, then you will lose the account and be sued by the client. You estimate the total cost for this error to be $2 million. If, on the other hand, you certify the accounts when irregularities exist, you will be sued for $10 million by the stockholders for malpractice.

a. Formulate the payoff table for this problem.

b. Describe how you would assess the state probabilities for this decision problem.

c. Assume you have assessed that the probability that the records are in order is .9. Which action would decision analysis prescribe?

d. What should the auditor be willing to pay for perfect information about the records?

19.23 Refer to Exercise 19.16, in which a hospital was considering purchasing 100 color television sets. On the basis of its prior information, how much should the hospital be willing to pay for perfect information about the number of seriously defective sets they would receive?

19.24 Refer to Exercise 19.17, in which an auto parts manufacturer is considering whether to stay in business or to lease its plant to another company. On the basis of its prior information, how much should the company be willing to pay for perfect information about whether Congress will pass the bill restricting the import of foreign cars?

19.4 The Expected Value of Sample Information: Preposterior Analysis (Optional)

We now want to make a realistic assessment of the expected worth of sample information. Of course, for the information to be of any use to us in deciding whether to obtain sample information, we must make the assessment *before* the sample is taken. Accordingly, the analysis is referred to as *preposterior analysis.*

For example, consider the smoke detector example of the previous sections. We repeat the payoff table with the prior state probabilities in Table 19.14 (next page). The expected payoff criterion using the prior probabilities yields $EP(a_1) = \$10,000$ and $EP(a_2) = 0$, so we would not market the detector (action a_2) based on the prior information.

Table 19.14

Payoff Table for the Smoke Detector Example

		STATE OF NATURE (PRIOR PROBABILITIES IN PARENTHESES)			
		$S_1: p = .01\,(.10)$	$S_2: p = .05\,(.40)$	$S_3: p = .10\,(.40)$	$S_4: p = .15\,(.10)$
ACTION	a_1: Market detector	−$1,500,000	−$200,000	$300,000	$1,000,000
	a_2: Do not market detector	0	0	0	0

Table 19.15

Probability Revision Table for Each Sample Outcome in the Smoke Detector Example

(1) State	(2) Prior probability	(3) Conditional probability of sample outcome given state	(4) Intersection of states and sample outcome (2) × (3)	(5) Posterior probability (4) ÷ Total of (4)
		$x = 0$		
$S_1: p = .01$	.10	.9801	.0980	.1146
$S_2: p = .05$	.40	.9025	.3610	.4221
$S_3: p = .10$	.40	.8100	.3240	.3789
$S_4: p = .15$	.10	.7225	.0722	.0844
Total:	1.00		.8552	1.0000
		$x = 1$		
$S_1: p = .01$	.10	.0198	.0020	.0145
$S_2: p = .05$	.40	.0950	.0380	.2764
$S_3: p = .10$	.40	.1800	.0720	.5236
$S_4: p = .15$	.10	.2550	.0255	.1855
Total:	1.00		.1375	1.0000
		$x = 2$		
$S_1: p = .01$	.10	.0001	.0000	.0000
$S_2: p = .05$	.40	.0025	.0010	.1389
$S_3: p = .10$	.40	.0100	.0040	.5556
$S_4: p = .15$	.10	.0225	.0022	.3056
Total:	1.00		.0072	1.0001*

* Rounding error.

    Now suppose the company is considering taking a sample of two consumers to obtain their opinions about the detector. (We choose a small sample size to reduce the computational difficulty.) The value of x, the number of the sampled consumers who state they will purchase the detector, will be either 0, 1, or 2. *Preposterior analysis involves examining the decision problem for each possible sample outcome.* Thus, in Table 19.15 we use a probability revision table to derive the posterior probabilities for each of the three possible sample outcomes. The first two columns show the states and prior probabilities, respectively. Column 3 presents the conditional probability of observing the sample outcome given a particular state of nature. For the smoke detector example, these are binomial probabilities with $n = 2$ and a value of p corresponding to the market share of each state. Thus, for the first two entries in column 3 under the heading $x = 0$, we find

$$P(x = 0|p = .01) = \binom{2}{x}p^x(1-p)^{2-x} = \binom{2}{0}(.01)^0(.99)^2 = (.99)^2 = .9801$$

$$P(x = 0|p = .05) = \binom{2}{0}(.05)^0(.95)^2 = (.95)^2 = .9025$$

and so on. In column 4 we find the probability of the intersection of the states and the sample outcome using the formula

$$P(x \cap S_i) = P(S_i)P(x|S_i)$$

which is the product of the respective entries in columns 2 and 3. Finally, we find the revised state probabilities — the posterior probabilities — in column 5 by applying Bayes' rule:

$$P(S_i|x) = \frac{P(x \cap S_i)}{\sum_{\text{All states}} P(x \cap S_j)} = \frac{P(S_i)P(x|S_i)}{\sum_{\text{All states}} P(S_j)P(x|S_j)}$$

Then each element in column 5 is equal to the corresponding element in column 4 divided by the column 4 total.

We now determine which action is dictated by each posterior distribution. That is, if none of the two sampled consumers will buy the detector (i.e., $x = 0$), which action should be selected? We use the expected payoff criterion with the posterior probabilities corresponding to $x = 0$:

$$EP(a_1|x = 0) = \sum_{\text{All states}} (\text{Payoff})(\text{Posterior probability of state for } x = 0)$$

$$= (-1,500,000)(.1146) + (-200,000)(.4221) + (300,000)(.3789) + (1,000,000)(.0844) = -\$58,250$$

$$EP(a_2|x = 0) = 0(.1146) + 0(.4221) + 0(.3789) + 0(.0844) = 0$$

Thus, the expected payoff criterion selects action a_2: Do not market the detector when $x = 0$ is the sample outcome.

Now suppose we observe $x = 1$ when the sample information is collected:

$$EP(a_1|x = 1) = \sum_{\text{All states}} (\text{Payoff})(\text{Posterior probability of state for } x = 1)$$

$$= (-1,500,000)(.0145) + (-200,000)(.2764) + (300,000)(.5236) + (1,000,000)(.1855) = \$265,550$$

$$EP(a_2|x = 1) = 0$$

So we choose a_1: Market the detector if $x = 1$.

Finally,

$$EP(a_1|x = 2) = (-1,500,000)(.0000) + (-200,000)(.1389) + (300,000)(.5556) + (1,000,000)(.3056) = \$444,500$$

$$EP(a_2|x = 2) = 0$$

So the expected payoff criterion selects action a_1: Market the detector when $x = 2$.

Table 19.16 (next page) summarizes our work to this point. Note that we included the probability of observing each of the sample outcomes in the last column of Table 19.16. These probabilities are the sums of the column 4 entries for each sample outcome in the probability revision table (Table 19.15). Thus,

$$P(x = 0) = \sum_{\text{All states}} P[(x = 0) \cap S_i]$$

$$= .0980 + .3610 + .3240 + .0722 = .8552$$

$P(x = 1)$ and $P(x = 2)$ can be computed in a similar manner. They form the *marginal (or predictive) probability distribution* for the random variable x. Note that the marginal probabilities are not dependent on the state, and they will sum to 1 if no rounding errors are present.

Table19.16

Actions Selected and
Expected Payoffs for the
Smoke Detector Example

SAMPLE OUTCOME	ACTION SELECTED	EXPECTED PAYOFF	MARGINAL PROBABILITY OF SAMPLE OUTCOME
$x = 0$	a_2	0	.8552
$x = 1$	a_1	$265,550	.1375
$x = 2$	a_1	$444,500	.0072
			.9999* ≈ 1.0

* Rounding error.

Now recall our ultimate objective. We are trying to determine how much is to be gained from sampling. Since we now know the expected payoff and the marginal probability of each sample outcome (Table 19.16), we can calculate the expected payoff of sampling (EPS):

$$\text{EPS} = \sum_x (EP|x)p(x) = \sum_{\substack{\text{All sample} \\ \text{outcomes}}} \begin{pmatrix} \text{Maximum expected} \\ \text{payoff for} \\ \text{sample outcome} \end{pmatrix} \begin{pmatrix} \text{Marginal} \\ \text{probability of} \\ \text{sample outcome} \end{pmatrix}$$

$$= (0)(.8552) + (265,550)(.1375) + (444,500)(.0072)$$
$$= \$39,713.53$$

or $39,700, rounding to the nearest hundred dollars. Thus, the mean payoff is $39,700 when $n = 2$ consumers are sampled.

To determine the expected gain attributed to sampling, we compare the EPS to the expected payoff for no sampling (EPNS). But EPNS is the expected payoff of the action selected by the expected payoff criterion using prior probabilities. We showed in previous sections that action a_2 is chosen using prior decision analysis, so that

$$\text{EPNS} = EP(a_2) = 0$$

Finally, the expected value of sample information (EVSI) is the expected payoff of sampling less the expected payoff with no sampling; i.e.,

$$\text{EVSI} = \text{EPS} - \text{EPNS} = \$39,700 - \$0 = \$39,700$$

This figure represents the mean dollar amount the company will gain from sampling and therefore provides a figure it will be reluctant to exceed in the cost of obtaining the sample information.

The steps for computing the expected value of sample information are summarized in the box. The calculation of EVSI becomes very tedious when the number of possible sample outcomes is large. However, because the method is the same no matter how many possible outcomes exist, computers can be useful aids in determining EVSI.

Computing the Expected Value of Sample Information (EVSI)

Step 1 Obtain the posterior state probabilities for each possible sample outcome using a probability revision table.

Step 2 Use the expected payoff criterion with the posterior probabilities to determine the action with the maximum expected payoff *for each sample outcome.*

Step 3 Find the marginal probability distribution for the sample outcomes by using

$$P(x) = \sum_{\text{All states}} P(x \cap S_i)$$

For each sample outcome, the marginal probability will be the sum of column 4 in the probability revision table (step 1).

Step 4 Find the expected payoff of sampling (EPS) by combining the results of steps 2 and 3:

$$EPS = \sum_{\substack{\text{All sample} \\ \text{outcomes}}} \left(\begin{array}{c} \text{Maximum} \\ \text{expected payoff} \\ \text{for sample outcome} \end{array} \right) \left(\begin{array}{c} \text{Marginal} \\ \text{probability of} \\ \text{sample outcome} \end{array} \right)$$

Step 5 Calculate the EVSI by

$$EVSI = EPS - EPNS$$

where EPNS is the expected payoff of no sampling, computed using the prior probabilities.

After the EVSI has been determined, it should be compared with the cost of sampling (CS) by computing the expected net gain for sampling (ENGS). For example, if the smoke detector company determines that a total cost of $500 will be incurred during the sampling of two consumers, the expected net gain of sampling is

$$ENGS = EVSI - CS = \$39,700 - \$500 = \$39,200$$

As long as the net gain is positive, the company can expect to gain by obtaining the sample information. We thus have the preposterior expected gain decision rule given in the box.

Preposterior Expected Gain Decision Rule

If the ENGS is greater than 0, the decision analyst should obtain the sample information before making a decision. The ENGS is calculated from the formula

$$ENGS = EVSI - CS$$

where CS is the cost of sampling.

Decision trees (Section 18.2) are often used to summarize the results of a preposterior analysis. The decision tree for the smoke detector example is shown in Figure 19.1. The first decision fork (always reading from left to right) represents the decision of whether to sample.

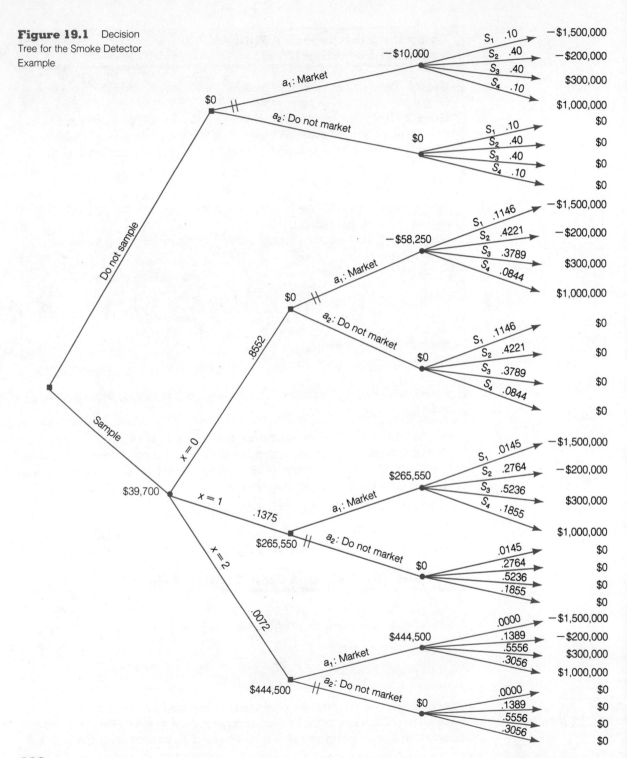

Figure 19.1 Decision Tree for the Smoke Detector Example

Along the upper branch (Do not sample) we place a decision fork representing the two possible actions of the decision problem. Beside this fork we write the expected payoff of no sampling (EPNS), which is 0 for this example. At the ends of the action branches, we place chance forks and branch into the four states of nature. Beside each chance fork we write the expected payoff for the associated action, where the expected payoffs are computed using the prior probabilities. The expected payoff is $-\$10,000$ for action a_1 and $\$0$ for action a_2 in our example. On the state branches, we write the prior probabilities, and at the ends of the branches are the outcomes corresponding to the action/state combinations.

The lower branch of the decision tree in Figure 19.1, the Sample branch, has an extra chance fork corresponding to the possible sample outcomes. The expected payoff of sampling (EPS), which is $\$39,700$ for this example, is written beside the sampling chance fork. The marginal probability for each sample outcome is written on the appropriate sample outcome branch, and the expected payoff for the optimal action corresponding to each sample outcome is recorded beside the decision fork at the end of each sample outcome branch. The remainder of the branching is into actions and then into states, just as for the Do not sample branch. The only difference is that posterior rather than prior probabilities are recorded on each state of nature branch. Note that two vertical lines are used to block the

---

Drawing a Decision Tree

Step 1 Beginning at the left of the page, form two branches, the upper one corresponding to Do not sample and the lower to Sample. At the ends of the branches, record the expected payoff of no sampling (EPNS) and the expected payoff of sampling (EPS), respectively.

Step 2 At the first decision fork of the upper branch (Do not sample), draw a branch corresponding to each action of the decision problem. At the ends of each of these action branches, record the expected payoff corresponding to that action using the prior probabilities.

Step 3 At the chance fork of each action branch (still in the upper branch), create a branch for each state of nature. On each of the branches record the prior probability of each state. At the end of each branch, record the payoff corresponding to each action/state combination.

Step 4 At the sampling chance fork of the lower branch (Sample), draw a branch corresponding to each possible outcome of the sample. Place the marginal probability of each outcome on the corresponding branch. At the end of each sample branch, record the maximum expected payoff corresponding to the sample outcome.

Step 5 Repeat steps 2 and 3 for the lower branch, creating action and state of nature branches. The only change is that the posterior state probabilities (rather than the prior probabilities) corresponding to each sample outcome are recorded on the state of nature branches.

Step 6 Draw two vertical lines through any action branch with an expected payoff that is less than the expected payoff for another action branch originating from the same decision fork. These vertical lines are intended to block the branch, indicating that the action should not be taken.

branches corresponding to actions with expected payoffs that are not maximum. This reminds us which action should be chosen at each decision fork.*

The steps to follow in drawing a decision tree are summarized in the previous box.

Example 19.4

In Section 18.2, we introduced the decision problem facing the promoter of a rock concert. The payoff table characterizing this decision problem is reproduced in Table 19.17. Suppose the promoter has the option of purchasing a long-range weather forecast for the night of the concert from a well-known meteorologist for $15,000. The meteorologist's track record in terms of the percentage of times in the past her predictions have or have not been accurate is shown in Table 19.18.

Table 19.17
Payoff Table for the Rock Concert Example

		STATE OF NATURE (PRIOR PROBABILITIES IN PARENTHESES)	
		Rain, S_1 $(\frac{1}{3})$	No rain, S_2 $(\frac{2}{3})$
ACTION	a_1: Rent stadium	−$40,000	$350,000
	a_2: Rent Civic Center	$150,000	$150,000

Table 19.18
Long-Range Prediction Record for Meteorologist

		ACTUAL WEATHER	
		Rain	No rain
METEOROLOGIST'S PREDICTION	Rain	85%	30%
	No rain	15%	70%

Eighty-five percent of the rainy days have been correctly predicted by the meteorologist and 70% of the days without rain have been correctly predicted by her. Should the promoter purchase this sample information (the meteorologist's opinion) or make a decision concerning which facility to rent utilizing just the prior information?

a. Calculate the EVSI.
b. Calculate the ENGS and make the decision about whether to obtain the meteorologist's prediction.
c. Summarize the results of this preposterior analysis using a decision tree.

Solution   **a.** We will follow the five-step approach for finding the EVSI.

Step 1 The first step is to construct a probability revision table to obtain the posterior probability distribution corresponding to each sample outcome. The two possible sample outcomes in this decision problem are that the meteorologist will predict no rain and that she will predict rain. The probability revision tables corresponding to these outcomes are shown in Table 19.19. Thus, the posterior probability of rain is .586 if the meteorologist predicts rain, but it is only .097 if the meteorologist predicts no rain.

* The computations for EVSI are often performed directly from a decision tree such as Figure 19.1. Both EPNS and EPS can be determined by starting at the far right-hand side of the tree and taking expectations backward through the tree.

Table 19.19

Probability Revision Tables
for the Rock Concert
Example

(1) State	(2) Prior probability	(3) Conditional probability of sample outcome given state	(4) Intersection of sample outcome and state (2) × (3)	(5) Posterior probability (4) ÷ Total of (4)
Predicts rain				
S_1: Rain	.333	.85	.283	.586
S_2: No rain	.667	.30	.200	.414
Total:	1.000		.483	1.000
Predicts no rain				
S_1: Rain	.333	.15	.050	.097
S_2: No rain	.667	.70	.466	.903
Total:	1.000		.516	1.000

Step 2 We now use the expected payoff criterion and the posterior probabilities to determine the preferred action for each sample outcome.

$$EP(a_1|\text{Predicts rain}) = (-40{,}000)(.586) + (350{,}000)(.414) = \$121{,}460$$
$$EP(a_2|\text{Predicts rain}) = (150{,}000)(.586) + (150{,}000)(.414) = \$150{,}000$$
$$EP(a_1|\text{Predicts no rain}) = (-40{,}000)(.097) + (350{,}000)(.903) = \$312{,}170$$
$$EP(a_2|\text{Predicts no rain}) = (150{,}000)(.097) + (150{,}000)(.903) = \$150{,}000$$

Thus, if the meteorologist predicts rain, the expected payoff criterion selects action a_2: Rent Civic Center. But if the meteorologist predicts no rain, the criterion selects a_1: Rent stadium.

Step 3 We now find the marginal probabilities for each sample outcome by summing the probabilities of the combinations of sample outcome and state over all states. These are the column 4 sums in the probability revision table (Table 19.19). We find

$$P(\text{Predicts rain}) = .483$$
$$P(\text{Predicts no rain}) = .516$$

Step 4 We summarize the results of steps 2 and 3 in Table 19.20.

Table 19.20

Summary for the Rock
Concert Example

SAMPLE OUTCOME	ACTION SELECTED	EXPECTED PAYOFF	MARGINAL PROBABILITY OF SAMPLE OUTCOME
Predicts rain	a_2	$150,000	.483
Predicts no rain	a_1	$312,170	.516

We now want to obtain the expected payoff of sampling:

$$EPS = \sum_{\substack{\text{All sample} \\ \text{outcomes}}} \left(\begin{array}{c}\text{Maximum expected payoff} \\ \text{for sample outcome}\end{array}\right)\left(\begin{array}{c}\text{Marginal probability of} \\ \text{sample outcome}\end{array}\right)$$

$$= (150{,}000)(.483) + (312{,}170)(.516)$$
$$= \$233{,}530 \quad \text{(rounding to the nearest dollar)}$$

Step 5 Finally, the EVSI is the difference between the EPS and the EPNS. Using the prior probabilities from Table 19.17, we find

$$EP(a_1) = (-40,000)(\tfrac{1}{3}) + (350,000)(\tfrac{2}{3}) = \$220,000$$
$$EP(a_2) = (150,000)(\tfrac{1}{3}) + (150,000)(\tfrac{2}{3}) = \$150,000$$

so that based on prior information we select action a_1, and the EPNS is $220,000. Thus,

$$\begin{aligned} \text{EVSI} &= \text{EPS} - \text{EPNS} \\ &= \$233,530 - \$220,000 = \$13,530 \end{aligned}$$

The expected gain from sampling is $13,530.

b. We now want to decide whether the promoter should hire the meteorologist. The ENGS is

$$\text{ENGS} = \text{EVSI} - \text{CS}$$

The meteorologist will charge $15,000 for her prediction, so

$$\text{ENGS} = \$13,530 - \$15,000 = -\$1,470$$

Since the ENGS is negative, the promoter should not pay for the sample information.

c. The decision tree summarizing the results of the preposterior analysis is shown in Figure 19.2. Note that the upper branch represents the Do not sample decision. The action and state branches emanate from the Do not sample fork. The expected payoff of no sampling, the expected payoffs for each action, the prior probabilities, and finally, the payoffs are also shown. The fact that a_1 is the preferred action is indicated by the vertical lines through the a_2 branch.

In the lower (Sample) branch, the first branching consists of the two possible sample outcomes, Predicts rain and Predicts no rain. The action and state branches emanate from the sample outcome branches. The expected payoff of sampling, the maximum expected payoff for each sample outcome, the expected payoff for each action, the posterior probabilities, and the actual payoffs are also recorded. We have again drawn vertical lines through action branches with expected payoffs that are exceeded by other actions emanating from the same decision fork.   ■

In the context of decision analysis, the term *sampling* means any procedure or process for gathering information. This includes statistical sampling, such as random sampling, as well as less technical methods, such as obtaining an expert opinion, as in the preceding example. If we are interested in random sampling, the optimal sample size can be determined by conducting a preposterior analysis for each potential sample size and choosing the sample size with the maximum ENGS. If this optimal sample size is 0 (or negative), the decision should be based on presently available information. Otherwise, the decision-maker should select a sample of the optimal size and then repeat the analysis to determine whether further sampling is expected to yield a positive net gain. Considerable effort is required to conduct a preposterior analysis when the sample size is moderate or large. Because the methodology remains the same for any sample size, computer programs have been written to conduct preposterior analyses.

Figure 19.2   Decision Tree for the Rock Concert Example

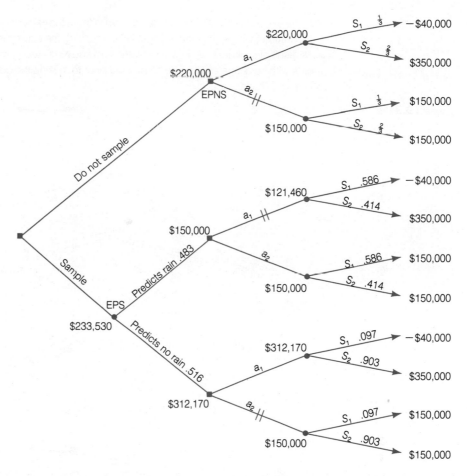

Case Study 19.1

An Example of the Benefits of Additional Information

In addition to studying whether hurricanes should be seeded (see Case Study 18.2) Howard, Matheson, and North (1972) addressed the question of whether more evidence on the effects of hurricane seeding should be gathered before the government policy decision on seeding is made. Would the expected loss from a representative hurricane be reduced by carrying out an additional seeding experiment?

First, the authors looked at the cost and possible outcomes of a seeding experiment. The cost to seed a hurricane and observe the results is $250,000. The possible outcomes are the same as those given in Case Study 18.2 for a seeded hurricane; the prior probabilities for these outcomes are also given in Case Study 18.2. Using the probabilities of each experimental outcome conditioned on each of the states of nature, the prior probabilities of the outcomes of seeding can be revised using Bayes' rule. The resulting posterior probabilities can then be used to evaluate the expected loss (EL) for seeding and not seeding. The decision to experiment or not can be made by comparing the expected loss of the "best" strategy *with* an experiment with the expected loss of the "best" strategy *without* an experiment. A condensed decision tree is shown in Figure 19.3. The tree indicates that the expected loss with the experiment is $2.83 million lower than without the experiment. Since the net gain from the experiment is greater than the cost ($0.25 million), the experiment should be conducted. As a result of their analysis, Howard, Matheson, and North recommended that further experiments with hurricane seeding be conducted prior to making the government policy decision on seeding hurricanes.

Figure 19.3

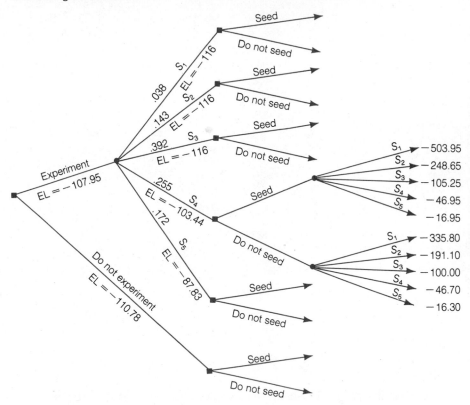

Learning the Mechanics

19.25 Consider the following payoff table (prior probabilities are shown in parentheses):

		STATE OF NATURE	
		S_1 (.30)	S_2 (.70)
ACTION	a_1	$500	−$50
	a_2	−$100	$250

The decision-maker would like to decide whether to purchase sample information about the true state of nature prior to choosing an action. The sample information would cost $100. The reliability of the sample information is described by the following conditional probabilities:

P(Sample information indicates S_1 true$|S_1$ is true) = .8
P(Sample information indicates S_2 true$|S_1$ is true) = .2
P(Sample information indicates S_1 true$|S_2$ is true) = .1
P(Sample information indicates S_2 true$|S_2$ is true) = .9

a. Find the expected payoff of sampling (EPS) and the expected payoff from no sampling (EPNS).
b. Use the results of part a to find the expected value of sample information (EVSI).
c. Find the expected net gain of sampling (ENGS).
d. According to the ENGS, should the decision-maker purchase the sample information prior to making a decision? Explain.

19.26 Refer to Exercise 19.25. Suppose a second source of sample information was also available to the decision-maker. This information costs only $10, but it is much less reliable than the first source (as indicated by the following conditional probabilities):

P(Sample information indicates S_1 true$|S_1$ is true) = .6
P(Sample information indicates S_2 true$|S_1$ is true) = .4
P(Sample information indicates S_1 true$|S_2$ is true) = .4
P(Sample information indicates S_2 true$|S_2$ is true) = .6

a. Find the expected net gain of sampling (ENGS) for the second source of sample information.
b. From which source should the decision-maker purchase sample information? Explain.

19.27 Consider the following decision tree with outcomes expressed as payoffs and prior probabilities in parentheses:

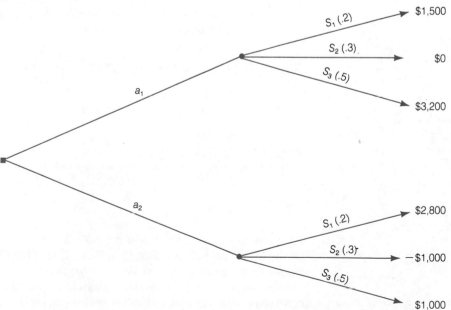

The decision-maker is considering purchasing sample information about the true state of nature prior to choosing an action. The sample information costs $250. The reliability of the sample information is described by the following conditional probabilities:

P(Sample information indicates S_1 true|S_1 true) = .7

P(Sample information indicates S_2 true|S_1 true) = .2

P(Sample information indicates S_3 true|S_1 true) = .1

P(Sample information indicates S_1 true|S_2 true) = .05

P(Sample information indicates S_2 true|S_2 true) = .9

P(Sample information indicates S_3 true|S_2 true) = .05

P(Sample information indicates S_1 true|S_3 true) = .1

P(Sample information indicates S_2 true|S_3 true) = .1

P(Sample information indicates S_3 true|S_3 true) = .8

a. What are the prior probabilities for S_1, S_2, and S_3?

b. Find the posterior probabilities for S_1, S_2, and S_3 when the sample information indicates S_1 is true.

c. Repeat part b for the case when the sample information indicates S_2 is true.

d. Repeat part b for the case when the sample information indicates S_3 is true.

e. Find the predictive (marginal) probabilities for the three sample results.

f. Expand the decision tree to include the decision-maker's sampling decision. Enter the payoffs on the tree along with all the probabilities you found in parts a – e. (For an example of such a tree, see Figure 19.2.)

g. Find EPNS and EPS, and enter them on your tree.

h. Find EVSI.

i. Use the preposterior expected gain decision rule to determine whether the decision-maker should purchase the sample information.

Applying the Concepts

19.28 The decision problem for a company that may market a new product is characterized in the following payoff table (prior probabilities in parentheses):

	PRODUCT'S STATUS AFTER 1 YEAR ON THE MARKET		
	Failure (.6)	Successful (.3)	Very successful (.1)
Market	− $200,000	$300,000	$600,000
Do not market	0	0	0

The company is considering whether to conduct a $30,000 market survey to gain information concerning the product's potential for success. One of four different conclusions would be yielded by the survey: "Product will be very successful," "Product will be successful," "Product will be a failure," or "Product's status after 1 year is uncertain." The reliability of the conclusions yielded by the survey can be described by the following conditional probabilities:

P(Survey concludes "very successful"|Product is very successful) = .6

P(Survey concludes "successful"|Product is very successful) = .2

P(Survey concludes "failure"|Product is very successful) = .1

P(Survey concludes "uncertain"|Product is very successful) = .1

P(Survey concludes "very successful"|Product is successful) = .2

P(Survey concludes "successful"|Product is successful) = .4

P(Survey concludes "failure"|Product is successful) = .2

P(Survey concludes "uncertain"|Product is successful) = .2

P(Survey concludes "very successful"|Product is a failure) = .1

P(Survey concludes "successful"|Product is a failure) = .1

P(Survey concludes "failure"|Product is a failure) = .5

P(Survey concludes "uncertain"|Product is a failure) = .3

a. Find the expected value of perfect information (EVPI), and interpret your result in the context of the problem.

b. Find the expected value of sample information (EVSI), and interpret your result in the context of the problem.

c. Find the expected net gain of sampling (ENGS), and use it to determine whether the company should undertake the proposed market survey.

19.29 Reconsider Exercises 18.18 and 18.32. The dress buyer expects to sell between three and eight dozen dresses with the prior probabilities shown in the table in the margin. A market research firm can be hired to forecast the demand for the new style of dress. Past records indicate that the research firm's conditional probabilities of forecasts, given the various states of nature (sales), are as shown in the following table:

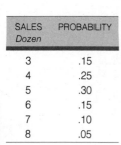

SALES *Dozen*	PROBABILITY
3	.15
4	.25
5	.30
6	.15
7	.10
8	.05

		ACTUAL SALES (DOZENS)					
		3	4	5	6	7	8
	3	.70	.10	.06	.04	0	0
	4	.20	.50	.10	.05	.05	0
FORECAST	5	.10	.20	.50	.11	.05	.05
SALES (DOZENS)	6	0	.10	.20	.40	.20	.10
	7	0	.10	.04	.30	.60	.15
	8	0	0	.10	.10	.10	.70

Perform a preposterior analysis and indicate how much the buyer should be willing to spend for the sample information.

19.30 A computer company has the capacity to produce seven computers per year. Its assessment of the prior probability distribution of next year's demand and the payoff table (in millions of dollars) constructed by the company's accounting department are shown at the top of the next page.

DEMAND	PROBABILITY
0	.05
1	.15
2	.22
3	.22
4	.16
5	.10
6	.05
7	.02
>7	.03

		STATE OF NATURE Number of computers demanded								
		0	1	2	3	4	5	6	7	>7
	Produce 0	0	−1	−2	−3	−4	−5	−6	−7	−7
	Produce 1	−.2	1	0	−1	−2	−3	−4	−5	−5
	Produce 2	−.4	.8	2	1	0	−1	−2	−3	−3
ACTION	Produce 3	−.6	.6	1.8	3	2	1	0	−1	−1
	Produce 4	−.8	.4	1.6	2.8	4	3	2	1	1
	Produce 5	−1.0	.2	1.4	2.6	3.8	5	4	3	3
	Produce 6	−1.2	0	1.2	2.4	3.6	4.8	6	5	5
	Produce 7	−1.4	−.2	1.0	2.2	3.4	4.6	5.8	7	7

The computer company is considering hiring a market forecaster to predict the demand for computers in the coming year. The following table reflects his reliability:

		ACTUAL DEMAND								
		0	1	2	3	4	5	6	7	>7
	0	.70	.30	.15	0	0	0	0	0	0
	1	.20	.50	.20	.10	.05	0	0	0	0
	2	.10	.10	.40	.30	.20	.20	0	0	0
FORECAST DEMAND	3	0	.05	.15	.40	.50	.40	.05	0	0
	4	0	.05	.05	.15	.20	.30	.10	.05	0
	5	0	0	.05	.05	.05	.10	.20	.05	0
	6	0	0	0	0	0	0	.40	.10	0
	7	0	0	0	0	0	0	.20	.50	.10
	>7	0	0	0	0	0	0	.05	.30	.90

The market forecaster will provide the computer company with a demand forecast for $10,000. Should the computer company spend $10,000 for the forecast?

19.31 A shoe manufacturer is considering the possibility of introducing a new line of athletic shoes. The company's management estimates profit from the new shoes to be

$$\pi = 100p - 2.5$$

where π is profit in millions of dollars and p is the proportion of the market the new shoes will capture. Management's assessments of the probabilities of capturing different proportions of the market are given in the table. If the shoe company's management would like to purchase some marketing research, what should it be willing to spend for the information?

MARKET SHARE	PROBABILITY
0	.10
0.01	.22
0.02	.30
0.03	.24
0.04	.13
0.05	.01

19.32 Refer to Exercise 19.16, in which a hospital was considering purchasing 100 color television sets. On the basis of its prior information, what is it worth to the hospital to be able to test one of the 100 television sets before selecting a purchase agreement?

19.5 An Example of a Two-Action, Infinite-State Decision Problem (Optional)

The smoke detector example of the previous sections allowed us to introduce the concepts of posterior and preposterior decision analysis. However, the small number of different possible market shares used as states of nature made the example somewhat unrealistic. A better approach would be to permit the market share, p, of a product to take on any value between 0 and 1, inclusive. Then a company would be faced with a decision problem with two actions — Market the product and Do not market the product — and an infinite number of possible states of nature corresponding to the infinite number of values p could assume. In this section, we discuss an approach to solving a decision problem with two actions and an infinite number of states.

Clearly, a payoff table or a decision tree cannot be used to enumerate the potential outcomes associated with the two actions of this decision problem because the number of potential states of nature that could occur is infinite. Thus, it is necessary to describe the outcomes for each action as a function of the market share, p.

Suppose a company has estimated the total demand for a newly developed product to be 10,000 units and that its accountants have determined that (1) the company incurs a fixed production cost (setup cost) of $50,000 whether it produces one unit or one million units, (2) it incurs a variable production cost of $10 per unit, and (3) the price it would sell the product for would be $35. Accordingly, the product's contribution to the profit, π, is

$$\pi = \text{Revenue} - \text{Expenditures}$$

where

$$\text{Revenue} = (\text{Market share})(\text{Total market})(\text{Sale price})$$
$$= p(10,000)(\$35)$$
$$= \$350,000p$$

$$\text{Expenditures} = \text{Fixed cost} + \text{Total variable cost}$$
$$= \$50,000 + (\text{Market share})(\text{Total market})(\text{Variable cost})$$
$$= \$50,000 + (p)(10,000)(\$10)$$
$$= \$50,000 + \$100,000p$$

Thus,

$$\pi = \$350,000p - (\$50,000 + \$100,000p)$$
$$= -\$50,000 + \$250,000p$$

Like the first row of the payoff table for the smoke detector example, this straight-line function describes the possible outcomes that could occur if the company chooses action a_1: Market the product. Thus, we will denote this function by π_{a_1}. If the company chooses action a_2: Do not market the product, the function describing the possible outcomes that could occur is simply $\pi_{a_2} = 0$ because there will be no profit or loss. Both these payoff functions are shown in Figure 19.4 (next page). Note that for p values greater than .20, action a_1 yields the higher contribution to profit, while action a_2 yields higher contributions when p is less than .20. The point at which the payoff functions intersect, $p = .20$, is referred to as the *breakeven value of p, p_{BE}.*

Figure 19.4   Payoff
Functions for the Two-
Action, Infinite-State
Marketing Example

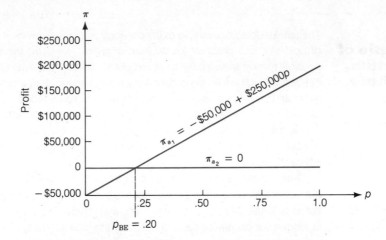

Although the best strategy is clear if the value of p is known, the market share will not be known in most realistic decision problems. We therefore need to specify a probability distribution for p to characterize our uncertainty concerning p. An important difference between the finite-state decision problems we discussed earlier and the infinite-state problem is that in the infinite-state problem we must utilize a continuous probability distribution rather than a discrete distribution to characterize the uncertainty about the potential states of nature. However, it can be shown that in the case of two-action decision problems with linear payoff functions, the analysis requires only that we know the mean of the prior distribution of p. Thus, in the above example, the decision-maker need only assess $E(p)$.

If the expected value of p exceeds its breakeven value, then the expected payoff for action a_1 will exceed that for a_2. Conversely, if the expected value of p is less than the breakeven value, the expected payoff for action a_1 is less than that for a_2. Thus,

1. If $E(p) > p_{BE}$, then $EP(a_1) > EP(a_2)$ and we prefer action a_1 to action a_2.
2. If $E(p) < p_{BE}$, then $EP(a_1) < EP(a_2)$ and we prefer action a_2 to action a_1.
3. If $E(p) = p_{BE}$, then $EP(a_1) = EP(a_2)$ and both actions yield the same expected payoffs.

Suppose in the product marketing example the company assigns a prior distribution to p that is normal with a mean of .15 and a standard deviation of .05, as shown in Figure 19.5. Note that the mean is less than the breakeven value, $p_{BE} = .20$. Based on the prior information, the company should select action a_2: Do not market the product.

Figure 19.5   Prior
Distribution for Market
Share, p

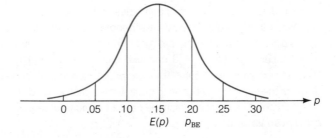

Exercises
19.33–19.38

Learning the Mechanics

19.33 Consider the two profit functions for the actions A and B,

$$\pi_A = -8 + 2x \qquad \pi_B = -1 + 1x$$

and the prior distribution for x given in the table.

x	5	10	15	20	25
$p(x)$	.05	.10	.30	.40	.15

a. Graph the profit functions.
b. Find the breakeven point—the point where the decision-maker would be indifferent between actions A and B.
c. Find the expected value of x. Which action should the decision-maker take?

19.34 Refer to Exercise 19.33. Formulate the payoff table for the decision problem, and apply the expected payoff criterion. Does the action prescribed by the expected payoff criterion agree with your answer in part c of Exercise 19.33?

19.35 Consider the two profit functions for the actions A and B,

$$\pi_A = -1,000 + 5x \qquad \pi_B = .5x$$

and the prior distribution for x given in the table.

x	100	200	300	400	500
$p(x)$	.1	.2	.3	.2	.2

a. Find the breakeven value for x.
b. Find $E(x)$.
c. Should the decision-maker select action A or action B? Justify your answer.

19.36 Refer to Exercise 19.35. Suppose the prior distribution for x were normal with mean 320 and standard deviation 75. Which action should the decision-maker select? Justify your answer.

Applying the Concepts

19.37 A company is considering whether to replace a damaged bottling machine with a brand A machine or a brand B machine. Brand A costs $15,000 and brand B costs $10,000. The following cost functions describe the total cost (TC) of operating each brand for the next 3 years:

$$TC_A = 15,000 + 11x \qquad TC_B = 10,000 + 17x$$

where x is the number of hours the machine is used over the next 3 years. The company believes the probability distribution in the table characterizes the number of hours the new bottling machine would be used over the next 3 years.

x	2,000	2,500	3,000	3,500	4,000
$p(x)$	.1	.2	.3	.2	.2

a. Graph the total cost functions.
b. Find the breakeven point for this decision problem, and use it to construct a decision rule involving $E(x)$ for deciding which brand to purchase.
c. Compute $E(x)$.
d. According to the decision rule you constructed in part b, which brand should the company purchase?

19.38 The manager of a doughnut shop believes the shop's daily sales of glazed doughnuts (in dozens) can be characterized by a normal distribution with unknown mean and variance. Prior experience suggests that the probability of the sales being greater than 20 dozen is .50 and the probability of sales being greater than 30 dozen is .05.

a. Determine the mean and variance of the prior normal probability distribution of doughnut sales.
b. The manager is considering purchasing one of two automatic doughnut machines. The first machine can be purchased for $10,000 and costs 10¢ per dozen to operate. The second machine can be purchased for $15,000 and costs 5¢ per dozen to operate. If the shop is open 365 days per year, which machine should the manager order to minimize expected costs over the first year?

Summary

In Chapter 18, we solved decision-making problems under uncertainty by assigning probabilities to the various states of nature and selecting the action that maximized the expected payoff or minimized the expected opportunity loss. Because the assessment of state probabilities is based on a limited amount of information, we may wish to collect additional information — a sample — and revise these probabilities. The state probabilities assessed before sampling are called *prior probabilities*. Their revised values, obtained using *sample information* and the procedures of this chapter, are called *posterior probabilities*. The decision analyst can compute the *expected value of sample information* before actually obtaining the sample; this is called a *preposterior analysis*. This quantity can then be compared to the *cost of sampling* to determine whether the sample information is worth its cost. If we decide to sample, we observe the sample outcome and use the appropriate posterior probabilities to make a decision.

We showed that the procedures for making decisions based on prior analysis (Chapter 18) or posterior analysis (Chapter 19) are identical once the probabilities of the states of nature have been assigned to the payoff table. In either case, use of the *expected utility criterion* will lead to decisions that are consistent with the decision-maker's preferences for outcomes and attitudes toward risk. Since the *expected payoff criterion* and the *expected utility criterion* are equivalent for risk-neutral decision-makers, the expected payoff criterion is frequently used as an approximation to the expected utility criterion.

Although most of the examples we considered are decision problems with a finite number of states of nature, the basic concepts of decision analysis remain unchanged when the number of states is infinite. Like most of the other topics we have discussed in this text, decision analysis embodies a variety of methods, criteria, and analytic techniques. Our objective was to present an introduction to this important area of business statistics. Consult the references at the end of this chapter for more detailed treatments.

Supplementary Exercises 19.39–19.50

[*Note: Starred (*) exercises refer to the optional sections.*]

19.39 Suppose you are sitting on a jury and hear the following evidence: A woman's body is found in a ditch in an urban creek following a violent argument with her boyfriend the previous evening. Investigation of the murder weapon shows a palm print that matches the boyfriend's print, but such evidence is not conclusive. A fingerprint expert asserts that such prints are possessed by one person in a thousand (Finkelstein & Fairley, 1977).

a. What is the posterior probability of the boyfriend's guilt if the prior probability of guilt is .10? Repeat this procedure for each of the following prior probabilities: .2, .3, .4, .5, .6, .7, .8, and .9.

b. Graph the posterior probabilities you computed in part a versus their respective prior probabilities. Graphs of this type can be used to examine the sensitivity of a particular posterior probability to different prior probabilities. Comment on the importance of such sensitivity analyses for decision analysis.

19.40 The management of a bank must decide whether to install a commercial loan decision-support system (an on-line management information system) to aid its analysts in making commercial loan decisions. Experience suggests that each correct loan decision (accepting good loan applications and rejecting those that will eventually be defaulted) adds, on the average, approximately $25,000 per decision to the bank's profit. Further, it is estimated that the additional number, x, of correct loan decisions (per year) that could be attributed to the decision-support system has the probability distribution given in the table.

x	0	10	20	30	40	50	60	70	80	90
$p(x)$	.01	.04	.10	.15	.20	.15	.10	.10	.10	.05

a. If the decision-support system is estimated to have a useful life of 5 years, what would be the expected increase in profits that could be attributed to it?

b. The increase in profits will accrue only if the system is used by the analysts. Past experience with this type of system has shown that for various behavioral and political reasons the system was not used by analysts in 80% of the installations. Given this information and the fact that the system costs $1,500,000 to purchase, install, and maintain over a 5-year period, should the bank purchase the system?

*c. The bank is considering hiring a consulting firm to interview its loan analysts and then predict whether this particular group of analysts will use the decision-support system. The reliability of the firm's predictions is measured by the probabilities given in the table. The consulting firm charges $50,000 for its survey. Should the bank purchase the survey? Explain.

		ACTUAL OUTCOME	
		Used system	*Did not use system*
FORECAST	*Will use system*	.7	.1
	Will not use system	.3	.9

19.41 *Acceptance sampling*[†] is commonly used by manufacturers to screen incoming lots of material for an excessive number of defective units. A sample is selected from each incoming lot of units, the number of defective units is counted, and the lot is either rejected or accepted depending on whether the number of defectives, *x*, exceeds a predetermined acceptance number. As an example of the decision analysis approach to acceptance sampling, assume the proportion of the number of defectives in an incoming lot is either 5% or 10%. The prior probability that the proportion of defectives will be 5% is .80. Suppose the cost of rejecting a lot with 5% defectives is $1,000, while the cost of accepting a lot with 10% defectives is $4,100. There are no costs for making a correct decision (i.e., accepting a lot with 5% defectives or rejecting a lot with 10% defectives).

a. Formulate the payoff table for this problem.

b. If no sample is drawn, should the lot be accepted or rejected?

c. Calculate the EVPI for this problem. Should management consider a sampling inspection program?

d. Assume a unit is drawn at random from the lot and is found to be defective. Should the lot be accepted or rejected?

e. If the unit drawn in part d was not defective, should the lot be accepted or rejected?

* f. Calculate the EVSI when the sample size is 1. Draw the corresponding decision tree.

*g. A frequent measure of the goodness of a statistical procedure is its efficiency. In decision analysis, the *efficiency* of the sampling plan is

$$\text{Efficiency} = \left(\frac{\text{EVSI}}{\text{EVPI}}\right)100\%$$

What is the efficiency of a sampling plan if the sample size is 1?

*h. It will cost management $10 in fixed costs plus $10 for every item inspected. Should management use a sample size equal to 1?

[†] Acceptance sampling is discussed in Section 2.6 in Wetherill (1977).

*19.42 Assume the same basic facts given in Exercise 19.41, but now consider a sample size of 3.

a. Draw a decision tree for a preposterior analysis and calculate EVSI.
b. What is the efficiency of this sampling plan?
c. What is the ENGS?

*19.43 Repeat Exercise 19.41 with a sample size of 5. Then, using these results and the results of Exercises 19.41 and 19.42, draw the following graphs:

a. Efficiency of sample versus sample size
b. ENGS versus sample size

*19.44 A winery is considering the possibility of producing and marketing a new low-cost dinner wine. Introduction of the wine will cost $3 million in promotional and fixed costs per year, and each bottle sold will contribute 30¢ to profits. Management believes that sales would be below 5 million bottles with probability .10 and greater than 25 million bottles with probability .05. It also believes sales are approximately normally distributed. Given the winery's assessed probabilities, should it produce and market the new variety of dinner wine?

19.45 Given the payoff table shown here (state probabilities in parentheses), find the EVPI. Interpret this number.

		STATE OF NATURE		
		S_1 (.3)	S_2 (.5)	S_3 (.2)
ACTION	a_1	$5,000	$2,000	$6,000
	a_2	$7,000	$0	$8,000

19.46 Repeat Exercise 19.45 for the following payoff table:

		STATE OF NATURE			
		S_1 (.1)	S_2 (.3)	S_3 (.4)	S_4 (.2)
ACTION	a_1	$10,000	$3,000	$0	−$4,000
	a_2	$6,000	$3,000	$1,000	$2,000
	a_3	$3,000	$6,000	$1,000	$0
	a_4	$5,000	$3,000	$1,000	−$1,000

19.47 The chief forester of a large midwestern city must plan for the identification and removal next year of elm trees infected with Dutch elm disease. State law requires that all elms identified as being diseased must be removed and disposed of by October 30. For each diseased tree left standing after October 30, the city loses $300 in state funds that have been budgeted for its reforestation program. Since the forester's staff can cut only 15,000 trees per season, private contractors must be hired to cut the trees in excess of 15,000. Unfortunately, the private contractors must be hired at the beginning of the disease season (May) before the seriousness of the disease epidemic is known. There is a fixed cost of $2,000 per contract signed, and each contractor is paid $250 for each tree removed. Assume each contractor has the capacity to remove 6,000 trees per season. The forester has hired a consultant to help determine how many contractors to hire. The first action taken by the consultant is to assess a probability distribution that characterizes local disease experts' prior opinions regarding the number of elms that will be infected in the coming season. This distribution is given in the table.

NUMBER OF TREES	PROBABILITY
0– 5,000	.05
5,001–10,000	.20
10,001–20,000	.30
20,001–30,000	.20
30,001–40,000	.10
40,001–50,000	.08
50,001–60,000	.07

a. Using the midpoints of the intervals in the probability distribution as the states of nature, formulate the payoff table for this decision problem.
b. From your payoff table, construct a decision tree for the forester's decision problem.
c. Based on the prior probabilities, how many contractors should be hired to maximize the expected payoff?
d. How much should the forester be willing to pay for perfect information about the number of trees to be infected?

*19.48 Refer to Exercise 19.47. The consultant reports to the forester that a statistical model can be developed to predict the number of trees that will be infected. The conditional probabilities of the forecasts given the various states of nature are shown in the table. It will cost $5 million to develop the model. Conduct a preposterior analysis to determine whether the model should be developed.

		ACTUAL NUMBER OF TREES INFECTED						
		0– 5,000	5,001– 10,000	10,001– 20,000	20,001– 30,000	30,001– 40,000	40,001– 50,000	50,001– 60,000
	0–5,000	.5	.3	.1	0	0	0	0
	5,001–10,000	.35	.4	.2	.1	0	0	0
	10,001–20,000	.15	.2	.5	.2	.1	0	0
FORECAST	20,001–30,000	0	.1	.2	.5	.2	0	0
	30,001–40,000	0	0	0	.2	.5	.1	.1
	40,001–50,000	0	0	0	0	.2	.5	.4
	50,001–60,000	0	0	0	0	0	.4	.5

19.49 Consider the following payoff table:

		STATE OF NATURE		
		S_1	S_2	S_3
	a_1	12	40	−5
ACTION	a_2	5	50	−10
	a_3	20	20	20

Given the prior probabilities

$$P(S_1) = .5 \qquad P(S_2) = .3 \qquad P(S_3) = .2$$

what is the EVPI for this problem?

19.50 Refer to Exercise 19.49.

a. Use the prior probabilities to determine which action is selected by the expected payoff criterion.

b. Suppose sample information has been purchased and the prior probabilities have been revised to yield the following posterior probabilities:

$$P(S_1) = .5 \qquad P(S_2) = .4 \qquad P(S_3) = .1$$

Use the posterior probabilities to determine which action is selected by the expected payoff criterion.

c. In which decision do you place more trust, the action selected using the prior probabilities in part a, or the action selected using the posterior probabilities in part b? Why?

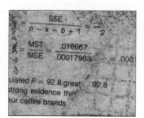

On Your Own . . .

Refer to the "On Your Own" section of Chapter 18, in which you were to decide whether to promote a spring event that requires good weather. Ask a local meteorologist for a long-range forecast based on a careful study of all pertinent data. You need to know the meteorologist's prediction 60 days in advance of the scheduled date of the event. Before you can assess the worth of the meteorologist's prediction, you have to ask for two conditional probabilities: the probability that the meteorologist will predict rain 60 days in advance *given that* it actually will rain, and the probability that he or she will predict no rain *given that* it will not rain. Conduct a complete preposterior analysis using the meteorologist's conditional probabilities and your own prior probabilities from the Chapter 18 "On Your Own" section. Will the meteorologist's prediction affect the action selected by the expected payoff criterion? How much would you be willing to pay the meteorologist for the prediction? Explain.

References

Baird, B. F. *Introduction to decision analysis.* North Scituate, Mass.: Duxbury, 1978.

Brown, R. V., Kahr, A. S., & Peterson, C. *Decision analysis for the manager.* New York: Holt, Rinehart and Winston, 1974.

Bunn, D. *Applied decision analysis.* New York: McGraw-Hill, 1984.

Finkelstein, M. O., & Fairley, W. "A comment on 'Trial by mathematics.'" Reprinted in *Statistics and public policy.* W. Fairley & F. Mosteller, eds. Reading, Mass.: Addison-Wesley, 1977.

Howard, R. A., Matheson, J. E., & North, D. W. "The decision to seed hurricanes." *Science,* June 1972, *176,* 1191–1202.

Raiffa, H. *Decision analysis. Introductory lectures on choices under uncertainty.* Reading, Mass.: Addison-Wesley, 1968.

Raiffa, H., & Schlaifer, R. *Applied statistical decision theory.* Cambridge, Mass.: MIT Press, 1961.

Wetherill, G. B. *Sampling inspection and quality control.* New York: Halsted, 1977.

Winkler, R. L. *An introduction to Bayesian inference and decision.* New York: Holt, Rinehart and Winston, 1972.

Winkler, R. L., & Hays, W. L. *Statistics: Probability, inference, and decision.* 2d ed. New York: Holt, Rinehart and Winston, 1975. Chapters 8 and 9.

CHAPTER 20

Survey Sampling

Where We've Been . . .

Although many methods are available for selecting a sample, the statistical methods described in the preceding chapters were based primarily on simple random sampling from populations of measurements that were large in relation to the sample size. Three exceptions to this method of data collection — the paired difference experiment and its generalization, the randomized block design (Chapters 9 and 15), and the factorial design (Chapter 15) — demonstrated the power of experimental design to increase the amount of information in sample data.

Where We're Going . . .

The term *sample survey* is usually used in conjunction with sampling of people, households, businesses, etc. The Current Population Survey and the Gallup Poll are examples of such surveys. Special problems arise in survey sampling that may require more elaborate sampling designs than simple random sampling. This chapter introduces some of the problems encountered in survey sampling and the sampling designs and methods that have been developed to handle them.

Contents

Almost all the statistical methods we have covered were based on simple random sampling (Section 4.6). Three exceptions to this method of data collection, the paired difference experiment, the randomized block design, and the factorial design, demonstrated that sampling designs other than simple random sampling can be used to increase the amount of information obtained in a sample. In this chapter, we present sampling designs and estimation procedures of a specific type, those used in *sample surveys.*

The term *sample survey* is usually used in conjunction with the sampling of collections of people, households, businesses, etc. A consumer preference poll is an example of a sample survey. Samplings conducted to estimate the general level of business inventories or to estimate the proportion of households that watched a particular television program are also examples of sample surveys. Sample survey designs may apply to either finite populations or infinite (conceptual) populations, which are sometimes called *processes* (refer to Case Study 3.2, page 62).

Most sample surveys are conducted to estimate one or more of three population parameters. For example, suppose we are interested in the market for seafood. One population parameter we might want to estimate is the mean amount, μ, of money spent monthly per household on seafood in a given market. A second population parameter of interest would be the total money, τ, spent on seafood per month in the market (i.e., the sum of the expenditures for all households in the market). Third, we might be interested in the proportion, p, of households that consume some seafood each month. Procedures for estimating μ and p for simple random samples were discussed in Chapter 8. We will discuss the estimation of the population total, τ, in this chapter. We present a summary of these estimation objectives in the box.

Common Objectives of Sample Surveys

1. Estimation of the population mean μ
2. Estimation of population total τ
3. Estimation of population proportion p

Sample surveys cost time and money, and sometimes they are almost impossible to conduct. For example, suppose we want to obtain an estimate of the proportion of households in the United States that plan to purchase new television sets next year, and we plan to base our estimate on the intentions of a random sample of 3,000 households. What are the problems associated with collecting these data? In order to use a random number table (Chapter 4) to select the sample, we would need a list of all the households in the United States. Obtaining such a list would be a monumental obstacle. After we obtain a list of households, we need to contact each of the 3,000 selected for the sample. Will all be at home when the surveyor reaches the household? And will all answer the surveyor's question? You can see that collecting a random sample is easier said than done. The large body of knowledge called *survey sampling* or *sample survey design* was developed to help solve some of the problems we have noted. It includes sample survey designs that will aid in reducing the cost and time involved in conducting a sample survey, and it includes the statistical estimation procedures associated with those designs. Since survey sampling is a course in itself (or several courses), we will present only a few of the most widely used sample survey designs and address only a few of the problems you might encounter. Further information on this important subject can be found in the references at the end of the chapter.

Case Study 20.1

Who Does Sample Surveys?*

We all know of the public opinion polls that are reported in the press and broadcast media. The Gallup Poll and the Harris Survey issue reports periodically, describing national public opinion on a wide range of current issues. State polls and metropolitan area polls, often supported by a local newspaper or television station, are reported regularly in many localities. The major broadcasting networks and national news magazines also conduct polls and report their findings.

But the great majority of surveys are not exposed to public view. The reason is that, unlike the public opinion polls, most surveys are directed to a specific administrative or commercial purpose. The wide variety of issues with which surveys deal is illustrated by the following listing of actual uses:

1. The U.S. Department of Agriculture conducted a survey to find out how poor people use food stamps.
2. Major television networks rely on surveys to tell them how many and what types of people are watching their programs.
3. Auto manufacturers use surveys to find out if people are satisfied with their cars.
4. The U.S. Bureau of the Census compiles a survey every month — the Current Population Survey (see Case Study 1.3 for more details) — to obtain information on employment and unemployment in the nation.
5. The National Center for Health Statistics sponsors a survey every year to determine how much money people are spending for different types of medical care.
6. Local housing authorities conduct surveys to ascertain satisfaction of people in public housing with their living accommodations.
7. The Illinois Board of Higher Education surveys the interest of Illinois residents in adult education.
8. Local, state, and national transportation authorities conduct surveys to acquire information on residents' commuting and travel habits.
9. Magazines and trade journals utilize surveys to find out what their subscribers are reading.
10. Surveys are used to ascertain the characteristics of people who use our national parks and other recreation facilities.
11. Sample surveys are used by marketing researchers to uncover new uses for products already on the market. Such information is helpful in redirecting existing advertising campaigns or creating new ones, as illustrated in the following examples (Cox, 1979):
   a. The producer of Ben-Gay, a topical analgesic, believed that consumers used Ben-Gay primarily for the relief of simple muscle aches. Data collected from a large sample of consumers revealed, however, that more than 50% of all consumers use Ben-Gay for arthritis relief (Davis, 1977).

* Most of this case study has been reproduced from the American Statistical Association's pamphlet, *What Is a Survey?* by R. Ferber, P. Sheatsley, A. Turner, and J. Waksberg (1980).

b. More than 4,000 consumers are surveyed weekly by Lever Brothers. The sample information they obtained regarding Wisk detergent indicated that many consumers were using Wisk as a ''pretreater'' of shirt collars. This information spawned the familiar ''ring-around-the-collar'' advertising campaign (*Marketing News,* Feb. 10, 1978).

20.1 Terminology

The terminology used in statistical survey sampling is slightly different from that used in other statistical applications. For example, the object upon which a measurement is taken is called an *element* instead of an *experimental unit.* The term *population* retains the same meaning: It is the collection of measurements about which we wish to make an inference.

> ### Definition 20.1
>
> The object upon which a measurement is made is called an *element.*

Sometimes we may want to reduce the cost of sampling by taking measurements on collections of elements that are physically near one another or bear some other relationship that makes them more easily observed as a group. For example, if we plan to sample the opinions of all adults regarding some particular product, we might wish to randomly select households and then interview all the adults in the households. When nonoverlapping sets of elements are randomly selected and each element in the set is measured, the sets are called *sampling units.* For the product preference survey just described, a household would be a sampling unit and the adults in the household would be the elements. Note that each element in a sampling unit (a household) is measured and that the elements in one sampling unit do not occur in the elements of another.

In the preceding chapters, we randomly selected experimental units and made a single observation on each. Thus, the earlier chapters were restricted to the special case where each sampling unit contained only one element.

> ### Definition 20.2
>
> A *sampling unit* is a collection of elements. The elements must satisfy the condition that those in any one sampling unit do not overlap with the elements in other sampling units.

In order to select a sample of sampling units from the total of those available, we must have a listing of them. Such a listing, which must include *all* the sampling units in the population of interest (to enable us to draw a sample that is representative of the population), is called a *frame.* Then, a *sample* is a subset of sampling units selected from a frame. The plan that specifies which sampling units will be included in a sample is called a *sampling design* or, for sample surveys, a *sample survey design.*

> **Definition 20.3**
>
> A *frame* is a list of sampling units.
>
> **Definition 20.4**
>
> A *sample* is a collection of sampling units selected from a frame.

We summarize the terminology in the box.

Term	Definition	Example: Product Preference Survey
Element	Object on which a measurement is made	Individual consumer
Sampling unit	Collection of elements	Household
Frame	List of sampling units	List of all households in relevant population
Sample	Collection of sampling units selected from frame	Set of households from which product preferences are obtained

20.2 Sample Survey Designs

Several useful sampling designs are available for sample surveys. Two of the most common (in addition to random sampling), *stratified random sampling* and *cluster sampling,* are described in this section, and the appropriate procedures for estimating the population mean, μ, a proportion, p, and the total, τ, of all measurements in the population are presented in Sections 20.6 and 20.7. Two other sampling designs, *systematic sampling* and *randomized response sampling,* are discussed briefly in this section, but we refer you to the references at the end of the chapter for the associated estimation procedures.

Stratified random sampling is used when the sampling units associated with the population are physically separated into two or more groups of sampling units (called *strata*) where the within-strata response variation is less than the variation within the entire population. For example, if y is the rent paid for a two-bedroom apartment in a city, we might want to divide the city into regions (strata) where the rents within each stratum are relatively homogeneous. Then we would estimate a population mean, proportion, or total by selecting random samples from within each stratum and combining the strata estimates as explained in Section 20.6. Stratified random sampling often produces estimators with smaller standard errors than those achieved using simple random sampling. Furthermore, by sampling from each stratum we are more likely to obtain a sample representative of the entire population. In addition, the administrative and labor costs of selecting the strata samples are often less than those for simple random sampling.

It is often less costly to use *cluster sampling,* where we randomly select groups (or *clusters*) of sampling units rather than individual units. For example, suppose we wish to sample the opinions of voters in a city. It would cost approximately the same amount of money to have pollsters contact a random sample of 1,000 households as it would to contact 1,000 individual voters. Since each household could contain two or more voters, sampling 1,000 clusters (households) could produce the opinions of several thousand voters and do so at approximately the same cost as randomly sampling the opinions of 1,000 voters. The estimation procedures for cluster sampling are discussed in Section 20.7.

Sometimes it is difficult or too costly to select random samples. For example, it would be easier to obtain a sample of student opinions at a large university by selecting every hundredth name from the student directory, with the first name selected randomly from the first 100 names in the directory. Although *systematic samples* are usually easier to select than other types of samples, one difficulty is the possibility of a systematic sampling bias. For example, if every fifth item in an assembly line is selected for quality control inspection, and if five different machines are sequentially producing the items, all the items sampled may have been manufactured by the same machine. If we use systematic sampling we must be certain that no cycles (like every fifth item manufactured by the same machine) exist in the list of the sampling units.

Randomized response sampling is particularly useful when the questions of the pollsters are likely to elicit false answers. For example, suppose each person in a sample of wage earners is asked whether he or she cheated on his or her income tax return. A person who has not cheated most likely would give an honest answer to this question. A cheater might lie, thus biasing an estimate of the proportion of persons who cheat on their income tax return.

One method of coping with the false responses produced by sensitive questions is randomized response sampling. Each person is presented *two* questions; one question is the object of the survey and the other is an innocuous question to which the interviewee will give an honest answer. For example, each person might be asked these two questions:

1. Did you cheat on your income tax return?
2. Did you drink coffee this morning?

Then a procedure is used to randomly select which of the two questions the person is to answer. For example, the interviewee might be asked to flip a coin. If the coin shows a head, the interviewee answers the sensitive question, #1. If the coin shows a tail, the interviewee answers the innocuous question, #2. Since the interviewer never has the opportunity to see the coin, the interviewee can answer the question and feel assured that his or her guilt (if guilty) will not be exposed. Consequently, the random response procedure can elicit an honest response to a sensitive question.

Four of the most important sampling designs are discussed in this chapter. In each case, we will present the methodology for selecting the sample, calculating the estimates of population parameters, and measuring the standard error of the estimates. The size of the standard error will serve as a measure of the amount of information on a parameter that is provided by a specific sampling design.

**Case Study
20.2**

Methods of Data
Collection in
Sample Surveys*

The survey designs described in this chapter prescribe methods for selecting elements from a frame. Once selected, the attribute of interest must be measured for each of the elements. That is, the data must be collected. Surveys that involve human populations can be classified by their method of data collection. Thus, there are *mail surveys, telephone surveys,* and *personal interview surveys.*

Mail surveys require the development of questionnaires that respondents complete on their own (i.e., self-enumeration). Mail surveys are seldom used to collect information from the general public because names and addresses are not often available and response rates tend to be low. However, this method may be effective with members of particular groups, such as subscribers to specialized magazines or members of a professional organization.

Telephone interviewing is an efficient method of collecting some types of data and is being increasingly used. Random samples of telephone numbers may be randomly or systematically selected from telephone directories, or a recent innovation called *random-digit dialing* may be employed. This approach involves using a random number generator to mechanically create the sample of phone numbers to be called. Random-digit dialing was developed to help overcome the sampling biases introduced into survey results by sampling from telephone directories (Glasser & Metzger, 1972).

Personal interviews are generally conducted in a respondent's home or office. They are much more expensive than either mail or telephone surveys, but may be necessary when complex information is being collected.

There are also newer methods of data collection by which information is recorded directly into computers. This includes the A. C. Nielsen Company's measurement of TV audiences using electronic devices—called *audimeters*—attached to a sample of TV sets. Nielsen places an audimeter in each of a sample of about 1,700 homes across the United States. The audimeter, usually located in a closet or in the basement, is wired to every TV set in the home and records when the sets are on or off and which channels are tuned in. The audimeter is connected via special telephone lines to Nielsen's computer. When you read in your newspaper that a particular TV show received, say, a "20 rating" for the week by A. C. Nielsen, it means that 20% of the sample of Nielsen families tuned in to that show for at least 6 minutes (Chagall, 1978).

Some surveys combine various methods. Survey workers may use the telephone to screen eligible respondents (say, women of a particular age group) and then make appointments for a personal interview. The U.S. Bureau of the Census' monthly Current Population Survey (see Case Study 1.3) uses both telephone and personal interviews.

Because changes in attitude or behavior cannot be reliably ascertained from a single interview, some surveys use a *panel* of respondents who are interviewed two or more times. Such surveys are often used during election campaigns, or to chart a family's health or purchasing pattern over a period of time. The Nielsen families, for example, constitute a panel of respondents whose TV watching patterns are monitored over time. Panels are also used to trace changes in behavior over time, as with social experiments that study changes in the work behavior of low-income families in response to an income maintenance plan.

---

* Portions of this case study have been reproduced from the American Statistical Association's pamphlet, *What Is a Survey?* by R. Ferber, P. Sheatsley, A. Turner, and J. Waksberg (1980).

Case Study 20.3

The *Literary Digest* Poll: FDR versus Alf Landon

Regardless of the survey design and data collection method employed, great care must be exercised in implementing the survey. Poorly implemented surveys may yield disastrous results, as this case study illustrates.

In 1936, the *Literary Digest,* a popular magazine, mailed 10 million questionnaires to voters in the United States. The questionnaire asked which presidential candidate was preferred, the Democratic incumbent, F. D. Roosevelt, or the Republican governor of Kansas, Alfred Landon. The *Digest* had previously predicted the winner of the presidency in every election since 1916. Prior to receiving the responses to its questionnaire, the *Digest* boasted, "When the last figure has been totted and checked, if past experience is a criterion, the country will know to within a fraction of 1% the actual popular vote of forty million" (Aug. 22, 1936, p. 3). The *Digest* received 2.4 million responses — a sample size approximately 800 times larger than is currently used by the Gallup Poll. The sample results indicated Landon would win by a landslide: Landon 57% and FDR 43%. Unfortunately for Landon and the *Literary Digest,* the actual election results yielded a landslide for FDR: FDR 62% and Landon 38%. What went wrong? How could such a large sample generate such misleading results? Part of the answer lies in the *Digest*'s choice of a sampling frame. The frame was constructed from sources such as telephone directories, club membership lists, magazine subscriber lists, and lists of car owners. Although use of such lists might not yield such misleading results today, the country was split politically along economic lines in 1936 — Republicans were generally wealthier than Democrats. As a result, the vast majority of people listed in the *Digest*'s frame were Republicans. Accordingly, the sample was not representative of the population of voters in the United States; it was heavily biased in favor of Republican voters.

If you have never heard of the *Literary Digest,* there is a reason: It is now defunct — thanks in part to the credibility lost as a result of its 1936 presidential poll (Huff, 1954; Freedman, Pisani & Purves, 1978; Bryson, 1976).

20.3 Estimation in Survey Sampling: Bounds on the Error of Estimation

Estimation procedures developed for the various sample survey designs may differ from those presented in earlier chapters for two reasons. The standard errors of estimators presented in earlier chapters were based on the assumption that the number of sampling units, N, in the population is large relative to the sample size, n. This assumption may not hold in survey sampling and thus will necessitate a modification of the formulas given for the standard errors of the estimators.

The second difference is that the sampling distributions of estimators are often unknown. For this reason, it is difficult to construct exact confidence intervals for population parameters. The usual procedure (see Scheaffer, Mendenhall, & Ott, 1979) is to give an estimate along with an approximate upper limit on the error of estimation — i.e., on the difference that might occur between the estimate and the unknown value of the population parameter. This upper limit, which we call a *bound on the error of estimation,* is calculated using the Empirical Rule of Section 3.7. The logic is that, according to the Empirical Rule, most (approximately 95%) of the estimates produced by an unbiased estimator should lie within *two standard errors* of the estimated population parameter. Or, we could form an approximate large-sample confidence interval for a parameter using the logic of Section 8.1; that is, we will find the endpoints of the confidence interval by adding and subtracting two standard errors to the estimate. Consequently, we will present the formulas for estimators, the estimated bounds on the error of estimation, and approximate confidence intervals for each sample survey design using the procedure shown in the box.

General Procedure for Estimating Population Parameters Based on Sample Surveys

1. Present a formula for calculating the estimate.
2. Give a bound on the error of estimation equal to 2 standard errors (or the sample estimate thereof) of the estimator.
3. Calculate an approximate 95% confidence interval for the parameter by forming the interval given by:

    Estimate ± (Bound on error)

    that is,

    Estimate ± (2 estimated standard errors)

Case Study 20.4
Sampling Error versus Nonsampling Error*

In Chapter 7, we learned that the behavior of the sample mean, $\bar{x}$, in repeated sampling can be described by its sampling distribution. We described the difference between a particular value of the estimator, $\bar{x}$, and the true value of the population parameter, μ, as *estimation error*. This difference is also known as *sampling error*. It is not error in the sense that anyone or anything is at fault or deserves blame; it is simply due to the fact that $\bar{x}$ is computed from a subset of the population rather than from the entire population. The standard error of the sampling distribution of $\bar{x}$ is a measure of the magnitude of the sampling error (estimation error) that may be present in the results of a survey that has been conducted to estimate μ. Accordingly, the standard error of $\bar{x}$ is used to place a bound on the sampling error associated with $\bar{x}$. As we will see in Section 20.8, this bound can be tightened simply by increasing the sample size of the survey.

Unfortunately, the other types of errors that plague surveys—known as *nonsampling errors*—are not so easily measured or controlled. Nonsampling errors are any phenomena other than sampling errors that cause a difference between an estimate and the true value of the population parameter. Nonsampling errors can be classified into two groups: *random errors* whose effects approximately cancel out if large samples are used and *biases* that tend to create errors in the same direction and thus do not cancel out over the entire sample.

Biases can arise from any aspect of the survey operation. Some of the main contributing causes are the following:

1. *Sampling operations.* There may be mistakes made in drawing the sample, or part of the population may be omitted from the sampling frame (as was the case in the *Literary Digest* poll, discussed in Case Study 20.3).
2. *Noninterviews.* Information may be obtained for only part of the sample due to, for example, "not-at-homes" or nonresponse to mail questionnaires. This causes a problem because, typically, there are differences between the noninterviewed part of the sample and the part that is interviewed.

* Portions of this case study have been reproduced from the American Statistical Association's pamphlet, *What Is a Survey?* by R. Ferber, P. Sheatsley, A. Turner, and J. Waksberg (1980).

3. *Adequacy of respondent.* Sometimes respondents cannot be interviewed, and information is obtained about them from others; the proxy respondent is not always as knowledgeable about the facts.

4. *Understanding the concepts.* Some respondents may not understand what is wanted.

5. *Lack of knowledge.* Respondents in some cases do not know the information requested or do not try to obtain the correct information.

6. *Concealment of the truth.* Out of fear or suspicion of the survey, respondents may conceal the truth. In some instances, this concealment may reflect a respondent's desire to answer in a way that is socially acceptable, such as indicating that he or she is carrying out an energy conservation program when this is not actually so.

7. *Loaded questions.* The question may be worded to influence the respondents to answer in a specific (not necessarily correct) way.

8. *Processing errors.* These can include coding errors, data keying, computer programming errors, etc.

9. *Conceptual problems.* There may be differences between what is desired and what the survey actually covers. For example, the population or the time period may not be the one for which information is needed, but had to be used to meet a deadline.

10. *Interviewer errors.* Interviewers may misread the question or twist the answers in their own words and thereby introduce bias.

Although not every survey will be subject to all these biases, a good survey statistician would be aware of their possible existence and attempt to control as many as possible.

In the case of the U.S. Bureau of the Census' Current Population Survey (see Case Study 1.3), many safeguards have been built into the survey process to protect against biases due to interviewer errors (Taeuber, 1978):

1. The survey's 1,100 interviewers are continuously trained and retrained.

2. Each interviewer's work is reviewed each month.

3. Periodically, interviewers are accompanied by supervisory personnel.

4. Approximately twice each year, a sample of the addresses assigned to an interviewer is reinterviewed by a supervisor. The interviewers have no way of knowing when their work will be checked or which addresses will be reinterviewed.

These precautions not only protect against interviewer error but also provide a measure of quality of the Current Population Survey.

20.4 Estimation for Simple Random Sampling

We discussed the estimation of a population mean, μ, and a proportion, p, based on simple random sampling in Chapter 8. The confidence intervals for these parameters were based on the assumption that the sample size, n, is sufficiently large and, although we did not state it, that the number, N, of sampling units in the population is large relative to the sample size, n.

In some sample surveys, the sample size, n, may represent 5% or perhaps 10% of the total number, N, of sampling units in the population. When the sample size is large relative to the number of measurements in the population, the standard errors of the estimators of μ and p (given in Chapter 8) should be multiplied by a *finite population correction factor.*

The form of the finite population correction factor depends on how the population variance σ^2 is defined. In order to simplify the formulas of the standard errors that are used in sample surveys, it is common to define σ^2 as division of the sum of squares of deviations by $N - 1$ rather than by N (analogous to the way we defined the sample variance). If we adopt this convention, the finite population correction factor becomes $\sqrt{(N - n)/N}$. Then the point estimators and the estimated bounds on the errors of estimation for μ and p are as shown in the boxes.*

Estimation of the Population Mean, μ: Simple Random Sampling

Estimator of μ: $\bar{x} = \dfrac{\sum x_i}{n}$

Estimated bound on the error of estimation: $2\hat{\sigma}_{\bar{x}} = 2\dfrac{s}{\sqrt{n}}\sqrt{\dfrac{N - n}{N}}$

where

$$s = \sqrt{\dfrac{\sum (x_i - \bar{x})^2}{n - 1}}$$

$N =$ Number of sampling units in the population

$n =$ Number of sampling units in the sample

[*Note:* In simple random sampling, each sampling unit contains only one element.]

Approximate 95% confidence interval: $\bar{x} \pm 2\hat{\sigma}_{\bar{x}}$

Estimation of the Population Proportion, p: Simple Random Sampling

Estimator of p: $\hat{p} = \dfrac{x}{n}$

where x is the number of sampling units that possess a specific attribute (in terms of the binomial distribution, x is the number of "successes").

Estimated bound on the error of estimation: $2\hat{\sigma}_{\hat{p}} = 2\sqrt{\dfrac{\hat{p}(1 - \hat{p})}{n}}\sqrt{\dfrac{N - n}{N}}$

where

$N =$ Number of sampling units in the population

$n =$ Number of sampling units in the sample

Approximate 95% confidence interval: $\hat{p} \pm 2\hat{\sigma}_{\hat{p}}$

---

* For most sample surveys, the finite population correction factor is approximately equal to 1 and, if desired, can be safely ignored. However, if $n/N > .05$, the finite population correction factor should be included in the calculation of the standard error and the bound on the error of estimation.

The point estimator and the estimated bound on the error for estimating a population total, τ, were not presented in Chapter 8. Their formulas are shown in the box.

Estimation of the Population Total, τ: Simple Random Sampling

Estimator of τ: $\hat{\tau} = N\bar{x}$

where

N = Number of sampling units in the population

n = Number of sampling units in the sample

$\bar{x}$ = Sample mean

Estimated bound on the error of estimation: $2\hat{\sigma}_{\hat{\tau}} = 2\sqrt{N^2 \dfrac{s^2}{n}\left(\dfrac{N-n}{N}\right)}$

where s^2 is the sample variance; i.e.,

$$s^2 = \frac{\sum (x_i - \bar{x})^2}{n - 1}$$

Approximate 95% confidence interval: $\hat{\tau} \pm 2\hat{\sigma}_{\hat{\tau}}$

Example 20.1

A specialty manufacturer wants to purchase remnants of sheet aluminum foil. The foil, all of which is the same thickness, is stored on 7,462 rolls, each containing a varying amount of foil. To obtain an estimate of the total number of square feet of foil on all the rolls, the manufacturer randomly sampled 100 rolls and measured the number of square feet on each roll. The sample mean was 47.4, and the sample variance was 153.1. Find an approximate 95% confidence interval for the total amount of foil on the 7,462 rolls.

Solution

Each roll of foil is a sampling unit, and there are $N = 7,462$ units in the population and $n = 100$ in the sample. Further,

$$\bar{x} = 47.4 \qquad \text{and} \qquad s^2 = 153.1$$

Substituting these quantities into the formula for the confidence interval, we obtain (for $\hat{\tau} = N\bar{x}$):

$$\hat{\tau} \pm 2\sqrt{N^2 \frac{s^2}{n}\left(\frac{N-n}{N}\right)} = (7,462)(47.4) \pm 2\sqrt{(7,462)^2 \frac{153.1}{100}\left(\frac{7,462 - 100}{7,462}\right)}$$

or, the approximate 95% confidence interval is

$$353,698.8 \pm 18,341.8$$

Consequently, the manufacturer estimates the total amount of foil to be in the interval 335,357.0 square feet to 372,040.6 square feet. If the manufacturer wants to adopt a conservative approach, the bid for the foil will be based on the lower confidence limit, 335,357 square feet of foil. ■

Examples of the estimation of a population mean, μ, and sample proportion, p, are not presented in this section because the examples would be identical to those presented in Chapter 8, except for the use of the finite population correction factor. We include exercises of this type at the end of this section.

Exercises 20.1–20.13

Learning the Mechanics

20.1 Calculate the percentage of the population sampled and the finite population correction factor for each of the following situations:

a. $n = 1,000$, $N = 2,500$ **b.** $n = 1,000$, $N = 5,000$
c. $n = 1,000$, $N = 10,000$ **d.** $n = 1,000$, $N = 100,000$

20.2 Suppose the standard deviation of the population is known to be $\sigma = 100$. Calculate the standard error of $\bar{x}$ for each of the situations described in Exercise 20.1.

20.3 Suppose $N = 5,000$, $n = 36$, and $s = 12$.

a. Compare the size of the standard error of $\bar{x}$ computed with and without the finite population correction factor.
b. Repeat part a, but this time assume $n = 500$.
c. Theoretically, when sampling from a finite population, the finite population correction factor should always be used in computing the standard error of $\bar{x}$. However, when n is small relative to N, the finite population correction factor is close to 1 and can safely be ignored. Explain how parts a and b illustrate this point.

20.4 Suppose you want to estimate a population mean, μ, and $\bar{x} = 375$, $s = 11$, $N = 305$, and $n = 30$. Find an approximate 95% confidence interval for μ.

20.5 Suppose you want to estimate a population proportion, p, and $\hat{p} = .37$, $N = 4,000$, and $n = 900$. Find an approximate 95% confidence interval for p.

20.6 Suppose you want to estimate a population total, τ, and $\bar{x} = 39.4$, $s = 4.0$, $N = 3,500$, and $n = 100$. Find an approximate 95% confidence interval for τ.

20.7 A random sample of size $n = 30$ was drawn from a population of size $N = 2,000$. The following measurements were obtained:

21	33	19	29	22	38
58	29	52	36	18	35
42	36	41	35	36	33
38	29	38	39	54	42
42	37	30	53	37	29

a. Estimate τ and place a bound on the error of estimation.
b. Estimate μ and place a bound on the error of estimation.

c. Estimate p, the proportion of measurements in the population that are greater than 30. Place a bound on the error of estimation.

Applying the Concepts

20.8 Organizations hire independent public accountants to perform audit examinations of their financial statements and to judge the fairness with which the financial statements characterize the financial position of the organization. The audit examination includes numerous reviews and tests that are designed to provide the auditor with evidence from which an opinion about the financial statements can be developed. In addition, this evidence provides the auditor with a basis for deciding whether the organization's financial statements have been prepared according to "generally accepted accounting principles." Since the early 1950's, auditors have relied to a great extent on sampling techniques, rather than 100% audits, to help them test and evaluate financial records. For example, sampling is frequently used to obtain an estimate of the total dollar value of an account — the account balance. The estimate can be used to check the account balance reported in the organization's financial statements. Such an examination of an account balance is known as a *substantive test* (Arkin, 1982). In order to evaluate the reasonableness of a firm's stated total value of its parts inventory, an auditor randomly samples 100 of the total of 5,000 parts in stock, prices each part, and reports the results shown in the table.

PART SERIAL NUMBER	PART PRICE	NUMBER IN SAMPLE
002	$ 108	3
101	55	2
832	500	1
077	73	10
688	300	1
910	54	4
839	92	6
121	833	5
271	50	9
399	125	12
761	1,000	2
093	62	8
505	205	7
597	88	11
830	100	19

a. Find a point estimate of the total value of the parts inventory.

b. Estimate the bound on the error of estimation associated with your point estimate of part a. [*Hint:* $s = \$209.10$]

c. Construct an approximate 95% confidence interval for the total value of the parts inventory.

d. The firm reported a total parts inventory value of $1,500,000. What does your confidence interval of part c suggest about the reasonableness of the firm's reported figure? Explain.

20.9 On Friday, February 3, 1984, the head of the Environmental Protection Agency (EPA), William Ruckelshaus, announced the banning of further use of the cancer-causing pesticide ethylene dibromide (EDB) as a fumigant for grain and flour-milling equipment. EDB is used to protect against infestation by microscopic roundworms called nematodes. In addition, Ruckelshaus announced maximum safe levels for EDB presence in raw grain, flour, cake mixes, cereals, bread, and other grain products now on supermarket shelves and in warehouses. Because the federal government does not have the authority to regulate the amount of chemicals in foods, these safe levels were intended as guidelines for state governments. Ruckelshaus estimated that, if state governments followed the EPA guidelines, approximately 7% of the existing corn products would have to be removed from supermarket and warehouse shelves. Following the announcement, state agriculture agencies began sampling the grain products sold in their respective states and testing for the presence of unsafe levels of EDB (Berg, Klauda, & Feyder, 1984). Of the 3,000 corn-related products sold in a particular state, tests indicated that 15 of a random sample of 175 had EDB residues above the safe level.

a. In the context of the problem, describe the population parameter, p, for which $\hat{p} = 15/175$ is a point estimate.
b. Estimate the bound on the error of estimation associated with $\hat{p}$ in part a. Interpret this bound in the context of the problem.
c. Construct an approximate 95% confidence interval for p.
d. Do the data provide sufficient evidence to indicate that more than 7% of the corn-related products in this state would have to be removed from shelves and warehouses? Test using $\alpha = .05$, and interpret your test results.

20.10 A sample survey is undertaken to determine the proportion of voters in a certain county who favor a proposal to create urban "enterprise job zones" that would seek to attract new business and job opportunities in declining areas of the county's cities. A random sample of 1,000 voters is selected from the 50,840 eligible voters in the county. Of the 1,000 voters, 620 said they would favor the proposal. Use the techniques outlined in this section to find an approximate 95% confidence interval for the true proportion of the county's voters who favor the creation of urban enterprise job zones.

20.11 A small grocery chain, which stocks 410 items, conducted an audit to compare the dollar value of the inventory shown on its books with the actual value of the inventory on hand. Sixty items were randomly selected from the 410, each of the sixty items was inventoried, and the difference between the book and actual values of the inventory was recorded. The difference between the book and actual inventories for the sixty items had a mean equal to $330 and a standard deviation equal to $546.

a. Estimate the mean difference per item between the book and actual inventories using a 95% confidence interval.
b. Estimate the total difference between the book and actual inventories for the chain. Use a 95% confidence interval.

20.12 A wholesale shipment contains 800 boxes of light bulbs, with ten bulbs per box (a total of 8,000 bulbs). Before accepting the shipment, a retailer wants to estimate the total number of defective light bulbs in the shipment. The retailer randomly selects fifty boxes and determines the number of defectives in each box. If the number of defectives per box has a mean of 0.4 and a variance of 1.2, estimate the total number of defective bulbs in the shipment and place bounds on the error of estimation.

20.13 In an urban industrial community, 70,500 persons are classified as potential members of the work force. An economist who wishes to investigate the unemployment rate in the community interviews 6,150 potential members of the work force and finds that 572 are currently jobless. Estimate the current unemployment rate in the community, and place a bound on the error of estimation.

20.5
Simple
Random
Sampling:
Nonresponse

We have explained in Section 4.6 how to draw a simple random sample, but we did not comment on the physical problem of actually doing it. For example, we mentioned in the introduction to this chapter that it would be extremely difficult to select a random sample of 3,000 households from all the households in the United States. And, even if we had a frame, it would be costly to contact the selected households.

Two methods for reducing the cost of random sampling are to use a telephone survey or a mailed survey. This type of sampling eliminates transportation costs and reduces labor costs, but it introduces a serious difficulty, the problem of *nonresponse.* By this, we mean that sampling units contained in a sample do not produce sample observations. For example, an individual may not be at home when telephoned or may refuse to complete and mail back a questionnaire.

Nonresponse is a serious problem because it may lead to very biased results. There may be a high correlation between the type of response and whether or not a person responds. For example, most citizens in a community might have an opinion on a school bond issue, but the respondents in a mail survey might very well be those with vested interests in the outcome of the survey — say, parents with children of school age, or school teachers, or those whose taxes might be substantially affected. Others with no vested interests might have opinions on the issue but might not take the time to respond. For this example, the absence of the nonrespondents' data could lead to a larger estimate of the percentage in favor of the issue than was actually the case. In other words, the absence of the nonrespondent data could lead to a biased estimate.

The problem of nonresponse identifies a very important sampling problem. If your sampling plan calls for a specific collection of sampling units, failure to acquire the responses from those units may violate your sampling plan and lead to biased estimates. If you intend to select a random sample and you cannot obtain the responses from some of the sampling units, then your sampling procedure is no longer random and the methodology based on it and the product of the methodology are suspect.

There are ways for coping with nonresponse. Most involve tracking down all or part of the nonrespondents and using the additional information to adjust for the missing nonrespondent data. For mailed surveys, however, it has been found that the inclusion of a monetary incentive with the questionnaire—even as little as 25¢—will substantially increase the response rate of the survey (Armstrong, 1975).

20.6 Stratified Random Sampling

Suppose you were in the wholesale seafood business in a city that had three distinctly different market areas. To plan your purchasing, you wish to obtain an estimate of the mean monthly seafood consumption per household in the city.

If you base your estimate of the mean monthly consumption, μ, of seafood per household on the mean, $\bar{x}$, of a random sample of n households selected within the city, the standard error that measures the variation associated with your estimate is

$$\sigma_{\bar{x}} = \frac{\sigma}{\sqrt{n}} \sqrt{\frac{N-n}{N}}$$

One way to reduce $\sigma_{\bar{x}}$ and reduce the costs of collecting the sample is to select samples within the three markets. The seafood consumption per household is likely to be less in some neighborhoods than in others. Consequently, there will be a substantial amount of variability in the household consumption, x, within the city. In contrast, the variation in consumption within one of the relatively homogeneous (socially and economically) neighborhoods is likely to be less, as is also the variation in consumption within each of the other neighborhoods. This suggests an alternative to simple random sampling. We select a random sample from within each of the three relatively homogeneous marketing areas (called *strata*), estimate the mean consumption within each, and then combine these estimates to obtain an estimate of the mean monthly consumption per household for the whole city. This type of sampling plan, called *stratified random sampling,* has three advantages:

1. Stratified sampling provides additional information; that is, it gives estimates of the mean for *each* stratum as well as of the mean for the entire population.
2. Stratified sampling usually provides more accurate estimates of the population mean than does a simple random sample of the same size because the variability within the strata is usually less than the variability over the entire population.
3. The transportation and administrative costs of sampling within strata are usually less than the costs of sampling within the entire population. This is because the sampling units are frequently geographically closer when selected within strata than when they are selected randomly from within the entire population.

To summarize, a stratified random sampling plan consists of partitioning the population into a group of k strata, each of which is more homogeneous than the population itself. This sampling plan usually results in more precise estimates (lower variability) at a lower cost. To implement a stratified sampling plan, select a random sample of n_1 sampling units from stratum 1, n_2 from stratum 2, . . . , and n_k from stratum k. Then, the total sample size selected from the population is $n = n_1 + n_2 + \cdots + n_k$. The notation and the formulas for parameter estimators are given in the following boxes.

Notation for Stratified Random Sampling

k = Number of strata

N_i = Number of sampling units in stratum i

N = Number of sampling units in the population
    $= N_1 + N_2 + \cdots + N_k$

n_i = Number of sampling units selected from stratum i

n = Total number of sampling units in the sample
    $= n_1 + n_2 + \cdots + n_k$

$\bar{x}_i$ = Mean of the sample for stratum $i = \dfrac{\sum\limits_{j=1}^{n_i} x_{ij}}{n_i}$

where x_{ij} is the jth measurement obtained from stratum i. Also,

s_i^2 = Sample variance for stratum $i = \dfrac{\sum\limits_{j=1}^{n_i} (x_{ij} - \bar{x}_i)^2}{n_i - 1}$

Estimation of the Population Mean, μ: Stratified Random Sampling

Estimator of μ: $\bar{x}_{st} = \dfrac{1}{N}(N_1\bar{x}_1 + N_2\bar{x}_2 + \cdots + N_k\bar{x}_k)$

Estimated bound on the error of estimation: $2\hat{\sigma}_{\bar{x}_{st}} = 2\sqrt{\dfrac{1}{N^2}\sum\limits_{i=1}^{k} N_i^2 \left(\dfrac{N_i - n_i}{N_i}\right)\dfrac{s_i^2}{n_i}}$

Approximate 95% confidence interval: $\bar{x}_{st} \pm 2\hat{\sigma}_{\bar{x}_{st}}$

Estimation of the Population Total, τ: Stratified Random Sampling

Estimator of τ: $\hat{\tau} = N\bar{x}_{st} = N_1\bar{x}_1 + N_2\bar{x}_2 + \cdots + N_k\bar{x}_k$

Estimated bound on the error of estimation: $2\hat{\sigma}_{\hat{\tau}} = 2\sqrt{\sum\limits_{i=1}^{k} N_i^2 \left(\dfrac{N_i - n_i}{N_i}\right)\dfrac{s_i^2}{n_i}}$

Approximate 95% confidence interval: $\hat{\tau} \pm 2\hat{\sigma}_{\hat{\tau}}$

Estimation of a Population Proportion, p: Stratified Random Sampling

Estimator of p: $\hat{p}_{st} = \dfrac{1}{N}(N_1\hat{p}_1 + N_2\hat{p}_2 + \cdots + N_k\hat{p}_k)$

where $\hat{p}_i$ is the sample proportion for stratum i ($i = 1, 2, \ldots, k$). Also,

Estimated bound on the error of estimation: $2\hat{\sigma}_{\hat{p}_{st}} = 2\sqrt{\dfrac{1}{N^2}\sum_{i=1}^{k} N_i^2\left(\dfrac{N_i - n_i}{N_i}\right)\dfrac{\hat{p}_i(1 - \hat{p}_i)}{n_i - 1}}$

Approximate 95% confidence interval: $\hat{p}_{st} \pm 2\hat{\sigma}_{\hat{p}_{st}}$

Example 20.2 The seafood wholesaler described earlier selected random samples of $n_1 = n_2 = n_3 = 400$ households from within each of the three markets (strata) and obtained from each household an estimate of the dollar amount spent per month on seafood. The number of households in each market along with the sample means and variances are shown in the table.

NEIGHBORHOOD	N_i	$\bar{x}_i$	s_i^2
1	20,800	$5.31	16.83
2	6,400	$9.49	15.10
3	12,600	$6.75	23.78
$N = 39,800$			

a. Estimate the total amount, τ, spent per month on seafood in the city.

b. Place bounds on the error of estimation.

Solution **a.** Substituting the values of N_i and $\bar{x}_i$ into the formula for $\hat{\tau}$, we obtain

$$\hat{\tau} = N\bar{x}_{st} = N_1\bar{x}_1 + N_2\bar{x}_2 + N_3\bar{x}_3$$
$$= (20,800)(5.31) + (6,400)(9.49) + (12,600)(6.75)$$
$$= \$256,234$$

b. The bound on the error of estimation is

$$2\hat{\sigma}_{\hat{\tau}} = 2\sqrt{\sum_{i=1}^{k} N_i^2\left(\frac{N_i - n_i}{N_i}\right)\frac{s_i^2}{n_i}}$$

$$= 2\sqrt{(20,800)^2\left(\frac{20,800 - 400}{20,800}\right)\left(\frac{16.83}{400}\right) + (6,400)^2\left(\frac{6,400 - 400}{6,400}\right)\left(\frac{15.10}{400}\right) + (12,600)^2\left(\frac{12,600 - 400}{12,600}\right)\left(\frac{23.78}{400}\right)}$$

$$= \$10,666$$

Thus, we estimate the total monthly expenditure for seafood in the city (for the month sampled) to be $256,234, and an approximate 95% confidence interval is $256,234 $\pm$ $10,666, or $245,568 to $266,900. ∎

Example 20.3 Refer to Example 20.2, and estimate the mean monthly expenditure for seafood per household in neighborhood 2.

Solution   Estimates of the mean expenditure per month per household for seafood for the three neighborhoods might play an important role in deciding how to allocate sales effort and in deciding where to locate retail markets. An estimate of the mean monthly expenditure per household for neighborhood 2 is

$$\bar{x}_2 = \$9.49$$

The estimated bound on the error of estimation is

$$2\hat{\sigma}_{\bar{x}_2} = 2\frac{s_2}{\sqrt{n_2}}\sqrt{\frac{N_2 - n_2}{N_2}} = 2\frac{\sqrt{15.10}}{\sqrt{400}}\sqrt{\frac{6,400 - 400}{6,400}} = \$0.38$$

Thus, we estimate the mean monthly expenditure per household in neighborhood 2 for the sampled month to be $9.49. We are reasonably certain that the true mean monthly expenditure per household in neighborhood 2 is between $9.11 and $9.87. ∎

Examples 20.2 and 20.3 illustrate the methods for estimating parameters based on the stratified random sampling of $n_1, n_2, \ldots, n_k$ sampling units from the k strata. Without being specific, we know that the standard errors of the estimators will decrease as the total sample size, $n = n_1 + n_2 + \cdots + n_k$ increases, but we have not commented on the relative magnitudes of $n_1, n_2, \ldots, n_k$. As a general rule, we select larger samples from strata with greater variability. More precise determination of the sample size requires numerical estimates of the strata variances. Also, the cost of sampling for each stratum will usually play a role in determining strata sample sizes because the total cost of sampling must be kept within the budget for the project. An example of sample size determination is given in Section 20.8.

Exercises 20.14–20.20

Learning the Mechanics

20.14 A survey based on a stratified random sample produced the data shown in the table.

	STRATUM		
	1	*2*	*3*
N_i	3,000	5,000	4,000
n_i	60	100	80
$\bar{x}_i$	39.5	28.6	33.4
s_i^2	4.8	9.1	3.3
$\hat{p}_i$	.4	.5	.3

a. Find an approximate 95% confidence interval for the population mean, μ.
b. Find an approximate 95% confidence interval for the population total, τ.
c. Find an approximate 95% confidence interval for the population proportion, p.

20.15 A survey based on a stratified random sample produced the data shown in the table.

STRATUM	NUMBER OF SAMPLING UNITS IN STRATUM	MEASUREMENTS
1	4,000	10, 15, 5, 30, 25, 26, 38, 50, 10, 28
2	6,000	5, 33, 15, 45, 47, 36, 25, 40, 17, 31, 62, 28, 33, 45, 68
3	10,000	28, 75, 62, 43, 31, 48, 35, 26, 5, 81, 66, 18, 33, 38, 40, 45, 46, 18, 62, 40
4	15,000	45, 43, 15, 78, 92, 105, 38, 45, 49, 10, 36, 48, 17, 82, 76, 51, 39, 46, 40, 52, 88, 20, 40, 41, 50

a. Estimate the population mean, μ, and place a bound on the error of estimation.

b. Estimate the population total, τ, and place a bound on the error of estimation.

c. Estimate the proportion of the measurements in the population, p, that are between 35 and 55, inclusive.

Applying the Concepts

20.16 In 1980, the U.S. Department of Labor classified approximately 185,000 persons as health care administrators and estimated that another 105,000 positions would be created during the 1980's. Health care administrators include hospital administrators, managers of nursing homes, and managers of health maintenance organizations (Wright, 1982). In order to estimate the mean 1980 income of the head administrators of the 6,965 hospitals in the United States, a labor economist used stratified random sampling to select thirty administrators to be questioned about their incomes. The population was stratified according to the number of beds in each administrator's hospital. The results of the survey are shown here.

INCOME ($ THOUSAND)		
Under 100 beds ($N_1 = 3,210$)	100–299 beds ($N_2 = 2,015$)	300 beds and over ($N_3 = 1,740$)
32.0	39.2	69.2
39.1	55.4	65.0
35.6	51.6	58.9
36.2	48.0	49.3
38.7	37.5	70.5
	48.9	60.0
	46.1	54.8
	44.6	68.8
	45.2	57.3
	27.3	71.1
		68.1
		62.4
		45.0
		56.7
		59.5

Source: Salary data based on Wright (1982), p. 608.

a. Find a point estimate for the mean 1980 income of hospital administrators.

b. Place bounds on the error of estimation associated with your point estimate in part a, and interpret the bounds in the context of the problem.

c. Find an approximate 95% confidence interval for the mean income of administrators of hospitals with 300 or more beds.

d. Examine the sample data and suggest a reason why the labor economist chose to allocate the sample size unevenly across the strata.

20.17 Since 1978, Internal Revenue Service (IRS) agents have been using sampling procedures to facilitate the auditing of tax returns of individuals and businesses. For example, sampling is used to estimate the total value of the error associated with a particular account balance reported on a tax return. Generally, agents use 95% confidence intervals to estimate such quantities. If substantial error is found, adjustments to the tax return will be suggested. For further details, see Brown (1982) and Hull and Everett (1982). In auditing the investment credit of a particular corporation, the IRS stratified the firm's population of 1,000 invoices containing the appropriate investment credit information into four strata according to the size of the expenditure involved: $0 to under $1,000, $1,000 to under $3,000, $3,000 to under $10,000, and $10,000 and over. Random samples of invoices of sizes $n_1 = 6$, $n_2 = 8$, $n_3 = 10$, and $n_4 = 15$ were drawn from each of the respective strata. Each sampled invoice was examined to determine whether it was properly treated by the firm in determining the firm's investment credit. The table describes the error associated with each sampled invoice as identified by the IRS. Positive errors reflect an overstatement by the firm of its investment credit and negative errors reflect an understatement.

INVESTMENT CREDIT ERRORS			
$0 to under $1,000 ($N_1 = 100$)	$1,000 to under $3,000 ($N_2 = 400$)	$3,000 to under $10,000 ($N_3 = 300$)	$10,000 and over ($N_4 = 200$)
$ 10	$ 0	$ 750	$ 0
0	0	0	0
0	100	0	5,000
−15	0	1,000	0
25	−50	0	0
20	0	0	0
	550	0	1,800
	0	1,500	0
		0	0
		2,000	0
			0
			0
			0
			0
			500

a. Find a point estimate for the total value of the error in the investment credit claimed by the firm.

b. Place bounds on the error of estimation associated with your point estimate of part a, and interpret the bounds in the context of the problem.

c. Find an approximate 95% confidence interval for the total value of the error.

d. The firm claimed an investment credit of $500,000. Based on your answers to parts a–c, approximately how much investment credit should the firm have claimed? Explain.

20.18 An economist wants to estimate the mean annual income of families in a mainly industrial community. Since one section of the city houses primarily factory workers, one mostly company executives, and the remaining area mostly farmers, the economist decides to use the three relatively homogeneous areas as strata. The economist selected random samples of thirty homes from within each of the three strata and gathered information on the annual income for each family. The number of households in each section of the city along with the sample means and variances are given in the table. Estimate the mean annual income for households in the community, and place a bound on the error of estimation.

CITY SECTION	N_i	$\bar{x}_i$ ($)	s_i^2
Factory workers	360	14,900	9,150,500
Executives	74	39,250	25,003,000
Farmers	95	23,800	16,801,100

20.19 The owners of a chain of department stores wish to estimate the proportion of customer accounts for which payments are 6 or more weeks overdue. A random sample of customers is taken in each of the chain's four stores, and the sample proportion of overdue accounts in each store is determined. These data and the total number of customer accounts are given in the table. Using the stores as strata, give an estimate of the true proportion of customer accounts that are 6 or more weeks overdue in this chain of department stores. Place a bound on the error of estimation.

STORE	N_i	n_i	$\hat{p}$, sample proportion of overdue accounts
1	1,572	100	.28
2	2,369	100	.31
3	3,007	120	.35
4	2,981	120	.10

20.20 Suppose you want to estimate the total amount of money spent on textbooks each quarter by students at your university. In order to reduce the variability in the data, you decide to consider student classes (freshman, sophomore, junior, senior) as strata. You randomly sample fifty students in each class and obtain an estimate of the total amount spent on textbooks during the quarter for each student. From the information given in the table, construct an approximate 95% confidence interval for the population total amount spent on textbooks per quarter by students at your university.

CLASS	N_i, total number of students	$\bar{x}_i$, average amount spent on textbooks	s_i^2, variance
Freshman	4,085	$75.20	62.50
Sophomore	3,520	62.00	86.50
Junior	5,525	45.15	31.40
Senior	5,070	42.85	39.70

20.7 Cluster Sampling

As explained in Section 20.2, *cluster sampling* involves the random selection of clusters of elements. Each sampling unit listed in the frame is a cluster of elements, and *all* the elements in a selected cluster are included in the sample.

Cluster sampling is often less costly than simple random sampling because it may be easier to construct a frame of clusters than a frame of the individual elements in a population. Second, it is frequently less costly when the elements within a cluster are geographically close to one another. This makes it easier and less costly for a pollster to obtain a response from each element. Sampling households rather than individual people is a good example of cluster sampling. If you are seeking the preferences, opinions, or buying habits of adult consumers in a city, it is easier to construct a frame of households than of individuals because all houses and apartment buildings would be listed at the local tax assessor's office. In contrast, no listing of the names of all adults in the city may be available. Also, it is less costly

---

Notation for Cluster Sampling

N = Number of clusters in the population

n = Number of clusters selected in a random sample

m_i = Number of elements in cluster i, $i = 1, 2, \ldots, n$

M = Number of elements in the population = $\displaystyle\sum_{i=1}^{N} m_i$

$\overline{m}$ = Average cluster size for the sample = $\dfrac{\displaystyle\sum_{i=1}^{n} m_i}{n}$

$\overline{M}$ = Average cluster size for the population = $\dfrac{M}{N}$

x_i = Total of all observations in cluster i

Estimation of the Population Mean, μ: Cluster Sampling

Estimator of μ: $\overline{x} = \dfrac{\displaystyle\sum_{i=1}^{n} x_i}{\displaystyle\sum_{i=1}^{n} m_i}$

Estimated bound on the error of estimation: $2\hat{\sigma}_{\overline{x}} = 2\sqrt{\left(\dfrac{N-n}{Nn\overline{M}^2}\right)\dfrac{\sum(x_i - \overline{x}m_i)^2}{n-1}}$

where

$$\sum(x_i - \overline{x}m_i)^2 = \sum x_i^2 - 2\overline{x}\sum x_i m_i + \overline{x}^2 \sum m_i^2$$

If $\overline{M}$ is unknown, use $\overline{m}$ to approximate its value.

Approximate 95% confidence interval: $\overline{x} \pm 2\hat{\sigma}_{\overline{x}}$

Estimation of the Population Total, τ: Cluster Sampling

Estimator of τ: $\quad \hat{\tau} = M\bar{x} = M\left(\dfrac{\sum x_i}{\sum m_i}\right)$

Estimated bound on the error of estimation: $\quad 2\hat{\sigma}_{\hat{\tau}} = 2\sqrt{N^2\left(\dfrac{N-n}{Nn}\right)\dfrac{\sum(x_i - \bar{x}m_i)^2}{n-1}}$

where

$$\sum(x_i - \bar{x}m_i)^2 = \sum x_i^2 - 2\bar{x}\sum x_i m_i + \bar{x}^2 \sum m_i^2$$

Approximate 95% confidence interval: $\quad M\bar{x} \pm 2\hat{\sigma}_{\hat{\tau}}$

Estimation of a Population Proportion, p: Cluster Sampling

Estimator of p: $\quad \hat{p} = \dfrac{\sum a_i}{\sum m_i}$

where a_i is the number of elements in cluster i that possess the characteristic of interest, $i = 1, 2, \ldots, n$.

Estimated bound on the error of estimation: $\quad 2\hat{\sigma}_{\hat{p}} = 2\sqrt{\left(\dfrac{N-n}{Nn\bar{M}^2}\right)\dfrac{\sum(a_i - \hat{p}m_i)^2}{n-1}}$

where

$$\sum(a_i - \hat{p}m_i)^2 = \sum a_i^2 - 2\hat{p}\sum a_i m_i + \hat{p}^2 \sum m_i^2$$

If $\bar{M}$ is unknown, use $\bar{m}$ to approximate its value.

Approximate 95% confidence interval: $\quad \hat{p} \pm 2\hat{\sigma}_{\hat{p}}$

to interview two adults within one household than to travel and interview two persons selected at random from within the city.

The notation and the formulas for estimations based on cluster sampling are shown in the accompanying boxes.

Example 20.4

A heavy equipment manufacturer wished to estimate the mean cost of maintenance and repair for a new model of bulldozer sold last year. Although the manufacturer can locate the construction companies that have purchased the bulldozers, it is unlikely that individual maintenance records are kept for each and every machine. Consequently, it is easier to construct a frame of construction companies and to treat the collection of bulldozers within each company as a cluster. The total number of bulldozers sold last year was $M = 1,804$. Twenty construction companies were randomly selected from a set of $N = 279$ that purchased the new bulldozer last year. A listing of the number of bulldozers purchased by each construction company along with the total cost of annual repair and maintenance (R&M) for the purchased bulldozers is shown in the table. Estimate the mean cost for the year per bulldozer for repair and maintenance.

COMPANY	NUMBER OF BULLDOZERS	R&M COST ($)	COMPANY	NUMBER OF BULLDOZERS	R&M COST ($)
1	3	1,270	11	2	494
2	10	5,860	12	6	1,980
3	6	4,310	13	10	7,740
4	10	7,940	14	3	1,144
5	2	500	15	15	12,130
6	3	968	16	3	1,770
7	4	1,490	17	4	1,052
8	3	2,710	18	4	2,617
9	2	390	19	12	3,985
10	5	1,785	20	6	2,463

Solution We are given

N = Number of construction companies (clusters) in the population = 279

n = Number of construction companies in the sample = 20

M = Total number of bulldozers in the population = 1,804

Then, the average cluster size for the population is

$$\overline{M} = \frac{M}{N} = \frac{1,804}{279} = 6.47$$

We need to calculate

$$\sum m_i = 3 + 10 + 6 + \cdots + 6 = 113$$
$$\sum x_i = 1,270 + 5,860 + \cdots + 2,463 = 62,598$$
$$\sum m_i^2 = (3)^2 + (10)^2 + \cdots + (6)^2 = 907$$
$$\sum x_i^2 = (1,270)^2 + (5,860)^2 + \cdots + (2,463)^2 = 377,214,308$$
$$\sum x_i m_i = (1,270)(3) + (5,860)(60) + \cdots + (2,463)(6) = 553,603$$

Then, the estimated mean expenditure per bulldozer per year is

$$\overline{x} = \frac{\sum x_i}{\sum m_i} = \frac{62,598}{113} = 553.96$$

To calculate the estimated bound on the error of estimation, we first need to calculate

$$\sum (x_i - \overline{x}m_i)^2 = \sum x_i^2 - 2\overline{x}\sum x_i m_i + \overline{x}^2 \sum m_i^2$$
$$= 377,214,308 - 613,347,835.8 + 278,332,615.2$$
$$= 42,199,087.4$$

Then,

$$2\hat{\sigma}_{\bar{x}} = 2\sqrt{\left(\frac{N-n}{Nn\overline{M}^2}\right)\frac{\sum(x_i - \bar{x}m_i)^2}{n-1}}$$

$$= 2\sqrt{\frac{279-20}{(279)(20)(6.47)^2}\left(\frac{42,199,087.4}{20-1}\right)}$$

$$= 2\sqrt{2,462.7} = 99.25$$

Therefore, we estimate the mean annual expenditure per bulldozer to be $553.96, and an approximate 95% confidence interval for the true mean annual expenditure per bulldozer is 553.96 ± 99.25, or $454.71 to $653.21.

Thus, the salespeople for the heavy equipment manufacturer can conservatively advertise the mean annual cost of maintenance and repairs to be less than $653.21, the upper limit on the estimate of μ. ∎

Exercises 20.21 – 20.28

Learning the Mechanics

20.21 The table shows the results of a sample survey based on cluster sampling with $N = 400$, $n = 10$, and $M = 1,240$.

	CLUSTER									
	1	2	3	4	5	6	7	8	9	10
m_i	2	2	2	3	3	3	4	4	1	5
x_i	6.4	6.7	5.8	17.2	19.4	18.7	24.0	25.8	6.2	32.3

a. Find an approximate 95% confidence interval for the population mean, μ.
b. Find an approximate 95% confidence interval for the population total, τ.

20.22 A population of 2,000 elements was divided into 200 clusters. Six clusters were randomly selected, and every element in each of the six clusters was measured. The data that resulted are shown in the table.

CLUSTER	MEASUREMENTS
1	5, 18, 33, 22, 19, 18, 20, 8, 9, 25
2	2, 25, 16, 38, 11, 14, 17
3	22, 18, 33, 50, 35, 40
4	28, 24, 19, 31, 27, 26, 26, 24, 24, 26
5	13, 21, 19, 15, 26, 41, 12
6	41, 28, 30, 15, 31, 29, 29, 40, 21, 25, 18, 50

a. Estimate the population mean, μ, and place a bound on the error of estimation.
b. Estimate the population total, τ, and place a bound on the error of estimation.
c. Estimate the proportion of measurements in the population that are less than 30, and place a bound on the error of estimation.

Applying the Concepts

20.23 An important figure in the financial statements of a business is the value of its inventory. Inventory value may be critical in determining both the profit and net worth of the business. Businesses typically conduct physical inventories once a year. As a result, it is not practical to maintain a year-round staff of trained inventory-takers. Instead, for a day or two each year, workers from various areas in the firm are enlisted to conduct the inventory. Because of the job's boring nature and the workers' lack of knowledge about the items in the firm's inventory, errors in item identification, counts, and pricing frequently occur, particularly when workers are asked to conduct *100% physical inventories.* Since such errors nearly always occur, even 100% physical inventories yield only estimates of inventory value, not the actual value. Furthermore, since the extent of such errors is not known, it is not possible to determine the accuracy of the estimate. These problems may be alleviated to a great extent by estimating inventory value by statistical sampling rather than by a 100% physical inventory. Since fewer workers would be required to complete the inventory, it may be possible to avoid using unqualified workers. In addition, the smaller number of items to be processed would mean less opportunity for human error to affect the estimate. Further, by using statistical sampling, it is possible to obtain a bound on the difference between the actual inventory value and the estimated inventory value. A cluster sampling procedure that has been used in large factories involves dividing the factory floor into small zones — clusters — and assigning a number to each zone. Then all items (parts, tools, machinery, etc.) in each of a randomly selected set of areas are counted and valued (Arkin, 1982). The results of such a process are described in the table.

FACTORY FLOOR ZONE NUMBER	NUMBER OF ITEMS	TOTAL VALUE ($ thousand)
98	25	1.2
33	101	4.0
76	83	1.8
59	455	6.7
81	90	0.5
3	22	0.2
21	66	2.5
62	14	0.1
42	299	5.0
17	387	10.2
6	46	1.1
70	33	0.9

Note: The total number of zones is 100 and the total number of items on the factory floor is 12,968.

α. Estimate the total value of the inventory on the factory floor, and place a bound on the error of estimation. [*Note:*   In practice, the number of items on the factory floor would probably not be known. We address this problem in Exercise 20.45.]

b. In the context of the problem, interpret the bound you obtained in part a.

c. A 100% physical inventory of the factory floor resulted in an estimate of $280,000 for the total inventory value. Does this seem reasonable given your result for part a? Explain.

20.24 Refer to Exercise 20.23. Estimate the mean dollar value per item on the factory floor, and place a bound on the error of estimation.

20.25 Managers are frequently faced with the need to change the behavior of the people within their organizations. One approach to effect such a change is to hire new people who bring new skills and interests to the organization or to retrain existing personnel. Another approach is to change the management system of the organization by implementing a program such as *management by objectives* (MBO). MBO is a technique "designed to create and maintain a routine of goal-setting at all levels of management, in order to facilitate motivation, evaluation, and decision-making" (Reitz, 1981, p. 148). MBO is characterized by goal-setting that starts at the top level of the organization and moves downward. Each level sets its goals consistent with the level immediately above. An essential feature of MBO is frequent performance review (feedback). Managers and nonmanagers alike are evaluated with respect to the specific goals they set for themselves rather than against the performance of other managers or employees. The personnel director of a large corporation that recently implemented an MBO program has been charged with the task of estimating the proportion of the corporation's employees who believe MBO is an improvement over their previous management style. The corporation is physically located in seventy different plants and branch offices worldwide. Since the corporation's personnel records are decentralized, the construction of a frame for simple random sampling is not feasible given the deadline for completion of the study. Accordingly, it has been decided to use cluster sampling with each different location as a cluster. Ten locations were randomly selected, and all employees at each location were mailed a questionnaire asking for their opinions of the MBO program. A 100% response rate was obtained at each location. The results of the survey are shown in the table. Estimate the proportion of employees who prefer MBO to the previous management style, and place a bound on the error of estimation.

LOCATION	NUMBER OF EMPLOYEES	NUMBER OF EMPLOYEES PREFERRING MBO
Hartford, Connecticut	550	401
London, England	163	80
Dallas, Texas	780	580
San Jose, California	333	300
Toronto, Canada	495	395
Ann Arbor, Michigan	87	80
Osaka, Japan	212	210
New York, New York	1,001	683
Phoenix, Arizona	199	172
Dover, New Jersey	47	38

20.26 Before implementing a plan designed to reduce flight time and hence conserve fuel and energy, the Air Force needs an estimate of the total number of miles flown by a certain type of aircraft during a given month. Air Force records show that a total of 1,500 planes of this type in the fleet are harbored at ninety-six different airfields across the country. The Air Force randomly selects six of the airfields and monitors the flight mileage of each plane at each airfield for 1 month. The data are shown in the table.

AIRFIELD	NUMBER OF AIRPLANES	MILES FLOWN (Thousands)
1	20	36
2	10	25
3	18	16
4	18	24
5	10	15
6	16	20

a. Treat the collection of all aircraft of this type at each airfield as a cluster. Estimate the total number of miles flown per month, and place a bound on the error of estimation.

b. What are the advantages or disadvantages of this method of sampling compared to taking a simple random sample from the total of 1,500 airplanes in the fleet?

20.27 A city is divided into 180 small neighborhoods (clusters) for the purpose of estimating the average utility bill of households during the month of July. Ten neighborhoods are selected at random, and the July utility bills of every household in each of the ten neighborhoods are recorded. The data are summarized in the table. Obtain an estimate for the average July utility bill of all households in the city, and place a bound on the error of estimation.

NEIGHBORHOOD	NUMBER OF HOUSEHOLDS	TOTAL OF JULY UTILITY BILLS
1	20	$530
2	18	486
3	20	704
4	25	775
5	30	861
6	18	666
7	30	960
8	19	494
9	21	823
10	19	665

20.28 A real estate appraiser wants to estimate the proportion of adult males who own their homes in a section of a city. This information will then be used as part of an appraisal of the retail value of the homes. The area is divided into 200 clusters, each containing five city blocks. Eight clusters are selected at random, and information on the number of adult males who live in the area and who also own their homes is collected. Given the data in the table, estimate the proportion of adult males who own their homes in this city section with an approximate 95% confidence interval.

CLUSTER	NUMBER OF ADULT MALES	NUMBER WHO OWN HOMES
1	98	66
2	92	74
3	106	65
4	80	51
5	90	30
6	29	19
7	60	45
8	63	40

20.8 Determining the Sample Size

To determine the sample size for sample surveys, you use essentially the same procedure as explained in Section 8.6. Generally speaking, the bound on the error of estimation will be approximately inversely proportional to the number of sampling units. This relationship does not hold exactly because of the effect of the finite population correction factor and because, for stratified random sampling, you are really selecting k random samples, one corresponding to each stratum. Nevertheless, doubling the sample size, n, will decrease (even for stratified random sampling if you keep $n_1, n_2, \ldots, n_k$ in the same proportions), approximately, the bound on the error of estimation to $1/\sqrt{2}$ times its original value. If you quadruple the sample size n, you will cut the bound on the error of estimation in half.

To select the sample size to estimate a population parameter based on a specific sample survey design, first decide on the accuracy you desire in your estimate; that is, decide on the bound on the error of estimation that you are willing to tolerate. Set this number equal to the estimated bound on the error of estimation and solve the resulting equation for n. We will illustrate with an example.

Example 20.5

Suppose the seafood wholesaler in Example 20.2 wanted to reduce the bound on the error of estimating the total, τ, of monthly seafood expenditure in the city to $5,000. That is, the wholesaler wants to estimate the total monthly expenditure to within $5,000 with approximate 95% confidence. If the wholesaler plans to use equal sample sizes, approximately how many households must be selected from within each stratum to estimate τ with a bound on the error of estimation of $5,000?

Solution

We found in Example 20.2 that the bound on the error of estimation for $n_1 = n_2 = n_3 = 400$ was $10,666. Since $5,000 is slightly less than half of this value, we know (without calculating) that it will require approximately four times as many households to reduce the bound on the error of estimation to $1/\sqrt{4} = 1/2$ its original size.

To solve the problem formally, let

$$2\hat{\sigma}_{\hat{\tau}} = 2\sqrt{\sum_{i=1}^{k} N_i^2\left(\frac{N_i - n_i}{N_i}\right)\frac{s_i^2}{n_i}} = \$5,000$$

where (since we want equal sample sizes) we will let $n_1 = n_2 = n_3 = n_s$. We will also assume, for a first approximation to n_s, that $(N_i - n_i)/N_i \approx 1$. Substituting these values, along with $N_1 = 20{,}800$, $N_2 = 6{,}400$, $N_3 = 12{,}600$, and the sample variances from the earlier samples into the formula for the bound on the error of estimation yields

$$2\sqrt{\frac{(20{,}800)^2(16.83)}{n_s} + \frac{(6{,}400)^2(15.10)}{n_s} + \frac{(12{,}600)^2(23.78)}{n_s}} = 5{,}000$$

and solving for n_s yields $n_s = 1{,}868$.

This solution will be larger than the actual strata sample sizes required to achieve a $5,000 bound on the error of estimation because the finite population correction factors will not equal 1. We now substitute $n_s = 1{,}868$ into the equation and re-solve it for n_s:

$$2\sqrt{(20{,}800)^2\left(\frac{20{,}800 - 1{,}868}{20{,}800}\right)\left(\frac{16.83}{n_s}\right) + (6{,}400)^2\left(\frac{6{,}400 - 1{,}868}{6{,}400}\right)\left(\frac{15.10}{n_s}\right) + (12{,}600)^2\left(\frac{12{,}600 - 1{,}868}{12{,}600}\right)\left(\frac{23.78}{n_s}\right)}$$
$$= 5{,}000$$

or $n_s = 1{,}645$.

This solution will be too small because we used $n_s = 1{,}868$ in the finite population correction factor. If we use this new value to calculate the finite population correction factors and re-solve the equation for n_s, we obtain $n_s = 1{,}672$. Thus, we would select approximately 1,672 households from each stratum in order to reduce the bound on the error of estimation to $5,000. ∎

Example 20.5 illustrates that although the finite population correction factor does affect the sample sizes required to obtain a specified bound on the error of estimation, the effect is not large. The solution, assuming the finite population correction factor equals 1, was 1,868—a value not much larger than the solution obtained using the correction factor.

Often previous sample data will not be available from which to obtain estimates of the strata variances. These must then be more crudely estimated, possibly by using each stratum range divided by 4, or by calculating s_i^2 from small pilot samples drawn from each stratum. Although this will produce only crude estimates of the required sample sizes, the procedure is still worthwhile, since the general magnitude of the sample size can be determined. This, in turn, allows the researcher to determine an approximate relationship between sampling costs and the bound on the error of estimation.

Exercises
20.29–20.33

Applying the Concepts

20.29 Refer to Exercise 20.8. Suppose the auditor wants to estimate the total value of the parts inventory to within $100,000 of the true value with approximately 95% confidence. In order to obtain this result, how many of the firm's 5,000 inventory items should be sampled?

20.30 Refer to Exercise 20.16. Suppose the labor economist wants to estimate the mean 1980 income of the head administrators to within $1,000 with approximately 95% confidence.

α. If an equal number of administrators is to be sampled from each stratum, what is the total number of administrators that should be sampled?

b. If thirty administrators are to be sampled from each of the first two strata, "under 100 beds" and "100 – 299 beds," approximately how many should be sampled from the third stratum?

20.31 Refer to Exercise 20.20. Suppose you want to estimate the total amount of money spent on textbooks per quarter to within $7,500 of the true value. If equal sample sizes are used, approximately how many students must be selected from each class in order to estimate the total with a bound on the error of estimation of $7,500 (with approximately 95% confidence)?

20.32 Refer to Exercise 20.18. The economist now desires to reduce the bound on the error of estimation to $600. Assuming equal sample sizes, how many homes from each city section should be sampled so that the economist estimates the mean annual income for households in the community to within $600 of the true value (with approximately 95% confidence)?

20.33 Refer to Exercise 20.10. It is desired to estimate the proportion of the county's voters who favor the creation of urban enterprise job zones to within 0.01 of the true value with approximate 95% confidence. In order to obtain this accuracy, how many of the county's 50,840 eligible voters should be sampled?

Summary

This chapter introduced the important topic of *survey sampling.* We presented several sampling designs for reducing the cost of conducting a sample survey and also presented the associated methods of estimation.

The objective of a sample survey is usually to estimate one or more of three population parameters: a *population mean, μ,* a *population total, τ,* and (or) a *population proportion, p.* We introduced three sample survey designs for collecting a sample: simple random sampling, stratified random sampling, and cluster sampling.

Simple random sampling is conceptually easy to understand, but it is often difficult to conduct, and it may be more costly than other sample survey designs. This is because it may be difficult and costly to construct the frame, and the cost of collecting the sample may be relatively large due to geographic separation of the sampling units.

Stratified random sampling is used when the population can be subdivided into groups (strata) of sampling units that possess smaller variability within strata than between strata. Random samples are selected from within each stratum, and the information contained in these samples is then pooled to obtain an estimate of the desired population parameter. Stratified sampling has the advantage that it enables the sampler to obtain estimates of the individual stratum parameters. In addition, it may be less costly than simple random sampling because the strata frames are often easier to construct and the sampling units are often geographically closer to one another in comparison to simple random sampling within the entire population. Finally, stratified samples often result in more precise estimates because the variance within strata is less than the variance of the entire population.

Cluster sampling is a design in which you select a random sample of clusters of elements from the population and then include in the sample every element in the cluster. Thus, each cluster of elements is a sampling unit. Cluster sampling is advantageous because it is often easier and less costly to construct a frame of clusters than to construct a frame of individual elements. We obtain the responses from more elements at lower cost, but the responses within a cluster may be highly correlated (for example, the opinions of people in the same household may be similar). Consequently, we must sample an adequate number of clusters if we wish to obtain a good estimate of the desired population parameter.

There are many other sampling designs available to a sample surveyor; some are variations on stratified random and cluster sampling, and other designs are completely different. In addition, different types of estimators can be used with these designs. In this introduction to survey sampling, our intent was to present only the basic elements of a sample survey and several of the most important sample survey designs. More thorough presentations are given in textbooks devoted to this topic (see the references at the end of this chapter).

Supplementary Exercises 20.34 – 20.45

20.34 Describe how cluster sampling could be used to estimate the damage to a citrus farmer's orange crop.

20.35 In recent years, corporations, labor unions and trade and medical associations have set up organizations known as *political action committees* — commonly called PAC's — to raise money from their members for support of political candidates believed to represent their best interests. Approximately 3,500 PAC's currently exist. Federal law limits the amount a PAC can contribute to a presidential candidate to $5,000 per election. However, a loophole in the law permits committees to spend as much as they want to elect or defeat a candidate as long as there is no cooperation or contact with the candidate or the candidate's authorized agents ("ABC's of How America Chooses a President," *U.S. News and World Report,* Feb. 20, 1984, pp. 39–46). In early 1984, in order to estimate the amount of money that would be spent in support of Ronald Reagan in the 1984 presidential election, a political economist hired by the Democratic party randomly sampled thirty PAC's and asked them how much they expected to spend in support of Reagan. The following results were obtained (in thousands of dollars):

10	0	5	18	0	5
22	0	50	60	35	0
0	18	35	0	40	10
50	20	150	15	0	0
30	15	0	20	15	10

a. Estimate the total amount that PAC's expected to spend in support of Reagan in 1984. Place a bound on the error of estimation.
b. Use an approximate 95% confidence interval to estimate the proportion of PAC's that planned to support Reagan.
c. In addition to sampling error, what might cause your estimate for part a to be inaccurate?

20.36 A company has a long-standing tradition of not charging its customers interest for late payment of bills. However, economic realities have forced the company to reconsider its payment policy. To guide them in establishing a new policy, the company has decided to estimate the mean number of days between the date an invoice is mailed to a customer and the date payment is received from the customer. Because of the large variance in the number of days until payment and the wide range of invoice amounts, the company has decided to use stratified sampling to estimate this mean. The population of invoices for which full payment was received during the first 6 months of the year was sampled and the data shown in the table were obtained.

INVOICE AMOUNT	NUMBER OF INVOICES PER STRATUM	NUMBER OF DAYS UNTIL PAYMENT
Under $100	20,000	60, 50, 95, 30, 15, 92, 100, 65, 48, 49, 63, 82, 91, 110, 68, 30, 40, 35, 38, 50
$100 to under $500	15,000	40, 28, 33, 42, 61, 48, 31, 25, 33, 48, 51, 26, 15, 35, 63
$500 to under $1,000	5,000	38, 53, 61, 35, 36, 41, 41, 43, 20, 21
$1,000 and over	2,000	28, 15, 10, 30, 32, 27, 33, 35, 34, 30

a. Estimate the mean number of days until payment, and place a bound on the error of estimation.

b. In the context of the problem, interpret the bound you obtained in part a.

c. Construct an approximate 95% confidence interval for the mean number of days until payment of invoices whose amounts are under $100.

d. Use an approximate 95% confidence interval to estimate the proportion of invoices that are paid in full within 60 days. Within 90 days.

20.37 A large manufacturing company is considering a new health insurance plan for its employees. Before putting the plan into effect, the company wants to estimate the proportion of its employees who favor the new health insurance proposal. The company's sampling scheme is to randomly select nine of its forty-five manufacturing plants scattered throughout the country and to use each plant as a cluster. The employees at each of the nine plants are interviewed, and their opinions regarding the new health insurance plan are recorded. Use the data in the table to obtain an estimate of the true proportion of this company's employees who favor the new health insurance plan. Place a bound on the error of estimation.

PLANT	NUMBER OF EMPLOYEES	NUMBER FAVORING THE NEW PLAN
1	112	98
2	75	65
3	83	71
4	154	123
5	108	97
6	68	61
7	102	92
8	85	90
9	83	65

20.38 Refer to Exercise 20.23. If the actual total value of the inventory on the factory floor differs from the value derived from a 100% physical inventory, is the difference due to sampling error or nonsampling error? Explain.

20.39 When a poll reports, for example, that 61% of the public supports a program of national health insurance, it usually also reports the sampling error. For example, a poll might report that the estimate is accurate to within plus or minus 3%. An essay in *Time* magazine ("How Not to Read the Polls," Apr. 28, 1980, pp. 72–73) points out:

> Readers consistently misinterpret the meaning of this 'warning label.' . . . [The sampling error warning] says nothing about errors that might be caused by a sloppily worded question or a biased one or a single question that evokes complex feelings. Example: 'Are you satisfied with your job?' Most important of all, warning labels about sampling error say nothing about whether or not the public is conflict-ridden or has given a subject much thought. This is the most serious source of opinion poll misinterpretation.

Carefully explain the difference between sampling error and nonsampling error, both in general and in the context of the above quote.

20.40 Publishers of a weekly nationwide business magazine believe that a large proportion of their Florida subscribers invest in the stock market. They would like to be able to use this information to persuade brokerage firms in Florida to advertise in their magazine. The publishers send each of the 500,000 subscribers in Florida a questionnaire about their (the subscribers') stock market investments. A total of 10,000 of the questionnaires are returned, and of these, 9,296 subscribers responded that they do currently have stock market investments.

a. Use this information to estimate the proportion of Florida subscribers who invest in the stock market, and place a bound on the error of estimation.

b. As a brokerage firm in Florida, would you consider the resulting estimate in part a to be reliable? Explain.

20.41 Refer to Exercise 20.40. The publishers of the magazine have decided to alter their sampling scheme. Instead of sending out questionnaires, they will personally interview a random selection of their Florida subscribers. In order to estimate, with approximate 95% confidence, the true proportion investing in the stock market with a bound on the error of estimation of .05, how many of the magazine's 500,000 Florida subscribers should be included in the sample?

20.42 With the recent crackdown by many states on drunk drivers, the accuracy of devices used by state and local police to measure blood alcohol levels has been called into question. One particular device known as the *breathalyzer* has been under attack by lawyers in several states. As a result, state officials in Minnesota tested all 185 breathalyzers currently in use and found eight to yield inaccurate readings. Although only 4.2% of the devices failed to operate properly, lawyers argued that even 1% was too high and that a better instrument is needed (Homan, 1982). Anxious to demonstrate the reliability of its product, suppose the manufacturer of the breathalyzer subsidized the testing of the device in a random sample of ten other states, and all breathalyzers in use in those states were tested. The total number of breathalyzers in use in the United States is 6,000. The results obtained are shown in the table.

STATE	NUMBER OF DEVICES IN USE	NUMBER OF DEFECTIVE DEVICES
Nevada	50	2
New York	375	15
Virginia	150	4
Washington	105	0
South Carolina	60	1
Utah	100	5
Kansas	138	5
Wisconsin	155	6
Ohio	200	10
Georgia	105	2

a. Use an approximate 95% confidence interval to estimate the proportion of defective breathalyzers in use in the United States.

b. Does your confidence interval suggest that the Minnesota result was atypical? Explain.

c. Does your confidence interval indicate that the proportion defective could be as low as 1%? Explain.

20.43 A manufacturer of typewriters wants to estimate the average monthly repair cost of the typewriters sold by the company to certain businesses. Although a list of repair costs for each machine sold is not available, the company was able to obtain a list of businesses, how many typewriters they have purchased from the manufacturer, and the total amount spent on typewriter repairs during the past month. Of the total of sixty businesses that have dealt with the manufacturer, twelve were included in the list. The data are given in the table. Using each business as a cluster, construct an approximate 95% confidence interval for the true average monthly repair cost of the typewriters.

BUSINESS	NUMBER OF TYPEWRITERS	TOTAL REPAIR COST FOR THE PAST MONTH	BUSINESS	NUMBER OF TYPEWRITERS	TOTAL REPAIR COST FOR THE PAST MONTH
1	8	$ 45	7	3	$16
2	9	36	8	8	49
3	5	23	9	5	29
4	12	55	10	10	62
5	10	47	11	9	51
6	14	101	12	7	27

20.44 In its next advertising campaign, a tobacco company will use an estimate of the average number of cigarettes smoked per day by its employees. The company expects a difference in amounts smoked by men and women, so it has decided to stratify on sex. From the company's 535 male employees, 50 are selected, and of the 366 female employees, 40 are sampled. An estimate of the number of cigarettes smoked per day by each is recorded. The table at the top of the next page gives the respective means and variances of the samples. Estimate the average number of cigarettes smoked per day by the company employees, and place bounds on the error of estimation.

	N_i	n_i	$\bar{x}_i$	s_i^2
MEN	535	50	8.5	16.8
WOMEN	366	40	5.2	21.2

20.45 In Exercise 20.23, since the total number of items on the factory floor, M, was known to be 12,968, the point estimator $M\bar{x}$ could be used to estimate the total value, τ, of the inventory on the floor. In practice, however, it is unlikely that M would be known. As a result, a different point estimator must be used to estimate τ. It turns out that $N\bar{x}_t$ is also an unbiased estimator of τ, where $\bar{x}_t = \sum_{i=1}^{n} x_i/n$ is the average cluster total and N is the number of clusters in the population. The estimated bound on the error of estimation associated with $N\bar{x}_t$ is the same as the bound associated with $\hat{\tau}$ (see Section 20.7), except that the term $\bar{x}m_i$ is replaced by $\bar{x}_t$.

a. Assume M is unknown in Exercise 20.23, and estimate the total value of inventory on the factory floor using the approach described here. Place a bound on the error of estimation.

b. Compare your point estimate and bound with the results you obtained in part a of Exercise 20.23.

References

Arkin, H. *Sampling methods for the auditor.* New York: McGraw-Hill, 1982. Chapters 1, 3, and 4.

Armstrong, J. S. "Monetary incentives in mail surveys." *Public Opinion Quarterly,* 1975, *39,* 111–116.

Berg, A., Klauda, P., & Feyder, S. "EDB banned as grain pesticide." *Minneapolis Star and Tribune,* Feb. 4, 1984, 1A.

Brown, D. B. "Statistical sampling in the IRS examination of large cases." *The Tax Executive,* Apr. 1982, *34,* 175–179.

Bryson, M. C. "The *Literary Digest* poll: Making of a statistical myth." *American Statistician,* Nov. 1976.

Chagall, D. "Can you believe the ratings?" *TV Guide,* June 24, 1978, 3.

Cochran, W. G. *Sampling techniques.* 2d ed. New York: Wiley, 1953.

Cox, E. P., III. *Marketing research, information for decision-making.* New York: Harper & Row, 1979. P. 7.

Davis, L. A. "Grasp behavior before picking target market, says McC and McC exec." *Marketing News,* Nov. 18, 1977, 6.

Ferber, R., Sheatsley, P., Turner, A., & Waksberg, J. *What is a survey?* Washington, D.C.: American Statistical Association, 1980.

Freedman, D., Pisani, R., & Purves, R. *Statistics.* New York: Norton, 1978. Chapter 19.

Glasser, G. J., & Metzger, G. D. "Random-digit dialing as a method of telephone sampling." *Journal of Marketing Research,* Feb. 1972, *9,* 59–64.

Greenberg, B. G., Kuebler, R. T., Abernathy, J. R., & Horvitz, D. G. "Application of randomized response technique in obtaining quantitative data." *Journal of the American Statistical Association,* 1971, *66.*

Hansen, M. H., Hurwitz, W. N., & Madow, W. G. *Sampling survey methods and theory.* Vol. 1. New York: Wiley, 1953.

Homan, S. "Breathalyzer battle is uncorked in district court." *Minnesota Daily,* Oct. 14, 1982, 1.

Huff, D. *How to lie with statistics.* New York: Norton, 1954. P. 20.

Hull, R. P., & Everett, J. O. "On the use of statistical sampling in tax audits." *The Tax Executive,* Oct. 1982, *35,* 51–54.

Kish, L. *Survey sampling.* New York: Wiley, 1965.

"Marketing-oriented Lever uses research to capture bigger dentifrice market shares." *Marketing News,* Feb. 10, 1978, 9.

Reitz, H. J. *Behavior in organizations.* Rev. ed., Homewood, Ill.: Richard D. Irwin, 1981. Chapters 14 and 18.

Scheaffer, R., Mendenhall, W., & Ott, R. L. *Elementary survey sampling.* 2d ed. North Scituate, Mass.: Duxbury, 1979.

Taeuber, C. "Information for the nation from a sample survey." In Tanur, et al., eds. *Statistics: A guide to the unknown.* 2d ed. San Francisco: Holden-Day, 1978.

Wright, J. W. *The American almanac of jobs and salaries.* New York: Avon Books, 1982. P. 608.

APPENDIX A

Basic Counting Rules

Simple events associated with many experiments have identical characteristics. If you can develop a counting rule to count the number of simple events, it can be used to aid in the solution of many probability problems. For example, many experiments involve sampling n elements from a population of N. Then, as explained in Section 4.1, we can use the formula

$$\binom{N}{n} = \frac{N!}{n!(N-n)!}$$

to find the number of different samples of n elements that could be selected from the total of N elements. This gives the number of simple events for the experiment.

Here, we give you a few useful counting rules. You should learn the characteristics of the situation to which each rule applies. Then, when working a probability problem, carefully examine the experiment to see whether you can use one of the rules.

Learning how to decide whether a particular counting rule applies to an experiment takes patience and practice. If you want to develop this skill, try to use the rules to solve some of the exercises in Chapter 4. You will also find large numbers of exercises in the texts listed in the references at the end of Chapter 4. Proofs of the rules below can be found in the text by W. Feller listed in the references to Chapter 4.

1. *Multiplicative rule:* You have *k sets* of different elements, n_1 in the first set, n_2 in the second set, ... , and n_k in the kth set. Suppose you want to form a sample of k elements *by taking one element from each* of the k sets. The number of different samples that can be formed is the product

$$n_1 \cdot n_2 \cdot n_3 \cdot \cdots \cdot n_k$$

Example A.1 If a product can be shipped by four different airlines and each airline can ship via three different routes, how many ways can you ship the product?

Solution A method of shipment corresponds to a pairing of one airline and one route. Therefore, $k = 2$, the number of airlines is $n_1 = 4$, the number of routes is $n_2 = 3$, and the number of ways to ship the product is $n_1 \cdot n_2 = (4)(3) = 12$. ∎

How the multiplicative rule works can be seen by using a **decision tree.** The airline choice is shown by three branching lines in Figure A.1.

Figure A.1   Decision Tree for Example A.1

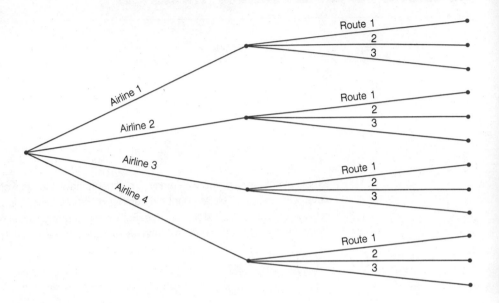

Example A.2   You have twenty candidates for three different executive positions, E_1, E_2, and E_3. How many different ways could you fill the positions?

Solution   For this example, there are $k = 3$ sets of elements:

Set 1:   The candidates available to fill position E_1

Set 2:   The candidates remaining (after filling E_1) that are available to fill E_2

Set 3:   The candidates remaining (after filling E_1 and E_2) that are available to fill E_3

The numbers of elements in the sets are $n_1 = 20$, $n_2 = 19$, $n_3 = 18$. Thus, the number of different ways to fill the three positions is $n_1 \cdot n_2 \cdot n_3 = (20)(19)(18) = 6{,}840$.   ■

2. **Partitions rule:**   You have a **single set** of N distinctly different elements, and you want to partition them into k sets, the first set containing n_1 elements, the second containing n_2 elements, ... , and the kth containing n_k elements. The number of different partitions is

$$\frac{N!}{n_1! n_2! \cdots n_k!} \qquad \text{where} \quad n_1 + n_2 + n_3 + \cdots + n_k = N$$

Example A.3   You have twelve construction workers and you want to assign three to job 1, four to job 2, and five to job 3. How many different ways could you make this assignment?

Solution   For this example, $k = 3$ (corresponding to the $k = 3$ job sites), $N = 12$, and $n_1 = 3$, $n_2 = 4$, $n_3 = 5$. Then, the number of different ways to assign the workers to the job sites is

$$\frac{N!}{n_1!n_2!n_3!} = \frac{12!}{3!4!5!} = \frac{12 \cdot 11 \cdot 10 \cdot \cdots \cdot 3 \cdot 2 \cdot 1}{(3 \cdot 2 \cdot 1)(4 \cdot 3 \cdot 2 \cdot 1)(5 \cdot 4 \cdot 3 \cdot 2 \cdot 1)}$$
$$= 27{,}720$$

3. *Combinations rule:*   The combinations rule given in Chapter 4 is a special case ($k = 2$) of the partitions rule. That is, sampling is equivalent to partitioning a set of N elements into $k = 2$ groups: elements that appear in the sample and those that do not. Let $n_1 = n$, the number of elements in the sample, and $n_2 = N - n$, the number of elements remaining. Then the number of different samples of n elements that can be selected from N is

$$\frac{N!}{n_1!n_2!} = \frac{N!}{n!(N-n)!} = \binom{N}{n}$$

This formula was given in Section 4.1.

Example A.4   How many samples of four firemen can be selected from a group of ten?

Solution   We have $N = 10$ and $n = 4$; then,

$$\binom{N}{n} = \binom{10}{4} = \frac{10!}{4!6!} = \frac{10 \cdot 9 \cdot 8 \cdot \cdots \cdot 3 \cdot 2 \cdot 1}{(4 \cdot 3 \cdot 2 \cdot 1)(6 \cdot 5 \cdot \cdots \cdot 2 \cdot 1)}$$
$$= 210$$

APPENDIX B

Tables

Contents

Table I Random Numbers

COLUMN ROW	1	2	3	4	5	6	7	8	9	10	11	12	13	14
1	10480	15011	01536	02011	81647	91646	69179	14194	62590	36207	20969	99570	91291	90700
2	22368	46573	25595	85393	30995	89198	27982	53402	93965	34095	52666	19174	39615	99505
3	24130	48360	22527	97265	76393	64809	15179	24830	49340	32081	30680	19655	63348	58629
4	42167	93093	06243	61680	07856	16376	39440	53537	71341	57004	00849	74917	97758	16379
5	37570	39975	81837	16656	06121	91782	60468	81305	49684	60672	14110	06927	01263	54613
6	77921	06907	11008	42751	27756	53498	18602	70659	90655	15053	21916	21825	44394	42880
7	99562	72905	56420	69994	98872	31016	71194	18738	44013	48840	63213	21069	10634	12952
8	96301	91977	05463	07972	18876	20922	94595	56869	69014	60045	18425	84903	42508	32307
9	89579	14342	63661	10281	17453	18103	57740	84378	25331	12566	58678	44947	05585	56941
10	85475	36857	53342	53988	53060	59533	38867	62300	08158	17983	16439	11458	18593	64952
11	28918	69578	88231	33276	70997	79936	56865	05859	90106	31595	01547	85590	91610	78188
12	63553	40961	48235	03427	49626	69445	18663	72695	52180	20847	12234	90511	33703	90322
13	09429	93969	52636	92737	88974	33488	36320	17617	30015	08272	84115	27156	30613	74952
14	10365	61129	87529	85689	48237	52267	67689	93394	01511	26358	85104	20285	29975	89868
15	07119	97336	71048	08178	77233	13916	47564	81056	97735	85977	29372	74461	28551	90707
16	51085	12765	51821	51259	77452	16308	60756	92144	49442	53900	70960	63990	75601	40719
17	02368	21382	52404	60268	89368	19885	55322	44819	01188	65255	64835	44919	05944	55157
18	01011	54092	33362	94904	31273	04146	18594	29852	71585	85030	51132	01915	92747	64951
19	52162	53916	46369	58586	23216	14513	83149	98736	23495	64350	94738	17752	35156	35749
20	07056	97628	33787	09998	42698	06691	76988	13602	51851	46104	88916	19509	25625	53104
21	48663	91245	85828	14346	09172	30168	90229	04734	59193	22178	30421	61666	99904	32812
22	54164	58492	22421	74103	47070	25306	76468	26384	58151	06646	21524	15227	96909	44592
23	32639	32363	05597	24200	13363	38005	94342	28728	35806	06912	17012	64161	18296	22851
24	29334	27001	87637	87308	58731	00256	45834	15398	46557	41135	10367	07684	36138	18510
25	02488	33062	28834	07351	19731	92420	60952	61280	50001	67658	32586	86679	50720	94953

(continued)

Table I Continued

COLUMN ROW	1	2	3	4	5	6	7	8	9	10	11	12	13	14
26	81525	72295	04839	96423	24878	82651	66566	14778	76797	14780	13300	87074	79666	95725
27	29676	20591	68086	26432	46901	20849	89768	81536	86645	12659	92259	57102	80428	25280
28	00742	57392	39064	66432	84673	40027	32832	61362	98947	96067	64760	64584	96096	98253
29	05366	04213	25669	26422	44407	44048	37937	63904	45766	66134	75470	66520	34693	90449
30	91921	26418	64117	94305	26766	25940	39972	22209	71500	64568	91402	42416	07844	69618
31	00582	04711	87917	77341	42206	35126	74087	99547	81817	42607	43808	76655	62028	76630
32	00725	69884	62797	56170	86324	88072	76222	36086	84637	93161	76038	65855	77919	88006
33	69011	65795	95876	55293	18988	27354	26575	08625	40801	59920	29841	80150	12777	48501
34	25976	57948	29888	88604	67917	48708	18912	82271	65424	69774	33611	54262	85963	03547
35	09763	83473	73577	12908	30883	18317	28290	35797	05998	41688	34952	37888	38917	88050
36	91576	42595	27958	30134	04024	86385	29880	99730	55536	84855	29080	09250	79656	73211
37	17955	56349	90999	49127	20044	59931	06115	20542	18059	02008	73708	83517	36103	42791
38	46503	18584	18845	49618	02304	51038	20655	58727	28168	15475	56942	53389	20562	87338
39	92157	89634	94824	78171	84610	82834	09922	25417	44137	48413	25555	21246	35509	20468
40	14577	62765	35605	81263	39667	47358	56873	56307	61607	49518	89656	20103	77490	18062
41	98427	07523	33362	64270	01638	92477	66969	98420	04880	45585	46565	04102	46880	45709
42	34914	63976	88720	82765	34476	17032	87589	40836	32427	70002	70663	88863	77775	69348
43	70060	28277	39475	46473	23219	53416	94970	25832	69975	94884	19661	72828	00102	66794
44	53976	54914	06990	67245	68350	82948	11398	42878	80287	88267	47363	46634	06541	97809
45	76072	29515	40980	07391	58745	25774	22987	80059	39911	96189	41151	14222	60697	59583
46	90725	52210	83974	29992	65831	38857	50490	83765	55657	14361	31720	57375	56228	41546
47	64364	67412	33339	31926	14883	24413	59744	92351	97473	89286	35931	04110	23726	51900
48	08962	00358	31662	25388	61642	34072	81249	35648	56891	69352	48373	45578	78547	81788
49	95012	68379	93526	70765	10592	04542	76463	54328	02349	17247	28865	14777	62730	92277
50	15664	10493	20492	38391	91132	21999	59516	81652	27195	48223	46751	22923	32261	85653
51	16408	81899	04153	53381	79401	21438	83035	92350	36693	31238	59649	91754	72772	02338
52	18629	81953	05520	91962	04739	13092	97662	24822	94730	06496	35090	04822	86774	98289
53	73115	35101	47498	87637	99016	71060	88824	71013	18735	20286	23153	72924	35165	43040
54	57491	16703	23167	49323	45021	33132	12544	41035	80780	45393	44812	12515	98931	91202
55	30405	83946	23792	14422	15059	45799	22716	19792	09983	74353	68668	30429	70735	25499
56	16631	35006	85900	98275	32388	52390	16815	69298	82732	38480	73817	32523	41961	44437
57	96773	20206	42559	78985	05300	22164	24369	54224	35083	19687	11052	91491	60383	19746
58	38935	64202	14349	82674	66523	44133	00697	35552	35970	19124	63318	29686	03387	59846
59	31624	76384	17403	53363	44167	64486	64758	75366	76554	31601	12614	33072	60332	92325
60	78919	19474	23632	27889	47914	02584	37680	20801	72152	39339	34806	08930	85001	87820
61	03931	33309	57047	74211	63445	17361	62825	39908	05607	91284	68833	25570	38818	46920
62	74426	33278	43972	10119	89917	15665	52872	73823	73144	88662	88970	74492	51805	99378

63	09066	00903	20795	95452	92648	45454	09552	88815	16553	51125	79375	97596	16296	66092
64	42238	12426	87025	14267	20979	04508	64535	31355	86064	29472	47689	05974	52468	16834
65	16153	08002	26504	41744	81959	65642	74240	56302	00033	67107	77510	70625	28725	34191
66	21457	40742	29820	96783	29400	21840	15035	34537	33310	06116	95240	15957	16372	06004
67	21581	57802	02050	89728	17937	37621	47075	42080	97403	48626	68995	43805	33386	21597
68	55612	78095	83197	33732	05810	24813	86902	60397	16489	03264	88525	42786	05269	92532
69	44657	66999	99324	51281	84463	60563	79312	93454	63876	25471	93911	25650	12382	73572
70	91340	84979	46949	81973	37949	61023	43997	15263	80644	43942	89203	71795	99533	50501
71	91227	21199	31935	27022	84067	05462	35216	14486	29891	68607	41867	14951	91396	85065
72	50001	38140	66321	19924	72163	09538	12151	06878	91903	18749	34405	56087	82790	70925
73	65390	05224	72958	28609	81406	39147	25549	48542	42627	45233	57202	94617	23772	07896
74	27504	96131	83944	41575	10573	08619	64482	73923	36152	05184	94142	25299	84387	34925
75	37169	94851	39117	89632	00959	16487	65536	49071	39782	17095	02330	74301	00275	48280
76	11508	70225	51111	38351	19444	66499	71945	05422	13442	78675	84081	66938	93354	59894
77	37449	30362	06694	54690	04052	53115	62757	95348	78662	11163	81651	50245	34971	52924
78	46515	70331	85922	38329	57015	15765	97161	17869	45349	61796	66345	81073	49106	79860
79	30986	81223	42416	58353	21532	30502	32305	86482	05174	07901	54339	58861	74818	46942
80	63798	64995	46583	09785	44160	78128	83991	42865	92520	83531	80377	35909	81250	54238
81	82486	84846	99254	67632	43218	50076	21361	64816	51202	88124	41870	52689	51275	83556
82	21885	32906	92431	09060	64297	51674	64126	62570	26123	05155	59194	52799	28225	85762
83	60336	98782	07408	53458	13564	59089	26445	29789	85205	41001	12535	12133	14645	23541
84	43937	46891	24010	25560	86355	33941	25786	54990	71899	15475	95434	98227	21824	19585
85	97656	63175	89303	16275	07100	92063	21942	18611	47348	20203	18534	03862	78095	50136
86	03299	01221	05418	38982	55758	92237	26759	86367	21216	98442	08303	56613	91511	75928
87	79626	06486	03574	17668	07785	76020	79924	25651	83325	88428	85076	72811	22717	50585
88	85636	68335	47539	03129	65651	11977	02510	26113	99447	68645	34327	15152	55230	93448
89	18039	14367	61337	06177	12143	46609	32989	74014	64708	00533	35398	58408	13261	47908
90	08362	15656	60627	36478	65648	16764	53412	09013	07832	41574	17639	82163	60859	75567
91	79556	29068	04142	16268	15387	12856	66227	38358	22478	73373	88732	09443	82558	05250
92	92608	82674	27072	32534	17075	27698	98204	63863	11951	34648	88022	56148	34925	57031
93	23982	25835	40055	67006	12293	02753	14827	23235	35071	99704	37543	11601	35503	85171
94	09915	96306	05908	97901	28395	14186	00821	80703	70426	75647	76310	88717	37890	40129
95	59037	33300	26695	62247	69927	76123	50842	43834	86654	70959	79725	93872	28117	19233
96	42488	78077	69882	61657	34136	79180	97526	43092	04098	73571	80799	76536	71255	64239
97	46764	86273	63003	93017	31204	36692	40202	35275	57306	55543	53203	18098	47625	88684
98	03237	45430	55417	63282	90816	17349	88298	90183	36600	78406	06216	95787	42579	90730
99	86591	81482	52667	61582	14972	90053	89534	76036	49199	43716	97548	04379	46370	28672
100	38534	01715	94964	87288	65680	43772	39560	12918	86537	62738	19636	51132	25739	56947

Source: Abridged from W. H. Beyer, Ed., *CRC Standard Mathematical Tables*, 24th ed.(Cleveland: The Chemical Rubber Company), 1976. Reproduced by permission of the publisher.

Table II   Binomial Probabilities

Tabulated values are $\sum_{x=0}^{k} p(x)$. (Computations are rounded at the third decimal place.)

a. $n = 5$

k \ p	0.01	0.05	0.10	0.20	0.30	0.40	0.50	0.60	0.70	0.80	0.90	0.95	0.99
0	.951	.774	.590	.328	.168	.078	.031	.010	.002	.000	.000	.000	.000
1	.999	.977	.919	.737	.528	.337	.188	.087	.031	.007	.000	.000	.000
2	1.000	.999	.991	.942	.837	.683	.500	.317	.163	.058	.009	.001	.000
3	1.000	1.000	1.000	.993	.969	.913	.812	.663	.472	.263	.081	.023	.001
4	1.000	1.000	1.000	1.000	.998	.990	.969	.922	.832	.672	.410	.226	.049

b. $n = 6$

k \ p	0.01	0.05	0.10	0.20	0.30	0.40	0.50	0.60	0.70	0.80	0.90	0.95	0.99
0	.941	.735	.531	.262	.118	.047	.016	.004	.001	.000	.000	.000	.000
1	.999	.967	.886	.655	.420	.233	.109	.041	.011	.002	.000	.000	.000
2	1.000	.998	.984	.901	.744	.544	.344	.179	.070	.017	.001	.000	.000
3	1.000	1.000	.999	.983	.930	.821	.656	.456	.256	.099	.016	.002	.000
4	1.000	1.000	1.000	.998	.989	.959	.891	.767	.580	.345	.114	.033	.001
5	1.000	1.000	1.000	1.000	.999	.996	.984	.953	.882	.738	.469	.265	.059

c. $n = 7$

k \ p	0.01	0.05	0.10	0.20	0.30	0.40	0.50	0.60	0.70	0.80	0.90	0.95	0.99
0	.932	.698	.478	.210	.082	.028	.008	.002	.000	.000	.000	.000	.000
1	.998	.956	.850	.577	.329	.159	.063	.019	.004	.000	.000	.000	.000
2	1.000	.996	.974	.852	.647	.420	.227	.096	.029	.005	.000	.000	.000
3	1.000	1.000	.997	.967	.874	.710	.500	.290	.126	.033	.003	.000	.000
4	1.000	1.000	1.000	.995	.971	.904	.773	.580	.353	.148	.026	.004	.000
5	1.000	1.000	1.000	1.000	.996	.981	.937	.841	.671	.423	.150	.044	.002
6	1.000	1.000	1.000	1.000	1.000	.998	.992	.972	.918	.790	.522	.302	.068

d. $n = 8$

k \ p	0.01	0.05	0.10	0.20	0.30	0.40	0.50	0.60	0.70	0.80	0.90	0.95	0.99
0	.923	.663	.430	.168	.058	.017	.004	.001	.000	.000	.000	.000	.000
1	.997	.943	.813	.503	.255	.106	.035	.009	.001	.000	.000	.000	.000
2	1.000	.994	.962	.797	.552	.315	.145	.050	.011	.001	.000	.000	.000
3	1.000	1.000	.995	.944	.806	.594	.363	.174	.058	.010	.000	.000	.000
4	1.000	1.000	1.000	.990	.942	.826	.637	.406	.194	.056	.005	.000	.000
5	1.000	1.000	1.000	.999	.989	.950	.855	.685	.448	.203	.038	.006	.000
6	1.000	1.000	1.000	1.000	.999	.991	.965	.894	.745	.497	.187	.057	.003
7	1.000	1.000	1.000	1.000	1.000	.999	.996	.983	.942	.832	.570	.337	.077

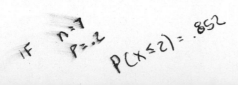

e. $n = 9$

k	0.01	0.05	0.10	0.20	0.30	0.40	0.50	0.60	0.70	0.80	0.90	0.95	0.99
0	.914	.630	.387	.134	.040	.010	.002	.000	.000	.000	.000	.000	.000
1	.997	.929	.775	.436	.196	.071	.020	.004	.000	.000	.000	.000	.000
2	1.000	.992	.947	.738	.463	.232	.090	.025	.004	.000	.000	.000	.000
3	1.000	.999	.992	.914	.730	.483	.254	.099	.025	.003	.000	.000	.000
4	1.000	1.000	.999	.980	.901	.733	.500	.267	.099	.020	.001	.000	.000
5	1.000	1.000	1.000	.997	.975	.901	.746	.517	.270	.086	.008	.001	.000
6	1.000	1.000	1.000	1.000	.996	.975	.910	.768	.537	.262	.053	.008	.000
7	1.000	1.000	1.000	1.000	1.000	.996	.980	.929	.804	.564	.225	.071	.003
8	1.000	1.000	1.000	1.000	1.000	1.000	.998	.990	.960	.866	.613	.370	.086

f. $n = 10$

k	0.01	0.05	0.10	0.20	0.30	0.40	0.50	0.60	0.70	0.80	0.90	0.95	0.99
0	.904	.599	.349	.107	.028	.006	.001	.000	.000	.000	.000	.000	.000
1	.996	.914	.736	.376	.149	.046	.011	.002	.000	.000	.000	.000	.000
2	1.000	.988	.930	.678	.383	.167	.055	.012	.002	.000	.000	.000	.000
3	1.000	.999	.987	.879	.650	.382	.172	.055	.011	.001	.000	.000	.000
4	1.000	1.000	.998	.967	.850	.633	.377	.166	.047	.006	.000	.000	.000
5	1.000	1.000	1.000	.994	.953	.834	.623	.367	.150	.033	.002	.000	.000
6	1.000	1.000	1.000	.999	.989	.945	.828	.618	.350	.121	.013	.001	.000
7	1.000	1.000	1.000	1.000	.998	.988	.945	.833	.617	.322	.070	.012	.000
8	1.000	1.000	1.000	1.000	1.000	.998	.989	.954	.851	.624	.264	.086	.004
9	1.000	1.000	1.000	1.000	1.000	1.000	.999	.994	.972	.893	.651	.401	.096

g. $n = 15$

k	0.01	0.05	0.10	0.20	0.30	0.40	0.50	0.60	0.70	0.80	0.90	0.95	0.99
0	.860	.463	.206	.035	.005	.000	.000	.000	.000	.000	.000	.000	.000
1	.990	.829	.549	.167	.035	.005	.000	.000	.000	.000	.000	.000	.000
2	1.000	.964	.816	.398	.127	.027	.004	.000	.000	.000	.000	.000	.000
3	1.000	.995	.944	.648	.297	.091	.018	.002	.000	.000	.000	.000	.000
4	1.000	.999	.987	.836	.515	.217	.059	.009	.001	.000	.000	.000	.000
5	1.000	1.000	.998	.939	.722	.403	.151	.034	.004	.000	.000	.000	.000
6	1.000	1.000	1.000	.982	.869	.610	.304	.095	.015	.001	.000	.000	.000
7	1.000	1.000	1.000	.996	.950	.787	.500	.213	.050	.004	.000	.000	.000
8	1.000	1.000	1.000	.999	.985	.905	.696	.390	.131	.018	.000	.000	.000
9	1.000	1.000	1.000	1.000	.996	.966	.849	.597	.278	.061	.002	.000	.000
10	1.000	1.000	1.000	1.000	.999	.991	.941	.783	.485	.164	.013	.001	.000
11	1.000	1.000	1.000	1.000	1.000	.998	.982	.909	.703	.352	.056	.005	.000
12	1.000	1.000	1.000	1.000	1.000	1.000	.996	.973	.873	.602	.184	.036	.000
13	1.000	1.000	1.000	1.000	1.000	1.000	1.000	.995	.965	.833	.451	.171	.010
14	1.000	1.000	1.000	1.000	1.000	1.000	1.000	1.000	.995	.965	.794	.537	.140

(continued)

Table II   Continued

h. $n = 20$

k \ p	0.01	0.05	0.10	0.20	0.30	0.40	0.50	0.60	0.70	0.80	0.90	0.95	0.99
0	.818	.358	.122	.012	.001	.000	.000	.000	.000	.000	.000	.000	.000
1	.983	.736	.392	.069	.008	.001	.000	.000	.000	.000	.000	.000	.000
2	.999	.925	.677	.206	.035	.004	.000	.000	.000	.000	.000	.000	.000
3	1.000	.984	.867	.411	.107	.016	.001	.000	.000	.000	.000	.000	.000
4	1.000	.997	.957	.630	.238	.051	.006	.000	.000	.000	.000	.000	.000
5	1.000	1.000	.989	.804	.416	.126	.021	.002	.000	.000	.000	.000	.000
6	1.000	1.000	.998	.913	.608	.250	.058	.006	.000	.000	.000	.000	.000
7	1.000	1.000	1.000	.968	.772	.416	.132	.021	.001	.000	.000	.000	.000
8	1.000	1.000	1.000	.990	.887	.596	.252	.057	.005	.000	.000	.000	.000
9	1.000	1.000	1.000	.997	.952	.755	.412	.128	.017	.001	.000	.000	.000
10	1.000	1.000	1.000	.999	.983	.872	.588	.245	.048	.003	.000	.000	.000
11	1.000	1.000	1.000	1.000	.995	.943	.748	.404	.113	.010	.000	.000	.000
12	1.000	1.000	1.000	1.000	.999	.979	.868	.584	.228	.032	.000	.000	.000
13	1.000	1.000	1.000	1.000	1.000	.994	.942	.750	.392	.087	.002	.000	.000
14	1.000	1.000	1.000	1.000	1.000	.998	.979	.874	.584	.196	.011	.000	.000
15	1.000	1.000	1.000	1.000	1.000	1.000	.994	.949	.762	.370	.043	.003	.000
16	1.000	1.000	1.000	1.000	1.000	1.000	.999	.984	.893	.589	.133	.016	.000
17	1.000	1.000	1.000	1.000	1.000	1.000	1.000	.996	.965	.794	.323	.075	.001
18	1.000	1.000	1.000	1.000	1.000	1.000	1.000	.999	.992	.931	.608	.264	.017
19	1.000	1.000	1.000	1.000	1.000	1.000	1.000	1.000	.999	.988	.878	.642	.182

i. $n = 25$

k \ p	0.01	0.05	0.10	0.20	0.30	0.40	0.50	0.60	0.70	0.80	0.90	0.95	0.99
0	.778	.277	.072	.004	.000	.000	.000	.000	.000	.000	.000	.000	.000
1	.974	.642	.271	.027	.002	.000	.000	.000	.000	.000	.000	.000	.000
2	.998	.873	.537	.098	.009	.000	.000	.000	.000	.000	.000	.000	.000
3	1.000	.966	.764	.234	.033	.002	.000	.000	.000	.000	.000	.000	.000
4	1.000	.993	.902	.421	.090	.009	.000	.000	.000	.000	.000	.000	.000
5	1.000	.999	.967	.617	.193	.029	.002	.000	.000	.000	.000	.000	.000
6	1.000	1.000	.991	.780	.341	.074	.007	.000	.000	.000	.000	.000	.000
7	1.000	1.000	.998	.891	.512	.154	.022	.001	.000	.000	.000	.000	.000
8	1.000	1.000	1.000	.953	.677	.274	.054	.004	.000	.000	.000	.000	.000
9	1.000	1.000	1.000	.983	.811	.425	.115	.013	.000	.000	.000	.000	.000
10	1.000	1.000	1.000	.994	.902	.586	.212	.034	.002	.000	.000	.000	.000
11	1.000	1.000	1.000	.998	.956	.732	.345	.078	.006	.000	.000	.000	.000
12	1.000	1.000	1.000	1.000	.983	.846	.500	.154	.017	.000	.000	.000	.000
13	1.000	1.000	1.000	1.000	.994	.922	.655	.268	.044	.002	.000	.000	.000
14	1.000	1.000	1.000	1.000	.998	.966	.788	.414	.098	.006	.000	.000	.000
15	1.000	1.000	1.000	1.000	1.000	.987	.885	.575	.189	.017	.000	.000	.000
16	1.000	1.000	1.000	1.000	1.000	.996	.946	.726	.323	.047	.000	.000	.000
17	1.000	1.000	1.000	1.000	1.000	.999	.978	.846	.488	.109	.002	.000	.000
18	1.000	1.000	1.000	1.000	1.000	1.000	.993	.926	.659	.220	.009	.000	.000
19	1.000	1.000	1.000	1.000	1.000	1.000	.998	.971	.807	.383	.033	.001	.000
20	1.000	1.000	1.000	1.000	1.000	1.000	1.000	.991	.910	.579	.098	.007	.000
21	1.000	1.000	1.000	1.000	1.000	1.000	1.000	.998	.967	.766	.236	.034	.000
22	1.000	1.000	1.000	1.000	1.000	1.000	1.000	1.000	.991	.902	.463	.127	.002
23	1.000	1.000	1.000	1.000	1.000	1.000	1.000	1.000	.998	.973	.729	.358	.026
24	1.000	1.000	1.000	1.000	1.000	1.000	1.000	1.000	1.000	.996	.928	.723	.222

Table III Exponentials

λ	$e^{-\lambda}$	λ	$e^{-\lambda}$	λ	$e^{-\lambda}$
0.00	1.000000	2.35	.095369	4.70	.009095
0.05	.951229	2.40	.090718	4.75	.008652
0.10	.904837	2.45	.086294	4.80	.008230
0.15	.860708	2.50	.082085	4.85	.007828
0.20	.818731	2.55	.078082	4.90	.007447
0.25	.778801	2.60	.074274	4.95	.007083
0.30	.740818	2.65	.070651	5.00	.006738
0.35	.704688	2.70	.067206	5.05	.006409
0.40	.670320	2.75	.063928	5.10	.006097
0.45	.637628	2.80	.060810	5.15	.005799
0.50	.606531	2.85	.057844	5.20	.005517
0.55	.576950	2.90	.055023	5.25	.005248
0.60	.548812	2.95	.052340	5.30	.004992
0.65	.522046	3.00	.049787	5.35	.004748
0.70	.496585	3.05	.047359	5.40	.004517
0.75	.472367	3.10	.045049	5.45	.004296
0.80	.449329	3.15	.042852	5.50	.004087
0.85	.427415	3.20	.040762	5.55	.003887
0.90	.406570	3.25	.038774	5.60	.003698
0.95	.386741	3.30	.036883	5.65	.003518
1.00	.367879	3.35	.035084	5.70	.003346
1.05	.349938	3.40	.033373	5.75	.003183
1.10	.332871	3.45	.031746	5.80	.003028
1.15	.316637	3.50	.030197	5.85	.002880
1.20	.301194	3.55	.028725	5.90	.002739
1.25	.286505	3.60	.027324	5.95	.002606
1.30	.272532	3.65	.025991	6.00	.002479
1.35	.259240	3.70	.024724	6.05	.002358
1.40	.246597	3.75	.023518	6.10	.002243
1.45	.234570	3.80	.022371	6.15	.002133
1.50	.223130	3.85	.021280	6.20	.002029
1.55	.212248	3.90	.020242	6.25	.001930
1.60	.201897	3.95	.019255	6.30	.001836
1.65	.192050	4.00	.018316	6.35	.001747
1.70	.182684	4.05	.017422	6.40	.001661
1.75	.173774	4.10	.016573	6.45	.001581
1.80	.165299	4.15	.015764	6.50	.001503
1.85	.157237	4.20	.014996	6.55	.001430
1.90	.149569	4.25	.014264	6.60	.001360
1.95	.142274	4.30	.013569	6.65	.001294
2.00	.135335	4.35	.012907	6.70	.001231
2.05	.128735	4.40	.012277	6.75	.001171
2.10	.122456	4.45	.011679	6.80	.001114
2.15	.116484	4.50	.011109	6.85	.001059
2.20	.110803	4.55	.010567	6.90	.001008
2.25	.105399	4.60	.010052	6.95	.000959
2.30	.100259	4.65	.009562	7.00	.000912

λ	$e^{-\lambda}$	λ	$e^{-\lambda}$	λ	$e^{-\lambda}$
7.05	.000867	8.05	.000319	9.05	.000117
7.10	.000825	8.10	.000304	9.10	.000112
7.15	.000785	8.15	.000289	9.15	.000106
7.20	.000747	8.20	.000275	9.20	.000101
7.25	.000710	8.25	.000261	9.25	.000096
7.30	.000676	8.30	.000249	9.30	.000091
7.35	.000643	8.35	.000236	9.35	.000087
7.40	.000611	8.40	.000225	9.40	.000083
7.45	.000581	8.45	.000214	9.45	.000079
7.50	.000553	8.50	.000204	9.50	.000075
7.55	.000526	8.55	.000194	9.55	.000071
7.60	.000501	8.60	.000184	9.60	.000068
7.65	.000476	8.65	.000175	9.65	.000064
7.70	.000453	8.70	.000167	9.70	.000061
7.75	.000431	8.75	.000158	9.75	.000058
7.80	.000410	8.80	.000151	9.80	.000056
7.85	.000390	8.85	.000143	9.85	.000053
7.90	.000371	8.90	.000136	9.90	.000050
7.95	.000353	8.95	.000130	9.95	.000048
8.00	.000336	9.00	.000123	10.00	.000045

Table IV Normal Curve Areas

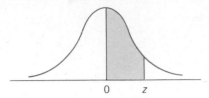

z	.00	.01	.02	.03	.04	.05	.06	.07	.08	.09
0.0	.0000	.0040	.0080	.0120	.0160	.0199	.0239	.0279	.0319	.0359
0.1	.0398	.0438	.0478	.0517	.0557	.0596	.0636	.0675	.0714	.0753
0.2	.0793	.0832	.0871	.0910	.0948	.0987	.1026	.1064	.1103	.1141
0.3	.1179	.1217	.1255	.1293	.1331	.1368	.1406	.1443	.1480	.1517
0.4	.1554	.1591	.1628	.1664	.1700	.1736	.1772	.1808	.1844	.1879
0.5	.1915	.1950	.1985	.2019	.2054	.2088	.2123	.2157	.2190	.2224
0.6	.2257	.2291	.2324	.2357	.2389	.2422	.2454	.2486	.2517	.2549
0.7	.2580	.2611	.2642	.2673	.2704	.2734	.2764	.2794	.2823	.2852
0.8	.2881	.2910	.2939	.2967	.2995	.3023	.3051	.3078	.3106	.3133
0.9	.3159	.3186	.3212	.3238	.3264	.3289	.3315	.3340	.3365	.3389
1.0	.3413	.3438	.3461	.3485	.3508	.3531	.3554	.3577	.3599	.3621
1.1	.3643	.3665	.3686	.3708	.3729	.3749	.3770	.3790	.3810	.3830
1.2	.3849	.3869	.3888	.3907	.3925	.3944	.3962	.3980	.3997	.4015
1.3	.4032	.4049	.4066	.4082	.4099	.4115	.4131	.4147	.4162	.4177
1.4	.4192	.4207	.4222	.4236	.4251	.4265	.4279	.4292	.4306	.4319
1.5	.4332	.4345	.4357	.4370	.4382	.4394	.4406	.4418	.4429	.4441
1.6	.4452	.4463	.4474	.4484	.4495	.4505	.4515	.4525	.4535	.4545
1.7	.4554	.4564	.4573	.4582	.4591	.4599	.4608	.4616	.4625	.4633
1.8	.4641	.4649	.4656	.4664	.4671	.4678	.4686	.4693	.4699	.4706
1.9	.4713	.4719	.4726	.4732	.4738	.4744	.4750	.4756	.4761	.4767
2.0	.4772	.4778	.4783	.4788	.4793	.4798	.4803	.4808	.4812	.4817
2.1	.4821	.4826	.4830	.4834	.4838	.4842	.4846	.4850	.4854	.4857
2.2	.4861	.4864	.4868	.4871	.4875	.4878	.4881	.4884	.4887	.4890
2.3	.4893	.4896	.4898	.4901	.4904	.4906	.4909	.4911	.4913	.4916
2.4	.4918	.4920	.4922	.4925	.4927	.4929	.4931	.4932	.4934	.4936
2.5	.4938	.4940	.4941	.4943	.4945	.4946	.4948	.4949	.4951	.4952
2.6	.4953	.4955	.4956	.4957	.4959	.4960	.4961	.4962	.4963	.4964
2.7	.4965	.4966	.4967	.4968	.4969	.4970	.4971	.4972	.4973	.4974
2.8	.4974	.4975	.4976	.4977	.4977	.4978	.4979	.4979	.4980	.4981
2.9	.4981	.4982	.4982	.4983	.4984	.4984	.4985	.4985	.4986	.4986
3.0	.4987	.4987	.4987	.4988	.4988	.4989	.4989	.4989	.4990	.4990

Source: Abridged from Table I of A. Hald, *Statistical Tables and Formulas* (New York: John Wiley & Sons, Inc.), 1952. Reproduced by permission of A. Hald and the publisher, John Wiley & Sons, Inc.

Table V Critical Values of *t*

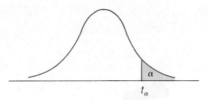

DEGREES OF FREEDOM	$t_{.100}$	$t_{.050}$	$t_{.025}$	$t_{.010}$	$t_{.005}$
1	3.078	6.314	12.706	31.821	63.657
2	1.886	2.920	4.303	6.965	9.925
3	1.638	2.353	3.182	4.541	5.841
4	1.533	2.132	2.776	3.747	4.604
5	1.476	2.015	2.571	3.365	4.032
6	1.440	1.943	2.447	3.143	3.707
7	1.415	1.895	2.365	2.998	3.499
8	1.397	1.860	2.306	2.896	3.355
9	1.383	1.833	2.262	2.821	3.250
10	1.372	1.812	2.228	2.764	3.169
11	1.363	1.796	2.201	2.718	3.106
12	1.356	1.782	2.179	2.681	3.055
13	1.350	1.771	2.160	2.650	3.012
14	1.345	1.761	2.145	2.624	2.977
15	1.341	1.753	2.131	2.602	2.947
16	1.337	1.746	2.120	2.583	2.921
17	1.333	1.740	2.110	2.567	2.898
18	1.330	1.734	2.101	2.552	2.878
19	1.328	1.729	2.093	2.539	2.861
20	1.325	1.725	2.086	2.528	2.845
21	1.323	1.721	2.080	2.518	2.831
22	1.321	1.717	2.074	2.508	2.819
23	1.319	1.714	2.069	2.500	2.807
24	1.318	1.711	2.064	2.492	2.797
25	1.316	1.708	2.060	2.485	2.787
26	1.315	1.706	2.056	2.479	2.779
27	1.314	1.703	2.052	2.473	2.771
28	1.313	1.701	2.048	2.467	2.763
29	1.311	1.699	2.045	2.462	2.756
∞	1.282	1.645	1.960	2.326	2.576

Source: From M. Merrington, "Table of Percentage Points of the *t*-Distribution," *Biometrika*, 1941, *32*, 300. Reproduced by permission of the *Biometrika* Trustees.

Table VI   Percentage Points of the F Distribution, $\alpha = .10$

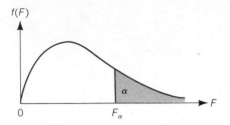

	v_1	NUMERATOR DEGREES OF FREEDOM $= V_i = n_i - 1$								
	v_2	1	2	3	4	5	6	7	8	9
	1	39.86	49.50	53.59	55.83	57.24	58.20	58.91	59.44	59.86
	2	8.53	9.00	9.16	9.24	9.29	9.33	9.35	9.37	9.38
	3	5.54	5.46	5.39	5.34	5.31	5.28	5.27	5.25	5.24
	4	4.54	4.32	4.19	4.11	4.05	4.01	3.98	3.95	3.94
	5	4.06	3.78	3.62	3.52	3.45	3.40	3.37	3.34	3.32
	6	3.78	3.46	3.29	3.18	3.11	3.05	3.01	2.98	2.96
	7	3.59	3.26	3.07	2.96	2.88	2.83	2.78	2.75	2.72
	8	3.46	3.11	2.92	2.81	2.73	2.67	2.62	2.59	2.56
	9	3.36	3.01	2.81	2.69	2.61	2.55	2.51	2.47	2.44
	10	3.29	2.92	2.73	2.61	2.52	2.46	2.41	2.38	2.35
	11	3.23	2.86	2.66	2.54	2.45	2.39	2.34	2.30	2.27
	12	3.18	2.81	2.61	2.48	2.39	2.33	2.28	2.24	2.21
	13	3.14	2.76	2.56	2.43	2.35	2.28	2.23	2.20	2.16
	14	3.10	2.73	2.52	2.39	2.31	2.24	2.19	2.15	2.12
	15	3.07	2.70	2.49	2.36	2.27	2.21	2.16	2.12	2.09
	16	3.05	2.67	2.46	2.33	2.24	2.18	2.13	2.09	2.06
	17	3.03	2.64	2.44	2.31	2.22	2.15	2.10	2.06	2.03
	18	3.01	2.62	2.42	2.29	2.20	2.13	2.08	2.04	2.00
	19	2.99	2.61	2.40	2.27	2.18	2.11	2.06	2.02	1.98
	20	2.97	2.59	2.38	2.25	2.16	2.09	2.04	2.00	1.96
	21	2.96	2.57	2.36	2.23	2.14	2.08	2.02	1.98	1.95
	22	2.95	2.56	2.35	2.22	2.13	2.06	2.01	1.97	1.93
	23	2.94	2.55	2.34	2.21	2.11	2.05	1.99	1.95	1.92
	24	2.93	2.54	2.33	2.19	2.10	2.04	1.98	1.94	1.91
	25	2.92	2.53	2.32	2.18	2.09	2.02	1.97	1.93	1.89
	26	2.91	2.52	2.31	2.17	2.08	2.01	1.96	1.92	1.88
	27	2.90	2.51	2.30	2.17	2.07	2.00	1.95	1.91	1.87
	28	2.89	2.50	2.29	2.16	2.06	2.00	1.94	1.90	1.87
	29	2.89	2.50	2.28	2.15	2.06	1.99	1.93	1.89	1.86
	30	2.88	2.49	2.28	2.14	2.05	1.98	1.93	1.88	1.85
	40	2.84	2.44	2.23	2.09	2.00	1.93	1.87	1.83	1.79
	60	2.79	2.39	2.18	2.04	1.95	1.87	1.82	1.77	1.74
	120	2.75	2.35	2.13	1.99	1.90	1.82	1.77	1.72	1.68
	∞	2.71	2.30	2.08	1.94	1.85	1.77	1.72	1.67	1.63

DENOMINATOR DEGREES OF FREEDOM $= V_2 = n_2 - 1$

ν_1	NUMERATOR DEGREES OF FREEDOM									
ν_2	10	12	15	20	24	30	40	60	120	∞
1	60.19	60.71	61.22	61.74	62.00	62.26	62.53	62.79	63.06	63.33
2	9.39	9.41	9.42	9.44	9.45	9.46	9.47	9.47	9.48	9.49
3	5.23	5.22	5.20	5.18	5.18	5.17	5.16	5.15	5.14	5.13
4	3.92	3.90	3.87	3.84	3.83	3.82	3.80	3.79	3.78	3.76
5	3.30	3.27	3.24	3.21	3.19	3.17	3.16	3.14	3.12	3.10
6	2.94	2.90	2.87	2.84	2.82	2.80	2.78	2.76	2.74	2.72
7	2.70	2.67	2.63	2.59	2.58	2.56	2.54	2.51	2.49	2.47
8	2.54	2.50	2.46	2.42	2.40	2.38	2.36	2.34	2.32	2.29
9	2.42	2.38	2.34	2.30	2.28	2.25	2.23	2.21	2.18	2.16
10	2.32	2.28	2.24	2.20	2.18	2.16	2.13	2.11	2.08	2.06
11	2.25	2.21	2.17	2.12	2.10	2.08	2.05	2.03	2.00	1.97
12	2.19	2.15	2.10	2.06	2.04	2.01	1.99	1.96	1.93	1.90
13	2.14	2.10	2.05	2.01	1.98	1.96	1.93	1.90	1.88	1.85
14	2.10	2.05	2.01	1.96	1.94	1.91	1.89	1.86	1.83	1.80
15	2.06	2.02	1.97	1.92	1.90	1.87	1.85	1.82	1.79	1.76
16	2.03	1.99	1.94	1.89	1.87	1.84	1.81	1.78	1.75	1.72
17	2.00	1.96	1.91	1.86	1.84	1.81	1.78	1.75	1.72	1.69
18	1.98	1.93	1.89	1.84	1.81	1.78	1.75	1.72	1.69	1.66
19	1.96	1.91	1.86	1.81	1.79	1.76	1.73	1.70	1.67	1.63
20	1.94	1.89	1.84	1.79	1.77	1.74	1.71	1.68	1.64	1.61
21	1.92	1.87	1.83	1.78	1.75	1.72	1.69	1.66	1.62	1.59
22	1.90	1.86	1.81	1.76	1.73	1.70	1.67	1.64	1.60	1.57
23	1.89	1.84	1.80	1.74	1.72	1.69	1.66	1.62	1.59	1.55
24	1.88	1.83	1.78	1.73	1.70	1.67	1.64	1.61	1.57	1.53
25	1.87	1.82	1.77	1.72	1.69	1.66	1.63	1.59	1.56	1.52
26	1.86	1.81	1.76	1.71	1.68	1.65	1.61	1.58	1.54	1.50
27	1.85	1.80	1.75	1.70	1.67	1.64	1.60	1.57	1.53	1.49
28	1.84	1.79	1.74	1.69	1.66	1.63	1.59	1.56	1.52	1.48
29	1.83	1.78	1.73	1.68	1.65	1.62	1.58	1.55	1.51	1.47
30	1.82	1.77	1.72	1.67	1.64	1.61	1.57	1.54	1.50	1.46
40	1.76	1.71	1.66	1.61	1.57	1.54	1.51	1.47	1.42	1.38
60	1.71	1.66	1.60	1.54	1.51	1.48	1.44	1.40	1.35	1.29
120	1.65	1.60	1.55	1.48	1.45	1.41	1.37	1.32	1.26	1.19
∞	1.60	1.55	1.49	1.42	1.38	1.34	1.30	1.24	1.17	1.00

DENOMINATOR DEGREES OF FREEDOM

Table VII Percentage Points of the F Distribution, $\alpha = .05$

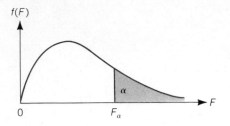

ν_2 \ ν_1	NUMERATOR DEGREES OF FREEDOM								
	1	2	3	4	5	6	7	8	9
1	161.4	199.5	215.7	224.6	230.2	234.0	236.8	238.9	240.5
2	18.51	19.00	19.16	19.25	19.30	19.33	19.35	19.37	19.38
3	10.13	9.55	9.28	9.12	9.01	8.94	8.89	8.85	8.81
4	7.71	6.94	6.59	6.39	6.26	6.16	6.09	6.04	6.00
5	6.61	5.79	5.41	5.19	5.05	4.95	4.88	4.82	4.77
6	5.99	5.14	4.76	4.53	4.39	4.28	4.21	4.15	4.10
7	5.59	4.74	4.35	4.12	3.97	3.87	3.79	3.73	3.68
8	5.32	4.46	4.07	3.84	3.69	3.58	3.50	3.44	3.39
9	5.12	4.26	3.86	3.63	3.48	3.37	3.29	3.23	3.18
10	4.96	4.10	3.71	3.48	3.33	3.22	3.14	3.07	3.02
11	4.84	3.98	3.59	3.36	3.20	3.09	3.01	2.95	2.90
12	4.75	3.89	3.49	3.26	3.11	3.00	2.91	2.85	2.80
13	4.67	3.81	3.41	3.18	3.03	2.92	2.83	2.77	2.71
14	4.60	3.74	3.34	3.11	2.96	2.85	2.76	2.70	2.65
15	4.54	3.68	3.29	3.06	2.90	2.79	2.71	2.64	2.59
16	4.49	3.63	3.24	3.01	2.85	2.74	2.66	2.59	2.54
17	4.45	3.59	3.20	2.96	2.81	2.70	2.61	2.55	2.49
18	4.41	3.55	3.16	2.93	2.77	2.66	2.58	2.51	2.46
19	4.38	3.52	3.13	2.90	2.74	2.63	2.54	2.48	2.42
20	4.35	3.49	3.10	2.87	2.71	2.60	2.51	2.45	2.39
21	4.32	3.47	3.07	2.84	2.68	2.57	2.49	2.42	2.37
22	4.30	3.44	3.05	2.82	2.66	2.55	2.46	2.40	2.34
23	4.28	3.42	3.03	2.80	2.64	2.53	2.44	2.37	2.32
24	4.26	3.40	3.01	2.78	2.62	2.51	2.42	2.36	2.30
25	4.24	3.39	2.99	2.76	2.60	2.49	2.40	2.34	2.28
26	4.23	3.37	2.98	2.74	2.59	2.47	2.39	2.32	2.27
27	4.21	3.35	2.96	2.73	2.57	2.46	2.37	2.31	2.25
28	4.20	3.34	2.95	2.71	2.56	2.45	2.36	2.29	2.24
29	4.18	3.33	2.93	2.70	2.55	2.43	2.35	2.28	2.22
30	4.17	3.32	2.92	2.69	2.53	2.42	2.33	2.27	2.21
40	4.08	3.23	2.84	2.61	2.45	2.34	2.25	2.18	2.12
60	4.00	3.15	2.76	2.53	2.37	2.25	2.17	2.10	2.04
120	3.92	3.07	2.68	2.45	2.29	2.17	2.09	2.02	1.96
∞	3.84	3.00	2.60	2.37	2.21	2.10	2.01	1.94	1.88

(Label on left side vertical: DENOMINATOR DEGREES OF FREEDOM)

Source: From M. Merrington and C. M. Thompson, "Tables of Percentage Points of the Inverted Beta (F)-Distribution," *Biometrika*, 1943, *33*, 73–88. Reproduced by permission of the *Biometrika* Trustees.

ν_2 \ ν_1	NUMERATOR DEGREES OF FREEDOM									
	10	12	15	20	24	30	40	60	120	∞
1	241.9	243.9	245.9	248.0	249.1	250.1	251.1	252.2	253.3	254.3
2	19.40	19.41	19.43	19.45	19.45	19.46	19.47	19.48	19.49	19.50
3	8.79	8.74	8.70	8.66	8.64	8.62	8.59	8.57	8.55	8.53
4	5.96	5.91	5.86	5.80	5.77	5.75	5.72	5.69	5.66	5.63
5	4.74	4.68	4.62	4.56	4.53	4.50	4.46	4.43	4.40	4.36
6	4.06	4.00	3.94	3.87	3.84	3.81	3.77	3.74	3.70	3.67
7	3.64	3.57	3.51	3.44	3.41	3.38	3.34	3.30	3.27	3.23
8	3.35	3.28	3.22	3.15	3.12	3.08	3.04	3.01	2.97	2.93
9	3.14	3.07	3.01	2.94	2.90	2.86	2.83	2.79	2.75	2.71
10	2.98	2.91	2.85	2.77	2.74	2.70	2.66	2.62	2.58	2.54
11	2.85	2.79	2.72	2.65	2.61	2.57	2.53	2.49	2.45	2.40
12	2.75	2.69	2.62	2.54	2.51	2.47	2.43	2.38	2.34	2.30
13	2.67	2.60	2.53	2.46	2.42	2.38	2.34	2.30	2.25	2.21
14	2.60	2.53	2.46	2.39	2.35	2.31	2.27	2.22	2.18	2.13
15	2.54	2.48	2.40	2.33	2.29	2.25	2.20	2.16	2.11	2.07
16	2.49	2.42	2.35	2.28	2.24	2.19	2.15	2.11	2.06	2.01
17	2.45	2.38	2.31	2.23	2.19	2.15	2.10	2.06	2.01	1.96
18	2.41	2.34	2.27	2.19	2.15	2.11	2.06	2.02	1.97	1.92
19	2.38	2.31	2.23	2.16	2.11	2.07	2.03	1.98	1.93	1.88
20	2.35	2.28	2.20	2.12	2.08	2.04	1.99	1.95	1.90	1.84
21	2.32	2.25	2.18	2.10	2.05	2.01	1.96	1.92	1.87	1.81
22	2.30	2.23	2.15	2.07	2.03	1.98	1.94	1.89	1.84	1.78
23	2.27	2.20	2.13	2.05	2.01	1.96	1.91	1.86	1.81	1.76
24	2.25	2.18	2.11	2.03	1.98	1.94	1.89	1.84	1.79	1.73
25	2.24	2.16	2.09	2.01	1.96	1.92	1.87	1.82	1.77	1.71
26	2.22	2.15	2.07	1.99	1.95	1.90	1.85	1.80	1.75	1.69
27	2.20	2.13	2.06	1.97	1.93	1.88	1.84	1.79	1.73	1.67
28	2.19	2.12	2.04	1.96	1.91	1.87	1.82	1.77	1.71	1.65
29	2.18	2.10	2.03	1.94	1.90	1.85	1.81	1.75	1.70	1.64
30	2.16	2.09	2.01	1.93	1.89	1.84	1.79	1.74	1.68	1.62
40	2.08	2.00	1.92	1.84	1.79	1.74	1.69	1.64	1.58	1.51
60	1.99	1.92	1.84	1.75	1.70	1.65	1.59	1.53	1.47	1.39
120	1.91	1.83	1.75	1.66	1.61	1.55	1.50	1.43	1.35	1.25
∞	1.83	1.75	1.67	1.57	1.52	1.46	1.39	1.32	1.22	1.00

DENOMINATOR DEGREES OF FREEDOM

Table VIII   Percentage Points of the F Distribution, $\alpha = .025$

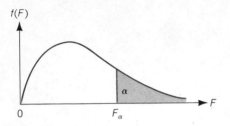

$f(F)$

v_1	NUMERATOR DEGREES OF FREEDOM								
v_2	1	2	3	4	5	6	7	8	9
1	647.8	799.5	864.2	899.6	921.8	937.1	948.2	956.7	963.3
2	38.51	39.00	39.17	39.25	39.30	39.33	39.36	39.37	39.39
3	17.44	16.04	15.44	15.10	14.88	14.73	14.62	14.54	14.47
4	12.22	10.65	9.98	9.60	9.36	9.20	9.07	8.98	8.90
5	10.01	8.43	7.76	7.39	7.15	6.98	6.85	6.76	6.68
6	8.81	7.26	6.60	6.23	5.99	5.82	5.70	5.60	5.52
7	8.07	6.54	5.89	5.52	5.29	5.12	4.99	4.90	4.82
8	7.57	6.06	5.42	5.05	4.82	4.65	4.53	4.43	4.36
9	7.21	5.71	5.08	4.72	4.48	4.32	4.20	4.10	4.03
10	6.94	5.46	4.83	4.47	4.24	4.07	3.95	3.85	3.78
11	6.72	5.26	4.63	4.28	4.04	3.88	3.76	3.66	3.59
12	6.55	5.10	4.47	4.12	3.89	3.73	3.61	3.51	3.44
13	6.41	4.97	4.35	4.00	3.77	3.60	3.48	3.39	3.31
14	6.30	4.86	4.24	3.89	3.66	3.50	3.38	3.29	3.21
15	6.20	4.77	4.15	3.80	3.58	3.41	3.29	3.20	3.12
16	6.12	4.69	4.08	3.73	3.50	3.34	3.22	3.12	3.05
17	6.04	4.62	4.01	3.66	3.44	3.28	3.16	3.06	2.98
18	5.98	4.56	3.95	3.61	3.38	3.22	3.10	3.01	2.93
19	5.92	4.51	3.90	3.56	3.33	3.17	3.05	2.96	2.88
20	5.87	4.46	3.86	3.51	3.29	3.13	3.01	2.91	2.84
21	5.83	4.42	3.82	3.48	3.25	3.09	2.97	2.87	2.80
22	5.79	4.38	3.78	3.44	3.22	3.05	2.93	2.84	2.76
23	5.75	4.35	3.75	3.41	3.18	3.02	2.90	2.81	2.73
24	5.72	4.32	3.72	3.38	3.15	2.99	2.87	2.78	2.70
25	5.69	4.29	3.69	3.35	3.13	2.97	2.85	2.75	2.68
26	5.66	4.27	3.67	3.33	3.10	2.94	2.82	2.73	2.65
27	5.63	4.24	3.65	3.31	3.08	2.92	2.80	2.71	2.63
28	5.61	4.22	3.63	3.29	3.06	2.90	2.78	2.69	2.61
29	5.59	4.20	3.61	3.27	3.04	2.88	2.76	2.67	2.59
30	5.57	4.18	3.59	3.25	3.03	2.87	2.75	2.65	2.57
40	5.42	4.05	3.46	3.13	2.90	2.74	2.62	2.53	2.45
60	5.29	3.93	3.34	3.01	2.79	2.63	2.51	2.41	2.33
120	5.15	3.80	3.23	2.89	2.67	2.52	2.39	2.30	2.22
∞	5.02	3.69	3.12	2.79	2.57	2.41	2.29	2.19	2.11

DENOMINATOR DEGREES OF FREEDOM

v_2 \ v_1	NUMERATOR DEGREES OF FREEDOM									
	10	12	15	20	24	30	40	60	120	∞
1	968.6	976.7	984.9	993.1	997.2	1001	1006	1010	1014	1018
2	39.40	39.41	39.43	39.45	39.46	39.46	39.47	39.48	39.49	39.50
3	14.42	14.34	14.25	14.17	14.12	14.08	14.04	13.99	13.95	13.90
4	8.84	8.75	8.66	8.56	8.51	8.46	8.41	8.36	8.31	8.26
5	6.62	6.52	6.43	6.33	6.28	6.23	6.18	6.12	6.07	6.02
6	5.46	5.37	5.27	5.17	5.12	5.07	5.01	4.96	4.90	4.85
7	4.76	4.67	4.57	4.47	4.42	4.36	4.31	4.25	4.20	4.14
8	4.30	4.20	4.10	4.00	3.95	3.89	3.84	3.78	3.73	3.67
9	3.96	3.87	3.77	3.67	3.61	3.56	3.51	3.45	3.39	3.33
10	3.72	3.62	3.52	3.42	3.37	3.31	3.26	3.20	3.14	3.08
11	3.53	3.43	3.33	3.23	3.17	3.12	3.06	3.00	2.94	2.88
12	3.37	3.28	3.18	3.07	3.02	2.96	2.91	2.85	2.79	2.72
13	3.25	3.15	3.05	2.95	2.89	2.84	2.78	2.72	2.66	2.60
14	3.15	3.05	2.95	2.84	2.79	2.73	2.67	2.61	2.55	2.49
15	3.06	2.96	2.86	2.76	2.70	2.64	2.59	2.52	2.46	2.40
16	2.99	2.89	2.79	2.68	2.63	2.57	2.51	2.45	2.38	2.32
17	2.92	2.82	2.72	2.62	2.56	2.50	2.44	2.38	2.32	2.25
18	2.87	2.77	2.67	2.56	2.50	2.44	2.38	2.32	2.26	2.19
19	2.82	2.72	2.62	2.51	2.45	2.39	2.33	2.27	2.20	2.13
20	2.77	2.68	2.57	2.46	2.41	2.35	2.29	2.22	2.16	2.09
21	2.73	2.64	2.53	2.42	2.37	2.31	2.25	2.18	2.11	2.04
22	2.70	2.60	2.50	2.39	2.33	2.27	2.21	2.14	2.08	2.00
23	2.67	2.57	2.47	2.36	2.30	2.24	2.18	2.11	2.04	1.97
24	2.64	2.54	2.44	2.33	2.27	2.21	2.15	2.08	2.01	1.94
25	2.61	2.51	2.41	2.30	2.24	2.18	2.12	2.05	1.98	1.91
26	2.59	2.49	2.39	2.28	2.22	2.16	2.09	2.03	1.95	1.88
27	2.57	2.47	2.36	2.25	2.19	2.13	2.07	2.00	1.93	1.85
28	2.55	2.45	2.34	2.23	2.17	2.11	2.05	1.98	1.91	1.83
29	2.53	2.43	2.32	2.21	2.15	2.09	2.03	1.96	1.89	1.81
30	2.51	2.41	2.31	2.20	2.14	2.07	2.01	1.94	1.87	1.79
40	2.39	2.29	2.18	2.07	2.01	1.94	1.88	1.80	1.72	1.64
60	2.27	2.17	2.06	1.94	1.88	1.82	1.74	1.67	1.58	1.48
120	2.16	2.05	1.94	1.82	1.76	1.69	1.61	1.53	1.43	1.31
∞	2.05	1.94	1.83	1.71	1.64	1.57	1.48	1.39	1.27	1.00

DENOMINATOR DEGREES OF FREEDOM

Table IX Percentage Points of the F Distribution, $\alpha = .01$

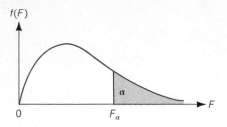

v_2	NUMERATOR DEGREES OF FREEDOM v_1								
	1	2	3	4	5	6	7	8	9
1	4,052	4,999.5	5,403	5,625	5,764	5,859	5,928	5,982	6,022
2	98.50	99.00	99.17	99.25	99.30	99.33	99.36	99.37	99.39
3	34.12	30.82	29.46	28.71	28.24	27.91	27.67	27.49	27.35
4	21.20	18.00	16.69	15.98	15.52	15.21	14.98	14.80	14.66
5	16.26	13.27	12.06	11.39	10.97	10.67	10.46	10.29	10.16
6	13.75	10.92	9.78	9.15	8.75	8.47	8.26	8.10	7.98
7	12.25	9.55	8.45	7.85	7.46	7.19	6.99	6.84	6.72
8	11.26	8.65	7.59	7.01	6.63	6.37	6.18	6.03	5.91
9	10.56	8.02	6.99	6.42	6.06	5.80	5.61	5.47	5.35
10	10.04	7.56	6.55	5.99	5.64	5.39	5.20	5.06	4.94
11	9.65	7.21	6.22	5.67	5.32	5.07	4.89	4.74	4.63
12	9.33	6.93	5.95	5.41	5.06	4.82	4.64	4.50	4.39
13	9.07	6.70	5.74	5.21	4.86	4.62	4.44	4.30	4.19
14	8.86	6.51	5.56	5.04	4.69	4.46	4.28	4.14	4.03
15	8.68	6.36	5.42	4.89	4.56	4.32	4.14	4.00	3.89
16	8.53	6.23	5.29	4.77	4.44	4.20	4.03	3.89	3.78
17	8.40	6.11	5.18	4.67	4.34	4.10	3.93	3.79	3.68
18	8.29	6.01	5.09	4.58	4.25	4.01	3.84	3.71	3.60
19	8.18	5.93	5.01	4.50	4.17	3.94	3.77	3.63	3.52
20	8.10	5.85	4.94	4.43	4.10	3.87	3.70	3.56	3.46
21	8.02	5.78	4.87	4.37	4.04	3.81	3.64	3.51	3.40
22	7.95	5.72	4.82	4.31	3.99	3.76	3.59	3.45	3.35
23	7.88	5.66	4.76	4.26	3.94	3.71	3.54	3.41	3.30
24	7.82	5.61	4.72	4.22	3.90	3.67	3.50	3.36	3.26
25	7.77	5.57	4.68	4.18	3.85	3.63	3.46	3.32	3.22
26	7.72	5.53	4.64	4.14	3.82	3.59	3.42	3.29	3.18
27	7.68	5.49	4.60	4.11	3.78	3.56	3.39	3.26	3.15
28	7.64	5.45	4.57	4.07	3.75	3.53	3.36	3.23	3.12
29	7.60	5.42	4.54	4.04	3.73	3.50	3.33	3.20	3.09
30	7.56	5.39	4.51	4.02	3.70	3.47	3.30	3.17	3.07
40	7.31	5.18	4.31	3.83	3.51	3.29	3.12	2.99	2.89
60	7.08	4.98	4.13	3.65	3.34	3.12	2.95	2.82	2.72
120	6.85	4.79	3.95	3.48	3.17	2.96	2.79	2.66	2.56
∞	6.63	4.61	3.78	3.32	3.02	2.80	2.64	2.51	2.41

ν_1				NUMERATOR DEGREES OF FREEDOM						
ν_2	10	12	15	20	24	30	40	60	120	∞
1	6,056	6,106	6,157	6,209	6,235	6,261	6,287	6,313	6,339	6,366
2	99.40	99.42	99.43	99.45	99.46	99.47	99.47	99.48	99.49	99.50
3	27.23	27.05	26.87	26.69	26.60	26.50	26.41	26.32	26.22	26.13
4	14.55	14.37	14.20	14.02	13.93	13.84	13.75	13.65	13.56	13.46
5	10.05	9.89	9.72	9.55	9.47	9.38	9.29	9.20	9.11	9.02
6	7.87	7.72	7.56	7.40	7.31	7.23	7.14	7.06	6.97	6.88
7	6.62	6.47	6.31	6.16	6.07	5.99	5.91	5.82	5.74	5.65
8	5.81	5.67	5.52	5.36	5.28	5.20	5.12	5.03	4.95	4.86
9	5.26	5.11	4.96	4.81	4.73	4.65	4.57	4.48	4.40	4.31
10	4.85	4.71	4.56	4.41	4.33	4.25	4.17	4.08	4.00	3.91
11	4.54	4.40	4.25	4.10	4.02	3.94	3.86	3.78	3.69	3.60
12	4.30	4.16	4.01	3.86	3.78	3.70	3.62	3.54	3.45	3.36
13	4.10	3.96	3.82	3.66	3.59	3.51	3.43	3.34	3.25	3.17
14	3.94	3.80	3.66	3.51	3.43	3.35	3.27	3.18	3.09	3.00
15	3.80	3.67	3.52	3.37	3.29	3.21	3.13	3.05	2.96	2.87
16	3.69	3.55	3.41	3.26	3.18	3.10	3.02	2.93	2.84	2.75
17	3.59	3.46	3.31	3.16	3.08	3.00	2.92	2.83	2.75	2.65
18	3.51	3.37	3.23	3.08	3.00	2.92	2.84	2.75	2.66	2.57
19	3.43	3.30	3.15	3.00	2.92	2.84	2.76	2.67	2.58	2.49
20	3.37	3.23	3.09	2.94	2.86	2.78	2.69	2.61	2.52	2.42
21	3.31	3.17	3.03	2.88	2.80	2.72	2.64	2.55	2.46	2.36
22	3.26	3.12	2.98	2.83	2.75	2.67	2.58	2.50	2.40	2.31
23	3.21	3.07	2.93	2.78	2.70	2.62	2.54	2.45	2.35	2.26
24	3.17	3.03	2.89	2.74	2.66	2.58	2.49	2.40	2.31	2.21
25	3.13	2.99	2.85	2.70	2.62	2.54	2.45	2.36	2.27	2.17
26	3.09	2.96	2.81	2.66	2.58	2.50	2.42	2.33	2.23	2.13
27	3.06	2.93	2.78	2.63	2.55	2.47	2.38	2.29	2.20	2.10
28	3.03	2.90	2.75	2.60	2.52	2.44	2.35	2.26	2.17	2.06
29	3.00	2.87	2.73	2.57	2.49	2.41	2.33	2.23	2.14	2.03
30	2.98	2.84	2.70	2.55	2.47	2.39	2.30	2.21	2.11	2.01
40	2.80	2.66	2.52	2.37	2.29	2.20	2.11	2.02	1.92	1.80
60	2.63	2.50	2.35	2.20	2.12	2.03	1.94	1.84	1.73	1.60
120	2.47	2.34	2.19	2.03	1.95	1.86	1.76	1.66	1.53	1.38
∞	2.32	2.18	2.04	1.88	1.79	1.70	1.59	1.47	1.32	1.00

DENOMINATOR DEGREES OF FREEDOM

Table X Critical Values of T_L and T_U for the Wilcoxon Rank Sum Test: Independent Samples

Test statistic is rank sum associated with smaller sample (if equal sample sizes, either rank sum can be used).

a. $\alpha = .025$ one-tailed; $\alpha = .05$ two-tailed

n_2	n_1 3		4		5		6		7		8		9		10	
	T_L	T_U	T_L	T_U	T_L	T_U	T_L	T_U	T_L	T_U	T_L	T_U	T_L	T_U	T_L	T_U
3	5	16	6	18	6	21	7	23	7	26	8	28	8	31	9	33
4	6	18	11	25	12	28	12	32	13	35	14	38	15	41	16	44
5	6	21	12	28	18	37	19	41	20	45	21	49	22	53	24	56
6	7	23	12	32	19	41	26	52	28	56	29	61	31	65	32	70
7	7	26	13	35	20	45	28	56	37	68	39	73	41	78	43	83
8	8	28	14	38	21	49	29	61	39	73	49	87	51	93	54	98
9	8	31	15	41	22	53	31	65	41	78	51	93	63	108	66	114
10	9	33	16	44	24	56	32	70	43	83	54	98	66	114	79	131

b. $\alpha = .05$ one-tailed; $\alpha = .10$ two-tailed

n_2	n_1 3		4		5		6		7		8		9		10	
	T_L	T_U	T_L	T_U	T_L	T_U	T_L	T_U	T_L	T_U	T_L	T_U	T_L	T_U	T_L	T_U
3	6	15	7	17	7	20	8	22	9	24	9	27	10	29	11	31
4	7	17	12	24	13	27	14	30	15	33	16	36	17	39	18	42
5	7	20	13	27	19	36	20	40	22	43	24	46	25	50	26	54
6	8	22	14	30	20	40	28	50	30	54	32	58	33	63	35	67
7	9	24	15	33	22	43	30	54	39	66	41	71	43	76	46	80
8	9	27	16	36	24	46	32	58	41	71	52	84	54	90	57	95
9	10	29	17	39	25	50	33	63	43	76	54	90	66	105	69	111
10	11	31	18	42	26	54	35	67	46	80	57	95	69	111	83	127

Source: From F. Wilcoxon and R. A. Wilcox, "Some Rapid Approximate Statistical Procedures," 1964, 20–23. Reproduced with the permission of American Cyanamid Company.

Table XI   Critical Values of T_0 in the Wilcoxon Paired Difference Signed Rank Test

ONE-TAILED	TWO-TAILED	$n = 5$	$n = 6$	$n = 7$	$n = 8$	$n = 9$	$n = 10$
$\alpha = .05$	$\alpha = .10$	1	2	4	6	8	11
$\alpha = .025$	$\alpha = .05$		1	2	4	6	8
$\alpha = .01$	$\alpha = .02$			0	2	3	5
$\alpha = .005$	$\alpha = .01$				0	2	3
		$n = 11$	$n = 12$	$n = 13$	$n = 14$	$n = 15$	$n = 16$
$\alpha = .05$	$\alpha = .10$	14	17	21	26	30	36
$\alpha = .025$	$\alpha = .05$	11	14	17	21	25	30
$\alpha = .01$	$\alpha = .02$	7	10	13	16	20	24
$\alpha = .005$	$\alpha = .01$	5	7	10	13	16	19
		$n = 17$	$n = 18$	$n = 19$	$n = 20$	$n = 21$	$n = 22$
$\alpha = .05$	$\alpha = .10$	41	47	54	60	68	75
$\alpha = .025$	$\alpha = .05$	35	40	46	52	59	66
$\alpha = .01$	$\alpha = .02$	28	33	38	43	49	56
$\alpha = .005$	$\alpha = .01$	23	28	32	37	43	49
		$n = 23$	$n = 24$	$n = 25$	$n = 26$	$n = 27$	$n = 28$
$\alpha = .05$	$\alpha = .10$	83	92	101	110	120	130
$\alpha = .025$	$\alpha = .05$	73	81	90	98	107	117
$\alpha = .01$	$\alpha = .02$	62	69	77	85	93	102
$\alpha = .005$	$\alpha = .01$	55	61	68	76	84	92
		$n = 29$	$n = 30$	$n = 31$	$n = 32$	$n = 33$	$n = 34$
$\alpha = .05$	$\alpha = .10$	141	152	163	175	188	201
$\alpha = .025$	$\alpha = .05$	127	137	148	159	171	183
$\alpha = .01$	$\alpha = .02$	111	120	130	141	151	162
$\alpha = .005$	$\alpha = .01$	100	109	118	128	138	149
		$n = 35$	$n = 36$	$n = 37$	$n = 38$	$n = 39$	
$\alpha = .05$	$\alpha = .10$	214	228	242	256	271	
$\alpha = .025$	$\alpha = .05$	195	208	222	235	250	
$\alpha = .01$	$\alpha = .02$	174	186	198	211	224	
$\alpha = .005$	$\alpha = .01$	160	171	183	195	208	
		$n = 40$	$n = 41$	$n = 42$	$n = 43$	$n = 44$	$n = 45$
$\alpha = .05$	$\alpha = .10$	287	303	319	336	353	371
$\alpha = .025$	$\alpha = .05$	264	279	295	311	327	344
$\alpha = .01$	$\alpha = .02$	238	252	267	281	297	313
$\alpha = .005$	$\alpha = .01$	221	234	248	262	277	292
		$n = 46$	$n = 47$	$n = 48$	$n = 49$	$n = 50$	
$\alpha = .05$	$\alpha = .10$	389	408	427	446	466	
$\alpha = .025$	$\alpha = .05$	361	379	397	415	434	
$\alpha = .01$	$\alpha = .02$	329	345	362	380	398	
$\alpha = .005$	$\alpha = .01$	307	323	339	356	373	

Source: From F. Wilcoxon and R. A. Wilcox, "Some Rapid Approximate Statistical Procedures," 1964, 28. Reproduced with the permission of American Cyanamid Company.

Table XII Critical Values of χ^2

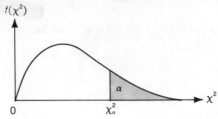

DEGREES OF FREEDOM	$\chi^2_{.995}$	$\chi^2_{.990}$	$\chi^2_{.975}$	$\chi^2_{.950}$	$\chi^2_{.900}$
1	0.0000393	0.0001571	0.0009821	0.0039321	0.0157908
2	0.0100251	0.0201007	0.0506356	0.102587	0.210720
3	0.0717212	0.114832	0.215795	0.351846	0.584375
4	0.206990	0.297110	0.484419	0.710721	1.063623
5	0.411740	0.554300	0.831211	1.145476	1.61031
6	0.675727	0.872085	1.237347	1.63539	2.20413
7	0.989265	1.239043	1.68987	2.16735	2.83311
8	1.344419	1.646482	2.17973	2.73264	3.48954
9	1.734926	2.087912	2.70039	3.32511	4.16816
10	2.15585	2.55821	3.24697	3.94030	4.86518
11	2.60321	3.05347	3.81575	4.57481	5.57779
12	3.07382	3.57056	4.40379	5.22603	6.30380
13	3.56503	4.10691	5.00874	5.89186	7.04150
14	4.07468	4.66043	5.62872	6.57063	7.78953
15	4.60094	5.22935	6.26214	7.26094	8.54675
16	5.14224	5.81221	6.90766	7.96164	9.31223
17	5.69724	6.40776	7.56418	8.67176	10.0852
18	6.26481	7.01491	8.23075	9.39046	10.8649
19	6.84398	7.63273	8.90655	10.1170	11.6509
20	7.43386	8.26040	9.59083	10.8508	12.4426
21	8.03366	8.89720	10.28293	11.5913	13.2396
22	8.64272	9.54249	10.9823	12.3380	14.0415
23	9.26042	10.19567	11.6885	13.0905	14.8479
24	9.88623	10.8564	12.4011	13.8484	15.6587
25	10.5197	11.5240	13.1197	14.6114	16.4734
26	11.1603	12.1981	13.8439	15.3791	17.2919
27	11.8076	12.8786	14.5733	16.1513	18.1138
28	12.4613	13.5648	15.3079	16.9279	18.9392
29	13.1211	14.2565	16.0471	17.7083	19.7677
30	13.7867	14.9535	16.7908	18.4926	20.5992
40	20.7065	22.1643	24.4331	26.5093	29.0505
50	27.9907	29.7067	32.3574	34.7642	37.6886
60	35.5346	37.4848	40.4817	43.1879	46.4589
70	43.2752	45.4418	48.7576	51.7393	55.3290
80	51.1720	53.5400	57.1532	60.3915	64.2778
90	59.1963	61.7541	65.6466	69.1260	73.2912
100	67.3276	70.0648	74.2219	77.9295	82.3581

Source: From C. M. Thompson, "Tables of the Percentage Points of the χ^2-Distribution," *Biometrika*, 1941, *32*, 188–189. Reproduced by permission of the *Biometrika* Trustees.

$\alpha =$	.10	.05	.025	.01	.005
DEGREES OF FREEDOM	$\chi^2_{.100}$	$\chi^2_{.050}$	$\chi^2_{.025}$	$\chi^2_{.010}$	$\chi^2_{.005}$
1	2.70554	3.84146	5.02389	6.63490	7.87944
2	4.60517	5.99147	7.37776	9.21034	10.5966
3	6.25139	7.81473	9.34840	11.3449	12.8381
4	7.77944	9.48773	11.1433	13.2767	14.8602
5	9.23635	11.0705	12.8325	15.0863	16.7496
6	10.6446	12.5916	14.4494	16.8119	18.5476
7	12.0170	14.0671	16.0128	18.4753	20.2777
8	13.3616	15.5073	17.5346	20.0902	21.9550
9	14.6837	16.9190	19.0228	21.6660	23.5893
10	15.9871	18.3070	20.4831	23.2093	25.1882
11	17.2750	19.6751	21.9200	24.7250	26.7569
12	18.5494	21.0261	23.3367	26.2170	28.2995
13	19.8119	22.3621	24.7356	27.6883	29.8194
14	21.0642	23.6848	26.1190	29.1413	31.3193
15	22.3072	24.9958	27.4884	30.5779	32.8013
16	23.5418	26.2962	28.8454	31.9999	34.2672
17	24.7690	27.5871	30.1910	33.4087	35.7185
18	25.9894	28.8693	31.5264	34.8053	37.1564
19	27.2036	30.1435	32.8523	36.1908	38.5822
20	28.4120	31.4104	34.1696	37.5662	39.9968
21	29.6151	32.6705	35.4789	38.9321	41.4010
22	30.8133	33.9244	36.7807	40.2894	42.7956
23	32.0069	35.1725	38.0757	41.6384	44.1813
24	33.1963	36.4151	39.3641	42.9798	45.5585
25	34.3816	37.6525	40.6465	44.3141	46.9278
26	35.5631	38.8852	41.9232	45.6417	48.2899
27	36.7412	40.1133	43.1944	46.9630	49.6449
28	37.9159	41.3372	44.4607	48.2782	50.9933
29	39.0875	42.5569	45.7222	49.5879	52.3356
30	40.2560	43.7729	46.9792	50.8922	53.6720
40	51.8050	55.7585	59.3417	63.6907	66.7659
50	63.1671	67.5048	71.4202	76.1539	79.4900
60	74.3970	79.0819	83.2976	88.3794	91.9517
70	85.5271	90.5312	95.0231	100.425	104.215
80	96.5782	101.879	106.629	112.329	116.321
90	107.565	113.145	118.136	124.116	128.299
100	118.498	124.342	129.561	135.807	140.169

Table XIII Percentage Points of the Studentized Range, $q(k, v)$, Upper 5%

v \ k	2	3	4	5	6	7	8	9	10	11	12	13	14	15	16	17	18	19	20
1	17.97	26.98	32.82	37.08	40.41	43.12	45.40	47.36	49.07	50.59	51.96	53.20	54.33	55.36	56.32	57.22	58.04	58.83	59.56
2	6.08	8.33	9.80	10.88	11.74	12.44	13.03	13.54	13.99	14.39	14.75	15.08	15.38	15.65	15.91	16.14	16.37	16.57	16.77
3	4.50	5.91	6.82	7.50	8.04	8.48	8.85	9.18	9.46	9.72	9.95	10.15	10.35	10.52	10.69	10.84	10.98	11.11	11.24
4	3.93	5.04	5.76	6.29	6.71	7.05	7.35	7.60	7.83	8.03	8.21	8.37	8.52	8.66	8.79	8.91	9.03	9.13	9.23
5	3.64	4.60	5.22	5.67	6.03	6.33	6.58	6.80	6.99	7.17	7.32	7.47	7.60	7.72	7.83	7.93	8.03	8.12	8.21
6	3.46	4.34	4.90	5.30	5.63	5.90	6.12	6.32	6.49	6.65	6.79	6.92	7.03	7.14	7.24	7.34	7.43	7.51	7.59
7	3.34	4.16	4.68	5.06	5.36	5.61	5.82	6.00	6.16	6.30	6.43	6.55	6.66	6.76	6.85	6.94	7.02	7.10	7.17
8	3.26	4.04	4.53	4.89	5.17	5.40	5.60	5.77	5.92	6.05	6.18	6.29	6.39	6.48	6.57	6.65	6.73	6.80	6.87
9	3.20	3.95	4.41	4.76	5.02	5.24	5.43	5.59	5.74	5.87	5.98	6.09	6.19	6.28	6.36	6.44	6.51	6.58	6.64
10	3.15	3.88	4.33	4.65	4.91	5.12	5.30	5.46	5.60	5.72	5.83	5.93	6.03	6.11	6.19	6.27	6.34	6.40	6.47
11	3.11	3.82	4.26	4.57	4.82	5.03	5.20	5.35	5.49	5.61	5.71	5.81	5.90	5.98	6.06	6.13	6.20	6.27	6.33
12	3.08	3.77	4.20	4.51	4.75	4.95	5.12	5.27	5.39	5.51	5.61	5.71	5.80	5.88	5.95	6.02	6.09	6.15	6.21
13	3.06	3.73	4.15	4.45	4.69	4.88	5.05	5.19	5.32	5.43	5.53	5.63	5.71	5.79	5.86	5.93	5.99	6.05	6.11
14	3.03	3.70	4.11	4.41	4.64	4.83	4.99	5.13	5.25	5.36	5.46	5.55	5.64	5.71	5.79	5.85	5.91	5.97	6.03
15	3.01	3.67	4.08	4.37	4.60	4.78	4.94	5.08	5.20	5.31	5.40	5.49	5.57	5.65	5.72	5.78	5.85	5.90	5.96
16	3.00	3.65	4.05	4.33	4.56	4.74	4.90	5.03	5.15	5.26	5.35	5.44	5.52	5.59	5.66	5.73	5.79	5.84	5.90
17	2.98	3.63	4.02	4.30	4.52	4.70	4.86	4.99	5.11	5.21	5.31	5.39	5.47	5.54	5.61	5.67	5.73	5.79	5.84
18	2.97	3.61	4.00	4.28	4.49	4.67	4.82	4.96	5.07	5.17	5.27	5.35	5.43	5.50	5.57	5.63	5.69	5.74	5.79
19	2.96	3.59	3.98	4.25	4.47	4.65	4.79	4.92	5.04	5.14	5.23	5.31	5.39	5.46	5.53	5.59	5.65	5.70	5.75
20	2.95	3.58	3.96	4.23	4.45	4.62	4.77	4.90	5.01	5.11	5.20	5.28	5.36	5.43	5.49	5.55	5.61	5.66	5.71
24	2.92	3.53	3.90	4.17	4.37	4.54	4.68	4.81	4.92	5.01	5.10	5.18	5.25	5.32	5.38	5.44	5.49	5.55	5.59
30	2.89	3.49	3.85	4.10	4.30	4.46	4.60	4.72	4.82	4.92	5.00	5.08	5.15	5.21	5.27	5.33	5.38	5.43	5.47
40	2.86	3.44	3.79	4.04	4.23	4.39	4.52	4.63	4.73	4.82	4.90	4.98	5.04	5.11	5.16	5.22	5.27	5.31	5.36
60	2.83	3.40	3.74	3.98	4.16	4.31	4.44	4.55	4.65	4.73	4.81	4.88	4.94	5.00	5.06	5.11	5.15	5.20	5.24
120	2.80	3.36	3.68	3.92	4.10	4.24	4.36	4.47	4.56	4.64	4.71	4.78	4.84	4.90	4.95	5.00	5.04	5.09	5.13
∞	2.77	3.31	3.63	3.86	4.03	4.17	4.29	4.39	4.47	4.55	4.62	4.68	4.74	4.80	4.85	4.89	4.93	4.97	5.01

Table XIV   Percentage Points of the Studentized Range, $q(k, v)$, Upper 1%

v \ k	2	3	4	5	6	7	8	9	10	11	12	13	14	15	16	17	18	19	20
1	90.03	135.0	164.3	185.6	202.2	215.8	227.2	237.0	245.6	253.2	260.0	266.2	271.8	277.0	281.8	286.3	290.0	294.3	298.0
2	14.04	19.02	22.29	24.72	26.63	28.20	29.53	30.68	31.69	32.59	33.40	34.13	34.81	35.43	36.00	36.53	37.03	37.50	37.95
3	8.26	10.62	12.17	13.33	14.24	15.00	15.64	16.20	16.69	17.13	17.53	17.89	18.22	18.52	18.81	19.07	19.32	19.55	19.77
4	6.51	8.12	9.17	9.96	10.58	11.10	11.55	11.93	12.27	12.57	12.84	13.09	13.32	13.53	13.73	13.91	14.08	14.24	14.40
5	5.70	6.98	7.80	8.42	8.91	9.32	9.67	9.97	10.24	10.48	10.70	10.89	11.08	11.24	11.40	11.55	11.68	11.81	11.93
6	5.24	6.33	7.03	7.56	7.97	8.32	8.61	8.87	9.10	9.30	9.48	9.65	9.81	9.95	10.08	10.21	10.32	10.43	10.54
7	4.95	5.92	6.54	7.01	7.37	7.68	7.94	8.17	8.37	8.55	8.71	8.86	9.00	9.12	9.24	9.35	9.46	9.55	9.65
8	4.75	5.64	6.20	6.62	6.96	7.24	7.47	7.68	7.86	8.03	8.18	8.31	8.44	8.55	8.66	8.76	8.85	8.94	9.03
9	4.60	5.43	5.96	6.35	6.66	6.91	7.13	7.33	7.49	7.65	7.78	7.91	8.03	8.13	8.23	8.33	8.41	8.49	8.57
10	4.48	5.27	5.77	6.14	6.43	6.67	6.87	7.05	7.21	7.36	7.49	7.60	7.71	7.81	7.91	7.99	8.08	8.15	8.23
11	4.39	5.15	5.62	5.97	6.25	6.48	6.67	6.84	6.99	7.13	7.25	7.36	7.46	7.56	7.65	7.73	7.81	7.88	7.95
12	4.32	5.05	5.50	5.84	6.10	6.32	6.51	6.67	6.81	6.94	7.06	7.17	7.26	7.36	7.44	7.52	7.59	7.66	7.73
13	4.26	4.96	5.40	5.73	5.98	6.19	6.37	6.53	6.67	6.79	6.90	7.01	7.10	7.19	7.27	7.35	7.42	7.48	7.55
14	4.21	4.89	5.32	5.63	5.88	6.08	6.26	6.41	6.54	6.66	6.77	6.87	6.96	7.05	7.13	7.20	7.27	7.33	7.39
15	4.17	4.84	5.25	5.56	5.80	5.99	6.16	6.31	6.44	6.55	6.66	6.76	6.84	6.93	7.00	7.07	7.14	7.20	7.26
16	4.13	4.79	5.19	5.49	5.72	5.92	6.08	6.22	6.35	6.46	6.56	6.66	6.74	6.82	6.90	6.97	7.03	7.09	7.15
17	4.10	4.74	5.14	5.43	5.66	5.85	6.01	6.15	6.27	6.38	6.48	6.57	6.66	6.73	6.81	6.87	6.94	7.00	7.05
18	4.07	4.70	5.09	5.38	5.60	5.79	5.94	6.08	6.20	6.31	6.41	6.50	6.58	6.65	6.72	6.79	6.85	6.91	6.97
19	4.05	4.67	5.05	5.33	5.55	5.73	5.89	6.02	6.14	6.25	6.34	6.43	6.51	6.58	6.65	6.72	6.78	6.84	6.89
20	4.02	4.64	5.02	5.29	5.51	5.69	5.84	5.97	6.09	6.19	6.28	6.37	6.45	6.52	6.59	6.65	6.71	6.77	6.82
24	3.96	4.55	4.91	5.17	5.37	5.54	5.69	5.81	5.92	6.02	6.11	6.19	6.26	6.33	6.39	6.45	6.51	6.56	6.61
30	3.89	4.45	4.80	5.05	5.24	5.40	5.54	5.65	5.76	5.85	5.93	6.01	6.08	6.14	6.20	6.26	6.31	6.36	6.41
40	3.82	4.37	4.70	4.93	5.11	5.26	5.39	5.50	5.60	5.69	5.76	5.83	5.90	5.96	6.02	6.07	6.12	6.16	6.21
60	3.76	4.28	4.59	4.82	4.99	5.13	5.25	5.36	5.45	5.53	5.60	5.67	5.73	5.78	5.84	5.89	5.93	5.97	6.01
120	3.70	4.20	4.50	4.71	4.87	5.01	5.12	5.21	5.30	5.37	5.44	5.50	5.56	5.61	5.66	5.71	5.75	5.79	5.83
∞	3.64	4.12	4.40	4.60	4.76	4.88	4.99	5.08	5.16	5.23	5.29	5.35	5.40	5.45	5.49	5.54	5.57	5.61	5.65

Source: From *Biometrika Tables for Statisticians*. Vol. I, 3d ed., edited by E. S. Pearson and H. O. Hartley (Cambridge University Press, 1966.) Reproduced by permission of Professor E. S. Pearson and the Biometrika Trustees.

Table XV Critical Values for the Durbin – Watson d Statistic, $\alpha = .05$

n	$k = 1$		$k = 2$		$k = 3$		$k = 4$		$k = 5$	
	d_L	d_U	d_L	d_U	d_L	d_U	d_L	d_U	d_L	d_U
15	1.08	1.36	0.95	1.54	0.82	1.75	0.69	1.97	0.56	2.21
16	1.10	1.37	0.98	1.54	0.86	1.73	0.74	1.93	0.62	2.15
17	1.13	1.38	1.02	1.54	0.90	1.71	0.78	1.90	0.67	2.10
18	1.16	1.39	1.05	1.53	0.93	1.69	0.82	1.87	0.71	2.06
19	1.18	1.40	1.08	1.53	0.97	1.68	0.86	1.85	0.75	2.02
20	1.20	1.41	1.10	1.54	1.00	1.68	0.90	1.83	0.79	1.99
21	1.22	1.42	1.13	1.54	1.03	1.67	0.93	1.81	0.83	1.96
22	1.24	1.43	1.15	1.54	1.05	1.66	0.96	1.80	0.86	1.94
23	1.26	1.44	1.17	1.54	1.08	1.66	0.99	1.79	0.90	1.92
24	1.27	1.45	1.19	1.55	1.10	1.66	1.01	1.78	0.93	1.90
25	1.29	1.45	1.21	1.55	1.12	1.66	1.04	1.77	0.95	1.89
26	1.30	1.46	1.22	1.55	1.14	1.65	1.06	1.76	0.98	1.88
27	1.32	1.47	1.24	1.56	1.16	1.65	1.08	1.76	1.01	1.86
28	1.33	1.48	1.26	1.56	1.18	1.65	1.10	1.75	1.03	1.85
29	1.34	1.48	1.27	1.56	1.20	1.65	1.12	1.74	1.05	1.84
30	1.35	1.49	1.28	1.57	1.21	1.65	1.14	1.74	1.07	1.83
31	1.36	1.50	1.30	1.57	1.23	1.65	1.16	1.74	1.09	1.83
32	1.37	1.50	1.31	1.57	1.24	1.65	1.18	1.73	1.11	1.82
33	1.38	1.51	1.32	1.58	1.26	1.65	1.19	1.73	1.13	1.81
34	1.39	1.51	1.33	1.58	1.27	1.65	1.21	1.73	1.15	1.81
35	1.40	1.52	1.34	1.58	1.28	1.65	1.22	1.73	1.16	1.80
36	1.41	1.52	1.35	1.59	1.29	1.65	1.24	1.73	1.18	1.80
37	1.42	1.53	1.36	1.59	1.31	1.66	1.25	1.72	1.19	1.80
38	1.43	1.54	1.37	1.59	1.32	1.66	1.26	1.72	1.21	1.79
39	1.43	1.54	1.38	1.60	1.33	1.66	1.27	1.72	1.22	1.79
40	1.44	1.54	1.39	1.60	1.34	1.66	1.29	1.72	1.23	1.79
45	1.48	1.57	1.43	1.62	1.38	1.67	1.34	1.72	1.29	1.78
50	1.50	1.59	1.46	1.63	1.42	1.67	1.38	1.72	1.34	1.77
55	1.53	1.60	1.49	1.64	1.45	1.68	1.41	1.72	1.38	1.77
60	1.55	1.62	1.51	1.65	1.48	1.69	1.44	1.73	1.41	1.77
65	1.57	1.63	1.54	1.66	1.50	1.70	1.47	1.73	1.44	1.77
70	1.58	1.64	1.55	1.67	1.52	1.70	1.49	1.74	1.46	1.77
75	1.60	1.65	1.57	1.68	1.54	1.71	1.51	1.74	1.49	1.77
80	1.61	1.66	1.59	1.69	1.56	1.72	1.53	1.74	1.51	1.77
85	1.62	1.67	1.60	1.70	1.57	1.72	1.55	1.75	1.52	1.77
90	1.63	1.68	1.61	1.70	1.59	1.73	1.57	1.75	1.54	1.78
95	1.64	1.69	1.62	1.71	1.60	1.73	1.58	1.75	1.56	1.78
100	1.65	1.69	1.63	1.72	1.61	1.74	1.59	1.76	1.57	1.78

Source: From J. Durbin and G. S. Watson, "Testing for Serial Correlation in Least Squares Regression, II," *Biometrika*, 1951, *30*, 159–178. Reproduced by permission of the *Biometrika* Trustees.

Table XVI   Critical Values for the Durbin–Watson d Statistic, $\alpha = .01$

n	$k=1$		$k=2$		$k=3$		$k=4$		$k=5$	
	d_L	d_U	d_L	d_U	d_L	d_U	d_I	d_U	d_L	d_U
15	0.81	1.07	0.70	1.25	0.59	1.46	0.49	1.70	0.39	1.96
16	0.84	1.09	0.74	1.25	0.63	1.44	0.53	1.66	0.44	1.90
17	0.87	1.10	0.77	1.25	0.67	1.43	0.57	1.63	0.48	1.85
18	0.90	1.12	0.80	1.26	0.71	1.42	0.61	1.60	0.52	1.80
19	0.93	1.13	0.83	1.26	0.74	1.41	0.65	1.58	0.56	1.77
20	0.95	1.15	0.86	1.27	0.77	1.41	0.68	1.57	0.60	1.74
21	0.97	1.16	0.89	1.27	0.80	1.41	0.72	1.55	0.63	1.71
22	1.00	1.17	0.91	1.28	0.83	1.40	0.75	1.54	0.66	1.69
23	1.02	1.19	0.94	1.29	0.86	1.40	0.77	1.53	0.70	1.67
24	1.04	1.20	0.96	1.30	0.88	1.41	0.80	1.53	0.72	1.66
25	1.05	1.21	0.98	1.30	0.90	1.41	0.83	1.52	0.75	1.65
26	1.07	1.22	1.00	1.31	0.93	1.41	0.85	1.52	0.78	1.64
27	1.09	1.23	1.02	1.32	0.95	1.41	0.88	1.51	0.81	1.63
28	1.10	1.24	1.04	1.32	0.97	1.41	0.90	1.51	0.83	1.62
29	1.12	1.25	1.05	1.33	0.99	1.42	0.92	1.51	0.85	1.61
30	1.13	1.26	1.07	1.34	1.01	1.42	0.94	1.51	0.88	1.61
31	1.15	1.27	1.08	1.34	1.02	1.42	0.96	1.51	0.90	1.60
32	1.16	1.28	1.10	1.35	1.04	1.43	0.98	1.51	0.92	1.60
33	1.17	1.29	1.11	1.36	1.05	1.43	1.00	1.51	0.94	1.59
34	1.18	1.30	1.13	1.36	1.07	1.43	1.01	1.51	0.95	1.59
35	1.19	1.31	1.14	1.37	1.08	1.44	1.03	1.51	0.97	1.59
36	1.21	1.32	1.15	1.38	1.10	1.44	1.04	1.51	0.99	1.59
37	1.22	1.32	1.16	1.38	1.11	1.45	1.06	1.51	1.00	1.59
38	1.23	1.33	1.18	1.39	1.12	1.45	1.07	1.52	1.02	1.58
39	1.24	1.34	1.19	1.39	1.14	1.45	1.09	1.52	1.03	1.58
40	1.25	1.34	1.20	1.40	1.15	1.46	1.10	1.52	1.05	1.58
45	1.29	1.38	1.24	1.42	1.20	1.48	1.16	1.53	1.11	1.58
50	1.32	1.40	1.28	1.45	1.24	1.49	1.20	1.54	1.16	1.59
55	1.36	1.43	1.32	1.47	1.28	1.51	1.25	1.55	1.21	1.59
60	1.38	1.45	1.35	1.48	1.32	1.52	1.28	1.56	1.25	1.60
65	1.41	1.47	1.38	1.50	1.35	1.53	1.31	1.57	1.28	1.61
70	1.43	1.49	1.40	1.52	1.37	1.55	1.34	1.58	1.31	1.61
75	1.45	1.50	1.42	1.53	1.39	1.56	1.37	1.59	1.34	1.62
80	1.47	1.52	1.44	1.54	1.42	1.57	1.39	1.60	1.36	1.62
85	1.48	1.53	1.46	1.55	1.43	1.58	1.41	1.60	1.39	1.63
90	1.50	1.54	1.47	1.56	1.45	1.59	1.43	1.61	1.41	1.64
95	1.51	1.55	1.49	1.57	1.47	1.60	1.45	1.62	1.42	1.64
100	1.52	1.56	1.50	1.58	1.48	1.60	1.46	1.63	1.44	1.65

Source: From J. Durbin and G. S. Watson, "Testing for Serial Correlation in Least Squares Regression, II," *Biometrika*, 1951, *30*, 159–178. Reproduced by permission of the *Biometrika* Trustees.

Table XVII   Critical Values of Spearman's Rank Correlation Coefficient

The α values correspond to a one-tailed test of H_0: $\rho_s = 0$. The value should be doubled for two-tailed tests.

n	$\alpha = .05$	$\alpha = .025$	$\alpha = .01$	$\alpha = .005$
5	.900	—	—	—
6	.829	.886	.943	—
7	.714	.786	.893	—
8	.643	.738	.833	.881
9	.600	.683	.783	.833
10	.564	.648	.745	.794
11	.523	.623	.736	.818
12	.497	.591	.703	.780
13	.475	.566	.673	.745
14	.457	.545	.646	.716
15	.441	.525	.623	.689
16	.425	.507	.601	.666
17	.412	.490	.582	.645
18	.399	.476	.564	.625
19	.388	.462	.549	.608
20	.377	.450	.534	.591
21	.368	.438	.521	.576
22	.359	.428	.508	.562
23	.351	.418	.496	.549
24	.343	.409	.485	.537
25	.336	.400	.475	.526
26	.329	.392	.465	.515
27	.323	.385	.456	.505
28	.317	.377	.448	.496
29	.311	.370	.440	.487
30	.305	.364	.432	.478

Source: From E. G. Olds, "Distribution of Sums of Squares of Rank Differences for Small Samples," *Annals of Mathematical Statistics*, 1938, 9. Reproduced with the permission of the Editor, *Annals of Mathematical Statistics*.

ANSWERS TO SELECTED EXERCISES

Chapter 2

2.1a. Quantitative   **b.** Qualitative   **c.** Quantitative   **d.** Quantitative   **e.** Qualitative   **f.** Quantitative
2.2a. Qualitative   **b.** Quantitative   **c.** Quantitative   **d.** Quantitative
2.3a. Qualitative   **b.** Quantitative   **c.** Quantitative   **d.** Qualitative   **e.** Quantitative
2.4a. Qualitative   **b.** Quantitative   **c.** Qualitative
2.5a. Quantitative   **b.** Quantitative   **c.** Quantitative   **d.** Qualitative   **2.10c.** Burnsville; St. Paul
2.16a. $3.18 billion; $1.85 billion   **2.19c.** 14¢   **2.27b.** .64   **2.31b.** .65   **2.33b.** Yes   **2.38a.** .9   **b.** .1
2.41a. Qualitative   **b.** Quantitative   **c.** Quantitative   **2.47a.** Frequency bar chart   **2.48b.** No   **2.50a.** Pie chart

Chapter 3

3.1a. 34.35%   **b.** 30.6%   **3.2a.** 56.63; 34.7   **b.** No   **3.3b.** .1625; .125; 0   **3.4** 26.303
3.5a. $1.3158; $1.3265; $1.336   **b.** $1.3072; $1.324; $1.336   **c.** $1.3149
3.6a. McDonald's: $1,068,493.2; Burger King: $705,882.35   **b.** 41.67; 9.62; 1.37   **3.7** $39.592
3.10a. Skewed to the right; mean is 33.42; median is 29   **c.** Mean is 35.41; median is 29
3.11a. 2; 37.5; 6.124   **b.** 1.25; 1.835; 1.355
3.12a. 30; 200; 900   **b.** 9; 39; 81   **c.** 157; 10,069; 24,649   **d.** 9; 43; 81   **e.** 12; 102; 144
3.13a. 6; 5; 2.236   **b.** 1.5; 5.1; 2.258   **c.** 39.25; 1,302.25; 36.087   **d.** 1.8; 6.7; 2.588   **e.** 2; 15.6; 3.950
3.14a. 3.6; 5.3; 2.3   **b.** 4.33; 7.07; 2.66   **c.** 3.33; 4.27; 2.07   **d.** 2.25; 4.92; 2.22
3.15a. 6.2; 77.2; 8.786   **b.** 28.25; 2,304.92; 48.010
3.16a. 5.6; 17.3; 4.16   **b.** 13.75 feet; 152.25 square feet; 12.34 feet   **c.** -2.5; 4.3; 2.07
d. .33 ounce; .059 square ounce; .24 ounce
3.21a. 8.38%   **b.** 6.910; 2.629   **c.** Yes   **d.** No   **3.22** Increase; decrease
3.23a. 276.44; 288.17   **b.** 29.4; 42.9   **c.** 16.03   **d.** Minneapolis/St. Paul
3.24a. Worker A, 33.14; Worker B, 34.57   **b.** Worker A, 3.98; Worker B, .98   **d.** Worker A, .82; Worker B, 2.12
3.25a. Germany: 14.2; Italy: 4.7; France: 5.5; U.K.: 11.1; Belgium: 4.9
b. Germany: 22.662; Italy: 1.978; France: 3.108; U.K.: 14.933; Belgium: 2.71
c. Germany (greatest), U.K., France, Belgium, Italy (least)
d. Germany (greatest), U.K., France, Belgium, Italy (least)   **e.** Yes; no
3.26 Between 104.17 and 156.25
3.27b. 39.67; 4.16; 2.04   **d.** Approx. 68%; approx. 95%; approx. 100% (graph is mound-shaped)   **e.** 70%; 93%; 100%
3.28a. 103.9   **b.** 12,396.2; 111.3   **d.** At least 0%; at least 75%; at least 88.9%   **e.** 85%; 95%; 100%
3.29a. .1488; .0273; .1652   **b.** At least 0%; at least 75%; at least 88.89%   **d.** 88%; 96%; 96%
3.30a. Yes   **b.** At most $\frac{1}{4}$ **c.** 1.96%   **3.31** At most 13 weeks   **3.32** .025
3.33a. Revenues: 88.44, 7,144.53; profits: -5.5556, 95.53; miles: 833.89, 1,193,296.6   **3.34** At least 88.9%
3.35 2.5%; 2.5%; 0%   **3.36a.** At least $\frac{8}{9}$ **b.** Approx. .16   **c.** Yes   **3.37** 11:30; 4:00   **3.38** Do not buy
3.41 $Q_L = 46$; $M = 54$; $Q_U = 68$ **3.42** $Q_L = 1.28$; $Q_U = 1.55$
3.43a. 1; sample   **b.** -1.5; sample   **c.** 1.765; population   **d.** $-.6$; population
3.44a. 19.375; 18.261   **b.** 3.92   **c.** Yes   **3.45a.** 3.8; 4.082   **b.** 21.36   **c.** Yes
3.51a. $Q_L = 15.0$; $M = 15.9$; $Q_U = 16.8$ **b.** $\frac{12}{50}$; $\frac{38}{50}$ **c.** 4.25; -1.90; 0
3.53a. 5.111%; 2.309%   **b.** U.S.: .86; Australia: .43; Japan: -1.35 **3.54a.** Greenspan: $-.20$; Wilson: 1.95
3.55b. 12 and 20   **3.56** 1982: 84th percentile; 1981: 71.2th percentile   **3.57a.** .4   **b.** .4   **c.** No

3.58a. 10.96 and 14.12   **b.** 2.3; 3.18   **3.59b.** 47, 49, 50, and 64   **c.** 1.92, 2.06, 2.13, and 3.14   **3.60b.** No
3.61a. 68%; 100%   **b.** 31   **c.** First store   **3.62** 60; 10   **3.63a.** $1,090,900
3.64a. 239; 29; 841   **b.** 634; 50; 2,500   **c.** 254; 2; 4   **d.** 10,004; 102; 10,404
3.65a. 17.7; 4.21   **b.** 33.5; 5.79   **c.** 50.67; 7.12   **d.** 2,467.67; 49.68   **3.66a.** 3.12   **b.** 9.02   **c.** 9.79
3.67a. 6; 27; 5.20   **b.** 6.25; 28.25; 5.32   **c.** 7; 37.67; 6.14   **d.** 3; 0; 0
3.68a. 12   **b.** 13   **c.** 15   **d.** 0
3.69a. 5.67; 1.066; 1.03   **b.** $-$1.5; 11.5 dollars squared; $3.39   **c.** .4125 lb.; .088 lb. squared; .30 lb.
3.71a. 12.4; 19.42   **b.** 1.03; .08   **3.75a.** 533.5   **b.** $1,456.5 million   **3.77a.** At least 0%   **b.** At most 25%
3.78a. Approx. 68%   **b.** Approx. 2.5%
3.80a. 5.1; 5.5; 6; 9; 7.43; 2.73   **b.** 2.25   **c.** Central tendency: mean, median, mode
3.82a. $7,500   **b.** Over $120,000   **c.** Very unlikely   **3.83c.** 35.6; 33; 28   **3.84** At least $\frac{8}{9}$
3.85a. .56; 3.30   **b.** No   **3.86** No information; $V = 0$ for all data sets
3.87a. -3.0 **b.** Approx. 0%   **c.** 90 or above   **3.88a.** At least $\frac{3}{4}$ **b.** At least $\frac{8}{9}$ **c.** At least 55.6%
3.89a. August, $R = 11$, while for June, $R = 10$; June, $s^2 = 17.48$, while for August, $s^2 = 11.9$; s^2 since R is affected by extreme values
b. $s^2 = 17.48$; no effect   **c.** $s^2 = 157.3$; s^2 is multiplied by the square of the constant
3.90a.

	U.S.	CANADA	U.K.	SWEDEN	FRANCE	W. GERMANY
MEAN	41.08%	70.83%	60.42%	83.42%	66.33%	56.08%
VARIANCE	330.08	529.24	634.26	511.17	1,051.88	907.17

b.

	MEAN	VARIANCE
Brewing	54.17	640.97
Cigarettes	91.00	142.00
Fabric	35.67	365.07
Paints	40.67	727.47
Petroleum	62.50	666.70
Shoes	20.33	71.87
Glass	85.83	210.97
Cement	67.67	805.07
Steel	60.67	352.67
Bearings	80.67	390.27
Refrigerators	77.50	202.70
Batteries	79.67	269.87

c. U.S., Sweden; antifriction bearings

d. Most competitive: shoes, fabric, paints; least competitive: cigarettes, glass bottles, antifriction bearings

Chapter 4

4.2a. .4   **b.** .25   **c.** .6   **4.3a.** .25   **b.** .4   **4.4a.** 120   **b.** 15   **c.** 56   **d.** 1   **e.** 1
4.5a. 10   **b.** 21   **c.** 15   **d.** 1   **e.** 1   **4.6b.** .152   **c.** .252   **4.7** $P(A) = .16$; $P(B) = .64$ **4.8** $\frac{1}{20}$
4.9 $P(A) = \frac{1}{6}$; $P(B) = \frac{5}{6}$ **4.11a.** $\frac{10}{35}$ **b.** $\frac{20}{35}$ **c.** $\frac{5}{35}$ **4.12a.** .5   **b.** .225   **c.** .2
4.13 $P(A) = .25$; $P(B) = .15$; $P(C) = .60$ **4.14b.** $\frac{1}{18}$ **c.** $\frac{6}{18}$ **4.15a.** $\frac{1}{15}, \frac{1}{15}, \frac{1}{15}$ **b.** 0   **c.** $\frac{3}{15}; \frac{12}{15}$ **d.** $\frac{2}{15}; \frac{6}{15}$
4.16a. $\frac{1}{3}$ **b.** $\frac{1}{3}$ **c.** $\frac{1}{6}$ **d.** $\frac{1}{6}$ **4.17a.** $\frac{3}{4}$ **b.** $\frac{13}{20}$ **c.** 1   **d.** $\frac{2}{5}$ **e.** $\frac{1}{4}$ **f.** $\frac{7}{20}$ **g.** 1   **h.** $\frac{1}{4}$
4.18a. .5   **b.** .19   **c.** .5   **d.** 1   **e.** .31   **f.** .69
4.19a. $A = \{(1, 4), (2, 3), (3, 2), (4, 1)\}$;
   $B = \{(1, 3), (2, 3), (3, 3), (4, 3), (5, 3), (6, 3), (3, 1), (3, 2), (3, 4), (3, 5), (3, 6)\}$;
   $A \cap B = \{(2, 3), (3, 2)\}$;
   $A \cup B = \{(1, 3), (2, 3), (3, 3), (4, 3), (5, 3), (6, 3), (3, 1), (3, 2), (3, 4), (3, 5), (3, 6), (1, 4), (4, 1)\}$
b. $\frac{4}{36}; \frac{11}{36}$ **c.** $\frac{2}{36}; \frac{13}{36}$

4.20a. $\frac{7}{8}$ **b.** $\frac{3}{8}$ **c.** $\frac{3}{8}$ **d.** 0
4.22a. Yes   **b.** $P(A) = .26$; $P(B) = .35$; $P(C) = .72$; $P(D) = .28$; $P(E) = .05$ **c.** .56; .05; .77   **d.** .74
4.23a. (1, R), (2, R), (3, R), (1, S), (2, S), (3, S), (1, E), (2, E), (3, E)   **b.** Sample space   **c.** .46   **d.** .05   **e.** .30
f. .61   **g.** .34
4.25a. .76   **b.** .03   **c.** .62   **d.** 0   **e.** 0   **4.27b.** .152   **c.** .004   **d.** .514   **e.** .392
4.29a. $P(A) = .48$; $P(B) = .52$; $P(C) = .16$; $P(D) = .26$; $P(E) = .35$; $P(F) = .23$ **b.** 1   **c.** .05   **d.** .05   **e.** 0   **f.** 0
4.31a. $P(A) = .7$; $P(B) = .41$; $P(C) = .18$; $P(D) = .16$ **b.** .74   **c.** .59   **d.** .37   **e.** .11
4.32b. .30   **c.** .59   **d.** .41   **e.** .96   **4.33a.** .112   **b.** .839   **c.** 0   **d.** .683
4.34a. .65   **b.** 0   **c.** 0   **d.** .60   **4.35** No   **4.36a.** .37   **b.** .68   **c.** .15   **d.** .2206   **e.** 0   **f.** 0
4.37 All pairs are dependent   **4.38a.** $\frac{7}{8}$ **b.** $\frac{3}{8}$ **c.** $\frac{7}{8}$ **d.** $\frac{3}{8}$ **e.** 0   **f.** $\frac{1}{4}$ **4.39a.** $\frac{3}{7}$ **b.** $\frac{3}{4}$ **c.** $\frac{3}{4}$
4.40 $P(R|S) = 0$; $P(S|R) = 0$ **4.41** Yes   **4.42a.** .02426   **b.** .011; .978   **c.** .0874; .2170   **d.** .0568
4.43a. .9883   **b.** .0117   **c.** .7917   **d.** .1183   **4.44** a   **4.45** .005
4.46a. .568   **b.** .24   **c.** .75   **d.** 1   **4.47** No   **4.48** .6
4.49a. .18   **b.** .82   **c.** .31   **d.** .69   **e.** .26   **4.50a.** .2778   **b.** .58   **4.51a.** 45   **b.** $\frac{1}{45}$
4.59 Yes   **4.60** .5   **4.61a.** .8145   **b.** .0135   **d.** No   **4.62** 462
4.63a. $\frac{150}{200}$ **b.** $\frac{23}{80}$ **c.** $\frac{90}{150}$ **d.** $\frac{12}{200}$ **4.64a.** No   **c.** Yes   **4.65** 252
4.66 N: Noticed ad; N^c: Did not notice ad; L: Under 30; M: 30–50; H: Over 50
a. (L, N), (M, N), (H, N), (L, N^c), (M, N^c), (H, N^c)   **b.** Sample space
c. $P(L, N) = .25$; $P(M, N) = .20$; $P(H, N) = .10$; $P(L, N^c) = .05$; $P(M, N^c) = .15$; $P(H, N^c) = .25$
4.68a. .60   **b.** .05   **c.** .70   **d.** 0   **e.** 1   **4.71a.** .26   **4.73a.** $\frac{6}{30}$ **b.** $\frac{6}{29}$ **c.** .634   **4.75b.** .05
4.76a. $\frac{1}{15}$ **b.** $\frac{6}{15}$ **c.** $\frac{14}{15}$ **d.** $\frac{6}{14}$ **e.** $\frac{5}{14}$ **4.77a.** .429   **b.** .24   **c.** .221   **d.** .875
4.79a. .236   **b.** .671   **4.81a.** .0000106   **b.** .07887   **c.** .0704   **4.82** .79   **4.85** False

Chapter 5

5.3a. Discrete   **b.** Continuous   **c.** Continuous   **d.** Discrete
5.4a. Discrete   **b.** Discrete   **c.** Continuous   **d.** Discrete   **e.** Continuous

5.11a. HHH, THH, HTH, HHT, TTH, THT, HTT, TTT   **b.**

x	0	1	2	3
$p(x)$	$\frac{1}{8}$	$\frac{3}{8}$	$\frac{3}{8}$	$\frac{1}{8}$

5.12a.

x	1	2	3	4	5	6
$p(x)$	$\frac{1}{6}$	$\frac{1}{6}$	$\frac{1}{6}$	$\frac{1}{6}$	$\frac{1}{6}$	$\frac{1}{6}$

5.13a. Invalid   **b.** Valid   **c.** Invalid   **d.** Invalid

5.14a. .10   **b.** 0   **c.** .25   **d.** .70   **e.** .90   **f.** .80
5.15a. .65   **b.** .75   **c.** .80   **d.** .85   **e.** .60   **f.** .65   **5.16b.** .56; .32

5.17a.

x	.0	1	2	3
$p(x)$	.000125	.007125	.135375	.857375

c. .99275   **5.18a.** .118   **b.** .302   **c.** .580

5.19

x	0	1	2
$p(x)$	.2	.3	.5

5.21a. 4.25   **5.22a.** .5   **5.23a.** 31; 169; 13   **c.** .95

5.24a. .3; .011; .105   **c.** .85   **d.** 1.0
5.25a. Expected total loss is $2,450 for both firms   **b.** Firm B   **c.** Pure risk   **5.26a.** .8   **b.** No
5.27a. 4.978   **b.** 2.984   **c.** Approximately .949   **5.28a.** 3.26   **b.** 1.6324; 1.2777   **d.** .95

5.29 $E(x) = 13,000$; market new line   **5.30** $1,000   **5.31** $7,200   **5.32** $11,000   **5.33** Too little

5.34a.

Total cost	$1,000	$2,000	$3,000
P(Total cost)	.25	.25	.50

b. .25   **c.** $2,250   **d.** $2,250

5.35a. 10   **b.** 20   **c.** 1   **d.** 1   **e.** 6

5.36

x	0	1	2	3	4	5
p(x)	.3277	.4096	.2048	.0512	.0064	.0003

5.37a. .1852   **b.** .3456   **c.** .04

5.38a.

x	0	1	2	3	4	5	6
p(x)	.0467	.1866	.3110	.2765	.1382	.0369	.0041

b. 2.4; 1.44   **c.** 2.4 ± 2.4 **d.** .9590

5.39a.

x	0	1	2	3	4	5
p(x)	.031	.156	.313	.313	.156	.031

b. 2.5; 1.25   **c.** 2.5 ± 2.24 **d.** .938

5.40a. .813   **b.** 1.00   **c.** .187   **5.41a.** .005   **b.** .973   **c.** .403   **d.** .966   **e.** .009   **f.** .207
5.42e. $p = .5$, symmetric; $p < .5$, skewed to the right; $p > .5$, skewed to the left   **5.43** .009   **5.44** .0005
5.45a. Approx. 0   **b.** .151   **5.46a.** .013   **b.** .783
5.47b. 2.4; 1.47   **c.** Binomial with $p = .90$, $q = .10$, and $n = 24$; 21.6; 1.47   **5.48** .098
5.49 $\mu = .5$; $\sigma = .707$; no; guarantee is probably inaccurate
5.50a. 0   **b.** Approx. 0   **c.** Approx. 0   **d.** .098   **e.** .873   **f.** 1.0
5.51a. 0   **b.** Approx. 0   **c.** Approx. 0   **d.** .234   **e.** .966   **f.** 1.0   **5.52** $\mu = 48$; $\sigma = 6.5$; no; no
5.53a. .049787   **b.** .011109   **c.** .182684   **d.** .002479   **e.** .224042   **f.** .213763   **g.** .041937
5.54a. .919698   **b.** .073264   **c.** .864665   **d.** .000336   **5.55b.** $\mu = 2$; $\sigma = 1.414$; 2 ± 2.828 **c.** .947345
5.56b. $\mu = 4$; $\sigma = 2$; 4 ± 4 **c.** .978656   **5.57** a, c, and e not within interval
5.58 $p(0) = .277$, $p(1) = .365$, $p(2) = .231$ from binomial table; $p(0) \approx .287$, $p(1) \approx .358$, $p(2) \approx .224$ using Poisson approximation
5.59a. .0262   **b.** 10.33; 3.214   **c.** 1.76   **d.** .11067
5.60a. .0006688   **b.** 7.31; 2.704   **c.** Very small probability since 20 is approx. 4.69 standard deviations above μ
5.61a. .7764   **b.** .1118   **5.62** .1929; .6602   **5.63** .090; .91   **5.64** .2510; .5578; .0111   **5.65** .0803; yes
5.66 .632   **5.70a.** .267857   **b.** .017857   **c.** .178571   **d.** 0   **5.71a.** .3   **b.** .1190   **c.** .1667   **d.** .1667

5.72a.

x	2	3	4	5
p(x)	$\frac{21}{252}$	$\frac{105}{252}$	$\frac{105}{252}$	$\frac{21}{252}$

b. 3.5; .5833   **c.** 3.5 ± 1.53 **d.** 1

5.73a.

x	2	3	4	5	6
p(x)	$\frac{15}{495}$	$\frac{120}{495}$	$\frac{225}{495}$	$\frac{120}{495}$	$\frac{15}{495}$

b. 4; .8528   **c.** 4 ± 1.71 **d.** .9394

5.74a. 0   **b.** .4545   **c.** .7273   **d.** .2727   **e.** .0303   **f.** 0   **5.75a.** Hypergeometric   **b.** Binomial
5.76 .25   **5.77** .6; .333; .167; .0714

5.80

x	0	1	2	3	4
p(x)	$\frac{70}{495}$	$\frac{224}{495}$	$\frac{168}{495}$	$\frac{32}{495}$	$\frac{1}{495}$

5.81 .467; .533   **5.82a.** 113.24; 4.19

5.83a. .16   **b.** .128   **c.** .488   **d.** 1   **e.** .1024   **f.** .64   **5.84b.** 1.429; .612   **c.** .91
5.85b. 3.333; 7.778   **c.** .8824   **5.86a.** .51   **b.** .343   **c.** 1   **d.** .8824
5.87a. .0625   **b.** .9375   **c.** 2; 1.414   **5.88** .2401   **5.89** .7536

5.90a. .995 **b.** Claim probably not valid **5.91** .729; 10 **5.92** .0819 **5.93a.** .1536 **b.** .0768 **c.** .125
5.94a. .5357 **b.** .0667 **c.** .8 **5.95a.** .147 **b.** .0384 **c.** .16
5.96a. .2240 **b.** .1804 **c.** .0126
5.97a. .0183 **b.** .1954 **c.** .0733 **d.** .1563 **e.** .2381 **f.** .9084
5.98a. .3 **b.** .4599 **c.** .51 **d.** .1029 **e.** .2401 **f.** .5820

5.99a.

x	1	2	3	4	5	6	7
$p(x)$	.4	.24	.144	.086	.052	.031	.019

b. 2.5; 1.936; -1.37 to 6.37 **c.** .953

5.100a. Discrete **b.** Continuous **c.** Continuous **d.** Continuous
5.101 y has the largest variance; x has smallest variance

5.102

x	0	1	2
$p(x)$	$\frac{4}{9}$	$\frac{4}{9}$	$\frac{1}{9}$

5.103a.

x	0	1	2	3	4	5
$p(x)$	.590	.329	.072	.009	.000	.000

b. .5; .45

5.104a. True **b.** .017 **5.105** .512
5.106a. A: 4.6; B: 3.7 **b.** A: $46,000; B: $55,500 **c.** A: $\sigma^2 = 1.34$, $\sigma = 1.16$; B: $\sigma^2 = 1.21$, $\sigma = 1.10$ **d.** A: .95; B: .95
5.107 .4019; .1608 **5.108** $33,333.33 **5.109** .0996; .0738 **5.110** .033; .985; claim probably invalid
5.111 $\frac{11}{12}$; $\frac{1}{30}$ **5.112** .303 **5.113a.** .001 **d.** Yes; $P(x = 20) = .012$ **5.114** .1024 **5.115** .042
5.116 .051 **5.117** .0315; .1067 **5.118a.** .277 **b.** .723 **c.** 2.11; 2.34 **d.** No **5.119** .343
5.120 .0039 **5.121** .657; .027 **5.122** .1715 **5.123** .265; .1755 **5.124a.** 5; 4 **b.** .617 **c.** .006
5.125 .346; .683 **5.126** 4.664%

Chapter 6

6.1a. .4772 **b.** .4987 **c.** .4332 **d.** .2881 **6.2a.** .7745 **b.** .9544 **c.** .6247 **d.** .9974
6.3a. .0919 **b.** .4895 **c.** .4772 **d.** .9179 **e.** .2417 **f.** .2857
6.4a. .0013 **b.** .0548 **c.** .05 **d.** .5 **e.** .1587 **f.** .05 **6.5a.** .6826 **b.** .95 **c.** .9 **d.** .9544
6.6a. 1.645 **b.** 1.96 **c.** -1.96 **d.** 1.28
6.7a. -2.5 **b.** 0 **c.** $-.625$ **d.** -3.75 **e.** 1.25 **f.** -1.25
6.8a. 1.25 below **b.** 1.875 above **c.** 0 **d.** 1.5 above
6.9a. -1.88 **b.** 1.96 **c.** 1.645 **d.** 1.0 **e.** $-.42$ **f.** 1.47
6.10a. .9544 **b.** .0918 **c.** .0228 **d.** .8607 **e.** .0927 **f.** .7049
6.11a. .1151 **b.** .6554 **c.** 10.50 **6.12** .0024 **6.13a.** XYZ **b.** ABC: $105; XYZ: $107 **c.** ABC
6.14a. .0307 **b.** .0893 **6.15a.** .0301 **b.** .0301 **6.16a.** .2843 **b.** .0228 **6.17** 5.068
6.18a. 50% **b.** 4.75% **c.** 32.987 oz.
6.19a. $-.675$; .675 **b.** 1.35 standard deviations **c.** -2.70; 2.70 **d.** -4.73; 4.73 **e.** .0026
f. .0070 **g.** Approx. 0
6.20a. .04, $20 \leq x \leq 45$ **b.** 32.5; 52.08 **c.** 1 **6.21a.** .6 **b.** .2 **c.** .2 **d.** .2 **e.** 0 **f.** .8 **g.** .36
6.22a. $\frac{1}{3}$, $2 \leq x \leq 5$ **b.** 3.5; .75 **c.** .577 **6.23a.** 3.5 **b.** 2.6 **c.** 2.0 **d.** 4
6.25b. .5; .083 **c.** .05; .95 **d.** Uniform distribution with $c = .90$ and $d = .95$ **6.26** 2, 1.33; .3125
6.27 .333; 15 min. **6.28a.** Continuous **c.** 7; .289; $\mu \pm 2\sigma$ is 6.423 to 7.577
6.30a. .002479 **b.** .011109 **c.** .000123 **d.** .25924
6.31a. .999447 **b.** .999955 **c.** .981684 **d.** .632121 **6.32** .5; .25; .950213 **6.33** .2231 **6.34** .095
6.35 .1353; .3935 **6.36a.** .367879; .211882 **b.** .049787 **c.** Less **d.** 40.6
6.37a. $\mu = \sigma = 23.81$ **b.** 23.81 **c.** .716346 **d.** .8647 **e.** .9502
6.41a. Yes **b.** 10; 6 **c.** .692 **d.** Approx. .6962 **6.42a.** .5; .5 **b.** .212; .2119 **c.** .345; .3446
6.43a. .5398 **b.** .7330 **c.** .9345 **6.44a.** No **b.** Yes **c.** No **d.** Yes **e.** Yes **f.** Yes
6.45 .9732 **6.46** Approx. .0559 **6.47a.** Binomial **b.** 30; 4.58 **c.** Approx. 0

6.48b. Approx. 0　　**c.** No　　**d.** Yes　　**6.49** Approx. .0559; yes　　**6.50** Approx. 0
6.51a. Approx. .0516　　**b.** Approx. .8324　　**6.52a.** .0885　　**b.** .7123
6.53a. $\frac{1}{80}$　　**b.** 50; 23.1　　**c.** 3.8 to 96.2　　**d.** .625　　**e.** 0　　**f.** .875　　**g.** .5775　　**h.** .1875
6.54a. .45119　　**b.** .40657　　**c.** 0　　**d.** .87754　　**e.** .27387　　**f.** 0
6.55a. .95　　**b.** .90　　**c.** .9974　　**d.** .9925　　**e.** .0606　　**f.** .9270
6.56a. .3446　　**b.** .6179　　**c.** .9989　　**d.** .3612　　**6.57a.** −.13　　**b.** .02　　**c.** 1.04　　**d.** −.69
6.58a. .6915　　**b.** .1587　　**c.** .1915　　**d.** .3085　　**e.** 0　　**f.** Approx. 1.0
6.59a. .9441　　**b.** .9429　　**c.** .9988　　**d.** .0031　　**6.60a.** .0918　　**b.** 0　　**c.** Lowered 4.87 decibels (to 95.13)
6.61 .0122; .0062　　**6.62** .6065; .6321　　**6.63a.** 288　　**b.** .2483　　**c.** Not possible
6.65 .9922; .6618　　**6.66** .1056
6.67 Ranked high to low:　　**a.** Range: bank 3, bank 1, bank 2　　**b.** Standard deviation: bank 3, bank 1, bank 2
c. Coefficient of variation: bank 1, bank 3, bank 2
6.68a. 1.4 days　　**b.** .082　　**c.** No　　**6.69a.** .095　　**b.** .9987　　**c.** .3085　　**6.70** .6321
6.71 Approx. .9817　　**6.72a.** .1922　　**b.** .4681　　**c.** $(.4681)^3$　　**6.73a.** .135　　**b.** .5940
6.74a. .0548　　**b.** .6006　　**c.** .3446　　**d.** 6,503.80　　**6.75a.** .2033　　**b.** 12,800　　**6.76** 320, 16; $P(x \geq 400) \approx 0$

Chapter 7

7.1a. 20; .949　　**b.** 100; 1.581　　**c.** 25; .577　　**d.** 400; .90　　**7.2a.** 15; .60　　**b.** .83　　**c.** −1.67
7.3a. .0475　　**b.** .9525　　**c.** .9082　　**d.** .9050　　**e.** .0475　　**7.4d.** 4.78; 1.642　　**7.5b.** 4.5; 1.172
7.6b. 4.84; 1.313　　**7.7b.** 4.68; .8270　　**7.8a.** 6; .3536　　**b.** .5222　　**c.** .0793　　**d.** Smaller standard deviation
7.9a. 12; .8　　**b.** 10; .6　　**c.** 2; 1　　**d.** Yes　　**7.10a.** −.5　　**b.** .6915　　**c.** .3085　　**d.** .8426
7.11a. 6; (chip #1, chip #2), (chip #1, chip #3), (chip #1, chip #4), (chip #2, chip #3), (chip #2, chip #4), (chip #3, chip #4),
where chip #1 is marked 1, chip #2 is marked 2, chip #3 is marked 2, and chip #4 is marked 3

b. $\frac{1}{6}$　　**c.** 1.5, 1.5, 2, 2, 2.5, 2.5　　**d.**

$\bar{x}$	1.5	2	2.5
$p(\bar{x})$	$\frac{2}{6}$	$\frac{2}{6}$	$\frac{2}{6}$

7.12a. Two 0's; one 0 and one 1; two 1's　　**b.** 0; .5; 1　　**c.**

$\bar{x}$	0	.5	1
$p(\bar{x})$	$\frac{1}{4}$	$\frac{2}{4}$	$\frac{1}{4}$

7.13a. Three 0's; three 1's; two 0's and one 1; one 0 and two 1's　　**b.** 0; 1; $\frac{1}{3}$; $\frac{2}{3}$　　**c.**

$\bar{x}$	0	$\frac{1}{3}$	$\frac{2}{3}$	1
$p(\bar{x})$	$\frac{1}{8}$	$\frac{3}{8}$	$\frac{3}{8}$	$\frac{1}{8}$

7.15 No　　**7.16a.** Approximately normal with $\mu_{\bar{x}} = 10$ and $\sigma_{\bar{x}} = 2.05$　　**b.** $P(\bar{x} \geq 13.49) \approx P(z \geq 1.70) = .0446$
7.17 .0456　　**7.18a.** .35; .6538　　**b.** Approx. normal with $\mu_{\bar{x}} = .35$ and $\sigma_{\bar{x}} = .03269$　　**c.** .35; .03269　　**d.** .0630
7.19a. .0013　　**b.** No　　**7.20** .4514　　**7.21** .0082
7.22a. Approx. normal with unknown mean and $\sigma_{\bar{x}} = .0717$　　**b.** Approx. normal with unknown mean and $\sigma_{\bar{y}} = .0536$　　**c.** 501
7.23a. $\mu \pm 1.342$　　**b.** Approx. .0026　　**7.24a.** $\mu \pm .7357$　　**b.** Approx. .7224; approx. .7995
7.25a. .05　　**b.** 1　　**c.** .000625　　**7.26a.** Approx. normal with $\mu_{\bar{x}} = 75.05$ and $\sigma_{\bar{x}} = .02$　　**b.** .0062　　**c.** Yes

7.27a. 45; {(1, 2), (1, 3), (1, 4), . . . , (9, 10)}　　**b.** $\frac{21}{45}$　　**c.**

x	0	1	2
$p(x)$	$\frac{3}{45}$	$\frac{21}{45}$	$\frac{21}{45}$

7.28 60,000 to 75,000; $\sigma_B \approx 1,666.7$; $\mu_A = 22,500$; $\mu_B = 45,000$; 61,910 to 73,090　　**7.29** .9332
7.30a. Approx. normal with mean 7,500 and variance 60,750　　**b.** .9576　　**c.** .0075

Chapter 8

8.1a. 5 ± 1.176 **8.2a.** $3.125 \pm .115$ **8.3a.** $14.1 \pm .570$ **b.** $14.1 \pm .749$ **c.** Increases   **d.** Yes
8.4a. $14.1 \pm .901$ **b.** Increases; decreases   **8.8a.** $.65\%$ **b.** $4.3 \pm .154$ **8.9a.** 28.9 ± 2.72
8.10 $.72 \pm .11$ **8.11** 480 ± 3.016 **8.12** 19.8 ± 1.225 **8.13a.** $3.23 \pm .041$
8.19a. $.025$ **b.** $.05$ **c.** $.005$ **d.** $.0985$ **e.** $.10$ **f.** $.01$ **8.20** No
8.21a. $z = -1.57$; reject H_0 **b.** $z = -1.57$; reject H_0 **8.22a.** Reject H_0 if $z > 1.5$ **b.** $.0668$
8.23a. $z = 2.5$; reject H_0 **b.** $z = 2.5$; reject H_0 **8.24a.** $.0183$ **b.** $.0015$ **c.** $z = 4.23$; yes
8.25a. $H_a: \mu > 35$ mpg; $H_0: \mu = 35$ mpg   **b.** $z = 1.8$; yes
8.26a. $H_0: \mu = \$8.00$; $H_a: \mu > \$8.00$ **c.** $z = .87$; do not reject H_0 **8.27** $z = -4.49$; yes   **8.28** $z = -3.16$; yes
8.29a. $z = -3.74$; yes   **8.30** $z = 3.54$; yes   **8.31** $.7764$ **8.32** $.4522$ **8.33** $.0643$ **8.34** $.0930$
8.35a. $H_0: \mu = \$4,627$; $H_a: \mu > \$4,627$ **b.** $.1075$ **8.36a.** $H_0: \mu = \$58,380$; $H_a: \mu > \$58,380$ **b.** $.0071$
8.37 $.0359$ **8.39** Approx. 0   **8.42a.** 2.306 **b.** 2.764 **c.** -2.898 **d.** -1.761
8.43a. $t = -1.63$; do not reject H_0 **b.** $t = -1.63$; do not reject H_0
8.44a. $.05 \le p\text{-value} \le .10$ **b.** $.10 \le p\text{-value} \le .20$ **8.45a.** 4.8 ± 2.040 **b.** 2.132
8.46a. $t = -1.40$; do not reject H_0 **b.** $t = -1.40$; do not reject H_0 **8.47a.** $p\text{-value} > .10$ **b.** $p\text{-value} > .20$
8.48a. 1.833 ± 2.141 **b.** 2.015 **8.49a.** $t = -3.0$; yes   **b.** $.01 < p\text{-value} < .02$ **d.** $19.7 \pm .186$
8.50 $\$32,846.80 \pm \$2,452.15$ **8.51** $\$69,644.86 \pm \$29,330.03$ **8.52** $t = -4.19$; yes   **8.53** $t = 2.66$; yes
8.54 43.5 ± 6.21 **8.55a.** $t = 1.50$; no   **b.** $.05 < p\text{-value} < .10$
8.56a. $t = 1.11$ (perceived minus chronological); no   **8.57** $t = .87$; no; $p\text{-value} > .10$ **8.58** 8.42 ± 3.74
8.61 $.42 \pm .048$ **8.62** $.76 \pm .059$ **8.63b.** $z = -1.53$; do not reject H_0 **c.** $.063$
8.64a. $z = -2.33$ **c.** Reject H_0 **d.** $.0099$ **8.65a.** $z = 2.31$; reject H_0 **b.** $.0104$
8.66b. $z = 1.72$; yes   **c.** $.1209 \pm .0065$ **8.67** $.0427$
8.68a. Yes; $.12 \pm .0674$ does not contain 0 or 1   **b.** $.12 \pm .0288$ **8.69a.** $z = 2.30$; yes   **b.** $.0107$
8.70 $.0833 \pm .0242$ **8.71** $.06 \pm .02$ **8.72a.** $z = -1.24$; no   **b.** $.1075$
8.73a. Oklahoma City: $.773 \pm .0753$; New York: $.6 \pm .1623$; Atlanta: $.446 \pm .0732$ **b.** $z = 2.91$; yes
8.74b. Normal by the Central Limit Theorem   **c.** $.3174$ **8.75** 586 **8.76** $.98, .784, .56, .392, .196$
8.77a. 68 **b.** 31 **8.78a.** $1,083$ **b.** $1,692$ **8.79a.** 722 **b.** 174 **8.80** 97 **8.81** 55
8.82 $8,068$ **8.83** 543 **8.84** 139 **8.85** 322 **8.86** 260
8.87a. -1.725 **b.** 3.250 **c.** 1.860 **d.** 2.898
8.88a. $.025 < p\text{-value} < .05$ **b.** $.005 < p\text{-value} < .01$ **c.** $.10 < p\text{-value} < .20$ **d.** $.01 < p\text{-value} < .02$
8.89 Small   **8.92a.** 12.2 ± 1.645 **b.** 166 **c.** $z = 1.3$; no   **8.93** $.04 \pm .022$ **8.94** $1,476$
8.95a. $.075 \pm .0365$ **b.** $z = 1.62$; reject H_0 **8.96** $.0526$ **8.97** 667 **8.98a.** $z = 1.41$; no   **c.** $.0793$
8.99 $z = 1.07$; no   **8.100** $.1423$ **8.101** 65 **8.102a.** $12,522 \pm 784$ **8.103** $.5625 \pm .0154$
8.104a. $z = -3.03$; yes   **8.105** $.0012$ **8.106** $z = 3.79$; discount store's claim is supported   **8.107** $4.5 \pm .122$

Chapter 9

9.1a. $.1140$ **d.** $z < -1.96$ or $z > 1.96$ **e.** $z = -5.26$; reject H_0 **f.** Approx. 0   **9.3** $-.6 \pm .1875$
9.4a. 1.77 **c.** $z > 1.28$ **d.** $z = 2.88$; reject H_0 **e.** $.002$ **9.5** 5.1 ± 4.12
9.6a. $z = -2.78$; yes   **b.** $.0027$ **9.7** -1.9 ± 1.12 **9.8a.** Yes; $z = 12.71$; $p\text{-value} \approx 0$; reject H_0
9.10 $z = 1.96$; reject H_0; workers with belief in class system are more satisfied with their jobs
9.11b. $z = 4.27$; yes   **c.** Approx. 0   **9.12** $1.9 \pm .87$; wider   **9.13a.** $z = 2.77$; yes   **9.14** $z = 2.17$; yes
9.17a. $.443$ **b.** $t = -2.18$; reject H_0 **c.** $.025 < p\text{-value} < .05$ **9.18** $-.88 \pm .739$
9.19a. 15.36 **b.** $t = -5.35$ **c.** Approx. 0   **9.20** -8 ± 3.077 **9.22a.** $t = 3.19$; yes   **b.** 5 ± 2.68
9.23a. $t = 2.10$; no   **c.** 4 ± 3.304 **9.24a.** $t = -8.81$; no   **b.** $-.0184 \pm .0446$
9.25a. $t = -1.96$; yes   **c.** Approx. $.05$ **d.** -7.4 ± 6.224 **9.26a.** $t = 4.46$; yes   **b.** $p\text{-value} < .005$

9.27a. $t = -.66$; no   **9.28a.** $s_1^2 = 88.62$; $s_2^2 = 68.49$ **c.** $t = .61$; no

9.29a. AFC: $\bar{x}_1 = 120.5$, $s_1^2 = 510.42$; NFC: $\bar{x}_2 = 115.1$, $s_2^2 = 364.23$ **b.** $t = .68$; no

9.31a. 4.10   **b.** ≈ 3.57 **c.** 8.80   **d.** 3.21   **9.32a.** .01   **b.** .95   **c.** .95   **d.** .01

9.33a. $F = 2.26$; no   **b.** $.10 < p\text{-value} < .20$ **9.34a.** $F = 4.29$; no   **b.** $.10 \leq p\text{-value} \leq .20$

9.35 $F = 2.63$; yes   **9.36** $F = 10$; yes   **9.37** $F = 1.53$; no

9.38a. $F = 5.03$; not appropriate   **d.** $.02 \leq p\text{-value} \leq .05$ **9.39a.** $F = 1.11$; do not reject H_0 **b.** Type II error

9.40a. -7.6; 4.56   **b.** $74.8 - 82.4 = -7.6$ **c.** -3.73; yes   **d.** $.02 < p\text{-value} < .05$ **9.41** -7.6 ± 5.66

9.42a. $t < -1.333$ **b.** $t = -3.24$; reject H_0 **9.43** -3.5 ± 1.88 **9.45a.** $t = -.10$; no   **b.** $p\text{-value} > .10$

9.46a. $t = -1.92$; yes   **9.47a.** $.239 \pm .0731$ **9.48a.** $t = .078$; no   **b.** 3.3 ± 1.874

9.49a. $t = 7.68$; yes   **b.** $p\text{-value} < .01$ **d.** $.4167 \pm .1395$ **9.50a.** $t = .40$; no   **b.** $.417 \pm 2.2963$

9.51a. 662.5 ± 995.35

9.54a. .19; .323   **b.** $z < -1.645$ or $z > 1.645$ **c.** $z = -3.10$; reject H_0 **d.** $p\text{-value} < .002$

9.55 $-.133 \pm .0978$ **9.56a.** $z < -1.96$ **b.** $z = -3.49$; reject H_0 **c.** Approx. 0   **9.57** $-.104 \pm .0379$

9.60a. $z = .88$; no   **b.** $.03 \pm .056$ **9.61a.** $z = 4.48$; reject H_0 **b.** Approx. 0   **9.62a.** $.17 \pm .0353$

9.63 $z = 7.79$; yes   **9.64a.** $z = 2.04$; yes   **b.** $.173 \pm .179$

9.65a. $.1732 \pm .0076$ (95% confidence interval)   **b.** $.0756 \pm .0064$ (95% confidence interval)   **c.** $.0976 \pm .0099$

9.66 $z = 17.97$; yes; B   **9.67** Less   **9.69** $z = .79$; do not reject H_0 **9.70** $n_1 = n_2 = 41$ **9.71** $n_1 = n_2 = 376$

9.72 $n_1 = n_2 = 812$ **9.73** $n_1 = n_2 = 34$, so 24 additional observations required   **9.74** $n_1 = n_2 = 4{,}802$

9.75 $n_1 = n_2 = 542$ **9.76** $n_1 = n_2 = 769$ **b.** Yes; $n = 385$ **9.77** 34   **9.78** $n_1 = 260$, $n_2 = 520$

9.79 $z = -.86$; no   **9.80** $F = 2.79$; do not reject H_0 **9.81a.** $z = -2.60$; yes   **b.** .0047   **9.83** $n_1 = n_2 = 542$

9.84a. $t = 1.06$; do not reject H_0 **b.** $p\text{-value} > .20$ **9.85** $F = 1.21$; do not reject H_0 **9.86a.** $.52 \pm .1128$

9.87 $n_1 = n_2 = 49$ **9.88** $n_1 = n_2 = 195$ **9.89a.** $t = -4.02$; yes   **b.** $p\text{-value} < .005$ **9.90** $z = 1.67$; yes

9.91 $.4 \pm .616$ **9.92a.** $-.0913 \pm .0518$ **b.** $.308 \pm .0405$ **9.93** $z = -4$; yes   **9.94** $n_1 = n_2 = 193$

9.95a. $t = 2.27$; yes   **9.96** 9.9 ± 8.937 **9.97** $.0308 \pm .0341$ **9.98a.** $z = -1.3$; no   **b.** .1936

9.99a. $-1{,}141.67 \pm 2{,}018.76$ **9.100** $.047 \pm .0839$ **9.101a.** $t = -1.38$; no   **9.102** $F = 1.82$; no

Chapter 10

10.2 $y = 3.25 + .25x$ **10.3a.** $y = -4 + 4x$ **b.** $y = 3 + \frac{4}{3}x$ **c.** $y = -\frac{5}{2} + \frac{3}{2}x$ **d.** $y = 11 - 4x$

10.5a. 3; 1   **b.** -1; 2   **c.** 2; 1   **d.** 3; 0   **e.** 2; -3 **f.** -1; 0   **10.6a.** $-.4286$; 1   **10.7a.** 4; 1.55

10.8a. -2.4583; 1.632   **10.9d.** $y = 1 + x$ **e.** $\hat{y} = 1 + x$ **10.10a.** $\hat{y} = 25.883 + 3.115x$ **c.** 88.2 cents/gallon

10.11b. 24.45; 2.38   **c.** 33.38   **10.12b.** $-.125$; 3.125   **d.** 15.5   **10.13a.** Positive   **b.** $\hat{y} = -52.3 + 389x$

10.14a. $\hat{y} = 133.1 - .2647x$ **10.15** .0507   **10.16a.** 57.5; 3.59375   **b.** 248.57143; 7.53247   **c.** 9.2882; .516

10.17a. 1.7143; .3429   **b.** 1.95; .65   **c.** 9.097; 1.137   **d.** 1.5; 1.5   **e.** 88.62; 14.77   **f.** 52.476; 8.746

g. 11; 3.667   **h.** 278.56; 23.21

10.18a. 14.77; 3.843   **b.** 72.61 cents; 3.843 cents   **c.** $1.19; 3.843 cents   **10.19b.** 69.221; 3.846

10.20a. $\hat{y} = 18.890 + .0109x$ **b.** 23.25   **c.** 19.43; 3.886   **10.21a.** $\hat{y} = -45.78 + 1.562x$ **c.** 19.60; 4.9

10.22a. $\hat{y} = -.2462 + 1.3152x$ **c.** 7.645; 11.591   **d.** 12.4366; 2.487

10.23a. 5   **b.** 3   **c.** 8   **d.** 6   **e.** 18   **f.** 5

10.24a. $t = 9.04$; yes   **b.** $t = 8.60$; yes   **c.** $t = 11.61$; yes   **d.** $t = 22.61$; yes   **e.** $t = 5.94$; yes   **f.** $t = 8.12$; yes

10.25a. 31 ± 1.17; $31 \pm .94$ **b.** 64 ± 5.08; 64 ± 4.16 **c.** $-8.4 \pm .75$; $-8.4 \pm .62$

10.26a. $\hat{y} = 12.71 + 1.50x$ **b.** $t = 18.26$; yes

10.27a. For each firm, reject H_0 and conclude market model is useful   **b.** .14; .076   **10.28** $3.115 \pm .268$

10.29 $t = 5.94$; yes   **10.30** 5.638 ± 1.448 **10.31** $\hat{\beta}_1 = 7.70$; $t = 2.56$; yes $(\alpha = .05)$ **10.33** $t = 3.23$; yes

10.34 $t = 8.12$; yes   **10.35a.** $\hat{y} = 40.926 - .1343x$ **b.** $t = -4.21$; yes   **c.** $-.1343 \pm .0578$

10.36a. .976; .9528   **b.** $-.988$; .9759   **10.38a.** .9582; .9181   **b.** $-.9676$; .9362

10.39a. .9423   **b.** .961   **c.** .944   **10.41** $r_1 = -.9674$; $r_2 = -.1105$; x_1

10.42a. .6382; .407   **b.** $t = 2.87$; yes   **10.43** .0787; $-.2806$ **10.44c.** $r_1 = .965$; $r_2 = .996$

10.45a. $\hat{y} = -768.6 + 6.20x_1$ **b.** $t = 3.35$; yes   **c.** .584

10.46a. $\hat{y} = -235.1 + 1.2735x_2$ **b.** $t = 18.30$; yes   **c.** .977   **10.47a.** .815   **b.** $t = 3.98$; yes

10.48a. $\hat{y} = 44.17 - .0255x$ **c.** $t = -.03$; do not reject H_0 **d.** No   **e.** Approx. 0

10.49a. $2.45 \pm .949$ **b.** 2.45 ± 2.12 **10.50a.** 5.70 ± 1.456 **b.** $-.83 \pm .780$

10.51a. $\hat{y} = 1.4 + .8x$ **c.** 1   **d.** .1   **e.** $2.2 \pm .247$ **f.** $2.6 \pm .737$

10.52a. $\hat{y} = 9.5538 + 2.671x$ **c.** $t = 8.48$; yes   **d.** 18.10 ± 1.189 **e.** $17.57 \pm .426$ **10.53** 119.33 ± 5.64

10.54a. $\hat{y} = 5.325 + .5861x$ **c.** $t = 15.35$; model is useful   **d.** 28.18 ± 1.273; 28.18 ± 4.629

10.55 $1,091.4 \pm 908.59$ **10.56** $1,091.4 \pm 3,012.90$

10.59b. $\hat{y} = -.0817 + .1253x$ **c.** $t = 8.21$; yes   **d.** .9455; .894   **e.** $1.798 \pm .206$ **f.** $1.798 \pm .624$

10.60a. $\hat{y} = 27.78 - .6x$ **c.** 7   **d.** .5385   **e.** $-.6 \pm .1838$ **f.** $26.7 \pm .3479$ **g.** 26.7 ± 1.3453

10.61a. $\hat{y} = -1,064,378 + 180.5x$ **b.** $t = 9.56$; yes   **c.** Approx. 0   **d.** .8208

10.62a. $\hat{y} = -1.081 + .6757x$ **b.** $t = 2.5$; yes   **c.** $.6757 \pm .860$ **d.** 15.81 ± 1.334 **e.** 14.46 ± 3.689

10.63a. $-.814$; .6636   **b.** $t = -4.44$; yes

10.64a. $\hat{y} = 22.32 + 2.650x$ **c.** $t = 6.28$; yes   **d.** .9421; .8875   **e.** 109.76 ± 2.155 **f.** 109.76 ± 6.088

10.65a. $\hat{y} = 46.40x$ **b.** $\hat{y} = 478 + 45.2x$ **d.** $t = .91$; no   **10.66a.** .8429   **b.** $t = 2.71$; no

10.67a. $\hat{y} = 16.28 + 2.078x$ **c.** $t = 6.67$; yes   **d.** p-value $< .01$ **e.** 57.84 ± 6.146

10.68a. $\hat{y} = 13.48 + .056x$ **c.** .7402; .5479   **d.** 17.40 ± 2.474

10.69a. $\hat{y} = 18.223 + 1.166x$ **c.** $t = 4.97$; yes   **d.** p-value $< .01$ **e.** .8044   **f.** 123.2 ± 19.09

10.70a. $\hat{y} = 4,060 + 31.1x$ **b.** .988   **d.** $t = 41.87$; yes   **e.** 31.1 ± 1.539 **f.** p-value $< .005$

g. $63,075 \pm 530.79$

10.72 $-.491$ **10.73a.** $t = -2.59$; yes; $.005 < p$-value $< .01$

Chapter 11

11.1a. $t = 1.45$; do not reject H_0 **b.** $t = 3.21$; reject H_0

11.2a. $t = 3.13$; reject H_0 **b.** $t = 3.13$; reject H_0 if $t > 1.717$; yes   **c.** 9.82

11.4a. $\hat{y} = 1.433 + .010x_1 + .379x_2$ **b.** $t = 3.15$; yes   **e.** .07669613

11.5a. 55.62   **b.** $t = -2.8$; yes   **c.** $.005 < p$-value $< .01$

11.6a. $\hat{y} = 20.09 - .67x + .0095x^2$ **c.** $t = 1.51$; do not reject H_0 **d.** $\hat{y} = 19.279 - .445x_1$ **e.** $-.445 \pm .0728$

11.7a. $t = -3.33$; yes   **11.8** $t = 2.11$; reject H_0 **11.9** $t = 3.04$; reject H_0 ($\alpha = .05$)   **11.10b.** $F = 48.53$; yes

11.11a. .4615   **b.** $F = 7.28$; yes

11.12a. Expense per vehicle mile: $F = 1.616$, do not reject H_0; expense per ton mile: $F = 2.148$, do not reject H_0

b. Greater

11.13a. $F = 31.98$; yes   **b.** $t = -2.27$; yes

11.14a. $\hat{y} = 131.924 + 2.726x_1 + .047x_2 - 2.587x_3$ **b.** $F = 17.87$; reject H_0; model useful   **c.** $t = .51$; do not reject H_0

d. .770104   **e.** Will save the company $19.41 per week

11.15 $F = 1.06$; do not reject H_0 **11.16b.** $\hat{y} = 95.75 - .3199x$ **11.17b.** $F = 58.56$; yes   **c.** $t = 50$; yes

11.18a. $\hat{y} = 2.41 + 1.43x_1 - .366x_2$ **b.** $F = 54.83$; reject H_0 **c.** $R^2 = .94$

d. $\hat{y} = -.349 + 2.07x_1 + .0215x_2 - .0919x_1x_2$ **e.** $R^2 = .986$ **g.** $t = -4.54$; yes

11.19b. $\hat{y} = 51,653 - 32.7x + .0206x^2$ **c.** $R^2 = .98$ **d.** $F = 563.5$; reject H_0 **e.** $t = 5.61$; yes

11.20a. $\hat{y} = 90.1 - 1.836x_1 + .285x_2$ **b.** $R^2 = .916$ **c.** $F = 65.43$; yes   **d.** $t = -5.01$; reject H_0

11.21a. $\hat{y} = -13.062 + .742x_1 + 18.603x_2 + 13.410x_3$ **b.** $F = 188.33$; reject H_0

11.22a. $\hat{y} = .601 + .595x_1 - 3.725x_2 - 16.232x_3 + .235x_1x_2 + .308x_1x_3$ **b.** $F = 139.42$; reject H_0

11.23a. $F = 165.84$; reject H_0 **c.** $t = 3.64$, yes; $t = -2.25$, no   **11.25** $t = -2.06$; no

11.26a. $\hat{y} = .0562 + .273x_1 + .0006x_2$ **b.** $F = 163.17$; reject H_0 **c.** $t = 4.34$; reject H_0 **d.** 14.25

11.28a. $\hat{y} = .5950 + .0125x_1 + .0300x_2 + .0025x_1x_2$ **b.** $F = 12.67$; yes ($\alpha = .05$)   **c.** $t = .23$; no

11.29a. $H_0: \beta_2 = \beta_3 = 0$ **c.** $t = -3.33$; yes   **11.30** $F = 15.32$; reject H_0

11.31a. $\hat{y} = 53.6 - .198x + .0003x^2$ **b.** $t = .78$; no   **11.32a.** $F = 1.28$; do not reject H_0 **11.33a.** 13.68

11.34a. $\hat{y} = -1,187 + 1,333x - 45.6x^2$ **b.** $R^2 = .973$ **c.** $F = 216.22$; reject H_0 **d.** $t = -5.84$; reject H_0

11.35 $t = -1.10$; do not reject H_0 **11.36b.** $F = 52.21$; reject H_0 **c.** $t = -3.33$; yes ($\alpha = .05$)   **d.** $t = 4$; yes ($\alpha = .05$)

11.38b. $t = 40.54$; reject H_0 **c.** 17.79   **11.39b.** $F = 16.10$; yes   **c.** $t = 2.5$; yes   **d.** 945

11.40b. $t = 5$; yes   **c.** 825   **11.42a.** $F = 6.61$; yes

11.43a. $\hat{y} = 1.68 + .444x_1 - .0793x_2$ **b.** $F = 148.67$; reject H_0 **c.** $R^2 = .977$ **d.** $-.0793 \pm .0113$ **e.** 1.20 hours

f. 12 hours

11.44a. $\hat{y} = -1.5705 + .02573x_1 + .03361x_2$; $R^2 = .681$; $F = 39.49$; reject H_0

11.45a. $R^2 = .937$; $F = 101.14$; reject H_0 **c.** $t = 1.67$; reject H_0

Chapter 12

12.1a. Quantitative   **b.** Qualitative   **c.** Qualitative   **d.** Qualitative   **e.** Quantitative

12.2a. Quantitative   **b.** Quantitative   **c.** Qualitative   **d.** Qualitative   **e.** Qualitative   **f.** Qualitative

g. Quantitative   **h.** Qualitative

12.5a. First-order; $\beta_0 = 10$; $\beta_1 = .5$ **b.** First-order; $\beta_0 = 80$; $\beta_1 = -.5$

12.6a. Second-order; $\beta_0 = 4$; β_2 is negative   **b.** Second-order; $\beta_0 = 8$; β_2 is positive

12.7a. First   **b.** Second   **c.** Third   **d.** Third   **e.** Second   **f.** First

12.10a. $E(y) = \beta_0 + \beta_1 x + \beta_2 x^2$ **b.** Expect $\beta_0 > 0$, $\beta_2 > 0$ **12.11a.** $E(y) = \beta_0 + \beta_1 x + \beta_2 x^2$ **b.** $\beta_0 > 0$, $\beta_2 < 0$

12.12 $E(y) = \beta_0 + \beta_1 x + \beta_2 x^2$ **12.13** $t = -6.60$; yes   **12.14a.** $E(y) = \beta_0 + \beta_1 x + \beta_2 x^2$

12.15b. First-order; first-order; second-order   **12.16b.** $\hat{y} = 79.75 + 6.48x - .81x^2$ **c.** $t = -4.08$; yes

12.17a. $\hat{y} = 18.1984 - 1.804x$; $R^2 = .242$ **d.** $\hat{y} = 18.1397 - 2.39x + .451x^2$; $R^2 = .253$ **f.** $t = .56$; no

12.18a. $E(y) = \beta_0 + \beta_1 x_1 + \beta_2 x_1^2$ **b.** $F = 44.5$; yes   **c.** From printout: .0001   **d.** $t = -4.68$; yes

e. From printout: .0001

12.19 $E(y) = \beta_0 + \beta_1 x_1 + \beta_2 x_2$ **12.20** $E(y) = \beta_0 + \beta_1 x_1 + \beta_2 x_2 + \beta_3 x_1 x_2$

12.21 $E(y) = \beta_0 + \beta_1 x_1 + \beta_2 x_2 + \beta_3 x_1 x_2 + \beta_4 x_1^2 + \beta_5 x_2^2$ **12.23a.** Second-order

12.25a. Both quantitative   **b.** $E(y) = \beta_0 + \beta_1 x_1 + \beta_2 x_2$ **c.** $E(y) = \beta_0 + \beta_1 x_1 + \beta_2 x_2 + \beta_3 x_1 x_2 + \beta_4 x_1^2 + \beta_5 x_2^2$

d. $H_0: \beta_3 = 0$; $H_a: \beta_3 \neq 0$

12.26 $E(y) = \beta_0 + \beta_1 x_1 + \beta_2 x_2 + \beta_3 x_1 x_2 + \beta_4 x_1^2 + \beta_5 x_2^2$

12.27a. Both quantitative   **b.** $E(y) = \beta_0 + \beta_1 x_1 + \beta_2 x_2$ **c.** $E(y) = \beta_0 + \beta_1 x_1 + \beta_2 x_2 + \beta_3 x_1 x_2$

d. $E(y) = \beta_0 + \beta_1 x_1 + \beta_2 x_2 + \beta_3 x_1 x_2 + \beta_4 x_1^2 + \beta_5 x_2^2$

12.30a. At least one of the parameters β_3, β_4, β_5 differs from 0   **c.** $\nu_1 = 3$, $\nu_2 = 24$ **12.31** $F = 1.15$; do not reject H_0

12.33a. $H_0: \beta_1 = \beta_2 = \beta_3 = \beta_4 = \beta_5 = 0$; $H_a:$ At least one of the parameters β_1, β_2, β_3, β_4, β_5 differs from 0

b. $H_0: \beta_3 = \beta_4 = \beta_5 = 0$; $H_a:$ At least one of the parameters β_3, β_4, β_5 differs from 0   **c.** $F = 18.29$; reject H_0

d. $F = 8.46$; reject H_0

12.34a. $\hat{y} = -215 - .910x_1 + 78.7x_2 + .143x_1 x_2 - .0001x_1^2 - 5.99x_2^2$ **b.** $F = 298.8$; yes   **c.** 173,240

12.35 $F = 24.19$; yes   **12.36a.** $F = 31.55$; reject H_0 **b.** p-value $< .01$

12.37a. $\hat{y} = 1.119 - .0026x_1 + .7x_2 + .00018x_1^2 - .03026x_2^2 - .00149x_1 x_2$ **b.** $F = 77.05$; yes   **c.** $F = 6.933$; yes

d. $t = -.65$; no

12.38a. $E(y) = \beta_0 + \beta_1 x_1 + \beta_2 x_2 + \beta_3 x_3 + \beta_4 x_1 x_2 + \beta_5 x_1 x_3 + \beta_6 x_2 x_3 + \beta_7 x_1^2 + \beta_8 x_2^2 + \beta_9 x_3^2$

b. $\hat{y} = 655.81 - 57.33x_1 - 3.39x_2 - 28.27x_3 + .22x_1 x_2 + 2.20x_1 x_3 + .09x_2 x_3 + .45x_1^2 + .004x_2^2 + .21x_3^2$ **c.** $F = 10.25$; yes

d. $F = 2.25$; no

12.41a. 10.2   **b.** 6.2   **c.** 22.2   **d.** 12.2

12.42 $H_0: \beta_1 = \beta_2 = \beta_3 = 0$; $H_a:$ At least one of the parameters β_1, β_2, β_3 differs from 0

12.45a. $F = 4.81$; yes   **b.** \$11,400   **c.** \$20,000   **12.46** 3.80 ± 7.306 **12.47a.** Qualitative
12.48a. 60   **b.** 510
12.49b. $\hat{y} = 25.1 + 3.85x_1 + 6.55x_2 - 2.65x_3 - 4.75x_4$ (variety A is the base level)   **c.** $F = 24.03$; yes
12.50a. $E(y) = \beta_0 + \beta_1 x_1 + \beta_2 x_2 + \beta_3 x_3$ where $x_1 = \begin{cases} 1 \text{ if publishing company} \\ 0 \text{ otherwise} \end{cases}$ $x_2 = \begin{cases} 1 \text{ if electric utility} \\ 0 \text{ otherwise} \end{cases}$ $x_3 = \begin{cases} 1 \text{ if bank} \\ 0 \text{ otherwise} \end{cases}$
b. $F = 31.82$; reject H_0 **c.** $t = 8.93$; yes
12.56b. $E(y) = \beta_0 + \beta_1 x_1 + \beta_2 x_2$, where $x_1 =$ size of orange and $x_2 = 1$ if brand A and $x_2 = 0$ if brand B
c. $E(y) = \beta_0 + \beta_1 x_1 + \beta_2 x_2 + \beta_3 x_1 x_2$ **e.** $H_0: \beta_3 = 0$; $H_a: \beta_3 \neq 0$
12.57a. $F = 25.96$; yes   **b.** 10,390
12.58a. $E(y) = \beta_0 + \beta_1 x_1 + \beta_2 x_2 + \beta_3 x_3$ **b.** $E(y) = \beta_0 + \beta_1 x_1 + \beta_2 x_2 + \beta_3 x_3 + \beta_4 x_1 x_2 + \beta_5 x_1 x_3$
c. $\hat{y} = -10.8 + .101x_1 + 3.48x_2 - 4.36x_3$; $\hat{y} = -8.27 + .0884x_1 - 1.75x_2 - 7.52x_3 + .0246x_1 x_2 + .0151x_1 x_3$
d. $F = .22$; no   **e.** $H_0: \beta_2 = \beta_3 = \beta_4 = \beta_5 = 0$
12.59a. $E(y) = \beta_0 + \beta_1 x$ **b.** Include $\beta_2 x_2 + \beta_3 x_3$ **c.** Include $\beta_4 x_1 x_2 + \beta_5 x_1 x_3$
12.60a. $E(y) = \beta_0 + \beta_1 x_1 + \beta_2 x_2 + \beta_3 x_3$ **b.** $H_0: \beta_2 = \beta_3 = 0$ **12.61** $F = 2.60$; do not reject H_0
12.62a. $H_0: \beta_2 = \beta_3 = 0$ **b.** $F = 6.99$; reject H_0 **12.64** $E(y) = \beta_0 + \beta_1 x_1 + \beta_2 x_1^2$ **12.65** Include $\beta_3 x_2 + \beta_4 x_3$
12.66 Include $\beta_5 x_1 x_2 + \beta_6 x_1^2 x_2 + \beta_7 x_1 x_3 + \beta_8 x_1^2 x_3$
12.71a. $F = 4.90$; reject H_0 **b.** $H_0: \beta_4 = \beta_5 = 0$ **c.** $F = 2.36$; no   **12.72** $F = 6.71$; yes
12.73a. $F = 149$; reject H_0 **12.74a.** $H_0: \beta_4 = \beta_5 = 0$ **b.** $H_0: \beta_3 = \beta_4 = \beta_5 = 0$ **12.76** $F = 9.99$; yes
12.79a. $E(y) = \beta_0 + \beta_1 x_1 + \beta_2 x_2 + \beta_3 x_1 x_2$ **c.** $H_0: \beta_3 = 0$ **d.** $H_0: \beta_2 = \beta_3 = 0$
12.81a. Qualitative: x_7, x_8, x_9, x_{10}; quantitative: x_1 through x_6, x_{11}
b. 5; not employed, white-collar, blue-collar, farm-related, other   **d.** $F = 11.96$; model is useful
e. $H_0: \beta_7 = \beta_8 = \beta_9 = \beta_{10} = 0$
   H_a: At least one of the parameters β_7, β_8, β_9, β_{10} differs from 0
12.82a. $F = 221.4$; reject H_0 **b.** $F = 13.49$; yes
f. $\hat{y} = .709 + .109x_1 - .252x_2 - .618x_3 - 1.20x_4 - .0156x_1 x_2 + .0055x_1 x_3 + .0049x_1 x_4$ **g.** $F = 1.78$; no
12.83a. $H_0: \beta_2 = \beta_5 = 0$ **b.** $H_0: \beta_3 = \beta_4 = \beta_5 = 0$ **12.84** $F = 2.15$; do not reject H_0
12.85a. $\hat{y} = 10.2 + .683x_1 + 2.02x_2 + .5x_3$ **b.** $F = 62.78$; yes   **12.86a.** $E(y) = \beta_0 + \beta_1 x + \beta_2 x^2$ **b.** No
12.87a. $E(y) = \beta_0 + \beta_1 x_1 + \beta_2 x^2 + \beta_3 x_2 + \beta_4 x_3 + \beta_5 x_1 x_2 + \beta_6 x_1^2 x_2 + \beta_7 x_1 x_3 + \beta_8 x_1^2 x_3$
12.88a. $\hat{y} = -.0353 + 1.88x_1 + .0334x_2 - 1.24x_1 x_2$ **b.** Bull: 1.88; bear: .64   **c.** $t = -1.77$; do not reject H_0
d. $F = 2.39$; do not reject H_0
12.90a. Two   **b.** $E(y) = \beta_0 + \beta_1 x_1 + \beta_2 x_2$
12.92a. $E(y) = \beta_0 + \beta_1 x_1 + \beta_2 x_2$ **b.** $E(y) = \beta_0 + \beta_1 x_1 + \beta_2 x_2 + \beta_3 x_1^2 + \beta_4 x_1 x_2 + \beta_5 x_1^2 x_2$ **c.** $H_0: \beta_3 = \beta_4 = \beta_5 = 0$
12.93a. $F = 2.49$; no   **b.** $F = 209$; reject H_0

Chapter 13

	1970	1971	1972	1973	1974	1975	1976	1977	1978	1979	1980	1981	1982
13.2	78.06	80.59	82.87	87.16	91.61	94.19	96.01	100.00	105.04	108.04	113.84	113.61	115.07
13.4	68.57	70.79	72.80	76.56	80.47	82.74	84.34	87.84	92.27	94.90	100.00	99.79	101.08

13.5a.	1970	1971	1972	1973	1974	1975	1976	1977	1978	1979	1980	1981	1982	1983
	94.14	79.69	100.00	119.92	132.81	147.27	153.52	121.09	69.53	89.84	134.38	165.23	141.41	186.72

b. 86.72%; 38.95%

13.6a.

	1973	1974	1975	1976	1977	1978	1979	1980	1981
Jan.	100.0	129.8	167.1	184.9	191.0	202.1	270.3	445.3	524.3
Feb.	98.0	142.5	166.9	182.6	193.0	201.7	276.8	470.6	561.6
Mar.	102.5	150.5	167.0	180.0	195.9	201.6	289.4	484.4	566.8
Apr.	104.0	156.1	169.1	181.4	198.7	202.4	305.2	485.6	564.2
May	104.7	164.7	173.2	182.2	201.5	204.4	321.7	487.6	553.2
June	105.8	172.2	178.6	189.2	204.4	207.2	347.0	488.3	551.8
July	106.0	172.3	187.2	191.8	204.3	210.6	367.8	487.9	546.2
Aug.	105.9	172.8	189.8	192.3	204.3	210.6	382.6	487.2	543.9
Sept.	105.6	170.1	189.8	192.5	203.4	215.4	391.3	482.3	551.6
Oct.	109.4	161.5	189.9	192.5	202.8	216.1	394.2	480.8	541.7
Nov.	112.8	160.7	187.9	191.9	202.5	218.8	399.4	484.0	540.9
Dec.	119.7	162.6	187.9	190.9	202.0	222.7	422.8	487.0	539.5

d. Price index

13.7a.

YEAR	WHITE-COLLAR	BLUE-COLLAR	SERVICE
1972	85.6	93.6	87.6
1973	88.6	98.0	89.0
1974	91.8	97.9	91.3
1975	93.1	92.2	93.7
1976	96.5	95.7	96.7
1977	100.0	100.0	100.0
1978	104.6	104.5	103.7
1979	109.5	106.5	103.9
1980	112.9	102.5	105.1
1981	115.2	101.9	106.8
1982	116.3	96.5	109.1

b. White-collar; blue-collar   **c.** Quantity indexes

13.9

JAN.	FEB.	MAR.	APR.	MAY	JUNE	JUL.	AUG.	SEPT.	OCT.
89.10	92.10	98.09	95.10	100.00	100.82	94.01	94.01	97.28	100.0

13.11a.

1961	1962	1963	1964	1965	1966	1967	1968	1969	1970	1971	1972
68.33	72.47	76.40	81.64	87.72	94.80	100.00	109.32	118.23	126.19	136.28	149.48

1973	1974	1975	1976	1977	1978	1979	1980	1981	1982
164.92	180.69	198.49	220.21	246.75	275.48	308.14	340.85	375.93	402.00

b.

1961	1962	1963	1964	1965	1966	1967	1968	1969	1970	1971
37.82	40.11	42.28	45.18	48.55	52.47	55.34	60.50	65.43	69.84	75.42

1972	1973	1974	1975	1976	1977	1978	1979	1980	1981	1982
82.73	91.27	100.00	109.85	121.87	136.56	152.46	170.54	188.64	208.06	222.49

13.13.

1961	1962	1963	1964	1965	1966	1967	1968	1969	1970	1971	1972
71.5	74.8	77.8	82.6	88.2	95.5	100.0	108.5	116.8	125.4	132.8	143.9

1973	1974	1975	1976	1977	1978	1979	1980	1981	1982
159.9	178.6	195.4	212.4	234.3	259.8	293.7	328.8	360.0	379.1

13.15

	JAN.	FEB.	MAR.	APR.	MAY	JUNE	JULY	AUG.	SEPT.	OCT.	NOV.	DEC.
a. Price	100.0	99.3	99.7	98.6	98.0	96.5	98.1	97.0	96.8	95.8	95.1	94.6
Quantity	100.0	92.7	102.4	88.7	87.6	79.1	80.5	73.9	71.2	69.7	60.6	62.2
b.	100.0	100.0	100.0	99.9	99.9	99.7	99.9	99.8	99.8	99.5	99.4	99.4

13.16

JAN.	FEB.	MAR.	APR.	MAY	JUNE	JULY	AUG.	SEPT.	OCT.	NOV.	DEC.
100.00	99.95	99.98	99.88	99.84	99.67	99.85	99.70	99.68	99.32	99.21	99.13

13.17 7-point

13.18

	1971	1972	1973	1974	1975	1976	1977	1978	1979
$N = 3$	45.42	65.89	105.37	139.64	148.63	144.83	155.53	216.53	369.10
$N = 5$		78.76	103.75	120.46	138.40	157.54	187.16	276.08	

13.20

	1971	1972	1973	1974	1975	1976	1977	1978	1979	1980	1981
3-pt.	137.27	142.43	148.70	155.13	160.17	164.93	171.10	177.93	185.80	190.67	194.67
5-pt.		143.32	148.82	154.08	159.92	166.02	171.62	178.32	184.32	189.46	

13.21a. (centered)

	1977		1978				1979			
	III	IV	I	II	III	IV	I	II	III	IV
	487.39	469.27	447.83	423.85	413.19	415.27	413.60	405.97	391.69	352.89

13.22

YEAR	3-POINT	5-POINT	7-POINT
1967			
1968	108.30		
1969	109.77	110.36	
1970	111.70	115.86	116.17
1971	119.67	119.30	116.91
1972	126.43	119.62	117.99
1973	123.73	121.74	120.77
1974	119.57	123.70	125.23
1975	119.03	125.32	128.81
1976	129.17	128.06	129.30
1977	136.97	133.20	130.44
1978	139.57	136.74	132.91
1979	138.60	136.62	134.80
1980	133.30	135.14	
1981	132.40		
1982			

13.23b.

1981	JAN.	FEB.	MAR.	APR.	MAY	JUNE	JULY	AUG.	SEPT.	OCT.	NOV.	DEC.
3-pt.		1211.3	1330.7	1433.7	1494.3	1451.3	1400.7	1392.0	1554.7	1559.0	1641.3	1502.3
5-pt.			1348.8	1367.0	1437.0	1462.4	1403.8	1509.6	1501.2	1517.8	1570.6	1689.6
7-pt.				1375.4	1380.6	1407.1	1522.6	1478.4	1496.1	1526.0	1587.6	1646.9

1982	JAN.	FEB.	MAR.	APR.	MAY	JUNE	JULY	AUG.	SEPT.	OCT.	NOV.	DEC.
3-pt.	1706.0	1752.3	1856.3	1845.7	1907.0	1985.3	2294.3	2382.0	2451.0	2207.0	2227.0	
5-pt.	1636.4	1749.0	1812.2	1879.2	1916.6	2137.4	2194.6	2279.8	2317.4	2339.6		
7-pt.	1725.0	1712.3	1796.0	1872.4	2051.7	2085.7	2171.9	2202.0	2249.1			

13.24

Jan. 1973		1975	41.72	1977	48.73	1979	64.69	1981	132.81
Feb.			42.15		49.08		69.07		136.87
Mar.	25.77		42.68		49.61		74.08		140.22
Apr.	26.07		43.27		50.29		77.96		141.61
May	26.47		44.29		50.86		82.56		140.83
June	26.64		45.45		51.29		87.28		139.68
July	26.73		46.49		51.53		91.64		139.04
Aug.	26.97		47.34		51.59		95.31		138.46
Sept.	27.32		47.81		51.50		97.97		137.91
Oct.	28.02		47.85		51.38		100.75		137.57
Nov.	29.23		47.60		51.27		103.92		
Dec.	31.09		47.24		51.18		107.93		
Jan. 1974	33.18	1976	46.74	1978	51.12	1980	112.50		
Feb.	35.36		46.41		51.11		116.86		
Mar.	37.64		46.12		51.24		120.14		
Apr.	39.79		46.34		51.50		122.32		
May	41.30		46.80		51.94		123.20		
June	42.42		47.42		52.40		123.34		
July	43.13		47.99		53.06		123.17		
Aug.	42.97		48.51		53.65		122.83		
Sept.	42.38		48.64		54.24		122.61		
Oct.	41.89		48.60		54.85		122.56		
Nov.	41.61		48.53		57.88		124.45		
Dec.	41.44		48.56		60.98		128.46		

13.25b.

YEAR, QTR.	1979,3	1979,4	1980,1	1980,2	1980,3	1980,4	1981,1	1981,2
$100(Y_t/M_t)$	79.94	49.63	135.77	117.78	99.31	54.77	127.91	115.96

YEAR, QTR.	1981,3	1981,4	1982,1	1982,2	1982,3	1982,4	1983,1	1983,2
$100(Y_t/M_t)$	94.60	67.95	123.06	116.19	89.21	75.88	117.51	113.78

13.26 $w = .2$

13.27a.

YEAR	QUARTER	
1977	I	367.40
	II	474.25
	III	517.88
	IV	497.49
1978	I	394.87
	II	453.08
	III	456.44
	IV	421.72
1979	I	359.36
	II	441.28
	III	437.94
	IV	394.52
1980	I	306.61
	II	298.86

13.28

YEAR	$w = .2$	$w = .8$
1970	133.10	133.10
1971	133.96	136.54
1972	135.43	140.35
1973	138.06	146.95
1974	141.69	154.35
1975	145.47	159.35
1976	149.12	162.83
1977	153.39	168.97
1978	158.54	177.07
1979	163.67	182.77
1980	169.75	191.83
1981	174.54	193.33
1982	178.87	195.63

13.29a.

1971	100.31	1976	100.28	1981	133.08
	99.53		103.08		130.27
	98.70		104.59		122.22
	101.07		106.60		120.06
1972	105.36	1977	100.87	1982	117.98
	106.61		100.60		112.27
	109.37		97.75		118.93
	115.45		95.90		132.92
1973	112.70	1978	91.22	1983	145.62
	106.79		94.24		159.26
	107.94		100.05		165.84
	100.67		97.29		164.64
1974	95.99	1979	100.30		
	89.00		102.13		
	71.18		107.16		
	69.35		107.71		
1975	79.16	1980	106.06		
	90.38		111.42		
	85.82		122.42		
	94.48		128.74		

13.30

YEAR	
1970	36.41
1971	38.83
1972	48.72
1973	73.27
1974	116.48
1975	138.94
1976	131.87
1977	140.09
1978	166.79
1979	237.30
1980	421.65

13.31

YEAR	WHITE-COLLAR	BLUE-COLLAR	SERVICE
1972	39.33	28.72	11.03
1973	39.89	29.26	11.10
1974	40.81	29.58	11.26
1975	41.60	29.07	11.47
1976	42.71	29.18	11.75
1977	44.01	29.78	12.09
1978	45.64	30.70	12.48
1979	47.52	31.49	12.72
1980	49.26	31.47	12.92
1981	50.74	31.39	13.13
1982	51.83	30.67	13.37

13.32a.

YEAR	$w = .2$	$w = .8$	YEAR	$w = .2$	$w = .8$
1960	42.40	42.40	1972	77.21	102.26
1961	42.88	44.32	1973	84.69	112.13
1962	43.78	46.78	1974	91.33	116.75
1963	44.93	48.96	1975	98.94	126.87
1964	46.80	53.23	1976	110.20	149.53
1965	49.12	57.37	1977	124.02	173.35
1966	51.38	59.79	1978	138.83	193.15
1967	53.76	62.60	1979	154.95	214.15
1968	56.87	67.96	1980	171.86	234.43
1969	60.64	74.15	1981	189.65	255.53
1970	64.63	79.31	1982	205.70	267.03
1971	70.16	89.70			

13.33a. and **13.34a.**

YEAR	COLD ROLLED		HOT ROLLED		GALVANIZED	
	$w = .5$	3-pt.	$w = .5$	3-pt.	$w = .5$	3-pt.
1971	10.00		7.48		9.61	
1972	10.39	10.62	7.94	8.09	10.25	10.36
1973	10.73	11.54	8.17	8.63	10.42	11.29
1974	11.76	13.30	8.64	9.54	11.40	12.59
1975	13.89	15.66	9.88	10.81	13.10	14.42
1976	16.03	18.19	11.04	12.37	14.59	16.32
1977	18.21	20.55	12.42	13.84	16.34	18.21
1978	20.66	23.02	13.97	15.46	18.41	20.30
1979	23.10	25.05	15.51	17.01	20.36	22.22
1980	24.80	27.85	16.99	18.55	22.12	24.36
1981	28.15	30.42	18.57	19.80	24.50	25.84
1982	30.70		19.68		25.63	

13.35a.

YEAR	
1971	51.82
1972	57.48
1973	57.52
1974	65.55
1975	80.26
1976	88.81
1977	100.00
1978	113.06
1979	124.18
1980	131.68
1981	150.21
1982	154.55

b. Price index

13.36a.

	1981	1982
Jan.	100.00	78.18
Feb.	95.23	76.61
Mar.	92.74	74.95
Apr.	86.60	73.58
May	90.71	75.11
June	82.33	72.92
July	77.81	71.84
Aug.	75.82	71.67
Sept.	75.53	71.09
Oct.	76.57	70.30
Nov.	78.56	67.81
Dec.	79.26	67.03

13.37

YEAR		YEAR	
1960	32.77	1972	81.45
1961	34.62	1973	88.56
1962	36.63	1974	91.11
1963	38.25	1975	100.00
1964	41.96	1976	119.94
1965	45.13	1977	138.56
1966	46.68	1978	153.09
1967	48.92	1979	169.55
1968	53.55	1980	185.09
1969	58.50	1981	201.55
1970	62.29	1982	208.58
1971	71.33		

13.38 and **13.39**

YEAR	SIMPLE COMPOSITE INDEX (1972 BASE)	SIMPLE COMPOSITE INDEX (1980 BASE)	3-PT. MOVING AVERAGE	$w = .3$	SIMPLE INDEX FOR AUTO LOANS (1980 BASE)
1972	100.00	36.86		36.86	40.44
1973	119.09	43.90	43.44	38.97	47.27
1974	134.50	49.57	48.44	42.15	52.51
1975	140.69	51.86	53.15	45.06	54.98
1976	157.39	58.01	61.02	48.95	61.88
1977	198.54	73.18	72.61	56.22	73.55
1978	235.08	86.65	86.32	65.35	87.29
1979	268.97	99.14	95.26	75.49	99.54
1980	271.30	100.00	101.92	82.84	100.00
1981	289.26	106.62	106.52	89.97	106.35
1982	306.39	112.93		96.86	112.37

13.40a.

YEAR	LASPEYRES INDEX
1980	100.00
1981	106.89
1982	113.81

13.41a.

YEAR	PAASCHE INDEX
1980	100.00
1981	106.81
1982	113.39

13.42

YEAR	BUSINESS FORMATION INDEX	HOUSING INDEX	STOCK INDEX	SIMPLE COMPOSITE INDEX
1967	100.57	74.37	105.82	90.67
1968	111.02	78.63	118.16	98.96
1969	109.12	65.40	101.12	88.02
1970	100.00	100.00	100.00	100.00
1971	109.40	120.66	110.10	114.46
1972	113.77	134.60	130.41	127.33
1973	108.26	71.66	105.20	91.60
1974	100.95	48.35	74.49	70.97
1975	110.16	60.68	98.47	85.57
1976	114.91	84.05	116.12	101.90
1977	128.02	97.61	104.18	108.35
1978	127.07	94.77	106.63	107.51
1979	127.16	65.40	110.00	95.76
1980	115.19	65.14	136.12	99.27
1981	100.85	54.49	126.33	87.77

13.43a.

	$w = .2$	$w = .8$
1967	103.70	103.70
1968	106.12	113.38
1969	104.72	101.96
1970	103.37	98.79
1971	104.28	106.08
1972	108.98	123.46
1973	107.81	107.17
1974	100.84	79.83
1975	99.98	93.17
1976	102.74	109.67
1977	102.61	103.61
1978	102.99	104.32
1979	103.95	107.10
1980	109.84	128.14
1981	112.63	124.67

b. $w = .2$

13.44a. 1970 real income: \$17,196.90; 1980 real income: \$14,181.52   **b.** \$42,441.97

Chapter 14

14.2a. $w = .3$: forecast $= 185.9$, error $= 10.3$; $w = .7$: forecast $= 193.4$, error $= 2.8$
b. $w = .7$, $v = .3$: forecast $= 201.2$, error $= -5.0$; $w = .3$, $v = .7$: forecast $= 203.4$; error $= -7.2$
14.3 $w = .3$: forecast $= 189.5$; $w = .7$: forecast $= 195.9$

14.4a.

QTR.	FORECAST
I	137.11
II	137.11
III	137.11
IV	137.11

b.

QTR.	ERROR
I	13.96
II	28.00
III	31.55
IV	27.01

c.

QTR.	FORECAST	ERROR
I	129.00	22.07
II	129.00	36.11
III	129.00	39.66
IV	129.00	35.12

d. $w = .7$, $v = .5$:

QTR.	FORECAST
I	140.84
II	149.04
III	157.24
IV	165.44

$w = .3$, $v = .5$:

QTR.	FORECAST
I	120.63
II	120.72
III	120.81
IV	120.90

14.5a.

QTR.	$w = .3$	$w = .7$
I	154.43	164.28
II	152.43	164.28
III	151.43	164.28
IV	151.43	164.28

b.

QTR.	$w = .3$, $v = .5$	$w = .7$, $v = .5$
I	178.56	173.90
II	189.42	178.35
III	200.28	182.80
IV	211.14	187.25

14.6a. and **b.**

MONTH	FORECAST	ERROR
Jan.	436.5	43.4
Feb.	436.5	53.9
Mar.	436.5	-16.8
Apr.	436.5	-4.5
May	436.5	1.2
June	436.5	-23.7
July	436.5	-13.1
Aug.	436.5	-20.1
Sept.	436.5	-25.0
Oct.	436.5	-42.6
Nov.	436.5	-53.8
Dec.	436.5	-48.5

c. and **d.**

MONTH	FORECAST	ERROR
Jan.	436.5	43.4
Feb.	467.0	23.4
Mar.	481.4	-61.7
Apr.	432.9	-0.9
May	435.5	2.2
June	438.1	-25.3
July	419.2	4.2
Aug.	424.0	-7.6
Sept.	418.5	-7.0
Oct.	413.8	-19.9
Nov.	399.5	-16.8
Dec.	388.3	-0.3

14.8

YEAR	FORECAST	PREDICTION INTERVAL
1983	32.59	$32.59 \pm .927$
1984	34.32	34.32 ± 1.040

14.9a. $Y = \beta_0 + \beta_1 t + \beta_2 x_1 + \beta_3 x_2 + \beta_4 x_4 + \varepsilon$ where $x_1 = \begin{cases} 1 \text{ if Qtr. 1} \\ 0 \text{ otherwise} \end{cases}$ $x_2 = \begin{cases} 1 \text{ if Qtr. 2} \\ 0 \text{ otherwise} \end{cases}$ $x_3 = \begin{cases} 1 \text{ if Qtr. 3} \\ 0 \text{ otherwise} \end{cases}$ $t = 1, \ldots, 40$

b. $\hat{Y} = 11.49 + .51t - 3.95x_1 - 2.09x_2 - 4.52x_3$; $F = 1,241.25$; model is useful

c.

QTR.	FORECAST
1	28.45
2	30.82
3	28.90
4	33.93

14.10a. $\hat{Y} = 4.81 + 10.3t$ **b.**

YEAR	FORECAST	PREDICTION INTERVAL
1983	241.71	241.71 ± 54.27
1984	252.01	252.01 ± 56.80
1985	262.31	262.31 ± 57.42

14.11a. $\hat{Y} = 119.85 + 16.51t + 262.3Q_1 + 222.8Q_2 + 105.5Q_3$ $(t = 1, 2, \ldots, 20)$; $F = 117.22$; model is useful

b.

QTR.	FORECAST
I	728.9
II	705.9
III	605.1
IV	516.1

14.12a. $\hat{Y} = 106.665 + 2.056t$ $(t = 1, 2, \ldots, 16)$

b.

YEAR	FORECAST	PREDICTION INTERVAL
1983	141.617	141.617 ± 19.857
1984	143.673	143.673 ± 20.265

14.14b. Reject H_0 ($\alpha = .05$)

14.15b. $d = .0128$; reject H_0 **c.** Residuals are normally distributed

14.16a. $\hat{Y} = 493.28 + 11.24t$ **b.** $d = 1.054$; reject H_0

14.20

FORECAST	ERROR
983.07	-84.06
996.38	50.16
1,008.44	250.20

14.21 1981: 983.07 ± 205.97; 1982: 996.38 ± 212.217; 1983: $1,008.44 \pm 212.596$

14.22a. White-collar: 52.99; blue-collar: 30.07; service: 13.62   **b.** White-collar: 55.61; blue-collar: 30.26; service: 13.95

14.23

YEAR	FORECAST
1983	301.7
1984	322.8
1985	343.9

14.24a. 1984: $59.21; 1985: $59.21; Expected loss = $0.54 per share

b. 1984: $64.19; 1985: $70.46; Expected gain = $10.71 per share

14.25a. $\hat{Y} = -2,866 + 1.47t$ $(t = 1970, 1971, \ldots, 1983)$ **b.** 1984: $50.48 \pm $23.49; 1985: $51.95 \pm $24.11

14.26 Residuals: .0107, -6.0843, -1.0544, 3.8505, 6.5055, 9.6604, 10.1904, -1.6547, -19.6247, -14.5948, -1.8148, 6.5901, -2.5049, 10.5250; $d = 1.021$; test is inconclusive

14.27

QTR.	FORECAST	ERROR
1	3,139.1	32.4
2	3,156.4	115.6
3	3,173.7	188.5
4	3,191.0	241.0

14.28a. $\hat{Y} = 799.10 + 47.15t$ $(t = 1, 2, \ldots , 48)$;

QTR.	FORECAST
1	$3,109.45 \pm 215.8$
2	$3,156.60 \pm 216.3$
3	$3,203.75 \pm 216.8$
4	$3,298.05 \pm 217.4$

b. $\hat{Y} = 793.22 + 47.17t + 11.7Q_1 + 4.8Q_2 + 4.7Q_3$; $F = .023$; yes

c.

QTR.	FORECAST
1	3,116.3
2	3,156.5
3	3,203.6
4	3,246.1

14.29a. $d = .071$; reject H_0

14.30a. $\hat{Y} = 6.9147 + .0247t$; $\hat{Y} = 6.9116 + .0247t + .0056Q_1 + .0030Q_2 + .0024Q_3$

b.

	QTR. I	QTR. II	QTR. III	QTR. IV
Simple	$3,377.9 \pm 145$	$3,462.3 \pm 149$	$3,548.9 \pm 153$	$3,637.7 \pm 157.2$
Seasonal	3,386.3	3,462.0	3,546.4	3,626.4

14.31a. Auto: $\hat{Y} = -47,818,194 + 24,308t$ $(t = 1972, 1973, \ldots , 1982)$;
Home: $\hat{Y} = -1,431,148 + 731.6t$ $(t = 1972, 1973, \ldots , 1982)$;
Credit: $\hat{Y} = 13,808,574 + 7,003t$ $(t = 1972, 1973, \ldots , 1982)$

	AUTO	HOME	CREDIT
1983	$\$384,570 \pm 37,357$	$\$19,615 \pm 2,780$	$\$78,375 \pm 16,225$
1984	$\$408,878 \pm 38,882$	$\$20,346 \pm 2,894$	$\$85,378 \pm 16,887$

b.

	AUTO	HOME	CREDIT
1983	367,904	19,900	72,020
1984	383,140	20,702	75,793

14.32 Jan.: $121.822; Feb.: $121.882; Mar.: $121.882

14.33 $\hat{Y} = 39.85 + 2.267t$ $(t = 1, 2, \ldots , 36)$; Jan.: $\$123.729 \pm 24.299$; Feb.: $\$125.996 \pm 24.400$; Mar.: $\$128.263 \pm 24.512$

14.34 $d = .181$; reject H_0

Chapter 15

15.1a. 19.00 **b.** 99.00 **c.** 1.61 **d.** 3.87 **15.2a.** .99 **b.** .01 **c.** .05 **d.** .95

15.3a.

SOURCE	df	SS	MS	F
Treatments	2	5.00	2.50	1.18
Error	6	12.72	2.12	
Total	8	17.72		

b. $F = 1.18$; do not reject H_0 **c.** 2 ± 2.583 **d.** Narrower **e.** 3.7 ± 2.519 **f.** 51

15.4a.

SOURCE	df	SS	MS	F
Treatments	6	16.9	2.817	3.48
Error	35	28.3	.809	
Total	41	45.2		

b. 7 **c.** $F = 3.48$; yes **d.** p-value $< .01$ **e.** $t = -.83$; no **f.** $-.4 \pm .79$ **g.** $3.7 \pm .56$
15.8b. $F = 8.44$; reject H_0 **c.** p-value $< .01$ **d.** 206 ± 126.14

15.9b.

SOURCE	df	SS	MS	F
Treatments	3	6.816	2.272	8.03
Error	105	29.710	.283	
Total	108	36.526		

c. $F = 8.03$; yes **d.** $-.187 \pm .343$ **e.** $t = 2.34$; yes

15.10a. $F = 16.95$; reject H_0 **b.** -72 ± 26.08 **15.11b.** $F = 31.75$; yes
15.12a. $F = 3.17$; no **b.** 473.3 ± 22.93 **c.** 37.05 ± 30.76
15.13a. $T_1 = 953.91$; $T_2 = 1,831.95$; $T_3 = 689.04$; CM $= 109,772.091$; SST $= 593.936$ **b.** SSE $= 7,719.83$

c.

SOURCE	df	SS	MS	F
Treatments	2	593.936	296.968	4.12
Error	107	7,719.830	72.148	
Total	109	8,313.766		

d. $F = 4.12$; yes **e.** 6.62 ± 3.92 **f.** $t = 2.17$; yes

15.14a. $T_1 = -1.3257$; $T_2 = -.9580$; $T_3 = -.7061$; $T_4 = -.4818$; $T_5 = -.0765$ **b.** SSE $= .48605$

c.

SOURCE	df	SS	MS	F
Treatments	4	.02301	.00575	1.08
Error	91	.48605	.00534	
Total	95	.50906		

d. $F = 1.08$; no **e.** $-.0387 \pm .0569$

15.15a. $F = 17.32$; yes **b.** p-value $< .01$ **c.** $t = 4.24$; yes **d.** $-.6 \pm 1.21$

15.16a.

SOURCE	df	SS	MS	F
Treatments	2	23.167	11.583	12.64
Block	3	14.250	4.75	5.18
Error	6	5.500	.917	
Total	11	42.917		

b. $F = 12.64$; yes **c.** $F = 5.18$; yes **d.** $.025 < p$-value $< .05$ **e.** -2.5 ± 1.32

15.17a.

SOURCE	df	SS	MS	F
Treatments	3	28.2	9.40	4.141
Block	5	69.0	13.80	6.079
Error	15	34.1	2.27	
Total	23	131.3		

b. $F = 4.141$; no **c.** $F = 6.079$; yes **d.** -2.4 ± 1.525

15.21a.

SOURCE	df	SS	MS	F
Treatments	3	3.740	1.247	8.43
Block	2	29.622	14.811	100.07
Error	6	.885	.148	
Total	11	34.247		

$F = 8.43$; reject H_0

b. $.01 < p$-value $< .025$ **d.** $-1.3 \pm .767$
15.22a. $F = 39.46$; yes   **b.** $F = 1.93$; no   **c.** -27 ± 6.85
15.23a. $F = 12.25$; yes   **c.** $t = 3.5$; reject H_0 **d.** $12.25 = (3.5)^2$; $7.71 = (2.776)^2$

15.24a. Randomized block design   **b.**

SOURCE	df	SS	MS	F
Treatments	2	.1821	.0911	9.0811
Block	11	29.2598	2.6600	265.1563
Error	22	.2207	.010032	
Total	34	29.6626		

c. $F = 9.0811$; yes   **d.** $t = -.0489$; no
15.25a. $F = .34$; no   **b.** p-value $> .10$

c.

SOURCE	df	SS	MS	F
Treatments	2	.941	.471	.34
Block	5	10,239.969	2,047.994	1,471.38
Error	10	13.919	1.392	
Total	17	10,254.829		

d. $-.1833 \pm 1.234$

15.26a. $F = 78.176$; reject H_0 **b.**

SOURCE	df	SS	MS	F
Treatments	4	129,778.9	32,444.725	78.716
Block	5	40,726.8	8,145.360	19.762
Error	20	8,243.5	412.175	
Total	29	178,749.2		

15.27a.

SOURCE	df	SS	MS	F
Treatments	3	.1858	.0619	21.34
Block	9	5.0607	.5623	193.897
Error	27	.0778	.0029	
Total	39	5.3243		

b. $F = 21.34$; reject H_0 **c.** $t = -1.29$; no

15.28b.

SOURCE	df	SS	MS	F
A	2	.8	.400	3.704
B	3	5.3	1.767	16.361
AB	6	9.6	1.600	14.815
Error	12	1.3	.108	
Total	23	17.0		

d. $F = 14.815$; yes

15.29a. *A*: 4; *B*: 2   **b.** 3   **c.**

SOURCE	df	SS	MS	F
A	3	2.25	.75	5.000
B	1	.95	.95	6.333
AB	3	.90	.30	2.000
Error	16	2.40	.15	
Total	23	6.50		

d. Interaction: $F = 2.0$, do not reject H_0; factor A: $F = 5.0$, reject H_0; factor B: $F = 6.333$, reject H_0

15.30a.

SOURCE	df	SS	MS	F
A	1	4.441	4.441	18.075
B	2	4.127	2.064	8.400
AB	2	18.007	9.0035	36.644
Error	6	1.474	0.2457	
Total	11	28.049		

b. $F = 36.644$; yes   **d.** $-2.05 \pm .963$

15.31a.

SOURCE	df	SS	MS	F
A	1	658.845	658.845	46.650
B	1	255.380	255.380	18.083
AB	1	2.000	2.000	.142
Error	4	56.490	14.123	
Total	7	972.715		

b. $F = .142$; no   **c.** $F = 46.650$; yes   **d.** $F = 18.083$; yes   **e.** -11.3 ± 7.377

15.32a.

SOURCE	df	SS	MS	F
Agency	1	39.967	39.967	7.011
Medium	2	198.332	99.166	17.394
Agency-Medium	2	77.345	38.673	6.784
Error	6	34.205	5.701	
Total	11	349.849		

b. $F = 6.784$; yes

15.33a.

	LIGHT	HEAVY
FEMALE	146.40	116.00
MALE	104.00	98.00

b. 6,739.605   **c.** SS(Sex) = 114.005; SS(Weight) = 41.405; SS(Sex–Weight) = 18.605

d.

	SAMPLE VARIANCE	SS DEVIATIONS WITHIN
Female, Light	46.3761	324.6327
Female, Heavy	8.5849	60.0943
Male, Light	25.4016	177.8112
Male, Heavy	32.4900	227.4300

e. SSE = 789.968   **f.** SS(Total) = 963.983

g.

SOURCE	df	SS	MS	F
Sex	1	114.005	114.005	4.041
Weight	1	41.405	41.405	1.4676
Sex–Weight	1	18.605	18.605	0.6594
Error	28	789.968	28.213	
Total	31	963.983		

h. $F = .6594$; no   **i.** $t = -1.996$; yes   **j.** $t = .847$; no

15.34a.

SOURCE	df	SS	MS	F
Sex	1	10,686.361	10,686.361	68.7358
Weight	1	538.756	538.756	3.4653
Sex–Weight	1	831.744	831.744	5.350
Error	36	5,596.908	155.470	
Total	39	17,653.769		

b. $F = 5.350$; yes   **c.** $t = -7.50$; yes   **d.** $t = -4.23$; yes

15.35a. 3.95   **b.** 5.56   **c.** 6.20   **d.** 4.20

15.36a. 15   **b.** .048   **c.** .479

d. Means of the following treatment pairs appear to differ: (4 and 1), (4 and 5), (4 and 2), (3 and 5), (3 and 2), (1 and 2), (5 and 2).

15.37a. 6   **b.** 5.19   **c.** 5.19

15.38 $\omega = 152.574$; means of the following treatment pairs appear to differ: (C and A), (B and A)

15.40 $\omega = 1.973$; means of the following treatment pairs appear to differ: (A2, B2 and A2, B1), (A2, B2 and A1, B3), (A2, B3 and A2, B1), (A2, B3 and A1, B3), (A1, B1 and A2, B1), (A1, B1 and A1, B3), (A1, B2 and A1, B3)

15.41 $\omega = 15.306$; means of the following treatment pairs appear to differ: (A2, B1 and A1, B1), (A2, B1 and A1, B2), (A2, B2 and A1, B2)

15.42 $\omega = 9.505$; means of the following treatment pairs appear to differ: (2, T and 2, N), (2, T and 2, R), (1, N and 2, R), (1, T and 2, R)

15.43a. $F = 8.77$; yes   **b.** $.89 \pm .362$ **15.44a.** $F = 4.81$; no   **b.** -10 ± 10.35

15.45a. $F = 4.88$; yes   **b.** p-value $< .01$ **c.** 1.66 ± 2.369 **d.** 11.99 ± 1.061

e. $\omega = 2.336$; only treatment pair B and D appear to differ

15.46a. Completely randomized   **b.** $F = 6.30$; yes   **c.** 25 ± 2.34

d. $\omega = 5.523$; means of the following treatment pairs appear to differ: (C and D), (B and D)

15.47a. $F = 3.64$; no   **b.** $F = 46.85$

15.49a. df: 1, 98; MS: 3,237.2, 164.98; $F = 19.62$ **b.** Yes   **c.** No; need the sample means

15.50a.

SOURCE	df	SS	MS	F
Extractor	5	84.71	16.94	12.46
Truckload	14	159.29	11.38	8.37
Error	70	95.33	1.36	
Total	89			

b. $F = 12.46$; yes

15.51a.

SOURCE	df	SS	MS	F
A	3	2.6	.867	1.113
B	5	9.2	1.840	2.361
AB	15	46.5	3.100	3.978
Error	24	18.7	.7792	
Total	47	77.0		

b. A: 4, B: 6, $r = 2$ **c.** $F = 3.978$; yes

15.52a.

SOURCE	df	SS	MS	F
A	3	74.333	24.778	16.519
B	2	4.083	2.042	1.361
AB	6	168.917	28.153	18.769
Error	12	18.000	1.500	
Total	23	265.333		

b. $F = 18.769$; yes   **c.** $\omega = 4.858$

15.53a.

SOURCE	df	SS	MS	F
Payment	1	1,444	1,444	29.469
Schedule	1	361	361	7.367
Payment–Schedule	1	1	1	.020
Error	12	588	49	
Total	15	2,394		

b. $F = .020$; no   **c.** $\omega = 14.7$; yes, flexible schedule/hourly & piece rate

15.54a. $F = 22.23$; yes   **b.** $F = 20.45$; yes   **c.** 1.59 ± 4.088 **15.55a.** $F = 83.87$; yes   **b.** $-1.64 \pm .49$

15.56a. $F = 7.61$; yes   **b.** $8.067 \pm .4491$ **15.57a.** $F = 15.59$; yes   **15.58** $F = 2.95$; no

15.59a. Completely randomized   **b.**

SOURCE	df	SS	MS	F
Treatment	2	57.60	28.80	.34
Error	13	1,109.33	85.33	
Total	15	1,166.93		

c. $F = .34$; no

15.60 81 ± 7.32 **15.61a.** $F = .19$; no   **b.**

SOURCE	df	SS	MS	F
Treatment	2	.632	.316	.19
Block	3	.856	.285	.17
Error	6	9.842	1.640	
Total	11	11.329		

c. $F = .17$; no

15.62 $.55 \pm 3.36$ **15.63a.** Completely randomized   **b.** $F = 7.02$; yes   **c.** $8.15 \pm .44$

15.64a. $F = 9.75$; yes   **b.** $F = 4.88$; yes   **c.**

SOURCE	df	SS	MS	F
Treatment	2	1,277.2	638.6	9.75
Block	4	1,279.1	319.78	4.88
Error	8	524.1	65.52	
Total	14	3,080.4		

15.65 11.6 ± 11.8 **15.66a.** Completely randomized   **b.** $F = 7.79$; yes   **c.** -5.65 ± 3.25

15.67a. $t = -.46$; do not reject H_0 **b.** $t = .46$; do not reject H_0 **c.** $(.46)^2 = .2116$; $(2.145)^2 = 4.60$; do not reject H_0

15.68a.

SOURCE	df	SS	MS	F
Checklist	1	114.568	114.568	2.768
Error	42	1,738.409	41.391	
Total	43	1,852.977		

c. $t = 1.66$

15.69a.

SOURCE	df	SS	MS	F
Market	2	5,643.075	2,821.538	22.475
Error	78	9,792.176	125.541	
Total	80	15,435.251		

p-value $< .01$; yes

b. NYSE – ASE: 16.2938 ± 4.5564; NYSE – OTC: 17.7146 ± 5.6643; ASE – OTC: 1.4208 ± 5.8285

15.71a.

SOURCE	df	SS	MS	F
Category	2	198,772.467	99,386.234	3.4819
Error	27	770,670.900	28,543.367	
Total	29	969,443.367		

15.72a.

SOURCE	df	SS	MS	F
Incentive	2	52,003.11	26,001.56	17.4293
Union	1	10,706.72	10,706.72	7.1679
Incentive – Union	2	69.78	34.89	0.0234
Error	12	17,902.00	1,491.83	
Total	17	80,681.61		

b. $F = .0234$; no

Chapter 16

16.1a. $T_B \leq 32$ or $T_B \geq 58$ **b.** $T_A \geq 40$ **c.** $T_B \geq 98$ **16.2b.** $T_B \geq 39$ **16.3** $T_B = 42.5$; reject H_0
16.5 $T_{U.S.} = 39$; yes   **16.6** $T_{After} = 86$; reject H_0 **16.7** $T_{Young} = 55.5$; no   **16.8a.** $T_{Twin} = 82$; no
16.9 $T_{Previous} = 35$; no   **16.10a.** $t = -1.26$; do not reject H_0 ($\alpha = .05$)   **b.** $T_A = 37.5$; do not reject H_0 ($\alpha = .05$)
16.11 $T_B = 29$; no   **16.12a.** $z = -4.82$ **c.** $.05$ **16.13a.** $z = 1.77$; reject H_0
16.14a. $T \leq 101$ **b.** $T_- \leq 303$ **c.** $T_+ \leq 0$ **16.15b.** $T_- \leq 8$ **16.16** $T_- = 4.50$; reject H_0

16.18a. $T = 17$; do not reject H_0 **16.19** $T_+ = 2$; reject H_0 **16.20a.** $T_+ = 1$; reject H_0 ($\alpha = .05$)
16.21 $T_+ = 3$; yes   **16.22** $T_+ = 6$; no   **16.23** $T_- = 8$; no
16.24a. $t = .98$; do not reject H_0 **b.** $T_- = 6$; do not reject H_0
16.25a. 31.4104   **b.** 27.4884   **c.** 58.5713 (by interpolation)   **d.** 96.5782   **e.** 5.99147   **f.** 25.1882
16.26a. .995   **b.** .025   **c.** .100   **d.** .975   **e.** .025   **f.** .100
16.27a. Completely randomized design   **c.** Reject H_0 if $H > 9.21034$ **16.28** $H = 15.9445$; reject H_0
16.30c. $H = 14.74854$; reject H_0 **16.31a.** $H = 11.415$; reject H_0 **b.** Completely randomized design
16.32 $H = 2.03$; no   **16.33** $H = 5.85$; no   **16.34** $H = 7.971$; yes
16.35a. $F = 1.33$; do not reject H_0 **b.** $H = 1.22$; do not reject H_0
16.36b. $H = 17.7310$; reject H_0 **c.** Wilcoxon rank sum test for independent samples   **16.37b.** $F_r > 4.60517$
16.38 $F_r = 6.9286$; reject H_0 **16.39** $F_r = 12.8$; reject H_0 **16.40b.** $F_r = 20.1333$; reject H_0 **c.** p-value $< .005$
16.41a. $F_r = 4.75$; reject H_0 **b.** $T_- = 0$; reject H_0 **16.42** $F_r = 6.35$; yes   **16.43** $F_r = 12.3$; yes
16.44 $F_r = 7.85$; reject H_0 **16.45a.** $F_r = 12.2$; yes   **c.** $.005 < p$-value $< .01$
16.46a. $r_s < -0.683$ or $r_s > 0.683$ **b.** $r_s > .400$ **c.** $r_s < -.478$
16.47a. $r_s = 1$ **b.** $r_s = -.9$ **c.** $r_s = 1$ **d.** $r_s = .2$ **16.49a.** $r_s = .66986$ **b.** Reject H_0
16.50a. $r_s = .3459$ **b.** Reject H_0 **16.51a.** .861   **b.** Yes   **16.52a.** .4524   **b.** No   **16.53** $r_s = .9341$
16.54 $r_s = -.8536$; yes   **16.55** $r_s = .657$; no   **16.57a.** $T_{After} = 19$; yes   **16.58a.** x and y_1: .9848; x and y_2: .9879
16.59 $T_A = 21$; no   **16.60** $T_1 = 135$; yes   **16.61** $H = 14.61$; yes   **16.62** $T_1 = 38.5$; reject H_0
16.63 $T_- = 3$; yes   **16.64** $F_r = 6.21$; no   **16.65** $r_s = .4091$; no   **16.66a.** $T_+ = 1$; yes   **b.** $t = -2.96$; reject H_0
16.67 $T_- = 3.5$; yes   **16.68** $H = 14.27$; yes   **16.69** $T_{Before} = 132.5$; yes   **16.70** $F_r = 11.77$; yes
16.71 $T_+ = 2.5$; do not reject H_0 **16.72** $H = 16.39$; yes   **16.73** $T_1 = 59$; reject H_0 **16.74** $r_s = .9286$; yes
16.75 $F_r = 1.55$; no   **16.76** $r_s = .28$; no   **16.77** $H = 12.79$; yes   **16.78** $T_{Door} = 28.5$; do not reject H_0
16.79 $r_s = .7714$; no   **16.80** $F_r = 6.35$; yes   **16.81** $T_- = 17.5$; no   **16.82** $r_s = .86053$

Chapter 17

17.1a. 24.9958   **b.** 70.0648   **c.** 18.5494   **d.** 10.5966   **17.2a.** .01   **b.** .01   **c.** .90   **d.** .005
17.3a. $X^2 > 4.60517$ **b.** $X^2 > 13.2767$ **c.** $X^2 > 7.81473$ **17.5a.** $X^2 = 3.941$; no   **b.** p-value $> .10$
17.6a. $X^2 = 12.374$; do not reject H_0 **b.** $.05 < p$-value $< .10$
17.7a. $X^2 = 60.569$; yes   **c.** p-value $< .005$ **d.** $.278 \pm .039$, $.632 \pm .042$
17.8a. $X^2 = 1,038$; yes   **b.** Approx. 0   **17.9** $X^2 = 10.3$; yes   **17.10** $X^2 = 9.48$; yes   **17.11** $X^2 = 17.36$; yes
17.12 $X^2 = 3.92$; no   **17.13** $X^2 = 10.44$; yes   **17.14a.** $X^2 > 26.2962$ **b.** $X^2 > 15.9871$ **c.** $X^2 > 9.21034$
17.15 $X^2 = 15.27$; reject H_0 **17.16** $X^2 = 38.02$; reject H_0
17.18a. Union members: $X^2 = 13.36$, reject independence; nonunion workers: $X^2 = 9.16$, do not reject independence
b. Union members: $.025 < p$-value $< .05$; nonunion workers: p-value $> .10$
17.19b. $X^2 = 89.09$; reject H_0 **17.20a.** $X^2 = 4.97$; yes   **c.** $.05 < p$-value $< .10$ **17.21** $X^2 = 40.70$; yes
17.22 $X^2 = 9.50$; yes   **17.23** $X^2 = 43.72$; reject H_0 **17.24a.** $X^2 = 1.35$; no   **b.** p-value $> .10$
17.25a. $X^2 = 87.38$; yes   **17.26a.** $X^2 = 8.13$; yes   **b.** $.01 < p$-value $< .025$
17.27a. $X^2 = 18.54$; yes   **b.** p-value $< .005$ **17.28** $X^2 = 6.58$; yes
17.29a. $X^2 = 6.66$; reject H_0 **b.** $.025 < p$-value $< .05$ **d.** $.56 \pm .12$ **17.30** $X^2 = 2.40$; no
17.31 $X^2 = 31.85$; yes   **17.32** $.12 \pm .0947$ **17.33** $X^2 = 5.51$; no
17.34b. Reject H_0 **c.** p-value $< .005$ **17.35** $X^2 = 2.60$; no

b. $X^2 = 895.79$; yes   **c.** $z = 12.5$; yes

17.36a.

| | PERFORMANCE | | | | |
	1	2	3	4	Quit or fired
JOB-MATCHED	178	792	634	277	99
NOT JOB-MATCHED	79	673	990	1,228	991

17.37 $X^2 = 42.54$; yes   **17.38** $X^2 = 103.08$; yes   **17.39** $X^2 = 7.384$; no ($\alpha = .05$)
17.40a. $X^2 = 47.979$; yes   **b.** $.125 \pm .046$ **17.41** $X^2 = 30.507$; yes   **17.42** $X^2 - 6.93$; no
17.43 $.284 \pm .0571$ **17.44** $X^2 = 38.68$; yes   **17.45** $X^2 = 7.4$; do not reject H_0 **17.46** $X^2 = 3.13$; no
17.47 $.095 \pm .128$ **17.48a.** $X^2 = 269.91$; yes   **b.** p-value $< .005$ **17.49** $X^2 = 6.74$; yes
17.50a. $X^2 = 46.25$ **b.** p-value $< .005$ **17.51** $.143 \pm .042$
17.52a. $X^2 = 9.647$ **b.** 11.0705 **c.** $\chi^2_{.05}$ with $(6 - 3) = 3$ df is 7.81473; yes   **d.** $.01 < p$-value $< .025$
17.53 $X^2 = 9.47$; no ($\alpha = .05$)   **17.54** $X^2 = 67.15$; reject H_0

Chapter 18

18.3a. Uncertainty   **b.** Conflict   **c.** Certainty   **18.4a.** Certainty   **b.** Uncertainty
18.5 Actions, States of nature, Outcomes, Objective variable

18.13 a_3 is inadmissible;   **18.14** a_2 and a_4 are inadmissible

	S_1	S_2	S_3	S_4
a_1	0	0	40	35
a_2	5	5	0	5
a_4	20	35	50	0

18.15a. a_4 inadmissible   **18.16** a_1, S_1: \$200; a_1, S_2: \$500; a_2, S_1: \$1,400; a_2, S_2: \$0; a_3, S_1: \$0; a_3, S_2: \$700

18.17a. Payoffs in millions of dollars:

	STATE OF NATURE		
	1%	2%	3%
Market	14	16	18
Do not market	15	15	15

b. Opportunity losses in millions of dollars:

	1%	2%	3%
Market	1	0	0
Do not market	0	1	3

18.18a.

		STATE OF NATURE					
		3 doz.	4 doz.	5 doz.	6 doz.	7 doz.	8 doz.
	3 doz.	720	720	720	720	720	720
	4 doz.	660	960	960	960	960	960
ACTION	5 doz.	600	900	1,200	1,200	1,200	1,200
	6 doz.	540	840	1,140	1,440	1,440	1,440
	7 doz.	480	780	1,080	1,380	1,680	1,680
	8 doz.	420	720	1,020	1,320	1,620	1,920

b.

ACTION		STATE OF NATURE					
		3 doz.	4 doz.	5 doz.	6 doz.	7 doz.	8 doz.
	3 doz.	0	240	480	720	960	1,200
	4 doz.	60	0	240	480	720	960
	5 doz.	120	60	0	240	480	720
	6 doz.	180	120	60	0	240	480
	7 doz.	240	180	120	60	0	240
	8 doz.	300	240	180	120	60	0

18.19a.

	STATE OF NATURE	
	Successful	Unsuccessful
Increase advertising	600,000	−600,000
Do not increase advertising	200,000	200,000

b. No

18.20a.

	STATE OF NATURE		
	5%	10%	50%
Purchase	−1,250	−1,500	−1,500
Do not purchase	−250	−500	−2,500

18.21a. Payoffs in millions of dollars:

	STATE OF NATURE	
	Win	Lose
Court	−1	−101
No court	−50	−50

18.22a. Payoffs in millions of dollars:

	STATE OF NATURE				
	.5	10	15	20	25
Introduce	−2.85	0	1.50	3	4.5
Do not introduce	0	0	0	0	0

b. Opportunity losses in millions of dollars:

	STATE OF NATURE				
	.5	10	15	20	25
Introduce	2.85	0	0	0	0
Do not introduce	0	0	1.5	3	4.5

18.23 a_2 **18.24a.** a_2 **c.** a_1 **18.26a.** a_2 **b.** a_2 **18.27** a_1

18.28a.

	STATE OF NATURE		
	Major	Moderate	Minor
Y	−8,000	−5,400	−4,400
Z	−9,000	−5,000	−3,500

b. Z

18.29a. A   **b.** A   **18.30** Yes   **18.31** Do not purchase   **18.32** 6 doz.
18.33a. Both actions have the same expected payoff

b.

	Successful	Unsuccessful
Increase advertising	0	800,000
Do not increase advertising	400,000	0

c. Both actions have the same expected opportunity loss.

18.34a. a_2 and a_3 are inadmissible   **b.** a_4 **c.** a_4 **18.35a.** a_1 **b.** a_3 **18.36a.** a_2 **b.** a_2
18.37a. a_3 **b.** a_1 **18.38a.** Z   **b.** Y   **18.39a.** Market   **b.** Do not market
18.40a. 8 doz.   **b.** 3 doz.   **18.41a.** Do not purchase   **b.** Purchase

18.42a. $U(100) = .2$; $U(500) = .7$; $U(800) = .95$ **18.43a.**

	S_1	S_2	S_3
a_1	5,625	2,500	900
a_2	3,600	6,400	9

b. a_2

18.44a. None inadmissible   **b.**

	S_1	S_2	S_3
a_1	.672	.835	.896
a_2	.712	.772	.772
a_3	.672	.852	.835
a_4	.672	0	1.000

c. a_3 **d.** Yes

18.45a.

	S_1	S_2	S_3	S_4
a_1	.2	.8	0	0
a_2	.05	.65	.90	.50
a_3	0	.20	.60	1.00

b. a_2 **18.46a.** $U(600,000) = .9$; $U(0) = .8$

18.47a.

	Dry well	Moderate success	Gusher
Invest	−500,000	600,000	1,500,000
Do not invest	0	0	0

b. Invest   **c.** Do not invest

18.48 6 doz.   **18.49a.** Risk-taking   **b.** Risk-neutral   **c.** Risk-avoiding   **d.** Risk-neutral
18.50b. Risk-avoiding   **c.** a_1 **18.51b.** Risk-taking   **c.** a_2 **18.52a.** Risk-neutral   **b.** a_3; no
18.53b. Risk-avoider   **18.54b.** Risk-avoider

18.55b. Payoffs in millions of dollars:

	Bill will pass	Bill won't pass
Don't lease	2.5	−1.5
Lease	.5	.5

c. Opportunity losses in millions of dollars:

	Bill will pass	Bill won't pass
Don't lease	0	2
Lease	2	0

d. Don't lease

18.56b. Risk-neutral   **c.** Don't lease

18.57a. a_2 inadmissible   **b.**

	S_1	S_2	S_3
a_1	28	0	107
a_3	60	36	0
a_4	15	72	10
a_5	0	27	70

c.

	EXPECTED PAYOFF	EXPECTED OPPORTUNITY LOSS
a_1	23.7	35.4
a_3	18.3	40.8
a_4	28.0	31.1
a_5	37.0	22.1

18.58a. Relative frequency   **b.** Subjective   **c.** Subjective   **d.** Both

18.59a.

	S_1	S_2	S_3
Loan	7,500	6,500	−30,000
Don't loan	6,000	6,000	6,000

b.

	S_1	S_2	S_3
Loan	0	0	36,000
Don't loan	1,500	500	0

18.60a. $P(S_1) = .8625$; $P(S_2) = .09375$; $P(S_3) = .04375$ **b.** Don't make loan   **18.61a.** Make loan   **b.** Don't make loan

18.62a. Risk-avoiding   **b.**

	S_1	S_2	S_3		No
Loan	.3279	.3263	.2646		
Don't loan	.3256	.3256	.3256		

18.63a.

	1	2
$0.99	7.94	11.92
$1.98	11.96	16.00
$2.75	12.38	13.75
$3.50	10.50	7.00

b.

	1	2
$0.99	4.44	4.08
$1.98	0.42	0
$2.75	0	2.25
$3.50	1.88	9.00

c. $1.98

18.64a. Payoffs in thousands of dollars:

	Win	Lose
Settle	−250	−250
Court	0	−1,000

c. Settle

18.65a. Go to court   **b.** Settle

18.66a.

	Win	Lose
Settle	.6186	.6186
Court	.7143	0

b. Settle

18.67a. Payoffs in millions of dollars:

	Use	Don't use
Install	2.75	−1
Don't install	0	0

b. Opportunity losses in millions of dollars:

	Use	Don't use
Install	0	1
Don't install	2.75	0

c. Don't install

18.68a. Risk-neutral   **b.** Risk-avoider   **c.** Risk-taker   **d.** Risk-taker

18.69b.

	S_1	S_2	S_3
a_1	.24	.95	.09
a_2	0	.55	1.00
a_3	.35	.19	.90
a_4	.55	.66	.22

c. a_4; same under expected payoff criterion

Chapter 19

19.2

(4)	(5)
.150	.297
.320	.634
.035	.069
.505	1.000

19.3

(4)	(5)
.315	.538
.015	.026
.195	.333
.060	.103
.585	1.000

19.4 $\frac{2}{3}$; 0

19.7a.

x	5	10	15	20	25
$p(x)$	.196	.627	.118	.039	.020

b. 10.3; 16.16

19.8a. .1025; .000179

b.

p	POSTERIOR PROBABILITY
.09	.377
.10	.253
.11	.158
.12	.107
.13	.105
	1.000

c. .1031; .000181   **19.9** .5263   **19.10** .9174

19.11a.

p	POSTERIOR PROBABILITY
.01	.25
.05	.50
.10	.25

b.

p	POSTERIOR PROBABILITY
.01	.00096
.05	.21767
.10	.78137

19.12a.

MEAN DEMAND	POSTERIOR PROBABILITY
2	.145
3	.541
4	.314

b.

MEAN DEMAND	POSTERIOR PROBABILITY
2	.190
3	.586
4	.224

19.13 a_2 **19.14a.** a_3 **b.** $P(S_1) = .888$, $P(S_2) = .056$, $P(S_3) = .056$ **c.** 9.226; -12.376; 19.845; 7.392   **d.** a_3

19.15a. a_3 **b.** $P(S_1) = .25$, $P(S_2) = .5625$, $P(S_3) = .1875$ **c.** a_1

19.16a.

		STATE OF NATURE				
		.00	.05	.10	.15	.20
ACTION	Agreement 1	$-46,000$	$-46,000$	$-46,000$	$-46,000$	$-46,000$
	Agreement 2	$-40,000$	$-42,000$	$-44,000$	$-46,000$	$-48,000$

b. Agreement 2   **c.** Agreement 2 in both cases

19.17a. Payoffs in millions of dollars:

		STATE OF NATURE	
		(.6)	(.4)
		Bill passes	Bill doesn't pass
ACTION	Don't lease	2.5	-1.5
	Lease	.5	.5

b.

STATE OF NATURE	POSTERIOR PROBABILITY
Bill passes	.923
Bill doesn't pass	.077

d. Don't lease

19.18a.

	S_1	S_2	S_3
a_1	$ 40	$250	$ 0
a_2	$115	$ 0	$125
a_3	$ 0	$210	$ 20

b. $45.00

19.19a.

	S_1	S_2	S_3
a_1	0	0	5,000
a_2	3,000	500	0

b. $1,125   **c.** S_2 **d.** $P(S_1) = .061$; $P(S_2) = .864$; $P(S_3) = .075$ **e.** $375

19.20a. $1,800   **b.** $4,584   **c.** $744   **19.21a.** Do not install   **b.** $1,550

19.22a. Payoffs in millions of dollars:

		STATE OF NATURE	
		Error	No error
ACTION	Certify	-10	0
	Don't certify	0	-2

c. Certify   **d.** $1 million

19.23 $200   **19.24** $.8 million

19.25a. EPS = $267.96; EPNS = $145   **b.** EVSI = $122.96   **c.** ENGS = $22.96   **d.** Yes

19.26a. $13.97   **b.** First source

19.27a. Prior probabilities: $P(S_1) = .2$; $P(S_2) = .3$; $P(S_3) = .5$

b. Posterior probabilities: $P(S_1) = .6829$; $P(S_2) = .0732$; $P(S_3) = .2439$

c. Posterior probabilities: $P(S_1) = .1111$; $P(S_2) = .75$; $P(S_3) = .1389$

d. Posterior probabilities: $P(S_1) = .0460$; $P(S_2) = .0345$; $P(S_3) = .9195$

e. P(Sample information indicates S_1 true) = .205; P(Sample information indicates S_2 true) = .360;
P(Sample information indicates S_3 true) = .435

g. EPNS = $1,900; EPS = $1,956.94   **h.** EVSI = $56.94   **i.** Should not purchase

19.28a. $120,000   **b.** $47,958   **c.** $17,958; purchase survey   **19.29** $49.17

19.30 ENGS = $350,000; yes

19.31 Up to $.34 million   **19.32** $0   **19.33b.** $x = 7$ **c.** $E(x) = 17.5$; A

19.34a.

		STATE OF NATURE				
		5	10	15	20	25
ACTION	A	2	12	22	32	42
	B	4	9	14	19	24

b. Choose action A; yes

19.35a. $x = 222.22 **b.** $E(x) = 320 **c.** A   **19.36** A   **19.37b.** $x = 833.33$ **c.** 3,100   **d.** Brand A

19.38a. $\mu = 20$; $\sigma^2 = 36.95$ **b.** First machine

19.39a.

PRIOR PROBABILITY OF GUILT	POSTERIOR PROBABILITY OF GUILT
.1	.9911
.2	.9960
.3	.9977
.4	.9985
.5	.9990
.6	.9993
.7	.9996
.8	.9998
.9	.9999

19.40a. $5,987,500   **b.** No   **c.** Purchase survey

19.41a.

		STATE OF NATURE	
		(.8)	(.2)
		$p = .05$	$p = .1$
ACTION	Accept	0	−4,100
	Reject	−1,000	0

b. Rejected   **c.** 800   **d.** Rejected   **e.** Accepted

f. $22   **g.** 2.75%   **h.** Yes

19.42a. $89.22   **b.** 11.15%   **c.** $49.22   **19.44** Yes   **19.45** $1,000   **19.46** $1,100

19.47α. Payoffs in thousands of dollars:

		STATE OF NATURE						
		(.05) S_1	(.20) S_2	(.30) S_3	(.20) S_4	(.10) S_5	(.08) S_6	(.07) S_7
	a_1	0	0	0	−3,000	−6,000	−9,000	−12,000
	a_2	−2	−2	−2	−2,702	−5,702	−8,702	−11,702
	a_3	−4	−4	−4	−2,504	−5,404	−8,404	−11,404
ACTION	a_4	−6	−6	−6	−2,506	−5,106	−8,106	−11,106
	a_5	−8	−8	−8	−2,508	−5,008	−7,808	−10,808
	a_6	−10	−10	−10	−2,510	−5,010	−7,510	−10,510
	a_7	−12	−12	−12	−2,512	−5,012	−7,512	−10,212
	a_8	−14	−14	−14	−2,514	−5,014	−7,514	−10,014

c. 7   **d.** $10,620

19.48 Develop the model   **19.49** 9   **19.50α.** a_3 **b.** a_1 or a_2

Chapter 20

20.1α. 40%; .77   **b.** 20%; .89   **c.** 10%; .95   **d.** 1%; .99   **20.2α.** 77   **b.** 89   **c.** 95   **d.** 99
20.3α. 1.99; 2   **b.** .509; .537   **20.4** 375 ± 3.814   **20.5** .37 ± .028   **20.6** 137,900 ± 2,759.71
20.7α. 72,066.67 ± 7,115.52   **b.** 36.03 ± 3.56   **c.** .7 ± .166
20.8α. $782,300   **b.** $206,993.77   **c.** $782,300 ± $206,993.77   **d.** Unreasonable
20.9b. .041   **c.** .086 ± .041   **d.** $z = .81$; no   **20.10** .62 ± .0304
20.11α. $330 ± $130.25   **b.** $135,300 ± $53,403.90   **20.12** $\hat{\tau} = 320$; bound = 240
20.13 $\hat{p} = .093$; bound = .0071   **20.14α.** 32.925 ± .3154   **b.** 395,100 ± 3,785.18   **c.** .4083 ± .0622
20.15α. 42.13 ± 5.21   **b.** 1,474,400 ± 182,206.5   **c.** .45 ± .119
20.16α. $44,844   **b.** $2,128   **c.** $44,840 ± $2,128
20.17α. $285,500.00   **b.** $200,377.33   **c.** $285,500 ± $200,377.33   **20.18** $\bar{x}_{st} = $19,905$; bound = $779
20.19 $\hat{p}_{st} = .2543$; bound = .0399   **20.20** $992,135.25 ± $17,993.29
20.21α. 5.6034 ± .7225   **b.** 6,948.2 ± 895.9
20.22α. $\bar{x} = 24.17$; bound = 4.297   **b.** $\hat{\tau} = 48,346.15$; bound = 8,594.65   **c.** $\hat{p} = .75$; bound = .1433
20.23α. $\hat{\tau} = $273,600$; bound = $75,822   **20.24** $\bar{x} = 21; bound = $5.85   **20.25** $\hat{p} = .76$; bound = .0597
20.26α. $\hat{\tau} = 2,217$; bound = 566.42   **20.27** $\bar{x} = 31.65; bound = $2.65   **20.28** .631 ± .110   **20.29** 402
20.31 274   **20.32** 48   **20.33** 8,001   **20.35α.** $\hat{\tau} = $73,850$; bound = $37,845.89   **b.** .7 ± .167
20.36α. $\bar{x}_{st} = 48.55$; bound = 6.31   **c.** 60.55 ± 11.996   **20.37** $\hat{p} = .876$; bound = .047
20.40α. $\hat{p} = .9296$; bound = .005   **20.41** Approx. 400   **20.42α.** .035 ± .009   **c.** No   **20.43** $5.41 ± $0.64
20.44 $\bar{x}_{st} = 7.16$; bound = .861   **20.45α.** $N\bar{x}_t = $285,000

INDEX

Text designer: Janet Bollow
Cover designer: John Williams
Technical artist: Reese Thornton
Production coordinators: Susan Reiland and Phyllis Niklas
Typesetter: Progressive Typographers, Inc.

Symbol	Description	Page
σ (lowercase sigma)	Population standard deviation	76
σ^2	Population variance	76
σ_{β_1}	Standard deviation of the sampling distribution of β_1	412
$\sigma_{\hat{p}}$	Standard deviation of the sampling distribution of $\hat{p}$	314
$\sigma_{(\hat{p}_1 - \hat{p}_2)}$	Standard deviation of the sampling distribution of $(\hat{p}_1 - \hat{p}_2)$	375
$\sigma_{\bar{x}}$	Standard deviation of the sampling distribution of $\bar{x}$	255
$\sigma_{(\bar{x}_1 - \bar{x}_2)}$	Standard deviation of the sampling distribution of $(\bar{x}_1 - \bar{x}_2)$	264
$\sigma_{\hat{y}}$	Standard deviation of the sampling distribution of $\hat{y}$	429
$\sigma_{(y - \hat{y})}$	Standard deviation of prediction error when $\hat{y}$ is used to predict a particular value of y	429
Σ (capital sigma)	Symbol for summation	59
t	Statistic used for small-sample tests of hypotheses	305
t_α	Value of t distribution with an area α to its right	302
T_A, T_B	Rank sums corresponding to the two samples in a Wilcoxon rank sum test	738
T_i	Total of observations for treatment i in an analysis of variance	672
T_L, T_U	Upper and lower rejection region values in a Wilcoxon rank sum test	738
T_t	Secular trend of a time series	628
T_0	Rejection region value in a Wilcoxon signed rank test	747
T_+, T_-	Sum of the ranks of the positive and negative differences in a Wilcoxon signed rank test	747
τ (tau)	Population total	912
$\hat{\tau}$	Estimator of population total τ	922
$U(O_{ij})$	Utility value corresponding to action i and state of nature j outcome in a decision analysis	850
$\bar{x}$	(1) Sample mean	61
	(2) Estimator of population mean μ computed from a cluster sample	934
$\bar{\bar{x}}$	Mean of all observations in an analysis of variance	672
x_i	(1) ith sample measurement	60
	(2) Total of all observations in cluster i of a cluster sample	934
$\bar{x}_i$	(1) Sample mean for ith treatment in an analysis of variance	672
	(2) Sample mean for stratum i in a stratified random sample	928
$\bar{x}_D$	Sample mean of differences in a paired difference experiment	364
$\bar{x}_{st}$	Estimator of population mean μ computed from a stratified random sample	928
X^2	Test statistic for multinomial and contingency table tests	791
Y_t	Value of a time series Y at time t	594
$\hat{y}$	Least squares prediction of y using a regression model	401
z	z-score	95
$z_{\alpha/2}$	Value of standard normal variable with an area $\alpha/2$ to its right	279